THE FA CUP CLUB BY CLUB RECORD SINCE 1945

COMPILED BY: JAMES WRIGHT

ASSISTANT COMPILER: KERRY MILLER

EDITORIAL ASSISTANT: MICHAEL WILLIAMS

Published by:
Tony Williams

ISBN 1-869833-41-4

Typeset by:
Inky Mad Spider

Printed and bound in Great Britain by R.Booth (Bookbinder) Ltd., Mabe, Penryn, Cornwall.

Distributed by Little Red Witch Book Distribution 0823 491 069

Cover design: Bob Bickerton

Editorial Address:
24a Queen Square, North Curry, Taunton, Somerset, TA3 6LE.
Tel: 0823 490 469 Fax: 0823 490 281

INTRODUCTION

The idea of a compiling this book first came to me in February 1991 as I was travelling back on the train to Taunton having visited the Football Association headquarters at Lancaster Gate. I had spent the day looking at micro-film records in the Competitions Department, gathering various statistics that 'Football Directories' required for the 'Guinness Non-League Fact Book' we were then compiling, and I had been greatly intrigued by the results on film of ties in the qualifying rounds of the F.A. Challenge Cup.

Why this fascination? Well, as far as I know, results of the qualifying rounds have never appeared en bloc in in any publication. When the 'Rothmans Yearbook' arrived on the scene in 1970 it started printing qualifying rounds scores, and has done ever since, whilst our own 'Non-League Club Directory' has provided extensive coverage of the early Cup rounds since its inauguration in the late Seventies. But, the qualifying rounds of the Challenge Cup prior to the 1969-70 season are an uncharted blank, and I strongly felt that a complete record of our oldest and best-loved competition was needed.

So I returned to North Curry and put the idea to Tony Williams, and, never one to dampen enthusiasm if a new publication is in prospect, he gave it the thumbs-up.

Having decided to undertake the project, the next step was to work out a format. The answer, I felt, lay in the initial intrigue of the results. When I first scanned the scores on the F.A. micro-film it was the clubs rather than the scorelines that fascinated. 'Who on earth are Luddenden Foot?' 'Did Nanpean Rovers really once play in the F.A. Cup?' - These were questions that immediately sprang to mind, so I soon plumped for a 'club-by-club' formula rather than the more traditional 'year-by-year, round-by-round' listing. This has the advantage that anyone interested in one particular club will be able to turn straight to the appropriate page and at a glance see which years the club participated in the Cup, what its longest run was, at what round it entered and what results were gained against any particular opposition.

The disadvantage of this format was that it meant the book would take a lot longer to compile. The 'raw material' was the Football Association's micro-film record which, largely, consisted of printed draw sheets with results penned on. I worked backwards from the Nineties building up alphabetic files of clubs. For each year, and each round, scores had to be added to the appropriate club's page and crossed off the draw sheet. When this task had been completed it was then a matter of filling gaps. Many scores, particurlary mid-week replays, had not been inked in, and two complete years, 1945-46 and 1952-53, were missing from the Lancaster Gate records. Fortunately, I came across an invaluable contact in Tony Brown who had been conducting similar research on behalf of the Association of Football Statisticians. We merged our respective records which whittled the list of missing scores down to a 'double-figures' total, then put out appeals in 'Team Talk' magazine, wrote to clubs involved in 'missing matches' and visited libraries - and finally the goal was achieved.

I am indebted to a large number of people, in addition to Tony Brown, for their assistance in this project, and their names should all appear in Appendix II at the rear of the book. Kerry Miller must receive special praise for the huge amount of work that he has accomplished on this book. In addition to researching results and current club whereabouts, he undertook the mammoth task of cross-referencing every score in the book - an onerous but crucially important job.

The lay-out of the book is very simple. All clubs that have competed in the F.A. Challenge Cup between 1945 and 1993 are listed alphabetically, starting on page five. Each club's results are listed chronologically, and a comprehensive key to the annotation appears in Appendix I. Clubs are listed by the last name under which they entered the F.A. Cup, but cross-references are made if the stem of the name differs from the current name, e.g. 'Abbey United' is cross-referenced to 'Cambridge United' but 'Whitby United' is not cross-referenced to 'Whitby Town'. Where a club has been the subject of an amalgamation it is treated as a separate entity (e.g. Dagenham & Redbridge are regarded as a new club from 1992 onwards) but appropriate cross-references are always made.

Of course, one of the problems of a work such as this is that it is immediately dated. By the time you first read it, several rounds of the 1993-94 F.A. Cup will have been contested. All I can do is humbly point you in the direction of 'Team Talk' magazine which will list all F.A. Cup results involving non-League clubs, and hope that an updated edition of this book will appear in a few years time.

Because it is envisaged that this book will be of interest not only for the Cup results, but as a potted history of many little-known clubs, the current playing status of each club is listed under the heading 'Currently'. It should be remembered, however, that this information is only up-to-date for September 1993 - many clubs will change leagues, cease to exist, merge, reform etc in the coming years. Which leads conveniently to the next point - after much soul-searching it was decided to refer to leagues under their original titles, i.e. with sponsors names omitted, for the sake of historical continuity. League sponsors names, however, are listed in Appendix III.

Finally, while every conceivable effort has been made to ensure accuracy, it would be extremely rash to assume that none of the 27,000 results in this book are incorrect. As I stated at the beginning, the aim of this project was to provide a long-overdue complete record of Post-War F.A. Cups ties, so if you do spot any errors please inform me at the address opposite.

JAMES WRIGHT

Arsenal's Ian Wright holds the 1992/93 F.A. Cup aloft. Photo: Colorsport.

ABBEY UNITED
See Cambridge United

ABERAMAN & ABERDARE ATH.
Currently: (Aberaman F.C.) Welsh League

45-46 Q1: Llanelly (H) 6-1 - *expelled*

46-47 Q1: Lovells Athletic (A) 0-1

47-48 PR: Barry Town (A) 0-2

ABERGAVENNY THURSDAYS
Currently: League of Wales

63-64 Q1: Cheltenham Town (A) 2-7

64-65 Q1: Gloucester City (A) 1-3

65-66 Q1: Stonehouse (A) 1-2

66-67 Q1: Gloucester City (A) 1-4

67-68 Q1: Llanelly (H) 0-2

68-69 Q1: Stonehouse (H) 4-1
Q2: Cheltenham Town (H) 2-2, (A) 2-3

69-70 Q1: Cinderford Town (A) 3-2
Q2: Merthyr Tydfil (A) 2-3

70-71 Q1: Ton Pentre (A) 1-4

71-72 Q1: Barry Town (H) 1-0
Q2: Ton Pentre (H) 0-2

ABINGDON TOWN
Currently: Isthmian League

47-48 EX: Aylesbury United (H) 2-4

48-49 EX: St Frideswides (H) 4-3
PR: Wallingford Town (H) 2-2, (A) 0-2

49-50 EX: Osberton Radiator (A) 0-5

50-51 EX: Slough Centre (A) 2-2, (H) 4-3
PR: Chesham United (A) 0-5

51-52 PR: Huntley & Palmers (A) 2-6

52-53 Q1: Hemel Hempstead Town (A) 0-6

53-54 PR: Oxford City (H) 0-5

54-55 PR: Bicester Town (A) 2-5

55-56 Q1: Slough Town (H) 0-3

56-57 PR: Banbury Spencer (H) 0-3

57-58 PR: Maidenhead United (H) 1-0
Q1: Chesham United (A) 1-5

58-59 PR: Maidenhead United (H) 0-2

59-60 PR: Maidenhead United (H) 1-1, (A) 1-3

60-61 Q1: Banbury Spencer (H) 4-1
Q2: Oxford City (A) 1-1, (H) 2-1
Q3: Chesham United (A) 2-1
Q4: Hitchin Town (A) 0-2

61-62 Q1: Huntley & Palmers (H) 2-0
Q2: Banbury Spencer (A) 1-4

64-65 Q1: Newbury Town (A) 0-2

65-66 Q1: Hemel Hempstead Town (A) 0-6

81-82 PR: Hendon (H) 1-2

82-83 PR: Aylesbury United (H) 3-2
Q1: St Albans City (A) 1-4

83-84 Q1: Wokingham Town (H) 0-3

84-85 PR: Baldock Town (H) 1-3

85-86 Q1: Tring Town (H) 0-1

86-87 PR: Clandown (A) 1-3

87-88 Q1: Bracknell Town (A) 2-3

88-89 PR: Havant Town (H) 4-2
Q1: Basingstoke Town (A) 1-3

89-90 Q1: Thame United (A) 3-0
Q2: Cwmbran Town (H) 0-0, (A) 4-3
Q3: Maidenhead United (H) 3-1
Q4: Slough Town (H) 0-3

90-91 Q1: Bournemouth (A) 1-2

91-92 PR: Bournemouth (A) 2-1
Q1: Thame United (A) 0-2

92-93 PR: Fleet Town (A) 2-1
Q1: Devizes Town (H) 4-0
Q2: Maidenhead United (H) 2-0
Q3: Bashley (H) 4-2
Q4: Merthyr Tydfil (H) 0-0, (A) 1-2

ABINGDON UNITED
Currently: Hellenic League

86-87 Q1: Stourbridge (A) 1-1, (H) 0-0, (A) 1-2

87-88 PR: Oxford City (H) 1-1, (A) 0-3

88-89 Q1: Hungerford Town (H) 1-2

89-90 PR: Newport IOW (H) 1-4

90-91 PR: Sholing Sports (A) 3-1
Q1: Farnborough Town (H) 0-1

91-92 PR: Buckingham Town (A) 0-1

92-93 PR: Poole Town (A) 1-0
Q1: Bemerton Heath Harlequins (H) 0-5

ACCRINGTON
Currently: Defunct

64-65 Q1: Horwich R.M.I. (A) 2-5

ACCRINGTON STANLEY
Currently: Defunct

45-46 R1: Chorley (A) 1-2, (H) 2-0 (*agg: 3-2*)
R2: Oldham Ath. (A) 1-2, (H) 3-1 (*agg: 4-3*)
R3: Manchester U. (H) 2-2, (A) 1-5 (*agg: 3-7*)

46-47 R1: Doncaster Rovers (A) 2-2, (H) 0-5

47-48 R1: Stockport County (A) 1-3

48-49 R1: Hull City (A) 1-3

49-50 R1: Hartlepools United (H) 0-1

50-51 R1: Wrexham (A) 0-1

51-52 R1: Chester (H) 1-2

52-53 R1: Horden Colliery Welfare (A) 2-1
R2: Mansfield Town (H) 0-2

53-54 R1: Blyth Spartans (A) 1-0
R2: Tranmere Rovers (H) 2-2, (A) 1-5

54-55 R1: Creswell Colliery (H) 7-1
R2: Millwall (A) 2-3

55-56 R1: Wrexham (H) 3-1
R2: Darlington (A) 1-0
R3: Liverpool (A) 0-2

56-57 R1: Morecambe (H) 4-1
R2: Oldham Athletic (H) 2-1
R3: Bournemouth & Boscombe Ath. (A) 0-2

57-58 R1: Wrexham (A) 1-0
R2: Carlisle United (A) 1-1, (H) 3-2
R3: Bristol City (H) 2-2, (A) 1-3

58-59 R1: Workington (H) 5-1
R2: Buxton (H) 6-1
R3: Darlington (H) 3-0
R4: Portsmouth (H) 0-0, (A) 1-4

59-60 R1: Mansfield Town (H) 1-2

60-61 R1: Barrow (H) 2-1
R2: Mansfield Town (H) 3-0
R3: Preston North End (A) 1-1, (H) 0-4

61-62 R1: Stockport County (A) 1-0
R2: Hartlepools United (A) 1-2

ACCRINGTON STANLEY '68
Currently: Northern Premier League

71-72 Q1: Morecambe (A) 0-2

72-73 Q1: Darwen (H) 1-1, (A) 4-2
Q2: Runcorn (H) 1-1, (A) 1-2

73-74 Q1: Barrow (A) 4-0
Q2: Netherfield (A) 1-2

74-75 PR: Bacup Borough (A) 3-3, (H) 4-1
Q1: Radcliffe Borough (H) 1-1, (A) 1-0
Q2: Chorley (H) 2-0
Q3: Horwich R.M.I. (A) 2-0
Q4: Altrincham (A) 0-3

75-76 Q1: Hyde United (H) 2-3

76-77 Q1: Bacup Borough (H) 5-0
Q2: Formby (H) 0-3

77-78 PR: Skelmersdale United (A) 3-0
Q1: Burscough (A) 2-2, (H) 0-1

78-79 PR: Lancaster City (H) 1-2

79-80 PR: Farsley Celtic (A) 2-0
Q1: Netherfield (A) 0-4

80-81 Q1: Darwen (H) 2-0
Q2: Fleetwood Town (H) 1-1, (A) 2-3

81-82 PR: South Liverpool (H) 2-1
Q1: Chorley (A) 0-0, (H) 0-0, (A) 0-2

82-83 Q1: Harrogate Town (H) 1-1, (A) 1-3

83-84 PR: Crook Town (H) 3-1
Q1: Willington (A) 1-1, (H) 3-0
Q2: Gateshead (H) 1-1, (A) 2-1
Q3: Bishop Auckland (A) 1-4

84-85 Q1: Ilkeston Town (H) 2-1
Q2: Witton Albion (A) 0-4

85-86 PR: Darwen (H) 2-0
Q1: Droylsden (H) 4-1
Q2: Runcorn (H) 1-1, (A) 1-9

86-87 PR: Lancaster City (H) 0-1

87-88 PR: Bridlington Town (A) 0-1

88-89 Q1: Seaham Red Star (A) 0-0, (H) 2-1
Q2: Billingham Synthonia (H) 1-1, (A) 1-5

89-90 PR: Atherton Laburnum R. (A) 1-1, (H) 5-2
Q1: Borrowash Victoria (H) 4-0
Q2: Mossley (A) 1-3

90-91 PR: Blackpool (Wren) Rovers (A) 4-2
Q1: West Auckland Town (H) 3-0
Q2: Blyth Spartans (H) 2-1
Q3: Gretna (H) 2-1
Q4: Fleetwood Town (H) 0-2

91-92 Q1: Prescot A.F.C. (A) 5-0
Q2: Knowsley United (H) 2-2, (A) 1-2

92-93 Q1: Hyde United (A) 5-1
Q2: Bradford Park Avenue (H) 2-0
Q3: Stalybridge Celtic (A) 2-1
Q4: Northallerton Town (H) 3-1
R1: Gateshead (H) 3-2
R2: Crewe Alex. (H - *at Blackburn Rvrs*) 1-6

Below: *Stanley's Ashley Hoskins gets in a cross against Crewe at Ewood Park. Photo: Paul Dennis.*

ACHILLES (IPSWICH)
Currently: Suffolk & Ipswich League

48-49 PR: Old Grammarians (Ipswich) (A) 9-1
Q1: Norwich C.E.Y.M.S. (A) 4-3
Q2: Gothic (A) 0-4

49-50 PR: Leiston (H - *played away*) 5-0
Q1: Gorleston (A) 1-5

ACTON TOWN
Currently: Defunct

46-47 EX: Twickenham (A) 2-1
PR: Wood Green Town (A) 0-4

47-48 EX: Edgware Town (H - *played away*) 0-9

48-49 EX: Wingate (H) 1-8

49-50 EX: Ruislip Manor (H - *played away*) 2-4

ADDLESTONE & WEYBRIDGE TOWN
Currently: Defunct * - As Addlestone F.C.

65-66 * Q1: Woking (A) 0-9

66-67 * Q1: Oxford City (A) 0-8

68-69 * Q1: Dorking (A) 2-1
Q2: Woking (A) 2-5

69-70 * Q1: Woking (A) 3-3, (H) 2-0
Q2: Wokingham Town (H) 0-1

70-71 * Q1: Dulwich Hamlet (A) 2-2, (H) 1-2

71-72 * Q1: Hemel Hempstead T. (A) 2-2, (H) 1-1, 4-1
Q2: Tilbury (A) 0-3

72-73 * Q1: Croydon Amateurs (H) 1-0
Q2: St Albans City (H) 0-1

73-74 * Q1: Boreham Wood (H) 1-3

74-75 * PR: Egham Town (A) 3-1
Q1: Wokingham Town (H) 0-0, (A) 1-1, 1-3

75-76 * Q1: Bye
Q2: Feltham (A) 6-2
Q3: Tooting & Mitcham United (A) 2-4

76-77 * Q1: Letchworth Garden City (A) 0-1

77-78 * Q1: Clapton (H) 0-1

78-79 * PR: Epsom & Ewell (A) 0-2

79-80 * PR: Egham Town (A) 2-0
Q1: Molesey (A) 3-2
Q2: Sutton United (H) 0-0, (A) 3-0
Q3: Welling United (A) 1-3

80-81 Q1: Boreham Wood (H) 2-2, (A) 2-0
Q2: Carshalton Athletic (H) 1-0
Q3: Maidenhead United (A) 0-0, (H) 5-0
Q4: Bideford (H) 3-0
R1: Brentford (H - *played away*) 2-2, (A) 0-2

81-82 Q1: Ruislip Manor (H) 3-1
Q2: Bognor Regis Town (A) 0-0, (H) 2-0
Q3: Fareham Town (H) 2-0
Q4: Taunton Town (H) 2-2, (A) 0-0, (A) 2-4

82-83 Q1: Ringmer (A) 1-2

83-84 PR: Kingsbury Town (A) 1-0
Q1: Cray Wanderers (H) 3-1
Q2: Hendon (H) 2-1
Q3: Harrow Borough (A) 0-1

84-85 PR: Letchworth Garden City (H) 7-0
Q1: Corinthian-Casuals (A - *played away*) 3-0
Q2: Welling United (A) 1-2

ALDERSHOT
Currently: Defunct

45-46 R1: Reading (A) 1-3, (H) 7-3 (*agg: 8-6*)
R2: Newport I.W. (H) 7-0, (A) 5-0 (*agg: 12-0*)
R3: Plymouth A. (H) 2-0, (A) 1-0 (*agg: 3-0*)
R4: Brighton (A) 0-3, (H) 1-4 (*agg: 1-7*)

46-47 R1: Cheltenham Town (H) 4-2
R2: Bournemouth & Boscombe Ath. (A) 2-4

47-48 R1: Bromsgrove Rovers (H) 2-0
R2: Swindon T. (H) 0-0, (A) 0-0, 0-2

48-49 R1: Ipswich Town (A) 3-0
R2: Chester (H) 1-0
R3: Gateshead (A) 1-3

49-50 R1: Weymouth (A) 2-2, (H) 2-3

50-51 R1: Bromley (H) 2-2, (A) 1-0
R2: Bournemouth & Boscombe Ath. (H) 3-0
R3: Bristol Rovers (A) 1-5

51-52 R1: Tonbridge (A) 0-0, (H) 3-2
R2: Buxton (A) 3-4

52-53 R1: Millwall (H) 0-0, (A) 1-7

53-54 R1: Wellington Town (H) 5-3
R2: Peterborough United (A) 1-2

54-55 R1: Chelmsford City (H) 3-1
R2: Hartlepools United (A) 0-4

55-56 R1: Yeovil T. (A) 1-1, (H) 1-1, 3-0
R2: Reading (A) 2-2, (H) 3-0
R3: Barnsley (H) 1-2

56-57 R1: Hereford United (A) 2-3

57-58 R1: Worcester City (H) 0-0, (A) 2-2, 3-2
R2: Coventry City (H) 4-1
R3: Portsmouth (A) 1-5

58-59 R1: Swindon Town (A) 0-5

59-60 R1: King's Lynn (A) 1-3

60-61 R1: Notts County (H) 2-0
R2: Colchester United (H) 3-1
R3: Shrewsbury (H) 1-1, (A) 2-2, 2-0
R4: Stoke City (A) 0-0, (H) 0-0, 0-3

61-62 R1: Tunbridge Wells United (H) 3-1
R2: Brentford (H) 2-2, (A) 0-2

62-63 R1: Brentford (H) 1-0
R2: Port Vale (A) 0-2

63-64 R1: Sutton United (A) 4-0
R2: Torquay United (A) 3-2
R3: Aston Villa (A) 0-0, (H) 2-1
R4: Swindon Town (H) 1-2

64-65 R1: Dartford (A) 1-1, (H) 1-0
R2: Reading (H) 1-3

65-66 R1: Wellingborough Town (H) 2-1
R2: Walsall (H) 0-2

66-67 R1: Torquay United (H) 2-1
R2: Reading (H) 1-0
R3: Brighton & Hove A. (H) 0-0, (A) 1-3

67-68 R1: Reading (A) 2-6

68-69 R1: Dartford (A) 1-3

69-70 R1: Margate (A) 7-2
R2: Bristol Rovers (H) 3-1
R3: Huddersfield Town (A) 1-1, (H) 3-1
R4: Carlisle United (A) 2-2, (H) 1-4

70-71 R1: Hendon (A) 2-0
R2: Bristol Rovers (H) 1-1, (A) 3-1
R3: Liverpool (A) 0-1

71-72 R1: Alvechurch (H) 4-2
R2: Reading (A) 0-1

72-73 R1: Southend United (A) 2-0
R2: Watford (A) 0-2

73-74 R1: Dagenham (A) 4-0
R2: Cambridge United (H) 1-2

74-75 R1: Brighton & Hove Albion (A) 1-3

75-76 R1: Wealdstone (H) 4-3
R2: Bishop's Stortford (H) 2-0
R3: Lincoln City (H) 1-2

76-77 R1: Portsmouth (H) 1-1, (A) 1-2

77-78 R1: Reading (A) 1-3

78-79 R1: Weymouth (H) 1-1, (A) 2-0
R2: Barking (A) 2-1
R3: Sheffield United (A) 0-0, (H) 1-0
R4: Swindon Town (H) 2-1
R5: Shrewsbury Town (H) 2-2, (A) 1-3

79-80 R1: Exeter City (H) 4-1
R2: Hereford United (A) 2-1
R3: Everton (A) 1-4

80-81 R1: Oxford United (A) 0-1

81-82 R1: Leytonstone-Ilford (H) 2-0
R2: Oxford United (H) 2-2, (A) 2-4

82-83 R1: Wimborne Town (H) 4-0
R2: Portsmouth (A) 3-1
R3: Swindon Town (A) 0-7

83-84 R1: Worcester City (H) 1-1, (A) 1-2

84-85 R1: Newport County (A) 1-1, (H) 4-0
R2: Burton Albion (H) 0-3

85-86 R1: Plymouth Argyle (A) 0-1

86-87 R1: Torquay United (H) 1-0
R2: Colchester United (H) 3-2
R3: Oxford United (H) 3-0
R4: Barnsley (H) 1-1, (A) 0-3

87-88 R1: Sutton United (A) 0-3

88-89 R1: Hayes (H) 1-0
R2: Bristol C. (H) 1-1, (A) 0-0, (H) 2-2, (A) 0-1

89-90 R1: Cambridge United (H) 0-1

90-91 R1: Tiverton Town (H) 6-2
R2: Maidstone United (H) 2-1
R3: West Ham (H - *played away*) 0-0, (A) 1-6

91-92 R1: Enfield (A) 0-1

Below: *Aldershot Football Club's last ever appearance in the F.A. Cup was an ignominious home defeat at the hands of Diadora League Isthmian League side Enfield on 16th November 1991. In this action their goalkeeper John Granville is under pressure. Photo: Eric Marsh.*

ALFORD UNITED

Currently: Defunct

49-50 EX: Skegness Town (H) 6-4
PR: Bourne Town (H) 3-3, (A) 3-5

51-52 Q1: Skegness Town (H) 1-3

52-53 Q1: Boston United (H) 4-5

54-55 Q1: Ashby Institute (H) 4-2
Q2: Skegness Town (H) 2-2, (A) 2-5

55-56 Q2: Grantham (H) 0-3

56-57 Q1: Barton Town (A) 1-0
Q2: Louth United (A) 1-1, (H) 2-1
Q3: Grantham (H) 1-2

57-58 Q1: Bourne Town (H) 1-0
Q2: Gainsborough Trinity (H) 2-1
Q3: Grantham (H) 1-0
Q4: Boston United (A) 0-4

58-59 PR: Boston United (A) 0-3

59-60 Q1: Gainsborough Trinity (A) 1-4

60-61 Q1: Holbeach United (A) 1-7

61-62 Q1: Ransome & Marles (A) 5-2
Q2: Skegness Town (A) 1-6

62-63 Q1: Holbeach United (H) 1-1, (A) 4-6

ALFRETON TOWN

Currently: Northern Premier League

60-61 Q1: Shirebrook Miners Welfare (A) *W/O*
Q2: Belper Town (H) 1-7

61-62 Q1: Shirebrook Miners Welfare (A) 8-1
Q2: Sutton Town (A) 0-5

62-63 Q1: Heanor Town (H) 1-0
Q2: Arnold St Mary's (H) 0-4

63-64 Q1: Belper Town (A) 3-5

64-65 Q1: Belper Town (A) 2-2, (H) 0-3

65-66 Q1: Heanor Town (A) 3-5

66-67 Q1: Macclesfield Town (A) 1-2

67-68 Q1: Matlock Town (H) 1-2

68-69 Q1: Matlock Town (H) 1-2

69-70 Q1: Sutton Town (H) 2-1
Q2: Wombwell Sporting (A) 1-1, (H) 2-1
Q3: Rawmarsh Welfare (H) 3-1
Q4: Goole Town (H) 3-0
R1: Barrow (H) 1-1, (A) 0-0, (*at Chesterfield*) 2-2
(*at Preston North End*) 0-2

70-71 Q1: Arnold (H) 3-1
Q2: Gainsborough Trinity (H) 1-2

71-72 Q1: Bilston (H) 4-0
Q2: Heanor Town (H) 3-1
Q3: Nuneaton Borough (H) 0-4

72-73 Q1: Belper Town (A) 1-1, (H) 4-1
Q2: Sutton Town (H) 3-0
Q3: Eastwood Town (A) 4-0
Q4: Nuneaton Borough (H) 0-2

73-74 Q1: Burton Albion (H) 3-1
Q2: Bilston (A) 2-0
Q3: Worksop Town (H) 2-1
Q4: Buxton (A) 2-2, (H) 2-1
R1: Blyth Spartans (H) 0-0, (A) 1-2

74-75 PR: Bedworth United (A) 1-0
Q1: Tamworth (H) 1-1, (A) 0-1

75-76 Q1: Gresley Rovers (H) 2-0
Q2: Bilston (A) 2-2, (H) 2-1
Q3: Tividale (A) 0-0, (H) 0-1

76-77 Q1: Belper Town (H) 2-0
Q2: Droylsden (H) 0-1

77-78 Q1: Leek Town (H) 0-1

78-79 PR: Mexborough Town (H) 2-5

79-80 PR: Denaby United (A) 2-0
Q1: Louth United (A) 2-2, (H) 4-2
Q2: Worksop Town (H) 3-1
Q3: Burton Albion (A) 0-2

80-81 Q1: Brigg Town (H) 2-1
Q2: Eastwood Town (H) 1-0
Q3: Northwich Victoria (A) 2-3

81-82 PR: Ashby Institute (H - *Matlock Town*) 5-0
Q1: Arnold (A) 2-1
Q2: Boston United (H - *played away*) 0-2

82-83 Q1: Shepshed Charterhouse (H) 0-4

83-84 PR: Ashton United (H) 0-1

84-85 PR: Eastwood Hanley (H) 4-2
Q1: Morecambe (A) 1-0
Q2: Southport (A) 1-1, (H) 3-0
Q3: Burscough (A) 2-2, (H) 2-3

85-86 Q1: Bourne Town (H) 6-0
Q2: Matlock Town (H) 2-0
Q3: Gresley Rovers (H) 0-1

86-87 Q1: Gainsborough Trinity (H) 0-0, (A) 1-2

87-88 PR: Formby (H) 3-0
Q1: Witton Albion (H) 4-2
Q2: Irlam Town (H) 2-0
Q3: Colwyn Bay (H) 1-1, (A) 0-1

88-89 PR: Bilston Town (A) 0-4

89-90 PR: Princes End United (A) 2-0
Q1: Rocester (H) 1-0
Q2: Boston United (A) 0-1

90-91 PR: Rushall Olympic (H) 2-2, (A) 0-3

91-92 PR: Sandwell Borough (A) 2-1
Q1: Hinckley Athletic (H) 1-0
Q2: Frickley Athletic (A) 1-4

92-93 PR: Oakham United (H) 2-1
Q1: Stafford Rangers (H) 0-0, (A) 0-3

ALMA SWANLEY

Currently: Kent League

85-86 Q1: Chelmsford City (A) 0-2

86-87 PR: Southall (H) 4-0
Q1: Yeading (A) 4-4, (H - *at Greenwich B.*) 0-1

87-88 PR: Feltham (A - *at Hounslow*) 0-5

90-91 PR: Purfleet (H) 1-2

92-93 PR: Three Bridges (A) 3-0
Q1: Bedfont (H) 1-0
Q2: Yeading (A) 1-7

ALMONDSBURY GREENWAY

Currently: (Almondsbury Town) Hellenic League

80-81 Q1: Barnstaple Town (H) 0-1

81-82 PR: Wellington (H) 1-1, (A) 0-3

ALNWICK TOWN

Currently: Northern League

48-49 EX: Shankhouse (A) 1-4

49-50 PR: Ashington (H) 2-4

50-51 EX: Newbiggin Central Welfare (H) 4-0
PR: Newburn (H) 10-2
Q1: Hexham Hearts (A) 1-2

51-52 Q1: Cramlington Welfare (H) 5-0
Q2: Shankhouse (H) 2-0
Q3: Blyth Spartans (A) 3-4

52-53 Q1: West Sleekburn (H) 4-1
Q2: Newburn (H) 0-1

53-54 Q1: Shankhouse (H) 9-0
Q2: Hexham Hearts (A) 2-3

54-55 PR: Shankhouse (A) 1-5

55-56 Q1: South Shields (A) 0-5

56-57 Q1: South Shields (A) 0-3

57-58 Q1: South Bank (H) 8-3
Q2: Newburn (A) 2-0
Q3: Easington Colliery Welfare (A) 4-6

58-59 Q1: Cockfield (H) 3-3, (A) 2-3

85-86 Q1: Bridlington Trinity (A) 0-1

86-87 PR: Guisborough Town (H) 1-0
Q1: Annfield Plain (A) 3-2
Q2: Easington Colliery (H) 0-3

87-88 PR: Durham C. (H) 1-1, (A) 1-1, (H) 0-0, (A) 2-1
Q1: Billingham Synthonia (A) 0-2

88-89 Q1: Guisborough Town (A) 0-3

89-90 PR: Peterlee Newtown (H) 1-1, (A) 2-1
Q1: Ashington (A) 5-0
Q2: Barrow (A) 1-3

90-91 Q1: Fleetwood Town (H) 0-5

91-92 PR: Chester-le-Street Town (H) 4-3
Q1: Brandon United (H) 1-1, (A) 1-0
Q2: Gateshead (A) 0-6

92-93 PR: Esh Winning (A) 0-0, (H) 2-1
Q1: Consett (H) 0-0, (A) 0-2

ALTON TOWN

Currently: Merged with Bass (Alton). Playing as Bass Alton Town in the Hampshire League

50-51 EX: Basingstoke Town (A) 2-1
PR: Shaftesbury (A) 5-1
Q1: Hamworthy (H) 9-0
Q2: Blandford United (H) 9-0
Q3: Dorchester (H) 2-2, (A) 2-2 *ab.*, (A) 0-1

51-52 Q1: Winchester City (A) 2-2, (H) 3-1
Q2: Basingstoke Town (A) 5-2
Q3: Newport Isle of Wight (A) 1-5

52-53 Q1: Ryde Sports (A) 4-3
Q2: Basingstoke Town (A) 0-2

53-54 Q1: Gosport Borough Athletic (H) 3-2
Q2: Cowes Isle of Wight (A) 0-5

57-58 Q1: Basingstoke Town (H) 2-3

58-59 Q1: Basingstoke Town (A) 2-2, (H) 3-2
Q2: Cowes Isle of Wight (A) 2-1
Q3: Andover (A) 2-3

59-60 Q1: Basingstoke Town (A) 2-5

60-61 Q1: Fareham Town (A) 3-4

61-62 Q1: Andover (A) 1-5

62-63 Q1: Newport Isle of Wight (H) 2-0
Q2: Newbury Town (A) 9-1
Q3: Andover (H) 1-1, (A) 1-4

63-64 Q1: Cowes Isle of Wight (A) 1-5

64-65 Q1: Andover (A) 1-4

65-66 Q1: Fareham Town (A) 3-7

66-67 Q1: Fleet Town (A) 1-6

67-68 Q1: Crawley Town (A) 0-1

69-70 Q1: East Grinstead (A) 3-1
Q2: Crawley Town (A) 0-1

70-71 Q1: Gosport Borough (A) 1-5

71-72 Q1: Cowes (H) 3-2
Q2: Fareham Town (H) 0-1

72-73 Q1: Farnborough Town (H) 2-0
Q2: Gosport Borough (H) 8-1
Q3: Basingstoke Town (H) 2-0
Q4: Devizes Town (H) 2-0
R1: Newport County (A) 1-5

73-74 Q1: Cowes (H) 2-0
Q2: Gosport Borough (A) 1-1, (H) 2-1
Q3: Bognor Regis Town (H) 1-2

74-75 Q1: Newport I.O.W. (H) 3-2
Q2: Gosport Borough (H) 2-2, (A) 1-0
Q3: Salisbury (H) 1-3

75-76 Q1: Horsham (H) 2-1
Q2: Basingstoke Town (A) 0-5

76-77 Q1: Andover (H) 1-0
Q2: Fareham Town (H) 0-0, (A) 0-1

77-78 PR: Yeovil Town (A) 2-2, (H) 0-4

78-79 PR: Burgess Hill Town (A) 3-1
Q1: Worthing (A) 1-4

79-80 PR: Didcot Town (A) 0-0, (H) 0-2

80-81 Q1: Andover (H) 0-3

ALTRINCHAM

Currently: Alliance Premier League

47-48 PR: Nantwich (A) 8-1
Q1: Hyde United (H) 4-1
Q2: Droylsden (H) 4-1
Q3: Witton Albion (A) 2-4

48-49 PR: Witton Albion (H) 0-4

Above: *Altrincham's historic 1-1 draw at Tottenham in 1979 - 'keeper Peter Eales punches clear under pressure from Peter Taylor. Photo: Press Association.*

49-50 PR: Mossley (H) 2-3

50-51 PR: Glossop (A) 4-1
Q1: Macclesfield Town (H) 3-1
Q2: Winsford United (H) 3-2
Q3: Hyde United (A) 1-1, (H) 1-2

51-52 Q1: Winsford United (A) 0-2

52-53 Q1: Bye
Q2: Stalybridge Celtic (A) 2-2, (H) 2-1
Q3: Winsford United (A) 1-0
Q4: Ashton United (A) 1-3

53-54 Q2: Stalybridge Celtic (H) 2-1
Q3: Winsford United (A) 1-3

54-55 Q1: Northwich Victoria (H) 3-2
Q2: Stalybridge Celtic (A) 1-2

55-56 PR: Northwich Victoria (A) 2-2, (H) 0-2

56-57 PR: Northwich Victoria (H) 4-3
Q1: Macclesfield Town (H) 1-3

57-58 PR: Lostock Gralam (A) 4-3
Q1: Macclesfield Town (H) 4-3
Q2: Ellesmere Port Town (H) 2-0
Q3: Witton Albion (A) 2-3

59-60 Q1: Droylsden (H) 7-1
Q2: Mossley (H) 3-2
Q3: Lytham (A) 1-1, (H) 3-0
Q4: Prescot Cables (A) 0-1

60-61 Q1: Earlestown (A) 3-4

61-62 PR: Earlestown (H) 6-1
Q1: Marine (H) 3-3, (A) 2-2, 1-0
Q2: Ashton United (A) 3-3, (H) 3-1
Q3: Wigan Athletic (H) 1-1, (A) 1-3

62-63 Q1: Marine (H) 1-0
Q2: Ashton United (H) 4-2
Q3: St Helens Town (A) 3-1
Q4: Rhyl (H) 2-3

63-64 Q1: Earlestown (A - *played home*) 10-0
Q2: Skelmersdale United (A) 3-0
Q3: South Liverpool (H) 3-0
Q4: Rhyl (H) 3-1
R1: Wrexham (H) 1-1, (A) 0-0, 0-3

64-65 Q1: Marine (H) 3-1
Q2: St Helens Town (H) 4-1
Q3: South Liverpool (H) 0-3

65-66 Q1: Prescot Town (A) 2-1
Q2: Marine (H) 4-0
Q3: Skelmersdale United (H) 4-1
Q4: Bangor City (A) 3-3, (H) 3-2
R1: Scarborough (H) 6-0
R2: Rochdale (A) 3-1
R3: Wolverhampton Wanderers (A) 0-5

66-67 Q4: Wigan Athletic (H) 2-4

67-68 Q4: Great Harwood (A) 1-0
R1: Grantham (A) 3-0
R2: Barrow (H) 1-2

68-69 Q4: Wigan Athletic (H) 2-0
R1: Crewe Alexandra (H) 0-1

69-70 Q4: Macclesfield Town (A) 0-2

70-71 Q4: Great Harwood (H) 1-1, (A) 1-2

71-72 Q1: Buxton (H) 1-0
Q2: Eastwood Hanley (H) 4-1
Q3: Nantwich (H) 1-1, (A) 4-1
Q4: Oswestry Town (A) 3-0
R1: Rossendale United (A) 0-1

72-73 Q1: Buxton (A) 0-0, (H) 4-1
Q2: Radcliffe Borough (H) 3-2
Q3: Ashton United (A) 3-1
Q4: Ellesmere Port Town (H) 1-1, (A) 2-1
R1: Notts County (H) 0-1

73-74 Q1: Glossop (H) 3-1
Q2: Nantwich (A) 3-0
Q3: Horwich R.M.I. (H) 4-0
Q4: Lancaster City (A) 1-1, (H) 1-0
R1: Hartlepool United (H) 2-0
R2: Blackburn Rovers (A) 0-0, (H) 0-2

74-75 Q4: Accrington Stanley (H) 3-0
R1: Scunthorpe United (A) 1-1, (H) 3-1
R2: Gateshead United (H) 3-0
R3: Everton (A) 1-1, (H - *at Man. Utd*) 0-2

75-76 R1: Halifax Town (A) 1-3

76-77 Q4: Grantham (H) 1-0
R1: Rotherham United (A) 0-5

77-78 Q4: Runcorn (A) 1-2

78-79 R1: Southport (H) 4-3
R2: Droylsden (A) 2-0
R3: Tottenham (A) 1-1, (H - *at Man. C.*) 0-3

79-80 R1: Crewe Alexandra (H) 3-0
R2: Rotherham United (A) 2-0
R3: Orient (H) 1-1, (A) 1-2

80-81 R1: Burscough (A) 2-1
R2: Scunthorpe United (A) 0-0, (H) 1-0
R3: Liverpool (A) 1-4

81-82 R1: Sheffield United (A) 2-2, (H) 3-0
R2: York City (A) 0-0, (H) 4-3
R3: Burnley (A) 1-6

82-83 R1: Rochdale (H) 2-1
R2: Huddersfield Town (H) 0-1

83-84 R1: Frickley Athletic (A) 1-0
R2: Darlington (A) 0-0, (H) 0-2

84-85 R1: Blackpool (A) 1-0
R2: Doncaster Rovers (H) 1-3

85-86 R1: Chorley (A) 2-0
R2: Blackpool (A) 2-1
R3: Birmingham City (A) 2-1
R4: York City (A) 0-2

86-87 R1: Frickley Athletic (A) 0-0, (H) 4-0
R2: Telford United (A) 0-1

87-88 R1: Wigan Athletic (H) 0-2

88-89 Q4: Macclesfield Town (A) 0-0, (H) 4-0
R1: Lincoln City (H) 3-2
R2: Halifax Town (H) 0-3

89-90 Q4: Tow Law Town (A) 0-2

90-91 Q1: Rhyl (H) 3-2
Q2: Maine Road (A) 1-0
Q3: Bangor City (H) 3-0
Q4: Macclesfield Town (A) 2-2, (H) 3-0
R1: Huddersfield Town (H) 1-2

91-92 Q4: Winsford United (A) 2-3

92-93 Q1: Curzon Ashton (H) 3-0
Q2: Sheffield (H) 3-1
Q3: Colwyn B. (A - *at Northwich*) 3-3, (H) 1-1, (H) 3-1
Q4: Gainsborough Trinity (A) 2-0
R1: Chester City (A) 1-1, (H) 2-0
R2: Port Vale (H) 1-4

ALVECHURCH

Currently: Defunct (reformed in West Midlands (Regional) League)

68-69 Q1: Redditch (H) 3-2
Q2: Worcester City (A) 0-0, (H) 0-1

69-70 Q1: Lye Town (A) 3-2
Q2: Stourbridge (A) 1-1, (H) 1-3

70-71 Q1: Bilston (A) 0-2

71-72 Q1: Moor Green (H) 4-0
Q2: Darlaston (A) 4-0
Q3: Atherstone Town (H) 3-0
Q4: Oxford City (H) 2-2, (A) 1-1, (*at Birmingham C.*) 1-1, (*at Oxford U.*) 0-0, (*at Oxford U.*) 0-0, (*at Aston Villa*) 1-0
R1: Aldershot (A) 2-4

72-73 Q1: Oldbury United (H) 3-1
Q2: Lye Town (H) 4-0
Q3: Nuneaton Borough (A) 0-2

73-74 Q1: Halesowen Town (H) 2-0
Q2: Bromsgrove Rovers (A) 2-1
Q3: Stourbridge (H) 3-2
Q4: Stafford Rangers (A) 1-1, (H) 2-0
R1: Exeter City (A) 1-0
R2: King's Lynn (H) 6-1
R3: Bradford City (A) 2-4

74-75 Q1: Sutton Coldfield Town (H) 3-0
Q2: Nuneaton Borough (H) 1-3

75-76 PR: Evesham United (H) 1-1, (A) 1-0
Q1: Welton Rovers (A) 3-1
Q2: Ton Pentre (H) 1-0
Q3: Barry Town (H) 3-1
Q4: Stafford Rangers (A) 1-1, (H) 1-2

76-77 Q1: Redditch United (A) 0-2

77-78 Q1: Kidderminster Harriers (H) 2-2, (A) 1-1, 0-1

78-79 PR: Brierley Hill Alliance (A) 2-0
Q1: Wolverton Town & B.R. (A) 2-1
Q2: Redditch United (A) 0-1

79-80 PR: Halesowen Town (A) 1-1, (H) 6-0
Q1: Lye Town (A) 1-1, (H) 1-2

80-81 Q1: Banbury United (H) 0-2

81-82 Q1: Evesham United (H) 2-0
Q2: Bedworth United (A) 1-0
Q3: Burton Albion (A) 0-2

82-83 Q1: Worcester City (H) 2-4

83-84 Q1: Racing Club Warwick (A) 2-2, (H) 5-1
Q2: Buckingham Town (A) 1-2

84-85 Q1: Boreham Wood (H) 4-1
Q2: V.S. Rugby (A) 0-5

85-86 Q1: Basildon United (A) 3-1
Q2: Braintree Town (A) 1-2

86-87 Q1: Bedworth United (H) 1-1, (A) 0-1

87-88 Q1: Redditch United (H) 1-1, (A) 3-1
Q2: Rothwell Town (A) 2-1
Q3: Atherstone United (A) 3-4

88-89 Q1: March Town United (A) 2-1
Q2: Bromsgrove Rovers (A) 2-2, (H) 3-3, (A) 0-2

89-90 Q1: Bedworth United (H) 0-1

90-91 PR: Desborough Town (H) 2-1
Q1: Wellingborough Town (H) 4-1
Q2: Witton Albion (H) 2-7

91-92 Q1: A.P.V. Peterborough City (A) 0-0, (H) 3-2
Q2: Malvern Town (H) 3-0
Q3: Corby Town (H) 2-0
Q4: Welling United (A) 1-5

92-93 Q1: V.S. Rugby (A) *withdrew*

AMBLE
Currently: (Amble Town) Northern Alliance

45-46 Q1: Newburn (A) 1-3

46-47 PR: Gosforth & Coxlodge (A) 2-6

47-48 EX: Annfield Plain (A) 2-5

48-49 PR: Blyth Spartans (H) 0-4

49-50 EX: Newbiggin Central Welfare (H) 0-2

50-51 PR: Hexham Hearts (H) 1-1 *then withdrew*

51-52 Q1: Shankhouse (H) 3-4

52-53 Q1: Ashington (H) 0-4

53-54 Q1: Newburn (H) 3-3 *then withdrew*

AMERSHAM TOWN
Currently: London Spartan League

50-51 EX: Wycombe Wanderers (H) 0-13

65-66 Q1: Wolverton Town & B.R. (A) 2-2, (H) 0-2

66-67 Q1: Hayes (A) 1-4

67-68 Q1: Dulwich Hamlet (A) 1-2

68-69 PR: Erith & Belvedere (H) 1-5

69-70 Q1: Cheshunt (A) 0-3

AMMANFORD TOWN
Currently: Merged with Ammanford Athletic
Playing as Ammanford A.F.C. in Welsh League

76-77 Q1: Evesham United (H) 1-0, *replay ordered (at Worcester City FC)* 1-5

AMPTHILL TOWN
Currently: South Midlands League

81-82 Q1: Hendon (H) 0-1

82-83 PR: Great Yarmouth Town (A) 0-2

83-84 PR: Rushden Town (H) 2-1
Q1: Thame United (A) 1-2

84-85 PR: Barton Rovers (H) 1-0
Q1: Oxford City (H) 1-4

86-87 Q1: Halesowen Town (A - *at Lye Town*) 0-4

ANDOVER
Currently: Wessex League

46-47 PR: Thornycroft Athletic (A) 0-2

47-48 EX: Pirelli General Cable Works (H) 7-0
PR: Salisbury Corinthians (A) 2-1
Q1: Poole Town (A) 1-2

48-49 PR: Weymouth (A) 0-3

49-50 EX: Ryde Sports (A) 0-1

50-51 EX: Ryde Sports (A) 1-2

51-52 PR: Westbury United (A) 1-5

52-53 PR: Frome Town (H) 2-3

53-54 PR: Melksham (A) 5-1
Q1: Salisbury (A) 1-2

54-55 Q1: Basingstoke Town (A) 1-3

55-56 Q1: Gosport Borough Athletic (H) 5-0
Q2: Winchester City (H) 2-1
Q3: Fareham Town (A) 2-2, (H) 0-2

56-57 Q1: Chichester City (A) 3-2
Q2: Bournemouth Gasworks Athletic (H) 3-2
Q3: Winchester City (A) 2-0
Q4: Cheltenham Town (A) 1-2

57-58 Q1: Chichester City (H) 2-3

58-59 Q1: Winchester City (H) 4-1
Q2: Fareham Town (H) 1-0
Q3: Alton Town (H) 3-2
Q4: Guildford City (A) 0-1

59-60 Q1: Gosport Borough Ath. (H) 0-0, (A) 1-0
Q2: Cowes Isle of Wight (A) 0-3

60-61 Q2: Fareham Town (A) 3-3, (H) 3-2
Q3: Chichester City (A) 1-2

61-62 Q1: Alton Town (H) 5-1
Q2: Basingstoke Town (H) 7-1
Q3: Cowes Isle of Wight (H) 2-1
Q4: Yeovil Town (A) 0-4

62-63 Q1: Cowes Isle of Wight (H) 4-1
Q2: Basingstoke Town (H) 2-1
Q3: Alton Town (A) 1-1, (H) 4-1
Q4: Hendon (A) 1-1, (H) 5-4
R1: Gillingham (H) 0-1

63-64 Q1: Newport Isle of Wight (H) 2-0
Q2: Cowes Isle of Wight (H) 1-1, (A) 2-4

64-65 Q1: Alton Town (H) 4-1
Q2: Fareham Town (A) 1-2

65-66 Q1: Warminster Town (A) 4-0
Q2: Salisbury (H) 0-3

66-67 Q1: Newbury Town (A) 3-0
Q2: Fareham Town (A) 0-1

67-68 Q1: Newport Isle of Wight (A) 3-4

68-69 PR: Selsey (A) 0-1

69-70 Q1: Newport I.O.W. (H) 4-1
Q2: Waterlooville (H) 2-1
Q3: Salisbury (H) 0-0, (A) 0-3

70-71 Q1: Bath City (H) 0-1

71-72 Q1: Melksham Town (A) 3-1
Q2: Basingstoke Town (H) 1-3

72-73 Q1: Dorchester Town (A) 1-1, (H) 2-1
Q2: Salisbury (H) 0-1

73-74 Q1: Bath City (A) 0-3

74-75 PR: Basingstoke Town (A) 0-1

75-76 Q1: Frome Town (H) 1-1, (A) 3-5

76-77 Q1: Alton Town (A) 0-1

77-78 Q1: Three Bridges (H) 2-0
Q2: Horsham (A) 2-3

78-79 PR: Newbury Town (H) 1-1, (A) 2-1
Q1: Yeovil Town (A) 0-4

79-80 PR: Gosport Borough (A) 1-2

80-81 Q1: Alton Town (A) 3-0
Q2: Poole Town (H) 0-2

81-82 Q1: Pagham (A - *played at home*) 1-2

82-83 PR: Wokingham Town (A) 1-6

83-84 Q1: A.F.C. Totton (H) 1-3

84-85 PR: Calne Town (H) 6-0
Q1: Fareham Town (A) 1-2

85-86 Q1: Hungerford Town (H) 1-3

86-87 PR: Sholing Sports (H) 1-0
Q1: Devizes Town (A) 2-5

87-88 PR: Melksham Town (A) 0-2

88-89 PR: Chippenham Town (A) 0-4

89-90 PR: Camberley Town (H) 2-2, (A) 5-1
Q1: Devizes Town (H) 2-0
Q2: Marlow (A) 2-3

90-91 PR: Croydon Athletic (A) 2-2, (H) 7-1
Q1: Horsham Y.M.C.A. (H) 3-0
Q2: Bromley (H) 2-0
Q3: Marlow (H) 0-1

91-92 Q1: Selsey (A) 1-2

92-93 PR: Ringmer (H) 5-0
Q1: Hampton (H) 0-6

ANNFIELD PLAIN
Currently: Wearside League

45-46 Q1: Ashington (H) 1-2

46-47 Q1: Newburn (H) 1-2

47-48 PR: Amble (H) 5-2
Q1: South Shields (H) 2-4

48-49 PR: Gosforth & Coxlodge (H) 2-1
Q1: Shankhouse (H) 7-1
Q2: Murton Colliery Welfare (A) 2-1
Q3: Blyth Spartans (A) 2-0
Q4: Billingham Synthonia Recreation (A) 1-2

49-50 PR: Blyth Spartans (A) 0-3

50-51 EX: S. Shields Ex-Schoolboys (H) 1-1, (A) 3-1
PR: Ashington (A) 1-3

51-52 Q1: Dawdon Colliery Welfare (A) 0-3

52-53 Q1: Boldon Colliery Welfare (H) 6-2
Q2: South Shields (A) 1-3

53-54 Q1: Dawdon Colliery Welfare (A) 4-1
Q2: Consett (A) 3-2
Q3: South Shields (H) 0-1

54-55 Q1: Seaham Colliery Welfare (A) 2-1
Q2: Boldon Colliery Welfare (A) 3-1
Q3: Easington Colliery Welfare (H) 5-1
Q4: Blyth Spartans (H) 1-2

55-56 Q1: Silksworth Colliery (A) 5-9

56-57 Q2: Consett (H) 4-2
Q3: Shotton Colliery Welfare (A) 3-2
Q4: Blyth Spartans (A) 0-3

57-58 Q1: North Shields (A) 1-4

58-59 Q1: Whitley Bay Ath. (H) 1-1, (A) 1-2

59-60 Q2: Bedlington Mechanics (H) 4-1
Q3: Scarborough (H) 2-3

60-61 Q1: West Auckland Town (A) 4-2
Q2: Shildon (H) 1-4

61-62 PR: South Bank (A) 2-4

62-63 Q1: Evenwood Town (A) 0-0, (H) 2-1
Q2: Whitley Bay (H) 2-2, (A) 1-0
Q3: Horden Colliery Welfare (A) 1-2

63-64 Q1: Stanley United (H) 1-2

64-65 Q1: Durham City (H) 2-0
Q2: Ryhope Coll. Welfare (A) 1-1, (H) 2-1
Q3: Tow Law Town (H) 3-2
Q4: Horden Colliery Welfare (H) 3-2
R1: Southport (A) 1-6

65-66 Q1: Whitley Bay Athletic (A) 0-11

66-67 Q1: Ferryhill Athletic (H) 2-2, (A) 2-2, 3-2
Q2: Murton Colliery Welfare (H) 4-0
Q3: Billingham Synthonia (A) 0-4

67-68 Q1: West Auckland Town (H) 2-2, (A) 0-2

68-69 Q1: Evenwood Town (A) 1-7

69-70 Q1: Consett (A) 3-2
Q2: Whitley Bay (A) 1-7

70-71 Q1: Gateshead (H) 1-5

71-72 Q1: Durham City (H) 0-5

72-73 Q1: Evenwood Town (A) 0-2

73-74 Q1: Murton Colliery Welfare (H) 0-1

76-77 Q1: Billingham Synthonia (H) 3-2
Q2: Netherfield (H) 1-1, (A) 0-6

77-78 PR: Wingate (A) 1-2

78-79 PR: Carlisle City (A) 2-4

79-80 PR: Crook Town (A) 2-5

80-81 Q1: Billingham Synthonia (H) 2-3

81-82 Q1: Durham City (H) 2-3

82-83 Q1: Wingate (A) 3-1
Q2: Bishop Auckland (A) 3-2
Q3: Barrow (A) 0-8

83-84 Q1: Gretna (A) 0-1

86-87 PR: Consett (A) 0-0, (H) 3-1
Q1: Alnwick Town (H) 2-3

87-88 PR: West Auckland Town (H) 0-4

88-89 PR: Denaby United (H) 1-0
Q1: Brandon United (A) 0-2

89-90 PR: Shotton Comrades (H) 2-3

90-91 PR: West Auckland Town (A) 2-4

91-92 Q1: North Shields (H) 0-4

92-93 PR: Hebburn (A) 1-1, (H) 5-1
Q1: Newcastle Blue Star (H) 0-1

A.P. LEAMINGTON
See Leamington

APPLEBY
Currently: Westmorland League

47-48 PR: Milnthorpe Corinthians (H) 3-9

48-49 PR: Florence & Ullcoats United (H) 3-6

APPLEBY FRODINGHAM ATH.

Currently: Merged with Winterton Rangers. Playing as Winterton Rangers in Northern Counties (East) League

47-48 EX: Dinnington Athletic (H) 4-1
PR: Maltby Main (A) 4-1
Q1: Denaby United (A) 1-4

48-49 EX: Laceby (H) 2-4

49-50 EX: Brigg Town (H) 1-1, (A) 1-4

50-51 PR: Farsley Celtic (A) 0-1

76-77 Q1: Bridlington Town (H) 5-3
Q2: Goole Town (H) 0-0, (A) 0-1

77-78 PR: Winterton Rangers (A) 1-0
Q1: Bridlington Trinity (A) 2-1
Q2: Frickley Athletic (A) 2-1
Q3: Brigg Town (H) 2-2, (A) 2-1
Q4: Mossley (H) 0-2

78-79 PR: Eastwood Town (H) 1-2

79-80 PR: Bridlington Trinity (A) 0-6

80-81 Q1: Ashby Institute (H) 5-0
Q2: Worksop Town (H) 0-2

81-82 PR: Buxton (H) 2-2, (A) 0-3

82-83 Q1: Gainsborough Tr. (A) 2-2, (H) 0-0, (A) 1-2

83-84 PR: Wren Rovers (A) 2-3

84-85 PR: Glossop (H) 2-0
Q1: Horwich R.M.I. (A) 0-3

APSLEY

Currently: Merged with Hemel Hempstead United Playing as Hemel Hempstead in Isthmian League
See also Hemel Hemstead

46-47 PR: St Albans City (A) 1-5

A.P.V. PETERBOROUGH CITY

See Peterborough City

ARLESEY TOWN

Currently: South Midlands League

46-47 PR: Biggleswade Town (H) 1-2

47-48 PR: Leighton United (H) 2-0
Q1: Bedford Town (A) 1-2

48-49 EX: Bedford Avenue (H) 5-2
PR: Hitchin Town (A) 0-0, (H) 2-3

49-50 EX: Huntingdon United (H) 4-5

50-51 EX: Letchworth Town (A) 2-3

84-85 PR: Cheshunt (H) 2-2, (A) 1-0
Q1: Corby Town (A) 1-2

85-86 Q1: Aylesbury United (H) 1-2

86-87 Q1: Dudley Town (A - *at Hednesford*) 2-5

87-88 PR: Chalfont St Peter (A) 1-1, (H) 1-0
Q1: Buckingham Town (H) 0-4

88-89 PR: Hoddesdon Town (H) 1-1, (A) 3-1
Q1: Metropolitan Police (A) 1-1, (H) 2-0
Q2: Wealdstone (A) 0-1

89-90 Q1: Lowestoft Town (A) 1-1, (H) 0-4

90-91 PR: Walthamstow Pennant (H) 0-4

91-92 PR: Clapton (H) 0-1

92-93 Q1: Shepshed Albion (H) 0-1

ARMITAGE

Currently: Defunct (reformed in Southern League)

75-76 Q1: Leek Town (H) 0-3

76-77 Q1: Bedworth United (H) 2-1
Q2: Darlaston (H) 1-1, (A) 0-1

80-81 Q1: Belper Town (H) 1-2

81-82 Q1: Nantwich Town (H) 0-2

82-83 Q1: Willenhall Town (H) 3-2
Q2: Belper Town (H) 1-1, (A) 1-0
Q3: Grantham (A) 1-3

83-84 PR: Ely City (A) 2-3

84-85 Q1: Witton Albion (H) 0-4

85-86 PR: Leek Town (A) 0-0, (H) 0-2

86-87 Q1: Worksop Town (A) 0-7

ARMTHORPE WELFARE

Currently: Northern Counties (East) League

47-48 EX: Matlock Town (H) 3-1
PR: Norton Woodseats (H) 1-4

48-49 EX: South Kirkby Colliery (H) 2-5

49-50 EX: Farsley Celtic (H) 4-5

50-51 EX: Ashby Institute (A) 1-8

85-86 Q1: Burscough (A) 1-1, (H) 0-1

86-87 PR: Curzon Ashton (A) 2-2, (H) 4-1
Q1: Ashton United (H) 2-1
Q2: St Helens Town (H) 1-1, (A) 1-0
Q3: Chorley (H) 0-2

87-88 PR: Guisborough Town (A) 0-2

88-89 PR: Darlington Cleveland B. (H) 3-1
Q1: Fleetwood Town (H) 2-2, (A) 0-5

89-90 PR: Sheffield (A) 0-1

90-91 PR: Sheffield (H) 3-0
Q1: Southport (H) 1-2

91-92 PR: Vauxhall GM (H) 1-1, (A) 2-1
Q1: Heanor Town (A) 2-0
Q2: Eastwood Hanley (A) 2-3

92-93 PR: Brandon United (H) 2-0
Q1: Billingham Town (H) 2-2, (A) 0-2

ARNOLD

Currently: Merged with Arnold Kingswell
Playing as Arnold Town in Northern Co's (East) Lge
See also Arnold Town
* - As Arnold St Mary's

61-62 * Q1: Matlock Town (H) 1-5

62-63 * Q1: Matlock Town (H) 3-2
Q2: Alfreton Town (A) 4-0
Q3: Buxton (A) 3-6

63-64 * Q1: Matlock Town (A) 1-4

64-65 Q1: Sutton United (A) 2-2, (H) 2-0
Q2: Matlock Town (A) 3-1
Q3: Belper Town (A) 3-3, (H) 1-0
Q4: Corby Town (H) 0-2

65-66 Q1: Matlock T. (H) 1-1, (A) 2-2, (H) 1-2

66-67 Q1: Burton Albion (A) 0-2

67-68 Q1: Heanor Town (H) 3-0
Q2: Atherstone Town (H) 2-1
Q3: Long Eaton United (H) 1-0
Q4: Stourbridge (H) 4-2
R1: Bristol Rovers (H) 0-3

68-69 Q1: Gresley Rovers (A) 0-1

69-70 Q1: Bedworth United (A) 0-0, (H) 6-1
Q2: Rugby Town (H) 0-3

70-71 Q1: Alfreton Town (A) 1-3

71-72 Q1: Brigg Town (H) 2-0
Q2: Eastwood Town (H) 2-4

72-73 Q1: Eastwood Town (A) 3-3, (H) 0-5

73-74 Q1: Matlock Town (H) 1-1, (A) 4-3
Q2: Worksop Town (A) 0-1

74-75 Q1: Ilkeston Town (H) 0-0, (A) 1-0
Q2: Enderby Town (H) 0-0, (A) 0-1

75-76 Q1: Long Eaton United (H) 2-1
Q2: Darlaston (A) 1-0
Q3: Macclesfield Town (A) 1-3

76-77 Q1: Atherstone Town (H) 1-0
Q2: Hednesford Town (H) 0-0, (A) 0-3

77-78 PR: Spalding United (A) 3-2
Q1: Chatteris Town (A) 6-1
Q2: March Town United (A) 8-3
Q3: Boston (H) 2-0
Q4: Telford United (H) 3-0
R1: Port Vale (H) 0-0, (A) 2-5

78-79 PR: Bourne Town (A) 4-1
Q1: Wellingborough Town (A) 1-1, (H) 2-1
Q2: Hinckley Athletic (A) 0-1

79-80 Q1: Worksop Town (H) 2-3

80-81 Q1: Barton Town (H) 0-1

81-82 Q1: Alfreton Town (H) 1-2

82-83 PR: Hinckley Athletic (H) 0-1

83-84 Q1: Bilston (H) 1-2

84-85 PR: Ilkeston Town (H) 1-4

85-86 PR: Shifnal T. (H - *at Eastwood Town*) 4-0
Q1: Tividale (H) 6-1
Q2: Witton Albion (H) 0-2

86-87 PR: Brigg Town (A) 4-5

87-88 PR: Hednesford T. (H - *played away*) 1-0
Q1: Eastwood Town (A) 2-1
Q2: Matlock Town (H) 2-3

88-89 PR: Bootle (H - *played away*) 1-0
Q1: Northwich Victoria (A) 0-5

ARNOLD TOWN

Currently: Northern Counties (East) League
See also Arnold

89-90 Q1: Belper Town (A) 2-2, (H) 3-1
Q2: Southport (A) 1-2

90-91 PR: Wednesfield (H) 1-1, (A) 0-1

91-92 PR: Belper Town (H - *played away*) 0-2

92-93 PR: Liversedge (H - *at Kimberley Town*) 4-0
Q1: Worksop Town (A) 3-5

ARSENAL

Currently: F.A. Premier League

45-46 R3: West Ham (A) 0-6, (H) 1-0 (*agg: 1-6*)

46-47 R3: Chelsea (A) 1-1, (H) 1-1, 0-2

47-48 R3: Bradford (Park Avenue) (H) 0-1

48-49 R3: Tottenham Hotspur (H) 3-0
R4: Derby County (A) 0-1

49-50 R3: Sheffield Wednesday (H) 1-0
R4: Swansea Town (H) 2-1
R5: Burnley (H) 2-0
R6: Leeds United (H) 1-0
SF: Chelsea (*both at Tottenham*) 2-2, 1-0
F: Liverpool (*at Wembley*) 2-0

50-51 R3: Carlisle United (H) 0-0, (A) 4-1
R4: Northampton Town (H) 3-2
R5: Manchester United (A) 0-1

51-52 R3: Norwich City (A) 5-0
R4: Barnsley (H) 4-0
R5: Leyton Orient (A) 3-0
R6: Luton Town (A) 3-2
SF: Chelsea (*both at Tottenham*) 1-1, 3-0
F: Newcastle United (*at Wembley*) 0-1

52-53 R3: Doncaster Rovers (H) 4-0
R4: Bury (H) 6-2
R5: Burnley (A) 2-0
R6: Blackpool (H) 1-2

53-54 R3: Aston Villa (H) 5-1
R4: Norwich City (H) 1-2

54-55 R3: Cardiff City (H) 1-0
R4: Wolverhampton Wanderers (A) 0-1

55-56 R3: Bedford Town (H) 2-2, (A) 2-1
R4: Aston Villa (H) 4-1
R5: Charlton Athletic (A) 2-0
R6: Birmingham City (H) 1-3

56-57 R3: Stoke City (H) 4-2
R4: Newport County (A) 2-0
R5: Preston North End (A) 3-3, (H) 2-1
R6: West Bromwich Albion (A) 2-2, (H) 1-2

57-58 R3: Northampton Town (A) 1-3

58-59 R3: Bury (A) 1-0
R4: Colchester United (A) 2-2, (H) 4-0
R5: Sheffield United (H) 2-2, (A) 0-3

59-60 R3: Rotherham Utd (A) 2-2, (H) 1-1, 0-2

60-61 R3: Sunderland (A) 1-2

61-62 R3: Bradford City (H) 3-0
R4: Manchester United (A) 0-1

62-63 R3: Oxford United (H) 5-1
R4: Sheffield Wednesday (H) 2-0
R5: Liverpool (H) 1-2

Above: *George Graham shoots past Ray Clemence to score Arsenal's first goal in their 2-1 victory over Liverpool in the 1971 final. The win completed a League & Cup double for the Gunners. Photo: Colorsport.*

63-64 R3: Wolverhampton Wanderers (H) 2-1
R4: West Bromwich Albion (A) 3-3, (H) 2-0
R5: Liverpool (H) 0-1

64-65 R3: Darlington (A) 2-0
R4: Peterborough United (A) 1-2

65-66 R3: Blackburn Rovers (A) 0-3

66-67 R3: Bristol Rovers (A) 3-0
R4: Bolton Wanderers (A) 0-0, (H) 3-0
R5: Birmingham City (A) 0-1

67-68 R3: Shrewsbury Town (A) 1-1, (H) 2-0
R4: Swansea Town (A) 1-0
R5: Birmingham City (H) 1-1, (A) 1-2

68-69 R3: Cardiff City (A) 0-0, (H) 2-0
R4: Charlton Athletic (H) 2-0
R5: West Bromwich Albion (A) 0-1

69-70 R3: Blackpool (H) 1-1, (A) 2-3

70-71 R3: Yeovil Town (A) 3-0
R4: Portsmouth (A) 1-1, (H) 3-2
R5: Manchester City (H) 2-1
R6: Leicester City (A) 0-0, (H) 1-0
SF: Stoke (*at Sheff. W.*) 2-2, (*at Aston V.*) 2-0
F: Liverpool (*at Wembley*) 2-1

71-72 R3: Swindon Town (A) 2-0
R4: Reading (A) 2-1
R5: Derby (A) 2-2, (H) 0-0, (*at Leicester*) 1-0
R6: Orient (A) 1-0
SF: Stoke (*at Aston V.*) 1-1, (*at Everton*) 2-1
F: Leeds United (*at Wembley*) 0-1

72-73 R3: Leicester City (H) 2-2, (A) 2-1
R4: Bradford City (H) 2-0
R5: Carlisle United (A) 2-1
R6: Chelsea (A) 2-2, (H) 2-1
SF: Sunderland (*at Sheffield Wednesday*) 1-2
TP: Wolverhampton Wanderers (H) 1-3

73-74 R3: Norwich City (A) 1-0
R4: Aston Villa (H) 1-1, (A) 0-2

74-75 R3: York City (H) 1-1, (A) 3-1
R4: Coventry City (A) 1-1, (H) 3-0
R5: Leicester City (H) 0-0, (A) 1-1, 1-0
R6: West Ham United (H) 0-2

75-76 R3: Wolverhampton Wanderers (A) 0-3

76-77 R3: Notts County (A) 1-0
R4: Coventry City (H) 3-1
R5: Middlesbrough (A) 1-4

77-78 R3: Sheffield United (A) 5-0
R4: Wolverhampton Wanderers (H) 2-1
R5: Walsall (H) 4-1
R6: Wrexham (A) 3-2
SF: Orient (*at Chelsea*) 3-0
F: Ipswich Town (*at Wembley*) 0-1

78-79 R3: Sheff. W. (H) 1-1, (A) 1-1, (*at Leicester*) 2-2, (*at Leicester*) 3-3, (*at Leicester*) 2-0
R4: Notts County (H) 2-0
R5: Nottingham Forest (A) 1-0
R6: Southampton (A) 1-1, (H) 2-0
SF: Wolverhampton W. (*at Aston Villa*) 2-0
F: Manchester United (*at Wembley*) 3-2

79-80 R3: Cardiff City (A) 0-0, (H) 2-1
R4: Brighton & Hove Albion (H) 2-0
R5: Bolton Wanderers (A) 1-1, (H) 3-0
R6: Watford (A) 2-1
SF: Liverpool (*at Sheff W.*) 0-0, (*at Aston Villa*) 1-1, (*at Aston Villa*) 1-1, (*at Coventry*) 1-0
F: West Ham United (*at Wembley*) 0-1

80-81 R3: Everton (A) 0-2

81-82 R3: Tottenham Hotspur (A) 0-1

82-83 R3: Bolton Wanderers (H) 2-1
R4: Leeds United (H) 1-1, (A) 1-1, (H) 2-1
R5: Middlesbrough (A) 1-1, (H) 3-2
R6: Aston Villa (H) 2-0
SF: Manchester United (*at Aston Villa*) 1-2

83-84 R3: Middlesbrough (A) 2-3

84-85 R3: Hereford United (A) 1-1, (H) 7-2
R4: York City (A) 0-1

85-86 R3: Grimsby Town (A) 4-3
R4: Rotherham United (H) 5-1
R5: Luton Town (A) 2-2, (H) 0-0, (A) 0-3

86-87 R3: Reading (A) 3-1
R4: Plymouth Argyle (H) 6-1
R5: Barnsley (H) 2-0
R6: Watford (H) 1-3

87-88 R3: Millwall (H) 2-0
R4: Brighton & Hove Albion (A) 2-1
R5: Manchester United (H) 2-1
R6: Nottingham Forest (H) 1-2

88-89 R3: West Ham United (A) 2-2, (H) 0-1

89-90 R3: Stoke City (A) 1-0
R4: Queens Park Rangers (H) 0-0, (A) 0-2

90-91 R3: Sunderland (H) 2-1
R4: Leeds (H) 0-0, (A) 1-1, (H) 0-0, (A) 2-1
R5: Shrewsbury Town (A) 1-0
R6: Cambridge United (H) 2-1
SF: Tottenham Hotspur (*at Wembley*) 1-3

91-92 R3: Wrexham (A) 1-2

92-93 R3: Yeovil Town (A) 3-1
R4: Leeds United (H) 2-2, (A) 3-2
R5: Nottingham Forest (H) 2-0
R6: Ipswich Town (A) 4-2
SF: Tottenham Hotspur (*at Wembley*) 1-0
F: Sheff. Wed. (*both at Wembley*) 1-1, 2-1

ARUNDEL

Currently: Sussex County League

50-51 PR: Bognor Regis Town (H) 1-0
Q1: Hastings United (H) 0-2

54-55 PR: Wigmore Athletic (H) 4-0
Q1: Horsham (A) 0-2

58-59 PR: Bexhill Town (A) 3-2
Q1: Newhaven (H) 5-3
Q2: Horsham (A) 1-5

59-60 PR: Littlehampton Town (A) 2-1
Q1: Lancing Athletic (A) 3-2
Q2: Hastings United (H) 2-5

60-61 Q1: Crawley Town (H) 3-0
Q2: Littlehampton Town (A) 2-3

69-70 Q1: Southwick (A) 1-2

70-71 Q1: Ringmer (A) 2-5

71-72 Q1: Bognor Regis Town (H) 1-0
Q2: Chichester City (H) 0-0, (A) 1-1, 2-7

72-73 Q1: Eastbourne Town (A) 5-0
Q2: Haywards Heath (H) 1-2

73-74 Q1: Newport I.O.W. (H) 0-2

74-75 PR: Burgess Hill Town (A) 2-2, (H) 1-1, 0-1

75-76 PR: Guildford & Dorking United (A) 0-7

78-79 Q1: Bognor Regis Town (H) 2-3

79-80 PR: Epsom & Ewell (A) 1-1, (H) 0-1

80-81 PR: Kingstonian (H) 0-2

81-82 PR: Wick (H) 1-4

82-83 PR: Dorking Town (A) 1-2

83-84 PR: Eastbourne United (A) 0-1

84-85 Q1: Worthing (H) 2-2, (A) 1-4

85-86 Q1: Basingstoke Town (H) 1-3

86-87 PR: Ringmer (H) 0-0, (A) 3-0 (*ab. in ET*), (A) 3-0
Q1: Camberley Town (A) 1-0
Q2: Herne Bay (H) 1-3

87-88 PR: Epsom & Ewell (A) 0-4

88-89 PR: Whyteleafe (A) 0-6

89-90 PR: Chertsey Town (A) 1-3

90-91 PR: Chatham Town (H) 2-3

91-92 PR: Canterbury City (A) 0-1

92-93 PR: Croydon Athletic (A) 3-7

ASHBY INSTITUTE

Currently: Defunct

49-50 EX: Winterton Rangers (A) 4-1
PR: Bentley Colliery (A) 1-3

50-51 EX: Armthorpe Welfare (H) 8-1
PR: Thorne Colliery (H) 2-1
Q1: Brigg Town (H) 0-3

51-52 PR: Skegness Town (H) 3-6

52-53 PR: Brigg Town (H) 2-3

53-54 Q1: Grantham (A) 2-2, (H) 2-1
Q2: Brigg Town (H) 4-3
Q3: Boston United (H) 2-3

54-55 Q1: Alford United (A) 2-4

55-56 Q1: Grantham (A) 2-4

56-57 Q1: Louth United (H) 0-0, (A) 0-5

57-58 Q1: Brigg Town (H) 2-5

58-59 Q1: Brigg Town (A) 1-3

59-60 Q1: Brigg Town (A) 1-1, (H) 1-5

68-69 Q1: Selby Town (H) 0-3

69-70 Q1: Bridlington Trinity (H) 1-0
Q2: Scarborough (H) 0-2

70-71 Q1: Frickley Colliery Athletic (A) 0-1

71-72 Q1: Scarborough (H) 0-6

72-73 Q1: Bridlington Trinity (A) 1-2

73-74 Q1: Frickley Colliery (H) 0-0, (A) 1-2

74-75 Q1: Worksop Town (H) 0-1

75-76 Q1: Mexborough Town (H) 0-1

77-78 Q1: Gainsborough Trinity (A) 0-1

78-79 Q1: Grantham (A) 3-5

79-80 PR: Eastwood Town (A) 1-3

80-81 Q1: Appleby Frodingham (A) 0-5

81-82 PR: Alfreton Town (A - *at Matlock Town*) 0-5

ASHFORD TOWN

Currently: Southern League
* - As Ashford F.C.

46-47 * PR: Whitstable (A) 10-3
Q1: Maidstone United (A) 5-3
Q2: Gravesend & Northfleet (H) 1-1, (A) 2-3

47-48 * PR: Whitstable (H) 4-1
Q1: Gravesend & Northfleet (A) 0-4

48-49 * EX: Woolwich Poly (A - *played home*) 2-0
PR: Whitstable (A) 1-0
Q1: Ramsgate Athletic (A) 0-4

49-50 * EX: Sheppey United (A) 0-1

50-51 * EX: Margate (A) 2-1
PR: Whitstable (A) 2-0
Q1: Betteshanger Colliery Welfare (A) 1-2

51-52 PR: Hastings United (A) 3-1
Q1: Redhill (A) 3-2
Q2: Eastbourne (A) 2-2, (H) 4-0
Q3: Tonbridge (H) 1-1, (A) 0-4

52-53 PR: Newhaven (A) 4-2
Q1: Hastings United (H) 1-3

53-54 Q1: East Grinstead (H) 4-0
Q2: Lancing Athletic (A) 3-1
Q3: Hastings United (A) 1-2

54-55 PR: Deal Town (A) 2-0
Q1: Snowdown Coll. Welfare (H) 1-1, (A) 0-5

55-56 PR: Tooting & Mitcham United (H) 1-0
Q1: Ramsgate Athletic (H) 2-5

56-57 PR: Whitstable (H) 3-1
Q1: Canterbury City (H) 1-2

57-58 PR: Gravesend & Northfleet (A) 1-3

58-59 PR: Betteshanger Colliery Welfare (H) 10-1
Q1: Snowdown Colliery Welfare (H) 6-0
Q2: Whitstable (A) 2-1
Q3: Canterbury City (H) 1-1, (A) 4-2
Q4: Hastings United (A) 1-1, (H) 2-1
R1: Crystal Palace (H) 0-1

59-60 Q1: Deal Town (A) 1-0
Q2: Folkestone Town (H) 1-0
Q3: Betteshanger Colliery Welfare (H) 3-0
Q4: Gravesend & Northfleet (A) 2-1
R1: Brentford (A) 0-5

60-61 Q4: Margate (H) 1-1, (A) 2-1
R1: Gillingham (H) 1-2

61-62 Q4: Dover (H) 3-1
R1: Wycombe Wanderers (A) 0-0, (H) 3-0
R2: Queens Park Rangers (H) 0-3

62-63 Q4: Margate (A) 0-2

63-64 Q4: Folkestone Town (A) 0-3

64-65 Q1: Sheppey United (A) 1-0
Q2: Deal Town (H) 2-2, (A) 2-4

65-66 Q1: Tunbridge Wells United (A) 1-4

66-67 Q1: Leytonstone (A) 2-2, (H) 4-0
Q2: Dulwich Hamlet (A) 4-1
Q3: Margate (H) 1-0
Q4: Guildford City (A) 1-1, (H) 2-0
R1: Cambridge City (H) 4-1
R2: Swindon Town (A) 0-5

67-68 Q4: Wimbledon (A) 0-3

68-69 Q1: Maidstone United (A) 2-1
Q2: Dover (A) 5-2
Q3: Canterbury City (H) 3-4

69-70 Q1: Dover (H) 0-0, (A) 4-2
Q2: Maidstone United (H) 1-0
Q3: Canterbury City (H) 1-1, (A) 4-1
Q4: Walton & Hersham (H) 0-1

70-71 Q1: Herne Bay (A) 1-2

71-72 Q1: Bexhill Town (H) 2-0
Q2: Tonbridge (H) 3-1
Q3: Dover (H) 0-2

72-73 Q1: Chatham Town (A) 2-0
Q2: Herne Bay (H) 6-0
Q3: Dover (A) 2-1
Q4: Guildford City (H) 3-4

73-74 Q1: Eastbourne United (H) 4-0
Q2: Maidstone United (A) 1-1, (H) 0-2

74-75 PR: Deal Town (A) 4-0
Q1: Sittingbourne (H) 0-0, (A) 2-1
Q2: Dover (H) 1-0
Q3: Canterbury City (A) 2-2, (H) 4-0
Q4: Hillingdon Borough (A) 2-1
R1: Walsall (H) 1-3

75-76 Q1: Lewes (H) 2-1
Q2: Crawley Town (A) 1-4

76-77 Q1: Canterbury City (H) 1-0
Q2: Hastings United (H) 0-1

77-78 PR: Whitstable Town (A) 1-0
Q1: Lewes (A) 0-1

78-79 PR: Eastbourne United (A) 0-1

79-80 PR: Peacehaven & Telscombe (A) 0-0, (H) 2-1
Q1: Three Bridges (A) 2-0
Q2: Croydon (H) 0-2

80-81 Q1: Corinthian-Casuals (H) 4-1
Q2: Crawley Town (H) 3-0
Q3: Epsom & Ewell (A) 0-1

81-82 Q1: Hastings Town (H) 1-0
Q2: Deal Town (A) 2-1
Q3: Dover (A) 1-2

82-83 PR: Sheppey United (H) 0-2

83-84 PR: Beckenham Town (A) 3-1
Q1: Deal Town (H) 5-0
Q2: Hailsham Town (A) 3-1
Q3: Gravesend & Northfleet (A) 1-1, (H) 3-2
Q4: Barking (A) 0-3

84-85 Q1: Lewes (H) 1-2

85-86 PR: Faversham Town (H) 5-1
Q1: Hythe Town (A) 0-1

86-87 PR: Steyning Town (H) 1-0
Q1: Portfield (A) 7-1
Q2: Southwick (H) 0-0, (A) 0-1

87-88 Q1: Bromley (A) 2-5

88-89 Q1: Dorking (H) 2-1
Q2: Hastings Town (H) 2-1
Q3: Dover Athletic (A) 0-3

89-90 Q1: Ruislip Manor (A) 3-1
Q2: Erith & Belvedere (H) 0-1

90-91 PR: Leatherhead (H) 3-1
Q1: Dover Athletic (A) 0-1

91-92 PR: Whyteleafe (A) 0-2

92-93 PR: Wick (A) 1-1, (H) 3-1
Q1: Faversham Town (H) 1-1, (A) 2-0
Q2: Windsor & Eton (H) 2-2, (A) 3-2
Q3: Deal Town (H) 3-1
Q4: Slough Town (H) 1-2

ASHFORD TOWN (MIDDX)

Currently: Combined Counties League

92-93 PR: Rayners Lane (A) 2-2, (H) 0-1

ASHINGTON

Currently: Northern League

45-46 Q1: Annfield Plain (A) 2-1
Q2: Consett (H) 1-1, (A) 0-3

46-47 Q1: Murton Colliery Welfare (A) 3-1
Q2: Newburn (A) 3-3, (H) 6-1
Q3: Crook Colliery Welfare (H) 7-1
Q4: North Shields (A) 1-1, (H) 1-3

47-48 Q1: West Stanley (H - *played home*) 4-3
Q2: South Shields (A) 1-3

48-49 PR: West Stanley (A) 1-0
Q1: Blyth Spartans (A) 1-2

49-50 EX: Wardley Welfare (A - *played home*) 5-2
PR: Alnwick Town (A) 4-2
Q1: Heaton Stannington (A) 2-3

50-51 PR: Annfield Plain (H) 3-1
Q1: West Stanley (H) 2-1
Q2: Hexham Hearts (H) 0-0, (A) 6-2
Q3: Cramlington Welfare (H) 3-1
Q4: Farsley Celtic (H) 2-1
R1: Halifax Town (A) 3-2
R2: Rochdale (H) 1-2

51-52 Q4: Blyth Spartans (H) 0-2

52-53 Q1: Amble (A) 4-0
Q2: Hexham Hearts (A) 5-3
Q3: Newburn (A) 4-1
Q4: Billingham Synthonia Recreation (H) 4-0
R1: Tranmere Rovers (A) 1-8

53-54 Q1: West Sleekburn Colliery Welfare (H) 1-2

54-55 PR: Newburn (A) 6-1
Q1: Heaton Stannington (A) 6-1
Q2: North Shields (H) 2-0
Q3: West Sleekburn Welfare (H) 2-1
Q4: Scarborough (H) 2-3

55-56 Q1: Gosforth & Coxlodge (A - *played home*) 7-0
Q2: North Shields (A) 1-3

56-57 Q1: Whitley Bay Athletic (A) 3-1
Q2: North Shields (A) 0-1

57-58 Q2: North Shields (A) 0-0, (H) 3-1
Q3: Horden Colliery Welfare (A) 1-3

58-59 Q2: Consett (A) 2-3

59-60 Q1: Scarborough (A) 2-2, (H) 0-0, 0-1

60-61 Q1: Newburn (A - *played home*) 2-1
Q2: Silksworth Colliery Welfare (H) 6-1
Q3: Ferryhill Athletic (A) 1-2

61-62 PR: Spennymoor United (H) 3-2
Q1: Silksworth Colliery Welfare (H) 4-1
Q2: Stanley United (A) 4-1
Q3: Bedlington Mechanics (H) 2-2, (A) 4-1
Q4: Scarborough (A) 2-2, (H) 2-0
R1: Chester (A) 1-4

62-63 Q1: Willington (H) 4-3
Q2: Stockton - *withdrew*

63-64 Q1: Billingham Synthonia (H) 1-1, (A) 2-0
Q2: Stanley United (A) 0-3

64-65 Q2: Tow Law Town (H) 0-0, (A) 0-0, 1-2

65-66 Q1: West Auckland Town (H) 3-1
Q2: Stockton (A) 1-3

66-67 Q1: North Shields (H) 2-2, (A) 4-2
Q2: Horden Colliery Welfare (A) 1-2

67-68 Q1: Horden Colliery Welfare (H) 3-2
Q2: West Auckland Town (A) 1-0
Q3: Tow Law Town (A) 2-3

68-69 Q1: Billingham Synthonia (A) 0-2

69-70 Q1: Ryhope Colliery (A) 1-0
Q2: Bishop Auckland (A) 0-3

72-73 Q1: Crook Town (A) 0-2

73-74 Q1: Billingham Synthonia (A) 4-1
Q2: Murton Colliery Welfare (H) 2-1
Q3: Horden Colliery Welfare (A) 1-1, (H) 2-1
Q4: Willington (A) 0-1

74-75 Q1: Horden Colliery Welfare (H) 2-1
Q2: Tow Law Town (A) 4-0
Q3: Willington (H) 2-2, (A) 5-1
Q4: Gateshead United (H) 1-3

75-76 Q1: Netherfield (H) 0-2

78-79 Q1: Bishop Auckland (H) 0-1

79-80 Q1: Boldon C.A. (A) 1-0
Q2: Crook Town (A) 3-2
Q3: North Shields (A) 1-2

80-81 Q1: Bishop Auckland (H) 0-3

81-82 Q1: Crook Town (H) 4-2
Q2: Lancaster City (A) 3-1
Q3: Horden Colliery Welfare (A) 0-0, (H) 1-3

82-83 PR: Chester-le-Street (H) 2-2, (A) 1-2

83-84 PR: Durham City (A) 1-3

84-85 Q1: Whitley Bay (H) 3-1
Q2: Bishop Auckland (H) 0-5

85-86 PR: Durham City (H) 0-2

86-87 PR: Seaham Colliery Welfare Red Star (H) 3-2
Q1: Bridlington Town (A - *played home*) 2-4

87-88 PR: Guiseley (H) 3-1
Q1: Ryhope C.A. (A) 1-1, (H) 1-2

88-89 PR: Rossendale United (H) 2-4

89-90 PR: Harworth Colliery Institute (A) 3-0
Q1: Alnwick Town (H) 0-5

90-91 PR: Prudhoe East End (H) 1-4

91-92 PR: Crook Town (H) 3-1
Q1: Consett (H) 0-4

ASHTON UNITED

Currently: Northern Premier League
* - As Hurst F.C.

45-46 * Q1: Earle (H) 9-3
Q2: Witton Albion (A) 1-6

46-47 * Q1: Chorley (A) 1-4

47-48 PR: Winsford United (H) 2-0
Q1: Witton Albion (H) 2-6

48-49 EX: Mossley (H) 3-0
PR: Hyde United (A) 1-2

49-50 EX: Mossley (A) 1-2

50-51 PR: Winsford United (A) 0-2

51-52 Q1: Skelmersdale United (A) 1-5

52-53 Q1: Skelmersdale United (H) 7-2
Q2: Horwich R.M.I. (H) 2-1
Q3: Mossley (H) 2-1
Q4: Altrincham (H) 3-1
R1: Halifax Town (A) 1-1, (H) 1-2

53-54 PR: Leyland Motors (A) 5-1
Q1: Mossley (A) 2-3

54-55 PR: Chorley (A) 1-2

55-56 Q1: Nelson (H) 1-1, (A) 4-1
Q2: Leyland Motors (H) 2-1
Q3: Rossendale United (H) 1-0
Q4: Wigan Athletic (H) 5-0
R1: Southport (A) 1-6

56-57 PR: Skelmersdale United (A) 0-5

57-58 PR: Skelmersdale United (H) 3-1
Q1: Rossendale United (A) 2-2, (H) 1-0
Q2: Crompton Recreation (H) 4-1
Q3: Chorley (H) 2-3

58-59 PR: Leyland Motors (H) 4-1
Q1: Skelmersdale United (H) 1-3

59-60 PR: Nelson (A) 0-0, (H) 1-2

60-61 Q1: Wigan Athletic (A) 2-3

61-62 Q1: Horwich R.M.I. (A) 2-0
Q2: Altrincham (H) 3-3, (A) 1-3

62-63 Q1: Prescot Cables (H) 2-0
Q2: Altrincham (A) 2-4

63-64 Q1: St Helens Town (H) 5-2
Q2: South Liverpool (H) 2-2, (A) 1-3

64-65 Q1: South Liverpool (A) 1-2

65-66 Q1: St Helens Town (H) 2-4

68-69 Q1: Witton Albion (H) 1-6

70-71 Q1: Formby (A) 0-2

71-72 Q1: Clitheroe (H) 2-1
Q2: Great Harwood (H) 3-2
Q3: Hyde United (H) 2-2, (A) 1-3

72-73 Q1: Droylsden (A) 2-1
Q2: Hyde United (H) 1-1, (A) 2-2, 2-1
Q3: Altrincham (H) 1-3

73-74 Q1: Macclesfield Town (H) 0-3

74-75 Q1: Great Harwood (H) 1-0
Q2: Horwich R.M.I. (H) 0-2

75-76 Q1: Skelmersdale United (H) 1-2

76-77 Q1: Hyde United (A) 1-4

77-78 PR: Winsford United (A) 1-1, (H) 0-2

78-79 PR: Formby (A) 1-3

79-80 PR: Hyde United (A) 3-1
Q1: Stalybridge Celtic (A) 2-1
Q2: Buxton (H) 1-1, (A) 1-1, 2-2, 3-1
Q3: Marine (A) 0-4

81-82 Q1: Lytham (H) 1-1, (A) 1-3

82-83 Q1: Leyland Motors (H) 6-2
Q2: Bootle (H) 0-0, (A) 1-0
Q3: Macclesfield Town (H) 0-2

83-84 PR: Alfreton Town (A) 1-0
Q1: Runcorn (H) 0-1

84-85 PR: Prescot Cables (A) 0-0, (H) 3-1
Q1: Hyde United (H) 0-0, (A) 4-2
Q2: Hednesford Town (A) 0-3

85-86 PR: Chadderton (A) 2-2, (H) 2-1
Q1: Stalybridge Celtic (H) 0-1

86-87 PR: Ossett Albion (H) 3-2
Q1: Armthorpe Welfare (A) 1-2

87-88 PR: Kirkby Town (H) 2-0
Q1: Bootle (A) 0-1

88-89 PR: St Helens Town (A) 1-0
Q1: Colwyn Bay (A) 0-0, (H) 2-1
Q2: Bangor City (H) 1-3

89-90 PR: Belper Town (A) 0-1

90-91 PR: Denaby United (H) 0-2

91-92 PR: Rhyl (H) 0-0, (A) 0-1

92-93 PR: Garforth Town (H) 1-2

ASHTREE HIGHFIELD

See Sandwell Borough

ASPATRIA SPARTANS

Currently: (Aspatria F.C.) Carlisle & Dist. Lge

49-50 PR: Cleator Moor Celtic (H) 3-1
Q1: Milnthorpe Corinthians (H) 6-1
Q2: Scalegill (H) 1-0
Q3: Netherfield (H) 2-4

50-51 Q1: Florence & Ullcoats United (A) 5-2
Q2: Cleator Moor Celtic (A) 3-8

ASTON VILLA

Currently: F.A. Premier League

45-46 R3: Coventry C. (A) 1-2, (H) 2-0 (*agg: 3-2*)
R4: Millwall (A) 4-2, (H) 9-1 (*agg: 13-3*)
R5: Chelsea (A) 1-0, (H) 1-0 (*agg: 2-0*)
R6: Derby Co. (H) 3-4, (A) 1-1 (*agg: 4-5*)

46-47 R3: Burnley (A) 1-5

47-48 R3: Manchester United (H) 4-6

48-49 R3: Bolton Wdrs (H) 1-1, (A) 0-0, 2-1
R4: Cardiff City (H) 1-2

49-50 R3: Middlesbrough (H) 2-2, (A) 0-0, 0-3

50-51 R3: Burnley (H) 2-0
R4: Wolverhampton Wanderers (A) 1-3

51-52 R3: Newcastle United (A) 2-4

52-53 R3: Middlesbrough (H) 3-1
R4: Brentford (H) 0-0, (A) 2-1
R5: Rotherham United (A) 3-1
R6: Everton (H) 0-1

53-54 R3: Arsenal (A) 1-5

54-55 R3: Brighton & Hove A. (A) 2-2, (H) 4-2
R4: Doncaster Rovers (A) 0-0, (H) 2-2, 1-1, 0-0 *abandoned after 90 minutes*, 1-3

55-56 R3: Hull City (H) 1-1, (A) 2-1
R4: Arsenal (A) 1-4

56-57 R3: Luton Town (A) 2-2, (H) 2-0
R4: Middlesbrough (A) 3-2
R5: Bristol City (H) 2-1
R6: Burnley (A) 1-1, (H) 2-0
SF: West Bromwich Albion (*at Wolverhampton Wanderers*) 2-2, (*at Birmingham City*) 1-0
F: Manchester United (*at Wembley*) 2-1

57-58 R3: Stoke City (A) 1-1, (H) 3-3, 0-2

58-59 R3: Rotherham United (H) 2-1
R4: Chelsea (A) 2-1
R5: Everton (A) 4-1
R6: Burnley (H) 0-0, (A) 2-0
SF: Nottingham Forest (*at Sheffield Wed.*) 0-1

59-60 R3: Leeds United (H) 2-1
R4: Chelsea (A) 2-1
R5: Port Vale (A) 2-1
R6: Preston North End (H) 2-0
SF: Wolverhampton Wanderers (*at West Bromwich Albion*) 0-1

60-61 R3: Bristol Rovers (A) 1-1, (H) 4-0
R4: Peterborough United (A) 1-1, (H) 2-1
R5: Tottenham Hotspur (H) 0-2

61-62 R3: Crystal Palace (H) 4-3
R4: Huddersfield Town (H) 2-1
R5: Charlton Athletic (H) 2-1
R6: Tottenham Hotspur (A) 0-2

62-63 R3: Bristol City (A) 1-1, (H) 3-2
R4: Manchester United (A) 0-1

63-64 R3: Aldershot (H) 0-0, (A) 1-2

64-65 R3: Coventry City (H) 3-0
R4: Sheffield United (A) 2-0
R5: Wolverhampton W. (H) 1-1, (A) 0-0, 1-3

65-66 R3: Leicester City (H) 1-2

66-67 R3: Preston North End (A) 1-0
R4: Liverpool (A) 0-1

67-68 R3: Millwall (H) 3-0
R4: Rotherham United (H) 0-1

68-69 R3: Queens Park Rangers (H) 2-1
R4: Southampton (A) 2-2, (H) 2-1
R5: Tottenham Hotspur (A) 2-3

69-70 R3: Charlton Athletic (H) 1-1, (A) 0-1

70-71 R1: Torquay United (A) 1-3

71-72 R1: Southend United (A) 0-1

72-73 R3: Everton (A) 2-3

73-74 R3: Chester (H) 3-1
R4: Arsenal (A) 1-1, (H) 2-0
R5: Burnley (A) 0-1

74-75 R3: Oldham Athletic (A) 3-0
R4: Sheffield United (H) 4-1
R5: Ipswich Town (A) 2-3

75-76 R3: Southampton (A) 1-1, (H) 1-2

76-77 R3: Leicester City (A) 1-0
R4: West Ham United (H) 3-0
R5: Port Vale (H) 3-0
R6: Manchester United (A) 1-2

77-78 R3: Everton (A) 1-4

78-79 R3: Nottingham Forest (A) 0-2

79-80 R3: Bristol Rovers (A) 2-1
R4: Cambridge United (A) 1-1, (H) 4-1
R5: Blackburn Rovers (A) 1-1, (H) 1-0
R6: West Ham United (A) 0-1

80-81 R3: Ipswich Town (A) 0-1

81-82 R3: Notts County (A) 6-0
R4: Bristol City (A) 1-0
R5: Tottenham Hotspur (A) 0-1

82-83 R3: Northampton Town (A) 1-0
R4: Wolverhampton Wanderers (H) 1-0
R5: Watford (H) 4-1
R6: Arsenal (A) 0-2

83-84 R3: Norwich City (H) 1-1, (A) 0-3

84-85 R3: Liverpool (A) 0-3

85-86 R3: Portsmouth (A) 2-2, (H) 3-2
R4: Millwall (H) 1-1, (A) 0-1

86-87 R3: Chelsea (H) 2-2, (A) 1-2

87-88 R3: Leeds United (A) 2-1
R4: Liverpool (H) 0-2

88-89 R3: Crewe Alexandra (A) 3-2
R4: Wimbledon (H) 0-1

89-90 R3: Blackburn Rovers (A) 2-2, (H) 3-1
R4: Port Vale (H) 6-0
R5: West Bromwich Albion (A) 2-0
R6: Oldham Athletic (A) 0-3

90-91 R3: Wimbledon (H) 1-1, (A) 0-1

91-92 R3: Tottenham Hotspur (H) 0-0, (A) 1-0
R4: Derby County (A) 4-3
R5: Swindon Town (A) 2-1
R6: Liverpool (A) 0-1

92-93 R3: Bristol Rvrs (H) 1-1, (A - *at Bath*) 3-0
R4: Wimbledon (H) 1-1, (A) 0-0 (*5-6 pens*)

ATHERSTONE TOWN

Currently: Defunct

46-47 PR: Boldmere St Michaels (H) 4-2
Q1: Nuneaton Borough (H) 1-4

47-48 Q1: Coalville Town Amateurs (A) 0-1

49-50 PR: Shepshed Albion (A) 0-0, (H) 8-2
Q1: Barwell Athletic (A) 2-2, (H) 4-3
Q2: Nuneaton Borough (H) 2-2, (A) 1-1, 1-2

50-51 PR: Coventry Amateurs (A) 3-2
Q1: Lockheed-Leamington (H) 2-4

51-52 PR: Darlaston (A) 1-1, (H) 1-4

52-53 Q1: Sutton Coldfield Town (A) 2-1
Q2: Rugby Town (H) 2-0
Q3: Bedworth Town (H) 1-1, (A) 0-2

53-54 Q1: Tamworth (A) 1-0
Q2: Burton Albion (A) 0-3

54-55 Q1: Birch Coppice Colliery (A) 3-0
Q2: Rugby Town (H) 2-1
Q3: Burton Albion (H) 1-2

55-56 PR: Burton Albion (A) 1-2

56-57 Q1: Boldmere St Michaels (H) 4-0
Q2: Lockheed-Leamington (H) 4-4, (A) 1-2

57-58 Q1: Bedworth Town (A) 1-2

58-59 PR: Burton Albion (A) 2-3

59-60 Q1: Gresley Rovers (A) 2-2, (H) 2-0
Q2: Ilkeston Town (H) 0-2

60-61 Q1: Hinckley Athletic (H) 0-3

61-62 Q1: Long Eaton United (H) 3-2
Q2: Hinckley Athletic (A) 1-5

62-63 Q1: Ilkeston Town (H) 1-1, (A) 2-1
Q2: Burton Albion (H) 2-1
Q3: Hinckley Athletic (A) 1-3

63-64 Q1: Long Eaton United (A) 2-2, (H) 1-3

64-65 Q1: Gresley Rovers (A) 5-3
Q2: Ilkeston Town (H) 4-2
Q3: Nuneaton Borough (H) 1-1, (A) 5-2
Q4: Hereford United (H) 1-3

65-66 Q1: Long Eaton United (A) 2-7

66-67 Q1: Nuneaton Borough (H) 1-6

67-68 Q1: Belper Town (H) 2-0
Q2: Arnold (A) 1-2

68-69 Q1: Long Eaton United (H) 4-2
Q2: Gresley Rovers (A) 2-0
Q3: Heanor Town (H) 3-2
Q4: Kettering Town (A) 0-2

69-70 Q1: Rugby Town (H) 1-2

70-71 PR: Gresley Rovers (A) 1-0
Q1: Bedworth United (A) 2-1
Q2: Long Eaton United (A) 1-2

71-72 Q1: Bromsgrove Rovers (H) 3-1
Q2: Worcester City (A) 0-0, (H) 1-0
Q3: Alvechurch (A) 0-3

72-73 Q1: Burton Albion (A) 0-1

73-74 Q1: Darlaston (H) 1-0
Q2: Ilkeston Town (A) 0-2

74-75 Q1: Hinckley Athletic (H) 5-1
Q2: Coventry Sporting (H) 5-0
Q3: Nuneaton Borough (H) 1-1, (A) 0-2

75-76 PR: Enderby Town (A) 1-2

76-77 Q1: Arnold (A) 0-1

77-78 Q1: Cheltenham Town (H) 0-0, (A) 0-1

78-79 Q1: Belper Town (H) 2-0
Q2: Irthlingborough Diamonds (H) 1-3

ATHERSTONE UNITED

Currently: Southern League

85-86 PR: Boston (A) 2-0
Q1: Bilston Town (H) 3-3, (A) 2-0
Q2: Bromsgrove Rovers (H) 4-0
Q3: Grantham (A) 2-0
Q4: Dagenham (A) 1-5

86-87 Q1: Moor Green (H) 2-1
Q2: Stafford Rangers (H) 2-4

87-88 PR: Northampton Spencer (A) 5-2
Q1: Malvern Town (H) 1-1, (A) 2-0
Q2: Lye Town (H) 1-0
Q3: Alvechurch (H) 4-3
Q4: Leyton Wingate (A) 0-0, (H) 4-2
R1: V.S. Rugby (A) 0-0, (H) 0-2

88-89 Q1: Wisbech Town (H) 4-0
Q2: Redditch United (A) 1-2

89-90 Q1: Desborough Town (A) 0-1

90-91 Q1: Wolverton (A) 2-2, (H) 4-1
Q2: Evesham United (A) 2-1
Q3: Shepshed Charterhouse (A) 3-2
Q4: Bishop's Stortford (A) 1-0
R1: Fleetwood Town (H) 3-1
R2: Crewe Alexandra (A) 0-1

91-92 Q4: Grays Athletic (A) 2-0
R1: Hereford United (H) 0-0, (A) 0-3

Above: *Atherstone United striker Mark Tolley evades a tackle from Greg Downs to get in a shot at home to Hereford United in 1991. Photo: Paul Barber.*

92-93 Q4: Kidderminster Harriers (A) 0-2

ATHERTON COLLIERIES

Currently: North West Counties League

48-49 PR: Lytham (H) 4-1
Q1: Darwen (A) 2-3

49-50 EX: Shell (A) 1-5

50-51 PR: Hyde United (A) 0-5

ATHERTON LABURNUM R.

Currently: North West Counties League

89-90 PR: Accrington Stanley (H) 1-1, (A) 2-5

90-91 PR: Rossendale United (H) 3-1
Q1: Harworth Colliery Institute (A) 2-1
Q2: Bangor City (H) 0-0, (A) 0-4

91-92 PR: Knowsley United (A) 1-5

92-93 PR: Irlam Town (A) 2-1
Q1: Great Harwood Town (H) 1-1, (A) 2-1
Q2: Colwyn Bay (H) 1-2

AVELEY

Currently: Isthmian League

54-55 PR: Ilford (H) 0-0, (A) 0-3

55-56 PR: Brentwood & Warley (H) 5-1
Q1: Leyton (A) 0-3

56-57 PR: Leytonstone (A) 2-6

57-58 PR: Rainham Town (A) 1-2

58-59 PR: Barking (H) 0-1

59-60 PR: Leytonstone (H) 1-2

60-61 Q1: Brentwood & Warley (H) 2-5

61-62 Q1: Ilford (H) 2-2, (A) 0-3

62-63 Q1: Woodford Town (H) 1-0
Q2: Tilbury (A) 1-2

63-64 Q1: Brentwood & Warley (A) 4-2
Q2: Tilbury (A) 3-3, (H) 2-1
Q3: Ilford (H) 0-1

64-65 Q1: Tilbury (A) 1-1, (H) 2-0
Q2: Hornchurch (A) 0-4

65-66 Q1: Walthamstow Avenue (A) 0-4

66-67 Q1: Kingstonian (A) 2-5

67-68 Q1: Hillingdon Borough (A) 0-4

68-69 Q1: Tooting & Mitcham United (H) 0-1

69-70 Q1: Bromley (H) 1-2

70-71 Q1: Braintree & Crittall Athletic (H) 2-1
Q2: Boreham Wood (H) 3-3, (A) 3-0
Q3: Hayes (A) 3-2
Q4: Leytonstone (H) 0-0, (A) 3-2
R1: Yeovil Town (A) 0-1

71-72 Q1: Banstead Athletic (H) 1-0
Q2: Southall (H) 0-0, (A) 3-3, 2-1
Q3: Maidenhead United (H) 1-1, (A) 2-3

72-73 Q1: Clapton (A) 2-1
Q2: Sutton United (H) 1-2

73-74 Q1: Harlow Town (H) 2-1
Q2: Crawley Town (A) 3-2
Q3: Harrow Borough (H) 1-0
Q4: Boreham Wood (A) 2-2, (H) 1-2

74-75 PR: Cray Wanderers (A) 2-4

75-76 Q1: Hornchurch (H) 1-1, (A) 1-3

76-77 Q1: Rainham Town (A) 2-1
Q2: Grays Athletic (H) 1-0
Q3: Woking (H) 1-1, (A) 0-4

77-78 Q1: Leytonstone (H) 0-2

78-79 PR: Gravesend & Northfleet (A) 2-6

79-80 PR: Epping Town (A) 2-2, (H) 0-1

80-81 Q1: Basildon United (H) 2-0
Q2: Walthamstow Avenue (H) 2-0
Q3: Grays Athletic (A) 1-0
Q4: Gravesend & Northfleet (A) 0-4

81-82 Q1: Welling (H) 1-1, (A) 1-1, (H) 0-0, (A) 2-3

82-83 Q1: Haverhill Rovers (H) 5-0
Q2: Walthamstow Avenue (H) 1-3

83-84 Q1: Woodford Town (A) 2-0
Q2: Wealdstone (H) 1-1, (A) 0-2

84-85 Q1: March Town United (H) 5-0
Q2: Cambridge City (H) 2-1
Q3: Gorleston (A) 4-0
Q4: Dagenham (H) 0-1

85-86 Q1: Harefield United (A) 0-0, (H) 2-0
Q2: Grays Athletic (A) 1-2

86-87 PR: Hornchurch (H) 0-1

87-88 PR: Tiptree United (A) 4-0
Q1: Bury Town (H) 2-2, (A) 1-3

88-89 PR: Halstead (H) 2-2, (A) 3-3 *abandoned in extra-time* (H) 1-4

89-90 PR: Chesham United (H) 0-0, (A) 1-0
Q1: Boreham Wood (H) 0-1

90-91 PR: Barkingside (A) 1-2

91-92 PR: Felixstowe Town (H) 2-0
Q1: Heybridge Swifts (H) 0-2

92-93 PR: Brook House (A) 1-1, (H) 1-0
Q1: Leighton Town (A) 4-2
Q2: Boston United (A) 2-1
Q3: Corby Town (A) 1-4

AYLESBURY UNITED

Currently: Isthmian League

45-46 EX: Chesham United (H) 5-0
PR: Osberton Radiators (H) 5-0
Q1: Oxford City (H) 1-2

46-47 EX: Morris Motors (H) 2-1
PR: Osberton Radiators (H) 6-2
Q1: Headington United (H) 2-3

47-48 EX: Abingdon Town (A) 4-2
PR: Huntley & Palmers Recreation (A) 1-4

48-49 EX: Pressed Steel (H) 4-1
PR: Huntley & Palmers Recreation (A) 2-3

49-50 EX: Bicester Town (H) 5-2
PR: Slough Town (A) 2-3

50-51 EX: Marlow (A) 4-2
PR: Uxbridge (H) 2-2, (A) 1-1, 4-1
Q1: Yiewsley (A) 2-2, (H) 2-0
Q2: Wycombe Wanderers (H) 0-2

51-52 Q1: Marlow (H) 4-1
Q2: Banbury Spencer (A) 4-0
Q3: Wycombe Wanderers (A) 2-1
Q4: Hendon (H) 4-3
R1: Watford (H) 0-5

52-53 PR: Chesham United (H) 4-1
Q1: Headington United (A) 2-4

53-54 Q1: Headington United (H) 1-2

54-55 PR: Wycombe Wanderers (H) 0-1

55-56 PR: Slough Centre (H) 3-1
Q1: Banbury Spencer (A) 0-7

56-57 Q1: Slough Town (H) 3-0
Q2: Oxford City (H) 2-0
Q3: Witney Town (H) 7-0
Q4: Tooting & Mitcham United (A) 1-3

57-58 PR: Headington United (A) 0-3

58-59 PR: Wokingham Town (H) 2-2, (A) 2-4

59-60 PR: Windsor & Eton (A) 3-2
Q1: Oxford City (H) 1-4

60-61 Q1: Chesham United (A) 1-5

61-62 Q1: Oxford City (A) 2-5

62-63 Q1: Huntley & Palmers (H) 6-0
Q2: Hemel Hempstead Town (A) 0-2

63-64 Q1: Maidenhead United (H) 2-3

64-65 Q1: Chesham United (A) 0-5

65-66 Q1: Huntley & Palmers (H) 3-3, (A) 0-1

66-67 Q1: Hillingdon Borough (A) 0-6

67-68 Q1: Maidenhead United (H) 2-2, (A) 2-4

68-69 Q1: Wembley (H) 1-0
Q2: Maidenhead United (H) 2-1
Q3: Wealdstone (A) 1-2

69-70 Q1: Wealdstone (A) 0-0, (H) 1-3

70-71 Q1: Banbury United (H) 0-3

71-72 Q1: Guildford City (A) 0-2

72-73 Q1: Oxford City (H) 1-1, (A) 0-3

73-74 Q1: Hatfield Town (H) 3-2
Q2: Ware (A) 0-1

74-75 PR: Marlow (A) 3-3, (H) 1-1, 0-1

75-76 Q1: Redditch United (H) 2-1
Q2: A.P. Leamington (A) 1-3

76-77 Q1: Banbury United (H) 1-3

77-78 Q1: Kempston Rovers (H) 0-3

78-79 PR: Didcot Town (A) 1-1, (H) 2-1
Q1: Wokingham Town (A) 0-2

79-80 PR: Grays Athletic (A) 2-0
Q1: Hayes (A) 0-2

80-81 Q1: Burnham (H) 2-0
Q2: Uxbridge (H) 6-0
Q3: Hendon (A) 1-1, (H) 1-0
Q4: Barnet (H) 1-1, (A) 0-0, (H) 0-1

81-82 Q1: Feltham (H) 0-1

82-83 PR: Abingdon Town (A) 2-3

83-84 PR: Harefield United (H) 2-0
Q1: Boreham Wood (H) 2-0
Q2: Harrow Borough (A) 0-0, (H) 1-2

84-85 Q1: Hayes (H) 3-2
Q2: Buckingham Town (H) 0-0, (A) 0-4

85-86 Q1: Arlesey Town (A) 2-1
Q2: Hampton (A) 1-0
Q3: Grays Ath. (A) 2-2, (H - *at Tring T.*) 1-0
Q4: Harlow T. (H - *at RAF Halton*) 0-0, (A) 2-1
R1: Slough T. (A) 2-2, (H - *at Tring T.*) 2-5

86-87 Q1: Barking (H) 1-0
Q2: Harefield United (A) 2-2, (H) 2-0
Q3: Boreham Wood (A) 1-0
Q4: Yeading (A) 3-1
R1: Bath City (A) 2-3

87-88 Q1: Wycombe Wanderers (H) 2-0
Q2: Sudbury Town (A) 1-1, (H) 2-1
Q3: Hertford Town (A) 4-0
Q4: Enfield (A) 2-1
R1: Bristol City (A) 0-1

88-89 Q4: Sudbury Town (H) 1-1, (A) 1-0
R1: Waterlooville (A) 4-1
R2: Sutton United (H) 0-1

89-90 Q4: Hendon (H) 4-1
R1: Southend United (H) 1-0
R2: Northampton Town (A) 0-0, (H) 0-1

90-91 Q4: Dagenham (A) 2-0
R1: Walsall (H) 0-1

91-92 Q4: Chesham United (H) 1-1, (A) 3-1
R1: Kidderminster Harriers (A) 1-0
R2: Hereford United (H) 2-3

Above: *Aylesbury United striker Cliff Hercules celebrates his second goal, the equaliser, against Hereford United in 1991. Photo: Paul Dennis.*

92-93 Q4: Enfield (A) 0-0, (H) 2-1
R1: West Bromwich Albion (A) 0-8

AYLESFORD PAPER MILLS

Currently: Kent County League

47-48 EX: Betteshanger Colliery Welfare (A) 2-3

48-49 EX: Callender Athletic (A) 0-6

49-50 PR: Bowater Lloyds (H) 1-10

50-51 PR: Tonbridge (H) 0-3

BACUP BOROUGH

Currently: North West Counties League

47-48 PR: Lytham (A) 1-0
Q1: Morecambe (H) 2-3

48-49 PR: Rossendale United (A) 0-2

49-50 PR: Great Harwood (A) 1-1, (H) 5-1
Q1: Chorley (A) 1-3

50-51 PR: Morecambe (A) 4-0
Q1: Darwen (H) 2-0
Q2: Rossendale United (H) 3-2
Q3: Nelson (H) 0-2

51-52 Q1: Lancaster City (A) 0-2

52-53 Q1: Netherfield (A) 0-5

53-54 Q1: Burscough (A) 1-4

54-55 PR: Rossendale United (H) 1-0
Q1: Chorley (H) 1-2

55-56 PR: Leyland Motors (A) 1-2

56-57 Q1: Mossley (H) 2-8

57-58 PR: Lytham (H) 3-0
Q1: Mossley (H) 1-1, (A) 1-3

58-59 PR: Droylsden (A) 4-1
Q1: Nelson (H) 2-3

59-60 Q1: Horwich R.M.I. (A) 2-1
Q2: Lytham (A) 1-2

60-61 Q1: Darwen (A) 1-0
Q2: Nelson (H) 0-3

61-62 PR: Darwen (H) 1-5

62-63 Q1: Stalybridge Celtic (H) 0-3

63-64 Q1: Nelson (A) 1-5

64-65 Q1: Hyde United (A) 0-9

65-66 Q1: Lytham St Annes (A) 0-2

66-67 Q1: Darwen (A) 3-2
Q2: Chorley (A) 0-2

67-68 Q1: Macclesfield Town (A) 0-7

68-69 Q1: Rossendale United (H) 0-1

70-71 Q1: Droylsden (H) 1-3

71-72 Q1: Fleetwood (H) 0-0, (A) 0-3

72-73 Q1: Morecambe (H) 1-0
Q2: Lancaster City (A) 1-2

73-74 Q1: Fleetwood (H) 2-3

74-75 PR: Accrington Stanley (H) 3-3, (A) 1-4

75-76 PR: New Brighton (A) 1-3

76-77 Q1: Accrington Stanley (A) 0-5

77-78 PR: Runcorn (A) 0-4

BAKER PERKINS

See Peterborough City

BALDOCK TOWN

Currently: Southern League

48-49 EX: St Neots St Marys (A) 4-0
PR: Vauxhall Motors (A) 1-1, (H) 2-5

49-50 PR: Leighton United (H) 2-0
Q1: Huntingdon United (A) 3-2
Q2: Hitchin Town (A) 1-4

50-51 PR: Huntingdon United (H) 1-3

67-68 Q1: Harrow Borough (A) 0-1

68-69 Q1: Hoddesdon Town (A) 1-1, (H) 0-2

69-70 Q1: Harrow Borough (H) 3-0
Q2: Hoddesdon Town (H) 0-1

70-71 PR: Wolverton Town & B.R. (A) 0-1

84-85 PR: Abingdon Town (A) 3-1
Q1: Moor Green (A) 1-2

85-86 Q1: Harrow Borough (H) 0-2

86-87 PR: Hemel Hempstead (A) 2-2, (H) 1-0
Q1: Saffron Walden Town (H) 1-0
Q2: Bromsgrove Rovers (H) 0-1

87-88 PR: Hampton (H) 1-0
Q1: Canvey Island (A) 1-0
Q2: Uxbridge (H) 0-1

88-89 PR: Felixstowe Town (A) 1-1, (H) 4-0
Q1: Hemel Hempstead (A) 1-5

89-90 PR: Cray Wanderers (H) 3-0
Q1: Wycombe Wanderers (H) 0-2

90-91 PR: Chesham United (A) 1-4

91-92 PR: Barkingside (A) 1-1, (H) 5-0
Q1: Halstead Town (A) 3-2
Q2: Hendon (A) 2-1
Q3: Dartford (H) 2-2, (A) 3-2
Q4: Halesowen Town (H) 1-1, (A) 0-1

92-93 Q1: Waltham Abbey (A - *played home*) 3-2
Q2: Newmarket Town (A) 2-2, (H) 2-6

BAMBER BRIDGE

Currently: Northern Premier League

92-93 PR: Prudhoe East End (H) 4-0
Q1: Peterlee Newtown (H) 1-1, (A) 2-0
Q2: Spennymoor United (H) 0-4

BANBURY UNITED

Currently: Hellenic League
* - As Banbury Spencer

45-46 * EX: Headington United (H) 8-1
PR: Newbury Town (A) 8-0

Q1: Windsor & Eton (A) 3-0
Q2: Slough United (H) 2-5

46-47 * PR: Headington United (A) 2-3

47-48 * EX: Oxford City (H) 5-0
PR: Osberton Radiator (H) 8-2
Q1: Metal & Produce Recovery Depot (A) 3-0
Q2: Maidenhead United (H) 4-0
Q3: Southall (A) 4-3
Q4: Grays Athletic (A) 1-0
R1: Colchester United (A) 1-2

48-49 * PR: Headington United (A) 3-1
Q1: Berkhamsted Town (A) 2-1
Q2: Uxbridge (H) 3-1
Q3: Oxford City (H) 2-3

49-50 * PR: Hayes (A) 0-1

50-51 * EX: Hemel Hempstead Town (A) 1-1, (H) 5-1
PR: Huntley & Palmers Recreation (A) 2-1
Q1: Bicester Town (H) 4-0
Q2: Slough Town (H) 1-5

51-52 * Q1: Huntley & Palmers Recreation (H) 2-1
Q2: Aylesbury United (H) 0-4

52-53 * PR: Maidenhead United (H) 1-1, (A) 0-3

53-54 * PR: Wycombe Wanderers (H) 2-1
Q1: Oxford City (H) 2-0
Q2: Chesham United (A) 0-1

54-55 * PR: Huntley & Palmers (A) 3-0
Q1: Chesham United (A) 0-1

55-56 * Q1: Aylesbury United (H) 7-0
Q2: Oxford City (H) 3-1
Q3: Wycombe Wanderers (H) 1-2

56-57 * PR: Abingdon Town (A) 3-0
Q1: Witney Town (A) 0-1

57-58 * Q1: Headington United (A) 0-1

58-59 * PR: Oxford City (H) 0-3

59-60 * Q1: Marlow (A) 3-0
Q2: Oxford City (A) 1-5

60-61 * Q1: Abingdon Town (A) 1-4

61-62 * Q1: Chesham United (A) 4-1
Q2: Abingdon Town (H) 4-1
Q3: Oxford City (H) 3-1
Q4: Yiewsley (H) 4-0
R1: Shrewsbury Town (A) 1-7

62-63 * Q1: Oxford City (H) 0-2

63-64 * Q1: Huntley & Palmers (H) 4-0
Q2: Maidenhead United (H) 2-3

64-65 * Q1: Oxford City (A) 1-2

65-66 * Q1: Chesham United (H) 2-0
Q2: Hemel Hempstead Town (A) 1-5

66-67 Q1: Hitchin Town (A) 4-1
Q2: Hemel Hempstead Town (A) 3-6

67-68 Q1: Dunstable Town (H) 2-0
Q2: Maidenhead United (A) 3-1
Q3: Wembley (H) 3-2
Q4: Chelmsford City (A) 0-2

68-69 PR: Marlow (A) 4-1
Q1: Letchworth Town (A) 3-2
Q2: Wealdstone (A) 1-3

69-70 Q1: Wembley (H) 2-1
Q2: Wealdstone (A) 0-1

70-71 Q1: Aylesbury United (A) 3-0
Q2: Wycombe Wanderers (H) 0-3

71-72 Q1: Bedford Town (H) 2-2, (A) 0-1

72-73 Q1: Wokingham Town (H) 4-1
Q2: Slough Town (H) 2-1
Q3: Witney Town (H) 0-0, (A) 2-1
Q4: Frome Town (A) 1-1, (H) 3-0
R1: Barnet (H) 0-2

73-74 Q1: Evesham United (A) 2-2, (H) 2-0
Q2: Witney Town (A) 2-1
Q3: Cinderford Town (A) 2-2, (H) 4-1
Q4: Tamworth (H) 2-0
R1: Northampton (H) 0-0, (A) 2-3

74-75 Q1: Nuneaton Borough (A) 0-3

75-76 Q1: Lye Town (H) 1-0
Q2: Cheltenham Town (A) 0-2

76-77 Q1: Aylesbury United (A) 3-1
Q2: Didcot Town (H) 3-2
Q3: Chesham United (H) 1-4

77-78 PR: Wolverton Town & B.R. (A) 1-1, (H) 4-1
Q1: Lye Town (A) 3-3, (H) 2-1
Q2: Wellingborough Town (A) 2-1
Q3: Oxford City (H) 1-0
Q4: Bideford (A) 0-1

78-79 PR: Thame United (H) 4-2
Q1: Witney Town (A) 2-0
Q2: Willenhall Town (A) 0-2

79-80 PR: Chalfont St Peter (A) 2-1
Q1: Hertford Town (A) 1-3

80-81 Q1: Alvechurch (A) 2-0
Q2: V.S. Rugby (H) 3-3, (A) 3-1
Q3: Moor Green (A) 2-0
Q4: Kettering Town (A) 0-3

81-82 Q1: Hemel Hempstead (H) 2-1
Q2: Hendon (A) 2-2, (H) 3-4

82-83 Q1: Kidderminster Harriers (H) 0-2

83-84 PR: Racing Club Warwick (A) 1-3

84-85 Q1: Willenhall Town (H) 1-4

85-86 PR: Chalfont St Peter (A) 1-2

86-87 PR: Highgate United (A) 3-1
Q1: Coventry Sporting (H) 4-2
Q2: Malvern Town (H) 1-2

87-88 PR: Edgware (H) 3-0
Q1: Irthlingborough Diamonds (A) 1-3

88-89 PR: Holbeach United (A) 4-1
Q1: Leighton Town (A) 0-0, (H) 2-1
Q2: Nuneaton Borough (A) 1-1, (H) 1-0
Q3: Redditch United (H) 2-3

89-90 Q1: Maidenhead United (H) 1-3

90-91 PR: Solihull (A) 0-0, (H) 1-1, (A) 2-2, (H) 3-4

91-92 PR: Stratford Town (H) 4-1
Q1: Hednesford Town (H) 2-1
Q2: Chasetown (A) 1-1, (H) 1-2

92-93 PR: Boston (A) 1-4

BANGOR CITY

Currently: League of Wales

45-46 Q1: Rhyl (H) 4-1 - *expelled*

46-47 Q1: Foden Motors Works (A) 6-3
Q2: Stalybridge Celtic (H) 4-1
Q3: Rhyl (H) 5-3
Q4: South Liverpool (A) 2-2, (H) 0-4

47-48 PR: Burscough (A) 1-3

48-49 EX: Orrell (A) 8-1
PR: Crossens (H) 6-0
Q1: Burscough (H) 4-2
Q2: St Helens Town (A) 3-0
Q3: Rhyl (H) 0-2

49-50 PR: Haydock C. & B. (A) 2-1
Q1: St Helens Town (A) 3-0
Q2: Rhyl (A) 1-4

50-51 PR: Skelmersdale United (A) 0-1

51-52 PR: South Liverpool (A) 1-1, (H) 2-1
Q1: Bootle (A) 1-1, (H) 2-0
Q2: Runcorn (H) 1-0
Q3: Prescot Cables (H) 1-0
Q4: New Brighton (H) 2-1
R1: Southport (H) 2-2, (A) 0-3

52-53 PR: Runcorn (A) 2-2, (H) 3-2
Q1: St Helens Town (H) 2-0
Q2: New Brighton (H) 2-0
Q3: Flint Town United (H) 4-2
Q4: Witton Albion (A) 2-0
R1: Southport (A) 1-3

53-54 PR: St Helens Town (A) 2-2, (H) 5-1
Q1: Prescot Cables (H) 1-2

54-55 PR: South Liverpool (A) 3-1
Q1: Pwllheli & District (A) 1-2

55-56 PR: Llandudno (H) 3-3, (A) 0-1

56-57 PR: Pwllheli & District (H) 2-2, (A) 1-4

57-58 Q1: Flint Town United (A) 1-1, (H) 5-1
Q2: Prescot Cables (A) 2-4

58-59 Q1: New Brighton (H) 0-0, (A) 2-3

59-60 Q1: New Brighton (H) 3-2
Q2: Runcorn (H) 4-1
Q3: Prescot Cables (A) 1-4

60-61 Q1: Flint Town United (A) 2-1
Q2: Runcorn (H) 2-1
Q3: New Brighton (H) 3-0
Q4: Netherfield (H) 1-0
R1: Wrexham (H) 1-0
R2: Southport (H) 1-1, (A) 1-3

61-62 Q1: Runcorn (A) 0-2

62-63 Q1: New Brighton (H) 4-0
Q2: Ellesmere Port Town (H) 1-2

63-64 Q1: Ellesmere Port Town (A) 1-0
Q2: Runcorn (A) 2-1
Q3: New Brighton (H) 2-0
Q4: Wigan Athletic (A) 1-1, (H) 1-0
R1: Barrow (A) 2-3

64-65 Q4: Lancaster City (A) 3-2
R1: York City (A) 1-5

65-66 Q4: Altrincham (H) 3-3, (A) 2-3

66-67 Q1: Llandudno (A) 1-0
Q2: Kirkby Town (A) 1-0
Q3: New Brighton (H) 6-6, (A) 1-0
Q4: Chorley (A) 3-3, (H) 4-3
R1: Mansfield Town (A) 1-4

67-68 Q1: Pwllheli & District (H) 6-0
Q2: Holyhead Town (H) 3-1
Q3: Rhyl (H) 4-0
Q4: Goole Town (A) 0-2

68-69 Q1: Holyhead Town (A) 3-2
Q2: Portmadoc (A) 8-1
Q3: South Liverpool (H) 3-1
Q4: Runcorn (A) 4-1
R1: Morecambe (H) 2-3

69-70 Q4: Fleetwood (H) 2-1
R1: Kirkby Town (H) 6-0
R2: York City (H) 0-0, (A) 0-2

70-71 Q4: Witton Albion (H) 1-1, (A) 3-2
R1: Darlington (A) 1-5

71-72 Q4: Hyde United (A) 3-1
R1: Bolton Wanderers (A) 0-3

72-73 Q4: Rossendale United (A) 2-1
R1: Rochdale (A) 2-1
R2: York City (H) 2-3

73-74 Q4: Runcorn (A) 2-2, (H) 1-2

74-75 Q4: Matlock Town (A) 0-3

75-76 Q1: Pwllheli & District (H) 2-0
Q2: Marine (A) 0-1

76-77 Q1: Prescot Town (H) 6-0
Q2: Bethesda Athletic (H) 4-2
Q3: Winsford United (A) 1-1, (H) 4-1
Q4: Boston (A) 0-1

77-78 PR: Witton Albion (A) 1-1, (H) 2-1
Q1: Nantwich Town (A) 1-1, (H) 4-1
Q2: South Liverpool (A) 2-2, (H) 1-0
Q3: Rhyl (H) 1-0
Q4: Spennymoor United (A) 1-2

78-79 PR: Leek Town (A) 2-2, (H) 1-2

79-80 PR: Formby (A) 2-2, (H) 0-1

80-81 Q1: Bootle (H) 0-2

81-82 Q1: Glossop (H) 6-0
Q2: Caernarfon Town (A) 2-3

82-83 Q1: Macclesfield Town (A) 1-3

83-84 Q1: Bootle (A) 1-0
Q2: Chorley (A) 4-2
Q3: South Liverpool (H) 1-0
Q4: Scarborough (H) 2-1
R1: Northwich Victoria (A) 1-1, (H) 1-0
R2: Blackpool (H) 1-1, (A) 1-2

84-85 R1: Tranmere Rovers (H) 1-1, (A) 0-7

85-86 Q4: South Liverpool (H) 1-1, (A) 2-3

87-88 Q1: Marine (H) 2-2, (A) 1-3

88-89 Q1: Irlam Town (H) 2-2, (A) 4-1
Q2: Ashton United (A) 3-1
Q3: Southport (A) 0-3

89-90 Q1: Heanor Town (H) 3-1
Q2: Hyde United (A) 1-2

90-91 Q1: Farsley Celtic (A) 0-0, (H) 3-0
Q2: Atherton Lab. Rovers (A) 0-0, (H) 4-0

Q3: Altrincham (A) 0-3

91-92 Q1: Curzon Ashton (A) 1-1, (H) 1-2

BANSTEAD ATHLETIC

Currently: Isthmian League

50-51 EX: Sutton United (A) 1-3

68-69 Q1: Uxbridge (H) 1-1, (A) 1-3

69-70 Q1: Carshalton Athletic (A) 1-2

70-71 PR: Dorking (A) 0-2

71-72 Q1: Aveley (A) 0-1

78-79 PR: Hampton (A) 0-2

79-80 Q1: Sutton United (H) 0-2

80-81 Q1: Kingstonian (A) 0-1

81-82 Q1: Horsham (H) 2-0
Q2: Pagham (A) 2-2, (H) 7-1
Q3: Farnborough Town (A) 0-4

82-83 Q1: Southwick (A) 2-2, (H) 0-1

83-84 PR: St Albans City (A) 0-10

84-85 PR: Lewes (H) 2-3

85-86 Q1: Sittingbourne (A) 2-1
Q2: Hastings Town (H) 0-1

86-87 Q1: Hendon (A) 2-2, (H) 0-1

87-88 Q1: Beckenham Town (H) 5-3
Q2: Woking (H) 0-0, (A) 0-1

88-89 PR: Horndean (A) 3-2
Q1: Windsor & Eton (H) 0-2

89-90 PR: Three Bridges (A) 0-1

90-91 PR: Malden Vale (H) 1-0
Q1: Molesey (H) 3-3, (A) 0-2

91-92 Q1: Wokingham Town (H) 1-2

92-93 PR: Eastbourne United (H) 2-1
Q1: Herne Bay (H) 4-1
Q2: Dover Athletic (A) 0-0, (H) 1-2

BANSTEAD MENTAL HOSP.

Currently: Defunct

45-46 PR: Metropolitan Police (H) 0-2

BARKING

Currently: Isthmian League

46-47 EX: London Tran. (C.B.) (A - *played home*) 9-0
PR: Severalls Athletic (H) *W/O*
Q1: Harwich & Parkeston (A) 3-0
Q2: Crittall Athletic (H) 3-0
Q3: Tilbury (H) 3-0
Q4: Leytonstone (H) 1-4

47-48 PR: Romford (A) 3-1
Q1: Crittall Athletic (H) 3-1
Q2: Brentwood & Warley (H) 0-0, (A) 3-2
Q3: Grays Athletic (H) 0-2

48-49 PR: Dagenham British Legion (H) 4-0
Q1: Harwich & Parkeston (H) 2-1
Q2: Leyton (H) 3-0
Q3: Romford (A) 2-3

49-50 PR: Eton Mnr (A - *played home*) 1-1, (H) 5-3
Q1: Clapton (H) 4-1
Q2: Grays Athletic (H) 4-0
Q3: Tilbury (H) 1-2

50-51 PR: Eton Manor (A) 4-2
Q1: Briggs Sports (H) 2-2, (A) 1-2

51-52 Q1: Romford (A) 0-1

52-53 PR: Ilford (H) 1-1, (A) 2-4

53-54 Q1: Erith & Belvedere (H) 1-2

54-55 PR: Woodford Town (H) 3-2
Q1: Rainham Town (H) 1-1, (A) 2-1
Q2: Chelmsford City (A) 2-2, (H) 1-1, 2-3

55-56 PR: Leyton (H) 2-2, (A) 0-1

56-57 PR: Tilbury (H) 4-1
Q1: Brentwood & Warley (H) 2-2, (A) 1-2

58-59 PR: Aveley (A) 1-0
Q1: Tilbury (H) 3-1
Q2: Woodford Town (A) 1-2

59-60 Q1: Leytonstone (H) 0-1

60-61 Q1: Grays Athletic (A) 3-2
Q2: Tilbury (H) 3-3, (A) 1-3

61-62 Q1: Rainham Town (A) 1-0
Q2: Tilbury (A) 0-2

62-63 Q1: Ilford (H) 0-4

63-64 Q1: Rainham Town (H) 3-1
Q2: Ilford (H) 1-2

64-65 Q1: Walthamstow Avenue (H) 1-2

65-66 Q1: Ilford (A) 4-2
Q2: Grays Athletic (H) 0-1

66-67 Q1: Leatherhead (A) 0-1

67-68 Q1: Huntley & Palmers (A) 2-1
Q2: Windsor & Eton (A) 1-2

68-69 Q1: Windsor & Eton (H) 0-1

69-70 Q1: Clapton (A) 5-0
Q2: Malden Town (A) 2-2, (H) 4-0
Q3: Walton & Hersham (A) 1-4

70-71 Q1: Leatherhead (A) 1-3

71-72 Q1: Bishop's Stortford (H) 0-1

72-73 Q1: Rainham Town (H) 1-0
Q2: Hertford Town (H) 1-0
Q3: St Albans City (H) 3-2
Q4: Hayes (H) 1-2

73-74 Q1: Egham Town (H) 0-2

74-75 PR: Corinthian-Casuals (A) 2-4

75-76 PR: Harrow Borough (A) 2-2, (H) 2-0
Q1: Stevenage Athletic (A) 1-2

76-77 Q1: Chertsey Town (H) 6-1
Q2: Sutton United (H) 1-1, (A) 4-1
Q3: Wokingham Town (H) 3-1
Q4: Tooting & Mitcham Utd (A) 1-1, (H) 1-2

77-78 Q1: Chalfont St Peter (H) 5-2
Q2: Hillingdon Borough (H) 1-3

78-79 PR: Clapton (A) 6-1
Q1: Ware (A) 2-0
Q2: Leytonstone (A) 2-1
Q3: Billericay Town (H) 2-0
Q4: Bedford Town (H) 3-1
R1: Yeovil Town (A) 1-0
R2: Aldershot (H) 1-2

79-80 Q1: Cheshunt (A) 5-1
Q2: Tilbury (A) 1-0
Q3: Edgware (A) 3-0
Q4: Dagenham (A) 4-2
R1: Oxford United (H) 1-0
R2: Reading (A) 1-3

80-81 Q4: Maidstone United (A) 0-2

81-82 Q4: Maidstone United (A) 1-0
R1: Bideford (A) 2-1
R2: Gillingham (A) 1-1, (H - *played away*) 1-3

82-83 Q4: Folkestone (H) 0-2

83-84 Q4: Ashford Town (H) 3-0
R1: Farnborough Town (H) 2-1
R2: Plymouth Argyle (A) 1-2

84-85 Q4: Buckingham Town (A) 1-3

85-86 Q1: Cheshunt (H) 4-1
Q2: Chalfont St Peter (H) 0-2

86-87 Q1: Aylesbury United (A) 0-1

87-88 Q1: Uxbridge (A) 1-4

88-89 Q1: Beckenham Town (H) 0-0, (A) 1-0
Q2: Grays Athletic (A) 1-1, (H) 0-3

89-90 Q1: Hendon (H) 1-1, (A) 2-2, (H) 1-2

90-91 Q1: Enfield (A) 1-4

91-92 PR: Sudbury Town (A) 2-2, (H) 2-2, (A) 1-2

92-93 PR: Biggleswade Town (A - *at Langford*) 3-1
Q1: Norwich United (A) 1-2

BARKINGSIDE

Currently: London Spartan League

88-89 PR: Uxbridge (H) 1-2

89-90 PR: Harlow Town (H) 2-5

90-91 PR: Aveley (H) 2-1
Q1: Redbridge Forest (H) 1-3

91-92 PR: Baldock Town (H) 1-1, (A) 0-5

92-93 PR: Harefield United (A) 1-0
Q1: Wembley (H) 1-3

BARNET

Currently: Football League

45-46 PR: Edgware Town (A) 4-1
Q1: Tufnell Park (A) 1-1, (H) 3-1
Q2: Enfield (H) 5-0
Q3: Wealdstone (H) 3-0
Q4: Ilford (H) 5-2
R1: Queens Park R. (H) 2-6, (A) 1-2 (*agg: 3-8*)

46-47 R1: Sutton United (H) 3-0
R2: Southend United (H) 2-9

47-48 Q4: Gillingham (A) 1-3

48-49 Q4: Hendon (H) 5-4
R1: Exeter City (H) 2-6

49-50 Q4: Chelmsford City (H) 2-6

50-51 PR: Hendon (H) 2-3

51-52 Q1: Slough Town (A) 1-1, (H) 1-6

52-53 PR: Berkhamsted Town (A) 4-1
Q1: St Albans City (H) 1-2

53-54 PR: Wealdstone (H) 1-2

54-55 PR: Royston (H) 11-0
Q1: Hitchin Town (H) 2-0
Q2: Hoddesdon Town (H) 3-0
Q3: Clapton (A) 1-0
Q4: Great Yarmouth Town (H) 2-0
R1: Southampton (H) 1-4

55-56 PR: Stevenage Town (A) 3-1
Q1: Eton Manor (A) 2-3

56-57 PR: Stevenage Town (H) 2-1
Q1: Eton Manor (H) 0-3

57-58 PR: Letchworth Town (A) 1-2

58-59 Q1: St Albans City (H) 1-2

59-60 R1: Salisbury (A) 0-1

60-61 Q1: Hounslow Town (H) 5-1
Q2: Bishop's Stortford (A) 2-4

61-62 Q1: Hounslow Town (A) 4-2
Q2: Wealdstone (A) 1-1, (H) 8-0
Q3: Enfield (A) 4-2
Q4: Hitchin Town (H) 3-2
R1: Weymouth (A) 0-1

62-63 Q1: Hertford Town (H) 2-0
Q2: Enfield (A) 1-4

63-64 Q1: Stevenage Town (H) 4-2
Q2: Hertford Town (H) 3-1
Q3: Ware (A) 6-1
Q4: Wycombe Wanderers (H) 6-3
R1: Torquay United (A) 2-6

64-65 Q1: Harlow Town (A) 2-0
Q2: Hertford Town (H) 0-0, (A) 2-0
Q3: Stevenage Town (H) 2-0
Q4: Walthamstow Avenue (H) 3-3, (A) 4-1
R1: Cambridge United (H) 2-1
R2: Enfield (A) 4-4, (H) 3-0
R3: Preston North End (H) 2-3

65-66 R1: Dartford (H) 0-2

66-67 Q1: Ilford (A) 2-0
Q2: Cray Wanderers (A) 4-1
Q3: Edgware Town (H) 4-1
Q4: Enfield (H) 1-2

67-68 Q1: Walton & Hersham (H) 3-2
Q2: Clapton (H) 9-0
Q3: Windsor & Eton (H) 7-1
Q4: Sutton United (A) 2-2, (H) 3-1
R1: Hereford United (A) 2-3

68-69 Q4: Enfield (H) 4-2
R1: Brentwood Town (H) 1-1, (A) 0-1

69-70 Q4: Wycombe Wanderers (A) 0-0, (H) 3-0
R1: Walton & Hersham (A) 1-0
R2: Sutton United (H) 0-2

70-71 Q4: Lowestoft Town (A) 0-0, (H) 2-0
R1: Newport County (H) 6-1
R2: Slough Town (A) 1-0
R3: Colchester United (H) 0-1

71-72 Q4: Hendon (A) 2-2, (H) 2-0
R1: Kettering Town (A) 4-2
R2: Torquay United (H) 1-4

Above: *The players of non-League Barnet celebrate forcing First Division Brighton & Hove Albion to a draw in 1982. The players pictured are, from left to right; Gary Phillips, Danny Westwood, Graham Pearce, Steve Robinson, Terry Voyce, Mike Pittaway, Colin Barnes, Kevin Millett. Photo: Formula One Pictures.*

72-73 R1: Banbury United (A) 2-0
R2: Bilston (H) 1-1, (A) 1-0
R3: Queens Park Rangers (A) 0-0, (H) 0-3

73-74 Q4: Hendon (H) 2-2, (A) 0-3

74-75 Q4: Hitchin Town (H) 1-1, (A) 0-2

75-76 PR: Grays Athletic (A) 2-1
Q1: Sutton United (A) 1-1, (H) 1-2

76-77 Q1: Egham Town (H) 6-1
Q2: Hatfield Town (H) 3-0
Q3: Slough Town (H) 0-1

77-78 Q1: Camberley Town (H) 4-1
Q2: Erith & Belvedere (H) 2-1
Q3: St Albans City (A) 4-2
Q4: Hampton (A) 2-1
R1: Peterborough United (H) 1-2

78-79 Q1: Bracknell Town (H) 2-1
Q2: Feltham (H) 3-2
Q3: Wokingham Town (A) 4-0
Q4: Edgware (A) 1-0
R1: Woking (H) 3-3, (A) 3-3, (*at Brentford*) 0-3

79-80 Q4: Wycombe Wanderers (H) 0-2

80-81 Q4: Aylesbury (A) 1-1, (H) 1-1, (A) 1-0
R1: Minehead (H) 2-2, (A) 2-1
R2: Peterborough United (H) 0-1

81-82 Q4: Corinthian-Casuals (H) 2-0
R1: Harlow Town (A) 0-0, (H) 1-0
R2: Wycombe Wanderers (H) 2-0
R3: Brighton & Hove A. (H) 0-0, (A) 1-3

82-83 R1: Carshalton Athletic (A) 0-4

83-84 Q4: Harlow Town (A) 1-1, (H) 5-1
R1: Bristol Rovers (H) 0-0, (A) 1-3

84-85 Q4: Boston United (H) 3-1
R1: Plymouth Argyle (A) 0-3

85-86 Q4: Enfield (H) 0-7

86-87 Q1: Dulwich Hamlet (H) 0-2

87-88 Q1: Witney Town (A) 3-0
Q2: Irthlingborough Diamonds (A) 4-0
Q3: Berkhamsted Town (A) 3-0
Q4: Willenhall Town (A) 6-0
R1: Hereford United (H) 0-1

88-89 Q1: Epsom & Ewell (H) 7-0
Q2: Leatherhead (H) 4-3
Q3: Grays Athletic (H) 0-1

89-90 Q1: Bishop's Stortford (A) 1-0
Q2: Newmarket Town (H) 4-2
Q3: Cambridge City (A) 4-3
Q4: Burton Albion (A) 2-2, (H) 1-0
R1: Bristol City (A) 0-2

90-91 Q1: Clapton (A - *at Dagenham*) 2-0
Q2: Braintree Town (A) 2-0
Q3: Harlow Town (A) 3-1
Q4: Heybridge Swifts (H) 3-1
R1: Chelmsford City (H) 2-2, (A) 2-0
R2: Northampton Town (H) 0-0, (A) 1-0
R3: Portsmouth (H) 0-5

91-92 R1: Tiverton Town (H) 5-0
R2: Enfield (A) 4-1
R3: Charlton Ath. (A - *at West Ham U.*) 1-3

92-93 R1: A.F.C. Bournemouth (A) 0-0, (H) 1-2

BARNOLDSWICK & DIST.

Currently: Defunct

48-49 PR: Darwen (A) 0-2

49-50 PR: Nelson (H) 1-3

50-51 PR: Lancaster City (A) 1-5

BARNSLEY

Currently: Football League

45-46 R3: Newcastle U. (A) 2-4, (H) 3-0 (*agg: 5-4*)
R4: Rotherham U. (H) 3-0, (A) 1-2 (*agg: 4-2*)
R5: Bradford P.A. (H) 0-1, (A) 1-1 (*agg: 1-2*)

46-47 R3: Huddersfield Town (A) 4-3
R4: Preston North End (A) 0-6

47-48 R3: Manchester City (A) 1-2

48-49 R3: Blackpool (H) 0-1

49-50 R3: Stockport County (A) 2-4

50-51 R3: Northampton Town (A) 1-3

51-52 R3: Colchester United (H) 3-0
R4: Arsenal (A) 0-4

52-53 R3: Brighton & Hove Albion (H) 4-3
R4: Plymouth Argyle (A) 0-1

53-54 R1: York City (H) 5-2
R2: Norwich City (A) 1-2

54-55 R1: Wigan Athletic (H) 3-2
R2: Gateshead (A) 3-3, (H) 0-1

55-56 R3: Aldershot (A) 2-1
R4: Blackburn Rovers (H) 0-1

56-57 R3: Port Vale (H) 3-3, (A) 1-0
R4: Cardiff City (A) 1-0
R5: Nottingham Forest (H) 1-2

57-58 R3: Hull City (A) 1-1, (H) 0-2

58-59 R3: Brentford (A) 0-2

59-60 R1: Bradford City (H) 3-3, (A) 1-2

60-61 R1: Gateshead (A) 0-0, (H) 2-0
R2: Bradford City (A) 2-1
R3: Reading (A) 1-1, (H) 3-1
R4: Huddersfield Town (A) 1-1, (H) 1-0
R5: Luton Town (H) 1-0
R6: Leicester City (A) 0-0, (H) 1-2

61-62 R1: West Auckland Town (A) 3-3, (H) 2-0
R2: Carlisle United (H) 1-2

62-63 R1: Rhyl (H) 4-0
R2: Chesterfield (H) 2-1
R3: Everton (H) 0-3

63-64 R1: Stockport County (H) 1-0
R2: Rochdale (H) 3-1
R3: Scunthorpe United (A) 2-2, (H) 3-2
R4: Bury (H) 2-1
R5: Manchester United (H) 0-4

64-65 R1: Netherfield (A) 3-1
R2: Chester (H) 2-5

65-66 R1: Lincoln City (A) 3-1
R2: Grimsby Town (H) 1-1, (A) 0-2

66-67 R1: Southport (H) 3-1
R2: Port Vale (H) 1-1, (A) 3-1
R3: Cardiff City (H) 1-1, (A) 1-2

67-68 R1: Chesterfield (A) 0-2

68-69 R1: Rochdale (H) 0-0, (A) 1-0
R2: Darlington (A) 0-0, (H) 1-0
R3: Leicester City (H) 1-1, (A) 1-2

69-70 R1: Darlington (A) 0-0, (H) 2-0
R2: Barrow (H) 3-0
R3: Mansfield Town (A) 2-3

70-71 R1: Bradford (Park Avenue) (H) 1-0
R2: Rhyl (A) 0-0, (H) 1-1, 0-2

71-72 R1: Rochdale (A) 3-1
R2: Chesterfield (H) 0-0, (A) 0-1

72-73 R1: Halifax Town (H) 1-1, (A) 1-2

73-74 R1: Chesterfield (A) 0-0, (H) 2-1
R2: Bradford City (H) 1-1, (A) 1-2

74-75 R1: Halifax Town (H) 1-2

75-76 R1: Marine (A) 1-3

76-77 R1: Boston (H) 3-1
R2: Port Vale (A) 0-3

77-78 R1: Huddersfied Town (H) 1-0
R2: Grimsby Town (A) 0-2

78-79 R1: Worksop Town (H) 5-1
R2: Rotherham United (H) 1-1, (A) 1-2

79-80 R1: Hartlepool United (H) 5-2
R2: Chester (A) 0-1

80-81 R1: Chester (A) 2-1
R2: Rotherham United (A) 1-0
R3: Torquay United (H) 2-1
R4: Enfield (H) 1-1, (A - *at Tottenham*) 3-0
R5: Middlesbrough (A) 1-2

81-82 R3: Blackpool (H) 0-2

82-83 R3: Bradford City (A) 1-0
R4: Cambridge United (A) 0-1

83-84 R3: Sheffield Wednesday (A) 0-1

84-85 R3: Reading (H) 4-3
R4: Brighton & Hove Albion (H) 2-1
R5: Southampton (A) 2-1
R6: Liverpool (H) 0-4

85-86 R3: Bury (A) 0-2

86-87 R3: Caernarfon Town (A) 0-0, (H) 1-0
R4: Aldershot (A) 1-1, (H) 3-0
R5: Arsenal (A) 0-2

87-88 R3: Bolton Wanderers (H) 3-1
R4: Birmingham City (H) 0-2

88-89 R3: Chelsea (H) 4-0
R4: Stoke City (A) 3-3, (H) 2-1
R5: Everton (H) 0-1

89-90 R3: Leicester City (A) 2-1
R4: Ipswich Town (H) 2-0
R5: Sheffield U. (A) 2-2, (H) 0-0, (H) 0-1

90-91 R3: Leeds United (H) 1-1, (A) 0-4

91-92 R3: Norwich City (A) 0-1

92-93 R3: Leicester City (A) 2-2, (H) 1-1 (*5-4 pens*)
R4: West Ham United (H) 4-1
R5: Manchester City (A) 0-2

BARNSTAPLE TOWN

Currently: Western League

48-49 EX: Tiverton Town (A) 3-2
PR: Gloucester City (A) 2-5

49-50 PR: Tavistock Town (A) 4-0
Q1: Wells City (A) 0-1

50-51 PR: Oak Villa (A) 6-2
Q1: Bideford (A) 2-2, (H) 3-1
Q2: Glastonbury (A) 0-3

51-52 PR: Tiverton Town (A) 2-1
Q1: Truro City (A) 3-2
Q2: Bridgwater Town (A) 3-1
Q3: Bideford (H) 2-1
Q4: Lymington (A) 1-1, (H) 3-1
R1: Folkestone (H) 2-2, (A) 2-5

52-53 PR: Dartmouth United (H) 5-1
Q1: Taunton (H) 1-1, (A) 5-3
Q2: Bridgwater Town (H) 4-2
Q3: Ilfracombe Town (H) 0-0, (A) 0-1

53-54 PR: Tavistock (A) 3-1
Q1: Penzance (A) 6-0
Q2: Wadebridge Town (H) 2-2, (A) 4-3
Q3: St Blazey (A) 5-3
Q4: Bath City (A) 1-2

54-55 PR: Taunton (A) 3-3, (H) 6-0
Q1: Truro City (A) 3-1
Q2: Ilfracombe Town (H) 2-0
Q3: Tavistock (H) 12-1
Q4: Yeovil Town (H) 3-1
R1: Bournemouth & Boscombe Ath. (H) 1-4

55-56 PR: Taunton (A) 1-2

57-58 PR: Ilfracombe Town (A) 7-1
Q1: Minehead (H) 5-1
Q2: Truro City (A) 5-2
Q3: Bideford (H) 2-3

58-59 Q1: Truro City (H) 3-0
Q2: Bideford (H) 0-2

59-60 Q1: Newquay (A) 3-3, (H) *W/O*
Q2: Wadebridge Town (H) 9-1
Q3: Bideford (H) 1-1, (A) 5-1
Q4: Trowbridge Town (H) 1-0
R1: Exeter City (A) 0-4

60-61 Q2: St Blazey (H) 1-1, (A) 2-1
Q3: Bideford (H) 1-0
Q4: Bath City (H) 1-2

61-62 Q2: Penzance (A) 3-2
Q3: Bideford (H) 1-2

62-63 Q1: Falmouth Town (A) 1-1, (H) 1-3

63-64 Q1: St Austell (H) 4-2
Q2: Bideford (A) 0-2

64-65 Q2: Bideford (H) 0-0, (A) 0-3

65-66 Q2: Bideford (A) 2-2, (H) 2-2, 1-4

66-67 Q1: Bridgwater Town (A) 1-0
Q2: Minehead (H) 1-2

67-68 Q1: Wadebridge Town (A) 1-7

68-69 Q1: Bideford (A) 2-2, (H) 0-1

69-70 Q1: St Blazey (H) 3-1
Q2: Wadebridge Town (A) 2-4

70-71 Q1: Bideford (H) 1-7

71-72 Q1: Bideford (H) 1-3

72-73 Q1: Bodmin Town (H) 3-1
Q2: Wadebridge Town (H) 3-0
Q3: Bideford (A) 2-1
Q4: Weymouth (H) 1-0
R1: Bilston (H) 0-2

73-74 Q1: Minehead (H) 2-1
Q2: Falmouth Town (A) 1-4

74-75 Q1: Wadebridge Town (H) 0-4

75-76 Q1: St Blazey (H) 9-1
Q2: Falmouth Town (A) 0-4

76-77 Q1: Bath City (H) 2-1
Q2: Minehead (H) 1-2

77-78 PR: Wadebridge Town (A) 7-0
Q1: Chard Town (A) 0-1

78-79 PR: Liskeard Athletic (A) 0-1

79-80 PR: Falmouth Town (A) 2-1
Q1: St Blazey (A) 2-0
Q2: Dorchester Town (H) 0-0, (A) 3-1
Q3: Tiverton Town (A) 1-2

80-81 Q1: Almondsbury Greenway (A) 1-0
Q2: Bath City (H) 0-1

81-82 PR: Tiverton Town (H) 3-1
Q1: Chard Town (A) 2-1
Q2: Bideford (H) 0-1

82-83 Q1: Glastonbury (A) 1-1, (H) 4-1
Q2: Bath City (A) 2-4

83-84 PR: Saltash United (A) 1-3

84-85 PR: St Blazey (H) 4-1
Q1: Bath City (A) 1-4

85-86 PR: Saltash United (A) 0-1

86-87 Q1: St Blazey (A) 1-1, (H) 0-0, (A) 2-0
Q2: Minehead (A) 1-2

87-88 PR: Llanelli (A) 2-1
Q1: Minehead (A) 1-1, (H) 1-0
Q2: Forest Green Rovers (H) 1-2

88-89 PR: Paulton Rovers (A) 1-2

89-90 Q1: Weymouth (A) 2-6

90-91 PR: Ilfracombe Town (A) 0-4

91-92 PR: Torrington (A) 1-3

92-93 PR: Forest Green Rovers (A) 2-4

BARNTON

Currently: Mid-Cheshire League

48-49 EX: Nantwich (H) 5-1
PR: Fodens Motor Works (H) *W/O*
Q1: Hyde United (H) 0-2

49-50 EX: Knutsford (H) 2-2, (A) 1-2

BARRI

Currently: (Barry Town) Welsh League
* - As Barry Town

45-46 * Q1: Clevedon (H) 10-0
Q2: Cardiff Corinthians (H) 6-1
Q3: Llanelly (A) 7-1
Q4: Lovells Athletic (H) 1-5

46-47 * Q1: Clevedon (H) 4-1
Q2: St Philips Marsh Adult School (A) 6-1
Q3: Merthyr Tydfil (A) 0-3

47-48 * PR: Aberaman & Aberdare Athletic (H) 2-0
Q1: Soundwell (A) 10-0
Q2: Ebbw Vale (H) 2-0
Q3: Merthyr Tydfil (H) 3-4

48-49 * Q1: Ebbw Vale (H) 4-1
Q2: Llanelly (H) 3-1
Q3: Lovells Athletic (H) 1-3

49-50 * PR: Soundwell (H) 3-0
Q1: Gloucester City (H) 1-1, (A) 0-1

50-51 * PR: Soundwell (H) 4-0
Q1: Cinderford Town (A) 2-0
Q2: Stonehouse (A) 3-2
Q3: Llanelly (A) 1-2

51-52 * Q1: Troedrhiw (A) 3-1
Q2: Llanelly (H) 2-2, (A) 2-2, 4-0
Q3: Ebbw Vale (H) 4-2
Q4: Bath City (A) 2-0
R1: Newport County (A) 0-4

52-53 * Q1: Troedrhiw (A) 8-3
Q2: Cheltenham Town (A) 3-0
Q3: Llanelly (H) 1-1, (A) 0-3

53-54 * Q1: Stonehouse (A) 6-0
Q2: Gloucester City (H) 2-1
Q3: Merthyr Tydfil (A) 3-3, (H) 2-3

54-55 * Q1: Cheltenham Town (H) 1-1, (A) 2-1
Q2: Gloucester City (H) 1-4

55-56 * Q1: Stonehouse (A) 4-3
Q2: Gloucester City (H) 5-2
Q3: Lovells Athletic (H) 1-3

56-57 * Q1: Gloucester City (A) 1-3

57-58 * Q1: Stonehouse (A) 2-0
Q2: Cinderford Town (H) 3-0
Q3: Llanelly (A) 1-1, (H) 1-0
Q4: Bath City (H) 1-2

58-59 * PR: Cheltenham Town (H) 2-0
Q1: Merthyr Tydfil (H) 1-4

59-60 * Q1: Ebbw Vale (A) 2-2, (H) 6-1
Q2: Llanelly (H) 2-0
Q3: Cheltenham Town (H) 1-4

60-61 * Q1: Ebbw Vale (H) 9-0
Q2: Llanelly (A) 0-0, (H) 1-2

61-62 * Q1: Lovells Athletic (A) 3-2
Q2: Gloucester City (A) 1-1, (H) 2-1
Q3: Merthyr Tydfil (H) 2-0
Q4: Bideford (H) 2-1
R1: Queens Park Rangers (H) 1-1, (A) 0-7

62-63 * Q1: Stonehouse (H) 2-0
Q2: Gloucester City (A) 0-3

63-64 * Q1: Lovells Athletic (H) 1-1, (A) 3-1
Q2: Llanelly (H) 1-2

64-65 * Q1: Stonehouse (A) 2-1
Q2: Merthyr Tydfil (A) 0-4

65-66 * Q1: Lovells Athletic (A) 1-6

66-67 * Q1: Merthyr Tydfil (H) 0-1

67-68 * Q1: Cinderford Town (H) 1-0
Q2: Llanelly (A) 0-0, (H) 4-0
Q3: Cheltenham Town (H) 2-2, (A) 1-3

69-70 * Q1: Merthyr Tydfil (A) 1-2

70-71 * Q1: Llanelly (A) 0-1

71-72 * Q1: Abergavenny Thursdays (A) 0-1

72-73 * Q1: Llanelli (A) 1-0
Q2: Merthyr Tydfil (H) 1-0
Q3: Taunton Town (H) 0-0, (A) 0-2

73-74 * Q1: Merthyr Tydfil (H) 0-3

74-75 * Q1: Cinderford Town (A) 2-2, (H) 0-2 *(aban. in extra-time)*, (H) 0-2

75-76 * Q1: Everwarm (H) 1-1, (A) 1-0
Q2: Merthyr Tydfil (H) 5-2
Q3: Alvechurch (A) 1-3

76-77 * PR: Glastonbury (A) 0-1

77-78 * Q1: Melksham Town (H) 4-1
Q2: Worcester City (A) 0-1

78-79 * PR: Mangotsfield United (H) 2-0
Q1: Ton Pentre (A) 1-0
Q2: Paulton Rovers (A) 2-1
Q3: Merthyr Tydfil (H) 0-2

79-80 * Q1: Bath City (H) 2-1
Q2: Newbury Town (A) 2-1
Q3: Hungerford Town (A) 1-3

80-81 * Q1: Bromsgrove Rovers (H) 1-0
Q2: Lye Town (H) 1-1, (A) 2-1
Q3: Worcester City (A) 1-1, (H) 2-3

81-82 * PR: Ton Pentre (H) 2-0
Q1: Cheltenham Town (A) 0-4

82-83 * PR: Haverfordwest County (H) 2-0
Q1: Forest Green Rovers (A) 3-2
Q2: Merthyr Tydfil (A) 1-3

83-84 * PR: Calne Town (H) 4-1
Q1: Chard Town (H) 2-0
Q2: Mangotsfield United (H) 4-2
Q3: Cheltenham Town (A) 1-3

84-85 * Q1: Forest Green Rovers (H) 3-2
Q2: Mangotsfield United (A) 1-1, (H) 3-1
Q3: Gloucester City (A) 3-1
Q4: Merthyr Tydfil (A) 1-1, (H) 1-1, (H) 3-2
R1: Reading (H) 1-2

85-86 * Q1: Paulton Rovers (H) 2-2, (A) 2-0
Q2: Minehead (H) 5-1
Q3: Chippenham Town (H) 2-2, (A) 1-0
Q4: Yeovil Town (A) 1-4

86-87 * Q1: Dorchester Town (A) 1-1, (H) 3-4

87-88 * PR: Salisbury (A) 1-0
Q1: Clevedon Town (H) 5-1
Q2: Merthyr Tydfil (H) 0-1

88-89 * PR: Bristol Manor Farm (A) 1-0
Q1: Worcester City (H) 0-2

89-90 * Q1: Malvern Town (A) 5-1
Q2: Gloucester City (H) 2-2, (A) 0-2

90-91 * PR: Minehead (H) 2-1
Q1: Clevedon Town (H) 0-0, (A) 3-0
Q2: Bashley (H) 0-2

91-92 * PR: Ton Pentre (H) 3-1
Q1: Yate Town (A) 3-0
Q2: Weymouth (A) 1-1, (H) 2-3

92-93 PR: Taunton Town (A) 3-0
Q1: Clevedon Town (H - *at Worcester*) 1-3

BARROW

Currently: Northern Premier League

45-46 R1: Netherfield (H) 1-0, (A) 2-2 (*agg: 3-2*)
R2: Carlisle Utd (H) 4-2, (A) 4-3 (*agg: 8-5*)
R3: Manchester C. (A) 2-6, (H) 2-2 (*agg: 4-8*)

46-47 R1: Halifax Town (H) 0-0, (A) 0-1

47-48 R1: Carlisle United (H) 3-2
R2: Runcorn (A) 1-0
R3: Chelsea (A) 0-5

48-49 R1: Rochdale (A) 1-1, (H) 2-0
R2: Notts County (A) 2-3

49-50 R1: Southport (A) 1-1, (H) 0-1

50-51 R1: Carlisle United (A) 1-2

51-52 R1: Chesterfield (H) 0-2

52-53 R1: York City (A) 2-1
R2: Millwall (H) 2-2, (A) 1-4

53-54 R1: Spennymoor United (A) 3-0
R2: Great Yarmouth Town (H) 5-2
R3: Swansea Town (H) 2-2, (A) 2-4

54-55 R1: Darlington (H) 1-1, (A) 1-2

55-56 R1: Crewe Alexandra (H) 0-0, (A) 3-2
R2: Tranmere Rovers (A) 3-0
R3: Sheffield United (A) 0-5

56-57 R1: Chester (A) 0-0, (H) 3-1
R2: Chesterfield (A) 1-4

57-58 R1: Stockport County (A) 1-2

58-59 R1: Notts County (A) 2-1
R2: Hartlepools United (H) 2-0
R3: Wolverhampton Wanderers (H) 2-4

59-60 R1: York City (A) 1-3

60-61 R1: Accrington Stanley (A) 1-2

61-62 R1: Wrexham (A) 2-3

62-63 R1: Buxton (A) 2-2, (H) 3-1
R2: Wrexham (A) 2-5

63-64 R1: Bangor City (H) 3-2
R2: Chester (A) 2-0
R3: Swansea Town (A) 1-4

64-65 R1: Grimsby Town (A) 1-1, (H) 2-2, 0-2

65-66 R1: Grimsby Town (H) 1-2

66-67 R1: Rochdale (A) 3-1
R2: Tranmere Rovers (H) 2-1
R3: Southampton (H) 2-2, (A) 0-3

67-68 R1: Oldham Athletic (H) 2-0
R2: Altrincham (A) 2-1
R3: Leicester City (H) 1-2

68-69 R1: Goole Town (A) 3-1
R2: Stockport County (A) 0-2

69-70 R1: Alfreton Town (A) 1-1, (H) 0-0, (*at Chesterfield*) 2-2, (*at Preston North End*) 2-0
R2: Barnsley (A) 0-3

70-71 R1: Lincoln City (A) 1-2

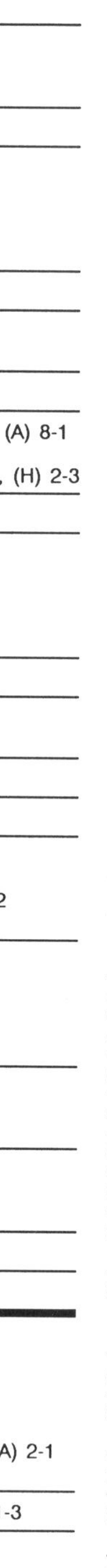

71-72 R1: Darlington (H) 0-2

72-73 Q4: Lancaster City (A) 1-3

73-74 Q1: Accrington Stanley (H) 0-4

74-75 PR: Clitheroe (A) 8-4
Q1: Rossendale United (H) 1-0
Q2: Darwen (H) 0-2

75-76 PR: Crook Town (A) 0-3

76-77 Q1: Washington (A) 2-0
Q2: Shildon (H) 2-1
Q3: Whitby Town (H) 2-2, (A) 4-3
Q4: Marine (A) 1-1, (H) 3-1
R1: Goole Town (H) 0-2

77-78 Q1: Horwich R.M.I. (A) 0-1

78-79 PR: Lytham (A) 2-0
Q1: Chorley (A) 1-2

79-80 PR: Emley (A) 0-1

80-81 Q1: Boldon Community Association (A) 8-1
Q2: Whitby Town (H) 1-1, (A) 2-1
Q3: Horden Colliery Welfare (A) 0-0, (H) 2-3

81-82 Q1: South Bank (A) 2-3

82-83 PR: Crook Town (H) 2-0
Q1: Ferryhill Athletic (A) 1-0
Q2: Lancaster City (A) 0-0, (H) 1-0
Q3: Annfield Plain (H) 8-0
Q4: North Shields (A) 1-2

83-84 Q1: Chester-le-Street (A) 0-1

84-85 Q1: Colwyn Bay (H) 4-0
Q2: Marine (A) 0-3

85-86 Q1: Brandon United (A) 0-5

86-87 Q1: Easington Colliery (H) 0-3

87-88 Q1: North Shields (A) 1-1, (H) 3-0
Q2: Crook Town (A) 1-0
Q3: Fleetwood Town (A) 0-0, (H) 3-2
Q4: Runcorn (A) 1-2

88-89 Q1: Lancaster City (H) 3-1
Q2: South Bank (A) 0-0, (H) 1-0
Q3: Morecambe (A) 0-0, (H) 5-1
Q4: Whitby Town (H) 1-1, (A) 3-1
R1: Rotherham United (A) 1-3

89-90 Q1: Cleator Moor Celtic (A) 4-1
Q2: Alnwick Town (H) 3-1
Q3: Whitley Bay (H) 2-2, (A) 1-3

90-91 R1: Bishop Auckland (A) 1-0
R2: Whitley Bay (A) 1-0
R3: Bolton Wanderers (A) 0-1

91-92 Q4: Bridlington Town (H) 0-1

92-93 Q4: Southport (H) 0-0, (A) 2-3

BARTON ROVERS

Currently: Isthmian League

76-77 Q1: Cambridge City (H) 3-0
Q2: Soham Town Rangers (H) 5-0
Q3: Wellingborough Town (H) 1-1, (A) 2-1
Q4: Nuneaton Borough (H) 2-3

77-78 Q1: Hemel Hempstead (H) 1-1, (A) 1-3

78-79 PR: Corby Town (A) 1-0
Q1: Wisbech Town (A) 2-0
Q2: Rushden Town (A) 1-1, (H) 3-1
Q3: Bedford Town (H) 1-2

79-80 PR: Leyton Wingate (A) 1-3

80-81 Q1: Camberley Town (H) 3-0
Q2: Walton & Hersham (H) 1-0
Q3: Slough Town (A) 1-0
Q4: A.P. Leamington (A) 1-0
R1: Torquay United (A) 0-2

81-82 Q1: Haverhill Rovers (H) 1-0
Q2: Bedford Town (A) 0-2

82-83 PR: Cheshunt (H) 2-0
Q1: Grays Athletic (A) 0-1

83-84 Q1: Kidderminster Harriers (H) 0-1

84-85 PR: Ampthill Town (A) 0-1

85-86 PR: Chesham United (H) 2-1
Q1: Walthamstow Avenue (H) 1-2

86-87 PR: Saffron Walden Town (H) 1-1, (A) 1-3

87-88 PR: Coventry Sporting (A) 1-2

88-89 Q1: Saffron Walden Town (H) 1-0
Q2: Bedworth United (H) 1-3

89-90 PR: Chipstead (H) 0-0, (A) 3-2
Q1: Windsor & Eton (H) 2-0
Q2: Burnham (H) 1-1, (A) 2-3

90-91 PR: Wisbech Town (A) 1-1, (H) 2-1
Q1: Redditch United (H) 0-2

91-92 PR: Bourne Town (H) 3-4

92-93 Q1: Moor Green (H) 2-3

BARTON TOWN

Currently: Lincolnshire League

47-48 EX: Grimethorpe Athletic (H) 3-4

48-49 EX: Thorne Colliery (A) 0-2

49-50 PR: Goole Town (A) 1-3

50-51 EX: Upton Colliery (H) 5-3
PR: Frickley Colliery (H) 1-3

51-52 Q1: Boston United (A) 3-5

52-53 PR: Boston United (H) 1-7

53-54 Q1: Lysaght's Spts (A) 2-2, (H) 1-4 ab., 1-2

54-55 Q1: Grantham (A) 2-5

55-56 Q1: Skegness Town (A) 2-7

56-57 Q1: Alford Town (H) 0-1

66-67 Q1: Harrogate Town (A) 4-0
Q2: Goole Town (A) 3-3, (H) 0-2

67-68 Q1: Hull Brunswick (H) 5-2
Q2: Brigg Town (H) 3-3, (A) 2-2, 1-0
Q3: Goole Town (H) 1-1, (A) 1-4

68-69 PR: Goole Town (A) 1-4

69-70 Q1: Bridlington Town (A) 5-3
Q2: Hull Brunswick (A) 1-1, (H) 1-2

70-71 Q1: Brigg Town (H) 1-1, (A) 0-3

71-72 Q1: Bridlington Town (H) 1-0
Q2: Goole Town (A) 2-3

72-73 Q1: Brigg Town (A) 3-1
Q2: Gainsborough Trinity (H) 2-2, (A) 1-3

73-74 Q1: Bradford Park Avenue (H) 1-2

74-75 Q1: Winterton Rangers (H) 2-2, (A) 0-1

75-76 Q1: Louth United (A) 0-0, (H) 1-3

76-77 Q1: Brigg Town (H) 2-2, (A) 2-3

77-78 PR: Yorkshire Amateur (A) 2-0
Q1: Emley (A) 2-3

78-79 Q1: Boston (H) 1-3

79-80 Q1: Goole Town (H) 0-1

80-81 Q1: Arnold (A) 1-0
Q2: Desborough Town (H) 4-1
Q3: Boston United (A) 0-2

81-82 Q1: Buxton (H) 1-3

Left: *Bishop Auckland 'keeper Phil Owens collects a cross under pressure from Colin Cowperthwaite as Barrow win 1-0 in 1990. Photo: Ged Rule.*

BARWELL

Currently: Midland Combination
See also Barwell Athletic and Hinckley F.C.

92-93 PR: Lye Town (A - *at Dudley T.*) 1-1, (H) 1-3

BARWELL ATHLETIC

Currently: Merged with Hinckley F.C.
Playing as Barwell in Midland Combination
See also Barwell

49-50 PR: Coalville Town (H) 3-0
Q1: Atherstone Town (H) 2-2, (A) 3-4

50-51 PR: Whitwick Colliery (H) 1-2

51-52 Q1: Hinckley Athletic (A) 1-1, (H) 2-7

52-53 Q1: South Normanton (A) 0-4

BASFORD UNITED

Currently: Notts Alliance

45-46 Q2: Grantham (A) 1-6

46-47 Q1: Ollerton Colliery (H) 2-1
Q2: Ransome & Marles (H) 0-7

47-48 Q1: Stamford (H) 3-1
Q2: Grantham (A) 0-7

48-49 PR: Ollerton Colliery (H) 0-3

49-50 EX: Stanton Ironworks (H) 0-1

50-51 EX: Langold W.M.C. (H) 1-5

51-52 Q1: Boots Athletic (A) 2-2, (H) 2-0
Q2: Newhall United (H) 1-1, (A) 0-3

52-53 Q1: Boots Athletic (H) 0-1

53-54 Q1: Newhall United (H) 0-0, (A) 3-2
Q2: Sth Normanton Miners Welfare (H) 0-5

54-55 Q1: Gresley Rovers (H) 1-7

BASHLEY

Currently: Southern League

88-89 Q1: Newport I.O.W. (A) 1-1, (H) 1-0
Q2: Pagham (H) 4-3
Q3: Fareham Town (H) 1-2

89-90 Q1: Basingstoke Town (A) 1-1, (H) 2-3

90-91 Q1: Mangotsfield United (A) 2-2, (H) 6-3
Q2: Barry Town (A) 2-0
Q3: Weymouth (H) 2-2, (A) 3-2
Q4: Welling United (A) 0-1

91-92 Q1: A.F.C. Lymington (A) 4-2
Q2: Maidenhead United (H) 1-1, (A) 0-1

92-93 Q1: Thame United (A) 3-2
Q2: Wimborne Town (H) 3-1
Q3: Abingdon Town (A) 2-4

BASILDON UNITED

Currently: Essex Senior League

79-80 PR: Cambridge City (A) 2-1
Q1: Harwich & Parkeston (A) 0-2

80-81 Q1: Aveley (A) 0-2

81-82 Q1: Walthamstow Avenue (H) 1-2

82-83 PR: Wellingborough Town (A) 2-5

83-84 PR: Wootton Blue Cross (A) 1-1, (H) 2-0
Q1: Leytonstone-Ilford (H) 1-0
Q2: Saffron Walden Town (A) 4-2
Q3: Wealdstone (A) 1-3

84-85 Q1: Felixstowe Town (H) 4-0
Q2: Harlow Town (A) 1-1, (H) 2-3

85-86 Q1: Alvechurch (H) 1-3

86-87 PR: Potton United (H) 3-1
Q1: Hornchurch (H) 0-2

87-88 PR: Cray Wanderers (H) 1-3

88-89 PR: Braintree Town (H) 2-4

89-90 PR: Stowmarket (H) 0-1

90-91 PR: Witham Town (A) 3-2
Q1: Hounslow (A) 3-4

91-92 PR: Brimsdown Rovers (H) 0-1

92-93 PR: Tring Town (H) 1-0
Q1: Ruislip Manor (A) 1-3

BASINGSTOKE TOWN

Currently: Isthmian League

46-47 PR: Salisbury Corinth. (H) 1-1, (A) 2-2, 1-2

47-48 PR: Salisbury (A) 1-5

48-49 EX: Bitterne Nomads (H) 1-2

49-50 EX: Totton (A) 0-3

50-51 EX: Alton Town (H) 1-2

51-52 Q1: Cowes Isle of Wight (H) 4-3
Q2: Alton Town (H) 2-5

52-53 Q1: Totton (H) 3-1
Q2: Alton Town (H) 2-0
Q3: Newport Isle of Wight (H) 2-4

53-54 Q1: Newport Isle of Wight (H) 0-5

54-55 Q1: Andover (H) 3-1
Q2: Winchester City (H) 0-2

55-56 Q1: Fareham Town (H) 3-3, (A) 2-3

57-58 Q1: Alton Town (A) 3-2
Q2: Cowes Isle of Wight (H) 2-5

58-59 Q1: Alton Town (H) 2-2, (A) 2-3

59-60 Q1: Alton Town (H) 5-2
Q2: Fareham Town (H) 4-1
Q3: Cowes Isle of Wight (H) 2-1
Q4: Salisbury (A) 2-2, (H) 1-2

61-62 Q1: Chichester City (H) 5-0
Q2: Andover (A) 1-7

62-63 Q1: Fareham Town (H) 4-2
Q2: Andover (A) 1-2

63-64 Q1: Fareham Town (H) 4-3
Q2: Chichester City (A) 2-1
Q3: Cowes Isle of Wight (A) 1-3

64-65 Q2: Cowes Isle of Wight (H) 4-2
Q3: Fareham Town (A) 3-3, (H) 1-2

65-66 Q1: Littlehampton Town (H) 6-0
Q2: Fareham Town (H) 0-2

66-67 Q1: Woking (H) 1-2

67-68 Q1: Woking (H) 5-1
Q2: Chichester City (H) 3-4

68-69 Q1: Waterlooville (A) 1-2

69-70 Q1: Wokingham Town (H) 1-2

70-71 PR: Fleet (A) 3-0
Q1: Cowes Isle of Wight (A) 3-1
Q2: Newport I.O.W. (A) 2-2, (H) 1-0
Q3: Waterlooville (H) 0-0, (A) 0-1

71-72 Q1: Welton Rovers (H) 2-1
Q2: Andover (A) 3-1
Q3: Salisbury (H) 5-2
Q4: Fareham Town (H) 2-2, (A) 1-1, 2-1
R1: Northampton Town (H) 1-5

72-73 Q1: Winchester C. (H) 1-1, (A) 1-1, 0-0, 3-0
Q2: Fareham Town (H) 3-1
Q3: Alton Town (H) 0-2

73-74 Q1: Frome Town (H) 2-0
Q2: Melksham Town (A) 6-0
Q3: Trowbridge Town (H) 0-1

74-75 PR: Andover (H) 1-0
Q1: Waterlooville (H) 3-1
Q2: Salisbury (H) 1-1, (A) 1-3

75-76 Q1: Farnborough Town (H) 2-1
Q2: Alton Town (H) 5-0
Q3: Southwick (A) 1-2

76-77 Q1: Chichester City (H) 10-0
Q2: Horsham (H) 2-0
Q3: Waterlooville (H) 1-2

77-78 Q1: Marlow (H) 2-0
Q2: Hampton (A) 1-1, (H) 0-2

78-79 Q1: Newport I.O.W. (A) 1-0
Q2: Dorchester Town (A) 0-1

79-80 PR: Clapton (A) 0-3

80-81 PR: Worthing (A) 1-0
Q1: Egham Town (H) 2-3

81-82 PR: Dorking Town (A) 2-0
Q1: Tooting & Mitcham United (H) 2-1
Q2: Hillingdon Borough (H) 4-2
Q3: Wembley (A) 1-5

82-83 PR: Poole Town (A) 0-0, (H) 2-0
Q1: Chippenham Town (A) 1-1, (H) 3-2
Q2: Slough Town (H) 2-2, (A) 0-2

83-84 Q1: Llanelli (H) 2-1
Q2: Clandown (H) 1-1, (A) 2-0
Q3: Witney Town (A) 2-2, (H) 3-2
Q4: Worcester City (H) 1-1, (A) 1-3

84-85 PR: Dorking (H) 2-0
Q1: Bognor Regis Town (A) 2-2, (H) 0-1

85-86 Q1: Arundel (A) 3-1
Q2: A.F.C. Totton (A) 1-1, (H) 1-2

86-87 Q1: Ton Pentre (H) 0-2

87-88 Q1: Dulwich Hamlet (H) 3-0
Q2: Marlow (A) 1-1, (H) 2-1
Q3: Tooting & Mitcham (A) 0-0, (H) 4-1
Q4: Sutton United (A) 0-3

88-89 Q1: Abingdon Town (H) 3-1
Q2: Fareham Town (A) 0-3

89-90 Q1: Bashley (H) 1-1, (A) 3-2
Q2: Chertsey Town (H) 3-1
Q3: Witney Town (A) 2-0
Q4: Marlow (H) 1-1, (A) 2-1
R1: Bromsgrove Rovers (H) 3-0
R2: Torquay United (H) 2-3

90-91 Q4: Wycombe Wanderers (A) 0-6

91-92 Q1: Pagham (A) 3-1
Q2: Horsham (H) 1-1, (A) 1-2

92-93 Q1: Brockenhurst (A) 0-1

BATH CITY

Currently: Alliance Premier League

45-46 R1: Cheltenham (H) 3-2, (A) 2-0 *(agg: 5-2)*
R2: Lovells Ath. (A) 1-2, (H) 2-5 *(agg: 3-7)*

46-47 Q4: Merthyr Tydfil (A) 1-7

47-48 Q4: Merthyr Tydfil (A) 1-2

48-49 Q4: Gloucester City (H) 2-3

49-50 PR: Roundway Hospital (A - *played home*) 7-1
Q1: Salisbury (H) 0-2

50-51 PR: Chippenham Town (H) 2-0
Q1: Welton Rovers (A) 1-2

51-52 PR: Clevedon (A) 3-1
Q1: Glastonbury (A) 2-2, (H) 3-1
Q2: Clandown (A) 3-1
Q3: Chippenham United (A) 3-0
Q4: Barry Town (H) 0-2

52-53 Q1: Paulton Rovers (A) 7-2
Q2: Wells City (H) 2-0
Q3: Glastonbury (A) 3-0
Q4: Trowbridge Town (H) 3-0
R1: Southend United (H) 3-1
R2: Grimsby Town (A) 0-1

53-54 Q4: Barnstaple Town (H) 2-1
R1: Walsall (H) 0-3

54-55 Q4: Merthyr Tydfil (A) 1-3

55-56 PR: Clandown (A) 0-0, (H) 4-0
Q1: Chippenham United (H) 0-1

56-57 Q1: Clandown (H) 2-0
Q2: Bridgwater Town (H) 1-2

57-58 Q1: Borough of Weston-super-Mare (H) 5-0
Q2: Clevedon (A) 1-1, (H) 4-1
Q3: Glastonbury (H) 2-1
Q4: Barry Town (A) 2-1
R1: Exeter City (H) 2-1
R2: Yeovil Town (A) 0-2

58-59 Q4: Trowbridge Town (H) 3-1
R1: Colchester United (A) 0-2

59-60 Q4: Yeovil Town (A) 2-0
R1: Millwall (H) 3-1
R2: Notts County (A) 1-0
R3: Brighton & Hove Albion (H) 0-1

60-61 Q4: Barnstaple Town (A) 2-1
R1: Swindon Town (A) 2-2, (H) 4-6

61-62 Q4: Bridgwater Town (H) 0-2

62-63 Q4: Falmouth Town (A) 1-2

63-64 Q4: Falmouth Town (H) 2-0

R1: Maidenhead United (A) 2-0
R2: Wimbledon (A) 2-2, (H) 4-0
R3: Bolton Wanderers (H) 1-1, (A) 0-3

64-65 Q4: Merthyr Tydfil (H) 4-1
R1: Queens Park Rangers (A) 0-2

65-66 Q4: Welton Rovers (H) 3-1
R1: Newport County (H) 2-0
R2: Bournemouth & Boscombe Ath. (A) 3-5

66-67 Q4: Weymouth (H) 2-2, (A) 1-0
R1: Sutton United (H) 1-0
R2: Brighton & Hove Albion (H) 0-5

67-68 Q4: Weymouth (A) 1-1, (H) 0-1

68-69 Q4: Yeovil Town (H) 0-2

69-70 Q1: Taunton (A) 4-2
Q2: Frome Town (A) 4-1
Q3: Minehead (A) 0-3

70-71 Q1: Andover (A) 1-0
Q2: Trowbridge Town (H) 3-0
Q3: Poole Town (A) 0-1

71-72 Q1: Chippenham Town (H) 2-1
Q2: Salisbury (A) 1-2

72-73 Q1: Cheltenham Town (H) 0-0, (A) 0-3

73-74 Q1: Andover (H) 3-0
Q2: Trowbridge Town (A) 0-0, (H) 2-4

74-75 PR: Devizes Town (A) 3-2
Q1: Weston-super-Mare (H) 3-0
Q2: Hungerford Town (H) 6-1
Q3: Mangotsfield United (A) 3-1
Q4: Yeovil Town (H) 2-1
R1: Wimbledon (A) 0-1

75-76 PR: Fareham Town (A) 0-1

76-77 Q1: Barnstaple Town (A) 1-2

77-78 PR: Taunton Town (A) 2-1
Q1: Bridport (A) 3-0
Q2: Swaythling (A) 1-1, (H) 3-0
Q3: Dorchester Town (H) 2-0
Q4: Merthyr Tydfil (A) 2-1
R1: Plymouth Argyle (H) 0-0, (A) 0-2

78-79 PR: Glastonbury (A) 3-0
Q1: Weston-super-Mare (A) 2-1
Q2: Salisbury (A) 2-0
Q3: Bridgwater Town (H) 7-1
Q4: Worcester City (H) 1-1, (A) 1-2

79-80 Q1: Barry Town (A) 1-2

80-81 PR: Glastonbury (H) 7-1
Q1: Weston-super-Mare (A) 2-1
Q2: Barnstaple Town (A) 1-0
Q3: Ton Pentre (A) 3-1
Q4: Leatherhead (A) 0-1

81-82 Q1: Mangotsfield United (H) 3-0
Q2: Cheltenham Town (A) 2-2, (H) 1-2

82-83 Q1: Taunton Town (H) 2-2, (A) 4-2
Q2: Barnstaple Town (H) 4-2
Q3: Wimborne Town (A) 0-1

83-84 Q1: Shepton Mallet Town (H) 4-0
Q2: Merthyr Tydfil (H) 0-1

84-85 Q1: Barnstaple Town (H) 4-1
Q2: Minehead (A) 0-0, (H) 3-0
Q3: Frome Town (A) 1-3

85-86 Q1: Taunton Town (H) 4-1
Q2: Clevedon Town (H) 1-0
Q3: Exmouth Town (H) 2-0
Q4: Croydon (H) 4-1
R1: Farnborough Town (A) 4-0
R2: Peterborough United (A) 0-1

86-87 Q4: Yeovil Town (H) 2-1
R1: Aylesbury United (H) 3-2
R2: Bristol C. (A) 1-1, (H - *played away*) 0-3

87-88 Q4: Slough Town (H) 3-1
R1: Chelmsford City (A) 2-1
R2: Welling United (A) 1-0
R3: Mansfield Town (A) 0-4

88-89 R1: Grays Athletic (H) 2-0
R2: Welling United (H) 0-0, (A) 2-3

89-90 Q4: Poole Town (A) 2-2, (H) 3-0
R1: Fulham (H) 2-2, (A) 1-2

90-91 Q4: Woking (A) 1-2

91-92 Q1: Stroud (A) 3-1
Q2: Maesteg Park Athletic (H) 5-2
Q3: Worcester City (H) 1-2

92-93 Q1: Glastonbury (A) 4-0
Q2: Falmouth Town (A) 3-0
Q3: Weymouth (H) 2-0
Q4: Tiverton Town (A) 0-0, (H) 2-1
R1: Cardiff City (A) 3-2
R2: Northampton Town (H) 2-2, (A) 0-3

BECCLES

Currently: (Beccles Town) Anglian Combination

50-51 EX: Diss Town (H) 4-2
PR: Stowmarket (A) 3-7

51-52 Q1: Gorleston (A) 1-5

52-53 Q1: Bungay Town (H) 3-1
Q2: Sheringham (A) 2-2, (H) 2-1
Q3: Great Yarmouth Town (A) 1-2

53-54 Q1: Sheringham (H) 7-1
Q2: Gorleston (H) 1-5

54-55 Q1: Wymondham Town (H) 2-0
Q2: Gothic (H) 3-1
Q3: Gorleston (A) 0-4

55-56 Q1: Bungay Town (A) 2-0
Q2: Wymondham Town (H) 2-2, (A) 2-1
Q3: Great Yarmouth Town (H) 1-4

56-57 Q2: Bungay Town (A) 2-2, (H) 4-4, 0-3

57-58 Q2: Great Yarmouth Town (A) 0-4

BECKENHAM TOWN

Currently: Kent League

83-84 PR: Ashford Town (H) 1-3

84-85 Q1: Hitchin Town (H) 0-2

85-86 Q1: Sutton United (A) 0-5

87-88 PR: Hailsham Town (H) 2-2, (A) 4-2
Q1: Banstead Athletic (A) 3-5

88-89 PR: Kempston Rovers (A) 1-0
Q1: Barking (A) 0-0, (H) 0-1

89-90 PR: Walthamstow Pennant (H) 0-5

90-91 Q1: Flackwell Heath (H) 0-2

91-92 PR: Wingate & Finchley (H) 1-0
Q1: Fisher Athletic (A) 0-4

92-93 PR: Feltham & Hounslow Borough (H) 2-0
Q1: Kingsbury Town (A) 3-2
Q2: Berkhamsted Town (A) 0-0, (H) 0-1

BEDFONT

Currently: Combined Counties League

92-93 PR: Haywards Heath Town (A) 1-0
Q1: Alma Swanley (A) 0-1

BEDFORD AVENUE

Currently: Merged with Bedford North End. Playing as Bedford North End Avenue in Bedford & Dist. Lge.

45-46 Q1: Bedford Town (H) 0-0, (A) 4-0
Q2: Hitchin Town (A) 2-0
Q3: Letchworth Town (H) 1-0
Q4: Grantham (A) 1-6

46-47 Q1: Biggleswade Town (A) 7-1
Q2: Hitchin Town (H) 0-8

47-48 PR: Kempston Rovers (A) 1-4

48-49 EX: Arlesey Town (A) 2-5

49-50 EX: Bedford St Cuth. (H) 1-1, (A) 0-0, 3-2
PR: Huntingdon United (A) 2-4

50-51 EX: Bedford St Cuthberts (A) 6-1
PR: Wootton Blue Cross (H) 0-4

BEDFORD CORINTHIANS

Currently: (Corinthians F.C.) Bedford & Dist. Lge

49-50 EX: Houghton Rangers (A - *played home*) 1-4

50-51 EX: Marston Shelton Rovers (A) 0-3

BEDFORD QUEENS WORKS

Currently: Defunct

47-48 PR: Letchworth Town (H) 1-8

48-49 PR: Stewartby Works (H) 1-2

50-51 EX: Lynton Works (Bedford) (H) 6-5
PR: Leighton United (A) 1-5

BEDFORD ST CUTHBERTS

Currently: Defunct

49-50 EX: Bedford Ave. (A) 1-1, (H) 0-0, 2-3

50-51 EX: Bedford Avenue (H) 1-6

BEDFORD TOWN

Currently: Defunct (reformed in Sth Mids Lge)

45-46 Q1: Bedford Avenue (A) 0-0, (H) 0-4

46-47 PR: Wolverton Town (H) 1-1, (A) 2-1
Q1: Luton Amateur (A) 5-1
Q2: Leighton United (A) 5-2
Q3: Hitchin Town (H) 2-2, (A) 2-3

47-48 PR: Eynesbury Rovers (H) 7-4
Q1: Arlesey Town (H) 2-1
Q2: Hitchin Town (A) 3-2
Q3: Vauxhall Motors (A) 1-1, (H) 0-2

48-49 PR: Kempston Rovers (H) 7-1
Q1: Vauxhall Motors (H) 1-2

49-50 PR: Kempston Rovers (A - *played home*) 2-0
Q1: Luton Amateur (H) 2-0
Q2: St Neots & District (H) 3-0
Q3: Hitchin Town (H) 2-0
Q4: Hastings United (A) 0-2

50-51 PR: Potton United (A) 6-2
Q1: Leighton United (H) 8-2
Q2: Wolverton Town (H) 5-1
Q3: Hitchin Town (A) 3-2
Q4: Guildford City (A) 0-0, (H) 1-2

51-52 Q1: Biggleswade Town (H) 3-2
Q2: Eynesbury Rovers (H) 3-0
Q3: Wolverton Town (H) 5-1
Q4: Bromsgrove Rovers (A) 5-2
R1: Swindon Town (A) 0-2

52-53 Q1: Potton United (H) 6-0
Q2: Eynesbury Rovers (A) 4-0
Q3: Hitchin Town (A) 3-2
Q4: Peterborough United (A) 1-2

53-54 Q1: Potton United (A) 5-1
Q2: Biggleswade Town (A) 0-0, (H) 5-0
Q3: Dunstable Town (A) 4-2
Q4: Gorleston (A) 2-0
R1: Weymouth (A) 0-2

54-55 Q4: March Town United (H) 5-2
R1: Dorchester Town (A) 0-2

55-56 Q1: Biggleswade Town (H) 4-0
Q2: Dunstable Town (A) 4-0
Q3: Eynesbury Rovers (A) 4-1
Q4: Walthamstow Avenue (H) 6-0
R1: Leyton (H) 3-0
R2: Watford (H) 3-2
R3: Arsenal (A) 2-2, (H) 1-2

56-57 R1: Norwich City (A) 4-2
R2: Reading (A) 0-1

57-58 Q4: Walthamstow Avenue (H) 1-1, (A) 0-1

58-59 Q4: Wisbech Town (H) 3-4

59-60 Q4: Hayes (H) 5-3
R1: Gillingham (H) 0-4

60-61 Q4: King's Lynn (H) 1-4

61-62 Q1: Letchworth Town (H) 6-0
Q2: Hitchin Town (A) 2-3

62-63 Q1: Wolverton Town & B.R. (H) 8-0
Q2: Hitchin Town (A) 5-3
Q3: Cambridge City (H) 2-1
Q4: Wisbech Town (H) 1-0
R1: Cambridge United (H) 2-1
R2: Gillingham (A) 0-3

63-64 Q4: Cambridge City (H) 2-2, (A) 3-2
R1: Weymouth (A) 1-1, (H) 1-0
R2: Chelmsford City (A) 1-0
R3: Newcastle United (A) 2-1
R4: Carlisle United (H) 0-3

64-65 Q4: Cambridge United (H) 1-4

65-66 Q4: Cambridge United (A) 2-1
R1: Exeter City (A) 2-1
R2: Brighton & Hove A. (A) 1-1, (H) 2-1
R3: Hereford United (H) 2-1
R4: Everton (H) 0-3

66-67 Q4: Romford (H) 1-1, (A) 2-1
R1: Wycombe (A) 1-1, (H) 3-3, 1-1, 3-2
R2: Oxford United (A) 1-1, (H) 1-0
R3: Peterborough United (H) 2-6

67-68 Q4: Boston United (A) 1-1, (H) 2-3

68-69 Q1: Histon (H) 5-0
Q2: Stamford (A) 0-1

69-70 Q1: Corby Town (H) 2-3

70-71 Q1: Letchworth Town (A) 3-0
Q2: St Albans City (A) 1-1, (H) 2-3

71-72 Q1: Banbury United (A) 2-2, (H) 1-0
Q2: Biggleswade Town (H) 3-0
Q3: Witney Town (H) 2-2, (A) 0-2

72-73 PR: Slough Town (A) 0-1

73-74 Q1: Cambridge City (H) 2-0
Q2: Histon (A) 1-2

74-75 Q1: Wellingborough Town (H) 2-1
Q2: Rushden Town (H) 2-0
Q3: Potton United (A) 2-1
Q4: Kettering (A) 3-3, (H) 0-0, (H) 0-2

75-76 Q1: Ely City (H) 2-0
Q2: Bourne Town (A) 5-1
Q3: Stamford (A) 2-0
Q4: Lowestoft Town (H) 6-1
R1: Wycombe Wdrs (A) 0-0, (H) 2-2, 1-2

76-77 Q1: Chatteris Town (H) 7-1
Q2: Potton United (H) 4-1
Q3: St Neots Town (H) 3-0
Q4: Dudley Town (A) 0-1

77-78 PR: Willesden (A) 3-4

78-79 Q1: Bishop's Stortford (H) 2-1
Q2: Rothwell Town (H) 5-2
Q3: Barton Rovers (A) 2-0
Q4: Barking (A) 1-3

79-80 Q1: Berkhamsted Town (A) 4-1
Q2: Hertford Town (A) 2-0
Q3: Chesham United (A) 0-0, (H) 0-1

80-81 Q1: Bishop's Stortford (H) 3-2
Q2: Bury Town (H) 4-0
Q3: Hitchin Town (A) 2-3

81-82 PR: Hoddesdon Town (H) 4-0
Q1: Potton United (A) 1-1, (H) 4-1
Q2: Barton Rovers (H) 2-0
Q3: Ely City (H) 1-0
Q4: Wisbech Town (H) 3-0
R1: Wimbledon (H) 0-2

82-83 Q1: Edgware (A) *Scratched*

BEDLINGTON TERRIERS

Currently: Northern League
* - As Bedlington Colliery Welfare
+ - As Bedlington Mechanics

59-60 + Q2: Annfield Plain (A) 1-4

60-61 + Q1: Billingham Synthonia Recreation (H) 3-2
Q2: Horden Colliery Welfare (A) 1-3

61-62 + Q1: Whitby Town (H) 4-2
Q2: Billingham Synthonia Recreation (H) 1-0
Q3: Ashington (A) 2-2, (H) 1-4

62-63 + Q1: Whitby Town (H) 3-1
Q2: Shildon (A) 0-4

67-68 * Q1: Ferryhill Athletic (A) 1-2

69-70 * Q1: Whitby Town (H) 0-1

70-71 * Q1: Spennymoor United (A) 0-2

71-72 * Q1: Ryhope Colliery Welfare (H) 5-1
Q2: Consett (H) 0-0, (A) 1-4

86-87 Q1: Chester-le-Street Town (H) 1-2

87-88 PR: Crook Town (A) 1-2

88-89 PR: Evenwood Town (A) 0-2

89-90 PR: Clitheroe (A) 0-4

90-91 PR: Norton & Stockton Ancients (H) 0-4

91-92 PR: Prudhoe East End (A) 2-0
Q1: Spennymoor United (A) 1-0
Q2: Gretna (A) 1-3

92-93 PR: South Bank (A) 0-5

BEDWORTH UNITED

Currently: Southern League
* - As Bedworth Town

48-49 * PR: Ibstock Penistone Rovers (A) 4-1
Q1: Whitwick Colliery (H) 1-3

49-50 * PR: Nuneaton Borough (H) 1-3

50-51 * PR: Morris Sports (H) 3-1
Q1: Gresley Rovers (A) 2-0
Q2: Brush Sports (A) 2-3

51-52 * PR: Rugby Town (H) 2-2, (A) 6-1
Q1: Darlaston (A) 2-1
Q2: Hednesford (H) 3-0
Q3: Nuneaton Borough (H) 1-1, (A) 2-1
Q4: Kettering Town (A) 2-4

52-53 * Q1: Burton Albion (A) 2-1
Q2: Hednesford (A) 3-0
Q3: Atherstone Town (A) 1-1, (H) 2-0
Q4: Kidderminster Harriers (A) 1-1, (H) 0-2

53-54 * Q1: Burton Albion (A) 1-2

54-55 * PR: Rugby Town (H) 2-3

55-56 * Q1: Rugby Town (A) 2-2, (H) 2-2, 3-1
Q2: Burton Albion (H) 1-1, (A) 2-3

56-57 * Q1: Bournville Athletic (A) 4-0
Q2: Tamworth (A) 4-1
Q3: Lockheed-Leamington (H) 2-4

57-58 * Q1: Atherstone Town (H) 2-1
Q2: Worcester City (H) 1-1, (A) 0-3

58-59 * PR: Halesowen Town (A) 2-2, (H) 4-2
Q1: Sutton Coldfield Town (H) 1-1, (A) 3-2
Q2: Bilston (H) 0-1

59-60 * Q1: Evesham United (A) 1-3

60-61 * Q1: Brierley Hill Alliance (H) 4-1
Q2: Halesowen Town (A) 2-5

61-62 * Q1: Halesowen Town (H) 3-0
Q2: Brierley Hill Alliance (A) 0-2

65-66 * Q1: Stourbridge (A) 0-8

66-67 * Q1: Loughborough United (A) 2-2, (H) 1-2

67-68 * Q1: Rugby Town (H) 2-0
Q2: Long Eaton United (A) 0-2

68-69 * PR: Belper Town (A) 3-2
Q1: Rugby Town (H) 3-3, (A) 2-0
Q2: Heanor Town (H) 2-2, (A) 0-1

69-70 PR: Loughborough United (A) 1-1, (H) 2-1
Q1: Arnold (H) 0-0, (A) 1-6

70-71 Q1: Atherstone Town (H) 1-2

71-72 Q1: Ilkeston Town (A) 2-1
Q2: Sutton Town (A) 2-2, (H) 0-1

72-73 Q1: Rugby Town (H) 0-3

73-74 Q1: A.P. Leamington (H) 1-0
Q2: Stourbridge (A) 2-5

74-75 PR: Alfreton Town (H) 0-1

75-76 PR: Kidderminster Harriers (A) 1-0
Q1: Rothwell Town (A) 0-1

76-77 Q1: Armitage (A) 1-2

77-78 PR: Valley Sports Rugby (A) 0-0, (H) 0-1

78-79 Q1: Brereton Social (H) 0-0, (A) 2-3

79-80 PR: Desborough Town (A) 1-1, (H) 6-0
Q1: Olney Town (A) 4-0
Q2: Corby Town (H) 1-0
Q3: Enderby Town (A) 0-0, (H) 0-1

80-81 Q1: Gornal Athletic (H) 2-0
Q2: Witton Albion (H) 1-2

81-82 Q1: Hednesford Town (A) 1-1, (H) 3-0
Q2: Alvechurch (H) 0-1

82-83 Q1: Flackwell Heath (A) 1-0
Q2: Corby Town (A) 0-1

83-84 Q1: Dunstable (H) 3-2
Q2: Kidderminster Harriers (H) 2-1
Q3: Moor Green (H) 0-0 *ab. 20 mins*, (H) 2-1
Q4: Chelmsford City (A) 1-2

84-85 Q1: Coventry Sporting (H) 0-0, (A) 3-2
Q2: Willenhall Town (A) 0-3

85-86 Q1: Berkhamsted Town (A) 1-1, (H) 1-2

86-87 Q1: Alvechurch (A) 1-1, (H) 1-0
Q2: March Town United (A) 0-1

87-88 Q1: Hinckley Athletic (A) 3-2
Q2: Racing Club Warwick (H) 1-2

88-89 Q1: Bourne Town (H) 1-1, (A) 4-3
Q2: Barton Rovers (A) 3-1
Q3: Bromsgrove Rovers (A) 1-3

89-90 Q1: Alvechurch (A) 1-0
Q2: Stratford Town (H) 3-0
Q3: Sutton Coldfield Town (A) 2-1
Q4: Redditch United (A) 1-1, (H) 0-2

90-91 Q1: Sutton Coldfield Town (H) 1-5

91-92 Q1: Bromsgrove Rovers (H) 0-2

92-93 PR: Walsall Wood (H) 1-0
Q1: West Midlands Police (A) 2-1
Q2: Stafford Rangers (H) 1-1, (A) 0-1

BEIGHTON MINERS WELF.

Currently: Defunct

48-49 EX: Maltby Main (A) 3-1
PR: Dinnington Athletic (A) 1-5

49-50 PR: Grimethorpe Athletic (H) 5-1
Q1: Denaby United (A) 2-0
Q2: Hoyland Common Albion (A) 2-3

50-51 PR: Kilnhurst Colliery (A) 3-0
Q1: Worksop Town (H) 1-1, (A) 3-5

51-52 Q1: Rawmarsh Welfare (A) 0-2

52-53 Q1: Brunswick Institute (A) 2-0
Q2: Rawmarsh Welfare (H) 6-0
Q3: Norton Woodseat (H) 1-1, (A) 3-1
Q4: Buxton (A) 3-2
R1: Wrexham (H) 0-3

53-54 Q1: Langold W.M.C. (H) 5-2
Q2: Norton Woodseats Amateur (H) 2-1
Q3: Worksop Town (A) 2-3

54-55 Q1: Brunswick Institute (H) 6-0
Q2: Rawmarsh Welfare (A) 0-1

55-56 Q1: Norton Woodseats Amateur (A) 2-1
Q2: Worksop Town (A) 0-3

56-57 Q2: Stocksbridge Works (A) 3-4

57-58 Q2: Norton Woodseats Amateur (H) 1-2

58-59 PR: Belper Town (H) 2-5

BELPER TOWN

Currently: Northern Counties (East) League

56-57 Q1: Gresley Rovers (A) 3-7

57-58 Q1: Clay Cross & Danesmoor (H) 3-1
Q2: Ilkeston Town (A) 4-2
Q3: Gresley Rovers (H) 2-1
Q4: Spalding United (A) 1-2

58-59 PR: Beighton Miners Welfare (A) 5-2
Q1: Sheffield (H) 2-3

59-60 Q2: Norton Woodseats Amateur (H) 3-2
Q3: Matlock Town (H) 2-3

60-61 Q1: South Normanton Welfare (H) 3-2
Q2: Alfreton Town (A) 7-1
Q3: Sutton Town (H) 1-2

61-62 Q1: Heanor Town (A) 2-4

62-63 Q2: Buxton (H) 3-4

63-64 Q1: Alfreton Town (H) 5-3
Q2: Matlock Town (H) 2-3

64-65 Q1: Alfreton Town (H) 2-2, (A) 3-0
Q2: Heanor Town (H) 2-1
Q3: Arnold (H) 3-3, (A) 0-1

65-66 Q1: Buxton (H) 1-1, (A) 3-6

66-67 Q1: Gresley Rovers (H) 4-2
Q2: Burton Albion (H) 1-3

67-68 Q1: Atherstone Town (A) 0-2

68-69 PR: Bedworth Town (H) 2-3

69-70 Q1: Gresley Rovers (H) 0-3

70-71 PR: Heanor Town (A) 1-3

71-72 Q1: Burton Albion (H) 0-0, (A) 0-2

72-73 Q1: Alfreton Town (H) 1-1, (A) 1-4

73-74 Q1: Eastwood Town (H) 0-0, (A) 3-0
Q2: Tamworth (A) 0-3

74-75 Q1: Stafford Rangers (H) 0-0, (A) 0-4

75-76 Q1: Ilkeston Town (H) 1-0
Q2: Gornal Athletic (A) 0-2

76-77 Q1: Alfreton Town (A) 0-2

77-78 PR: Sutton Town (A) 1-2

78-79 Q1: Atherstone Town (A) 0-2

79-80 PR: Brierley Hill Alliance (A) 2-0
Q1: Coventry Sporting (A) 0-1

80-81 Q1: Armitage (A) 2-1
Q2: Winsford United (H) 2-2, (A) 0-5

81-82 PR: Congleton Town (A) 2-0
Q1: Telford United (H) 0-6

82-83 Q1: Mexborough Town Ath. (H) 1-1, (A) 3-0
Q2: Armitage (A) 1-1, (H) 0-1

83-84 PR: Bilston (H) 3-3, (A) 0-1

84-85 Q1: Rhyl (H) 1-1, (A) 0-1

85-86 PR: Emley (A) 1-1, (H) 0-1

86-87 PR: Bootle (A) 0-2

87-88 PR: Droylsden (A) 2-4

88-89 PR: Harworth Colliery I. (A) 0-0, (H) 1-5

89-90 PR: Ashton United (H) 1-0
Q1: Arnold Town (H) 2-2, (A) 1-3

90-91 PR: St Helens Town (H) 2-3

91-92 PR: Arnold Town (A - *played home*) 2-0
Q1: Borrowash Victoria (A) 0-2

92-93 PR: Mickleover R.B.L. (A - *played home*) 2-0
Q1: Bradford Park Avenue (A) 0-2

BEMERTON HEATH HARLEQUINS

Currently: Wessex League

92-93 PR: Sholing Sports (A) 2-1
Q1: Abingdon United (A) 5-0
Q2: Bognor (A) 1-1, (H) 2-2, (A) 1-1, (H) 1-0
Q3: Witney Town (A) 0-1

BENTINCK COLLIERY

Currently: (Bentinck M.W.) Notts Sunday Lge

50-51 EX: Holbeach United (A) 0-2

51-52 PR: Cresswell Colliery (H) 1-2

BENTLEY COLLIERY

Currently: Defunct

47-48 EX: Winterton Rangers (H) 2-4

48-49 EX: Upton Colliery (H) 3-1
PR: South Kirkby Colliery (H) 1-3

49-50 EX: Upton Colliery (H) 9-1
PR: Ashby Institute (H) 3-1
Q1: Farsley Celtic (H) 4-2
Q2: Goole Town (A) 1-1, (H) 2-4

50-51 PR: Brigg Town (A) 0-4

51-52 Q1: Worksop Town (A) 1-5

52-53 Q1: Langold W.M.C. (A) 0-2

53-54 Q1: Brunswick Institute (A) 4-0
Q2: Worksop Town (H) 1-2

54-55 Q1: Rawmarsh Welfare (A) 1-2

55-56 Q2: Langold W.M.C. (A) 2-1
Q3: Worksop Town (A) 2-9

56-57 Q2: Upton Colliery (H) 2-1
Q3: Frickley Colliery (H) 1-2

BERKHAMSTED TOWN

Currently: Isthmian League

45-46 PR: Harrow Town (A) 0-8

46-47 EX: Welwyn Garden City (A) 2-2, (H) 4-2
PR: Hoddesdon Town (A) 3-4

47-48 EX: Hemel Hempstead Town (A) 4-3
PR: Sawbridgeworth (A) 6-1
Q1: Harrow Town (H) 3-4

48-49 EX: Rickmansworth Town (H) 3-1
PR: Slough Town (H) 3-1
Q1: Banbury Spencer (H) 1-2

49-50 EX: Southall (A) 0-1

50-51 PR: Bicester Town (H) 1-1, (A) 1-2

51-52 PR: Edgware Town (H) 3-1
Q1: Hayes (A) 0-5

52-53 PR: Barnet (H) 1-4

53-54 PR: Hemel Hempstead Town (H) 3-3, (A) 2-4

54-55 PR: Hendon (H) 0-3

55-56 PR: Kingstonian (H) 2-2, (A) 0-6

56-57 PR: Uxbridge (A) 2-3

57-58 PR: Wembley (A) 0-3

58-59 Q1: Hemel Hempstead Town (H) 2-2, (A) 2-1
Q2: Enfield (A) 0-6

77-78 Q1: Gravesend & Northfleet (H) 0-1

78-79 PR: Chesham United (A) 3-3, (H) 1-0
Q1: Uxbridge (A) 1-2

79-80 Q1: Bedford Town (H) 1-4

80-81 Q1: Finchley (H) 1-2

81-82 Q1: Hampton (H) 0-3

82-83 PR: Dulwich Hamlet (H) 3-3, (A) 0-6

83-84 PR: Dorking (A) 0-1

84-85 Q1: V.S. Rugby (H) 0-0, (A) 1-3

85-86 Q1: Bedworth United (H) 1-1, (A) 2-1
Q2: Stamford (A) 0-3

86-87 PR: Tiptree United (H) 1-1, (A) 1-2

87-88 PR: Wootton Blue Cross (A) 0-0, (H) 2-0
Q1: Hitchin Town (H) 3-1
Q2: Hemel Hempstead (H) 3-3, (A) 4-1
Q3: Barnet (H) 0-3

88-89 PR: March Town United (H) 2-2, (A) 2-4

89-90 PR: Hoddesdon T. (A - *at Hertford Town*) 3-2
Q1: East Thurrock United (H) 1-0
Q2: Gravesend & Northfleet (A) 0-1

90-91 PR: Harwich & Parkeston (A) 1-4

91-92 Q1: Harrow Borough (H) 3-2
Q2: Leighton Town (H) 2-0
Q3: Slough Town (H) 1-4

92-93 Q1: Harrow Borough (A) 2-0
Q2: Beckenham Town (H) 0-0, (A) 1-0
Q3: Chesham United (A) 0-3

BESTWOOD COLLIERY

Currently: (Bestwood Miners Welfare) Notts Alliance

49-50 EX: Worksop Town (H) 1-2

51-52 PR: Cinderhill Colliery (H) 1-1, (A) 0-4

52-53 Q1: Linby Colliery (A) 0-3

53-54 Q1: Cinderhill Colliery (H) 3-1
Q2: Cresswell Colliery (H) 0-7

54-55 Q1: Linby Colliery (A) 0-5

BETHESDA ATHLETIC

Currently: Caernarfon & District League

69-70 Q1: Pwllheli & District (A) 6-0
Q2: Rhyl (H) 2-2 *aban. after 70 mins*, (H) 1-3

74-75 Q1: South Liverpool (H) 1-0
Q2: Rhyl (H) 2-2, (A) 2-2, 0-3

75-76 PR: Porthmadog (A) 2-3

76-77 Q1: Oswestry Town (H) 2-1
Q2: Bangor City (A) 2-4

BETTESHANGER C.W.

Currently: Defunct

47-48 EX: Aylesford Paper Mills (H) 3-2
PR: Woolwich Polytechnic (H) 2-1
Q1: Folkestone Town (A) 1-5

48-49 PR: Ramsgate Athletic (A) 1-6

49-50 PR: Ramsgate Athletic (A) 0-6

50-51 EX: Folkestone Town (H) 1-0
PR: Erith & Belvedere (H) 2-1
Q1: Ashford Town (H) 2-1
Q2: Snowdown Colliery W. (H) 0-0, (A) 0-1

51-52 PR: Sheppey United (A) 3-1
Q1: Gravesend & Northfleet (H) 3-1
Q2: Snowdown Colliery Welfare (A) 2-0
Q3: Folkestone Town (A) 0-2

52-53 PR: Deal Town (H) 2-0
Q1: Ramsgate Athletic (H) 1-2

53-54 PR: Walton & Hersham (H) 3-2
Q1: Tooting & Mitcham United (H) 1-0
Q2: Tunbridge Wells United (H) 1-2

55-56 PR: Tonbridge (H) 2-8

56-57 PR: Maidstone United (H) 1-0
Q1: Gravesend & Northfleet (A) 1-7

57-58 PR: Snowdown Colliery Welfare (H) 2-0
Q1: Ramsgate Athletic (H) 1-0
Q2: Whitstable (A) 0-2

58-59 PR: Ashford Town (A) 1-10

59-60 PR: Ramsgate Athletic (H) 2-2, (A) 1-0
Q1: Dover (A) 0-0, (H) 3-1
Q2: Canterbury City (H) 6-0
Q3: Ashford Town (A) 0-3

60-61 Q1: Deal Town (H) 1-7

BEXHILL TOWN

Currently: Sussex County League

45-46 Q1: Hastings & St Leonards (H) *withdrew*

46-47 PR: Hove (A - *played home*) 5-2
Q1: East Grinstead (H) 3-1
Q2: Bognor Regis Town (A) 1-2

47-48 Q1: East Grinstead (A) 1-7

48-49 PR: Chichester City (A) 5-3
Q1: Shoreham (A - *played home*) 5-1
Q2: Horsham (A) 0-4

49-50 PR: Littlehampton Town (H) 3-4

50-51 PR: Haywards Heath (H) 0-1

51-52 PR: Bognor Regis Town (A) 1-1, (H) 3-0
Q1: Tonbridge (H) 0-4

52-53 PR: Shoreham (H) 2-0
Q1: Lancing Athletic (H) 1-2

53-54 PR: Haywards Heath (H) 0-3

54-55 PR: Haywards Heath (H) 2-5

55-56 PR: Littlehampton Town (H) 2-3

56-57 Q1: Eastbourne (A) 1-4

57-58 PR: Littlehampton Town (A) 1-3

58-59 PR: Arundel (H) 2-3

59-60 Q1: Hastings United (A) 1-4

60-61 Q1: Tonbridge (A) 2-2, (H) 1-2

61-62 Q1: Eastbourne United (A) 2-5

62-63 Q1: Newhaven (H - *played away*) 0-0, (A) 2-0
Q2: Maidstone United (A) 0-5

63-64 Q1: Maidstone United (A) 0-1

64-65 Q1: Eastbourne (A) 0-4

65-66 Q1: Maidstone United (A) 0-4

66-67 Q1: Haywards Heath (A) 1-0
Q2: Eastbourne United (A) 2-3

67-68 Q1: Herne Bay (A) 2-0
Q2: Ramsgate Athletic (A) 1-4

70-71 Q1: Brett Sports (H) 1-1, (A) 2-0
Q2: Folkestone (H) 1-1, (A) 2-4

71-72 Q1: Ashford Town (A) 0-2

72-73 Q1: Faversham Town (H) 2-0
Q2: Sittingbourne (H) 0-0, (A) 0-1

73-74 Q1: Ramsgate Athletic (H) 0-2

74-75 PR: Eastbourne United (A) 3-2
Q1: Southwick (H) 0-6

75-76 Q1: Margate (H) 0-8

76-77 Q1: Bognor Regis T. (H - *played away*) 2-1
Q2: Lewes (H) 0-3

77-78 PR: Sheppey United (A) 2-1
Q1: Burgess Hill Town (A) 1-2

78-79 Q1: Crawley Town (H - *played away*) 1-1, (A)

1-1, (*at Hastings United*) 0-1

79-80 Q1: Croydon (H) 0-2

80-81 Q1: Bromley (H) 0-7

81-82 Q1: Croydon (H) *Scratched*

BEXLEY

Currently: Defunct

47-48 EX: Sittingbourne (A) 4-3
PR: Sheppey United (A) 2-3

48-49 EX: Tonbridge (H - *played away*) 0-5

49-50 PR: Dover (A) 2-7

BEXLEY UNITED

Currently: Defunct
* - As Bexleyheath & Welling

52-53 * PR: Carshalton Athletic (H) 1-5

53-54 * PR: Dulwich Hamlet (H) 1-3

54-55 * PR: Tooting & Mitcham Utd (H) 3-3, (A) 1-4

55-56 * PR: Sittingbourne (A) 2-4

56-57 * PR: Epsom (A) 3-1
Q1: Carshalton Athletic (A) 9-4
Q2: Bromley (H) 2-5

57-58 * PR: Tonbridge (H) 1-0
Q1: Tunbridge Wells United (A) 4-1
Q2: Dulwich Hamlet (H) 3-1
Q3: Walton & Hersham (A) 1-3

58-59 * Q1: Tonbridge (H) 1-1, (A) 5-6

59-60 * Q1: Sittingbourne (H) 5-1
Q2: Gravesend & Northfleet (A) 3-4

60-61 * Q1: Erith & Belvedere (A) 6-3
Q2: Sittingbourne (H) 1-0
Q3: Dartford (H) 5-0
Q4: Sutton United (H) 1-3

61-62 * Q1: Gravesend & Northfleet (A) 2-2, (H) 4-1
Q2: Dartford (A) 0-4

62-63 * Q1: Bromley (A) 1-2

63-64 Q2: Bromley (H) 0-0, (A) 2-2, (H) 1-0
Q3: Sittingbourne (A) 2-0
Q4: Guildford City (A) 0-0, (H) 3-0
R1: Wimbledon (H) 1-5

64-65 Q1: Sittingbourne (A) 3-0
Q2: Sutton United (A) 1-1, (H) 2-1
Q3: Dartford (A) 1-3

65-66 Q1: Chatham Town (H) 6-2
Q2: Sheppey United (A) 3-1
Q3: Sittingbourne (H) 4-2
Q4: Folkestone Town (A) 1-4

66-67 Q1: Woodford Town (H) 5-1
Q2: Brentwood Town (H) 3-2
Q3: Hornchurch (A) 2-2, (H) 0-3

67-68 Q1: Tilbury (H) 2-0
Q2: Stevenage Town (H) 1-2

68-69 Q1: Sutton United (H) 1-0
Q2: Tooting & Mitcham United (A) 1-0
Q3: Hillingdon Borough (A) 0-3

69-70 Q1: Walthamstow Ave. (A) 1-1, (H) 2-2, 0-2

70-71 Q1: Hertford Town (H) 2-2, (A) 2-1
Q2: Grays Athletic (H) 1-3

71-72 Q1: Clapton (H) 2-1
Q2: Leatherhead (H) 3-2
Q3: Tilbury (H) 1-1, (A) 1-2

72-73 Q1: Bracknell Town (H) 1-0
Q2: Walthamstow Avenue (H) 1-0
Q3: Hampton (A) 0-0, (H) 4-1
Q4: Bognor Regis Town (A) 0-1

73-74 Q1: Edmonton & Haringey (H) 3-0
Q2: Romford (A) 2-2, (H) 3-1
Q3: Boreham Wood (A) 0-1

74-75 Q1: Grays Athletic (H) 0-1

75-76 Q1: Hillingdon Borough (H) 0-2

BICESTER TOWN

Currently: Hellenic League

46-47 EX: Headington United (H) 2-3

47-48 PR: Metal & Produce Recovery Depot (H) 1-3

48-49 PR: Oxford City (A) 1-6

49-50 EX: Aylesbury United (A) 2-5

50-51 PR: Berkhamsted (A) 1-1, (H) 2-1
Q1: Banbury Spencer (A) 0-4

51-52 PR: Windsor & Eton (A) 2-3

52-53 Q1: Maidenhead United (A) 0-2

53-54 PR: Maidenhead United (H) 0-5

54-55 PR: Abingdon Town (H) 5-2
Q1: Maidenhead (A) 2-3

55-56 PR: Slough Town (A) 0-4

BIDEFORD

Currently: Western League

48-49 EX: Ilminster Town (A) 5-1
PR: Oak Villa (H) 6-0
Q1: Street (A) 1-4

49-50 PR: Newton Spurs (H) 1-1, (A) 4-2
Q1: Ilminster Town (H) 6-0
Q2: Wells City (A) 1-1, (H) 3-2
Q3: Dartmouth United (A) 4-2
Q4: Gloucester City (H) 1-1, (A) 1-3

50-51 PR: Dartmouth United (H) 7-1
Q1: Barnstaple Town (H) 2-2, (A) 1-3

51-52 PR: Taunton (A) 1-1, (H) 8-2
Q1: St Austell (A) 1-1, (H) 5-0
Q2: Dartmouth United (H) 7-0
Q3: Barnstaple Town (A) 1-2

52-53 PR: Minehead (A) 4-1
Q1: Ilfracombe Town (A) 0-3

53-54 Q1: Ilfracombe Town (A) 4-0
Q2: St Blazey (H) 1-3

54-55 PR: Newquay Amateur (A) 1-5

55-56 Q1: Minehead (H) 4-0
Q2: St Blazey (H) 4-1
Q3: Penzance (A) 2-2, (H) 2-0
Q4: Yeovil Town (H) 0-3

56-57 PR: St Blazey (A) 5-2
Q1: Ilfracombe Town (A) 2-1
Q2: Newquay (H) 4-0
Q3: Taunton (A) 7-1
Q4: Dorchester Town (H) 1-1, (A) 0-3

57-58 Q1: Wadebridge Town (A) 2-0
Q2: Penzance (H) 5-1
Q3: Barnstaple Town (A) 3-2
Q4: Yeovil Town (A) 1-3

58-59 PR: Minehead (A) 4-3
Q1: Tavistock (H) 3-0
Q2: Barnstaple Town (A) 2-0
Q3: Wadebridge Town (H) 7-1
Q4: Yeovil Town (H) 1-4

59-60 PR: Tavistock (H) 4-3
Q1: Penzance (A) 5-3
Q2: Truro City (H) 6-2
Q3: Barnstaple Town (A) 1-1, (H) 1-5

60-61 Q1: Truro City (A) 2-2, (H) 4-2
Q2: Penzance (H) 5-2
Q3: Barnstaple Town (A) 0-1

61-62 Q1: Truro City (H) 5-3
Q2: Wadebridge Town (A) 4-1
Q3: Barnstaple Town (A) 2-1
Q4: Barry Town (A) 1-2

62-63 Q1: Truro City (A) 3-0
Q2: Wadebridge Town (H) 0-0, (A) 5-2
Q3: Falmouth Town (A) 1-1, (H) 0-3

63-64 Q2: Barnstaple Town (H) 2-0
Q3: St Blazey (H) 3-1
Q4: Trowbridge Town (A) 2-2, (H) 2-4

64-65 Q1: St Austell (A) 5-3
Q2: Barnstaple Town (A) 0-0, (H) 3-0
Q3: St Blazey (A) 3-0
Q4: Cheltenham Town (H) 1-0
R1: Colchester United (A) 3-3, (H) 1-2

65-66 Q2: Barnstaple Town (H) 2-2, (A) 2-2, 4-1
Q3: St Blazey (A) 2-2, (H) 3-0
Q4: Weymouth (A) 1-1, (H) 1-3

66-67 Q1: Falmouth Town (A) 3-0
Q2: St Austell (H) 5-0
Q3: Minehead (A) 0-5

67-68 Q1: St Blazey (H) 3-2
Q2: St Austell (H) 2-0
Q3: Falmouth Town (A) 1-3

68-69 Q1: Barnstaple Town (H) 2-2, (A) 1-0
Q2: Falmouth Town (A) 1-2

69-70 Q1: Falmouth Town (H) 1-2

70-71 Q1: Barnstaple Town (A) 7-1
Q2: Saltash United (H) 3-1
Q3: St Blazey (A) 6-2
Q4: Weymouth (A) 0-3

71-72 Q1: Barnstaple Town (A) 3-1
Q2: Falmouth Town (H) 3-1
Q3: Wadebridge Town (H) 4-1
Q4: Weymouth (A) 1-3

72-73 Q1: Penzance (H) 3-2
Q2: Truro City (H) 8-0
Q3: Barnstaple Town (H) 1-2

73-74 Q1: Penzance (H) 4-1
Q2: Newquay (A) 1-1, (H) 6-1
Q3: Falmouth (A) 3-3, (H) 1-1, 2-2, 2-2, 2-1
Q4: Trowbridge (H) 2-2, (A) 1-1, 1-1, 3-2
R1: Bristol Rovers (H) 0-2

74-75 Q1: Penzance (A) 2-1
Q2: Wadebridge Town (A) 3-3, (H) 4-2
Q3: Minehead (A) 1-2

75-76 PR: Penzance (A) 1-5

76-77 Q1: Welton Rovers (A) 2-1
Q2: Taunton Town (A) 2-4

77-78 Q1: St Blazey (A) 1-0
Q2: Newquay (A) 3-2
Q3: Tiverton Town (A) 0-0, (H) 3-0
Q4: Banbury United (H) 1-0
R1: Portsmouth (A) 1-3

Below: *Bideford attack during their First Round tie at Fratton Park in 1977.*

78-79 Q1: Falmouth Town (H) 2-1
Q2: Saltash United (H) 2-0
Q3: Taunton Town (A) 0-3

79-80 PR: Frome Town (A) 1-0
Q1: Liskeard Athletic (A) 1-3

80-81 Q1: Bridgwater Town (H) 1-0
Q2: Clevedon Town (H) 2-1
Q3: Trowbridge Town (A) 3-2
Q4: Addlestone & Weybridge Town (A) 0-3

81-82 Q1: St Blazey (H) 4-1
Q2: Barnstaple Town (A) 1-0
Q3: Falmouth Town (H) 1-0
Q4: Kingstonian (H) 1-0
R1: Barking (H) 1-2

82-83 Q1: Weston-super-Mare (A) 4-1
Q2: Shepton Mallet Town (H) 3-1
Q3: Liskeard Athletic (A) 2-1
Q4: Slough Town (A) 1-7

83-84 Q1: Tiverton Town (A) 6-1
Q2: Frome Town (A) 0-0, (H) 0-2

84-85 PR: Bristol Manor Farm (H) 2-1
Q1: Cheltenham Town (A) 0-0, (H) 0-2

85-86 Q1: Merthyr Tydfil (H) 1-1, (A) 1-1, (H) 2-0
Q2: Exmouth Town (A) 1-2

86-87 Q1: Cheltenham Town (A) 4-3
Q2: Saltash United (A) 2-1
Q3: Forest Green Rovers (H) 2-1
Q4: Dartford (H) 0-2

87-88 Q1: Exmouth (H) 1-1, (A) 2-0
Q2: Tiverton Town (A) 2-4

88-89 PR: Shortwood United (H) 1-1, (A) 1-2

89-90 Q1: Taunton Town (A) 0-3

90-91 PR: Wimborne Town (A) 2-3

91-92 PR: Falmouth Town (H) 2-3

92-93 PR: Torrington (A) 0-1

BIGGLESWADE TOWN

Currently: South Midlands League

46-47 PR: Arlesey Town (A) 2-1
Q1: Bedford Avenue (H) 1-7

47-48 PR: St Neots & District (H) 9-1
Q1: Kempston Rovers (H) 4-5

48-49 PR: Eynesbury Rovers (H) 3-1
Q1: Letchworth Town (H) 4-4, (A) 3-3, 4-0
Q2: Vauxhall Motors (H) 1-4

50-51 EX: Dunstable Town (H) 6-0
PR: Letchworth Town (A) 2-2, (H) 3-2
Q1: Wootton Blue Cross (H) 1-2

51-52 Q1: Bedford Town (A) 2-3

52-53 Q1: Wolverton Town & B.R. (H) 0-3

53-54 Q1: Wolverton Town & B.R. (A) 2-0
Q2: Bedford Town (H) 0-0, (A) 0-5

54-55 Q1: Dunstable Town (A) 3-2
Q2: Potton United (A) 5-2
Q3: Eynesbury Rovers (A) 2-3

55-56 Q1: Bedford Town (A) 0-4

56-57 Q1: Vauxhall Motors (H) 2-3

57-58 Q2: Wolverton Town & B.R. (A) 0-7

58-59 Q1: Vauxhall Motors (H) 1-2

59-60 Q2: Letchworth Town (H) 1-2

60-61 Q1: Hitchin Town (A) 0-4

61-62 Q1: Hitchin Town (A) 1-2

62-63 Q1: Letchworth Town (H) 3-3, (A) 1-1 *aban. after 106 minutes*, (A) 3-0
Q2: Cambridge City (H - *played away*) 0-5

63-64 Q1: Wolverton Town & B.R. (H) 4-1
Q2: St Albans City (H) 5-4
Q3: Hitchin Town (H) 2-2, (A) 1-5

64-65 Q1: Hitchin Town (A) 2-2, (H) 2-4

65-66 Q1: Wellingborough Town (A) 0-3

66-67 Q1: Cambridge United (A) 0-6

67-68 Q1: Rothwell Town (H) 1-1, (A) 2-5

68-69 Q1: Rothwell Town (A) 3-2
Q2: Cambridge City (H) 2-1
Q3: Stamford (H) 1-2

69-70 Q1: St Neots Town (A) 3-2
Q2: Cambridge City (A) 0-2

70-71 Q1: Leighton Town (H) 1-4

71-72 Q1: Rushden Town (H) 2-1
Q2: Bedford Town (A) 0-3

72-73 Q1: Hatfield Town (A) 4-1
Q2: Woking (H) 0-2

73-74 Q1: Letchworth Town (H) 2-0
Q2: Corby Town (A) 0-1

74-75 Q1: Potton United (H) 0-0, (A) 1-2

75-76 Q1: Maidenhead United (H) 0-1

90-91 Q1: Hornchurch (H) 2-2, (A) 1-3

91-92 PR: Newmarket T. (A) 1-1, (H) 2-2, (H) 1-0
Q1: Brimsdown Rovers (H) 0-2

92-93 PR: Barking (H - *at Langford*) 1-3

BILLERICAY TOWN

Currently: Isthmian League

77-78 Q1: Harwich & Parkeston (H) 1-1, (A) 4-1
Q2: Haringey Borough (A) 3-1
Q3: Walthamstow Avenue (H) 3-1
Q4: Hendon (A) 2-3

78-79 Q1: Chelmsford City (H) 2-1
Q2: Letchworth City (H) 5-1
Q3: Barking (A) 0-2

79-80 Q1: Bishop's Stortford (A) 2-1
Q2: Harwich & Parkeston (A) 1-3

80-81 Q1: Chalfont St Peter (H) 1-1, (A) 3-0
Q2: Dulwich Hamlet (H) 1-2

81-82 PR: Tiptree United (H) 1-0
Q1: Cray Wanderers (A) 4-0
Q2: Welling United (H) 3-1
Q3: Leytonstone-Ilford (H) 0-0, (A) 0-1

82-83 Q1: Wisbech Town (H) 3-1
Q2: Soham Town Rangers (H) 5-3
Q3: Wellingborough Town (A) 1-1, (H) 1-2

83-84 Q1: Thetford Town (H) 1-0
Q2: Walthamstow Av. (H) 2-2, (A) 0-0, (A) 1-2

84-85 Q1: Cambridge C. (H) 1-1, (A - *pl. home*) 1-3

85-86 Q1: Ware (A) 0-1

86-87 PR: Stowmarket Town (H) 0-2

87-88 Q1: Kingsbury Town (H) 0-3

88-89 PR: Haverhill Rovers (H) 0-1

89-90 PR: Dunstable (H) 0-1

90-91 PR: Hanwell Town (H) 3-2
Q1: Leyton-Wingate (A) 1-1, (H) 1-0
Q2: Edgware Town (H) 1-0
Q3: Egham Town (A) 1-1, (H) 1-2

91-92 Q1: Clacton Town (A) 2-1
Q2: Sudbury Town (H) 3-1
Q3: Enfield (H) 1-3

92-93 Q1: Dagenham & Redbridge (A) 1-1, (H) 1-4

BILLINGHAM ST JOHN

Currently: Defunct

48-49 PR: Cargo Fleet Works (H) 4-5

BILLINGHAM SYNTHONIA

Currently: Northern League
* - As Billingham Synthonia Recreation

45-46 * Q2: Bye
Q3: Stockton (A) 1-4

46-47 * Q1: Brigham & Cowan (A) 2-2, (H) *W/O*
Q2: Portrack Shamrocks (A) 1-2

47-48 * Q1: Portrack Shamrocks (H) 1-3

48-49 * PR: Guisborough (A) 5-1
Q1: Cargo Fleet Works (H) 11-1
Q2: Smith's Dock (A) 5-2
Q3: Portrack Shamrocks (H) 5-0
Q4: Annfield Plain (H) 2-1
R1: Crewe Alexandra (A) 0-5

49-50 * Q1: Whitby United (A) 2-2, (H) 5-0
Q2: South Bank (A) 1-0
Q3: Portrack Shamrocks (H) 3-1
Q4: Horden Colliery Welfare (H) 1-1, (A) 1-0
R1: Stockport County (A) 0-3

50-51 * Q4: Scarborough (H) 0-3

51-52 * Q1: Skinningrove Works (H) 6-0
Q2: Bridlington Trinity United (A) 6-0
Q3: Whitby Town (A) 3-2
Q4: North Shields (H) 2-1
R1: Scunthorpe United (A) 0-5

52-53 * Q1: South Bank (H) 3-2
Q2: Head Wrightsons (H) 6-1
Q3: Ferryhill Athletic (H) 5-0
Q4: Ashington (A) 0-4

53-54 * Q1: Whitby Town (H) 2-1
Q2: Bridlington Central United (H) 4-1
Q3: Ferryhill Athletic (H) 1-2

54-55 * Q1: Bridlington Central (H) 2-2, (A) 2-3

55-56 * Q2: South Bank (A) 1-0
Q3: Bridlington Central United (A) 0-1

56-57 * Q1: Bridlington Central United (H) 2-1
Q2: North Skelton Athletic (A) 3-1
Q3: Whitby Town (A) 3-2
Q4: Crook Town (H) 8-3
R1: Carlisle United (A) 1-6

57-58 * Q4: Easington Colliery Welfare (A) 3-2
R1: Boston United (A) 2-5

58-59 * Q1: Tow Law Town (H) 2-4

59-60 * Q1: Murton Colliery Welfare (H) 3-5

60-61 * Q1: Bedlington Mechanics (A) 2-3

61-62 * Q1: Ryhope Colliery Welfare (A) 2-1
Q2: Bedlington Mechanics (A) 0-1

62-63 * Q1: Horden Colliery Welfare (H) 2-2, (A) 2-4

63-64 Q1: Ashington (A) 1-1, (H) 0-2

64-65 Q1: Ferryhill Athletic (A) 0-5

65-66 Q1: Whitby Town (H) 1-2

66-67 Q1: Evenwood Town (H) 1-0
Q2: Whitby Town (A) 1-1, (H) 1-0
Q3: Annfield Plain (H) 4-0
Q4: South Shields (A) 0-2

67-68 Q1: Whitby Town (H) 2-6

68-69 Q1: Ashington (H) 2-0
Q2: Blyth Spartans (A) 2-1
Q3: Bishop Auckland (H) 0-2

70-71 Q1: Whitley Bay (H) 2-4

71-72 Q1: Ferryhill Athletic (H) 0-2

72-73 Q1: Stanley United (H) 3-2
Q2: Evenwood Town (A) 0-0, (H) 2-1
Q3: Crook Town (A) 3-0
Q4: South Shields (H) 1-1, (A) 1-2

73-74 Q1: Ashington (H) 1-4

75-76 Q1: Shildon (H) 1-1, (A) 2-3

76-77 Q1: Annfield Plain (A) 2-3

77-78 Q1: Eppleton Colliery Welfare (H) 2-0
Q2: Whitley Bay (A) 1-3

78-79 PR: Tow Law Town (H) 2-1
Q1: Willington (A) 1-0
Q2: Easington Colliery Welfare (A) 3-1
Q3: Boldon C.A. (H) 0-0, (A) 4-2
Q4: Blyth Spartans (H) 0-1

79-80 PR: Evenwood Town (A) 2-1
Q1: Wallsend Town (A) 4-1
Q2: Bishop Auckland (H) 0-1

80-81 Q1: Annfield Plain (A) 3-2
Q2: Farsley Celtic (H) 2-0
Q3: Gateshead (A) 0-3

81-82 Q1: Lancaster City (A) 0-1

82-83 Q1: Seaham Colliery Welfare Red Star (H) 0-1

83-84 Q1: Lancaster City (H) 0-1

84-85 Q1: Brandon United (H) 2-1
Q2: Blue Star (A) 0-1

85-86 Q1: Gateshead (H) 0-4

86-87 Q1: Workington (A) 1-2

87-88 Q1: Alnwick Town (H) 2-0
Q2: Chester-le-Street T. (A) 1-1, (H) 4-3
Q3: Blyth Spartans (H) 5-2

Q4: Caernarfon Town (A) 2-0
R1: Halifax T. (H - *at Hartlepool Utd*) 2-4

88-89 Q1: Harrogate Town (A) 3-1
Q2: Accrington Stanley (A) 1-1, (H) 5-1
Q3: Billingham Town (H) 3-0
Q4: Northwich Victoria (A) 0-2

89-90 Q1: Guisborough Town (H) 2-0
Q2: Netherfield (H) 0-0, (A) 2-1
Q3: Gateshead (A) 2-0
Q4: North Shields (H) 2-1
R1: Lincoln City (A) 0-1

90-91 Q1: Northallerton Town (A) 0-2

91-92 Q1: Netherfield (A) 2-3

92-93 Q1: Gateshead (A) 1-3

BILLINGHAM TOWN

Currently: Northern League

84-85 PR: Coundon Three Tuns (H) 2-0
Q1: North Shields (A) 2-7

85-86 PR: Easington Colliery (A) 3-2
Q1: Shildon (A) 2-1
Q2: Morecambe (H) 0-5

86-87 Q1: South Bank (A) 1-1, (H) 0-2

87-88 Q1: Bridlington Town (H) 0-3

88-89 Q1: Guiseley (H) 1-0
Q2: Newcastle Blue Star (H) 2-1
Q3: Billingham Synthonia (A) 0-3

89-90 Q1: Spennymoor United (H) 1-1, (A) 1-2

90-91 PR: Brandon United (H) 1-0
Q1: Guisborough Town (H) 1-2

91-92 PR: Stockton (A) 4-2
Q1: Penrith (A) 2-4

92-93 PR: Chester-le-Street Town (A) 1-0
Q1: Armthorpe Welfare (A) 2-2, (H) 2-0
Q2: Guisborough Town (A) 0-3

BILSTON TOWN

Currently: Southern League
* - As Bilston F.C.

49-50 * EX: Oswestry Town (H) 1-0
PR: Darlaston (H) 2-1
Q1: Bromsgrove Rovers (A) 1-2

50-51 * PR: Wellington Town (H) 1-3

51-52 * PR: Stourbridge (A) 0-5

52-53 * PR: Stafford Rangers (A) 1-0
Q1: Cradley Heath (A) 2-2, (H) 3-1
Q2: Bromsgrove Rovers (A) 0-1

53-54 * PR: Dudley Town (A) 2-1
Q1: Kidderminster Harriers (H) 0-2

54-55 * Q1: Lye Town (H) 4-2
Q2: Hednesford (H) 1-4

55-56 * PR: Stafford Rangers (H) 1-5

56-57 * PR: Wellington Town (H) 1-1, (A) 2-3

57-58 * PR: Darlaston (H) 2-0
Q1: Nuneaton Borough (A) 0-2

58-59 * PR: Lockheed-Leamington (H) 6-1
Q1: Rugby Town (H) 2-1
Q2: Bedworth Town (A) 1-0
Q3: Brierley Hill Alliance (H) 2-2, (A) 2-4

59-60 * PR: Lockheed-Leamington (H) 3-2
Q1: Halesowen Town (A) 4-2
Q2: Rugby Town (H) 5-1
Q3: Evesham United (A) 1-2

60-61 * Q1: Evesham United (A) 3-1
Q2: Lockheed Leamington (H) 1-3

61-62 * Q1: Hednesford (A) 6-3
Q2: Rugby Town (A) 0-1

62-63 * Q1: Hednesford (H) 2-3

63-64 * Q1: Rugby Town (H) 1-4

64-65 * Q1: Halesowen Town (A) 1-1, (H) 0-3

65-66 * Q1: Rugby Town (H) 2-1
Q2: Stourbridge (H) 0-1

66-67 * Q1: Hednesford (A) 4-4, (H) 2-3

67-68 * Q1: Dudley Town (H) 0-1

68-69 * Q1: Dudley Town (A) 2-0
Q2: Lower Gornal Athletic (H) 3-0
Q3: Stafford Rangers (H) 3-2
Q4: Matlock Town (H) 2-0
R1: Halifax Town (H) 1-3

69-70 * Q1: Stafford Rangers (H) 0-1

70-71 * Q1: Alvechurch (H) 2-0
Q2: Kidderminster Harriers (H) 2-2, (A) 1-7

71-72 * Q1: Alfreton Town (A) 0-4

72-73 * Q1: Halesowen Town (A) 4-1
Q2: Stourbridge (H) 3-2
Q3: Bromsgrove Rovers (A) 1-1, (H) 1-0
Q4: Brierley Hill Alliance (H) 3-0
R1: Barnstaple Town (A) 2-0
R2: Barnet (A) 1-1, (H) 0-1

73-74 * Q1: Long Eaton United (A) 3-1
Q2: Alfreton Town (H) 0-2

74-75 * PR: Darlaston (A) 2-1
Q1: Stourbridge (H) 3-0
Q2: Redditch United (H) 0-2

75-76 * Q1: Eastwood Town (H) 3-1
Q2: Alfreton Town (H) 2-2, (A) 1-2

76-77 * Q1: Valley Sports (A) 4-1
Q2: Dudley Town (A) 1-4

77-78 * Q1: Brierley Hill Alliance (H) 1-2

78-79 * PR: Halesowen Town (A) 0-2

79-80 * Q1: Telford United (H) 1-2

80-81 * PR: Congleton Town (H) 3-2
Q1: Winsford United (A) 2-4

81-82 * PR: Rushall Olympic (H) 0-0, (A) 3-1
Q1: Halesowen Town (H) 2-3

82-83 * Q1: Blakenall (H) 2-2, (A) 2-1
Q2: Witton Albion (A) 2-4

83-84 * PR: Belper Town (A) 3-3, (H) 1-0
Q1: Arnold (A) 2-1
Q2: Frickley Athletic (H) 1-1, (A) 0-2

84-85 Q1: South Liverpool (H - *at Darlaston*) 3-2
Q2: Chorley (H) 0-1

85-86 Q1: Atherstone United (A) 3-3, (H) 0-2

86-87 PR: Lye Town (H) 1-2

87-88 PR: Highgate Utd (A) 1-1, (H) 0-0, (H) 2-0
Q1: Friar Lane Old Boys (A) 2-2, (H) 3-2
Q2: Willenhall Town (H) 0-3

88-89 PR: Alfreton Town (H) 4-0
Q1: Warrington Town (H) 0-0, (A) 2-3

89-90 PR: Desborough Town (H) 1-1, (A) 1-2

90-91 Q1: Wednesfield (H) 6-0
Q2: Buxton (H) 2-1
Q3: Witton Albion (A) 0-4

91-92 Q1: Chasetown (A) 0-0, (H) 0-1

92-93 PR: Newcastle Town (H) 1-3

BIRCH COPPICE COLLIERY

Currently: Defunct

54-55 Q1: Atherstone Town (H) 0-3

BIRMINGHAM CITY

Currently: Football League

45-46 R3: Portsmouth (H) 1-0, (A) 0-0 (*agg: 1-0*)
R4: Watford (H) 5-0, (A) 1-1 (*agg: 6-1*)
R5: Sunderland (A) 0-1, (H) 3-1 (*agg: 3-2*)
R6: Bradford P.A. (A) 2-2, (H) 6-0 (*agg: 8-2*)
SF: Derby (*at Sheff. W.*) 1-1, (*at Man. City*) 0-4

46-47 R3: Fulham (A) 2-1
R4: Portsmouth (H) 1-0
R5: Manchester City (H) 5-0
R6: Liverpool (A) 1-4

47-48 R3: Notts County (H) 0-6

48-49 R3: Leicester C. (H) 1-1, (A) 1-1, 1-2

49-50 R3: Swansea Town (A) 0-3

50-51 R3: Manchester City (H) 2-0
R4: Derby County (A) 3-1
R5: Bristol City (H) 2-0
R6: Manchester United (H) 1-0
SF: Blackpool (*at Man. C.*) 0-0, (*at Everton*) 1-2

51-52 R3: Fulham (A) 1-0
R4: Leyton Orient (H) 0-1

52-53 R3: Oldham Athletic (A) 3-1
R4: Sheffield United (A) 1-1, (H) 3-1
R5: Chelsea (A) 4-0
R6: Tottenham H. (H) 1-1, (A) 2-2, 0-1

53-54 R3: Wolverhampton Wanderers (A) 2-1
R4: Ipswich Town (A) 0-1

54-55 R3: Hull City (A) 2-0
R4: Bolton Wanderers (H) 2-1
R5: Doncaster Rovers (H) 2-1
R6: Manchester City (H) 0-1

55-56 R3: Torquay United (A) 7-1
R4: Leyton Orient (A) 4-0
R5: West Bromwich Albion (A) 1-0
R6: Arsenal (A) 3-1
SF: Sunderland (*at Sheffield Wed.*) 3-0
F: Manchester City (*at Wembley*) 1-3

56-57 R3: Carlisle United (A) 3-3, (H) 4-0
R4: Southend United (A) 6-1
R5: Millwall (A) 4-1
R6: Nottingham Forest (H) 0-0, (A) 1-0
SF: Manchester Utd (*at Sheffield Wed.*) 0-2

57-58 R3: York City (A) 0-3

58-59 R3: Middlesbrough (A) 1-1, (H) 1-0
R4: Fulham (H) 1-1, (A) 3-2
R5: Nottingham F. (H) 1-1, (A) 1-1, 0-5

59-60 R3: Watford (A) 1-2

Below: *Birmingham 'keeper David Seaman is beaten by a Ronnie Ellis shot giving Altrincham their first goal in 1986, the last time a non-League won away to a First Division club in the Cup. Photo - John Rooney.*

60-61 R3: Nottingham Forest (A) 2-0
R4: Rotherham United (H) 4-0
R5: Leicester City (H) 1-1, (A) 1-2

61-62 R3: Tottenham Hotspur (H) 3-3, (A) 2-4

62-63 R3: Bury (H) 3-3, (A) 0-2

63-64 R3: Port Vale (H) 1-2

64-65 R3: West Ham United (A) 2-4

65-66 R3: Bristol City (H) 3-2
R4: Leicester City (H) 1-2

66-67 R3: Blackpool (H) 2-1
R4: Rotherham United (A) 0-0, (H) 2-1
R5: Arsenal (H) 1-0
R6: Tottenham Hotspur (H) 0-0, (A) 0-6

67-68 R3: Halifax Town (A) 4-2
R4: Leyton Orient (H) 3-0
R5: Arsenal (A) 1-1, (H) 2-1
R6: Chelsea (H) 1-0
SF: West Bromwich Albion (N) 0-2

68-69 R3: Lincoln City (H) 2-1
R4: Sheffield Wednesday (A) 2-2, (H) 2-1
R5: Manchester United (H) 2-2, (A) 2-6

69-70 R3: Chelsea (A) 0-3

70-71 R3: Huddersfield Town (A) 1-1, (H) 0-2

71-72 R3: Port Vale (H) 3-0
R4: Ipswich Town (H) 1-0
R5: Portsmouth (H) 3-1
R6: Huddersfield Town (H) 3-1
SF: Leeds Utd (*at Sheffield Wednesday*) 0-3

72-73 R3: Swindon Town (A) 0-2

73-74 R3: Cardiff City (H) 5-2
R4: Queens Park Rangers (A) 0-2

74-75 R3: Luton Town (A) 1-0
R4: Chelsea (A) 1-0
R5: Walsall (H) 2-1
R6: Middlesbrough (H) 1-0
SF: Fulham (*at Sheff. W.*) 1-1, (*at Man. C.*) 0-1

75-76 R3: Portsmouth (A) 1-1, (H) 0-1

76-77 R3: Portsmouth (H) 1-0
R4: Leeds United (H) 1-2

77-78 R3: Wigan Athletic (H) 4-0
R4: Derby County (A) 1-2

78-79 R3: Burnley (H) 0-2

79-80 R3: Southampton (H) 2-1
R4: Middlesbrough (H) 2-1
R5: Tottenham Hotspur (A) 1-3

80-81 R3: Sunderland (H) 1-1, (A) 2-1
R4: Coventry City (A) 2-3

81-82 R3: Ipswich Town (H) 2-3

82-83 R3: Walsall (A) 0-0, (H) 1-0
R4: Crystal Palace (A) 0-1

83-84 R3: Sheffield United (A) 1-1, (H) 2-0
R4: Sunderland (A) 2-1
R5: West Ham United (H) 3-0
R6: Watford (H) 1-3

84-85 R3: Norwich (H) 0-0, (A) 1-1, (H) 1-1, (A) 0-1

85-86 R3: Altrincham (H) 1-2

86-87 R3: Ipswich Town (A) 1-0
R4: Walsall (A) 0-1

87-88 R3: Gillingham (A) 3-0
R4: Barnsley (A) 2-0
R5: Nottingham Forest (H) 0-1

88-89 R3: Wimbledon (H) 0-1

89-90 R1: Leyton Orient (A) 1-0
R2: Colchester United (A) 2-0
R3: Oldham Athletic (H) 1-1, (A) 0-1

90-91 R1: Cheltenham Town (H) 1-0
R2: Brentford (H) 1-3

91-92 R1: Torquay United (A) 0-3

92-93 R1: Reading (A) 0-1

BIRMINGHAM CITY TRANSPORT

Currently: Defunct

45-46 Q1: Worcester City (A) 0-8

46-47 PR: Stourbridge (H) 0-5

47-48 PR: Bourneville Athletic (A) 3-0
Q1: Halesowen Town (A) 1-2

48-49 PR: Worcester City (A) 0-4

49-50 PR: Cradley Heath (H) 1-5

BIRTLEY

Currently: Wearside League
* - As Birtley Town

47-48 * PR: Blyth Spartans (H) 0-2

48-49 * PR: Hexham Hearts (A) 0-5

49-50 * EX: Heaton Stannington (H) 2-2, (A) 2-2, 3-4

50-51 * PR: Gosforth & Coxlodge (H) 1-4

54-55 Q1: Easington Colliery Welfare (H) 2-7

BISHOP AUCKLAND

Currently: Northern Premier League

45-46 R1: Willington (A) 5-0, (H) 0-2 (*agg: 5-2*)
R2: York City (H) 1-2, (A) 0-3 (*agg: 1-5*)

46-47 R1: Rochdale (A) 1-6

47-48 Q4: North Shields (H) 3-2
R1: Chester (A) 1-3

48-49 Q4: Scarborough (A) 0-3

49-50 Q4: Stockton (A) 0-7

50-51 Q4: Horden Colliery (H) 2-0
R1: York City (H) 2-2, (A) 1-2

51-52 R1: Blyth Spartans (A) 1-2

52-53 Q4: Spennymoor United (A) 1-1, (H) 2-1
R1: Selby Town (A) 5-1
R2: Coventry City (H) 1-4

53-54 Q4: Spennymoor United (A) 1-3

54-55 R1: Kettering Town (H) 5-1
R2: Crystal Palace (A) 4-2
R3: Ipswich Town (A) 2-2, (H) 3-0
R4: York City (H) 1-3

55-56 R1: Durham City (H) 3-1
R2: Scunthorpe United (H) 0-0, (A) 0-2

56-57 R1: Tranmere Rovers (H) 2-1
R2: Rhyl (A) 1-3

57-58 R1: Bury (H) 0-0, (A) 1-4

58-59 Q4: Stanley United (H) 4-1
R1: Tranmere Rovers (A) 1-8

59-60 Q4: Scarborough (H) 1-2

60-61 Q4: Crook Town (A) 2-1
R1: Bridlington Town (H) 3-2
R2: Stockport County (A) 0-2

61-62 Q4: South Shields (A) 1-2

62-63 Q4: South Shields (A) 1-2

63-64 Q1: Horden Colliery Welfare (H) 0-0, (A) 1-2

64-65 Q1: Shildon (H) 4-1
Q2: North Shields (H) 2-3

65-66 Q1: South Bank (H) 5-1
Q2: Spennymoor United (A) 0-0, (H) 1-4

66-67 Q1: Willington (A) 3-0
Q2: South Bank (H) 3-1
Q3: Horden Colliery Welfare (A) 1-0
Q4: Crook Town (A) 4-4, (H) 2-0
R1: Blyth S. (H) 1-1, (A) 0-0, (*at Sunderland*) 3-3, (*at Sunderland*) 4-1
R2: Halifax Town (H) 0-0, (A) 0-7

67-68 Q4: Ryhope Colliery Welfare (H) 2-2, (A) 1-4

68-69 Q1: Gateshead (H) 2-1
Q2: Horden Colliery Welfare (H) 2-1
Q3: Billingham Synthonia (A) 2-0
Q4: Goole Town (H) 2-3

69-70 Q1: Washington (H) 4-1
Q2: Ashington (H) 3-0
Q3: Shildon (H) 2-1
Q4: South Shields (A) 2-2, (H) 1-3

70-71 PR: Boldon Colliery Welfare (H) 3-0
Q1: North Shields (A) 0-2

71-72 Q1: Stanley United (H) 4-1
Q2: Gateshead (A) 2-3

72-73 Q1: Whitley Bay (A) 1-0
Q2: Ferryhill Athletic (A) 2-3

73-74 Q1: Gateshead (H) *W/O*
Q2: Shildon (A) 3-1
Q3: Tow Law Town (H) 3-1
Q4: South Shields (H) 0-1

74-75 Q1: Stanley United (A) *W/O*
Q2: Whitley Bay (A) 2-2, (H) 4-3
Q3: Spennymoor United (H) 4-2
Q4: Lancaster City (A) 1-1, (H) 2-1
R1: Morecambe (H) 5-0
R2: Preston North End (H) 0-2

75-76 PR: North Shields (H) 0-1

76-77 Q1: Lancaster City (A) 1-1, (H) 2-0
Q2: Consett (H) 3-0
Q3: Crook Town (H) 1-1, (A) 0-1

77-78 Q1: West Auckland Town (H) 3-1
Q2: Netherfield (A) 1-1, (H) 1-1, (A) 4-3
Q3: Boldon C.A. (H) 3-2
Q4: Blyth Spartans (H) 0-1

78-79 Q1: Ashington (A) 1-0
Q2: Consett (A) 0-0, (A) 1-2

79-80 Q1: Carlisle City (A) 2-2, (H) 2-2, 5-0
Q2: Billingham Synthonia (A) 1-0
Q3: Horden Colliery Welfare (A) 1-4

80-81 Q1: Ashington (A) 3-0
Q2: Bridlington Trinity (H) 1-0
Q3: Evenwood Town (A) 1-0
Q4: Workington (A) 1-4

81-82 Q1: Ossett Albion (H) 4-0
Q2: Emley (A) 4-1
Q3: Frickley Athletic (H) 3-0
Q4: Caernarfon Town (A) 2-0
R1: Nuneaton Borough (H) 4-1
R2: Carlisle Utd (A) 0-0 *abandoned after 69 minutes*, (A - *at Workington*) 0-1

82-83 Q1: Yorkshire Amateur (A) 1-0
Q2: Annfield Plain (H) 2-3

83-84 Q1: Thackley (H) 2-2, (A) 4-1
Q2: Clitheroe (H) 1-0
Q3: Accrington Stanley (H) 4-1
Q4: Whitby Town (A) 2-4

84-85 Q1: Chester-le-Street Town (H) 4-3
Q2: Ashington (A) 5-0
Q3: Gretna (A) 2-0
Q4: Macclesfield Town (H) 1-2

85-86 Q1: Ferryhill Athletic (A) 3-0
Q2: Blue Star (A) 3-1
Q3: Bridlington Trinity (H) 3-2
Q4: Scarborough (A) 1-4

86-87 Q1: Gateshead (H) 2-0
Q2: North Shields (A) 0-0, (H) 4-2
Q3: Morecambe (A) 2-1
Q4: Chorley (A) 2-3

87-88 Q1: Workington (H) 5-2
Q2: Seaham Red Star (A) 1-0
Q3: Harrogate Town (A) 1-1, (H) 2-0
Q4: Guisborough Town (A) 2-1
R1: Blackpool (H) 1-4

88-89 Q1: Evenwood Town (H) 4-0
Q2: Bridlington Town (A) 1-2

89-90 Q1: Chester-le-Street Town (H) 3-2
Q2: Langley Park Welfare (A) 5-2
Q3: South Bank (H) 1-1, (A) 3-1
Q4: Mossley (A) 1-1, (H) 3-0
R1: Tow Law Town (H) 2-0
R2: Crewe Alexandra (A) 1-1, (H) 0-2

90-91 Q4: South Liverpool (H) 1-0
R1: Barrow (H) 0-1

91-92 Q4: Guiseley (A) 1-2

92-93 Q1: Durham City (A) 1-1, (H) 5-2
Q2: Newcastle Blue Star (A) 1-0
Q3: Blyth Spartans (H) 1-3

BISHOP'S STORTFORD

Currently: Isthmian League

45-46 PR: Hoddesdon Town (A) 0-0, (H) 4-1
Q1: Enfield (A) 1-8

46-47 PR: Chipperfield (H) 2-1
Q1: Hoddesdon Town (A) 2-3

48-49 EX: Harlow Town (A) 4-1

Above: *Lyndon Lynch gives Bishop's Stortford the lead in their replay against Middlesbrough in 1983. However the then Second Division side came back to win 2-1. Photo: Eric Marsh.*

PR: Woodford Town (A) 2-3

50-51 EX: Leyton (H) 2-1
PR: Harwich & Parkeston (A) 3-5

54-55 PR: Enfield (A) 1-3

55-56 PR: Eton Manor (H) 1-2

56-57 PR: Enfield (H) 3-0
Q1: Hoddesdon Town (H) 1-0
Q2: Eton Manor (H) 0-2

57-58 PR: Tufnell Park Edmonton (A) 1-2

58-59 PR: Cheshunt (A) 2-3

59-60 Q2: Hertford Town (H) 0-1

60-61 Q1: Cheshunt (A) 2-0
Q2: Barnet (H) 4-2
Q3: Harrow Town (A) 4-8

61-62 Q1: Harrow Town (A) 1-7

62-63 Q1: Ware (H) 1-0
Q2: Wealdstone (H) 0-2

63-64 Q1: Harrow Town (H) 1-2

64-65 Q1: Ware (A) 3-1
Q2: Stevenage Town (A) 1-4

65-66 Q1: Stevenage Town (H) 1-1, (A) 0-2

66-67 Q1: Soham Town Rangers (H) 2-0
Q2: Bury Town (H) 2-5

67-68 Q1: Hatfield Town (A) 2-1
Q2: Wolverton Town & B.R. (A) 3-1
Q3: Slough Town (A) 1-5

68-69 Q1: Wolverton Town & B.R. (H) 6-0
Q2: Corinthian-Casuals (H) 9-0
Q3: Slough Town (A) 0-2

69-70 Q1: Hendon (H) 1-2

70-71 Q1: Canvey Island (H) 5-3
Q2: Bromley (H) 2-1
Q3: Dartford (A) 1-1, (H) 3-1
Q4: Cheshunt (H) 5-2
R1: Reading (A) 1-6

71-72 Q1: Barking (A) 1-0
Q2: Harlow Town (H) 4-2
Q3: Guildford City (H) 2-2, (A) 1-1, 1-2

72-73 Q1: Epping Town (H) 1-0
Q2: Hitchin Town (H) 4-1
Q3: Vauxhall Motors (H) 2-0
Q4: Dagenham (H) 1-1, (A) 4-0
R1: Enfield (A) 1-1, (H) 1-0
R2: Peterborough Town (H) 2-2, (A) 1-3

73-74 Q4: Dagenham (H) 1-1, (A) 1-2

74-75 R1: Leatherhead (H) 0-0, (A) 0-2

75-76 Q4: Chelmsford City (A) 2-0
R1: Dartford (A) 4-1
R2: Aldershot (A) 0-2

76-77 Q4: Wealdstone (A) 2-3

77-78 Q4: Lowestoft Town (A) 0-2

78-79 Q1: Bedford Town (A) 1-2

79-80 Q1: Billericay Town (H) 1-2

80-81 Q1: Bedford Town (A) 2-3

81-82 R1: Sutton United (H) 2-2, (A) 1-2

82-83 Q4: Harlow Town (A) 1-1, (H) 4-0
R1: Reading (A) 2-1
R2: Slough Town (A) 4-1
R3: Middlesbrough (A) 2-2, (H) 1-2

83-84 Q4: Wealdstone (A) 0-1

84-85 Q4: Maidstone United (H) 1-0
R1: Brentford (A) 0-4

85-86 Q4: Kidderminster Harriers (A) 4-3
R1: Peterborough United (H) 2-2, (A) 1-3

86-87 Q4: Fisher Athletic (H) 2-0
R1: Colchester United (H) 1-1, (A) 0-2

87-88 Q4: Halesowen Town (A) 0-1

88-89 Q1: Heybridge Swifts (H) 3-1
Q2: Witham Town (A) 3-2
Q3: Hendon (A) 3-5

89-90 Q1: Barnet (H) 0-1

90-91 Q1: Stevenage Borough (A) 3-2
Q2: Hounslow (A) 5-1
Q3: Redbridge Forest (H) 2-1
Q4: Atherstone United (H) 0-1

91-92 Q1: Mirrlees Blackstone (H) 1-1, (A) 0-2

92-93 PR: Viking Sports (A) 1-0
Q1: Burnham (A - *at Windsor & Eton*) 2-3

BITTERNE NOMADS

Currently: Defunct

47-48 PR: Thornycroft Athletic (H) 2-3

48-49 EX: Basingstoke Town (A) 2-1
PR: Newport I.O.W. (H - *played away*) 0-4

BLACKBURN ROVERS

Currently: F.A. Premier League

45-46 R3: Bolton Wdrs (A) 0-1, (H) 3-3 (*agg: 3-4*)

46-47 R3: Hull City (H) 1-1, (A) 3-0
R4: Port Vale (H) 2-0
R5: Charlton Athletic (A) 0-1

47-48 R3: West Ham Utd (H) 0-0, (A) 0-0, 4-2
R4: Southampton (A) 2-3

48-49 R3: Hull City (H) 1-2

49-50 R3: Liverpool (H) 0-0, (A) 1-2

50-51 R3: Bristol City (A) 1-2

51-52 R3: Nottingham Forest (A) 2-2, (H) 2-0
R4: Hull City (H) 2-0
R5: West Bromwich Albion (H) 1-0
R6: Burnley (H) 3-1
SF: Newcastle (*at Sheff. W.*) 0-0, (*at Leeds*) 1-2

52-53 R3: Luton Town (A) 1-6

53-54 R3: Bristol Rovers (A) 1-0
R4: Hull City (H) 2-2, (A) 1-2

54-55 R3: Swansea Town (H) 0-2

55-56 R3: Northampton Town (A) 2-1
R4: Barnsley (A) 1-0
R5: West Ham United (A) 0-0, (H) 2-3

56-57 R3: Everton (A) 0-1

57-58 R3: Rotherham United (A) 4-1
R4: Everton (A) 2-1
R5: Cardiff City (A) 0-0, (H) 2-1
R6: Liverpool (H) 2-1
SF: Bolton Wdrs (*at Manchester City*) 1-2

58-59 R3: Leyton Orient (H) 4-2
R4: Burnley (H) 0-0, (A) 1-2

59-60 R3: Sunderland (A) 1-1, (H) 4-1
R4: Blackpool (H) 1-1, (A) 3-0
R5: Tottenham Hotspur (A) 3-1
R6: Burnley (A) 3-3, (H) 2-0
SF: Sheffield Wednesday (*at Man. City*) 2-1
F: Wolverhampton Wdrs (*at Wembley*) 0-3

60-61 R3: Chesterfield (A) 0-0, (H) 3-0
R4: Bolton Wanderers (A) 3-3, (H) 4-0
R5: Sheffield United (A) 1-2

61-62 R3: Brighton & Hove Albion (A) 3-0
R4: Stoke City (A) 1-0
R5: Middlesbrough (H) 2-1
R6: Fulham (A) 2-2, (H) 0-1

62-63 R3: Middlesbrough (H) 1-1, (A) 1-3

63-64 R3: Grimsby Town (H) 4-0
R4: Fulham (H) 2-0
R5: Oxford United (A) 1-3

64-65 R3: Leicester City (A) 2-2, (H) 1-2

65-66 R3: Arsenal (H) 3-0
R4: West Ham United (A) 3-3, (H) 4-1
R5: Norwich City (A) 2-2, (H) 3-2
R6: Sheffield Wednesday (H) 1-2

66-67 R3: Carlisle United (H) 1-2

67-68 R3: Swindon Town (A) 0-1

68-69 R3: Stockport County (H) 2-0
R4: Portsmouth (H) 4-0
R5: Manchester City (A) 1-4

69-70 R3: Swindon Town (H) 0-4

70-71 R3: Everton (A) 0-2

71-72 R1: Port Vale (H) 1-1, (A) 1-3

72-73 R1: Lincoln City (A) 2-2, (H) 4-1
R2: Crewe Alexandra (H) 0-1

73-74 R1: Willington (A) 0-0, (H) 6-1
R2: Altrincham (H) 0-0, (A) 2-0
R3: Everton (A) 0-3

74-75 R1: Matlock Town (A) 4-1
R2: Darlington (H) 1-0
R3: Bristol Rovers (H) 1-2

75-76 R3: Luton Town (A) 0-2

76-77 R3: Charlton Athletic (A) 1-1, (H) 2-0
R4: Orient (H) 3-0
R5: Derby County (A) 1-3

77-78 R3: Shrewsbury Town (H) 2-1
R4: Orient (A) 1-3

78-79 R3: Millwall (A - *played home*) 2-1
R4: Liverpool (A) 0-1

79-80 R1: Kidderminster Harriers (A) 2-0
R2: Stafford Rangers (H) 2-0
R3: Fulham (H) 1-1, (A) 1-0

Season	Results
	R4: Coventry City (H) 1-0 R5: Aston Villa (H) 1-1, (A) 0-1
80-81	R3: Notts County (A) 1-2
81-82	R3: West Bromwich Albion (A) 2-3
82-83	R3: Liverpool (H) 1-2
83-84	R3: Chelsea (H) 1-0 R4: Swindon Town (A) 2-1 R5: Southampton (H) 0-1
84-85	R3: Portsmouth (A) 0-0, (H) 2-1 R4: Oxford United (A) 1-0 R5: Manchester United (H) 0-2
85-86	R3: Nottingham Forest (A) 1-1, (H) 3-2 R4: Everton (A) 1-3
86-87	R3: Portsmouth (A) 0-2
87-88	R3: Portsmouth (H) 1-2
88-89	R3: Welling United (A) 1-0 R4: Sheffield Wednesday (H) 2-1 R5: Brentford (H) 0-2
89-90	R3: Aston Villa (H) 2-2, (A) 1-3
90-91	R3: Liverpool (H) 1-1, (A) 0-3
91-92	R3: Kettering Town (H) 4-1 R4: Notts County (A) 1-2
92-93	R3: A.F.C. Bournemouth (H) 3-1 R4: Crewe Alexandra (A) 3-0 R5: Newcastle United (H) 1-0 R6: Sheffield U. (H) 0-0, (A) 2-2 *(4-5 pens)*

BLACKHALL COLLIERY WELF.

Currently: Defunct

Season	Results
45-46	Q1: Seaham C.W. (H) 4-2 Q2: Shildon (A) 1-6
46-47	PR: Ferryhill Athletic (A) 1-2
47-48	EX: Willington (H) 2-1 PR: West Auckland Town (A) 3-5
48-49	EX: Spennymoor United (A) 0-3
49-50	EX: Tow Law Town (H) 1-0 PR: Consett (H) 1-4
50-51	EX: Spennymoor United (A) 2-1 PR: Dawdon Colliery (A) 1-1, (H) 3-1 Q1: Ushaw Moor (A) 3-1 Q2: Tow Law Town (A) 0-0, (H) 3-0 Q3: Horden Colliery Welfare (A) 1-4
51-52	Q1: Ushaw Moor (H) 2-1 Q2: Chilton Athletic (A) 0-0, (H) 1-0 Q3: Horden Colliery Welfare (H) 3-1 Q4: Scarborough (A) 0-0, (H) 5-3 R1: Workington (H) 2-5
52-53	Q2: Horden Colliery Welfare (A) 0-3
53-54	Q1: Murton Colliery Welfare (A) 1-2
54-55	Q1: Murton Colliery Welfare (H) 2-0 Q2: Durham City (H) 2-2, (A) 1-4
55-56	Q1: Murton Colliery Welfare (A) 2-4
56-57	Q1: Spennymoor United (A) 1-1, (H) 0-4
57-58	Q1: Boldon Colliery Welfare (A) 2-4
58-59	Q2: Cockfield (A) 2-1 Q3: Whitley Bay Athletic (H) 2-2, (A) 0-5

Above: *Stanley Matthews, and his Blackpool team-mates, celebrate with the Cup after the fabulous match against Bolton Wanderers in 1953. Photo: Colorsport.*

BLACKPOOL

Currently: Football League

Season	Results
45-46	R3: Wrexham (A) 4-1, (H) 4-1 *(agg: 8-2)* R4: Middlesbrough (H) 3-2, (A) 2-3, 0-1
46-47	R3: Sheffield Wednesday (A) 1-4
47-48	R3: Leeds United (H) 4-0 R4: Chester (H) 4-0 R5: Colchester United (H) 5-0 R6: Fulham (A) 2-0 SF: Tottenham Hotspur *(at Aston Villa)* 3-1 F: Manchester United *(at Wembley)* 2-4
48-49	R3: Barnsley (A) 1-0 R4: Stoke City (A) 1-1, (H) 0-1
49-50	R3: Southend United (H) 4-0 R4: Doncaster Rovers (H) 2-1 R5: Wolverhampton Wdrs (A) 0-0, (H) 1-0 R6: Liverpool (A) 1-2
50-51	R3: Charlton Athletic (A) 2-2, (H) 3-0 R4: Stockport County (H) 2-1 R5: Mansfield Town (H) 2-0 R6: Fulham (H) 1-0 SF: Birm. City *(at Man. C.)* 0-0, *(at Everton)* 2-1 F: Newcastle United *(at Wembley)* 0-2
51-52	R3: West Ham United (A) 1-2
52-53	R3: Sheffield Wednesday (A) 2-1 R4: Huddersfield Town (H) 1-0 R5: Southampton (H) 1-1, (A) 2-1 R6: Arsenal (A) 2-1 SF: Tottenham Hotspur *(at Aston Villa)* 2-1 F: Bolton Wanderers *(at Wembley)* 4-3
53-54	R3: Luton (H) 1-1, (A) 0-0, *(Aston V.)* 1-1, 2-0 R4: West Ham United (A) 1-1, (H) 3-1 R5: Port Vale (A) 0-2
54-55	R3: York City (H) 0-2
55-56	R3: Manchester City (A) 1-2
56-57	R3: Bolton Wanderers (A) 3-2 R4: Fulham (H) 6-2 R5: West Bromwich Albion (H) 0-0, (A) 1-2
57-58	R3: West Ham United (A) 1-5
58-59	R3: Southampton (A) 2-1 R4: Bristol City (A) 1-1, (H) 1-0 R5: West Bromwich Albion (H) 3-1 R6: Luton Town (H) 1-1, (A) 0-1
59-60	R3: Mansfield Town (H) 3-0 R4: Blackburn Rovers (A) 1-1, (H) 0-3
60-61	R3: Scunthorpe United (A) 2-6
61-62	R3: West Bromwich Albion (H) 0-0, (A) 1-2
62-63	R3: Norwich City (A) 1-1, (H) 1-3
63-64	R3: West Bromwich Albion (A) 2-2, (H) 0-1
64-65	R3: Stoke City (A) 1-4
65-66	R3: Manchester City (H) 1-1, (A) 1-3
66-67	R3: Birmingham City (A) 1-2
67-68	R3: Chesterfield (H) 2-1 R4: Sheffield United (A) 1-2
68-69	R3: Coventry City (A) 1-3
69-70	R3: Arsenal (A) 1-1, (H) 3-2 R4: Mansfield Town (H) 0-2
70-71	R3: West Ham United (H) 4-0 R4: Hull City (A) 0-2
71-72	R3: Chelsea (H) 0-1
72-73	R3: Bradford City (A) 1-2
73-74	R3: Southampton (A) 1-2
74-75	R3: Plymouth Argyle (A) 0-2
75-76	R3: Burnley (H) 1-0 R4: Southampton (A) 1-3
76-77	R3: Derby County (H) 0-0, (A) 2-3
77-78	R3: West Bromwich Albion (A) 1-4
78-79	R1: Lincoln City (H) 2-1 R2: Bury (A) 1-3
79-80	R1: Wigan Athletic (H) 1-1, (A) 0-2
80-81	R1: Fleetwood T. (A - *played home*) 4-0 R2: Doncaster Rovers (A) 1-2
81-82	R1: Horden C.W. (A - *at Hartlepool Utd*) 1-0 R2: Kettering Town (A) 3-0 R3: Barnsley (A) 2-0 R4: Queens Park Rangers (H) 0-0, (A) 1-5
82-83	R1: Horwich R.M.I. (H) 3-0 R2: Preston North End (A) 1-2
83-84	R1: Gainsborough Trinity (A) 2-0 R2: Bangor City (A) 1-1, (H) 2-1 R3: Manchester City (H) 2-1 R4: Oxford United (A) 1-2
84-85	R1: Altrincham (H) 0-1
85-86	R1: Lincoln City (A) 1-0 R2: Altrincham (H) 1-2
86-87	R1: Middlesbrough (A) 0-3
87-88	R1: Bishop Auckland (A) 4-1 R2: Northwich Victoria (A) 2-0 R3: Scunthorpe United (A) 0-0, (H) 1-0 R4: Manchester City (H) 1-1, (A) 1-2
88-89	R1: Scunthorpe United (H) 2-1 R2: Bury (H) 3-0 R3: A.F.C. Bournemouth (H) 0-1
89-90	R1: Bolton Wanderers (H) 2-1 R2: Chester City (H) 3-0 R3: Burnley (H) 1-0 R4: Torquay United (H) 1-0 R5: Queens Pk R. (H) 2-2, (A) 0-0, (A) 0-3
90-91	R1: Grimsby Town (H) 2-0 R2: Huddersfield Town (A) 2-0 R3: Tottenham Hotspur (H) 0-1
91-92	R1: Grimsby Town (H) 2-1 R2: Hull City (H) 0-1
92-93	R1: Rochdale (H) 1-1, (A) 0-1

BLACKPOOL MECHANICS

Currently: North West Counties League

Season	Results
90-91	PR: Ferryhill Athletic (A) 1-3

BLACKPOOL ROVERS

Currently: North West Counties League
* - As Wren Rovers FC

83-84 * PR: Appleby Frodingham (H) 3-2
Q1: Oswestry Town (H) 0-2

84-85 * Q1: Easington Colliery (A) 2-2, (H) 4-2
Q2: Ryhope C.A. (H) 2-3

85-86 * Q1: Rhyl (A) 1-3

86-87 * Q1: Thackley (H) 3-1
Q2: Peterlee Newtown (H) 2-2, (A) 0-2

87-88 * Q1: Farsley Celtic (H) 1-2

88-89 * PR: Whitley Bay (H) 0-3

89-90 PR: Droylsden (A) 2-3

90-91 PR: Accrington Stanley (H) 2-4

91-92 PR: Thackley (H) 3-2
Q1: Fleetwood Town (A) 2-3

92-93 PR: Shildon (A) 0-2

BLAENAU FFESTINIOG

Currently: Defunct

72-73 Q1: Oswestry Town (H) 1-2

73-74 Q1: Marine (A) 0-0, (H) 0-0, 0-1

74-75 Q1: Oswestry Town (H) 0-0, (A) 0-1

BLAKENALL

Currently: West Midlands (Regional) League

81-82 PR: Desborough Town (H) 1-1, (A) 6-2
Q1: Bromsgrove Rovers (A) 0-2

82-83 PR: Winsford United (A) 2-1
Q1: Bilston (A) 2-2, (H) 1-2

83-84 PR: Buckingham Town (H) 0-1

84-85 PR: Mile Oak Rovers & Youth (H) 2-0
Q1: Chorley (A) 1-5

85-86 PR: Tamworth (H) 0-4

90-91 Q1: Rushall Olympic (H) 3-2
Q2: Nuneaton Borough (H) 3-3, (A) 0-3

91-92 PR: Oldbury United (A) 2-1
Q1: Boston United (H) 1-2

92-93 Q1: Droylsden (H) 4-3
Q2: Nantwich Town (A) 0-1

BLANDFORD UNITED

Currently: Dorset Combination

49-50 EX: Dorchester Town (A) 1-2

50-51 PR: Gosport Borough Athletic (H) 4-1
Q1: Bournemouth (H) 6-2
Q2: Alton Town (A) 0-9

51-52 Q1: Lymington (H) 1-3

52-53 PR: Dorchester Town (H) 2-5

BLETCHLEY (TOWN UTD)

See Milton Keynes City

BLETCHLEY & W.I.P.A.C. SPTS

Currently: Defunct (Merged with Bletchley Boys Brigade Old Boys to form Bletchley Town United). See also Bletchley Town United
* - As Bletchley Town

54-55 * Q1: Wolverton Town & B.R. (A) 0-1

55-56 Q2: Eynesbury Rovers (A) 0-5

BLOXWICH STROLLERS

Currently: West Midlands (Regional) League

54-55 PR: Sutton Coldfield Town (A) 3-0
Q1: Burton Albion (H) 1-6

55-56 PR: Moor Green (A) 2-2, (H) 0-2

BLUE STAR

See Newcastle Blue Star

BLYTH SPARTANS

Currently: Northern League

47-48 PR: Birtley Town (A) 2-0
Q1: Throckley Welfare (H) 4-0
Q2: Newburn (A) 5-1
Q3: South Shields (H) 0-3

48-49 PR: Amble (A) 4-0
Q1: Ashington (H) 2-1
Q2: North Shields (H) 2-1
Q3: Annfield Plain (H) 0-2

49-50 PR: Annfield Plain (H) 3-0
Q1: Gosforth & Coxlodge (A) 4-0
Q2: Heaton Stannington (H) 5-1
Q3: North Shields (H) 1-5

50-51 PR: Shilbottle Colliery Welfare (A) 6-1
Q1: South Shields (A) 2-0
Q2: Cramlington Welfare (A) 0-2

51-52 Q1: Newburn (A) 1-1, (H) 1-0
Q2: Hexham Hearts (H) 4-0
Q3: Alnwick Town (H) 4-3
Q4: Ashington (A) 2-0
R1: Bishop Auckland (H) 2-1
R2: Tranmere R. (A) 1-1, (H) 1-1 *abandoned in extra-time*, (H) 2-2, 1-5

52-53 Q4: Horden Colliery Welfare (A) 1-2

53-54 Q4: North Shields (H) 4-2
Q1: Accrington Stanley (H) 0-1

54-55 Q4: Annfield Plain (A) 2-1
R1: Boston United (A) 1-1, (H) 5-4
R2: Torquay United (H) 1-3

55-56 Q4: Shildon (H) 2-4

56-57 Q4: Annfield Plain (H) 3-0
R1: Ilkeston Town (A) 5-1
R2: Hartlepools United (H) 0-1

57-58 Q4: Crook Town (A) 0-3

58-59 Q4: Durham City (H) 1-0
R1: Morecambe (A) 2-1
R2: Stockport County (H) 3-4

59-60 Q4: Spennymoor United (H) 4-0
R1: Wrexham (A) 1-2

60-61 Q4: Horden Colliery Welfare (A) 3-1
R1: Mansfield Town (A) 1-3

61-62 Q4: North Shields (A) 2-1
R1: Hartlepools United (A) 1-5

62-63 Q4: Horden Colliery Welfare (H) 2-1
R1: Morecambe (H) 2-1
R2: Carlisle United (H) 0-2

63-64 Q4: Tow Law Town (H) 1-0
R1: Chester (A) 2-3

64-65 Q4: Scarborough (A) 3-4

65-66 Q1: Ryhope Colliery Welfare (H) 4-3
Q2: Horden Colliery Welfare (H) 0-2

66-67 Q1: Whitley Bay (H) 4-1
Q2: Tow Law Town (H) 3-3, (A) 3-2
Q3: Stockton (H) 4-2
Q4: Gateshead (A) 3-1
R1: Bishop Auckland (A) 1-1, (H) 0-0, (*at Sunderland*) 3-3, (*at Sunderland*) 1-4

67-68 Q1: Gateshead (A) 1-1, (H) 2-1
Q2: Whitby Town (A) 0-2

68-69 Q1: Spennymoor United (H) 4-3
Q2: Billingham Synthonia (H) 1-2

69-70 Q1: Stockton (A) 3-3, (H) 8-2
Q2: Evenwood Town (H) 1-1, (A) 1-2

70-71 Q1: Willington (H) 2-1
Q2: West Auckland Town (H) 6-1
Q3: Evenwood Town (H) 2-1
Q4: South Shields (H) 1-1, (A) 0-3

71-72 Q1: Boldon Colliery Welfare (H) 3-2
Q2: Willington (H) 3-1
Q3: Consett (H) 8-1
Q4: Whitley Bay (A) 1-1, (H) 2-1
R1: Crewe Alexandra (A) 1-0
R2: Stockport County (H) 1-0
R3: Reading (H) 2-2, (A) 1-6

72-73 Q4: Scarborough (A) 1-2

73-74 Q4: Netherfield (H) 2-0
R1: Alfreton Town (A) 0-0, (H) 2-1
R2: Grimsby Town (A) 1-1, (H) 0-2

74-75 Q4: Scarborough (H) 3-1
R1: Preston North End (H) 1-1, (A) 1-5

Right: *Blyth hero John Lang keeps a steady hand on the ball to foil Preston striker Mike Elwiss.*

75-76 Q4: Rossendale United (H) 0-0, (A) 0-1

76-77 Q4: Gateshead United (H) 0-3

77-78 Q1: Shildon (A) 3-0
Q2: Crook Town (A) 1-1, (H) 3-0
Q3: Consett (A) 4-1
Q4: Bishop Auckland (A) 1-0
R1: Burscough (H) 1-0
R2: Chesterfield (H) 1-0
R3: Enfield (H) 1-0
R4: Stoke City (A) 3-2
R5: Wrexham (A) 1-1, (H - *at Newcastle U.*) 1-2

78-79 Q4: Billingham Synthonia (A) 1-0
R1: York City (A) 1-1, (H) 3-5

79-80 Q4: Marine (H) 2-2, (A) 5-0
R1: Mansfield Town (H) 0-2

80-81 Q4: Horden Colliery Welfare (H) 7-0
R1: Burton Albion (H) 2-1
R2: Hull C. (H) 1-1, (A) 2-2, (*at Leeds Utd*) 1-2

81-82 Q4: Scarborough (A) 3-2
R1: Walsall (H) 1-2

82-83 Q4: Northwich Victoria (A) 0-3

83-84 Q4: Hyde United (A) 1-1, (H) 2-4

84-85 Q1: Guisborough Town (H) 1-1, (A) 1-3

85-86 Q1: Farsley Celtic (A) 2-1
Q2: Whitley Bay (A) 2-1
Q3: Scarborough (H) 1-1, (A) 1-3

86-87 Q1: Crook Town (H) 1-1, (A) 1-0
Q2: Guiseley (A) 2-0
Q3: Gretna (A) 2-5

87-88 Q1: Gateshead (H) 2-1
Q2: Bridlington Town (A) 2-1
Q3: Billingham Synthonia (A) 2-5

88-89 Q1: Rossendale United (H) 1-0
Q2: Brandon United (A) 2-4

89-90 Q1: Murton (A) 3-0
Q2: Durham City (H) 4-1
Q3: North Shields (H) 0-3

90-91 Q1: Bridlington Town (H) 2-0
Q2: Accrington Stanley (A) 1-2

91-92 Q1: Bridlington Town (A) 2-3

92-93 Q1: Penrith (A) 2-1
Q2: Workington (H) 6-0
Q3: Bishop Auckland (A) 3-1
Q4: Stockton (H) 1-1, (A) 2-1
R1: Southport (H) 1-2

BODMIN TOWN

Currently: South Western League

54-55 PR: Wadebridge Town (H) 2-0
Q1: Minehead (H) 3-3, (A) 2-2, 2-3

55-56 PR: Ilfracombe Town (H) 4-3
Q1: Wadebridge Town (A) 5-2
Q2: Penzance (A) 3-4

72-73 Q1: Barnstaple Town (A) 1-3

BOGNOR REGIS TOWN

Currently: Isthmian League

45-46 Q1: Southwick (A) 1-4

46-47 PR: Littlehampton Town (A) 2-1
Q1: Haywards Heath (A) 1-0
Q2: Bexhill Town (H) 2-1
Q3: Eastbourne (A) 1-4

47-48 Q1: Shoreham (H) 1-1, (A) 5-2
Q2: Worthing (H) 1-3

48-49 Q1: Littlehampton Town (H) 8-0
Q2: Worthing (A) 4-1
Q3: Horsham (A) 2-1
Q4: Dulwich Hamlet (H) 1-8

49-50 Q1: Haywards Heath (A) 0-7

50-51 PR: Arundel (A) 0-1

51-52 PR: Bexhill Town (H) 1-1, (A) 0-3

52-53 PR: Littlehampton Town (A) 3-4

53-54 PR: Redhill (A) 0-2

54-55 PR: Redhill (H) 3-2
Q1: Worthing (A) 3-3, (H) 4-1
Q2: Eastbourne (H) 4-2
Q3: Tunbridge Wells United (A) 0-4

55-56 PR: Shoreham (A) 6-1
Q1: East Grinstead (H) 3-1
Q2: Redhill (H) 2-2, (A) 0-4

56-57 PR: Newhaven (A) 5-1
Q1: Lancing Athletic (A) 2-0
Q2: Redhill (H) 0-3

57-58 Q1: Littlehampton Town (A) 3-3, (H) 5-4
Q2: Newhaven (H) 5-1
Q3: Redhill (H) 0-3

58-59 PR: Littlehampton Town (H) 5-1
Q1: Haywards Heath (H) 0-2

59-60 PR: Eastbourne (H) 1-2

60-61 Q1: Horsham (A) 1-3

61-62 Q2: Littlehampton Town (H) 1-1, (A) 2-0
Q3: Crawley Town (A) 1-2

62-63 Q1: Worthing (A) 2-1
Q2: Haywards Heath (H) 2-5

63-64 Q1: Lewes (H) 0-4

64-65 Q1: Redhill (H) 1-3

65-66 Q1: Newport Isle of Wight (A) 1-2

66-67 Q1: Littlehampton Town (A) 3-3, (H) 1-4

67-68 Q1: Haywards Heath (A) 1-2

68-69 PR: Horsham (A) 3-2
Q1: Haywards Heath (A) 1-1, (H) 2-3

69-70 Q1: Littlehampton Town (A) 0-1

70-71 Q1: Dorking (H) 2-1
Q2: Eastbourne (A) 4-2
Q3: Ringmer (H) 1-2

71-72 Q1: Arundel (A) 0-1

72-73 Q1: Dorking (H) 3-0
Q2: Leatherhead (H) 2-0
Q3: Lewes (A) 1-1, (H) 3-1
Q4: Bexley United (H) 1-0
R1: Colchester United (A) 0-6

73-74 Q1: Ryde Sports (H) 3-0
Q2: Newport I.O.W. (H) 1-0
Q3: Alton Town (A) 2-1
Q4: Hitchin Town (A) 1-2

74-75 Q1: Horsham (H) 1-2

75-76 Q1: Newport I.O.W. (H) 1-3

76-77 Q1: Bexhill Town (A - *played home*) 1-2

77-78 Q1: Farnborough Town (H) 0-2

78-79 Q1: Arundel (A) 3-2
Q2: Waterlooville (H) 0-2

79-80 Q1: Redhill (A) 5-0
Q2: Worthing (A) 2-1
Q3: Croydon (H) 0-1

80-81 Q1: Bridport (H) 3-1
Q2: Newbury Town (H) 1-2

81-82 PR: Haywards Heath (H) 5-1
Q1: Worthing (A) 0-0, (H) 1-0
Q2: Addlestone & Weybridge (H) 0-0, (A) 0-2

82-83 PR: Herne Bay (A) 1-0
Q1: Eastbourne Town (A) 3-1
Q2: Whitstable Town (A) 3-0
Q3: Margate (H) 3-0
Q4: Yeovil Town (A) 2-4

83-84 Q1: Canterbury City (A) 3-0
Q2: Hertford Town (A) 1-1, (H) 2-0
Q3: Corinthian-Casuals (A) 1-3

84-85 Q1: Basingstoke Town (H) 2-2, (A) 1-0
Q2: Wokingham Town (A) 2-1
Q3: Epsom & Ewell (A) 5-4
Q4: Frome Town (H) 2-0
R1: Swansea City (A) 1-1, (H) 3-1
R2: Reading (A) 2-6

85-86 Q4: Worthing (A) 2-1
R1: Enfield (A) 2-0
R2: Gillingham (A) 1-6

86-87 Q4: Wimborne Town (A) 5-2
R1: Slough Town (A) 1-1, (H) 0-1

87-88 Q4: Thanet United (A) 4-0
R1: Torquay United (H) 0-3

88-89 Q4: Whitehawk (H) 2-2, (A - *at Brighton*) 2-0
R1: Exeter City (H) 2-1
R2: Cambridge United (H) 0-1

Above: *Goalscorers Paul Pullen (left) and Steve Guille toast Vauxhall-Opel League Bognor Regis' 2-1 win over Exeter City in 1988. Photo: Nigel Bowles.*

89-90 Q4: Dorchester Town (H) 1-1, (A) 1-5

90-91 Q1: Folkestone (A) 2-1
Q2: Peacehaven & Telscombe (A) 1-3

91-92 Q1: Steyning Town (A) 1-0
Q2: Burgess Hill Town (H) 1-2

92-93 Q1: Romsey Town (H) 9-2
Q2: Bemerton (H) 1-1, (A) 2-2, (H) 1-1, (A) 0-1

BOLDMERE ST MICHAELS

Currently: Midland Combination

46-47 PR: Atherstone Town (A) 2-4

47-48 PR: Hednesford (H) 0-1

48-49 EX: Lye Town (A) 5-2
PR: Hereford United (A) 1-6

49-50 EX: Moor Green (A) 2-3

50-51 PR: Lye Town (A) 1-2

51-52 Q1: Sutton Coldfield Town (A) 0-2

52-53 PR: Rugby Town (H) 2-2, (A) 1-2

53-54 PR: Lockheed-Leamington (A) 0-7

54-55 Q1: Rugby Town (A) 1-5

55-56 PR: Sutton Coldfield Town (H) 2-2, (A) 2-4

56-57 Q1: Atherstone Town (A) 0-4

57-58 PR: Moor Green (A) 1-0
Q1: Lye Town (A) 2-4

58-59 Q1: Evesham United (H) 2-4

83-84 PR: Dudley Town (H) 0-2

84-85 PR: Halesowen T. (H) 2-2, (A) 1-1, (A) 0-1

85-86 PR: Heanor Town (A - *played home*) 2-0
Q1: South Liverpool (H) 1-1, (A) 0-5

86-87 PR: Oldswinford (A) 3-3, (H) 3-1
Q1: Rothwell Town (H) 0-1

87-88 Q1: Chatteris Town (H) 2-2, (A) 3-0
Q2: Shepshed Charterhouse (H) 1-2

88-89 Q1: Frickley Athletic (A) 1-2

89-90 Q1: Tamworth (H) 2-3

90-91 PR: Paget Rangers (A) 0-2

91-92 PR: Hinckley Town (A) 1-3

92-93 PR: Nuneaton Borough (A) 1-2

BOLDON COMMUNITY ASSOC.

Currently: Northern League
***** - As Boldon Colliery Welfare

49-50 * EX: Usworth Colliery (A) 2-0
PR: Heaton Stannington (H) 1-2

50-51 * EX: Morpeth Town (A) 3-1
PR: West Stanley (H) 1-4

51-52 * Q1: Consett (H) 3-5

52-53 * Q1: Annfield Plain (A) 2-6

53-54 * Q1: Heaton Stannington (H) 2-1
Q2: South Shields (H) 3-3, (A) 2-9

54-55 * Q1: Silksworth Colliery Welfare (H) 2-0
Q2: Annfield Plain (H) 1-3

55-56 * Q2: Consett (H) 1-2

56-57 * Q2: Shotton Colliery Welfare (A) 0-3

57-58 * Q1: Blackhall Colliery Welfare (H) 4-2
Q2: Easington Colliery Welfare (A) 1-2

58-59 * Q2: Tow Law Town (A) 1-4

59-60 * Q2: Easington Colliery Welfare (A) 2-0
Q3: Consett (H) 0-4

60-61 * Q2: Stockton (A) 2-2, (H) 3-1
Q3: Bridlington Town (A) 2-11

61-62 * Q1: Whitley Bay (A) 2-5

62-63 * Q1: Ferryhill Athletic (H) 1-2

63-64 * Q1: West Auckland T. (H - *played away*) 1-4

64-65 * Q1: Consett (A) 1-5

65-66 * Q1: Tow Law Town (H) 2-1
Q2: Consett (H) 1-1, (A) 0-5

66-67 * Q1: Stockton (A) 2-2, (H) 0-0, 1-4

67-68 * PR: Spennymoor United (A) 0-5

68-69 * Q1: North Shields (A) 0-3

69-70 * PR: Ferryhill Athletic (A) 0-2

70-71 * PR: Bishop Auckland (A) 0-3

71-72 * Q1: Blyth Spartans (A) 2-3

72-73 * Q1: Tow Law Town (A) 1-1, (H) 0-3

73-74 * Q1: Evenwood Town (H) 0-1

74-75 * PR: West Auckland Town (H) 4-0
Q1: Shildon (H) 2-3

75-76 * Q1: Consett (H) 2-0
Q2: Netherfield (H) 1-1, (A) 2-3

76-77 Q1: Whitley Bay (A) 0-5

77-78 Q1: Carlisle City (H) 3-1
Q2: Whitby Town (H) 2-1
Q3: Bishop Auckland (A) 2-3

78-79 Q1: Durham City (H) 2-0
Q2: Washington (H) 3-2
Q3: Billingham Synthonia (A) 0-0, (H) 2-4

79-80 Q1: Ashington (H) 0-1

80-81 Q1: Barrow (A) 1-8

81-82 PR: Tow Law Town (H) 1-5

BOLSOVER COLLIERY

Currently: Defunct

48-49 EX: Steel, Peech & Tozer Social S. (A) 2-4

49-50 EX: Kiveton Park Colliery (H) 2-1
PR: Cresswell Colliery (H) 4-5

BOLTON WANDERERS

Currently: Football League

45-46 R3: Blackburn R. (H) 1-0, (A) 3-3 (*agg: 4-3*)
R4: Liverpool (H) 5-0, (A) 0-2 (*agg: 5-2*)
R5: Middlesbrough (H) 1-0, (A) 1-1 (*agg: 2-1*)
R6: Stoke City (A) 2-0, (H) 0-0 (*agg: 2-0*)
SF: Charlton Athletic (*at Aston Villa*) 0-2

46-47 R3: Stockport County (H) 5-1
R4: Manchester City (H) 3-3, (A) 0-1

47-48 R3: Tottenham Hotspur (H) 0-2

48-49 R3: Aston Villa (A) 1-1, (H) 0-0, 1-2

49-50 R3: Coventry City (A) 2-1
R4: Leeds United (A) 1-1, (H) 2-3

50-51 R3: York City (H) 2-0
R4: Newcastle United (A) 2-3

51-52 R3: West Bromwich Albion (A) 0-4

52-53 R3: Fulham (H) 3-1
R4: Notts County (H) 1-1, (A) 2-2, 1-0
R5: Luton Town (A) 1-0
R6: Gateshead (A) 1-0
SF: Everton (*at Manchester City*) 4-3
F: Blackpool (*at Wembley*) 3-4

53-54 R3: Liverpool (H) 1-0
R4: Headington United (A) 4-2
R5: Portsmouth (H) 0-0, (A) 2-1
R6: Sheffield Wednesday (A) 1-1, (H) 0-2

54-55 R3: Millwall (H) 1-0
R4: Birmingham City (A) 1-2

55-56 R3: Huddersfield Town (H) 3-0
R4: Sheffield United (H) 1-2

56-57 R3: Blackpool (H) 2-3

57-58 R3: Preston North End (A) 3-0
R4: York City (A) 0-0, (H) 3-0
R5: Stoke City (H) 3-1
R6: Wolverhampton Wanderers (H) 2-1
SF: Blackburn R. (*at Manchester City*) 2-1
F: Manchester United (*at Wembley*) 2-0

58-59 R3: Scunthorpe United (A) 2-0
R4: Wolverhampton Wanderers (A) 2-1
R5: Preston N.E. (H) 2-2, (A) 1-1, 1-0
R6: Nottingham Forest (A) 1-2

59-60 R3: Bury (A) 1-1, (H) 4-2
R4: West Bromwich Albion (A) 0-2

60-61 R3: Hull City (A) 1-0
R4: Blackburn Rovers (H) 3-3, (A) 0-4

61-62 R3: Manchester United (A) 1-2

62-63 R3: Sheffield United (A) 1-3

63-64 R3: Bath City (A) 1-1, (H) 3-0
R4: Preston North End (H) 2-2, (A) 1-2

64-65 R3: Workington (H) 4-1
R4: Preston North End (A) 2-1
R5: Liverpool (H) 0-1

65-66 R3: West Bromwich Albion (H) 3-0
R4: Preston North End (H) 1-1, (A) 2-3

66-67 R3: Crewe Alexandra (H) 1-0
R4: Arsenal (H) 0-0, (A) 0-3

67-68 R3: Nottingham Forest (A) 2-4

68-69 R3: Northampton Town (H) 2-1
R4: Bristol Rovers (H) 1-2

69-70 R3: Watford (H) 1-2

70-71 R3: York City (A) 0-2

71-72 R1: Bangor City (H) 3-0
R2: Rossendale Utd (A - *at Bury*) 4-1
R3: Torquay United (H) 2-1
R4: Chelsea (A) 0-3

72-73 R1: Chester (H) 1-1, (A) 1-0
R2: Shrewsbury Town (H) 3-0
R3: Charlton Athletic (A) 1-1, (H) 4-0
R4: Cardiff (H) 2-2, (A) 1-1, (*at W. Brom.*) 1-0
R5: Luton Town (H) 0-1

73-74 R3: Stoke City (H) 3-2
R4: Southampton (A) 3-3, (H) 0-2

74-75 R3: West Bromwich Albion (H) 0-0, (A) 0-4

75-76 R3: Brentford (A) 0-0, (H) 2-0
R4: Huddersfield Town (A) 1-0
R5: Newcastle (H) 3-3, (A) 0-0, (*at Leeds*) 1-2

76-77 R3: West Ham United (A) 1-2

77-78 R3: Tottenham Hotspur (A) 2-2, (H) 2-1
R4: Mansfield Town (H) 1-0
R5: Middlesbrough (A) 0-2

78-79 R3: Bristol City (A) 1-3

79-80 R3: Sunderland (A) 1-0
R4: Halifax Town (H) 2-0
R5: Arsenal (H) 1-1, (A) 0-3

80-81 R3: Nottingham Forest (A) 3-3, (H) 0-1

81-82 R3: Derby County (H) 3-1
R4: Crystal Palace (A) 0-1

82-83 R3: Arsenal (A) 1-2

83-84 R1: Tranmere Rovers (A) 2-2, (H) 4-1
R2: Mansfield Town (H) 2-0
R3: Sunderland (H) 0-3

84-85 R1: Hull City (A) 1-2

85-86 R1: Wrexham (A) 1-3

86-87 R1: Halifax T. (A) 1-1, (H) 1-1, (A) 3-1
R2: Tranmere Rovers (H) 2-0
R3: Coventry City (A) 0-3

87-88 R1: Burnley (A) 1-0
R2: Wrexham (A) 2-1
R3: Barnsley (A) 1-3

88-89 R1: Chesterfield (H) 0-0, (A) 3-2
R2: Port Vale (H) 1-2

89-90 R1: Blackpool (A) 1-2

90-91 R1: Witton Albion (A) 2-1
R2: Chesterfield (A) 4-3
R3: Barrow (H) 1-0
R4: Manchester United (A) 0-1

91-92 R1: Emley (A - *at Huddersfield Town*) 3-0
R2: Bradford City (H) 3-1
R3: Reading (H) 2-0
R4: Brighton & Hove Albion (H) 2-1
R5: Southampton (H) 2-2, (A) 2-3

92-93 R1: Sutton Coldfield Town (H) 2-1
R2: Rochdale (H) 4-0
R3: Liverpool (H) 2-2, (A) 2-0
R4: Wolverhampton Wanderers (A) 2-0
R5: Derby County (A) 1-3

Above: *Nat Lofthouse scores Bolton's first goal in the 1958 final. Photo: Colorsport.*

BOOTLE

Currently: North West Counties League

80-81 Q1: Bangor City (A) 2-0
Q2: Chorley (H) 0-1

81-82 Q1: Prescot Cables (A) 1-3

82-83 PR: Droylsden (H) 3-0
Q1: St Helens Town (A) 4-0
Q2: Ashton United (A) 0-0, (H) 0-1

83-84 Q1: Bangor City (H) 0-1

84-85 Q1: Marine (H) 0-2

85-86 Q1: Chorley (H) 0-1

86-87 PR: Belper Town (H) 2-0
Q1: Burscough (A) 2-2, (H) 2-1
Q2: Eastwood T. (H) 2-2, (A) 1-1, (H) 1-1, (A) 0-1

87-88 Q1: Ashton United (H) 1-0
Q2: Marine (H) 2-2, (A) 0-1

88-89 PR: Arnold (A - *played home*) 1-0

89-90 PR: Burscough (A) 0-2

90-91 PR: Winsford United (H) 1-0
Q1: Ilkeston Town (A) 3-2
Q2: Southport (H) 2-0
Q3: Chorley (A) 2-6

91-92 Q1: Newcastle Town (H) 2-1
Q2: Droylsden (A) 1-1, (H) 1-3

92-93 PR: Formby (A) 2-1
Q1: Chadderton (A) 0-3

BOOTLE ATHLETIC

Currently: Defunct

49-50 EX: Stoneycroft (H) 5-1
PR: Earlestown (H) 5-1
Q1: Prescot Cables (H) 2-1
Q2: Wigan Athletic (A) 1-6

50-51 PR: Earle (H) 2-1
Q1: Burscough (A) 0-2

51-52 Q1: Bangor City (H) 1-1, (A) 0-2

52-53 PR: Llandudno (A) 1-1, (H) 1-0
Q1: New Brighton (H) 1-1, (A) 0-1

53-54 PR: Pwllheli & District (H) 0-2

BOOTS ATHLETIC

Currently: Notts Alliance

46-47 Q1: Ransome & Marles (A) 1-3

47-48 PR: Ilkeston Town (H) 0-4

48-49 PR: Ransome & Marles (H) 0-6

49-50 EX: Measham Imperial (H) 1-2

50-51 EX: Retford Town (A) 0-2

51-52 Q1: Basford United (H) 2-2, (A) 0-2

52-53 Q1: Basford United (A) 1-0
Q2: Newhall United (H) 2-2, (A) 2-0
Q3: Ilkeston Town (H) 0-4

53-54 Q1: Matlock Town (H) 0-5

54-55 Q1: Ilkeston Town (H) 0-6

55-56 Q2: Gresley Rovers (A) 1-0
Q3: Ilkeston Town (H) 0-9

56-57 Q2: Ilkeston Town (A) 0-2

57-58 Q2: Gresley Rovers (H) 1-3

58-59 Q1: Hallam (A) 1-3

59-60 Q1: Norton Woodseats Amateur (A) 1-2

BOREHAM WOOD

Currently: Isthmian League

70-71 Q1: Leyton (A) 4-2
Q2: Aveley (A) 3-3, (H) 0-3

71-72 Q1: Cheshunt (H) 2-1
Q2: Wealdstone (H) 1-1, (A) 2-0
Q3: Walthamstow Avenue (H) 2-2, (A) 1-2

73-74 Q1: Addlestone (A) 3-1
Q2: Finchley (A) 1-0
Q3: Bexley United (H) 1-0
Q4: Aveley (H) 2-2, (A) 2-1
R1: Southend United (A) 0-3

74-75 PR: Epping Town (A) 0-3

75-76 Q1: Hounslow (H) 2-0
Q2: Dagenham (A) 0-4

76-77 Q1: Hertford Town (A) 2-1
Q2: Epsom & Ewell (H) 1-1, (A) 1-2

77-78 Q1: Hoddesdon Town (A) 1-0
Q2: Edgware (A) 2-2, (H) 4-2
Q3: Finchley (A) 5-1
Q4: Dartford (H) 3-2
R1: Swindon Town (H) 0-0, (A) 0-2

78-79 Q1: Burnham (H) 3-2
Q2: Hillingdon Borough (H) 0-2

79-80 Q1: Chesham United (A) 0-2

80-81 Q1: Addlestone & Weybridge (A) 2-2, (H) 0-2

81-82 Q1: Kingstonian (A) 0-2

82-83 Q1: Newmarket Town (A) 3-0
Q2: Hayes (H) 3-0
Q3: Tring Town (H) 3-0
Q4: Dartford (H) 1-1, (A) 1-2

83-84 Q1: Aylesbury United (A) 0-2

84-85 PR: Haverhill Rovers (H) 2-1
Q1: Alvechurch (A) 1-4

85-86 Q1: Wembley (A) 0-2

86-87 PR: Egham Town (H) 2-2, (A) 3-1
Q1: Rayners Lane (A) 5-2
Q2: Kingstonian (H) 2-2, (A) 1-0
Q3: Aylesbury United (H) 0-1

87-88 Q1: Vauxhall Motors (H) 2-0
Q2: Buckingham Town (A) 0-0, (H) 2-1
Q3: Worcester City (H) 1-3

88-89 Q1: Hitchin Town (H) 2-0
Q2: Bury Town (H) 0-0, (A) 4-1
Q3: Kettering Town (A) 0-4

89-90 PR: Harefield United (H) 1-0
Q1: Aveley (A) 1-0
Q2: Wycombe Wanderers (A) 1-3

90-91 PR: Gorleston (H) 2-0
Q1: Baker Perkins (H) 0-0, (A) 2-1
Q2: Rushden Town (H) 1-0
Q3: Boston United (H) 1-1, (A) 0-4

91-92 Q1: Lowestoft Town (A) 1-2

92-93 PR: Redhill (A) 5-1
Q1: Chesham United (H) 2-2, (A) 1-9

BOROUGH UNITED

Currently: Defunct

62-63 Q1: Stork (H) 4-0
Q2: Runcorn (A) 1-0
Q3: Ellesmere Port Town (H) 0-1

63-64 Q1: Pwllheli & District (H) 7-2
Q2: New Brighton (H) 1-1, (A) 1-3

64-65 Q1: Stork (A) 4-0
Q2: Runcorn (A) 2-0
Q3: Ellesmere Port Town (A) 0-4

65-66 Q1: Rhyl (A) 1-1, (H) 1-0
Q2: New Brighton (H) 3-0
Q3: Colwyn Bay (H) 1-1, (A) 1-2

66-67 Q1: Oswestry Town (H) 2-3

BORROWASH VICTORIA

Currently: Central Midlands League

88-89 PR: Grantham (A) 1-2

89-90 Q1: Accrington Stanley (A) 0-4

90-91 PR: Gresley Rovers (H) 1-2

91-92 PR: St Helens Town (A) 3-1
Q1: Belper Town (H) 2-0
Q2: Macclesfield Town (A) 2-1
Q3: Emley (H) 0-3

92-93 Q1: Mossley (A) 0-0, (H) 0-1

BOSTON

Currently: United Counties League

65-66 Q1: Stamford (A) 1-0
Q2: Grantham (A) 0-7

66-67 Q1: Louth United (A) 3-0
Q2: King's Lynn (A) 1-2

67-68 Q1: Louth United (H) 0-0, (A) 0-4

68-69 Q1: Louth United (A) 1-3

69-70 Q1: King's Lynn (H) 2-3

70-71 Q1: Louth United (A) 1-0
Q2: Spalding United (A) 2-2, (H) 3-0
Q3: Boston United (H) 0-4

71-72 Q1: Bourne Town (H) 1-5

72-73 Q1: Corby Town (A) 1-3

73-74 Q1: Holbeach United (H) 0-2

74-75 Q1: Spalding United (H) 4-0
Q2: Skegness Town (H) 1-1, (A) 2-1
Q3: King's Lynn (A) 0-1

75-76 PR: Corby Town (A) 0-0, (H) 1-2

76-77 Q1: Bourne Town (H) 2-0
Q2: King's Lynn (H) 2-1
Q3: Stamford (H) 1-0
Q4: Bangor City (H) 1-0
R1: Barnsley (A) 1-3

77-78 Q1: Parson Drove (A) 2-0
Q2: Holbeach United (A) 1-0
Q3: Arnold (A) 0-2

78-79 Q1: Barton Town (A) 3-1
Q2: Grantham (H) 0-1

79-80 Q1: Bourne Town (A) 2-0
Q2: North Ferriby United (A) 3-1
Q3: Skegness Town (A) 1-1, (H) 2-2, 1-0
Q4: A.P. Leamington (H) 2-2, (A) 0-1

80-81 Q1: Spalding United (H) 6-1
Q2: Holbeach United (A) 3-0
Q3: Corby Town (H) 0-1

81-82 PR: Holbeach United (H) 5-0
Q1: Gainsborough Trinity (H) 0-0, (A) 2-1
Q2: North Ferriby United (H) 1-2

82-83 PR: Bourne Town (H) 1-3

83-84 PR: Gresley Rovers (H) 1-3

84-85 Q1: Matlock Town (H) 1-4

85-86 PR: Atherstone United (H) 0-2

88-89 Q1: Sutton Town (H) 2-0
Q2: Witton Albion (A) 0-0, (H) 0-2

89-90 Q1: Dudley Town (A) 1-0
Q2: Grantham Town (H) 1-2

90-91 PR: King's Lynn (H) 2-0
Q1: Bromsgrove Rovers (H) 0-3

91-92 PR: Harrogate Town (H) 2-3

92-93 PR: Banbury United (H) 4-1
Q1: Stourbridge (H) 3-4

BOSTON UNITED

Currently: Northern Premier League

45-46 Q2: Ollerton Colliery (A) 2-4

46-47 Q2: Grantham (A) 2-1
Q3: Ransome & Marles (H) 3-1
Q4: Scunthorpe United (A) 1-4

47-48 Q1: Gedling Colliery (A) 5-3
Q2: Ilkeston Town (A) 0-1

48-49 PR: Spalding United (A) 1-2

49-50 EX: Holbeach United (H) 7-0
PR: Teversal & Silverhill C.W. (H) 2-1
Q1: Grantham (H) 2-3

50-51 EX: Stamford (A) 1-1, (H) 10-2
PR: South Normanton Miners Welfare (H) 3-2
Q1: Grantham (A) 0-0, (H) 4-1
Q2: Linby Colliery (H) 0-4

51-52 Q1: Barton Town (H) 5-3
Q2: Retford Town (H) 6-1
Q3: Skegness Town (A) 1-2

52-53 PR: Barton Town (A) 7-1
Q1: Alford United (A) 5-4
Q2: Retford Town (A) 4-1
Q3: Skegness Town (H) 3-2
Q4: Frickley Colliery (H) 3-2
R1: Oldham Athletic (H) 1-2

53-54 Q1: Bourne Town (A) 4-1
Q2: Lysaght's Sports (A) 4-0
Q3: Ashby Institute (A) 3-2
Q4: Shirebrook Miners Welfare (A) 5-2
R1: Scunthorpe United (A) 0-9

54-55 Q1: Brigg Town (A) 2-0
Q2: Grantham (A) 2-2, (H) 1-0
Q3: Skegness Town (A) 6-2
Q4: Peterborough United (A) 2-1
R1: Blyth Spartans (H) 1-1, (A) 4-5

55-56 Q4: Sutton Town (H) 8-2
R1: Northwich Victoria (H) 3-2
R2: Derby County (A) 6-1
R3: Tottenham Hotspur (A) 0-4

56-57 Q4: Grantham (H) 6-3
R1: Bradford (Park Avenue) (H) 0-2

57-58 Q4: Alford United (H) 4-0
R1: Billingham Synthonia Recreation (H) 5-2
R2: Darlington (A) 3-5

58-59 PR: Alford United (H) 3-0
Q1: Louth United (H) 5-2
Q2: Skegness United (A) 3-0
Q3: Gainsborough Trin. (H) 1-1, (A) 2-2, 3-1
Q4: Sheffield (A) 3-0
R1: Chester (A) 2-3

59-60 Q4: Kettering Town (A) 0-1

60-61 Q4: Kettering Town (A) 1-1, (H) 1-3

61-62 Q1: Louth United (H) 3-4

62-63 Q1: Spalding United (A) 3-1
Q2: Grantham (H) 3-2
Q3: Skegness Town (H) 1-0
Q4: Kettering Town (H) 2-0
R1: King's Lynn (H) 1-2

63-64 Q1: Holbeach United (A) 2-2, (H) 0-1

64-65 Q1: Spalding United (H) 0-14

65-66 Q1: Skegness Town (A) 2-3

66-67 Q1: Stamford (H) 4-0
Q2: Spalding United (H) 2-0
Q3: King's Lynn (A) 5-2
Q4: Grantham (H) 1-4

67-68 Q1: Holbeach United (H) 1-1, (A) 2-0
Q2: Louth United (A) 1-0
Q3: King's Lynn (H) 2-0
Q4: Bedford Town (H) 1-1, (A) 3-2
R1: Corby Town (A) 3-0
R2: Leyton Orient (H) 1-1, (A) 1-2

68-69 Q4: Grantham (H) 2-2, (A) 1-2

69-70 PR: Wisbech Town (H) 2-1
Q1: Spalding United (A) 4-0
Q2: Bourne Town (H) 0-0, (A) 2-0
Q3: King's Lynn (A) 1-2

70-71 Q1: Holbeach United (H) 4-0
Q2: Lincoln United (H) 1-0
Q3: Boston (A) 4-0
Q4: Frickley Colliery Athletic (A) 3-1
R1: Southport (A) 2-0
R2: York City (H) 1-2

71-72 Q4: Winterton Rangers (A) 3-0
R1: Ellesmere Port Town (A) 3-0
R2: Hartlepool United (H) 2-1
R3: Portsmouth (H) 0-1

72-73 Q4: Bury Town (A) 3-1
R1: Lancaster City (H) 1-2

73-74 Q4: Corby Town (A) 2-1
R1: Hayes (H) 0-0, (A) 2-1
R2: Hitchin Town (H) 1-0
R3: Derby County (A) 0-0, (H) 1-6

74-75 Q4: Enderby Town (A) 2-1
R1: Chesterfield (A) 1-3

75-76 Q4: Kettering Town (A) 4-3

R1: Lincoln City (H) 0-1

76-77 Q4: Goole Town (A) 1-1, (H) 1-3

77-78 Q4: A.P. Leamington (H) 1-2

78-79 PR: Heanor Town (A) 3-0
Q1: Sutton Town (A) 0-0, (H) 4-0
Q2: Retford Town (A) 4-1
Q3: Gainsborough Trinity (H) 3-0
Q4: Kettering Town (A) 3-1
R1: Tranmere Rovers (A) 1-2

79-80 Q1: Ely City (A) 2-1
Q2: Stamford (A) 5-0
Q3: Wisbech Town (A) 5-1
Q4: Nuneaton Borough (H) 1-1, (A) 1-2

80-81 Q1: Skegness Town (H) 3-0
Q2: Grantham (A) 3-1
Q3: Barton Town (H) 2-0
Q4: Corby Town (A) 1-0
R1: Rotherham United (H) 0-4

81-82 Q1: Sutton Town (H) 2-1
Q2: Alfreton Town (A - *played home*) 2-0
Q3: North Ferriby United (H) 4-0
Q4: Dunstable (H) 3-1
R1: Kettering Town (H) 0-1

82-83 Q4: Shifnal Town (H) 4-1
R1: Crewe Alexandra (H) 3-1
R2: Sheffield United (H) 1-1, (A) 1-5

Above: *Jim Lumby shoots against Sheffield United 'keeper Keith Waugh. The ball rebounded for him to put Boston United ahead in the Second Round in 1982. Photo: Bob Whitaker.*

83-84 Q4: Stafford Rangers (H) 3-1
R1: Bury (H) 0-3

84-85 Q4: Barnet (A) 1-3

85-86 Q4: Runcorn (A) 2-2, (H) 1-1, (A) 1-4

86-87 Q4: Gainsborough Trinity (H) 6-0
R1: Runcorn (A) 1-1, (H) 1-2

87-88 Q4: Welling United (H) 1-1, (A) 2-3

88-89 Q1: Coventry Sporting (H) 8-1
Q2: Mile Oak Rovers & Youth (H) 5-0
Q3: Hinckley Town (H) 3-4

89-90 Q1: Leek Town (H) 3-3, (A) 3-0
Q2: Alfreton Town (H) 1-0
Q3: Matlock Town (A) 1-1, (H) 0-1

90-91 Q1: Lowestoft Town (H) 7-0
Q2: V.S. Rugby (H) 3-1
Q3: Boreham Wood (A) 1-1, (H) 4-0
Q4: Dartford (A) 1-1, (H) 2-1
R1: Wycombe Wanderers (H) 1-1, (A) 0-4

91-92 Q1: Blakenall (A) 2-1
Q2: Tamworth (H) 1-1, (A) 0-1

92-93 Q1: King's Lynn (H) 2-1
Q2: Aveley (H) 1-2

BOTLEY

Currently: Southampton Senior League

48-49 EX: Winchester City (H) 1-3

(A.F.C.) BOURNEMOUTH

Currently: Football League
***** - As Bournemouth & Boscombe Athletic

45-46 * R1: Lovells Ath. (A) 1-4, (H) 3-2 (*agg: 4-6*)

46-47 * R1: Exeter City (H) 4-2
R2: Aldershot (H) 4-2
R3: Derby County (H) 0-2

47-48 * R1: Guildford City (H) 2-0
R2: Bradford City (H) 1-0
R3: Wolverhampton Wanderers (H) 1-2

48-49 * R3: Manchester United (A) 0-6

49-50 * R3: Bradford (Park Avenue) (A) 1-0
R4: Northampton Town (H) 1-1, (A) 1-2

50-51 * R1: Colchester United (H) 1-0
R2: Aldershot (A) 0-3

51-52 * R1: Southend United (A) 1-6

52-53 * R1: Ipswich Town (A) 2-2, (H) 2-2, 2-3

53-54 * R1: Southampton (A) 1-1, (H) 3-1
R2: Scunthorpe United (A) 0-1

54-55 * R1: Barnstaple Town (A) 4-1
R2: Oldham Athletic (H) 1-0
R3: West Bromwich Albion (H) 0-1

55-56 * R1: Reading (A) 0-1

56-57 * R1: Burton Albion (H) 8-0
R2: Swindon Town (A) 1-0
R3: Accrington Stanley (H) 2-0
R4: Wolverhampton Wanderers (A) 1-0
R5: Tottenham Hotspur (H) 3-1
R6: Manchester United (H) 1-2

57-58 * R1: Oswestry Town (A) 5-1
R2: Northampton Town (A) 1-4

58-59 * R1: Tooting & Mitcham United (A) 1-3

59-60 * R1: Walthamstow Avenue (A) 3-2
R2: Enfield (A) 5-1
R3: York City (H) 1-0
R4: Bradford City (A) 1-3

60-61 * R1: Exeter City (A) 1-1, (H) 3-1
R2: Yeovil Town (H) 2-1
R3: Burnley (A) 0-1

61-62 * R1: Margate (H) 0-3

62-63 * R1: Coventry City (A) 0-1

63-64 * R1: Bristol Rovers (H) 1-3

64-65 * R1: Gravesend & Northfleet (H) 7-0
R2: Bristol City (H) 0-3

65-66 * R1: Weymouth (H) 0-0, (A) 4-1
R2: Bath City (H) 5-3
R3: Burnley (H) 1-1, (A) 0-7

66-67 * R1: Welton Rovers (H) 3-0
R2: Queens Park Rangers (A) 0-2

67-68 * R1: Northampton Town (H) 2-0
R2: Walthamstow Avenue (A) 3-1
R3: Liverpool (H) 0-0, (A) 1-4

68-69 R1: Bury Town (A) 0-0, (H) 3-0
R2: Bristol Rovers (H) 0-0, (A) 0-1

69-70 R1: Luton Town (H) 1-1, (A) 1-3

70-71 R1: Oxford City (A) 1-1, (H) 8-1
R2: Yeovil Town (H) 0-1

71-72 R1: Margate (H) 11-0
R2: Southend United (H) 2-0
R3: Walsall (A) 0-1

72-73 R1: Cambridge United (H) 5-1
R2: Colchester United (H) 0-0, (A) 2-0
R3: Newcastle United (A) 0-2

73-74 R1: Charlton Athletic (H) 1-0
R2: Watford (A) 1-0
R3: Orient (A) 1-2

74-75 R1: Southwick (H) 5-0
R2: Wycombe Wanderers (A) 0-0, (H) 1-2

75-76 R1: Sutton United (A) 1-1, (H) 1-0
R2: Hereford United (H) 2-2, (A) 0-2

76-77 R1: Newport County (H) 0-0, (A) 0-3

77-78 R1: Colchester (A) 1-1, (H) 0-0, (*Watford*) 1-4

78-79 R1: Hitchin Town (H) 2-1
R2: Wimbledon (A) 1-1, (H) 1-2

79-80 R1: Peterborough United (A) 2-1
R2: Colchester United (A) 0-1

80-81 R1: Wycombe Wanderers (A) 3-0
R2: Charlton Athletic (A) 1-2

81-82 R1: Reading (H) 1-0
R2: Dorchester Town (A) 1-1, (H) 2-1
R3: Oxford United (H) 0-2

82-83 R1: Southend United (H) 0-2

83-84 R1: Walsall (H) 4-0
R2: Windsor & Eton (A) 0-0, (H) 2-0
R3: Manchester United (H) 2-0
R4: Middlesbrough (A) 0-2

84-85 R1: Kettering Town (A) 0-0, (H) 3-2
R2: Dartford (A) 1-1, (H) 4-1
R3: Manchester United (A) 0-3

85-86 R1: Dartford (H) 0-0, (A) 2-0
R2: Dagenham (H) 4-1
R3: Wigan Athletic (A) 0-3

86-87 R1: Fareham Town (H) 7-2
R2: Orient (H) 0-1

87-88 R3: Brighton & Hove Albion (A) 0-2

88-89 R3: Blackpool (A) 1-0
R4: Hartlepool United (A) 1-1, (H) 5-2
R5: Manchester United (H) 1-1, (A) 0-1

89-90 R3: Sheffield United (A) 0-2

90-91 R1: Gillingham (H) 2-1
R2: Hayes (H) 1-0
R3: Chester City (A - *at Macclesfield*) 3-2
R4: Portsmouth (A) 1-5

91-92 R1: Bromsgrove Rovers (H) 3-1
R2: Brentford (H) 2-1
R3: Newcastle United (H) 0-0, (A) 0-0 *aband. (fog) after 17 mins*, (A) 2-2 (*4-3 pens*)
R4: Ipswich Town (A) 0-3

92-93 R1: Barnet (H) 0-0, (A) 2-1
R2: Cheltenham Town (A) 1-1, (H) 3-0
R3: Blackburn Rovers (A) 1-3

BOURNEMOUTH

Currently: Wessex League

46-47 PR: Poole Town (H) 2-4

47-48 PR: Poole Town (A) 2-3

48-49 EX: Weymouth (A) 3-8

49-50 EX: Bournemouth Gasworks Athletic (H) 1-0
PR: Thornycroft Athletic (H) 5-2
Q1: Portland United (H) 3-1
Q2: Cowes (H) 3-3, (A) 0-4

50-51 PR: Cowes (A) 1-1, (H) 4-2
Q1: Blandford United (A) 2-6

89-90 PR: Bracknell Town (H) 2-0
Q1: Witney Town (A) 0-1

90-91 PR: Thatcham Town (H) 1-0
Q1: Abingdon Town (H) 2-1
Q2: Salisbury (A) 0-4

91-92 PR: Abingdon Town (H) 1-2

92-93 PR: Wimborne Town (A) 1-1, (H) 1-3

BOURNEMOUTH GASWORKS ATHLETIC

Currently: Defunct

46-47 PR: Weymouth S.A.A. (H) *W/O*
Q1: Newport Isle of Wight (A) 1-0
Q2: R.A.O.C. (Hilsea) (A) 2-2, (H) 6-2
Q3: Poole Town (A) 2-4 *protested*, (A) 2-3

47-48 PR: Portland United (H) 4-0
Q1: Gosport Borough Athletic (H) 0-3

48-49 PR: Gosport Borough Athletic (A) 1-0
Q1: East Cowes Victoria (A) 1-3

49-50 EX: Bournemouth (A) 0-1

50-51 EX: Shaftesbury (H) 1-2

51-52 Q1: Bridport (A) 2-2, (H) 3-1
Q2: Portland United (H) 1-3

52-53 Q1: Poole Town (H) 3-1
Q2: Portland United (H) 5-1
Q3: Dorchester Town (A) 1-2

53-54 Q1: Bridport (H) 8-0
Q2: Ilminster Town (A) 4-0
Q3: Portland United (A) 1-4

54-55 Q2: Dorchester Town (A) 0-4

55-56 Q1: Cowes Isle of Wight (A) 1-4

56-57 Q2: Andover (A) 2-3

BOURNE TOWN
Currently: United Counties League

47-48 PR: Stamford Town (A) 0-4

48-49 PR: Raleigh Athletic (H) 0-5

49-50 EX: Rufford Colliery (A - *played home*) 5-3
PR: Alford United (A) 3-3, (H) 5-3
Q1: South Normanton Miners Welf. (A) 2-3

50-51 EX: Heanor Athletic (A) 1-3

51-52 Q1: Retford Town (H) 2-4

52-53 Q1: Grantham (H) 0-5

53-54 Q1: Boston United (H) 1-4

54-55 Q1: Symington's Recreation (H) 3-2
Q2: Corby Town (H) 1-3

55-56 Q1: Brigg Town (A) 2-2, (H) 2-3

56-57 Q1: Brigg Town (H) 2-0
Q2: Grantham (H) 2-8

57-58 Q1: Alford United (A) 0-1

58-59 Q1: Skegness Town (H) 1-2

59-60 Q1: Louth United (H) 4-1
Q2: Gainsborough Trinity (A) 1-4

61-62 Q1: Rushden Town (H) 2-1
Q2: Rothwell Town (A) 2-1
Q3: Corby Town (H) 1-5

62-63 Q1: Rushden Town (H) 4-1
Q2: Stamford (H) 5-1
Q3: Corby Town (A) 1-4

63-64 Q1: Desborough Town (H) 6-1
Q2: Corby Town (A) 2-4

64-65 Q1: Desborough Town (A) 0-2

65-66 Q1: Rushden Town (A) 4-4, (H) 4-1
Q2: Rothwell Town (H) 3-1
Q3: Wellingborough (H) 2-2, (A) 2-3

67-68 Q1: Wisbech Town (H) 4-0
Q2: King's Lynn (A) 1-3

68-69 Q1: Wisbech Town (H) 2-3

69-70 Q1: Holbeach United (A) 2-1
Q2: Boston United (A) 0-0, (H) 0-2

70-71 Q1: Wisbech Town (A) 1-2

71-72 Q1: Boston (A) 5-1
Q2: Stamford (H) 3-1
Q3: King's Lynn (H) 0-3

72-73 Q1: Holbeach United (A) 1-0
Q2: Kettering Town (H) 1-5

73-74 Q1: Histon (A) 0-1

74-75 Q1: Louth United (H) 1-0
Q2: King's Lynn (H) 2-2, (A) 0-1

75-76 Q1: Chatteris Town (H) 4-0
Q2: Bedford Town (H) 1-5

76-77 Q1: Boston (A) 0-2

77-78 Q1: Rothwell Town (A) 1-4

78-79 PR: Arnold (H) 1-4

79-80 Q1: Boston (H) 0-2

80-81 Q1: Cambridge City (H) 0-0, (A) 1-0
Q2: Great Yarmouth Town (H) 0-2

81-82 Q1: North Ferriby United (H) 1-2

82-83 PR: Boston (A) 3-1
Q1: Winterton Rangers (A) 3-4

83-84 PR: Chipping Norton Town (H) 4-2
Q1: Shifnal Town (H) 1-4

84-85 PR: Wembley (A) 1-2

85-86 Q1: Alfreton Town (A) 0-6

86-87 PR: Tamworth (H) 0-2

87-88 PR: Milton Keynes Borough (H) 1-4

88-89 PR: Baker Perkins (H) 1-1, (A) 1-0
Q1: Bedworth United (A) 1-1, (H) 3-4

90-91 PR: Ely City (H) 3-0
Q1: Wembley (A) 1-4

91-92 PR: Barton Rovers (A) 4-3
Q1: Braintree Town (H) 0-3

92-93 PR: Peterborough City (H) 4-3
Q1: Milton Keynes Borough (H) 3-2
Q2: Moor Green (H) 4-8

BOURNVILLE ATHLETIC
Currently: Defunct

45-46 Q1: Tamworth (A) 5-2
Q2: Moor Green (H) 6-5
Q3: Nuneaton B. (A) 1-8 - *Nuneaton expelled*
Q4: Shrewsbury Town (A) 2-6

46-47 Q1: Hereford United (A) 0-1

47-48 PR: Birmingham City Transport (H) 0-3

48-49 EX: Hednesford (H) 2-3

49-50 EX: Cradley Heath (H) 1-6

50-51 PR: Hereford United (H) 1-5

51-52 PR: Tamworth (H) 1-3

52-53 Q1: Rugby Town (H) 0-2

53-54 PR: Sutton Coldfield Town (A) 2-3

54-55 PR: Lockheed-Leamington (A) 1-7

55-56 Q1: Sutton Coldfield Town (A) 2-2, (H) 1-4

56-57 Q1: Bedworth Town (H) 0-4

57-58 Q1: Stourbridge (A) 1-3

58-59 PR: Lye Town (A) 0-1

59-60 Q1: Kidderminster Harriers (A) 1-7

BOWATER LLOYDS
Currently: Defunct
* - As Lloyds (Sittingbourne) F.C.

45-46 * Q1: Woolwich Polytechnic (A) 1-1, (H) 4-0
Q2: Ramsgate Athletic (A) 3-3, (H) 3-1
Q3: Bromley (H) 3-4

46-47 * PR: Shorts Sports (H) 4-2
Q1: Gravesend & Northfleet (H) 1-4

47-48 * EX: Chatham Town (H) 2-4

48-49 * PR: Erith & Belvedere (H) 5-1
Q1: Dartford (H) 1-2

49-50 PR: Aylesford Paper Mills (A) 10-1
Q1: Canterbury City (H) 2-3

50-51 PR: Faversham Town (H) 4-1
Q1: Snowdown Coll. Welf. (H) 1-1, (A) 0-2

51-52 PR: Ramsgate Athletic (H) 2-2, (A) 0-7

52-53 PR: Sheppey United (A) 1-5

53-54 PR: Ramsgate Athletic (H) *withdrew*

BOWTHORN UNITED
Currently: Defunct

47-48 PR: Kells Centre (H) 2-2, (A) 3-1
Q1: Lowca (H) 4-2
Q2: Parton United (H) 3-4

48-49 PR: Penrith (A) 2-9

49-50 Q1: Cockermouth (A) 2-8

50-51 PR: Milnthorpe Corinthians (A) 2-5

BRACKLEY TOWN
Currently: United Counties League

87-88 PR: Wisbech Town (A) 0-1

88-89 PR: Spalding United (H) 1-0
Q1: Rushall Olympic (H) 1-2

89-90 PR: Coventry Sporting (H) *W/O*
Q1: Shepshed Charterhouse (H) 2-1
Q2: Sutton Coldfield Town (H) 1-2

90-91 PR: Walsall Wood (H) 1-0
Q1: Buckingham T. (H) 1-1, (A) 1-1, (A) 0-2

BRACKNELL TOWN
Currently: Isthmian League

72-73 Q1: Bexley United (A) 0-1

73-74 Q1: Finchley (A) 0-1

74-75 Q1: Wimbledon (H) 1-3

75-76 Q1: Feltham (H) 1-1, (A) 2-3

76-77 Q1: Uxbridge (A) 1-0
Q2: Enfield (A) 2-5

77-78 Q1: Tilbury (H) 1-2

78-79 Q1: Barnet (A) 1-2

79-80 PR: Marlow (A) 3-2
Q1: Thame United (A) 5-6

80-81 PR: Poole Town (H) 1-5

81-82 Q1: Wokingham Town (H) 1-2

82-83 PR: Waterlooville (A) 2-1
Q1: Gosport Borough (A) 0-1

83-84 PR: Burnham (A - *played home*) 0-2

84-85 Q1: Tooting & Mitcham United (H) 0-3

85-86 Q1: Hayes (H) 1-1, (A) 1-2

86-87 Q1: Croydon (H) 2-0
Q2: Welling United (A) 1-2

87-88 PR: Peacehaven & Telscombe (H) 1-0
Q1: Abingdon Town (H) 3-2
Q2: Chichester City (H) 4-0
Q3: Newport I.O.W. (H) 4-1
Q4: Cheltenham Town (A) 1-2

88-89 Q1: Whitehawk (H) 1-2

89-90 PR: Bournemouth (A) 0-2

90-91 PR: Hampton (H) 2-3

91-92 PR: Portfield (H) 2-2, (A) 1-2

92-93 PR: Canterbury City (A) 1-4

BRADFORD CITY
Currently: Football League

45-46 R1: Notts County (A) 2-2, (H) 1-2 *(agg: 3-4)*

46-47 R1: Gateshead (A) 1-3

47-48 R1: Gateshead (A) 3-1
R2: Bournemouth & Boscombe Ath. (A) 0-1

48-49 R1: Doncaster Rovers (H) 4-3
R2: New Brighton (H) 0-0, (A) 0-1

49-50 R1: Fleetwood (H) 9-0
R2: Southport (A) 1-2

50-51 R1: Oldham Athletic (H) 2-2, (A) 1-2

51-52 R1: Carlisle United (H) 6-1
R2: Bradford (Park Avenue) (A) 2-3

52-53 R1: Rhyl (H) 4-0
R2: Ipswich Town (H) 1-1, (A) 1-5

53-54 R1: Crewe Alexandra (A) 0-0, (H) 0-1

54-55 R1: Mansfield Town (H) 3-1
R2: Merthyr Tydfil (H) 7-1
R3: Brentford (A) 1-1, (H) 2-2, 0-1

55-56 R1: Oldham Athletic (H) 3-1
R2: Worksop Town (H) 2-2, (A) 0-1

56-57 R1: Derby County (A) 1-2

57-58 R1: Scarborough (H) 6-0
R2: Chester (A) 3-3, (H) 3-1
R3: Scunthorpe United (A) 0-1

58-59 R1: Mansfield Town (A) 4-3
R2: Bradford (Park Avenue) (A) 2-0
R3: Brighton & Hove Albion (A) 2-0
R4: Preston North End (A) 2-3

59-60 R1: Barnsley (A) 3-3, (H) 2-1
R2: Rochdale (A) 1-1, (H) 2-1
R3: Everton (H) 3-0
R4: Bournemouth & Boscombe Ath. (H) 3-1
R5: Burnley (H) 2-2, (A) 0-5

60-61 R1: Scarborough (H) 0-0, (A) 3-1
R2: Barnsley (H) 1-2

61-62 R1: York City (H) 1-0
R2: Hull City (A) 2-0
R3: Arsenal (A) 0-3

62-63 R1: Oldham Athletic (A) 5-2
R2: Gateshead (H) 3-2
R3: Newcastle United (H) 1-6

63-64 R1: Port Vale (H) 1-2

64-65 R1: Scarborough (A) 0-1

65-66 R1: Darlington (A) 2-3

66-67 R1: Port Vale (H) 1-2

67-68 R1: Wrexham (H) 7-1
R2: Bury (H) 2-3

68-69 R1: Chester (H) 1-2

69-70 R1: Grimsby Town (H) 2-1
R2: Lincoln City (H) 3-0
R3: Tottenham Hotspur (H) 2-2, (A) 0-5

70-71 R1: Macclesfield Town (H) 3-2
R2: Lincoln C. (A) 2-2, (H) 2-2, 1-4

71-72 R1: Wrexham (A) 1-5

72-73 R1: Grantham (H) 3-0
R2: Tranmere Rovers (H) 2-1
R3: Blackpool (H) 2-1
R4: Arsenal (A) 0-2

73-74 R1: Workington (H) 2-0
R2: Barnsley (A) 1-1, (H) 2-1
R3: Alvechurch (H) 4-2
R4: Luton Town (A) 0-3

74-75 R1: Hartlepool United (A) 0-1

75-76 R1: Chesterfield (H) 1-0
R2: Rotherham United (A) 3-0
R3: Shrewsbury Town (A) 2-1
R4: Tooting & Mitcham United (H) 3-1
R5: Norwich City (A) 2-1
R6: Southampton (H) 0-1

76-77 R1: Walsall (A) 0-0, (H) 0-1

77-78 R1: Crewe Alexandra (H) 0-1

78-79 R1: Port Vale (H) 1-0
R2: Stockport County (A) 2-4

79-80 R1: Brandon Utd (A - *at Spennymoor*) 3-0
R2: Darlington (A) 1-0
R3: Carlisle United (A) 2-3

80-81 R1: Port Vale (A) 2-4

81-82 R1: Scunthorpe United (A) 0-1

82-83 R1: Port Vale (A) 1-0
R2: Mansfield Town (A) 1-1, (H) 3-2
R3: Barnsley (H) 0-1

83-84 R1: Wigan Athletic (H) 0-0, (A) 2-4

84-85 R1: Tow Law Town (H) 7-2
R2: Mansfield Town (H) 2-1
R3: Telford United (A) 1-2

85-86 R3: Ipswich (A) 4-4, (H - *at Leeds Utd*) 0-1

86-87 R3: Oldham Athletic (A) 1-1, (H) 5-1
R4: Everton (H) 0-1

87-88 R3: Wolverhampton Wanderers (H) 2-1
R4: Oxford United (H) 4-2
R5: Portsmouth (A) 0-3

88-89 R3: Tottenham Hotspur (H) 1-0
R4: Hull City (H) 1-2

89-90 R3: Charlton (A - *at Crystal P.*) 1-1, (H) 0-3

90-91 R1: Shrewsbury Town (H) 0-0, (A) 1-2

91-92 R1: Bury (A) 1-0
R2: Bolton Wanderers (A) 1-3

92-93 R1: Preston North End (H) 1-1, (A) 5-4
R2: Huddersfield Town (H) 0-2

BRADFORD PARK AVENUE

Currently: Defunct

45-46 R3: Port Vale (H) 2-1, (A) 1-1 (*agg: 3-2*)
R4: Manchester C. (H) 1-3, (A) 8-2 (*agg: 9-5*)
R5: Barnsley (A) 1-0, (H) 1-1 (*agg: 2-1*)
R6: Birmingham C. (H) 2-2, (A) 0-6 (*agg: 2-8*)

46-47 R3: Manchester United (H) 0-3

47-48 R3: Arsenal (A) 1-0
R4: Colchester United (A) 2-3

48-49 R3: Newcastle United (A) 2-0
R4: Manchester Utd (H) 1-1, (A) 1-1, 5-0

49-50 R3: Bournemouth & Boscombe Ath. (H) 0-1

50-51 R1: Chester (A) 2-1
R2: Millwall (A) 1-1, (H) 0-1

51-52 R1: York City (A) 1-1, (H) 1-1, 4-0
R2: Bradford City (H) 3-2
R3: Sheffield Wednesday (H) 2-1
R4: Leeds United (A) 0-2

52-53 R1: Rochdale (H) 2-1
R2: Gateshead (H) 1-2

53-54 R1: Selby Town (A) 2-0
R2: Cambridge United (A) 2-1
R3: Manchester City (H) 2-5

54-55 R1: Southport (H) 2-0
R2: Southend United (H) 2-3

55-56 R1: Rhyl (A) 3-0
R2: Workington (H) 4-3
R3: Middlesbrough (H) 0-4

56-57 R1: Boston United (A) 2-0
R2: Peterborough United (A) 0-3

57-58 R1: Oldham Athletic (A) 0-2

58-59 R1: Gateshead (A) 4-1
R2: Bradford City (H) 0-2

59-60 R1: Scarborough (H) 6-1
R2: South Shields (A) 5-1
R3: Chelsea (A) 1-5

60-61 R1: York City (A) 0-0, (H) 0-2

61-62 R1: Port Vale (H) 0-1

62-63 R1: Halifax Town (A) 0-1

63-64 R1: Heanor Town (H) 3-1
R2: Oldham Athletic (A) 0-2

64-65 R1: Doncaster Rovers (H) 2-3

65-66 R1: Hull City (H) 2-3

66-67 R1: Witton Albion (H) 3-2
R2: Workington (H) 3-1
R3: Fulham (H) 1-3

67-68 R1: Grimsby Town (A) 1-1, (H) 4-1
R2: Tranmere Rovers (H) 2-3

68-69 R1: Stockport County (A) 0-3

69-70 R1: South Shields (A) 1-2

70-71 Q4: Washington (A) 3-0
R1: Barnsley (A) 0-1

71-72 Q4: South Shields (H) 0-1

72-73 Q1: Stocksbridge Works Social (A) 3-1
Q2: Stalybridge Celtic (H) 2-1
Q3: Macclesfield Town (A) 0-1

73-74 Q1: Barton Town (A) 2-0
Q2: Mexborough Town (A) 1-1, (H) 4-2
Q3: Goole Town (H) 3-3, (A) 1-4

BRADFORD PARK AVENUE

Currently: North West Counties League

92-93 PR: Burscough (H - *played away*) 1-1, (A) 2-1
Q1: Belper Town (H) 2-0
Q2: Accrington Stanley (A) 0-2

BRADFORD UNITED

Currently: Defunct

46-47 PR: Thorne Colliery (A) 0-0, (H) 1-2

47-48 PR: Luddenden Foot (H) 1-0
Q1: South Kirkby Colliery (H) 4-2
Q2: Selby Town (A) 1-3

48-49 EX: Harrogate Hotspurs (H) 4-2
PR: New Waltham (H) 8-4
Q1: Goole Town (A) 2-4

51-52 Q1: Ossett Town (A) *withdrew*

BRAINTREE TOWN

Currently: Southern League
* - As Braintree & Crittall Athletic
See also Crittall Athletic

69-70 * Q1: Finchley (A) 1-1, (H) 2-0
Q2: Hounslow (A) 2-2, (H) 2-0
Q3: Hoddesdon Town (A) 1-1, (H) 3-1
Q4: Kettering Town (A) 0-4

70-71 * Q1: Aveley (A) 1-2

71-72 * Q1: Chertsey Town (H) 2-1
Q2: Cray Wanderers (H) 1-0
Q3: Romford (H) 0-2

84-85 PR: Hillingdon B. (H) 0-0, (A) 0-0, (A) 2-0
Q1: Buckingham Town (A) 2-2, (H) 1-2

85-86 Q1: Lowestoft Town (A) 2-1
Q2: Alvechurch (H) 2-1
Q3: Chalfont St Peter (A) 1-1, (H) 2-0
Q4: Halesowen Town (A) 1-2

86-87 Q1: Cambridge City (H) 1-1, (A) 0-3

87-88 Q1: Sudbury Town (H) 0-4

88-89 PR: Basildon United (A) 4-2
Q1: Corby Town (H) 2-0
Q2: Hendon (A) 1-3

89-90 PR: Newmarket Town (H) 1-1, (A) 0-1

90-91 PR: Collier Row (H) 1-0
Q1: Hitchin Town (A) 1-0
Q2: Barnet (H) 0-2

91-92 PR: Bury Town (H) 2-1
Q1: Bourne Town (A) 3-0
Q2: Kettering Town (A) 1-3

92-93 PR: March Town United (A) 3-1
Q1: Letchworth Garden City (A) 4-0
Q2: Chasetown (A) 2-0
Q3: Solihull Borough (A) 1-4

BRANDON COLLIERY WELF.

Currently: Defunct

46-47 PR: Stanley United (H) 3-3, (A) 3-1
Q1: Evenwood Town (H) 2-1
Q2: Seaham Colliery Welf. (H) 1-1, (A) 0-2

47-48 PR: Easington Colliery Welfare (A) 0-2

50-51 EX: Ushaw Moor (H) 0-1

BRANDON UNITED

Currently: Northern League

79-80 Q1: Spennymoor United (H) 3-2
Q2: Tow Law Town (A) 4-0
Q3: South Bank (A) 2-1
Q4: North Shields (A) 2-1
R1: Bradford City (H - *at Spennymoor*) 0-3

80-81 Q1: Shildon (H) 0-0, (A) 0-1

81-82 Q1: Horden Colliery Welfare (A) 1-1, (H) 1-3

82-83 Q1: Willington (A) 5-0
Q2: South Bank (A) 1-2

83-84 Q1: Guisborough Town (H) 0-0, (A) 2-1
Q2: Gretna (H) 1-0
Q3: North Shields (A) 0-2

84-85 PR: Harrogate Town (H) 3-0
Q1: Billingham Synthonia (A) 1-2

85-86 Q1: Barrow (H) 5-0
Q2: Bridlington Trinity (A) 2-6

86-87 Q1: Eppleton C.W. (A) 1-1, (H) 2-1
Q2: Workington (A) 0-0, (H) 0-1

87-88 Q1: Penrith (A) 1-2

88-89 Q1: Annfield Plain (H) 2-0
Q2: Blyth Spartans (H) 4-2
Q3: Whitley Bay (A) 1-0
Q4: Caernarfon Town (A) 1-1, (H) 2-0
R1: Doncaster (A) 0-0, (H - *played away*) 1-2

89-90 Q1: Langley Park Welfare (A) 1-3

90-91 PR: Billingham Town (A) 0-1

91-92 PR: Shotton Comrades (H) 7-1
Q1: Alnwick Town (A) 1-1, (H) 0-1

92-93 PR: Armthorpe Welfare (A) 0-2

BRENTFORD

Currently: Football League

45-46 R3: Tottenham H. (A) 2-2, (H) 2-0 (*agg: 4-2*)
R4: Bristol City (A) 1-2, (H) 5-0 (*agg: 6-2*)
R5: Queens Pk Rgrs (A) 3-1, (H) 0-0 (*agg: 3-1*)
R6: Charlton Ath. (A) 3-6, (H) 1-3 (*agg: 4-9*)

46-47 R3: Cardiff City (H) 1-0
R4: Leicester City (H) 0-0, (A) 0-0, 1-4

47-48 R3: Rotherham United (A) 3-0
R4: Middlesbrough (H) 1-2

48-49 R3: Middlesbrough (H) 3-2
R4: Torquay United (H) 1-0
R5: Burnley (H) 4-2
R6: Leicester City (H) 0-2

49-50 R3: Chelsea (H) 0-1

50-51 R3: Stockport County (A) 1-2

51-52 R3: Queens Park Rangers (H) 3-1
R4: Luton Town (A) 2-2, (H) 0-0, 2-3

52-53 R3: Leeds United (H) 2-1
R4: Aston Villa (A) 0-0, (H) 1-2

53-54 R3: Hull (A) 0-0, (A) 2-2, (*at Doncaster*) 2-5

54-55 R1: Nuneaton Borough (H) 2-1
R2: Crook Town (H) 4-1
R3: Bradford City (A) 1-1, (H) 2-2, 1-0
R4: Newcastle United (A) 2-3

55-56 R1: March Town United (H) 4-0
R2: Leyton Orient (A) 1-4

56-57 R1: Guildford City (H) 3-0
R2: Crystal Palace (H) 1-1, (A) 2-3

57-58 R1: Millwall (A) 0-1

58-59 R1: Exeter City (H) 3-2
R2: King's Lynn (H) 3-0
R3: Barnsley (H) 2-0
R4: West Bromwich Albion (A) 0-2

59-60 R1: Ashford Town (H) 5-0
R2: Exeter City (A) 1-3

60-61 R1: Watford (A) 2-2, (H) 0-2

61-62 R1: Oxford United (H) 3-0
R2: Aldershot (A) 2-2, (H) 2-0
R3: Leyton Orient (H) 1-1, (A) 1-2

62-63 R1: Aldershot (A) 0-1

63-64 R1: Margate (H) 2-2, (A) 2-0
R2: Gravesend & Northfleet (H) 1-0
R3: Middlesbrough (H) 2-1
R4: Oxford United (A) 2-2, (H) 1-2

64-65 R1: Wisbech Town (A) 2-0
R2: Notts County (H) 4-0
R3: Burnley (A) 1-1, (H) 0-2

65-66 R1: Yeovil Town (H) 2-1
R2: Reading (A) 0-5

66-67 R1: Chelmsford City (H) 1-0
R2: Leyton Orient (A) 0-0, (H) 3-1
R3: Sunderland (A) 2-5

67-68 R1: Guildford City (H) 2-2, (A) 1-2

68-69 R1: Woking (H) 2-0
R2: Watford (A) 0-1

69-70 R1: Plymouth Argyle (H) 0-0, (A) 0-2

70-71 R1: Gillingham (H) 2-1
R2: Walsall (H) 1-0
R3: Workington (A) 1-0
R4: Cardiff City (A) 2-0
R5: Hull City (A) 0-1

71-72 R1: Swansea City (A) 1-1, (H) 2-3

72-73 R1: Yeovil Town (A) 1-2

73-74 R1: Plymouth Argyle (A) 1-2

74-75 R1: Slough Town (A) 4-1
R2: Brighton & Hove Albion (A) 0-1

75-76 R1: Northampton Town (H) 2-0
R2: Wimbledon (A) 2-0
R3: Bolton Wanderers (H) 0-0, (A) 0-2

76-77 R1: Chesham United (H) 2-0
R2: Colchester (A) 0-0 *ab. 52 mins*, (A) 2-3

77-78 R1: Folkestone & Shepway (H) 2-0
R2: Swindon Town (A) 1-2

78-79 R1: Exeter City (A) 0-1

79-80 R1: Swindon Town (A) 1-4

80-81 R1: Addlestone & W. (A - *pl. home*) 2-2, (H) 2-0
R2: Fulham (A) 0-1

81-82 R1: Exeter City (H) 2-0
R2: Colchester United (H) 1-1, (A) 0-1

82-83 R1: Windsor & Eton (A - *played home*) 7-0
R2: Swindon Town (A) 2-2, (H) 1-3

83-84 R1: Dagenham (H) 2-1
R2: Wimbledon (H) 3-2
R3: Gillingham (A) 3-5

84-85 R1: Bishop's Stortford (H) 4-0
R2: Northampton (H) 2-2, (A) 0-0 *ab.*, (A) 2-0
R3: Oldham Athletic (A) 1-2

85-86 R1: Bristol Rovers (H) 1-3

86-87 R1: Bristol Rvrs (A - *at Bath*) 0-0, (H) 2-0
R2: Cardiff City (A) 0-2

87-88 R1: Brighton & Hove Albion (H) 0-2

88-89 R1: Halesowen Town (H) 2-0
R2: Peterborough United (A) 0-0, (H) 3-2
R3: Walsall (A) 1-1, (H) 1-0
R4: Manchester City (H) 3-1
R5: Blackburn Rovers (A) 2-0
R6: Liverpool (A) 0-4

89-90 R1: Colchester United (H) 0-1

90-91 R1: Yeovil Town (H) 5-0
R2: Birmingham City (A) 3-1
R3: Oldham Athletic (A) 1-3

91-92 R1: Gillingham (H) 3-3, (A) 3-1
R2: A.F.C. Bournemouth (A) 1-2

92-93 R3: Grimsby Town (H) 0-2

BRENTWOOD TOWN

Currently: Merged with Chelmsford City
* - As Brentwood & Warley
See also Chelmsford City

46-47 * EX: Tilbury (H) 3-4

47-48 * PR: Woodford Town (A) 8-1
Q1: Harwich & Parkeston (A) 4-1
Q2: Barking (A) 0-0, (H) 2-3

48-49 * EX: Hoffmann Ath. (A - *played home*) 8-0
PR: Eton Manor (H) 2-1
Q1: Woodford Town (H) 5-0
Q2: Romford (A) 1-3

49-50 * PR: Harwich & Parkeston (A) 2-4

50-51 * PR: Tilbury (H) 0-1

51-52 * PR: Ilford (A) 1-1, (H) 3-3, 3-2
Q1: Grays Athletic (A) 2-1
Q2: Dagenham (H) 3-3, (A) 2-1
Q3: Romford (A) 1-3

52-53 * PR: Dagenham (H) 1-3

53-54 * PR: Dagenham (A) 0-4

54-55 * PR: Rainham Town (H) 0-1

55-56 * PR: Aveley (A) 1-5

56-57 * PR: Dagenham (A) 1-0
Q1: Barking (A) 2-2, (H) 2-1
Q2: Clacton Town (H) 0-1

57-58 * PR: Harwich & Park. (H) 0-0, (A) 1-1, 2-0
Q1: Rainham Town (A) 0-2

58-59 * Q1: Leyton (A) 2-2, (H) 2-1
Q2: Rainham Town (A) 1-3

59-60 * PR: Tilbury (H) 1-2

60-61 * Q1: Aveley (A) 5-2
Q2: Ilford (A) 2-0
Q3: Tilbury (A) 3-1
Q4: Oxford United (H) 1-4

61-62 * Q1: Grays Athletic (A) 2-3

62-63 * Q1: Rainham Town (H) 3-2
Q2: Ilford (A) 1-4

63-64 * Q1: Aveley (H) 2-4

64-65 * Q1: Grays Athletic (A) 2-0
Q2: Walthamstow Avenue (A) 0-1

65-66 * Q1: Tilbury (H) 0-2

66-67 Q1: Tooting & Mitcham United (A) 3-2
Q2: Bexley United (A) 2-3

67-68 Q1: Harlow Town (A) 2-0
Q2: Uxbridge (A) 4-1
Q3: Carshalton Athletic (A) 2-0
Q4: Walthamstow Avenue (H) 1-3

68-69 PR: Hayes (A) 3-1
Q1: Harlow Town (A) 3-0
Q2: Croydon Amateurs (A) 2-0
Q3: Metropolitan Police (H) 2-1
Q4: Hillingdon Borough (A) 0-0, (H) 2-0
R1: Barnet (A) 1-1, (H) 1-0
R2: Southend United (A) 1-10

69-70 Q4: Lowestoft Town (H) 1-0
R1: Reading (H) 1-0
R2: Hendon (A) 2-0
R3: Northampton Town (H) 0-1

BRERETON SOCIAL

Currently: Staffordshire Senior League

73-74 Q1: Ilkeston Town (A) 2-2, (H) 1-1, 0-1

75-76 PR: Hednesford (A) 1-1, (H) 1-1, 3-3, 0-2

76-77 Q1: New Mills (A) 2-5

78-79 Q1: Bedworth United (A) 0-0, (H) 3-2
Q2: Sutton Coldfield Town (H) 3-2
Q3: Redditch United (A) 0-0, (H) 0-1

79-80 Q1: Highgate United (A) 2-0
Q2: Moor Green (A) 1-2

80-81 PR: Evesham United (H) 1-1, (A) 2-3

81-82 PR: Tamworth (H) 0-3

BRETT SPORTS

Currently: Defunct

69-70 Q1: Sheppey United (A) 1-3

70-71 Q1: Bexhill Town (A) 1-1, (H) 0-2

BRIDGEND TOWN

Currently: Welsh League
* - As Everwarm F.C.

73-74 * PR: Mangotsfield United (H) 0-4

74-75 * Q1: Stonehouse (A) 1-1, (H) 4-1
Q2: Cinderford Town (A) 1-2

75-76 * Q1: Barry Town (A) 1-1, (H) 0-1

76-77 * PR: Llanelli (H) 0-1

77-78 Q1: Clevedon Town (H) 4-3
Q2: Cinderford Town (A) 4-0
Q3: Merthyr Tydfil (H) 1-3

78-79 Q1: Merthyr Tydfil (A) 0-4

79-80 PR: Gloucester City (A) 2-0
Q1: Oxford City (A) 0-0, (H) 5-2
Q2: Redditch United (H) 0-0, (A) 3-2
Q3: Clevedon Town (A) 2-0
Q4: Hungerford Town (H) 1-1, (A) 0-5

80-81 Q1: Ton Pentre (H) 0-1

81-82 PR: Paulton Rovers (H) 6-0
Q1: Calne Town (A) 2-1
Q2: Worcester City (H) 1-3

82-83 Q1: Cinderford Town (H) 2-1
Q2: Bridgwater Town (H) 1-0
Q3: Merthyr Tydfil (H) 1-3

83-84 Q1: Redditch United (H) 1-0
Q2: Cheltenham Town (H) 0-2

84-85 Q1: Witney Town (H) 0-2

85-86 PR: Poole Town (H) 0-1

86-87 Q1: Salisbury (A) 1-2

87-88 PR: Weston-super-Mare (H) 1-3

88-89 PR: Tiverton Town (A) 2-7

89-90 PR: Cwmbran Town (A - *played home*) 0-1

90-91 PR: Ton Pentre (H) 2-1
Q1: Bristol Manor Farm (A) 1-1, (H) 3-0
Q2: Worcester City (H) 1-7

91-92 PR: Chippenham Town (H) 2-0
Q1: Cheltenham Town (H) 3-3, (A) 0-5

BRIDGNORTH TOWN

Currently: Southern League

82-83 PR: Lye Town (A) 2-0
Q1: Rushden Town (A) 2-0
Q2: A.P. Leamington (A) 1-6

83-84 PR: Highgate United (A) 2-1
Q1: Sutton Town (A) 2-0
Q2: Leicester United (H) 2-1
Q3: Gainsborough Trinity (A) 1-1, (H) 1-4

84-85 Q1: Redditch United (H) 3-2
Q2: Rushden Town (A) 1-0
Q3: Kidderminster Harriers (A) 2-3

85-86 Q1: Mile Oak Rovers & Youth (H) 0-1

86-87 PR: Congleton Town (A) 0-0, (H) 4-0
Q1: Rossendale United (H) 1-1, (A) 2-3

87-88 PR: Hinckley Town (A) 1-2

88-89 PR: Long Eaton United (A) 5-0
Q1: Mossley (A - *at Curzon Ashton*) 0-2

89-90	PR: Radcliffe Borough (A) 2-2, (H) 0-2
90-91	PR: Vauxhall G.M. (H) 1-1, (A) 1-4
91-92	PR: Hinckley (A) 4-2 Q1: Matlock Town (H) 1-2
92-93	PR: West Midlands Police (A) 2-5

BRIDGWATER TOWN

Currently: Defunct (reformed in Somerset Snr Lge)

49-50	PR: Taunton (H) 1-1, (A) 3-1 Q1: Dartmouth United (A) 0-2
50-51	PR: Glastonbury (H) 1-1, (A) 0-7
51-52	PR: Minehead (H) 2-1 Q1: Ilminster Town (A) 1-1, (H) 4-2 Q2: Barnstaple Town (H) 1-3
52-53	PR: Tavistock (A) 2-1 Q1: St Austell (A) 3-2 Q2: Barnstaple Town (A) 2-4
53-54	Q1: Chippenham United (A) 1-3
54-55	PR: Clevedon (A) 4-0 Q1: Wells City (A) 1-2
55-56	PR: Wells City (A) 1-2
56-57	Q1: Clevedon (H) 4-0 Q2: Bath City (A) 2-1 Q3: Glastonbury (A) 3-4
58-59	Q1: Street (H) 2-0 Q2: Borough of Weston-super-Mare (A) 3-1 Q3: Taunton (H) 1-2
59-60	Q1: Minehead (H) 2-1 Q2: Ilminster Town (A) 3-1 Q3: Glastonbury (H) 3-1 Q4: Cheltenham Town (A) 0-0, (H) 0-1
60-61	Q2: Minehead (H) 4-1 Q3: Borough of Weston-super-Mare (A) 1-0 Q4: Cheltenham Town (H) 0-0, (A) 2-1 R1: Hereford United (H) 3-0 R2: Oxford United (A) 1-2
61-62	Q4: Bath City (A) 2-0 R1: Boro. of Weston-s-Mare (H) 0-0, (A) 1-0 R2: Crystal Palace (H) 0-3
62-63	Q1: Boro. of Weston-s-M. (H) 1-1, (A) 0-0, 3-1 Q2: Taunton (H) 5-1 Q3: Minehead (H) 1-3
63-64	Q2: Taunton (A) 3-1 Q3: Minehead (A) 1-0 Q4: Llanelly (H) 0-0, (A) 1-0 R1: Luton Town (H) 0-3
64-65	Q4: Welton Rovers (A) 0-1
65-66	Q1: Taunton (H) 1-0 Q2: Frome Town (A) 1-1, (H) 0-1
66-67	Q1: Barnstaple Town (H) 0-1
68-69	Q1: Street (A) 2-2, (H) 3-1 Q2: Trowbridge Town (A) 3-2 Q3: Frome Town (H) 0-1
69-70	Q1: Minehead (A) 0-2
70-71	Q1: Minehead (A) 1-1, (H) 2-3
71-72	Q1: Bridport (H) 1-0 Q2: Dorchester Town (H) 1-0 Q3: Trowbridge Town (H) 2-1 Q4: Yeovil Town (H) 2-0 R1: Reading (H) 0-3
72-73	Q1: Ferndale Athletic (H) 3-0 Q2: Taunton Town (H) 0-4
73-74	Q1: Dorchester Town (H) 3-3, (A) 1-0 Q2: Taunton Town (A) 0-1
74-75	PR: Dorchester Town (A) 2-3
75-76	Q1: Minehead (H) 1-2
76-77	Q1: Falmouth Town (H) 2-4
77-78	Q1: Newbury Town (A) 1-0 Q2: Dorchester (A) 3-4
78-79	Q1: Chard Town (H) 1-0 Q2: Tiverton Town (H) 5-1 Q3: Bath City (A) 1-7
79-80	Q1: Yeovil Town (H) 0-0, (A) 0-2
80-81	Q1: Bideford (A) 0-1
81-82	Q1: Wellington (H) 2-0 Q2: Taunton Town (H) 1-1, (A) 0-1
82-83	Q1: Mangotsfield United (H) 1-1, (A) 2-1 Q2: Bridgend Town (A) 0-1
83-84	PR: Falmouth Town (A) 1-0 Q1: St Blazey (A) 1-3
84-85	PR: Dorchester Town (A) *Scratched*

BRIDLINGTON TOWN

Currently: Northern Premier League
***** - As Bridlington Central United

48-49 *	PR: Whitby United (H) 4-1 Q1: South Bank (A) 0-10
49-50 *	PR: Cargo Fleet Works (A) 8-0 Q1: Portrack Shamrocks (A) 0-1
50-51 *	PR: Smith's Dock (A) 6-3 Q1: Head Wrightsons (H) 4-5
51-52 *	Q1: Whitby Town (A) 2-6
52-53 *	Q1: Head Wrightsons (A) 0-2
53-54 *	Q1: South Bank (H) 4-0 Q2: Billingham Sythonia Recreation (A) 1-4
54-55 *	Q1: Billingham Syn. Rec. (A) 2-2, (H) 3-2 Q2: North Skelton Athletic (H) 1-6
55-56 *	Q1: North Skelton Athletic (H) 3-0 Q2: Whitby Town (H) 4-4, (A) 1-0 Q3: Billingham Synthonia Recreation (H) 1-0 Q4: Durham City (A) 1-5
56-57 *	Q1: Billingham Synthonia Recreation (A) 1-2
57-58 *	Q2: Shildon (H) 0-3
58-59 *	Q1: Chilton Athletic (H) 2-3
59-60	Q1: Ferryhill Athletic (A) 0-0, (H) 1-2
60-61	Q1: Durham City (H) 6-0 Q2: Murton Colliery Welfare (H) 5-0 Q3: Boldon Colliery Welfare (H) 11-2 Q4: South Shields (H) 5-3 R1: Bishop Auckland (A) 2-3
61-62	Q1: Stockton (A) 3-2 Q2: North Shields (H) 1-2
62-63	Q1: Scarborough (H) 1-1, (A) 2-5
63-64	Q1: Harrogate Town (H) 3-3, (A) 2-0 Q2: Goole Town (H) 4-1 Q3: Frickley Colliery (A) 0-1
64-65	Q1: Yorkshire Amateur (A) 1-0 Q2: Bridlington Trinity (A) 4-4, (H) 3-1 Q3: Scarborough (A) 1-3
65-66	Q1: Ossett Albion (A) 0-0, (H) 1-2
66-67	Q1: Selby Town (H) 4-0 Q2: Bridlington Trinity (H) 0-2
67-68	Q1: Brigg Town (H) 0-0, (A) 0-1
68-69	Q1: Hull Brunswick (H) 1-1, (A) 2-3
69-70	PR: Barton Town (H) 3-5
70-71	Q1: Scarborough (A) 0-1
71-72	PR: Bridlington Trinity (H) 2-1 Q1: Barton Town (A) 0-1
72-73	Q1: Farsley Celtic (A) 2-3
73-74	Q1: Rawmarsh Welfare (H) 5-0 Q2: Goole Town (A) 1-3
74-75	Q1: South Bank (H) 1-0 Q2: Goole Town (H) 1-0 Q3: Winterton Rangers (H) 1-1, (A) 2-0 Q4: Farsley Celtic (H) 0-4
75-76	PR: Horden C.W. (A) 1-1, (H) 4-1 Q1: Willington (A) 2-4
76-77	Q1: Appleby Frodingham Athletic (A) 3-5
77-78	Q1: Durham City (H) 1-1, (A) 0-1
78-79	PR: Farsley Celtic (A) 1-0 Q1: Yorkshire Amateur (A) 0-0, (H) 2-3
79-80	Q1: Frickley Athletic (A) 0-5
80-81	Q1: Blue Star (A) 1-3
81-82	PR: Thackley (H) 1-3
85-86	Q1: Scarborough (H) 0-1
86-87	PR: Murton (H) 2-0 Q1: Ashington (H - *played away*) 4-2 Q2: Morecambe (H) 0-1
87-88	PR: Accrington Stanley (H) 1-0 Q1: Billingham Town (A) 3-0 Q2: Blyth Spartans (H) 1-2
88-89	PR: Cleator Moor Celtic (A) 0-0, (H) 4-1 Q1: North Shields (A) 1-1, (H) 1-1, (H) 2-1 Q2: Bishop Auckland (H) 2-1 Q3: Guisborough Town (A) 1-1, (H) 0-1
89-90	Q1: Shotton Comrades (A) 5-0 Q2: Seaham Red Star (H) 2-1 Q3: Tow Law Town (H) 0-0, (A) 0-0, (A) 2-3
90-91	Q1: Blyth Spartans (A) 0-2
91-92	PR: Evenwood Town (H) 5-1 Q1: Blyth Spartans (H) 3-2 Q2: Northallerton Town (H) 4-0 Q3: North Shields (A) 2-0 Q4: Barrow (A) 1-0 R1: York City (H) 1-2
92-93	Q1: Brigg Town (A) 1-2

Below: *Action from Bridlington Town's F.A. Cup derby against York in 1991. Brid's Wayne Noteman (4) outjumps Nigel Pepper with Paul Stevenson (6) in support. Photo: Simon Kench.*

BRIDLINGTON TRINITY

Currently: Defunct
* - As Bridlington Trinity United

50-51 * PR: South Bank East End (A) 1-1, (H) 4-2
Q1: Scarborough (A) 2-7

51-52 * Q1: Head Wrightsons (A) 3-2
Q2: Billingham Synthonia Recreation (H) 0-6

54-55 * Q1: North Skelton Athletic (A) 1-9

64-65 Q1: Selby Town (A) 6-1
Q2: Bridlington Town (H) 4-4, (A) 1-3

65-66 Q1: Selby Town (H) 3-2
Q2: Hull Brunswick (H) 6-0
Q3: Ossett Albion (A) 0-2

66-67 Q1: Scarborough (A) 2-1
Q2: Bridlington Town (A) 2-0
Q3: Goole Town (A) 0-4

67-68 Q1: Selby Town (H) 1-2

68-69 Q1: Scarborough (A) 0-0, (H) 1-1, (A) 1-3

69-70 Q1: Ashby Institute (A) 0-1

70-71 Q1: Farsley Celtic (H) 1-0
Q2: Goole Town (H) 0-0, (A) 0-0, 4-1
Q3: Scarborough (A) 2-2, (H) 0-5

71-72 PR: Bridlington Town (A) 1-2

72-73 Q1: Ashby Institute (H) 2-1
Q2: Worksop Town (H) 0-1

73-74 Q1: Mexborough Town (A) 2-3

74-75 Q1: Whitby Town (A) 1-1, (H) 0-1

75-76 PR: Evenwood Town (A) 3-2
Q1: Tow Law Town (A) 0-1

76-77 Q1: Selby Town (A) 2-0
Q2: Mexborough Town (A) 2-3

77-78 Q1: Appleby Frodingham Athletic (H) 1-2

78-79 Q1: Emley (H) 1-0
Q2: Winterton Rangers (H) 2-2, (A) 1-2

79-80 PR: Appleby Frodingham Athletic (H) 6-0
Q1: Selby Town (A) 1-0
Q2: Goole Town (H) 0-2

80-81 PR: Eppleton Colliery Welfare (H) 3-0
Q1: Netherfield (A) 2-1
Q2: Bishop Auckland (A) 0-1

81-82 PR: Winterton Rangers (H) 3-1
Q1: Denaby United (H) 2-0
Q2: Curzon Ashton (H) 0-1

82-83 PR: Whitley Bay (H) 3-1
Q1: Farsley Celtic (A) 0-3

83-84 PR: Seaham C.W. Red Star (A) 0-7

84-85 PR: Easington Colliery (H) 0-2

85-86 PR: Netherfield (H) 4-0
Q1: Alnwick Town (H) 1-0
Q2: Brandon United (H) 6-2
Q3: Bishop Auckland (A) 2-3

86-87 Q1: Peterlee Newtown (H) 1-1, (A) 0-2

87-88 PR: Clitheroe (A) 0-4

88-89 PR: Leyland Motors (A) 1-0
Q1: Spennymoor United (A) 0-3

89-90 PR: Darlington C.B. (H) *Scratched*

BRIDPORT

Currently: Western League

51-52 Q1: Bournemouth Gasworks (H) 2-2, (A) 1-3

52-53 Q1: Dorchester Town (H) 0-2

53-54 PR: Bournemouth Gasworks Athletic (A) 0-8

54-55 Q2: Portland United (A) 2-4

55-56 Q2: Poole Town (A) 1-3

57-58 Q2: Ilminster Town (A) 2-1
Q3: Portland United (A) 1-2

58-59 Q1: Salisbury (H) 2-5

59-60 Q2: Poole Town (A) 0-4

60-61 Q1: Poole Town (A) 3-6

61-62 Q1: Swanage Town (H) 3-1
Q2: Portland United (A) 3-4

62-63 Q1: Portland United (H) 1-5

63-64 Q1: Portland United (A) 4-2
Q2: Dorchester Town (A) 0-1

64-65 Q1: Poole Town (A) 0-2

65-66 Q1: Poole Town (A) 2-3

66-67 Q1: Poole Town (A) 0-7

67-68 Q1: Portland United (A) 1-3

68-69 Q1: Warminster Town (H) 9-1
Q2: Frome Town (H) 1-4

69-70 Q1: Warminster Town (H) 9-3
Q2: Minehead (A) 0-2

70-71 Q1: Glastonbury (H) 0-0, (A) 0-2

71-72 Q1: Bridgwater Town (A) 0-1

72-73 Q1: Frome Town (A) 2-4

73-74 Q1: Salisbury (H) 0-1

74-75 Q1: Poole Town (H) 1-6

75-76 Q1: Dorchester Town (H) 4-3
Q2: Frome Town (H) 0-3

76-77 Q1: Minehead (H) 2-4

77-78 Q1: Bath City (H) 0-2

78-79 Q1: Dorchester Town (H) 0-1

79-80 Q1: Glastonbury (A) 1-2

80-81 Q1: Bognor Regis Town (A) 1-3

81-82 PR: Ottery St Mary (H) 5-0
Q1: Liskeard Athletic (H) 2-2, (A) 1-3

82-83 PR: Wimborne Town (H) 2-3

BRIERLEY HILL ALLIANCE

Currently: Defunct

48-49 EX: Cradley Heath (A) 1-4

49-50 PR: Lye Town (A) 0-2

50-51 PR: Darlaston (H) 7-1
Q1: Wellington Town (A) 1-3

51-52 PR: Lye Town (H) 4-2
Q1: Cradley Heath (A) 5-1
Q2: Kidderminster Harriers (H) 1-2

52-53 PR: Halesowen Town (A) 4-1
Q1: Lye Town (A) 3-1
Q2: Kidderminster Harr. (A) 1-1, (H) 1-2

53-54 PR: Cradley Heath (A) 6-0
Q1: Stourbridge (A) 5-0
Q2: Worcester City (H) 2-0
Q3: Kidderminster Harriers (A) 0-2

54-55 PR: Stourbridge (H) 0-3

55-56 PR: Kidderminster Harr. (H) 1-1, (A) 2-4

56-57 PR: Stourbridge (H) 0-2

57-58 PR: Lockheed-Leamington (A) 4-1
Q1: Halesowen Town (H) 3-2
Q2: Nuneaton Borough (H) 4-2
Q3: Worcester City (A) 0-4

58-59 Q1: Hednesford (A) 6-0
Q2: Evesham United (H) 4-0
Q3: Bilston (A) 2-2, (H) 4-2
Q4: Worcester City (A) 0-3

59-60 Q1: Rugby Town (H) 2-2, (A) 0-1

60-61 Q1: Bedworth Town (A) 1-4

61-62 Q1: Evesham United (A) 5-1
Q2: Bedworth Town (H) 2-0
Q3: Rugby Town (H) 2-1
Q4: Worcester City (A) 1-0
R1: Grantham (H) 3-0
R2: Shrewsbury Town (A) 0-3

62-63 Q4: Hinckley Athletic (H) 1-3

63-64 Q1: Halesowen Town (A) 0-1

64-65 Q1: Stourbridge (A) 2-3

65-66 Q1: Hednesford (H) 1-1, (A) 3-1
Q2: Lockheed-Leamington (A) 3-2
Q3: Stourbridge (H) 1-2

66-67 Q1: Wellington Town (H) 2-1
Q2: Stourbridge (H) 5-0
Q3: Hednesford (A) 0-6

67-68 Q1: Burton Albion (H) 1-1, (A) 1-2

68-69 Q1: Lower Gornal Athletic (H) 1-5

69-70 PR: Lower Gornal Athletic (A) 2-4

70-71 PR: Stafford Rangers (A) 2-1
Q1: Stourbridge (A) 0-3

71-72 PR: Bromsgrove Rovers (H) 0-2

72-73 Q1: Tamworth (H) 2-1
Q2: Warley (H) 5-2
Q3: Burton Albion (A) 1-0
Q4: Bilston (A) 0-3

73-74 Q1: Hednesford (H) 1-1, (A) 1-2

74-75 Q1: Kidderminster Harriers (H) 1-2

75-76 Q1: Gloucester City (H) 2-1
Q2: Cinderford Town (A) 1-0
Q3: Coventry Sporting (A) 1-2

76-77 Q1: Nuneaton Borough (A) 0-2

77-78 Q1: Bilston (A) 2-1
Q2: Halesowen Town (H) 0-1

78-79 PR: Alvechurch (H) 0-2

79-80 PR: Belper Town (H) 0-2

80-81 PR: Darlaston (H) 0-2

81-82 PR: Wellingborough Town (H) *Scratched*

BRIGGS SPORTS

Currently: Merged with Ford Sports
Playing as Ford United in Essex Senior League
See also Ford United

48-49 EX: Clacton Town (A) 0-1

49-50 EX: Crittall Athletic (H) 7-0
PR: Dagenham British Legion (H) 10-1
Q1: Harwich & Parkeston (A) 0-0, (H) 0-3

50-51 PR: Clacton Town (H) 2-0
Q1: Barking (A) 2-2, (H) 2-1
Q2: Romford (A) 2-2, (H) 1-2

51-52 PR: Tilbury (A) 4-0
Q1: Clacton Town (A) 1-0
Q2: Romford (H) 1-1, (A) 2-6

52-53 Q1: Dagenham (A) 2-2, (H) 0-0 *ab. in ET*, (H) 1-3

53-54 PR: Clacton Town (H) 4-3
Q1: Dagenham (A) 3-1
Q2: Ilford (A) 1-1, (H) 5-0
Q3: Chelmsford City (A) 0-1

54-55 PR: Leytonstone (H) 1-4

55-56 PR: Ilford (H) 3-0
Q1: Grays Athletic (H) 0-0, (A) 0-0, 1-0
Q2: Dagenham (A) 1-0
Q3: Leyton (H) 1-2

56-57 PR: Leyton (H) 4-0
Q1: Romford (H) 0-1

57-58 PR: Chelmsford City (A) 0-3

58-59 PR: Clapton (H) 2-2, (A) 3-1
Q1: Hornchurch & Upminster (H) 4-4, (A) 2-3

BRIGG TOWN

Currently: Northern Counties (East) League

48-49 EX: Winterton Rangers (H) 3-2
PR: Goole Town (A) 3-6

49-50 EX: Appleby Frodingham (A) 1-1, (H) 4-1
PR: Luddington (A) 7-1
Q1: Selby Town (A) 1-2

50-51 EX: Lysaght's Sports (H) 3-1
PR: Bentley Colliery (H) 4-0
Q1: Ashby Institute (A) 3-0
Q2: Goole Town (A) 1-3

52-53 PR: Ashby Institute (A) 3-2
Q1: Retford Town (A) 2-8

53-54 Q1: Skegness Town (H) 4-1
Q2: Ashby Institute (A) 3-4

54-55 Q1: Boston United (H) 0-2

55-56 Q1: Bourne Town (H) 2-2, (A) 3-2

	Q2: Skegness Town (H) 1-3
56-57	Q1: Bourne Town (A) 0-2
57-58	Q1: Ashby Institute (A) 5-2 Q2: Grantham (H) 1-1, (A) 0-2
58-59	Q1: Ashby Institute (H) 3-1 Q2: Gainsborough Trinity (A) 2-6
59-60	Q1: Ashby Institute (H) 1-1, (A) 5-1 Q2: Skegness Town (H) 0-3
67-68	Q1: Bridlington Town (A) 0-0, (H) 1-0 Q2: Barton Town (A) 3-3, (H) 2-2, 0-1
68-69	Q1: Goole Town (H) 1-5
69-70	Q1: Scarborough (H - *played away*) 1-4
70-71	Q1: Barton Town (A) 1-1, (H) 3-0 Q2: Dinnington Athletic (H) 1-1, (A) 1-0 Q3: Frickley Colliery Athletic (A) 2-4
71-72	Q1: Arnold (A) 0-2
72-73	Q1: Barton Town (H) 1-3
73-74	Q1: Retford Town (H) 1-0 Q2: Sutton Town (A) 1-1, (H) 0-1
74-75	Q1: Matlock Town (H) 0-1
75-76	Q1: Goole Town (H) 2-1 Q2: Mexborough Town (H) 2-3
76-77	Q1: Barton Town (A) 2-2, (H) 3-2 Q2: Emley (H) 1-2
77-78	Q1: Farsley Celtic (H) 2-0 Q2: Gainsborough Trinity (H) 1-0 Q3: Appleby Frodingham (A) 2-2, (H) 1-2
78-79	Q1: Spalding United (H) 1-1, (A) 4-3 Q2: Worksop (H) 1-1, (A) 1-1, (*Gainsboro.*) 0-2
79-80	Q1: Gainsborough Trinity (A) 1-1, (H) 1-5
80-81	Q1: Alfreton Town (A) 1-2
81-82	Q1: Curzon Ashton (H) 0-0, (A) 1-4
82-83	Q1: Goole Town (H) 1-1, (A) 2-7
83-84	PR: Hednesford Town (H) 0-0, (A) 0-3
84-85	PR: Tamworth (H) 0-2
85-86	Q1: Worksop Town (H) 0-1
86-87	PR: Arnold (H) 5-4 Q1: Lye Town (H) 0-2
87-88	PR: Oakham United (H) 4-0 Q1: Mile Oak Rovers & Youth (A) 2-1 Q2: Goole Town (A) 3-1 Q3: Leek Town (H) 3-2 Q4: Lincoln City (H - *played away*) 1-4
88-89	Q1: Eastwood Town (A) 1-3
89-90	PR: St Helens Town (H) 0-2
90-91	PR: Willenhall T. (A) 1-1, (H) 1-1, (H) 1-3
91-92	PR: Worksop Town (A - *at Gainsborough*) 0-1
92-93	Q1: Bridlington Town (H) 2-1 Q2: North Ferriby United (A) 2-0 Q3: Southport (H) 0-1

BRIGHAM & COWAN (HULL)

Currently: Defunct

46-47	Q1: Billingham S.R. (H) 2-2, (A) *withdrew*

BRIGHTLINGSEA UTD

Currently: Eastern Counties League

48-49	EX: Harwich & Parkeston (H) 1-3
49-50	EX: Clapton (A) 0-4
92-93	PR: Fisher Athletic (A - *played home*) 1-2

BRIGHTON & HOVE ALBION

Currently: Football League

45-46	R1: Romford (H) 3-1, (A) 1-1 (*agg: 4-2*) R2: Walthamstow (A) 1-1, (H) 4-2 (*agg: 5-3*) R3: Norwich City (A) 2-1, (H) 4-1 (*agg: 6-2*) R4: Aldershot (H) 3-0, (A) 4-1 (*agg: 7-1*) R5: Derby Co. (H) 1-4, (A) 0-6 (*agg: 1-10*)
46-47	R1: Norwich City (A) 2-7
47-48	R1: Trowbridge Town (A) 1-1, (H) 5-0 R2: Hartlepools Utd (A) 1-1, (H) 1-1, 2-1 R3: Portsmouth (A) 1-4
48-49	R1: Newport County (A) 1-3
49-50	R1: Ipswich Town (A) 1-2
50-51	R1: Tooting & Mitcham United (A) 3-2 R2: Ipswich Town (H) 2-0 R3: Chesterfield (H) 2-1 R4: Bristol City (A) 0-1
51-52	R1: Bristol City (H) 1-2
52-53	R1: Yeovil Town (A) 4-1 R2: Norwich City (H) 2-0 R3: Barnsley (A) 3-4
53-54	R1: Coventry City (H) 5-1 R2: Wrexham (A) 1-1, (H) 1-1, 1-3
54-55	R1: Tunbridge Wells United (H) 5-0 R2: Norwich City (A) 0-0, (H) 5-1 R3: Aston Villa (A) 2-2, (H) 2-4
55-56	R1: Newport County (H) 8-1 R2: Norwich City (H) 1-2
56-57	R1: Millwall (H) 1-1, (A) 1-3
57-58	R1: Walsall (H) 2-1 R2: Norwich City (A) 1-1, (H) 1-2
58-59	R3: Bradford City (H) 0-2
59-60	R3: Bath City (A) 1-0 R4: Rotherham Utd (A) 1-1, (H) 1-1, 6-0 R5: Preston North End (A) 1-2
60-61	R3: Derby County (H) 3-1 R4: Burnley (H) 3-3, (A) 0-2
61-62	R3: Blackburn Rovers (H) 0-3
62-63	R1: Southend United (A) 1-2
63-64	R1: Colchester United (H) 0-1
64-65	R1: Bristol City (A) 0-1
65-66	R1: Wisbech Town (H) 10-1 R2: Bedford Town (H) 1-1, (A) 1-2
66-67	R1: Newport County (A) 2-1 R2: Bath City (A) 5-0 R3: Aldershot (A) 0-0, (H) 3-1 R4: Chelsea (H) 1-1, (A) 0-4
67-68	R1: Southend United (H) 1-0 R2: Swansea Town (A) 1-2
68-69	R1: Kidderminster H. (H) 2-2, (A) 1-0 R2: Northampton Town (H) 1-2
69-70	R1: Enfield (H) 2-1 R2: Walsall (H) 1-1, (A) 1-1, (N) 0-0, (*at Coventry City*) 1-2
70-71	R1: Cheltenham Town (H) 4-0 R2: Hereford United (A) 2-1 R3: Cardiff City (A) 0-1
71-72	R1: Hillingdon Borough (H) 7-1 R2: Walsall (H) 1-1, (A) 1-2
72-73	R3: Chelsea (H) 0-2
73-74	R1: Walton & Hersham (A) 0-0, (H) 0-4
74-75	R1: Aldershot (H) 3-1 R2: Brentford (H) 1-0 R3: Leatherhead (H) 0-1
75-76	R1: Watford (A) 3-0 R2: Gillingham (A) 1-0 R3: Southend United (A) 1-2
76-77	R1: C. Palace (H) 2-2, (A) 1-1, (*at Chelsea*) 0-1
77-78	R3: Scarborough (H) 3-0 R4: Notts County (H) 1-2
78-79	R3: Wolverhampton Wanderers (H) 2-3
79-80	R3: Mansfield Town (A) 2-0 R4: Arsenal (A) 0-2
80-81	R3: Manchester United (A) 2-2, (H) 0-2
81-82	R3: Barnet (A) 0-0, (H) 3-1 R4: Oxford United (H) 0-3
82-83	R3: Newcastle United (H) 1-1, (A) 1-0 R4: Manchester City (H) 4-0 R5: Liverpool (A) 2-1 R6: Norwich City (H) 1-0 SF: Sheffield Wednesday (*at Arsenal*) 2-1 F: Manchester U. (*at Wembley*) 2-2, 4-0
83-84	R3: Swansea City (H) 2-0 R4: Liverpool (H) 2-0 R5: Watford (A) 1-3
84-85	R3: Hull City (H) 1-0 R4: Barnsley (A) 1-2
85-86	R3: Newcastle United (A) 2-0 R4: Hull City (A) 3-2 R5: Peterborough United (A) 2-2, (H) 1-0 R6: Southampton (H) 0-2
86-87	R3: Sheffield United (A) 0-0, (H) 1-2
87-88	R1: Brentford (A) 2-0 R2: Northampton Town (A) 2-1 R3: A.F.C. Bournemouth (H) 2-0 R4: Arsenal (H) 1-2
88-89	R3: Leeds United (H) 1-2
89-90	R3: Luton Town (H) 4-1 R4: Oldham Athletic (A) 1-2
90-91	R3: Scunthorpe United (H) 3-2 R4: Liverpool (A) 2-2, (H) 2-3
91-92	R3: Crawley Town (H) 5-0 R4: Bolton Wanderers (A) 1-2
92-93	R1: Hayes (H) 2-0 R2: Woking (H) 1-1, (A) 2-1 R3: Portsmouth (H) 1-0 R4: Manchester United (A) 0-1

Above: *Brighton's Gary Howlett beats Kevin Moran of Manchester United in the 1983 final. Photo: Colorsport.*

BRIMSDOWN ROVERS

Currently: Spartan League

91-92 PR: Basildon United (A) 1-0
Q1: Biggleswade Town (A) 2-0
Q2: St Albans City (A) 1-1, (H) 2-0
Q3: Chesham United (H) 2-2, (A) 1-2

92-93 Q1: St Albans City (A) 1-3

BRISTOL AERO. CO.

Currently: Defunct

47-48 EX: Soundwell (A) 0-2

48-49 EX: Hoffmann Ath. (Stonehouse) (H) 0-4

49-50 PR: Troedrhiw (A) 0-3

BRISTOL CITY

Currently: Football League

45-46 R1: Yeovil & P. (A) 2-2, (H) 3-0 (*agg: 5-2*)
R2: Bristol R. (H) 4-2, (A) 2-0 (*agg: 6-2*)
R3: Swansea T. (H) 5-1, (A) 2-2 (*agg: 7-3*)
R4: Brentford (H) 2-1, (A) 0-5 (*agg: 2-6*)

46-47 R1: Hayes (H) 9-3
R2: Gillingham (H) 1-2

47-48 R1: Dartford (A) 0-0, (H) 9-2
R2: Crystal Palace (H) 0-1

48-49 R1: Crystal Palace (A) 1-0
R2: Swansea Town (H) 3-1
R3: Chelsea (H) 1-3

49-50 R1: Nottingham Forest (A) 0-1

50-51 R1: Gloucester City (H) 4-0
R2: Wrexham (H) 2-1
R3: Blackburn Rovers (H) 2-1
R4: Brighton & Hove Albion (H) 1-0
R5: Birmingham City (A) 0-2

51-52 R1: Brighton & Hove Albion (A) 2-1
R2: Colchester United (A) 0-2

52-53 R1: Coventry City (A) 0-2

53-54 R1: Torquay United (A) 3-1
R2: Rhyl (A) 3-0
R3: Rotherham United (H) 1-3

54-55 R1: Southend United (H) 1-2

55-56 R3: Everton (A) 1-3

56-57 R3: Rotherham United (H) 4-1
R4: Rhyl (H) 3-0
R5: Aston Villa (A) 1-2

57-58 R3: Accrington Stanley (A) 2-2, (H) 3-1
R4: Notts County (A) 2-1
R5: Bristol Rovers (H) 3-4

58-59 R3: Doncaster Rovers (A) 2-0
R4: Blackpool (H) 1-1, (A) 0-1

59-60 R3: Charlton Athletic (H) 2-3

60-61 R1: Chichester City (A - *played home*) 11-0
R2: King's Lynn (A) 2-2, (H) 3-0
R3: Plymouth Argyle (A) 1-0
R4: Leicester City (A) 1-5

61-62 R1: Hereford United (H) 1-1, (A) 5-2
R2: Dartford (H) 8-2
R3: Walsall (H) 0-0, (A) 1-4

62-63 R1: Wellington Town (H) 4-2
R2: Wimbledon (H) 2-1
R3: Aston Villa (H) 1-1, (A) 2-3

63-64 R1: Corby Town (A) 3-1
R2: Exeter City (A) 2-0
R3: Doncaster Rovers (A) 2-2, (H) 2-0
R4: Sunderland (A) 1-6

64-65 R1: Brighton & Hove Albion (H) 1-0
R2: Bournemouth & Boscombe Ath. (A) 3-0
R3: Sheffield United (H) 1-1, (A) 0-3

65-66 R3: Birmingham City (A) 2-3

66-67 R3: Halifax Town (A) 1-1, (H) 4-1
R4: Southampton (H) 1-0
R5: Tottenham Hotspur (A) 0-2

67-68 R3: Bristol Rovers (H) 0-0, (A) 1-0
R4: Middlesbrough (A) 1-1, (H) 2-1
R5: Leeds United (A) 0-2

68-69 R3: West Ham United (A) 2-3

Above: *In 1986 Bristol City entertained local rivals Bath City in the Second Round, and were held to a 1-1 draw before eventually winning 3-0. The above action shows their defenders Glyn Riley and Rob Newman (2) crowding out Bath's Mike England.*

69-70 R3: Chester (A) 1-2

70-71 R3: Southampton (A) 0-3

71-72 R3: Preston North End (A) 2-4

72-73 R3: Portsmouth (A) 1-1, (H) 4-1
R4: Wolverhampton Wanderers (A) 0-1

73-74 R3: Hull City (H) 1-1, (A) 1-0
R4: Hereford United (A) 1-0
R5: Leeds United (A) 1-1, (A) 1-0
R6: Liverpool (H) 0-1

74-75 R3: Sheffield United (A) 0-2

75-76 R3: Coventry City (A) 1-2

76-77 R3: Ipswich Town (A) 1-4

77-78 R3: Wrexham (H) 4-4, (A) 0-3

78-79 R3: Bolton Wanderers (H) 3-1
R4: Crystal Palace (A) 0-3

79-80 R3: Derby County (H) 6-2
R4: Ipswich Town (H) 1-2

80-81 R3: Derby County (A) 0-0, (H) 2-0
R4: Carlisle United (A) 1-1, (H) 5-0
R5: Nottingham Forest (A) 1-2

81-82 R1: Torquay United (H) 0-0, (A) 2-1
R2: Northampton Town (H) 3-0
R3: Peterborough United (A) 1-0
R4: Aston Villa (H) 0-1

82-83 R1: Orient (A) 1-4

83-84 R1: Cor.-Casuals (A - *at Dulwich*) 0-0, (H) 4-0
R2: Bristol Rovers (A) 2-1
R3: Notts County (A) 2-2, (H) 0-2

84-85 R1: Fisher Athletic (A) 1-0
R2: Bristol Rovers (H) 1-3

85-86 R1: Swindon Town (A) 0-0, (H) 4-2
R2: Exeter City (H) 1-2

86-87 R1: V.S. Rugby (H) 3-1
R2: Bath C. (H) 1-1, (A - *played home*) 3-0
R3: Plymouth Argyle (H) 1-1, (A) 1-3

87-88 R1: Aylesbury United (H) 1-0
R2: Torquay United (H) 0-1

88-89 R1: Southend United (H) 3-1
R2: Aldershot (A) 1-1, (H) 0-0, (A) 2-2, (H) 1-0
R3: Hartlepool United (A) 0-1

89-90 R1: Barnet (H) 2-0
R2: Fulham (H) 2-1
R3: Swindon Town (H) 2-1
R4: Chelsea (H) 3-1
R5: Cambridge Utd (H) 0-0, (A) 1-1, (A) 1-5

90-91 R3: Norwich City (A) 1-2

91-92 R3: Wimbledon (H) 1-1, (A - *at Crystal P.*) 1-0
R4: Leicester City (A) 2-1
R5: Nottingham Forest (A) 1-4

92-93 R3: Luton Town (A) 0-2

BRISTOL MANOR FARM

Currently: Western League

82-83 PR: Paulton Rovers (A) 2-0
Q1: Welton Rovers (A) 0-0, (H) 1-0
Q2: Trowbridge Town (A) 0-3

83-84 PR: Glastonbury (H) 0-1

84-85 PR: Bideford (H) 1-2

85-86 PR: Chard Town (H) 2-0
Q1: Gosport Borough (H) 1-1, (A) 2-2, (A) 3-4

86-87 PR: Evesham United (H) 0-2

87-88 Q1: Weston-super-Mare (H) 0-3

88-89 PR: Barry Town (A) 0-1

89-90 PR: Newbury Town (A) 2-2, (H) 3-1
Q1: Cwmbran Town (H) 0-1

90-91 Q1: Bridgend Town (H) 1-1, (A) 0-3

91-92 PR: Yate Town (A) 1-4

92-93 PR: Paulton Rovers (A) 2-0
Q1: AFC Lymington (A) 3-3, (H - *at Keynsham Town*) 0-2

BRISTOL ROVERS

Currently: Football League

45-46 R1: Swindon T. (A) 0-1, (H) 4-1 (*agg: 4-2*)
R2: Bristol C. (A) 2-4, (H) 0-2 (*agg: 2-6*)

46-47 R1: Merthyr Tydfil (A) 1-3

47-48 R1: Leytonstone (H) 3-2
R2: New Brighton (H) 4-0
R3: Swansea Town (H) 3-0
R4: Fulham (A) 2-8

48-49 R1: Walsall (A) 1-2

49-50 R1: Swindon Town (A) 0-1

50-51 R1: Llanelly (H) 1-1, (A) 1-1, 3-1
R2: Gillingham (H) 2-2, (A) 1-1, (*at Tottenham Hotspur*) 2-1
R3: Aldershot (H) 5-1
R4: Luton Town (A) 2-1
R5: Hull City (H) 3-0
R6: Newcastle United (A) 0-0, (H) 1-3

51-52 R1: Kettering Town (H) 3-0

R2: Weymouth (H) 2-0
R3: Preston North End (H) 2-0
R4: Southend United (A) 1-2

52-53 R1: Leyton Orient (A) 1-1, (H) 1-0
R2: Peterborough United (A) 1-0
R3: Huddersfield Town (A) 0-2

53-54 R3: Blackburn Rovers (H) 0-1

54-55 R3: Portsmouth (H) 2-1
R4: Chelsea (H) 1-3

55-56 R3: Manchester United (H) 4-0
R4: Doncaster Rovers (H) 1-1, (A) 0-1

56-57 R3: Hull City (A) 4-3
R4: Preston North End (H) 1-4

57-58 R3: Mansfield Town (H) 5-0
R4: Burnley (H) 2-2, (A) 3-2
R5: Bristol City (A) 4-3
R6: Fulham (A) 1-3

58-59 R3: Charlton Athletic (H) 0-4

59-60 R3: Doncaster Rovers (H) 0-0, (A) 2-1
R4: Preston North End (H) 3-3, (A) 1-5

60-61 R3: Aston Villa (H) 1-1, (A) 0-4

61-62 R3: Oldham Athletic (H) 1-1, (A) 0-2

62-63 R1: Port Vale (H) 0-2

63-64 R1: Bournemouth & Boscombe Ath. (A) 3-1
R2: Coventry City (A) 2-1
R3: Norwich City (H) 2-1
R4: Manchester United (A) 1-4

64-65 R1: Walsall (A) 2-0
R2: Weymouth (H) 4-1
R3: Stockport County (H) 0-0, (A) 2-3

65-66 R1: Reading (A) 2-3

66-67 R1: Oxford City (A) 2-2, (H) 4-0
R2: Luton Town (H) 3-2
R3: Arsenal (H) 0-3

67-68 R1: Arnold (A) 3-0
R2: Wimbledon (A) 4-0
R3: Bristol City (A) 0-0, (H) 0-1

68-69 R1: Peterborough United (H) 3-1
R2: A.F.C. Bournemouth (A) 0-0, (H) 1-0
R3: Kettering Town (H) 1-1, (A) 2-1
R4: Bolton Wanderers (A) 2-1
R5: Everton (H) 0-1

69-70 R1: Telford United (A) 3-0
R2: Aldershot (A) 1-3

70-71 R1: Fulham (A) 2-1
R2: Aldershot (A) 1-1, (H) 1-3

71-72 R1: Telford United (H) 3-0
R2: Cambridge United (H) 3-0
R3: Leeds United (A) 1-4

72-73 R1: Hayes (A) 0-1

73-74 R1: Bideford (A) 2-0
R2: Northampton Town (A) 2-1
R3: Nottingham Forest (A) 3-4

74-75 R3: Blackburn Rovers (A) 2-1
R4: Derby County (A) 0-2

75-76 R3: Chelsea (A) 1-1, (H) 0-1

76-77 R3: Nottm F. (A) 1-1, (H) 1-1, (*Aston V.*) 0-6

77-78 R3: Sunderland (A) 1-0
R4: Southampton (H) 2-0
R5: Ipswich Town (H) 2-2, (A) 0-3

78-79 R3: Swansea City (A) 1-0
R4: Charlton Athletic (H) 1-0
R5: Ipswich Town (A) 1-6

79-80 R3: Aston Villa (H) 1-2

80-81 R3: Preston North End (A) 4-3
R4: Southampton (A) 1-3

81-82 R1: Fulham (H) 1-2

82-83 R1: Wycombe Wanderers (H) 1-0
R2: Plymouth Argyle (H) 2-2, (A) 0-1

83-84 R1: Barnet (A) 0-0, (H) 3-1
R2: Bristol City (H) 1-2

84-85 R1: King's Lynn (H) 2-1
R2: Bristol City (A) 3-1
R3: Ipswich Town (H) 1-2

85-86 R1: Brentford (A) 3-1
R2: Swansea City (A) 2-1
R3: Leicester City (H) 3-1
R4: Luton Town (A) 0-4

86-87 R1: Brentford (H - *at Bath*) 0-0, (A) 0-2

87-88 R1: Merthyr Tydfil (H - *at Bath*) 6-0
R2: V.S. Rugby (A) 1-1, (H - *at Bath*) 4-1
R3: Shrewsbury Town (A) 1-2

88-89 R1: Fisher Athletic (H - *at Bath*) 3-0
R2: Kettering Town (A) 1-2

89-90 R1: Reading (H - *at Bath*) 1-1, (A) 0-0, (H - *at Bath*) 0-1

90-91 R3: Crewe Alexandra (H - *at Bath*) 0-2

91-92 R3: Plymouth Argyle (H - *at Bath*) 5-0
R4: Liverpool (H - *at Bath*) 1-1, (A) 1-2

92-93 R3: Aston Villa (A) 1-1, (H - *at Bath*) 0-3

BRISTOL ST GEORGE

Currently: Avon Premier Combination

48-49 EX: Hanham Athletic (A) 0-2

50-51 PR: Merthyr Tydfil (A) 3-11

51-52 PR: Peasedown Miners Welfare (A) 1-3

52-53 PR: Street (A) 0-2

53-54 PR: Radstock Town (H) 4-3
Q1: Hanham Athletic (A) 2-0
Q2: Chippenham United (A) 2-4

BROCKENHURST

Currently: Wessex League

82-83 Q1: A.F.C. Totton (H) 1-2

83-84 PR: Clandown (H) 1-1, (A) 0-3

84-85 PR: Chippenham Town (H) 1-3

85-86 PR: Warminster Town (H) 1-3

86-87 PR: Westbury United (H) 2-0
Q1: Havant Town (H) 1-2

91-92 Q1: Dorchester Town (H) 1-2

92-93 PR: Shortwood United (A) 4-0
Q1: Basingstoke Town (H) 1-0
Q2: Calne Town (A) 1-0
Q3: Salisbury (H) 1-3

BRODSWORTH MAIN COLLIERY

Currently: (Brod. Miners Welf.) N. Co's (East) Lge

45-46 Q1: Firbeck Colliery (H) 1-1, (A) 4-3
Q2: Denaby United (H) 2-3

46-47 PR: Lysaght's Sports (H) 9-1
Q1: Denaby United (H) 1-1, (A) 1-2

47-48 EX: Monckton Athletic (A) 2-1
PR: Rawmarsh Welfare (H) 3-4

48-49 EX: Frickley Colliery (A) 3-4

49-50 EX: Meltham (A - *played home*) 3-2
PR: South Kirkby Colliery (H) 2-0
Q1: Ossett Town (A) 3-1
Q2: Selby Town (A) 1-0
Q3: Goole Town (H) 1-1, (A) 2-8

50-51 PR: Goole Town (A) 0-5

51-52 Q1: Langold W.M.C. (A) 2-3

52-53 Q1: Norton Woodseats (H) 0-5

53-54 Q1: Worksop Town (H) 1-4

54-55 Q1: Norton Woodseats Amateur (H) 0-4

55-56 Q1: Langold W.M.C. (H) 1-2

BROMLEY

Currently: Isthmian League

45-46 Q1: Sheppey United (A) 5-1
Q2: Gravesend & Northfleet (H) 2-0
Q3: Lloyds (Sittingbourne) (A) 4-3
Q4: Shorts Sports (H) 2-0
R1: Slough U. (H) 2-1 *abandoned after 80 minutes*, (H) 6-1, (A) 0-1 (*agg: 6-2*)
R2: Watford (H) 1-3, (A) 1-1 (*agg: 2-4*)

46-47 Q4: Sutton United (A) 0-2

47-48 Q4: Wealdstone (A) 2-0
R1: Reading (H) 3-3, (A) 0-3

48-49 PR: Folkestone Town (H) 2-1
Q1: Gravesend & Northfleet (A) 1-4

49-50 R1: Watford (H) 1-2

50-51 Q4: Leytonstone (H) 3-1
R1: Aldershot (A) 2-2, (H) 0-1

51-52 R1: Torquay United (A) 2-3

52-53 PR: Maidstone United (A) 6-0
Q1: Gravesend & Northfleet (H) 0-1

53-54 PR: Wimbledon (A) 1-2

54-55 PR: Maidstone United (A) 3-1
Q1: Margate (A) 2-4

55-56 PR: Margate (H) 0-1

56-57 PR: Metropolitan Police (H) 5-3
Q1: Erith & Belvedere (H) 6-0
Q2: Bexleyheath & Welling (A) 5-2
Q3: Tooting & Mitcham United (A) 0-4

57-58 PR: Epsom (H) 4-2
Q1: Woking (A) 5-1
Q2: Walton & Hersham (A) 0-1

58-59 Q1: Tooting & Mitcham U. (H) 2-2, (A) 1-5

59-60 PR: Redhill (H) 5-0
Q1: Wimbledon (A) 0-3

60-61 Q1: Kingstonian (H) 2-3

61-62 Q1: Metropolitan Police (H) 4-0
Q2: Kingstonian (A) 1-2

62-63 Q1: Bexleyheath & Welling (H) 2-1
Q2: Erith & Belvedere (H) 2-3

63-64 Q1: Chatham Town (H) 4-1
Q2: Bexley United (A) 0-0, (H) 2-2, 0-1

64-65 Q1: Chatham Town (A) 1-3

65-66 Q1: Erith & Belvedere (H) 3-2
Q2: Sittingbourne (H) 0-2

66-67 Q1: Tunbridge Wells Rangers (H) 0-1

67-68 Q1: Dover (A) 0-4

68-69 Q1: Hillingdon Borough (A) 0-7

69-70 Q1: Aveley (A) 2-1
Q2: Hillingdon Borough (A) 1-4

70-71 PR: Uxbridge (A) 0-0, (H) 3-1
Q1: Walthamstow Avenue (A) 4-1
Q2: Bishop's Stortford (A) 1-2

71-72 Q1: Civil Service (A - *played home*) 10-0
Q2: Stevenage Athletic (H) 1-1, (A) 4-2
Q3: Hayes (H) 3-0
Q4: Guildford City (H) 0-1

72-73 PR: Hertford Town (A) 1-2

73-74 Q1: Southall (H) 0-1

74-75 PR: Dagenham (A) 2-2, (H) 2-4

75-76 Q1: Leytonstone (H) 3-1
Q2: Croydon (A) 1-2

76-77 Q1: Redhill (A) 1-0
Q2: Faversham Town (H) 2-0
Q3: Cray Wanderers (A) 2-0
Q4: Walton & Hersham (H) 9-3
R1: Swindon Town (A) 0-7

77-78 Q1: Herne Bay (A) 2-2, (H) 5-0
Q2: Crawley Town (A) 2-3

78-79 PR: Folkestone & Shepway (A) 1-2

79-80 PR: Faversham Town (A) 2-0
Q1: Margate (A) 1-4

80-81 Q1: Bexhill Town (A) 7-0
Q2: Chatham Town (H) 4-0
Q3: Maidstone United (A) 0-2

81-82 Q1: Fareham Town (H) 0-5

82-83 PR: Chertsey Town (A) 12-1
Q1: Whitstable Town (A) 0-1

83-84 Q1: Horley Town (H) 3-1
Q2: Gravesend & Northfleet (H) 0-4

84-85 PR: Cray Wanderers (H) 4-0
Q1: Heybridge Swifts (H) 1-1, (A) 1-2

85-86 PR: Camberley Town (A) 2-2, (H) 4-0
Q1: Thanet Town (A) 2-2, (H) 2-1

Q2: Ruislip Manor (H) 3-2
Q3: Gravesend & Northfleet (A) 3-2
Q4: Maidstone United (H) 0-2

86-87 Q1: Carshalton Athletic (H) 2-2, (A) 2-4

87-88 Q1: Ashford Town (H) 5-2
Q2: Harefield United (A) 3-2
Q3: Sutton United (A) 0-0, (H) 1-2

88-89 Q1: Sheppey United (A) 4-1
Q2: Carshalton Athletic (A) 1-1, (H) 4-2
Q3: Crawley Town (H) 2-2, (A) 0-1

89-90 Q1: Kingsbury T. (H) 1-1, (A) 2-2, (A) 2-0
Q2: Royston Town (H) 3-0
Q3: Hampton (A) 1-0
Q4: Welling United (A) 2-5

90-91 Q1: Walton & Hersham (A) 3-2
Q2: Andover (A) 0-2

91-92 Q1: Whitehawk (A) 2-0
Q2: Worthing (H) 3-1
Q3: Dover Athletic (H) 0-3

92-93 Q1: Hailsham Town (A) 3-2
Q2: Worthing (A) 1-2

BROMSGROVE ROVERS

Currently: Alliance Premier League

46-47 PR: Dudley Town (H) 0-3

47-48 PR: Oswestry Town (A) 4-1
Q1: Worcester City (H) 3-2
Q2: Halesowen Town (H) 1-1, (A) 2-1
Q3: Stourbridge (H) 2-0
Q4: Brush Sports (H) 5-2
R1: Aldershot (A) 0-2

48-49 PR: Oswestry Town (H) 5-0
Q1: Stourbridge (H) 3-2
Q2: Hednesford (H) 8-3
Q3: Hereford United (H) 2-4

49-50 PR: Moor Green (A) 2-2, (H) 4-1
Q1: Bilston (H) 2-1
Q2: Cradley Heath (A) 2-1
Q3: Dudley Town (H) 3-1
Q4: Shrewsbury Town (H) 5-2
R1: Hereford United (A) 0-3

50-51 Q4: Kettering Town (H) 3-2
R1: Hereford United (H) 1-3

51-52 Q4: Bedford Town (H) 2-5

52-53 Q1: Darlaston (H) 3-2
Q2: Bilston (H) 1-0
Q3: Kidderminster Harriers (H) 0-2

53-54 Q1: Stafford Rangers (A) 3-2
Q2: Kidderminster Harriers (A) 1-2

54-55 PR: Darlaston (H) 4-3
Q1: Oswestry Town (A) 1-1, (H) 3-0
Q2: Stourbridge (H) 3-1
Q3: Hednesford (A) 2-1
Q4: Hinckley Athletic (A) 1-2

55-56 PR: Halesowen Town (A) 1-2

56-57 PR: Cradley Heath (H) 3-3, (A) 1-0
Q1: Worcester City (A) 1-0
Q2: Kidderminster Harriers (H) 4-0
Q3: Wellington Town (H) 1-0
Q4: Nuneaton Borough (A) 2-1
R1: Tooting & Mitcham United (A) 1-2

57-58 Q4: Worcester City (H) 3-3, (A) 1-2

58-59 Q1: Lye Town (H) 4-2
Q2: Oswestry Town (A) 0-3

59-60 PR: Stafford Rangers (H) 2-1
Q1: Moor Green (A) 4-2
Q2: Stourbridge (H) 4-0
Q3: Oswestry Town (A) 1-3

60-61 Q1: Oswestry Town (A) 2-3

61-62 PR: Moor Green (H) 2-0
Q1: Redditch (H) 4-0
Q2: Kidderminster Harriers (A) 2-0
Q3: Sankey of Wellington (H) 1-2

62-63 Q1: Oswestry Athletic (H) 7-1
Q2: Kidderminster H. (H) 0-0, (A) 3-1
Q3: Wellington Town (A) 0-2

63-64 Q1: Wellington Town (H) 1-3

64-65 Q1: Worcester City (A) 0-4

65-66 Q1: Stafford Rangers (A) 1-1, (H) 1-2

66-67 Q1: Rugby Town (A) 2-4

67-68 Q1: Lower Gornal Athletic (H) 2-0
Q2: Darlaston (A) 0-0, (H) 5-0
Q3: Burton Albion (A) 1-5

68-69 PR: Burton Albion (A) 3-1
Q1: Stafford Rangers (H) 1-1, (A) 1-2

69-70 Q1: Dudley Town (H) 0-1

70-71 PR: Lockheed Leamington (A) 3-1
Q1: Halesowen Town (A) 2-1
Q2: Redditch (A) 2-2, (H) 3-0
Q3: Kidderminster H. (H) 2-2, (A) 1-2

71-72 PR: Brierley Hill Alliance (A) 2-0
Q1: Atherstone Town (A) 1-3

72-73 Q1: Hednesford (A) 5-1
Q2: Highgate United (H) 2-1
Q3: Bilston (H) 1-1, (A) 0-1

73-74 Q1: Moor Green (A) 1-1, (H) 1-0
Q2: Alvechurch (H) 1-2

74-75 Q1: Worcester City (H) 0-3

75-76 PR: Coventry Sporting (A) 0-3

76-77 Q1: Stourbridge (A) 3-1
Q2: A.P. Leamington (A) 1-1, (H) 2-1
Q3: Nuneaton Borough (A) 0-2

77-78 Q1: Thame United (A) 3-1
Q2: Oxford City (A) 1-2

78-79 PR: Lye Town (H) 3-1
Q1: Worcester City (A) 0-1

79-80 Q1: Dudley Town (H) 0-1

80-81 Q1: Barry Town (A) 0-1

81-82 Q1: Blakenall (H) 2-0
Q2: Sutton Coldfield Town (H) 1-0
Q3: Malvern Town (H) 4-1
Q4: Nuneaton Borough (A) 1-2

82-83 Q1: Tividale (A) 1-0
Q2: Moor Green (H) 2-2, (A) 0-1

83-84 PR: March Town United (A) 2-3

84-85 Q1: Shepshed Charterhouse (H) 2-5

85-86 Q1: Gainsborough Trinity (H) 1-1, (H) 2-1
Q2: Atherstone United (A) 0-4

86-87 Q1: Holbeach United (H) 2-0
Q2: Baldock Town (A) 1-0
Q3: March Town United (H) 1-0
Q4: Buckingham Town (H) 2-0
R1: Newport County (H) 0-1

87-88 Q1: Willenhall Town (A) 2-3

88-89 Q1: Chalfont St Peter (H) 1-1, (A) 3-0
Q2: Alvechurch (H) 2-2, (A) 3-3, (H) 2-0
Q3: Bedworth United (H) 3-1
Q4: Moor Green (H) 2-0
R1: Welling United (A) 0-3

89-90 Q1: King's Lynn (A) 3-0
Q2: March Town United (H) 4-0
Q3: Tamworth (H) 2-0
Q4: V.S. Rugby (H) 1-0
R1: Basingstoke Town (A) 0-3

90-91 Q1: Boston (A) 3-0
Q2: Sandwell Borough (A) 2-0
Q3: Sutton Coldfield T. (A) 0-0, (H) 4-2
Q4: Kidderminster Harriers (H) 1-2

91-92 Q1: Bedworth United (A) 2-0
Q2: Rushden Town (H) 1-0
Q3: Redditch United (H) 2-0
Q4: Tamworth (A) 1-0
R1: A.F.C. Bournemouth (A) 1-3

92-93 Q4: Stafford Rangers (A) 0-3

Above: *A Shaun O'Meara penalty puts Bromsgrove ahead at Bournemouth in 1991. Photo: Gavin Ellis.*

BROOK HOUSE

Currently: London Spartan League

92-93 PR: Aveley (H) 1-1, (A) 0-1

BROOKWOOD HOSPITAL

Currently: Defunct

47-48 PR: Epsom (A) 3-4

48-49 PR: Redhill (A) 1-11

BRUNSWICK INSTITUTE

See Hull Brunswick

BRUSH SPORTS

See Loughborough United

BUCKINGHAM TOWN

Currently: Southern League

50-51 EX: Yiewsley (H) 1-5

79-80 Q1: Hendon (H) 0-7

80-81 Q1: Evesham United (A) 1-0
Q2: Cheltenham Town (H) 2-1
Q3: Kidderminster Harriers (A) 1-2

81-82 Q1: Sutton Coldfield Town (A) 1-2

82-83 PR: Desborough Town (H) 1-0
Q1: Mile Oak Rovers & Youth (A) 0-2

83-84 PR: Blakenall (A) 1-0
Q1: Wigston Fields (A) 4-1
Q2: Alvechurch (H) 2-1
Q3: Sutton Coldfield Town (A) 1-2

84-85 Q1: Braintree Town (H) 2-2, (A) 2-1
Q2: Aylesbury United (A) 0-0, (H) 4-0
Q3: Heybridge Swifts (A) 0-0, (H) 1-0
Q4: Barking (H) 3-1
R1: Orient (H) 0-2

85-86 Q1: Uxbridge (A) 1-0
Q2: Chelmsford City (A) 0-1

86-87 Q1: Dunstable (H) 2-2, (A) 2-1
Q2: Redhill (A) 4-2
Q3: Haringey Borough (A) 2-1
Q4: Bromsgrove Rovers (A) 0-2

87-88 Q1: Arlesey Town (A) 4-0
Q2: Boreham Wood (H) 0-0, (A) 1-2

88-89 Q1: Finchley (H) 0-3

89-90 PR: Yeading (A) 0-4

90-91 PR: Irthlingborough Diamonds (A) 4-3
Q1: Brackley Town (A) 1-1, (H) 1-1, (H) 2-0
Q2: Shepshed Charterhouse (H) 2-4

91-92 PR: Abingdon United (H) 1-0

Q1: Horsham (A) 0-1

92-93 Q1: Maidenhead United (H) 1-1, (A) 1-2

BULFORD UNITED

Currently: Defunct

54-55 PR: Calne & Harris United (A) 1-1, (H) 6-3
Q1: Swindon Victoria (A) 2-2, (H) 1-3

55-56 PR: Welton Rovers (H) 1-1, (A) 3-1
Q1: Calne & Harris United (H) 4-1
Q2: Salisbury (A) 0-3

BUNGAY TOWN

Currently: Anglian Combination

50-51 EX: Haverhill Rovers (A) 2-2, (H) 2-1
PR: Leiston (H) 1-4

51-52 Q1: Great Yarmouth Town (A) 2-4

52-53 Q1: Beccles (A) 1-3

53-54 Q1: Wymondham Town (A) 3-3, (H) 4-1
Q2: Cromer (A) 0-2

54-55 Q1: North Walsham Athletic (A) 2-3

55-56 Q1: Beccles (H) 0-2

56-57 Q2: Beccles (H) 2-2, (A) 4-4, 3-0
Q3: Great Yarmouth Town (H) 1-4

57-58 Q1: Great Yarmouth Town (H) 0-2

58-59 Q1: Sheringham (H) 4-3
Q2: Great Yarmouth Town (A) 1-2

59-60 Q2: Gorleston (H) 1-0
Q3: Great Yarmouth Town (H) 1-4

60-61 Q1: Gorleston (A) 1-0
Q2: Sudbury Town (H) 4-2
Q3: Clacton Town (H) 0-1

61-62 Q1: Clacton Town (H) 0-2

62-63 Q1: Great Yarmouth Town (A) 2-3

63-64 Q2: Great Yarmouth Town (H) 2-2, (A) 1-2

BURGESS HILL TOWN

Currently: Sussex County League

71-72 Q1: Eastbourne United (A) 2-0
Q2: Hastings United (H) 1-4

72-73 Q1: Peacehaven & Telscombe (H) 1-3

74-75 PR: Arundel (H) 2-2, (A) 1-1, 1-0
Q1: Worthing (H) 2-0
Q2: Chichester City (H) 4-1
Q3: Horsham (A) 0-5

75-76 PR: Haywards Heath (A) 4-0
Q1: Redhill (A) 0-1

76-77 Q1: Woking (A) 1-3

77-78 Q1: Bexhill Town (H) 2-1
Q2: Maidstone United (A) 0-5

78-79 PR: Alton Town (H) 1-3

79-80 Q1: Erith & Belvedere (A) 0-0, 0-0, 0-2

80-81 Q1: Canterbury City (H) 1-2

81-82 PR: Molesey (H) 4-0
Q1: Crawley Town (A) 1-0
Q2: Walton & Hersham (H) 2-1
Q3: Carshalton Athletic (H) 1-5

82-83 Q1: Canterbury City (H) 2-2, (A) 1-2

83-84 PR: Horsham (A) 0-0, (H - *played away*) 0-2

84-85 PR: Whitstable Town (A) 0-1

85-86 PR: Hastings Town (A) 0-1

86-87 PR: Staines Town (H) 0-2

87-88 PR: Witham Town (A) 0-1

88-89 PR: Harefield United (H) 2-1
Q1: Wembley (A) 1-3

89-90 PR: Wandsworth & Norwood (H) 1-2

90-91 PR: Sittingbourne (A) 0-2

91-92 PR: Tunbridge Wells (A) 2-0
Q1: Cove (A) 1-1, (H) 4-0
Q2: Bognor Regis Town (A) 2-1
Q3: Gravesend & Northfleet (H) 0-1

92-93 Q1: Hastings Town (H) 0-2

BURNHAM

Currently: Merged with Hillingdon
Playing as Burnham in Southern League
See also Burnham (2).

74-75 PR: Hampton (A) 0-2

75-76 PR: Hertford Town (A) 2-0
Q1: Windsor & Eton (A) 1-1, (H) 1-0
Q2: Wealdstone (H) 0-2

76-77 Q1: Molesey (A) 1-2

77-78 Q1: Chertsey Town (H) 0-1

78-79 Q1: Boreham Wood (A) 2-3

79-80 Q1: Feltham (A) 2-1
Q2: Metropolitan Police (A) 1-1, (H) 3-3, 0-1

80-81 Q1: Aylesbury United (A) 0-2

81-82 PR: Newbury Town (H - *played away*) 3-4

82-83 Q1: Folkestone (A) 0-2

83-84 PR: Bracknell Town (H - *played away*) 2-0
Q1: Hitchin Town (H) 1-2

84-85 PR: Leyton-Wingate (A) 0-1

85-86 Q1: Grays Athletic (A) *Scratched*

BURNHAM

Currently: Southern League
* - As Burnham & Hillingdon
See also Burnham (1) and Hillingdon

85-86 * PR: Great Yarmouth Town (A) 0-2

86-87 * PR: Rayners Lane (H - *played away*) 0-1

87-88 Q1: Cray Wanderers (H - *played away*) 1-1, (A - *played home*) 2-1
Q2: Harrow Borough (H) 2-1
Q3: Welling United (A) 1-3

88-89 Q1: Rainham T. (H) 2-2, (A) 1-1, (A) 3-1
Q2: Stevenage Borough (A) 2-3 *Stevenage expelled for fielding ineligible player*
Q3: Dulwich Hamlet (A) 1-1, (H) 2-3

89-90 PR: Edgware Town (A) 3-1
Q1: Hertford Town (A) 1-0
Q2: Barton Rovers (A) 1-1, (H) 3-2
Q3: Staines Town (H) 0-1

90-91 Q1: Dagenham (A) 1-1, (H) 1-2

91-92 PR: Feltham & H. (H - *at Windsor*) 1-1, (A) 4-0
Q1: Dulwich H. (A - *at Tooting & Mitcham*) 0-1

Above: *Burnham forwards Trevor Argrave and Rowan Dodds challenge Dulwich goalkeeper Julian Gray as the visitors slip to a First Qualifying Round defeat in 1991. Photo: Dave West*

92-93 PR: Canvey Island (H - *at Windsor*) 1-0
Q1: Bishop's Stortford (H - *at Windsor*) 3-2
Q2: Hendon (A) 0-6

BURNHAM RAMBLERS

Currently: Essex Senior League

89-90 PR: Saffron Walden Town (A) 1-2

90-91 PR: Hornchurch (H) 0-2

91-92 PR: Wisbech Town (A) 3-4

92-93 PR: Watton United (A) 0-1

BURNLEY

Currently: Football League

45-46 R3: Stoke City (A) 1-3, (H) 2-1 (*agg: 3-4*)

46-47 R3: Aston Villa (H) 5-1
R4: Coventry City (H) 2-0
R5: Luton Town (A) 0-0, (H) 3-0
R6: Middlesbrough (A) 1-1, (H) 1-0
SF: Liverpool (*at Blackburn Rvrs*) 0-0, (*at Man. City*) 1-0
F: Charlton Athletic (*at Wembley*) 0-1

47-48 R3: Swindon Town (H) 0-2

48-49 R3: Charlton Athletic (H) 2-1
R4: Rotherham United (A) 1-0
R5: Brentford (A) 2-4

49-50 R3: Notts County (A) 4-1
R4: Port Vale (H) 2-1
R5: Arsenal (A) 0-2

50-51 R3: Aston Villa (A) 0-2

51-52 R3: Hartlepools United (H) 1-0
R4: Coventry City (H) 2-0
R5: Liverpool (H) 2-0
R6: Blackburn Rovers (A) 1-3

52-53 R3: Portsmouth (A) 1-1, (H) 3-1
R4: Sunderland (H) 2-0
R5: Arsenal (H) 0-2

53-54 R3: Manchester United (H) 5-3
R4: Newcastle United (H) 1-1, (A) 0-1

54-55 R3: Sunderland (A) 0-1

55-56 R3: Bury (A) 1-0
R4: Chelsea (H) 1-1, (A) 1-1, 2-2, 0-0, 0-2

56-57 R3: Chesterfield (H) 7-0
R4: New Brighton (H) 9-0
R5: Huddersfield Town (A) 2-1
R6: Aston Villa (H) 1-1, (A) 0-2

57-58 R3: Swansea Town (H) 4-2
R4: Bristol Rovers (A) 2-2, (H) 2-3

58-59 R3: Stockport County (A) 3-1
R4: Blackburn Rovers (A) 0-0, (H) 2-1
R5: Portsmouth (H) 1-0
R6: Aston Villa (A) 0-0, (H) 0-2

59-60 R3: Lincoln City (A) 1-1, (H) 2-0
R4: Swansea Town (A) 0-0, (H) 2-1
R5: Bradford City (A) 2-2, (H) 5-0
R6: Blackburn Rovers (H) 3-3, (A) 0-2

60-61 R3: Bournemouth & Boscombe Ath. (H) 1-0
R4: Brighton & Hove A. (A) 3-3, (H) 2-0
R5: Swansea Town (H) 4-0
R6: Sheffield Wednedsay (A) 0-0, (H) 2-0
SF: Tottenham Hotspur (*at Aston Villa*) 0-3

61-62 R3: Queens Park Rangers (H) 6-1
R4: Leyton Orient (H) 1-1, (A) 1-0
R5: Everton (H) 3-1
R6: Sheffield United (A) 1-0
SF: Fulham (*at Aston V.*) 1-1, (*at Leicester*) 2-1
F: Tottenham Hotspur (*at Wembley*) 1-3

62-63 R3: Tottenham Hotspur (A) 3-0
R4: Liverpool (H) 1-1, (A) 1-2

63-64 R3: Rotherham United (H) 1-1, (A) 3-2
R4: Newport County (H) 2-1
R5: Huddersfield Town (H) 3-0
R6: West Ham United (A) 2-3

64-65 R3: Brentford (H) 1-1, (A) 2-0
R4: Reading (A) 1-1, (H) 1-0
R5: Manchester United (A) 1-2

65-66 R3: Bournemouth & B.A. (A) 1-1, (H) 7-0
R4: Tottenham Hotspur (A) 3-4

66-67 R3: Everton (H) 0-0, (A) 1-2

67-68 R3: West Ham United (H) 1-3

68-69 R3: Derby County (H) 3-1
R4: Liverpool (A) 1-2

69-70 R3: Wolverhampton Wanderers (H) 3-0
R4: Chelsea (A) 2-2, (H) 1-3

70-71 R3: Oxford United (A) 0-3

71-72 R3: Huddersfield Town (H) 0-1

72-73 R3: Liverpool (H) 0-0, (A) 0-3

73-74 R3: Grimsby Town (A) 2-0
R4: Oldham Athletic (A) 4-1

R5: Aston Villa (H) 1-0
R6: Wrexham (H) 1-0
SF: Newcastle Utd (*at Sheffield Wed.*) 0-2
TP: Leicester City (A) 1-0

74-75 R3: Wimbledon (H) 0-1

75-76 R3: Blackpool (A) 0-1

76-77 R3: Lincoln City (H) 2-2, (A) 1-0
R4: Port Vale (A) 1-2

77-78 R3: Fulham (H) 1-0
R4: Chelsea (A) 2-6

78-79 R3: Birmingham City (A) 2-0
R4: Sunderland (H) 1-1, (A) 3-0
R5: Liverpool (A) 0-3

79-80 R3: Stoke City (H) 1-0
R4: Bury (A) 0-1

80-81 R1: Scarborough (H) 1-0
R2: Port Vale (H) 1-1, (A) 0-2

81-82 R1: Runcorn (H) 0-0, (A) 2-1
R2: Bury (A) 1-1, (H) 2-1
R3: Altrincham (H) 6-1
R4: Shrewsbury Town (A) 0-1

82-83 R3: Carlisle United (A) 2-2, (H) 3-1
R4: Swindon Town (H) 3-1
R5: Crystal Palace (A) 0-0, (H) 1-0
R6: Sheffield Wednesday (H) 1-1, (A) 0-5

83-84 R1: Hyde United (A) 2-0
R2: Chesterfield (A) 2-2, (H) 3-2
R3: Oxford United (H) 0-0, (A) 1-2

84-85 R1: Penrith (A) 9-0
R2: Halifax Town (H) 3-1
R3: Wimbledon (A) 1-3

85-86 R1: Nuneaton Borough (A) 3-2
R2: Rotherham United (A) 1-4

86-87 R1: Telford United (A) 0-3

87-88 R1: Bolton Wanderers (H) 0-1

88-89 R1: Chester City (H) 0-2

89-90 R1: Stockport County (H) 1-1, (A) 2-1
R2: Scunthorpe Utd (A) 2-2, (H) 1-1, (H) 5-0
R3: Blackpool (A) 0-1

90-91 R1: Stafford Rangers (A) 3-1
R2: Stoke City (H) 2-0
R3: Manchester City (H) 0-1

91-92 R1: Doncaster Rovers (H) 1-1, (A) 3-1
R2: Rotherham United (H) 2-0
R3: Derby Co. (H) 2-2, (A) 0-2 *abandoned (fog) after 76 minutes*, (A) 0-2

92-93 R1: Scarborough (H) 2-1
R2: Shrewsbury Town (H) 1-1, (A) 2-1
R3: Sheffield United (A) 2-2, (H) 2-4

BURSCOUGH

Currently: North West Counties League

47-48 PR: Bangor City (H) 3-1
Q1: Rhyl (H) 0-3

48-49 PR: Marine (H) 4-2
Q1: Bangor City (A) 2-4

49-50 PR: Marine (H) 2-1
Q1: Wigan Athletic (A) 1-1, (H) 1-5

50-51 EX: St Helens Town (H) 3-1
PR: Haydock C. & B. (A) 3-1
Q1: Bootle (H) 2-0
Q2: Skelmersdale United (H) 3-2
Q3: Wigan Athletic (H) 0-2

51-52 Q1: Morecambe (H) 2-2, (A) 1-0
Q2: Netherfield (A) 2-4

52-53 PR: Penrith (A) 4-4, (H) 3-1
Q1: Lancaster City (H) 1-0
Q2: Netherfield (H) 2-4

53-54 Q1: Bacup Borough (H) 4-1
Q2: Lancaster City (H) 2-1
Q3: Morecambe (A) 1-0
Q4: Wigan Athletic (A) 1-2

54-55 Q1: Penrith (H) 4-0
Q2: Lancaster City (A) 3-2
Q3: Netherfield (H) 0-1

55-56 Q1: Lancaster City (A) 0-2

56-57 Q1: Milnethorpe Corinthians (A) 1-2

57-58 Q1: Fleetwood (H) 4-3
Q2: Netherfield (A) 2-0
Q3: Morecambe (A) 2-6

58-59 Q1: Netherfield (H) 2-2, (A) 1-2

59-60 Q1: Lancaster City (A) 4-2
Q2: Netherfield (H) 4-1
Q3: Clitheroe (A) 2-1
Q4: Ellesmere Port Town (A) 2-1
R1: Crewe Alexandra (H) 1-3

60-61 Q1: Corinthians Milnthorpe (H) 2-1
Q2: Morecambe (A) 2-2, (H) 1-2

61-62 Q1: Lancaster City (H) 2-0
Q2: Fleetwood (A) 1-1, (H) 5-2
Q3: Morecambe (H) 1-8

62-63 Q1: Fleetwood (H) 1-4

63-64 Q1: Horwich R.M.I. (A) 3-0
Q2: Netherfield (A) 0-2

64-65 Q1: Lancaster City (A) 1-1, (H) 1-2

65-66 Q1: Horwich R.M.I. (A) 1-2

66-67 Q1: Rossendale United (H) 2-3

67-68 Q1: Droylsden (A) 1-1, (H) 5-2
Q2: Stalybridge Celtic (A) 1-1, (H) 3-1
Q3: Ellesmere Port Town (A) 2-3

68-69 Q1: Ellesmere Port Town (H) 3-1
Q2: Stalybridge Celtic (A) 2-2, (H) 2-3

69-70 Q1: Leyland Motors (H) 5-2
Q2: Hyde United (A) 1-0
Q3: Wigan Athletic (A) 1-1, (H) 2-3

70-71 Q1: Prestwich Heys (A) 3-2
Q2: South Liverpool (H) 0-3

71-72 Q1: Radcliffe Borough (A) 3-2
Q2: Chorley (H) 2-1
Q3: Ellesmere Port Town (H) 0-1

72-73 Q1: Wigan Rovers (H) 2-0
Q2: Chorley (H) 1-1, (A) 2-1
Q3: Runcorn (H) 2-2, (A) 3-2
Q4: Wigan Athletic (H) 1-3

73-74 Q1: Formby (H) 1-1, (A) 1-4

74-75 Q1: Lancaster City (H) 0-1

75-76 PR: Great Harwood (A) 1-2

76-77 Q1: Winsford United (A) 0-0, (H) 1-3

77-78 Q1: Accrington Stanley (H) 2-2, (A) 1-0
Q2: Great Harwood (A) 1-0
Q3: Chorley (H) 3-0
Q4: Morecambe (H) 0-0, (A) 1-0
R1: Blyth Spartans (A) 0-1

78-79 PR: Mossley (A) 1-2

79-80 Q1: Chorley (H) 6-1
Q2: Netherfield (A) 2-0
Q3: Rossendale United (A) 4-0
Q4: Horden Colliery Welfare (A) 2-0
R1: Sheffield Utd (H - *played away*) 0-3

80-81 Q1: Prestwich Heys (H) 2-1
Q2: Hyde United (A) 2-1
Q3: Prescot Cables (H) 4-0
Q4: Morecambe (H) 2-0
R1: Altrincham (H) 1-2

81-82 Q1: Darwen (H) 4-0
Q2: Telford United (A) 0-3

82-83 PR: Stalybridge Celtic (A) 1-1, (H) 4-1
Q1: Oswestry Town (A) 1-2

83-84 Q1: Chorley (A) 0-2

84-85 PR: Emley (H) 2-1
Q1: Skelmersdale United (H) 3-0
Q2: Leek Town (H) 2-0
Q3: Alfreton Town (H) 2-2, (A) 3-2
Q4: Blue Star (A) 0-0, (H) 0-4

85-86 Q1: Armthorpe Welfare (H) 1-1, (A) 1-0
Q2: Mossley (H) 0-3

86-87 PR: Kirkby Town (H) 2-0
Q1: Bootle (H) 2-2, (A) 1-2

87-88 PR: Warrington Town (H - *at Southport*) 1-2

88-89 PR: Emley (H) 0-1

89-90 PR: Bootle (H) 2-0
Q1: Maine Road (H) 1-2

90-91 Q1: Maine Road (H) 0-3

91-92 PR: Leyland DAF SGL (A) *W/O*
Q1: Buxton (A) 2-4

92-93 PR: Bradford P.A. (A - *pl. home*) 2-2, (H) 1-2

BURTON ALBION

Currently: Southern League

51-52 PR: Moor Green (A) 4-2
Q1: Nuneaton Borough (A) 2-2, (H) 2-4

52-53 PR: Moor Green (A) 1-1, (H) 3-0
Q1: Bedworth Town (H) 1-2

53-54 Q1: Bedworth Town (H) 2-1
Q2: Atherstone Town (H) 3-0
Q3: Nuneaton Borough (H) 1-1, (A) 1-3

54-55 PR: Tamworth (H) 1-0
Q1: Bloxwich Strollers (A) 6-1
Q2: Moor Green (H) 3-2
Q3: Atherstone Town (A) 2-1
Q4: Wellington Town (H) 0-1

55-56 PR: Atherstone Town (H) 2-1
Q1: Tamworth (H) 2-0
Q2: Bedworth Town (A) 1-1, (H) 3-2
Q3: Sutton Coldfield (A - *played home*) 6-3
Q4: Brush Sports (A) 2-0
R1: Wycombe Wanderers (A) 3-1
R2: Halifax Town (A) 0-0, (H) 1-0
R3: Charlton Athletic (A) 0-7

56-57 Q4: Hinckley Athletic (H) 6-1
R1: Bournemouth & Boscombe Ath. (A) 0-8

57-58 Q4: Oswestry Town (A) 1-5

58-59 PR: Atherstone Town (H) 3-2
Q1: Nuneaton Borough (H) 0-3

59-60 Q1: Nuneaton Borough (H) 1-4

60-61 Q1: Ilkeston Town (A) 1-3

61-62 Q1: Loughborough United (A) 3-1
Q2: Nuneaton Borough (A) 0-1

62-63 Q1: Long Eaton United (H) 1-1, (A) 3-0
Q2: Atherstone Town (A) 1-2

63-64 Q1: Tamworth (H) 0-1

64-65 Q1: Tamworth (A) 0-2

65-66 Q1: Loughborough United (H) 1-0
Q2: Hinckley Athletic (H) 8-1
Q3: Long Eaton United (A) 2-1
Q4: Gainsborough Trinity (H) 3-2
R1: Corby Town (A) 3-6

66-67 Q1: Arnold (H) 2-0
Q2: Belper Town (A) 3-1
Q3: Nuneaton Borough (H) 0-1

67-68 Q1: Brierley Hill Alliance (A) 1-1, (H) 2-1
Q2: Dudley Town (A) 4-1
Q3: Bromsgrove Rovers (H) 5-1
Q4: Kidderminster Harriers (H) 1-4

68-69 PR: Bromsgrove Rovers (H) 1-3

69-70 Q1: Eastwood Town (A) 1-0
Q2: Gresley Rovers (A) 3-0
Q3: Rugby Town (A) 0-1

70-71 PR: Loughborough United (H) 1-0
Q1: Rugby Town (A) 2-0
Q2: Newhall United (A) 3-1
Q3: Long Eaton United (A) 3-1
Q4: Cheltenham Town (A) 2-2, (H) 0-3

71-72 Q1: Belper Town (A) 0-0, (H) 2-0
Q2: Stafford Rangers (H) 1-2

72-73 Q1: Atherstone Town (H) 1-0
Q2: Moor Green (H) 2-1
Q3: Brierley Hill Alliance (H) 0-1

73-74 Q1: Alfreton Town (A) 1-3

74-75 Q1: Heanor Town (H) 0-0, (A) 3-1
Q2: Gresley Rovers (H) 0-0, (A) 1-0
Q3: Stafford Rangers (H) 0-0, (A) 0-2

75-76 Q1: Darlaston (H) 1-3

76-77 Q1: Eastwood Town (H) 1-1, (A) 2-1
Q2: Hyde United (A) 1-0
Q3: Long Eaton United (H) 5-0
Q4: Northwich Victoria (H) 0-1

77-78 Q1: Stratford Town (H) 1-0
Q2: Cheltenham Town (H) 2-1

Above: *Tumultuous Burton Albion celebrations at the Baseball Ground after their equaliser in the controversial Third Round tie against Leicester City in 1985. Burton eventually lost 1-6, but the result was annulled and the match replayed behind closed doors at Coventry. Photo: Dave Fretwell.*

	Q3: Halesowen Town (H) 1-0 Q4: Grantham (A) 2-0 R1: Wrexham (A) 0-2
78-79	PR: Oxford City (H) 0-1
79-80	Q1: Gresley Rovers (A) 3-1 Q2: Sutton Town (A) 1-1, (H) 3-2 Q3: Alfreton Town (H) 2-0 Q4: Parson Drove United (H) 1-0 R1: Bury (H) 0-2
80-81	Q1: Willenhall Town (H) 2-2, (A) 2-1 Q2: Stourbridge (A) 1-1, (H) 2-1 Q3: Winsford United (H) 2-2, (A) 3-1 Q4: Penrith (H) 1-0 R1: Blyth Spartans (A) 1-2
81-82	Q1: Coventry Sporting (H) 3-1 Q2: Halesowen Town (A) 0-0, (H) 2-0 Q3: Alvechurch (H) 2-0 Q4: Willenhall Town (A) 1-2
82-83	Q1: Oldbury United (A) 0-0, (H) 1-0 Q2: Shifnal Town (H) 2-4
83-84	Q1: Rothwell Town (A) 5-1 Q2: Wednesfield Social (A) 2-1 Q3: Oldbury United (A) 3-0 Q4: Walthamstow Avenue (A) 0-0, (H) 3-1 R1: Windsor & Eton (H) 1-2
84-85	Q1: Wootton Blue Cross (A) 4-0 Q2: Stevenage Borough (A) 2-0 Q3: Willenhall Town (H) 2-1 Q4: Wycombe Wanderers (A) 1-1, (H) 1-0 R1: Staines Town (H) 2-0 R2: Aldershot (A) 3-0 R3: Leicester City (H - *at Derby County*) 1-6 (*Replayed at Coventry City*) 0-1
85-86	Q4: Wycombe Wanderers (A) 0-1
86-87	Q1: Letchworth Garden C. (A) 1-1, (H) 5-2 Q2: Halesowen Town (A) 0-2
87-88	R1: York City (A) 0-0, (H) 1-2
88-89	Q4: Dagenham (A) 0-2
89-90	Q4: Barnet (H) 2-2, (A) 0-1
90-91	Q1: Halesowen Harriers (H) 2-0 Q2: Hinckley Athletic (H) 4-0 Q3: Corby Town (A) 1-0 Q4: Tamworth (H) 0-0, (A) 2-3
91-92	Q1: West Midlands Police (A) 1-0 Q2: Willenhall Town (H) 4-1 Q3: Shepshed Albion (H) 3-2 Q4: Colchester United (A) 0-5
92-93	Q1: Leek Town (A) 2-3

BURY

Currently: Football League

45-46	R3: Rochdale (H) 3-3, (A) 4-2 (*agg: 7-5*) R4: Sunderland (A) 1-3, (H) 5-4 (*agg: 6-7*)
46-47	R3: Southampton (A) 1-5
47-48	R3: Leicester City (A) 0-1
48-49	R3: Yeovil Town (A) 1-3
49-50	R3: Rotherham United (H) 5-4 R4: Derby County (H) 2-2, (A) 2-5
50-51	R3: Newcastle United (A) 1-4
51-52	R3: Rotherham United (A) 1-2
52-53	R3: Grimsby Town (A) 3-1 R4: Arsenal (A) 2-6
53-54	R3: Chesterfield (A) 0-2
54-55	R3: Stoke C. (H) 1-1, (A) 1-1, 3-3, 2-2, 2-3
55-56	R3: Burnley (H) 0-1
56-57	R3: Portsmouth (H) 1-3
57-58	R1: Bishop Auckland (A) 0-0, (H) 4-1 R2: Scunthorpe United (A) 0-2
58-59	R1: York City (H) 0-0, (A) 1-0 R2: Chester (A) 1-1, (H) 2-1 R3: Arsenal (H) 0-1
59-60	R1: Hartlepools United (H) 5-0 R2: Oldham Athletic (H) 2-1 R3: Bolton Wanderers (H) 1-1, (A) 2-4
60-61	R1: Tranmere Rovers (A) 0-1
61-62	R3: Sheffield United (H) 0-0, (A) 2-2, 0-2
62-63	R3: Birmingham City (A) 3-3, (H) 2-0 R4: Manchester City (A) 0-1
63-64	R3: Yeovil Town (A) 2-0 R4: Barnsley (A) 1-2
64-65	R3: Crystal Palace (A) 1-5
65-66	R3: Leeds United (A) 0-6
66-67	R3: Walsall (H) 2-0 R4: Swindon Town (A) 1-2
67-68	R1: Hartlepools United (A) 3-2 R2: Bradford City (A) 3-2 R3: Leyton Orient (A) 0-1
68-69	R3: Huddersfield Town (H) 1-2
69-70	R1: Mansfield Town (H) 2-2, (A) 0-2
70-71	R1: Grimsby Town (A) 1-0 R2: Notts County (H) 1-1, (A) 0-3
71-72	R1: Lincoln City (A) 2-1 R2: Workington (A) 3-1 R3: Rotherham United (H) 1-1, (A) 1-2
72-73	R1: Doncaster Rovers (A) 1-3
73-74	R1: Tranmere Rovers (A) 1-2
74-75	R1: Southport (H) 4-2 R2: Grimsby Town (A) 1-1, (H) 2-1 R3: Millwall (H) 2-2, (A) 1-1, (*at West Brom. Albion*) 2-0 R4: Mansfield Town (H) 1-2
75-76	R1: Doncaster Rovers (H) 4-2 R2: Spennymoor United (H) 3-0 R3: Middlesbrough (A) 0-0, (H) 3-2 R4: Leicester City (A) 0-1
76-77	R1: Workington (H) 6-0 R2: Shrewsbury Town (H) 0-0, (A) 1-2
77-78	R1: Sheffield Wednesday (A) 0-1
78-79	R1: Wigan Athletic (A) 2-2, (H) 4-1 R2: Blackpool (H) 3-1 R3: Orient (A) 2-3
79-80	R1: Burton Albion (A) 2-0 R2: York City (H) 0-0, (A) 2-0 R3: Rochdale (A) 1-1, (H) 3-2 R4: Burnley (H) 1-0 R5: Liverpool (A) 0-2
80-81	R1: Darlington (A) 2-0 R2: Lincoln City (H) 2-0 R3: Fulham (H) 1-1, (A) 0-0, (*at W. Brom.*) 0-1
81-82	R1: Tranmere Rovers (A) 1-1, (H) 3-1 R2: Burnley (H) 1-1, (A) 1-2
82-83	R1: York City (A) 1-3
83-84	R1: Boston United (A) 3-0 R2: Scunthorpe United (A) 0-2
84-85	R1: Preston North End (A) 3-4
85-86	R1: Chester City (H) 2-0 R2: Tranmere Rovers (A) 1-1, (H) 2-1 R3: Burnley (H) 2-0 R4: Reading (A) 1-1, (H) 3-0 R5: Watford (A) 1-1, (H) 0-3
86-87	R1: Preston North End (A) 1-5
87-88	R1: Scunthorpe United (A) 1-3
88-89	R1: Guisborough (A - *at Middlesbrough*) 1-0 R2: Blackpool (A) 0-3
89-90	R1: Rotherham United (A) 0-0, (H) 1-2
90-91	R1: Chorley (A) 1-2
91-92	R1: Bradford City (H) 0-1
92-93	R1: Witton Albion (H) 2-0 R2: Wigan Athletic (A) 1-1, (H) 1-0 R3: Manchester United (A) 0-2

BURY TOWN

Currently: Southern League

47-48	Q1: Chatteris Town (A) 5-2 Q2: Cambridge Town (H) 2-1 Q3: March Town United (H) 3-0 Q4: Great Yarmouth Town (A) 0-3
48-49	Q1: King's Lynn (A) 0-7
49-50	PR: Royston Town (A) 6-0 Q1: Cambridge Town (H) 0-1
50-51	PR: Wisbech Town (A) 0-1
51-52	Q1: Stowmarket (A) 3-0 Q2: Lowestoft Town (H) 2-0 Q3: Sudbury Town (H) 1-1, (A) 2-2, 2-4
52-53	Q1: Leiston (H) 9-1 Q2: Stowmarket (H) 1-1, (A) 4-2 Q3: Sudbury Town (H) 3-0 Q4: Great Yarmouth Town (A) 0-2
53-54	Q1: Lowestoft Town (A) 1-2
54-55	Q1: Haverhill Rovers (A) 6-4 Q2: Stowmarket (A) 3-2 Q3: Sudbury Town (A) 1-3
55-56	Q1: Whitton United (H) 4-2 Q2: Lowestoft Town (H) 2-3
56-57	Q1: Haverhill Rovers (H) 1-1, (A) 6-1 Q2: Diss Town (A) 4-2 Q3: Sudbury Town (H) 0-0, (A) 1-3
57-58	Q1: Leiston (A) 8-1 Q2: Lowestoft Town (H) 2-1 Q3: Stowmarket (A) 3-2 Q4: Clapton (A) 2-3
59-60	Q2: Clacton Town (H) 6-5 Q3: Harwich & Parkeston (H) 2-0 Q4: Peterborough United (A) 1-7
60-61	Q1: Cambridge City (H) 0-3

61-62 Q1: Histon (A) 3-2
Q2: Newmarket Town (A) 6-2
Q3: Cambridge United (A) 2-3

62-63 Q1: Chatteris Town (H) 4-1
Q2: Cambridge United (H) 0-2

63-64 Q1: Ely City (A) 4-0
Q2: Chatteris Town (A) 5-0
Q3: Cambridge City (H) 0-3

64-65 Q1: Soham Town Rangers (H) 2-1
Q2: Cambridge City (H) 0-2

65-66 Q1: March Town United (A) 2-1
Q2: Ely City (H) 5-0
Q3: Wisbech Town (H) 0-3

66-67 Q1: Newmarket Town (A) 1-1, (H) 2-1
Q2: Bishop's Stortford (A) 5-2
Q3: Cambridge City (A) 3-3, (H) 0-1

67-68 Q1: Harwich & Parkeston (H) 2-1
Q2: Clacton Town (H) 3-2
Q3: Lowestoft Town (H) 0-1

68-69 Q1: Great Yarmouth T. (A) 0-0, (H) 1-0
Q2: Sudbury Town (A) 1-1, (H) 3-2
Q3: Gorleston (H) 4-1
Q4: Stamford (A) 2-0
R1: A.F.C. Bournemouth (H) 0-0, (A) 0-3

69-70 Q1: Gorleston (A) 2-1
Q2: Clacton Town (H) 3-1
Q3: Lowestoft Town (H) 1-3

70-71 Q1: Clacton Town (H) 0-2

71-72 Q1: Clacton Town (H) 2-0
Q2: Sudbury Town (H) 2-0
Q3: Harwich & Parkeston (H) 1-0
Q4: King's Lynn (H) 1-3

72-73 Q1: Clacton Town (A) 4-1
Q2: Sudbury Town (H) 1-1, (A) 3-1
Q3: Cambridge City (A) 1-0
Q4: Boston United (H) 1-3

73-74 Q1: Thetford Town (H) 0-4

74-75 Q1: Thetford Town (H) 4-1
Q2: Sudbury Town (H) 0-2

75-76 Q1: St Neots Town (H) 1-1, (A) 0-2

76-77 Q1: Clacton Town (H - *played away*) 2-1
Q2: Lowestoft Town (H - *played away*) 2-3

77-78 PR: Sudbury Town (A) 1-1, (A) 2-0
Q1: Cambridge City (A) 1-1, (H) 1-2

78-79 PR: King's Lynn (H) 1-2

79-80 Q1: Clacton Town (A) 2-0
Q2: Harlow Town (A) 1-2

80-81 PR: Felixstowe Town (H) 2-1
Q1: Wisbech Town (A) 2-1
Q2: Bedford Town (A) 0-4

81-82 PR: Spalding United (H) 2-0
Q1: Cambridge C. (A) 1-1, (H) 1-1, (A) 2-1
Q2: King's Lynn (H) 0-5

83-84 PR: Tiptree United (H) 3-3, (A) 1-0
Q1: V.S. Rugby (H) 0-2

84-85 PR: Great Yarmouth Town (H) 3-0
Q1: Saffron Walden Town (H) 0-2

85-86 PR: Lowestoft Town (A) 0-2

86-87 Q1: Stamford (A) 3-2
Q2: Sudbury Town (A) 2-0
Q3: Harlow Town (H) 2-1
Q4: Enfield (A) 1-1, (H) 0-1

87-88 Q1: Aveley (A) 2-2, (H) 3-1
Q2: Letchworth Garden C. (H) 1-1, (A) 1-3

88-89 Q1: Wivenhoe Town (H) 0-0, (A) 2-0
Q2: Boreham Wood (A) 0-0, (H) 1-4

89-90 PR: Clapton (H) 0-5

90-91 PR: Wembley (A) 0-1

91-92 PR: Braintree Town (A) 1-2

92-93 PR: Haringey Borough (A) 2-5

BUXTON

Currently: Northern Premier League

46-47 PR: Hyde United (H) 2-2, (A) 3-2 *expelled*

47-48 PR: Macclesfield Town (H) 6-1
Q1: Northwich Victoria (H) 2-0
Q2: Witton Albion (A) 3-6

48-49 PR: Lostock Gralam (A) 4-1
Q1: Witton Albion (A) 0-3

49-50 EX: Ellesmere Port Town (A) 3-2
PR: Lostock Gralam (A) 2-1
Q1: Hyde United (H) 3-0
Q2: Mossley (A) 1-2

50-51 PR: Congleton Town (A) 1-3

51-52 PR: Hyde United (H) 2-1
Q1: Macclesfield Town (A) 0-0, (H) 2-0
Q2: Winsford United (H) 4-0
Q3: Congleton Town (H) 2-0
Q4: Frickley Colliery (A) 1-1, (H) 3-1
R1: Rawmarsh Welfare (A) 4-1
R2: Aldershot (H) 4-3
R3: Doncaster Rovers (A) 0-2

52-53 Q4: Beighton Miners Welfare (H) 2-3

53-54 Q4: Kettering Town (H) 0-3

54-55 Q1: Hyde United (A) 0-3

55-56 Q1: Lostock Gralam (H) 2-1
Q2: Winsford United (A) 1-5

56-57 PR: Witton Albion (A) 1-2

57-58 PR: Northwich Vitoria (A) 2-4

58-59 Q1: Congleton Town (A) 5-1
Q2: Hyde United (H) 3-0
Q3: Ellesmere Port Town (A) 2-2, (H) 4-1
Q4: New Brighton (H) 4-0
R1: Crook Town (H) 4-1
R2: Accrington Stanley (A) 1-6

59-60 Q1: Linotype & Machinery (H) 4-1
Q2: Witton Albion (H) 1-2

60-61 Q1: Linotype & Machinery (H) 1-3

61-62 Q1: Linotype & Machinery (A) 1-1, (H) 6-1
Q2: Congleton Town (H) 2-3

62-63 Q1: Sutton Town (H) 2-1
Q2: Belper Town (A) 4-3
Q3: Arnold St Marys (H) 6-3
Q4: Gainsborough Trinity (A) 0-0, (H) 4-1
R1: Barrow (H) 2-2, (A) 1-3

63-64 Q1: Sutton Town (H) 1-1, (A) 0-2

64-65 Q1: Heanor Town (A) 1-2

65-66 Q1: Belper Town (A) 1-1, (H) 6-3
Q2: Heanor Town (A) 1-5

66-67 Q1: Worksop Town (H) 1-2

67-68 Q1: Eastwood (Hanley) (H) 4-6

68-69 Q1: Norton Woodseats Amateur (A) 3-0
Q2: Ilkeston Town (H) 1-0
Q3: Matlock Town (H) 0-3

69-70 PR: Norton Woodseats Amateur (A) 0-1

70-71 PR: Northwich Victoria (A) 0-2

71-72 Q1: Altrincham (A) 0-1

72-73 Q1: Altrincham (H) 0-0, (A) 1-4

73-74 Q1: Farsley Celtic (H) 1-0
Q2: Emley (A) 2-1
Q3: Mossley (H) 2-1
Q4: Alfreton Town (H) 2-2, (A) 1-2

74-75 Q1: Runcorn (H) 0-1

75-76 PR: Eastwood Hanley (A) 3-2
Q1: Northwich Victoria (A) 0-2

76-77 Q1: Rossendale United (A) 5-0
Q2: Worksop Town (A) 0-3

77-78 Q1: Mexborough Town (A) 3-1
Q2: Hednesford Town (A) 0-1

78-79 Q1: Glossop (H) 3-1
Q2: Rhyl (H) 2-0
Q3: Runcorn (A) 1-1, (H) 0-4

79-80 Q1: Matlock Town (H) 3-1
Q2: Ashton U. (A) 1-1, (H) 1-1, 2-2, 1-3

80-81 PR: Eastwood Town (H) 1-2

81-82 PR: Appleby Frodingham A. (A) 2-2, (H) 3-0
Q1: Barton Town (A) 3-1
Q2: Stalybridge Celtic (H) 1-0
Q3: Curzon Ashton (H) 4-1
Q4: Workington (A) 1-4

82-83 Q1: Telford United (A) 0-3

83-84 Q1: Curzon Ashton (H) 2-1
Q2: Horwich R.M.I. (H) 0-1

84-85 Q1: Denaby United (A) 3-3, (H) 0-1

85-86 Q1: Ilkeston Town (A) 2-2, (H) 4-1
Q2: Goole Town (A) 1-3

86-87 Q1: Leek Town (H) 1-0
Q2: Oldbury United (A) 1-3

87-88 Q1: Rhyl (H) 6-3
Q2: Colwyn Bay (A) 2-2, (H) 2-5

88-89 Q1: Hinckley Athletic (A) 3-1
Q2: Frickley Athletic (A) 0-1

89-90 Q1: Emley (H) 3-1
Q2: Sandwell B. (H) 1-1, (A) 1-1, (H) 3-2
Q3: Witton Albion (A) 1-1, (H) 4-6

90-91 Q1: Stratford Town (A) 4-1
Q2: Bilston Town (A) 1-2

91-92 Q1: Burscough (H) 4-2
Q2: Curzon Ashton (A) 0-1

92-93 Q1: Southport (A) 0-0, (H) 1-2

CAERNARFON TOWN

Currently: Northern Premier League
* - As Caernarvon Town

79-80 * Q1: Northwich Victoria (H) 0-0, (A) 0-4

80-81 * PR: Chorley (H) 0-2

81-82 * Q1: Winsford United (A) 3-2
Q2: Bangor City (H) 3-2
Q3: Telford United (A) 2-1
Q4: Bishop Auckland (H) 0-2

82-83 Q1: Colwyn Bay (A) 3-0
Q2: Prescot Cables (H) 4-1
Q3: Horwich R.M.I. (A) 2-2, (H) 0-2

83-84 PR: Congleton Town (A) 0-1

84-85 PR: Garforth Miners (H) 4-1
Q1: Frickley Athletic (A) 0-3

85-86 PR: Congleton Town (H) 1-1, (A) 0-1

86-87 Q1: Marine (H) 2-0
Q2: Winsford United (A) 3-1
Q3: Eastwood Town (A) 4-1
Q4: Chester-le-Street Town (A) 3-2
R1: Stockport County (H) 1-0
R2: York City (H) 0-0, (A) 2-1
R3: Barnsley (H) 0-0, (A) 0-1

Below: *Caernarfon captain Phil Wilson beats Barnsley's Larry May (left) to a high cross as the North Wales side hold their Second Division visitors to a draw in 1987.*

87-88 Q4: Billingham Synthonia (H) 0-2

88-89 Q4: Brandon United (H) 1-1, (A) 0-2

89-90 Q1: Horwich R.M.I. (H) 3-1
Q2: Congleton Town (H) 1-2

90-91 Q1: Denaby Utd (H) *Denaby failed to arrive*
Q2: Colwyn Bay (H) 2-6

91-92 Q1: Colwyn Bay (H) 1-1, (A) 1-2

92-93 Q1: Colwyn Bay (H - *at Curzon Ashton*) 1-4

CALLENDER ATHLETIC

Currently: Defunct

46-47 PR: Woolwich Polytechnic (H) 2-3

47-48 PR: Folkestone Town (A) 0-6

48-49 EX: Aylesford Paper Mills (H) 6-0
PR: Dartford (H) 1-2

49-50 EX: Folkestone Town (H) 0-7

CALNE TOWN

Currently: Western League
* - As Calne & Harris United

46-47 * EX: Warminster Town (H) 3-4

48-49 * EX: Peasedown Miners Welfare (H) 1-3

49-50 * EX: Swindon G.W.R. Corinthians (A) 2-3

50-51 * PR: Clandown (A) 0-3

51-52 * PR: Melksham (H) 4-0
Q1: Salisbury (A) 0-2

52-53 * PR: Trowbridge Town (H) 0-4

53-54 * PR: Chippenham Town (H) 0-2

54-55 * PR: Bulford United (H) 1-1, (A) 3-6

55-56 * Q1: Bulford United (A) 1-4

56-57 * PR: Chippenham Town (A) 2-9

57-58 * Q1: Warminster Town (H) 1-2

58-59 * Q1: Trowbridge Town (H) 2-7

59-60 * Q2: Devizes Town (H) 7-2
Q3: Trowbridge Town (H) 1-6

60-61 * Q1: Devizes Town (H) 2-5

61-62 * Q1: Melksham Town (A) 0-6

76-77 Q1: Llanelli (A) 1-2

77-78 Q1: Chippenham Town (H) 3-1
Q2: Merthyr Tydfil (H) 0-4

78-79 PR: Forest Green Rovers (A) 1-8

79-80 Q1: Hungerford Town (A) 1-3

80-81 PR: Chippenham Town (H) 0-1

81-82 Q1: Bridgend Town (H) 1-2

82-83 PR: Salisbury (A) 2-3

83-84 PR: Barry Town (A) 1-4

84-85 PR: Andover (A) 0-6

85-86 PR: Horndean (A) 1-1, (H) 0-0, (H) 1-2

86-87 Q1: A.F.C. Totton (A) 0-1

87-88 Q1: Oxford City (H) 1-5

88-89 PR: Thatcham Town (H) 0-1

89-90 PR: Littlehampton Town (A) 1-1, (H) 0-1

90-91 PR: Paulton Rovers (H) 2-0
Q1: Melksham Town (A) 1-2

91-92 PR: Westbury United (H) 1-2

92-93 PR: Gosport Borough (A) 4-0
Q1: Welton Rovers (A) 4-1
Q2: Brockenhurst (H) 0-1

CAMBERLEY

Currently: Merged with Yorktown F.C.
Playing as Camberley Town in Isthmian League
See also Camberley Town

48-49 PR: Metropolitan Police (A) 2-7

49-50 EX: McLaren Sports (A) 1-3

50-51 PR: Cobham (H) 3-0
Q1: Tooting & Mitcham United (A) 2-3

CAMBERLEY TOWN

Currently: Isthmian League
See also Camberley F.C.

76-77 Q1: Epsom & Ewell (H) 1-1, (A) 0-1

77-78 Q1: Barnet (A) 1-4

78-79 PR: Egham Town (A) 3-2
Q1: Walton & Hersham (A) 3-2
Q2: Southall & Ealing B. (A) 2-2, (H) 1-3

79-80 Q1: Waterlooville (H) 1-2

80-81 Q1: Barton Rovers (A) 0-3

81-82 Q1: Newbury Town (H) 0-2

82-83 Q1: Devizes Town (A) 0-1

83-84 Q1: Corinthian-Casuals (A) 0-2

84-85 PR: Eastbourne Town (H) 0-0, (A) 1-2

85-86 PR: Bromley (H) 2-2, (A) 0-4

86-87 PR: Shoreham (H) 4-0
Q1: Arundel (H) 0-1

87-88 PR: Corinthian-Casuals (A) 1-1, (H) 2-0
Q1: Welling United (H) 0-2

88-89 PR: Flackwell Heath (A) 2-3

89-90 PR: Andover (A) 2-2, (H) 1-5

90-91 PR: Oakwood (H - *played away*) 0-5

91-92 Q1: Marlow (H) 1-3

92-93 PR: Herne Bay (A) 3-3, (H) 2-3

CAMBRIDGE CITY

Currently: Southern League
* - As Cambridge Town

45-46 * Q1: Abbey United (A) 8-0
Q2: King's Lynn (H) 4-1
Q3: Wisbech Town (A) 1-3

46-47 * Q2: King's Lynn (A) 2-0
Q3: Chatteris Town (A) 6-1
Q4: Chelmsford City (A) 4-0
R1: Swindon Town (A) 1-4

47-48 * Q1: King's Lynn (H) 3-1
Q2: Bury Town (A) 1-2

48-49 * Q1: Wisbech Town (A) 4-4, (H) 5-2
Q2: Parson Drove (A) 3-1
Q3: King's Lynn (A) 5-4
Q4: Gothic (H) 6-1
R1: Walthamstow Avenue (A) 2-3

49-50 * Q1: Bury Town (A) 1-0
Q2: Newmarket Town (H) 1-0
Q3: King's Lynn (A) 1-3

52-53 Q1: Huntingdon United (A) 3-0
Q2: King's Lynn (H) 3-3, (A) 1-5

53-54 Q1: Histon (A) 5-2
Q2: Cambridge United (H) 1-3

54-55 PR: Exning United (H) 2-1
Q1: March Town United (A) 0-1

55-56 PR: March Town United (H) 2-2, (A) 1-3

56-57 PR: Warboys Town (H) 2-1
Q1: Thetford Town (A) 2-0
Q2: Ely City (H) 0-1

57-58 PR: Histon (A) 2-1
Q1: King's Lynn (H) 1-6

58-59 Q1: Cambridge United (A) 1-2

59-60 Q1: Histon (A) 4-1
Q2: March Town United (H) 5-1
Q3: Cambridge United (A) 1-0
Q4: Headington United (H) 2-3

60-61 Q1: Bury Town (A) 3-0
Q2: Ely City (A) 8-1
Q3: Cambridge U. (A) 1-1, (H) 1-1, (H) 2-3

61-62 Q1: St Albans City (A) 2-1
Q2: Vauxhall Motors (A - *played home*) 7-0
Q3: Hitchin Town (A) 1-2

62-63 Q1: St Albans City (H) 3-0
Q2: Biggleswade T. (A - *played home*) 5-0
Q3: Bedford Town (A) 1-2

63-64 Q2: Sudbury Town (A) 4-2
Q3: Bury Town (A) 3-0
Q4: Bedford Town (A) 2-2, (H) 2-3

64-65 Q1: Chatteris Town (A) 2-1
Q2: Bury Town (A) 2-0
Q3: Wisbech Town (H) 1-2

65-66 Q1: Soham Town Rangers (H) 8-1
Q2: Wisbech Town (H) 1-1, (A) 0-1

66-67 Q1: Letchworth Town (H) 5-3
Q2: Cambridge United (H) 1-0
Q3: Bury Town (H) 3-3, (A) 1-0
Q4: Corby Town (A) 2-0
R1: Ashford Town (A) 1-4

67-68 Q1: Desborough Town (H) 4-0
Q2: Rothwell Town (A) 7-1
Q3: Rushden Town (H) 1-0
Q4: Corby Town (A) 2-2, (H) 0-1

68-69 Q1: St Neots T. (H) 0-0, (A) 3-3, (H) 3-0
Q2: Biggleswade Town (A) 1-2

69-70 Q1: Stamford (H) 7-0
Q2: Biggleswade Town (A) 2-0
Q3: Rushden Town (H) 4-1
Q4: Hendon (A) 0-1

70-71 Q1: Desborough Town (H) 5-1
Q2: Wellingborough Town (H) 2-2, (A) 3-2 *ab.*, (*at Peterborough United*) 2-1
Q3: Irthlingborough Diamonds (A) 2-2, (H) 3-0
Q4: Oxford City (A) 1-4

71-72 Q1: Kettering Town (A) 1-6

72-73 Q1: Harwich & Parkeston (A) 3-1
Q2: Potton United (H) 3-1
Q3: Bury Town (H) 0-1

73-74 Q1: Bedford Town (A) 0-2

74-75 PR: Corby Town (A) 1-2

75-76 Q1: March Town United (H) 5-1
Q2: Letchworth Town (A) 1-0
Q3: Lowestoft Town (A) 0-1

76-77 Q1: Barton Rovers (A) 0-3

77-78 Q1: Bury Town (H) 1-1, (A) 2-1
Q2: Harlow Town (A) 0-1

78-79 PR: Gorleston (A) 0-1

79-80 PR: Basildon United (H) 1-2

80-81 Q1: Bourne Town (A) 0-0, (H) 0-1

81-82 Q1: Bury Town (H) 1-1, (A) 1-1, (H) 1-2

82-83 PR: March Town United (H) 0-0, (A) 2-3

83-84 Q1: Wealdstone (H) 1-2

84-85 PR: Hoddesdon Town (H - *at Royston*) 3-1
Q1: Billericay (A) 1-1, (H - *played away*) 3-1
Q2: Aveley (A) 1-2

85-86 Q1: Harlow Town (A) 1-2

86-87 Q1: Braintree Town (A) 1-1, (H) 3-0
Q2: Newmarket Town (A) 2-1
Q3: King's Lynn (A) 0-1

87-88 Q1: Harwich & Parkeston (H) 2-0
Q2: Great Yarmouth Town (A) 1-3

88-89 Q1: Potton United (H) 5-1
Q2: Sudbury Town (A) 1-2

89-90 Q1: Stevenage Borough (A) 5-3
Q2: Canvey Island (H) 3-0
Q3: Barnet (H) 3-4

90-91 Q1: Newmarket Town (A) 2-1
Q2: Great Yarmouth Town (A) 4-0
Q3: Heybridge Swifts (A) 0-1

91-92 Q1: King's Lynn (A) 3-3, (H) 1-2

92-93 Q1: Heybridge Swifts (A) 4-2
Q2: Norwich United (H) 6-1
Q3: Leyton (A) 0-3

CAMBRIDGE UNITED

Currently: Football League
* - As Abbey United

45-46 * Q1: Cambridge Town (H) 0-8

47-48 * PR: Histon Institute (A) 4-6

48-49 * PR: Wisbech Town (H) 1-1, (A) 0-8

49-50 * PR: Wisbech Town (H) 2-1
Q1: Newmarket Town (A) 0-1

50-51 * Q1: King's Lynn (A) 2-2, (H) 0-1

51-52 Q1: March Town United (A) 1-1, (H) 3-4

52-53 PR: Chatteris Town (A) 4-0
Q1: March Town United (H) 3-1
Q2: Wisbech Town (H) 0-0, (A) 3-2
Q3: King's Lynn (H) 0-0, (A) 0-4

53-54 Q1: St Neots & District (A) 3-0
Q2: Cambridge City (A) 3-1
Q3: Wisbech Town (H) 1-0
Q4: Stowmarket (A) 5-0
R1: Newport County (H) 2-2, (A) 2-1
R2: Bradford (Park Avenue) (H) 1-2

54-55 Q4: Eynesbury Rovers (H) 3-1
R1: Torquay United (A) 0-4

55-56 PR: Chatteris Town (A) 1-2

56-57 PR: Holbeach United (A) 2-2, (H) 4-0
Q1: Ely City (H) 2-5

57-58 Q1: St Neots Town (H) 6-2
Q2: March Town United (A) 1-4

58-59 Q1: Cambridge City (H) 2-1
Q2: Holbeach United (H) 1-2

59-60 Q1: Ely City (A) 3-0
Q2: Holbeach United (H) 3-0
Q3: Cambridge City (H) 0-1

60-61 Q1: Newmarket Town (H) 5-1
Q2: March Town United (H) 7-3
Q3: Cambridge C. (H) 1-1, (A) 1-1, (A) 3-2
Q4: Clacton Town (A) 1-2

61-62 Q1: Chatteris Town (A) 5-1
Q2: Sudbury Town (H) 5-1
Q3: Bury Town (H) 3-2
Q4: Romford (A) 1-2

62-63 Q2: Bury Town (A) 2-0
Q3: Sudbury Town (H) 6-0
Q4: Lowestoft Town (H) 4-0
R1: Bedford Town (A) 1-2

63-64 Q4: Hitchin Town (H) 4-1
R1: Chelmsford City (H) 0-1

64-65 Q4: Bedford Town (A) 4-1
R1: Barnet (A) 1-2

65-66 Q4: Bedford Town (H) 1-2

66-67 Q1: Biggleswade Town (H) 6-0
Q2: Cambridge City (A) 0-1

67-68 Q1: March Town United (H) 6-0
Q2: Ely City (H) 3-1
Q3: Kettering Town (H) 3-0
Q4: Lowestoft Town (A) 2-2, (H) 1-2

68-69 PR: March Town United (A) 1-1, (H) 5-0
Q1: Kettering Town (A) 0-1

69-70 Q1: Wellingborough (H) 7-0
Q2: Potton United (A) 10-0
Q3: Newmarket Town (H) 6-0
Q4: Chelmsford City (A) 2-3

70-71 R1: Enfield (A) 1-0
R2: Colchester United (A) 0-3

71-72 R1: Weymouth (H) 2-1
R2: Bristol Rovers (A) 0-3

72-73 R1: A.F.C. Bournemouth (A) 1-5

73-74 R1: Gillingham (H) 3-2
R2: Aldershot (A) 2-1
R3: Oldham (H) 2-2, (A) 3-3, (*at Nottm F.*) 1-2

74-75 R1: Hitchin Town (A) 0-0, (H) 3-0
R2: Hereford United (H) 2-0
R3: Mansfield Town (A) 0-1

75-76 R1: Leatherhead (A) 0-2

76-77 R1: Colchester United (H) 1-1, (A) 0-2

77-78 R1: Lowestoft Town (A) 2-0
R2: Plymouth Argyle (A) 0-1

78-79 R3: Shrewsbury Town (A) 1-3

79-80 R3: Chesham United (A) 2-0
R4: Aston Villa (H) 1-1, (A) 1-4

80-81 R3: Norwich City (A) 0-1

81-82 R3: Doncaster Rovers (A) 1-2

82-83 R3: Weymouth (H) 1-0
R4: Barnsley (H) 1-0
R5: Sheffield Wednesday (H) 1-2

83-84 R3: Derby County (H) 0-3

84-85 R1: Peterborough United (H) 0-2

85-86 R1: Dagenham (A) 1-2

86-87 R1: Exeter City (A) 1-1, (H) 2-0
R2: Maidstone United (A) 0-1

87-88 R1: Farnborough Town (H) 2-1
R2: Yeovil Town (H) 0-1

88-89 R1: Woking (A) 4-1
R2: Bognor Regis Town (A) 1-0
R3: Plymouth Argyle (A) 0-2

89-90 R1: Aldershot (A) 1-0
R2: Woking (H) 3-1
R3: Darlington (H) 0-0, (A) 3-1
R4: Millwall (A) 1-1, (H) 1-0
R5: Bristol C. (A) 0-0, (H) 1-1, (H) 5-1
R6: Crystal Palace (H) 0-1

90-91 R1: Exeter City (A) 2-1
R2: Fulham (A) 0-0, (H) 2-1
R3: Wolverhampton Wanderers (A) 1-0
R4: Middlesbrough (H) 2-0
R5: Sheffield Wednesday (H) 4-0
R6: Arsenal (A) 1-2

91-92 R3: Coventry City (A) 1-1, (H) 1-0
R4: Swindon Town (H) 0-3

92-93 R3: Sheffield Wednesday (H) 1-2

CANTERBURY CITY

Currently: Southern League

48-49 EX: Margate (A) 1-2

49-50 PR: Chatham Town (H) 2-1
Q1: Bowater Lloyds (A) 3-2
Q2: Gravesend & Northfleet (A) 1-5

50-51 PR: Sittingbourne (H) 0-1

51-52 PR: Margate (A) 1-6

52-53 PR: Tunbridge Wells United (A) 1-2

53-54 PR: Tunbridge Wells United (H) 0-2

54-55 PR: Sutton United (H) 3-0
Q1: Dulwich Hamlet (H) 2-2, (A) 2-0
Q2: Carshalton Athletic (H) 2-1
Q3: Sittingbourne (H) 2-1
Q4: Hounslow Town (A) 0-3

55-56 PR: Sutton United (H) 2-1
Q1: Deal Town (A) 2-2, (H) 2-1
Q2: Ramsgate Athletic (A) 1-1, (H) 2-5

56-57 PR: Folkestone Town (A) 1-0
Q1: Ashford Town (A) 2-1
Q2: Margate (A) 0-2

57-58 Q1: Whitstable Town (A) 2-2, (H) 1-5

58-59 Q1: Dover (A) 2-0
Q2: Ramsgate Athletic (A) 2-0
Q3: Ashford Town (A) 1-1, (H) 2-4

59-60 Q1: Snowdown Colliery Welfare (H) 1-0
Q2: Betteshanger Colliery Welfare (A) 0-6

60-61 Q1: Dover (A) 1-4

61-62 Q1: Whitstable Town (A - *played home*) 4-0
Q2: Ramsgate Athletic (A) 1-2

62-63 Q1: Folkestone Town (H) 0-3

63-64 Q1: Whitstable (H) 7-1
Q2: Ramsgate Athletic (H) 0-1

64-65 Q1: Dover (A) 2-0
Q2: Folkestone Town (H) 3-1
Q3: Deal Town (H) 4-1
Q4: Crawley Town (H) 3-0
R1: Torquay United (H) 0-6

65-66 Q1: Ramsgate Athletic (H) 2-1
Q2: Herne Bay (H) 1-0
Q3: Folkestone Town (A) 0-1

66-67 Q1: Herne Bay (A) 4-0
Q2: Hastings United (A) 0-2

67-68 Q1: Tonbridge (H) 1-2

68-69 Q1: Whitstable Town (H) 1-0
Q2: Sittingbourne (H) 2-0
Q3: Ashford Town (A) 4-3
Q4: Eastbourne (A) 2-2, (H) 4-2
R1: Swindon Town (H) 0-1

69-70 Q1: Chatham Town (A) 6-1
Q2: Tunbridge Wells (A) 4-3
Q3: Ashford Town (A) 1-1, (H) 1-4

70-71 PR: Hastings United (A) 0-2

71-72 Q1: Chatham Town (H) 5-1
Q2: Folkestone (H) 1-3

72-73 Q1: Cray Wanderers (A) 1-2

73-74 Q1: Maidstone United (A) 2-4

74-75 Q1: Herne Bay (H) 4-0
Q2: Ramsgate (H) 2-1
Q3: Ashford Town (H) 2-2, (A) 0-4

75-76 PR: Folkestone & Shepway (A) 2-1
Q1: Sidley United (A) 2-0
Q2: Sheppey United (H) 6-2
Q3: Margate (H) 2-0
Q4: Hendon (A) 0-1

76-77 Q1: Ashford Town (A) 0-1

77-78 PR: Tunbridge Wells (A) 0-5

78-79 PR: East Grinstead (A) 2-1
Q1: Sheppey United (A) 4-1
Q2: Ramsgate (A) 0-1

79-80 Q1: Dulwich Hamlet (H) 1-1, (A) 0-4

80-81 Q1: Burgess Hill Town (A) 2-1
Q2: Tilbury (H) 2-1
Q3: Dover (A) 2-2, (H) 3-3, (H) 0-2

81-82 Q1: Eastbourne Town (A) 2-0
Q2: Hastings United (A) 1-4

82-83 PR: Tunbridge Wells (A) 3-0
Q1: Burgess Hill T. (A) 2-2, (H) 2-1
Q2: Tooting & Mitcham United (A) 0-2

83-84 PR: Haringey Borough (A) 4-1
Q1: Bognor Regis Town (H) 0-3

84-85 PR: Littlehampton Town (A) 1-1, (H) 6-0
Q1: Faversham Town (H) 3-0
Q2: Croydon (H) 2-1
Q3: Worthing (H) 2-1
Q4: Enfield (H) 0-1

85-86 Q1: Cray Wanderers (A) 1-1, (H) 5-0
Q2: Whyteleafe (A) 2-1
Q3: Hastings Town (A) 0-3

86-87 Q1: Folkestone (H) 0-1

87-88 PR: Thanet United (A) 0-3

88-89 PR: Tonbridge A.F.C. (A) 3-2
Q1: Woking (A) 0-3

89-90 PR: Lancing (A) 1-0
Q1: Tooting & Mitcham (H) 2-0
Q2: Dover Athletic (A) 0-0, (H) 0-2

90-91 PR: Dorking (H) 0-0, (A) 1-4

91-92 PR: Arundel (H) 1-0
Q1: Gravesend & Northfleet (A) 1-2

92-93 PR: Bracknell Town (H) 4-1
Q1: Croydon (A) 0-0, (H) 2-1
Q2: Hastings Town (A) 2-1
Q3: Worthing (A) 1-3

CANVEY ISLAND

Currently: Essex Senior League

69-70 PR: Tooting & Mitcham U. (H) 0-0, (A) 1-4

70-71 Q1: Bishop's Stortford (A) 3-5

87-88 Q1: Baldock Town (H) 0-1

88-89 PR: Stowmarket Town (H) 2-3

89-90 PR: Langford (A) 3-0
Q1: Purfleet (H) 3-0
Q2: Cambridge City (A) 0-3

90-91 PR: Halstead Town (A) 1-1, (H) 1-7

91-92 PR: Harwich & Parkeston (H) 0-2

92-93 PR: Burnham (A - *at Windsor & Eton*) 0-1

CARDIFF CITY

Currently: Football League

45-46 R3: W. Bromwich A. (H) 1-1, (A) 0-4 (*agg: 1-5*)

46-47 R3: Brentford (A) 0-1

47-48 R3: Sheffield Wednesday (H) 1-2

48-49 R3: Oldham Athletic (A) 3-2
R4: Aston Villa (A) 2-1
R5: Derby County (A) 1-2

49-50 R3: West Bromwich Albion (H) 2-2, (A) 1-0
R4: Charlton Athletic (A) 1-1, (H) 2-0
R5: Leeds United (A) 1-3

50-51 R3: West Ham United (A) 1-2

51-52 R3: Swindon Town (H) 1-1, (A) 0-1

52-53 R3: Halifax Town (A) 1-3

53-54 R3: Peterborough United (H) 3-1
R4: Port Vale (H) 0-2

54-55 R3: Arsenal (A) 0-1

55-56 R3: Leeds United (A) 2-1
R4: West Ham United (A) 1-2

56-57 R3: Leeds United (A) 2-1
R4: Barnsley (H) 0-1

57-58 R3: Leeds United (A) 2-1
R4: Leyton Orient (H) 4-1
R5: Blackburn Rovers (H) 0-0, (A) 1-2

58-59 R3: Plymouth Argyle (A) 3-0
R4: Norwich City (A) 2-3

59-60 R3: Port Vale (H) 0-2

60-61 R3: Manchester City (H) 1-1, (A) 0-0, 0-2

61-62 R3: Middlesbrough (A) 0-1

62-63 R3: Charlton Athletic (A) 0-1

63-64 R3: Leeds United (H) 0-1

64-65 R3: Charlton Athletic (H) 1-2

65-66 R3: Port Vale (H) 2-1
R4: Southport (A) 0-2

66-67 R3: Barnsley (A) 1-1, (H) 2-1
R4: Manchester City (H) 1-1, (A) 1-3

67-68 R3: Stoke City (A) 1-4

68-69 R3: Arsenal (H) 0-0, (A) 0-2

69-70 R3: York (A) 1-1, (H) 1-1, (*at Birm. City*) 1-3

70-71 R3: Brighton & Hove Albion (H) 1-0
R4: Brentford (H) 0-2

71-72 R3: Sheffield United (A) 3-1
R4: Sunderland (H) 1-1, (A) 1-1, (*at Manchester City*) 3-1
R5: Leeds United (H) 0-2

72-73 R3: Scunthorpe United (A) 3-2
R4: Bolton (A) 2-2, (H) 1-1, (*at West Brom.*) 0-1

73-74 R3: Birmingham City (A) 2-5

74-75 R3: Leeds United (A) 1-4

75-76 R1: Exeter City (H) 6-2
R2: Wycombe Wanderers (H) 1-0
R3: Orient (A) 1-0
R4: Southend United (A) 1-2

76-77 R3: Tottenham Hotspur (H) 1-0
R4: Wrexham (H) 3-2
R5: Everton (H) 1-2

77-78 R3: Ipswich Town (H) 0-2

78-79 R3: Swindon Town (A) 0-3

79-80 R3: Arsenal (H) 0-0, (A) 1-2

80-81 R3: Leicester City (A) 0-3

81-82 R3: Manchester City (A) 1-3

82-83 R1: Wokingham Town (A) 1-1, (H) 3-0
R2: Weymouth (H) 2-3

83-84 R3: Ipswich Town (H) 0-3

84-85 R3: Gillingham (A) 1-2

85-86 R1: Exeter City (A) 1-2

86-87 R1: Ton Pentre (A) 4-1
R2: Brentford (H) 2-0
R3: Millwall (A) 0-0, (H) 2-2, (H) 1-0
R4: Stoke City (A) 1-2

87-88 R1: Peterborough United (A) 1-2

88-89 R1: Hereford United (H) 3-0
R2: Enfield (A) 4-1
R3: Hull City (H) 1-2

89-90 R1: Halesowen Town (H) 1-0
R2: Gloucester City (H) 2-2, (A) 1-0
R3: Queens Park Rangers (H) 0-0, (A) 0-2

90-91 R1: Hayes (H) 0-0, (A - *at Brentford*) 0-1

91-92 R1: Swansea City (A) 1-2

92-93 R1: Bath City (H) 2-3

CARDIFF CORINTHIANS

Currently: Welsh League

45-46 Q1: Ebbw Vale (A) *W/O*
Q2: Barry Town (A) 1-6

46-47 PR: Merthyr Tydfil (A) 1-4

47-48 PR: Llanelly (A) 0-3

48-49 Q1: Llanelly (A) 1-1, (H) 0-2

49-50 PR: Mount Hill Enterprise (H) 0-1

CARGO FLEET WORKS

Currently: Teesside League

47-48 PR: Guisborough (A) 1-4

48-49 PR: Billingham St John (A) 5-4
Q1: Billingham Synthonia Rec. (A) 1-11

49-50 PR: Bridlington Central United (H) 0-8

50-51 Q1: Whitby Town (A) 2-10

CARLISLE CITY

Currently: Northern Alliance

76-77 Q1: South Bank (A) 0-3

77-78 Q1: Boldon Community Association (A) 1-3

78-79 PR: Annfield Plain (H) 4-2
Q1: Spennymoor United (A) 1-2

79-80 Q1: Bishop Auckland (H) 2-2, (A) 2-2, 0-5

80-81 PR: Farsley Celtic (H) 1-4

CARLISLE UNITED

Currently: Football League

45-46 R1: North Shields (H) 5-1, (A) 3-2 (*agg: 8-4*)
R2: Barrow (A) 2-4, (H) 3-4 (*agg: 5-8*)

46-47 R1: Runcorn (H) 4-0
R2: South Liverpool (A) 3-2
R3: Sheffield United (A) 0-3

47-48 R1: Barrow (A) 2-3

48-49 R1: New Brighton (A) 0-1

49-50 R1: Lincoln City (H) 1-0
R2: Swindon Town (H) 2-0
R3: Leeds United (H) 2-5

50-51 R1: Barrow (H) 2-1
R2: Southport (A) 3-1
R3: Arsenal (A) 0-0, (H) 1-4

51-52 R1: Bradford City (A) 1-6

52-53 R1: Scunthorpe United (A) 0-1

53-54 R1: Southport (A) 0-1

54-55 R1: Stockport County (A) 1-0
R2: Watford (H) 2-2, (A) 1-4

55-56 R1: Darlington (A) 0-0, (H) 0-0, 1-3

Above: *Nicky Platnauer (left) holds off Enfield's Robin Lewis as Cardiff City record an emphatic 4-1 F.A. Cup win. Photo: R J Vallence.*

56-57 R1: Billingham Synthonia Recreation (H) 6-1
R2: Darlington (H) 2-1
R3: Birmingham City (H) 3-3, (A) 0-4

57-58 R1: Rhyl (H) 5-1
R2: Accrington Stanley (H) 1-1, (A) 2-3

58-59 R1: Heanor Town (A) 5-1
R2: Chesterfield (H) 0-0, (A) 0-1

59-60 R1: Rochdale (A) 2-2, (H) 1-3

60-61 R1: Chester (A) 1-0
R2: Port Vale (A) 1-2

61-62 R1: Darlington (A) 4-0
R2: Barnsley (A) 2-1
R3: Wolverhampton Wanderers (A) 1-3

62-63 R1: Hartlepools United (H) 2-1
R2: Blyth Spartans (A) 2-0
R3: Gravesend & Northfleet (H) 0-1

63-64 R1: York City (A) 5-2
R2: Gateshead (H) 4-3
R3: Queens Park Rangers (H) 2-0
R4: Bedford Town (A) 3-0
R5: Preston North End (H) 0-1

64-65 R1: Crook Town (A) 0-1

65-66 R3: Crystal Palace (H) 3-0
R4: Shrewsbury Town (A) 0-0, (H) 1-1, 3-4

66-67 R3: Blackburn Rovers (A) 2-1
R4: Ipswich Town (A) 0-2

67-68 R3: Newcastle United (A) 1-0
R4: Everton (H) 0-2

68-69 R3: Chelsea (A) 0-2

69-70 R3: Nottingham Forest (A) 0-0, (H) 2-1
R4: Aldershot (H) 2-2, (A) 4-1
R5: Middlesbrough (A) 1-2

70-71 R3: Southend United (A) 3-0
R4: Tottenham Hotspur (H) 2-3

71-72 R3: Tottenham Hotspur (A) 1-1, (H) 1-3

72-73 R3: Huddersfield Town (H) 2-2, (A) 1-0
R4: Sheffield United (H) 2-1
R5: Arsenal (H) 1-2

73-74 R3: Sunderland (H) 0-0, (A) 1-0
R4: Liverpool (A) 0-0, (H) 0-2

74-75 R3: Preston North End (A) 1-0
R4: West Bromwich Albion (H) 3-2
R5: Mansfield Town (A) 1-0
R6: Fulham (H) 0-1

75-76 R3: West Bromwich Albion (A) 1-3

76-77 R3: Matlock Town (H) 5-1
R4: Liverpool (A) 0-3

77-78 R1: Stafford Rangers (H) 2-0
R2: Chester (H) 3-1
R3: Manchester United (H) 1-1, (A) 2-4

78-79 R1: Halifax Town (H) 1-0
R2: Hull City (H) 3-0
R3: Ipswich Town (A) 2-3

79-80 R1: Hull City (H) 3-3, (A) 2-0
R2: Sheffield Wednesday (H) 3-0
R3: Bradford City (H) 3-2
R4: Wrexham (H) 0-0, (A) 1-3

80-81 R1: Workington (A) 0-0, (H) 4-1
R2: Walsall (H) 3-0
R3: Mansfield Town (A) 2-2, (H) 2-1
R4: Bristol City (H) 1-1, (A) 0-5

81-82 R1: Darlington (A) 2-2, (H) 3-1
R2: Bishop Auckland (H) 0-0 *abandoned after 69 minutes*, (*at Workington*) 1-0
R3: Huddersfield Town (H) 2-3

82-83 R3: Burnley (H) 2-2, (A) 1-3

83-84 R3: Swindon Town (H) 1-1, (A) 1-3

84-85 R3: Dagenham (H) 1-0
R4: Leicester City (A) 0-1

85-86 R3: Queens Park Rangers (H) 1-0
R4: Peterborough United (A) 0-1

86-87 R1: Notts County (A) 1-1, (H) 0-3

87-88 R1: Macclesfield Town (A) 2-4

88-89 R1: Telford United (A) 1-1, (H) 4-1
R2: Scarborough (A) 1-0

R3: Liverpool (H) 0-3

89-90 R1: Wrexham (H) 3-0
R2: Wigan Athletic (A) 0-2

90-91 R1: Wigan Athletic (A) 0-5

91-92 R1: Crewe Alexandra (H) 1-1, (A) 3-5

92-93 R1: Wigan Athletic (A) 1-3

CARSHALTON ATHLETIC

Currently: Isthmian League

46-47 PR: Wimbledon (A) 0-3

47-48 Q1: Sutton United (A) 3-1
Q2: Redhill (A) 2-5

48-49 PR: Woking (A) 1-1, (H) 4-7

49-50 PR: Walton & Hersham (A) 2-2, (H) 0-8

50-51 EX: Woking (A) 2-2, (H) 7-4
PR: Vickers Armstrong (H) 4-2
Q1: Hounslow Town (H) 1-0
Q2: Kingstonian (H) 1-1, (A) 4-2
Q3: Tooting & Mitcham United (H) 1-3

51-52 PR: Sutton United (A) 3-3, (H) 2-3

52-53 PR: Bexleyheath & Welling (A) 5-1
Q1: Kingstonian (H) 3-0
Q2: Sutton United (A) 2-0
Q3: Wimbledon (H) 3-4

53-54 PR: Sittingbourne (A) 1-2

54-55 Q1: Walton & Hersham (A) 0-0, (H) 2-0
Q2: Canterbury City (A) 1-2

55-56 PR: Dulwich Hamlet (H) 3-1
Q1: Snowdown Colliery Welfare (A) 1-0
Q2: Sittingbourne (A) 0-0, (H) 1-2

56-57 Q1: Bexleyheath & Welling (H) 4-9

57-58 Q1: Dulwich Hamlet (A) 0-4

58-59 PR: Kingstonian (A) 5-1
Q1: Metropolitan Police (H) 5-0
Q2: Sutton United (A) 1-1, (H) 3-4

59-60 PR: Metropolitan Police (A) 3-1
Q1: Kingstonian (H) 2-4

60-61 Q1: Epsom (A) 1-0
Q2: Slough Town (H) 5-2
Q3: Sutton United (H) 2-2, (A) 0-3

61-62 Q1: Redhill (A) 0-1

62-63 Q1: Marlow (H) 4-0
Q2: Dulwich Hamlet (H) 2-5

63-64 Q1: Redhill (H) 2-0
Q2: Tooting & Mitcham United (H) 0-3

64-65 Q1: Tooting & Mitcham United (A) 4-1
Q2: Slough Town (A) 0-2

65-66 Q1: Redhill (A) 2-2, (H) 3-0
Q2: Lancing (A) 2-0
Q3: Crawley Town (A) 0-3

66-67 Q1: Ware (H) 2-4

67-68 Q1: Staines Town (H) 2-2, (A) 1-1, 3-2
Q2: Hayes (H) 3-2
Q3: Brentwood Town (H) 0-2

68-69 Q1: Metropolitan Police (H) 4-5

69-70 Q1: Banstead Athletic (H) 2-1
Q2: Metropolitan Police (A) 4-1
Q3: Staines Town (A) 2-1
Q4: Ramsgate (H) 1-0
R1: Hendon (A) 3-5

70-71 Q1: Lancing (A) 2-1
Q2: Littlehampton Town (A) 3-2
Q3: Crawley Town (H) 0-4

71-72 Q1: Chesham United (H) 2-1
Q2: Walton & Hersham (H) 0-0, (A) 1-5

72-73 Q1: Molesey (H) 0-0, (A) 1-4

73-74 Q1: Horsham (H) 0-3

74-75 Q1: Leytonstone (H) 0-1

75-76 Q1: Kingstonian (H) 0-2

76-77 Q1: Marlow (H) 2-1
Q2: Epping T. (H) 1-1, (A) 1-1, 4-2
Q3: Dagenham (H) 3-3, (A) 1-2

77-78 Q1: St Albans City (H) 2-3

78-79 Q1: Chertsey Town (H) 3-0
Q2: Slough Town (H) 1-2

79-80 PR: Dunstable (A) 2-1
Q1: Hounslow (A) 0-2

80-81 PR: Feltham (H) 2-0
Q1: Willesden (A) 2-0
Q2: Addlestone (A) 0-1

81-82 Q1: Littlehampton Town (A) 3-0
Q2: Uxbridge (A) 3-0
Q3: Burgess Hill Town (A) 5-1
Q4: Leytonstone-Ilford (A) 0-2

82-83 Q1: Horley Town (A) 2-1
Q2: Southwick (H) 3-1
Q3: Egham Town (A) 2-0
Q4: Walthamstow Avenue (A) 1-1, (H) 2-1
R1: Barnet (H) 4-0
R2: Torquay United (A) 1-4

83-84 Q1: Southall (A) 3-3, (H) 3-4

84-85 Q1: Lancing (H) 4-0
Q2: Staines Town (A) 2-4

85-86 Q1: Herne Bay (A) 5-1
Q2: Tonbridge A.F.C. (A) 2-0
Q3: Kingstonian (A) 0-2

86-87 Q1: Bromley (A) 2-2, (H) 4-2
Q2: Eastbourne Town (A) 1-0
Q3: Dover Athletic (A) 3-3, (H) 1-3

87-88 Q1: Kingstonian (H) 1-0
Q2: Saffron Walden Town (A) 5-1
Q3: Gravesend & Northfleet (A) 6-2
Q4: Wokingham Town (H) 2-1
R1: Welling United (A) 2-3

88-89 Q1: Lewes (H) 3-1
Q2: Bromley (H) 1-1, (A) 2-4

89-90 Q1: Wandsworth & Norwood (A) 1-1, (H) 3-1
Q2: Slough Town (H) 0-2

90-91 Q1: Erith & Belvedere (H) 3-0
Q2: Dorking (A) 0-2

91-92 Q1: Faversham Town (A) 2-3

92-93 Q1: Erith & Belvedere (H) 1-2

CHADDERTON

Currently: North West Counties League

83-84 PR: Denaby United (H) 1-0
Q1: South Liverpool (H) 1-4

84-85 PR: Shifnal Town (A) 2-2, (H) 2-1
Q1: Oswestry Town (H) 0-0, (A) 0-4

85-86 PR: Ashton United (H) 2-2, (A) 1-2

86-87 PR: Irlam Town (H) 0-1

87-88 Q1: Heanor Town (H) 1-0
Q2: Macclesfield Town (A) 0-5

88-89 Q1: Stalybridge Celtic (A) 4-1
Q2: Hyde United (H) 1-5

89-90 PR: Gresley Rovers (H) 1-2

90-91 PR: Radcliffe Borough (H) 1-2

91-92 Q1: Prescot A.F.C. (A) 2-3

92-93 PR: Lancaster City (H) 2-1

Q1: Bootle (H) 3-0
Q2: Southport (A) 0-2

CHALFONT ST PETER

Currently: Isthmian League

77-78 Q1: Barking (A) 2-5

78-79 Q1: Epping T. (H) 0-0, (A) 1-1, (*at Hoddesdon*) 0-0, (*at Hounslow*) 2-1
Q2: Sutton United (H) 0-2

79-80 PR: Banbury United (H) 1-2

80-81 Q1: Billericay Town (H) 1-1, (H) 0-3

81-82 Q1: Slough Town (A) 1-2

82-83 PR: Rainham Town (H) 2-1
Q1: Clapton (A) 1-3

83-84 PR: Finchley (H) 2-1
Q1: Uxbridge (A) 2-4

84-85 Q1: Oldbury U. (H) 0-0, (A) 1-1, (H) 1-3

85-86 PR: Banbury United (H) 2-1
Q1: King's Lynn (H) 1-1, (A) 2-1
Q2: Barking (A) 2-0
Q3: Braintree Town (H) 1-1, (A) 0-2

86-87 Q1: Hayes (H) 0-3

87-88 PR: Arlesey Town (H) 1-1, (A) 0-1

88-89 Q1: Bromsgrove Rovers (A) 1-1, (H) 0-3

89-90 Q1: Yeading (A) 0-0, (H) 0-5

90-91 PR: Welwyn Garden City (A) 2-1
Q1: Malvern Town (H) 2-6

91-92 PR: Flackwell Heath (H) 2-0
Q1: Nuneaton Borough (H) 0-4

92-93 PR: Hoddesdon Town (H) 1-0
Q1: Cheshunt (A) 0-1

CHARD TOWN

Currently: Western League

77-78 Q1: Barnstaple Town (H) 1-0
Q2: Tiverton Town (A) 0-2

78-79 Q1: Bridgwater Town (A) 0-1

79-80 Q1: Tiverton Town (A) 1-2

80-81 PR: Clevedon Town (H) 1-1, (A) 1-4

81-82 Q1: Barnstaple Town (H) 1-2

82-83 Q1: Penzance (H) 2-1
Q2: Liskeard Athletic (A) 0-3

83-84 PR: Taunton Town (H) 2-1
Q1: Barry Town (A) 0-2

84-85 PR: Shepton Mallet Town (H) 0-2

85-86 PR: Bristol Manor Farm (A) 0-2

88-89 Q1: Poole Town (H) 0-3

89-90 PR: Yate Town (H) 2-1
Q1: Dorchester Town (H) 0-2

90-91 Q1: Romsey Town (H) 4-4, (A) 0-3

91-92 PR: Witney Town (H) 1-2

Below: *A typical early season F.A. Cup scene as Chard Town entertain Dorchester. Photo: Allan J Spurway.*

CHARLTON ATHLETIC

Currently: Football League

45-46 R3: Fulham (H) 3-1, (A) 1-2 (*agg: 4-3*)
R4: Wolves (H) 5-2, (A) 1-1 (*agg: 6-3*)
R5: Preston N.E. (A) 1-1, (H) 6-0 (*agg: 7-1*)
R6: Brentford (H) 6-3, (A) 3-1 (*agg: 9-3*)
SF: Bolton Wanderers (*at Aston Villa*) 2-0
F: Derby County (*at Wembley*) 1-4

46-47 R3: Rochdale (H) 3-1
R4: West Bromwich Albion (A) 2-1
R5: Blackburn Rovers (H) 1-0
R6: Preston North End (H) 2-1
SF: Newcastle United (*at Leeds United*) 4-0
F: Burnley (*at Wembley*) 1-0

47-48 R3: Newcastle United (H) 2-1
R4: Stockport County (H) 3-0
R5: Manchester United (A) 0-2

48-49 R3: Burnley (A) 1-2

49-50 R3: Fulham (H) 2-2, (A) 2-1
R4: Cardiff City (H) 1-1, (A) 0-2

50-51 R3: Blackpool (H) 2-2, (A) 0-3

51-52 R3: Luton Town (A) 0-1

52-53 R3: Hull City (A) 1-3

53-54 R3: Portsmouth (A) 3-3, (H) 2-3

54-55 R3: Rochdale (A) 3-1
R4: West Bromwich Albion (A) 4-2
R5: Wolverhampton Wanderers (A) 1-4

55-56 R3: Burton Albion (H) 7-0
R4: Swindon Town (H) 2-1
R5: Arsenal (H) 0-2

56-57 R3: Middlesbrough (A) 1-1, (H) 2-3

57-58 R3: Huddersfield Town (A) 2-2, (H) 1-0
R4: Fulham (A) 1-1, (H) 0-2

58-59 R3: Bristol Rovers (A) 4-0
R4: Everton (H) 2-2, (A) 1-4

59-60 R3: Bristol City (A) 3-2
R4: Wolverhampton Wanderers (A) 1-2

60-61 R3: Tottenham Hotspur (A) 2-3

61-62 R3: Scunthorpe United (H) 1-0
R4: Derby County (H) 2-1
R5: Aston Villa (A) 1-2

62-63 R3: Cardiff City (H) 1-0
R4: Chelsea (H) 0-3

63-64 R3: West Ham United (A) 0-3

64-65 R3: Cardiff City (A) 2-1
R4: Middlesbrough (H) 1-1, (A) 1-2

65-66 R3: Preston North End (H) 2-3

66-67 R3: Sheffield United (H) 0-1

67-68 R3: Coventry City (A) 0-3

68-69 R3: Crystal Palace (H) 0-0, (A) 2-0
R4: Arsenal (A) 0-2

69-70 R3: Aston Villa (A) 1-1, (H) 1-0
R4: Queens Park Rangers (H) 2-3

70-71 R3: Hull City (A) 0-3

71-72 R3: Tranmere Rovers (H) 0-0, (A) 2-4

72-73 R1: Tonbridge (A) 5-0
R2: Walsall (A) 2-1
R3: Bolton Wanderers (H) 1-1, (A) 0-4

73-74 R1: A.F.C. Bournemouth (A) 0-1

74-75 R1: Chelmsford United (A) 1-0
R2: Peterborough United (A) 0-3

75-76 R3: Sheffield Wednesday (H) 2-1
R4: Portsmouth (H) 1-1, (A) 3-0
R5: Wolverhampton Wanderers (A) 0-3

76-77 R3: Blackburn Rovers (H) 1-1, (A) 0-2

77-78 R3: Notts County (H) 0-2

78-79 R3: Maidstone United (H) 1-1, (A) 2-1
R4: Bristol Rovers (A) 0-1

79-80 R3: Wrexham (A) 0-6

80-81 R1: Harlow Town (A) 2-0
R2: A.F.C. Bournemouth (H) 2-1
R3: Plymouth Argyle (A) 2-1

Above: *Charlton's Colin Pates (left) is pursued by Kettering's Robbie Cooke as the First Division side scrape a narrow win over their non-League opposition in 1989. Photo: Mick Cheney.*

R4: Fulham (A) 2-1
R5: Ipswich Town (A) 0-2

81-82 R3: Orient (A) 0-1

82-83 R3: Ipswich Town (H) 2-3

83-84 R3: Colchester United (A) 1-0
R4: Watford (H) 0-2

84-85 R3: Tottenham Hotspur (A) 1-1, (H) 1-2

85-86 R3: West Ham Utd (H - *at Crystal Pal.*) 0-1

86-87 R3: Walsall (H - *at Crystal Palace*) 1-2

87-88 R3: West Ham United (A) 0-2

88-89 R3: Oldham A. (H - *at Crystal Palace*) 2-1
R4: Kettering (H - *at Crystal Palace*) 2-1
R5: West Ham Utd (H - *at Crystal Pal.*) 0-1

89-90 R3: Bradford C. (H - *at C. Pal.*) 1-1, (A) 3-0
R4: West Bromwich Albion (A) 0-1

90-91 R3: Everton (H - *at Crystal Palace*) 1-2

91-92 R3: Barnet (H - *at West Ham United*) 3-1
R4: Sheffield U. (H - *at W. Ham*) 0-0, (A) 1-3

92-93 R3: Leeds United (A) 1-1, (H) 1-3

CHASETOWN

Currently: West Midlands (Regional) League

87-88 PR: Evesham United (H) 0-2

88-89 PR: Wednesfield Social (A) 3-2
Q1: Wellingborough Town (A) 2-1
Q2: Tamworth (H) 0-1

89-90 PR: Spalding United (H) 2-2, (A) 0-3

90-91 PR: Evesham United (H) 0-2

91-92 PR: Highgate United (A) 3-0
Q1: Bilston Town (H) 0-0, (A) 1-0
Q2: Banbury United (H) 1-1, (A) 2-1
Q3: V.S. Rugby (H) 0-0, (A) 0-3

92-93 Q1: Redditch United (H) 1-0
Q2: Braintree Town (H) 0-2

CHATHAM

Currently: Defunct

46-47 PR: Folkestone (H) 0-8

47-48 EX: Whitstable (H) *Withdrew*

CHATHAM TOWN

Currently: Kent League
* - As Medway F.C.

47-48 EX: Lloyds (Sittingbourne) (A) 4-2
PR: Margate (A) 0-3

48-49 EX: Dover (H) 2-3

49-50 PR: Canterbury City (A) 1-2

50-51 EX: Whitstable (A) 0-1

51-52 PR: Folkestone Town (A) 0-4

52-53 PR: Dover (H) 0-6

53-54 PR: Tooting & Mitcham United (H) 1-3

54-55 PR: Walton & Hersham (A) 1-1, (H) 0-4

55-56 PR: Ramsgate Athletic (H) 1-6

56-57 PR: Ramsgate Athletic (H) 2-4

57-58 PR: Ramsgate Athletic (A) 1-5

58-59 PR: Erith & Belvedere (A) 0-8

59-60 PR: Sheppey United (H) 0-3

62-63 Q1: Gravesend & Northfleet (A) 1-2

63-64 Q1: Bromley (A) 1-4

64-65 Q1: Bromley (H) 3-1
Q2: Dartford (H) 2-4

65-66 Q1: Bexley United (A) 2-6

66-67 Q1: Margate (A) 1-2

67-68 Q1: Maidstone United (H) 4-2
Q2: Tonbridge (A) 1-2

68-69 Q1: Sittingbourne (H) 1-6

69-70 Q1: Canterbury City (H) 1-6

70-71 Q1: Gravesend & Northfleet (H) 1-4

71-72 Q1: Canterbury City (A) 1-5

72-73 Q1: Ashford Town (H) 0-2

73-74 Q1: Molesey (H) 3-0
Q2: Fleet Town (A) 4-2
Q3: Wycombe Wanderers (H) 0-7

74-75 * Q1: Whitstable Town (H) 4-2
Q2: Faversham Town (H) 2-1
Q3: Maidstone United (A) 0-7

75-76 * Q1: Tunbridge Wells (H) 1-3

76-77 * PR: Rainham Town (H) 3-3, (A) 1-2

77-78 * Q1: Sutton United (H) 0-1

78-79 * Q1: Sidley United (H) 4-1
Q2: Eastbourne United (H) 0-0, (A) 0-0, (*at Maidstone United*) 0-6

79-80 Q1: Horsham (H) 2-2, (A) 2-1
Q2: Dover (H) 1-1, (A) 1-0
Q3: Margate (H) 0-1

80-81 PR: Eastbourne United (H) 2-1
Q1: Tonbridge A.F.C. (A) 1-1, (H) 1-0
Q2: Bromley (A) 0-4

81-82 PR: Hastings United (H) 1-4

82-83 PR: Woking (A) 0-0, (H) 2-1
Q1: Hastings Town (A) 7-2
Q2: Southall (A) 2-2, (H) 4-2
Q3: Folkestone (H) 1-1, (A) 0-5

83-84 Q1: Epsom & Ewell (H) 1-2

84-85 PR: Metropolitan Police (H) 2-3

85-86 PR: Southall (H) 1-1, (A) 0-2

86-87 PR: Vauxhall Motors (H) 0-0, (A) 2-0
Q1: Staines Town (H) 1-2

87-88 PR: Collier Row (H) 4-1
Q1: Crawley Town (A) 3-1
Q2: Fisher Athletic (H) 0-3

88-89 PR: Dorking (H) 1-5

89-90 PR: Erith & Belvedere (A) 1-5

90-91 PR: Arundel (A) 3-2
Q1: Worthing (A) 0-3

91-92 PR: Steyning Town (H) 1-3

92-93 PR: Worthing (A) 0-8

CHATTERIS TOWN

Currently: Eastern Counties League

45-46 Q1: Newmarket Town (H) 0-1

46-47 Q2: Newmarket Town (A) 2-0
Q3: Cambridge Town (H) 1-6

47-48 Q1: Bury Town (H) 2-5

48-49 PR: Newmarket Town (A) 2-9

49-50 PR: Newmarket Town (A) 4-4, (H) 1-4

50-51 PR: South Lynn (A) 1-0
Q1: Newmarket Town (H) 0-2

51-52 Q1: King's Lynn (A) 1-14

52-53 PR: Cambridge United (H) 0-4

53-54 Q1: Wisbech Town (A) 0-6

54-55 PR: March Town United (H) 1-3

55-56 PR: Cambridge United (H) 2-1
Q1: King's Lynn (H) 2-4

56-57 PR: St Neots & District (H) 1-3

57-58 PR: Ely City (H) 1-1, (A) 1-0
Q1: Wisbech Town (H) 0-5

58-59 PR: March Town United (A) 2-5

59-60 Q1: March Town United (H) 1-2

60-61 Q1: Ely City (A) 2-6

61-62 Q1: Cambridge United (H) 1-5

62-63 Q1: Bury Town (A) 1-4

63-64 Q1: March Town United (H) 4-0
Q2: Bury Town (H) 0-5

64-65 Q1: Cambridge City (H) 1-2

65-66 Q1: Ely City (H) 2-3

66-67 Q1: March Town United (A) 3-4

67-68 Q1: St Neots Town (H) 1-2

68-69 PR: Desborough Town (A) 0-3

69-70 PR: St Neots Town (A) 0-3

70-71 Q1: March Town United (A) 1-2

71-72 Q1: Soham Town Rangers (H) 3-0
Q2: Kettering Town (A) 0-2

72-73 Q1: Gorleston (A) 2-0
Q2: Wisbech Town (H) 3-1
Q3: Ely City (A) 3-3, (H) 2-4

73-74 Q1: Harwich & Parkeston (H) 0-4

74-75 Q1: St Neots Town (H) 0-2

75-76 Q1: Bourne Town (A) 0-4

76-77 Q1: Bedford Town (A) 1-7

77-78 Q1: Arnold (H) 1-6

78-79 Q1: March Town United (A) 1-4

79-80 PR: Potton United (A) 1-1, (H) 1-2

80-81 PR: Great Yarmouth Town (H) 1-1, (A) 2-3

81-82 PR: Felixstowe Town (H) 3-1
Q1: Ely City (H) 3-3, (A) 1-2

82-83 Q1: Great Yarmouth Town (H) 1-6

83-84 Q1: Wellingborough Town (H) 0-2

84-85 PR: Oldswinford (H) 1-4

85-86 PR: Newmarket Town (H) 0-3

86-87 Q1: Harlow Town (H) 2-2, (A) 0-1

87-88 PR: Grantham (A) 2-2, (H) 1-0
Q1: Boldmere St Michael (A) 2-2, (H) 0-3

88-89 PR: R.C. Warwick (H) 2-2, (A) 0-6

89-90 PR: March Town United (A) 0-5

92-93 PR: Hitchin Town (A) 1-3

CHELMSFORD CITY

Currently: Merged with Brentwood Town
Playing as Chelmsford City in Southern League
See also Chelmsford City (2)

45-46 Q4: Leiston (H) 9-0
R1: Northampton (A) 1-5, (H) 0-5 *(agg: 1-10)*

46-47 Q4: Cambridge Town (H) 0-4

47-48 Q4: Colchester United (A) 1-3

48-49 Q4: Guildford City (A) 2-0
R1: Weymouth (A) 1-2

49-50 Q4: Barnet (A) 6-2
R1: Leytonstone (A) 2-1
R2: Ipswich Town (H) 1-1, (A) 0-1

50-51 Q4: Wycombe Wanderers (A) 4-0
R1: Tonbridge (H) 2-2, (A) 1-0
R2: Mansfield Town (H) 1-4

51-52 Q4: Leytonstone (A) 1-2

52-53 Q4: Finchley (H) 0-0, (A) 0-3

53-54 PR: Woodford Town (A) 3-0
Q1: Romford (H) 3-2
Q2: Erith & Belvedere (H) 2-1
Q3: Briggs Sports (H) 1-0
Q4: Great Yarmouth Town (H) 0-0, (A) 0-1

54-55 PR: Clacton Town (H) 2-0
Q1: Leytonstone (A) 0-0, (H) 2-1
Q2: Barking (H) 2-2, (A) 1-1, 3-2
Q3: Leyton (A) 1-0
Q4: Gorleston (A) 2-1
R1: Aldershot (A) 1-3

55-56 PR: Grays Athletic (A) 0-1

56-57 PR: Ilford (H) 1-0
Q1: Rainham Town (H) 6-0
Q2: Romford (H) 4-0
Q3: Clacton Town (H) 2-2, (A) 0-0, 1-2

57-58 PR: Briggs Sports (H) 3-0
Q1: Clacton Town (H) 4-0
Q2: Leyton (H) 5-0
Q3: Rainham Town (H) 6-0
Q4: Gorleston (A) 0-1

58-59 Q4: Harwich & Parkeston (H) 2-0
R1: Worcester City (H) 0-0, (A) 1-3

59-60 Q4: Grays Athletic (A) 3-1
R1: Crystal Palace (A) 1-5

60-61 Q4: Wisbech Town (H) 3-3, (A) 4-1
R1: Port Vale (H) 2-3

61-62 Q4: Wisbech Town (A) 3-3, (H) 1-0
R1: King's Lynn (H) 1-2

62-63 Q4: Romford (H) 2-0
R1: Shrewsbury Town (H) 2-6

63-64 Q4: Romford (H) 2-0
R1: Cambridge United (A) 1-0
R2: Bedford Town (H) 0-1

64-65 Q4: Oxford City (H) 6-2
R1: Notts County (A) 0-2

65-66 Q4: Romford (A) 1-2

66-67 Q4: Hornchurch (A) 4-0
R1: Brentford (A) 0-1

67-68 Q4: Banbury United (H) 2-0
R1: Oxford Utd (H) 3-3, (A) 3-3, 1-0
R2: Colchester United (H) 0-2

68-69 Q4: Kingstonian (A) 3-3, (H) 5-3
R1: Grantham (A) 1-2

69-70 Q4: Cambridge United (H) 3-2
R1: Hereford United (H) 1-2

Right: *Chelmsford's best recent Cup win was in 1990 over Conference leaders Kettering. Here Dean Murphy towers over Kettering's Andy Hunt. Photo: Mick Cheney.*

CHELMSFORD CITY

Currently: Southern League
See also Chelmsford City (1) and Brentwood Town

70-71 Q4: King's Lynn (H) 2-0
R1: Crawley (A) 1-1, (H) 6-1
R2: Torquay United (H) 0-1

71-72 Q4: Kettering Town (A) 1-4

72-73 Q4: Crawley Town (A) 2-0
R1: Hillingdon Borough (H) 2-0
R2: Telford United (H) 5-0
R3: Ipswich Town (H) 1-3

73-74 Q4: Epping Town (A) 2-1
R1: Watford (A) 0-1

74-75 Q4: Horsham (A) 3-1
R1: Charlton Athletic (H) 0-1

75-76 Q4: Bishop's Stortford (H) 0-2

76-77 Q4: Leatherhead (H) 0-4

77-78 Q1: Histon (A) 1-0
Q2: Gorleston (A) 1-1, (H) 5-0
Q3: Harlow Town (A) 1-1, (H) 2-1
Q4: Folkestone & Shepway (H) 0-3

78-79 Q1: Billericay Town (A) 1-2

79-80 PR: Great Yarmouth Town (A) 3-1
Q1: Parson Drove (A) 0-2

80-81 Q1: Clacton Town (H) 0-0, (A) 2-1
Q2: Edgware (H) 3-1
Q3: Wembley (A) 1-3

81-82 PR: Gorleston (A) 0-2

82-83 PR: Finchley (H) 3-1
Q1: Sudbury Town (A) 1-1, (H) 3-1
Q2: Grays Athletic (H) 3-2
Q3: Leytonstone-Il. (H) 0-0, (A) 0-0, (H) 2-1
Q4: Chesham United (H) 1-3

83-84 Q1: Gorleston (H) 5-1
Q2: Great Yarmouth Town (H) 4-2
Q3: V.S. Rugby (H) 2-2, (A) 2-1
Q4: Bedworth United (H) 2-1
R1: Wycombe Wanderers (H) 0-0, (A) 2-1
R2: Gillingham (A) 1-6

84-85 Q1: Royston Town (A) 3-0
Q2: Hornchurch (A) 1-1, (H) 6-1
Q3: Harlow Town (H) 1-2

85-86 Q1: Alma Swanley (H) 2-0
Q2: Buckingham Town (H) 1-0
Q3: Ware (H) 1-0
Q4: Kettering Town (H) 1-0
R1: Weymouth (H) 1-0
R2: Wycombe Wanderers (A) 0-2

86-87 Q4: Kidderminster Harriers (H) 2-1
R1: Woking (A) 1-1, (H) 2-1
R2: Gillingham (A) 0-2

87-88 Q4: Letchworth Garden City (A) 1-0
R1: Bath City (H) 1-2

88-89 Q4: Halesowen Town (H) 1-3

89-90 Q4: Kidderminster H. (A) 2-2, (H) 1-3

90-91 Q1: Walthamstow Pennant (A) 3-0
Q2: Hornchurch (A) 2-1
Q3: Enfield (A) 1-1, (H) 1-0
Q4: Kettering Town (H) 0-0, (A) 2-1
R1: Barnet (A) 2-2, (H) 0-2

91-92 Q1: Clapton (A) 5-1
Q2: Enfield (H) 1-1, (A) 1-2

92-93 Q1: Grays Athletic (H) 0-0, (A) 1-2

CHELSEA

Currently: F.A. Premier League

45-46	R3: Leicester C. (H) 1-1, (A) 2-0 (*agg: 3-1*) R4: West Ham Utd (H) 2-0, (A) 0-1 (*agg: 1-2*) R5: Aston Villa (H) 0-1, (A) 0-1 (*agg: 0-2*)
46-47	R3: Arsenal (H) 1-1, (A) 1-1, 2-0 R4: Derby County (H) 2-2, (A) 0-1
47-48	R3: Barrow (H) 5-0 R4: Manchester City (A) 0-2
48-49	R3: Bristol City (A) 3-1 R4: Everton (H) 2-0 R5: West Bromwich Albion (A) 0-3
49-50	R3: Brentford (A) 1-0 R4: Newcastle United (H) 3-0 R5: Chesterfield (A) 1-1, (H) 3-0 R6: Manchester United (H) 2-0 SF: Arsenal (*both at Tottenham*) 2-2, 0-1
50-51	R3: Rochdale (A) 3-2 R4: Exeter City (A) 1-1, (H) 2-0 R5: Fulham (H) 1-1, (A) 0-3
51-52	R3: Chester (H) 2-2, (A) 3-2 R4: Tranmere Rovers (H) 4-0 R5: Leeds United (A) 1-1, (H) 1-1, 5-1 R6: Sheffield United (A) 1-0 SF: Arsenal (*both at Tottenham*) 1-1, 0-3
52-53	R3: Derby County (A) 4-4, (H) 1-0 R4: W. Bromwich A. (H) 1-1, (A) 0-0, 1-1, 4-0 R5: Birmingham City (H) 0-4
53-54	R3: West Bromwich Albion (A) 0-1
54-55	R3: Walsall (H) 2-0 R4: Bristol Rovers (A) 3-1 R5: Notts County (A) 0-1
55-56	R3: Hartlepools United (A) 1-0 R4: Burnley (A) 1-1, (H) 1-1, 2-2, 0-0, 2-0 R5: Everton (A) 0-1
56-57	R3: Leyton Orient (A) 2-0 R4: Tottenham Hotspur (A) 0-4
57-58	R3: Doncaster Rovers (A) 2-0 R4: Darlington (H) 3-3, (A) 1-4
58-59	R3: Newcastle United (A) 4-1 R4: Aston Villa (H) 1-2
59-60	R3: Bradford (Park Avenue) (H) 5-1 R4: Aston Villa (H) 1-2
60-61	R3: Crewe Alexandra (H) 1-2
61-62	R3: Liverpool (A) 3-4
62-63	R3: Tranmere Rovers (A) 2-2, (H) 3-1 R4: Charlton Athletic (A) 3-0 R5: Manchester United (A) 1-2
63-64	R3: Tottenham Hotspur (A) 1-1, (H) 2-0 R4: Huddersfield Town (H) 1-2
64-65	R3: Northampton Town (H) 4-1 R4: West Ham United (A) 1-0 R5: Tottenham Hotspur (H) 1-0 R6: Peterborough United (H) 5-1 SF: Liverpool (*at Aston Villa*) 0-2
65-66	R3: Liverpool (A) 2-1 R4: Leeds United (H) 1-0 R5: Shrewsbury Town (H) 3-2 R6: Hull City (H) 2-2, (A) 3-1 SF: Sheffield Wednesday (*at A. Villa*) 0-2
66-67	R3: Huddersfield Town (A) 2-1 R4: Brighton & Hove A. (A) 1-1, (H) 4-0 R5: Sheffield United (H) 2-0 R6: Sheffield Wednesday (H) 1-0 SF: Leeds United (*at Aston Villa*) 1-0 F: Tottenham Hotspur (*at Wembley*) 1-2
67-68	R3: Ipswich Town (H) 3-0 R4: Norwich City (H) 1-0 R5: Sheffield Wednesday (A) 2-2, (H) 2-0 R6: Birmingham City (A) 0-1
68-69	R3: Carlisle United (H) 2-0 R4: Preston North End (A) 0-0, (H) 2-1 R5: Stoke City (H) 3-2 R6: West Bromwich Albion (H) 1-2
69-70	R3: Birmingham City (H) 3-0 R4: Burnley (H) 2-2, (A) 3-1 R5: Crystal Palace (H) 4-1 R6: Queens Park Rangers (H) 4-2 SF: Watford (*at Tottenham Hotspur*) 5-1 F: Leeds (*at Wembley*) 2-2, (*at Man. U.*) 2-1
70-71	R3: Crystal Palace (A) 2-2, (H) 2-0 R4: Manchester City (H) 0-3
71-72	R3: Blackpool (A) 1-0 R4: Bolton Wanderers (H) 3-0 R5: Orient (A) 2-3
72-73	R3: Brighton & Hove Albion (A) 2-0 R4: Ipswich Town (H) 2-0 R5: Sheffield Wednesday (A) 2-1 R6: Arsenal (H) 2-2, (A) 1-2
73-74	R3: Queens Park Rangers (H) 0-0, (A) 0-1
74-75	R3: Sheffield Wednesday (H) 3-2 R4: Birmingham City (H) 0-1
75-76	R3: Bristol Rovers (H) 1-1, (A) 1-0 R4: York City (A) 2-0 R5: Crystal Palace (H) 2-3
76-77	R3: Southampton (A) 1-1, (H) 0-3
77-78	R3: Liverpool (H) 4-2 R4: Burnley (H) 6-2 R5: Orient (A) 0-0, (H) 1-2
78-79	R3: Manchester United (A) 0-3
79-80	R3: Wigan Athletic (H) 0-1
80-81	R3: Southampton (A) 1-3
81-82	R3: Hull City (H) 0-0, (A) 2-0 R4: Wrexham (H) 0-0, (A) 1-1, (A) 2-1 R5: Liverpool (H) 2-0 R6: Tottenham Hotspur (H) 2-3
82-83	R3: Huddersfield Town (A) 1-1, (H) 2-0 R4: Derby County (A) 1-2
83-84	R3: Blackburn Rovers (A) 0-1
84-85	R3: Wigan Athletic (H) 2-2, (A) 5-0 R4: Millwall (H) 2-3
85-86	R3: Shrewsbury Town (A) 1-0 R4: Liverpool (H) 1-2
86-87	R3: Aston Villa (A) 2-2, (H) 2-1 R4: Watford (A) 0-1
87-88	R3: Derby County (A) 3-1 R4: Manchester United (A) 0-2
88-89	R3: Barnsley (A) 0-4
89-90	R3: Crewe Alexandra (H) 1-1, (A) 2-0 R4: Bristol City (A) 1-3
90-91	R3: Oxford United (H) 1-3
91-92	R3: Hull City (A) 2-0 R4: Everton (H) 1-0 R5: Sheffield United (H) 1-0 R6: Sunderland (H) 1-1, (A) 1-2
92-93	R3: Middlesbrough (A) 1-2

Above: *David Webb scores Chelsea's winner with a far post header in the 1970 final replay. Photo: Colorsport.*

CHELTENHAM TOWN

Currently: Southern League

45-46	Q4: Peasedown M.W. (H) 1-1, (A) 1-0 R1: Bath C. (A) 2-3, (H) 0-2 (*agg: 2-5*)
46-47	Q4: Hereford United (A) 1-1, (H) 4-3 R1: Aldershot (A) 2-4
47-48	Q4: Kidderminster Harriers (A) 4-2 R1: Street (H) 5-0 R2: Hull City (A) 2-4
48-49	Q4: Wellington Town (A) 1-2
49-50	Q4: Hereford Utd (A) 1-1, (H) 2-2, 2-4
50-51	Q4: Yeovil Town (A) 4-2 R1: Reading (A) 1-3
51-52	Q4: Merthyr Tydfil (H) 2-3
52-53	Q1: Cinderford Town (A) 1-1, (H) 5-0 Q2: Barry Town (H) 0-3
53-54	Q1: Merthyr Tydfil (A) 2-3
54-55	Q1: Barry Town (A) 1-1, (H) 1-2
55-56	Q1: Lovells Athletic (H) 1-2
56-57	PR: Lovells Athletic (H) 3-0 Q1: Ebbw Vale (A) 5-2 Q2: Gloucester City (A) 2-1 Q3: Llanelly (H) 4-0 Q4: Andover (H) 2-1 R1: Reading (H) 1-2
57-58	Q1: Lovells Ath. (H) 0-0, (A) 0-0, 2-4
58-59	PR: Barry Town (A) 0-2
59-60	PR: Lovells Athletic (H) 1-0 Q1: Gloucester City (A) 3-1 Q2: Merthyr Tydfil (H) 2-2, (A) 1-0 Q3: Barry Town (A) 4-1 Q4: Bridgwater Town (H) 0-0, (A) 1-0 R1: Watford (H) 0-0, (A) 0-3
60-61	Q1: Gloucester City (A) 4-1 Q2: Merthyr Tydfil (H) 4-0 Q3: Llanelly (H) 2-0 Q4: Bridgwater Town (A) 0-0, (H) 1-2
61-62	Q1: Chippenham United (A) 6-2 Q2: Melksham Town (H) 5-2 Q3: Chippenham Town (H) 2-0 Q4: Borough of Weston-super-Mare (H) 0-1
62-63	Q1: Llanelly (A) 3-2 Q2: Lovells Athletic (H) 5-1 Q3: Gloucester City (A) 2-1 Q4: Minehead (A) 1-0 R1: Enfield (H) 3-6
63-64	Q1: Abergavenny Thursdays (H) 7-2 Q2: Gloucester City (A) 2-1 Q3: Llanelly (H) 0-1
64-65	Q1: Melksham Town (A) 4-0 Q2: Trowbridge Town (A) 3-1 Q3: Devizes Town (H) 6-1 Q4: Bideford (A) 0-1
65-66	Q2: Chippenham Town (H) 4-1 Q3: Devizes Town (A) 8-2 Q4: Hereford United (H) 0-1

66-67	Q1: Lovells Athletic (A) 3-0 Q2: Merthyr Tydfil (A) 3-1 Q3: Cinderford Town (A) 3-2 Q4: Yeovil Town (H) 3-3, (A) 1-3
67-68	Q1: Merthyr Tydfil (H) 2-1 Q2: Gloucester City (A) 1-0 Q3: Barry Town (A) 2-2, (H) 3-1 Q4: Hereford United (A) 2-3
68-69	Q1: Lovells Athletic (H) 2-1 Q2: Abergavenny Thur. (A) 2-2, (H) 3-2 Q3: Cinderford Town (A) 3-1 Q4: Frome Town (A) 2-1 R1: Watford (H) 0-4
69-70	Q4: Glastonbury (A) 0-0, (H) 4-1 R1: Oxford City (H) 0-2
70-71	Q4: Burton Albion (H) 2-2, (A) 3-0 R1: Brighton & Hove Albion (A) 0-4
71-72	Q4: Hereford United (A) 0-3
72-73	Q1: Bath City (A) 0-0, (H) 3-2 Q2: Trowbridge Town (H) 4-0 Q3: Devizes Town (A) 0-1
74-75	Q1: Llanelli (H) 3-2 Q2: Gloucester City (H) 4-1 Q3: Cinderford Town (H) 3-2 Q4: Salisbury (H) 4-1 R1: Wycombe Wanderers (A) 1-3
75-76	Q1: Desborough Town (H) 1-1, (A) 3-2 Q2: Banbury United (H) 2-0 Q3: Oxford City (A) 0-0, (H) 2-0 Q4: Nuneaton Borough (A) 1-2
76-77	Q1: Ton Pentre (A) 1-1, (H) 4-0 Q2: Merthyr Tydfil (A) 3-3, (H) 1-1, 0-4
77-78	PR: Moor Green (H) 4-1 Q1: Atherstone Town (A) 0-0, (H) 1-0 Q2: Burton Albion (A) 1-2
78-79	Q1: Clevedon Town (H) 6-1 Q2: Melksham Town (H) 6-0 Q3: Trowbridge Town (A) 4-0 Q4: Yeovil Town (H) 1-2
79-80	PR: Devizes Town (A) 1-0 Q1: Paulton Rovers (A) 2-0 Q2: Merthyr Tydfil (H) 0-2
80-81	PR: Oxford City (A) 2-0 Q1: Forest Green Rovers (H) 3-2 Q2: Buckingham Town (A) 1-2
81-82	Q1: Barry Town (H) 4-0 Q2: Bath City (H) 2-2, (A) 2-1 Q3: Haverfordwest County (H) 4-0 Q4: Dorchester Town (H) 1-3
82-83	Q1: Thame United (A) 3-2 Q2: Gloucester Town (H) 5-1 Q3: Trowbridge Town (A) 1-1, (H) 1-0 Q4: Weymouth (H) 0-0, (A) 0-4
83-84	Q1: Glastonbury (A) 0-0, (H) 4-0 Q2: Bridgend Town (A) 2-0 Q3: Barry Town (H) 3-1 Q4: Windsor & Eton (A) 0-1
84-85	Q1: Bideford (H) 0-0, (A) 2-0 Q2: Ton Pentre (A) 3-2 Q3: Merthyr Tydfil (A) 1-4
85-86	Q1: Minehead (A) 1-1, (H) 1-2
86-87	Q1: Bideford (H) 3-4
87-88	Q1: Dorchester Town (H) 4-1 Q2: Mangotsfield Utd (A) 1-1, (H) 2-0 Q3: Weston-super-Mare (A) 2-1 Q4: Bracknell Town (H) 2-1 R1: Wolverhampton Wanderers (A) 1-5
88-89	Q1: Radstock Town (A) 2-0 Q2: Gloucester City (A) 0-3
89-90	Q1: Saltash United (H) 1-0 Q2: Weston-super-Mare (H) 7-0 Q3: Dorchester Town (A) 1-2
90-91	Q1: Exmouth Town (H) 2-2, (A) 3-3, (H) 3-0 Q2: Weston-super-Mare (A) 2-0 Q3: Worcester City (H) 4-2 Q4: Dorking (A) 3-2 R1: Birmingham City (A) 0-1
91-92	Q1: Bridgend Town (A) 3-3, (H) 5-0 Q2: Taunton Town (H) 8-0 Q3: Weymouth (A) 0-4
92-93	Q1: Waterlooville (A) 0-0, (H) 2-0 Q2: Cinderford Town (H) 3-0 Q3: A.F.C. Lymington (A) 1-0 Q4: Worthing (H) 3-2 R1: St Albans City (A) 2-1 R2: A.F.C. Bournemouth (H) 1-1, (A) 0-3

Above: *Jubilant scenes in the home dressing room at Whaddon Road after Cheltenham Town had snatched a late equaliser to take Second Division Bournemouth to a replay in 1992. Photo: Eric Marsh.*

CHERTSEY TOWN

Currently: Isthmian League

50-51	EX: Wimbledon (H) 1-3
64-65	Q1: Walton & Hersham (A) 1-4
65-66	Q1: Leatherhead (A) 3-3, (H) 2-5
66-67	Q1: Walthamstow Avenue (H) 0-3
69-70	PR: Wolverton Town & B.R. (H) 0-2
70-71	Q1: Walton & Hersham (A) 0-5
71-72	Q1: Braintree & Crittall Ath. (A) 1-2
75-76	PR: Gravesend & Northfleet (A) 1-1, (H) 0-2
76-77	Q1: Barking (A) 1-6
77-78	Q1: Burnham (A) 1-0 Q2: Ilford (H) 1-1, (A) 1-6
78-79	Q1: Carshalton Athletic (A) 0-3
79-80	Q1: Hillingdon Borough (H) 0-1
80-81	PR: Dunstable (H) 2-1 Q1: Walton & Hersham (A) 0-1
81-82	PR: Lewes (H) 2-5
82-83	PR: Bromley (H) 1-12
83-84	PR: Peacehaven & Telscombe (H) 0-5
84-85	PR: Lancing (H) 0-0, (A) 0-1
85-86	PR: Hampton (A) 0-2
86-87	PR: Tring Town (A) 3-1 Q1: Leytonstone-Ilf. (H) 1-1, (A - *at Leyton-Wingate*) 1-0 Q2: Hendon (H) 0-1
87-88	Q1: Haywards Heath (H) 3-1 Q2: Newport I.O.W. (H) 0-1
88-89	Q1: Feltham (H) 0-0, (A) 0-1
89-90	PR: Arundel (H) 3-1 Q1: Eastleigh (H) 4-0 Q2: Basingstoke Town (A) 1-3
90-91	PR: Walton & Hersham (H) 0-3
91-92	PR: Worthing (H) 2-2, (A) 1-4
92-93	Q1: Gravesend & Northfleet (H) 3-2 Q2: Margate (A) 4-1 Q3: Kingstonian (H) 1-3

CHESHAM UNITED

Currently: Isthmian League

45-46	EX: Aylesbury United (A) 0-5
46-47	EX: Metal & Prod. Rec. Depot (A) 1-1, (H) 5-0 PR: Uxbridge (A) 2-7
47-48	EX: Wallingford Town (A) 2-4
48-49	EX: Hemel Hempstead Town (H) 6-2 PR: Maidenhead United (H) 1-4
49-50	EX: Dickinson (Apsley) (H) 3-0 PR: Uxbridge (A) 0-2
50-51	EX: Witney Town (H) 4-2 PR: Abingdon Town (H) 5-0 Q1: Wycombe Wanderers (H) 1-1, (A) 2-4
51-52	PR: Witney Town (A) 3-1 Q1: Headington United (A) 2-5
52-53	PR: Aylesbury United (A) 1-4
53-54	PR: Huntley & Palmers Recreation (H) 3-1 Q1: Marlow (H) 2-0 Q2: Banbury Spencer (H) 1-0 Q3: Headington United (A) 0-2
54-55	Q1: Banbury Spencer (H) 1-0 Q2: Maidenhead United (H) 5-5, (A) 3-5
55-56	PR: Windsor & Eton (A) 2-2, (H) 2-0 Q1: Oxford City (A) 1-2
57-58	Q1: Abingdon Town (H) 5-1 Q2: Marlow (H) 2-2, (A) 1-5
58-59	PR: Huntley & Palmers (H) 3-0 Q1: Oxford City (A) 2-5
59-60	Q1: Wokingham Town (A) 1-4
60-61	Q1: Aylesbury United (H) 5-1 Q2: Wokingham Town (H) 1-1, (A) 2-1 Q3: Abingdon Town (H) 1-2
61-62	Q1: Banbury Spencer (H) 1-4
62-63	Q1: Hemel Hempstead Town (A) 2-3
63-64	Q1: Oxford City (A) 0-5
64-65	Q1: Aylesbury United (H) 5-0 Q2: Hemel Hempstead Town (H) 1-1, (A) 2-3
65-66	Q1: Banbury Spencer (A) 0-2
66-67	Q1: Wembley (H) 1-0 Q2: Southall (H) 4-3 Q3: Hemel Hempstead Town (A) 3-2 Q4: Leatherhead (A) 2-1 R1: Enfield (A) 0-6
67-68	Q1: Leytonstone (H) 0-3

68-69 R1: Colchester United (A) 0-5

69-70 Q1: Hitchin Town (A) 0-5

70-71 Q1: Cheshunt (H) 0-1

71-72 Q1: Carshalton Athletic (A) 1-2

72-73 Q1: Witney Town (H) 0-1

73-74 Q1: Wealdstone (H) 1-1, (A) 4-2
Q2: Hertford Town (A) 0-2

74-75 Q1: Vauxhall Motors (H) 1-0
Q2: Oxford City (H) 4-1
Q3: Wycombe Wanderers (H) 1-3

75-76 Q1: Epping Town (H) 3-0
Q2: Hornchurch (H) 2-0
Q3: Sutton United (A) 1-3

76-77 Q1: Tring Town (A) 3-0
Q2: Thame United (A) 1-0
Q3: Banbury United (A) 4-1
Q4: Worcester City (H) 4-2
R1: Brentford (A) 0-2

Below: *When Chesham visited Brentford in 1976, Stuart Atkins (left), seen giving a Bees defender the slip, had three good chances of scoring, but the luck was not with him. Photo: Bucks Examiner.*

77-78 Q1: Willesden (H) 5-0
Q2: Finchley (A) 2-2, (H) 0-0, (*at Hendon*) 2-3

78-79 PR: Berkhamsted Town (H) 3-3, (A) 0-1

79-80 Q1: Boreham Wood (H) 2-0
Q2: Haverhill Rovers (A) 0-0, (H) 3-0
Q3: Bedford Town (H) 0-0, (A) 1-0
Q4: Maidstone United (H) 3-1
R1: Minehead (A) 2-1
R2: Merthyr Tydfil (H) 1-1, (A) 3-1
R3: Cambridge United (H) 0-2

80-81 Q1: St Albans City (H) 0-1

81-82 Q1: Irthlingborough Diamonds (A) 0-1

82-83 Q1: Cray Wanderers (H) 3-2
Q2: Clapton (H) 3-1
Q3: Feltham (H) 1-0
Q4: Chelmsford City (A) 3-1
R1: Yeovil Town (H) 0-1

83-84 Q1: Tilbury (A) 1-0
Q2: Wembley (A) 0-0, (H) 3-2
Q3: Hitchin Town (H) 0-2

84-85 Q1: Leyton-Wingate (A) 2-2, (H) 1-0
Q2: Heybridge Swifts (A) 0-0, (H) 1-2

85-86 PR: Barton Rovers (A) 1-2

86-87 PR: Metropolitan Police (H) 1-8

87-88 PR: Gorleston (A) 0-1

88-89 PR: Hornchurch (H) 1-1, (A) 6-5
Q1: Hayes (A) 0-1

89-90 PR: Aveley (A) 0-0, (H) 0-1

90-91 PR: Baldock Town (H) 4-1
Q1: Hertford Town (H) 0-0, (A) 5-1
Q2: Enfield (H) 0-3

91-92 Q1: Wolverton (H) 2-0
Q2: Wealdstone (A - *at Watford F.C.*) 4-2
Q3: Brimsdown Rovers (A) 2-2, (H) 2-1
Q4: Aylesbury United (A) 1-1, (H) 1-3

92-93 Q1: Boreham Wood (A) 2-2, (H) 9-1
Q2: Molesey (A) 4-0
Q3: Berkhamsted Town (H) 3-0
Q4: Solihull Borough (A) 1-3

CHESHUNT

Currently: Isthmian League

50-51 EX: Hoddesdon Town (H) 4-2
PR: Ware (H) 2-1
Q1: Hayes (A) 1-7

51-52 Q1: Leyton (H) 1-2

52-53 Q1: Tufnell Park Edmonton (H) 2-1
Q2: Eton Manor (H) 0-1

53-54 Q1: Stevenage Town (A) 1-6

57-58 PR: Enfield (A) 0-3

58-59 PR: Bishop's Stortford (H) 3-2
Q1: Hoddesdon Town (H) 4-0
Q2: St Albans (A) 2-1 *ab. 45 mins*, (A) 3-2
Q3: Enfield (H) 3-1
Q4: King's Lynn (H) 0-6

59-60 Q1: Hertford Town (A) 0-7

60-61 Q1: Bishop's Stortford (H) 0-2

64-65 Q1: Vauxhall Motors (A) 2-0
Q2: Bletchley Town Utd (H) 1-1, (A) 0-1

65-66 Q1: Ware (A) 1-3

66-67 Q1: Ford United (A) 1-0
Q2: Rainham Town (H) 5-2
Q3: Hertford Town (A) 0-0, (H) 1-0
Q4: Wycombe Wanderers (A) 0-8

67-68 Q1: Erith & Belvedere (H) 4-4, (A) 3-4

68-69 Q1: Hitchin Town (A) 1-3

69-70 Q1: Amersham Town (H) 3-0
Q2: Hitchin Town (A) 1-3

70-71 Q1: Chesham United (A) 1-0
Q2: Stevenage Athletic (H) 3-1
Q3: Guildford City (A) 1-1, (H) 2-0
Q4: Bishop's Stortford (A) 2-5

71-72 Q1: Boreham Wood (A) 1-2

72-73 Q1: Wimbledon (H) 0-4

73-74 Q1: Dagenham (H) 2-2, (A) 2-2, 0-0, 1-2

74-75 PR: Edmonton & Haringey (A) 1-2

75-76 Q1: Hemel Hempstead (H) 2-2, (A) 2-0
Q2: Clapton (A) 2-1
Q3: Romford (A) 0-1

76-77 Q1: Windsor & Eton (A) 2-3

77-78 Q1: Walton & Hersham (H) 3-2
Q2: Clapton (H) 2-1
Q3: Hillingdon Borough (H) 1-0
Q4: Leatherhead (A) 1-4

78-79 PR: Grays Athletic (A) 1-5

79-80 Q1: Barking (H) 1-5

80-81 PR: Clapton (H) 0-1

81-82 Q1: Lewes (H) 2-2, (A) 3-3, (H) 0-2

82-83 PR: Barton Rovers (A) 0-2

83-84 PR: Stowmarket Town (A) 0-1

84-85 PR: Arlesey Town (A) 2-2, (H) 0-1

85-86 PR: Barking (A) 1-4

86-87 PR: Rainham Town (H) 1-2

88-89 Q1: Letchworth Garden City (A) 2-1
Q2: Staines Town (H) 1-2

89-90 PR: Wootton Blue Cross (A) 2-0
Q1: Ware (A) 0-2

90-91 PR: Newmarket Town (A) 1-2

91-92 PR: Tilbury (H) 0-3

92-93 PR: Spalding United (H) 0-0, (A) 5-0
Q1: Chalfont St Peter (H) 1-0
Q2: Solihull Borough (H) 0-0, (A) 0-4

CHESTER CITY

Currently: Football League
* - As Chester F.C.

45-46 * R3: Liverpool (H) 0-2, (A) 1-2 (*agg: 1-4*)

46-47 * R3: Plymouth Argyle (H) 2-0
R4: Stoke City (H) 0-0, (A) 2-3

47-48 * R1: Bishop Auckland (H) 3-1
R2: Tranmere Rovers (A) 1-0
R3: Crystal Palace (A) 1-0
R4: Blackpool (A) 0-4

48-49 * R1: Hartlepools United (A) 3-1
R2: Aldershot (A) 0-1

49-50 * R1: Goole Town (H) 4-1
R2: Exeter City (A) 0-2

50-51 * R1: Bradford (Park Avenue) (H) 1-2

51-52 * R1: Accrington Stanley (A) 2-1
R2: Leyton (H) 5-2
R3: Chelsea (A) 2-2, (H) 2-3

52-53 * R1: Hartlepools United (H) 0-1

53-54 * R1: Stockport County (A) 2-4

54-55 * R1: Gateshead (A) 0-6

55-56 * R1: Chesterfield (A) 0-1

56-57 * R1: Barrow (H) 0-0, (A) 1-3

57-58 * R1: Gateshead (H) 4-3
R2: Bradford City (H) 3-3, (A) 1-3

58-59 * R1: Boston United (H) 3-2
R2: Bury (H) 1-1, (A) 1-2

59-60 * R1: Tranmere Rovers (A) 1-0
R2: Mansfield Town (A) 0-2

60-61 * R1: Carlisle United (H) 0-1

61-62 * R1: Ashington (H) 4-1
R2: Morecambe (H) 0-1

62-63 * R1: Tranmere Rovers (H) 0-2

63-64 * R1: Blyth Spartans (H) 3-2
R2: Barrow (H) 0-2

64-65 * R1: Crewe Alexandra (H) 5-0
R2: Barnsley (A) 5-2
R3: Manchester United (A) 1-2

65-66 * R1: Chesterfield (A) 2-0
R2: Wigan Athletic (H) 2-1
R3: Newcastle United (H) 1-3

66-67 * R1: Middlesbrough (H) 2-5

67-68 * R1: Port Vale (A) 2-1
R2: Chesterfield (H) 0-1

68-69 * R1: Bradford City (A) 2-1
R2: Lincoln City (H) 1-1, (A) 1-2

69-70 * R1: Halifax Town (A) 3-3, (H) 1-0
R2: Doncaster Rovers (H) 1-1, (A) 2-0
R3: Bristol City (H) 2-1
R4: Swindon Town (A) 2-4

70-71 * R1: Preston North End (A) 1-1, (H) 1-0
R2: Crewe Alexandra (H) 1-0
R3: Derby County (H) 1-2

71-72 * R1: Mansfield Town (H) 1-1, (A) 3-4

72-73 * R1: Bolton Wanderers (A) 1-1, (H) 0-1

73-74 * R1: Telford United (H) 1-0
R2: Huddersfield Town (H) 3-2
R3: Aston Villa (A) 1-3

74-75 * R1: Rotherham United (A) 0-1

75-76 * R1: Darlington (A) 0-0, (H) 2-0
R2: Shrewsbury Town (A) 1-3

76-77 * R1: Hartlepool United (H) 1-0
R2: Grimsby Town (A) 1-0
R3: Southend United (A) 4-0
R4: Luton Town (H) 1-0
R5: Wolverhampton Wanderers (A) 0-1

77-78 * R1: Darlington (H) 4-1
R2: Carlisle United (A) 1-3

78-79 * R1: Runcorn (H) 1-1, (A) 5-0
R2: Darlington (A) 1-2

79-80 * R1: Workington (H) 5-1
R2: Barnsley (H) 1-0
R3: Newcastle United (A) 2-0
R4: Millwall (H) 2-0
R5: Ipswich Town (A) 1-2

80-81 * R1: Barnsley (H) 1-2

81-82 * R1: Penrith (A) 0-1

82-83 * R1: Northwich Victoria (H) 1-1, (A) 1-3

83-84 R1: Chesterfield (H) 1-2

84-85 R1: Darlington (A) 2-3

85-86 R1: Bury (A) 0-2

86-87 R1: Rotherham Utd (H) 1-1, (A) 1-1, (H) 1-0
R2: Doncaster Rovers (H) 3-1
R3: Wrexham (A) 2-1
R4: Sheffield Wednesday (H) 1-1, (A) 1-3

87-88 R1: Runcorn (H) 0-1

88-89 R1: Burnley (A) 2-0
R2: Huddersfield Town (A) 0-1

89-90 R1: Macclesfield Town (A) 1-1, (H) 3-2
R2: Blackpool (A) 0-3

90-91 R1: Doncaster (H - *at Mac'field*) 2-2, (A) 2-1
R2: Leek Town (A) 1-1, (H - *at Mac'field*) 4-0
R3: A.F.C. Bournemouth (H - *at Mac'field*) 2-3

91-92 R1: Guiseley (H - *at Macclesfield*) 1-0
R2: Crewe Alexandra (A) 0-2

92-93 R1: Altrincham (H) 1-1, (A) 0-2

CHESTERFIELD

Currently: Football League

45-46 R3: York City (H) 1-1, (A) 2-3 (*agg: 3-4*)

46-47 R3: Sunderland (H) 2-1
R4: Middlesbrough (A) 1-2

47-48 R3: Derby County (A) 0-2

48-49 R3: Wolverhampton Wanderers (A) 0-6

49-50 R3: Yeovil Town (H) 3-1
R4: Middlesbrough (H) 3-2
R5: Chelsea (H) 1-1, (A) 0-3

50-51 R3: Brighton & Hove Albion (A) 1-2

51-52 R1: Barrow (A) 2-0
R2: Norwich City (A) 1-3

52-53 R1: Workington (H) 1-0
R2: Shrewsbury Town (A) 0-0, (H) 2-4

53-54 R1: Gainsborough Trinity (A) 4-1
R2: Southend United (A) 2-1
R3: Bury (H) 2-0
R4: Sheffield Wednesday (A) 0-0, (H) 2-4

54-55 R1: Hartlepools United (A) 0-1

55-56 R1: Chester (H) 1-0
R2: Hartlepools United (H) 1-2

56-57 R1: South Shields (A) 2-2, (H) 4-0
R2: Barrow (H) 4-1
R3: Burnley (A) 0-7

57-58 R1: York City (A) 0-1

58-59 R1: Rhyl (H) 3-0
R2: Carlisle United (A) 0-0, (H) 1-0
R3: Colchester United (A) 0-2

59-60 R1: South Shields (A) 1-2

60-61 R1: Doncaster Rovers (H) 3-3, (A) 1-0
R2: Oldham Athletic (H) 4-4, (A) 3-0
R3: Blackburn Rovers (H) 0-0, (A) 0-3

61-62 R1: Doncaster Rovers (A) 4-0
R2: Oldham Athletic (H) 2-2, (A) 2-4

62-63 R1: Stockport County (H) 4-1
R2: Barnsley (A) 1-2

63-64 R1: Crook Town (A) 2-1
R2: Netherfield (A) 1-1, (H) 4-1
R3: Oxford United (A) 0-1

64-65 R1: South Shields (H) 2-0
R2: York City (H) 2-1
R3: Peterborough United (H) 0-3

65-66 R1: Chester (H) 0-2

66-67 R1: Wrexham (A) 2-3

67-68 R1: Barnsley (H) 2-0
R2: Chester (A) 1-0
R3: Blackpool (A) 1-2

68-69 R1: Skelmersdale United (H) 2-0
R2: Wrexham (H) 2-1
R3: Portsmouth (A) 0-3

69-70 R1: Tranmere Rovers (A) 0-3

70-71 R1: Halifax Town (H) 2-0
R2: Workington (H) 0-0, (A) 2-3

71-72 R1: Oldham Athletic (H) 3-0
R2: Barnsley (A) 0-0, (H) 1-0
R3: Stoke City (A) 1-2

72-73 R1: Rhyl (H) 4-2
R2: Grimsby Town (A) 2-2, (H) 0-1

73-74 R1: Barnsley (H) 0-0, (A) 1-2

74-75 R1: Boston United (H) 3-1
R2: Doncaster Rovers (H) 1-0
R3: Sunderland (A) 0-2

75-76 R1: Bradford City (A) 0-1

76-77 R1: Scunthorpe United (A) 2-1
R2: Walsall (H) 1-1, (A) 0-0, (*at Derby*) 0-1

77-78 R1: Halifax Town (H) 1-0
R2: Blyth Spartans (A) 0-1

78-79 R1: Darlington (A) 1-1, (H) 0-1

79-80 R1: Grimsby Town (A) 1-1, (H) 2-3

80-81 R1: Wigan Athletic (A) 2-2, (H) 2-0
R2: Sheffield United (A) 1-1, (H) 1-0
R3: Peterborough United (A) 1-1, (H) 1-2

81-82 R1: Preston North End (H) 4-1
R2: Huddersfield Town (H) 0-1

82-83 R1: Peterborough United (H) 2-2, (A) 1-3

83-84 R1: Chester City (A) 2-1
R2: Burnley (H) 2-2, (A) 2-3

84-85 R1: Whitby Town (A) 3-1
R2: Walsall (A) 0-1

85-86 R1: Tranmere Rovers (A) 2-2, (H) 0-1

86-87 R1: Walsall (A) 0-2

87-88 R1: Notts County (A) 3-3, (H) 0-1

88-89 R1: Bolton Wanderers (A) 0-0, (H) 2-3

89-90 R1: Shrewsbury Town (A) 3-2
R2: Huddersfield Town (H) 0-2

90-91 R1: Spennymoor United (H) 3-2
R2: Bolton Wanderers (H) 3-4

91-92 R1: Darlington (A) 1-2

92-93 R1: Macclesfield (A) 0-0, (H) 2-2 (*2-3 pens*)

CHESTER-LE-STREET TOWN

Currently: Northern League
* - As Chester-le-Street F.C.

81-82 * PR: West Auckland Town (H) 1-0
Q1: Ferryhill Athletic (A) 2-2, (H) 2-1
Q2: Spennymoor United (H) 1-1, (A) 0-1

82-83 * PR: Ashington (A) 2-2, (H) 2-1
Q1: Guisborough Town (A) 0-0, (H) 3-0
Q2: Morecambe (H) 1-5

83-84 * PR: Shildon (H) 2-0
Q1: Barrow (A) 1-0
Q2: Horden Colliery Welfare (A) 1-6

84-85 * PR: Lancaster City (H) 3-0
Q1: Bishop Auckland (A) 3-4

85-86 * Q1: Durham City (A) 3-2
Q2: South Bank (A) 0-2

86-87 Q1: Bedlington Terriers (A) 2-1
Q2: Harrogate Town (A) 1-1, (H) 3-1
Q3: Easington Colliery (A) 1-1, (H) 5-3
Q4: Caernarfon Town (H) 2-3

87-88 PR: Ossett Albion (A) 1-1, (H) 2-1
Q1: Consett (H) 2-1
Q2: Billingham Synthonia (H) 1-1, (A) 3-4

88-89 Q1: Gretna (A) 0-5

89-90 PR: Washington (A) 0-0, (H) 2-1
Q1: Bishop Auckland (A) 2-3

90-91 PR: Easington Colliery (H) 0-2

91-92 PR: Alnwick Town (A) 3-4

92-93 PR: Billingham Town (H) 0-1

CHICHESTER CITY

Currently: Sussex County League

47-48 PR: Eastbourne Comrades (H) 5-2
Q1: Worthing (A) 2-3

48-49 PR: Bexhill Town (H) 3-5

49-50 PR: Eastbourne Comrades (H) 2-2, (A) 0-6

51-52 PR: Redhill (A) 0-3

52-53 PR: Hastings United (A) 2-4

54-55 Q1: Cowes Isle of Wight (A) 0-6

55-56 Q1: Winchester City (A) 2-2, (H) 1-3

56-57 Q1: Andover (H) 2-3

57-58 Q1: Andover (A) 3-2
Q2: Gosport Borough Athletic (H) 5-3
Q3: Cowes Isle of Wight (A) 1-3

58-59 Q1: Cowes Isle of Wight (A) 4-5

60-61 Q2: Cowes I.O.W. (H) 6-3
Q3: Andover (H) 2-1
Q4: Dorchester Town (H) 4-1
R1: Bristol City (H - *played away*) 0-11

61-62 Q1: Basingstoke Town (A) 0-5

62-63 Q1: Newbury Town (H) 2-3

63-64 Q2: Basingstoke Town (H) 1-2

64-65 Q1: Cowes Isle of Wight (A) 4-5

65-66 Q1: Cowes Isle of Wight (H) 3-5

66-67 Q1: Waterlooville (H) 2-2, (A) 1-4

67-68 Q1: Dorking (H) 2-0
Q2: Basingstoke Town (A) 4-3
Q3: Crawley Town (H) 1-0
Q4: Guildford City (A) 0-0, (H) 0-3

68-69 Q1: Fleet (H) 1-0
Q2: Wokingham Town (A) 0-5

69-70 PR: Woking (A) 0-4

70-71 PR: Horsham (H) 5-2
Q1: Selsey (A) 4-2
Q2: Ringmer (A) 0-4

71-72 Q1: Haywards Heath (H) 3-1
Q2: Arundel (A) 0-0, (H) 1-1, 7-2
Q3: Hastings United (H) 1-1, (A) 1-9

72-73 Q1: Pagham (H) 0-0, (A) 2-1
Q2: Redhill (H) 1-2

73-74 Q1: Gosport Borough (A) 0-8

74-75 Q1: Pagham (A) 3-3, (H) 5-4
Q2: Burgess Hill Town (A) 1-4

75-76 Q1: Littlehampton Town (A) 1-1, (H) 0-2

76-77 Q1: Basingstoke Town (A) 0-10

78-79 Q1: Dorking (H) 1-1, (A) 2-3

79-80 Q1: Horsham Y.M.C.A. (A) 2-4

80-81 PR: Devizes Town (H) 1-1, (A) 3-1
Q1: Newbury Town (A) 0-2

81-82 PR: Poole Town (H) 1-5

82-83 Q1: Maidenhead United (A) 2-4

83-84 Q1: Tonbridge A.F.C. (H) 1-2

84-85 PR: Kingstonian (H) 0-1

85-86 PR: Thanet United (A) 1-3

86-87 PR: Sheppey United (A) 1-2

87-88 Q1: Egham Town (H) 1-1, (A) 2-0
Q2: Bracknell Town (A) 0-4

88-89 PR: Petersfield United (H) 2-1
Q1: Fareham Town (A) 0-3

89-90 PR: Witney Town (A) 1-4

90-91 PR: A.F.C. Lymington (H) 1-5

91-92 PR: Chipstead (H) 0-3

92-93 PR: Whitehawk (A) 2-5 - *extra-time erroneously played, replay:* (H) 1-3

CHILTON ATHLETIC

Currently: Defunct
* - As Chilton & Windlestone Senior Boys

46-47 * PR: Tow Law Town (A) 3-1
Q1: Ferryhill Athletic (A) 1-3

47-48 PR: Shildon (H) 2-3

48-49 PR: Evenwood Town (A) 2-3

49-50 EX: Langley Park C.W. (H) 4-1
PR: South Hetton C.W. (A) 1-5

50-51 EX: West Auckland Town (A) 1-2

51-52 Q1: Eppleton Colliery Welfare (H) 4-2
Q2: Blackhall C.W. (H) 0-0, (A) 0-1

52-53 Q1: Ushaw Moor (A) 0-2

53-54 Q1: Seaham Colliery (A) 2-2, (H) 0-2

54-55 Q1: Wolsingham Welfare (A) 3-7

55-56 Q1: Durham City (A) 2-4

56-57 Q2: Horden Colliery Welfare (A) 0-10

57-58 Q1: Stanley United (A) 1-3

58-59 Q1: Bridlington Central United (A) 3-2
Q2: Stanley United (A) 2-4

CHINGFORD TOWN

Currently: Defunct

48-49 EX: Clapton (A) 1-0
PR: Ilford (A) 3-2
Q1: Leyton (A) 2-3

49-50 EX: Harwich & Parkeston (A) 2-4

50-51 PR: Ilford (H) 1-0
Q1: Crittall Athletic (H) 3-2
Q2: Woodford Town (A) 1-1, (H) 0-4

CHIPPENHAM TOWN

Currently: Western League

45-46 PR: Devizes Town (H) 9-0
Q1: Clandown (A) 1-0
Q2: Trowbridge Town (A) 1-3

46-47 PR: Trowbridge Town (A) 0-6

47-48 EX: Odd Down (H) 4-2
PR: Westbury United (A) 0-3

49-50 EX: Timsbury Athletic (A) 7-0
PR: Devizes Town (A) 4-4, (H) 4-3
Q1: Trowbridge Town (A) 1-3

50-51 PR: Bath City (A) 0-2

51-52 PR: Spencer Moulton (H) 4-0
Q1: Trowbridge Town (A) 2-2, (H) 2-1
Q2: Welton Rovers (H) 5-1
Q3: Salisbury (A) 1-1, (H) 2-1
Q4: Newport Isle of Wight (H) 3-1
R1: Leyton (A) 0-3

52-53 PR: Corsham Town (A) 4-1
Q1: Spencer Moulton (A) 3-0
Q2: Salisbury (A) 1-3

53-54 PR: Calne & Harris United (A) 2-0
Q1: Frome Town (A) 6-2
Q2: Salisbury (H) 4-2
Q3: Trowbridge Town (H) 3-2
Q4: Weymouth (H) 2-4

54-55 PR: Frome Town (A) 2-4

55-56 Q1: Westbury United (A) 1-1, (H) 0-1

56-57 PR: Calne & Harris United (H) 9-2
Q1: Devizes Town (A) 2-0
Q2: Salisbury (A) 2-1
Q3: Trowbridge Town (H) 4-1
Q4: Weymouth (H) 0-0, (A) 1-4

57-58 Q2: Trowbridge Town (H) 1-1, (A) 0-3

58-59 Q1: Devizes Town (A) 6-2
Q2: Westbury United (H) 3-0
Q3: Trowbridge Town (H) 2-2, (A) 0-3

59-60 Q1: Westbury United (A) 1-3

60-61 Q1: Trowbridge Town (A) 1-1, (H) 0-1

61-62 Q2: Trowbridge Town (H) 1-1, (A) 2-0
Q3: Cheltenham Town (A) 0-2

62-63 Q1: Salisbury (A) 2-2, (H) 3-1
Q2: Westbury United (H) 4-1
Q3: Trowbridge Town (H) 0-1

63-64 Q1: Melksham Town (A) 2-0
Q2: Trowbridge Town (A) 1-1, (H) 2-4

64-65 Q1: Trowbridge Town (A) 1-3

65-66 Q1: Melksham Town (H) 5-1
Q2: Cheltenham Town (A) 1-4

66-67 Q1: Westbury United (H) 4-2
Q2: Welton Rovers (H) 0-4

67-68 Q1: Westbury United (A) 0-0, (H) 3-2
Q2: Dorchester Town (A) 1-4

68-69 Q1: Welton Rovers (H) 2-4

69-70 Q1: Westbury United (H) 3-2
Q2: Welton Rovers (A) 2-2, (H) 2-1
Q3: Glastonbury (H) 2-2, (A) 0-7

71-72 PR: Frome Town (H) 1-0
Q1: Bath City (A) 1-2

72-73 Q1: Devizes Town (H) 0-4

73-74 Q1: Melksham Town (A) 2-4

74-75 Q1: Melksham Town (H) 3-0
Q2: Mangotsfield United (H) 0-2

75-76 Q1: Cinderford Town (H) 2-4

76-77 Q1: Devizes Town (H) 1-3

77-78 Q1: Calne Town (A) 1-3

78-79 Q1: Cinderford Town (H) 2-2, (A) 1-2

79-80 Q1: Merthyr Tydfil (H) 0-3

80-81 PR: Calne Town (A) 1-0
Q1: Lye Town (A) 1-1, (H) 0-2

81-82 PR: Hungerford Town (A) 0-4

82-83 Q1: Basingstoke Town (H) 1-1, (A) 2-3

83-84 PR: Romsey Town (A) 1-1, (H) 0-1

84-85 PR: Brockenhurst (A) 3-1
Q1: Sholing Sports (H) 3-0
Q2: Road Sea Southampton (H) 2-2, (A) 2-1
Q3: Slough Town (H) 1-0
Q4: Farnborough Town (A) 1-2

85-86 Q1: Trowbridge Town (A) 3-1
Q2: Sharpness (A) 3-2
Q3: Barry Town (A) 2-2, (H) 0-1

86-87 Q1: Poole Town (H) 3-1
Q2: Wimborne Town (A) 1-1, (H) 0-1

87-88 PR: Ottery St Mary (A) 1-3

88-89 PR: Andover (H) 4-0
Q1: Waterlooville (A) 0-2

89-90 PR: Sharpness (A) 1-1, (H) 1-0
Q1: Weston-super-Mare (H) 1-2

90-91 Q1: A.F.C. Lymington (H) 1-1, (A) 0-1

91-92 PR: Bridgend Town (A) 0-2

92-93 PR: Petersfield United (A) 1-0
Q1: Thatcham Town (H) 1-2

CHIPPENHAM UNITED

Currently: Defunct

48-49 EX: Radstock Town (H) 6-1
PR: Trowbridge Town (H) 1-2

49-50 EX: Frome Town (A) 3-1
PR: Westbury United (A) 2-1
Q1: Clandown (A) 0-3

50-51 PR: Purton (H) 4-1
Q1: Salisbury (A) 1-2

51-52 PR: Weston-super-Mare (H) 4-0
Q1: Street (A) 3-0
Q2: Wells City (A) 5-1
Q3: Bath City (H) 0-3

52-53 Q1: Wells City (H) 2-2, (A) 1-3

53-54 Q1: Bridgwater Town (H) 3-1
Q2: Bristol St George (H) 4-2
Q3: Street (H) 4-1
Q4: Newport Isle of Wight (A) 1-3

54-55 Q1: Peasedown Miners Welfare (A) 1-3

55-56 PR: Clevedon (A) 2-1
Q1: Bath City (A) 1-0
Q2: Street (A) 6-3
Q3: Borough of Weston-super-Mare (H) 3-2
Q4: Salisbury (H) 2-6

56-57 Q1: Street (A) 2-1
Q2: Glastonbury (A) 2-3

57-58 Q1: Wells City (A) 1-2

58-59 Q1: Melksham Town (A) 6-1
Q2: Trowbridge Town (H) 1-2

59-60 Q1: Devizes Town (A) 2-3

60-61 Q2: Melksham Town (A) 5-2
Q3: Trowbridge Town (A) 1-2

61-62 Q1: Cheltenham Town (H) 2-6

CHIPPERFIELD

Currently: Merged with Tudor Corinthians
Playing as Chipperfield Corinthians in Herts Senior Lge

46-47 EX: Hatfield United (A) 3-2
PR: Bishop's Stortford (A) 1-2

47-48 EX: Wood Green Town (A) 4-1
PR: St Albans City (A) 0-1

48-49 EX: Willesden (A) 1-7

CHIPPING NORTON TOWN

Currently: Oxfordshire Senior League

82-83 PR: Highgate United (A) 0-3

83-84 PR: Bourne Town (A) 2-4

CHIPSTEAD

Currently: Combined Counties League

89-90 PR: Barton Rovers (A) 0-0, (H) 2-3

90-91 PR: Littlehampton Town (H) 2-3

91-92 PR: Chichester City (A) 3-0
Q1: Dover Athletic (A) 0-6

92-93 PR: East Thurrock United (A) 0-1

CHORLEY

Currently: Northern Premier League

45-46 Q2: Wigan Athletic (H) 5-2
Q3: Darwen (H) 1-0
Q4: Workington (A) 2-1
R1: Accrington S. (H) 2-1, (A) 0-2 *(agg: 2-3)*

46-47 Q1: Hurst (H) 4-1
Q2: Skelmersdale U. (A) 1-1, (H) 1-1, 0-1

47-48 Q1: Nelson (A) 1-2

48-49 PR: Leyland Motors (A) 0-1

49-50 PR: De Havilland (Bolton) (H) 5-0

Q1: Bacup Borough (H) 3-1
Q2: Rossendale United (H) 2-3

50-51 PR: Darwen (H) 1-2

51-52 PR: Horwich R.M.I. (H) 2-5

52-53 Q1: Horwich R.M.I. (A) 3-5

53-54 Q1: Skelmersdale United (A) 1-1, (H) 0-2

54-55 PR: Ashton United (H) 2-1
Q1: Bacup Borough (A) 2-1
Q2: Nelson (H) 4-2
Q3: Darwen (A) 1-1, (H) 5-4
Q4: Netherfield (H) 1-4

55-56 PR: Darwen (H) 4-0
Q1: Lytham (A) 4-1
Q2: Rossendale United (A) 1-2

56-57 Q1: Nelson (H) 4-1
Q2: Horwich R.M.I. (A) 0-3

57-58 Q1: Nelson (H) 5-1
Q2: Mossley (A) 4-1
Q3: Ashton United (A) 3-2
Q4: Wigan Athletic (H) 1-2

58-59 PR: Mossley (H) 1-0
Q1: Horwich R.M.I. (H) 2-1
Q2: Darwen (A) 1-1, (H) 3-0
Q3: Skelmersdale United (A) 2-2, (H) 3-0
Q4: Morecambe (A) 0-2

59-60 Q1: Mossley (A) 1-2

60-61 Q1: Mossley (A) 1-0
Q2: Hyde United (A) 1-1, (H) 3-1
Q3: Nelson (A) 4-7

61-62 Q1: Hyde United (A) 0-3

62-63 Q1: Lytham St Annes (H) 10-2
Q2: Hyde United (H) 2-2, (A) 0-3

63-64 Q1: Stalybridge Celtic (H) 2-1
Q2: Nelson (H) 6-1
Q3: Hyde United (H) 2-0
Q4: Morecambe (A) 4-3
R1: Rochdale (A) 1-2

64-65 Q1: Stalybridge Celtic (A) 1-5

65-66 Q1: Nelson (H) 6-0
Q2: Rossendale United (H) 1-1, (A) 3-0
Q3: Hyde United (A) 1-1, (H) 4-1
Q4: Wigan Athletic (A) 0-4

66-67 Q1: Horwich R.M.I. (H) 1-0
Q2: Bacup Borough (H) 2-0
Q3: Lancaster City (H) 3-0
Q4: Bangor City (H) 3-3, (A) 3-4

67-68 Q1: St Helens Town (H) 1-1, (A) 3-0
Q2: Ellesmere Port Town (H) 2-2, (A) 2-3

68-69 Q1: St Helens Town (A) 0-0, (H) 0-1

69-70 Q1: Wigan Athletic (A) 1-1, (H) 2-5

70-71 PR: New Mills (A) 2-0
Q1: Witton Albion (A) 1-4

71-72 Q1: Marine (H) 3-0
Q2: Burscough (A) 1-2

72-73 PR: Ormskirk (A) 3-3, (H) 1-0
Q1: Formby (H) 2-1
Q2: Burscough (A) 1-1, (H) 1-2

73-74 Q1: Penrith (A) 1-0
Q2: Fleetwood (H) 0-0, (A) 1-1, 3-2
Q3: Netherfield (H) 0-1

74-75 Q1: Prestwich Heys (A) 0-0, (H) 6-1
Q2: Accrington Stanley (A) 0-2

75-76 Q1: Nantwich Town (H) 1-0
Q2: Skelmersdale United (H) 3-1
Q3: Winsford United (A) 0-2

76-77 Q1: Mossley (A) 2-5

77-78 Q1: Clitheroe (H) 5-1
Q2: Horwich R.M.I. (H) 1-0
Q3: Burscough (A) 0-3

78-79 Q1: Darwen (H) 3-0
Q2: Barrow (H) 2-1
Q3: Fleetwood Town (A) 1-0
Q4: Yorkshire Amateur (H) 4-2
R1: Scarborough (H) 0-1

79-80 Q1: Burscough (A) 1-6

80-81 PR: Caernarvon Town (A) 2-0
Q1: Skelmersdale United (A) 1-0
Q2: Bootle (A) 1-0
Q3: Marine (A) 0-3

81-82 Q1: Accrington S. (H) 0-0, (A) 0-0, (H) 2-0
Q2: Penrith (H) 0-1

82-83 PR: Formby (H) 5-0
Q1: Rossendale United (A) 3-0
Q2: Darwen (H) 0-0, (A) 3-0
Q3: Runcorn (H) 2-2, (A) 0-4

83-84 Q1: Burscough (H) 2-0
Q2: Bangor City (H) 2-4

84-85 Q1: Blakenall (H) 5-1
Q2: Bilston Town (A) 1-0
Q3: Formby (A) 2-3

85-86 Q1: Bootle (A) 1-0
Q2: Emley (A) 4-1
Q3: Southport (A) 3-1
Q4: Marine (H) 4-2
R1: Altrincham (H) 0-2

86-87 Q1: Horwich R.M.I. (H) 2-1
Q2: Penrith (A) 2-1
Q3: Armthorpe Welfare (A) 2-0
Q4: Bishop Auckland (H) 3-2
R1: Wolverhampton W. (H - *at Bolton*) 1-1, (A) 1-1, (H - *at Bolton*) 3-0
R2: Preston (H - *at Blackburn*) 0-0, (A) 0-5

87-88 Q4: Frickley Athletic (H) 2-0
R1: Hartlepool United (H) 0-2

88-89 Q4: Frickley Athletic (A) 1-1, (H) 0-1

89-90 Q4: Marine (H) 1-1, (A) 0-0, (A) 0-3

90-91 Q1: Mossley (H) 4-0
Q2: Emley (A) 1-0
Q3: Bootle (H) 6-2
Q4: Harrogate Railway Athletic (H) 3-1
R1: Bury (H) 2-1
R2: Shrewsbury Town (A) 0-1

Below: *Peter King of Chorley (striped shirt) grimaces as he contests a high ball with Emley's Steve Codd as the Magpies head for a 1-0 Second Qualifying Round win on 29th September 1990. Photo: Barry Lockwood.*

91-92 Q4: Emley (H) 2-2, (A) 1-1 *ab. (fog) 90 mins*, (H) 0-1

92-93 Q1: Knowsley United (H) 1-1, (A) 1-2

CHURCHMAN SPORTS (IPSWICH)

Currently: Defunct

49-50 PR: Whitton United (H - *played away*) 0-3

50-51 EX: Sudbury Town (A) 0-4

CINDERFORD TOWN

Currently: Hellenic League

48-49 EX: Gloucester City (A) 0-4

50-51 PR: St Philips Marsh Adult School (H) 2-1
Q1: Barry Town (H) 0-2

51-52 Q1: Ebbw Vale (H) 1-5

52-53 Q1: Cheltenham Town (H) 1-1, (A) 0-5

53-54 PR: Lovells Athletic (A) 3-1
Q1: Gloucester City (A) 1-2

54-55 Q1: Gloucester City (H) 0-3

55-56 Q1: Llanelly (A) 0-5

56-57 Q1: Stonehouse (A) 4-1
Q2: Llanelly (A) 0-3

57-58 Q1: Gloucester City (H) 2-1
Q2: Barry Town (A) 0-3

58-59 Q1: Gloucester City (A) 2-3

59-60 Q1: Merthyr Tydfil (H) 1-1, (A) 0-2

64-65 Q1: Merthyr Tydfil (A) 1-4

65-66 Q1: Merthyr Tydfil (H) 1-1, (A) 0-4

66-67 Q1: Llanelly (H) 2-0
Q2: Gloucester City (H) 2-2, (A) 3-0
Q3: Cheltenham Town (H) 2-3

67-68 Q1: Barry Town (A) 0-1

68-69 Q1: Merthyr Tydfil (A) 4-1
Q2: Llanelly (H) 3-0
Q3: Cheltenham Town (H) 1-3

69-70 Q1: Abergavenny Thursdays (H) 2-3

70-71 Q1: Gloucester City (H) 3-2
Q2: Ton Pentre (H) 0-1

71-72 Q1: Ton Pentre (H) 1-1, (A) 1-3

72-73 PR: Stonehouse (A) 0-4

73-74 Q1: Kidderminster H. (H) 1-1, (A) 3-1
Q2: Stonehouse (A) 2-1
Q3: Banbury United (H) 2-2, (A) 1-4

74-75 PR: Barry (H) 2-2, (A) 2-0 *ab. in E.T.*, (A) 2-0
Q1: Ton Pentre (H) 3-2
Q2: Everwarm (H) 2-1
Q3: Cheltenham Town (A) 2-3

75-76 Q1: Chippenham Town (A) 4-2
Q2: Brierley Hill Alliance (H) 0-1

76-77 Q1: Melksham Town (H) 1-1, (A) 1-0
Q2: Llanelli (A) 2-3

77-78 Q1: Bye
Q2: Bridgend Town (H) 0-4

78-79 Q1: Chippenham Town (A) 2-2, (H) 2-1
Q2: Merthyr Tydfil (H) 0-1

79-80 Q1: Redditch United (H) 1-2

80-81 PR: Forest Green (H) 0-0, (A) 0-0, (H) 1-2

81-82 PR: Llanelli (H) 1-2

82-83 PR: Melksham Town (H) 3-0
Q1: Bridgend Town (A) 1-2

83-84 Q1: Merthyr Tydfil (H) 1-2

84-85 PR: Forest Green Rovers (H) 1-2

92-93 PR: Newbury Town (H) 3-0
Q1: Swanage Town & Herston (A) 2-1
Q2: Cheltenham Town (A) 0-3

CINDERHILL COLLIERY

Currently: Defunct

49-50 EX: Heanor Athletic (H) 0-7

51-52 PR: Bestwood Colliery (A) 1-1, (H) 4-0
Q1: Shirebrook (A) 1-5

52-53 Q1: Ransome & Marles (A) 0-1

53-54 Q1: Bestwood Colliery (A) 1-3

54-55 Q1: Shirebrook Miners Welfare (A) 0-5

CITY OF NORWICH SCHOOL OLD BOYS UNION

Currently: Anglian Combination

48-49 PR: Stowmarket Corinthians (A) 0-8

49-50 PR: Felixstowe Utd (H - *played away*) 5-0
Q1: Stowmarket (H - *pl. away*) 3-3, (A) 3-3, 0-3

50-51 EX: Wymondham Town (A) 5-1
Q1: Great Yarmouth Town (A) 2-3

CIVIL SERVICE

Currently: Southern Amateur League

47-48 EX: Harlow Town (H) 2-0
PR: Finchley (A) 2-3

48-49 EX: Enfield (H - *played away*) 0-8

49-50 PR: Hatfield United (H) 0-3

50-51 PR: Hatfield Town (A) 2-1
Q1: Enfield (H) 2-5

71-72 Q1: Bromley (H - *played away*) 0-10

CLACTON TOWN

Currently: Eastern Counties League

46-47 PR: Tilbury (A) 0-3

48-49 EX: Briggs Sports (H) 1-0
PR: Harwich & Parkeston (A) 2-2, (H) 2-3

49-50 EX: Eton Manor (A) 1-2

50-51 PR: Briggs Sports (A) 0-2

51-52 Q1: Briggs Sports (H) 0-1

52-53 Q1: Romford (H) 1-1, (A) 3-1
Q2: Tilbury (H) 6-2
Q3: Grays Athletic (A) 1-2

53-54 PR: Briggs Sports (A) 3-4

54-55 PR: Chelmsford City (A) 0-2

55-56 PR: Rainham Town (A) 3-1
Q1: Woodford Town (H) 3-0
Q2: Leyton (A) 0-4

56-57 PR: Harwich & Parkeston (H) 0-0, (A) 0-2
Q1: Leytonstone (H) 1-1, (A) 1-0
Q2: Brentwood & Warley (A) 1-0
Q3: Chelmsford City (A) 2-2, (H) 0-0, 2-1
Q4: Yiewsley (H) 2-3

57-58 PR: Romford (A) 1-1, (H) 2-2, 4-2
Q1: Chelmsford City (A) 0-4

58-59 PR: Harwich & Parkeston (H) 0-1

59-60 Q1: Newmarket Town (A) 4-1
Q2: Bury Town (A) 5-6

60-61 Q1: Harwich & Parkeston (A) 4-0
Q2: Lowestoft Town (H) 6-2
Q3: Bungay Town (A) 1-0
Q4: Cambridge United (H) 2-1
R1: Southend United (H) 1-3

61-62 Q1: Bungay Town (A) 2-0
Q2: Harwich & Parkeston (H) 3-4

62-63 Q1: Lowestoft Town (A) 2-4

63-64 Q1: Harwich & Parkeston (A) 2-5

64-65 Q1: Gorleston (H) 9-1
Q2: Sudbury Town (H) 0-0, (A) 2-4

65-66 Q1: Harwich & Parkeston (A) 2-2, (H) 0-5

66-67 Q1: Harwich & Parkeston (A) 2-4

67-68 Q1: Gothic (H) 3-2
Q2: Bury Town (A) 2-3

68-69 Q1: Thetford Town (H) 4-2
Q2: Gorleston (H) 2-3

69-70 Q1: Thetford Town (H) 2-1
Q2: Bury Town (A) 1-3

70-71 Q1: Bury Town (A) 2-0
Q2: Thetford Town (H) 2-0
Q3: Lowestoft Town (A) 1-2

71-72 Q1: Bury Town (A) 0-2

72-73 Q1: Bury Town (H) 1-4

73-74 Q1: Lowestoft Town (H) 2-1
Q2: King's Lynn (A) 1-3

74-75 Q1: Harwich & Parkeston (H) 1-0
Q2: Lowestoft Town (H) 3-0
Q3: Sudbury Town (H) 2-1
Q4: Romford (H) 1-2

75-76 PR: Harlow Town (A) 3-2
Q1: Ruislip Manor (A) 2-0
Q2: Romford (H) 1-1, (A) 2-3

76-77 Q1: Bury Town (A - *played home*) 1-2

77-78 PR: Wisbech Town (A) 0-5

78-79 Q1: Ely City (H) 0-4

79-80 Q1: Bury Town (H) 0-2

80-81 Q1: Chelmsford City (A) 0-0, (H) 1-2

81-82 Q1: Ware (H) 1-0
Q2: Ely City (A) 1-2

88-89 PR: Wivenhoe Town (A) 0-3

89-90 PR: Witham Town (A) 1-2

90-91 PR: Hertford Town (H) 0-1

91-92 Q1: Billericay (H) 1-2

CLANDOWN

Currently: Somerset Senior League

45-46 Q1: Chippenham Town (H) 0-1

46-47 PR: Purton (H) 8-3
Q1: Hoffman Ath. (Stonehouse) (A) 1-2

47-48 EX: Warminster Town (A) 4-3
PR: Peasedown Miners Welfare (A) 3-2
Q1: Paulton R. (A) 3-4 - *replay ordered after protest over size of pitch,* (H) 4-1
Q2: Trowbridge Town (A) 3-4

48-49 PR: Coleford Athletic (A) 4-1
Q1: Welton Rovers (H) 2-1
Q2: Westbury United (H) 0-0, (A) 1-2

49-50 PR: Peasedown Miners Welfare (H) 3-1
Q1: Chippenham United (H) 3-0
Q2: Salisbury (H) 6-1
Q3: Trowbridge Town (A) 0-1

50-51 PR: Calne & Harris United (H) 3-0
Q1: Devizes Town (H) 2-0
Q2: Salisbury (A) 2-4

51-52 Q1: Paulton Rovers (H) 3-1
Q2: Bath City (H) 1-3

52-53 PR: Glastonbury (H) 0-4

53-54 PR: Wells City (H) 1-0
Q1: Glastonbury (H) 2-4

54-55 Q1: Street (H) 2-0
Q2: Wells City (H) 0-2

55-56 PR: Bath City (H) 0-0, (A) 0-4

56-57 Q1: Bath City (A) 0-2

57-58 Q1: Clevedon (H) 2-4

58-59 Q1: Taunton (H) 1-3

79-80 Q1: Forest Green Rovers (A) 2-3

80-81 Q1: Llanelli (A) 0-2

81-82 PR: Gloucester City (H) 1-3

82-83 PR: St Blazey (A) 1-3

83-84 PR: Brockenhurst (A) 1-1, (H) 3-0
Q1: Trowbridge Town (H) 4-2
Q2: Basingstoke Town (A) 1-1, (H) 0-2

84-85 PR: Haverfordwest County (H) 0-1

85-86 PR: Dorchester T. (A) 0-0, (H) 0-0, (A) 2-1
Q1: Forest Green Rovers (A) 1-0
Q2: Road Sea Southampton (H) 1-2

86-87 PR: Abingdon Town (H) 3-1
Q1: Wimborne Town (A) 2-2, (H) 1-2

87-88 PR: Taunton Town (A) 0-2

88-89 PR: Yate Town (H) 0-2

89-90 Q1: Worcester City (A) 0-3

90-91 PR: Trowbridge Town (A) 1-7

91-92 PR: Ilfracombe Town (H) 0-3

CLAPTON

Currently: Isthmian League

45-46 Q4: Walthamstow Avenue (A) 0-4

46-47 PR: Ford Sports (A) 4-2
Q1: Crittall Athletic (A) 1-3

47-48 EX: Rainham Town (A - *played home*) 2-1
PR: West Thurrock Athletic (A) 1-4

48-49 EX: Chingford Town (H) 0-1

49-50 EX: Brightlingsea United (H) 4-0
PR: Harlow Town (H) 7-1
Q1: Barking (A) 1-4

50-51 PR: Woodford Town (A) 0-4

51-52 PR: Letchworth Town (A) 2-0
Q1: Eton Manor (A) 0-1

52-53 Q1: Finchley (H) 1-2

53-54 PR: Eton Manor (A) 3-4

54-55 PR: Tufnell Park Edmonton (A) 4-0
Q1: St Albans City (H) 1-1, (A) 1-0
Q2: Enfield (H) 2-1
Q3: Barnet (H) 0-1

55-56 PR: Welwyn Garden City (A) 3-0
Q1: St Albans City (H) 0-0, (A) 1-4

57-58 PR: Shefford Town (A) 8-2
Q1: St Albans City (H) 3-1
Q2: Enfield (A) 3-2
Q3: Ware (H) 2-0
Q4: Bury Town (H) 3-2
R1: Queens Park Rangers (H) 1-1, (A) 1-3

58-59 PR: Briggs Sports (A) 2-2, (H) 1-3

59-60 Q1: Hornchurch & Upminster (H) 2-4

60-61 Q1: Leyton (H) 1-0
Q2: Hornchurch & Upminster (A) 1-2

61-62 Q1: Leytonstone (A) 1-1, (H) 1-2

62-63 Q1: Hornchurch (H) 2-3

63-64 Q1: Ford United (A) 3-2
Q2: Hendon (A) 0-8

64-65 Q1: Ford United (A) 1-3

65-66 Q1: Leytonstone (H) 0-5

66-67 Q1: Walton & Hersham (H) 3-2
Q2: Slough Town (H) 0-2

67-68 Q1: Leatherhead (H) 2-1
Q2: Barnet (A) 0-9

68-69 Q1: Malden Town (H) 1-1, (A) 1-2

69-70 Q1: Barking (H) 0-5

70-71 Q1: Feltham (H) 3-0
Q2: Hayes (A) 0-1

71-72 Q1: Bexley United (A) 1-2

72-73 Q1: Aveley (H) 1-2

73-74 Q1: Kingstonian (H) 0-1

75-76 Q1: Finchley (H) 2-0
Q2: Cheshunt (H) 1-2

76-77 Q1: Wealdstone (A) 1-5

77-78 PR: Metropolitan Police (H) 4-1
Q1: Addlestone (A) 1-0
Q2: Cheshunt (A) 1-2

78-79 PR: Barking (H) 1-6

79-80 PR: Basingstoke Town (H) 3-0
Q1: Maidenhead United (A) 0-1

80-81 PR: Cheshunt (A) 1-0
Q1: Walthamstow Avenue (A) 0-5

81-82 PR: Whyteleafe (H) 1-0
Q1: Corinthian-Casuals (A) 3-3, (H) 1-2

82-83 Q1: Chalfont St Peter (H) 3-1
Q2: Chesham United (A) 1-3

83-84 PR: Cray Wanderers (H) 2-3

84-85 PR: Dunstable (H) 0-2

85-86 PR: Leytonstone-Ilford (H) 3-2 - *expelled*

86-87 PR: Yeading (H) 0-1

87-88 Q1: Great Yarmouth Town (H) 1-2

88-89 PR: Merstham (A) 3-3, (H) 2-1
Q1: Leytonstone-Ilford (H) 0-1

89-90 PR: Bury Town (A) 5-0
Q1: Sudbury Town (H) 1-2

90-91 PR: Felixstowe Town (H) 5-2
Q1: Barnet (H - *at Dagenham F.C.*) 0-2

91-92 PR: Arlesey Town (A) 1-0
Q1: Chelmsford City (H) 1-5

92-93 PR: Gorleston (A) 2-5

CLAPTON ORIENT
See Leyton Orient

CLAY CROSS & DANESMOOR
Currently: Defunct

56-57 Q1: South Normanton Welfare (A) 5-3
Q2: Gresley Rovers (H) 3-1
Q3: Ilkeston Town (H) 1-8

57-58 Q1: Belper Town (A) 1-3

58-59 Q1: South Normanton Welfare (H) 2-3

CLEATOR MOOR CELTIC
Currently: Wearside League

46-47 PR: Penrith (A) 5-1
Q1: Parton United (A) 4-2
Q2: Lowca (H) 3-3, (A) 0-5

47-48 PR: Parton United (A) 1-3

48-49 PR: Moss Bay (A) 2-6

49-50 PR: Aspatria Spartans (A) 1-3

50-51 PR: Holmehead Works (H) 1-0
Q1: Penrith (A) 2-1
Q2: Aspatria Spartans (H) 8-3
Q3: Netherfield (H) 2-1
Q4: Workington (A) 1-0
R1: Tranmere Rov. (H - *at Workington*) 0-5

88-89 PR: Bridlington Town (H) 0-0, (A) 1-4

89-90 PR: Thackley (H) 1-1, (A) 3-1
Q1: Barrow (H) 1-4

90-91 PR: Willington (A) 1-0
Q1: Shildon (A) 1-2

91-92 Q1: Gretna (H) 0-7

CLEVEDON
Currently: Merged with Ashtonians
Playing as Clevedon Town in Southern League
See also Clevedon Town

45-46 Q1: Barry Town (A) 0-10

46-47 Q1: Barry Town (A) 1-4

47-48 PR: Merthyr Tydfil (A) 1-2

48-49 EX: Wells Amateur (A) *W/O*
PR: Dartmouth United (A) 3-1
Q1: Gloucester City (A) 2-8

49-50 PR: Hanham Athletic (H) 2-1
Q1: Troedrhiw (H) 2-1
Q2: Gloucester City (A) 0-3

50-51 PR: Douglas (Kingswood) (H) 5-0
Q1: Llanelly (H) 2-2, (A) 1-7

51-52 PR: Bath City (H) 1-3

52-53 PR: Peasedown Miners Welfare (A) 2-6

53-54 PR: Glastonbury (H) 0-1

54-55 PR: Bridgwater Town (H) 0-4

55-56 PR: Chippenham United (H) 1-2

56-57 Q1: Bridgwater Town (A) 0-4

57-58 Q1: Clandown (A) 4-2
Q2: Bath City (H) 1-1, (A) 1-4

58-59 Q1: Glastonbury (A) 0-0, (H) 0-2

CLEVEDON TOWN
Currently: Southern League
See also Clevedon F.C.

76-77 Q1: Weston-super-Mare (H) 1-1, (A) 0-3

77-78 PR: Mangotsfield United (H) 4-0
Q1: Bridgend Town (A) 3-4

78-79 Q1: Cheltenham Town (A) 1-6

79-80 Q1: Mangotsfield United (A) 6-2
Q2: Stourbridge (A) 3-2
Q3: Bridgend Town (H) 0-2

80-81 PR: Chard Town (A) 1-1, (H) 4-1
Q1: Shepton Mallet Town (A) 4-0
Q2: Bideford (A) 1-2

81-82 Q1: Welton Rovers (H) 3-1
Q2: Haverfordwest County (A) 2-3

82-83 Q1: St Blazey (H) 0-2

83-84 PR: Llanelli (A) 0-3

84-85 PR: Welton Rovers (A) 0-0, (H) 1-0
Q1: Waterlooville (H) 3-2
Q2: Glastonbury (A) 2-1
Q3: Witney Town (H) 2-3

85-86 Q1: St Blazey (A) 4-2
Q2: Bath City (A) 0-1

86-87 PR: Paulton Rovers (H) 1-0
Q1: Evesham United (A) 1-1, (H) 2-1
Q2: Mangotsfield United (H) 2-0
Q3: Ton Pentre (H) 0-4

87-88 Q1: Barry Town (A) 1-5

88-89 Q1: Tiverton Town (H) 1-2

89-90 PR: Ilfracombe Town (H) 0-1

90-91 PR: Dawlish Town (H) 3-3, (A) 3-2
Q1: Barry Town (A) 0-0, (H) 0-3

91-92 PR: Gosport Borough (A) 3-1
Q1: Witney Town (H) 2-2, (A) 0-1

92-93 PR: Yate Town (H) 4-1
Q1: Barri (A - *at Worcester City*) 3-1
Q2: Weston-super-Mare (A) 4-0
Q3: Newport A.F.C. (A - *at Gloucester*) 1-1, (H) 1-1, (A - *at Gloucester*) 2-4

CLITHEROE
Currently: North West Counties League

48-49 PR: Great Harwood (H) 5-2
Q1: Horwich R.M.I. (H) 3-1
Q2: Fleetwood (H) 0-3

49-50 PR: Lytham (H) 4-2
Q1: Fleetwood (A) 0-3

50-51 PR: Leyland Motors (H) 1-1, (A) 0-2

51-52 Q1: Netherfield (A) 0-2

52-53 Q1: Fleetwood (H) 1-1, (A) 2-1
Q2: Morecambe (H) 0-1

57-58 Q1: Milnthorpe Corinthians (H) 4-0
Q2: Morecambe (A) 0-1

58-59 Q1: Fleetwood (A) 2-6

59-60 Q1: Fleetwood (A) 2-2, (H) 1-0
Q2: Penrith (H) 6-3
Q3: Burscough (H) 1-2

60-61 Q1: Fleetwood (A) 2-3

61-62 Q1: Morecambe (A) 2-4

62-63 Q1: Lancaster City (H) 4-1
Q2: Netherfield (H) 0-4

63-64 Q1: Netherfield (H) 0-1

64-65 Q1: Morecambe (H) 1-2

65-66 Q1: Lancaster City (H) 2-0
Q2: Morecambe (H) 2-1
Q3: Fleetwood (A) 1-3

66-67 Q1: Lancaster City (A) 1-1, (H) 0-1

68-69 Q1: Great Harwood (H) 0-0, (A) 1-0
Q2: Fleetwood (A) 0-2

69-70 Q1: Fleetwood (H) 1-5

70-71 Q1: Fleetwood (H) 3-1
Q2: Penrith (H) 0-2

71-72 Q1: Ashton United (A) 1-2

72-73 Q1: Great Harwood (A) 1-4

73-74 Q1: Ormskirk (H) 1-4

74-75 PR: Barrow (H) 4-8

75-76 Q1: Lancaster City (H) 1-2

76-77 Q1: Formby (H) 0-0, (A) 1-3

77-78 Q1: Chorley (A) 1-5

78-79 Q1: Curzon Ashton (H) 0-1

79-80 Q1: Droylsden (H) 0-2

80-81 Q1: Curzon Ashton (H) 1-1, (A) 2-2, (H) 0-1

81-82 PR: Netherfield (H) 0-1

82-83 PR: Leyland Motors (H) 0-1

83-84 Q1: South Bank (H) 0-0, (A) 0-0, (H) 1-0
Q2: Bishop Auckland (A) 0-1

84-85 PR: Radcliffe Borough (A) 0-1

85-86 Q1: Southport (A) 2-4

86-87 PR: Fleetwood Town (A) 0-2

87-88 PR: Bridlington Trinity (H) 4-0
Q1: Whitley Bay (H) 2-0
Q2: Harrogate Town (H) 0-0, (A) 1-2

88-89 PR: Lancaster City (H) 2-2, (A) 0-1

89-90 PR: Bedlington Terriers (H) 4-0
Q1: Ferryhill A. (H) 2-2, (A) 1-1, (H) 3-4

90-91 PR: Northallerton Town (A) 2-4

91-92 PR: Langley Park (H) 4-4, (A - *played home*) 1-1, (A - *at Consett*) 0-1

92-93 PR: Immingham Town (H) 2-1
Q1: Hucknall Town (H) 1-3

COALVILLE TOWN
Currently: Defunct
* - As Coalville Town Amateurs

45-46 * Q2: Bye
Q3: Gresley Rovers (A) 7-0
Q4: Kettering Town (A) 1-2

46-47 * Q2: Ibstock Penistone Rovers (H) 14-0
Q3: Brush Sports (A) 3-4

47-48 * Q1: Atherstone Town (H) 1-0
Q2: Gresley Rovers (H) 0-3

48-49 * Q1: Brush Sports (H) 0-4

49-50 PR: Barwell Athletic (A) 0-3

50-51 PR: Brush Sports (H) 2-2, (A) 1-2

51-52 Q1: South Normanton Welfare (A) 0-6

52-53 Q1: Moira United (H) 7-1
Q2: Brush Sports (A) 1-3

53-54 Q1: Brush Sports (A) 0-2

54-55 Q1: Whitwick Colliery (A) 0-14

COBHAM
Currently: Combined Counties League

48-49 EX: Post Office Telecoms (H) 2-2, (A) 6-1
PR: Leatherhead (H - *played away*) 2-6

49-50 PR: Epsom (A) 2-4

50-51 PR: Camberley (A) 0-3

COCKERMOUTH
Currently: Defunct

47-48 EX: Pica (H) 6-1
PR: Netherfield (A) 2-10

48-49 PR: Moresby Welfare Centre (H) 6-3
Q1: Milnethorpe Corinthians (A) 0-11

49-50 PR: Bowthorn United (H) 8-2
Q1: Kells Welfare Centre (H) 1-3

COCKFIELD
Currently: Defunct (reformed in Auckland & Dist. Lge)

48-49 EX: Dawdon Colliery Welfare (A) 1-4

49-50 EX: Silksworth Colliery Welfare (A) 0-1

50-51 EX: Shildon (H) 0-3

54-55 Q1: Ferryhill Athletic (H) 1-1, (A) 1-2

55-56 Q1: Willington (A) 1-3

56-57 Q1: Stanley United (H) 2-3

57-58 Q1: Cramlington Welfare (H) 5-0
Q2: Evenwood Town (H) 2-5

58-59 Q1: Alnwick Town (A) 3-3, (H) 3-2
Q2: Blackhall Colliery Welfare (H) 1-2

COLCHESTER CASUALS
Currently: Defunct

48-49 EX: Dagenham British Legion (A) 2-3

49-50 EX: Saffron Walden Town (A) 3-2
PR: Grays Athletic (H - *played away*) 1-5

COLCHESTER UNITED

Currently: Football League

45-46 Q4: Wisbech Town (A) 0-5

46-47 Q4: Gothic (A - *played home*) 5-1
R1: Reading (A) 0-5

47-48 Q4: Chelmsford City (H) 3-1
R1: Banbury Spencer (H) 2-1
R2: Wrexham (H) 1-0
R3: Huddersfield Town (H) 1-0
R4: Bradford (Park Avenue) (H) 3-2
R5: Blackpool (A) 0-5

48-49 R1: Reading (H) 2-4

49-50 Q4: Wealdstone (A) 0-1

50-51 Q4: Woodford Town (A) 7-1
R1: Bournemouth & Boscombe Ath. (A) 0-1

51-52 R1: Port Vale (H) 3-1
R2: Bristol City (H) 2-1
R3: Barnsley (A) 0-3

52-53 R1: Weymouth (A) 1-1, (H) 4-0
R2: Llanelli (H) 3-2
R3: Rotherham United (A) 2-2, (H) 0-2

53-54 R1: Millwall (H) 1-1, (A) 0-4

54-55 R1: Reading (A) 3-3, (H) 1-2

55-56 R1: Torquay United (A) 0-2

56-57 R1: Southend United (H) 1-4

57-58 R1: Wisbech Town (A) 0-1

58-59 R1: Bath City (H) 2-0
R2: Yeovil Town (H) 1-1, (A) 7-1
R3: Chesterfield (H) 2-0
R4: Arsenal (H) 2-2, (A) 0-4

59-60 R1: Queens Park Rangers (H) 2-3

60-61 R1: Maidenhead United (H) 5-0
R2: Aldershot (A) 1-3

61-62 R1: Peterborough Utd (A) 3-3, (H) 2-2, 0-3

62-63 R1: Wimbledon (A) 1-2

63-64 R1: Brighton & Hove Albion (A) 1-0
R2: Queens Park Rangers (H) 0-1

64-65 R1: Bideford (H) 3-3, (A) 2-1
R2: Torquay United (A) 0-2

65-66 R1: Queens Park Rangers (H) 3-3, (A) 0-4

66-67 R1: Gainsborough Trinity (A) 1-0
R2: Peterborough United (H) 0-3

67-68 R1: Torquay United (A) 1-1, (H) 2-1
R2: Chelmsford City (A) 2-0
R3: West Bromwich Albion (H) 1-1, (A) 0-4

68-69 R1: Chesham United (H) 5-0
R2: Exeter City (H) 0-1

69-70 R1: Newport County (A) 1-2

70-71 R1: Ringmer (H) 3-0
R2: Cambridge United (H) 3-0
R3: Barnet (A) 1-0
R4: Rochdale (A) 3-3, (H) 5-0
R5: Leeds United (H) 3-2
R6: Everton (A) 0-5

71-72 R1: Shrewsbury Town (H) 1-4

72-73 R1: Bognor Regis Town (H) 6-0
R2: A.F.C. Bournemouth (A) 0-0, (H) 0-2

73-74 R1: Peterborough United (H) 2-3

74-75 R1: Watford (A) 1-0
R2: Leatherhead (A) 0-1

75-76 R1: Dover (H) 3-3, (A) 1-4

76-77 R1: Cambridge United (A) 1-1, (H) 2-0
R2: Brentford (H) 0-0 *ab. 62 mins*, (H) 3-2
R3: Kettering Town (A) 3-2
R4: Derby County (H) 1-1, (A) 0-1

77-78 R1: A.F.C. Bournemouth (H) 1-1, (A) 0-0, (*at Watford*) 4-1
R2: Watford (A) 0-2

78-79 R1: Oxford United (H) 4-2
R2: Leatherhead (A) 1-1, (H) 4-0
R3: Darlington (A) 1-0
R4: Newport County (A) 0-0, (H) 1-0
R5: Manchester United (H) 0-1

Above: *Colchester's John Froggatt (right) takes on Colin Todd of Derby in the 1977 tie. Photo: Colorsport.*

79-80 R1: Plymouth Argyle (H) 1-1, (A) 1-0
R2: A.F.C. Bournemouth (H) 1-0
R3: Reading (A) 0-2

80-81 R1: Portsmouth (H) 3-0
R2: Yeovil Town (H) 1-1, (A) 2-0
R3: Watford (H) 0-1

81-82 R1: Newport County (H) 2-0
R2: Brentford (A) 1-1, (H) 1-0
R3: Newcastle United (A) 1-1, (H) 3-4

82-83 R1: Torquay United (H) 0-2

83-84 R1: Torquay United (A) 2-1
R2: Wealdstone (H) 4-0
R3: Charlton Athletic (H) 0-1

84-85 R1: Southend United (A) 2-2, (H) 3-2
R2: Gillingham (H) 0-5

85-86 R1: Wycombe Wanderers (A) 0-2

86-87 R1: Bishop's Stortford (A) 1-1, (H) 2-0
R2: Aldershot (A) 2-3

87-88 R1: Tamworth (H) 3-0
R2: Hereford United (H) 3-2
R3: Plymouth Argyle (A) 0-2

88-89 R1: Fulham (A) 1-0
R2: Swansea City (H) 2-2, (A) 3-1
R3: Shrewsbury Town (A) 3-0
R4: Sheffield United (A) 3-3, (H) 0-2

89-90 R1: Brentford (A) 1-0
R2: Birmingham City (H) 0-2

90-91 R1: Reading (H) 2-1
R2: Leyton Orient (H) 0-0, (A) 1-4

91-92 Q4: Burton Albion (H) 5-0
R1: Exeter C. (H) 0-0, (A) 0-0 (*2-4 pens*)

92-93 R1: Slough Town (H) 4-0
R2: Gillingham (A) 1-1, (H) 2-3

COLEFORD ATHLETIC

Currently: Mid-Somerset League

48-49 EX: Somerton Amateur (A) 4-0
PR: Clandown (H) 1-4

49-50 EX: Swindon Victoria (H) 2-5

COLESHILL TOWN

Currently: Midland Combination

83-84 Q1: Gresley Rovers (H) 1-3

84-85 PR: St Helens Town (A) 1-6

COLLIER ROW

Currently: Isthmian League

86-87 PR: Harwich & Parkeston (A) 0-2

87-88 PR: Chatham Town (A) 1-4

88-89 PR: Rainham Town (H) 0-3

89-90 PR: Corinthian (H) 3-1
Q1: Dulwich Hamlet (H) 1-2

90-91 PR: Braintree Town (A) 0-1

91-92 PR: Saffron Walden Town (H) 2-2, (A) 3-2
Q1: Purfleet (A) 2-2, (H) 0-1

92-93 PR: Tilbury (A) 2-3

COLNE DYNAMOES

Currently: Defunct

90-91 Q1: Easington Colliery (A) *Scratched*

COLWYN BAY

Currently: Northern Premier League

65-66 Q1: Stork (A) 2-0
Q2: Ellesmere Port Town (A) 2-1
Q3: Borough United (A) 1-1, (H) 2-1
Q4: Fleetwood (A) 1-2

66-67 Q1: New Brigton (A) 1-3

79-80 Q1: Nantwich Town (A) 0-2

80-81 Q1: Oswestry Town (A) 1-0
Q2: Marine (H) 2-2, (A) 0-4

81-82 PR: Matlock (H) 3-3, (A) 2-2, (*at Mossley*) 1-4

82-83 Q1: Caernarfon Town (H) 0-3

83-84 PR: Emley (H) 2-3

84-85 PR: Lytham (H) 1-0
Q1: Barrow (A) 0-4

85-86 PR: Leyland Motors (H) 3-1
Q1: St Helens Town (H) 0-3

86-87 PR: Rossendale United (H) 1-1, (A) 2-3

87-88 PR: Winsford United (H) 3-0
Q1: Prescot Cables (A) 1-0
Q2: Buxton (H) 2-2, (A) 5-2
Q3: Alfreton Town (A) 1-1, (H) 1-0
Q4: Tow Law Town (H) 2-1
R1: Northwich Victoria (A) 0-1

88-89 Q1: Ashton United (H) 0-0, (A) 1-2

89-90 PR: Ilkeston Town (H - *at Rhyl*) 5-1
Q1: Morecambe (H - *at Rhyl*) 4-1
Q2: Maine Road (H - *at Rhyl*) 2-1
Q3: Congleton T. (H - *at Rhyl*) 1-1, (A) 0-4

90-91 Q1: Knowsley United (A) 0-0, (H) 3-0
Q2: Caernarfon Town (A) 6-2
Q3: Horwich R.M.I. (A) 3-1
Q4: Whitley Bay (H) 1-4

91-92 Q1: Caernarfon Town (A) 1-1, (H) 2-1
Q2: Rhyl (H) 2-0
Q3: Marine (H) 4-3
Q4: Morecambe (H) 0-2

92-93 Q1: Caernarfon (A - *at Curzon Ashton*) 4-1
Q2: Atherton Laburnum Rovers (A) 2-1
Q3: Altrincham (H - *at Northwich Vict.*) 3-3, (A) 1-1, (A) 1-3

CONGLETON TOWN

Currently: Northern Premier League

47-48 PR: Witton Albion (H) 3-3, (A) 0-7

48-49 PR: Matlock Town (A) 8-3
Q1: Winsford United (H) 2-2, (A) 0-2

49-50 EX: Wilmslow Albion (H) 8-2
PR: Shell (A) 6-3
Q1: Macclesfield Town (A) 2-1
Q2: Droylsden United (H) 1-2

50-51 PR: Buxton (H) 3-1
Q1: Winsford United (A) 0-4

51-52 Q1: Nantwich (A) 2-2, (H) 3-2
Q2: Northwich Victoria (H) 1-0
Q3: Buxton (A) 0-2

52-53 Q1: Macclesfield Town (A) 0-3

53-54 Q1: Hyde United (H) 5-5, (A) 1-0
Q2: Winsford United (A) 0-1

54-55 PR: Northwich Victoria (H) 2-5

55-56 PR: Nantwich (A) 1-0
Q1: Hyde United (H) 1-3

56-57 Q1: Hyde United (H) 3-3, (A) 2-6

57-58 PR: Stalybridge Celtic (H) 2-0
Q1: Witton Albion (A) 0-4

58-59 Q1: Buxton (H) 1-5

59-60 PR: Stockton Heath (A) 3-0
Q1: Northwich Victoria (H) 0-3

60-61 Q1: Lostock Gralam (A) 0-0, (H) 2-0
Q2: Winsford United (H) 3-1
Q3: Macclesfield Town (H) 0-3

61-62 PR: Mossley (A) 2-1
Q1: Lostock Gralam (H) 4-2
Q2: Buxton (A) 3-2
Q3: Northwich Victoria (H) 1-2

62-63 Q1: Wellington Town (H) 1-1, (A) 0-2

64-65 Q1: Winsford United (A) 1-2

65-66 Q1: Oswestry Town (A) 0-6

66-67 Q1: Northwich Victoria (A) 0-5

67-68 Q1: Tamworth (H) 0-5

68-69 Q1: Winsford United (H) 0-1

69-70 PR: Winsford United (H) 0-6

70-71 Q1: Skelmersdale United (A) 0-3

72-73 Q1: Eastwood Hanley (A) 1-2

73-74 Q1: Hyde United (H) 2-0
Q2: Horwich R.M.I. (A) 0-2

74-75 Q1: Macclesfield Town (A) 0-2

75-76 Q1: Curzon Ashton (H) 4-3
Q2: Leek Town (H) 1-3

76-77 PR: Worksop Town (H) 1-2

77-78 Q1: Rhyl (A) 0-0, (H) 0-2

78-79 Q1: Droylsden (H) 1-2

79-80 Q1: Marine (A) 0-4

80-81 PR: Bilston (A) 2-3

81-82 PR: Belper Town (H) 0-2

82-83 Q1: Hednesford Town (A) 2-1
Q2: Telford United (A) 2-3

83-84 PR: Caernarfon Town (H) 1-0
Q1: Leyland Motors (A) 3-1
Q2: Oswestry Town (H) 3-0
Q3: Macclesfield Town (A) 0-6

84-85 Q1: St Helens Town (A) 0-2

85-86 PR: Caernarfon Town (A) 1-1, (H) 1-0
Q1: Curzon Ashton (H) 1-0
Q2: Horwich R.M.I. (H) 2-2, (A) 0-2

86-87 PR: Bridgnorth Town (H) 0-0, (A) 0-4

87-88 PR: Stalybridge Celtic (A) 0-2

88-89 PR: Formby (H) 7-0
Q1: Harworth C.I. (H) 1-1, (A) 0-1

89-90 PR: Irlam Town (H) 1-1, (A) 2-0
Q1: Denaby United (H) 2-1
Q2: Caernarfon Town (A) 2-1
Q3: Colwyn Bay (A - *at Rhyl*) 1-1, (H) 4-0
Q4: Witton Albion (H) 1-0
R1: Crewe Alexandra (A) 0-2

90-91 Q1: Witton Albion (A) 0-2

91-92 PR: Sheffield (A) 0-2

92-93 PR: Eastwood Town (H) 2-0
Q1: Nantwich Town (H) 0-0, (A) 1-2

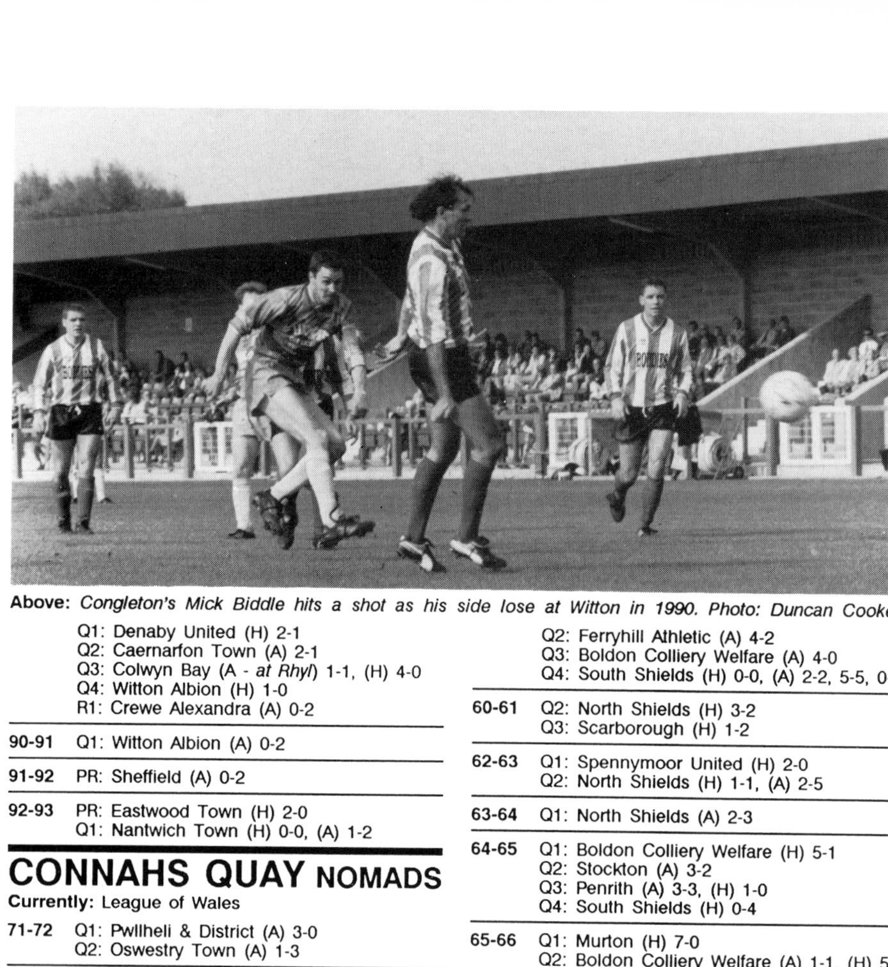

Above: *Congleton's Mick Biddle hits a shot as his side lose at Witton in 1990. Photo: Duncan Cooke.*

CONNAHS QUAY NOMADS

Currently: League of Wales

71-72 Q1: Pwllheli & District (A) 3-0
Q2: Oswestry Town (A) 1-3

72-73 Q1: Nantwich (A) 2-3

73-74 Q1: Prescot Town (H) 5-1
Q2: Portmadoc (A) 0-2

CONSETT

Currently: Northern League

45-46 Q1: Shankhouse (H) 6-0
Q2: Ashington (A) 1-1, (H) 3-0
Q3: Throckley Welfare (A) 4-2
Q4: Stockton (H) 2-3

46-47 Q1: Gosforth & Coxlodge (H) 7-0
Q2: Crook Colliery Welfare (A) 1-2

47-48 PR: Ferryhill Athletic (A) 2-3

48-49 EX: Stanley U. (A) 3-3, (H) 2-1 *protest*, 2-3

49-50 EX: Eppleton Colliery Welfare (A) 3-2
PR: Blackhall Colliery Welfare (A) 4-1
Q1: Evenwood Town (A) 4-1
Q2: Silksworth Colliery Welfare (A) 1-2

50-51 PR: Shotton Colliery Welfare (A) 8-1
Q1: Horden Colliery Welfare (A) 0-4

51-52 Q1: Boldon Colliery Welfare (A) 5-3
Q2: Dawdon Colliery Welfare (A) 3-0
Q3: South Shields (H) 4-0
Q4: Stockton (A) 0-2

52-53 Q1: Gosforth & Coxlodge (A) 5-0
Q2: Easington C.W. (A) 2-2, (H) 3-0
Q3: South Shields (H) 4-0
Q4: North Shields (H) 1-3

53-54 Q1: Easington C.W. (H) 2-2, (A) 3-1
Q2: Annfield Plain (H) 2-3

54-55 Q1: Dawdon Colliery Welfare (A) 1-2

55-56 Q1: Dawdon Colliery Welfare (H) 4-0
Q2: Boldon Colliery Welfare (A) 2-1
Q3: Easington Colliery Welfare (H) 1-4

56-57 Q1: Dawdon Colliery Welfare (A) 2-0
Q2: Annfield Plain (A) 2-4

57-58 Q1: Crook Town (A) 3-4

58-59 Q1: Whitby Town (H) 2-1
Q2: Ashington (H) 3-2
Q3: Willington (H) 0-0, (A) 2-1
Q4: Whitley Bay Athletic (H) 3-0
R1: Doncaster Rovers (A) 0-5

59-60 Q1: Evenwood Town (H) 2-1
Q2: Ferryhill Athletic (A) 4-2
Q3: Boldon Colliery Welfare (A) 4-0
Q4: South Shields (H) 0-0, (A) 2-2, 5-5, 0-1

60-61 Q2: North Shields (H) 3-2
Q3: Scarborough (H) 1-2

62-63 Q1: Spennymoor United (H) 2-0
Q2: North Shields (H) 1-1, (A) 2-5

63-64 Q1: North Shields (A) 2-3

64-65 Q1: Boldon Colliery Welfare (H) 5-1
Q2: Stockton (A) 3-2
Q3: Penrith (A) 3-3, (H) 1-0
Q4: South Shields (H) 0-4

65-66 Q1: Murton (H) 7-0
Q2: Boldon Colliery Welfare (A) 1-1, (H) 5-0
Q3: Stockton (H) 2-0
Q4: South Shields (A) 0-3

66-67 Q1: Whitby Town (H) 2-3

67-68 Q1: Crook Town (H) 1-2

68-69 Q1: Ryhope Colliery Welfare (H) 2-0
Q2: Evenwood Town (H) 4-3
Q3: Stockton (A) 3-0
Q4: South Shields (A) 1-1, (H) 0-6

69-70 Q1: Annfield Plain (H) 2-3

70-71 Q1: Durham City (A) 0-0, (H) 0-3

71-72 Q1: Crook Town (A) 4-1
Q2: Bedlington C.W. (A) 0-0, (H) 4-1
Q3: Blyth Spartans (A) 1-8

72-73 Q1: Ryhope Colliery Welfare (H) 3-1
Q2: Willington (H) 1-2

73-74 Q1: Durham City (H) 2-2, (A) 1-3

74-75 Q1: Willington (A) 1-4

75-76 Q1: Boldon Colliery Welfare (A) 0-2

76-77 Q1: Easington Colliery Welfare (H) 1-0
Q2: Bishop Auckland (A) 0-3

77-78 Q1: Wingate (H) 1-1, (A) 4-1
Q2: Washington (A) 3-0
Q3: Blyth Spartans (H) 1-4

78-79 PR: Eppleton Colliery Welf. (H) 1-1, (A) 7-0
Q1: Guisborough Town (A) 2-2, (H) 3-2
Q2: Bishop Auckland (A) 0-0, (H) 2-1
Q3: Spennymoor United (A) 0-0, (H) 1-2

79-80 Q1: Easington Colliery Welfare (A) 4-0
Q2: North Shields (A) 0-3

80-81 PR: Crook Town (H) 0-2

81-82 Q1: Morecambe (A) 3-2
Q2: Whitley Bay (A) 0-1

82-83 PR: Lancaster City (H) 0-3

83-84 PR: Gretna (A) 1-3

84-85 PR: Yorkshire Amateur (A) 1-0
Q1: Gateshead (H) 0-2

85-86 Q1: Tow Law Town (A) 0-1

86-87 PR: Annfield Plain (H) 0-0, (A) 1-3

87-88 Q1: Chester-le-Street Town (A) 1-2

88-89 Q1: Tow Law Town (A) 0-2

89-90 PR: Ferryhill Athletic (H) 1-3

90-91 Q1: Ryhope Community Association (A) 2-1
Q2: Seaham Red Star (A) 1-1, (H) 2-0
Q3: Newcastle Blue Star (A) 0-3

91-92 PR: Willington (H) 5-0
Q1: Ashington (A) 4-0
Q2: North Shields (A) 1-3

92-93 PR: Darlington Cleveland Bridge (A) 1-0
Q1: Alnwick Town (A) 0-0, (H) 2-0
Q2: Netherfield (H) 1-1 *ab. (fog) 58m*, (H) 3-4

CORBY TOWN

Currently: Southern League
* - As Stewarts & Lloyds

46-47 * Q2: Kettering Town (H) 1-1, (A) 2-4

47-48 * Q1: Desborough Town (A) 0-1

48-49 * Q1: Wellingborough Town (A) 0-1

49-50 PR: Rothwell Town (H) 7-1
Q1: Wellingborough Town (A) 5-0
Q2: Symington's Recreation (H) 6-1
Q3: Peterborough United (H) 1-0
Q4: Gravesend & Northfleet (H) 1-6

50-51 Q2: Wellingborough Town (H) 5-0
Q3: Kettering Town (H) 1-5

51-52 Q1: Rushden Town (A) 6-0
Q2: Kettering Town (H) 1-2

52-53 Q1: Desborough Town (A) 4-1
Q2: Kettering Town (H) 1-1, (A) 2-0
Q3: Peterborough United (H) 0-0, (A) 3-5

53-54 Q1: Spalding United (H) 6-2
Q2: Stamford (A) 2-3

54-55 Q1: Spalding United (A) 3-2
Q2: Bourne Town (A) 3-1
Q3: Wellingborough Town (H) 8-0
Q4: Worksop Town (H) 3-1
R1: Watford (H) 0-2

55-56 Q1: Kettering Town (H) 2-1
Q2: Spalding United (A) 3-1
Q3: Rothwell Town (H) 3-1
Q4: Worksop Town (A) 0-1

56-57 Q1: Rothwell Town (A) 1-0
Q2: Wellingborough Town (H) 6-0
Q3: Spalding United (H) 3-1
Q4: Peterborough United (H) 1-5

57-58 Q1: Rothwell Town (H) 2-1
Q2: Kettering Town (H) 3-1
Q3: Spalding United (A) 0-4

58-59 Q1: Stamford (H) 7-2
Q2: Kettering Town (A) 1-5

59-60 Q2: Spalding United (A) 2-1
Q3: Rushden Town (H) 2-2, (A) 1-2

60-61 Q1: Kettering Town (H) 1-2

61-62 Q1: St Neots Town (A) 2-0
Q2: Stamford (A) 1-1, (H) 3-1
Q3: Bourne Town (A) 5-1
Q4: Worksop Town (H) 2-2, (A) 1-2

62-63 Q1: Wellingborough Town (A) 0-0, (H) 1-0
Q2: St Neots Town (H) 1-0
Q3: Bourne Town (H) 4-1
Q4: King's Lynn (A) 1-2

63-64 Q1: St Neots Town (H) 3-0
Q2: Bourne Town (H) 4-2
Q3: Wellingborough Town (H) 3-1
Q4: Lockheed-Leamington (A) 2-2, (H) 2-0
R1: Bristol City (H) 1-3

64-65 Q4: Arnold (A) 2-0
R1: Hartlepools United (H) 1-3

65-66 Q4: King's Lynn (H) 2-1
R1: Buxton (H) 6-3
R2: Luton Town (H) 2-2, (A) 1-0
R3: Plymouth Argyle (A) 0-6

66-67 Q4: Cambridge City (H) 0-2

67-68 Q4: Cambridge City (H) 2-2, (A) 1-0
R1: Boston United (H) 0-3

68-69 Q4: St Albans City (H) 0-1

69-70 Q1: Bedford Town (A) 3-2
Q2: Rushden Town (A) 1-2

70-71 PR: St Neots Town (A) 4-1
Q1: Wellingborough Town (A) 1-4

71-72 Q1: Irthlingborough Diamonds (H) 0-1

72-73 Q1: Boston (H) 3-1
Q2: Skegness Town (H) 0-2

73-74 Q1: Wellingborough Town (H) 1-0
Q2: Biggleswade Town (H) 1-0
Q3: Histon (A) 2-0
Q4: Boston United (H) 1-2

74-75 PR: Cambridge City (H) 2-1
Q1: Wisbech Town (H) 2-0
Q2: Histon (H) 3-2
Q3: March Town United (A) 4-0
Q4: A.P. Leamington (A) 0-1

75-76 PR: Boston (H) 0-0, (A) 2-1
Q1: Stamford (A) 2-3

76-77 Q1: Spalding United (A) 3-0
Q2: St Neots Town (A) 0-3

77-78 Q1: Valley Sports (H) 1-1, (A) 2-0
Q2: Irthlingborough Diamonds (A) 2-1
Q3: Enderby Town (H) 1-2

78-79 PR: Barton Rovers (H) 0-1

79-80 Q1: Irthlingborough Diamonds (H) 1-0
Q2: Bedworth United (A) 0-1

80-81 Q1: Ely City (H) 1-0
Q2: Gainsborough Trinity (H) 2-0
Q3: Boston (A) 1-0
Q4: Boston United (H) 0-1

81-82 Q1: Enderby Town (H) 2-1
Q2: Grantham (A) 1-0
Q3: Ilkeston Town (H) 8-1
Q4: Harlow Town (A) 0-1

82-83 Q1: Halesowen Town (A) 2-1
Q2: Bedworth United (H) 1-0
Q3: Kidderminster Harriers (A) 3-1
Q4: Holbeach United (H) 0-1

83-84 Q1: Mile Oak Rovers & Youth (A) 1-0
Q2: Wisbech Town (A) 2-2, (H) 3-2
Q3: A.P. Leamington (H) 2-2, (A) 0-3

84-85 Q1: Arlesey Town (H) 2-1
Q2: Wellingborough Town (A) 4-1
Q3: King's Lynn (A) 0-0, (H) 0-3

85-86 Q1: Letchworth Garden City (A) 3-2
Q2: Histon (A) 1-0
Q3: V.S. Rugby (A) 0-2

86-87 Q1: Irthlingborough Diamonds (H) 3-0
Q2: Ware (A) 2-1
Q3: Kettering Town (A) 0-2

87-88 Q1: Worcester City (H) 1-1, (A) 1-3

88-89 Q1: Braintree Town (A) 0-2

89-90 Q1: Haverhill Rovers (A) 1-1, (H) 2-3

90-91 PR: Dudley Town (A) 1-1, (H) 1-0
Q1: Solihull Borough (H) 3-0
Q2: Matlock Town (H) 2-0
Q3: Burton Albion (H) 0-1

91-92 Q1: Hemel Hempstead (H) 1-0
Q2: Nuneaton Borough (A) 2-2, (H) 1-0
Q3: Alvechurch (A) 0-2

92-93 Q1: Rainham Town (A - *at Purfleet*) 1-0
Q2: Purfleet (A) 2-2, (H) 1-0
Q3: Aveley (H) 4-1
Q4: Kettering Town (A) 1-2

Below: *Corby's Ian McInerney (left) battles with Mark Smalley during the latest of his club's numerous Cup clashes with Kettering Town. Photo: Dave West.*

CORINTHIAN

Currently: Kent League

88-89 PR: Wick (H) 2-1
Q1: Steyning Town (A) 1-5

89-90 PR: Collier Row (A) 1-3

90-91 PR: Southwick (A) 0-1

91-92 PR: Merstham (H) 6-0
Q1: Erith & Belvedere (H) 1-3

92-93 PR: Cove (H) 1-0
Q1: Margate (A) 0-0, (H) 1-1, (H) 0-4

CORINTHIAN-CASUALS

Currently: London Spartan League

64-65 Q1: Windsor & Eton (A) 2-2, (H) 1-2

65-66 Q1: Hillingdon Borough (A) 2-1
Q2: Windsor & Eton (A) 8-0
Q3: Southall (A) 2-2, (H) 3-2
Q4: Enfield (A) 3-0
R1: Watford (H) 1-5

66-67 Q1: Vauxhall Motors (H) 2-1
Q2: Malden Town (H) 1-1, (A) 3-2
Q3: Leatherhead (A) 1-2

67-68 Q1: Slough Town (H) 0-3

68-69 Q1: Rainham Town (H) 6-4
Q2: Bishop's Stortford (A) 0-9

69-70 Q1: Harlow Town (A) 2-2, (H) 4-1
Q2: Hertford Town (H) 1-2

70-71 Q1: Hornchurch (A) 2-3

71-72 Q1: Harlow Town (H) 0-2

72-73 PR: Sutton United (A) 1-3

73-74 Q1: Epping Town (H) 0-2

74-75 PR: Barking (H) 4-2
Q1: Wembley (H) 1-2

75-76 PR: Epsom & Ewell (A) 2-4

76-77 Q1: Grays Athletic (H) 0-1

77-78 Q1: Epping Town (H) 5-1
Q2: Walthamstow Avenue (H) 0-1

78-79 Q1: Edgware (H) 0-0, (A) 0-4

79-80 Q1: Woking (H) 1-6

80-81 Q1: Ashford Town (A) 1-4

81-82 Q1: Clapton (H) 3-3, (A) 2-1
Q2: Hayes (H) 2-1
Q3: Hertford Town (H) 2-0
Q4: Barnet (A) 0-2

82-83 Q1: Wick (A) 2-1
Q2: Ramsgate (H - *at Dulwich*) 1-0
Q3: Dartford (A) 1-2

83-84 Q1: Camberley Town (H) 2-0
Q2: Southall (H - *at Leatherhead*) 3-2
Q3: Bognor Regis Town (H) 3-1
Q4: Merthyr Tydfil (H) 1-0
R1: Bristol C. (H - *at Dulwich*) 0-0, (A) 0-4

84-85 Q1: Addlestone & W. (H - *played away*) 0-3

85-86 PR: Uxbridge (A) 0-3

86-87 PR: Edgware (A) 2-2, (H - *at Molesey*) 1-0
Q1: Harefield United (A) 0-3

87-88 PR: Camberley Town (H) 1-1, (A) 0-2

88-89 PR: Hanwell Town (H - *played away*) 0-4

89-90 PR: Peacehaven (A) 0-0, (H - *Leatherhead*) 1-2

90-91 PR: Ware (A) 0-0, (H - *played away*) 1-0
Q1: Grays Athletic (H) 1-5

91-92 PR: Leatherhead (A) 1-3

92-93 Q1: Slough Town (H) 1-1, (A) 3-4

CORINTHIANS (MILNTHORPE)

See Milnthorpe Corinthians

CORSHAM TOWN

Currently: Wiltshire League

50-51 PR: Warminster Town (H) 3-2
Q1: Trowbridge Town (A) 1-6

51-52 PR: Warminster Town (A) 5-3
Q1: Frome Town (H) 2-7

52-53 PR: Chippenham Town (H) 1-4

COUNDON THREE TUNS

Currently: Auckland & District League

84-85 PR: Billingham Town (A) 0-2

COVE

Currently: Isthmian League

90-91 PR: Haywards Heath Town (H) 4-0
Q1: Windsor & Eton (H) 1-3

91-92 PR: Slade Green (H) 2-1
Q1: Burgess Hill Town (H) 1-1, (A) 0-4

92-93 PR: Corinthian (A) 0-1

COVENTRY CITY

Currently: F.A. Premier League

45-46 R3: Aston Villa (H) 2-1, (A) 0-2 *(agg: 2-3)*

46-47 R3: Newport County (H) 5-2
R4: Burnley (A) 0-2

47-48 R3: Walsall (H) 2-1
R4: Luton Town (A) 2-3

48-49 R3: Torquay United (A) 0-1

49-50 R3: Bolton Wanderers (H) 1-2

50-51 R3: Sunderland (A) 0-2

51-52 R3: Leicester City (A) 1-1, (H) 4-1
R4: Burnley (A) 0-2

52-53 R1: Bristol City (H) 2-0
R2: Bishop Auckland (A) 4-1
R3: Plymouth Argyle (A) 1-4

53-54 R1: Brighton & Hove Albion (A) 1-5

54-55 R1: Northampton Town (A) 1-0
R2: Scunthorpe United (H) 4-0
R3: Huddersfield Town (A) 3-3, (H) 1-2

55-56 R1: Exeter City (H) 0-1

56-57 R1: Swindon Town (A) 1-2

57-58 R1: Walthamstow Avenue (H) 1-0
R2: Aldershot (A) 1-4

58-59 R1: Weymouth (A) 5-2
R2: Plymouth Argyle (H) 1-3

59-60 R1: Southampton (H) 1-1, (A) 1-5

60-61 R1: Worcester City (A) 4-1
R2: Queens Park Rangers (A) 2-1
R3: Liverpool (A) 2-3

61-62 R1: Gillingham (H) 2-0
R2: King's Lynn (H) 1-2

62-63 R1: Bournemouth & Boscombe Ath. (H) 1-0
R2: Millwall (A) 0-0, (H) 2-1
R3: Lincoln City (A) 5-1
R4: Portsmouth (A) 1-1, (H) 2-2, 2-1
R5: Sunderland (H) 2-1
R6: Manchester United (H) 1-3

63-64 R1: Trowbridge Town (A) 6-1
R2: Bristol Rovers (H) 1-2

64-65 R3: Aston Villa (A) 0-3

65-66 R3: Swindon Town (A) 2-1
R4: Crewe Alexandra (A) 1-1, (H) 4-1
R5: Everton (A) 0-3

66-67 R3: Newcastle United (H) 3-4

67-68 R3: Charlton Athletic (H) 3-0
R4: Tranmere Rovers (H) 1-1, (A) 0-2

68-69 R3: Blackpool (H) 3-1
R4: Everton (H) 0-2

69-70 R3: Liverpool (H) 1-1, (A) 0-3

70-71 R3: Rochdale (A) 1-2

71-72 R3: West Bromwich Albion (A) 2-1
R4: Hull City (H) 0-1

72-73 R3: Orient (A) 4-1
R4: Grimsby Town (H) 1-0
R5: Hull City (H) 3-0
R6: Wolverhampton Wanderers (A) 0-2

73-74 R3: Sheffield Wednesday (A) 0-0, (H) 3-1
R4: Derby County (H) 0-0, (A) 1-0
R5: Queens Park Rangers (H) 0-0, (A) 2-3

74-75 R3: Norwich City (H) 2-0
R4: Arsenal (H) 1-1, (A) 0-3

75-76 R3: Bristol City (H) 2-1
R4: Newcastle United (H) 1-1, (A) 0-5

76-77 R3: Millwall (H) 1-0
R4: Arsenal (A) 1-3

77-78 R3: Middlesbrough (A) 0-3

78-79 R3: West Bromwich Albion (H) 2-2, (A) 0-4

79-80 R3: Oldham Athletic (A) 1-0
R4: Blackburn Rovers (A) 0-1

80-81 R3: Leeds United (A) 1-1, (H) 1-0
R4: Birmingham City (H) 3-2
R5: Tottenham Hotspur (A) 1-3

81-82 R3: Sheffield Wednesday (H) 3-1
R4: Manchester City (A) 3-1
R5: Oxford United (H) 4-0
R6: West Bromwich Albion (A) 0-2

82-83 R3: Worcester City (H) 3-1
R4: Norwich City (H) 2-2, (A) 1-2

83-84 R3: Wolves (H) 1-1, (A) 1-1, (H) 3-0
R4: Sheffield Wednesday (A) 2-3

84-85 R3: Manchester City (H) 2-1
R4: Manchester United (A) 1-2

85-86 R3: Watford (H) 1-3

86-87 R3: Bolton Wanderers (H) 3-0
R4: Manchester United (A) 1-0
R5: Stoke City (A) 1-0
R6: Sheffield Wednesday (A) 3-1
SF: Leeds United *(at Sheffield Wed.)* 3-2
F: Tottenham Hotspur *(at Wembley)* 3-2

87-88 R3: Torquay United (H) 2-0
R4: Watford (H) 0-1

88-89 R3: Sutton United (A) 1-2

89-90 R3: Northampton Town (A) 0-1

90-91 R3: Wigan Athletic (H) 1-1, (A) 1-0
R4: Southampton (H) 1-1, (A) 0-2

91-92 R3: Cambridge United (H) 1-1, (A) 0-1

92-93 R3: Norwich City (A) 0-1

COVENTRY SPORTING

Currently: Defunct
* - As Coventry Amateurs

50-51 * PR: Atherstone Town (H) 2-3

70-71 * Q1: Dudley Town (H) 1-2

74-75 Q1: Moor Green (H) 1-0
Q2: Atherstone Town (A) 0-5

75-76 PR: Bromsgrove Rovers (H) 3-0
Q1: Oldbury United (A) 0-0, (H) 3-1
Q2: Halesowen Town (H) 2-0
Q3: Brierley Hill Alliance (H) 2-1
Q4: Spalding United (H) 2-0
R1: Tranmere R. (H - *at Coventry City*) 2-0
R2: Peterbrough U. (H - *at Cov'try City*) 0-4

76-77 Q1: Tamworth (A) 1-1, (H) 2-0
Q2: Sutton Coldfield Town (A) 1-2

77-78 Q1: Enderby Town (H) 1-1, (A) 0-1

78-79 Q1: Milton Keynes City (A) 0-2

79-80 Q1: Belper Town (H) 1-0
Q2: Telford United (H) 2-4

80-81 Q1: Hinckley Athletic (H) 2-3

81-82 Q1: Burton Albion (A) 1-3

82-83 Q1: A.P. Leamington (H) 0-4

83-84 PR: Wigston Fields (A) 1-3

84-85 PR: Spalding United (H) 0-0, (A) 3-2
Q1: Bedworth United (A) 0-0, (H) 2-3

85-86 PR: Spalding United (A) 2-1 - *expelled*

86-87 PR: Racing Club Warwick (H) 3-1
Q1: Banbury United (A) 2-4

87-88 PR: Barton Rovers (H) 2-1
Q1: Leamington (A) 1-2

88-89 Q1: Boston United (A) 1-8

89-90 PR: Brackley Town (A) *Scratched*

COWES (ISLE OF WIGHT)

Currently: (Cowes Sports) Hampshire League

45-46 Q1: Ryde Sports (A) 3-1
Q2: East Cowes Victoria (H) 4-2
Q3: Newport I.O.W. (A) 1-0 - *expelled*

46-47 PR: R.A.O.C. Hilsea (A) 3-4

47-48 EX: Newport Isle of Wight (H) 1-3

48-49 PR: East Cowes Victoria (H) 1-2

49-50 EX: Lymington (H) 4-0
PR: Pirelli General (A) 4-3
Q1: Dorchester Town (H) 5-1
Q2: Bournemouth (A) 3-3, (H) 4-0
Q3: Weymouth (H) 1-5

50-51 PR: Bournemouth (H) 1-1, (A) 2-4

51-52 Q1: Basingstoke Town (A) 3-4

52-53 Q1: Newport Isle of Wight (H) 0-1

53-54 Q2: Alton Town (H) 5-0
Q3: Newport Isle of Wight (A) 2-4

54-55 Q1: Chichester City (H) 6-0

Above: *Coventry City captain Brian Kilcline (5) prepares to tackle Lenny Dennis of Sutton United in the historic 1989 tie at Gander Green Lane.*

Q2: Gosport Borough Athletic (A) 1-2

55-56 Q1: Bournemouth Gasworks Athletic (H) 4-1
Q2: Fareham Town (H) 2-3

56-57 Q1: Gosport Borough Athletic (H) 1-4

57-58 Q1: Winchester City (H) 0-0, (A) 1-0
Q2: Basingstoke Town (A) 5-2
Q3: Chichester City (H) 3-1
Q4: Trowbridge Town (H) 2-2, (A) 1-4

58-59 Q1: Chichester City (H) 5-4
Q2: Alton Town (H) 1-2

59-60 Q1: Newport Isle of Wight (H) 2-0
Q2: Andover (H) 3-0
Q3: Basingstoke Town (A) 1-2

60-61 Q1: Newport Isle of Wight (A) 2-1
Q2: Chichester City (A) 3-6

61-62 Q1: Newbury Town (H) 3-1
Q2: Newport Isle of Wight (A) 0-0, (H) 5-1
Q3: Andover (A) 1-2

62-63 Q1: Andover (A) 1-4

63-64 Q1: Alton Town (H) 5-1
Q2: Andover (A) 1-1, (H) 4-2
Q3: Basingstoke Town (H) 3-1
Q4: Yeovil Town (H) 0-1

64-65 Q1: Chichester City (H) 5-4
Q2: Basingstoke Town (A) 2-4

65-66 Q1: Chichester City (A) 5-3
Q2: Newport Isle of Wight (H) 3-3, (A) 3-0
Q3: Fareham Town (A) 2-4

66-67 Q1: Salisbury (A) 2-4

67-68 Q1: Thornycroft Athletic (H) 2-1
Q2: Salisbury (H) 1-1, (A) 1-5

68-69 Q1: Thornycroft Athletic (H) 0-1

69-70 Q1: Fareham Town (A) 0-3

70-71 Q1: Basingstoke Town (H) 1-3

71-72 Q1: Alton Town (A) 2-3

72-73 PR: Newport Isle of Wight (A) 0-2

73-74 Q1: Alton Town (A) 0-2

74-75 Q1: Salisbury (A) 0-3

75-76 Q1: Gosport Borough (H) 0-2

76-77 Q1: Waterlooville (A) 0-9

77-78 Q1: Salisbury (A) 1-5

78-79 PR: Fareham Town (H) 0-0, (A) 0-2

CRADLEY HEATH

Currently: Kidderminster League

47-48 PR: Halesowen Town (A) 1-4

48-49 EX: Brierley Hill Alliance (H) 4-1
PR: Halesowen Town (A) 0-2

49-50 EX: Bournville Athletic (A) 6-1
PR: Birmingham City Transport (A) 5-1
Q1: Lye Town (H) 1-0
Q2: Bromsgrove Rovers (H) 1-2

50-51 PR: Stourbridge (H) 0-1

51-52 Q1: Brierley Hill Alliance (H) 1-5

52-53 Q1: Bilston (H) 2-2, (A) 1-3

53-54 PR: Brierley Hill Alliance (H) 0-6

54-55 PR: Lye Town (A) 2-3

56-57 PR: Bromsgrove Rovers (A) 3-3, (H) 0-1

57-58 Q1: Wellington Town (A) 1-7

58-59 PR: Moor Green (A) 3-5

59-60 Q1: Stourbridge (H) 0-5

60-61 Q1: Redditch (H) 1-3

CRAMLINGTON WELFARE

Currently: Defunct

48-49 EX: Hexham Hearts (H) 3-4

49-50 EX: West Sleekburn Welfare (H) 3-1
PR: Newbiggin Central Welfare (A) 0-3

50-51 EX: Shankhouse (A) 6-2
PR: West Sleekburn Welfare (H) 5-1
Q1: Gosforth & Coxlodge (H) 5-2
Q2: Blyth Spartans (H) 2-0
Q3: Ashington (A) 1-3

51-52 Q1: Alnwick Town (A) 0-5

52-53 Q1: Hexham Hearts (H) 0-1

53-54 Q1: Hexham (A) 3-3, (H) 3-4 *ab. in E.T.*, 2-5

54-55 Q1: Gosforth & Coxlodge (A) 5-1
Q2: West Sleekburn Welfare (H) 1-7

55-56 Q1: Newburn (A) 2-1
Q2: South Shields (A) 3-5

56-57 Q1: Gosforth & Coxlodge (H) 3-1
Q2: South Shields (H) 0-6

57-58 Q1: Cockfield (A) 0-5

58-59 Q2: Whitley Bay Athletic (H) 3-4

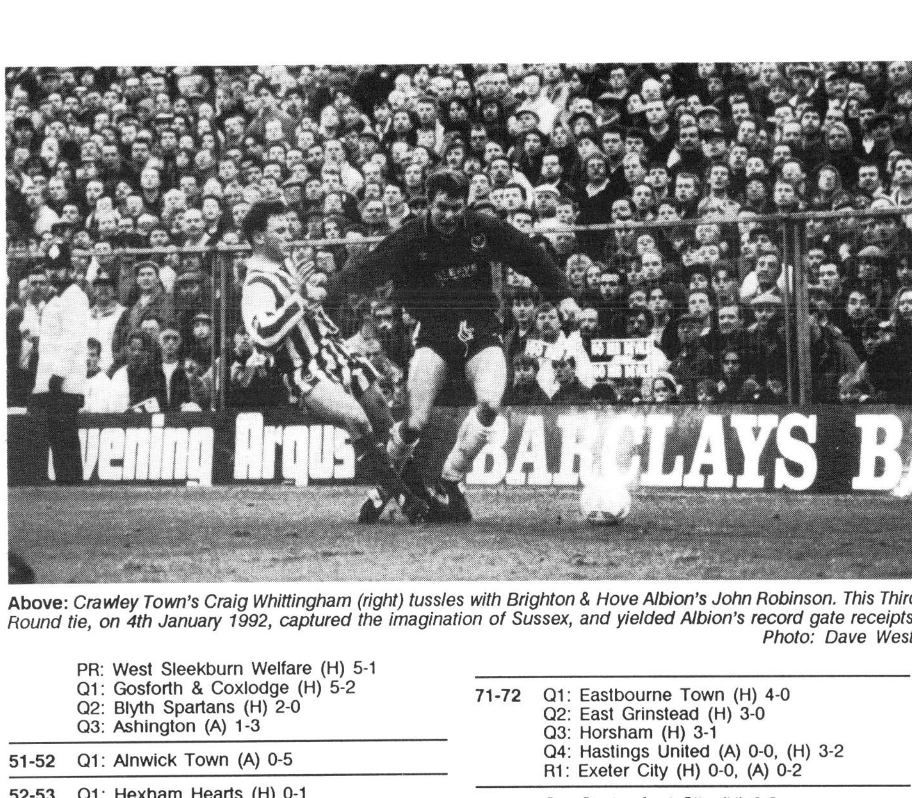

Above: *Crawley Town's Craig Whittingham (right) tussles with Brighton & Hove Albion's John Robinson. This Third Round tie, on 4th January 1992, captured the imagination of Sussex, and yielded Albion's record gate receipts.* Photo: *Dave West.*

CRAWLEY TOWN

Currently: Southern League

58-59 PR: Horsham (H) 0-1

59-60 PR: Southwick (H) 6-1
Q1: Worthing (A) 6-1
Q2: Eastbourne (H) 2-2, (A) 2-1
Q3: Hastings United (H) 2-2, (A) 2-5

60-61 Q1: Arundel (A) 0-3

61-62 Q1: Worthing (H) 5-0
Q2: Haywards Heath (H) 3-2
Q3: Bognor Regis Town (H) 2-1
Q4: Tunbridge Wells United (H) 1-2

63-64 Q1: Haywards Heath (A) 3-3, (H) 7-2
Q2: Littlehampton Town (A) 4-0
Q3: Lewes (H) 0-2

64-65 Q2: Horsham (H) 5-0
Q3: Redhill (A) 6-1
Q4: Canterbury City (A) 0-3

65-66 Q1: Haywards Heath (H) 3-0
Q2: Sutton United (A) 1-0
Q3: Carshalton Athletic (H) 3-0
Q4: Gravesend & Northfleet (A) 0-1

66-67 Q1: Worthing (H) 4-0
Q2: Maidstone United (H) 1-0
Q3: Eastbourne Utd (A) 1-1, (H) 2-2, 2-3

67-68 Q1: Alton Town (H) 1-0
Q2: Wokingham Town (A) 5-1
Q3: Chichester City (A) 0-1

68-69 Q1: Woking (A) 1-2

69-70 Q1: Dorking (H) 4-0
Q2: Alton Town (H) 1-0
Q3: Wokingham Town (A) 5-2
Q4: Wimbledon (A) 0-0, (H) 0-0, 0-2

70-71 Q1: Haywards Heath (H) 3-0
Q2: Woking (H) 3-1
Q3: Carshalton Athletic (A) 4-0
Q4: Folkestone (A) 0-0, (H) 3-0
R1: Chelmsford City (H) 1-1, (A) 1-6

71-72 Q1: Eastbourne Town (H) 4-0
Q2: East Grinstead (H) 3-0
Q3: Horsham (H) 3-1
Q4: Hastings United (A) 0-0, (H) 3-2
R1: Exeter City (H) 0-0, (A) 0-2

72-73 Q4: Chelmsford City (H) 0-2

73-74 Q1: Leyton (A) 2-2, (H) 2-1
Q2: Aveley (H) 2-3

74-75 Q1: Peacehaven & Telscombe (H) 3-0
Q2: Ringmer (H) 2-2, (A) 1-2

75-76 Q1: Hastings United (H) 2-1
Q2: Ashford Town (H) 4-1
Q3: Redhill (A) 1-1, (H) 1-0
Q4: Dover (H) 0-0, (A) 0-6

76-77 Q1: Tunbridge Wells (A) 0-2

77-78 Q1: Deal Town (H) 3-1
Q2: Bromley (H) 3-2
Q3: Maidstone (A) 1-1, (H) 1-1, (*Bromley*) 1-4

78-79 Q1: Bexhill Town (A - *played home*) 1-1, (H) 1-1, (*at Hastings United*) 1-0
Q2: Hastings United (H) 1-2

79-80 Q1: Slough Town (H) 0-0, (A) 0-3

80-81 PR: Deal Town (H) 2-1
Q1: Haywards Heath (H) 1-0
Q2: Ashford Town (A) 0-3

81-82 Q1: Burgess Hill Town (H) 0-1

82-83 Q1: Worthing (H) 1-2

83-84 PR: Hornchurch (A) 0-1

84-85 Q1: Ruislip Manor (H) 2-1
Q2: Walthamstow Avenue (A) 0-1

85-86 Q1: Erith & Belvedere (A) 1-1, (H) 3-0
Q2: Egham Town (A) 6-0
Q3: Leyton-Wingate (H) 2-3

86-87 Q1: Gravesend & Northfleet (H) 1-0
Q2: Eastleigh (A) 1-0
Q3: Woking (A) 1-3

87-88 Q1: Chatham Town (H) 1-3

88-89 Q1: Hailsham Town (H) 2-1
Q2: Tring Town (A) 2-1
Q3: Bromley (A) 2-2, (H) 1-0
Q4: Merthyr Tydfil (H) 3-3, (A) 1-3

89-90 Q1: Staines Town (H) 0-1

90-91 Q1: Eastbourne United (A) 2-0
Q2: Worthing (A) 2-3

91-92 Q1: Molesey (A) 5-1
Q2: Sheppey United (H) 2-0
Q3: Erith & Belvedere (A) 2-1
Q4: Horsham (A) 0-0, (H) 3-0
R1: Northampton Town (H) 4-2
R2: Hayes (A) 2-0
R3: Brighton & Hove Albion (A) 0-5

92-93 Q4: Yeovil Town (H) 1-2

CRAY WANDERERS

Currently: Kent League

60-61 Q1: Dartford (H) 4-5

61-62 Q2: Erith & Belvedere (H) 3-4

62-63 Q1: Sutton United (A) 1-4

63-64 Q1: Dartford (H) 1-0
Q2: Sittingbourne (A) 1-1, (H) 0-1

64-65 Q1: Dartford (A) 0-5

65-66 Q1: Sheppey United (H) 0-1

66-67 Q1: Harlow Town (A) 0-0, (H) 3-1
Q2: Barnet (H) 1-4

67-68 Q1: Ford United (A) 2-1
Q2: Hornchurch (A) 4-2
Q3: Dagenham (A) 0-1

68-69 Q1: Gravesend & Northfleet (A) 3-1
Q2: Redhill (A) 0-1

69-70 Q1: Dagenham (A) 0-3

70-71 Q1: Wokingham Town (A) 3-1
Q2: Ilford (A) 0-3

71-72 Q1: Ware (H) 3-0
Q2: Braintree & Crittall Athletic (A) 0-1

72-73 Q1: Canterbury City (H) 2-1
Q2: Dover (H) 0-2

73-74 Q1: Hampton (A) 3-3, (H) 1-3

74-75 PR: Aveley (H) 4-2
Q1: Walthamstow Avenue (H) 2-0
Q2: Sutton United (H) 1-5

75-76 Q1: Dulwich Hamlet (H) 1-3

76-77 Q1: Erith & Belvedere (H) 2-2, (A) 3-2
Q2: Maidstone United (H) 2-1
Q3: Bromley (H) 0-2

77-78 Q1: Snowdown Colliery Welfare (A) 1-2

78-79 Q1: Dulwich Hamlet (H) 1-2,

79-80 Q1: Farnborough Town (A) 1-0
Q2: Kingstonian (A) 0-1

80-81 PR: Dorking Town (H) 1-1, (A) 2-0
Q1: Tilbury (A) 1-4

81-82 Q1: Billericay Town (H) 0-4

82-83 PR: Hounslow (A) 5-2
Q1: Chesham United (A) 2-3

83-84 PR: Clapton (A) 3-2
Q1: Addlestone & Weybridge Town (A) 1-3

84-85 PR: Bromley (A) 0-4

85-86 Q1: Canterbury City (H) 1-1, (A) 0-5

86-87 Q1: Kingstonian (A) 0-2

87-88 PR: Basildon United (A) 3-1
Q1: Burnham (A - *played home*) 1-1, (H - *played away*) 1-2

88-89 PR: Tilbury (H) 1-4

89-90 PR: Baldock Town (A) 0-3

90-91 PR: Waltham Abbey (H) 3-1
Q1: Ruislip Manor (H) 2-3

CRESSWELL COLLIERY

Currently: Defunct

48-49 EX: Hardwick Colliery Sports (A) *W/O*
PR: Sheffield (H) 2-0
Q1: Dinnington Athletic (A) 1-3

49-50 EX: Maltby Main (H) 3-0
PR: Bolsover Colliery (A) 5-4
Q1: Hoyland Common Albion (A) 1-1, (H) 0-2

50-51 PR: Staveley Welfare (H) 9-0
Q1: Parkhouse Colliery (A) 2-1
Q2: Stocksbridge Works (A) 3-6

51-52 PR: Bentinck Colliery (A) 2-1
Q1: Raleigh Athletic (A) 4-2
Q2: Shirebrook (A) 2-2, (H) 1-0
Q3: Linby Colliery (H) 2-0
Q4: Gainsborough Trinity (A) 2-5

52-53 Q1: Sutton Town (H) 2-0
Q2: Ransome & Marles (H) 3-0
Q3: Linby Colliery (A) 0-0, (H) 0-0, 0-5

53-54 Q1: Ransome & Marles (H) 1-0
Q2: Bestwood Colliery (A) 7-0
Q3: Shirebrook Miners Welfare (H) 3-4

54-55 Q1: Parliament Street Methodists (A) 5-2
Q2: Sutton Town (H) 6-0
Q3: Linby Colliery (H) 3-1
Q4: Denaby United (A) 5-2
R1: Accrington Stanley (A) 1-7

55-56 Q1: Ransome & Marles (A) 1-6

56-57 Q1: Langwith Miners Welfare (A) 2-1
Q2: Ransome & Marles (H) 0-6

57-58 Q2: Ransome & Marles (A) 4-3
Q3: Sutton Town (A) 1-2

58-59 Q1: Sutton Town (H) 0-3

59-60 Q2: Heanor Town (H) 2-5

60-61 PR: Matlock Town (A) 0-6

61-62 Q1: Worksop Town (H) 1-2

62-63 Q1: Frickley Colliery (H) 1-4

63-64' Q1: Retford Town (A) 0-4

64-65 Q1: Matlock Town (A) 1-4

CREWE ALEXANDRA

Currently: Football League

45-46 R1: Wrexham (H) 4-2, (A) 0-3 (*agg: 4-5*)

46-47 R1: Rotherham United (A) 0-2

47-48 R1: South Shields (H) 4-1
R2: Workington (A) 2-1
R3: Sheffield United (H) 3-1
R4: Derby County (H) 0-3

48-49 R1: Billingham Synthonia Recreation (H) 5-0
R2: Millwall (H) 3-2
R3: Sunderland (H) 0-2

49-50 R1: Darlington (A) 2-2, (H) 1-0
R2: Oldham Athletic (H) 1-1, (A) 0-0, 0-3

50-51 R1: North Shields (H) 4-0
R2: Plymouth Argyle (H) 2-2, (A) 0-3

51-52 R1: Lincoln City (H) 2-4

52-53 R1: Gateshead (A) 0-2

53-54 R1: Bradford City (H) 0-0, (A) 1-0
R2: Walsall (A) 0-3

54-55 R1: Oldham Athletic (A) 0-1

55-56 R1: Barrow (A) 0-0, (H) 2-3

56-57 R1: Wrexham (H) 2-2, (A) 1-2

57-58 R1: Hull City (A) 1-2

58-59 R1: South Shields (H) 2-2, (A) 0-5

59-60 R1: Burscough (A) 3-1
R2: Stockport County (A) 0-0, (H) 2-0
R3: Workington (H) 2-0
R4: Tottenham Hotspur (H) 2-2, (A) 2-13

60-61 R1: Rochdale (H) 1-1, (A) 2-1
R2: Halifax Town (A) 2-2, (H) 4-0
R3: Chelsea (A) 2-1
R4: Tottenham Hotspur (A) 1-5

61-62 R1: Lincoln City (H) 2-0
R2: Port Vale (H) 1-1, (A) 0-3

62-63 R1: Scarborough (H) 1-1, (A) 3-2
R2: York City (A) 1-2

63-64 R1: Hull City (A) 2-2, (H) 0-3

64-65 R1: Chester (A) 0-5

65-66 R1: Scunthorpe United (H) 3-0
R2: South Shields (H) 3-1
R3: Folkestone Town (A) 5-1
R4: Coventry City (H) 1-1, (A) 1-4

66-67 R1: Grimsby Town (H) 1-1, (A) 1-0
R2: Darlington (H) 2-1
R3: Bolton Wanderers (A) 0-1

67-68 R1: Halifax Town (A) 2-3

68-69 R1: Altrincham (A) 1-0
R2: Halifax Town (A) 1-1, (H) 1-3

69-70 R1: Doncaster Rovers (A) 1-1, (H) 0-1

70-71 R1: Doncaster Rovers (H) 0-0, (A) 3-1
R2: Chester (A) 0-1

71-72 R1: Blyth Spartans (H) 0-1

72-73 R1: Stafford Rangers (H) 1-0
R2: Blackburn Rovers (A) 1-0
R3: Luton Town (A) 0-2

73-74 R1: Scarborough (H) 0-0, (A) 1-2

74-75 R1: Gateshead United (H) 2-2, (A) 0-1

75-76 R1: Rotherham United (A) 1-2

76-77 R1: Preston (H) 1-1, (A) 2-2, (*at Liverpool*) 0-3

77-78 R1: Bradford City (A) 1-0
R2: Scarborough (H) 0-0, (A) 0-2

78-79 R1: Nuneaton Borough (A) 2-0
R2: Hartlepool United (H) 0-1

79-80 R1: Altrincham (A) 0-3

80-81 R1: Mossley (A) 0-1

81-82 R1: Willenhall Town (A) 1-0
R2: Scunthorpe United (H) 1-3

82-83 R1: Boston United (A) 1-3

83-84 R1: Rochdale (A) 0-1

84-85 R1: Northwich Victoria (A) 1-3

85-86 R1: Derby County (A) 1-5

86-87 R1: York City (A) 1-3

87-88 R1: Lincoln City (A) 1-2

88-89 R1: Stafford Rangers (A) 2-2, (H) 3-2
R2: Runcorn (A) 3-0
R3: Aston Villa (H) 2-3

89-90 R1: Congleton Town (H) 2-0
R2: Bishop Auckland (H) 1-1, (A) 2-0
R3: Chelsea (A) 1-1, (H) 0-2

90-91 R1: Lincoln City (A) 4-1
R2: Atherstone United (H) 1-0
R3: Bristol Rovers (A - *at Bath*) 2-0
R4: Rotherham United (H) 1-0
R5: West Ham United (A) 0-1

91-92 R1: Carlisle United (A) 1-1, (H) 5-3
R2: Chester City (H) 2-0
R3: Liverpool (H) 0-4

92-93 R1: Wrexham (H) 6-1
R2: Accrington S. (A - *at Blackburn*) 6-1
R3: Marine (H) 3-1
R4: Blackburn Rovers (H) 0-3

Left: *One of Crewe's blackest moments in the Cup; John Rogers stretches to convert a Barry Howard cross and put Altrincham three up in 1979. Photo: John Rooney.*

CRITTALL ATHLETIC

Currently: Merged with Braintree.
Playing as Braintree Town in Southern League.
See also Braintree Town

45-46 Q2: Romford (A) 1-7

46-47 PR: Woodford Town (H) 4-2
Q1: Clapton (H) 3-1
Q2: Barking (A) 0-3

47-48 PR: Tilbury (H) 3-2
Q1: Barking (A) 1-3

48-49 PR: Upminster (H) 2-2, (A) 0-2

49-50 EX: Briggs Sports (A) 0-7

50-51 PR: Rainham Town (A) 0-0, (H) 2-1
Q1: Chingford Town (A) 2-3

66-67 Q1: Tilbury (H) 1-0
Q2: Sutton United (H) 1-2

67-68 Q1: Vauxhall Motors (H) 3-1
Q2: Hoddesdon Town (H) 2-0
Q3: Ware (H) 1-2

68-69 Q1: Ware (H) 1-1, (A) 1-2

CROCKENHILL

Currently: Kent League

84-85 PR: Grays Athletic (H) 0-3

85-86 PR: Hounslow (H) 0-1

86-87 PR: Feltham (H) 1-5

87-88 PR: Flackwell Heath (A) 3-0
Q1: Harefield United (A) 1-3

88-89 PR: Ruislip (A) 0-2

CROMER

Currently: (Cromer Town) Anglian Combination

47-48 PR: Norwich C.E.Y.M.S. (A) 0-0, (H) 1-3

48-49 PR: Norwich C.E.Y.M.S. (A) 0-2

49-50 PR: Great Yarmouth Town (A) 1-1, (H) 3-4

50-51 PR: Sudbury Town (H) 0-4

51-52 Q1: Wymondham Town (A) 4-1
Q2: Gorleston (A) 0-3

52-53 Q1: Great Yarmouth Town (A) 0-13

53-54 Q2: Bungay Town (H) 2-0
Q3: Gorleston (H) 2-6

54-55 Q1: Gothic (A) 2-7

55-56 Q1: Wymondham Town (H) 1-2

CROMPTON RECREATION

Currently: Defunct

50-51 EX: U.G.B. St Helens (H) 3-0
PR: Formby (H) 2-1
Q1: Marine (A) 1-0
Q2: Wigan Athletic (A) 0-1

57-58 PR: Leyland Motors (A) 2-2, (H) 5-1
Q1: Darwen (H) 2-1
Q2: Ashton United (A) 1-4

58-59 PR: Horwich R.M.I. (H) 1-4

CROOK TOWN

Currently: Northern League
***** - As Crook Colliery Welfare

46-47 * PR: Eden Colliery (A) 8-2
Q1: Throckley Welfare (A) 5-2
Q2: Consett (H) 2-1
Q3: Ashington (A) 1-7

47-48 * PR: Murton Colliery Welfare (H) 1-2

48-49 * EX: Horden Colliery Welfare (H) 0-3

49-50 * EX: Dawdon Colliery Welfare (A) 1-0
PR: Easington Colliery Welfare (H) 3-6

50-51 EX: Ferryhill Ath. (A) 2-2, (H) 4-4, 4-0
PR: Ushaw Moor (H) 2-2, (A) 2-3

51-52 Q1: Evenwood Town (A) 3-1
Q2: Willington (H) 2-1
Q3: Spennymoor United (H) 0-2

52-53 Q1: Shildon (A) 4-0
Q2: Spennymoor United (H) 1-2

53-54 Q1: Stanley United (H) 0-1

54-55 R1: Stanley United (H) 5-3
R2: Brentford (A) 1-4

55-56 Q4: Spennymoor United (A) 2-2, (H) 5-0
R1: Derby County (H) 2-2, (A) 1-5

56-57 Q4: Billingham Sythonia Recreation (A) 3-8

57-58 Q1: Consett (H) 4-3
Q2: Whitley Bay Athletic (A) 5-0
Q3: Stanley United (H) 1-1, (A) 4-0
Q4: Blyth Spartans (H) 3-0
R1: Workington (A) 1-8

58-59 Q4: Evenwood Town (H) 3-0
R1: Buxton (A) 1-4

59-60 R1: Matlock Town (H) 2-2, (A) 1-0
R2: York City (H) 0-1

60-61 Q4: Bishop Auckland (H) 1-2

61-62 Q4: Shildon (H) 1-2

62-63 R1: Hull City (A) 4-5

63-64 Q4: Stanley United (A) 2-0
R1: Chesterfield (H) 1-2

64-65 R1: Carlisle United (H) 1-0
R2: Oldham Athletic (H) 0-1

65-66 Q4: Whitby Town (A) 1-1, (H) 4-1
R1: Gateshead (A) 2-4

66-67 Q4: Bishop Auckland (H) 4-4, (A) 0-2

67-68 Q1: Consett (A) 2-1
Q2: Tow Law Town (A) 0-2

68-69 Q1: Stockton (H) 2-3

69-70 Q1: Ferryhill Athletic (H) 3-3, (A) 1-0
Q2: Shildon (H) 0-4

70-71 Q1: Ferryhill Athletic (A) 1-3

71-72 Q1: Consett (H) 1-4

72-73 Q1: Ashington (H) 2-0
Q2: Tow Law Town (H) 4-2
Q3: Billingham Synthonia (H) 0-3

73-74 Q1: Horden Colliery Welfare (H) 1-3

74-75 Q1: Wingate (H) 1-4

75-76 PR: Barrow (H) 3-0
Q1: Spennymoor United (A) 1-1, (H) 1-2

76-77 PR: Eppleton Colliery Welfare (H) 4-1
Q1: Penrith (A) 2-0
Q2: South Bank (H) 1-0
Q3: Bishop Auckland (A) 1-1, (H) 1-0
Q4: Netherfield (H) 2-1
R1: Nuneaton Borough (H) 1-4

77-78 Q1: Evenwood Town (H) 3-0
Q2: Blyth Spartans (H) 1-1, (A) 0-3

78-79 PR: South Bank (H) 1-2

79-80 PR: Annfield Plain (H) 5-2
Q1: Gateshead (A) 2-2, (H) 2-0
Q2: Ashington (H) 2-3

80-81 PR: Consett (A) 2-0
Q1: Thackley (A) 0-1

81-82 Q1: Ashington (A) 2-4

82-83 PR: Barrow (A) 0-2

83-84 PR: Accrington Stanley (A) 1-3

84-85 PR: Shildon (A) 1-0
Q1: Durham City (H) 3-1
Q2: Gateshead (H) 1-2

85-86 PR: Evenwood Town (A - *played home*) 5-1
Q1: Horden Colliery Welfare (A) 3-2
Q2: Scarborough (H) 0-1

86-87 Q1: Blyth Spartans (A) 1-1, (H) 0-1

87-88 PR: Bedlington Terriers (H) 2-1
Q1: Netherfield (A) 1-1, (H) 2-1
Q2: Barrow (H) 0-1

88-89 PR: Ferryhill Athletic (H) 0-4

89-90 PR: Workington (H) 0-0, (A) 1-0
Q1: West Auckland Town (H) 5-1
Q2: Tow Law Town (A) 2-4

90-91 PR: Horden Colliery Welfare (H) 1-2

91-92 PR: Ashington (A) 1-3

92-93 PR: Norton & Stockton Ancients (H) 0-3

CROSSENS (SOUTHPORT)

Currently: Southport & District League

46-47 PR: Wigan Athletic (H - *played away*) 2-3

47-48 PR: Rhyl (A) 0-10

48-49 PR: Bangor City (A) 0-6

49-50 EX: Earlestown (A) 1-2

50-51 EX: Skelmersdale United (H) 0-12

CROWN & MANOR

Currently: Defunct

47-48 EX: Sawbridgeworth (A) 1-4

48-49 PR: Harrow Town (A) 1-7

49-50 EX: Tufnell Park (H - *at Ilford F.C.*) 2-1
PR: Lyons Club (A) 4-0
Q1: St Albans City (A) 1-4

CROYDON

Currently: Isthmian League
***** - As Croydon Amateurs

66-67 * Q1: Hornchurch (H) 1-2

67-68 * Q1: Hayes (H) 0-1

68-69 * Q1: Staines Town (A) 4-0
Q2: Brentwood Town (H) 0-2

69-70 * Q1: Whyteleafe (A) 1-1, (H) 1-1, 0-1

72-73 * Q1: Addlestone (A) 0-1

73-74 Q1: Staines Town (A) 0-2

74-75 Q1: Leatherhead (H) 0-2

75-76 Q1: Erith & Belvedere (H) 1-1, (A) 3-1
Q2: Bromley (H) 2-1
Q3: Molesey (A) 4-0
Q4: Wycombe Wanderers (H) 2-2, (A) 2-5

76-77 PR: Guildford & Dorking United (H) 1-0
Q1: Tonbridge (A) 1-0
Q2: Woking (H) 0-0, (A) 0-2

77-78 Q1: Tunbridge Wells (H) 3-3, (A) 2-0
Q2: Sutton United (A) 0-2

78-79 Q1: Erith & Belvedere (H) 1-0
Q2: Margate (H) 0-2

79-80 Q1: Bexhill Town (A) 2-0
Q2: Ashford Town (A) 2-0
Q3: Bognor Regis Town (A) 1-0
Q4: Leatherhead (A) 1-1, (H) 3-0
R1: Wycombe Wanderers (A) 3-0
R2: Millwall (H - *at C. Palace*) 1-1, (A) 2-3

80-81 Q1: Southwick (H) 1-0
Q2: Littlehampton Town (A) 3-0
Q3: Gosport Borough (H) 0-1

81-82 PR: Ringmer (H) 1-0
Q1: Bexhill Town (A) *W/O*
Q2: Epsom & Ewell (H) 1-1, (A) 0-4

82-83 PR: Harefield United (A) 4-0
Q1: Hampton (A) 0-2

83-84 Q1: Three Bridges (A) 1-5

84-85 Q1: Whitstable Town (A) 0-0, (H) 5-0
Q2: Canterbury City (A) 1-2

85-86 Q1: Haywards Heath (A) 5-3
Q2: Hythe Town (A) 5-1
Q3: Southwick (A) 1-0
Q4: Bath City (A) 1-4

86-87 Q1: Bracknell Town (A) 0-2

87-88 Q1: Southwick (A) 3-1
Q2: Ramsgate (A) 1-0
Q3: Metropolitan Police (A) 1-0
Q4: Merthyr Tydfil (A) 0-3

88-89 Q1: Hastings Town (H) 1-2

89-90 PR: Havant Town (H - *at Met. Police*) 3-2
Q1: Wokingham T. (H - *at Sutton U.*) 0-3

90-91 PR: Egham Town (H) 0-4

91-92 PR: Darenth Heathside (H - *played away*) 3-0
Q1: Slough Town (A) 2-2, (H) 0-3

92-93 PR: Sheppey United (A - *at Faversham*) 1-0
Q1: Canterbury City (H) 0-0, (A) 1-2

Left: *The most significant moment in Croydon's F.A. Cup history. An open-mouthed John Jackson, the Millwall 'keeper, is beaten by a Rob Ward effort in the eigth minute of the Second Round tie at Selhurst Park on December 5th 1979. Photo: Press Association.*

CROYDON ATHLETIC

Currently: London Spartan League
* - As Wandsworth & Norwood

89-90 * PR: Burgess Hill Town (H) 2-1
Q1: Carshalton Athletic (H) 1-1, (A) 1-3

Below: *John McFadden fires a free-kick as Wandsworth & Norwood gain a surprise draw with Carshalton Athletic. Photo: Dave West.*

90-91 PR: Andover (H) 2-2, (A) 1-7

91-92 PR: Hythe Town (A) 4-4, (H) 2-1
Q1: Tonbridge A.F.C. (A) 1-2

92-93 PR: Arundel (H) 7-3
Q1: Dorking (H) 1-2

CROYDON ROVERS

Currently: Defunct

51-52 PR: Dorking (A) *Scratched*

CRYSTAL PALACE

Currently: Football League

45-46 R3: Queens P.R. (A) 0-0, (H) 0-0 *abandoned in extra-time*, (A) 0-1 (*agg: 0-1*)

46-47 R3: Newcastle United (A) 2-6

47-48 R1: Port Vale (H) 2-1
R2: Bristol City (A) 1-0
R3: Chester (H) 0-1

48-49 R1: Bristol City (H) 0-1

49-50 R1: Newport County (H) 0-3

50-51 R1: Millwall (H) 1-4

51-52 R1: Gillingham (H) 0-1

52-53 R1: Reading (H) 1-1, (A) 3-1
R2: Finchley (A) 1-3 *abandoned*, (H) 1-3

53-54 R1: Great Yarmouth Town (A) 0-1

54-55 R1: Swindon Town (A) 2-0
R2: Bishop Auckland (H) 2-4

55-56 R1: Southampton (H) 0-0, (A) 0-2

56-57 R1: Walthamstow Avenue (H) 2-0
R2: Brentford (A) 1-1, (H) 3-2
R3: Millwall (A) 0-2

57-58 R1: Margate (A) 3-2
R2: Southampton (H) 1-0
R3: Ipswich Town (H) 0-1

58-59 R1: Ashford Town (A) 1-0
R2: Shrewsbury T. (H) 2-2, (A) 2-2, 4-1
R3: Sheffield United (A) 0-2

59-60 R1: Chelmsford City (H) 5-1
R2: Margate (A) 0-0, (H) 3-0
R3: Scunthorpe United (A) 0-1

60-61 R1: Hitchin Town (H) 6-2
R2: Watford (H) 0-0, (A) 0-1

61-62 R1: Portsmouth (H) 3-0
R2: Bridgwater Town (A) 3-0

R3: Aston Villa (A) 3-4

62-63 R1: Hereford United (H) 2-0
R2: Mansfield Town (H) 2-2, (A) 2-7

63-64 R1: Harwich & Parkeston (H) 8-2
R2: Yeovil Town (A) 1-3

64-65 R3: Bury (H) 5-1
R4: Southampton (A) 2-1
R5: Nottingham Forest (H) 3-1
R6: Leeds United (H) 0-3

65-66 R3: Carlisle United (A) 0-3

66-67 R3: Leeds United (A) 0-3

67-68 R3: Walsall (A) 1-1, (H) 1-2

68-69 R3: Charlton Athletic (A) 0-0, (H) 0-2

69-70 R3: Walsall (H) 2-0
R4: Tottenham Hotspur (A) 0-0, (H) 1-0
R5: Chelsea (A) 1-4

70-71 R3: Chelsea (H) 2-2, (A) 1-2

71-72 R3: Everton (H) 2-2, (A) 2-3

72-73 R3: Southampton (H) 2-0
R4: Sheff. W. (A) 1-1, (H) 1-1, (*at Aston V.*) 2-3

73-74 R3: Wrexham (H) 0-2

74-75 R1: Tooting & Mitcham United (A) 2-1
R2: Plymouth Argyle (A) 1-2

Below: *Palace's Alan Whittle is flanked by two Tooting players during the historic derby in 1974.*

75-76 R1: Walton & Hersham (H) 1-0
R2: Millwall (A) 1-1, (H) 2-1
R3: Scarborough (A) 2-1
R4: Leeds United (A) 1-0
R5: Chelsea (A) 3-2
R6: Sunderland (A) 1-0
SF: Southampton (*at Chelsea*) 0-2

76-77 R1: Brighton (A) 2-2, (H) 1-1, (*at Chelsea*) 1-0
R2: Enfield (A - *played at home*) 4-0
R3: Liverpool (A) 0-0, (H) 2-3

77-78 R3: Hartlepool United (A) 1-2

78-79 R3: Middlesbrough (A) 1-1, (H) 1-0
R4: Bristol City (H) 3-0
R5: Wolverhampton Wanderers (H) 0-1

79-80 R3: Swansea (A) 2-2, (H) 3-3, (*at Cardiff C.*) 1-2

80-81 R3: Manchester City (A) 0-4

81-82 R3: Enfield (A) 3-2
R4: Bolton Wanderers (H) 1-0
R5: Orient (H) 0-0, (A) 1-0
R6: Queens Park Rangers (A) 0-1

82-83 R3: York City (H) 2-1
R4: Birmingham City (H) 1-0
R5: Burnley (H) 0-0, (A) 0-1

83-84 R3: Leicester City (H) 1-0
R4: West Ham United (H) 1-1, (A) 0-2

84-85 R3: Millwall (A) 1-1, (H) 1-2

85-86 R3: Luton Town (H) 1-2

86-87 R3: Nottingham Forest (H) 1-0
R4: Tottenham Hotspur (A) 0-4

87-88 R3: Newcastle United (A) 0-1

88-89 R3: Stoke City (A) 0-1

89-90 R3: Portsmouth (H) 2-1
R4: Huddersfield Town (H) 4-0
R5: Rochdale (H) 1-0
R6: Cambridge United (A) 1-0
SF: Liverpool (*at Aston Villa*) 4-3
F: Manchester U. (*both at Wembley*) 3-3, 0-1

90-91 R3: Nottingham F. (H) 0-0, (A) 2-2, (A) 0-3

91-92 R3: Leicester City (A) 0-1

92-93 R3: Hartlepool United (A) 0-1

CURZON ASHTON

Currently: Northern Premier League

75-76 Q1: Congleton Town (A) 3-4

76-77 Q1: Witton Albion (A) 1-3

77-78 Q1: New Mills (A) 2-1
Q2: Mossley (A) 0-1

78-79 Q1: Clitheroe (A) 1-0
Q2: Horwich R.M.I. (H) 1-2

79-80 Q1: Leyland Motors (A) 4-1
Q2: Rossendale United (A) 0-2

80-81 Q1: Clitheroe (A) 1-1, (H) 2-2, (A) 1-0
Q2: Prescot Cables (H) 1-4

81-82 Q1: Brigg Town (A) 0-0, (H) 4-1
Q2: Bridlington Trinity (A) 1-0
Q3: Buxton (A) 1-4

82-83 Q1: Rhyl (H) 4-1
Q2: Runcorn (A) 0-3

83-84 Q1: Buxton (A) 1-2

84-85 PR: Long Eaton United (A) 0-3

85-86 Q1: Congleton Town (A) 0-1

86-87 PR: Armthorpe Welfare (H) 2-2, (A) 1-4

87-88 PR: St Helens Town (A) 2-6

88-89 PR: Warrington Town (A) 2-3

89-90 PR: Skelmersdale United (A) 1-1, (H) 2-0
Q1: Prescot Cables (H) 2-0

Q2: Droylsden (A) 1-0
Q3: Mossley (H) 1-1, (A) 1-3

90-91 Q1: St Helens Town (A) 3-0
Q2: South Liverpool (A - *at Bootle*) 0-1

91-92 PR: Irlam Town (A) 0-0, (H) 4-1
Q1: Bangor City (H) 1-1, (A) 2-1
Q2: Buxton (H) 1-0
Q3: Knowsley United (A) 0-2

92-93 Q1: Altrincham (A) 0-3

CWMBRAN TOWN

Currently: League of Wales

88-89 PR: Radstock (H - *played away*) 2-2, (A) 0-1

89-90 PR: Bridgend Town (H - *played away*) 1-0
Q1: Bristol Manor Farm (A) 1-0
Q2: Abingdon Town (A) 0-0, (H) 3-4

90-91 PR: Mangotsfield Utd (H - *played away*) 0-4

91-92 PR: Paulton Rovers (H) 1-0
Q1: Mangotsfield United (A) 2-4

DAGENHAM

Currently: Merged with Redbridge Forest
Playing as Dagenham & Redbridge F.C. in the Alliance Premier League
See also Dagenham & Redbridge

51-52 Q1: Harwich & Parkeston (A) 2-2, (H) 2-1
Q2: Brentwood & Warley (H) 3-3, (A) 1-2

52-53 PR: Brentwood & Warley (A) 3-1
Q1: Briggs (H) 2-2, (A) 0-0 *ab. in E.T.*, (A) 3-1
Q2: Grays Athletic (H) 0-1

53-54 PR: Brentwood & Warley (H) 4-0
Q1: Briggs Sports (H) 1-3

54-55 PR: Tilbury (H) 3-1
Q1: Ilford (A) 3-3, (H) 3-4

55-56 PR: Romford (H) 2-1
Q1: Leytonstone (A) 3-0
Q2: Briggs Sports (H) 0-1

56-57 PR: Brentwood & Warley (H) 0-1

57-58 PR: Grays Athletic (A) 1-2

58-59 Q1: Edgware Town (A) 4-0
Q2: Hendon (A) 1-3

59-60 Q1: Walthamstow Avenue (H) 1-1, (A) 0-4

60-61 Q1: Leytonstone (A) 0-3

61-62 Q1: Hornchurch (A) 6-2
Q2: Hendon (H) 3-1
Q3: Romford (H) 1-1, (A) 1-4

62-63 Q1: Leyton (H) 0-3

63-64 Q1: Leyton (H) 2-1
Q2: Hornchurch (H) 2-0
Q3: Hendon (A) 0-3

64-65 Q1: Wembley (A) 2-2, (H) 3-0
Q2: Leytonstone (A) 0-4

65-66 Q1: Ford United (H) 2-2, (A) 2-1
Q2: Leyton (A) 2-3

66-67 Q1: Slough Town (A) 0-2

67-68 Q1: Redhill (H) 1-0
Q2: Dartford (H) 2-1
Q3: Cray Wanderers (H) 1-0
Q4: Wycombe Wanderers (A) 2-0
R1: Tonbridge (H) 1-0
R2: Reading (A) 1-1, (H) 0-1

68-69 Q1: Ruislip Manor (H) 2-2, (A) 6-1
Q2: Dartford (H) 1-2

69-70 Q1: Cray Wanderers (H) 3-0
Q2: Hornchurch (H) 2-0
Q3: Romford (A) 2-1
Q4: Leytonstone (A) 4-0
R1: Sutton United (H) 0-1

70-71 R1: Margate (H) 2-0
R2: Southend United (A) 0-1

71-72 R1: Walsall (A) 1-4

72-73 Q4: Bishop's Stortford (A) 1-1, (H) 0-4

73-74 Q1: Cheshunt (A) 2-2, (H) 2-2, 0-0, 2-1
Q2: Hampton (A) 5-0
Q3: Kingstonian (H) 3-2
Q4: Bishop's Stortford (A) 1-1, (H) 2-1
R1: Aldershot (H) 0-4

74-75 PR: Bromley (H) 2-2, (A) 4-2
Q1: Tilbury (H) 3-1
Q2: Redhill (H) 3-0
Q3: Leatherhead (A) 0-0, (H) 1-3

75-76 Q1: Edgware (H) 5-1
Q2: Boreham Wood (H) 4-0
Q3: Wealdstone (A) 0-2

76-77 Q1: Stevenage Athletic (A) *W/O*
Q2: Southall & Ealing Borough (A) 1-0
Q3: Carshalton Athletic (A) 3-3, (H) 2-1
Q4: Dartford (H) 1-1, (A) 2-3

77-78 R1: Walsall (A) 0-1

78-79 Q4: Irthlingborough (H) 0-0, (A) 2-1
R1: Watford (A) 0-3

79-80 Q4: Barking (H) 2-4

80-81 R1: Gillingham (A) 1-2

81-82 Q4: Gravesend & Northfleet (A) 0-0, (H) 6-3
R1: Yeovil Town (H) 2-2, (A) 1-0
R2: Millwall (H) 1-2

82-83 Q4: Tooting & Mitcham United (H) 2-0
R1: Gillingham (A) 0-1

83-84 Q4: Folkestone (A) 1-1, (H) 3-0
R1: Brentford (A) 1-2

84-85 Q4: Aveley (A) 1-0
R1: Swindon Town (H) 0-0, (A) 2-1
R2: Peterborough United (H) 1-0
R3: Carlisle United (A) 0-1

85-86 Q4: Atherstone United (H) 5-1
R1: Cambridge United (H) 2-1
R2: A.F.C. Bournemouth (A) 1-4

86-87 Q4: Wealdstone (H) 0-3

87-88 Q4: Great Yarmouth Town (A) 2-0
R1: Maidstone United (H) 0-2

88-89 Q4: Burton Albion (H) 2-0
R1: Sutton United (H) 0-4

89-90 Q4: Dartford (A) 1-3

90-91 Q1: Burnham (H) 1-1, (A) 2-1
Q2: Molesey (A) 2-1
Q3: Grays Athletic (H) 3-1
Q4: Aylesbury United (H) 0-2

91-92 Q1: Tiptree United (A) 0-1

DAGENHAM & REDBRIDGE

Currently: Alliance Premier League
See also Dagenham, Ilford, Leytonstone, Leytonstone-Ilford, Walthamstow Avenue and Redbridge Forest

92-93 Q1: Billericay Town (H) 1-1, (A) 4-1
Q2: Stowmarket Town (H) 6-1
Q3: Wealdstone (A - *at Watford*) 6-1
Q4: Hednesford Town (A) 2-1
R1: Leyton-Orient (H) 4-5

Below: *The newly amalgamated Dagenham & Redbridge club reached the First Round of the F.A. Cup at the first attempt, and in an enthralling derby against Leyton Orient, watched by a capacity 5,300 crowd, they twice held a two goal lead before succumbing 4-5. This action shows defender Paul Watts tackling Orient's Robert Taylor. Photo: Dave West.*

DAGENHAM BRITISH LEGION

Currently: Defunct

46-47 EX: Harwich & Parkeston (A) 1-8

47-48 PR: London Transport (C.B.) (H) 4-1
Q1: Ekco (A) 0-3

48-49 EX: Colchester Casuals (H) 3-2
PR: Barking (A) 0-4

49-50 PR: Briggs Sports (A) 1-10

DARENTH HEATHSIDE

Currently: Kent League

86-87 Q1: Welling United (A) 0-6

87-88 PR: Leatherhead (H) 2-1
Q1: Rayners Lane (A) 2-1
Q2: Hayes (A) 1-4

88-89 PR: Hertford Town (H) 0-1

89-90 PR: Hertford Town (H) 3-3, (A) 1-4

90-91 PR: Horsham Y.M.C.A. (A) 2-3

91-92 PR: Croydon (A - *played home*) 0-3

DARLASTON

Currently: West Midlands (Regional) League

46-47 PR: Nuneaton Borough (A) 1-3

47-48 PR: Worcester City (H) 1-2

48-49 PR: Moor Green (H) 2-1
Q1: Stafford Rangers (A) 3-4

49-50 EX: Thynnes Athletic (A) 6-0
PR: Bilston (A) 1-2

50-51 PR: Brierley Hill Alliance (A) 1-7

51-52 PR: Atherstone Town (H) 1-1, (A) 4-1
Q1: Bedworth Town (H) 1-2

52-53 PR: Stourbridge (H) 2-1
Q1: Bromsgrove Rovers (A) 2-3

53-54 Q1: Worcester City (H) 0-0, (A) 1-3

54-55 PR: Bromsgrove Rovers (A) 3-4

55-56 Q1: Stourbridge (H) 2-7

56-57 PR: Worcester City (H) 0-7

57-58 PR: Bilston (A) 0-2

58-59 PR: Evesham United (H) 1-3

67-68 Q1: Hinckley Athletic (A) 1-0
Q2: Bromsgrove Rovers (H) 0-0, (A) 0-5

68-69 Q1: Tamworth (A) 2-1
Q2: Stafford Rangers (A) 0-2

69-70 PR: Dudley Town (H) 1-2

71-72 Q1: Warley (H) 2-1
Q2: Alvechurch (H) 0-4

72-73 PR: Moor Green (A) 1-2

73-74 Q1: Atherstone Town (A) 0-1

74-75 PR: Bilston (H) 1-2

75-76 Q1: Burton Albion (H) 3-1
Q2: Arnold (H) 0-1

76-77 Q1: Highgate United (H) 2-1
Q2: Armitage (A) 1-1, (H) 1-0
Q3: Sutton Coldfield Town (H) 1-0
Q4: Kettering Town (H) 1-1, (A) 0-2

77-78 Q1: Eastwood Town (H) 3-0
Q2: Hinckley Athletic (H) 0-1

78-79 Q1: Evesham United (H) 1-1, (A) 4-2
Q2: Milton Keynes City (H) 5-0
Q3: Worcester City (A) 1-7

79-80 Q1: Hednesford Town (H) 1-2

80-81 PR: Brierley Hill Alliance (A) 2-0
Q1: V.S. Rugby (A) 1-3

81-82 Q1: Tamworth (H) 1-2

82-83 Q1: Rothwell Town (A) 0-3

DARLINGTON

Currently: Football League

45-46 R1: Stockton (H) 2-0, (A) 4-1 *(agg: 6-1)*
R2: Gateshead (H) 2-4, (A) 2-1 *(agg: 4-5)*

46-47 R1: Gainsborough Trinity (A) 2-1
R2: Hull City (H) 1-2

47-48 R1: Hartlepools United (A) 0-1

48-49 R1: Tranmere Rovers (A) 3-1
R2: Leyton Orient (H) 1-0
R3: Rotherham United (A) 2-4

49-50 R1: Crewe Alexandra (H) 2-2, (A) 0-1

50-51 R1: Rotherham United (H) 2-7

51-52 R1: Grimsby Town (A) 0-4

52-53 R1: Grimsby Town (H) 2-3

53-54 R1: Port Vale (H) 1-3

54-55 R1: Barrow (A) 1-1, (H) 2-1
R2: Walthamstow Avenue (A) 3-0
R3: Hartlepools U. (A) 1-1, (H) 2-2, 0-2

55-56 R1: Carlisle Utd (H) 0-0, (A) 0-0, 3-1
R2: Accrington Stanley (H) 0-1

56-57 R1: Evenwood Town (A - *played home*) 7-2
R2: Carlisle United (A) 1-2

57-58 R1: Rochdale (A) 2-0
R2: Boston United (H) 5-3
R3: Norwich City (A) 2-1
R4: Chelsea (A) 3-3, (H) 4-1
R5: Wolverhampton Wanderers (A) 1-6

58-59 R1: Wrexham (A) 2-1
R2: Halifax Town (A) 1-1, (H) 3-0
R3: Accrington Stanley (A) 0-3

59-60 R1: Prescot Cables (H) 4-0
R2: Doncaster Rovers (A) 2-3

60-61 R1: Grimsby Town (H) 2-0
R2: Hull C. (H) 1-1, (A) 1-1, 1-1, 0-0, 0-3

61-62 R1: Carlisle United (H) 0-4

62-63 R1: Lincoln City (A) 1-1, (H) 1-2

63-64 R1: Gateshead (H) 1-4

64-65 R1: Scunthorpe United (A) 2-1
R2: Hartlepools Utd (A) 0-0, (H) 4-1
R3: Arsenal (H) 0-2

65-66 R1: Bradford City (H) 3-2
R2: Oldham Athletic (H) 0-1

66-67 R1: Stockport Co. (H) 0-0, (A) 1-1, 4-2
R2: Crewe Alexandra (A) 1-2

67-68 R1: Shrewsbury Town (A) 0-3

68-69 R1: Grimsby Town (H) 2-0
R2: Barnsley (H) 0-0, (A) 0-1

69-70 R1: Barnsley (H) 0-0, (A) 0-2

70-71 R1: Bangor City (H) 5-1
R2: Rochdale (H) 0-2

71-72 R1: Barrow (A) 2-0
R2: Port Vale (A) 0-1

72-73 R1: Wrexham (H) 1-1, (A) 0-5

73-74 R1: Scunthorpe United (A) 0-1

74-75 R1: Workington (H) 1-0
R2: Blackburn Rovers (A) 0-1

75-76 R1: Chester (H) 0-0, (A) 0-2

76-77 R1: Scarborough (A) 0-0, (H) 4-1
R2: Sheffield Wednesday (H) 1-0
R3: Orient (H) 2-2, (A) 0-0, *(at Tottenham)* 0-3

77-78 R1: Chester (A) 1-4

78-79 R1: Chesterfield (H) 1-1, (A) 1-0
R2: Chester (H) 2-1
R3: Colchester United (H) 0-1

79-80 R1: Huddersfield Town (H) 1-1, (A) 1-0
R2: Bradford City (H) 0-1

80-81 R1: Bury (H) 0-2

81-82 R1: Carlisle United (H) 2-2, (A) 1-3

82-83 R1: Scunthorpe United (H) 0-1

Above: *Darlington's John Borthwick jumps with Cambridge United 'keeper John Vaughan in season 1989-90 when 'Darlo' reached the Third Round as a non-League club. Photo: Eric Marsh.*

83-84 R1: Mossley (H) 5-0
R2: Altrincham (H) 0-0, (A) 2-0
R3: Maidstone United (H) 4-1
R4: Plymouth Argyle (A) 1-2

84-85 R1: Chester City (H) 3-2
R2: Frickley Athletic (H) 1-0
R3: Middlesbrough (A) 0-0, (H) 2-1
R4: Telford United (H) 1-1, (A) 0-3

85-86 R1: Rochdale (A) 1-2

86-87 R1: Mansfield Town (H) 2-1
R2: Wigan Athletic (H) 0-5

87-88 R1: Sunderland (A) 0-2

88-89 R1: Notts County (H) 1-2

89-90 Q4: Runcorn (H) 4-2
R1: Northwich Victoria (H) 6-2
R2: Halifax Town (H) 3-0
R3: Cambridge United (A) 0-0, (H) 1-3

90-91 R1: York City (H) 1-1, (A) 0-1

91-92 R1: Chesterfield (H) 2-1
R2: Hartlepool United (H) 1-2

92-93 R1: Hull City (H) 1-2

DARLINGTON CLEVELAND BRIDGE

Currently: (D'gton Cleveland Social) Northern Lge

85-86 Q1: South Bank (H) 0-4

86-87 PR: Ferryhill Athletic (A) 2-1
Q1: Harrogate Town (A) 1-4

87-88 Q1: Shotton Comrades (H) 2-0
Q2: South Bank (H) 2-1
Q3: Tow Law Town (A) 0-4

88-89 PR: Armthorpe Welfare (A) 1-3

89-90 PR: Bridlington Trinity (A) *W/O*
Q1: Gateshead (H) 0-1

90-91 PR: Evenwood Town (H) 0-1

91-92 PR: Horden Colliery Welfare (H) 3-2
Q1: Murton (H) 1-3

92-93 PR: Consett (H) 0-1

DARTFORD

Currently: Kent League

46-47 PR: Sheppey United (H) 2-5

47-48 PR: Erith & Belvedere (H) 3-2
Q1: Margate (A) 3-0
Q2: Gravesend & Northfleet (A) 1-0
Q3: Folkestone Town (H) 1-0
Q4: Walthamstow Avenue (A) 1-0
R1: Bristol City (H) 0-0, (A) 2-9

48-49 PR: Callender Athletic (A) 2-1
Q1: Lloyds (Sittingbourne) (A) 2-1
Q2: Ramsgate Athletic (H) 2-0
Q3: Gravesend & Northfleet (A) 1-0
Q4: Wimbledon (A) 2-1
R1: Leyton Orient (H) 2-3

49-50 Q4: King's Lynn (A) 1-1, (H) 1-2

50-51 Q4: King's Lynn (A) 1-1, (H) 3-0
R1: Guildford City (A) 5-1
R2: Reading (A) 0-4

51-52 Q4: Guildford City (A) 1-2

52-53 Q4: Hendon (H) 0-3

53-54 Q1: Hounslow Town (A) 0-0, (H) 0-3

54-55 PR: Vickers (Weybridge) (A) 6-0
Q1: Dover (H) 1-2

55-56 PR: Gravesend & Northfleet (H) 0-3

56-57 PR: Gravesend & Northfleet (H) 2-2, (A) 2-3

57-58 PR: Deal Town (A) 1-1, (H) 2-1
Q1: Dover (A) 3-1
Q2: Gravesend & Northfleet (H) 0-1

58-59 Q1: Tunbridge Wells Utd (H) 3-3, (A) 2-1
Q2: Gravesend & Northfleet (A) 1-1, (H) 2-4

59-60 Q1: Sheppey United (H) 4-1
Q2: Tunbridge Wells United (H) 0-2

60-61 Q1: Cray Wanderers (A) 5-4
Q2: Maidstone United (A) 3-1
Q3: Bexleyheath & Welling (A) 0-5

61-62 Q1: Sittingbourne (H) 5-0
Q2: Bexleyheath & Welling (H) 4-0
Q3: Erith & Belvedere (H) 3-1
Q4: Hastings United (H) 4-1

R1: Exeter City (A) 3-3, (H) 2-1
R2: Bristol City (A) 2-8

62-63 Q4: Maidstone United (H) 2-0
R1: Yeovil Town (A) 2-3

63-64 Q1: Cray Wanderers (A) 0-1

64-65 Q1: Cray Wanderers (H) 5-0
Q2: Chatham Town (A) 4-2
Q3: Bexley United (H) 3-1
Q4: Tonbridge (H) 3-1
R1: Aldershot (H) 1-1, (A) 0-1

65-66 Q4: Tonbridge (A) 0-0, (H) 6-2
R1: Barnet (A) 2-0
R2: Port Vale (A) 0-1

66-67 Q4: Wimbledon (H) 2-2, (A) 0-3

67-68 Q1: Gravesend & Northfleet (H) 4-0
Q2: Dagenham (A) 1-2

68-69 Q1: Hornchurch (H) 4-0
Q2: Dagenham (A) 2-1
Q3: Redhill (H) 4-2
Q4: Guildford City (A) 1-0
R1: Aldershot (H) 3-1
R2: Kettering Town (A) 0-5

69-70 Q4: Hillingdon B. (A) 0-0, (H) 1-1, 1-4

70-71 Q1: Hampton (A) 1-0
Q2: Harrow Borough (A) 7-0
Q3: Bishop's Stortford (H) 1-1, (A) 1-3

71-72 Q1: Walton & Hersham (H) 1-1, (A) 0-1

72-73 Q1: Hemel Hempstead Town (H) 9-2
Q2: Tilbury (H) 4-3
Q3: Woking (H) 3-2
Q4: Walton & Hersham (A) 2-2, (H) 0-1

73-74 Q1: St Albans City (H) 4-1
Q2: Kingstonian (H) 1-3

74-75 R1: Plymouth Argyle (H) 2-3

75-76 Q4: Wembley (A) 1-0
R1: Bishop's Stortford (H) 1-4

76-77 Q4: Dagenham (A) 1-1, (H) 3-2
R1: Tooting & Mitcham (A) 2-4

77-78 Q4: Boreham Wood (A) 2-3

78-79 Q4: Sutton United (A) 2-0
R1: A.P. Leamington (H) 1-2

79-80 Q4: Leytonstone-Ilford (H) 0-2

80-81 Q1: Saffron Walden Town (H) 4-1
Q2: Grays Athletic (A) 0-2

81-82 PR: Redhill (H) 2-2, (A) 0-1

82-83 PR: Whitehawk (H) 5-2
Q1: Haywards Heath (A) 6-1
Q2: Tonbridge A.F.C. (A) 3-2
Q3: Corinthian-Casuals (H) 2-1
Q4: Boreham Wood (A) 1-1, (H) 2-1
R1: Worthing (A) 1-2

83-84 Q1: Hoddeson Town (A) 4-0
Q2: Epsom & Ewell (A) 2-1
Q3: Sittingbourne (H) 2-2, (A) 4-1
Q4: Tooting & Mitcham United (H) 2-0
R1: Millwall (A) 1-2

84-85 Q4: Grays Athletic (A) 3-1
R1: Metropolitan Police (A) 3-0
R2: A.F.C. Bournemouth (H) 1-1, (A) 1-4

85-86 Q4: Worcester City (H) 2-0
R1: A.F.C. Bournemouth (A) 0-0, (H) 0-2

86-87 Q4: Bideford (A) 2-0
R1: Enfield (H) 1-1, (A) 0-3

87-88 Q4: Maidstone United (A) 0-2

88-89 Q1: Flackwell Heath (H) 7-1
Q2: St Albans City (H) 1-1, (A) 4-2
Q3: Wokingham Town (A) 2-1
Q4: Slough Town (A) 2-1
R1: Kettering Town (A) 1-2

89-90 Q1: Redbridge Forest (A) 4-2
Q2: Witham Town (H) 3-1
Q3: Heybridge Swifts (A) 1-0
Q4: Dagenham (H) 3-1
R1: Exeter City (H) 1-1, (A) 1-4

90-91 Q4: Boston United (H) 1-1, (A) 1-2

91-92 Q1: Ware (H) 5-1
Q2: Ford United (A) 1-0
Q3: Baldock Town (A) 2-2, (H) 1-2

92-93 Q1: Horsham (A) *Scratched*

DARTMOUTH UNITED

Currently: South Devon League

46-47 Q1: Plymouth United (H) 5-2
Q2: Peasedown M.W. (A) 1-1, (H) 3-1
Q3: Radstock Town (A) 3-1
Q4: Yeovil Town (A) 2-10

47-48 Q1: Plymouth United (A) 2-1
Q2: St Austell (A) 2-5

48-49 PR: Clevedon (H) 1-3

49-50 PR: Tiverton Town (A) 2-2, (H) 2-0
Q1: Bridgwater Town (H) 2-0
Q2: St Austell (H) 2-1
Q3: Bideford (H) 2-4

50-51 PR: Bideford (A) 1-7

51-52 PR: Oak Villa (H) 4-1
Q1: Newquay (H) 1-0
Q2: Bideford (A) 0-7

52-53 PR: Barnstaple Town (A) 1-5

53-54 PR: St Austell (H) 2-1
Q1: Wadebridge Town (H) 2-3

54-55 PR: Minehead (A) 3-3, (H) 3-5

DARWEN

Currently: North West Counties League

45-46 Q2: Skelmersdale Utd (H) 2-2, (A) 3-2
Q3: Chorley (A) 0-1

46-47 Q1: Horwich R.M.I. (H) 1-1, (A) 2-0
Q2: Wigan Athletic (A) 2-1
Q3: Skelmersdale United (A) 1-1, (H) 6-4
Q4: Lancaster City (H) 2-5

47-48 Q1: Fleetwood (H) 1-3

48-49 PR: Barnoldswick & District (H) 2-0
Q1: Atherton Collieries (H) 3-2
Q2: Rossendale United (A) 0-4

49-50 Q1: Nelson (H) 0-5

50-51 PR: Chorley (A) 2-1
Q1: Bacup Borough (A) 0-2

51-52 PR: Stalybridge Celtic (A) 2-2, (H) 2-0
Q1: Lytham (A) 3-1
Q2: Mossley (H) 1-0
Q3: Skelmersdale United (A) 1-1, (H) 0-1

52-53 Q1: Rossendale United (A) 0-2

53-54 PR: Rossendale United (H) 2-0
Q1: Horwich R.M.I. (A) 1-1, (H) 3-2
Q2: Mossley (A) 0-2

54-55 Q1: Horwich R.M.I. (H) 1-0
Q2: Mossley (H) 3-1
Q3: Chorley (H) 1-1, (A) 4-5

55-56 PR: Chorley (A) 0-4

56-57 Q1: Leyland Motors (H) 1-0
Q2: Mossley (H) 1-1, (A) 0-3

57-58 Q1: Crompton Recreation (A) 1-2

58-59 Q1: Rossendale United (H) 3-1
Q2: Chorley (H) 1-1, (A) 0-3

59-60 PR: Droylsden (A) 1-2

60-61 Q1: Bacup Borough (H) 0-1

61-62 PR: Bacup Borough (A) 5-1
Q1: Lytham St Annes (H) 3-1
Q2: Hyde United (A) 1-5

65-66 Q1: Rossendale United (A) 2-3

66-67 Q1: Bacup Borough (H) 2-3

67-68 Q1: Ellesmere Port Town (H) 0-2

68-69 Q1: Skelmersdale United (H) 1-4

69-70 PR: Penrith (H) 3-0
Q1: Lancaster City (A) 0-1

72-73 Q1: Accrington Stanley (A) 1-1, (H) 2-4

73-74 Q1: Morecambe (A) 0-0, (H) 3-2
Q2: Formby (H) 0-1

74-75 Q1: Penrith (A) 3-0
Q2: Barrow (A) 2-0
Q3: Lancaster City (A) 0-3

75-76 PR: Droylsden (H) 2-3

76-77 PR: Radcliffe Borough (H) 3-1
Q1: Great Harwood (A) 1-1, (H) 0-3

77-78 Q1: Prescot Town (A) 1-0
Q2: Formby (A) 2-2, (H) 2-0
Q3: Runcorn (A) 0-2

78-79 Q1: Chorley (A) 0-3

79-80 Q1: Horwich R.M.I. (A) 1-4

80-81 Q1: Accrington Stanley (A) 0-2

81-82 Q1: Burscough (A) 0-4

82-83 Q1: Southport (H) 2-0
Q2: Chorley (A) 0-0, (H) 0-3

83-84 Q1: Hyde United (A) 0-3

84-85 PR: Thackley (A) 2-0
Q1: Gretna (H) 1-2

85-86 PR: Accrington Stanley (A) 0-2

86-87 PR: West Auckland Town (H) 2-0
Q1: Evenwood Town (A) 0-2

87-88 PR: Lancaster City (A) 4-0
Q1: Tow Law Town (H) 2-2, (A) 2-3

88-89 PR: Norton & Stockton Ancients (A) 0-1

89-90 Q1: Lancaster City (H) 0-3

90-91 PR: Peterlee Newtown (H) 2-0
Q1: Lancaster City (A) 0-1

91-92 PR: Hebburn (H) 1-1, (A) 1-2

92-93 Q1: Horden Colliery Welfare (A) 1-1, (H) 5-0
Q2: Northallerton Town (H) 1-6

DAVID BROWN ATHLETIC

Currently: Defunct

48-49 EX: Ossett Town (H) 0-11

Above: *Dartford under Bournemouth pressure in the snowy Watling Street 1985-86 replay. Photo: David Hills.*

DAWDON COLLIERY WELFARE
Currently: (Dawdon C.W. Mechanics) Washington Lge

46-47 PR: Seaham Colliery Welfare (A) 0-7

47-48 EX: Horden Colliery Welfare (H) 0-0, (A) 0-9

48-49 EX: Cockfield (H) 4-1
PR: Spennymoor United (H) 1-3

49-50 EX: Crook Colliery Welfare (H) 0-1

50-51 PR: Blackhall C.W. (H) 1-1, (A) 1-3

51-52 Q1: Annfield Plain (H) 3-0
Q2: Consett (H) 0-3

52-53 Q1: South Shields (H) 1-2

53-54 Q1: Annfield Plain (H) 1-4

54-55 Q1: Consett (H) 2-1
Q2: Easington Colliery Welfare (A) 2-3

55-56 Q1: Consett (A) 0-4

56-57 Q1: Consett (H) 0-2

DAWLISH TOWN
Currently: Western League

90-91 PR: Clevedon Town (A) 3-3, (H) 2-3

91-92 PR: Maesteg Park (H) 1-2

92-93 PR: Newport A.F.C. (H) 0-3

DEAL TOWN
Currently: Kent League

51-52 PR: Sittingbourne (A) 2-2, (H) 1-3

52-53 PR: Betteshanger Colliery Welfare (A) 0-2

53-54 PR: Sutton United (A) 5-3
Q1: Ramsgate Athletic (H) 0-0, (A) 0-1

54-55 PR: Ashford Town (H) 0-2

55-56 Q1: Canterbury City (H) 2-2, (A) 1-2

56-57 PR: Sittingbourne (H) 3-5

57-58 PR: Dartford (H) 1-1, (A) 1-2

58-59 Q1: Whitstable (H) 3-4

59-60 Q1: Ashford Town (H) 0-1

60-61 Q1: Betteshanger Colliery Welfare (A) 7-1
Q2: Folkestone Town (A) 1-5

61-62 Q1: Dover (A) 0-4

63-64 Q1: Ramsgate Athletic (A) 2-4

64-65 Q1: Whitstable (A) 7-2
Q2: Ashford Town (A) 2-2, (H) 4-2
Q3: Canterbury City (A) 1-4

65-66 Q1: Dover (H) 2-2, (A) 0-3

66-67 Q1: Sittingbourne (H) 1-1, (A) 2-6

67-68 Q1: Sheppey United (H) 2-0
Q2: Margate (H) 1-4

68-69 Q1: Snowdown C.W. (H) 2-2, (A) 1-2

69-70 Q1: Hastings United (A) 0-4

70-71 PR: Tunbridge Wells (A) 1-2

71-72 Q1: Tonbridge (H) 1-1, (A) 0-2

72-73 Q1: Folkestone (A) 1-4

73-74 Q1: Folkestone (H) 1-1, (A) 2-6

74-75 Q1: Ashford Town (H) 0-4

75-76 Q1: Eastbourne Utd (H) 1-1, (A) 0-1

76-77 Q1: Southwick (A) 0-2

77-78 Q1: Crawley Town (A) 1-3

80-81 PR: Crawley Town (A) 1-2

81-82 Q1: Thanet United (A) 2-2, (H) 2-1
Q2: Ashford Town (H) 1-2

82-83 Q1: Redhill (H) 3-1
Q2: Dover (A) 3-0
Q3: Tooting & Mitcham United (A) 1-8

83-84 Q1: Ashford Town (A) 0-5

84-85 PR: Hastings Town (H) 2-2, (A) 1-3

85-86 PR: Southwick (H) 1-4

89-90 PR: Tunbridge Wells (A) 1-1, (H) 2-1
Q1: Whitstable (H) 1-3

92-93 PR: Epsom & Ewell (H) 3-0
Q1: Malden Vale (H) 4-0
Q2: Horsham (A) 6-1
Q3: Ashford Town (A) 1-3

DE HAVILLAND (BOLTON)
Currently: Defunct

47-48 PR: Morecambe (H) 1-3

48-49 PR: Nelson (H) 0-1

49-50 PR: Chorley (A) 0-5

DE HAVILLAND VAMPIRES (BOREHAM WOOD)
Currently: Defunct

48-49 EX: St Albans City (H - *played away*) 0-5

DENABY UNITED
Currently: Northern Counties (East) League

45-46 Q1: Grimethorpe (A) 5-1
Q2: Brodsworth Main Colliery (A) 3-2
Q3: Rawmarsh Welfare (A) 1-5

46-47 PR: Maltby Main (H) 4-1
Q1: Brodsworth Main Colliery (A) 1-1, (H) 2-1
Q2: Wombwell Athletic (A) 2-4

47-48 PR: Winterton Rangers (A) 2-1
Q1: Appleby Frodingham Athletic (H) 4-1
Q2: Scunthorpe United (A) 0-1

48-49 PR: Kilnhurst Colliery (H) 1-0
Q1: Wombwell Athletic (H) 3-1
Q2: Harworth Colliery Inst. (A) 2-2, (H) 1-3

49-50 PR: Sheffield (H) 3-1
Q1: Beighton Miners Welfare (H) 0-2

50-51 PR: Parkgate Welfare (A) 0-2

51-52 Q1: Stocksbridge Works (A) 1-1, (H) 2-1
Q2: Frickley Colliery (A) 1-4

52-53 Q1: Stocksbridge Works (H) 2-1
Q2: Grimethorpe (H) 1-0
Q3: Frickley Colliery (A) 1-1, (H) 3-4

53-54 Q1: Frickley Colliery (H) 1-2

54-55 Q1: Retford Town (A) 4-1
Q2: Langwith Miners Welfare (H) 6-0
Q3: Upton Colliery (H) 2-0
Q4: Cresswell Colliery (H) 2-5

55-56 Q1: Retford Town (H) 5-0
Q2: Stocksbridge Works (H) 3-2
Q3: Frickley Colliery (A) 5-3
Q4: Northwich Victoria (A) 1-3

56-57 Q1: Retford Town (A) 3-3, (H) 3-0
Q2: Frickley Colliery (A) 2-3

57-58 Q2: Upton Colliery (H) 5-1
Q3: Frickley Colliery (A) 1-2

58-59 Q1: Yorkshire Amateur (H) 4-2
Q2: East End Park W.M.C. (H) 2-0
Q3: Stocksbridge Works (H) 2-1
Q4: Goole Town (A) 2-1
R1: Oldham Athletic (H) 0-2

59-60 Q1: Selby Town (A) 3-1
Q2: Farsley Celtic (H) 2-0
Q3: Goole Town (A) 1-0
Q4: Shildon (A) 1-6

60-61 Q1: Gainsborough Trinity (A) 3-0
Q2: Frickley Colliery (A) 0-3

61-62 Q1: Retford Town (A) 0-5

62-63 Q1: Retford Town (H) 4-0
Q2: Gainsborough Trinity (H) 1-2

63-64 Q1: Worksop Town (H) 0-5

65-66 Q1: Stocksbridge Works (A) 4-1
Q2: Gainsborough Trinity (A) 1-4

66-67 Q1: Mexborough Town (A) 2-0
Q2: Gainsborough Trinity (A) 1-2

67-68 Q1: Ossett Albion (H) 4-0
Q2: Farsley Celtic (H) 2-2, (A) 1-3

68-69 PR: Mexborough Town (A) 1-1, (H) 3-2
Q1: Gainsborough Trinity (A) 0-4

71-72 Q1: Emley (H) 3-0
Q2: Worksop Town (H) 1-2

72-73 Q1: Hatfield Main (H) 1-1, (A) 0-0, 1-2

73-74 Q1: Norton Woodseats Amateur (A) 4-0
Q2: Frickley Colliery (H) 0-3

74-75 Q1: Retford Town (A) 0-3

75-76 Q1: Stocksbridge Works Social (H) 4-1
Q2: Frickley Colliery (A) 2-2, (H) 0-2

76-77 Q1: Sutton Town (A) 1-0
Q2: Winterton Rangers (A) 1-2

77-78 Q1: Selby Town (A) 1-3

78-79 Q1: New Mills (A) 0-2

79-80 PR: Alfreton Town (H) 0-2

80-81 PR: Frickley Athletic (H) 1-3

81-82 Q1: Bridlington Trinity (A) 0-2

82-83 PR: Shepshed Charterhouse (H) 1-3

83-84 PR: Chadderton (A) 0-1

84-85 PR: Rossendale United (A) 2-1
Q1: Buxton (H) 3-3, (A) 1-0
Q2: Droylsden (A) 0-0, (H) 2-0
Q3: Marine (H) 0-1

85-86 Q1: Long Eaton United (H) 0-0, (A) 0-1

86-87 PR: North Shields (A) 1-3

87-88 PR: Peterlee Newtown (A) 3-1
Q1: Stockton (A) 0-1

88-89 PR: Annfield Plain (A) 0-1

89-90 Q1: Congleton Town (A) 1-2

90-91 PR: Ashton United (A) 2-0
Q1: Caernarfon Town (A) *Unable to fulfill*

91-92 PR: West Auckland Town (A) 5-3
Q1: Harrogate Railway Athletic (H) 1-0
Q2: Fleetwood Town (H) 1-0
Q3: Guiseley (A) 1-1, (H) 1-2

92-93 PR: Heanor Town (H) 2-5

DERBY COUNTY
Currently: Football League

45-46 R3: Luton Town (A) 6-0, (H) 3-0 (*agg: 9-0*)
R4: West Brom. A. (H) 1-0, (A) 3-1 (*agg: 4-1*)
R5: Brighton (A) 4-1, (H) 6-0, (*agg: 10-1*)
R6: Aston Villa (A) 4-3, (H) 1-1 (*agg: 5-4*)
SF: Birmingham City (*at Sheffield Wed.*) 1-1, (*at Manchester City*) 4-0
F: Charlton Athletic (*at Wembley*) 4-1

46-47 R3: Bournemouth & Boscombe Ath. (A) 2-0
R4: Chelsea (A) 2-2, (H) 1-0
R5: Liverpool (A) 0-1

47-48 R3: Chesterfield (H) 2-0
R4: Crewe Alexandra (A) 3-0
R5: Middlesbrough (A) 2-1
R6: Queens Park Rangers (A) 1-1, (H) 5-0
SF: Manchester United (*at Sheff. Wed.*) 1-3

48-49 R3: Southport (H) 4-1
R4: Arsenal (H) 1-0
R5: Cardiff City (H) 2-1
R6: Portsmouth (A) 1-2

49-50 R3: Manchester City (A) 5-3
R4: Bury (A) 2-2, (H) 5-2
R5: Northampton Town (H) 4-2
R6: Everton (H) 1-2

50-51 R3: West Bromwich Albion (H) 2-2, (H) 0-1
R4: Birmingham City (H) 1-3

51-52 R3: Middlesbrough (A) 2-2, (H) 0-2

52-53 R3: Chelsea (H) 4-4, (A) 0-1

53-54 R3: Preston North End (H) 0-2

54-55 R3: Manchester City (H) 1-3

55-56 R1: Crook Town (A) 2-2, (H) 5-1
R2: Boston United (H) 1-6

56-57 R1: Bradford City (H) 2-1
R2: New Brighton (H) 1-3

57-58 R3: Middlesbrough (A) 0-5

Above: *Derby's Kevin Hector (right) beats Brian Greenhoff to the ball in the 1976 Semi-Final. Photo: Colorsport*

58-59 R3: Preston North End (H) 2-2, (A) 2-4

59-60 R3: Manchester United (H) 2-4

60-61 R3: Brighton & Hove Albion (A) 1-3

61-62 R3: Leeds United (A) 2-2, (H) 3-1
R4: Charlton Athletic (A) 1-2

62-63 R3: Peterborough United (H) 2-0
R4: Leyton Orient (A) 0-3

63-64 R3: Liverpool (A) 0-5

64-65 R3: Plymouth Argyle (A) 2-4

65-66 R3: Manchester United (H) 2-5

66-67 R3: Norwich City (A) 0-3

67-68 R3: Leeds United (A) 0-2

68-69 R3: Burnley (A) 1-3

69-70 R3: Preston North End (A) 1-1, (H) 4-1
R4: Sheffield United (H) 3-0
R5: Queens Park Rangers (A) 0-1

70-71 R3: Chester (A) 2-1
R4: Wolverhampton Wanderers (H) 2-1
R5: Everton (A) 0-1

71-72 R3: Shrewsbury Town (H) 2-0
R4: Notts County (H) 6-0
R5: Arsenal (H) 2-2, (A) 0-0, (*at Leic. C.*) 0-1

72-73 R3: Peterborough United (A) 1-0
R4: Tottenham Hotspur (H) 1-1, (A) 5-3
R5: Queens Park Rangers (H) 4-2
R6: Leeds United (H) 0-1

73-74 R3: Boston United (H) 0-0, (A) 6-1
R4: Coventry City (A) 0-0, (H) 0-1

74-75 R3: Orient (A) 2-2, (H) 2-1
R4: Bristol Rovers (H) 2-0
R5: Leeds United (H) 0-1

75-76 R3: Everton (H) 2-1
R4: Liverpool (H) 1-0
R5: Southend United (H) 1-0
R6: Newcastle United (H) 4-2
SF: Manchester Utd (*at Sheffield Wed.*) 0-2

76-77 R3: Blackpool (A) 0-0, (H) 3-2
R4: Colchester United (A) 1-1, (H) 1-0
R5: Blackburn Rovers (H) 3-1
R6: Everton (A) 0-2

77-78 R3: Southend United (H) 3-2
R4: Birmingham City (H) 2-1
R5: West Bromwich Albion (H) 2-3

78-79 R3: Preston North End (A) 0-3

79-80 R3: Bristol City (A) 2-6

80-81 R3: Bristol City (H) 0-0, (A) 0-2

81-82 R3: Bolton Wanderers (A) 1-3

82-83 R3: Nottingham Forest (H) 2-0
R4: Chelsea (H) 2-1
R5: Manchester United (H) 0-1

83-84 R3: Cambridge United (A) 3-0
R4: Telford United (H) 3-2
R5: Norwich City (H) 2-1
R6: Plymouth Argyle (A) 0-0, (H) 0-1

84-85 R1: Hartlepool United (A) 1-2

85-86 R1: Crewe Alexandra (H) 5-1
R2: Telford United (H) 6-1
R3: Gillingham (A) 1-1, (H) 3-1
R4: Sheffield United (A) 1-0
R5: Sheffield Wednesday (H) 1-1, (A) 0-2

86-87 R3: Sheffield Wednesday (A) 0-1

87-88 R3: Chelsea (H) 1-3

88-89 R3: Southampton (H) 1-1, (A) 2-1
R4: Watford (A) 1-2

89-90 R3: Port Vale (A) 1-1, (H) 2-3

90-91 R3: Newcastle United (A) 0-2

91-92 R3: Burnley (A) 2-2, (H) 2-0 *abandoned (fog) after 76 minutes*, (H) 2-0
R4: Aston Villa (H) 3-4

92-93 R3: Stockport County (H) 2-1
R4: Luton Town (A) 5-1
R5: Bolton Wanderers (H) 3-1
R6: Sheffield Wednesday (H) 3-3, (A) 0-1

DESBOROUGH TOWN

Currently: United Counties League

47-48 Q1: Stewarts & Lloyds (H) 1-0
Q2: Peterborough United (H) 1-2

48-49 Q1: Westwood Works (A) *W/O*
Q2: Kettering Town (A) 2-2, (H) 0-3

49-50 Q1: Peterborough United (A) 1-5

50-51 Q1: Wellingborough Town (A) 0-2

51-52 Q1: Symington's Recreation (A) 3-1
Q2: Stamford (H) 2-1
Q3: Kettering Town (A) 0-2

52-53 Q1: Corby Town (H) 1-4

53-54 Q1: Symington's Recreation (A) 3-0
Q2: Kettering Town (H) 0-4

54-55 Q1: Rushden Town (A) 1-3

55-56 Q1: Rothwell Town (H) 0-0, (A) 0-5

63-64 Q1: Bourne Town (A) 1-6

64-65 Q1: Bourne Town (H) 2-0
Q2: St Neots Town (A) 0-3

65-66 Q1: St Neots Town (H) 3-0
Q2: Wellingborough Town (H) 1-2

66-67 Q1: Wellingborough Town (H) 2-1
Q2: St Neots Town (H) 1-2

67-68 Q1: Cambridge City (A) 0-4

68-69 PR: Chatteris Town (H) 3-0
Q1: Stamford (H) 0-4

69-70 Q1: Rushden Town (H) 1-2

70-71 Q1: Cambridge City (A) 1-5

71-72 PR: Irthlingborough Diamonds (H) 1-2

72-73 Q1: Enderby United (H) 1-2

73-74 Q1: Stamford Town (A) 0-1

74-75 Q1: Rushden Town (A) 1-2

75-76 Q1: Cheltenham Town (A) 1-1, (H) 2-3

76-77 Q1: Enderby Town (H) 0-1

78-79 PR: Friar Lane Old Boys (H) 0-3

79-80 PR: Bedworth United (H) 1-1, (A) 0-6

80-81 PR: Friar Lane Old Boys (H) 2-1
Q1: Normanby Park Works (A) 4-0
Q2: Barton Town (A) 1-4

81-82 PR: Blakenall (A) 1-1, (H) 2-6

82-83 PR: Buckingham Town (A) 0-1

83-84 PR: Eastwood Hanley (A) 0-1

84-85 PR: Racing Club Warwick (H) 3-0
Q1: Wigston F. (H) 0-0, (A) 1-1, (H) 1-2

85-86 PR: Oldbury United (H) 2-3

86-87 PR: Flackwell Heath (H) 1-1, (A) 2-1
Q1: Uxbridge (A) 0-4

87-88 Q1: Racing Club Warwick (H) 2-2, (A) 0-4

88-89 PR: Witney Town (H) 2-2, (A) 0-1

89-90 PR: Bilston Town (A) 1-1, (H) 2-1
Q1: Atherstone United (H) 1-0
Q2: Lye Town (H) 1-1, (A) 2-5

90-91 PR: Alvechurch (A) 1-2

91-92 PR: Vauxhall Motors (A) *W/O*
Q1: Rushden Town (H) 2-4

92-93 PR: Rushden & Diamonds (A) 0-2

DEVIZES TOWN

Currently: Western League

45-46 PR: Chippenham Town (A) 0-9

46-47 PR: Westbury United (H) 1-2

47-48 PR: Purton (H) 4-0
Q1: Trowbridge Town (A) 1-4

48-49 EX: Melksham (H) 2-1
PR: Salisbury Corinthians (H) 3-0
Q1: Westbury United (A) 2-3

49-50 EX: Spencer Moulton (A) 3-1
PR: Chippenham Town (H) 4-4, (A) 3-4

50-51 PR: Wootton Bassett Town (H) 4-0
Q1: Clandown (A) 0-2

51-52 PR: Frome Town (A) 0-1

52-53 Q1: Frome Town (A) 6-3
Q2: Trowbridge Town (H) 0-3

53-54 PR: Trowbridge Town (H) 2-11

54-55 Q1: Trowbridge Town (H) 2-5

55-56 Q1: Salisbury (H) 0-2

56-57 Q1: Chippenham Town (H) 0-2

58-59 Q1: Chippenham Town (H) 2-6

59-60 Q1: Chippenham United (H) 3-2
Q2: Calne & Harris United (A) 2-7

60-61 Q1: Calne & Harris United (A) 5-2
Q2: Trowbridge Town (A) 2-2, (H) 2-3

61-62 Q1: Trowbridge Town (A) 2-2, (H) 0-2

62-63 Q1: Melksham Town (A) 5-0
Q2: Trowbridge Town (H) 2-3

63-64 Q1: Trowbridge Town (H) 0-5

64-65 Q2: Westbury United (A) 3-0
Q3: Cheltenham Town (A) 1-6

65-66 Q2: Trowbridge Town (H) 3-2
Q3: Cheltenham Town (H) 2-8

66-67 Q1: Welton Rovers (A) 0-2

67-68 Q1: Poole Town (H) 0-4

68-69 Q1: Gloucester City (A) 1-3

69-70 PR: Poole Town (A) 1-6

70-71 Q1: Poole Town (H) 1-5

72-73 Q1: Chippenham Town (A) 4-0
Q2: Glastonbury (H) 7-2
Q3: Cheltenham Town (H) 1-0
Q4: Alton Town (A) 0-2

73-74 Q1: Taunton Town (A) 1-3

74-75 PR: Bath City (H) 2-3

75-76 PR: Melksham Town (A) 0-2

76-77 Q1: Chippenham Town (A) 3-1
Q2: Mangotsfield United (H) 0-1

79-80 PR: Cheltenham Town (H) 0-1

80-81 PR: Chichester City (A) 1-1, (H) 1-3

81-82 Q1: Shepton Mallet Town (H) 1-0
Q2: Gloucester City (A) 4-2
Q3: Worcester City (A) 1-4

82-83 Q1: Camberley Town (H) 1-0
Q2: Frome Town (A) 2-4

83-84 PR: Newbury Town (A) 2-4

84-85 PR: Wellington (A) 1-5

85-86 PR: Pagham (H) 2-2, (A) 1-4

86-87 PR: Farnham Town (H) 1-1, (A) 4-1
Q1: Andover (H) 5-2
Q2: Road Sea Southampton (H) 0-2

87-88 PR: Paulton Rovers (H) 0-0, (A) 0-1

88-89 PR: Sholing Sports (H) 3-2
Q1: Forest Green Rovers (A) 0-5

89-90 Q1: Andover (A) 0-2

90-91 PR: Swanage Town & Herston (A) 0-4

91-92 PR: Radstock Town (A) 2-0
Q1: Taunton Town (A) 0-2

92-93 PR: Oxford City (A) 3-2
Q1: Abingdon Town (A) 0-4

DICKINSONS (APSLEY)

Currently: Defunct

49-50 EX: Chesham United (A) 0-3

DIDCOT TOWN

Currently: Hellenic League

75-76 PR: Milton Keynes City (A) 1-3

76-77 Q1: Oxford City (H) 1-0
Q2: Banbury United (A) 2-3

77-78 PR: Leytonstone (H) 2-2, (A) 0-1

78-79 PR: Aylesbury United (H) 1-1, (A) 1-2

79-80 PR: Alton Town (H) 0-0, (A) 2-0
Q1: Newbury Town (A) 1-2

80-81 Q1: Halesowen Town (A) 1-1, (H) 0-1

81-82 PR: Willesden (H) *W/O*
Q1: Witney Town (A) 0-3

DILTON ROVERS

Currently: Defunct

46-47 EX: Wootton Bassett Town (A) 0-5

48-49 PR: Wilts County Mental Hospital (A) 0-4

DINNINGTON ATHLETIC

Currently: Defunct

46-47 Q1: Frickley Colliery (H) 3-4

47-48 EX: Appleby Frodingham Athletic (A) 1-4

48-49 PR: Beighton Miners Welfare (H) 5-1
Q1: Cresswell Colliery (H) 3-1
Q2: Norton Woodseats (H) 3-3, (A) 1-2

49-50 PR: Norton Woodseats (A) 1-3

70-71 Q1: Rawmarsh Welfare (A) 1-0
Q2: Brigg Town (A) 1-1, (H) 0-1

DISS TOWN

Currently: Eastern Counties League

50-51 EX: Beccles (A) 2-4

51-52 Q1: Sudbury Town (H) 0-4

52-53 Q1: Lowestoft Town (H) 1-4

53-54 Q1: Sudbury Town (A) 1-2

54-55 Q1: Stowmarket (H) 1-3

55-56 Q1: Stowmarket (A) 0-7

56-57 Q1: Whitton United (H) 6-3
Q2: Bury Town (H) 2-4

58-59 Q1: Gorleston (A) 2-3

59-60 Q1: Gorleston (A) 2-2, (H) 2-2, 1-2

DISTINGTON

See High Duty Alloys

DONCASTER ROVERS

Currently: Football League

45-46 R1: Rotherham (H) 0-1, (A) 1-2 (*agg: 1-3*)

46-47 R1: Accrington Stanley (H) 2-2, (A) 5-0
R2: Oldham Athletic (A) 2-1
R3: Portsmouth (H) 2-3

47-48 R3: Fulham (A) 0-2

48-49 R1: Bradford City (A) 3-4

49-50 R1: New Brighton (H) 5-1
R2: Mansfield Town (H) 1-0
R3: Reading (A) 3-2
R4: Blackpool (A) 1-2

50-51 R3: Rotherham United (A) 1-2

51-52 R3: Buxton (H) 2-0
R4: Middlesbrough (A) 4-1
R5: Portsmouth (A) 0-4

52-53 R3: Arsenal (A) 0-4

53-54 R3: Sunderland (A) 2-0
R4: Plymouth Argyle (A) 2-0
R5: Leyton Orient (A) 1-3

54-55 R3: Watford (A) 2-1
R4: Aston Villa (H) 0-0, (A) 2-2, 1-1, 0-0 *aband. after 90 minutes*, 3-1
R5: Birmingham City (A) 1-2

55-56 R3: Nottingham Forest (H) 3-0
R4: Bristol Rovers (A) 1-1, (H) 1-0
R5: Tottenham Hotspur (H) 0-2

56-57 R3: West Bromwich Albion (H) 1-1, (A) 0-2

57-58 R3: Chelsea (H) 0-2

58-59 R1: Consett (H) 5-0
R2: Tranmere Rovers (A) 2-1
R3: Bristol City (H) 0-2

59-60 R1: Gainsbrough Trinty (H) 3-3, (A) 1-0
R2: Darlington (H) 3-2
R3: Bristol Rovers (A) 0-0, (H) 1-2

60-61 R1: Chesterfield (A) 3-3, (H) 0-1

61-62 R1: Chesterfield (H) 0-4

62-63 R1: South Shields (A) 0-0, (H) 2-1
R2: Tranmere Rovers (H) 1-4

63-64 R1: Tranmere Rovers (H) 3-0
R2: Notts County (H) 1-1, (A) 2-1
R3: Bristol City (H) 2-2, (A) 0-2

64-65 R1: Bradford (Park Avenue) (A) 3-2
R2: Scarborough (H) 0-0, (A) 2-1
R3: Huddersfield Town (H) 0-1

65-66 R1: Wigan Athletic (H) 2-2, (A) 1-3

66-67 R1: Halifax Town (A) 2-2, (H) 1-3

67-68 R1: York City (A) 1-0
R2: Workington (H) 1-1, (A) 2-1
R3: Swansea Town (H) 0-2

68-69 R1: Notts County (H) 1-0
R2: Southport (H) 2-1
R3: Liverpool (A) 0-2

69-70 R1: Crewe Alexandra (H) 1-1, (A) 1-0
R2: Chester (A) 1-1, (H) 0-2

70-71 R1: Crewe Alexandra (A) 0-0, (H) 1-3

71-72 R1: Stockport County (H) 1-2

72-73 R1: Bury (H) 3-1
R2: Scarborough (A) 2-1
R3: Reading (A) 0-2

73-74 R1: Lincoln City (H) 1-0
R2: Tranmere Rovers (H) 3-0
R3: Liverpool (A) 2-2, (H) 0-2

74-75 R1: Oswestry Town (A) 3-1
R2: Chesterfield (A) 0-1

75-76 R1: Bury (A) 2-4

76-77 R1: Shrewsbury Town (H) 2-2, (A) 3-4

77-78 R1: Shrewsbury Town (H) 0-1

78-79 R1: Huddersfield Town (H) 2-1
R2: Shrewsbury Town (H) 0-3

79-80 R1: Port Vale (A) 3-1
R2: Mansfield Town (H) 1-2

80-81 R1: Sutton Coldfield Town (A) 2-0
R2: Blackpool (H) 2-1
R3: Hull City (A) 0-1

81-82 R1: Mansfield Town (A) 1-0
R2: Penrith (H) 3-0
R3: Cambridge United (H) 2-1
R4: Norwich City (A) 1-2

82-83 R1: Workington (A) 2-1
R2: Peterborough United (A) 2-5

83-84 R1: Mansfield Town (A) 0-3

84-85 R1: Rochdale (A) 2-1
R2: Altrincham (A) 3-1
R3: Queens Park Rangers (H) 1-0
R4: Everton (A) 0-2

85-86 R1: Wigan Athletic (A) 1-4

86-87 R1: Whitby Town (A) 2-2, (H) 3-2
R2: Chester City (A) 1-3

87-88 R1: Rotherham United (H) 1-1, (A) 0-2

88-89 R1: Brandon (H) 0-0, (A - *played home*) 2-1
R2: Sheffield United (H) 1-3

89-90 R1: Notts County (H) 1-0
R2: Grimsby Town (A) 0-1

90-91 R1: Chester C. (A - *at Macclesfield*) 2-2, (H) 1-2

91-92 R1: Burnley (A) 1-1, (H) 1-3

92-93 R1: Hartlepool United (H) 1-2

DORCHESTER TOWN

Currently: Southern League

48-49 EX: Hamworthy (H) 3-2
PR: Ryde Sports (H) 0-2

49-50 EX: Blandford United (H) 2-1
PR: Romsey Town (A) 4-1
Q1: Cowes (A) 1-5

50-51 EX: Portland United (H) 6-3
PR: Ryde Sports (A) 3-3, (H) 4-2
Q1: Romsey Town (A) 1-1, (H) 2-0
Q2: Poole Town (A) 3-1
Q3: Alton T. (A) 2-2, (H) 2-2 *abandoned*, 1-0
Q4: Glastonbury (H) 1-4

51-52 Q1: Portland United (A) 1-1, (H) 2-3

52-53 PR: Blandford United (A) 5-2
Q1: Bridport (A) 2-0
Q2: Ilminster Town (H) 6-1
Q3: Bournemouth Gasworks Athletic (H) 2-1
Q4: Weymouth (H) 1-5

53-54 Q1: Lymington (H) 9-0
Q2: Portland United (H) 1-3

54-55 Q1: Poole Town (H) 2-1
Q2: Bournemouth Gasworks Athletic (H) 4-0
Q3: Portland United (A) 5-1
Q4: Winchester City (A) 1-0
R1: Bedford Town (H) 2-0
R2: York City (H) 2-5

55-56 Q4: Newport Isle of Wight (H) 3-0
R1: Norwich City (A) 0-4

56-57 Q4: Bideford (A) 1-1, (H) 3-0
R1: Queens Park Rangers (A) 0-4

57-58 Q4: Weymouth (A) 2-2, (H) 2-1

R1: Wycombe Wanderers (H) 3-2
R2: Plymouth Argyle (A) 2-5

58-59 Q4: Weymouth (A) 0-3

59-60 Q4: Weymouth (A) 1-0
R1: Port Vale (H) 1-2

60-61 Q4: Chichester City (A) 1-4

61-62 Q1: Warminster Town (A) 6-1
Q2: Poole Town (A) 1-0
Q3: Portland United (A) 3-0
Q4: Weymouth (H) 3-3, (A) 0-2

62-63 Q2: Portland United (A) 3-1
Q3: Poole Town (H) 0-3

63-64 Q1: Poole Town (H) 1-0
Q2: Bridport (H) 1-0
Q3: Salisbury (H) 1-1, (A) 3-1
Q4: Weymouth (A) 0-3

64-65 Q1: Salisbury (A) 3-3, (H) 1-3

65-66 Q1: Portland United (A) 1-4

66-67 Q1: Warminster Town (H) 5-0
Q2: Street (H) 2-0
Q3: Poole Town (A) 0-1

67-68 Q1: Glastonbury (H) 1-0
Q2: Chippenham Town (H) 4-1
Q3: Poole Town (H) 3-2
Q4: Salisbury (H) 1-2

68-69 Q1: Poole Town (H) 2-5

69-70 Q1: Glastonbury (H) 1-2

71-72 Q1: Taunton Town (H) 3-2
Q2: Bridgwater Town (A) 0-1

72-73 Q1: Andover (H) 1-1, (A) 1-2

73-74 Q1: Bridgwater Town (A) 3-3, (H) 0-1

74-75 PR: Bridgwater Town (H) 3-2
Q1: Weymouth (H) 1-3

75-76 Q1: Bridport (A) 3-4

76-77 Q1: Poole Town (A) 0-2

77-78 Q1: Fareham Town (H) 0-0, (A) 2-1
Q2: Bridgwater Town (H) 4-3
Q3: Bath City (A) 0-2

78-79 Q1: Bridport (A) 1-0
Q2: Basingstoke Town (H) 1-0
Q3: Yeovil Town (A) 1-2

79-80 Q1: Wadebridge Town (H) 2-0
Q2: Barnstaple Town (A) 0-0, (H) 1-3

80-81 Q1: Gloucester City (A) 0-1

81-82 Q1: Hungerford Town (A) 2-1
Q2: Frome Town (H) 3-0
Q3: Eastleigh (A) 4-2
Q4: Cheltenham Town (A) 3-1
R1: Minehead (H) 3-3, (A) 4-0
R2: A.F.C. Bournemouth (H) 1-1, (A) 1-2

82-83 Q1: Oxford City (A) 2-2, (H) 1-0
Q2: Maidenhead United (H) 1-1, (A) 2-0
Q3: A.F.C. Totton (A) 0-1

83-84 Q1: Eastleigh (H) 0-0, (A) 2-0
Q2: Wokingham Town (H) 0-3

84-85 PR: Bridgwater Town (A) *W/O*
Q1: Weston-super-Mare (H) 4-2
Q2: Merthyr Tydfil (H) 0-0, (A) 0-3

85-86 PR: Clandown (H) 0-0, (A) 0-0, (H) 1-2

86-87 Q1: Barry Town (H) 1-1, (A) 4-3
Q2: Forest Green Rovers (A) 2-4

87-88 Q1: Cheltenham Town (A) 1-4

88-89 Q1: Frome Town (H) 3-1
Q2: Maesteg Park (A) 2-0
Q3: Worcester City (A) 1-1, (H) 1-2

89-90 Q1: Chard Town (A) 2-0
Q2: Trowbridge Town (H) 0-0, (A) 2-0
Q3: Cheltenham Town (H) 2-1
Q4: Bognor Regis Town (A) 1-1, (H) 5-1
R1: Gloucester City (A) 0-1

90-91 Q1: Falmouth Town (A) 4-2
Q2: Liskeard Athletic (A) 1-5

91-92 Q1: Brockenhurst (A) 2-1
Q2: Witney Town (H) 3-2
Q3: Trowbridge Town (H) 1-0
Q4: Hayes (A) 0-1

92-93 Q1: Mangotsfield United (A) 1-0
Q2: A.F.C. Lymington (A) 1-1, (H) 2-4

DORKING

Currently: Merged with Guildford City. Playing as Dorking in Isthmian Lge. See also Dorking (2)

48-49 EX: Epsom (H - *played away*) 0-3

49-50 PR: Redhill (A) 3-7

50-51 PR: Dulwich Hamlet (H) *W/O*
Q1: Kingstonian (A) 0-4

51-52 PR: Croydon Rovers (H) *W/O*
Q1: Woking (A) 1-5

52-53 PR: Woking (A) 1-4

53-54 PR: Epsom (A) 1-1, (H) 0-1

54-55 PR: Epsom (H) 1-3

55-56 PR: Erith & Bedvedere (A) 3-3, (H) 5-1
Q1: Folkestone Town (H) 3-1
Q2: Epsom (A) 2-3

56-57 PR: Tunbridge Wells United (H) 0-1

57-58 PR: Sutton United (H) 1-1, (A) 0-5

58-59 PR: Wimbledon (H) 2-1
Q1: Sutton United (H) 1-4

59-60 PR: Wimbledon (A) 0-6

60-61 Q1: Leatherhead (A) 2-1
Q2: Wimbledon (H) 4-3
Q3: Walton & Hersham (H) 1-1, (A) 1-2

61-62 Q1: Walton & Hersham (A) 2-2, (H) 1-3

62-63 Q1: Metropolitan Police (H) 2-3

63-64 Q1: Woking (H) 2-3

64-65 Q1: Kingstonian (A) 0-2

65-66 Q1: Walton & Hersham (H) 1-1, (A) 1-4

66-67 Q1: Horsham (H) 0-3

67-68 Q1: Chichester City (A) 0-2

68-69 Q1: Addlestone (H) 1-2

69-70 PR: Fleet (H) 1-0
Q1: Crawley Town (A) 0-4

70-71 PR: Banstead Athletic (H) 2-0
Q1: Bognor Regis Town (A) 1-2

72-73 Q1: Bognor Regis Town (A) 0-3

73-74 Q1: Maidenhead United (H) 0-2

DORKING

Currently: Isthmian League
* - As Guildford & Dorking Utd + - As Dorking Town
See also original Dorking and Guildford City

74-75 * Q4: Wimbledon (H) 0-3

75-76 * PR: Arundel (H) 7-0
Q1: Ryde Sports (A) 4-0
Q2: Southwick (H) 2-2, (A) 2-3

76-77 * PR: Croydon (A) 0-1

78-79 + Q1: Chichester City (A) 1-1, (H) 3-2
Q2: Horsham (H) 0-2

79-80 + Q1: Eastbourne United (H) 1-1, (A) 1-4

80-81 + PR: Cray Wanderers (A) 1-1, (H) 0-2

81-82 + PR: Basingstoke Town (H) 0-2

82-83 + PR: Arundel (H) 2-1
Q1: Staines Town (A - *played home*) 0-5

83-84 + PR: Berkhamsted Town (H) 1-0
Q1: Hendon (H) 1-1, (A) 1-4

84-85 PR: Basingstoke Town (A) 0-2

85-86 PR: Hailsham Town (A) 4-4, (H) 3-0
Q1: Welling United (H) 1-7

86-87 PR: Sittingbourne (A) 1-1, (H) 2-1
Q1: Wembley (A) 0-1

87-88 PR: Heybridge Swifts (A) 1-1, (H) 2-1
Q1: Fisher Athletic (H) 0-2

88-89 PR: Chatham Town (A) 5-1
Q1: Ashford Town (A) 1-2

89-90 Q1: Tilbury (H) 1-2

90-91 PR: Canterbury City (A) 0-0, (H) 4-1
Q1: Wick (A) 3-0
Q2: Carshalton Athletic (H) 2-0
Q3: Worthing (H) 1-1, (A) 4-2
Q4: Cheltenham Town (H) 2-3

91-92 Q1: Leatherhead (A) 2-1
Q2: Gravesend & Northfleet (H) 3-4

92-93 PR: Hythe Town (H) *W/O*
Q1: Croydon Athletic (A) 2-1
Q2: Walton & Hersham (H) 4-2
Q3: Dover Athletic (H) 1-0
Q4: Farnborough Town (A) 1-1, (H) 2-0
R1: Plymouth (H) 2-3

DOUGLAS (KINGSWOOD)

Currently: Defunct

50-51 PR: Clevedon (A) 0-5

DOVER

Currently: Defunct

46-47 PR: Ramsgate Athletic (A) 0-9

47-48 PR: Gravesend & Northfleet (H) 1-5

48-49 EX: Chatham Town (A) 3-2
PR: Tonbridge (H) 4-2
Q1: Sheppey United (A) 4-2
Q2: Gravesend & Northfleet (A) 1-4

49-50 PR: Bexley (H) 7-2
Q1: Snowdown Colliery Welfare (H) 2-0
Q2: Erith & Belvedere (H) 3-0
Q3: Gravesend & Northfleet (A) 0-5

Above: *Dorking's Carey Anderson contests a high ball with Plymouth's Andy Morrison (5). Photo: Dave West.*

50-51 PR: Snowdown Colliery Welfare (H) 1-2

51-52 PR: Whitstable (A) 4-0
Q1: Ramsgate Athletic (H) 4-0
Q2: Folkestone Town (H) 0-2

52-53 PR: Chatham Town (A) 6-0
Q1: Sheppey United (H) 2-0
Q2: Ramsgate Athletic (H) 5-3
Q3: Gravesend & Northfleet (A) 1-2

53-54 PR: Hounslow Town (H) 1-2

54-55 PR: Woking (H) 2-1
Q1: Dartford (A) 2-1
Q2: Whitstable (H) 2-1
Q3: Tonbridge (A) 2-3

55-56 PR: Whitstable (H) 5-1
Q1: Epsom (A) 2-3

56-57 PR: Snowdown C.W. (A) 0-0, (H) 1-2

57-58 PR: Folkestone Town (H) 2-1
Q1: Dartford (H) 1-3

58-59 Q1: Canterbury City (H) 0-2

59-60 Q1: Betteshanger C.W. (H) 0-0, (A) 1-3

60-61 Q1: Canterbury City (H) 4-1
Q2: Snowdown Colliery Welfare (H) 5-3
Q3: Folkestone Town (H) 1-0
Q4: Littlehampton Town (H) 2-1
R1: Peterborough United (H) 1-4

61-62 Q1: Deal Town (H) 4-0
Q2: Folkestone Town (A) 3-2
Q3: Ramsgate Athletic (H) 3-2
Q4: Ashford Town (A) 1-3

62-63 Q1: Sheppey United (A) 1-0
Q2: Ramsgate Athletic (H) 4-1
Q3: Sittingbourne (A) 1-2

63-64 Q1: Sheppey United (H) 1-2

64-65 Q1: Canterbury City (H) 0-2

65-66 Q1: Deal Town (A) 2-2, (H) 3-0
Q2: Folkestone Town (A) 1-1, (H) 2-3

66-67 Q1: Ramsgate Athletic (A) 1-2

67-68 Q1: Bromley (H) 4-0
Q2: Whitstable Town (A) 7-1
Q3: Tonbridge (A) 2-4

68-69 Q1: Tonbridge (A) 5-2
Q2: Ashford Town (H) 2-5

69-70 Q1: Ashford Town (A) 0-0, (H) 2-4

70-71 Q1: Hastings United (H) 0-1

71-72 Q1: Ramsgate Athletic (H) 2-1
Q2: Whitstable Town (A) 5-0
Q3: Ashford Town (A) 2-0
Q4: Walthamstow Avenue (A) 0-0, (H) 1-0
R1: Guildford City (A) 0-0, (H) 0-2

72-73 PR: Sheppey United (A) 2-2, (H) 1-0
Q1: Hastings United (H) 2-1
Q2: Cray Wanderers (A) 2-0
Q3: Ashford Town (H) 1-2

73-74 Q1: Tunbridge Wells (H) 5-0
Q2: Lewes (A) 1-1, (H) 1-2

74-75 Q1: Sheppey United (A) 3-1
Q2: Ashford Town (A) 0-1

75-76 Q1: Peacehaven & Telscombe (H) 4-1
Q2: Faversham Town (A) 4-0
Q3: Ramsgate (A) 2-0
Q4: Crawley Town (A) 0-0, (H) 6-0
R1: Colchester United (A) 3-3, (H) 4-1
R2: Southend United (A) 1-4

76-77 Q1: Eastbourne United (H) 3-1
Q2: Haywards Heath (H) 2-0
Q3: Margate (H) 3-2
Q4: Hitchin Town (H) 2-2, (A) 1-3

77-78 Q1: Maidstone United (H) 0-1

78-79 Q1: Eastbourne Town (H) 3-0
Q2: Maidstone United (H) 0-0, (A) 0-1

79-80 Q1: Haywards Heath (A) 3-0
Q2: Chatham Town (A) 1-1, (H) 0-1

80-81 Q1: Faversham Town (A) 2-0
Q2: Welling United (H) 2-0
Q3: Canterbury C. (H) 2-2, (A) 3-3, (H) 2-0
Q4: Wembley (A) 1-1, (H) 2-3

81-82 Q1: Folkestone Town (H) 4-1
Q2: Tonbridge A.F.C. (A) 2-2, (H) 5-2
Q3: Ashford Town (H) 2-1
Q4: Leatherhead (H) 1-1, (A) 1-0
R1: Oxford United (H) 0-2

82-83 Q1: Steyning Town (A) 4-3
Q2: Deal Town (H) 0-3

DOVER ATHLETIC

Currently: Alliance Premier League

83-84 Q1: Lewes (H) 1-4

84-85 PR: Horsham (H) 0-0, (A) 1-0
Q1: Three Bridges (H) 1-0
Q2: Leatherhead (H) 1-4

85-86 PR: Eastbourne United (A) 2-4

86-87 PR: Tunbridge Wells (H) 0-0, (A) 2-1
Q1: Wick (A) 4-0
Q2: Leyton-Wingate (H) 2-1
Q3: Carshalton Athletic (H) 3-3, (A) 3-1
Q4: Slough Town (A) 1-1, (H) 2-3

87-88 Q1: Metropolitan Police (A) 1-3

88-89 Q1: Egham Town (H) 2-0
Q2: Haywards Heath (H) 5-2
Q3: Ashford Town (H) 3-0
Q4: Fareham Town (A) 1-1, (H) 0-1

89-90 Q1: Herne Bay (A) 6-0
Q2: Canterbury City (H) 0-0, (A) 2-0
Q3: Folkestone (H) 0-1 .

90-91 Q1: Ashford Town (H) 1-0
Q2: Sittingbourne (H) 2-0
Q3: Windsor & Eton (A) 1-1, (H) 3-0
Q4: Merthyr Tydfil (H) 0-0, (A) 0-2

91-92 Q1: Chipstead (H) 6-0
Q2: Faversham Town (A) 0-0, (H) 2-1
Q3: Bromley (A) 3-0
Q4: Tiverton Town (A) 0-1

92-93 Q1: Tonbridge A.F.C. (A) 0-0, (H) 2-1
Q2: Banstead Athletic (H) 0-0, (A) 2-1
Q3: Dorking (A) 0-1

Below: *Athletic's Colin Blewden evades a Lloyd Hume tackle in the 0-0 draw at Tonbridge. Photo: Alan Coomes.*

DROYLSDEN

Currently: Northern Premier League

47-48 EX: Wilmslow Albion (H) 2-0
PR: Youlgrave (A) 6-6, (H) 2-1
Q1: Ellesmere Port Town (A) 2-2, (H) 3-1
Q2: Altrincham (A) 1-4

49-50 EX: Stork (A) 5-2
PR: Nantwich (H) 10-1
Q1: Winsford United (A) 3-2
Q2: Congleton Town (A) 2-1
Q3: Mossley (H) 1-3

50-51 PR: Macclesfield Town (H) 5-5, (A) 2-7

52-53 PR: Lytham (A) 0-2

53-54 Q1: Lytham (H) 2-4

54-55 Q1: Mossley (H) 1-2

55-56 Q1: Rossendale United (A) 3-4

58-59 PR: Bacup Borough (A) 1-4

59-60 PR: Darwen (H) 2-1
Q1: Altrincham (A) 1-7

61-62 Q1: Macclesfield Town (A) 0-4

62-63 Q1: Macclesfield (H) 3-3, (A) 2-2 *ab. in E.T.*, 3-2
Q2: Mossley (H) 0-0, (A) 2-1
Q3: Winsford United (A) 1-0
Q4: Morecambe (A) 0-1

63-64 Q1: Northwich Victoria (A) 1-2

64-65 Q1: Skelmersdale United (A) 0-0, (H) 1-2

65-66 Q1: Marine (H) 3-3, (A) 0-1

67-68 Q1: Burscough (H) 1-1, (A) 2-5

68-69 PR: Skelmersdale United (H) 0-3

69-70 Q1: St Helens Town (H) 1-0
Q2: Wigan Athletic (A) 1-4

70-71 Q1: Bacup Borough (A) 3-1
Q2: Witton Albion (H) 2-3

71-72 Q1: Ellesmere Port Town (H) 0-3

72-73 Q1: Ashton United (H) 1-2

73-74 Q1: Prestwich Heys (H) 1-4

74-75 Q1: Yorkshire Am. (H) 1-1, (A) 4-4, 0-1

75-76 Q1: Darwen (A) 3-2
Q2: Hyde United (H) 3-2
Q3: Gt Harwood (A) 1-1, (A) 1-1, 1-0
Q4: Gateshead United (H) 0-4

76-77 Q1: Glossop (H) 3-2
Q2: Alfreton Town (A) 1-0
Q3: Worksop Town (H) 1-0
Q4: Winterton Rangers (A) 3-3, (H) 3-2
R1: Grimsby Town (H) 0-0, (A) 3-5

77-78 Q1: Runcorn (H) 0-2

78-79 Q1: Congleton Town (A) 2-1
Q2: Porthmadog (H) 3-1
Q3: Stalybridge Celtic (A) 1-1, (H) 3-1
Q4: Goole Town (H) 2-0
R1: Rochdale (A) 1-0
R2: Altrincham (H) 0-2

79-80 Q1: Clitheroe (A) 2-0
Q2: Prescot Town (A) 2-2, (H) 1-0
Q3: Lancaster City (A) 0-0, (H) 2-0
Q4: Morecambe (A) 2-3

80-81 Q1: Stalybridge Celtic (H) 1-1, (A) 1-2

81-82 Q1: Southport (H) 1-0
Q2: Netherfield (A) 1-1, (H) 3-1
Q3: Penrith (A) 2-3

82-83 PR: Bootle (A) 0-3

83-84 PR: Prestwich Heys (H) 1-2

84-85 PR: Nantwich Town (A) 0-0, (H) 2-0
Q1: Fleetwood Town (H) 4-0
Q2: Denaby United (H) 0-0, (A) 0-2

85-86 Q1: Accrington Stanley (A) 1-4

86-87 PR: Formby (A) 1-1, (H) 3-1
Q1: Winsford United (A) 0-2

87-88 PR: Belper Town (H) 4-2
Q1: North Ferriby United (A) 3-2
Q2: Northwich Victoria (A) 1-2

88-89 PR: Peterlee Newtown (A) 2-1
Q1: Horwich R.M.I. (A) 3-3, (H) 1-2

89-90 PR: Blackpool (Wren) Rovers (H) 3-2
Q1: Fleetwood T. (H) 0-0, (A) 1-1, (A) 1-0
Q2: Curzon Ashton (H) 0-1

90-91 Q1: Stalybridge Celtic (H) 1-1, (A) 2-1
Q2: Leicester U. (A) 0-0, (H) 2-2, (A) 3-4

91-92 Q1: Harworth C.I. (A) 1-0
Q2: Bootle (H) 1-1, (A) 3-1
Q3: Winsford United (A) 2-3

92-93 Q1: Blakenall (A) 3-4

DUDLEY TOWN

Currently: Southern League

46-47 PR: Bromsgrove Rovers (A) 3-0
Q1: Stourbridge (H) 1-1, (A) 1-0
Q2: Nuneaton Borough (A) 1-2

47-48 PR: Stourbridge (A) 0-1

48-49 Q1: Stourbridge (A) 1-3

49-50 PR: Hednesford (A) 1-0
Q1: Sutton Coldfield T. (H) 0-0, (A) 1-0
Q2: Stafford Rangers (A) 2-2, (H) 1-0
Q3: Bromsgrove Rovers (A) 1-3

50-51 PR: Stafford Rangers (A) 2-1
Q1: Stourbridge (H) 0-0, (A) 3-1
Q2: Oswestry Town (H) 0-1

51-52 PR: Oswestry Town (A) 2-5

52-53 PR: Kidderminster Harriers (A) 0-4

53-54 PR: Bilston (H) 1-2

54-55 PR: Stafford Rangers (A) 1-3

55-56 PR: Hednesford (H) 1-4

56-57 PR: Kidderminster Harriers (H) 0-3

57-58 PR: Lye Town (A) 0-6

58-59 PR: Stafford Rgrs (H - *played away*) 0-11

64-65 Q1: Wellington Town (A) 3-1
Q2: Worcester City (H) 3-1
Q3: Kidderminster Harriers (A) 1-2

65-66 Q1: Wellington Town (H) 0-0, (A) 2-1
Q2: Worcester City (H) 0-3

66-67 Q1: Stourbridge (A) 3-5

67-68 Q1: Bilston (A) 1-0
Q2: Burton Albion (H) 1-4

68-69 Q1: Bilston (H) 0-2

69-70 PR: Darlaston (A) 2-1
Q1: Bromsgrove Rovers (A) 1-0
Q2: Highgate United (H) 3-0
Q3: Tamworth (A) 0-3

70-71 Q1: Coventry Amateur (A) 2-1
Q2: Stourbridge (H) 1-2

71-72 Q1: Worcester City (H) 0-1

72-73 Q1: Moor Green (A) 1-2

73-74 Q1: Tamworth (H) 1-2

74-75 Q1: A.P. Leamington (H) 1-3

75-76 PR: Hinckley Athletic (A) 4-0
Q1: Stourbridge (A) 1-0
Q2: Nuneaton Borough (H) 0-1

76-77 PR: Halesowen Town (H) 3-1
Q1: Stratford Town (A) 2-0
Q2: Bilston (H) 4-1
Q3: Enderby Town (A) 1-0
Q4: Bedford Town (H) 1-0
R1: York City (H) 1-1, (A) 1-4

77-78 Q1: Gloucester City (H) 1-1, (A) 2-1
Q2: A.P. Leamington (H) 0-2

78-79 Q1: Gresley Rovers (H) 3-0
Q2: Kidderminster Harriers (H) 2-0
Q3: Halesowen Town (A) 1-0
Q4: Worksop Town (H) 0-1

79-80 Q1: Bromsgrove Rovers (A) 1-0
Q2: Hinckley Ath. (A) 1-2 *(void)*, (H) 1-0
Q3: Sutton Coldfield Town (A) 1-4

80-81 Q1: Moreton Town (A) 1-0
Q2: Moor Green (H) 0-0, (A) 1-2

81-82 PR: Stourbridge (H) 3-0
Q1: Malvern Town (H) 0-2

82-83 PR: Matlock Town (A) 2-0
Q1: Rushall Olympic (A) 1-1, (H) 0-1

83-84 PR: Boldmere St Michael (A) 2-0
Q1: Irthlingborough Diamonds (H) 3-1
Q2: March Town United (A) 2-3

84-85 PR: Heanor Town (H) 4-0
Q1: Paget Rangers (H) 1-1, (A) 3-2
Q2: Stalybridge Celtic (H) 1-1, (A) 1-3

85-86 Q1: Wisbech Town (A) 0-2

86-87 Q1: Arlesey T. (H - *at Hednesford*) 5-2
Q2: Stevenage Borough (A) 0-2

87-88 PR: Rothwell (H - *at Tividale*) 1-1, (A) 1-2

88-89 PR: Harrisons (A) 2-0
Q1: Oldbury United (A) 3-2
Q2: Walsall Wood (H) 2-1
Q3: Sutton Coldfield Town (A) 1-0
Q4: Grays Athletic (H) 3-3, (A) 0-2

89-90 PR: Boston (H) 0-1

90-91 PR: Corby Town (H) 1-1, (A) 0-1

91-92 PR: Lincoln United (H) 1-4

92-93 PR: Leicester United (A) 0-3

DULWICH HAMLET

Currently: Isthmian League

45-46 Q4: Romford (H) 1-2

46-47 Q4: Hayes (A) 2-4

47-48 Q4: Guildford City (A) 2-5

48-49 Q4: Bognor Regis Town (A) 8-1
R1: Northampton Town (A) 1-2

49-50 Q4: Walthamstow Avenue (A) 3-3, (H) 1-3

50-51 PR: Dorking (A) *withdrew*

52-53 PR: Epsom (A) 2-2, (H) 4-2
Q1: Tooting & Mitcham United (H) 2-1
Q2: Wimbledon (H) 3-3, (A) 2-5

53-54 PR: Bexleyheath & Welling (A) 3-1
Q1: Tunbridge Wells United (A) 1-3

54-55 Q1: Canterbury City (A) 2-2, (H) 0-2

55-56 PR: Carshalton Athletic (A) 1-3

56-57 PR: Woking (H) 1-2

57-58 PR: Metropolitan Police (H) 8-0
Q1: Carshalton Athletic (H) 4-0
Q2: Bexleyheath & Welling (A) 1-3

58-59 PR: Epsom (H) 5-2
Q1: Redhill (A) 0-1

59-60 Q1: Woking (A) 0-3

60-61 Q1: Staines Town (A) 2-0
Q2: Sutton United (A) 2-4

61-62 Q1: Epsom & Ewell (A) 2-1
Q2: Tooting & Mitcham United (H) 3-1
Q3: Slough Town (H) 5-1
Q4: King's Lynn (H) 1-2

62-63 Q1: Redhill (H) 6-1
Q2: Carshalton Athletic (A) 5-2
Q3: Tooting & Mitcham United (A) 1-5

63-64 Q1: Walthamstow Avenue (H) 0-3

64-65 Q1: Wokingham Town (H) 0-0, (A) 0-2

65-66 Q1: Tooting & Mitcham United (H) 3-2
Q2: Wokingham Town (H) 1-2

66-67 Q1: Redhill (H) 2-1
Q2: Ashford Town (H) 1-4

67-68 Q1: Amersham Town (H) 2-1
Q2: Hitchin Town (A) 1-3

68-69 Q1: Woodford Town (H) 0-1

69-70 Q1: Wycombe Wanderers (A) 1-2

70-71 Q1: Addlestone (H) 2-2, (A) 2-1
Q2: Guildford City (A) 1-2

71-72 Q1: Dunstable Town (H) 1-0
Q2: Redhill (H) 0-1

72-73 PR: Southall (A) 1-0
Q1: Hampton (H) 1-2

73-74 Q1: Romford (H) 0-1

74-75 Q1: Sutton United (A) 2-4

75-76 Q1: Cray Wanderers (A) 3-1
Q2: Hillingdon Borough (H) 5-1
Q3: Southall & Ealing (A) 2-2, (H) 1-2

76-77 Q1: Hemel Hempstead (H) 0-0, (A) 2-1
Q2: Letchworth Garden City (A) 1-0
Q3: Wealdstone (H) 0-2

77-78 Q1: Egham Town (H) 1-0
Q2: Leyton-Wingate (H) 1-1, (A) 1-2

78-79 Q1: Cray Wanderers (A) 2-1
Q2: Ilford (H) 4-0
Q3: Gravesend & Northfleet (A) 1-1, (H) 0-1

79-80 Q1: Canterbury City (A) 1-1, (H) 4-0
Q2: Margate (A) 0-1

80-81 PR: Hampton (H) 3-1
Q1: Southall (A) 8-0
Q2: Billericay Town (A) 2-1
Q3: St Albans City (A) 1-2

81-82 Q1: Steyning Town (A) 1-1, (H) 3-0
Q2: Fareham Town (H) 1-2

82-83 PR: Berkhamsted Town (A) 3-3, (H) 6-0
Q1: Leyton-Wingate (A) 2-2, (H) 2-0
Q2: Hemel Hempstead (A) 2-1
Q3: Wealdstone (H) 0-0, (A) 1-2

83-84 Q1: Ramsgate (H) 5-0
Q2: Folkestone (H) 1-2

84-85 Q1: Kingstonian (H) 0-2

85-86 Q1: Eastbourne Town (H) 3-1
Q2: Southwick (H) 1-1, (A) 1-2

86-87 Q1: Barnet (A) 2-0
Q2: Wembley (A) 1-2

87-88 Q1: Basingstoke Town (A) 0-3

88-89 Q1: Three Bridges (H) 1-0
Q2: Marlow (H) 1-0
Q3: Burnham (H) 1-1, (A) 3-2
Q4: Fisher Athletic (A) 3-3, (H) 0-3

89-90 Q1: Collier Row (A) 2-1
Q2: Lewes (H) 4-1
Q3: Hailsham T. (H) 1-1, (A - *at Lewes*) 4-3
Q4: Merthyr T. (H - *at Fisher*) 1-1, (A) 2-4

90-91 Q1: Littlehampton Town (A) 0-2

91-92 PR: Harefield Utd (H - *at Tooting*) 2-1
Q1: Burnham (H - *at Tooting*) 1-0
Q2: Hertford Town (A) 1-2

92-93 Q1: Kingstonian (A) 0-4

Below: *Dulwich's Rudi Hedman shields the ball during the heavy defeat at Kingstonian. Photo: Paul Dennis.*

DUNSTABLE

Currently: Southern League
* - As Dunstable Town

50-51 * EX: Biggleswade Town (A) 0-6

52-53 * PR: Hitchin Town (H) 2-4

53-54 * Q1: Luton Amateur (A) 3-1
Q2: Vauxhall Motors (H) 3-2
Q3: Bedford Town (H) 2-4

54-55 * Q1: Biggleswade Town (H) 2-3

55-56 * Q1: Wolverton Town & B.R. (A) 2-0
Q2: Bedford Town (H) 0-4

56-57 * Q2: Vauxhall Motors (H) 3-0
Q3: Wolverton Town & B.R. (H) 3-1
Q4: Eton Manor (H) 5-1
R1: Margate (A) 1-3

57-58 * Q1: Eynesbury Rovers (A) 3-1
Q2: Vauxhall Motors (H) 1-6

58-59 * Q1: Hitchin Town (A) 2-6

59-60 * Q1: Letchworth Town (A) 0-5

60-61 * Q1: St Albans City (A) 1-2

65-66 * Q1: St Albans City (A) 0-3

66-67 * Q1: Southall (A) 0-3

67-68 * Q1: Banbury United (A) 0-2

68-69 * Q1: Wealdstone (A) 2-3

69-70 * Q1: Marlow (H) 4-2
Q2: Leighton Town (H) 3-1
Q3: Wealdstone (A) 0-4

70-71 * Q1: Maidenhead United (A) 1-0
Q2: Bletchley (H) 1-0
Q3: Wycombe Wanderers (H) 0-4

71-72 * Q1: Dulwich Hamlet (A) 0-1

72-73 * PR: Hitchin Town (A) 0-3

73-74 * Q1: Ware (A) 0-2

74-75 * Q1: Hertford Town (H) 3-2
Q2: Hitchin Town (H) 0-0, (A) 1-2

75-76 * PR: Hoddesdon Town (A) 2-1
Q1: Vauxhall Motors (A) 1-0
Q2: Wembley (H) 0-2

76-77 PR: Witney Town (H) 0-4

77-78 Q1: Edgware (A) 1-4

78-79 Q1: Valley Sports (Rugby) (A) 0-2

79-80 PR: Carshalton Athletic (H) 1-2

80-81 PR: Chertsey Town (A) 1-2

81-82 Q1: Sudbury Town (A) 1-1, (H) 3-1
Q2: Walthamstow Avenue (H) 3-2
Q3: St Albans City (A) 5-1
Q4: Boston United (A) 1-3

82-83 Q1: Tring Town (A) 0-1

83-84 Q1: Bedworth United (A) 2-3

84-85 PR: Clapton (A) 2-0
Q1: Hendon (A) 3-1
Q2: Wealdstone (A) 0-6

85-86 Q1: Hoddesdon Town (A) 3-1
Q2: Tring Town (H) 3-2
Q3: Walthamstow Avenue (A) 0-0, (H) 2-0
Q4: Nuneaton Borough (H) 0-2

86-87 Q1: Buckingham Town (A) 2-2, (H) 1-2

87-88 PR: Newmarket Town (A) 3-0
Q1: Stowmarket Town (A) 3-1
Q2: Leyton-Wingate (H) 0-1

88-89 PR: Tiptree (A) 1-1, (H) 1-1, (A) 0-0, (H) 0-1

89-90 PR: Billericay Town (A) 1-0
Q1: Vauxhall Motors (H) 3-0
Q2: Staines (A) 0-1 *withdrew after 38 mins*

DUNSTON FEDERATION BREWERY

Currently: Northern League

91-92 Q1: Guisborough Town (H) 1-0
Q2: Penrith (H) 2-2, (A) 6-6, (A) 1-2

92-93 PR: Ossett Town (A) 2-1
Q1: Norton & Stocton Ancients (H) 7-0
Q2: South Bank (H) 2-0
Q3: Northallerton Town (H) 0-3

DURHAM CITY

Currently: Northern League

54-55 Q1: Ushaw Moor (H) 4-3
Q2: Blackhall C.W. (A) 2-2, (H) 4-1
Q3: Wolsingham Welfare (H) 1-3

55-56 Q1: Chilton Athletic (H) 4-2
Q2: Wolsingham Welfare (A) 2-2, (H) 2-0
Q3: Ferryhill Athletic (H) 0-0, (A) 2-0
Q4: Bridlington Central United (H) 5-1
R1: Bishop Auckland (A) 1-3

56-57 Q2: Spennymoor United (A) 1-3

57-58 Q1: Gosforth & Coxlodge (H) 8-0
Q2: Morpeth Town (A) 2-1
Q3: Evenwood Town (A) 2-1
Q4: Willington (H) 2-0
R1: Spalding United (H) 3-1
R2: Tranmere Rovers (H) 0-3

58-59 Q4: Blyth Spartans (A) 0-1

59-60 Q4: West Auckland T. (A) 2-2, (H) 0-0, 1-4

60-61 Q1: Bridlington Town (A) 0-6

61-62 Q1: Stanley United (A) 1-5

62-63 Q1: Shildon (A) 1-3

63-64 Q1: Whitley Bay (A) 0-4

64-65 Q1: Annfield Plain (A) 0-2

65-66 Q1: Willington (H) 0-8

66-67 Q1: Murton Colliery Welfare (A) 2-4

67-68 Q1: Willington (A) 3-1
Q2: Murton Colliery Welfare (H) 3-0
Q3: Ryhope Colliery Welfare (A) 3-4

68-69 Q1: Willington (H) 1-0
Q2: Shildon (A) 1-3

69-70 Q1: Gateshead (A) 0-5

70-71 Q1: Consett (H) 0-0, (A) 3-1
Q2: Ferryhill Athletic (A) 0-1

71-72 Q1: Annfield Plain (A) 5-0
Q2: Spennymoor United (H) 2-0
Q3: Whitley Bay (A) 1-3

72-73 Q1: Ferryhill Athletic (H) 1-2

73-74 Q1: Consett (A) 2-2, (H) 3-1
Q2: Willington (A) 1-3

74-75 Q1: Spennymoor United (A) 2-6

75-76 Q1: Easington Colliery Welfare (H) 1-3

76-77 Q1: Willington (A) 3-3, (H) 3-3, 3-2
Q2: Tow Law Town (A) 2-1
Q3: Netherfield (A) 1-1, (H) 1-2

77-78 Q1: Bridlington Town (A) 1-1, (H) 1-0
Q2: Spennymoor United (H) 1-2

78-79 Q1: Boldon Community Association (A) 0-2

79-80 Q1: Horden Colliery Welfare (A) 0-6

80-81 Q1: Penrith (A) 0-6

81-82 Q1: Annfield Plain (A) 3-2
Q2: South Bank (A) 1-4

82-83 PR: Gateshead (A) 1-1, (H) 2-2, (*at Blyth*) 1-2

83-84 PR: Ashington (H) 3-1
Q1: Eppleton Colliery Welfare (A) 2-0
Q2: Whitby Town (H) 1-3

84-85 Q1: Crook Town (A) 1-3

85-86 PR: Ashington (A) 2-0
Q1: Chester-le-Street Town (H) 2-3

86-87 PR: Shildon (H) 2-1
Q1: Fleetwood Town (A) 0-2

87-88 PR: Alnwick (A) 1-1, (H) 1-1, (A) 0-0, (H) 1-2

88-89 PR: Guiseley (H) 1-2

89-90 PR: Evenwood Town (A) 1-0
Q1: Lancaster City (A) 1-0
Q2: Blyth Spartans (A) 1-4

90-91 Q1: Prudhoe East End (H) 0-3

91-92 PR: South Bank (H) 4-1
Q1: Tow Law Town (H) 1-0
Q2: Morecambe (H) 1-4

92-93 Q1: Bishop Auckland (H) 1-1, (A) 2-5

EARLE

Currently: Liverpool County Combination

45-46 Q1: Hurst (A) 3-9

46-47 Q2: Prescot Cables (H) 0-3

47-48 PR: Llandudno (A) 7-2
Q1: Skelmersdale United (A) 2-3

48-49 PR: St Helens Town (H) 1-2

49-50 EX: Newton Y.M.C.A. (A) 4-3
PR: Orrell (H) *W/O*
Q1: Rhyl (H) 1-3

50-51 PR: Bootle (A) 1-2

56-57 PR: South Liverpool (A) 0-7

EARLESTOWN

Currently: Defunct

47-48 PR: Haydock C. & B. Recreation (H) 3-0
Q1: Wigan Athletic (H) 0-1

48-49 EX: U.G.B. St Helens (H) 5-1
PR: Rhyl (A) 1-2

49-50 EX: Crossens (H) 2-1
PR: Bootle Athletic (A) 1-5

52-53 PR: Prescot Cables (H) 0-2

53-54 Q1: Runcorn (H) 1-4

54-55 PR: Marine (A) 0-4

55-56 Q1: South Liverpool (H) 1-1, (A) 1-3

56-57 Q1: Llandudno (A) 2-0
Q2: New Brighton (H) 1-6

57-58 PR: Prescot Cables (H) 1-6

58-59 PR: Prescot Cables (A) 3-4

59-60 PR: St Helens Town (A) 2-0
Q1: Pwllheli & District (H) 5-2
Q2: Prescot Cables (H) 0-1

60-61 Q1: Altrincham (H) 4-3
Q2: Skelmersdale United (H) 2-4

61-62 PR: Altrincham (A) 1-6

62-63 Q1: St Helens Town (H) 1-3

63-64 Q1: Altrincham (H - *played away*) 0-10

EASINGTON COLLIERY

Currently: Northern League
* - As Easington Colliery Welfare

46-47 * EX: Horden Colliery Welfare (A) 3-3, (H) 2-0
PR: Shildon (A) 2-2, (H) 2-4

47-48 * EX: Shotton Colliery Welfare (H) 4-1
PR: Brandon Colliery Welfare (H) 2-0
Q1: Murton Colliery Welfare (A) 3-2
Q2: West Auckland Town (A) 1-0
Q3: Ferryhill Athletic (H) 3-3, (A) 1-3

48-49 * PR: Eppleton Colliery Welfare (H) 6-1
Q1: Stanley United (A) 2-3

49-50 * PR: Crook Colliery Welfare (H) 6-3
Q1: Seaham Colliery Welfare (A) 1-1, (H) 2-1
Q2: Horden Colliery Welfare (A) 1-2

50-51 * PR: Wingate Welfare (H) 3-1
Q1: Evenwood Town (A) 2-3

51-52 * Q1: Gosforth & Coxlodge (A) 3-2
Q2: South Shields (A) 2-2, (H) 1-1, 1-2

52-53 * Q1: Heaton Stannington (H) 3-0
Q2: Consett (H) 2-2, (A) 0-3

53-54 * Q1: Consett (A) 2-2, (H) 1-3

54-55 * Q1: Birtley (A) 7-2
Q2: Dawdon Colliery Welfare (H) 3-2
Q3: Annfield Plain (A) 1-5

55-56 * Q1: Seaham Colliery Welfare (A) 2-1
Q2: Silksworth Colliery Welfare (H) 4-2
Q3: Consett (A) 4-1
Q4: Horden Colliery Welfare (A) 1-0
R1: Tranmere Rovers (H) 0-2

56-57 * Q4: Evenwood Town (H) 0-3

57-58 * Q1: Wolsingham Welfare (H) 11-2
Q2: Boldon Colliery (H) 2-1
Q3: Alnwick Town (H) 6-4

Q4: Billingham Synthonia Recreation (H) 2-3

58-59 * Q1: Evenwood Town (A) 1-8

59-60 * Q2: Boldon Colliery Welfare (H) 0-2

61-62 * Q1: North Shields (A) 0-3

62-63 * Q1: Stanley United (H) 1-5

75-76 * Q1: Durham City (A) 3-1
Q2: Shildon (H) 1-3

76-77 * Q1: Consett (A) 0-1

77-78 * Q1: Whitley Bay (H) 4-4, (A) 2-3

78-79 * Q1: West Auckland Town (H) 2-1
Q2: Billingham Synthonia (H) 1-3

79-80 * Q1: Consett (H) 0-4

80-81 PR: South Bank (H) 0-2

83-84 PR: Whitley Bay (H) 2-0
Q1: Peterlee Newtown (H) 2-1
Q2: Tow Law Town (H) 0-0, (A) 1-1, (H) 1-0
Q3: Horden Colliery Welfare (A) 2-3

84-85 PR: Bridlington Trinity (A) 2-0
Q1: Wren Rovers (H) 2-2, (A) 2-4

85-86 PR: Billingham Town (H) 2-3

86-87 Q1: Barrow (A) 3-0
Q2: Alnwick Town (A) 3-0
Q3: Chester-le-Street Town (H) 1-1, (A) 3-5

87-88 Q1: Leyland Motors (H) 2-1
Q2: Penrith (A) 2-1
Q3: Newcastle Blue Star (H) 3-0
Q4: Northwich Victoria (A) 0-3

88-89 PR: Northallerton Town (A) 0-2

89-90 Q1: Seaham Red Star (A) 0-1

90-91 PR: Chester-le-Street Town (A) 2-0
Q1: Colne Dynamoes (H) *W/O*
Q2: Langley Park (H) 1-1, (A) 1-0
Q3: Harrogate Railway Athletic (A) 0-2

91-92 PR: Spennymoor United (A) 0-1

92-93 PR: Shotton Comrades (H) 2-1
Q1: Workington (H) 1-1, (A) 0-1

EAST BIERLEY

Currently: Defunct

45-46 Q1: Thorne Colliery (H) 3-3, (A) 6-1
Q2: Yorkshire Amateur (A) 0-3

EASTBOURNE TOWN

Currently: Sussex County League
* - As Eastbourne F.C.

46-47 * PR: Newhaven (H) 4-1
Q1: Worthing (A) 5-3
Q2: Southwick (A) 5-5, (H) 4-1
Q3: Bognor Regis Town (H) 4-1
Q4: Finchley (H) 3-7

50-51 * PR: Shoreham (H) 2-1
Q1: Horsham (H) 3-2
Q2: Hastings United (H) 5-4
Q3: Haywards Heath (H) 4-2
Q4: Walthamstow Avenue (A) 0-2

51-52 * PR: Horsham (A) 3-2
Q1: Haywards Heath (A) 2-1
Q2: Ashford Town (H) 2-2, (A) 0-4

52-53 * PR: Lancing Athletic (A) 6-6, (H) 1-2

53-54 * PR: Worthing (A) 4-2
Q1: Redhill (A) 1-0
Q2: Hastings United (H) 2-7

54-55 * PR: Newhaven (A) 2-2, (H) 3-0
Q1: Littlehampton Town (H) 5-3
Q2: Bognor Regis Town (A) 2-4

55-56 * PR: Wigmore Athletic (H) 4-2
Q1: Redhill (H) 0-2

56-57 * PR: Haywards Heath (A) 3-2
Q1: Bexhill Town (H) 4-1
Q2: Horsham (A) 0-2

57-58 * PR: Newhaven (A) 1-2

58-59 * PR: Haywards Heath (H) 1-1, (A) 1-3

59-60 * PR: Bognor Regis Town (A) 2-1
Q1: Haywards Heath (A) 3-3, (H) 4-2
Q2: Crawley Town (A) 2-2, (H) 1-2

60-61 * Q1: Newhaven (H) 2-1
Q2: Hastings United (H) 0-7

62-63 * Q1: Tunbridge Wells United (H) 3-4

63-64 * Q1: Tunbridge Wells Utd (H) 1-1, (A) 0-2

64-65 * Q1: Bexhill Town (H) 4-0
Q2: Tonbridge (A) 0-2

65-66 * Q1: Tonbridge (H) 1-4

66-67 * Q1: Maidstone United (A) 2-2, (H) 1-3

67-68 * Q1: Littlehampton Town (H) 1-1, (A) 2-1
Q2: Eastbourne United (H) 2-0
Q3: Lancing Athletic (H) 5-0
Q4: Margate (H) 0-9

68-69 * Q1: Lancing (H) 2-0
Q2: Southwick (A) 2-1
Q3: Eastbourne United (A) 3-2
Q4: Canterbury City (H) 2-2, (A) 2-4

69-70 * Q1: Worthing (H) 5-1
Q2: Littlehampton Town (A) 0-2

70-71 * Q1: Eastbourne United (A) 3-1
Q2: Bognor Regis Town (H) 2-4

71-72 Q1: Crawley Town (A) 0-4

72-73 Q1: Arundel (H) 0-5

73-74 Q1: Peacehaven & Telscombe (H) 3-2
Q2: Littlehampton Town (A) 2-2, (H) 0-1

74-75 Q1: Maidstone United (H) 0-0, (A) 3-5

75-76 Q1: Deal Town (A) 1-1, (H) 1-0
Q2: Margate (H) 0-2

76-77 Q1: Lewes (H) 0-3

77-78 Q1: Redhill (A) 1-0
Q2: Folkestone & Shepway (A) 2-5

78-79 Q1: Dover (A) 0-3

79-80 PR: Herne Bay (A) 2-0
Q1: Ringmer (A) 3-3, (H) 2-0
Q2: Gravesend & Northfleet (H) 0-2

80-81 Q1: Epsom & Ewell (A) 0-1

81-82 Q1: Canterbury City (H) 0-2

82-83 Q1: Bognor Regis Town (H) 1-3

83-84 Q1: Hailsham Town (H) 0-1

84-85 PR: Camberley Town (A) 0-0, (H) 2-1
Q1: Wick (H) 9-2
Q2: Epsom & Ewell (H) 2-4

85-86 Q1: Dulwich Hamlet (A) 1-3

86-87 PR: Leatherhead (A) 1-1, (H - *E'bourne U.*) 3-1
Q1: Whitehawk (A) 3-2
Q2: Carshalton Athletic (H) 0-1

91-92 PR: Faversham (A) 0-0, (H - *E'bourne U.*) 0-4

92-93 PR: Horsham Y.M.C.A. (A) 3-4

EASTBOURNE UNITED

Currently: Sussex County League
* - As Eastbourne Comrades

47-48 * PR: Chichester City (A) 2-5

48-49 * PR: Worthing (A) 3-4

49-50 * PR: Chichester City (A) 2-2, (H) 6-0
Q1: Horsham (H) 0-1

50-51 * PR: Newhaven (H) 0-0, (A) 0-3

57-58 PR: Horsham (H) 1-1, (A) 0-2

58-59 Q1: Southwick (H) 3-1
Q2: Haywards Heath (H) 3-1
Q3: Horsham (A) 1-3

59-60 PR: Worthing (A) 1-3

60-61 Q1: Tunbridge Wells United (H) 1-2

61-62 Q1: Bexhill Town (H) 5-2
Q2: Newhaven (A) 6-1
Q3: Tunbridge Wells United (H) 1-5

62-63 Q1: Tonbridge (H) 4-3
Q2: Tunbridge Wells United (H) 0-1

63-64 Q1: Tonbridge (H) 0-1

64-65 Q2: Hastings United (H) 1-7

65-66 Q1: Hastings United (H) 0-4

66-67 Q1: Lancing (H) 2-0
Q2: Bexhill Town (H) 3-2
Q3: Crawley Town (H) 1-1, (A) 2-2, 3-2
Q4: Sutton United (A) 2-7

67-68 Q1: Horsham (H) 2-0
Q2: Eastbourne (A) 0-2

68-69 Q1: Littlehampton Town (A) 2-1
Q2: Haywards Heath (H) 3-0
Q3: Eastbourne Town (H) 2-3

69-70 PR: Littlehampton Town (A) 0-3

70-71 Q1: Eastbourne (H) 1-3

71-72 Q1: Burgess Hill Town (H) 0-2

72-73 PR: Lewes (A) 0-3

73-74 Q1: Ashford Town (A) 0-4

74-75 PR: Bexhill Town (H) 2-3

75-76 PR: Maidstone United (A) 0-5

76-77 Q1: Dover (A) 1-3

77-78 Q1: East Grinstead (H) 4-0
Q2: Horsham Y.M.C.A. (A) 1-4

78-79 PR: Ashford Town (H) 1-0
Q1: Sittingbourne (A) 4-1
Q2: Medway (A) 0-0, (H) 0-0, (*Maidstone*) 6-0
Q3: Hastings United (H) 2-1
Q4: Gravesend & Northfleet (A) 1-3

79-80 Q1: Dorking Town (A) 1-1, (H) 4-1
Q2: Gosport Borough (A) 0-1

80-81 PR: Chatham Town (A) 1-2

81-82 PR: Tonbridge A.F.C. (H) 0-2

82-83 Q1: Horndean (A) 1-1, (H) 3-2
Q2: Farnborough Town (A) 1-2

83-84 PR: Arundel (H) 1-0
Q1: Redhill (A) 1-1, (H) 2-1
Q2: Hastings United (H) 0-0, (A) 0-1

84-85 PR: Walton & Hersham (A) 0-1

85-86 PR: Dover (H) 4-2
Q1: Whyteleafe (A) 1-2

86-87 PR: Portfield (H) 1-1, (A) 0-1

87-88 PR: Ringmer (A) 5-1
Q1: Hythe Town (H) 6-2
Q2: Tonbridge A.F.C. (H) 0-0, (A) 1-3

88-89 PR: Shoreham (A) 3-1
Q1: Haywards Heath Town (A) 2-3

89-90 PR: Steyning Town (A - *played home*) 5-2
Q1: Malden Vale (H) 1-2

90-91 PR: Tunbridge Wells (H) 6-5
Q1: Crawley Town (H) 0-2

91-92 PR: Whitstable Town (A) 1-0
Q1: Lewes (H) 1-4

92-93 PR: Banstead Athletic (A) 1-2

Left: *Eastbourne United's Gary Gill makes a brave save to deny Crawley Town during the First Qualifying Round tie at the Oval in 1990. Photo: Graham Cotterill.*

EAST COWES VICTORIA

Currently: Merged with East Cowes Athletic
Playing as East Cowes Victoria Athletic in Wessex Lge

45-46	Q1: Sandown (H) 9-1 Q2: Cowes (A) 2-4
46-47	PR: Portsmouth Electricity (H) 4-1 Q1: Poole Town (A) 0-1
47-48	PR: Gosport Borough Athletic (A) 0-2
48-49	EX: Sandown (H) 6-1 PR: Cowes (A) 2-1 Q1: Bournemouth Gasworks Athletic (H) 3-1 Q2: Poole Town (H) 1-2
49-50	PR: Gosport Borough Athletic (H) 4-1 Q1: Poole Town (A) 1-5
50-51	PR: Romsey Town (A) 2-3

EAST END PARK W.M.C.

Currently: West Yorkshire League

58-59	Q1: Upton Colliery (H) 1-0 Q2: Denaby United (A) 0-2
59-60	Q1: Frickley Colliery (A) 0-1
60-61	Q1: Retford Town (H) 0-2
61-62	Q1: Yorkshire Amateur (H) 1-1, (A) 2-0 Q2: Goole Town (H) 1-1, (A) 1-2

EASTERN COACHWORKS (LOWESTOFT)

Currently: Defunct

50-51	EX: Fakenham Town (H) 8-2 PR: Gorleston (A) 1-0 Q1: Sudbury Town (H) 2-2, (A) 1-0 Q2: Lowestoft Town (H) 1-1, (A) 1-2

EAST GRINSTEAD

Currently: Sussex County League

45-46	PR: Horsham (H) 2-2, (A) 0-1
46-47	PR: Shoreham (H) 11-0 Q1: Bexhill Town (A) 1-3
47-48	PR: Newhaven (H) 5-2 Q1: Bexhill Town (H) 7-1 Q2: Horsham (A) 2-5
48-49	Q1: Worthing (A) 0-2
49-50	PR: Haywards Heath (A) 1-5
50-51	PR: Littlehampton Town (H) 6-1 Q1: Newhaven (A) 2-1 Q2: Haywards Heath (H) 1-5
51-52	PR: Haywards Heath (H) 3-5
52-53	PR: Redhill (H) 4-2 Q1: Haywards Heath (H) 1-0 Q2: Lancing Athletic (H) 0-1
53-54	PR: Southwick (H) 4-2 Q1: Ashford Town (A) 0-4
54-55	PR: Tunbridge Wells United (A) 0-5
55-56	PR: Newhaven (H) 2-1 Q1: Bognor Regis Town (A) 1-3
69-70	Q1: Alton Town (H) 1-3
70-71	PR: Woking (A) 0-2
71-72	Q1: Ringmer (H) 2-0 Q2: Crawley Town (A) 0-3
77-78	PR: Wigmore Athletic (A) 3-1 Q1: Eastbourne United (A) 0-4
78-79	PR: Canterbury City (H) 1-2
79-80	Q1: Gravesend & Northfleet (H) 1-4
80-81	Q1: Folkestone (A) 2-6
81-82	Q1: Wembley (A) 1-2

EASTLEIGH

Currently: Wessex League
* - As Swaythling F.C.

75-76 *	Q1: Fareham Town (H) 2-0 Q2: Salisbury (H) 0-1
76-77 *	Q1: Newport Isle of Wight (H) 4-0 Q2: Waterlooville (H) 0-3
77-78 *	Q1: Ilminster Town (A) 2-0 Q2: Bath City (H) 1-1, (A) 0-3
78-79 *	PR: Hungerford Town (A) 1-5
79-80 *	Q1: Gosport Borough (H) 1-4
81-82	Q1: Poole Town (H) 2-1 Q2: Melksham Town (H) 3-1 Q3: Dorchester Town (H) 2-4
82-83	Q1: Newport I.O.W. (H) 2-2, (A) 3-1 Q2: Worthing (A) 1-3
83-84	Q1: Dorchester Town (A) 0-0, (H) 0-2
84-85	Q1: A.F.C. Totton (H) 0-2
86-87	Q1: Lewes (H) 1-1, (A) 2-1 Q2: Crawley Town (H) 0-1
87-88	PR: Swanage T. & Herston (H) 1-1, (A) 1-3
88-89	PR: Hungerford Town (A) 0-0, (H) 0-1
89-90	Q1: Chertsey Town (A) 0-4
90-91	PR: Newbury Town (A) 1-2
91-92	PR: Thame United (A) 1-1, (H) 0-2
92-93	PR: Newport Isle of Wight (H) 1-2

EAST TANFIELD C.W.

Currently: Defunct

48-49	PR: Horden Colliery Welfare (H) *withdrew*

EAST THURROCK UNITED

Currently: Isthmian League

89-90	Q1: Berkhamsted Town (A) 0-1
90-91	PR: Stevenage Borough (H) 0-1
91-92	PR: Royston Town (H) 1-0 Q1: Grays Athletic (H) 1-1, (A) 1-2
92-93	PR: Chipstead (H) 1-0 Q1: Molesey (A) 2-4

EASTWOOD HANLEY

Currently: North West Counties League

67-68	Q1: Buxton (A) 6-4 Q2: Matlock Town (A) 1-4
68-69	Q1: Ilkeston Town (H) 2-3
69-70	Q1: Matlock Town (H) 2-3
70-71	PR: Mossley (A) 1-0 Q1: Ellesmere Port Town (A) 0-3
71-72	Q1: Winsford United (H) 1-0 Q2: Altrincham (A) 1-4
72-73	Q1: Congleton Town (H) 2-1 Q2: Witton Albion (H) 3-0 Q3: Ellesmere Port Town (A) 2-2, (H) 0-2
73-74	Q1: Northwich Victoria (H) 1-1, (A) 1-4
74-75	Q1: Mossley (H) 1-3
75-76	PR: Buxton (H) 2-3
76-77	PR: Heanor Town (H) 2-2, (A) 0-2
83-84	PR: Desborough Town (H) 1-0 Q1: Leicester United (H) 0-2
84-85	PR: Alfreton Town (A) 2-4
85-86	Q1: Hyde United (H) 0-0, (A) 2-1 Q2: St Helens Town (A) 0-2
86-87	PR: Radcliffe Borough (A) 3-3, (H) 1-0 Q1: Oldbury United (A) 0-0, (H) 0-1
87-88	Q1: Leek Town (H) 0-0, (A) 0-2
88-89	Q1: Prescot Cables (H) 2-0 Q2: Northwich Victoria (H) 0-1
89-90	Q1: Marine (A) 1-1, (H) 1-2
90-91	PR: West Midlands Police (H) 0-2
91-92	Q1: Northwich Victoria (H) 2-1 Q2: Armthorpe Welfare (H) 3-2 Q3: Stalybridge Celtic (H) 1-2
92-93	Q1: Racing Club Warwick (A) 2-0 Q2: Sutton Coldfield Town (A) 1-2

Left: *Third Qualifying Round action at Eastwood Hanley - Darren Twigg (9) challenges Stalybridge 'keeper Russ Hughes. Photo: Colin Stevens.*

EASTWOOD TOWN

Currently: Northern Premier League

68-69	Q1: Heanor Town (H) 2-2, (A) 1-5
69-70	Q1: Burton Albion (H) 0-1
70-71	Q1: Heanor Town (H) 0-1
71-72	Q1: Retford Town (H) 2-2, (A) 3-0 Q2: Arnold (A) 4-2 Q3: Winterton Rangers (H) 1-2
72-73	Q1: Arnold (H) 3-3, (A) 5-0 Q2: Heanor Town (H) 2-0 Q3: Alfreton Town (H) 0-4
73-74	PR: Sutton Coldfield Town (A) 2-0 Q1: Belper Town (A) 0-0, (H) 0-3
74-75	Q1: Sutton Town (A) 2-0 Q2: Tamworth (A) 1-1, (H) 5-3 Q3: Enderby Town (A) 0-1
75-76	Q1: Bilston (A) 1-3
76-77	Q1: Burton Albion (A) 1-1, (H) 1-2
77-78	Q1: Darlaston (A) 0-3
78-79	PR: Appleby Frodingham Athletic (A) 2-1 Q1: Worksop Town (A) 1-2
79-80	PR: Ashby Institute (H) 3-1 Q1: North Ferriby United (A) 1-2
80-81	PR: Buxton (A) 2-1 Q1: Nantwich Town (A) 0-0, (H) 1-0 Q2: Alfreton Town (A) 0-1
81-82	PR: Friar Lane Old Boys (H) 3-0 Q1: Grantham (A) 0-1
82-83	Q1: Prestwich Heys (H) 4-2 Q2: Worksop Town (A) 1-1, (H) 3-1 Q3: Telford United (H) 2-2, (A) 0-4
83-84	Q1: Winterton Rangers (A) 3-0 Q2: Gresley Rovers (A) 1-0 Q3: Winsford United (A) 1-0 Q4: Wycombe Wanderers (H) 2-2, (A) 1-2
84-85	Q1: Tamworth (H) 1-0 Q2: Matlock Town (A) 0-2
85-86	PR: Warrington Town (A) 1-3
86-87	Q1: Mossley (A) 3-3, (H) 1-1, (H) 2-0 Q2: Bootle (A) 2-2, (H) 1-1, (A) 1-1, (H) 1-0 Q3: Caernarfon Town (H) 1-4
87-88	Q1: Arnold (H) 1-2
88-89	PR: Hednesford Town (A) 3-1 Q1: Brigg Town (H) 3-1 Q2: Sutton Coldfield Town (A) 0-1
89-90	PR: Grantham Town (H) 1-2
90-91	PR: Newtown (H) 1-1, (H) 2-1 Q1: Hednesford (H) 1-1, (A) 1-1, (H) 2-3
91-92	PR: Farsley Celtic (H) 2-4
92-93	PR: Congleton Town (A) 0-2

EBBW VALE

Currently: League of Wales

45-46 Q1: Cardiff Corinthians (H) *scratched*

46-47 PR: Llanelly (H) 2-2, (A) 2-5

47-48 PR: Hoffmann Athletic (Stonehouse) (H) 2-0
Q1: Llanelly (H) 3-2
Q2: Barry Town (A) 0-2

48-49 Q1: Barry Town (A) 1-4

49-50 PR: Merthyr Tydfil (A) 1-5

50-51 PR: Llanelly (A) 0-2

51-52 Q1: Cinderford Town (A) 5-1
Q2: Gloucester City (H - *played away*) 2-1
Q3: Barry Town (A) 2-4

52-53 Q1: Stonehouse (A) 1-0
Q2: Llanelly (H) 0-3

53-54 Q1: Troedrhiw (A) 3-2
Q2: Merthyr Tydfil (A) 0-3

54-55 PR: Lovells Athletic (A) 2-3

55-56 Q1: Gloucester City (H) 2-2, (A) 1-4

56-57 Q1: Cheltenham Town (H) 2-5

57-58 Q1: Llanelly (H) 5-5, (A) 2-3

58-59 Q1: Stonehouse (H - *played away*) 0-1

59-60 Q1: Barry Town (H) 2-2, (A) 1-6

60-61 Q1: Barry Town (A) 0-9

61-62 Q2: Merthyr Tydfil (H) 1-2

62-63 Q1: Lovells Athletic (H) 1-1, (A) 1-4

ECCLESHILL UNITED

Currently: Northern Counties (East) League

91-92 PR: Great Harwood Town (A) 0-6

92-93 PR: Harworth Colliery Institute (H) 3-2
Q1: Seaham Red Star (A) 2-3

EDEN COLLIERY (LEADGATE)

Currently: Defunct

46-47 PR: Crook Colliery Welfare (H) 2-8

EDGWARE TOWN

Currently: Merged with Brent Green
Playing as Edgware Town in Isthmian League
See also Edgware Town (2)

45-46 PR: Barnet (H) 1-4

46-47 PR: Harrow Town (H) 1-2

47-48 EX: Acton Town (A - *played home*) 9-0
PR: Pinner (H) 7-0
Q1: Hoddesdon Town (A) 2-1
Q2: Wealdstone (H) 1-2

48-49 PR: Finchley (H) 0-0, (A) 1-2

49-50 EX: Hoddesdon (A - *played home*) 1-1, (H) 3-0
PR: Welwyn Garden City (A) 2-0
Q1: Ware (A) 2-0
Q2: Hatfield United (H) 5-1
Q3: Wealdstone (H) 0-1

50-51 PR: Tufnell Park (A) 2-0
Q1: Hendon (A) 1-7

51-52 PR: Berkhamsted Town (A) 1-3

52-53 PR: Southall (A) 3-1
Q1: Slough Centre (H) 2-1
Q2: Uxbridge (A) 1-2

53-54 PR: Southall (H) 0-1

54-55 PR: Hayes (H) 0-2

55-56 PR: Wimbledon (A) 1-4

56-57 PR: Wembley (A) 1-4

57-58 PR: Southall (A) 0-4

58-59 Q1: Dagenham (H) 0-4

59-60 Q1: Hendon (H) 0-1

60-61 Q1: Finchley (H) 3-1
Q2: Southall (A) 2-2, (H) 3-2
Q3: Maidenhead United (A) 3-3, (H) 0-2

61-62 Q1: Southall (H) 2-1
Q2: Maidenhead United (A) 0-1

62-63 Q1: Yiewsley (H) 0-3

63-64 Q1: Uxbridge (H) 1-2

66-67 Q1: Uxbridge (A) 2-1
Q2: Ware (A) 2-2, (H) 1-0
Q3: Barnet (A) 1-4

EDGWARE TOWN

Currently: Isthmian League
* - As Edgware F.C. See also Edgware Town (1)

73-74 * Q1: Hounslow (A) 0-2

74-75 * Q1: Harlow Town (H) 1-2

75-76 * Q1: Dagenham (A) 1-5

76-77 * Q1: Ware (A) 0-2

77-78 * Q1: Dunstable (H) 4-1
Q2: Boreham Wood (H) 2-2, (A) 2-4

78-79 * Q1: Corinthian-Casuals (A) 0-0, (H) 4-0
Q2: Metropolitan Police (H) 1-0
Q3: Leyton-Wingate (A) 1-1, (H) 3-1
Q4: Barnet (H) 0-1

79-80 * Q1: Hemel Hempstead (A) 2-1
Q2: Uxbridge (A) 2-0
Q3: Barking (H) 0-3

80-81 * PR: Hoddesdon Town (H) 4-3
Q1: Tiptree United (A) 1-0
Q2: Chelmsford City (A) 1-3

81-82 * PR: Staines Town (H) 3-1
Q1: Thame United (H) 1-3

82-83 * Q1: Bedford Town (H) *W/O*
Q2: Woodford Town (H) 0-1

83-84 * Q1: Windsor & Eton (H) 0-5

84-85 * PR: Sudbury Town (A) 1-8

85-86 * PR: Erith & Belvedere (H) 1-1, (A) 0-1

86-87 * PR: Corinthian-C. (H) 2-2, (A - *at Molesey*) 0-1

87-88 PR: Banbury United (A) 0-3

88-89 PR: Hitchin Town (H) 1-4

89-90 PR: Burnham (H) 3-1

90-91 PR: Eton Manor (A) 2-0
Q1: Harrow Borough (H) 1-0
Q2: Billericay Town (A) 0-1

91-92 PR: Southall (H) 4-0
Q1: Redditch United (A) 1-5

92-93 PR: Norwich United (A) 0-1

EDMONTON

See Haringey Borough

EDMONTON BOROUGH

Currently: Merged with Tufnell Park
Playing as Haringey Borough in London Spartan Lge
See also Haringey Borough

47-48 EX: Ware (A) 3-2
PR: Hoddesdon Town (A) 3-5

48-49 EX: Finchley (H) 0-2

EGHAM TOWN

Currently: Isthmian League

66-67 Q1: Wolverton Town & B.R. (H) 2-2, (A) 1-6

69-70 PR: Ruislip Manor (H) 1-1, (A) 2-1
Q1: Hornchurch (A) 1-1, (H) 0-0 *abandoned after 115 minutes*, 2-5

72-73 Q1: Letchworth Town (A) 2-1
Q2: Wycombe Wanderers (H) 2-6

73-74 Q1: Barking (A) 2-0
Q2: Staines Town (A) 0-2

74-75 PR: Addlestone (H) 1-3

75-76 Q1: Hampton (H) 2-0
Q2: Kingstonian (H) 0-1

76-77 Q1: Barnet (A) 1-6

77-78 Q1: Dulwich Hamlet (A) 0-1

78-79 PR: Camberley Town (H) 2-3

79-80 PR: Addlestone (H) 0-2

80-81 PR: Molesey (H) 3-1
Q1: Basingstoke Town (A) 3-2
Q2: Kingstonian (A) 1-2

81-82 PR: Marlow (H) 1-1, (A) 1-1, (H) 7-4
Q1: Maidenhead United (H) 1-2

82-83 Q1: Faversham Town (H) 0-0, (A) 3-1
Q2: Welling United (H) 2-0
Q3: Carshalton Athletic (H) 0-2

83-84 Q1: Sheppey United (H) 2-1
Q2: Leatherhead (H) 1-5

84-85 PR: Southwick (A) 1-1, (H) 2-1
Q1: Hailsham Town (H) 3-0
Q2: Gravesend & Northfleet (H) 1-0
Q3: Tooting & Mitcham (H) 0-0, (A) 0-1

85-86 Q1: Hornchurch (H) 1-1, (A) 1-0
Q2: Crawley Town (H) 0-6

86-87 PR: Boreham Wood (A) 2-2, (H) 1-3

87-88 PR: Portfield (H) 1-1, (A) 3-1
Q1: Chichester City (A) 1-1, (H) 0-2

88-89 Q1: Dover Athletic (A) 0-2

89-90 PR: Sheppey United (H) 4-1
Q1: Margate (H) 0-1

90-91 PR: Croydon (A) 4-0
Q1: Purfleet (H) 2-1
Q2: Witney Town (H) 1-0
Q3: Billericay Town (H) 1-1, (A) 2-1
Q4: Telford United (A) 0-2

91-92 PR: Wembley (H) 0-1

92-93 PR: Selsey (H) 2-1
Q1: Worthing (H) 1-1, (A) 1-7

EKCO (SOUTHEND-ON-SEA)

Currently: Essex Intermediate League

46-47 PR: Eton Manor (H) 2-0
Q1: Romford (A) 0-3

47-48 PR: Eton Manor (A) 3-2
Q1: Dagenham British Legion (H) 3-0
Q2: Grays Athletic (A) 0-1

ELDON ALBION

Currently: Defunct

48-49 EX: South Hetton Colliery Welfare (H) 0-6

ELLESMERE PORT TOWN

Currently: Defunct

46-47 PR: Nantwich (H) 9-0
Q1: Hyde United (A) 2-1
Q2: Rhyl (A) 4-4, (H) 1-3

47-48 PR: Lostock Gralam (H) 3-0
Q1: Droylsden (H) 2-2, (A) 1-3

48-49 EX: Northwich Victoria (H) 0-2

49-50 EX: Buxton (H) 2-3

50-51 EX: Wallasey Transport (A) *W/O*
PR: Nantwich (A) 3-4

51-52 Q1: Flint Town United (H) 2-2, (A) 1-3

52-53 PR: Marine (A) 3-3, (H) 2-1
Q1: South Liverpool (H) 4-0
Q2: Flint Town United (H) 1-2

53-54 Q1: Flint Town United (A) 2-3

54-55 Q1: Marine (A) 0-1

55-56 PR: South Liverpool (A) 2-4

56-57 PR: Macclesfield Town (A) 1-2

57-58 PR: Stockton Heath (H) 3-0
Q1: Hyde United (H) 5-0
Q2: Altrincham (A) 0-2

58-59 PR: Macclesfield Town (H) 3-1
Q1: Northwich Victoria (H) 3-1
Q2: Stockton Heath (A) 2-0
Q3: Buxton (H) 2-2, (A) 1-4

59-60 Q1: Macclesfield Town (A) 3-2
Q2: Northwich Victoria (A) 3-0
Q3: Witton Albion (H) 4-1
Q4: Burscough (H) 1-2

60-61	Q1: Pwllheli & District (A) 4-1 Q2: New Brighton (A) 0-0, (H) 0-1
61-62	PR: Llandudno (H) 5-3 Q1: Pwllheli & District (H) 2-0 Q2: New Brighton (A) 2-1 Q3: Runcorn (H) 4-3 Q4: Northwich Victoria (A) 0-1
62-63	Q1: Pwllheli & District (H) 3-0 Q2: Bangor City (A) 2-1 Q3: Borough United (A) 1-0 Q4: Wigan Athletic (A) 0-2
63-64	Q1: Bangor City (H) 0-1
64-65	Q1: Rhyl (H) 6-1 Q2: New Brighton (H) 4-0 Q3: Borough United (H) 4-0 Q4: Macclesfield Town (A) 1-2
65-66	Q1: Runcorn (H) 3-1 Q2: Colwyn Bay (H) 1-2
66-67	Q1: Witton Albion (H) 0-0, (A) 1-3
67-68	Q1: Darwen (A) 2-0 Q2: Chorley (A) 2-2, (H) 3-2 Q3: Burscough (H) 3-2 Q4: Runcorn (H) 1-2
68-69	Q1: Burscough (A) 1-3
69-70	Q1: Hyde United (H) 1-1, (A) 0-1
70-71	Q1: Eastwood (Hanley) (H) 3-0 Q2: New Brighton (A) 3-1 Q3: Skelmersdale United (H) 0-1
71-72	PR: Formby (H) 2-1 Q1: Droylsden (A) 3-0 Q2: Ormskirk (A) 1-0 Q3: Burscough (A) 1-0 Q4: Macclesfield Town (A) 2-1 R1: Boston United (H) 0-3
72-73	Q1: Leek Town (H) 2-1 Q2: Winsford Town (H) 1-0 Q3: Eastwood Hanley (H) 2-2, (A) 2-0 Q4: Altrincham (A) 1-1, (H) 1-2
73-74	Q1: Nantwich Town (A) 0-5
74-75	Q1: Rhyl (A) *scratched*

ELMORE

Currently: Western League

92-93	PR: Exmouth Town (A) 2-1 Q1: Falmouth Town (A) 0-2

ELY CITY

Currently: Eastern Counties League

54-55	PR: Thetford Town (H) 0-8
55-56	PR: Exning United (A) 4-2 Q1: Thetford Town (H) 4-3 Q2: Wisbech Town (A) 2-3
56-57	PR: Histon (A) 5-2 Q1: Cambridge United (A) 5-2 Q2: Cambridge City (A) 1-0 Q3: March Town United (H) 2-0 Q4: Sudbury Town (H) 1-0 R1: Torquay United (H) 2-6
57-58	PR: Chatteris Town (A) 1-1, (H) 0-1
58-59	PR: Holbeach United (H) 3-5
59-60	Q1: Cambridge United (H) 0-3
60-61	Q1: Chatteris Town (H) 6-2 Q2: Cambridge City (H) 1-8
61-62	Q1: Sudbury Town (A) 3-5
62-63	Q1: March Town United (A) 1-4
63-64	Q1: Bury Town (H) 0-4
64-65	Q1: Haverhill Rovers (H) 5-1 Q2: Wisbech Town (H) 0-2
65-66	Q1: Chatteris Town (A) 3-2 Q2: Bury Town (A) 0-5
66-67	Q1: St Neots Town (A) 2-4
67-68	Q1: Haverhill Rovers (H) 5-1 Q2: Cambridge United (A) 1-3
68-69	Q1: Newmarket Town (H) 4-1 Q2: Wellingborough Town (A) 1-3
69-70	PR: Soham Town Rangers (A) 1-1, (H) 2-3

Above: *Emley and Bolton attracted 9,035 to Leeds Road for a First Round tie on 17th November 1991. Here Bolton's Mark Winstanley outjumps Declan Duke (9). Photo: Barry Lockwood.*

70-71	Q1: King's Lynn (H) 1-2
71-72	Q1: Histon (H) 4-0 Q2: Wellingborough Town (A) 2-4
72-73	Q1: Great Yarmouth Town (A) 2-2, (H) 3-1 Q2: Thetford Town (H) 2-0 Q3: Chatteris Town (H) 3-3, (A) 4-2 Q4: Kettering Town (H) 1-2
73-74	PR: Letchworth Town (A) 1-2
74-75	Q1: Sudbury Town (A) 0-5
75-76	Q1: Bedford Town (A) 0-2
76-77	Q1: Wellingborough Town (A) 1-3
77-78	Q1: Holbeach United (H) 1-2
78-79	Q1: Clacton Town (A) 4-0 Q2: Lowestoft Town (H) 1-2
79-80	Q1: Boston United (H) 1-2
80-81	Q1: Corby Town (A) 0-1
81-82	Q1: Chatteris Town (A) 3-3, (H) 2-1 Q2: Clacton Town (H) 2-1 Q3: Bedford Town (A) 0-1
82-83	Q1: Lowestoft Town (H) 1-3
83-84	PR: Armitage (H) 3-2 Q1: Wednesfield Social (A) 0-4
86-87	PR: Felixstowe Town (A) 1-0 Q1: Tiptree United (H) 1-4
87-88	Q1: Hemel Hempstead (H) 1-1, (A) 1-2
88-89	PR: Saffron Walden Town (A) 0-2
89-90	Q1: Paget Rangers (A) 1-2
90-91	PR: Bourne Town (A) 0-3

EMLEY

Currently: Northern Premier League

71-72	Q1: Denaby United (A) 0-3
72-73	Q1: Macclesfield Town (H) 1-2
73-74	Q1: Radcliffe Borough (A) 2-1 Q2: Buxton (H) 1-2
74-75	Q1: Glossop (H) 4-1 Q2: Stalybridge Celtic (H) 3-1 Q3: Farsley Celtic (H) 1-2
75-76	PR: Mossley (A) 0-2
76-77	Q1: Gainsborough Trinity (A) 4-1 Q2: Brigg Town (A) 2-1 Q3: Winterton Rangers (H) 4-7
77-78	Q1: Barton Town (H) 3-2 Q2: Worksop Town (A) 2-4
78-79	Q1: Bridlington Trinity (A) 0-1
79-80	PR: Barrow (H) 1-0 Q1: Prescot Town (A) 0-1
80-81	PR: Fleetwood (H) 0-3
81-82	Q1: Thackley (H) 2-1 Q2: Bishop Auckland (H) 1-4
82-83	Q1: South Bank (H) 3-6
83-84	PR: Colwyn Bay (A) 3-2 Q1: Nantwich Town (A) 1-1, (H) 6-2 Q2: South Liverpool (H) 1-3
84-85	PR: Burscough (A) 1-2
85-86	PR: Belper Town (H) 1-1, (A) 1-0 Q1: Nantwich Town (H) 1-0 Q2: Chorley (H) 1-4
86-87	PR: Ilkeston Town (A) 3-1 Q1: Leyland Motors (A) 2-0 Q2: Hyde United (H) 2-2, (A) 4-1 Q3: Southport (A) 3-3, (H) 4-4, (A) 0-2
87-88	Q1: Southport (H) 2-0 Q2: Stockton (A) 1-0 Q3: Guisborough Town (A) 2-3
88-89	PR: Langley Park (H) 4-1 Q1: Burscough (A) 1-0 Q2: Horwich R.M.I. (H) 5-0 Q3: Fleetwood T. (A) 2-2, (H) 2-2, (A) 1-3
89-90	Q1: Buxton (A) 1-3
90-91	PR: Prescot A.F.C. (A) 1-1, (H) 2-1 Q1: Radcliffe Borough (A) 0-0, (H) 1-0 Q2: Chorley (H) 0-1
91-92	Q1: Farsley Celtic (A) 1-0 Q2: Horwich R.M.I. (H) 4-2 Q3: Borrowash Victoria (A) 3-0 Q4: Chorley (A) 2-2, (H) 1-1 *abandoned (fog) after 90 minutes*, (A) 1-0 R1: Bolton W. (*at Huddersfield Town*) 0-3
92-93	Q1: Marine (A) 0-5

ENDERBY TOWN

See Leicester United

ENFIELD

Currently: Isthmian League

45-46	PR: Hertford Town (A) 6-3 Q1: Bishop's Stortford (H) 8-1 Q2: Barnet (A) 0-5
46-47	EX: Wood Green Town (H) 1-1, (A) 3-4
47-48	EX: Welwyn Garden City (A) 5-1 PR: Wealdstone (A) 0-2
48-49	EX: Civil Service (A - *played home*) 8-0 PR: Lyon Club (Greenford) (A) 5-0 Q1: Ruislip Manor (A) 5-3 Q2: Hendon (A) 0-3

Above: *Peter Burton celebrates Enfield's equaliser at Barnsley. Photo: Mick Eason.*

49-50 PR: Finchley (A) 2-0
Q1: Wealdstone (H) 0-0, (A) 0-2

50-51 EX: Pinner (H) 5-0
PR: Willesden (H) 5-1
Q1: Civil Service (A) 5-2
Q2: St Albans City (H) 2-0
Q3: Hendon (H) 2-4

51-52 Q1: Woodford Town (H) 0-2

52-53 PR: Woodford Town (H) 3-3, (A) 2-4

53-54 Q1: Tufnell Park Edmonton (A) 0-2

54-55 PR: Bishop's Stortford (H) 3-1
Q1: Stevenage Town (A) 2-1
Q2: Clapton (A) 1-2

55-56 PR: Letchworth Town (H) 3-1
Q1: Hoddesdon Town (A) 5-2
Q2: St Albans City (H) 4-2
Q3: Hitchin Town (A) 1-3

56-57 PR: Bishop's Stortford (A) 0-3

57-58 PR: Cheshunt (H) 3-0
Q1: Eton Manor (H) 2-0
Q2: Clapton (H) 2-3

58-59 Q1: Hertford Town (A) 2-0
Q2: Berkhamsted Town (H) 6-0
Q3: Cheshunt (A) 1-3

59-60 Q1: Ware (A) 7-1
Q2: Hoddesdon Town (H) 15-0
Q3: Hertford Town (A) 3-2
Q4: Rushden Town (H) 3-0
R1: Headington United (H) 4-3
R2: Bournemouth & Boscombe Ath. (H) 1-5

60-61 Q4: Romford (A) 1-2

61-62 Q1: Hertford Town (H) 8-1
Q2: Harrow Town (A) 4-0
Q3: Barnet (H) 2-4

62-63 Q1: Stevenage Town (A) 2-0
Q2: Barnet (H) 4-1
Q3: Wealdstone (A) 5-1
Q4: Tooting & Mitcham United (A) 3-2
R1: Cheltenham Town (A) 6-3
R2: Peterborough United (A) 0-1

63-64 Q4: Hendon (H) 3-1
R1: Reading (A) 2-2, (H) 2-4

64-65 R1: Romford (A) 0-0, (H) 0-0, 4-2
R2: Barnet (H) 4-4, (A) 0-3

65-66 Q4: Corinthian-Casuals (H) 0-3

66-67 Q1: Leyton (H) 7-0
Q2: Hillingdon Borough (H) 3-0
Q3: Stevenage Town (H) 2-2, (A) 1-1, 2-0
Q4: Barnet (A) 2-1
R1: Chesham United (H) 6-0
R2: Watford (H) 2-4

67-68 R1: Swansea Town (A) 0-2

68-69 Q4: Barnet (A) 2-4

69-70 PR: Southall (H) 1-1, (A) 1-1, 6-2
Q1: Kingstonian (A) 3-1 *prot. upheld*, (A) 3-0
Q2: Grays Athletic (H) 7-1
Q3: Edmonton (A) 4-1
Q4: Wealdstone (A) 1-0
R1: Brighton & Hove Albion (A) 1-2

70-71 R1: Cambridge United (H) 0-1

71-72 Q4: Tilbury (A) 3-0
R1: Maidenhead United (H) 2-0
R2: Peterborough United (A) 0-4

72-73 R1: Bishop's Stortford (H) 1-1, (A) 0-1

73-74 Q4: Hayes (A) 1-1, (H) 0-1

74-75 Q1: Stevenage Athletic (A) 0-1

75-76 Q1: Hayes (H) 3-0
Q2: Maidenhead United (H) 6-0
Q3: Wembley (A) 0-1

76-77 PR: Hampton (H) 1-0
Q1: Tilbury (A) 2-2, (H) 3-0
Q2: Bracknell Town (H) 5-2
Q3: Epsom & Ewell (A) 1-1, (H) 1-0
Q4: Ilford (H) 2-2, (A) 4-0
R1: Harwich & Parkeston (H) 0-0, (A) 3-0
R2: Crystal Palace (H - *played away*) 0-4

77-78 Q1: Wembley (H) 6-0
Q2: Gravesend & Northfleet (H) 2-1
Q3: Leyton-Wingate (H) 4-0
Q4: Horsham (A) 4-0
R1: Wimbledon (H) 3-0
R2: Northampton Town (A) 2-0
R3: Blyth Spartans (A) 0-1

78-79 Q4: Gorleston (A) 6-2
R1: Wealdstone (A) 5-0
R2: Swindon Town (A) 0-3

79-80 Q4: Hitchin Town (A) 2-1
R1: Yeovil Town (H) 0-1

80-81 Q4: Epsom & Ewell (H) 5-0
R1: Wembley (H) 3-0
R2: Hereford United (H) 2-0
R3: Port Vale (A) 1-1, (H) 3-0
R4: Barnsley (A) 1-1, (H - *at Tottenham*) 0-3

81-82 R1: Hastings United (H) 2-0
R2: Wimbledon (H) 4-1
R3: Crystal Palace (H) 2-3

82-83 R1: Newport County (H) 0-0, (A) 2-4

83-84 R1: Wealdstone (A) 1-1, (H) 2-2, (A) 0-2

84-85 Q4: Canterbury City (A) 1-0
R1: Exeter City (A) 2-2, (H) 3-0
R2: Millwall (A) 0-1

85-86 Q4: Barnet (A) 7-0
R1: Bognor Regis Town (H) 0-2

86-87 Q4: Bury Town (H) 1-1, (A) 1-0
R1: Dartford (A) 1-1, (H) 3-0
R2: Swindon Town (A) 0-3

87-88 Q4: Aylesbury United (H) 1-2

88-89 R1: Leyton Orient (H) 1-1, (A) 2-2, (A) 1-0
R2: Cardiff City (H) 1-4

89-90 Q4: Matlock Town (A) 1-3

90-91 Q1: Barking (H) 4-1
Q2: Chesham United (A) 3-0
Q3: Chelmsford City (H) 1-1, (A) 0-1

91-92 Q1: Walthamstow Pennant (H) 4-0
Q2: Chelmsford City (A) 1-1, (H) 2-1
Q3: Billericay Town (A) 3-1
Q4: V.S. Rugby (H) 2-1
R1: Aldershot (A) 1-0
R2: Barnet (H) 1-4

92-93 Q4: Aylesbury United (H) 0-0, (A) 1-2

EPPING TOWN

Currently: Defunct

72-73 Q1: Bishop's Stortford (A) 0-1

73-74 Q1: Corinthian-Casuals (A) 2-0
Q2: Hounslow (A) 2-1
Q3: Maidenhead United (H) 3-0
Q4: Chelmsford City (H) 1-2

74-75 PR: Boreham Wood (H) 3-0
Q1: St Albans City (H) 0-0, (A) 2-2, 1-2

75-76 Q1: Chesham United (A) 0-3

76-77 Q1: Hoddesdon Town (H) 3-2
Q2: Carshalton A. (A) 1-1, (H) 1-1, 2-4

77-78 Q1: Corinthian-Casuals (A) 1-5

78-79 Q1: Chalfont St Peter (A) 0-0, (H) 1-1, (*at Hoddesdon T.*) 0-0, (*at Hounslow*) 1-2

79-80 PR: Aveley (H) 2-2, (A) 1-0
Q1: Tilbury (A) 0-3

80-81 PR: Haringey Borough (H) 2-1
Q1: Uxbridge (A) 0-1

81-82 PR: Sudbury Town (A) 3-3, (H) 2-4

82-83 PR: Haverhill Rovers (A) 0-3

83-84 PR: Royston Town (A) 1-4

84-85 PR: Tilbury (A) 1-0
Q1: Lowestoft Town (H) 3-4

EPPLETON COLLIERY WELF.

Currently: Northern League

48-49 EX: Langley Park C.W. (A) 4-3
PR: Easington Colliery Welfare (A) 1-6

49-50 EX: Consett (H) 2-3

50-51 EX: Seaham Colliery Welfare (A) 2-1
PR: Horden Colliery Welfare (A) 0-1

51-52 Q1: Chilton Athletic (A) 2-4

75-76 Q1: Ferryhill Athletic (H) 1-0
Q2: North Shields (H) 1-1, (A) 3-0
Q3: Willington (A) 1-2

76-77 PR: Crook Town (A) 1-4

77-78 PR: South Bank (H) 1-0
Q1: Billingham Synthonia (A) 0-2

78-79 PR: Consett (A) 1-1, (H) 0-7

79-80 Q1: Peterlee Newtown (A) 1-2

80-81 PR: Bridlington Trinity (A) 0-3

81-82 PR: Willington (A) 0-0, (H) 0-2

82-83 Q1: North Shields (A) 0-6

83-84 Q1: Durham City (H) 0-2

84-85 PR: Peterlee Newtown (A) 1-5

85-86 PR: Yorkshire Amateur (H) 5-1
Q1: Spennymoor United (H) 2-4

86-87 Q1: Brandon United (H) 1-1, (A) 1-2

EPSOM

Currently: Merged with Ewell & Stoneleigh F.C.
Playing as Epsom & Ewell in Isthmian League
See also Epsom & Ewell

45-46 PR: Woking (H) 1-8

46-47 PR: Metropolitan Police (H) 0-5

47-48 PR: Brookwood Hospital (H) 4-3
Q1: Kingstonian (A) 1-10

48-49 EX: Dorking (A - *played home*) 3-0
PR: Sutton United (H) 2-2, (A) 0-2

49-50 EX: Guildford (H) 6-0
PR: Cobham (H) 4-2
Q1: Woking (A) 2-1
Q2: Kingstonian (H) 1-3

51-52 PR: Woking (H) 3-4

52-53 PR: Dulwich Hamlet (H) 2-2, (A) 2-4

53-54 PR: Dorking (H) 1-1, (A) 1-0
Q1: Metropolitan Police (A) 2-1
Q2: Hounslow Town (A) 1-4

54-55 PR: Dorking (A) 3-1
Q1: Whitstable (A) 0-0, (H) 1-4

55-56 Q1: Dover (H) 3-2
Q2: Dorking (H) 3-2
Q3: Margate (H) 1-3

56-57 PR: Bexleyheath & Welling (H) 1-3

57-58 PR: Bromley (A) 2-4

58-59 PR: Dulwich Hamlet (A) 2-5

59-60 PR: Woking (A) 0-3

60-61 Q1: Carshalton Athletic (A) 0-1

EPSOM & EWELL

Currently: Isthmian League
See also Epsom F.C.

61-62 Q1: Dulwich Hamlet (H) 1-2

62-63 Q1: Slough Town (H) 1-3

63-64 Q1: Slough Town (H) 2-1
Q2: Walthamstow Avenue (H) 0-6

64-65 Q1: Marlow (A) 7-1
Q2: Wokingham Town (A) 4-2
Q3: Slough Town (H) 0-1

66-67 Q1: Hertford Town (A) 1-2

67-68 Q1: Stevenage Town (H) 1-3

68-69 Q1: Tilbury (A) 0-1

69-70 Q1: Tilbury (H) 0-1

70-71 Q1: Guildford City (A) 0-5

73-74 Q1: Wimbledon (H) 1-5

74-75 Q1: Redhill (A) 0-3

75-76 PR: Corinthian-Casuals (H) 4-2
Q1: Southall & Ealing (A) 1-1, (H) 3-3, 1-5

76-77 Q1: Camberley Town (A) 1-1, (H) 1-0
Q2: Boreham Wood (A) 1-1, (H) 2-1
Q3: Enfield (H) 1-1, (A) 0-1

77-78 Q1: Feltham (H) 1-1, (A) 1-2

78-79 PR: Addlestone (H) 2-0
Q1: Woking (A) 1-3

79-80 PR: Arundel (H) 1-1, (A) 1-0
Q1: Poole Town (A) 1-3

80-81 Q1: Eastbourne Town (H) 1-0
Q2: Margate (H) 3-1
Q3: Ashford Town (H) 1-0
Q4: Enfield (A) 0-5

81-82 Q1: Herne Bay (H) 2-1
Q2: Croydon (A) 1-1, (H) 4-0
Q3: Hastings United (H) 2-4

82-83 PR: Walton & Hersham (H) 1-2

83-84 Q1: Chatham Town (A) 2-1
Q2: Dartford (H) 1-2

84-85 Q1: Horndean (A) 3-1
Q2: Eastbourne Town (A) 4-2
Q3: Bognor Regis Town (H) 4-5

85-86 Q1: Hastings Town (A) 1-2

86-87 PR: Three Bridges (H) 1-2

87-88 PR: Arundel (H) 4-0
Q1: Molesey (A) 2-1
Q2: Metropolitan Police (A) 0-3

88-89 Q1: Barnet (A) 0-7

89-90 PR: Metropolitan Police (H) 0-0, (A) 2-0
Q1: Lewes (A) 0-2

90-91 PR: Horsham (A) 0-2

91-92 PR: Walton & Hersham (H) 1-5

92-93 PR: Deal Town (A) 0-3

EPSOM TOWN

Currently: Defunct

45-46 Q1: Walton & Hersham (A) 0-11

ERITH & BELVEDERE

Currently: Southern League

45-46 Q1: Gravesend & Northfleet (H) 3-3, (A) 1-4

46-47 PR: Gravesend & Northfleet (H) 3-3, (A) 1-4

47-48 PR: Dartford (A) 2-3

48-49 PR: Lloyds (Sittingbourne) (A) 1-5

49-50 EX: Sittingbourne (A) 2-0
PR: Faversham Town (A) 1-0
Q1: Tonbridge (H) 3-0
Q2: Dover (A) 0-3

50-51 PR: Betteshanger Colliery Welfare (A) 1-2

51-52 PR: Wimbledon (A) 1-0
Q1: Sutton United (A) 2-2, (H) 1-1, 0-3

52-53 PR: Kingstonian (A) 0-5

53-54 Q1: Barking (A) 2-1
Q2: Chelmsford City (A) 1-2

54-55 PR: Margate (H) 0-4

55-56 PR: Dorking (H) 3-3, (A) 1-5

56-57 PR: Sutton United (H) 4-3
Q1: Bromley (A) 0-6

57-58 PR: Tunbridge Wells United (H) 1-3

58-59 PR: Chatham Town (H) 8-0
Q1: Sittingbourne (H) 0-4

59-60 PR: Tonbridge (H) 0-2

60-61 Q1: Bexleyheath & Welling (H) 3-6

61-62 Q1: Sheppey United (A) 2-2, (H) 2-1
Q2: Cray Wanderers (A) 4-3
Q3: Dartford (A) 1-3

62-63 Q2: Bromley (A) 3-2
Q3: Gravesend & Northfleet (A) 0-5

63-64 Q1: Sittingbourne (A) 3-3, (H) 1-2

64-65 Q1: Sutton United (H) 0-4

65-66 Q1: Bromley (A) 2-3

66-67 Q1: Stevenage Town (A) 0-0, (H) 0-3

67-68 Q1: Cheshunt (A) 4-4, (H) 4-3
Q2: Leytonstone (A) 0-4

68-69 Q1: Amersham Town (A) 5-1
Q2: St Albans City (A) 2-3

69-70 Q1: St Albans City (H) 2-1
Q2: Wycombe Wanderers (A) 0-2

70-71 Q1: Metropolitan Police (A) 1-0
Q2: Romford (A) 0-0, (H) 1-1, 0-1

71-72 Q1: Leatherhead (H) 2-2, (A) 0-3

72-73 Q1: Harrow Borough (A) 0-0, (H) 2-1
Q2: Hayes (H) 1-2

73-74 Q1: Leatherhead (H) 1-6

74-75 Q1: Leyton (H) 5-0
Q2: Grays Athletic (A) 1-0
Q3: Sutton United (H) 1-5

75-76 Q1: Croydon (A) 1-1, (H) 1-3

76-77 Q1: Cray Wanderers (A) 2-2, (H) 2-3

77-78 Q1: Hounslow (H) 4-2
Q2: Barnet (A) 1-2

78-79 Q1: Croydon (A) 0-1

79-80 Q1: Burgess Hill (H) 0-0, (A) 0-0, 2-0
Q2: Welling United (A) 0-1

80-81 Q1: Grays Athletic (A) 0-0, (H) 1-3

81-82 PR: Rainham Town (H) 2-1
Q1: Leytonstone-Ilford (H) 2-2, (A) 0-3

82-83 Q1: Wembley (H) 1-2

83-84 PR: Molesey (A) 2-0
Q1: Hillingdon (A) 1-2

84-85 PR: Rainham Town (H) 2-2, (A) 1-3

85-86 PR: Edgware (H) 1-1, (H) 1-0
Q1: Crawley Town (H) 1-1, (A) 0-3

86-87 PR: Kingsbury Town (A) 0-0, (H) 1-0
Q1: Walton & Hersham (A) 2-2, (H) 0-1

87-88 PR: Wivenhoe Town (H) 0-0, (A) 2-4

88-89 Q1: Hanwell Town (H) 0-1

89-90 PR: Chatham Town (H) 5-1
Q1: Hornchurch (A) 2-1
Q2: Ashford Town (A) 1-0
Q3: Woking (H) 1-1, (A) 0-5

90-91 Q1: Carshalton Athletic (A) 0-3

91-92 PR: Horsham Y.M.C.A. (A) 2-1
Q1: Corinthian (A) 3-1
Q2: Wokingham Town (A) 2-1
Q3: Crawley Town (H) 1-2

92-93 Q1: Carshalton Athletic (A) 2-1
Q2: Havant Town (H) 1-1, (A) 4-5

ESH WINNING

Currently: Northern League

84-85 PR: Guisborough Town (H) 0-1

85-86 PR: Shildon (A) 1-3

86-87 Q1: Morecambe (A) 0-8

87-88 PR: Harrogate Town (A) 1-2

88-89 PR: Ryhope C.A. (H) 1-1, (A) 3-2
Q1: Farsley Celtic (H) 1-1, (A) 1-2

89-90 PR: North Shields (H) 2-6

90-91 PR: Shotton Comrades (A) 2-1
Q1: Harrogate Town (A) 3-1
Q2: Spennymoor United (H) 1-3

91-92 PR: Netherfield (H) 1-3

92-93 PR: Alnwick Town (H) 0-0, (A) 1-2

ETON MANOR

Currently: Essex Senior League

45-46 Q1: Romford (H) 1-1, (A) 3-4

46-47 PR: Ekco (A) 0-2

47-48 PR: Ekco (H) 2-3

48-49 EX: London Tran. (C.B.) (A - *played home*) 5-0
PR: Brentwood & Warley (A) 1-2

49-50 EX: Clacton Town (H) 2-1

PR: Barking (H - *played away*) 1-1, (A) 3-5

50-51 PR: Barking (H) 2-4

51-52 Q1: Clapton (H) 1-0
Q2: Leyton (H) 0-1

52-53 Q1: Letchworth Town (H) 1-1, (A) 1-1, (*at Barnet*) 3-0
Q2: Cheshunt (A) 1-0
Q3: Finchley (H) 0-1

53-54 Q1: Clapton (H) 4-3
Q2: Hitchin Town (H) 1-1, (A) 1-7

54-55 PR: St Albans City (H) 0-1

55-56 PR: Bishop's Stortford (A) 2-1
Q1: Barnet (H) 3-2
Q2: Hitchin Town (H) 3-3, (A) 1-2

56-57 Q1: Barnet (A) 3-0
Q2: Bishop's Stortford (A) 2-0
Q3: Hitchin Town (H) 3-1
Q4: Dunstable Town (A) 1-5

57-58 PR: Hertford Town (H) 3-1
Q1: Enfield (A) 0-2

58-59 Q1: Romford (H) 2-9

89-90 PR: Hailsham Town (A) 2-2, (H) 0-1

90-91 PR: Edgware Town (H) 0-2

EVENWOOD TOWN

Currently: Northern League

46-47 EX: Langley Park (A) 2-0
PR: Trimdon Grange (A) 3-3, (H) 2-1
Q1: Brandon Colliery Welfare (A) 1-2

47-48 PR: Tow Law Town (A) 6-4
Q1: Seaham Colliery Welfare (H) 3-1
Q2: Ferryhill Athletic (A) 0-4

48-49 PR: Chilton Athletic (H) 3-2
Q1: Seaham Colliery Welfare (H) 3-1
Q2: Horden Colliery Welfare (H) 1-2

49-50 PR: Stanley United (H) 5-1
Q1: Consett (H) 1-4

50-51 EX: Langley Park Colliery Welfare (H) 5-2
PR: Shildon (A) 5-3
Q1: Easington Colliery Welfare (H) 3-2
Q2: Horden Colliery Welfare (A) 0-4

51-52 Q1: Crook Town (H) 1-3

52-53 Q1: Tow Law Town (H) 1-0
Q2: West Auckland Town (A) 2-1
Q3: Spennymoor United (H) 1-1, (A) 1-4

53-54 Q1: Willington (A) 0-2

54-55 Q1: Stockton (H) 4-0
Q2: Ferryhill Athletic (A) 0-3

55-56 Q1: Tow Law Town (A) 1-3

56-57 Q1: Tow Law Town (H) 4-0
Q2: Willington (H) 2-1
Q3: Stanley United (H) 5-1
Q4: Easington Colliery Welfare (A) 3-0
R1: Darlington (H - *played away*) 2-7

57-58 Q2: Cockfield (A) 5-2
Q3: Durham City (H) 1-2

58-59 Q1: Easington Colliery Welfare (H) 8-1
Q2: Newburn (H) 7-2
Q3: North Shields (H) 1-0
Q4: Crook Town (A) 0-3

59-60 Q1: Consett (A) 1-2

60-61 Q1: Ferryhill Athletic (A) 2-3

61-62 Q1: Murton C.W. (H) 3-3, (A) 3-2
Q2: Shildon (A) 2-4

62-63 Q1: Annfield Plain (H) 0-0, (A) 1-2

64-65 Q1: South Bank (A) 4-1
Q2: Penrith (A) 1-3

65-66 Q1: Stockton (A) 0-3

66-67 Q1: Billingham Synthonia Recreation (A) 0-1

67-68 Q1: Ryhope Colliery Welfare (H) 0-6

68-69 Q1: Annfield Plain (H) 7-1
Q2: Consett (A) 3-4

69-70 Q1: Willington (A) 4-2
Q2: Blyth Spartans (A) 1-1, (H) 2-1
Q3: Whitby Town (H) 1-2

70-71 Q1: Tow Law Town (H) 3-0
Q2: Whitley Bay (H) 1-0
Q3: Blyth Spartans (A) 1-2

71-72 Q1: Shildon (A) 1-1, (H) 4-3
Q2: Whitley Bay (A) 1-3

72-73 Q1: Annfield Plain (H) 2-0
Q2: Billingham Synthonia (H) 0-0, (A) 1-2

73-74 Q1: Boldon Colliery Welfare (A) 1-0
Q2: Tow Law Town (H) 2-2, (A) 0-1

74-75 PR: Spennymoor United (H) 2-2, (A) 0-4

75-76 PR: Bridlington Trinity (H) 2-3

76-77 PR: Lancaster City (H) 1-1, (A) 0-4

77-78 Q1: Crook Town (A) 0-3

78-79 Q1: North Shields (H) 2-2, (A) 0-1

79-80 PR: Billingham Synthonia (H) 1-2

80-81 Q1: Ferryhill Athletic (A) 2-2, (H) 2-1
Q2: Shildon (H) 2-0
Q3: Bishop Auckland (H) 0-1

81-82 PR: Wallsend Town (A) 4-1
Q1: Tow Law Town (A) 2-4

82-83 Q1: Horden Colliery Welfare (H) 1-3

83-84 Q1: North Shields (H) 0-3

84-85 Q1: Peterlee Newtown (A) 0-4

85-86 PR: Crook Town (H - *played away*) 1-5

86-87 PR: Langley Park Welfare (A) 0-0, (H) 2-1
Q1: Darwen (H) 2-0
Q2: Spennymoor United (H) 0-5

87-88 PR: Leyland Motors (H) 0-2

88-89 PR: Bedlington Terriers (H) 2-0
Q1: Bishop Auckland (A) 0-4

89-90 PR: Durham City (H) 0-1

90-91 PR: Darlington Cleveland Bridge (A) 1-0
Q1: Seaham Red Star (A) 1-1, (H) 0-1

91-92 PR: Bridlington Town (A) 1-5

92-93 PR: Peterlee Newtown (A) 0-1

EVERTON

Currently: F.A. Premier League

45-46 R3: Preston N.E. (A) 1-2, (H) 2-2 (*agg: 3-4*)

46-47 R3: Southend United (H) 4-2
R4: Sheffield Wednesday (A) 1-2

47-48 R3: Grimsby Town (A) 4-1
R4: Wolverhampton W. (A) 1-1, (H) 3-2
R5: Fulham (A) 1-1, (H) 1-1, 0-1

48-49 R3: Manchester City (H) 1-0
R4: Chelsea (A) 0-2

49-50 R3: Queens Park Rangers (A) 2-0
R4: West Ham United (A) 2-1
R5: Tottenham Hotspur (H) 1-0
R6: Derby County (A) 2-1
SF: Liverpool (*at Manchester City*) 0-2

50-51 R3: Hull City (A) 0-2

51-52 R3: Leyton Orient (A) 0-0, (H) 1-3

52-53 R3: Ipswich Town (H) 3-2
R4: Nottingham Forest (H) 4-1
R5: Manchester United (H) 2-1
R6: Aston Villa (A) 1-0
SF: Bolton Wdrs (*at Manchester City*) 3-4

53-54 R3: Notts County (H) 2-1
R4: Swansea Town (H) 3-0
R5: Sheffield Wednesday (A) 1-3

54-55 R3: Southend United (H) 3-1
R4: Liverpool (H) 0-4

55-56 R3: Bristol City (H) 3-1
R4: Port Vale (A) 3-2
R5: Chelsea (H) 1-0
R6: Manchester City (A) 1-2

56-57 R3: Blackburn Rovers (H) 1-0
R4: West Ham United (H) 2-1
R5: Manchester United (A) 0-1

57-58 R3: Sunderland (A) 2-2, (H) 3-1
R4: Blackburn Rovers (H) 1-2

58-59 R3: Sunderland (H) 4-0
R4: Charlton Athletic (A) 2-2, (H) 4-1
R5: Aston Villa (H) 1-4

59-60 R3: Bradford City (A) 0-3

60-61 R3: Sheffield United (H) 0-1

61-62 R3: King's Lynn (H) 4-0
R4: Manchester City (H) 2-0
R5: Burnley (A) 1-3

62-63 R3: Barnsley (A) 3-0
R4: Swindon Town (A) 5-1
R5: West Ham United (A) 0-1

63-64 R3: Hull City (A) 1-1, (H) 2-1
R4: Leeds United (A) 1-1, (H) 2-0
R5: Sunderland (A) 1-3

64-65 R3: Sheffield Wednesday (H) 2-2, (A) 3-0
R4: Leeds United (A) 1-1, (H) 1-2

65-66 R3: Sunderland (H) 3-0
R4: Bedford Town (A) 3-0
R5: Coventry City (H) 3-0
R6: Manchester City (A) 0-0, (H) 0-0, 2-0
SF: Manchester Utd (*at Bolton Wdrs*) 1-0
F: Sheffield Wednesday (*at Wembley*) 3-2

66-67 R3: Burnley (A) 0-0, (H) 2-1
R4: Wolverhampton W. (A) 1-1, (H) 3-1
R5: Liverpool (H) 1-0
R6: Nottingham Forest (A) 2-3

67-68 R3: Southport (A) 1-0
R4: Carlisle United (A) 2-0
R5: Tranmere Rovers (H) 2-0
R6: Leicester City (H) 3-1
SF: Leeds United (N) 1-0
F: West Bromwich Albion (*at Wembley*) 0-1

68-69 R3: Ipswich Town (H) 2-1
R4: Coventry City (A) 2-0
R5: Bristol Rovers (A) 1-0
R6: Manchester United (A) 1-0
SF: Manchester City (*at Aston Villa*) 0-1

69-70 R3: Sheffield United (A) 1-2

70-71 R3: Blackburn Rovers (H) 2-0
R4: Middlesbrough (H) 3-0
R5: Derby County (H) 1-0
R6: Colchester United (H) 5-0
SF: Liverpool (*at Manchester Utd*) 1-2
TP: Stoke City (*at Crystal Palace*) 2-3

71-72 R3: Crystal Palace (A) 2-2, (H) 3-2
R4: Walsall (H) 2-1
R5: Tottenham Hotspur (H) 0-2

72-73 R3: Aston Villa (H) 3-2
R4: Millwall (H) 0-2

73-74 R3: Blackburn Rovers (H) 3-0
R4: West Bromwich Albion (H) 0-0, (A) 0-1

74-75 R3: Altrincham (H) 1-1, (A - *at Man. Utd*) 2-0
R4: Plymouth Argyle (A) 3-1
R5: Fulham (H) 1-2

75-76 R3: Derby County (A) 1-2

76-77 R3: Stoke City (H) 2-0
R4: Swindon Town (A) 2-2, (H) 2-1
R5: Cardiff City (A) 2-1
R6: Derby County (H) 2-0
SF: Liverpool (*both at Man. City*) 2-2, 0-3

77-78 R3: Aston Villa (H) 4-1
R4: Middlesbrough (A) 2-3

78-79 R3: Sunderland (A) 1-2

79-80 R3: Aldershot (H) 4-1
R4: Wigan Athletic (H) 3-0
R5: Wrexham (H) 5-2
R6: Ipswich Town (H) 2-1
SF: West Ham (*at A. Villa*) 1-1, (*at Leeds*) 1-2

80-81 R3: Arsenal (H) 2-0
R4: Liverpool (H) 2-1
R5: Southampton (A) 0-0, (H) 1-0
R6: Manchester City (H) 2-2, (A) 1-3

81-82 R3: West Ham United (A) 1-2

82-83 R3: Newport County (A) 1-1, (H) 2-1
R4: Shrewsbury Town (H) 2-1
R5: Tottenham Hotspur (H) 2-1
R6: Manchester United (A) 0-1

83-84 R3: Stoke City (A) 2-0
R4: Gillingham (H) 0-0, (A) 0-0, (A) 3-0
R5: Shrewsbury Town (H) 3-0

Above: *Everton's Graeme Sharp (9) is mobbed by ecstatic team-mates Andy Gray, Adrian Heath, Trevor Steven and Peter Reid, after scoring the opener in the 1984 final against Watford. Photo: Colorsport.*

R6: Notts County (A) 2-1
SF: Southampton (*at Arsenal*) 1-0
F: Watford (*at Wembley*) 2-0

84-85 R3: Leeds United (A) 2-0
R4: Doncaster Rovers (H) 2-0
R5: Telford United (H) 3-0
R6: Ipswich Town (H) 2-2, (A) 1-0
SF: Luton Town (*at Aston Villa*) 2-1
F: Manchester United (*at Wembley*) 0-1

85-86 R3: Exeter City (H) 1-0
R4: Blackburn Rovers (H) 3-1
R5: Tottenham Hotspur (A) 2-1
R6: Luton Town (A) 2-2, (H) 1-0
SF: Sheffield Wednesday (*at Aston Villa*) 2-1
F: Liverpool (*at Wembley*) 1-3

86-87 R3: Southampton (H) 2-1
R4: Bradford City (A) 1-0
R5: Wimbledon (A) 1-3

87-88 R3: Sheff. W. (A) 1-1, (H) 1-1, (H) 1-1, (A) 5-0
R4: Middlesbrough (H) 1-1, (A) 2-2, (H) 2-1
R5: Liverpool (H) 0-1

88-89 R3: West Bromwich Albion (A) 1-1, (H) 1-0
R4: Plymouth Argyle (A) 1-1, (H) 4-0
R5: Barnsley (A) 1-0
R6: Wimbledon (H) 1-0
SF: Norwich City (*at Aston Villa*) 1-0
F: Liverpool (*at Wembley*) 2-3

89-90 R3: Middlesbrough (A) 0-0, (H) 1-1, (H) 1-0
R4: Sheffield Wednesday (A) 2-1
R5: Oldham Ath (A) 2-2, (H) 1-1, (A) 1-2

90-91 R3: Charlton A. (A - *at Crystal Palace*) 2-1
R4: Woking (A - *played home*) 1-0
R5: Liverpool (A) 0-0, (H) 4-4, (H) 1-0
R6: West Ham United (A) 1-2

91-92 R3: Southend United (H) 1-0
R4: Chelsea (A) 0-1

92-93 R3: Wimbledon (A - *at Crystal P.*) 0-0, (H) 1-2

EVERWARM

See Bridgend Town

EVESHAM UNITED

Currently: Southern League

58-59 PR: Darlaston (A) 3-1
Q1: Boldmere St Michaels (A) 4-2
Q2: Brierley Hill Alliance (A) 0-4

59-60 Q1: Bedworth Town (H) 3-1
Q2: Hednesford (H) 3-1
Q3: Bilston (H) 2-1
Q4: Oswestry Town (A) 1-4

60-61 Q1: Bilston (H) 1-3

61-62 Q1: Brierley Hill Alliance (H) 1-5

73-74 Q1: Banbury United (H) 2-2, (A) 0-2

74-75 Q1: Warley County Borough (A) 0-2

75-76 PR: Alvechurch (A) 1-1, (H) 0-1

76-77 Q1: Ammanford Town (A) 0-1, *replay ordered, (at Worcester City)* 5-1
Q2: Worcester City (A) 1-3

77-78 Q1: Merthyr Tydfil (H) 0-0, (A) 0-2

78-79 Q1: Darlaston (A) 1-1, (H) 2-4

80-81 PR: Brereton Social (A) 1-1, (H) 3-2
Q1: Buckingham Town (H) 0-1

81-82 Q1: Alvechurch (A) 0-2

84-85 PR: Wisbech Town (A) 0-3

86-87 PR: Bristol Manor Farm (A) 2-0
Q1: Clevedon Town (H) 1-1, (A) 1-2

87-88 PR: Chasetown (A) 2-0
Q1: Lye Town (A) 0-1

88-89 PR: King's Lynn (H) 3-0
Q1: Redditch United (A) 1-2

89-90 PR: Malvern Town (H) 0-2

90-91 PR: Chasetown (A) 2-0
Q1: Racing Club Warwick (A) 0-0, (H) 5-1
Q2: Atherstone United (H) 0-2

91-92 PR: Rothwell Town (H) 3-1
Q1: Malvern Town (H) 2-4

92-93 PR: Stewarts & Lloyds (A) 2-4

EXETER CITY

Currently: Football League

45-46 R1: Trowbridge (A) 3-1, (H) 7-2 (*agg: 10-3*)
R2: Newport Co. (A) 1-5, (H) 1-3 (*agg: 2-8*)

46-47 R1: Bournemouth & Boscombe Ath. (A) 2-4

47-48 R1: Northampton Town (H) 1-1, (A) 0-2

48-49 R1: Barnet (A) 6-2
R2: Hereford United (H) 2-1
R3: Grimsby Town (A) 1-2

49-50 R1: Millwall (A) 5-3
R2: Chester (H) 2-0
R3: Nuneaton Borough (H) 3-0
R4: Liverpool (A) 1-3

50-51 R1: Glastonbury (A) 2-1
R2: Swindon Town (H) 3-0
R3: Grimsby Town (A) 3-3, (H) 4-2
R4: Chelsea (H) 1-1, (A) 0-2

51-52 R1: King's Lynn (A) 3-1
R2: Ipswich Town (A) 0-4

52-53 R1: Port Vale (A) 1-2

53-54 R1: Hereford United (H) 1-1, (A) 0-2

54-55 R1: Millwall (A) 2-3

55-56 R1: Coventry City (A) 1-0
R2: Hendon (H) 6-2
R3: Stoke City (H) 0-0, (A) 0-3

56-57 R1: Plymouth Argyle (H) 0-2

57-58 R1: Bath City (A) 1-2

58-59 R1: Brentford (A) 2-3

59-60 R1: Barnstaple Town (H) 3-1
R2: Brentford (H) 3-1
R3: Luton Town (H) 1-2

60-61 R1: Bournemouth & Bosc. (H) 1-1, (A) 1-3

61-62 R1: Dartford (H) 3-3, (A) 1-2

62-63 R1: Gravesend & Northfleet (A) 2-3

63-64 R1: Shrewsbury Town (H) 2-1
R2: Bristol City (H) 0-2

64-65 R1: Hayes (H) 1-0
R2: Shrewsbury Town (H) 1-2

65-66 R1: Bedford Town (H) 1-2

66-67 R1: Luton Town (H) 1-1, (A) 0-2

67-68 R1: Nuneaton Boro. (A) 0-0, (H) 0-0, 1-0
R2: Walsall (H) 1-3

68-69 R1: Newport County (H) 0-0, (A) 3-1
R2: Colchester United (A) 1-0
R3: Manchester United (H) 1-3

69-70 R1: Fulham (H) 2-0
R2: Northampton T. (A) 1-1, (H) 0-0, 1-2

70-71 R1: Swansea City (A) 1-4

71-72 R1: Crawley Town (A) 0-0, (H) 2-0
R2: Swansea City (A) 0-0, (H) 0-1

72-73 R1: Walton & Hersham (A) 1-2

73-74 R1: Alvechurch (H) 0-1

74-75 R1: Newport County (H) 1-2

75-76 R1: Cardiff City (A) 2-6

76-77 R1: Southend United (H) 1-1, (A) 1-2

77-78 R1: Newport County (A) 1-1, (H) 4-2
R2: Minehead (A) 3-0
R3: Wolverhampton W. (H) 2-2, (A) 1-3

78-79 R1: Brentford (H) 1-0
R2: Maidstone United (H) 0-1

79-80 R1: Aldershot (A) 1-4

80-81 R1: Leatherhead (H) 5-0
R2: Millwall (A) 1-0
R3: Maidstone United (A) 4-2
R4: Leicester City (A) 1-1, (H) 3-1
R5: Newcastle United (A) 1-1, (H) 4-0
R6: Tottenham Hotspur (A) 0-2

81-82 R1: Brentford (A) 0-2

82-83 R1: Plymouth Argyle (A) 0-2

83-84 R1: Maidstone United (H) 1-1, (A) 1-2

84-85 R1: Enfield (H) 2-2, (A) 0-3

85-86 R1: Cardiff City (H) 2-1
R2: Bristol City (A) 2-1
R3: Everton (A) 0-1

86-87 R1: Cambridge United (H) 1-1, (A) 0-2

87-88 R1: Leyton Orient (A) 0-2

88-89 R1: Bognor Regis Town (H) 1-2

89-90 R1: Dartford (A) 1-1, (H) 4-1
R2: Maidstone United (A - *at Dartford*) 1-1, (H) 3-2
R3: Norwich City (H) 1-1, (A) 0-2

90-91 R1: Cambridge United (H) 1-2

91-92 R1: Colchester (A) 0-0, (H) 0-0 (*4-2 pens*)
R2: Swansea City (H) 0-0, (A) 2-1
R3: Portsmouth (H) 1-2

92-93 R1: Kidderminster Harriers (H) 1-0
R2: Swansea City (H) 1-2 *abandoned (floodlight failure) after 84 minutes*, (H) 2-5

EXMOUTH TOWN

Currently: Western League

85-86 PR: Glastonbury (A) 5-0
Q1: Ottery St Mary (H) 2-0
Q2: Bideford (H) 2-1
Q3: Bath City (A) 0-2

86-87 Q1: Glastonbury (H) 5-0
Q2: Weston-super-Mare (A) 3-2
Q3: Minehead (H) 3-4

87-88 Q1: Bideford (A) 1-1, (H) 0-2

88-89 PR: Welton Rovers (A) 5-0
Q1: Ton Pentre (A) 1-0
Q2: Swanage Town & Herston (A) 1-1, (H) 3-0
Q3: Saltash United (A) 2-2, (H) 4-3
Q4: Woking (H) 1-5

89-90 Q1: Ilfracombe Town (H) 2-0
Q2: Taunton (A) 0-0, (H) 2-2, (A) 0-0, (H) 2-1
Q3: Weymouth (H) 2-0
Q4: Farnborough Town (H) 1-4

90-91 Q1: Cheltenham (A) 2-2, (H) 3-3, (A) 0-3

91-92 PR: Frome Town (A) 1-3

92-93 PR: Elmore (H) 1-2

EXNING UNITED

Currently: Cambridge & District Sunday League

54-55 PR: Cambridge City (A) 1-2

55-56 PR: Ely City (H) 2-4

EYNESBURY ROVERS

Currently: United Counties League

46-47 PR: Waterlows (H) 1-0
Q1: Leighton United (A) 1-2

47-48 PR: Bedford Town (A) 4-7

48-49 PR: Biggleswade Town (A) 1-3

49-50 PR: Wolverton Town & B.R. (H) 2-1
Q1: Hitchin Town (H) 0-1

50-51 EX: Wolverton Town & B.R. (A) 2-3

51-52 Q1: Hitchin Town (A) 7-1
Q2: Bedford Town (A) 0-3

52-53 Q1: Vauxhall Motors (A) 4-2
Q2: Bedford Town (H) 0-4

53-54 Q1: Vauxhall Motors (A) 2-6

54-55 Q2: Wolverton Town & B.R. (H) 3-2
Q3: Biggleswade Town (H) 3-2
Q4: Cambridge United (A) 1-3

55-56 Q1: Potton United (A) 2-0
Q2: Bletchley & Wipac Sports (H) 5-0
Q3: Bedford Town (H) 1-4

56-57 Q2: Wolverton Town & B.R. (A) 3-4

57-58 Q1: Dunstable Town (H) 1-3

58-59 Q1: Wolverton Town & B.R. (H) 3-0
Q2: Vauxhall Motors (H) 0-3

60-61 Q1: St Neots Town (H) 1-9

61-62 Q1: Rothwell Town (A) 2-6

62-63 Q1: St Neots Town (H) 0-5

63-64 Q1: Wellingborough Town (A) 0-3

64-65 Q2: Rothwell Town (H) 3-1
Q3: St Neots Town (A) 0-7

65-66 Q1: Rothwell Town (H) 0-2

66-67 Q1: Rushden Town (H) 0-0, (A) 3-6

67-68 Q1: Wellingborough Town (H) 0-4

68-69 Q1: Soham Town Rangers (A) 0-6

69-70 Q1: Newmarket Town (H) 2-3

89-90 PR: Wisbech Town (A) 0-5

90-91 PR: Haverhill Rovers (A) 1-1, (H) 0-2

91-92 PR: Leyton-Wingate (A) 0-6

92-93 PR: Milton Keynes Borough (H) 4-5

FAKENHAM TOWN

Currently: Eastern Counties League

50-51 EX: Eastern Coachworks (A) 2-8

FALMOUTH TOWN

Currently: South Western League

62-63 Q1: Barnstaple Town (H) 1-1, (A) 3-1
Q2: St Blazey (H) 1-0
Q3: Bideford (H) 1-1, (A) 3-0
Q4: Bath City (H) 2-1
R1: Oxford United (H) 1-2

63-64 Q4: Bath City (A) 0-2

64-65 Q1: Newton Abbot Spurs (A) 1-1, (H) 3-2
Q2: St Blazey (A) 1-2

65-66 Q2: St Blazey (A) 1-4

66-67 Q1: Bideford (H) 0-3

67-68 Q1: Penzance (H) 4-1
Q2: Wadebridge Town (H) 6-0
Q3: Bideford (H) 3-1
Q4: Minehead (A) 2-1
R1: Peterborough United (A) 2-5

68-69 Q1: Penzance (A) 4-3
Q2: Bideford (H) 2-1
Q3: Wadebridge Town (A) 2-2, (H) 3-1
Q4: Waterlooville (H) 2-2, (A) 1-1, 0-2

69-70 Q1: Bideford (A) 2-1
Q2: Penzance (H) 1-0
Q3: Wadebridge Town (A) 5-0
Q4: Ton Pentre (H) 1-1, (A) 1-1, 1-0
R1: Peterborough United (H) 1-4

70-71 Q1: Truro City (H) 5-1
Q2: St Blazey (A) 2-3

71-72 Q1: Truro City (H) 3-2
Q2: Bideford (A) 1-3

72-73 PR: Truro City (A) 0-1

73-74 Q1: St Blazey (A) 3-1
Q2: Barnstaple Town (H) 4-1
Q3: Bideford (H) 3-3, (A) 1-1, 2-2, 2-2, 1-2

74-75 Q1: Newquay (H) 2-0
Q2: Minehead (A) 2-3

75-76 Q1: Newquay (H) 5-1
Q2: Barnstaple Town (H) 4-0
Q3: Penzance (A) 3-0
Q4: Yeovil Town (H) 1-5

76-77 Q1: Bridgwater Town (A) 4-2
Q2: Newquay (H) 8-0
Q3: Yeovil Town (H) 2-0
Q4: Minehead (H) 1-1, (A) 0-3

77-78 Q1: Newquay (H) 0-1

78-79 Q1: Bideford (A) 1-2

79-80 PR: Barnstaple Town (H) 1-2

80-81 Q1: Liskeard Athletic (H) 1-1, (A) 3-2
Q2: Saltash United (H) 2-1
Q3: Taunton Town (A) 0-1

81-82 PR: Penzance (H) 2-2, (A) 2-2, (H) 1-0
Q1: Newquay (H) 2-0
Q2: Torrington (H) 1-0
Q3: Bideford (A) 0-1

82-83 Q1: Wimborne Town (H) 1-2

83-84 PR: Bridgwater Town (H) 0-1

88-89 Q1: Glastonbury (H) 3-0
Q2: Saltash United (H) 2-2, (A) 0-5

89-90 PR: Torrington (A) 1-1, (H) 4-2
Q1: St Blazey (H) 1-1, (A) 0-1

90-91 PR: St Austell (A) 4-0
Q1: Dorchester Town (H) 2-4

91-92 PR: Bideford (A) 3-2
Q1: Minehead (H) 2-0
Q2: Liskeard Athletic (A) 1-5

92-93 PR: St Blazey (A) 4-1
Q1: Elmore (H) 2-0
Q2: Bath City (H) 0-3

FAREHAM TOWN

Currently: Southern League

55-56 Q1: Basingstoke Town (A) 3-3, (H) 3-2
Q2: Cowes (A) 3-2
Q3: Andover (H) 2-2, (A) 2-0
Q4: Wycombe Wanderers (A) 1-3

58-59 PR: Ryde Sports (H) 4-2
Q1: Gosport Borough Athletic (H) 6-2
Q2: Andover (A) 0-1

59-60 Q1: Winchester City (A) 4-1
Q2: Basingstoke Town (A) 1-4

60-61 Q1: Alton Town (H) 4-3
Q2: Andover (H) 3-3, (A) 2-3

61-62 Q1: Newport I.O.W. (H) 2-3

62-63 Q1: Basingstoke Town (A) 2-4

63-64 Q1: Basingstoke Town (A) 3-4

64-65 Q1: Newport I.O.W. (A) 5-1
Q2: Andover (H) 2-1
Q3: Basingstoke Town (H) 3-3, (A) 2-1
Q4: Weymouth (A) 2-3

65-66 Q1: Alton Town (H) 7-3
Q2: Basingstoke Town (A) 2-0
Q3: Cowes Isle of Wight (H) 4-2
Q4: Wimbledon (H) 0-3

66-67 Q1: Newport Isle of Wight (H) 5-1
Q2: Andover (H) 1-0
Q3: Salisbury (H) 2-2, (A) 2-1
Q4: Welton Rovers (A) 1-4

67-68 Q1: Salisbury (H) 2-2, (A) 1-5

68-69 Q1: Wokingham Town (H) 2-3

69-70 Q1: Cowes (H) 3-0
Q2: Salisbury (A) 0-1

70-71 PR: Tornycroft Athletic (H) 1-5

71-72 Q1: Selsey (H) 8-2
Q2: Alton Town (A) 1-0
Q3: Thornycroft Athletic (H) 5-1
Q4: Basingstoke T. (A) 2-2, (H) 1-1, 1-2

72-73 Q1: Newport I.O.W. (A) 6-2
Q2: Basingstoke Town (A) 1-3

73-74 PR: Newport I.O.W. (A) 1-1, (H) 0-1

74-75 Q1: Littlehampton T. (H) 1-1, (A) 1-1, 0-1

75-76 PR: Bath City (H) 1-0
Q1: Swaythling (A) 0-2

76-77 Q1: Gosport Borough (H) 1-1, (A) 5-0
Q2: Alton Town (A) 0-0, (H) 1-0
Q3: Poole Town (H) 0-1

77-78 Q1: Dorchester Town (A) 0-0, (H) 1-2

78-79 PR: Cowes (A) 0-0, (H) 2-0
Q1: Waterlooville (A) 0-2

79-80 Q1: Littlehampton Town (A) 8-0
Q2: Tunbridge Wells (A) 2-1
Q3: Gosport Borough (H) 1-0
Q4: Tiverton Town (A) 2-1
R1: Merthyr Tydfil (H) 2-3

80-81 Q1: Newport I.O.W. (H) 2-0
Q2: Farnborough Town (A) 0-1

81-82 Q1: Bromley (A) 5-0
Q2: Dulwich Hamlet (A) 2-1
Q3: Addlestone & Weybridge T. (A) 0-2

82-83 Q1: Farnborough Town (H) 2-3

83-84 Q1: Maidenhead United (H) 1-1, (A) 1-0
Q2: A.F.C. Totton (H) 0-3

84-85 Q1: Andover (H) 2-1
Q2: Slough Town (A) 0-2

85-86 Q1: Salisbury (H) 2-2, (A) 5-0
Q2: Wokingham Town (H) 1-0
Q3: A.F.C. Totton (H) 0-0, (A) 3-0
Q4: Fisher Athletic (A) 2-1
R1: Maidstone United (H) 0-3

86-87 Q1: Oxford City (H) 2-1
Q2: Newbury Town (A) 5-0
Q3: Road Sea Southampton (A) 3-0
Q4: Trowbridge Town (A) 0-0, (H) 4-1
R1: A.F.C. Bournemouth (A) 2-7

87-88 Q1: Trowbridge Town (H) 1-0
Q2: Swanage Town & Herston (A) 2-0
Q3: Weymouth (A) 2-2, (H) 1-2

88-89 Q1: Chichester City (H) 3-0
Q2: Basingstoke Town (H) 3-0
Q3: Bashley (A) 2-1
Q4: Dover Athletic (H) 1-1, (A) 1-0

	R1: Torquay United (A) 2-2, (H) 2-3
89-90	Q1: Romsey Town (A) 1-1, (H) 1-2
90-91	PR: Hungerford Town (A) 0-1
91-92	PR: Thatcham Town (H) 1-5
92-93	Q1: Tooting & Mitcham United (H) 2-0 Q2: Sittingbourne (A) 2-3

FARNBOROUGH TOWN

Currently: Southern League

72-73	Q1: Alton Town (A) 0-2
73-74	Q1: Woking (H) 2-2, (A) 2-2, 1-2
74-75	Q1: Staines Town (H) 1-1, (A) 1-0 Q2: Tooting & Mitcham Utd (H) 2-2, (A) 1-6
75-76	Q1: Basingstoke Town (A) 1-2
76-77	PR: Salisbury (H) 4-0 Q1: Hungerford Town (A) 3-0 Q2: Poole Town (H) 1-1, (A) 1-3
77-78	Q1: Bognor Regis Town (A) 2-0 Q2: Newport I.O.W. (H) 3-0 Q3: Horsham (A) 0-2
78-79	PR: Maidenhead United (H) 1-0 Q1: Slough Town (A) 0-2
79-80	Q1: Cray Wanderers (H) 0-1
80-81	Q1: Frome Town (A) 1-1, (H) 1-0 Q2: Fareham Town (H) 1-0 Q3: Newbury Town (H) 4-1 Q4: Merthyr Tydfil (A) 1-0 R1: Yeovil Town (A) 1-2
81-82	Q1: Horndean (H) 5-0 Q2: Wick (A) 2-2, (H) 3-0 Q3: Banstead Athletic (H) 4-0 Q4: Weymouth (A) 0-3
82-83	Q1: Fareham Town (A) 3-2 Q2: Eastbourne United (H) 2-1 Q3: Worthing (A) 0-1
83-84	Q1: Wick (A) 2-1 Q2: Tonbridge A.F.C. (A) 2-1 Q3: Kingstonian (A) 4-2 Q4: Weymouth (A) 1-1, (H) 3-2 R1: Barking (A) 1-2
84-85	Q1: Fleet Town (H) 5-1 Q2: A.F.C. Totton (A) 1-1, (H) 5-1 Q3: Hungerford Town (A) 3-3, (H) 4-1 Q4: Chippenham Town (H) 2-1 R1: Hereford United (A) 0-3
85-86	Q4: Hastings Town (H) 3-2 R1: Bath City (H) 0-4
86-87	Q4: Herne Bay (H) 4-0 R1: Swindon Town (H - *played away*) 0-4
87-88	Q4: Saltash United (H) 4-2 R1: Cambridge United (A) 1-2
88-89	Q4: Waterlooville (H) 2-3
89-90	Q4: Exmouth Town (A) 4-1 R1: Hereford United (H) 0-1
90-91	Q1: Abingdon United (A) 1-0 Q2: Slough Town (A) 3-2 Q3: Salisbury (A) 3-0 Q4: Gloucester City (H) 4-1 R1: Fulham (A) 1-2
91-92	Q4: Salisbury (A) 7-1 R1: Halesowen Town (A) 2-2, (H) 4-0 R2: Torquay United (A) 1-1, (H) 4-3 R3: West Ham (H - *played away*) 1-1, (A) 0-1
92-93	Q4: Dorking (H) 1-1, (A) 0-2

FARNHAM TOWN

Currently: Combined Counties League

48-49	EX: McLaren Sports (H - *played away*) 4-2 PR: Hounslow Town (H) 2-4
49-50	PR: Tooting & Mitcham United (A) 0-4
50-51	PR: Kingstonian (A) 1-6
51-52	PR: Hounslow Town (H) 3-5
86-87	PR: Devizes Town (A) 1-1, (H) 1-4

FARSLEY CELTIC

Currently: Northern Premier League

48-49	EX: Liversedge (H) 6-0 PR: Thorne Colliery (H) 2-1 Q1: Ossett Town (A) 2-3
49-50	EX: Armthorpe Welfare (A) 5-4 PR: Brunswick Institute (A) 3-0 Q1: Bentley Colliery (A) 2-4
50-51	PR: Appleby Frodingham Athletic (H) 1-0 Q1: Frickley Colliery (H) 3-1 Q2: Selby Town (A) 3-2 Q3: Goole Town (H) 3-2 Q4: Ashington (A) 1-2
51-52	Q1: Selby Town (A) 1-1, (H) 4-2 Q2: Yorkshire Amateur (H) 2-3
52-53	Q1: Ossett Town (H) 1-0 Q2: Goole Town (A) 3-3, (H) 3-4
53-54	Q2: Goole Town (H) 0-1
54-55	Q2: Ossett Town (H) 2-1 Q3: Goole Town (H) 2-0 Q4: Wigan Athletic (A) 1-3
55-56	Q2: Ossett Town (A) 2-3
56-57	Q2: Yorkshire Amateur (H) 1-0 Q3: Goole Town (A) 0-9
57-58	Q2: Yorkshire Amateur (A) 1-1, (H) 1-2
58-59	Q1: Selby Town (H) 1-3
59-60	Q1: Upton Colliery (H) 5-2 Q2: Denaby United (A) 0-2
61-62	Q1: Goole Town (A) 1-5

Above: *Farnborough's ace striker Simon Read (right) contests a ball with Chris Hemming in the 1984 First Round tie against Hereford United. Photo: Eric Marsh.*

62-63	Q1: Goole Town (H) 1-0 Q2: Ossett Albion (A) 1-2
63-64	Q1: Yorkshire Amateur (H) 0-0, (A) 4-0 Q2: Frickley Colliery (A) 0-3
64-65	Q1: Scarborough (H) 0-0, (A) 0-0, (A) 0-5
65-66	Q1: Harrogate Town (H) 0-1
66-67	Q1: Yorkshire Amateur (H) 1-0 Q2: Retford Town (H) 2-0 Q3: Gainsborough Trinity (A) 1-1, (H) 0-1
67-68	Q1: Gainsborough Trinity (H) 2-1 Q2: Denaby United (A) 2-2, (H) 3-1 Q3: Retford Town (H) 0-1
68-69	Q1: Retford Town (H) 1-2
69-70	Q1: Frickley Colliery (H) 1-2
70-71	Q1: Bridlington Trinity (A) 0-1
71-72	Q1: Frickley Colliery (H) 0-1
72-73	Q1: Bridlington Town (H) 3-2 Q2: Scarborough (H) 0-1
73-74	Q1: Buxton (A) 0-1
74-75	Q1: Stocksbridge Works Social (A) 3-1 Q2: Yorkshire Amateur (A) 2-0 Q3: Emley (A) 2-1 Q4: Bridlington Town (A) 4-0 R1: Tranmere Rovers (H - *at Leeds Utd*) 0-2
75-76	PR: Horwich R.M.I. (A) 1-1, (H) 1-1, 1-2
76-77	Q1: Goole Town (H) 1-4
77-78	Q1: Brigg Town (A) 0-2
78-79	PR: Bridlington Town (H) 0-1
79-80	PR: Accrington Stanley (H) 0-2
80-81	PR: Carlisle City (A) 4-1 Q1: Peterlee Newtown (A) 2-0 Q2: Billingham Synthonia (A) 0-2
81-82	PR: Mexborough Town Ath. (H) 1-1, (A) 1-2
82-83	Q1: Bridlington Trinity (H) 3-0 Q2: Gateshead (A) 1-5
83-84	Q1: Horwich R.M.I. (H) 1-4
84-85	Q1: Radcliffe Borough (A) 2-5
85-86	PR: Seaham Colliery Welfare Red Star (H) 2-0 Q1: Blyth Spartans (H) 1-2
86-87	PR: Ryhope Community A. (A) 1-1, (H) 3-2 Q1: Newcastle Blue Star (H) 1-3
87-88	PR: Norton & Stockton Ancients (H) 5-4 Q1: Wren Rovers (A) 2-1 Q2: Tow Law Town (A) 1-2
88-89	PR: Netherfield (H) 2-2, (A) 3-0 Q1: Esh Winning (A) 1-1, (H) 2-1 Q2: Guisborough Town (A) 0-0, (H) 0-1
89-90	PR: Friar Lane Old Boys (A) 2-1 Q1: Goole Town (A) 0-1
90-91	PR: Ossett Albion (H) 1-1, (A) 2-0 Q1: Bangor City (H) 0-0, (A) 0-3
91-92	PR: Eastwood Town (A) 4-2 Q1: Emley (H) 0-1

FAVERSHAM TOWN

Currently: Kent League

49-50	EX: Margate (A) 3-1 PR: Erith & Belvedere (H) 0-1
50-51	PR: Bowater Lloyds (A) 1-4
51-52	PR: Snowdown Colliery Welfare (H) 0-3
52-53	PR: Sittingbourne (A) 1-3
65-66	Q1: Sittingbourne (A) 0-9
71-72	Q1: Herne Bay (A) 1-3
72-73	Q1: Bexhill Town (H) 0-2
73-74	Q1: Sheppey United (A) 3-2 Q2: Folkestone (H) 1-1, (A) 1-4
74-75	Q1: Tunbridge Wells (A) 0-0, (H) 3-2 Q2: Medway (A) 1-2
75-76	Q1: Herne Bay (H) 2-1

Q2: Dover (H) 0-4

76-77 Q1: Three Bridges (A) 3-3, (H) 2-1
Q2: Bromley (A) 0-2

77-78 Q1: Folkestone & Shepway (H) 0-3

78-79 PR: Hastings United (H) 1-3

79-80 PR: Bromley (H) 0-2

80-81 Q1: Dover (H) 0-2

81-82 Q1: Hastings United (A) 0-5

82-83 PR: Peacehaven & Telscombe Cliffs (H) 2-0
Q1: Egham Town (A) 0-0, (H) 1-3

83-84 PR: Lancing (A) 1-3

84-85 Q1: Canterbury City (A) 0-3

85-86 PR: Ashford Town (A) 1-5

86-87 Q1: Leyton-Wingate (A) 1-1, (H) 0-1

87-88 PR: Shoreham (H) 1-1, (A) 0-2

91-92 PR: Eastbourne T. (H) 0-0, (A - *E'bourne U.*) 4-0
Q1: Carshalton Athletic (H) 3-2
Q2: Dover Athletic (H) 0-0, (A) 1-2

92-93 PR: Portfield (A) 4-2
Q1: Ashford Town (A) 1-1, (H) 0-2

FELIXSTOWE TOWN

Currently: Eastern Counties League
* - As Felixstowe United

49-50 * PR: City of Norw. S.O.B.U. (A - *pl. home*) 0-5

50-51 * EX: Sheringham (A) 1-3

77-78 Q1: Gorleston (H) 2-4

78-79 PR: Hoddesdon Town (H) 1-0
Q1: Letchworth Garden City (A) 1-5

79-80 Q1: March Town United (H) 3-2
Q2: Parson Drove (A) 0-2

80-81 PR: Bury Town (A) 1-2

81-82 PR: Chatteris Town (A) 1-3

82-83 Q1: Irthlingborough D. (H) 1-1, (A) 1-3

83-84 Q1: Rainham Town (H) 3-1
Q2: Lowestoft Town (A) 0-3

84-85 PR: Harwich & Parkeston (H) 3-0
Q1: Basildon United (A) 0-4

85-86 Q1: Gorleston (H) 4-0
Q2: Woodford Town (A) 1-3

86-87 PR: Ely City (H) 0-1

87-88 PR: Walthamstow Avenue (H) 1-2

88-89 PR: Baldock Town (H) 1-1, (A) 0-4

89-90 PR: Tring Town (H) 0-2

90-91 PR: Clapton (A) 2-5

91-92 PR: Aveley (A) 0-2

92-93 PR: Leyton (A) 4-5

FELTHAM

Currently: Merged with Hounslow F.C. Playing as Feltham & Hounslow Borough in Isthmian League.
See also Feltham & Hounslow Borough.

66-67 Q1: Malden Town (A) 0-1

67-68 Q1: Hertford Town (H) 1-1, (A) 0-8

68-69 Q1: Slough Town (A) 1-2

70-71 Q1: Clapton (A) 0-3

71-72 Q1: Redhill (H) 1-3

73-74 PR: Edmonton & Haringey (H) 1-3

75-76 Q1: Bracknell Town (A) 1-1, (H) 3-2
Q2: Addlestone (H) 2-6

76-77 PR: Hornchurch (H) 0-1

77-78 Q1: Epsom & Ewell (A) 1-1, (H) 2-1
Q2: Maidenhead United (H) 3-2
Q3: Tilbury (A) 1-4

78-79 PR: Hayes (H) 2-0
Q1: Marlow (A) 1-1, (H) 3-0
Q2: Barnet (A) 2-3

79-80 Q1: Burnham (H) 1-2

80-81 PR: Carshalton Athletic (A) 0-2

81-82 Q1: Aylesbury United (A) 1-0
Q2: Thame United (A) 1-1, (H) 1-2

82-83 Q1: Tiptree United (H) 3-0
Q2: Harrow Borough (A) 3-2
Q3: Chesham United (A) 0-1

83-84 Q1: Whyteleafe (H) 0-1

86-87 PR: Crockenhill (A) 5-1
Q1: Metropolitan Police (H) 0-5

87-88 PR: Alma Swanley (H - *at Hounslow F.C.*) 5-0
Q1: Hayes (H - *at Brentford F.C.*) 1-3

88-89 PR: Hythe Town (H) 1-1, (A) 5-2
Q1: Chertsey Town (A) 0-0, (H) 1-0
Q2: Kingstonian (H) 0-0, (A) 0-3

89-90 Q1: Royston Town (A) 1-2

90-91 PR: Thame United (H) 2-0
Q1: Slough Town (A) 0-8

FELTHAM & HOUNSLOW BOROUGH

Currently: Isthmian League
See also Feltham F.C. and Hounslow F.C.

91-92 PR: Burnham (A - *at Windsor & E.*) 1-1, (H) 0-4

92-93 PR: Beckenham Town (A) 0-2

FERNDALE ATHLETIC

Currently: Welsh League

72-73 Q1: Bridgwater Town (A) 0-3

FERRYBRIDGE AMATEUR

Currently: West Riding County Amateur League

49-50 Q1: Brunswick Institute (A) 3-7

FERRYHILL ATHLETIC

Currently: Northern League

45-46 Q1: Shildon (H) 1-3

46-47 PR: Blackhall Colliery Welfare (H) 2-1
Q1: Chilton & Windlestone Senior Boys (H) 3-1
Q2: Spennymoor United (A) 0-2

47-48 PR: Consett (H) 3-2
Q1: Shildon (H) 1-0
Q2: Evenwood Town (H) 4-0
Q3: Easington Colliery Welf. (A) 3-3, (H) 3-1
Q4: Stockton (H) 1-3

48-49 PR: South Hetton C.W. (A) 1-1, (H) 1-2

49-50 PR: Horden Colliery Welfare (A) 4-8

50-51 EX: Crook Town (H) 2-2, (A) 4-4, 0-4

51-52 Q1: South Bank (H) 3-4

52-53 Q1: Skinningrove Works (H) 7-0
Q2: Whitby Town (H) 4-0
Q3: Billingham Synthonia Recreation (A) 0-5

53-54 Q1: Skinningrove Works (H) 18-0
Q2: Head Wrightsons (H) 7-1
Q3: Billingham Synthonia Recreation (A) 2-1
Q4: South Shields (H) 2-0
R1: Workington (A) 0-3

54-55 Q1: Cockfield (A) 1-1, (H) 2-1
Q2: Evenwood Town (H) 3-0
Q3: Stanley United (A) 1-3

55-56 Q2: Murton Colliery Welfare (A) 2-0
Q3: Durham City (A) 0-0, (H) 0-2

56-57 Q1: Horden Colliery Welfare (H) 0-3

57-58 Q1: Spennymoor United (A) 2-2, (H) 4-2
Q2: Horden Colliery Welfare (A) 1-3

58-59 Q1: Morpeth Town (H) 1-1, (A) 2-0
Q2: Spennymoor United (A) 3-3, (H) 2-1
Q3: Tow Law Town (A) 0-2

59-60 Q1: Bridlington Town (H) 0-0, (A) 2-1
Q2: Consett (H) 2-4

60-61 Q1: Evenwood Town (H) 3-2
Q2: South Bank (A) 4-3
Q3: Ashington (H) 2-1
Q4: Scarborough (A) 0-1

61-62 Q1: Horden Colliery Welfare (H) 0-1

62-63 Q1: Boldon Colliery Welfare (A) 2-1
Q2: Ryhope Colliery Welfare (H) 2-2, (A) 0-1

63-64 Q2: Ryhope Colliery Welfare (H) 4-1
Q3: Horden Colliery Welfare (A) 1-4

64-65 Q1: Billingham Synthonia Recreation (H) 5-0
Q2: Horden Colliery Welfare (A) 1-4

65-66 Q1: Stanley United (H) 1-3

66-67 Q1: Annfield Plain (A) 2-2, (H) 2-2, 2-3

67-68 Q1: Bedlington Colliery Welfare (H) 2-1
Q2: Spennymoor United (H) 0-0, (A) 2-4

68-69 Q1: Murton Colliery Welfare (A) 0-1

69-70 PR: Boldon Colliery Welfare (H) 2-0
Q1: Crook Town (A) 3-3, (H) 0-1

70-71 Q1: Crook Town (H) 3-1
Q2: Durham City (H) 1-0
Q3: Gateshead (A) 0-0, (H) 2-0
Q4: Scarborough (A) 0-3

71-72 Q1: Billingham Synthonia (A) 2-0
Q2: North Shields (A) 1-3

72-73 Q1: Durham City (A) 2-1
Q2: Bishop Auckland (H) 3-2
Q3: Willington (H) 1-5

73-74 Q1: Shildon (A) 1-2

74-75 Q1: Tow Law Town (H) 0-3

75-76 Q1: Eppleton Colliery Welfare (A) 0-1

76-77 Q1: Netherfield (H) 0-1

77-78 Q1: Spennymoor United (H) 2-4

78-79 Q1: Wallsend Town (A) 0-1

79-80 PR: Willington (H) 2-1
Q1: North Shields (A) 2-4

80-81 Q1: Evenwood Town (H) 2-2, (A) 1-2

81-82 Q1: Chester-le-Street (H) 2-2, (A) 1-2

82-83 Q1: Barrow (H) 0-1

83-84 PR: Guisborough Town (A) 1-2

84-85 PR: Guiseley (H) 1-2

85-86 PR: West Auckland Town (H) 2-2, (A) 2-1
Q1: Bishop Auckland (H) 0-3

86-87 PR: Darlington Cleveland Bridge (H) 1-2

87-88 PR: Langley Park Welfare (H) 3-0
Q1: Gretna (H) 1-2

88-89 PR: Crook Town (A) 4-0
Q1: Horden Colliery Welfare (A) 2-0
Q2: Spennymoor United (H) 0-2

89-90 PR: Consett (A) 3-1
Q1: Clitheroe (A) 2-2, (H) 1-1, (A) 4-3
Q2: Gateshead (A) 0-3

90-91 PR: Blackpool Mechanics (H) 3-1
Q1: South Bank (H) 1-1, (A) 0-1

91-92 PR: Penrith (A) 0-1

92-93 PR: Spennymoor United (H) 2-3

FILEY TOWN

Currently: Scarborough League

47-48 PR: South Bank East End (H) 3-2
Q1: Whitby United (A) 2-4

48-49 PR: Whitby Albion Rangers (H) 3-1
Q1: Portrack Shamrocks (H) 1-4

49-50 Q1: South Bank St Peters (A) 2-4

50-51 PR: Head Wrightsons (H) 3-7

FINCHLEY

Currently: Merged with Wingate. Playing as Wingate & Finchley in South Midlands League
See also Wingate & Finchley

45-46 PR: St Albans City (A) 3-4

46-47 EX: Polytechnic (A - *played home*) 2-0
PR: Hendon (H) 3-1
Q1: Wood Green Town (A) 4-2
Q2: Hoddesdon Town (H) 4-2
Q3: Harrow Town (H) 4-3
Q4: Eastbourne (A) 7-3
R1: Port Vale (A) 0-5

47-48 PR: Civil Service (H) 3-2
Q1: Wealdstone (A) 4-5

48-49 EX: Edmonton Borough (A) 2-0
PR: Edgware Town (A) 0-0, (H) 2-1
Q1: Hendon (H) 1-2

49-50 EX: Hertford Town (A) 5-3
PR: Enfield (H) 0-2

50-51 EX: Stevenage Town (H) 5-0
PR: St Albans City (A) 0-1

51-52 Q1: Tufnell Park Edmonton (H) 2-1
Q2: Woodford Town (A) 1-3

52-53 Q1: Clapton (A) 2-1
Q2: Woodford Town (H) 2-0
Q3: Eton Manor (A) 1-0
Q4: Chelmsford City (A) 0-0, (H) 3-0
R1: Kidderminster Harriers (A) 1-0
R2: Crystal Pal. (H) 3-1 *aband.*, (A) 3-1
R3: Shrewsbury Town (A) 0-2

53-54 Q4: Folkestone Town (A) 1-0
R1: Southend United (H) 1-3

54-55 PR: Kingstonian (H) 3-3, (A) 1-3

55-56 PR: Hayes (A) 4-1
Q1: Wimbledon (A) 1-0
Q2: Hemel Hempstead (A) 5-2
Q3: Southall (A) 0-3

56-57 PR: Hemel Hempstead (H) 5-0
Q1: Wembley (H) 1-0
Q2: Yiewsley (H) 1-2

57-58 PR: Hayes (H) 3-3, (A) 1-0
Q1: Hendon (H) 4-0
Q2: Yiewsley (A) 1-4

58-59 Q1: Hendon (A) 2-3

59-60 Q1: Romford (A) 3-1
Q2: Walthamstow Avenue (A) 0-4

60-61 Q1: Edgware Town (A) 1-3

61-62 Q1: Uxbridge (A) 2-1
Q2: Yiewsley (A) 0-2

62-63 Q1: Southall (H) 4-0
Q2: Hayes (H) 1-1, (A) 2-1
Q3: Maidenhead United (A) 1-3

63-64 Q1: Hounslow Town (H) 4-0
Q2: Hayes (A) 1-3

64-65 Q1: Hounslow (A) 4-1
Q2: Southall (H) 4-0
Q3: Hayes (H) 1-2

65-66 Q1: Uxbridge (A) 7-1
Q2: Southall (H) 2-2, (A) 1-2

66-67 Q1: Marlow (H) 4-1
Q2: Bletchley (H) 0-0, (A) 1-0
Q3: Slough Town (H) 3-2
Q4: Oxford City (A) 1-5

67-68 Q1: Hoddesdon Town (H) 0-1

68-69 Q1: Hounslow (H) 2-2, (A) 2-4

69-70 Q1: Braintree & Crittall A. (H) 1-1, (A) 0-2

70-71 Q1: Hitchin Town (H) 2-2, (A) 1-4

71-72 Q1: Stevenage Athletic (H) 0-1

72-73 Q1: Leyton (H) 2-0
Q2: Wealdstone (H) 0-2

73-74 Q1: Bracknell Town (H) 1-0
Q2: Boreham Wood (H) 0-1

74-75 Q1: Hoddesdon Town (H) 0-1

75-76 Q1: Clapton (A) 0-2

76-77 Q1: Slough Town (A) 2-2, (H) 0-4

77-78 Q1: Vauxhall Motors (H) 1-0
Q2: Chesham (H) 2-2, (A) 0-0, (*at Hendon*) 3-2
Q3: Boreham Wood (H) 1-5

78-79 PR: Hillingdon Borough (H) 0-1

79-80 Q1: Hampton (A) 1-2

80-81 Q1: Berkhamsted Town (A) 2-1
Q2: Hayes (H) 0-1

81-82 Q1: Sittingbourne (H) 4-3
Q2: Hertford Town (A) 3-4

82-83 PR: Chelmsford City (A) 1-3

83-84 PR: Chalfont St Peter (A) 1-2

84-85 PR: Hornchurch (H) 1-2

85-86 Q1: Histon (A) 1-3

86-87 PR: Royston Town (A) 3-2
Q1: Ware (A) 2-5

87-88 PR: Kempston Rovers (H) 1-0
Q1: Walton & Hersham (A) 0-3

88-89 PR: Wootton Blue Cross (H) 1-0
Q1: Buckingham Town (A) 3-0
Q2: Wycombe Wanderers (H) 0-3

89-90 Q1: Witham Town (A) 1-3

90-91 Q1: Great Yarmouth Town (H) 1-2

FIRBECK MAIN COLLIERY

Currently: Defunct

45-46 Q1: Brodsworth Main Coll. (A) 1-1, (H) 3-4

46-47 PR: Rawmarsh Colliery (A) 1-5

47-48 EX: Wombwell Athletic (A) 3-4

48-49 PR: Monckton Athletic (A) 2-1
Q1: Norton Woodseats (H) 1-2

49-50 PR: Staveley Welfare (H) 2-3

FISHER ATHLETIC

Currently: (Fisher '93 F.C.) Southern Lge

83-84 Q1: Peacehaven & Telscombe (A) 3-0
Q2: Lewes (A) 2-0
Q3: Leatherhead (A) 4-0
Q4: Harrow Borough (H) 1-1, (A) 2-4

84-85 Q1: Rainham Town (H) 6-1
Q2: Hitchin Town (A) 1-1, (H) 3-1
Q3: Tring Town (A) 1-1, (H) 5-0
Q4: Folkestone (A) 2-2, (H) 2-0
R1: Bristol City (H) 0-1

85-86 Q1: Sheppey United (A) 1-1, (H) 2-2, (A) 4-0
Q2: Redhill (A) 2-0
Q3: Tilbury (H) 2-1
Q4: Fareham Town (H) 1-2

86-87 Q1: Harrow Borough (H) 1-0
Q2: Walton & Hersham (A) 0-0, (H) 3-2
Q3: Hampton (A) 0-0, (H) 2-1
Q4: Bishop's Stortford (A) 0-2

87-88 Q1: Dorking (A) 2-0
Q2: Chatham Town (A) 3-0
Q3: Hayes (A) 0-2

88-89 Q1: Ramsgate (A) 2-1
Q2: Thanet United (A) 3-1
Q3: Kingstonian (H) 1-1, (A) 4-1
Q4: Dulwich Hamlet (H) 3-3, (A) 3-0
R1: Bristol Rovers (A - *at Bath*) 0-3

89-90 Q1: Hampton (A) 1-3

90-91 Q1: Harwich & Parkeston (H) 0-0, (A) 1-2

91-92 Q1: Beckenham Town (H) 4-0
Q2: Windsor & Eton (A) 2-3

92-93 PR: Brightlingsea Utd (H - *played away*) 2-1
Q1: Stevenage Borough (H - *played away*) 1-7

FLACKWELL HEATH

Currently: Isthmian League

82-83 Q1: Bedworth United (H) 0-1

83-84 PR: Salisbury (A) 0-1

84-85 Q1: Sudbury Town (A) 0-2

85-86 PR: Stowmarket (A) 0-3

86-87 PR: Desborough Town (A) 1-1, (H) 1-2

87-88 PR: Crockenhill (H) 0-3

88-89 PR: Camberley Town (H) 3-2
Q1: Dartford (A) 1-7

89-90 PR: Horndean (H) 3-0
Q1: Newport I.O.W. (H) 0-2

90-91 PR: Tring Town (H) 5-0
Q1: Beckenham Town (A) 2-0
Q2: Grays Athletic (H) 2-2, (A) 0-3

91-92 PR: Chalfont St Peter (A) 0-2

92-93 PR: Walthamstow Pennant (H) 2-0
Q1: Stowmarket Town (H) 0-5

FLEET TOWN

Currently: Wessex League
* - As Fleet F.C.

66-67 * Q1: Alton Town (H) 6-1
Q2: Horsham (A) 0-3

67-68 * Q1: Wokingham Town (A) 1-2

68-69 * Q1: Chichester City (A) 0-1

69-70 * PR: Dorking (A) 0-1

70-71 * PR: Basingstoke Town (H) 0-3

71-72 * Q1: Newport I.O.W. (H) 1-1, (A) 1-5

72-73 Q1: Hitchin Town (A) 1-2

73-74 Q1: Uxbridge (A) 1-1, (H) 3-1
Q2: Chatham Town (H) 2-4

82-83 PR: Worthing (A) 1-7

83-84 PR: Walton & Hersham (A) 1-1, (H) 0-4

84-85 PR: Petersfield United (H) 1-1, (A) 3-1
Q1: Farnborough Town (A) 1-5

85-86 PR: Sheppey United (H) 0-2

92-93 PR: Abingdon Town (H) 1-2

FLEETWOOD

Currently: Defunct

47-48 PR: Great Harwood (H) 7-1
Q1: Darwen (A) 3-1
Q2: Morecambe (H) 2-0
Q3: Nelson (H) 1-1, (A) 1-2

48-49 PR: Morecambe (A) 1-0
Q1: Nelson (H) 1-0
Q2: Clitheroe (A) 3-1
Q3: Rossendale United (H) 0-1

49-50 PR: Galgate (A - *played home*) 5-3
Q1: Clitheroe (H) 3-0
Q2: Nelson (H) 3-2
Q3: Rossendale United (H) 5-0
Q4: Lancaster City (H) 4-1
R1: Bradford City (A) 0-9

50-51 PR: Lytham (H) 3-1
Q1: Leyland Motors (A) 1-1, (H) 2-4

51-52 Q1: Great Harwood (A) 5-0
Q2: Lancaster City (A) 3-2
Q3: Netherfield (H) 3-0
Q4: Rhyl (A) 2-7

52-53 Q1: Clitheroe (A) 1-1, (H) 1-2

53-54 Q1: Netherfield (H) 3-1
Q2: Morecambe (H) 1-2

54-55 Q1: Morecambe (A) 2-2, (H) 3-1
Q2: Netherfield (A) 0-7

55-56 Q2: Milnthorpe Corinthians (H) 0-0, (A) 5-2
Q3: Lancaster City (H) 1-1, (A) 1-3

56-57 Q1: Lancaster City (H) 3-0
Q2: Penrith (H) 2-1
Q3: Morecambe (H) 3-3, (A) 1-2

57-58 Q1: Burscough (A) 3-4

58-59 Q1: Clitheroe (H) 6-2
Q2: Morecambe (A) 2-4

59-60 Q1: Clitheroe (H) 2-2, (A) 0-1

60-61 Q1: Clitheroe (H) 3-2
Q2: Netherfield (H) 0-4

61-62 Q1: Corinthians (Milnthorpe) (H) 5-0
Q2: Burscough (H) 1-1, (A) 2-5

62-63 Q1: Burscough (A) 4-1
Q2: Wigan Athletic (A) 1-8

63-64 Q2: Lancaster City (H) 1-2

64-65 Q1: Corinthians (Milnthorpe) (H) 3-0
Q2: Morecambe (A) 1-6

65-66 Q1: Milnethorpe Corinthians (H) 7-1
Q2: Horwich R.M.I. (A) 3-3, (H) 2-1
Q3: Clitheroe (H) 3-1
Q4: Colwyn Bay (H) 2-1
R1: Rochdale (H) 2-2, (A) 0-5

66-67 Q1: Penrith (H) 3-1
Q2: Netherfield (H) 2-2, (A) 1-2

67-68 Q1: Netherfield (H) 2-3

68-69 PR: Milnthorpe Corinthians (H) 5-0
Q1: Penrith (H) 0-0, (A) 5-0
Q2: Clitheroe (H) 2-0
Q3: Morecambe (A) 0-1

69-70 Q1: Clitheroe (A) 5-1
Q2: Netherfield (H) 3-0
Q3: Lancaster City (H) 3-1
Q4: Bangor City (A) 1-2

70-71 Q1: Clitheroe (A) 1-3

71-72 Q1: Bacup Borough (A) 0-0, (H) 3-0
Q2: Lancaster City (H) 0-2

72-73 Q1: Lancaster City (A) 1-3

73-74 Q1: Bacup Borough (A) 3-2
Q2: Chorley (A) 0-0, (H) 1-1, 2-3

74-75 Q1: Netherfield (H) 0-2

75-76 Q1: Glossop (H) 2-0
Q2: Lancaster City (H) 1-1, (A) 1-2

FLEETWOOD TOWN

Currently: Northern Premier League

78-79 Q1: Netherfield (H) 0-0, (A) 1-1, (H) 2-0
Q2: Lancaster City (H) 1-1, (A) 1-0
Q3: Chorley (H) 0-1

79-80 Q1: Mossley (H) 1-4

80-81 PR: Emley (A) 3-0
Q1: Worsbrough Bridge M.W. (A) 4-0
Q2: Accrington Stanley (A) 1-1, (H) 3-2
Q3: St Helens Town (A) 1-0
Q4: Stalybridge Celtic (H) 1-0
R1: Blackpool (H - *played away*) 0-4

81-82 Q1: Hyde United (H) 1-1, (A) 1-2

82-83 Q1: Spennymoor United (H) 1-2

83-84 PR: Blue Star (H) 2-1
Q1: Tow Law Town (H) 1-2

84-85 Q1: Droylsden (A) 0-4

85-86 PR: Thackley (A) 1-0
Q1: North Shields (H) 2-2, (A) 1-2

86-87 PR: Clitheroe (H) 2-0
Q1: Durham City (H) 2-0
Q2: Gretna (H) 1-3

87-88 Q1: West Auckland Town (H) 3-2
Q2: Gretna (A) 2-1
Q3: Barrow (H) 0-0, (A) 2-3

88-89 Q1: Armthorpe Welfare (A) 2-2, (H) 5-0
Q2: Marine (A) 4-2
Q3: Emley (H) 2-2, (A) 2-2, (H) 3-1
Q4: Runcorn (H) 1-3

89-90 Q1: Droylsden (A) 0-0, (H) 1-1, (H) 0-1

90-91 Q1: Alnwick Town (A) 5-0
Q2: Shildon (A) 4-0
Q3: North Shields (H) 2-0
Q4: Accrington Stanley (A) 2-0
R1: Atherstone United (A) 1-3

Above: *Mark Thornley spreads himself to deny Accrington's Andy Bondswell as Fleetwood Town secure a place in the First Round. Photo: John Rowbotham.*

91-92 Q1: Blackpool (Wren) Rovers (H) 3-2
Q2: Denaby United (A) 0-1

92-93 Q1: Guiseley (H) 3-2
Q2: Northallerton Town (H) 1-2

FLINT TOWN UNITED

Currently: League of Wales

50-51 EX: Liverpool Police (H) 4-2
PR: Llandudno (H) 2-0
Q1: Wigan Athletic (A) 1-1, (H) 1-3

51-52 Q1: Ellesmere Port Town (A) 2-2, (H) 3-1
Q2: Prescot Cables (A) 1-3

52-53 Q1: Prescot Cables (A) 1-1, (H) 3-0
Q2: Ellesmere Port Town (A) 2-1
Q3: Bangor City (A) 2-4

53-54 Q1: Ellesmere Port Town (H) 3-2
Q2: Runcorn (H) 1-3

54-55 Q1: St Helens Town (A) 2-2, (H) 5-2
Q2: Marine (H) 5-1
Q3: Pwllheli & District (H) 2-3

55-56 Q1: Runcorn (H) 0-0, (A) 3-4

56-57 PR: Runcorn (A) 1-1, (H) 1-2

57-58 Q1: Bangor City (H) 1-1, (A) 1-5

58-59 PR: Marine (H) 4-3
Q1: Runcorn (A) 1-0
Q2: New Brighton (A) 0-3

59-60 Q1: Prescot Cables (A) 0-4

60-61 Q1: Bangor City (H) 1-2

61-62 Q1: New Brighton (A) 0-7

FLIXTON

Currently: North West Counties League

91-92 Q1: Mossley (H) 1-1, (A) 1-2

92-93 PR: Worksop Town (H) 1-1, (A) 0-3

FLORENCE & ULLCOATS UTD

Currently: Defunct

47-48 PR: Frizington United (H) 1-3

48-49 PR: Appleby (A) 6-3
Q1: Netherfield (A) 0-10

49-50 PR: Scalegill (A) 4-6

50-51 PR: Millom Town (A) 3-2
Q1: Aspatria Spartans (H) 2-5

FODENS MOTOR WORKS (SANDBACH)

Currently: Defunct

45-46 Q1: Northwich Victoria (A) 4-0
Q2: Rhyl (A) 1-5

46-47 Q1: Bangor City (H) 3-6

47-48 PR: Hyde United (H) 1-2

48-49 PR: Barnton (A) *withdrew*

FOLKESTONE

Currently: Defunct
* - As Folkestone Town
\+ - As Folkestone & Shepway

46-47 * PR: Chatham (A) 8-0
Q1: Ramsgate Athletic (H) 2-1
Q2: Woolwich Polytechnic (A) 3-0
Q3: Gravesend & Northfleet (H) 1-2

47-48 * PR: Callender Athletic (H) 6-0
Q1: Betteshanger Colliery Welfare (H) 5-1
Q2: Ramsgate Athletic (H) 4-1
Q3: Dartford (A) 0-1

48-49 * PR: Bromley (A) 1-2

49-50 * EX: Callender Athletic (H) 7-0
PR: Snowdown C.W. (H) 1-1, (A) 1-2

50-51 * EX: Betteshanger Colliery Welfare (A) 0-1

51-52 * PR: Chatham Town (H) 4-0
Q1: Margate (H) 3-1
Q2: Dover (A) 2-0
Q3: Betteshanger Colliery Welfare (H) 2-0
Q4: Sutton United (H) 1-1, (A) 3-1
R1: Barnstaple Town (A) 2-2, (H) 5-2
R2: Stockton (A) 1-2

52-53 * Q4: Tonbridge (H) 0-0, (A) 4-4, 0-2

53-54 * Q4: Finchley (H) 0-1

54-55 * PR: Gravesend & Northfleet (A) 1-4

55-56 * PR: Woking (A) 1-1, (H) 2-1
Q1: Dorking (A) 1-3

56-57 * PR: Canterbury City (H) 0-1

57-58 * PR: Dover (A) 1-2

58-59 * Q1: Ramsgate Athletic (A) 2-3

59-60 * Q1: Whitstable (A) 6-1
Q2: Ashford Town (A) 0-1

60-61 * Q1: Ramsgate Athletic (A) 1-1, (H) 4-1
Q2: Deal Town (H) 5-1
Q3: Dover (A) 0-1

61-62 * Q2: Dover (H) 2-3

62-63 * Q1: Canterbury City (A) 3-0
Q2: Sittingbourne (A) 2-2, (H) 1-2

63-64 * Q2: Sheppey United (H) 2-0
Q3: Ramsgate Athletic (A) 3-1
Q4: Ashford Town (H) 3-0
R1: Oxford United (A) 0-2

64-65 * Q1: Ramsgate Athletic (A) 2-1
Q2: Canterbury City (A) 1-3

65-66 * Q1: Margate (H) 2-1
Q2: Dover (H) 1-1, (A) 3-2
Q3: Canterbury City (H) 1-0
Q4: Bexley United (H) 4-1
R1: Gillingham (A) 2-1
R2: Wimbledon (A) 1-0
R3: Crewe Alexandra (H) 1-5

66-67 * Q4: Gravesend & Northfleet (H) 3-2
R1: Swansea Town (H) 2-2, (A) 2-7

67-68 * Q4: Tonbridge (A) 1-5

68-69 Q1: Margate (A) 1-3

69-70 Q1: Herne Bay (H) 0-0, (A) 1-1, 1-0
Q2: Ramsgate Athletic (H) 1-1, (A) 0-1

70-71 PR: Snowdown Colliery Welfare (H) 4-3
Q1: Whitstable Town (A) 7-2
Q2: Bexhill Town (A) 1-1, (H) 4-2
Q3: Hastings United (A) 0-0, (H) 4-2
Q4: Crawley Town (H) 0-0, (A) 0-3

71-72 Q1: Sheppey United (H) 6-2
Q2: Canterbury City (A) 3-1
Q3: Maidstone United (H) 2-0
Q4: Romford (H) 0-2

72-73 Q1: Deal Town (H) 4-1
Q2: Tonbridge (H) 0-1

73-74 Q1: Deal Town (A) 1-1, (H) 6-2
Q2: Faversham Town (A) 1-1, (H) 4-1
Q3: Lewes (H) 5-1
Q4: Guildford City (H) 2-3

74-75 + Q1: Ramsgate (H) 0-0, (A) 0-2

75-76 + PR: Canterbury City (H) 1-2

76-77 + Q1: Sidley United (A - *played home*) 3-0

Q2: Margate (A) 2-2, (H) 2-4 *replayed* (H) 3-4

77-78 + Q1: Faversham Town (A) 3-0
Q2: Eastbourne Town (H) 5-2
Q3: Horsham Y.M.C.A. (A) 2-2, (H) 3-0
Q4: Chelmsford City (A) 3-0
R1: Brentford (A) 0-2

78-79 + PR: Bromley (H) 2-1
Q1: Whitstable Town (A) 1-1, (H) 5-0
Q2: Tonbridge A.F.C. (A) 3-2
Q3: Margate (H) 0-2

79-80 + Q1: Lewes (A) 1-2

80-81 Q1: East Grinstead (H) 6-2
Q2: Maidstone United (H) 0-2

81-82 Q1: Dover (A) 1-4

82-83 Q1: Burnham (H) 2-0
Q2: Ringmer (A) 2-0
Q3: Chatham Town (A) 1-1, (H) 5-0
Q4: Barking (A) 2-0
R1: Oxford United (A) 2-5

83-84 Q1: Haywards Heath (A) 6-2
Q2: Dulwich Hamlet (A) 2-1
Q3: Hastings United (H) 2-0
Q4: Dagenham (H) 1-1, (A) 0-3

84-85 Q1: Tonbridge A.F.C. (A) 1-0
Q2: Redhill (A) 3-0
Q3: Walthamstow Avenue (H) 1-0
Q4: Fisher Athletic (H) 2-2, (A) 0-2

85-86 Q1: Southwick (A) 1-1, (H) 1-1, (A) 1-3

86-87 Q1: Canterbury City (A) 0-1

87-88 PR: Tonbridge A.F.C. (A) 2-5

88-89 PR: Ringmer (H) 2-0
Q1: Kingstonian (A) 1-4

89-90 Q1: Leatherhead (H) 2-1
Q2: Redhill (H) 1-1, (A) 1-0
Q3: Dover Athletic (A) 1-0
Q4: Gloucester City (H) 0-1

90-91 Q1: Bognor Regis Town (H) 1-2

FORD SPORTS

Currently: Merged with Briggs Sports
Playing as Ford United in Essex Senior League
See also Ford United

45-46 Q1: Hoffmann Athletic (Chelmsford) (H) 4-2
Q2: Leyton (A) 2-6

46-47 PR: Clapton (H) 2-4

47-48 EX: West Thurrock Athletic (A) 0-3

48-49 EX: Romford (A) 0-5

49-50 PR: Ilford (A) 1-4

FORD UNITED

Currently: Essex Senior League
See also Ford Sports and Briggs Sports

59-60 PR: Hendon (H) 1-2

60-61 Q1: Hornchurch & Upminster (A) 0-1

62-63 Q1: Wembley (H) 8-1
Q2: Hendon (A) 1-2

63-64 Q1: Clapton (H) 2-3

64-65 Q1: Clapton (H) 3-1
Q2: Hendon (H) 2-5

65-66 Q1: Dagenham (A) 2-2, (H) 1-2

66-67 Q1: Cheshunt (H) 0-1

67-68 Q1: Cray Wanderers (H) 1-2

68-69 Q1: Redhill (A) 0-3

69-70 Q1: Romford (A) 2-2, (H) 2-4

70-71 Q1: Edmonton (A) 2-1
Q2: Leytonstone (H) 0-2

71-72 Q1: Staines Town (H) 1-4

72-73 Q1: Hertford Town (A) 0-2

89-90 PR: Heybridge Swifts (A) 1-1, (H) 0-2

90-91 PR: Kingsbury Town (H) 3-1
Q1: St Albans City (H) 3-1
Q2: Harlow Town (A) 0-1

91-92 PR: Hornchurch (H) 2-1
Q1: Wivenhoe Town (H) 3-1
Q2: Dartford (H) 0-1

92-93 PR: Metropolitan Police (A) 0-0, (H) 0-2

FOREST GREEN ROVERS

Currently: Southern League
* - As Stroud F.C.

77-78 Q1: Larkhall Athletic (H) 3-2
Q2: Weston-super-Mare (H) 0-2

78-79 PR: Calne Town (H) 8-1
Q1: Trowbridge Town (A) 0-1

79-80 Q1: Clandown (H) 3-2
Q2: Weston-super-Mare (A) 1-3

80-81 PR: Cinderford (A) 0-0, (H) 0-0, (A) 2-1
Q1: Cheltenham Town (A) 2-3

81-82 Q1: Gloucester City (A) 1-2

82-83 Q1: Barry Town (H) 2-3

83-84 Q1: Wimborne Town (H) 6-0
Q2: Witney Town (A) 2-2, (H) 1-2

84-85 PR: Cinderford Town (A) 2-1
Q1: Barry Town (A) 2-3

85-86 PR: Maesteg Park (A) 1-0
Q1: Clandown (H) 0-1

86-87 Q1: Yate Town (H) 2-0
Q2: Dorchester Town (H) 4-2
Q3: Bideford (A) 1-2

87-88 Q1: Torrington (A) 3-0
Q2: Barnstaple Town (A) 2-1
Q3: Merthyr Tydfil (A) 1-3

88-89 Q1: Devizes Town (H) 5-0
Q2: Poole Town (A) 4-2
Q3: Weymouth (A) 0-3

89-90 * Q1: Thatcham Town (A) 2-2, (H) 2-1
Q2: Maidenhead United (A) 0-2

90-91 * PR: Westbury United (A) 1-1, (H) 3-0
Q1: Gosport Borough (H) 4-1
Q2: Romsey Town (A) 0-1

91-92 * Q1: Bath City (H) 1-3

92-93 PR: Barnstaple Town (H) 4-2
Q1: Newport A.F.C. (H) 1-2

FORMBY

Currently: North West Counties League

47-48 PR: Wigan Athletic (H) 0-4

48-49 PR: Haydock C. & B. Recreation (H) 4-2
Q1: St Helens Town (H) 0-1

49-50 EX: Marine (A) 0-1

50-51 PR: Crompton's Recreation (A) 1-2

69-70 Q1: Wigan Rovers (A) 6-0
Q2: Horwich R.M.I. (H) 1-2

70-71 Q1: Ashton United (H) 2-0
Q2: Hyde United (A) 1-0
Q3: Witton Albion (H) 1-1, (A) 1-3

71-72 PR: Ellesmere Port Town (A) 1-2

72-73 Q1: Chorley (A) 1-2

73-74 Q1: Burscough (A) 1-1, (H) 4-1
Q2: Darwen (A) 1-0
Q3: Ormskirk (H) 1-0
Q4: Goole Town (H) 3-0
R1: Oldham Athletic (H) 0-2

74-75 Q1: Horwich R.M.I. (H) 0-2

75-76 Q1: Marine (H) 0-1

76-77 Q1: Clitheroe (A) 0-0, (H) 3-1
Q2: Accrington Stanley (A) 3-0
Q3: Great Harwood (H) 0-0, (A) 0-3

77-78 Q1: Lancaster City (H) 1-0
Q2: Darwen (H) 2-2, (A) 0-2

78-79 PR: Ashton United (H) 3-1
Q1: South Liverpool (A) 3-0
Q2: Hyde United (A) 2-2, (H) 2-1
Q3: Horwich R.M.I. (H) 0-0, (A) 1-5

79-80 PR: Bangor City (H) 2-2, (A) 1-0
Q1: Porthmadog (A) 2-0
Q2: Northwich Victoria (H) 1-1, (A) 0-2

80-81 PR: Glossop (H) 0-2

81-82 Q1: Marine (A) 0-4

82-83 PR: Chorley (A) 0-5

83-84 PR: North Ferriby United (H) 2-1
Q1: Stalybridge Celtic (A) 1-8

84-85 PR: Ossett Albion (A) 4-1
Q1: Lye Town (H) 5-2
Q2: St Helens Town (H) 1-0
Q3: Chorley (H) 3-2
Q4: Penrith (A) 2-3

85-86 Q1: Warrington Town (A) 3-1
Q2: Rhyl (A) 0-5

86-87 PR: Droylsden (H) 1-1, (A) 1-3

87-88 PR: Alfreton Town (A) 0-3

88-89 PR: Congleton Town (H) 0-7

89-90 PR: Heanor Town (A) 0-2

90-91 PR: Irlam Town (A) 0-2

92-93 PR: Bootle (H) 1-2

FRECHEVILLE COMMUNITY

Currently: County Senior League

76-77 PR: Winterton Rangers (H) 0-1

FRIAR LANE OLD BOYS

Currently: Leicestershire Senior League

76-77 PR: Warley County Borough (H) 2-0
Q1: Sutton Coldfield Town (A) 0-3

77-78 Q1: Telford United (H) 1-2

78-79 PR: Desborough Town (A) 3-0
Q1: Irthlingborough Diamonds (A) 0-3

79-80 Q1: Kidderminster Harriers (A) 0-2

80-81 PR: Desborough Town (H) 1-2

81-82 PR: Eastwood Town (A) 0-3

82-83 PR: Milton Keynes City (H) 1-1, (A) 4-1
Q1: Stourbridge (A) 0-3

83-84 PR: Winterton Rangers (A) 0-1

84-85 PR: Wednesfield (A) 0-0, (H) 0-0, (H) 2-1
Q1: Goole Town (H) 1-1, (A) 1-4

85-86 PR: Gresley Rovers (A) 0-8

86-87 PR: Leicester Utd (A - *played home*) 0-2

87-88 Q1: Bilston Town (H) 2-2, (A) 2-3

89-90 PR: Farsley Celtic (H) 1-2

90-91 PR: Hinckley Athletic (A) 1-3

91-92 Q1: Rushden Town (A) 2-3

FRICKLEY ATHLETIC

Currently: Northern Premier League
* - As Frickley Colliery

45-46 * Q1: Guiseley (A) 3-3, (H) *W/O*
Q2: South Kirkby Colliery (A) 2-0
Q3: Yorkshire Amateur (H) 0-4

46-47 * Q1: Dinnington Athletic (A) 4-3
Q2: South Kirkby Colliery (A) 1-2

47-48 * Q1: Selby Town (H) 1-3

48-49 * EX: Brodsworth Main Colliery (H) 4-3
PR: Lysaght's Sports (H) 4-0
Q1: South Kirkby Colliery (H) 3-0
Q2: Goole Town (H) 3-1
Q3: Selby Town (A) 0-2

49-50 * PR: Yorkshire Amateur (H) 1-0
Q1: Goole Town (H) 1-1, (A) 0-1

50-51 * PR: Barton Town (A) 3-1
Q1: Farsley Celtic (A) 1-3

51-52 * Q1: Hallam (H) 3-1
Q2: Denaby United (H) 4-1
Q3: Upton Colliery (H) 5-0
Q4: Buxton (H) 1-1, (A) 1-3

52-53 * Q1: Upton Colliery (H) 2-2, (A) 2-0
Q2: South Kirkby Colliery (H) 4-0
Q3: Denaby United (H) 1-1, (A) 4-3
Q4: Boston United (A) 2-3

Above: *Frickley forward Paul Wilson (right) in action during the Third Round tie against Rotherham in 1985.*
Photo: South Yorkshire Times.

53-54 * Q1: Denaby United (A) 2-1
Q2: Sheffield (H) 2-1
Q3: Upton Colliery (A) 3-2
Q4: Selby Town (A) 1-2

54-55 * Q1: Upton Colliery (A) 3-4

55-56 * Q1: Upton Colliery (A) 3-0
Q2: Hallam (A) 2-0
Q3: Denaby United (H) 3-5

56-57 * Q2: Denaby United (H) 3-2
Q3: Bentley Colliery (A) 2-1
Q4: Rhyl (A) 0-2

57-58 * Q2: Retford Town (H) 1-0
Q3: Denaby United (H) 2-1
Q4: Sutton Town (A) 1-0
R1: South Shields (A) 2-3

58-59 * Q1: Stocksbridge Works (A) 3-3, (H) 0-3

59-60 * Q1: East End Park W.M.C. (H) 1-0
Q2: Goole Town (H) 1-3

60-61 * Q1: Goole Town (A) 4-2
Q2: Denaby United (H) 3-0
Q3: Selby Town (A) 3-1
Q4: Sutton Town (A) 1-2

61-62 * Q1: Selby Town (A) 1-4

62-63 * Q1: Cresswell C.W. (A) 4-1
Q2: Worksop Town (A) 0-1

63-64 * Q1: Ossett Town (H) 3-0
Q2: Farsley Celtic (H) 3-0
Q3: Bridlington Town (H) 1-0
Q4: Macclesfield Town (A) 3-1
R1: Notts County (A) 1-2

64-65 * Q1: Stocksbridge Works (A) 4-1
Q2: Worksop Town (H) 2-0
Q3: Retford Town (A) 0-3

65-66 * Q1: Norton Woodseats Amateur (A) 3-0
Q2: Goole Town (H) 1-3

66-67 * Q1: Retford Town (A) 0-4

67-68 * Q1: Yorkshire Amateur (H) 5-0
Q2: Retford Town (A) 0-2

68-69 * Q1: Worksop Town (A) 4-2
Q2: Gainsborough Trinity (H) 2-1
Q3: Retford T. (H) 0-0, (A) 0-0, 0-3

69-70 * Q1: Farsley Celtic (A) 2-1
Q2: Retford Town (A) 1-1, (H) 3-0
Q3: Gainsborough Trinity (A) 2-3

70-71 * Q1: Ashby Institute (H) 1-0
Q2: Norton Woodseats A. (A) 0-0, (H) 2-1
Q3: Brigg Town (A) 0-0, (H) 2-1
Q4: Boston United (H) 1-3

71-72 * PR: Mexborough Town (H) 3-2
Q1: Farsley Celtic (A) 1-0
Q2: Yorkshire Amateur (A) 0-0, (H) 3-1
Q3: Worksop Town (A) 1-1, (H) 3-1
Q4: Grantham (H) 3-0
R1: Rotherham United (H) 2-2, (A) 0-4

72-73 * PR: Winterton Rangers (A) 0-2

73-74 * Q1: Ashby Institute (A) 0-0, (H) 2-1
Q2: Denaby United (A) 3-0
Q3: Sutton Town (H) 2-1
Q4: Rhyl (A) 4-0
R1: Halifax Town (A) 1-6

74-75 * Q1: Stalybridge Celtic (H) 2-2, (A) 0-2

75-76 * Q1: Gainsborough Trinity (H) 3-0
Q2: Denaby Utd (H) 2-2, (A) 2-0
Q3: Worksop Town (A) 1-1, (H) 1-1, 0-2

76-77 PR: Yorkshire Amateur (H) 3-0
Q1: Mexborough Town (A) 0-2

77-78 Q1: North Ferriby United (H) 3-1
Q2: Appleby Frodingham Ath. (H) 1-2

78-79 Q1: Hednesford Town (H) 0-2

79-80 Q1: Bridlington Town (H) 5-0
Q2: Whitby Town (A) 2-3

80-81 PR: Denaby United (A) 3-1
Q1: Worksop Town (A) 2-3

81-82 Q1: Whitby Town (H) 2-0
Q2: Goole Town (A) 3-2
Q3: Bishop Auckland (A) 0-3

82-83 PR: Shildon (H) 5-3
Q1: Netherfield (A) 2-0
Q2: Harrogate Town (H) 3-1
Q3: Spennymoor (H) 1-1, (A) 1-1, (H) 2-3

83-84 Q1: Hednesford Town (A) 2-1
Q2: Bilston (A) 1-1, (H) 2-0
Q3: Glossop (A) 3-2
Q4: North Shields (H) 1-0
R1: Altrincham (H) 0-1

84-85 Q1: Caernarfon Town (H) 4-1
Q2: Rhyl (A) 2-0
Q3: Oswestry Town (A) 1-1, (H) 2-0
Q4: Moor Green (H) 5-0
R1: Stalybridge Celtic (H) 2-1
R2: Darlington (A) 0-1

85-86 Q4: Northwich Victoria (H) 2-1
R1: Halesowen Town (H) 1-1, (A) 3-1
R2: Hartlepool United (A) 1-0
R3: Rotherham United (H) 1-3

86-87 R1: Altrincham (H) 0-0, (A) 0-4

87-88 Q4: Chorley (A) 0-2

88-89 Q1: Boldmere St Michael (H) 2-1
Q2: Buxton (H) 1-0
Q3: Witton Albion (H) 3-1
Q4: Chorley (H) 1-1, (A) 1-0
R1: Northwich Victoria (H) 0-2

89-90 Q1: Hinckley Athletic (A) 3-1
Q2: Goole Town (H) 1-1, (A) 0-1

90-91 Q1: Gainsborough Trinity (H) 4-3
Q2: Princes End United (A) 4-0
Q3: Nuneaton Borough (H) 1-0
Q4: Witton Albion (H) 0-2

91-92 Q1: Harrogate T. (A) 2-2, (H - *played away*), 3-3, (H) 3-2
Q2: Alfreton Town (H) 4-1
Q3: Lincoln United (H) 0-0, (A) 2-3

92-93 Q1: Lincoln United (H) 0-0, (A) 1-0
Q2: Halesowen Harriers (H) 8-2
Q3: Stafford Rangers (A) 0-3

FRIZINGTON UNITED

Currently: Defunct

46-47 PR: Haig United (A) 3-2
Q1: Netherfield (A) 2-7

47-48 PR: Florence & Ullcoats United (A) 3-1
Q1: Parton United (A) 2-3

48-49 PR: Milnethorpe Corinthians (A) 2-8

50-51 PR: Threlkeld (H) 5-1
Q1: Kells Welfare Centre (H) *W/O*
Q2: Netherfield (H) 1-2

FROME TOWN

Currently: Western League

46-47 EX: Hoffmann Athletic (Stonehouse) (A) 0-7

47-48 EX: Welton Rovers (H) 1-2

48-49 EX: Paulton Rovers (H) 2-0
PR: Peasedown Miners Welfare (H) 7-3
Q1: Salisbury (A) 2-3

49-50 EX: Chippenham United (H) 1-3

51-52 PR: Devizes Town (H) 1-0
Q1: Corsham Town (A) 7-2
Q2: Salisbury (H) 2-3

52-53 PR: Andover (A) 3-2
Q1: Devizes Town (H) 3-6

53-54 Q1: Chippenham Town (H) 2-6

54-55 PR: Chippenham (H) 4-2
Q1: Salisbury (A) 3-2
Q2: Trowbridge Town (A) 1-1, (H) 4-0
Q3: Melksham (A) 2-0
Q4: Weymouth (H) 3-1
R1: Leyton Orient (H) 0-3

55-56 PR: Trowbridge Town (H) 4-3
Q1: Warminster Town (H) 2-1
Q2: Westbury United (H) 2-2, (A) 2-1
Q3: Salisbury (A) 0-3

56-57 Q1: Trowbridge Town (A) 0-5

57-58 Q1: Melksham Town (A) 0-0, (H) 2-3

58-59 Q1: Poole Town (A) 1-7

59-60 Q1: Warminster Town (A) 1-1, (H) 1-2

60-61 Q2: Poole Town (A) 1-4

61-62 Q1: Street (A) 2-0
Q2: Minehead (A) 0-3

62-63 Q1: Glastonbury (A) 6-0
Q2: Minehead (H) 2-2, (A) 0-4

63-64 Q1: Minehead (H) 1-3

64-65 Q1: Taunton (A) 1-0
Q2: Minehead (H) 1-3

65-66 Q1: Glastonbury (A) 1-0
Q2: Bridgwater Town (H) 1-1, (A) 1-0
Q3: Welton Rovers (A) 1-4

66-67 Q1: Street (A) 1-1, (H) 1-3

67-68 Q1: Trowbridge Town (H) 1-0
Q2: Minehead (H) 1-1, (A) 1-2

68-69 Q1: Minehead (A) 2-1
Q2: Bridport (A) 4-1
Q3: Bridgwater Town (A) 1-0
Q4: Cheltenham Town (H) 1-2

69-70 PR: Street (A) 3-1
Q1: Portland United (A) 1-1, (H) 2-0
Q2: Bath City (H) 1-4

70-71 PR: Welton Rovers (A) 1-5

71-72 PR: Chippenham Town (A) 0-1

72-73 Q1: Bridport (H) 4-2

Q2: Welton Rovers (H) 1-1, (A) 1-0
Q3: Salisbury (H) 0-0, (A) 1-0
Q4: Banbury United (H) 1-1, (A) 0-3

73-74 Q1: Basingstoke Town (A) 0-2

74-75 Q1: Welton Rovers (A) 1-1, (H) 1-2

75-76 Q1: Andover (A) 1-1, (H) 5-3
Q2: Bridport (A) 3-0
Q3: Salisbury (A) 0-1

76-77 Q1: Mangotsfield United (H) 1-5

77-78 Q1: Yeovil Town (H) 2-1
Q2: Poole Town (A) 2-0
Q3: Salisbury (H) 2-2, (A) 0-1

78-79 PR: Gloucester City (H) 0-3

79-80 PR: Bideford (H) 0-1

80-81 Q1: Farnborough Town (H) 1-1, (A) 0-1

81-82 Q1: Trowbridge Town (H) 2-1
Q2: Dorchester Town (A) 0-3

82-83 Q1: Witney Town (H) 1-1, (A) 2-2, (H) 2-1
Q2: Devizes Town (H) 4-2
Q3: Slough Town (A) 0-3

83-84 Q1: Torrington (H) 1-1, (A) 3-0
Q2: Bideford (H) 0-0, (A) 2-0
Q3: Poole Town (H) 2-3

84-85 Q1: Torrington (A) 1-0
Q2: Wimborne Town (A) 3-1
Q3: Bath City (H) 3-1
Q4: Bognor Regis Town (A) 0-2

85-86 Q1: Mangotsfield United (A) 3-1
Q2: Ton Pentre (A) 1-2

86-87 Q1: Redditch United (H) 0-2

87-88 PR: Poole Town (H) 1-0
Q1: Weymouth (H) 2-2, (A) 0-3

88-89 PR: St Blazey (H) 4-1
Q1: Dorchester Town (A) 1-3

89-90 PR: Thame United (A) 0-7

90-91 PR: Romsey Town (A) 0-1

91-92 PR: Exmouth Town (H) 3-1
Q1: Maesteg Park (A) 0-4

92-93 Q1: Worcester City (H) 1-2

FULHAM

Currently: Football League

45-46 R3: Charlton Ath. (A) 1-3, (H) 2-1 *(agg: 3-4)*

46-47 R3: Birmingham City (H) 1-2

47-48 R3: Doncaster Rovers (H) 2-0
R4: Bristol Rovers (H) 8-2
R5: Everton (H) 1-1, (A) 1-1, 1-0
R6: Blackpool (H) 0-2

48-49 R3: Walsall (H) 0-1

49-50 R3: Charlton Athletic (A) 2-2, (H) 1-2

50-51 R3: Sheffield Wednesday (H) 1-0
R4: Millwall (A) 1-0
R5: Chelsea (A) 1-1, (H) 3-0
R6: Blackpool (A) 0-1

51-52 R3: Birmingham City (H) 0-1

52-53 R3: Bolton Wanderers (A) 1-3

53-54 R3: Grimsby T. (A) 5-5, (H) 0-0 *abandoned after 45 minutes*, (H) 3-1
R4: Leyton Orient (A) 1-2

54-55 R3: Preston North End (H) 2-3

55-56 R3: Notts County (A) 1-0
R4: Newcastle United (H) 4-5

56-57 R3: Ipswich Town (A) 3-2
R4: Blackpool (A) 2-6

57-58 R3: Yeovil Town (H) 4-0
R4: Charlton Athletic (H) 1-1, (A) 2-0
R5: West Ham United (A) 3-2
R6: Bristol Rovers (H) 3-1
SF: Man. Utd *(at A. Villa)* 2-2, *(at Arsenal)* 3-5

58-59 R3: Peterborough United (H) 0-0, (A) 1-0
R4: Birmingham City (A) 1-1, (H) 2-3

59-60 R3: Hull City (H) 5-0
R4: Leicester City (A) 1-2

Above: *Fulham's Alan Mullery is pursued by Billy Bonds of West Ham during the 1975 final. Photo: Colorsport*

60-61 R3: Newcastle United (A) 0-5

61-62 R3: Hartlepools United (H) 3-1
R4: Walsall (H) 2-2, (A) 2-1
R5: Port Vale (H) 1-0
R6: Blackburn Rovers (H) 2-2, (A) 1-0
SF: Burnley *(at Aston V.)* 1-1, *(at Leic. C.)* 1-2

62-63 R3: West Ham United (A) 0-0, (H) 1-2

63-64 R3: Luton Town (H) 4-1
R4: Blackburn Rovers (A) 0-2

64-65 R3: Millwall (H) 3-3, (A) 0-2

65-66 R3: Sheffield United (A) 1-3

66-67 R3: Bradford (Park Avenue) (A) 3-1
R4: Sheffield United (H) 1-1, (A) 1-3

67-68 R3: Macclesfield Town (H) 4-2
R4: Portsmouth (H) 0-0, (A) 0-1

68-69 R3: Sunderland (A) 4-1
R4: West Bromwich Albion (A) 1-2

69-70 R1: Exeter City (A) 0-2

70-71 R1: Bristol Rovers (H) 1-2

71-72 R3: Queens Park Rangers (A) 1-1, (H) 2-1
R4: Huddersfield Town (A) 0-3

72-73 R3: Sheffield Wednesday (A) 0-2

73-74 R3: Preston North End (H) 1-0
R4: Leicester City (H) 1-1, (A) 1-2

74-75 R3: Hull C. (H) 1-1, (A) 2-2, *(at Leic. C.)* 1-0
R4: Nottingham F. (H) 0-0, (A) 1-1, 1-1, 2-1
R5: Everton (A) 2-1
R6: Carlisle United (A) 1-0
SF: Birmingham City *(at Sheffield Wednesday)* 1-1, *(at Manchester City)* 1-0
F: West Ham United *(at Wembley)* 0-2

75-76 R3: Huddersfield Town (H) 2-3

76-77 R3: Swindon Town (H) 3-3, (A) 0-5

77-78 R3: Burnley (A) 0-1

78-79 R3: Queens Park Rangers (H) 2-0
R4: Manchester United (H) 1-1, (A) 0-1

79-80 R3: Blackburn Rovers (A) 1-1, (H) 0-1

80-81 R1: Reading (A) 2-1
R2: Brentford (H) 1-0
R3: Bury (A) 1-1, (H) 0-0, *(at West Brom.)* 1-0
R4: Charlton Athletic (H) 1-2

81-82 R1: Bristol Rovers (A) 2-1
R2: Hereford United (A) 0-1

82-83 R3: Oldham Athletic (A) 2-0
R4: Watford (A) 1-1, (H) 1-2

83-84 R3: Tottenham Hotspur (H) 0-0, (A) 0-2

84-85 R3: Sheffield Wednesday (H) 2-3

85-86 R3: Sheffield United (A) 0-2

86-87 R1: Hereford United (A) 3-3, (H) 4-0
R2: Newport County (H) 2-0
R3: Swindon Town (H) 0-1

87-88 R1: Gillingham (A) 1-2

88-89 R1: Colchester United (H) 0-1

89-90 R1: Bath City (A) 2-2, (H) 2-1
R2: Bristol City (A) 1-2

90-91 R1: Farnborough Town (H) 2-1
R2: Cambridge United (H) 0-0, (A) 1-2

91-92 R1: Hayes (H) 0-2

92-93 R1: Northampton Town (A) 1-3

GAINSBOROUGH TRINITY

Currently: Northern Premier League

45-46 Q4: Rawmarsh Welfare (A) 3-1
R1: Mansfield T. (A) 0-3, (H) 4-2 *(agg: 4-5)*

46-47 Q4: Yorkshire Amateur (A) 3-3, (H) 6-2
R1: Darlington (H) 1-2

47-48 Q4: Scunthorpe United (A) 2-4

48-49 Q4: Norton Woodseats (A) 4-2
R1: Witton Albion (H) 1-0
R2: Walsall (A) 3-4

49-50 Q4: Grantham (A) 0-2

50-51 Q4: Brush Sports (H) 3-1
R1: Plymouth Argyle (H) 0-3

51-52 Q4: Creswell Colliery (H) 5-2
R1: Witton Albion (A) 1-2

52-53 Q4: Ilkeston Town (H) 5-1
R1: Netherfield (H) 1-1, (A) 2-1
R2: Newport County (A) 1-2

53-54 Q4: Worksop Town (A) 2-2, (H) 2-1
R1: Chesterfield (H) 1-4

54-55 Q4: Selby Town (A) 2-4

55-56 Q4: Skegness Town (A) 1-1, (H) 0-2

56-57 Q4: Goole Town (A) 1-2

57-58 Q1: Louth United (H) 4-2
Q2: Alford United (A) 1-2

58-59 Q1: Grantham (A) 4-1
Q2: Brigg Town (H) 6-2
Q3: Boston United (A) 1-1, (H) 2-2, 1-3

59-60 Q1: Alford United (H) 4-1
Q2: Bourne Town (H) 4-1
Q3: Skegness Town (A) 0-0, (H) 3-0
Q4: Heanor Town (H) 4-2

R1: Doncaster Rovers (A) 3-3, (H) 0-1

60-61 Q1: Denaby United (H) 0-3

61-62 Q1: Norton Woodseats (H) 6-0
Q2: Worksop Town (A) 3-4

62-63 Q1: Stocksbridge Works (H) 3-1
Q2: Denaby United (A) 2-1
Q3: Worksop Town (A) 0-0, (H) 3-1
Q4: Buxton (H) 0-0, (A) 1-4

63-64 Q1: Stocksbridge Works (H) 5-0
Q2: Norton Woodseats Amateur (A) 6-1
Q3: Worksop Town (A) 3-1
Q4: Heanor Town (A) 0-2

64-65 Q1: Goole Town (H) 1-3

65-66 Q1: Retford Town (H) 1-0
Q2: Denaby United (H) 4-1
Q3: Goole Town (A) 4-3
Q4: Burton Albion (A) 2-3

66-67 Q1: Ossett Albion (H) 3-0
Q2: Denaby United (H) 2-1
Q3: Farsley Celtic (H) 1-1, (A) 1-0
Q4: Goole Town (H) 1-0
R1: Colchester United (H) 0-1

67-68 Q1: Farsley Celtic (A) 1-2

68-69 Q1: Denaby United (H) 4-0
Q2: Frickley Colliery Welfare (A) 1-2

69-70 Q1: Thackley (A) 4-1
Q2: Worksop Town (H) 2-1
Q3: Frickley Colliery Welfare (H) 3-2
Q4: Grantham (A) 0-5

70-71 PR: Sutton Town (H) 2-1
Q1: Worksop Town (A) 1-0
Q2: Alfreton Town (A) 2-1
Q3: Heanor Town (A) 2-0
Q4: Grantham (A) 1-1, (H) 3-3, 1-2

71-72 Q1: Lincoln United (H) 2-3

72-73 Q1: Winterton Rangers (A) 3-1
Q2: Barton Town (A) 2-2, (H) 3-1
Q3: Worksop Town (H) 1-0
Q4: Grantham (A) 1-2

73-74 Q1: Sutton Town (H) 1-2

74-75 Q1: Mexborough Town (H) 5-1
Q2: Matlock Town (A) 1-2

75-76 Q1: Frickley Colliery (A) 0-3

76-77 Q1: Emley (A) 1-4

77-78 Q1: Ashby Institute (H) 1-0
Q2: Brigg Town (A) 0-1

78-79 Q1: Enderby Town (A) 4-3
Q2: Louth United (H) 1-1, (A) 2-1
Q3: Boston United (A) 0-3

79-80 Q1: Brigg Town (H) 1-1, (A) 5-1
Q2: Skegness Town (A) 0-2

80-81 PR: Heanor Town (H) 3-1
Q1: March Town United (A) 2-1
Q2: Corby Town (A) 0-2

81-82 Q1: Boston (A) 0-0, (H) 1-2

82-83 Q1: Appleby Frod. (H) 2-2, (A) 0-0, (H) 2-1
Q2: Nuneaton Borough (A) 3-3, (H) 2-0
Q3: Shepshed Charterhouse (A) 0-3

83-84 Q1: Ilkeston Town (H) 6-0
Q2: Grantham (H) 2-0
Q3: Bridgnorth Town (H) 1-1, (A) 4-1
Q4: Hitchin Town (A) 1-0
R1: Blackpool (H) 0-2

84-85 Q1: Oldswinford (H) 3-0
Q2: Shepshed Charterhouse (A) 5-2
Q3: Nuneaton Borough (A) 0-2

85-86 Q1: Bromsgrove Rovers (H) 1-1, (A) 1-2

86-87 Q1: Alfreton Town (A) 0-0, (H) 2-1
Q2: Sutton Coldfield Town (A) 1-0
Q3: Grantham (A) 2-1
Q4: Boston United (A) 0-6

87-88 Q1: Matlock Town (A) 3-3, (H) 0-3

88-89 Q1: Gresley Rovers (H) 2-2, (A) 1-3

89-90 Q1: Sutton Coldfield Town (H) 1-2

90-91 Q1: Frickley Athletic (A) 3-4

91-92 Q1: Lincoln United (A) 1-3

92-93 Q1: Paget Rangers (A) 3-1
Q2: Gresley Rovers (A) 4-1
Q3: Pelsall Villa (H) 4-2
Q4: Altrincham (H) 0-2

GALGATE

Currently: Defunct

49-50 PR: Fleetwood (H - *played away*) 3-5

GARFORTH TOWN

Currently: Northern Counties (East) League
* - As Garforth Miners

84-85 * PR: Caernarfon Town (A) 1-4

85-86 PR: Northallerton Town (H) 1-2

86-87 Q1: Southport (A) 1-1, (H) 1-1 *ab. in E.T.* (A) 1-2

87-88 PR: Shotton Comrades (A) 1-2

90-91 PR: Shildon (A) 1-3

91-92 PR: Whickham (H) 4-1
Q1: Whitby Town (A) 1-0
Q2: Murton (A) 1-3

92-93 PR: Ashton United (A) 2-1
Q1: North Ferriby United (A) 0-1

GATESHEAD

Currently: Defunct

45-46 R1: Hartlepools U. (A) 2-1, (H) 6-2 (*agg: 8-3*)
R2: Darlington (A) 4-2, (H) 1-2 (*agg: 5-4*)
R3: Rotherham Utd (A) 2-2, (H) 0-2 (*agg: 2-4*)

46-47 R1: Bradford City (H) 3-1
R2: Lancaster City (H) 4-0
R3: Manchester City (A) 0-3

47-48 R1: Bradford City (H) 1-3

48-49 R1: Netherfield (H) 3-0
R2: Scarborough (H) 3-0
R3: Aldershot (H) 3-1
R4: West Bromwich Albion (H) 1-3

49-50 R1: York City (H) 3-1
R2: Newport County (A) 1-1, (H) 1-2

50-51 R3: Sheffield United (A) 0-1

51-52 R1: Stockport Co. (A) 2-2, (H) 1-1, 2-1
R2: Guildford City (H) 2-0
R3: Ipswich Town (A) 2-2, (H) 3-3, 2-1
R4: West Bromwich Albion (H) 0-2

52-53 R1: Crewe Alexandra (H) 2-0
R2: Bradford (Park Avenue) (A) 2-1
R3: Liverpool (H) 1-0
R4: Hull City (A) 2-1
R5: Plymouth Argyle (A) 1-0
R6: Bolton Wanferers (H) 0-1

53-54 R1: Tranmere Rovers (H) 1-2

54-55 R1: Chester (H) 6-0
R2: Barnsley (H) 3-3, (A) 1-0
R3: Tottenham Hotspur (H) 0-2

55-56 R1: Hartlepool United (A) 0-3

56-57 R1: Hull City (A) 0-4

57-58 R1: Chester (A) 3-4

58-59 R1: Bradford (Park Avenue) (H) 1-4

59-60 R1: Halifax Town (H) 3-4

60-61 R1: Barnsley (H) 0-0, (A) 0-2

61-62 Q4: Selby Town (H) 1-1, (A) 3-0
R1: Tranmere Rovers (A) 3-2
R2: Workington (H) 0-2

62-63 Q4: West Auckland Town (H) 2-2, (A) 2-0
R1: Wigan Athletic (H) 2-1
R2: Bradford City (A) 2-3

63-64 Q4: South Shields (H) 5-3
R1: Darlington (A) 4-1
R2: Carlisle United (A) 3-4

64-65 Q4: Netherfield (H) 1-4

65-66 Q4: Horden Colliery Welfare (H) 3-1
R1: Crook Town (H) 4-2
R2: Hull City (H) 0-4

66-67 Q4: Blyth Spartans (H) 1-3

67-68 Q1: Blyth Spartans (H) 1-1, (A) 1-2

68-69 Q1: Bishop Auckland (A) 1-2

69-70 Q1: Durham City (H) 5-0
Q2: Spennymoor United (H) 2-2, (H) 0-1

70-71 Q1: Annfield Plain (A) 5-1
Q2: Spennymoor United (A) 1-0
Q3: Ferryhill Athletic (H) 0-0, (A) 0-2

71-72 Q1: Tow Law Town (H) 3-0
Q2: Bishop Auckland (H) 3-2
Q3: North Shields (H) 0-1

72-73 Q1: West Auckland Town (H) 1-0
Q2: Murton Colliery Welfare (A) 4-2
Q3: Spennymoor United (H) 0-4

73-74 Q1: Bishop Auckland (A) *withdrew*

GATESHEAD

Currently: Alliance Premier League

78-79 Q1: Horden Colliery Welfare (H) 1-0
Q2: Wallsend Town (H) 6-0
Q3: Shildon (A) 8-1
Q4: Workington (H) 1-1, (A) 2-3

79-80 Q1: Crook Town (H) 2-2, (A) 0-2

80-81 Q1: Guisborough Town (A) 3-2
Q2: Tow Law Town (H) 2-0
Q3: Billingham Synthonia (H) 3-0
Q4: Marine (H) 0-1 - *Marine expelled*
R1: Lincoln City (A) 0-1

81-82 Q1: Spennymoor United (H) 1-1, (A) 0-3

82-83 PR: Durham C. (H) 1-1, (A) 2-2, (*at Blyth*) 2-1
Q1: Peterlee Newtown (A) 2-1
Q2: Farsley Celtic (H) 5-1
Q3: North Shields (A) 2-4

83-84 Q1: Seaham Colliery Welfare Red Star (A) 3-1
Q2: Accrington Stanley (A) 1-1, (H) 1-2

84-85 Q1: Consett (A) 2-0
Q2: Crook Town (A) 2-1
Q3: Blue Star (H) 1-1, (A) 1-3

85-86 Q1: Billingham Synthonia (A) 4-0
Q2: Spennymoor United (A) 2-1
Q3: South Bank (A) 2-2, (H) 1-1, (H) 1-2

86-87 Q1: Bishop Auckland (A) 0-2

87-88 Q1: Blyth Spartans (A) 1-2

88-89 Q1: Workington (A) 0-0, (H) 1-0
Q2: Tow Law Town (A) 2-3

89-90 Q1: Darlington Cleveland Bridge (A) 1-0
Q2: Ferryhill Athletic (H) 3-0
Q3: Billingham Synthonia (H) 0-2

90-91 Q1: North Shields (A) 1-1, (H) 0-1

91-92 Q1: Workington (A) 1-0
Q2: Alnwick Town (H) 6-0
Q3: Netherfield (H) 0-0, (A) 3-0
Q4: Runcorn (A) 0-1

92-93 Q1: Billingham Synthonia (H) 3-1
Q2: Whitby Town (H) 5-2
Q3: Spennymoor United (A) 7-0
Q4: Whitley Bay (H) 3-0
R1: Accrington Stanley (A) 2-3

GATESHEAD UNITED

Currently: Defunct
* - As South Shields

46-47 * PR: Murton Colliery Welfare (A) 2-3

47-48 * PR: Radcliffe Welfare United (H) 13-0
Q1: Annfield Plain (A) 4-2
Q2: Ashington (H) 3-1
Q3: Blyth Spartans (A) 3-0
Q4: Scarborough (A) 3-2
R1: Crewe Alexandra (A) 1-4

48-49 * PR: Shilbottle Colliery Welfare (A) 4-1
Q1: Newburn (H) 5-2
Q2: Stanley United (A) 3-2 *expelled*

49-50 * PR: Lynemouth Welfare (H) 9-2
Q1: Hexham Hearts (H) 3-1
Q2: North Shields (A) 0-2

50-51 * PR: Heaton Stannington (A) 3-0
Q1: Blyth Spartans (H) 0-2

51-52 * Q1: Heaton Stannington (H) 4-0
Q2: Easington C.W. (H) 2-2, (A) 1-1, 2-1
Q3: Consett (A) 0-4

52-53 * Q1: Dawdon Colliery Welfare (A) 2-1
Q2: Annfield Plain (H) 3-1
Q3: Consett (A) 0-4

53-54 * Q1: Gosforth & Coxlodge (A) 5-0
Q2: Boldon Colliery Welfare (A) 3-3, (H) 9-2
Q3: Annfield Plain (A) 1-0
Q4: Ferryhill Athletic (A) 0-2

54-55 * PR: North Shields (H) 1-4

55-56 * Q1: Alnwick Town (H) 5-0
Q2: Cramlington Welfare (H) 5-3
Q3: North Shields (A) 0-1

56-57 * Q1: Alnwick Town (H) 3-0
Q2: Cralmington Welfare (A) 6-0
Q3: North Shields (A) 1-1, (H) 2-1
Q4: Horden Colliery Welfare (H) 1-0
R1: Chesterfield (H) 2-2, (A) 0-4

57-58 * Q4: Horden Colliery Welfare (H) 4-2
R1: Frickley Colliery (H) 3-2
R2: York City (H) 1-3

58-59 * Q4: Tow Law Town (A) 3-2
R1: Crewe Alexandra (A) 2-2, (H) 5-0
R2: Oldham Athletic (A) 0-2

59-60 * Q4: Consett (A) 0-0, (H) 2-2, 5-5, 1-0
R1: Chesterfield (H) 2-1
R2: Bradford (Park Avenue) (H) 1-5

60-61 * Q4: Bridlington Town (A) 3-5

61-62 * Q4: Bishop Auckland (H) 2-1
R1: Morecambe (A) 1-2

62-63 * Q4: Bishop Auckland (H) 2-1
R1: Doncaster Rovers (H) 0-0, (A) 1-2

63-64 * Q4: Gateshead (A) 3-5

64-65 * Q4: Consett (A) 4-0
R1: Chesterfield (A) 0-2

65-66 * Q4: Consett (H) 3-0
R1: York City (H) 3-1
R2: Crewe Alexandra (A) 1-3

66-67 * Q4: Billingham Synthonia (H) 2-0
R1: Workington (H) 1-4

67-68 * Q4: Tow Law Town (H) 2-2, (A) 0-1

68-69 * Q4: Consett (H) 1-1, (A) 6-0
R1: York City (H) 0-6

69-70 * Q4: Bishop Auckland (H) 2-2, (A) 3-1
R1: Bradford (Park Avenue) (H) 2-1
R2: Oldham Athletic (H) 0-0, (A) 2-1
R3: Queens Park Rangers (A) 1-4

70-71 * Q4: Blyth Spartans (A) 1-1, (H) 3-0
R1: Wigan Athletic (H) 1-1, (A) 0-2

71-72 * Q4: Bradford (Park Avenue) (A) 1-0
R1: Scunthorpe United (H) 3-3, (A) 3-2
R2: Notts County (H) 1-3

72-73 * Q4: Billingham Synthonia (A) 1-1, (H) 2-1
R1: Rotherham United (A) 0-4

73-74 * Q4: Bishop Auckland (A) 1-0
R1: Rochdale (A) 0-2

74-75 Q4: Ashington (A) 3-1
R1: Crewe Alexandra (A) 2-2, (H) 1-0
R2: Altrincham (A) 0-3

75-76 Q4: Droylsden (A) 4-0
R1: Grimsby Town (A) 3-1
R2: Rochdale (H) 1-1, (A) 1-3

76-77 Q4: Blyth Spartans (A) 3-1
R1: Wrexham (A) 0-6

GEDLING COLLIERY

Currently: (Gedling Colliery Welfare) Notts Alliance

47-48 PR: Holbeach United (H) 6-1
Q1: Boston United (H) 3-5

48-49 PR: Grantham (A) 1-3

49-50 EX: Ollerton Colliery (A) 4-0
PR: Langold W.M.C. (H) 2-0
Q1: Ransome & Marles (A) 6-4
Q2: Spalding United (A) 2-5

50-51 PR: Raleigh Athletic (A) 1-1, (H) 8-1
Q1: Spalding United (A) 0-8

51-52 Q1: Ilkeston Town (A) 3-7

52-53 Q1: Gresley Rovers (A) 1-3

53-54 Q1: South Normanton M.W. (A) 1-1, (H) 2-4

54-55 Q1: Matlock Town (A) 1-1, (H) 6-1
Q2: Gresley Rovers (A) 2-3

GILLINGHAM

Currently: Football League

45-46 Q4: Sutton United (H) 3-9

46-47 Q4: Guildford City (A) 2-1
R1: Gravesend & Northfleet (H) 4-1
R2: Bristol City (A) 2-1
R3: Swansea Town (A) 1-4

47-48 Q4: Barnet (H) 3-1
R1: Leyton Orient (H) 1-0
R2: Rochdale (A) 1-1, (H) 1-1, 3-0
R3: Queens Park Rangers (H) 1-1, (A) 1-3

48-49 Q4: Romford (A) 1-2

49-50 Q4: Guildford City (A) 3-2
R1: Hastings United (A) 3-1
R2: Yeovil Town (A) 1-3

50-51 R1: Linby Colliery (A) 4-1
R2: Bristol R. (A) 2-2, (H) 1-1, (*at Tottenham Hotspur*) 1-2

51-52 R1: Crystal Palace (A) 1-0
R2: Rochdale (H) 0-3

52-53 R1: Wellington Town (A) 1-1, (H) 3-0
R2: Stockport County (A) 1-3

53-54 R1: Walthamstow Avenue (A) 0-1

54-55 R1: Newport County (H) 2-0
R2: Reading (H) 1-1, (A) 3-5

55-56 R1: Shrewsbury Town (H) 1-1, (A) 1-4

56-57 R1: Yiewsley (A) 2-2, (H) 2-0
R2: Newport County (H) 1-2

57-58 R1: Gorleston (H) 10-1
R2: Millwall (A) 1-1, (H) 6-1
R3: Nottingham Forest (A) 0-2

58-59 R1: Plymouth Argyle (A) 2-2, (H) 1-4

59-60 R1: Bedford Town (A) 4-0
R2: Torquay United (H) 2-2, (A) 2-1
R3: Swansea Town (H) 1-4

60-61 R1: Ashford Town (A) 2-1
R2: Southend United (H) 3-2
R3: Leyton Orient (H) 2-6

61-62 R1: Coventry City (A) 0-2

62-63 R1: Andover (A) 1-0
R2: Bedford Town (H) 3-0
R3: Port Vale (H) 2-4

63-64 R1: Queens Park Rangers (A) 1-4

64-65 R1: Guildford City (A) 2-2, (H) 1-0
R2: Luton Town (A) 0-1

65-66 R1: Folkestone Town (H) 1-2

66-67 R1: Tamworth (H) 4-1
R2: Walsall (A) 1-3

67-68 R1: Newport County (A) 0-3

68-69 R1: Leyton Orient (A) 1-1, (H) 2-1
R2: Luton Town (A) 1-3

69-70 R1: Southend United (A) 0-0, (H) 2-1
R2: Tamworth (H) 6-0
R3: Newport County (H) 1-0
R4: Peterborough United (H) 5-1
R5: Watford (A) 1-2

70-71 R1: Brentford (A) 1-2

71-72 R1: Plymouth Argyle (H) 3-2
R2: Romford (A) 1-0
R3: Swansea City (A) 0-1

72-73 R1: Reading (H) 1-2

73-74 R1: Cambridge United (A) 2-3

74-75 R1: Hereford United (A) 0-1

75-76 R1: Weymouth (A) 2-0
R2: Brighton & Hove Albion (H) 0-1

76-77 R1: Watford (H) 0-1

77-78 R1: Weymouth (H) 1-1, (A) 1-0
R2: Peterborough United (H) 1-1, (A) 0-2

78-79 R1: Reading (A) 0-0, (H) 1-2

79-80 R1: Wimbledon (H) 0-0, (A) 2-4

80-81 R1: Dagenham (H) 2-1
R2: Maidstone (H) 0-0, (A) 0-0, (H) 0-2

81-82 R1: Plymouth Argyle (A) 0-0, (H) 1-0
R2: Barking (H) 1-1, (A - *played home*) 3-1
R3: Oldham Athletic (H) 2-1
R4: West Bromwich Albion (H) 0-1

82-83 R1: Dagenham (H) 1-0
R2: Northampton Town (H) 1-1, (A) 2-3

83-84 R1: A.P. Leamington (A) 1-0
R2: Chelmsford City (H) 6-1
R3: Brentford (H) 5-3
R4: Everton (A) 0-0, (H) 0-0, (H) 0-3

84-85 R1: Windsor & Eton (H) 2-1
R2: Colchester United (A) 5-0
R3: Cardiff City (H) 2-1
R4: Ipswich Town (A) 2-3

85-86 R1: Northampton Town (H) 3-0
R2: Bognor Regis Town (H) 6-1
R3: Derby County (H) 1-1, (A) 1-3

86-87 R1: Kettering Town (A) 3-0
R2: Chelmsford City (H) 2-0
R3: Wigan Athletic (A) 1-2

87-88 R1: Fulham (H) 2-1
R2: Walsall (H) 2-1
R3: Birmingham City (H) 0-3

88-89 R1: Peterborough United (H) 3-3, (A) 0-1

89-90 R1: Welling United (H) 0-0, (A) 0-1

90-91 R1: A.F.C. Bournemouth (A) 1-2

91-92 R1: Brentford (A) 3-3, (H) 1-3

92-93 R1: Kettering Town (H) 3-2
R2: Colchester United (H) 1-1, (A) 3-2
R3: Huddersfield Town (H) 0-0, (A) 1-2

G.K.N. SANKEY

Currently: Defunct
* - As Sankey of Wellington

61-62 * Q1: Stafford Rangers (A) 2-2, (H) 5-1
Q2: Stourbridge (A) 2-0
Q3: Bromsgrove Rovers (A) 2-1
Q4: Hereford United (H) 0-1

62-63 * Q1: Kidderminster Harriers (A) 0-1

63-64 * Q1: Worcester City (H) 2-3

64-65 * Q1: Stafford Rangers (A) 3-3, (H) 3-0
Q2: Kidderminster Harriers (A) 0-3

85-86 Q1: Oswestry Town (A) 1-1, (H) 1-0
Q2: Leek Town (H) 1-1, (A) 4-5

86-87 Q1: South Liverpool (A) 3-2
Q2: Lye Town (A) 1-4

87-88 PR: Leek Town (A) 3-3, (H) 2-3

GLASTONBURY

Currently: Western League

46-47 Q1: Peasedown Miners Welfare (A) 0-1

47-48 Q1: St Austell (A) 1-2

48-49 PR: Weston-s-Mare St John's (A) 1-1, (H) 9-0
Q1: Soundwell (H) 4-3
Q2: Gloucester City (H) 1-1, (A) 1-3

49-50 PR: Wells City (H) 1-4

50-51 PR: Bridgwater Town (A) 1-1, (H) 7-0
Q1: Truro City (A) 4-2
Q2: Barnstaple Town (H) 3-0
Q3: Street (A) 1-0
Q4: Dorchester Town (A) 4-1
R1: Exeter City (H) 1-2

51-52 Q1: Bath City (H) 2-2, (A) 1-3

52-53 PR: Clandown (A) 4-0
Q1: Street (A) 2-1
Q2: Peasedown Miners Welfare (A) 1-0
Q3: Bath City (H) 0-3

53-54 PR: Clevedon (A) 1-0
Q1: Clandown (A) 4-2
Q2: Street (A) 1-2

55-56 Q1: Street (H) 0-1

56-57 Q1: Peasedown Miners Welfare (A) 2-0
Q2: Chippenham United (H) 3-2

Above: *Glastonbury defend a corner in their tie against Bath on 12th September 1992. Photo: Anthony Smith.*

	Q3: Bridgwater Town (H) 4-3 Q4: Yeovil Town (A) 1-3
57-58	Q1: Street (H) 5-0 Q2: Wells City (H) 3-0 Q3: Bath City (A) 1-2
58-59	Q1: Clevedon (H) 0-0, (A) 2-0 Q2: Taunton (H) 1-1, (A) 0-4
59-60	Q1: Street (H) 2-1 Q2: Taunton (A) 0-0, (H) 2-1 Q3: Bridgwater Town (A) 1-3
60-61	Q2: Borough of Weston-s-M. (H) 2-2, (A) 0-2
61-62	Q2: Borough of W.s.M. (H) 1-1, (A) 1-1, 0-3
62-63	Q1: Frome Town (H) 0-6
63-64	Q1: Borough of Weston-super-Mare (H) 2-5
64-65	Q2: Welton Rovers (A) 0-4
65-66	Q1: Frome Town (H) 0-1
66-67	Q1: Portland United (H) 2-2, (A) 2-4
67-68	Q1: Dorchester Town (A) 0-1
68-69	Q1: Westbury United (A) 1-3
69-70	PR: Melksham Town (H) 5-1 Q1: Dorchester Town (A) 2-1 Q2: Weston-super-Mare (H) 3-1 Q3: Chippenham Town (A) 2-2, (H) 7-0 Q4: Cheltenham Town (H) 0-0, (A) 1-4
70-71	Q1: Bridport (A) 0-0, (H) 2-0 Q2: Welton Rovers (H) 1-0 Q3: Minehead (A) 0-1
71-72	Q1: Poole Town (H) 2-1 Q2: Trowbridge Town (A) 0-0, (H) 0-5
72-73	Q1: Stonehouse (A) 1-0 Q2: Devizes Town (A) 2-7
73-74	Q1: Ton Pentre (A) 2-1 Q2: Merthyr Tydfil (H) 0-0, (A) 1-3
74-75	Q1: Taunton Town (H) 2-2, (A) 0-4
75-76	Q1: Hungerford Town (H) 2-1 Q2: Minehead (H) 0-4
76-77	PR: Barry Town (H) 1-0 Q1: Worcester City (A) 2-3
77-78	PR: Merthyr Tydfil (H) 0-1
78-79	PR: Bath City (H) 0-3
79-80	Q1: Bridport (H) 2-1 Q2: Saltash United (A) 0-4
80-81	PR: Bath City (A) 1-7
81-82	Q1: Weston-super-Mare (H) 3-1 Q2: Liskeard Athletic (A) 0-2
82-83	Q1: Barnstaple Town (H) 1-1, (A) 1-4
83-84	PR: Bristol Manor Farm (A) 1-0 Q1: Cheltenham Town (H) 0-0, (A) 0-4
84-85	Q1: Wellington (A) 3-2 Q2: Clevedon Town (H) 1-2
85-86	PR: Exmouth Town (H) 0-5
86-87	Q1: Exmouth Town (A) 0-5
87-88	PR: Torrington (A) 0-3
88-89	Q1: Falmouth Town (A) 0-3
89-90	PR: Maesteg Park (H) 0-1
90-91	PR: Yate Town (A) 0-4
91-92	PR: Keynsham Town (H) 1-0 Q1: Trowbridge Town (H) 0-4
92-93	Q1: Bath City (H) 0-4

GLOSSOP NORTH END

Currently: North West Counties League
* - As Glossop F.C.

45-46 *	Q1: Witton Albion (A) 2-8
46-47 *	Q1: Rhyl (H) 2-6
48-49 *	EX: Harrowby (A) 11-2 PR: Winsford United (A) 1-3
49-50 *	PR: Hyde United (H) 1-2
50-51 *	PR: Altrincham (H) 1-4
71-72 *	Q1: Worksop Town (H) 0-1
72-73 *	PR: Rawmarsh Welfare (A) 1-0 Q1: Mexborough Town (H) 3-2 Q2: Macclesfield Town (A) 0-3
73-74 *	Q1: Altrincham (A) 1-3
74-75 *	Q1: Emley (A) 1-4
75-76 *	Q1: Fleetwood (A) 0-2
76-77 *	Q1: Droylsden (A) 2-3
77-78 *	Q1: Winsford Town (H) 0-2
78-79 *	Q1: Buxton (A) 1-3
79-80 *	Q1: New Mills (A) 2-1 Q2: Winsford United (A) 0-2
80-81 *	PR: Formby (A) 2-0 Q1: Prescot Cables (A) 0-2
81-82 *	Q1: Bangor City (A) 0-6
82-83 *	Q1: Worksop Town (H) 2-5
83-84 *	Q1: Witton Albion (A) 1-1, (H) 2-0 Q2: Goole Town (H) 4-0 Q3: Frickley Athletic (A) 2-3
84-85 *	PR: Appleby Frodingham (A) 0-2
85-86 *	PR: Nantwich Town (A) 0-1
86-87 *	PR: Penrith (A) 2-6
87-88 *	PR: Heanor Town (H) 2-3
88-89 *	PR: Prescot Cables (H) 0-0, (A) 0-1
89-90 *	PR: Maine Road (H) 0-4
90-91 *	PR: Skelmersdale Utd (H) 1-1, (A) 2-0 Q1: Maine Road (A) 0-1
91-92 *	PR: Newtown (A) 2-4
92-93	Q1: Macclesfield Town (H) 0-1

GLOUCESTER CITY

Currently: Southern League

46-47	PR: Weston-super-Mare St Johns (A) 5-0 Q1: St Philips Marsh Adult School (A) 0-2
47-48	PR: Hanham Athletic (H) 3-4
48-49	EX: Cinderford Town (H) 4-0 PR: Barnstaple Town (H) 5-2 Q1: Clevedon (H) 8-2 Q2: Glastonbury (A) 1-1, (H) 3-1 Q3: Street (H) 4-1 Q4: Bath City (A) 3-2 R1: Mansfield Town (A) 0-4
49-50	PR: Weston-super-Mare (A) 3-2 Q1: Barry Town (A) 1-1, (H) 1-0 Q2: Clevedon (H) 3-0 Q3: Lovells Athletic (A) 3-0 Q4: Bideford (A) 1-1, (H) 3-1 R1: Norwich City (H) 2-3
50-51	Q4: Salisbury (H) 2-1 R1: Bristol City (A) 0-4
51-52	Q1: Stonehouse (A) 2-1 Q2: Ebbw Vale (A - *played home*) 1-2
52-53	PR: Llanelly (H) 1-1, (A) 0-5
53-54	Q1: Cinderford Town (H) 2-1 Q2: Barry Town (A) 1-2
54-55	Q1: Cinderford Town (A) 3-0 Q2: Barry Town (A) 4-1 Q3: Merthyr Tydfil (H) 0-1
55-56	Q1: Ebbw Vale (A) 2-2, (H) 4-1 Q2: Barry Town (A) 2-5
56-57	Q1: Barry Town (H) 3-1 Q2: Cheltenham Town (H) 1-2
57-58	Q1: Cinderford Town (A) 1-2
58-59	Q1: Cinderford Towm (H) 3-2 Q2: Lovells Athletic (A) 3-2 Q3: Merthyr Tydfil (A) 1-2
59-60	Q1: Cheltenham Town (H) 1-3
60-61	Q1: Cheltenham Town (H) 1-4
61-62	Q1: Stonehouse (H) 5-1 Q2: Barry Town (H) 1-1, (A) 1-2
62-63	Q1: Merthyr Tydfil (H) 3-2 Q2: Barry Town (A) 3-0 Q3: Cheltenham Town (H) 1-2
63-64	Q1: Merthyr Tydfil (H) 2-2, (A) 3-2 Q2: Cheltenham Town (H) 1-2
64-65	Q1: Abergavenny Thursdays (H) 3-1 Q2: Llanelly (H) 0-1
65-66	Q1: Llanelly (H) 1-0 Q2: Lovells Athletic (A) 2-1 Q3: Merthyr Tydfil (H) 1-1, (A) 1-1, 0-1
66-67	Q1: Abergavenny Thursdays (H) 4-1 Q2: Cinderford Town (A) 2-2, (H) 0-3
67-68	Q1: Lovells Athletic (A) 4-0 Q2: Cheltenham Town (H) 0-1
68-69	Q1: Devizes Town (H) 3-1 Q2: Welton Rovers (A) 2-1 Q3: Poole Town (A) 1-1, (H) 1-2
69-70	Q1: Ton Pentre (A) 2-2, (H) 0-1
70-71	Q1: Cinderford Town (A) 2-3
71-72	Q1: Merthyr Tydfil (H) 2-3
72-73	Q1: Trowbridge Town (H) 2-2, (A) 0-2
73-74	Q1: Stonehouse (A) 1-1, (H) 0-1
74-75	Q1: Merthyr Tydfil (H) 3-2 Q2: Cheltenham Town (A) 1-4
75-76	Q1: Brierley Hill Alliance (A) 1-2
76-77	PR: Trowbridge Town (H) 1-1, (A) 2-1 Q1: Merthyr Tydfil (A) 1-4
77-78	Q1: Dudley Town (A) 1-1, (H) 1-2
78-79	PR: Frome Town (A) 3-0 Q1: Melksham Town (A) 0-1
79-80	PR: Bridgend Town (H) 0-2
80-81	Q1: Dorchester Town (H) 1-0

Q2: Trowbridge Town (H) 0-1

81-82 PR: Clandown (A) 3-1
Q1: Forest Green Rovers (H) 2-1
Q2: Devizes Town (H) 2-4

82-83 Q1: Llanelli (H) 1-0
Q2: Cheltenham Town (A) 1-5

83-84 Q1: Haverfordwest County (A) 2-1
Q2: Welton Rovers (A) 4-1
Q3: Merthyr Tydfil (A) 2-3

84-85 Q1: Llanelli (A) 5-2
Q2: Haverfordwest County (A) *W/O*
Q3: Barry Town (H) 1-3

85-86 Q1: Ton Pentre (H) 0-0, (A) 3-3, (A) 1-2

86-87 PR: Saltash U. (A) 0-0, (H) 0-2

87-88 PR: Westbury United (H) 7-0
Q1: Ton Pentre (H) 1-2

88-89 Q1: Melksham Town (A) 5-0
Q2: Cheltenham Town (H) 3-0
Q3: Merthyr Tydfil (H) 0-1

89-90 Q1: Mangotsfield United (H) 4-0
Q2: Barry Town (A) 2-2, (H) 2-0
Q3: Worcester City (H) 4-2
Q4: Folkestone (A) 1-0
R1: Dorchester Town (H) 1-0
R2: Cardiff City (A) 2-2, (H) 0-1

90-91 Q4: Farnborough Town (A) 1-4

91-92 Q1: Shortwood Town (H) 4-1
Q2: Worcester City (A) 1-2

92-93 Q1: Weston-super-Mare (H) 2-3

GOOLE TOWN

Currently: Northern Premier League

45-46 Q1: Yorkshire Amateur (H) 0-1

46-47 Q1: Yorkshire Amateur (H) 2-4

47-48 PR: Upton Colliery (A) 3-1
Q1: Ossett Town (H) 3-1
Q2: Thorne Colliery (H) 2-0
Q3: Selby Town (A) 5-0
Q4: Grantham (A) 3-3, (H) 2-3

48-49 PR: Brigg Town (H) 6-3
Q1: Bradford United (H) 4-2
Q2: Frickley Colliery (A) 1-3

49-50 PR: Barton Town (H) 3-1
Q1: Frickley Colliery (A) 1-1, (H) 1-0
Q2: Bentley Colliery (H) 1-1, (A) 4-2
Q3: Brodsworth Main Coll. (A) 1-1, (H) 8-2
Q4: Scunthorpe United (A) 0-0, (H) 3-1
R1: Chester (A) 1-4

50-51 PR: Brodsworth Main Colliery (H) 5-0
Q1: Yorkshire Amateur (A) 4-0
Q2: Brigg Town (H) 3-1
Q3: Farsley Celtic (A) 2-3

51-52 Q1: Harrogate Town (H) 7-3
Q2: Ossett Town (A) 3-2
Q3: Yorkshire Amateur (H) 3-0
Q4: Spennymoor United (H) 4-3
R1: Tranmere Rovers (A) 2-4

52-53 Q2: Farsley Celtic (H) 3-3, (A) 4-3
Q3: Selby Town (A) 1-4

53-54 Q1: Ossett Town (H) 4-2
Q2: Farsley Celtic (A) 1-0
Q3: Selby Town (H) 1-3

54-55 Q2: Harrogate & Dist. Railway Ath. (H) 4-2
Q3: Farsley Celtic (A) 0-2

55-56 Q2: Harrogate & Dist. Railway Ath. (H) 6-0
Q3: Ossett Town (H) 2-1
Q4: Selby Town (A) 4-2
R1: Halifax Town (H) 1-2

56-57 Q2: Harrogate & Dist. Railwat Ath. (H) 4-0
Q3: Farsley Celtic (H) 9-0
Q4: Gainsborough Trinity (H) 2-1
R1: Wigan Athletic (A) 2-1
R2: Workington (H) 2-2, (A) 1-0
R3: Nottingham Forest (A) 0-6

57-58 Q4: Yorkshire Amateur (A) 2-1
R1: Scunthorpe United (A) 1-2

58-59 Q4: Denaby United (H) 1-2

59-60 Q1: Yorkshire Amateur (A) 3-1
Q2: Frickley Colliery (A) 3-1
Q3: Denaby United (H) 0-1

60-61 Q1: Frickley Colliery (H) 2-4

61-62 Q1: Farsley Celtic (H) 5-1
Q2: East End W.M.C. (A) 1-1, (H) 2-1
Q3: Selby Town (H) 2-2, (A) 0-1

62-63 Q1: Farsley Celtic (A) 0-1

63-64 Q1: Selby Town (A) 0-0, (H) 3-2
Q2: Bridlington Town (A) 1-4

64-65 Q1: Gainsborough Trinity (A) 3-1
Q2: Retford Town (H) 0-1

65-66 Q1: Mexborough Town (H) 4-2
Q2: Frickley Colliery (A) 3-1
Q3: Gainsborough Trinity (H) 3-4

66-67 Q1: Hull Brunswick (H) 3-1
Q2: Barton Town (H) 3-3, (A) 2-0
Q3: Bridlington Trinity (H) 4-0
Q4: Gainsborough Trinity (A) 0-1

67-68 Q1: Scarborough (A) 1-1, (H) 2-1
Q2: Selby Town (H) 2-0
Q3: Barton Town (A) 1-1, (H) 4-1
Q4: Bangor City (H) 2-0
R1: Spennymoor United (H) 0-0, (A) 1-3

68-69 PR: Barton Town (H) 4-1
Q1: Brigg Town (A) 5-1
Q2: Scarborough (A) 2-0
Q3: Selby Town (H) 5-0
Q4: Bishop Auckland (A) 3-2
R1: Barrow (H) 1-3

69-70 Q4: Alfreton Town (A) 0-3

70-71 Q1: Yorkshire Amateur (A) 2-1
Q2: Bridlington Trin. (A) 0-0, (H) 0-0, 1-4

71-72 Q1: Selby Town (H) 3-0
Q2: Barton Town (H) 3-2
Q3: Scarborough (A) 0-2

72-73 PR: Whitby Town (A) 1-0
Q1: Scarborough (H) 0-0, (A) 0-1

73-74 Q1: Winterton Rangers (H) 2-0
Q2: Bridlington Town (H) 3-1
Q3: Bradford Park Avenue (A) 3-3, (H) 4-1
Q4: Formby (A) 0-3

74-75 Q1: Stockton (H) 3-0
Q2: Bridlington Town (A) 0-1

75-76 Q1: Brigg Town (A) 1-2

76-77 Q1: Farsley Celtic (A) 4-1
Q2: Appleby Frodingham (A) 0-0, (H) 1-0
Q3: Mexborough Town (H) 7-1
Q4: Boston United (H) 1-1, (A) 3-1
R1: Barrow (A) 2-0
R2: Wrexham (A) 1-1, (H) 0-1

77-78 Q1: Louth United (H) 6-1
Q2: Selby Town (H) 7-0
Q3: Worksop (A) 2-2, (H) 2-2, (*at Donc. R.*) 3-1
Q4: Matlock Town (H) 2-1
R1: Spennymoor United (A) 1-3

78-79 Q4: Droylsden (A) 0-2

79-80 Q1: Barton Town (A) 1-0
Q2: Bridlington Trinity (A) 2-0
Q3: Whitby Town (A) 2-2, (H) 2-1
Q4: Mossley (A) 1-2

80-81 Q1: Whitley Bay (H) 1-0
Q2: Penrith (A) 0-2

81-82 Q1: Mexborough Town Athletic (A) 6-1
Q2: Frickley Athletic (H) 2-3

82-83 PR: North Ferriby United (H) 1-0
Q1: Brigg Town (A) 1-1, (H) 7-2
Q2: Shepshed Charterhouse (H) 0-2

83-84 Q1: Leek Town (A) 1-1, (H) 4-0
Q2: Glossop (A) 0-4

84-85 Q1: Friar Lane O.B. (A) 1-1, (H) 4-1
Q2: Gresley Rovers (A) 2-0
Q3: Matlock Town (H) 4-2
Q4: Mossley (A) 1-0
R1: Halifax Town (A) 0-2

85-86 Q1: Skegness Town (H) 3-2
Q2: Buxton (H) 3-1
Q3: Marine (H) 0-5

86-87 Q1: Scarborough (H) 2-1
Q2: Leicester United (A) 1-0
Q3: Lye Town (A) 3-1
Q4: Nuneaton Borough (H) 1-2

87-88 Q1: Sutton Town (A) 2-1
Q2: Brigg Town (H) 1-3

88-89 Q1: Mile Oak Rovers & Youth (A) 1-3

89-90 Q1: Farsley Celtic (H) 1-0
Q2: Frickley Athletic (A) 1-1, (H) 1-0
Q3: Grantham Town (H) 2-1
Q4: Northwich Victoria (A) 0-2

90-91 Q1: Nuneaton Borough (A) 0-1

91-92 Q1: Oakham United (H) 0-1

92-93 Q1: Horwich R.M.I. (H) 0-1

GORLESTON

Currently: Eastern Counties League

46-47 Q1: Gothic (A) 1-1, (H) 0-6

47-48 PR: Whitton United (H) 2-4

48-49 PR: Whitton United (H) 5-3
Q1: Lowestoft Town (A) 1-3

49-50 PR: Holt United (H) 4-1
Q1: Achilles (H) 5-1
Q2: Stowmarket (H) 4-2
Q3: Lowestoft Town (A) 3-0
Q4: Tilbury (H) 1-1, (A) 1-2

50-51 PR: Eastern Coachworks (H) 0-1

51-52 Q1: Beccles (H) 5-1
Q2: Cromer (H) 3-0
Q3: Gothic (H) 5-0
Q4: Romford (H) 1-0
R1: Leyton Orient (A) 2-2, (H) 0-0, 4-5

52-53 Q4: Leytonstone (H) 1-4

53-54 Q1: Gothic (A) 10-1
Q2: Beccles (A) 5-1
Q3: Cromer (A) 6-2
Q4: Bedford Town (H) 0-2

54-55 Q1: Sheringham (H) 4-0
Q2: North Walsham Athletic (A) 4-1
Q3: Beccles (H) 4-0
Q4: Chelmsford City (H) 1-2

55-56 Q2: Great Yarmouth Town (A) 0-2

56-57 Q1: Great Yarmouth Town (A) 1-5

57-58 Q2: Sheringham (H) 3-0
Q3: Great Yarmouth Town (H) 3-2
Q4: Chelmsford City (H) 1-0
R1: Gillingham (A) 1-10

58-59 Q1: Diss Town (H) 3-2
Q2: King's Lynn (A) 1-6

59-60 Q1: Diss Town (A) 2-2, (H) 2-2, 2-1
Q2: Bungay Town (A) 0-1

60-61 Q1: Bungay Town (H) 0-1

61-62 Q1: Great Yarmouth Town (A) 0-1

62-63 Q1: Stowmarket (A) 1-3

63-64 Q1: Lowestoft Town (A) 0-5

64-65 Q1: Clacton Town (A) 1-9

65-66 Q1: Great Yarmouth Town (A) 4-6

66-67 Q1: Sudbury Town (H) 1-3

67-68 Q1: Sudbury Town (H) 0-2

68-69 Q1: Harwich & Parkeston (H) 2-1
Q2: Clacton Town (A) 3-2
Q3: Bury Town (H) 1-4

69-70 PR: Sudbury Town (A) 3-1
Q1: Bury Town (H) 1-2

70-71 PR: Haverhill Rovers (A) 7-0
Q1: Great Yarmouth T. (A) 2-2, (H) 2-1
Q2: Lowestoft Town (A) 2-4

71-72 Q1: Sudbury Town (H) 0-3

72-73 Q1: Chatteris Town (H) 0-2

75-76 PR: King's Lynn (A) 0-2

76-77 Q1: Lowestoft Town (H) 1-1, (A) 0-2

77-78 Q1: Felixstowe Town (A) 4-2
Q2: Chelmsford City (H) 1-1, (A) 0-5

78-79 PR: Cambridge City (H) 1-0
Q1: Thetford Town (A) 5-1
Q2: Soham Town Rangers (A) 3-0

Q3: Lowestoft Town (H) 3-1
Q4: Enfield (H) 2-6

79-80 Q1: King's Lynn (A) 0-2

80-81 Q1: Haverhill Rovers (A) 3-2
Q2: Hitchin Town (H) 0-1

81-82 PR: Chelmsford City (H) 2-0
Q1: Heybridge Swifts (A) 1-2

82-83 Q1: King's Lynn (H) 2-3

83-84 Q1: Chelmsford City (A) 1-5

84-85 PR: Stowmarket (A) 1-1, (H) 3-0
Q1: Haringey Borough (H) 1-1, (A) 2-0
Q2: Lowestoft Town (H) 1-0
Q3: Aveley (H) 0-4

85-86 Q1: Felixstowe Town (A) 0-4

86-87 PR: Sudbury Town (A) 0-5

87-88 PR: Chesham United (H) 1-0
Q1: Letchworth Garden City (A) 0-1

88-89 PR: Heybridge Swifts (A) 1-3

89-90 PR: Lowestoft Town (A) 1-2

90-91 PR: Boreham Wood (A) 0-2

91-92 PR: Purfleet (A) 1-3

92-93 PR: Clapton (H) 5-2
Q1: Haringey Borough (A) 0-0, (H) 1-0
Q2: Leyton (H) 1-2

GORNAL ATHLETIC

Currently: West Midlands (Regional) League
* - As Lower Gornal Athletic

65-66 * Q1: Worcester City (A) 2-4

66-67 * Q1: Halesowen Town (A) 3-2
Q2: Hednesford (H) 0-3

67-68 * PR: Stafford Rangers (A) 1-0
Q1: Bromsgrove Rovers (A) 0-2

68-69 * PR: Hinckley Athletic (A) 1-1, (H) 3-2
Q1: Brierley Hill Alliance (A) 5-1
Q2: Bilston (A) 0-3

69-70 * PR: Brierley Hill Alliance (H) 4-2
Q1: Tamworth (H) 1-1, (A) 2-4

71-72 * Q1: Halesowen Town (H) 2-2, (A) 3-1
Q2: Redditch United (H) 0-0, (A) 1-3

72-73 * Q1: Highgate United (A) 0-6

73-74 Q1: Lye Town (H) 0-0, (A) 0-5

74-75 Q1: Redditch United (A) 1-2

75-76 Q1: Highgate United (H) 1-0
Q2: Belper Town (H) 2-0
Q3: Nuneaton Borough (A) 1-1, (H) 0-3

76-77 Q1: Lye Town (H) 1-3

77-78 Q1: Halesowen Town (H) 1-3

78-79 Q1: Kempston Rovers (H) 0-2

79-80 Q1: R.C. Warwick (A) 1-1, (H) 2-3

80-81 Q1: Bedworth United (A) 0-2

GOSFORTH & COXLODGE

Currently: Defunct

45-46 Q1: Throckley Welfare (H) 0-2

46-47 PR: Amble (H) 6-2
Q1: Consett (A) 0-7

47-48 Q1: Newburn (A) 0-2

48-49 PR: Annfield Plain (A) 1-2

49-50 EX: Shilbottle Colliery Welfare (A) 3-2
PR: Morpeth Town (A) 2-2, (H) 3-1
Q1: Blyth Spartans (H) 0-4

50-51 PR: Birtley Town (A) 4-1
Q1: Cramlington Welfare (A) 2-5

51-52 Q1: Easington Colliery Welfare (H) 2-3

52-53 Q1: Consett (H) 0-5

53-54 Q1: South Shields (H) 0-5

54-55 Q1: Cramlington Welfare (H) 1-5

55-56 Q1: Ashington (H - *played away*) 0-7

56-57 Q1: Cramlington Welfare (A) 1-3

57-58 Q1: Durham City (A) 0-8

GOSPORT BOROUGH

Currently: Wessex League
* - As Gosport Borough Athletic

45-46 * Q1: Salisbury Corinthians (A) 6-2
Q2: Newport Isle of Wight (A) 0-2

46-47 * PR: Ryde Sports (A) 8-1
Q1: Salisbury Corinthians (A) 2-2, (H) 2-1
Q2: Poole Town (A) 0-3

47-48 * PR: East Cowes Victoria (H) 2-0
Q1: Bournemouth Gasworks Athletic (A) 3-0
Q2: Newport Isle of Wight (H) 5-2
Q3: Ryde Sports (H) 1-2

48-49 * PR: Bournemouth Gasworks Athletic (H) 0-1

49-50 * PR: East Cowes Victoria (A) 1-4

50-51 * PR: Blandford United (A) 1-4

51-52 * Q1: Newport Isle of Wight (H) 2-3

52-53 * Q1: Winchester City (A) 0-1

53-54 * Q1: Alton Town (A) 2-3

54-55 * Q2: Cowes Isle of Wight (H) 2-1
Q3: Winchester City (A) 0-3

55-56 * Q1: Andover (A) 0-5

56-57 * Q1: Cowes Isle of Wight (A) 4-1
Q2: Winchester City (A) 0-3

57-58 * Q2: Chichester City (A) 3-5

58-59 * Q1: Fareham Town (A) 2-6

59-60 * Q1: Andover (A) 0-0, (H) 0-1

70-71 Q1: Alton Town (H) 5-1
Q2: Waterlooville (H) 2-3

71-72 PR: Newport I.O.W. (H) 0-0, (A) 0-4

72-73 Q1: Ryde Sports (H) 2-0
Q2: Alton Town (A) 1-8

73-74 Q1: Chichester City (H) 8-0
Q2: Alton Town (H) 1-1, (A) 1-2

74-75 Q1: Ryde Sports (H) 7-1
Q2: Alton Town (A) 2-2, (H) 0-1

75-76 Q1: Cowes (A) 2-0
Q2: Newport I.O.W. (H) 2-2, (A) 1-1, 2-0
Q3: Waterlooville (A) 0-4

76-77 Q1: Fareham Town (A) 1-1, (H) 0-5

77-78 Q1: Hungerford Town (H) 0-0, (A) 0-3

79-80 PR: Andover (H) 2-1
Q1: Swaythling (A) 4-1
Q2: Eastbourne United (H) 1-0
Q3: Fareham Town (A) 0-1

80-81 Q1: Hastings United (H) 0-0, (A) 4-3
Q2: Lewes (H) 2-1
Q3: Croydon (A) 1-0
Q4: Windsor & Eton (A) 0-2

81-82 Q1: Melksham Town (H) 0-1

82-83 Q1: Bracknell Town (H) 1-0
Q2: A.F.C. Totton (H) 2-2, (A) 1-2

83-84 Q1: Romsey Town (A) 2-0
Q2: Sholing Sports (A) 0-0, (H) 4-0
Q3: Wokingham Town (A) 1-2

84-85 Q1: Hungerford Town (A) 1-2

85-86 Q1: Bristol M.F. (A) 1-1, (H) 2-2, (H) 4-3
Q2: Oxford City (A) 1-2

86-87 Q1: Newport I.O.W. (H) 1-1, (A) 2-3

87-88 Q1: Yeovil Town (H) 0-1

88-89 Q1: Thatcham Town (A) 3-1
Q2: Thame United (A) 3-1
Q3: Waterlooville (H) 0-1

89-90 Q1: Hungerford Town (H) 2-0
Q2: Swanage Town & H. (H) 1-1, (A) 2-0
Q3: Poole Town (A) 0-1

90-91 Q1: Stroud (A) 1-4

91-92 PR: Clevedon Town (H) 1-3

92-93 PR: Calne Town (H) 0-4

GOTHIC (NORWICH)

Currently: Defunct

46-47 Q1: Gorleston (H) 1-1, (A) 6-0
Q2: Lowestoft Town (A) 5-2
Q3: Leiston (H) 4-4, (A) 2-0
Q4: Colchester United (H - *played away*) 1-5

47-48 Q1: Sheringham (H) 3-1
Q2: Leiston (H) 3-1
Q3: Great Yarmouth Town (H) 2-3

48-49 Q1: Leiston (H) 5-2
Q2: Achilles (H) 4-0
Q3: Great Yarmouth Town (H) 3-2
Q4: Cambridge Town (A) 1-6

49-50 Q1: Lowestoft Town (H) 1-3

50-51 PR: Sheringham (A) 3-0
Q1: Great Yarmouth Town (A) 0-3

51-52 Q1: Sheringham (A) 2-0
Q2: Great Yarmouth Town (A) 3-0
Q3: Gorleston (A) 0-5

52-53 Q1: Wymondham Town (H) 6-0
Q2: Great Yarmouth Town (H) 0-5

53-54 Q1: Gorleston (H) 1-10

54-55 Q1: Cromer (H) 7-2
Q2: Beccles (A) 1-3

66-67 Q1: Lowestoft Town (A) 0-6

67-68 Q1: Clacton Town (A) 2-3

68-69 Q1: Sudbury Town (A) 0-4

69-70 Q1: Harwich & Parkeston (H) 0-1

GRANTHAM TOWN

Currently: Southern League
* - As Grantham F.C.

45-46 * Q2: Basford United (H) 6-1
Q3: Ollerton Colliery (H) 2-1
Q4: Bedford Avenue (H) 6-1
R1: Kettering T. (A) 5-1, (H) 2-2 (*agg: 7-3*)
R2: Mansfield T. (H) 1-2, (A) 1-2 (*agg: 2-4*)

46-47 * Q2: Boston United (H) 1-2

47-48 * Q1: Spalding United (A) 4-0
Q2: Basford United (H) 7-0
Q3: Ilkeston Town (H) 11-1
Q4: Goole Town (H) 3-3, (A) 3-2
R1: Stockton (A) 1-2

48-49 * PR: Gedling Colliery (H) 3-1
Q1: Raleigh Athletic (H) 6-0
Q2: Linby Colliery (A) 2-1
Q3: Ransome & Marles (A) 0-2

49-50 * PR: Linby Colliery (A) 2-1
Q1: Boston United (A) 3-2
Q2: South Normanton Miners Welf. (A) 3-0
Q3: Spalding United (A) 2-0
Q4: Gainsborough Trinity (H) 2-0
R1: Wrexham (A) 1-4

50-51 * PR: Heanor Athletic (H) 5-1
Q1: Boston United (H) 0-0, (A) 1-4

51-52 * Q4: Ilkeston Town (A) 1-2

52-53 * Q1: Bourne Town (A) 5-0
Q2: Skegness Town (A) 0-2

53-54 * Q1: Ashby Institute (H) 2-2, (A) 1-2

54-55 * Q1: Barton Town (H) 5-2
Q2: Boston United (H) 2-2, (A) 0-1

55-56 * Q1: Ashby Institute (H) 4-2
Q2: Alford United (A) 3-0
Q3: Skegness Town (H) 3-3, (A) 0-3

56-57 * Q1: Skegness Town (H) 2-1
Q2: Bourne Town (A) 8-2
Q3: Alford United (A) 2-1
Q4: Boston United (A) 3-6

57-58 * Q1: Skegness Town (A) 1-1, (H) 2-0
Q2: Brigg Town (A) 1-1, (H) 2-0
Q3: Alford United (A) 0-1

58-59 * Q1: Gainsborough Trinity (H) 1-4

59-60 * Q1: Skegness Town (A) 0-5

60-61 * Q1: Skegness Town (H) 3-4

61-62 * Q1: Holbeach United (A) 2-0
Q2: Louth United (H) 2-1
Q3: Skegness Town (H) 3-1
Q4: Hinckley Athletic (H) 2-1
R1: Brierley Hill Alliance (A) 0-3

62-63 * Q1: Louth United (H) 5-2
Q2: Boston United (A) 2-3

63-64 * Q1: Louth United (H) 3-0
Q2: Holbeach United (H) 2-0
Q3: Stamford (H) 4-2
Q4: Kettering Town (A) 1-3

64-65 * Q2: Holbeach United (H) 1-1, (A) 1-0
Q3: Spalding United (A) 0-4

65-66 * Q1: Spalding United (H) 3-0
Q2: Boston (H) 7-0
Q3: Skegness Town (A) 7-0
Q4: Heanor Town (H) 4-4, (A) 2-1
R1: Hendon (H) 4-1
R2: Swindon Town (H) 1-4

66-67 * Q4: Boston United (A) 4-1
R1: Wimbledon (H) 2-1
R2: Oldham Athletic (H) 0-4

67-68 * Q4: Retford Town (A) 4-4, (H) 3-1
R1: Altrincham (H) 0-3

68-69 * Q4: Boston United (A) 2-2, (H) 2-1
R1: Chelmsford City (H) 2-1
R2: Swindon Town (H) 0-2

69-70 * Q4: Gainsborough Trinity (H) 5-0
R1: Oldham Athletic (A) 1-3

70-71 * Q4: Gainsborough Trin. (H) 1-1, (A) 3-3, 2-1
R1: Stockport County (H) 2-1
R2: Rotherham United (H) 1-4

71-72 * Q4: Frickley Colliery (A) 0-3

72-73 * Q4: Gainsborough Trinity (A) 2-1
R1: Bradford City (A) 0-3

73-74 * Q4: Kettering Town (H) 3-1
R1: Hillingdon Borough (A) 4-0
R2: Rochdale (H) 1-1, (A) 5-3
R3: Middlesbrough (H) 0-2

74-75 * Q4: Nuneaton Borough (A) 1-1, (H) 2-3

75-76 * Q4: Leek Town (H) 4-0
R1: Port Vale (H) 2-2, (A) 1-4

76-77 * Q4: Altrincham (A) 0-1

77-78 * Q4: Burton Albion (H) 0-2

78-79 * Q1: Ashby Institute (H) 5-3
Q2: Boston (A) 1-0
Q3: Worksop Town (A) 0-0, (H) 0-3

79-80 * Q1: St Neots Town (A) 2-4

80-81 * Q1: Long Eaton U. (A) 0-0, (H) 2-2, (A) 3-0
Q2: Boston United (H) 1-3

81-82 * Q1: Eastwood Town (H) 1-0
Q2: Corby Town (H) 0-1

82-83 * Q1: Hinckley Athletic (H) 2-0
Q2: Winterton Rangers (A) 0-0, (H) 4-0
Q3: Armitage (H) 3-1
Q4: Telford United (A) 0-3

83-84 * Q1: Rushall Olympic (A) 1-1, (H) 3-0
Q2: Gainsborough Trinity (A) 0-2

84-85 * Q1: Halesowen Town (H) 0-2

85-86 * Q1: Oldbury United (A) 1-1, (H) 2-1
Q2: Mile Oak Rovers & Youth (A) 3-1
Q3: Atherstone United (H) 0-2

86-87 * Q1: Wednesfield Social (H) 5-1
Q2: Rothwell Town (A) 1-0
Q3: Gainsborough Trinity (H) 1-2

87-88 * PR: Chatteris Town (H) 2-2, (A) 0-1

88-89 * PR: Borrowash Victoria (H) 2-1
Q1: North Ferriby United (A) 2-3

89-90 PR: Eastwood Town (A) 2-1
Q1: Louth United (H) 2-1
Q2: Boston (A) 2-1
Q3: Goole Town (A) 1-2

90-91 Q1: Hinckley Athletic (A) 1-2

91-92 PR: Ilkeston Town (H) 1-5

92-93 PR: Hucknall Town (A) 1-2

GRAVESEND & NORTHFLEET

Currently: Southern League

45-46 Q1: Erith & Belvedere (A) 3-3, (H) 4-1
Q2: Bromley (A) 0-2

46-47 PR: Erith & Belvedere (A) 3-3, (H) 4-1
Q1: Lloyds (Sittingbourne) (A) 4-1
Q2: Ashford (A) 1-1, (H) 3-2
Q3: Folkestone (A) 2-1
Q4: Walthamstow Avenue (H) 1-0
R1: Gillingham (A) 1-4

47-48 PR: Dover (A) 5-1
Q1: Ashford (H) 4-0
Q2: Dartford (H) 0-1

48-49 PR: Sittingbourne (H) 3-1
Q1: Bromley (H) 4-1
Q2: Dover (H) 4-1
Q3: Dartford (H) 0-1

49-50 PR: Sheppey United (H) 4-0
Q1: Ramsgate Athletic (A) 0-0, (H) 2-1
Q2: Canterbury City (H) 5-1
Q3: Dover (H) 5-0
Q4: Corby Town (A) 6-1
R1: Torquay United (H) 1-3

50-51 PR: Sheppey United (H) 5-2
Q1: Tonbridge (A) 0-1

51-52 PR: Maidstone United (H) 2-2, (A) 3-0
Q1: Betteshanger Colliery Welfare (A) 1-3

52-53 PR: Margate (A) 4-1
Q1: Bromley (A) 1-0
Q2: Sittingbourne (H) 3-0
Q3: Dover (H) 2-1
Q4: Wimbledon (A) 2-4

53-54 PR: Margate (A) 1-5

54-55 PR: Folkestone Town (H) 4-1
Q1: Tonbridge (H) 1-2

55-56 PR: Dartford (A) 3-0
Q1: Margate (H) 1-2

56-57 PR: Dartford (A) 2-2, (H) 3-2
Q1: Betteshanger Colliery Welfare (H) 7-1
Q2: Sittingbourne (A) 0-1

57-58 PR: Ashford Town (H) 3-1
Q1: Sittingbourne (H) 3-1
Q2: Dartford (A) 1-0
Q3: Whitstable (A) 3-0
Q4: Guildford City (A) 1-1, (H) 0-1

58-59 Q1: Sheppey United (A) 6-2
Q2: Dartford (H) 1-1, (A) 4-2
Q3: Sittingbourne (A) 4-4, (H) 2-0
Q4: Margate (H) 0-0, (A) 2-4

59-60 Q1: Tonbridge (H) 2-0
Q2: Bexleyheath & Welling (H) 4-3
Q3: Tunbridge Wells United (A) 3-0
Q4: Ashford Town (H) 1-2

60-61 Q1: Maidstone United (A) 1-2

61-62 Q1: Bexleyheath & Welling (H) 2-2, (A) 1-4

62-63 Q1: Chatham Town (H) 2-1
Q2: Sutton United (H) 2-1
Q3: Erith & Belvedere (H) 5-0
Q4: Lewes (H) 1-0
R1: Exeter City (H) 3-2
R2: Wycombe Wanderers (H) 3-1
R3: Carlisle United (A) 1-0
R4: Sunderland (H) 1-1, (A) 2-5

63-64 Q4: Lewes (H) 2-1
R1: Tooting & Mitcham United (A) 2-1
R2: Brentford (A) 0-1

64-65 Q4: Margate (H) 1-0
R1: Bournemouth & Boscombe Ath. (A) 0-7

65-66 Q4: Crawley Town (H) 1-0
R1: Wimbledon (A) 1-4

66-67 Q4: Folkestone Town (A) 2-3

67-68 Q1: Dartford (A) 0-4

68-69 Q1: Cray Wanderers (H) 1-3

69-70 Q1: Redhill (H) 0-1

70-71 Q1: Chatham Town (A) 4-1
Q2: Tonbridge (H) 0-1

71-72 Q1: Southall (H) 2-2, (A) 1-3

72-73 Q1: St Albans City (H) 1-1, (A) 0-1

73-74 Q1: Walthamstow Avenue (H) 6-1
Q2: Maidenhead United (H) 2-3

74-75 Q1: Romford (A) 0-2

75-76 PR: Chertsey Town (H) 1-1, (A) 2-0
Q1: Walthamstow Avenue (A) 1-2

76-77 Q1: Maidstone United (H) 0-0, (A) 0-3

77-78 PR: Staines Town (H) 4-0
Q1: Berkhamsted Town (A) 5-0
Q2: Enfield (A) 1-2

78-79 PR: Aveley (H) 6-2
Q1: Welling United (A) 2-1
Q2: Walthamstow Avenue (A) 3-2
Q3: Dulwich Hamlet (H) 1-1, (A) 1-0
Q4: Eastbourne United (H) 3-1
R1: Wimbledon (H) 0-0, (A) 0-1

79-80 Q1: East Grinstead (A) 4-1
Q2: Eastbourne Town (A) 2-0
Q3: Ramsgate (A) 2-2, (H) 2-1
Q4: Welling United (H) 2-1
R1: Torquay United (H) 0-1

80-81 Q4: Aveley (H) 4-0
R1: St Albans City (H) 1-2

81-82 Q4: Dagenham (H) 0-0, (A) 3-6

82-83 Q4: Maidstone United (H) 1-2

83-84 Q1: Herne Bay (A) 3-1
Q2: Bromley (A) 4-0
Q3: Ashford Town (H) 1-1, (A) 2-3

84-85 Q1: Walton & Hersham (A) 1-0
Q2: Egham Town (A) 0-1

85-86 Q1: Littlehampton T. (A - *played home*) 2-1
Q2: Sutton United (A) 1-0
Q3: Bromley (H) 2-3

86-87 Q1: Crawley Town (A) 0-1

87-88 PR: Three Bridges (A) 0-0, (H) 2-1
Q1: Herne Bay (H) 6-1
Q2: Witham Town (H) 1-0
Q3: Carshalton Athletic (H) 2-6

88-89 PR: Tunbridge Wells (H) 2-1
Q1: Hertford Town (H) 1-3

89-90 Q1: Harrow Borough (A) 2-1
Q2: Berkhamsted Town (H) 1-0
Q3: Wycombe W. (A) 1-1, (H) 1-1, (H) 0-3

90-91 Q1: Margate (A) 2-2, (H) 1-4

91-92 Q1: Canterbury City (H) 2-1
Q2: Dorking (A) 4-3
Q3: Burgess Hill Town (A) 1-0
Q4: Harlow Town (H) 1-1, (A) 0-1

92-93 Q1: Chertsey Town (A) 2-3

GRAYS ATHLETIC

Currently: Isthmian League

45-46 Q1: Leyton (A) 1-1, (H) 0-3

46-47 PR: Romford (A) 1-2

47-48 EX: Upminster (A) 1-0
PR: Ilford (H) 3-2
Q1: West Thurrock Athletic (H) 3-0
Q2: Ekco (H) 1-0
Q3: Barking (A) 2-0
Q4: Banbury Spencer (H) 0-1

48-49 PR: Romford (A) 0-3

49-50 EX: Stansted (A) 5-0
PR: Colchester Casuals (A - *played home*) 5-1
Q1: Ilford (A) 2-1
Q2: Barking (A) 0-4

50-51 PR: Romford (A) 1-7

51-52 Q1: Brentwood & Warley (H) 1-2

52-53 Q1: Harwich & Parkeston (H) 6-2
Q2: Dagenham (A) 1-0
Q3: Clacton Town (H) 2-1
Q4: King's Lynn (H) 0-0, (A) 2-0
R1: Llanelly (H) 0-5

53-54 Q4: Peterborough United (A) 1-4

54-55 PR: Leyton (A) 0-2

55-56 PR: Chelmsford City (H) 1-0
Q1: Briggs Sports (A) 0-0, (H) 0-0, (A) 0-1

56-57 PR: Romford (A) 2-4

Above: *Grays Athletic's most notable F.A. Cup achievement was their 1-0 away win over Barnet, then G.M.V. Conference leaders, in 1988. In this action, defenders Ian Brown (left) and Barry Fox sandwich a Barnet player.*

57-58	PR: Dagenham (H) 2-1 Q1: Ilford (A) 3-4
58-59	Q1: Woodford Town (H) 0-1
59-60	Q1: Tilbury (H) 2-1 Q2: Ilford (H) 2-2, (A) 4-2 Q3: Leyton (A) 1-1, (H) 6-2 Q4: Chelmsford City (H) 1-3
60-61	Q1: Barking (H) 2-3
61-62	Q1: Brentwood & Warley (H) 3-2 Q2: Ilford (H) 3-1 Q3: Tilbury (H) 1-1, (A) 1-2
62-63	Q1: Tilbury (H) 1-2
63-64	Q1: Tilbury (H) 1-3
64-65	Q1: Brentwood & Warley (H) 0-2
65-66	Q1: Hornchurch (H) 1-0 Q2: Barking (A) 1-0 Q3: Walthamstow Avenue (H) 1-3
66-67	Q1: Maidenhead United (H) 0-0, (A) 1-3
67-68	Q1: Ilford (A) 0-1
68-69	Q1: Southall (H) 1-4
69-70	Q1: Hampton (A) 2-1 Q2: Enfield (A) 1-7
70-71	PR: Ware (A) 1-0 Q1: Windsor & Eton (A) 1-0 Q2: Bexley United (A) 3-1 Q3: Leatherhead (A) 0-3
71-72	Q1: Sutton United (H) 2-4
73-74	PR: Kingstonian (A) 0-4
74-75	Q1: Bexley United (A) 1-0 Q2: Erith & Belvedere (H) 0-1
75-76	PR: Barnet (H) 1-2
76-77	Q1: Corinthian-Casuals (A) 1-0 Q2: Aveley (A) 0-1
77-78	Q1: Hillingdon Borough (H) 1-1, (A) 1-4
78-79	PR: Cheshunt (H) 5-1 Q1: Wembley (A) 0-0, (H) 4-1 Q2: Leyton-Wingate (A) 0-2
79-80	PR: Aylesbury United (H) 0-2
80-81	Q1: Erith & Belvedere (H) 0-0, (A) 3-1 Q2: Dartford (H) 2-0 Q3: Aveley (H) 0-1
81-82	Q1: St Albans City (A) 1-2
82-83	Q1: Barton Rovers (H) 1-0 Q2: Chelmsford City (A) 2-3
83-84	Q1: Staines Town (A) 0-1
84-85	PR: Crockenhill (A) 3-0 Q1: St Albans City (H) 3-0 Q2: Sutton United (H) 3-1 Q3: Wealdstone (H) 2-1 Q4: Dartford (H) 1-3
85-86	Q1: Burnham (H) *W/O* Q2: Aveley (H) 2-1 Q3: Aylesbury (H) 2-2, (A - *at Tring T.*) 0-1
86-87	Q1: Hitchin Town (H) 6-1 Q2: Woodford Town (A) 1-2
87-88	Q1: Hertford Town (H) 1-3
88-89	Q1: Tiptree United (H) 5-0 Q2: Barking (H) 1-1, (A) 3-0 Q3: Barnet (A) 1-0 Q4: Dudley Town (A) 3-3, (H) 2-0 R1: Bath City (A) 0-2
89-90	Q1: Heybridge Swifts (A) 1-2
90-91	Q1: Corinthian-Casuals (A) 5-1 Q2: Flackwell Heath (A) 2-2, (H) 2-0 Q3: Dagenham (A) 1-3
91-92	Q1: East Thurrock Utd (A) 1-1, (H) 2-1 Q2: Redbridge Forest (H) 3-1 Q3: Lowestoft Town (A) 2-1 Q4: Atherstone United (H) 0-2
92-93	Q1: Chelmsford City (A) 0-0, (H) 2-1 Q2: Sudbury Town (H) 1-0 Q3: Newmarket Town (A) 0-1

GREAT HARWOOD

Currently: Defunct

46-47	PR: Horwich R.M.I. (H) 2-6
47-48	PR: Fleetwood (A) 1-7
48-49	PR: Clitheroe (A) 2-5
49-50	PR: Bacup Borough (H) 1-1, (A) 1-5
50-51	PR: Horwich R.M.I. (H) 1-4
51-52	Q1: Fleetwood (H) 0-5
52-53	Q1: Morecambe (A) 0-1
53-54	Q1: Lancaster City (H) 1-4
54-55	Q1: Netherfield (H) 2-3
64-65	Q1: Rossendale United (A) 0-1
65-66	Q1: Hyde United (H) 1-4
67-68	Q1: Leyland Motors (H) 3-1 Q2: Netherfield (A) 2-1 Q3: Lancaster City (H) 3-1 Q4: Altrincham (H) 0-1
68-69	Q1: Clitheroe (A) 0-0, (H) 0-1
69-70	Q1: Netherfield (H) 1-3
70-71	Q1: Leyland Motors (H) 5-2 Q2: Lancaster City (A) 1-1, (H) 3-0 Q3: Penrith (H) 3-2 Q4: Altrincham (A) 1-1, (H) 2-1 R1: Rotherham United (H) 2-6
71-72	Q1: Prescot Town (H) 7-1 Q2: Ashton United (A) 2-3
72-73	Q1: Clitheroe (H) 4-1 Q2: Netherfield (H) 5-0 Q3: Lancaster City (A) 0-1
73-74	Q1: South Liverpool (H) 0-1
74-75	Q1: Ashton United (A) 0-1
75-76	PR: Burscough (H) 2-1 Q1: Prestwich Heys (A) 1-0 Q2: Prescot Town (H) 5-1 Q3: Droylsden (H) 1-1, (A) 1-1, 0-1
76-77	Q1: Darwen (H) 1-1, (A) 3-0 Q2: Mossley (H) 6-0 Q3: Formby (A) 0-0, (H) 3-0 Q4: Morecambe (A) 0-2
77-78	Q1: Prestwich Heys (H) 1-1, (A) 5-1 Q2: Burscough (H) 0-1

GREAT HARWOOD TOWN

Currently: Northern Premier League

90-91	PR: Harrogate Town (H) 2-2, (A) 1-2
91-92	PR: Eccleshill United (H) 6-0 Q1: Morecambe (A) 0-1
92-93	PR: Prescot A.F.C. (H) 2-1 Q1: Atherton L.R. (A) 1-1, (H) 1-2

GREAT YARMOUTH TOWN

Currently: Eastern Counties League

46-47	Q1: Old Grammarians (Ipswich) (H) 5-1 Q2: Leiston (A) 1-3
47-48	Q1: Norwich C.E.Y.M.S. (A) 6-1 Q2: Lowestoft Town (A) 3-2 Q3: Gothic (A) 3-2 Q4: Bury Town (H) 3-0 R1: Shrewsbury Town (H) 1-4
48-49	Q1: Stowmarket Corinthians (H) 3-2 Q2: Lowestoft Town (H) 2-0 Q3: Gothic (A) 2-3
49-50	PR: Cromer (H) 1-1, (A) 4-3 Q1: Whitton United (H) 4-1 Q2: Lowestoft Town (A) 2-3
50-51	PR: City of Norwich School O.B.U. (H) 3-2 Q1: Gothic (H) 3-0 Q2: Stowmarket (H) 2-1 Q3: Lowestoft Town (A) 2-1 Q4: Tooting & Mitcham United (A) 3-5

51-52 Q1: Bungay Town (H) 4-2
Q2: Gothic (H) 0-3

52-53 Q1: Cromer (H) 13-0
Q2: Gothic (A) 5-0
Q3: Beccles (H) 2-1
Q4: Bury Town (H) 2-0
R1: Guildford City (A) 2-2, (H) 1-0
R2: Wrexham (H) 1-2

53-54 Q4: Chelmsford City (A) 0-0, (H) 1-0
R1: Crystal Palace (H) 1-0
R2: Barrow (A) 2-5

54-55 Q4: Barnet (A) 0-2

55-56 Q1: Sheringham (A) 0-0, (H) 3-2
Q2: Gorleston (H) 2-0
Q3: Beccles (A) 4-1
Q4: March Town United (A) 0-1

56-57 Q1: Gorleston (H) 5-1
Q2: Sheringham (A) 2-0
Q3: Bungay Town (A) 4-1
Q4: Walthamstow Avenue (A) 0-6

57-58 Q1: Bungay Town (A) 2-0
Q2: Beccles (H) 4-0
Q3: Gorleston (A) 2-3

58-59 Q1: Thetford Town (H) 4-4, (A) 3-3, 5-4
Q2: Bungay Town (H) 2-1
Q3: King's Lynn (H) 0-1

59-60 Q1: Thetford Town (A) 4-2
Q2: Lowestoft Town (H) 6-2
Q3: Bungay Town (A) 4-1
Q4: Walthamstow Avenue (A) 1-2

60-61 Q1: Lowestoft Town (A) 1-4

61-62 Q1: Gorleston (H) 1-0
Q2: Lowestoft Town (H) 2-0
Q3: Harwich & Parkeston (A) 1-5

62-63 Q1: Bungay Town (H) 3-2
Q2: Harwich & Parkeston (H) 1-3

63-64 Q2: Bungay Town (A) 2-2, (H) 2-1
Q3: Harwich & Parkeston (A) 1-2

64-65 Q1: Sudbury Town (A) 0-1

65-66 Q1: Gorleston (H) 6-4
Q2: Lowestoft Town (A) 2-4

66-67 Q1: Haverhill Rovers (H) 0-3

67-68 Q1: Lowestoft Town (A) 0-3

68-69 Q1: Bury Town (H) 0-0, (A) 0-1

69-70 PR: Harwich & Parkeston (H) 0-1

70-71 Q1: Gorleston (H) 2-2, (A) 1-2

71-72 Q1: Harwich & Parkeston (H) 1-3

72-73 Q1: Ely City (H) 2-2, (A) 1-3

73-74 Q1: March Town Utd (A) 2-2, (H) 2-2, 1-0
Q2: Harwich & Parkeston (H) 1-2

74-75 Q1: Lowestoft Town (H) 3-3, (A) 2-3

75-76 Q1: Holbeach United (H) 1-0
Q2: St Neots Town (H) 3-2
Q3: Spalding United (A) 0-2

76-77 Q1: Sudbury Town (A) 1-1, (H) 0-1

77-78 Q1: Soham Town Rangers (A) 2-0
Q2: Lowestoft Town (A) 1-5

78-79 Q1: Harwich & Parkeston (H) 1-1, (A) 1-4

79-80 PR: Chelmsford City (H) 1-3

80-81 PR: Chatteris Town (A) 1-1, (H) 3-2
Q1: St Neots Town (A) 1-0
Q2: Bourne Town (A) 2-0
Q3: Harwich & Parkeston (A) 0-1

81-82 PR: Saffron Walden Town (H) 4-0
Q1: Parson Drove United (H) 3-2
Q2: Lowestoft Town (H) 3-1
Q3: King's Lynn (A) 1-5

82-83 PR: Ampthill Town (H) 2-0
Q1: Chatteris Town (A) 6-1
Q2: Wellingborough T. (H) 1-1, (A) 0-2

83-84 Q1: Holbeach United (H) 3-1
Q2: Chelmsford City (A) 2-4

84-85 PR: Bury Town (A) 0-3

85-86 PR: Burnham & Hillingdon (H) 2-0
Q1: Heybridge Swifts (H) 0-1

86-87 PR: Hoddesdon Town (A - *at Ware*) 2-0
Q1: Newmarket Town (A) 0-2

87-88 PR: Tilbury (H) 0-0, (A) 2-0
Q1: Clapton (A) 2-1
Q2: Cambridge City (H) 3-1
Q3: Uxbridge (A) 2-0
Q4: Dagenham (H) 0-2

88-89 Q1: Milton Keynes Borough (H) 3-0
Q2: Kettering Town (H) 0-3

89-90 PR: Stevenage Borough (H) 0-2

90-91 PR: Langford (H) 2-2, (A) 1-0
Q1: Finchley (A) 2-1
Q2: Cambridge City (H) 0-4

91-92 PR: Mirrlees Blackstone (A) 1-2

92-93 PR: Purfleet (A) 1-4

GREEN WAVES

Currently: Plymouth & District League

50-51 PR: Truro City (H) 2-3

GRESLEY ROVERS

Currently: Southern League

45-46 Q2: Bye
Q3: Coalville Town (H) 0-7

46-47 Q2: Brush Sports (A) 0-7

47-48 Q1: Nuneaton Borough (H) 3-2
Q2: Coalville Town Amateur (H) 3-0
Q3: Brush Sports (A) 1-5

48-49 Q1: Hinckley Athletic (H) 4-3
Q2: Whitwick Colliery (H) 0-3

49-50 Q1: Hinckley Athletic (A) 3-1
Q2: Brush Sports (H) 3-2
Q3: Nuneaton Borough (A) 2-2, (H) 2-3

50-51 Q1: Bedworth Town (H) 0-2

51-52 Q1: Long Eaton Town (A) 1-1, (H) 0-2

52-53 Q1: Gedling Colliery (H) 3-1
Q2: Ilkeston Town (H) 0-5

53-54 Q1: Ilkeston Town (H) 3-2
Q2: Matlock Town (H) 2-0
Q3: South Normanton Miners Welfare (H) 5-1
Q4: Nuneaton Borough (A) 1-4

54-55 Q1: Basford United (A) 7-1
Q2: Gedling Colliery (H) 3-2
Q3: Ilkeston Town (H) 2-2, (A) 4-5

55-56 Q2: Boots Athletic (H) 0-1

56-57 Q1: Belper Town (H) 7-3
Q2: Clay Cross & Danesmoor M.W. (A) 1-3

57-58 Q1: Matlock Town (A) 3-2
Q2: Boots Athletic (A) 3-1
Q3: Belper Town (A) 1-2

58-59 Q1: Tamworth (H) 1-3

59-60 Q1: Atherstone Town (H) 2-2, (A) 0-2

62-63 Q1: Tamworth (H) 2-2, (A) 1-4

63-64 Q1: Loughborough United (H) 1-3

64-65 Q1: Atherstone Town (H) 3-5

65-66 Q1: Ilkeston Town (H) 0-2

66-67 Q1: Belper Town (A) 2-4

67-68 Q1: Long Eaton United (A) 0-2

68-69 Q1: Arnold (H) 1-0
Q2: Atherstone Town (H) 0-2

69-70 PR: Long Eaton United (H) 3-0
Q1: Belper Town (A) 3-0
Q2: Burton Albion (H) 0-3

70-71 PR: Atherstone Town (H) 0-1

71-72 Q1: Stafford Rangers (H) 0-4

72-73 Q1: Warley (H) 0-1

73-74 Q1: Nuneaton Borough (A) 0-3

74-75 Q1: Hednesford (H) 1-0
Q2: Burton Albion (A) 0-0, (H) 0-1

75-76 Q1: Alfreton Town (A) 0-2

76-77 Q1: Telford United (A) 1-3

77-78 Q1: Sutton Town (H) 2-2, (A) 1-2

78-79 Q1: Dudley Town (A) 0-3

79-80 Q1: Burton Albion (H) 1-3

80-81 PR: Highgate United (H) 1-1, (A) 1-3

81-82 PR: Redditch United (H) 2-1
Q1: R.C. Warwick (H) 1-1, (A) 3-1
Q2: Willenhall Town (H) 3-3, (A) 0-1

82-83 PR: Worksop Town (H) 2-4

83-84 PR: Boston (A) 3-1
Q1: Coleshill Town (A) 3-1
Q2: Eastwood Town (H) 0-1

84-85 PR: Walsall Borough (A) 4-1
Q1: Lincoln United (H) 6-1
Q2: Goole Town (H) 0-2

85-86 PR: Friar Lane Old Boys (H) 8-0
Q1: Oldswinford (A) 2-2, (H) 5-3
Q2: Worksop Town (H) 1-0
Q3: Alfreton Town (A) 1-0
Q4: Leyton-Wingate (A) 0-2

86-87 PR: Wolverton Town (H) 0-1

87-88 PR: Tamworth (A) 2-3

88-89 PR: Paget Rangers (H) 2-0
Q1: Gainsborough Trin. (A) 2-2, (H) 3-1
Q2: Hinckley Town (A) 0-1

89-90 PR: Chadderton (A) 2-1
Q1: Witton Albion (H) 2-2, (A) 0-1

90-91 PR: Borrowash Victoria (A) 2-1
Q1: Worksop Town (A - *at Gainsborough*) 0-2

91-92 Q1: Raunds Town (A) 1-1, (H) 2-0
Q2: V.S. Rugby (H) 3-3, (A) 0-3

92-93 PR: Highgate United (H) 4-2
Q1: Newcastle Town (A) 1-0
Q2: Gainsborough Trinity (H) 1-4

Below: *Highgate United goalkeeper Mick Chapman claims a cross under pressure from Gresley's Stuart Evans (left) and Keiron Smith in the 1992 Preliminary Round. Photo: Derrick Kinsey.*

GRETNA

Currently: Northern Premier League

83-84 PR: Consett (H) 3-1
Q1: Annfield Plain (H) 1-0
Q2: Brandon United (A) 0-1

84-85 Q1: Darwen (A) 2-1
Q2: Peterlee Newtown (A) 0-0, (H) 2-0
Q3: Bishop Auckland (H) 0-2

85-86 Q1: Lancaster City (A) 4-0
Q2: Tow Law Town (A) 1-0
Q3: Morecambe (H) 0-2

86-87 Q1: Horden Colliery Welfare (H) 6-1
Q2: Fleetwood Town (A) 3-1
Q3: Blyth Spartans (H) 5-2
Q4: Spennymoor United (A) 0-2

87-88 Q1: Ferryhill Athletic (A) 2-1
Q2: Fleetwood Town (H) 1-2

88-89 Q1: Chester-le-Street Town (H) 5-0
Q2: Whitley Bay (H) 1-1, (A) 0-1

89-90 Q1: Tow Law Town (H) 3-5

90-91 Q1: Norton & Stockton Ancients (H) 5-1
Q2: Guisborough Town (H) 2-2, (A) 3-1
Q3: Accrington Stanley (A) 1-2

91-92 Q1: Cleator Moor Celtic (A) 7-0
Q2: Bedlington Terriers (H) 3-1
Q3: Murton (H) 3-0
Q4: Stalybridge Celtic (H) 3-2
R1: Rochdale (H) 0-0, (A) 1-3

Left: *Gretna created Cup history in 1991 when they became the first Scottish club for a century to compete in the Competition Proper. The tie against Rochdale received huge media coverage, including screening on B.B.C.'s 'Match of the Day', and this photo shows Tony Nelson spectacularly challenging 'Dale goalkeeper Gareth Gray. Photo: Alan Watson.*

92-93 Q1: Spennymoor United (A) 0-4

GRIMETHORPE ATHLETIC

Currently: Defunct
* - As Grimethorpe Rovers

45-46 * Q1: Denaby United (H) 1-5

46-47 * PR: Wombwell Main Colliery (A) 2-2, (H) *W/O*
Q1: Rawmarsh Welfare (A) 0-4

47-48 EX: Barton Town (A) 4-3
PR: Thurnscoe Victoria (A) *W/O*
Q1: Lysaght's Sports (H) 4-2
Q2: Norton Woodseats (A) 1-7

48-49 PR: Norton Woodseats (A) 1-2

49-50 PR: Beighton Miners Welfare (A) 1-5

50-51 PR: Stocksbridge Works (H) 1-2

51-52 Q1: South Kirkby Colliery (A) 0-4

52-53 Q1: Sheffield (H) 3-1
Q2: Denaby United (A) 0-1

GRIMSBY TOWN

Currently: Football League

45-46 R3: Sunderland (H) 1-3, (A) 1-2 *(agg: 2-5)*

46-47 R3: Reading (A) 2-2, (H) 3-1
R4: Liverpool (A) 0-2

47-48 R3: Everton (H) 1-4

48-49 R3: Exeter City (H) 2-1
R4: Hull City (H) 2-3

49-50 R3: Luton Town (A) 4-3
R4: Portsmouth (A) 0-5

50-51 R3: Exeter City (H) 3-3, (A) 2-4

51-52 R1: Darlington (H) 4-0
R2: Lincoln City (A) 1-3

52-53 R1: Darlington (A) 3-2
R2: Bath City (H) 1-0
R3: Bury (H) 1-3

53-54 R1: Rochdale (H) 2-0
R2: Witton Albion (A) 1-1, (H) 6-1
R3: Fulham (H) 5-5, (A) 0-0 *abandoned after 45 minutes*, (A) 1-3

54-55 R1: Halifax Town (H) 2-1
R2: Southampton (H) 4-1
R3: Wolverhampton Wanderers (H) 2-5

55-56 R1: Netherfield (A) 5-1
R2: Southport (A) 0-0, (H) 3-2
R3: Portsmouth (A) 1-3

56-57 R3: West Ham United (A) 3-5

57-58 R3: Sheffield United (A) 1-5

58-59 R3: Manchester City (H) 2-2, (A) 2-1
R4: Nottingham Forest (A) 1-4

59-60 R1: Rhyl (A) 2-1
R2: Wrexham (H) 2-3

60-61 R1: Darlington (A) 0-2

61-62 R1: Mansfield Town (A) 2-3

62-63 R3: Leicester City (H) 1-3

63-64 R3: Blackburn Rovers (A) 0-4

64-65 R1: Barrow (A) 1-1, (H) 2-2, 2-0
R2: Stockport County (A) 0-0, (H) 0-1

65-66 R1: Barrow (A) 2-1

R2: Barnsley (A) 1-1, (H) 2-0
R3: Portsmouth (H) 0-0, (A) 3-1
R4: Manchester City (A) 0-2

66-67 R1: Crewe Alexandra (A) 1-1, (H) 0-1

67-68 R1: Bradford (Park Ave.) (H) 1-1, (A) 1-4

68-69 R1: Darlington (A) 0-2

69-70 R1: Bradford City (A) 1-2

70-71 R1: Bury (H) 0-1

71-72 R1: York City (A) 2-4

72-73 R1: Wigan Athletic (H) 2-1
R2: Chesterfield (H) 2-2, (A) 1-0
R3: Preston North End (H) 0-0, (A) 1-0
R4: Coventry City (A) 0-1

73-74 R1: Runcorn (A) 1-0
R2: Blyth Spartans (H) 1-1, (A) 2-0
R3: Burnley (H) 0-2

74-75 R1: Huddersfield Town (H) 1-0
R2: Bury (H) 1-1, (A) 1-2

75-76 R1: Gateshead United (H) 1-3

76-77 R1: Droylsden (A) 0-0, (H) 5-3
R2: Chester (H) 0-1

77-78 R1: Workington (A) 2-0
R2: Barnsley (H) 2-0
R3: Southampton (H) 0-0, (A) 0-0, *(at Leicester City)* 1-4

78-79 R1: Hartlepool United (A) 0-1

79-80 R1: Chesterfield (H) 1-1, (A) 3-2
R2: Sheffield United (H) 2-0
R3: Liverpool (A) 0-5

80-81 R3: West Bromwich Albion (A) 0-3

81-82 R3: Millwall (A) 6-1
R4: Newcastle United (A) 2-1
R5: Queens Park Rangers (A) 1-3

82-83 R3: Scunthorpe United (A) 0-0, (H) 2-0
R4: Ipswich Town (A) 0-2

83-84 R3: Portsmouth (A) 1-2

84-85 R3: Notts County (A) 2-2, (H) 4-2
R4: Watford (H) 1-3

85-86 R3: Arsenal (H) 3-4

86-87 R3: Stoke City (H) 1-1, (A) 1-1, (A) 0-6

87-88 R1: Scarborough (A) 2-1
R2: Halifax Town (H) 0-0, (A) 0-2

88-89 R1: Wolverhampton Wanderers (H) 1-0
R2: Rotherham United (H) 3-2
R3: Middlesbrough (A) 2-1
R4: Reading (H) 1-1, (A) 2-1
R5: Wimbledon (A) 1-3

89-90 R1: York City (A) 2-1
R2: Doncaster Rovers (H) 1-0
R3: Huddersfield Town (A) 1-3

90-91 R1: Blackpool (A) 0-2

91-92 R1: Blackpool (A) 1-2

92-93 R3: Brentford (A) 2-0
R4: Swansea City (A) 0-0, (H) 2-0
R5: Ipswich Town (A) 0-4

GUILDFORD

Currently: Defunct

45-46 PR: Sutton United (A) 0-6

46-47 PR: Walton & Hersham (A) 0-11

47-48 PR: Redhill (A) 0-9

48-49 PR: Tooting & Mit. (H - *played away*) 1-6

49-50 EX: Epsom (A) 0-6

50-51 PR: Wimbledon (H) 3-9

GUILDFORD CITY

Currently: Merged with Dorking
Playing as Dorking in Isthmian League
See also Dorking (2)

45-46 Q4: Newport Isle of Wight (H) 1-2

46-47 Q4: Gillingham (H) 1-2

47-48 Q4: Dulwich Hamlet (H) 5-2
R1: Bournemouth & Boscombe Ath. (A) 0-2

48-49 Q4: Chelmsford City (H) 0-2

49-50 Q4: Gillingham (H) 2-3

50-51 Q4: Bedford Town (H) 0-0, (A) 2-1
R1: Dartford (H) 1-5

51-52 Q4: Dartford (H) 2-1
R1: Hereford United (H) 4-1
R2: Gateshead (A) 0-2

52-53 Q4: Headington United (H) 2-1
R1: Great Yarmouth Town (H) 2-2, (A) 0-1

53-54 PR: Snowdown Colliery Welfare (A) 3-1
Q1: Sittingbourne (H) 2-0
Q2: Ramsgate Athletic (A) 4-2
Q3: Tunbridge Wells United (A) 2-0
Q4: Tonbridge (H) 4-0
R1: Hastings United (A) 0-1

54-55 Q4: Hastings United (A) 0-1

55-56 Q4: Ramsgate Athletic (H) 2-2, (A) 2-3

56-57 Q4: Headington United (A) 2-0
R1: Brentford (A) 0-3

57-58 Q4: Gravesend & Northfleet (H) 1-1, (A) 1-0
R1: Yeovil Town (H) 2-2, (A) 0-1

58-59 Q4: Andover (H) 1-0
R1: Hereford United (H) 1-2

59-60 Q4: Margate (A) 0-1

60-61 Q4: Hastings United (A) 1-2

61-62 Q4: Margate (A) 2-6

62-63 Q4: Sittingbourne (H) 0-0, (A) 0-1

63-64 Q1: Petter Sports (A - *played home*) 8-2
Q2: Woking (A) 2-0
Q3: Leatherhead (H) 5-1

Q4: Bexley United (H) 0-0, (A) 0-3

64-65 Q1: Woking (A) 3-1
Q2: Walton & Hersham (A) 5-1
Q3: Leatherhead (A) 2-1
Q4: Maidenhead United (H) 9-0
R1: Gillingham (H) 2-2, (A) 0-1

65-66 Q1: Kingstonian (H) 3-2
Q2: Leatherhead (A) 2-2, (H) 3-0
Q3: Woking (H) 6-0
Q4: Bletchley (H) 4-0
R1: Wycombe Wanderers (H) 2-2, (A) 1-0
R2: Queens Park Rangers (A) 0-3

66-67 Q4: Ashford Town (H) 1-1, (A) 0-2

67-68 Q4: Chichester City (H) 0-0, (A) 3-0
R1: Brentford (A) 2-2, (H) 2-1
R2: Newport County (H) 0-1

68-69 Q4: Dartford (H) 0-1

69-70 PR: Uxbridge (H) 4-1
Q1: Metropolitan Police (A) 0-1

70-71 Q1: Epsom & Ewell (H) 5-0
Q2: Dulwich Hamlet (H) 2-1
Q3: Cheshunt (H) 1-1, (A) 0-2

71-72 Q1: Aylesbury United (H) 2-0
Q2: Hampton (A) 1-1, (H) 2-1
Q3: Bishop's Stortford (A) 2-2, (H) 1-1, 1-2
Q4: Bromley (A) 1-0
R1: Dover (H) 0-0, (A) 2-0
R2: Shrewsbury Town (A) 1-2

72-73 Q4: Ashford Town (A) 4-3
R1: Watford (A) 2-4

73-74 Q4: Folkestone (A) 3-2
R1: Hitchin Town (A) 1-1, (H) 1-4

GUINNESS EXPORTS

See Ormskirk

GUISBOROUGH

Currently: Defunct

47-48 PR: Cargo Fleet Works (H) 4-1
Q1: Whitby Albion Rangers (H) 1-2

48-49 PR: Billingham Synthonia Recreation (H) 1-5

GUISBOROUGH TOWN

Currently: Northern League

78-79 Q1: Consett (H) 2-2, (A) 2-3

79-80 PR: Blue Star (H) 3-2
Q1: Tow Law Town (A) 0-1

80-81 Q1: Gateshead (H) 2-3

81-82 PR: Shildon (H) 3-1
Q1: Seaham Colliery Welfare Red Star (H) 2-3

82-83 Q1: Chester-le-Street (H) 0-0, (A) 0-3

83-84 PR: Ferryhill Athletic (H) 2-1
Q1: Brandon United (A) 0-0, (H) 1-2

84-85 PR: Esh Winning (A) 1-0
Q1: Blyth Spartans (A) 1-1, (H) 3-1
Q2: Tow Law Town (A) 3-4

85-86 Q1: Blue Star (A) 1-2

86-87 PR: Alnwick Town (A) 0-1

87-88 PR: Armthorpe Welfare (H) 2-0
Q1: Thackley (A) 1-1, (H) 0-0, (H) 1-0
Q2: Rossendale United (A) 3-2
Q3: Emley (H) 3-2
Q4: Bishop Auckland (H) 1-2

88-89 Q1: Alnwick Town (H) 3-0
Q2: Farsley Celtic (H) 0-0, (A) 1-0
Q3: Bridlington Town (H) 1-1, (A) 1-0
Q4: Leek Town (A) 0-0, (H) 0-0, (H) 1-0
R1: Bury (H - *at Middlesbrough F.C.*) 0-1

89-90 Q1: Billingham Synthonia (A) 0-2

90-91 Q1: Billingham Town (A) 2-1
Q2: Gretna (A) 2-2, (H) 1-3

91-92 Q1: Dunston Federation Breweries (A) 0-1

92-93 Q1: Murton (A) 2-1
Q2: Billingham Town (H) 3-0
Q3: Netherfield (A) 1-4

GUISELEY

Currently: Northern Premier League

45-46 Q1: Frickley Colliery (H) 3-3, (A) *scratched*

83-84 Q1: Morecambe (A) 0-1

84-85 PR: Ferryhill Athletic (A) 2-1
Q1: West Auckland Town (H) 1-1, (A) 1-3

85-86 PR: Rossendale United (A) 0-1

86-87 PR: Northallerton Town (A) 4-0
Q1: Yorkshire Amateur (A) 1-0
Q2: Blyth Spartans (H) 0-2

87-88 PR: Ashington (A) 1-3

88-89 PR: Durham City (A) 2-1
Q1: Billingham Town (A) 0-1

89-90 PR: Langley Park (A) 4-5

90-91 PR: Hednesford Town (A) 0-2

91-92 Q1: Norton & Stockton Ancients (A) 4-0
Q2: Shildon (H) 5-1
Q3: Denaby United (H) 1-1, (A) 2-1
Q4: Bishop Auckland (H) 2-1
R1: Chester City (A - *at Macclesfield T.*) 0-1

92-93 Q1: Fleetwood Town (A) 2-3

HAIG UNITED

Currently: Defunct

46-47 PR: Frizington United (A) 2-3

HAILSHAM TOWN

Currently: Sussex County League

82-83 Q1: Thanet United (H) 0-3

83-84 PR: Woking (H - *played away*) 2-1
Q1: Eastbourne Town (A) 1-0
Q2: Ashford Town (H) 1-3

84-85 Q1: Egham Town (A) 0-3

85-86 PR: Dorking (H) 4-4, (A) 0-3

86-87 PR: Petersfield United (A) 1-2

87-88 PR: Beckenham Town (A) 2-2, (H) 2-4

88-89 PR: Ruislip Manor (H) 0-0, (A) 2-0
Q1: Crawley Town (A) 1-2

89-90 PR: Eton Manor (H) 2-2, (A) 1-0
Q1: Tonbridge A.F.C. (H) 2-0
Q2: Tilbury (A) 2-2, (H) 2-1 *abandoned in E.T.*, (H - *at Tonbridge*) 3-2
Q3: Dulwich H. (A) 1-1, (H - *at Lewes*) 3-4

90-91 Q1: Hampton (A) 1-0
Q2: Lewes (A) 3-0
Q3: Kingstonian (A) 0-4

91-92 Q1: Sheppey United (H) 1-1, (A) 1-4

92-93 PR: Steyning Town (H) 3-1
Q1: Bromley (H) 2-3

Below: *Hailsham's Dave Rowe raises a finger to celebrate his goal against Bromley. Photo: Roger Turner.*

HALESOWEN HARRIERS

Currently: West Midlands (Regional) League

87-88 Q1: Moor Green (H) 1-1, (A) 1-2

88-89 Q1: Stafford Rangers (A) 0-2

89-90 PR: Rushden Town (H) 2-5

90-91 PR: Heanor Town (A) 4-0
Q1: Burton Albion (A) 0-2

91-92 PR: Malvern Town (A) 2-3

92-93 PR: Wednesfield (H) 2-2, (A) 3-2
Q1: Lye Town (H) 2-1
Q2: Frickley Athletic (A) 2-8

HALESOWEN TOWN

Currently: Southern League

47-48 PR: Cradley Heath (H) 4-1
Q1: Birmingham City Transport (H) 2-1
Q2: Bromsgrove Rovers (A) 1-1, (H) 1-2

48-49 PR: Cradley Heath (H) 2-0
Q1: Hereford United (A) 0-2

49-50 EX: Sutton Coldfield Town (A) 0-3

50-51 PR: Kidderminster Harriers (A) 0-3

51-52 PR: Wellington Town (A) 0-4

52-53 PR: Brierley Hill Alliance (H) 1-4

53-54 PR: Stafford Rangers (H) 1-2

54-55 PR: Kidderminster Harriers (H) 1-4

55-56 PR: Bromsgrove Rovers (H) 2-1
Q1: Hednesford (A) 1-0
Q2: Stourbridge (H) 3-0
Q3: Kidderminster Harriers (A) 0-0, (H) 1-0
Q4: Hinckley Athletic (A) 4-1
R1: Hendon (H) 2-4

56-57 PR: Stafford Rangers (H) 2-3

57-58 Q1: Brierley Hill Alliance (A) 2-3

58-59 PR: Bedworth Town (H) 2-2, (A) 2-4

59-60 Q1: Bilston (H) 2-4

60-61 Q1: Hednesford (A) 3-2
Q2: Bedworth Town (H) 5-2
Q3: Lockheed Leamington (A) 1-6

61-62 Q1: Bedworth Town (A) 0-3

62-63 Q1: Nuneaton Borough (A) 0-6

63-64 Q1: Brierley Hill Alliance (H) 1-0
Q2: Nuneaton Borough (A) 1-2

64-65 Q1: Bilston (H) 1-1, (A) 3-0
Q2: Lockheed-Leamington (H) 2-4

66-67 Q1: Lower Gornal Athletic (H) 2-3

67-68 Q1: Redditch (A) 3-2
Q2: Worcester City (A) 1-1, (H) 0-0, 0-2

68-69 Q1: Wellington Town (H) 0-1

Above: *In front of a capacity crowd at Halesowen Town, Sean Flynn creates great excitement by firing the non-League locals into an early lead against Tranmere Rovers in the 1990-91 First Round. Photo: Mal Cobley.*

69-70	Q1: Telford United (A) 3-7
70-71	Q1: Bromsgrove Rovers (H) 1-2
71-72	Q1: Lower Gornal Ath. (A) 2-2, (H) 1-3
72-73	Q1: Bilston (H) 1-4
73-74	Q1: Alvechurch (A) 0-2
74-75	Q1: Lye Town (H) 1-2
75-76	Q1: Warley County Borough (H) 2-1 Q2: Coventry Sporting (A) 0-2
76-77	PR: Dudley Town (A) 1-3
77-78	PR: Oldbury United (H) 2-1 Q1: Gornal Athletic (A) 3-1 Q2: Brierley Hill Alliance (A) 1-0 Q3: Burton Albion (A) 0-1
78-79	PR: Bilston (H) 2-0 Q1: Telford United (A) 1-0 Q2: Tamworth (A) 2-0 Q3: Dudley Town (H) 0-1
79-80	PR: Alvechurch (H) 1-1, (A) 0-6
80-81	Q1: Didcot Town (H) 1-1, (A) 1-0 Q2: Kidderminster Harriers (H) 1-4
81-82	PR: Long Eaton United (A) 3-1 Q1: Bilston (A) 3-2 Q2: Burton Albion (H) 0-0, (A) 0-2
82-83	Q1: Corby Town (H) 1-2
83-84	Q1: King's Lynn (H) 6-0 Q2: Oldbury United (A) 0-2
84-85	PR: Boldmere S.M. (A) 2-2, (H) 1-1, (H) 1-0 Q1: Grantham (A) 2-0 Q2: Worksop Town (A) 3-0 Q3: Stourbridge (A) 1-1, (H) 3-4
85-86	Q1: R.C. Warwick (H) 2-0 Q2: Stafford Rangers (H) 3-2 Q3: Irthlingborough D. (H) 2-2, (A) 2-1 Q4: Braintree Town (H) 2-1 R1: Frickley Athletic (A) 1-1, (H) 1-3
86-87	Q1: Ampthill T. (H - *at Lye Town*) 4-0 Q2: Burton Albion (H) 2-0 Q3: Stevenage Borough (A) 3-1 Q4: Oldbury United (H) 2-2, (A) 2-1 R1: Southend United (A) 1-4
87-88	Q1: Ashtree Highfield (H) 1-1, (A) 1-0 Q2: Leicester United (H) 5-1 Q3: Racing Club Warwick (A) 3-1 Q4: Bishop's Stortford (H) 1-0 R1: Kidderminster Harriers (H) 2-2, (A) 0-4
88-89	Q4: Chelmsford City (A) 3-1 R1: Brentford (A) 0-2
89-90	Q4: Wivenhoe Town (A) 0-0, (H) 3-2 R1: Cardiff City (A) 0-1
90-91	Q4: Ruislip Manor (H) 5-2 R1: Tranmere Rovers (H) 1-2
91-92	Q4: Baldock Town (A) 1-1, (H) 1-0 R1: Farnborough Town (H) 2-2, (A) 0-4
92-93	Q4: V.S. Rugby (H) 1-2

HALIFAX TOWN

Currently: Alliance Premier League

45-46	R1: York City (H) 1-0, (A) 2-4 *(agg: 3-4)*
46-47	R1: Barrow (A) 0-0, (H) 1-0 R2: Stockport County (H) 1-1, (A) 1-2
47-48	R1: Wrexham (A) 0-5
48-49	R1: Scunthorpe United (H) 0-0, (A) 0-1
49-50	R1: Tranmere Rovers (A) 1-2
50-51	R1: Ashington (H) 2-3
51-52	R1: Wrexham (A) 0-3
52-53	R1: Ashton United (H) 1-1, (A) 2-1 R2: Southport (H) 4-2 R3: Cardiff City (H) 3-1 R4: Stoke City (H) 1-0 R5: Tottenham Hotspur (H) 0-3
53-54	R1: Rhyl (H) 0-0, (A) 3-4
54-55	R1: Grimsby Town (A) 1-2
55-56	R1: Goole Town (A) 2-1 R2: Burton Albion (H) 0-0, (A) 0-1
56-57	R1: Oldham Athletic (H) 2-3
57-58	R1: Mansfield Town (A) 0-2
58-59	R1: Southport (A) 2-0 R2: Darlington (H) 1-1, (A) 0-3
59-60	R1: Gateshead (A) 4-3 R2: Workington (A) 0-1
60-61	R1: Hartlepools United (H) 5-1 R2: Crewe Alexandra (H) 2-2, (A) 0-4
61-62	R1: Rochdale (A) 0-2
62-63	R1: Bradford Park Avenue (H) 1-0 R2: Lincoln City (A) 0-1
63-64	R1: Workington (A) 1-4
64-65	R1: South Liverpool (H) 2-2, (A) 2-4
65-66	R1: Southport (A) 0-2
66-67	R1: Doncaster Rovers (H) 2-2, (A) 3-1 R2: Bishop Auckland (A) 0-0, (H) 7-0 R3: Bristol City (H) 1-1, (A) 1-4
67-68	R1: Crewe Alexandra (H) 3-2 R2: Scunthorpe United (H) 1-0 R3: Birmingham City (H) 2-4
68-69	R1: Bilston (A) 3-1 R2: Crewe Alexandra (H) 1-1, (A) 3-1 R3: Swansea Town (A) 1-0 R4: Stoke City (A) 1-1, (H) 0-3
69-70	R1: Chester (H) 3-3, (A) 0-1
70-71	R1: Chesterfield (A) 0-2
71-72	R1: Wigan Athletic (A) 1-2
72-73	R1: Barnsley (A) 1-1, (H) 2-1 R2: Scunthorpe United (A) 2-3
73-74	R1: Frickley Colliery (H) 6-1 R2: Oldham Athletic (H) 0-1
74-75	R1: Barnsley (A) 2-1 R2: Stafford Rangers (A) 1-2
75-76	R1: Altrincham (H) 3-1 R2: Stafford Rangers (A) 3-1 R3: Ipswich Town (A) 1-3
76-77	R1: Stafford Rangers (A) 0-0, (H) 1-0 R2: Preston North End (H) 1-0 R3: Luton Town (H) 0-1
77-78	R1: Chesterfield (A) 0-1
78-79	R1: Carlisle United (A) 0-1
79-80	R1: Scarborough (H) 2-0 R2: Walsall (A) 1-1, (H) 1-1, (H) 2-0 R3: Manchester City (H) 1-0 R4: Bolton Wanderers (A) 0-2
80-81	R1: Hull City (A) 1-2
81-82	R1: Peterborough Utd (H) 0-3
82-83	R1: North Shields (H) 0-1
83-84	R1: Whitby Town (H) 2-3
84-85	R1: Goole Town (H) 2-0 R2: Burnley (A) 1-3
85-86	R1: Scunthorpe United (H) 1-3
86-87	R1: Bolton W. (H) 1-1, (A) 1-1, (H) 1-3
87-88	R1: Billingham Syn. (A - *Hartlepool U.*) 4-2 R2: Grimsby Town (A) 0-0, (H) 2-0 R3: Nottingham Forest (H) 0-4
88-89	R1: York City (H) 1-0 R2: Altrincham (A) 3-0 R3: Kettering Town (A) 1-1, (H) 2-3
89-90	R1: Stafford Rangers (A) 3-2 R2: Darlington (A) 0-3
90-91	R1: Wrexham (H) 3-2 R2: Rotherham United (A) 1-1, (H) 1-2
91-92	R1: Witton Albion (A) 1-1, (H) 1-2
92-93	R1: Marine (A) 1-4

HALLAM

Currently: Northern Counties (East) League

50-51	EX: Worksop Town (H) 2-4
51-52	Q1: Frickley Colliery (A) 1-3
52-53	Q1: South Kirkby Colliery (A) 1-2
53-54	Q1: South Kirkby Colliery (A) 2-1 Q2: Upton Colliery (H) 0-5
54-55	Q1: Sheffield (H) 1-3
55-56	Q1: Langwith Miners Welfare (A) 2-1 Q2: Frickley Colliery (H) 0-2
56-57	Q1: Norton Woodseats (H) 2-2, (A) 0-0, 1-3
57-58	Q2: Sheffield (H) 5-2 Q3: Norton Woodseats Amateur (A) 0-4
58-59	Q1: Boots Athletic (H) 3-1 Q2: Norton Woodseats Amateur (A) 1-4

HALSTEAD TOWN

Currently: Eastern Counties League

88-89	PR: Aveley (A) 2-2, (H) 3-3 *ab. in E.T.*, (A) 4-1 Q1: Uxbridge (A) 2-0 Q2: Leyton-Wingate (A) 1-7
89-90	PR: Welwyn Garden City (A) 1-1, (H) 4-2 Q1: Harlow Town (H) 3-2 Q2: Heybridge Swifts (A) 0-1
90-91	PR: Canvey Island (H) 1-1, (A) 7-1 Q1: Wivenhoe Town (A) 1-3
91-92	PR: Hoddesdon Town (H) 3-2 Q1: Baldock Town (H) 2-3

92-93 PR: Waltham Abbey (A - *pl. home*) 1-1, (H) 3-4

HAMPTON

Currently: Isthmian League

66-67 Q1: Metropolitan Police (H) 0-2

67-68 Q1: Southall (H) 2-0
Q2: Hemel Hempstead Town (H) 3-2
Q3: Walthamstow Avenue (H) 4-5

68-69 Q1: Kingstonian (H) 1-5

69-70 Q1: Grays Athletic (H) 1-2

70-71 Q1: Dartford (H) 0-1

71-72 Q1: Bletchley (H) 2-1
Q2: Guildford City (H) 1-1, (A) 1-2

72-73 Q1: Dulwich Hamlet (A) 2-1
Q2: Molesey (A) 0-0, (H) 1-0
Q3: Bexley United (H) 0-0, (A) 1-4

73-74 Q1: Cray Wanderers (H) 3-3, (A) 3-1
Q2: Dagenham (H) 0-5

74-75 PR: Burnham (H) 2-0
Q1: Wealdstone (H) 2-2, (A) 0-2

75-76 Q1: Egham Town (A) 0-2

76-77 PR: Enfield (A) 0-1

77-78 Q1: Wokingham Town (H) 3-0
Q2: Basingstoke Town (H) 1-1, (A) 2-0
Q3: Ilford (H) 1-1, (A) 1-1, (H) 2-0
Q4: Barnet (H) 1-2

78-79 PR: Banstead Athletic (H) 2-0
Q1: Windsor & Eton (A) 0-1

79-80 Q1: Finchley (H) 2-1
Q2: Walton & Hersham (A) 1-1, (H) 1-5

80-81 PR: Dulwich Hamlet (A) 1-3

81-82 Q1: Berkhamsted Town (A) 3-0
Q2: Kingstonian (A) 0-1

82-83 Q1: Croydon (H) 2-0
Q2: St Albans City (A) 3-1
Q3: Windsor & Eton (H) 1-2

83-84 Q1: Royston Town (A) 7-1
Q2: Uxbridge (A) 1-0
Q3: Slough Town (A) 2-3

84-85 Q1: Tring Town (A) 0-1

85-86 PR: Chertsey Town (H) 2-0
Q1: Southall (H) 3-1
Q2: Aylesbury United (H) 0-1

86-87 Q1: Tooting & Mitcham United (A) 2-1
Q2: Metropolitan Police (A) 2-2, (H) 2-0
Q3: Fisher Athletic (H) 0-0, (A) 1-2

87-88 PR: Baldock Town (A) 0-1

88-89 Q1: Leyton-Wingate (A) 1-1, (H) 0-1

89-90 PR: Northwood (A) 3-1
Q1: Fisher Athletic (H) 3-1
Q2: Hounslow (H) 2-0
Q3: Bromley (H) 0-1

90-91 PR: Bracknell Town (A) 3-2
Q1: Hailsham Town (H) 0-1

91-92 PR: Haywards Heath Town (H) 3-0
Q1: Lancing (A) 3-1
Q2: Littlehampton Town (A) 3-1
Q3: Tonbridge A.F.C. (H) 2-2, (A) 1-2 *aband. (floodlight failure) after 81 mins*, (A) 0-3

92-93 Q1: Andover (A) 6-0
Q2: Witney Town (A) 1-3

HAMWORTHY

Currently: (Hamworthy Utd) Dorset Combination

48-49 EX: Dorchester Town (A) 2-3

49-50 EX: Portland United (H) 0-1

50-51 EX: Longfleet St Mary's (A) 1-1, (H) 1-0
PR: Pirelli General (A) 2-1
Q1: Alton Town (A) 0-9

HANHAM ATHLETIC

Currently: Avon Premier Combination

46-47 EX: Soundwell (A - *played home*) 1-2

47-48 PR: Gloucester City (A) 4-3
Q1: Merthyr Tydfil (A) 0-9

48-49 EX: Bristol St George (H) 2-0
PR: Hoffmann Athletic (Stonehouse) (H) 3-1
Q1: Wells City (H) 4-3
Q2: Street (H) 2-5

49-50 PR: Clevedon (A) 1-2

50-51 PR: Troedrhiw (H) 0-2

51-52 PR: Paulton Rovers (H) 0-7

52-53 PR: Paulton Rovers (H) 0-1

53-54 PR: Paulton Rovers (H) 4-1
Q1: Bristol St George (H) 0-2

54-55 Q1: Radstock Town (A) 1-4

HANWELL TOWN

Currently: London Spartan League

88-89 PR: Corinthian-Casuals (A - *played home*) 4-0
Q1: Erith & Belvedere (A) 1-0
Q2: Wembley (H) 0-1

89-90 PR: Lewes (A) 1-2

90-91 PR: Billericay Town (A) 0-4

HARDWICK COLLIERY SPTS

Currently: Defunct

48-49 EX: Cresswell Colliery (H) *withdrew*

HAREFIELD UNITED

Currently: Isthmian League

79-80 PR: Walton & Hersham (H) 1-4

80-81 Q1: Leyton-Wingate (A) 3-0
Q2: Maidenhead United (H) 0-0, (A) 1-5

81-82 PR: Irthlingborough Diamonds (A) 1-2

82-83 PR: Croydon (H) 0-4

83-84 PR: Aylesbury United (A) 0-2

84-85 Q1: Sutton United (H) 0-3

85-86 PR: Hertford Town (A) 1-1, (H) 3-0
Q1: Aveley (H) 0-0, (A) 0-2

86-87 Q1: Corinthian-Casuals (H) 3-0
Q2: Aylesbury United (H) 2-2, (A) 0-2

87-88 Q1: Crockenhill (H) 3-1
Q2: Bromley (H) 2-3

88-89 PR: Burgess Hill Town (A) 1-2

89-90 PR: Boreham Wood (A) 0-1

90-91 PR: Merstham (H) 0-1

91-92 PR: Dulwich Hamlet (A - *at Tooting*) 1-2

92-93 PR: Barkingside (H) 0-1

HARINGEY BOROUGH

Currently: London Spartan League
x - As Tufnell Park Edmonton
* - As Edmonton
+ - As Edmonton & Haringey
See also Edmonton Borough and Tufnell Park

51-52 x Q1: Finchley (A) 1-2

52-53 x Q1: Cheshunt (A) 1-2

53-54 x Q1: Enfield (H) 2-0
Q2: Stevenage Town (H) 2-1
Q3: Hitchin Town (A) 1-5

54-55 x PR: Clapton (H) 0-4

57-58 x PR: Bishop's Stortford (H) 2-1
Q1: Letchworth Town (A) 1-1, (H) 0-1

68-69 * Q1: Ilford (A) 1-0
Q2: Leyton (A) 1-1, (H) 2-1
Q3: Kingstonian (H) 1-1, (A) 0-2

69-70 * Q1: Hemel Hempstead Town (H) 2-0
Q2: Ilford (H) 2-1
Q3: Enfield (H) 1-4

70-71 * Q1: Ford United (H) 1-2

72-73 * Q1: Vauxhall Motors (A) 0-0, (H) 0-2

73-74 + PR: Feltham (A) 3-1
Q1: Bexley United (A) 0-3

74-75 + PR: Cheshunt (H) 2-1
Q1: Ware (H) 0-1

75-76 + PR: Hatfield Town (A) 0-1

76-77 + PR: Kingstonian (H) 0-1

77-78 Q1: Ware (H) 2-2, (A) 3-3, (A) 1-0
Q2: Billericay Town (H) 1-3

78-79 PR: Ilford (H) 1-3

79-80 PR: Willesden (H) 0-1

80-81 PR: Epping Town (A) 1-2

81-82 PR: Thame United (A) 0-1

82-83 Q1: Hemel Hempstead (H) 0-3

83-84 Q1: Canterbury City (H) 1-4

84-85 Q1: Gorleston (A) 1-1, (H) 0-2

86-87 PR: Horsham Y.M.C.A. (A) 3-0
Q1: Three Bridges (H) 1-0
Q2: Wokingham Town (H) 4-2
Q3: Buckingham Town (H) 1-2

87-88 PR: Uxbridge (A) 2-2, (H) 2-3

91-92 PR: Watton United (H) 5-0
Q1: Redbridge Forest (A) 0-5

92-93 PR: Bury Town (H) 5-2
Q1: Gorleston (H) 0-0, (A) 0-1

Above: *Haringey's Leroy Rhodes attempts an ambitious overhead kick as his side record a comfortable Preliminary Round win over Watton United. Photo: Francis Short.*

HARLOW TOWN

Currently: Isthmian League

47-48	EX: Civil Service (A) 0-2
48-49	EX: Bishop's Stortford (H) 1-4
49-50	PR: Clapton (A) 1-7
62-63	Q1: Wealdstone (H) 0-2
63-64	Q1: Ware (H) 2-2, (A) 0-0, 1-2
64-65	Q1: Barnet (H) 0-2
65-66	Q1: Harrow Town (H) 3-1 Q2: Wealdstone (A) 1-5
66-67	Q1: Cray Wanderers (H) 0-0, (A) 1-3
67-68	Q1: Brentwood Town (H) 0-2
68-69	Q1: Brentwood Town (H) 0-3
69-70	Q1: Corinthian-Casuals (H) 2-2, (A) 1-4
70-71	Q1: Hayes (A) 0-3
71-72	Q1: Corinthian-Casuals (A) 2-0 Q2: Bishop's Stortford (A) 2-4
72-73	Q1: Uxbridge (H) 1-0 Q2: Vauxhall Motors (A) 1-2
73-74	Q1: Aveley (A) 1-2
74-75	Q1: Edgware (A) 2-1 Q2: Hoddesdon Town (H) 1-0 Q3: Stevenage Ath. (H) 0-0, (A) 2-0 Q4: Tooting & Mitcham United (A) 0-3
75-76	PR: Clacton Town (H) 2-3
76-77	Q1: Hillingdon Borough (H) 2-2, (A) 0-2
77-78	Q1: Stowmarket Town (H) 5-0 Q2: Cambridge City (H) 1-0 Q3: Chelmsford City (H) 1-1, (A) 1-2
78-79	PR: Hemel Hempstead (H) 1-1, (A) 4-0 Q1: Metropolitan Police (A) 0-1
79-80	PR: Lowestoft Town (H) 2-1 Q1: Hornchurch (A) 3-0 Q2: Bury Town (H) 2-1 Q3: Harwich & Parkeston (H) 1-0 Q4: Margate (H) 1-0 R1: Leytonstone-Ilford (H) 2-1 R2: Southend United (A) 1-1, (H) 1-0 R3: Leicester City (A) 1-1, (H) 1-0 R4: Watford (A) 3-4
80-81	Q4: Wealdstone (H) 1-1, (A) 1-0 R1: Charlton Athletic (H) 0-2
81-82	Q4: Corby Town (H) 1-0 R1: Barnet (H) 0-0, (A) 0-1
82-83	Q4: Bishop's Stortford (H) 1-1, (A) 0-4
83-84	Q4: Barnet (H) 1-1, (A) 1-5
84-85	Q1: Tiptree United (A) 4-0 Q2: Basildon United (H) 1-1, (A) 3-2 Q3: Chelmsford City (A) 2-1 Q4: Metropolitan Police (H) 1-3
85-86	Q1: Cambridge City (H) 2-1 Q2: Heybridge Swifts (H) 1-0 Q3: Woodford Town (H) 3-0 Q4: Aylesbury (A - *at RAF Halton*) 0-0, (H) 1-2
86-87	Q1: Chatteris Town (A) 2-2, (H) 1-0 Q2: Tilbury (A) 1-2 (*Tilbury expelled*) Q3: Bury Town (A) 1-2
87-88	PR: Tring Town (A) 2-0 Q1: Woodford Town (H) 1-0 Q2: Kingsbury (H) 1-1, (A) 2-2, (A) 2-3
88-89	PR: Thetford Town (A) 2-2, (H) 4-1 Q1: Sudbury Town (A) 1-3
89-90	PR: Barkingside (A) 5-2 Q1: Halstead Town (A) 2-3
90-91	PR: Tiptree United (A) 1-0 Q1: Rayners Lane (A) 3-0 Q2: Ford United (H) 1-0 Q3: Barnet (H) 1-3
91-92	Q1: Leyton-Wingate (H - *at Ware*) 4-1 Q2: Tiptree United (A) 6-0 Q3: King's Lynn (A) 3-2 Q4: Gravesend & Northfleet (A) 1-1, (H) 1-0 R1: Peterborough United (A) 0-7
92-93	Q1: Slade Green (A) *scratched*

Above: *With Penrith custodian Nicky Whitbread hopelessly out of position, Taj Singh rolls in Harrogate Railway's first F.A. Cup goal for 33 years. Photo: Colin Stevens.*

Above: *In the Third Round in 1980, Harlow Town created one of the biggest shocks of all time when they eliminated a Leicester City side destined to win the Second Division championship. Here goalscorer Peter McKenzie is chaired by ecstatic team-mates. Photo: Press Association.*

HARRISONS

Currently: Defunct

88-89	PR: Dudley Town (H) 0-2
89-90	PR: Sutton Coldfield Town (A) 0-7

HARROGATE RAILWAY ATH.

Currently: Northern Counties (East) League
* - As Harrogate & District Railway Athletic

54-55 *	Q2: Goole Town (A) 2-4
55-56 *	Q2: Goole Town (A) 0-6
56-57 *	Q1: Ossett Town (H) 3-2 Q2: Goole Town (A) 0-4
90-91	PR: Penrith (A) 5-0 Q1: Murton (H) 2-0 Q2: South Bank (H) 1-0 Q3: Easington Colliery (H) 2-0 Q4: Chorley (A) 1-3
91-92	Q1: Denaby United (A) 0-1
92-93	PR: Ilkeston Town (A) 0-7

HARROGATE TOWN

Currently: Northern Premier League
* - As Harrogate Hotspurs

48-49 *	EX: Bradford United (A) 2-4
50-51	EX: Yorkshire Amateur (A) 1-4
51-52	Q1: Goole Town (A) 3-7
61-62	Q2: Selby Town (H) 1-2
62-63	Q2: Scarborough (A) 1-5
63-64	Q1: Bridlington Town (A) 3-3, (H) 0-2
64-65	Q1: Ossett Albion (A) 0-3
65-66	Q1: Farsley Celtic (A) 1-0 Q2: Ossett Albion (A) 1-1, (H) 2-3
66-67	Q1: Barton Town (H) 0-4
82-83	PR: West Auckland Town (H) 3-0 Q1: Accrington Stanley (A) 1-1, (H) 3-1 Q2: Frickley Athletic (A) 1-3
83-84	Q1: Ryhope Community Association (A) 3-1 Q2: Whitby Town (H) 2-4
84-85	PR: Brandon United (A) 0-3
85-86	Q1: Morecambe (H) 0-2
86-87	Q1: Darlington Cleveland Bridge (H) 4-1 Q2: Chester-le-Street T. (H) 1-1, (A) 1-3
87-88	PR: Esh Winning (H) 2-1 Q1: Willington (A) 3-0 Q2: Clitheroe (A) 0-0, (H) 2-1 Q3: Bishop Auckland (H) 1-1, (A) 0-2
88-89	PR: Stockton (A - *played home*) 1-1, (H) 2-1 Q1: Billingham Synthonia (H) 1-3
89-90	PR: Prudhoe East End (A) 0-1
90-91	PR: Great Harwood Town (A) 2-2, (H) 2-1

Q1: Esh Winning (H) 1-3

91-92 PR: Boston (A) 3-2
Q1: Frickley Athletic (H) 2-2, (A - *played home*) 3-3, (A) 2-3

92-93 PR: Louth United (H) 4-3
Q1: Warrington Town (H) 1-2

HARROW BOROUGH

Currently: Isthmian League
* - As Harrow Town

45-46 * PR: Berkhamsted Town (H) 8-0
Q1: Kings Langley (H) 7-1
Q2: Wealdstone (H) 1-1, (A) 1-6

46-47 * PR: Edgware Town (A) 2-1
Q1: Wealdstone (H) 4-3
Q2: St Albans City (A) 5-2
Q3: Finchley (A) 3-4

47-48 * PR: Tufnell Park (H) 4-0
Q1: Berkhamsted Town (A) 4-3
Q2: Leavesden (A) 2-3

48-49 * PR: Crown & Manor (H) 7-1
Q1: Wealdstone (A) 1-2

49-50 * EX: Wingate (H) 0-2

50-51 * EX: Tufnell Park (A) 3-6

51-52 * PR: Uxbridge (A) 2-3

52-53 * PR: Uxbridge (H) 1-8

53-54 * PR: Hendon (H) 2-3

54-55 * PR: Metropolitan Police (A) 1-1, (H) 1-5

55-56 * PR: Uxbridge (H) 3-3, (A) 2-1
Q1: Wealdstone (H) 0-7

56-57 * Q1: Southall (H) 0-3

57-58 * PR: Hounslow Town (A) 0-2

58-59 * PR: Staines Town (A) 2-2, (H) 2-3

59-60 * Q1: Southall (A) 0-1

60-61 * Q1: Wealdstone (A) 2-1
Q2: Hertford Town (H) 3-2
Q3: Bishop's Stortford (H) 8-4
Q4: Maidenhead United (H) 2-3

61-62 * Q1: Bishop's Stortford (H) 7-1
Q2: Enfield (H) 0-4

62-63 * Q1: Wokingham Town (H) 5-2
Q2: Oxford City (A) 2-4

63-64 * Q1: Bishop's Stortford (A) 2-1
Q2: Ware (A) 1-2

64-65 * Q1: Hertford Town (A) 0-2

65-66 * Q1: Harlow Town (A) 1-3

66-67 Q1: Wokingham Town (A) 3-1
Q2: Wolverton Town & B.R. (A) 1-4

67-68 Q1: Baldock Town (H) 1-0
Q2: Ware (A) 1-4

68-69 Q1: Vauxhall Motors (A) 1-6

69-70 Q1: Baldock Town (A) 0-3

70-71 Q1: Hounslow (A) 1-0 *void - ineligible player*, (A) 2-2, (A) 1-1, *(at Southall)* 3-2
Q2: Dartford (H) 0-7

71-72 Q1: Wealdstone (H) 0-1

72-73 Q1: Erith & Belvedere (H) 0-0, (A) 1-2

73-74 Q1: Tooting & M.U. (H - *at Wealdstone*) 2-1
Q2: Horsham (H - *at Wealdstone*) 1-0
Q3: Aveley (A) 0-1

74-75 Q1: Molesey (H) 0-0, (A) 1-0
Q2: Leytonstone (A) 0-1

75-76 PR: Barking (H) 2-2, (A) 0-2

76-77 PR: Willesden (H) 3-1
Q1: Leytonstone (A) 0-2

77-78 Q1: Witney Town (H) 1-1, (A) 1-2

78-79 PR: Hertford Town (H) 0-2

79-80 Q1: Witney Town (H) 1-3

80-81 Q1: Marlow (A) 2-1
Q2: St Albans City (H) 3-4

Above: *David Pearce (left) scores Harrow's goal against Newport County in 1983. Photo: Eric Marsh.*

81-82 Q1: Oxford City (H) 4-2
Q2: Maidenhead United (A) 2-0
Q3: Wealdstone (A) 4-1
Q4: Hendon (A) 1-2

82-83 Q1: Letchworth Garden City (A) 6-0
Q2: Feltham (H) 2-3

83-84 Q1: Ware (H) 9-0
Q2: Aylesbury United (H) 0-0, (A) 2-1
Q3: Addlestone & Weybridge Town (H) 1-0
Q4: Fisher Athletic (A) 1-1, (H) 4-2
R1: Yeovil Town (A) 1-0
R2: Newport County (H) 1-3

84-85 Q4: Kettering Town (A) 1-1, (H) 0-2

85-86 Q1: Baldock Town (A) 2-0
Q2: Leyton-Wingate (A) 2-2, (H) 2-3

86-87 Q1: Fisher Athletic (A) 0-1

87-88 Q1: Yeading (H) 2-0
Q2: Burnham (A) 1-2

88-89 Q1: Staines Town (A) 0-2

89-90 Q1: Gravesend & Northfleet (H) 1-2

90-91 Q1: Edgware Town (A) 0-1

91-92 Q1: Berkhamsted Town (A) 2-3

92-93 Q1: Berkhamsted Town (H) 0-2

HARROWBY

Currently: Defunct

48-49 EX: Glossop (H) 2-11

HARTLEPOOL UNITED

Currently: Football League

45-46 R1: Gateshead (H) 1-2, (A) 2-6 *(agg: 3-8)*

46-47 R1: North Shields (H) 6-0
R2: Rochdale (A) 1-6

47-48 R1: Darlington (H) 1-0
R2: Brighton (H) 1-1, (A) 1-1, 1-2

48-49 R1: Chester (H) 1-3

49-50 R1: Accrington Stanley (A) 1-0
R2: Norwich City (H) 1-1, (A) 1-5

50-51 R1: Worcester City (A) 5-1
R2: Oldham Athletic (H) 1-2

51-52 R1: Rhyl (H) 2-0
R2: Watford (A) 2-1
R3: Burnley (A) 0-1

52-53 R1: Chester (A) 1-0
R2: Tranmere Rovers (A) 1-2

53-54 R1: Mansfield Town (H) 1-1, (A) 3-0
R2: Northampton Town (A) 1-1, (H) 1-0
R3: Stoke City (A) 2-6

54-55 R1: Chesterfield (H) 1-0
R2: Aldershot (H) 4-0
R3: Darlington (H) 1-1, (A) 2-2, 2-0
R4: Nottingham Forest (H) 1-1, (A) 1-2

55-56 R1: Gateshead (H) 3-0
R2: Chesterfield (A) 2-1
R3: Chelsea (H) 0-1

56-57 R1: Selby Town (H) 3-1
R2: Blyth Spartans (A) 1-0
R3: Manchester United (H) 3-4

57-58 R1: Prescot Cables (H) 5-0
R2: Stockport County (A) 1-2

58-59 R1: Rochdale (H) 1-1, (H) 3-3, 2-1
R2: Barrow (A) 0-2

59-60 R1: Bury (A) 0-5

60-61 R1: Halifax Town (A) 1-5

61-62 R1: Blyth Spartans (H) 5-1
R2: Accrington Stanley (H) 2-1
R3: Fulham (A) 1-3

62-63 R1: Carlisle United (A) 1-2

63-64 R1: Lincoln City (H) 0-1

64-65 R1: Corby Town (A) 3-1
R2: Darlington (H) 0-0, (A) 1-4

65-66 R1: Workington (H) 3-1
R2: Wrexham (H) 2-0
R3: Huddersfield Town (A) 1-3

66-67 R1: Shrewsbury Town (A) 2-5

67-68 R1: Bury (H) 2-3

68-69 R1: Rotherham United (H) 1-1, (A) 0-3

69-70 R1: North Shields (H) 3-0
R2: Wrexham (H) 0-1

70-71 R1: Rhyl (A) 0-1

71-72 R1: Scarborough (H) 6-1
R2: Boston United (A) 1-2

72-73 R1: Scunthorpe United (H) 0-0, (A) 0-0, *(at Sunderland F.C.)* 1-2

73-74 R1: Altrincham (A) 0-2

74-75 R1: Bradford City (H) 1-0
R2: Lincoln City (H) 0-0, (A) 0-1

75-76 R1: Stockport County (H) 3-0
R2: Marine (A) 1-1, (H) 6-3
R3: Manchester City (A) 0-6

76-77 R1: Chester (A) 0-1

77-78 R1: Tranmere Rovers (A) 1-1, (H) 3-1
R2: Runcorn (H) 4-2
R3: Crystal Palace (H) 2-1
R4: Ipswich Town (A) 1-4

78-79 R1: Grimsby Town (H) 1-0
R2: Crewe Alexandra (A) 1-0
R3: Leeds United (H) 2-6

79-80 R1: Barnsley (A) 2-5

80-81 R1: Scunthorpe United (A) 1-3

81-82 R1: Wigan Athletic (A) 2-2, (H) 1-0
R2: Hull City (A) 0-2

82-83 R1: Lincoln City (H) 3-0
R2: York City (H) 1-1, (A) 0-4

83-84 R1: Rotherham United (A) 0-0, (H) 0-1

84-85 R1: Derby County (H) 2-1
R2: York City (H) 0-2

85-86 R1: Macclesfield Town (A) 2-1
R2: Frickley Athletic (H) 0-1

86-87 R1: Wrexham (A) 1-2

87-88 R1: Chorley (A) 2-0
R2: York City (A) 1-1, (H) 3-1
R3: Luton Town (H) 1-2

Above: *Hartlepool's Lenny Johnrose can find no way through a packed Southport defence, but after being frustrated for an hour, his side ran in four late goals to qualify for their important home tie against Premier League Crystal Palace. Photo: Dennis Nicholson.*

88-89 R1: Wigan Athletic (H) 2-0
R2: Notts County (H) 1-0
R3: Bristol City (H) 1-0
R4: A.F.C. Bournemouth (H) 1-1, (A) 2-5

89-90 R1: Huddersfield Town (H) 0-2

90-91 R1: Runcorn (A) 3-0
R2: Wigan Athletic (A) 0-2

91-92 R1: Shrewsbury Town (H) 3-2
R2: Darlington (A) 2-1
R3: Ipswich Town (A) 1-1, (H) 0-2

92-93 R1: Doncaster Rovers (A) 2-1
R2: Southport (H) 4-0
R3: Crystal Palace (H) 1-0
R4: Sheffield United (A) 0-1

HARWICH & PARKESTON

Currently: Eastern Counties League

46-47 EX: Dagenham British Legion (H) 8-1
PR: Ilford (H) 3-2
Q1: Barking (H) 0-3

47-48 PR: Leyton (A) 2-1
Q1: Brentwood & Warley (H) 1-4

48-49 EX: Brightlingsea United (A) 3-1
PR: Clacton Town (H) 2-2, (A) 3-2
Q1: Barking (A) 1-2

49-50 EX: Chingford Town (H) 4-2
PR: Brentwood & Warley (H) 4-2
Q1: Briggs Sports (H) 0-0, (A) 3-0
Q2: Tilbury (H) 0-2

50-51 PR: Bishop's Stortford (H) 5-3
Q1: Woodford Town (A) 2-3

51-52 Q1: Dagenham (H) 2-2, (A) 1-2

52-53 Q1: Grays Athletic (A) 2-6

53-54 R1: Headington United (H) 2-3

54-55 PR: Romford (A) 1-3

55-56 PR: Leytonstone (A) 1-4

56-57 PR: Clacton Town (H) 0-0, (A) 0-2

57-58 PR: Brentwood & W. (A) 0-0, (H) 1-1, 0-2

58-59 PR: Clacton Town (A) 1-0
Q1: Sudbury Town (H) 1-1, (A) 2-0
Q2: Whitton United (A) 2-0
Q3: Stowmarket (H) 1-0
Q4: Chelmsford City (A) 0-2

59-60 Q1: Whitton United (A) 2-1
Q2: Sudbury Town (H) 4-2
Q3: Bury Town (A) 0-2

60-61 Q1: Clacton Town (H) 0-4

61-62 Q1: Stowmarket Town (A) 2-2, (H) 7-2
Q2: Clacton Town (A) 4-3
Q3: Great Yarmouth Town (H) 5-1
Q4: Kingstonian (H) 6-0
R1: Torquay United (A) 1-5

62-63 Q2: Great Yarmouth Town (A) 3-1
Q3: Lowestoft Town (A) 0-4

63-64 Q1: Clacton Town (H) 5-2
Q2: Lowestoft Town (H) 3-2
Q3: Great Yarmouth Town (H) 2-1
Q4: King's Lynn (H) 4-0
R1: Crystal Palace (A) 2-8

64-65 Q2: Lowestoft Town (H) 2-3

65-66 Q1: Clacton Town (H) 2-2, (A) 5-0
Q2: Sudbury Town (A) 2-1
Q3: Lowestoft Town (H) 4-2
Q4: Wellingborough Town (A) 0-1

66-67 Q1: Clacton Town (H) 4-2
Q2: Haverhill Rovers (A) 0-2

67-68 Q1: Bury Town (A) 1-2

68-69 Q1: Gorleston (A) 1-2

69-70 PR: Great Yarmouth Town (A) 1-0
Q1: Gothic (A) 1-0
Q2: Lowestoft Town (H) 0-1

70-71 PR: Sudbury Town (H) 1-2

71-72 PR: Lowestoft Town (H) 2-2, (A) 2-1
Q1: Great Yarmouth Town (A) 3-1
Q2: Thetford Town (A) 3-3, (H) 1-0
Q3: Bury Town (A) 0-1

72-73 Q1: Cambridge City (H) 1-3

73-74 Q1: Chatteris Town (A) 4-0
Q2: Great Yarmouth Town (A) 2-1
Q3: King's Lynn (H) 1-2

74-75 Q1: Clacton Town (A) 0-1

75-76 PR: Lowestoft Town (A) 3-4

76-77 PR: Thetford Town (H) 4-2
Q1: Newmarket Town (A) 1-1, (H) 8-1
Q2: Sudbury Town (H) 3-1
Q3: Lowestoft Town (A) 3-0
Q4: Lewes (A) 1-1, (H) 3-1
R1: Enfield (A) 0-0, (H) 0-3

77-78 PR: Southall & Ealing Borough (H) 4-0
Q1: Billericay Town (A) 1-1, (H) 1-4

78-79 Q1: Great Yarmouth Town (A) 1-1, (H) 4-1
Q2: March Town United (H) 1-1, (A) 1-2

79-80 Q1: Basildon United (H) 2-0
Q2: Billericay Town (H) 3-1
Q3: Harlow Town (A) 0-1

80-81 Q1: Lowestoft Town (A) 2-0
Q2: Stowmarket (H) 2-1
Q3: Great Yarmouth Town (H) 1-0
Q4: St Albans City (H) 2-2, (A) 0-3

81-82 Q1: Wisbech Town (H) 1-2

82-83 Q1: Hornchurch (A) 0-1

83-84 PR: Soham Town Rangers (A) 0-1

84-85 PR: Felixstowe Town (A) 0-3

85-86 PR: Hoddesdon Town (H) 2-3

86-87 PR: Collier Row (H) 2-0
Q1: Stowmarket Town (H) 2-2, (A) 3-1
Q2: Walthamstow Avenue (H) 4-1
Q3: Woodford Town (H) 1-2

87-88 Q1: Cambridge City (A) 0-2

88-89 Q1: Hendon (A) 1-5

89-90 PR: Wivenhoe Town (A) 0-2

90-91 PR: Berkhamsted Town (H) 4-1
Q1: Fisher Athletic (A) 0-0, (H) 2-1
Q2: Redbridge Forest (H) 1-3

Below: *Harwich's Tony Welch (centre) is thwarted by the Redbridge defence. The home team held an interval lead against the side on course for the Isthmian League title, but were eventually overhauled in an exciting tie. Photo: Gavin Ellis.*

91-92 PR: Canvey Island (A) 2-0
Q1: Potton United (H) 2-1
Q2: Lowestoft Town (A) 0-1

92-93 PR: Leighton Town (H) 3-3, (A) 0-2

HARWORTH COLLIERY INST.

Currently: Central Midlands League
* - As Harworth Colliery Athletic

46-47 * PR: Upton Colliery (H) 8-1
Q1: Scunthorpe United (A) 2-5

47-48 * EX: Pilkington Recreation (H) 7-3
PR: Wombwell Athletic (H) 4-1
Q1: Norton Woodseats (H) 0-1

48-49 * PR: Rawmarsh Welfare (A) 4-1
Q1: Steel, Peech & Tozer S.S. (A) 2-0
Q2: Denaby United (H) 2-2, (A) 3-1
Q3: Norton Woodseats (H) 1-6

49-50 * PR: Stocksbridge Works (H) 2-2, (A) 4-8

88-89 PR: Belper Town (H) 0-0, (A) 5-1
Q1: Congleton Town (A) 1-1, (H) 1-0
Q2: Southport (A) 0-2

89-90 PR: Ashington (H) 0-3

90-91 Q1: Atherton Laburnum Rovers (H) 1-2

91-92 PR: Maltby Miners Welfare (H) 2-1
Q1: Droylsden (H) 0-1

92-93 PR: Eccleshill United (A) 2-3

HASTINGS TOWN

Currently: Southern League
* - As Hastings & St Leonards

45-46 * Q1: Bexhill Town (A) *W/O*
Q2: Horsham (H) 6-1
Q3: Haywards Heath (A) 0-1

46-47 * PR: Worthing (H) 3-3, (A) 2-2, 2-3

47-48 * PR: Horsham (H) 1-2

48-49 * PR: Haywards Heath (H) *withdrew*

81-82 Q1: Ashford Town (A) 0-1

82-83 Q1: Chathham Town (H) 2-7

83-84 Q1: Tooting & Mitcham United (H) 3-4

84-85 PR: Deal Town (A) 2-2, (H) 3-1
Q1: Hastings United (A) 1-2

85-86 PR: Burgess Hill Town (H) 1-0
Q1: Epsom & Ewell (H) 2-1
Q2: Banstead Athletic (A) 1-0
Q3: Canterbury City (H) 3-0
Q4: Farnborough Town (A) 2-3

86-87 Q1: Horsham (H) 3-2
Q2: Woking (A) 0-4

87-88 PR: Lancing (H) 0-1

88-89 PR: Sittingbourne (A) 3-2
Q1: Croydon (A) 2-1
Q2: Ashford Town (A) 1-2

89-90 Q1: Walton & Hersham (H) 0-3

90-91 PR: Tooting & Mitcham U. (A) 1-1, (H) 1-2

91-92 PR: Metropolitan Police (A) 4-2
Q1: Peacehaven & Telscombe (A) 1-2

92-93 Q1: Burgess Hill Town (A) 2-0
Q2: Canterbury City (H) 1-2

HASTINGS UNITED

Currently: Defunct

49-50 PR: Shoreham (H) 3-0
Q1: Hove (A - *played home*) 14-2
Q2: Horsham (H) 4-1
Q3: Haywards Heath (A) 1-0
Q4: Bedford Town (H) 2-0
R1: Gillingham (H) 1-3

50-51 PR: Lancing Athletic (A) 3-2
Q1: Arundel (A) 2-0
Q2: Eastbourne (A) 4-5

51-52 PR: Ashford Town (H) 1-3

52-53 PR: Chichester City (H) 4-2
Q1: Ashford Town (A) 3-1
Q2: Worthing (A) 2-2, (H) 1-3

53-54 PR: Shoreham (A) 3-0
Q1: Horsham (H) 4-1
Q2: Eastbourne (A) 7-2
Q3: Ashford Town (H) 2-1
Q4: Hounslow Town (A) 2-1
R1: Guildford City (H) 1-0
R2: Swindon Town (H) 4-1
R3: Norwich City (H) 3-3, (A) 0-3

54-55 Q4: Guildford City (H) 1-0
R1: Hounslow Town (A) 4-2
R2: Selby Town (A) 2-0
R3: Sheffield Wednesday (A) 1-2

55-56 Q4: Redhill (A) 2-2, (H) 4-0
R1: Southall (H) 6-1
R2: Northampton Town (A) 1-4

56-57 Q4: Horsham (A) 2-0
R1: Ipswich Town (A) 0-4

57-58 Q4: Walton & Hersham (A) 1-3

58-59 Q4: Ashford Town (H) 1-1, (A) 1-2

59-60 PR: Horsham (A) 3-1
Q1: Bexhill Town (H) 4-1
Q2: Arundel (A) 5-2
Q3: Crawley Town (A) 2-2, (H) 5-2
Q4: Sutton United (A) 3-2
R1: Notts County (H) 1-2

60-61 Q2: Eastbourne (A) 7-0
Q3: Tonbridge (A) 2-1
Q4: Guildford City (H) 2-1
R1: Northampton Town (A) 1-2

61-62 Q4: Dartford (A) 1-4

62-63 Q1: Maidstone United (H) 0-0, (A) 2-4

63-64 Q2: Tonbridge (H) 2-5

64-65 Q1: Maidstone United (A) 3-1
Q2: Eastbourne United (A) 7-1
Q3: Tonbridge (A) 0-3

65-66 Q1: Eastbourne United (A) 4-0
Q2: Maidstone United (A) 5-1
Q3: Tonbridge (H) 1-1, (A) 1-3

66-67 Q1: Tonbridge (H) 1-0
Q2: Canterbury City (H) 2-0
Q3: Ramsgate Athletic (H) 2-1
Q4: Horsham (A) 1-2

67-68 Q1: Margate (H) 0-1

68-69 Q1: Ramsgate Athletic (H) 1-1, (A) 1-0
Q2: Snowdown Colliery Welfare (A) 7-3
Q3: Margate (A) 0-4

69-70 Q1: Deal Town (H) 4-0
Q2: Sheppey United (A) 6-0
Q3: Ramsgate Athletic (A) 1-2

70-71 PR: Canterbury City (H) 2-0
Q1: Dover (A) 1-0
Q2: Maidstone United (A) 2-0
Q3: Folkestone (H) 0-0, (A) 2-4

71-72 Q1: Southwick (H) 1-1, (A) 1-1, 2-1
Q2: Burgess Hill Town (H) 4-1
Q3: Chichester City (A) 1-1, (H) 9-1
Q4: Crawley Town (H) 0-0, (A) 2-3

72-73 Q1: Dover (A) 1-2

73-74 Q1: Sittingbourne (H) 3-5

74-75 Q1: Tonbridge (H) 0-0, (A) 2-1
Q2: Maidstone United (A) 0-6

75-76 Q1: Crawley Town (A) 1-2

76-77 Q1: Peacehaven & Telscombe (H) 5-0
Q2: Ashford Town (A) 1-0
Q3: Ramsgate (H) 2-0
Q4: Hillingdon Borough (A) 1-2

77-78 Q1: Margate (H) 2-2, (A) 2-1
Q2: Snowdown Colliery Welfare (H) 5-1
Q3: Sutton United (A) 0-1

78-79 PR: Faversham Town (A) 3-1
Q1: Ringmer (A) 2-0
Q2: Crawley Town (A) 2-1
Q3: Eastbourne United (A) 1-2

79-80 PR: Welling United (H) 0-4

80-81 Q1: Gosport Borough (A) 0-0, (H) 3-4

81-82 PR: Chatham Town (A) 4-1
Q1: Faversham Town (H) 5-0
Q2: Canterbury City (H) 4-1
Q3: Epsom & Ewell (A) 4-2
Q4: Wembley (H) 2-0
R1: Enfield (A) 0-2

82-83 Q1: Pagham (A) 3-1
Q2: Thanet United (H) 1-2

83-84 Q1: Lancing (A) 2-2, (H) 2-0
Q2: Eastbourne United (A) 0-0, (H) 1-0
Q3: Folkestone (A) 0-2

84-85 Q1: Hastings Town (H) 2-1
Q2: Sheppey United (A) 1-0
Q3: Leatherhead (A) 2-1
Q4: Staines Town (H) 1-1, (A) 1-2

85-86 Q1: Walton & Hersham (A) *Scratched*

HATFIELD MAIN

Currently: Northern Counties (East) League

68-69 Q1: Yorkshire Amateur (H) 5-0
Q2: Retford Town (H) 2-2, (A) 0-1

72-73 Q1: Denaby Utd (A) 1-1, (H) 0-0, 2-1
Q2: Yorkshire Amateur (H) 1-2

73-74 PR: Rawmarsh Welfare (A) 1-2

HATFIELD TOWN

Currently: Defunct
* - As Hatfield United

46-47 * EX: Chipperfield (H) 2-3

49-50 * EX: Ruislip Town (H) 6-2
PR: Civil Service (A) 3-0
Q1: Willesden (H) 4-1
Q2: Edgware Town (A) 1-5.

50-51 PR: Civil Service (H) 1-2

64-65 Q1: Stevenage Town (A) 0-5

66-67 Q1: Sutton United (A) 0-4

67-68 Q1: Bishop's Stortford (H) 1-2

69-70 PR: Windsor & Eton (H) 0-2

70-71 PR: Wealdstone (A) 0-2

71-72 Q1: Leytonstone (H) 0-4

72-73 Q1: Biggleswade Town (H) 1-4

73-74 Q1: Aylesbury United (A) 2-3

74-75 Q1: Letchworth Town (A) 0-1

75-76 PR: Edmonton & Haringey (H) 1-0
Q1: Tonbridge (A) 0-5

76-77 Q1: Hounslow (H) 2-0
Q2: Barnet (A) 0-3

77-78 PR: Marlow (H) 1-2

HAVANT TOWN

Currently: Southern League

86-87 PR: Radstock Town (H) 1-1, (A) 1-0
Q1: Brockenhurst (A) 2-1
Q2: A.F.C. Totton (H) 1-1, (A) 0-1

87-88 Q1: Waterlooville (H) 0-2

88-89 PR: Abingdon Town (A) 2-4

89-90 PR: Croydon (A - *at Metropolitan Police*) 2-3

90-91 PR: Horndean (H) 3-0
Q1: Langney Sports (H) 4-0
Q2: Kingstonian (H) 0-4

91-92 PR: Oakwood (A) 3-0
Q1: Portfield (A) 2-1
Q2: Marlow (A) 1-2

92-93 PR: A.F.C. Totton (A) 1-0
Q1: Horsham Y.M.C.A. (H) 2-1
Q2: Erith & Belvedere (A) 1-1, (H) 5-4
Q3: Sittingbourne (A) 2-3

Below: *Havant Town's efforts in reaching the Third Qualifying Round in 1992 represent their best ever showing in the Cup. Here their players Webbe (8), Riley (6), Rutherford (4) and goalkeeper Hards defend a corner during the 1-1 draw at Erith & Belvedere. Photo: V J Robertson.*

HAVERFORDWEST COUNTY

Currently: League of Wales

81-82 Q1: Llanelli (A) 2-1
Q2: Clevedon Town (H) 3-2
Q3: Cheltenham Town (A) 0-4

82-83 PR: Barry Town (A) 0-2

83-84 PR: Weston-super-Mare (H) 1-0
Q1: Gloucester City (H) 1-2

84-85 PR: Clandown (A) 1-0
Q1: Moreton Town (H) 2-2, (A) 1-1, (A) 5-3
Q2: Gloucester City (H) *Scratched*

HAVERHILL ROVERS

Currently: Eastern Counties League

50-51 EX: Bungay Town (H) 2-2, (A) 1-2

54-55 Q1: Bury Town (H) 4-6

55-56 Q1: Lowestoft Town (A) 0-9

56-57 Q1: Bury Town (A) 1-1, (H) 1-6

57-58 Q1: Lowestoft Town (H) 2-4

58-59 Q1: Long Melford (A) 2-2, (H) 4-2
Q2: Stowmarket (A) 1-5

64-65 Q1: Ely City (A) 1-5

65-66 Q1: Sudbury Town (A) 0-3

66-67 Q1: Great Yarmouth Town (A) 3-0
Q2: Harwich & Parkeston (H) 2-0
Q3: Lowestoft Town (H) 4-4, (A) 4-6

67-68 Q1: Ely City (A) 1-5

69-70 Q1: Lowestoft Town (A) 1-6

70-71 PR: Gorleston (H) 0-7

78-79 PR: Lowestoft Town (H) 0-0, (A) 0-2

79-80 PR: Wolverton Town & B.R. (H) 4-0
Q1: Letchworth G.C. (A) 1-1, (H) 1-0
Q2: Chesham United (H) 0-0, (A) 0-3

80-81 Q1: Gorleston (H) 2-3

81-82 Q1: Barton Rovers (A) 0-1

82-83 PR: Epping Town (H) 3-0
Q1: Aveley (A) 0-5

83-84 Q1: Lowestoft Town (H) 0-1

84-85 PR: Boreham Wood (A) 1-2

85-86 Q1: Hitchin (A) 1-1, (H) 0-0, (A) 0-3

86-87 Q1: King's Lynn (A) *Scratched*

87-88 Q1: Milton Keynes Boro. (H) 1-1, (A) 4-0
Q2: March Town United (H) 0-1

88-89 PR: Billericay Town (A) 1-0
Q1: Wycombe Wanderers (A) 1-4

89-90 PR: Racing Club Warwick (A) 1-1, (H) 1-0
Q1: Corby Town (H) 1-1, (A) 3-2
Q2: Hitchin Town (H) 2-3

90-91 PR: Eynesbury Rovers (H) 1-1, (A) 2-0
Q1: V.S. Rugby (H) 1-1, (A) 0-5

91-92 PR: King's Lynn (A) 2-5

92-93 PR: Letchworth Garden C. (A) 1-1, (H) 3-4

HAYDOCK C. & B. REC.

Currently: Defunct

46-47 Q2: Newton Y.M.C.A. (H) 1-1, (A) 3-1
Q3: Prescot Cables (A) 2-2, (H) 1-0
Q4: Marine (A) 0-7

47-48 PR: Earlestown (A) 0-3

48-49 PR: Formby (A) 2-4

49-50 EX: Prescot B.I. (H) 5-2
PR: Bangor City (H) 1-2

50-51 PR: Burscough (H) 1-3

HAYES

Currently: Isthmian League

45-46 PR: Maidenhead United (H) 4-1
Q1: Southall (H) 1-1, (A) 1-2

46-47 PR: Pressed Steel (H) 7-1
Q1: Wycombe Wanderers (A) 4-3
Q2: Slough United (H) 6-3
Q3: Uxbridge (H) 3-2
Q4: Dulwich Hamlet (H) 4-2
R1: Bristol City (A) 3-9

47-48 PR: Windsor & Eton (H) 3-1
Q1: Wycombe Wanderers (A) 0-1

48-49 EX: Slough Town (A) 1-2

49-50 EX: Windsor & Eton (A) 3-2
PR: Banbury Spencer (H) 1-0
Q1: Yiewsley (A) 2-2, (H) 3-2
Q2: Slough Town (A) 2-1
Q3: Southall (H) 4-1
Q4: Leytonstone (A) 2-3

50-51 PR: Southall (H) 3-0
Q1: Cheshunt (H) 7-1
Q2: Hendon (A) 0-2

51-52 Q1: Berkhamsted Town (H) 5-0
Q2: Wealdstone (A) 0-2

52-53 PR: Yiewsley (H) 6-1
Q1: Uxbridge (H) 0-3

53-54 PR: Uxbridge (A) 2-2, (H) 2-3

54-55 PR: Edgware Town (A) 2-0
Q1: Wimbledon (H) 1-1, (A) 2-0
Q2: Hendon (H) 3-3, (A) 3-2
Q3: Hounslow Town (A) 1-2

55-56 PR: Finchley (H) 1-4

56-57 PR: Wealdstone (A) 4-2
Q1: Hounslow Town (H) 0-2

57-58 PR: Finchley (A) 3-3, (H) 0-1

58-59 Q1: Southall (A) 2-0
Q2: Wealdstone (A) 4-1 *ab. 82m.*, (H) 1-2

59-60 PR: Wealdstone (H) 2-1
Q1: Staines Town (A) 2-1
Q2: Hounslow Town (H) 1-0
Q3: Southall (A) 1-1, (H) 4-1
Q4: Bedford Town (A) 3-5

60-61 Q1: Southall (A) 1-2

61-62 Q1: Maidenhead United (A) 2-8

62-63 Q1: Uxbridge (H) 3-0
Q2: Finchley (A) 1-1, (H) 1-2

63-64 Q1: Windsor & Eton (H) 2-1
Q2: Finchley (H) 3-1
Q3: Yiewsley (H) 2-0
Q4: Tooting & Mitcham United (H) 1-2

64-65 Q1: Hillingdon Borough (A) 2-1
Q2: Windsor & Eton (A) 1-0
Q3: Finchley (A) 2-1
Q4: Wycombe Wanderers (H) 7-0
R1: Exeter City (A) 0-1

65-66 Q1: Windsor & Eton (H) 1-2

66-67 Q1: Amersham Town (H) 4-1
Q2: Hornchurch (A) 0-1

67-68 Q1: Croydon Amateurs (A) 1-0
Q2: Carshalton Athletic (A) 2-3

68-69 PR: Brentwood Town (H) 1-3

69-70 Q1: Staines Town (H) 2-2, (A) 0-1

70-71 Q1: Harlow Town (H) 3-0
Q2: Clapton (H) 1-0
Q3: Aveley (H) 2-3

71-72 Q1: Kingstonian (H) 2-0
Q2: Wembley (A) 6-1
Q3: Bromley (A) 0-3

72-73 PR: Wembley (A) 3-1
Q1: Hoddesdon Town (H) 4-1
Q2: Erith & Belvedere (A) 2-1
Q3: Wealdstone (H) 3-1
Q4: Barking (A) 2-1
R1: Bristol Rovers (H) 1-0
R2: Reading (A) 0-0, (H) 0-1

73-74 Q4: Enfield (H) 1-1, (A) 1-0
R1: Boston United (A) 0-0, (H) 1-2

74-75 Q4: Southwick (A) 1-2

75-76 Q1: Enfield (A) 0-3

76-77 PR: Leyton-Wingate (H) 2-0
Q1: Staines Town (A) 1-3

77-78 Q1: Ilford (H) 0-2

78-79 PR: Feltham (A) 0-2

79-80 Q1: Aylesbury United (H) 2-0
Q2: Slough Town (H) 2-4

80-81 PR: Hemel Hempstead (H) 2-0
Q1: Newmarket Town (A) 1-1, (H) 5-0
Q2: Finchley (A) 1-0
Q3: Kempston Rovers (A) 2-0
Q4: Yeovil Town (H) 1-1, (A) 0-2

81-82 Q1: Tilbury (H) 1-1, (A) 0-0, (H) 0-0, (A) 1-1, (H) 4-0
Q2: Corinthian-Casuals (A) 1-2

82-83 Q1: Saffron Walden Town (H) 2-1
Q2: Boreham Wood (A) 0-3

83-84 Q1: Wembley (H) 1-3

84-85 Q1: Aylesbury United (A) 2-3

85-86 Q1: Bracknell Town (A) 1-1, (H) 2-1
Q2: Tilbury (A) 0-0, (H) 1-2

86-87 Q1: Chalfont St Peter (A) 3-0
Q2: Uxbridge (A) 1-3

87-88 Q1: Feltham (A - *at Brentford*) 3-1
Q2: Darenth Heathside (H) 4-1
Q3: Fisher Athletic (H) 2-0
Q4: Moor Green (H) 2-0
R1: Swansea City (H) 0-1

88-89 Q1: Chesham United (H) 1-0
Q2: Hemel Hempstead (A) 3-2
Q3: Wealdstone (A) 2-1
Q4: Redditch United (H) 1-0
R1: Aldershot (A) 0-1

89-90 Q4: Hythe Town (A) 0-0, (H) 3-0
R1: Peterborough United (A) 1-1, (H) 0-1

90-91 Q4: Kingstonian (H) 2-0
R1: Cardiff C. (A) 0-0, (H - *at Brentford*) 1-0
R2: A.F.C. Bournemouth (A) 0-1

91-92 Q4: Dorchester Town (H) 1-0
R1: Fulham (A) 2-0
R2: Crawley Town (H) 0-2

92-93 Q4: Newmarket Town (A) 2-0
R1: Brighton & Hove Albion (A) 0-2

Left: *Colin Day (partly hidden) rifles home a wonderful forty yard free-kick to start Hayes on their way to a famous win at Fulham in 1991. Photo: Dave West.*

HAYWARDS HEATH TOWN

Currently: Sussex County League
* - As Haywards Heath F.C.

45-46 * Q1: Newhaven (A) 2-2, (H) 5-0
Q2: Southwick (H) 5-1
Q3: Hastings & St Leonards (H) 1-0
Q4: Trowbridge Town (A) 0-6

46-47 * Q1: Bognor Regis Town (H) 0-1

47-48 * Q1: Horsham (A) 1-1, (H) 3-8

48-49 * PR: Hastings & St Leonards (A) *W/O*
Q1: Horsham (H) 0-1

49-50 * PR: East Grinstead (H) 5-1
Q1: Bognor Regis Town (H) 7-0
Q2: Worthing (A) 4-2
Q3: Hastings United (H) 0-1

50-51 * PR: Bexhill Town (A) 1-0
Q1: Worthing (A) 2-1
Q2: East Grinstead (A) 5-1
Q3: Eastbourne (A) 2-4

51-52 * PR: East Grinstead (A) 5-3
Q1: Eastbourne (H) 1-2

52-53 * PR: Southwick (H) 2-2, (A) 1-0
Q1: East Grinstead (A) 0-1

53-54 * PR: Bexhill Town (A) 3-0
Q1: Lancing Athletic (H) 1-3

54-55 * PR: Bexhill Town (A) 5-2
Q1: Tunbridge Wells United (A) 0-4

55-56 * Q1: Worthing (A) 1-4

56-57 * PR: Eastbourne (H) 2-3

57-58 * PR: Worthing (A) 1-1, (H) 3-3 *ab. in E.T.*, 1-7

58-59 * PR: Eastbourne (A) 1-1, (H) 3-1
Q1: Bognor Regis Town (A) 2-0
Q2: Eastbourne United (A) 1-3

59-60 * Q1: Eastbourne (H) 3-3, (A) 2-4

61-62 * Q1: Lancing Athletic (A) 4-1
Q2: Crawley Town (A) 2-3

62-63 * Q1: Lancing (H) 4-0
Q2: Bognor Regis Town (A) 5-2
Q3: Lewes (H) 0-3

63-64 * Q1: Crawley Town (H) 3-3, (A) 2-7

64-65 * Q1: Horsham (A) 3-3, (H) 1-2

65-66 * Q1: Crawley Town (A) 0-3

66-67 * Q1: Bexhill Town (H) 0-1

67-68 * Q1: Bognor Regis Town (H) 2-1
Q2: Lancing (A) 1-1, (H) 1-1, 0-3

68-69 * Q1: Bognor Regis Town (H) 1-1, (A) 3-2
Q2: Eastbourne United (A) 0-3

69-70 * Q1: Horsham (H) 1-2

70-71 * Q1: Crawley Town (A) 0-3

71-72 * Q1: Chichester City (A) 1-3

72-73 * PR: Ringmer (A) 1-0
Q1: Littlehampton Town (H) 2-2, (A) 2-1
Q2: Arundel (A) 2-1
Q3: Redhill (H) 1-2

73-74 * Q1: Waterlooville (H) 1-1, (A) 1-3

74-75 * Q1: Sidley United (A) 3-1
Q2: Southwick (A) 2-3

75-76 * PR: Burgess Hill Town (H) 0-4

76-77 * Q1: Ringmer (H) 3-1
Q2: Dover (A) 0-2

77-78 * Q1: Sittingbourne (A) 2-0
Q2: Ramsgate (A) 0-2

78-79 * Q1: Wigmore Athletic (H) 4-0
Q2: Worthing (H) 1-2

79-80 * Q1: Dover (H) 0-3

80-81 * PR: Whitstable Town (H) 1-0
Q1: Crawley Town (H) 0-1

81-82 * PR: Bognor Regis Town (A) 1-5

82-83 * Q1: Dartford (H) 1-6

83-84 * Q1: Folkestone (H) 2-6

84-85 * PR: Merstham (H) 2-0
Q1: Woking (H) 2-0
Q2: Sittingbourne (H) 0-3

85-86 * Q1: Croydon (H) 3-5

86-87 * PR: Tonbridge A.F.C. (A) 0-2

87-88 * PR: Steyning Town (H) 4-0
Q1: Chertsey Town (A) 1-3

88-89 PR: Yeading (A) 3-2
Q1: Eastbourne United (H) 3-2
Q2: Dover Athletic (A) 2-5

89-90 PR: A.F.C. Totton (H) 1-2

90-91 PR: Cove (A) 0-4

91-92 PR: Hampton (A) 0-3

92-93 PR: Bedfont (H) 0-1

HAZELLS (AYLESBURY)

Currently: Chiltonian League

69-70 PR: Ware (H) 3-2
Q1: Hounslow (A) 1-6

HEADINGTON UNITED

See Oxford United

HEAD WRIGHTSONS

Currently: Defunct

50-51 PR: Filey Town (A) 7-3
Q1: Bridlington Central United (A) 5-4
Q2: Whitby Town (A) 2-4

51-52 Q1: Bridlington Trinity United (H) 2-3

52-53 Q1: Bridlington Central United (H) 2-0
Q2: Billingham Synthonia Recreation (A) 1-6

53-54 Q2: Ferryhill Athletic (A) 1-7

54-55 Q1: Scarborough (A) 0-3

HEANOR TOWN

Currently: Central Midlands League
* - As Heanor Athletic

48-49 * EX: Linby Colliery (H) 0-1

49-50 * EX: Cinderhill Colliery (A) 7-0
PR: Spalding United (A) 2-3

50-51 * EX: Bourne Town (H) 3-1
PR: Grantham (A) 1-5

54-55 PR: Whitwick Colliery (H) 2-5

55-56 Q2: Brush Sports (H) 1-2

56-57 Q2: Whitwick Colliery (H) 2-0
Q3: Hinckley Athletic (A) 1-4

57-58 Q2: Players Athletic (A) 5-0
Q3: Hinckley Athletic (H) 3-1
Q4: Hereford United (H) 1-5

58-59 Q1: Ransome & Marles (A) 5-1
Q2: Retford Town (A) 1-1, (H) 7-1
Q3: Sutton Town (A) 3-1
Q4: Scarborough (H) 2-2, (A) 3-2
R1: Carlisle United (H) 1-5

59-60 Q1: Retford Town (A) 2-2, (H) 4-0
Q2: Cresswell Colliery (A) 5-2
Q3: South Normanton Welfare (H) 2-1
Q4: Gainsborough Trinity (A) 2-4

60-61 Q1: Matlock Town (A) 1-0
Q2: Sutton Town (A) 2-4

61-62 Q1: Belper Town (H) 4-2
Q2: Matlock Town (H) 4-2
Q3: Sutton Town (H) 5-1
Q4: Kettering Town (A) 0-2

62-63 Q1: Alfreton Town (A) 0-1

63-64 Q2: Sutton Town (H) 5-1
Q3: Matlock Town (A) 1-0
Q4: Gainsborough Trinity (H) 2-0
R1: Bradford Park Avenue (A) 1-3

64-65 Q1: Buxton (H) 2-1
Q2: Belper Town (A) 1-2

65-66 Q1: Alfreton Town (H) 5-3
Q2: Buxton (H) 5-1
Q3: Worksop Town (H) 3-2
Q4: Grantham (A) 4-4, (H) 1-2

67-68 Q1: Arnold (A) 0-3

68-69 Q1: Eastwood Town (A) 2-2, (H) 5-1
Q2: Bedworth Town (A) 2-2, (H) 1-0
Q3: Atherstone Town (A) 2-3

69-70 Q1: Rawmarsh Welfare (A) 1-1, (H) 0-1

70-71 PR: Belper Town (H) 3-1
Q1: Eastwood Town (A) 1-0
Q2: Retford Town (A) 2-1
Q3: Gainsborough Trinity (H) 0-2

71-72 Q1: Newhall United (H) 1-0
Q2: Alfreton Town (A) 1-3

72-73 PR: Norton Woodseats Amat. (A) 0-0, (H) 2-1
Q1: Ilkeston Town (H) 0-0, (A) 2-0
Q2: Eastwood Town (A) 0-2

73-74 PR: Matlock Town (A) 0-3

74-75 Q1: Burton Albion (A) 0-0, (H) 1-3

75-76 Q1: Tividale (H) 2-6

76-77 PR: Eastwood (Hanley) (A) 2-2, (H) 2-0
Q1: Long Eaton United (A) 0-3

77-78 PR: Leek Town (H) 2-2, (A) 0-2

78-79 PR: Boston United (H) 0-3

79-80 PR: Winterton Rangers (H) 0-5

80-81 PR: Gainsborough Trinity (A) 1-3

81-82 PR: Worksop Town (H) 1-3

82-83 PR: Sutton Town (A) 1-2

83-84 Q1: Marine (A) 2-3

84-85 PR: Dudley Town (A) 0-4

85-86 PR: Boldmere St M. (H - *played away*) 0-2

86-87 Q1: St Helens Town (A) 0-6

87-88 PR: Glossop (A) 3-2
Q1: Chadderton (A) 0-1

88-89 PR: Leek Town (A) 0-3

89-90 PR: Formby (H) 2-0
Q1: Bangor City (A) 1-3

90-91 PR: Halesowen Harriers (H) 0-4

91-92 PR: Rossendale United (A) 4-2
Q1: Armthorpe Welfare (H) 0-2

92-93 PR: Denaby United (A) 5-2
Q1: Ilkeston Town (H) 2-1
Q2: Marine (A) 0-2

HEATON STANNINGTON

Currently: Northern Alliance

49-50 EX: Birtley Town (A) 2-2, (H) 2-2, 4-3
PR: Boldon Colliery Welfare (A) 2-1
Q1: Ashington (H) 3-2
Q2: Blyth Spartans (A) 1-5

50-51 PR: South Shields (H) 0-3

51-52 Q1: South Shields (A) 0-4

52-53 Q1: Easington Colliery Welfare (A) 0-3

53-54 Q1: Boldon Colliery Welfare (A) 1-2

54-55 PR: Lynemouth Welfare (H) 3-3, (A) 3-2
Q1: Ashington (H) 1-6

76-77 Q1: Shildon (H) 0-3

HEBBURN

Currently: Northern League

89-90 Q1: Whitby Town (A) 3-1
Q2: South Bank (H) 0-0, (A) 0-3

90-91 PR: Ryhope C.A. (H - *at Washington*) 0-2

91-92 PR: Darwen (A) 1-1, (H) 2-1
Q1: Newcastle Blue Star (A) 1-5

92-93 PR: Annfield Plain (H) 1-1, (A) 1-5

HEDNESFORD TOWN

Currently: Southern League
* - As Hednesford F.C.

45-46 * Q1: Nuneaton Borough (H) 2-2, (A) 2-5

46-47 * PR: Hereford United (H) 0-3

47-48 * PR: Boldmere St Michaels (A) 1-0
Q1: Stourbridge (H) 2-3

48-49 * EX: Bournville Athletic (A) 3-2
PR: Thynnes Athletic (H) 10-0
Q1: Worcester City (H) 4-2
Q2: Bromsgrove Rovers (A) 0-3

49-50 * PR: Dudley Town (H) 0-1

50-51 * EX: Oswestry Town (A) 1-2

51-52 * Q1: Tamworth (H) 0-0, (A) 4-2
Q2: Bedworth Town (A) 0-3

52-53 * PR: Tamworth (A) 2-0
Q1: Nuneaton Borough (H) 1-1, (A) 5-2
Q2: Bedworth Town (H) 0-3

54-55 * PR: Worcester City (A) 3-2
Q1: Kidderminster Harriers (H) 3-2
Q2: Bilston (A) 4-1
Q3: Bromsgrove Rovers (H) 1-2

55-56 * PR: Dudley Town (A) 4-1
Q1: Halesowen Town (H) 0-1

56-57 * PR: Redditch (A) 1-4

57-58 * PR: Worcester City (A) 1-4

58-59 * Q1: Brierley Hill Alliance (H) 0-6

59-60 * Q1: Sutton Coldfield Town (A) 3-2
Q2: Evesham United (A) 1-3

60-61 * Q1: Halesowen Town (H) 2-3

61-62 * Q1: Bilston (H) 3-6

62-63 * Q1: Bilston (A) 3-2
Q2: Rugby Town (A) 0-2

63-64 * Q1: Nuneaton Borough (H) 3-4

64-65 * Q1: Lockheed-Leamington (A) 3-4

65-66 * Q1: Brierley Hill Alliance (A) 1-1, (H) 1-3

66-67 * Q1: Bilston (H) 4-4, (A) 3-2
Q2: Lower Gornal Athletic (A) 3-0
Q3: Brierley Hill Alliance (A) 6-0
Q4: Tamworth (A) 1-1, (H) 1-3

67-68 * Q1: Wellington Town (H) 0-5

68-69 * PR: Lockheed Leamington (A) 2-2, (H) 4-1
Q1: Worcester City (H) 1-2

69-70 * Q1: Worcester City (H) 2-1
Q2: Telford United (A) 3-4

70-71 * Q1: Nuneaton Borough (H) 1-2

71-72 * Q1: Redditch United (H) 0-2

72-73 * Q1: Bromsgrove Rovers (H) 1-5

73-74 * Q1: Brierley Hill Alliance (A) 1-1, (H) 2-1
Q2: Nuneaton Borough (A) 0-1

74-75 * Q1: Gresley Rovers (A) 0-1

75-76 * PR: Brereton (H) 1-1, (A) 1-1, 3-3, 2-0
Q1: Sutton Coldfield Town (A) 0-1

76-77 * Q1: Ilkeston Town (H) 1-0
Q2: Arnold (A) 0-0, (H) 3-0
Q3: Telford United (H) 0-0, (A) 0-3

77-78 Q1: Hyde United (H) 1-0
Q2: Buxton (H) 1-0
Q3: Stalybridge Celtic (A) 1-1, (H) 2-1
Q4: Nuneaton Borough (A) 1-2

78-79 Q1: Frickley Athletic (A) 2-0
Q2: New Mills (H) 4-0
Q3: Winsford United (A) 2-1
Q4: A.P. Leamington (A) 0-0, (H) 2-3

79-80 Q1: Darlaston (A) 2-1
Q2: Lye Town (A) 0-1

80-81 Q1: Kidderminster Harriers (A) 0-3

81-82 PR: Moor Green (H) 3-0
Q1: Bedworth United (H) 1-1, (A) 0-3

82-83 Q1: Congleton Town (H) 1-2

83-84 PR: Brigg Town (A) 0-0, (H) 3-0
Q1: Frickley Athletic (H) 1-2

84-85 Q1: Long Eaton United (A) 3-1
Q2: Ashton United (H) 3-0
Q3: Witton A. (H) 2-2, (A) 2-2, (A) 3-2
Q4: Nuneaton Borough (H) 0-4

85-86 Q1: Milton Keynes Borough (H) 2-1
Q2: Kidderminster Harriers (H) 1-5

86-87 Q1: Witton Albion (A) 2-0
Q2: Skelmersdale United (A) 1-2

87-88 PR: Arnold (A - *played home*) 0-1

88-89 PR: Eastwood Town (H) 1-3

89-90 PR: Lye Town (H) 0-2

90-91 PR: Guiseley (H) 2-0
Q1: Eastwood T. (A) 1-1, (H) 1-1, (A) 3-2
Q2: Hyde United (H) 2-2, (A) 2-5

91-92 PR: Northampton S. (H) 1-1, (A) 1-1, (H) 1-0
Q1: Banbury United (A) 1-2

92-93 Q1: Tamworth (H) 1-1, (A) 4-2
Q2: Rushden & Diamonds (H) 4-1
Q3: Shepshed Albion (A) 2-1
Q4: Dagenham & Redbridge (H) 1-2

HEMEL HEMPSTEAD

Currently: Isthmian League
* - As Hemel Hempstead Town
See also Hemel Hempstead United and Apsley

47-48 * EX: Berkhamsted Town (H) 3-4

48-49 * EX: Chesham United (A) 2-6

49-50 * EX: Marlow (H) 6-0
PR: Headington United (H) 3-1
Q1: Uxbridge (H) 1-4

50-51 * EX: Banbury Spencer (H) 1-1, (A) 1-5

51-52 * PR: Marlow (A) 3-4

52-53 * Q1: Abingdon Town (H) 6-0
Q2: Wycombe Wanderers (H) 1-2

53-54 * PR: Berkhamsted Town (A) 3-3, (H) 4-2
Q1: Hendon (A) 1-2

54-55 * PR: Wingate (H) 2-2, (A) 3-1
Q1: Metropolitan Police (H) 0-0, (A) 2-3

55-56 * Q1: Hounslow Town (H) 1-0
Q2: Finchley (H) 2-5

56-57 * PR: Finchley (A) 0-5

57-58 * Q1: Hounslow Town (H) 1-2

58-59 * PR: Ware (A) 2-2, (H) 1-0
Q1: Berkhamsted Town (A) 2-2, (H) 1-2

62-63 * Q1: Chesham United (H) 3-2
Q2: Aylesbury United (H) 2-0
Q3: Oxford City (A) 3-4

63-64 * Q1: Newbury Town (A) 0-0, (H) 6-0
Q2: Oxford City (H) 5-0
Q3: Maidenhead United (A) 1-2

64-65 * Q1: Huntley & Palmers (A) 6-0
Q2: Chesham United (A) 1-1, (H) 3-2
Q3: Oxford City (H) 1-1, (A) 2-4

65-66 * Q1: Abingdon Town (H) 6-0
Q2: Banbury Spencer (H) 5-1
Q3: Oxford City (H) 0-1

66-67 * Q1: Huntley & Palmers (H) 1-0
Q2: Banbury United (H) 6-3
Q3: Chesham United (H) 2-3

67-68 * Q1: Kingstonian (H) 1-0
Q2: Hampton (A) 2-3

68-69 * Q1: Leyton (A) 2-3

69-70 * Q1: Edmonton (A) 0-2

70-71 * Q1: Kingstonian (A) 0-2

71-72 * Q1: Addlestone (H) 2-2, (A) 1-1, 1-4

72-73 * Q1: Dartford (H) 2-9

73-74 * PR: Maidenhead United (A) 0-2

74-75 * Q1: Hitchin Town (H) 2-3

75-76 Q1: Cheshunt (A) 2-2, (H) 0-2

76-77 Q1: Dulwich Hamlet (A) 0-0, (H) 1-2

77-78 Q1: Barton Rovers (A) 1-1, (H) 3-1
Q2: Letchworth G.C. (H) 2-2, (A) 3-4

78-79 PR: Harlow Town (A) 1-1, (H) 0-4

79-80 Q1: Edgware (H) 1-2

80-81 PR: Hayes (A) 0-2

81-82 Q1: Banbury United (A) 1-2

82-83 PR: Hillingdon Borough (H) 0-0, (A) 0-1
Q1: Haringey Borough (A) 3-0
Q2: Dulwich Hamlet (H) 1-2

83-84 PR: Three Bridges (A) 2-3

84-85 Q1: King's Lynn (H) 0-2

85-86 PR: Rothwell Town (A) 3-3, (H) 1-0
Q1: Nuneaton Borough (H) 1-3

86-87 PR: Baldock Town (H) 2-2, (A) 0-1

87-88 PR: Soham Town Rangers (A) 0-0, (H) 1-0
Q1: Ely City (A) 1-1, (H) 2-1
Q2: Berkhamsted Town (A) 3-3, (H) 1-4

88-89 Q1: Baldock Town (H) 5-1
Q2: Hayes (H) 2-3

89-90 Q1: Uxbridge (A) 0-1

90-91 PR: Metropolitan Police (H) 1-2

91-92 PR: Tring Town (A) 3-0
Q1: Corby Town (A) 0-1

92-93 Q1: Solihull Borough (H) 1-2

HEMEL HEMPSTEAD UTD

Currently: Merged with Apsley
Playing as Hemel Hempstead in Isthmian League
See also Hemel Hemstead

45-46 PR: Kings Langley (H) 4-7

HENDON

Currently: Isthmian League

46-47 EX: Pinner (A) 3-2
PR: Finchley (A) 1-3

48-49 EX: Welwyn Garden City (A) 3-0
PR: Hoddesdon Town (H) 2-1
Q1: Finchley (A) 2-1
Q2: Enfield (H) 3-0
Q3: Wealdstone (H) 4-2
Q4: Barnet (A) 4-5

49-50 PR: Wealdstone (H) 0-4

50-51 PR: Barnet (A) 3-2
Q1: Edgware Town (H) 7-1
Q2: Hayes (H) 2-0
Q3: Enfield (A) 4-2
Q4: Tonbridge (A) 3-3, (H) 1-3

51-52 Q4: Aylesbury United (A) 3-4

52-53 Q1: Wealdstone (A) 1-0
Q2: St Albans City (A) 1-1, (H) 3-1
Q3: Uxbridge (H) 3-1
Q4: Dartford (A) 3-0
R1: Northampton Town (H) 0-0, (A) 0-2

53-54 PR: Harrow Town (A) 3-2
Q1: Hemel Hempstead Town (H) 2-1
Q2: Yiewsley (H) 2-2, (A) 0-2

54-55 PR: Berkhamsted Town (A) 3-0
Q1: Yiewsley (H) 2-1
Q2: Hayes (A) 3-3, (H) 2-3

55-56 R1: Halesowen Town (A) 4-2
R2: Exeter City (A) 2-6

56-57 PR: Yiewsley (A) 0-1

57-58 PR: Wealdstone (A) 5-0
Q1: Finchley (A) 0-4

58-59 Q1: Finchley (H) 3-2
Q2: Dagenham (H) 3-1
Q3: Hornchurch & Upminster (A) 1-0
Q4: Wycombe Wanderers (H) 1-3

59-60 PR: Ford United (A) 2-1
Q1: Edgware Town (A) 1-0
Q2: Hornchurch & Upminster (H) 0-2

60-61 R1: Oxford United (H) 2-2, (A) 2-3

61-62 Q1: Leyton (H) 9-1
Q2: Dagenham (A) 1-3

62-63 Q1: Leytonstone (H) 1-0
Q2: Ford United (H) 2-1
Q3: Leyton (H) 4-1
Q4: Andover (H) 1-1, (A) 4-5

63-64 Q1: Leytonstone (H) 4-2
Q2: Clapton (H) 8-0

Above: *The boot that did it! Rod Haider shows his appreciation, and is congratulated by Tony Jennings, in the dressing room after scoring the goal that gave Hendon their famous draw away to Newcastle United in 1974. The replay was held at Vicarage Road, Watford, on a weekday afternoon because it was during the 'Three-Day Week' and so floodlights could not be used.*

Q3: Dagenham (H) 3-0
Q4: Enfield (A) 1-3

64-65 Q1: Leyton (A) 3-2
Q2: Ford United (A) 5-2
Q3: Leytonstone (H) 2-1
Q4: Slough Town (H) 3-1
R1: Port Vale (A) 1-2

65-66 R1: Grantham (A) 1-4

66-67 R1: Reading (H) 1-3

67-68 Q4: Romford (H) 1-2

68-69 Q1: Hertford Town (A) 0-0, (H) 1-0
Q2: Slough Town (A) 1-2

69-70 Q1: Bishop's Stortford (A) 2-1
Q2: Rainham Town (A) 1-1, (H) 7-2
Q3: Hertford Town (A) 4-2
Q4: Cambridge City (H) 1-0
R1: Carshalton Athletic (H) 5-3
R2: Brentwood Town (H) 0-2

70-71 Q4: St Albans City (H) 0-0, (A) 2-1
R1: Aldershot (H) 0-2

71-72 Q4: Barnet (H) 2-2, (A) 0-2

72-73 R1: Plymouth Argyle (A) 0-1

73-74 Q4: Barnet (A) 2-2, (H) 3-0
R1: Leytonstone (H) 3-0
R2: Merthyr Tydfil (A) 3-0
R3: Newcastle U. (A) 1-1, (H - *at Watford*) 0-4

74-75 Q4: Maidstone United (H) 0-2

75-76 Q4: Canterbury City (H) 1-0
R1: Reading (H) 1-0
R2: Swindon Town (H) 0-1

Right: *The save of the match from Hendon goalkeeper, Malcolm Dalrymple. Ray Hiron, the Reading skipper wriggled clear of the defence, but Dalrymple made a superb stop to take his side to their most recent triumph over a League club. Photo: Denis Eaglefield, Reading Chronicle.*

76-77 Q4: Waterlooville (A) 1-4

77-78 Q4: Billericay Town (H) 3-2
R1: Watford (A) 0-2

78-79 Q4: Hitchin Town (H) 1-3

79-80 Q1: Buckingham Town (A) 7-0
Q2: Maidenhead United (A) 2-2, (H) 0-3

80-81 Q1: Hillingdon Borough (A) 0-0, (H) 3-2
Q2: Woking (H) 1-1, (A) 4-1
Q3: Aylesbury United (H) 1-1, (A) 0-1

81-82 PR: Abingdon Town (A) 2-1
Q1: Ampthill Town (A) 1-0
Q2: Banbury United (H) 2-2, (A) 4-3
Q3: Tring Town (H) 4-0
Q4: Harrow Borough (H) 2-1
R1: Wycombe Wanderers (H) 1-1, (A) 0-2

82-83 Q1: Merstham (A) 2-0
Q2: Wealdstone (H) 1-1, (A) 2-3

83-84 Q1: Dorking (A) 1-1, (H) 4-1
Q2: Addlestone & Weybridge Town (A) 1-2

84-85 Q1: Dunstable (H) 1-3

85-86 Q1: Ruislip Manor (A) 0-1

86-87 Q1: Banstead Athletic (H) 2-2, (A) 1-0
Q2: Chertsey Town (A) 1-0
Q3: Welling United (H) 0-1

87-88 Q1: Ware (A) 1-0
Q2: Hertford Town (H) 1-2

88-89 Q1: Harwich & Parkeston (H) 5-1
Q2: Braintree Town (H) 3-1
Q3: Bishop's Stortford (H) 5-3
Q4: V.S. Rugby (A) 1-1, (H) 2-0
R1: Reading (A) 2-4

89-90 Q1: Barking (A) 1-1, (H) 2-2, (A) 2-1
Q2: Lowestoft Town (H) 7-0
Q3: Sudbury Town (A) 2-1
Q4: Aylesbury United (A) 1-4

90-91 Q1: Metropolitan Police (A) 3-1
Q2: Ruislip Manor (A) 1-2

91-92 Q1: Stowmarket Town (A) 4-1
Q2: Baldock Town (H) 1-2

92-93 Q1: Hertford Town (A) 2-0
Q2: Burnham (H) 6-0
Q3: Wembley (A) 0-1

HENLEY TOWN

Currently: Chiltonian League

46-47 EX: Uxbridge (H) 6-6, (A) 1-3

47-48 EX: Lyons Club (H) 1-7

48-49 EX: Oxford City (A) 1-9

49-50 EX: Pressed Steel (H) 4-2
PR: Yiewsley (H) 0-3

HEREFORD UNITED

Currently: Football League

45-46 Q1: Moor Green (H) 0-8

46-47 PR: Hednesford (A) 3-0
Q1: Bournville Athletic (H) 1-0
Q2: Worcester City (H) 3-0
Q3: Nuneaton Borough (H) 5-0
Q4: Cheltenham Town (A) 1-1, (H) 3-4

47-48 PR: Thynnes Athletic (A) 11-0
Q1: Stafford Rangers (H) 2-1
Q2: Stourbridge (A) 0-4

48-49 PR: Boldmere St Michaels (H) 6-1
Q1: Halesowen Town (H) 2-0
Q2: Stafford Rangers (A) 5-3
Q3: Bromsgrove Rovers (A) 4-2
Q4: Oxford City (H) 4-3
R1: Kidderminster Harriers (A) 3-0
R2: Exeter City (A) 1-2

49-50 Q4: Cheltenham Town (H) 1-1, (A) 2-2, 4-2
R1: Bromsgrove Rovers (H) 3-0
R2: Weymouth (A) 1-2

50-51 PR: Bournville Athletic (A) 5-1
Q1: Kidderminster Harriers (A) 1-0
Q2: Wellington Town (A) 4-1
Q3: Oswestry Town (A) 2-1
Q4: Scunthorpe United (H) 1-0
R1: Bromsgrove Rovers (A) 3-1
R2: Newport County (H) 0-3

51-52 Q4: Peterborough United (A) 1-1, (H) 1-0
R1: Guildford City (A) 1-4

52-53 Q4: Brush Sports (A) 1-0
R1: Leyton (A) 0-0, (H) 3-2
R2: Scunthorpe United (H) 0-0, (A) 1-2

53-54 Q4: Brush Sports (A) 2-2, (H) 3-0
R1: Exeter City (A) 1-1, (H) 2-0
R2: Wigan Athletic (A) 1-4

54-55 Q4: Nuneaton Borough (A) 2-3

55-56 Q4: Nuneaton Borough (A) 8-1
R1: Swindon Town (A) 0-4

56-57 Q4: Lockheed-Leamington (A) 4-1
R1: Aldershot (H) 3-2

Above: *Brian Owen (10) reels away after scoring a seventeenth second goal against Newcastle at St James' Park. The then Southern League side eventually beat their First Division opponents in an historic televised replay at Edgar Street. Photo: Hereford Times.*

R2: Southend United (H) 2-3

57-58 Q4: Heanor Town (A) 5-1
R1: Newport Isle of Wight (A) 3-0
R2: Queens Park Rangers (H) 6-1
R3: Sheffield Wednesday (H) 0-3

58-59 Q4: Nuneaton Borough (A) 2-2, (H) 3-1
R1: Guildford City (A) 2-1
R2: Newport County (H) 0-2

59-60 Q4: Worcester City (A) 3-0
R1: Newport County (A) 2-4

60-61 Q4: Lockheed-Leamington (A) 2-1
R1: Bridgwater Town (A) 0-3

61-62 Q4: Sankey of Wellington (A) 1-0
R1: Bristol City (A) 1-1, (H) 2-5

62-63 Q4: Worcester City (A) 2-0
R1: Crystal Palace (A) 0-2

63-64 Q4: Hinckley Athletic (H) 1-1, (A) 1-1, 3-2
R1: Newport County (H) 1-1, (A) 0-4

64-65 Q4: Atherstone Town (A) 3-1
R1: Oldham Athletic (A) 0-4

65-66 Q4: Cheltenham Town (A) 1-0
R1: Leytonstone (A) 1-0
R2: Millwall (H) 1-0
R3: Bedford Town (A) 1-2

66-67 Q4: Kidderminster Harr. (H) 1-1, (A) 4-2
R1: Peterborough United (A) 1-4

67-68 Q4: Cheltenham Town (H) 3-2
R1: Barnet (H) 3-2
R2: Watford (A) 0-3

68-69 Q4: Worcester City (H) 4-1
R1: Torquay United (H) 0-0, (A) 2-4

69-70 Q4: Rugby Town (H) 3-1
R1: Chelmsford City (A) 2-1
R2: Newport County (A) 1-2

70-71 Q4: Kidderminster Harriers (H) 5-0
R1: Northampton Town (H) 2-2, (A) 2-1
R2: Brighton & Hove Albion (H) 1-2

71-72 Q4: Cheltenham Town (H) 3-0
R1: King's Lynn (A) 0-0, (H) 1-0
R2: Northampton T. (H) 0-0, (A) 2-2, (*at W. Bromwich Albion*) 2-1
R3: Newcastle United (A) 2-2, (H) 2-1
R4: West Ham United (H) 0-0, (A) 0-3

72-73 R1: Torquay United (A) 0-3

73-74 R1: Torquay United (H) 3-1
R2: Walton & Hersham (H) 3-0
R3: West Ham United (A) 1-1, (H) 2-1
R4: Bristol City (H) 0-1

74-75 R1: Gillingham (H) 1-0
R2: Cambridge United (A) 0-2

75-76 R1: Torquay United (H) 2-0
R2: A.F.C. Bournemouth (A) 2-2, (H) 2-0
R3: York City (A) 1-2

76-77 R3: Reading (H) 1-0
R4: Middlesbrough (A) 0-4

77-78 R1: Wealdstone (A) 0-0, (H) 2-3

78-79 R1: Newport County (H) 0-1

79-80 R1: Northampton Town (H) 1-0
R2: Aldershot (H) 1-2

80-81 R1: Southend United (A) 1-0
R2: Enfield (A) 0-2

81-82 R1: Southend United (H) 3-1
R2: Fulham (H) 1-0
R3: Scunthorpe United (A) 1-1, (H) 4-1
R4: Leicester City (H) 0-1

82-83 R1: Portsmouth (A) 1-4

83-84 R1: Reading (A) 0-2

84-85 R1: Farnborough Town (H) 3-0
R2: Plymouth Argyle (A) 0-0, (H) 2-0
R3: Arsenal (H) 1-1, (A) 2-7

85-86 R1: Yeovil Town (A) 4-2
R2: Reading (A) 0-2

86-87 R1: Fulham (H) 3-3, (A) 0-4

87-88 R1: Barnet (A) 1-0
R2: Colchester United (A) 2-3

Below: *Frenetic action from Hereford's First Round tie at Barnet. Photo: J B Vass.*

88-89 R1: Cardiff City (A) 0-3

89-90 R1: Farnborough Town (A) 1-0
R2: Merthyr Tydfil (H) 3-2
R3: Walsall (H) 2-1
R4: Manchester United (H) 0-1

90-91 R1: Peterborough United (H) 1-1, (A) 1-2

91-92 R1: Atherstone United (A) 0-0, (H) 3-0
R2: Aylesbury United (A) 3-2
R3: Woking (A) 0-0, (H) 2-1
R4: Nottingham Forest (A) 0-2

92-93 R1: Sutton United (A) 2-1
R2: Yeovil Town (A) 0-0, (H) 1-2

HERNE BAY

Currently: Kent League

65-66 Q1: Whitstable (A) 3-1
Q2: Canterbury City (A) 0-1

66-67 Q1: Canterbury City (H) 0-4

67-68 Q1: Bexhill Town (H) 0-2

68-69 Q1: Sheppey United (A) 1-1, (H) 3-5

69-70 Q1: Folkestone (A) 0-0, (H) 1-1, 0-1

70-71 Q1: Ashford Town (H) 2-1
Q2: Ramsgate Athletic (A) 0-0, (H) 3-1
Q3: Tonbridge (H) 4-1
Q4: Margate (H) 0-1

71-72 Q1: Faversham Town (H) 3-1
Q2: Maidstone United (A) 0-3

72-73 Q1: Tunbridge Wells (H) 5-0
Q2: Ashford Town (A) 0-6

73-74 PR: Ramsgate (A) 1-2

74-75 Q1: Canterbury City (A) 0-4

75-76 Q1: Faversham Town (A) 1-2

76-77 PR: Whitstable Town (H) 4-1
Q1: Ramsgate (A) 1-2

77-78 Q1: Bromley (H) 2-2, (A) 0-5

78-79 PR: Horsham Y.M.C.A. (H) 1-1, (A) 0-1

79-80 PR: Eastbourne Town (H) 0-2

80-81 PR: Tonbridge A.F.C. (H) 0-3

81-82 Q1: Epsom & Ewell (A) 1-2

82-83 PR: Bognor Regis Town (H) 0-1

83-84 Q1: Gravesend & Northfleet (H) 1-3

84-85 Q1: Walthamstow Avenue (H) 0-3

85-86 Q1: Carshalton Athletic (H) 1-5

86-87 Q1: Worthing (A) 1-0
Q2: Arundel (A) 3-1
Q3: Whitstable Town (H) 1-0
Q4: Farnborough Town (A) 0-4

87-88 Q1: Gravesend & Northfleet (A) 1-6

88-89 PR: Molesey (A) 0-7

89-90 PR: Horsham (H) 3-1
Q1: Dover Athletic (H) 0-6

90-91 Q1: Lewes (H) 0-1

91-92 Q1: Kingstonian (H) 0-2

92-93 PR: Camberley Town (H) 3-3, (A) 3-2
Q1: Banstead Athletic (A) 1-4

HERTFORD TOWN

Currently: Isthmian League

45-46 PR: Enfield (H) 3-6

46-47 EX: Leavesden (H) 6-2
PR: Saffron Walden Town (H) 7-2
Q1: St Albans City (A) 1-5

49-50 EX: Finchley (H) 3-5

50-51 EX: Polytechnic (A) 6-2
PR: Wealdstone (H) 1-3

55-56 PR: St Albans City (H) 1-2

56-57 Q1: Letchworth Town (A) 0-0, (H) 3-0
Q2: Hitchin Town (H) 0-1

57-58 PR: Eton Manor (A) 1-3

58-59 Q1: Enfield (H) 0-2

59-60 Q1: Cheshunt (H) 7-0
Q2: Bishop's Stortford (A) 1-0
Q3: Enfield (H) 2-3

60-61 Q1: Ware (H) 5-1
Q2: Harrow Town (A) 2-3

61-62 Q1: Enfield (A) 1-8

62-63	Q1: Barnet (A) 0-2
63-64	Q1: Wealdstone (A) 1-0 Q2: Barnet (A) 1-3
64-65	Q1: Harrow Town (H) 2-0 Q2: Barnet (A) 0-0, (H) 0-2
65-66	Q1: Wealdstone (H) 1-2
66-67	Q1: Epsom & Ewell (H) 2-1 Q2: Windsor & Eton (A) 2-2, (H) 4-1 Q3: Cheshunt (H) 0-0, (A) 0-1
67-68	Q1: Feltham (A) 1-1, (H) 8-0 Q2: Slough Town (A) 0-3
68-69	Q1: Hendon (H) 0-0, (A) 0-1
69-70	Q1: Slough Town (H) 1-0 Q2: Corinthian-Casuals (A) 2-1 Q3: Hendon (H) 2-4
70-71	Q1: Bexley United (A) 2-2, (H) 1-2
71-72	PR: Leytonstone (H) 1-1, (A) 1-2
72-73	PR: Bromley (H) 2-1 Q1: Ford United (H) 2-0 Q2: Barking (A) 0-1
73-74	Q1: Wokingham Town (H) 5-1 Q2: Chesham United (H) 2-0 Q3: Ware (A) 0-0, (H) 3-1 Q4: Hillingdon Borough (A) 1-2
74-75	Q1: Dunstable (A) 2-3
75-76	PR: Burnham (H) 0-2
76-77	PR: Romford (H) 1-1, (A) 2-1 Q1: Boreham Wood (H) 1-2
77-78	Q1: Tring Town (H) 1-1, (A) 3-2 Q2: Kempston Rovers (H) 1-0 Q3: Letchworth Garden City (H) 0-3
78-79	PR: Harrow Borough (A) 2-0 Q1: Sutton United (A) 1-2
79-80	Q1: Banbury United (H) 3-1 Q2: Bedford Town (H) 0-2
80-81	Q1: Kempston Rovers (A) 0-3
81-82	Q1: Redhill (A) 2-1 Q2: Finchley (H) 4-3 Q3: Corinthian-Casuals (A) 0-2
82-83	Q1: Wealdstone (A) 0-5
83-84	Q1: Horsham Y.M.C.A. (H) 1-1, (A) 2-2, (H) 2-0 Q2: Bognor Regis Town (H) 1-1, (A) 0-2
84-85	Q1: Sutton Coldfield Town (H) 2-2, (A) 1-2
85-86	PR: Harefield United (H) 1-1, (A) 0-3
86-87	PR: Soham Town Rangers (A) 1-0 Q1: Woodford Town (A) 0-2
87-88	PR: Potton United (H) 1-1, (A) 2-1 Q1: Grays Athletic (A) 3-1 Q2: Hendon (A) 2-1 Q3: Aylesbury United (H) 0-4
88-89	PR: Darenth Heathside (A) 1-0 Q1: Gravesend & Northfleet (A) 3-1 Q2: Wokingham Town (A) 1-3
89-90	PR: Darenth Heathside (A) 3-3, (H) 4-1 Q1: Burnham (H) 0-1
90-91	PR: Clacton Town (A) 1-0 Q1: Chesham United (A) 0-0, (H) 1-5
91-92	PR: Northwood (H) 3-2 Q1: Staines Town (H) 2-0 Q2: Dulwich Hamlet (H) 2-1 Q3: Windsor & Eton (H) 1-2

Right: *Hertford defend in their win over Diadora League Division One promotion contenders Dulwich.*
Photo: Paul Dennis.

92-93	Q1: Hendon (H) 0-2

HESSLE OLD BOYS (HULL)

Currently: Defunct

48-49	EX: Meltham Mills (H) 2-3

HEXHAM HEARTS

Currently: Defunct

48-49	EX: Cramlington Welfare (A) 4-3 PR: Birtley Town (H) 5-0 Q1: North Shields (A) 0-0, (H) 1-2
49-50	PR: W. Stanley (A - *at Annfield P.*) 0-0, (H) 2-1 Q1: South Shields (A) 1-3
50-51	PR: Amble (A) 1-1, (H) *Amble withdrew* Q1: Alnwick Town (H) 2-1 Q2: Ashington (A) 0-0, (H) 2-6
51-52	Q1: West Sleekburn Welfare (A) 2-2, (H) 6-0 Q2: Blyth Spartans (A) 0-4
52-53	Q1: Cramlington Welfare (A) 1-0 Q2: Ashington (H) 3-5
53-54	Q1: Cramlington (H) 3-3, (A) 4-3 *ab. in E.T.*, 5-2 Q2: Alnwick Town (H) 3-2 Q3: Newburn (H) 5-4 Q4: Horden Colliery Welfare (H) 2-2, (A) 0-2
54-55	Q1: West Sleekburn Welfare (A) 2-3
55-56	Q1: North Shields (H) 2-4

HEYBRIDGE SWIFTS

Currently: Isthmian League

81-82	Q1: Gorleston (H) 2-1 Q2: Wisbech Town (H) 2-2, (A) 1-2
82-83	PR: Thetford Town (H) 1-0 Q1: Woodford Town (A) 1-3
83-84	Q1: Soham Town Rangers (H) 1-0 Q2: V.S. Rugby (H) 2-2, (A) 0-2
84-85	Q1: Bromley (A) 1-1, (H) 2-1 Q2: Chesham United (H) 0-0, (A) 2-1 Q3: Buckingham Town (H) 0-0, (A) 0-1
85-86	Q1: Great Yarmouth Town (A) 1-0 Q2: Harlow Town (A) 0-1
86-87	Q1: Walthamstow A. (A - *at B. Stortford*) 2-3
87-88	PR: Dorking (H) 1-1, (A) 1-2
88-89	PR: Gorleston (H) 3-1 Q1: Bishop's Stortford (A) 1-3
89-90	PR: Ford United (H) 1-1, (A) 2-0 Q1: Grays Athletic (H) 2-1 Q2: Halstead Town (H) 1-0 Q3: Dartford (H) 0-1
90-91	Q1: Sudbury Town (A) 3-1 Q2: Wembley (A) 2-2, (H) 3-1 Q3: Cambridge City (H) 1-0 Q4: Barnet (A) 1-3
91-92	Q1: Aveley (A) 2-0 Q2: Mirrlees Blackstone (H) 1-1, (A) 1-0 Q3: Kettering Town (A) 0-3
92-93	Q1: Cambridge City (H) 2-4

HIGH DUTY ALLOYS (DISTINGTON)

Currently: Defunct
* - As Distington

46-47 *	PR: Lowca (H) 1-7
47-48 *	PR: William Colliery (A) 2-8
48-49	PR: Scalegill (A) 8-3 Q1: Moss Bay (A) 3-2 Q2: Penrith (H) 4-4, (A) 2-3
49-50	Q1: Scalegill (A) *withdrew*

HIGHGATE UNITED

Currently: Midland Combination

69-70	Q1: Moor Green (A) 1-1, (H) 3-2 Q2: Dudley Town (A) 0-3
70-71	PR: Worcester City (H) 1-1, (A) 1-5
71-72	Q1: Kidderminster Harriers (H) 3-1 Q2: Lockheed Leamington (A) 2-0 Q3: Redditch United (A) 0-3
72-73	PR: Sutton Coldfield Town (A) 0-0, (H) 2-0 Q1: Lower Gornal Athletic (H) 6-0 Q2: Bromsgrove Rovers (A) 1-2
73-74	Q1: Worcester City (H) 1-1, (A) 2-1 Q2: Lye Town (H) 1-0 Q3: Nuneaton Borough (A) 4-1 Q4: Telford United (A) 0-2
74-75	Q1: Oldbury United (H) 2-1 Q2: Kidderminster Harriers (A) 2-5
75-76	Q1: Gornal Athletic (A) 0-1
76-77	Q1: Darlaston (A) 1-2
77-78	Q1: Willenhall Town (H) 2-1 Q2: Kidderminster Harriers (H) 0-2
78-79	Q1: Stourbridge (H) 2-1 Q2: Worcester City (H) 0-0, (A) 2-3
79-80	Q1: Brereton Social (H) 0-2
80-81	PR: Gresley Rovers (A) 1-1, (H) 3-1 Q2: Witton Albion (A) 1-3
81-82	Q1: Kempston Rovers (H) 2-2, (A) 2-1 Q2: Malvern Town (A) 1-2
82-83	PR: Chipping Norton Town (H) 3-0 Q1: V.S. Rugby (A) 1-3
83-84	PR: Bridgnorth Town (H) 1-2
84-85	Q1: Mangotsfield United (A) 0-0, (H) 1-3
85-86	PR: Oldswinford (A) 1-2
86-87	PR: Banbury United (H) 1-3
87-88	PR: Bilston (H) 1-1, (A) 0-0, (A) 0-2
88-89	PR: Rushden Town (H) 0-4
89-90	PR: Hinckley Athletic (A) 0-2
90-91	PR: Stratford Town (A) 1-3
91-92	PR: Chasetown (H) 0-3
92-93	PR: Gresley Rovers (A) 2-4

HILLINGDON

Currently: Merged with Burnham
Playing as Burnham in Southern League
See also Burnham (2)

83-84	Q1: Erith & Belvedere (H) 2-1 Q2: Hitchin Town (H) 0-1
84-85	PR: Braintree (A) 0-0, (H) 0-0, (H) 0-2

HILLINGDON BOROUGH

Currently: Defunct
* - As Yiewsley

45-46 * PR: Marlow (A) 4-3
Q1: Slough United (H) 4-4, (A) 0-2

46-47 * EX: Wycombe Redfords (A) 7-3
PR: Maidehead United (H) 3-3, (A) 0-3

47-48 * EX: Windsor & Eton (H) 3-3, (A) 2-3

48-49 * EX: Uxbridge (A) 1-1, (H) 3-3, (A - *at Hayes*) 0-3

49-50 * EX: Rickmansworth Town (A) 2-2, (H) 2-0
PR: Henley Town (A) 3-0
Q1: Hayes (H) 2-2, (A) 2-3

50-51 * EX: Buckingham Town (A) 5-1
PR: Leavesden (A) 2-1
Q1: Aylesbury United (H) 2-2, (A) 0-2

51-52 * PR: Maidenhead United (A) 1-4

52-53 * PR: Hayes (A) 1-6

53-54 * PR: Windsor & Eton (A) 3-3, (H) 2-1
Q1: Uxbridge (A) 1-0
Q2: Hendon (A) 2-2, (H) 2-0
Q3: Wealdstone (H) 0-3

54-55 * PR: Southall (H) 1-0
Q1: Hendon (A) 1-2

55-56 * PR: Southall (H) 0-0, (A) 1-2

56-57 * PR: Hendon (A) 1-0
Q1: Uxbridge (A) 4-1
Q2: Finchley (A) 2-1
Q3: Southall (A) 1-0
Q4: Clacton Town (A) 3-2
R1: Gillingham (H) 2-2, (A) 0-2

57-58 * Q1: Wembley (A) 1-0
Q2: Finchley (H) 4-1
Q3: Hounslow Town (A) 1-3

58-59 * Q1: Hounslow Town (A) 2-0
Q2: Wembley (H) 3-1
Q3: Wealdstone (H) 1-2

59-60 * Q1: Uxbridge (H) 2-1
Q2: Southall (A) 1-1, (H) 1-2

60-61 * Q1: Uxbridge (A) 1-4

61-62 * Q1: Windsor & Eton (A) 2-0
Q2: Finchley (H) 2-0
Q3: Maidenhead United (A) 3-2
Q4: Banbury Spencer (A) 0-4

62-63 * Q1: Edgware Town (A) 3-0
Q2: Maidenhead United (A) 2-3

63-64 * Q1: Southall (H) 2-2, (A) 3-0
Q2: Uxbridge (A) 0-0, (H) 2-1
Q3: Hayes (A) 0-2

64-65 Q1: Hayes (H) 1-2

65-66 Q1: Corinthian-Casuals (H) 1-2

66-67 Q1: Aylesbury United (H) 6-0
Q2: Enfield (A) 0-3

67-68 Q1: Aveley (H) 4-0
Q2: Sutton United (A) 1-5

68-69 Q1: Bromley (H) 7-0
Q2: Tilbury (A) 3-0
Q3: Bexley United (H) 3-0
Q4: Brentwood Town (H) 0-0, (A) 0-2

69-70 Q1: Tooting & Mitcham U. (H) 0-0, (A) 2-1
Q2: Bromley (H) 4-1
Q3: Tilbury (A) 2-1
Q4: Dartford (H) 0-0, (A) 1-1, 4-1
R1: Wimbledon (H) 2-0
R2: Luton Town (H) 2-1
R3: Sutton United (H) 0-0, (A) 1-4

70-71 Q4: Slough Town (A) 2-2, (H) 0-2

71-72 R1: Brighton & Hove Albion (A) 1-7

72-73 Q4: Redhill (H) 0-0, (A) 1-0
R1: Chelmsford City (A) 0-2

73-74 Q4: Hertford Town (H) 2-1
R1: Grantham (H) 0-4

74-75 Q4: Ashford Town (H) 1-2

75-76 Q1: Bexley United (A) 2-0
Q2: Dulwich Hamlet (A) 1-5

76-77 Q1: Harlow Town (A) 2-2, (H) 2-0
Q2: Molesey (A) 1-1, (H) 2-1
Q3: Staines Town (H) 2-0
Q4: Hastings United (H) 2-0
R1: Torquay United (A) 2-1
R2: Watford (H) 2-3

77-78 PR: Slough Town (H) 3-3, (A) 1-0
Q1: Grays Athletic (A) 1-1, (H) 4-1
Q2: Barking (A) 3-1
Q3: Cheshunt (A) 0-1

78-79 PR: Finchley (A) 1-0
Q1: Molesey (A) 2-2, (H) 2-1
Q2: Boreham Wood (A) 2-0
Q3: Kingstonian (A) 0-0, (H) 3-2
Q4: Tooting & Mitcham United (H) 2-1
R1: Swansea City (A) 1-4

79-80 Q1: Chertsey Town (A) 1-0
Q2: Ware (A) 1-1, (H) 3-0
Q3: Leytonstone-Ilford (A) 1-2

80-81 Q1: Hendon (H) 0-0, (A) 2-3

81-82 Q1: Tunbridge Wells (H) 7-2
Q2: Basingstoke Town (A) 2-4

82-83 PR: Hemel Hempstead (A) 0-0, (H) 0-1

HINCKLEY

Currently: Merged with Barwell Athletic
Playing as Barwell in Midland Combination
See also Barwell

91-92 PR: Bridgnorth Town (H) 2-4

HINCKLEY ATHLETIC

Currently: West Midlands (Regional) League

48-49 PR: Morris Sports (A) 5-1
Q1: Gresley Rovers (A) 3-4

49-50 PR: Morris Sports (H) 11-0
Q1: Gresley Rovers (H) 1-3

50-51 PR: Newhall United (A) 2-2, (H) 2-1
Q1: Ibstock Penistone Rovers (H) 4-0
Q2: Lockheed-Leamington (H) 7-0
Q3: Brush Sports (H) 0-1

51-52 Q1: Barwell Athletic (H) 1-1, (A) 7-2
Q2: Sth Normanton Welfare (H) 2-2, (A) 2-1
Q3: Brush Sports (H) 2-3

52-53 Q1: Whitwick Colliery (H) 2-3

53-54 Q1: Players Athletic (H) 5-0
Q2: Raleigh Athletic (A) 3-0
Q3: Brush Sports (A) 1-2

54-55 Q1: Long Eaton Town (A) 7-1
Q2: Brush Sports (A) 4-3
Q3: Whitwick Colliery (A) 2-2, (H) 4-1
Q4: Bromsgrove Rovers (H) 2-1
R1: Newport Isle of Wight (H) 4-3
R2: Rochdale (A) 1-2

55-56 Q4: Halesowen Town (H) 1-4

56-57 Q1: Brush Sports (A) 2-2, (H) 5-1
Q2: Long Eaton Town (A) 4-3
Q3: Heanor Town (H) 4-1
Q4: Burton Albion (A) 1-6

57-58 Q1: Brush Sports (A) 1-0
Q2: Long Eaton Town (H) 4-4, (A) 9-1
Q3: Heanor Town (A) 1-3

58-59 Q1: Brush Sports (H) 1-2

59-60 Q1: Brush Sports (H) 0-1

60-61 Q1: Atherstone Town (A) 3-0
Q2: Loughborough United (A) 1-2

61-62 Q1: Ilkeston Town (A) 1-1, (H) 2-1
Q2: Atherstone Town (H) 5-1
Q3: Nuneaton Boro. (H) 2-2, (A) 1-1, 3-1
Q4: Grantham (A) 1-2

62-63 Q1: Loughborough United (H) 4-2
Q2: Tamworth (H) 0-0, (A) 1-0
Q3: Atherstone Town (H) 3-1
Q4: Brierley Hill Alliance (A) 3-1
R1: Sittingbourne (H) 3-0
R2: Queens Park Rangers (A) 2-7

63-64 Q4: Hereford Utd (A) 1-1, (H) 1-1, 2-3

64-65 Q4: Spalding United (A) 1-3

65-66 Q1: Tamworth (A) 1-1, (H) 4-2
Q2: Burton Albion (A) 1-8

66-67 Q1: Worcester City (H) 0-4

67-68 Q1: Darlaston (H) 0-1

68-69 PR: Lower Gornal Ath. (H) 1-1, (A) 2-3

70-71 Q1: Newhall United (H) 1-1, (A) 1-4

72-73 Q1: Irthlingborough D. (A) 1-1, (H) 1-2

73-74 Q1: Stourbridge (H) 2-4

74-75 Q1: Atherstone Town (A) 1-5

75-76 PR: Dudley Town (H) 0-4

76-77 PR: Tividale (H) 0-1

77-78 Q1: Tamworth (H) 0-0, (A) 1-1, (A) 2-1
Q2: Darlaston (A) 1-0
Q3: Telford United (A) 0-1

78-79 Q1: Long Eaton United (H) 5-0
Q2: Arnold (H) 1-0
Q3: Irthlingborough Diamonds (H) 1-2

79-80 Q1: Rushden Town (A) 3-2
Q2: Dudley Town (H) 2-1 *(void)*, (A) 0-1

80-81 Q1: Coventry Sporting (A) 3-2
Q2: Tamworth (H) 2-1
Q3: King's Lynn (A) 1-5

81-82 Q1: Ilkeston Town (A) 0-2

82-83 PR: Arnold (A) 1-0
Q1: Grantham (A) 0-2

83-84 Q1: Shepshed Charterhouse (H) 0-1

84-85 Q1: Stalybridge Celtic (H) 1-3

85-86 Q1: Willenhall Town (H) 2-1
Q2: March Town United (A) 2-1
Q3: Nuneaton Borough (A) 0-0, (H) 0-1

86-87 Q1: Kidderminster Harriers (H) 0-1

87-88 PR: Wednesfield Social (A) 1-0
Q1: Bedworth United (H) 2-3

88-89 PR: Winsford United (H) 3-0
Q1: Buxton (H) 1-3

89-90 PR: Highgate United (H) 2-0
Q1: Frickley Athletic (H) 1-3

90-91 PR: Friar Lane Old Boys (H) 3-1
Q1: Grantham (H) 2-1
Q2: Burton Albion (A) 0-4

91-92 PR: Holbeach United (A) 3-2
Q1: Alfreton Town (A) 0-1

92-93 PR: Stratford Town (A) 2-6

HINCKLEY TOWN

Currently: Southern League

87-88 PR: Bridgnorth Town (H) 2-1
Q1: Sutton Coldfield Town (A) 1-1, (H) 2-1
Q2: Oldbury United (A) 2-5

88-89 PR: Stourbridge (H) 2-0
Q1: Lye Town (A) 3-0
Q2: Gresley Rovers (H) 1-0
Q3: Boston United (A) 4-3
Q4: Welling United (A) 1-1, (H) 0-3

89-90 Q1: Stafford Rangers (A) 0-1

90-91 PR: Nuneaton Borough (A) 1-4

91-92 PR: Boldmere St Michaels (H) 3-1
Q1: Leicester United (H) 2-0
Q2: Shepshed Albion (H) 3-3, (A) 2-3

92-93 PR: Willenhall Town (H) 1-1, (A) 1-2

HISTON

Currently: Eastern Counties League
* - As Histon Institute

47-48 * PR: Abbey United (A) 6-4
Q1: Parson Drove United (H) 3-2
Q2: March Town United (A) 0-1

48-49 * Q1: March Town United (H) 2-1
Q2: King's Lynn (H) 3-4

49-50 * Q1: South Lynn (H) 4-2
Q2: King's Lynn (H) 2-2, (A) 2-5

50-51 * Q1: Parson Drove United (H) 1-0
Q2: Newmarket Town (A) 3-1
Q3: King's Lynn (A) 1-3

51-52 * Q1: St Neots & District (A) 3-6

52-53 * Q1: Wisbech Town (A) 0-3

53-54 PR: Holbeach United (A) 1-0
Q1: Cambridge City (H) 2-5

54-55 PR: Warboys Town (H) 4-2
Q1: Thetford Town (H) 1-2

55-56 PR: King's Lynn (A) 1-6

56-57 PR: Ely City (H) 2-5

57-58 PR: Cambridge City (H) 1-2

58-59 PR: Wisbech Town (H) 0-5

59-60 Q1: Cambridge City (H) 1-4

60-61 Q1: March Town United (H) 1-2

61-62 Q1: Bury Town (H) 2-3

67-68 Q1: Rushden Town (A) 0-8

68-69 Q1: Bedford Town (A) 0-5

70-71 Q1: Irthlingborough Diamonds (A) 1-2

71-72 PR: Rothwell Town (H) 4-2
Q1: Ely City (A) 0-4

72-73 PR: Soham Town Rangers (A) 2-0
Q1: Potton United (H) 1-3

73-74 Q1: Bourne Town (H) 1-0
Q2: Bedford Town (H) 2-1
Q3: Corby Town (H) 0-2

74-75 Q1: Stamford (A) 3-1
Q2: Corby Town (A) 2-3

75-76 Q1: Letchworth Town (H) 0-2

76-77 Q1: Potton United (H) 1-4

77-78 Q1: Chelmsford City (H) 0-1

78-79 Q1: Parson Drove (H) 3-1
Q2: St Neots Town (H) 0-1

79-80 PR: V.S. Rugby (H) 0-2

80-81 PR: Irthlingborough Diamonds (H) 3-0
Q1: Tamworth (A) 0-3

81-82 PR: Leyton-Wingate (H) 1-4

84-85 PR: Wootton Blue Cross (A) 2-3

85-86 PR: Soham Town Rangers (H) 3-0
Q1: Finchley (H) 3-1
Q2: Corby Town (H) 0-1

86-87 PR: March Town U. (A) 1-1, (H) 1-1, (A) 2-3

87-88 Q1: Walthamstow Avenue (H) 2-1
Q2: Leytonstone-Ilford (H) 1-2

88-89 PR: Wisbech Town (H) 0-1

89-90 Q1: Stratford Town (A) 0-2

90-91 Q1: Rothwell Town (H) 2-1
Q2: Redditch United (H) 1-1, (A) 0-1

91-92 PR: March Town Utd (A) 1-1, (H) 2-1
Q1: Sudbury Town (A) 0-1

92-93 PR: Long Buckby (H) 1-2

HITCHIN TOWN

Currently: Isthmian League

45-46 Q1: Vauxhall Motors (H) 3-2
Q2: Bedford Avenue (H) 0-2

46-47 Q1: Letchworth Town (A) 2-0
Q2: Bedford Avenue (A) 8-0
Q3: Bedford Town (A) 2-2, (H) 3-2
Q4: Peterborough United (A) 1-4

47-48 PR: Waterlows (H) 8-0
Q1: Wolverton Town (A) 2-1
Q2: Bedford Town (H) 2-3

48-49 PR: Arlesey Town (H) 0-0, (A) 3-2
Q1: Leighton United (H) 4-2
Q2: Potton United (A) 1-1, (H) 3-1
Q3: Vauxhall Motors (A) 1-2

49-50 PR: Houghton Rangers (H) 5-0
Q1: Eynesbury Rovers (A) 1-0
Q2: Baldock Town (H) 4-1
Q3: Bedford Town (A) 0-2

50-51 PR: Marston Shelton Rovers (H) 2-1
Q1: Huntingdon United (A) 5-1
Q2: Wootton Bassett Town (A) 4-3
Q3: Bedford Town (H) 2-3

51-52 Q1: Eynesbury Rovers (H) 1-7

52-53 PR: Dunstable Town (A) 4-2
Q1: Luton Amateurs (H) 5-0
Q2: Wolverton Town & B.R. (H) 6-2
Q3: Bedford Town (H) 2-3

53-54 Q1: Letchworth Town (H) 3-3, (A) 1-0
Q2: Eton Manor (A) 1-1, (H) 7-1
Q3: Tufnell Park Edmonton (H) 5-1
Q4: Leytonstone (A) 1-0
R1: Peterborough United (H) 1-3

54-55 PR: Ware (A) 3-2
Q1: Barnet (A) 0-2

55-56 Q1: Ware (H) 5-0
Q2: Eton Manor (A) 3-3, (H) 2-1
Q3: Enfield (H) 3-1
Q4: Leyton (A) 1-3

56-57 PR: Ware (A) 1-1, (H) 5-2
Q1: Shefford Town (A) 6-2
Q2: Hertford Town (A) 1-0
Q3: Eton Manor (A) 1-3

57-58 Q1: Ware (A) 1-3

58-59 Q1: Dunstable Town (H) 6-2
Q2: Stevenage Town (A) 1-1, (H) 4-3
Q3: Vauxhall Motors (A) 2-0
Q4: Woodford Town (H) 1-1, (A) 3-2
R1: Millwall (H) 1-1, (A) 1-2

59-60 Q1: Wolverton Town & B.R. (A) 1-2

60-61 Q1: Biggleswade Town (H) 4-0
Q2: Vauxhall Motors (H) 3-0
Q3: St Albans City (H) 4-0
Q4: Abingdon Town (H) 2-0
R1: Crystal Palace (A) 2-6

61-62 Q1: Biggleswade Town (H) 2-1
Q2: Bedford Town (H) 3-2
Q3: Cambridge City (H) 2-1
Q4: Barnet (A) 2-3

62-63 Q1: Vauxhall Motors (H) 0-0, (A) 3-0
Q2: Bedford Town (H) 3-5

63-64 Q1: Vauxhall Motors (H) 4-2
Q2: Letchworth Town (A) 2-1
Q3: Biggleswade Town (A) 2-2, (H) 5-1
Q4: Cambridge United (A) 1-4

64-65 Q1: Biggleswade Town (H) 2-2, (A) 4-2
Q2: St Albans City (H) 4-0
Q3: Bletchley Town United (H) 0-4

65-66 Q1: Letchworth Town (H) 4-1
Q2: St Albans City (A) 0-2

66-67 Q1: Banbury United (H) 1-4

67-68 Q1: St Albans City (A) 0-0, (H) 3-1
Q2: Dulwich Hamlet (H) 3-1
Q3: Leytonstone (A) 1-2

68-69 Q1: Cheshunt (H) 3-1
Q2: Woodford Town (H) 3-1
Q3: St Albans City (H) 0-2

69-70 Q1: Chesham United (H) 5-0
Q2: Cheshunt (H) 3-1
Q3: Wycombe Wanderers (A) 0-1

70-71 Q1: Finchley (A) 2-2, (H) 4-1
Q2: Walton & Hersham (H) 1-1, (A) 0-3

71-72 Q1: Tilbury (H) 2-2, (A) 2-3

72-73 PR: Dunstable (H) 3-0
Q1: Fleet Town (H) 2-1
Q2: Bishop's Stortford (A) 1-4

73-74 Q1: Stevenage A. (H) 1-1, (A) 1-1, 3-2
Q2: Rothwell Town (A) 7-1
Q3: Bletchley Town (A) 1-1, (H) 2-0
Q4: Bognor Regis Town (H) 2-1
R1: Guildford City (H) 1-1, (A) 4-1
R2: Boston United (A) 0-1

74-75 Q1: Hemel Hempstead (A) 3-2
Q2: Dunstable (A) 0-0, (H) 2-1
Q3: St Albans City (H) 2-1
Q4: Barnet (A) 1-1, (H) 2-0
R1: Cambridge United (H) 0-0, (A) 0-3

75-76 Q4: Romford (H) 0-1

76-77 Q4: Dover (A) 2-2, (H) 3-1
R1: Weymouth (A) 1-1, (H) 2-2, (*at Aldershot*) 3-3, (*at Salisbury*) 3-1
R2: Swindon T. (H) 1-1, (A) 0-1 *abandoned (fog) after 67 minutes*, (A) 1-3

77-78 Q4: Kettering Town (H) 2-2, (A) 1-2

78-79 Q4: Hendon (A) 3-1
R1: A.F.C. Bournemouth (A) 1-2

79-80 Q4: Enfield (H) 1-2

80-81 Q1: Rushden Town (H) 3-0
Q2: Gorleston (A) 1-0
Q3: Bedford Town (H) 3-2
Q4: Sutton Coldfield Town (H) 0-1

81-82 Q1: Southall (H) 1-2

82-83 Q1: Wellingborough Town (H) 0-4

83-84 Q1: Burnham (H) 2-1
Q2: Hillingdon (A) 1-0
Q3: Chesham United (A) 2-0
Q4: Gainsborough Trinity (H) 0-1

84-85 Q1: Beckenham Town (A) 2-0
Q2: Fisher Athletic (H) 1-1, (A) 1-3

85-86 Q1: Haverhill (H) 1-1, (A) 0-0, (H) 3-0
Q2: V.S. Rugby (H) 0-0, (A) 1-3

86-87 Q1: Grays Athletic (A) 1-6

87-88 Q1: Berkhamsted Town (A) 1-3

88-89 PR: Edgware Town (A) 4-1
Q1: Boreham Wood (A) 0-2

89-90 PR: Leicester United (H) 3-1
Q1: Wisbech Town (H) 3-2
Q2: Haverhill Rovers (A) 3-2
Q3: Redditch United (H) 0-2

90-91 Q1: Braintree Town (H) 0-1

91-92 PR: Tiptree United (H) 1-1, (A) 0-1

92-93 PR: Chatteris Town (H) 3-1
Q1: Wisbech Town (H) 4-2
Q2: V.S. Rugby (A) 0-3

Below: *More like an Olympic 100m than an F.A. Cup Preliminary Round tie; Hitchin's David Taylor is just outpaced by a Chatteris defender, but the home side win the tie. Photo: John Wood, Hitchin Herald & Post.*

HODDESDON TOWN

Currently: South Midlands League

45-46 PR: Bishop's Stortford (H) 0-0, (A) 1-4

46-47 PR: Berkhamsted Town (H) 4-3
Q1: Bishop's Stortford (H) 3-2
Q2: Finchley (A) 2-4

47-48 PR: Edmonton Borough (H) 5-3
Q1: Edgware Town (H) 1-2

48-49 EX: Pinner (A) 7-0
PR: Hendon (A) 1-2

49-50 EX: Edgware (H - *played away*) 1-1, (A) 0-3

50-51 EX: Cheshunt (A) 2-4

54-55 Q1: Shefford Town (A) 5-2
Q2: Barnet (A) 0-3

55-56 Q1: Enfield (H) 2-5

56-57 Q1: Bishop's Stortford (A) 0-1

57-58 Q1: St Albans City (H) 2-2, (A) 1-4

58-59 Q1: Cheshunt (A) 0-4

59-60 Q1: St Albans City (H) 2-0
Q2: Enfield (A) 0-15

66-67 Q1: Bletchley (H) 0-7

67-68 Q1: Finchley (A) 1-0
Q2: Crittall Athletic (A) 0-2

68-69 Q1: Baldock Town (H) 1-1, (A) 2-0
Q2: Vauxhall Motors (A) 0-1

69-70 Q1: Vauxhall Motors (H) 4-2
Q2: Baldock Town (A) 1-0
Q3: Braintree & Crittall Ath. (H) 1-1, (A) 1-3

70-71 Q1: Ilford (H) 1-1, (A) 0-2

71-72 Q1: Metropolitan Police (H) 2-1
Q2: Walthamstow Avenue (A) 0-2

72-73 Q1: Hayes (A) 1-4

74-75 Q1: Finchley (A) 1-0
Q2: Harlow Town (A) 0-1

75-76 PR: Dunstable Town (H) 1-2

76-77 Q1: Epping Town (A) 2-3

77-78 Q1: Boreham Wood (H) 0-1

78-79 PR: Felixstowe Town (A) 0-1

79-80 PR: Ruislip Manor (H) 1-2

80-81 PR: Edgware (A) 3-4

81-82 PR: Bedford Town (A) 0-4

82-83 Q1: Windsor & Eton (H) 0-2

83-84 PR: Merstham (H - *at Ware*) 1-0
Q1: Dartford (H) 0-4

84-85 PR: Cambridge City (A - *Royston Town*) 1-3

85-86 PR: Harwich & Parkeston (A) 3-2
Q1: Dunstable (H) 1-3

86-87 PR: Great Yarmouth T. (H - *at Ware*) 0-2

87-88 PR: Southall (H - *at Ware*) 2-0
Q1: Wembley (H) 1-3

88-89 PR: Arlesey Town (A) 1-1, (H) 1-3

89-90 PR: Berkhamsted T. (H - *at Hertford T.*) 2-3

90-91 PR: Rayners Lane (A) 1-2

91-92 PR: Halstead Town (A) 2-3

92-93 PR: Chalfont St Peter (A) 0-1

HOFFMANN ATHLETIC (CHELMSFORD)

Currently: Defunct

45-46 Q1: Ford Sports (A) 2-4

46-47 PR: Leyton (A) 0-3

48-49 EX: Brentwood & Warley (H - *played away*) 0-8

HOFFMANN ATHLETIC (STONEHOUSE)

Currently: Defunct

46-47 EX: Frome Town (H) 7-0
PR: Paulton Rovers (A) 4-2
Q1: Clandown (H) 2-1
Q2: Melksham (H) 5-1
Q3: Trowbridge Town (H) 3-4

47-48 PR: Ebbw Vale (A) 0-2

48-49 EX: Bristol Aero. Company (A) 4-0
PR: Hanham Athletic (A) 1-3

49-50 EX: Llanelly (A) 1-6

50-51 PR: Mount Hill Enterprise (A) 1-1, (H) 2-1
Q1: Merthyr Tydfil (A) 0-7

HOLBEACH UNITED

Currently: United Counties League

47-48 PR: Gedling Colliery (A) 1-6

48-49 PR: Sth Normanton Miners Welfare (A) 1-5

49-50 EX: Boston United (A) 0-7

50-51 EX: Bentinck Welfare (H) 2-0
PR: Langold W.M.C. (A) 1-2

51-52 Q1: Lysaght's Sports (H) 5-0
Q2: Skegness Town (A) 0-4

52-53 PR: Retford Town (A) 1-2

53-54 PR: Histon (H) 0-1

54-55 PR: St Neots & District (H) 4-1
Q1: Somersham Town (A) 7-1
Q2: King's Lynn (H) 2-2, (A) 1-3

55-56 PR: Newmarket Town (H) 6-0
Q1: Wisbech Town (A) 2-2, (H) 0-2

56-57 Q1: Cambridge United (H) 2-2, (A) 0-5

57-58 PR: King's Lynn (A) 1-3

58-59 PR: Ely City (A) 5-3
Q1: Soham Town Rangers (A) 3-1
Q2: Cambridge United (A) 2-1
Q3: Wisbech Town (A) 0-4

59-60 Q1: St Neots Town (A) 1-1, (H) 3-2
Q2: Cambridge United (A) 0-3

60-61 Q1: Alford United (H) 7-1
Q2: Louth United (A) 3-0
Q3: Skegness Town (H) 1-0
Q4: Loughborough United (H) 1-2

61-62 Q1: Grantham (H) 0-2

62-63 Q1: Alford United (A) 1-1, (H) 6-4
Q2: Skegness Town (H) 2-3

63-64 Q1: Boston United (H) 2-2, (A) 1-0
Q2: Grantham (A) 0-2

64-65 Q1: Louth United (A) 5-2
Q2: Grantham (A) 1-1, (H) 0-1

65-66 Q1: Louth United (H) 2-0
Q2: Skegness Town (A) 2-2, (H) 0-1

66-67 Q1: Spalding United (A) 2-5

67-68 Q1: Boston United (A) 1-1, (H) 0-2

68-69 Q1: Spalding United (H) 1-1, (A) 5-2
Q2: Wisbech Town (A) 1-3

69-70 Q1: Bourne Town (H) 1-2

70-71 Q1: Boston United (A) 0-4

71-72 Q1: Stamford (H) 1-4

72-73 Q1: Bourne Town (H) 0-1

73-74 Q1: Boston (A) 2-0
Q2: Stamford (A) 1-3

74-75 Q1: Skegness Town (A) 0-3

75-76 Q1: Great Yarmouth Town (A) 0-1

76-77 Q1: Stamford (A) 2-3

77-78 Q1: Ely City (A) 2-1
Q2: Boston (H) 0-1

78-79 PR: Louth United (H) 0-3

79-80 PR: Skegness Town (H) 2-2, (A) 1-2

80-81 Q1: Ilkeston Town (A) 0-0, (H) 1-0
Q2: Boston (H) 0-3

81-82 PR: Boston (A) 0-5

82-83 Q1: Long Eaton United (H) 3-1
Q2: Rushall Olympic (H) 1-0
Q3: Moor Green (H) 2-1
Q4: Corby Town (A) 1-0
R1: Wrexham (H - *at Peterborough Utd*) 0-4

83-84 Q1: Great Yarmouth Town (A) 1-3

84-85 PR: Stevenage Borough (A) 0-8

85-86 PR: Rushden Town (H) 1-1, (A) 3-3, (A) 0-1

86-87 Q1: Bromsgrove Rovers (A) 0-2

87-88 PR: Walsall Wood (H) 1-4

88-89 PR: Banbury United (H) 1-4

89-90 Q1: Rushden Town (A) 5-4
Q2: Tamworth (A) 0-1

90-91 PR: Potton United (H) 1-2

91-92 PR: Hinckley Athletic (H) 2-3

HOLMEHEAD WORKS

Currently: Defunct

50-51 PR: Cleator Moor Celtic (A) 0-1

HOLT UNITED

Currently: Anglian Combination

49-50 PR: Gorleston (A) 1-4

50-51 PR: Thetford Town (H) 1-5

HOLYHEAD TOWN

Currently: Anglesey League

64-65 Q1: Runcorn (A) 2-5

65-66 Q1: New Brighton (H) 2-4

67-68 Q1: Portmadoc (H) 4-0
Q2: Bangor City (A) 1-3

68-69 Q1: Bangor City (H) 2-3

70-71 Q1: Portmadoc (A) 0-6

HORDEN COLLIERY WELF.

Currently: Northern League

46-47 EX: Easington C.W. (H) 3-3, (A) 0-2

47-48 EX: Dawdon Colliery Welfare (A) 0-0, (H) 9-0
PR: Spennymoor United (H) 2-0
Q1: West Auckland Town (A) 0-1

48-49 EX: Crook Colliery Welfare (A) 3-0
PR: East Tanfield Colliery Welfare (H) *W/O*
Q1: Spennymoor United (H) 3-1
Q2: Evenwood Town (A) 2-1
Q3: Stanley United (A) 3-1
Q4: Stockton (A) 2-1
R1: Southport (A) 1-2

49-50 PR: Ferryhill Athletic (H) 8-4
Q1: Willington (A) 2-2, (H) 4-0
Q2: Easington Colliery Welfare (H) 2-1
Q3: Silksworth Colliery (H) 3-1
Q4: Billingham Syn. Rec. (A) 1-1, (H) 0-1

50-51 PR: Eppleton Colliery Welfare (H) 1-0
Q1: Consett (H) 4-0
Q2: Evenwood Town (H) 4-0
Q3: Blackhall Colliery Welfare (H) 4-1
Q4: Bishop Auckland (A) 0-2

51-52 Q1: Seaham Colliery Welfare (H) 9-1
Q2: Murton Colliery (A) 3-0
Q3: Blackhall Colliery Welfare (A) 1-3

52-53 Q1: Seaham Colliery Welfare (A) 3-1
Q2: Blackhall Colliery Welfare (H) 3-0
Q3: Ushaw Moor (H) 4-1
Q4: Blyth Spartans (H) 2-1
R1: Accrington Stanley (H) 1-2

53-54 Q1: Silksworth Colliery Welfare (H) 1-0
Q2: Seaham Colliery Welfare (A) 2-0
Q3: Ushaw Moor (H) 4-2
Q4: Hexham Hearts (A) 2-2, (H) 2-1
R1: Wrexham (H) 0-1

54-55 Q4: Spennymoor United (H) 1-0
R1: Scunthorpe United (H) 0-1

55-56 Q4: Easington Colliery Welfare (H) 0-1

56-57 Q1: Ferryhill Athletic (A) 3-0
Q2: Chilton Athletic (H) 10-0
Q3: Spennymoor United (H) 3-0
Q4: South Shields (A) 0-1

57-58 Q2: Ferryhill Athletic (H) 3-1
Q3: Ashington (H) 3-1
Q4: South Shields (A) 2-4

58-59 Q1: Shildon (A) 6-2
Q2: North Shields (A) 1-4

59-60 Q1: North Shields (H) 2-2, (A) 1-3

60-61 Q2: Bedlington Mechanics (H) 3-1
Q3: Shildon (H) 5-1
Q4: Blyth Spartans (H) 1-3

61-62 Q1: Ferryhill Athletic (A) 1-0
Q2: Whitley Bay (A) 4-0
Q3: Shildon (A) 0-1

62-63 Q1: Billingham Synthonia (A) 2-2, (H) 4-2
Q2: Stanley United (A) 1-0
Q3: Annfield Plain (H) 2-0
Q4: Blyth Spartans (A) 1-2

63-64 Q1: Bishop Auckland (A) 0-0, (H) 2-1
Q2: West Auckland Town (H) 1-0
Q3: Ferryhill Athletic (H) 3-2
Q4: Netherfield (H) 0-3

64-65 Q2: Ferryhill Athletic (H) 4-1
Q3: North Shields (A) 2-0
Q4: Annfield Plain (A) 2-3

65-66 Q1: Shildon (A) 4-0
Q2: Blyth Spartans (A) 2-0
Q3: Whitley Bay (H) 1-0
Q4: Gateshead (A) 1-3

66-67 Q1: Spennymoor United (A) 2-0
Q2: Ashington (H) 2-1
Q3: Bishop Auckland (H) 0-1

67-68 PR: North Shields (H) 1-0
Q1: Ashington (A) 2-3

68-69 Q1: Whitby Town (H) 2-1
Q2: Bishop Auckland (A) 1-2

69-70 Q1: Shildon (H) 0-1

70-71 Q1: Stanley Utd (H) 0-0, (A) 1-1, 1-2

71-72 Q1: Spennymoor United (A) 2-4

72-73 Q1: North Shields (H) 0-2

73-74 Q1: Crook Town (A) 3-1
Q2: Wingate (H) 3-2
Q3: Ashington (H) 1-1, (A) 1-2

74-75 Q1: Ashington (A) 1-2

75-76 Q1: Bridlington Town (H) 1-1, (A) 1-4

76-76 PR: Wingate (H) 2-3

77-78 PR: Spennymoor United (H) 2-2, (A) 1-3

78-79 Q1: Gateshead (A) 0-1

79-80 Q1: Durham City (H) 6-0
Q2: Washington (A) 5-0
Q3: Bishop Auckland (H) 4-1
Q4: Burscough (H) 0-2

80-81 Q1: Willington (H) 1-0
Q2: Spennymoor United (A) 2-1
Q3: Barrow (H) 0-0, (A) 3-2
Q4: Blyth Spartans (A) 0-7

81-82 Q1: Brandon United (H) 1-1, (A) 3-1
Q2: Tow Law Town (A) 4-1
Q3: Ashington (H) 0-0, (A) 3-1
Q4: Hyde United (H) 2-0
R1: Blackpool (H - *at Hartlepool Utd*) 0-1

82-83 Q1: Ferryhill Athletic (A) 3-1
Q2: North Shields (H) 0-1

83-84 Q1: West Auckland Town (H) 3-2
Q2: Chester-le-Street Town (H) 6-1
Q3: Easington Colliery (H) 3-2
Q4: Penrith (A) 0-3

84-85 Q1: Blue Star (A) 0-3

85-86 PR: Langley Park Welfare (A) 6-2
Q1: Crook Town (H) 2-3

86-87 Q1: Gretna (A) 1-6

87-88 PR: Penrith (A) 0-7

88-89 Q1: Ferryhill Athletic (H) 0-2

89-90 PR: Whitley Bay (H) 0-3

90-91 PR: Crook Town (A) 2-1
Q1: Workington (A) 1-1, (H) 2-1
Q2: Northallerton Town (H) 0-3

91-92 PR: Darlington Cleveland Bridge (A) 2-3

92-93 PR: Darwen (H) 1-1, (A) 0-5

HORLEY TOWN

Currently: Combined Counties League

82-83 Q1: Carshalton Athletic (H) 1-2

83-84 Q1: Bromley (A) 1-3

84-85 PR: Ruislip Manor (H) 0-3

85-86 PR: Walton & Hersham (H) 0-5

HORNCHURCH

Currently: Isthmian League
See also Hornchurch & Upminster

61-62 Q1: Dagenham (H) 2-6

62-63 Q1: Clapton (A) 3-2
Q2: Leyton (H) 1-2

63-64 Q1: Wembley (A) 2-0
Q2: Dagenham (A) 0-2

64-65 Q1: Ilford (A) 4-3
Q2: Aveley (H) 4-0
Q3: Walthamstow Avenue (A) 1-3

65-66 Q1: Grays Athletic (A) 0-1

66-67 Q1: Croydon Amateurs (A) 2-1
Q2: Hayes (H) 1-0
Q3: Bexley United (H) 2-2, (A) 3-0
Q4: Chelmsford City (H) 0-4

67-68 Q1: Ruislip Manor (A) 1-0
Q2: Cray Wanderers (H) 2-4

68-69 Q1: Dartford (A) 0-4

69-70 Q1: Egham (H) 1-1, (A) 0-0 *ab. 115m.*, 5-2
Q2: Dagenham (H) 0-2

70-71 Q1: Corinthian-Casuals (H) 3-2
Q2: Redhill (A) 0-0, (H) 2-1
Q3: Leytonstone (H) 1-2

71-72 PR: Metropolitan Police (H) 1-4

72-73 Q1: Walthamstow Avenue (H) 0-8

73-74 Q1: Sutton United (H) 0-0, (A) 0-2

74-75 Q1: Metropolitan Police (H) 2-1
Q2: Leatherhead (A) 0-5

75-76 Q1: Aveley (A) 1-1, (H) 3-1
Q2: Chesham United (A) 0-2

76-77 PR: Feltham (A) 1-0
Q1: Southall & Ealing Borough (A) 1-2

77-78 Q1: Leyton-Wingate (H) 0-1

78-79 Q1: Leytonstone (H) 1-1, (A) 1-4

79-80 Q1: Harlow Town (H) 0-3

80-81 PR: Walthamstow Avenue (H) 2-3

81-82 Q1: Woodford Town (H) 0-0, (A) 1-2

82-83 Q1: Harwich & Parkeston (H) 1-0
Q2: Tring T. (A) 2-2, (H) 0-0, (H) 0-3

83-84 PR: Crawley Town (H) 1-0
Q1: Tring Town (H) 3-2
Q2: St Albans City (A) 0-3

84-85 PR: Finchley (A) 2-1
Q1: Woodford Town (H) 2-1
Q2: Chelmsford City (H) 1-1, (A) 1-6

85-86 Q1: Egham Town (A) 1-1, (H) 0-1

86-87 PR: Aveley (A) 1-0
Q1: Basildon United (A) 2-0
Q2: King's Lynn (H) 1-1, (A) 0-2

87-88 PR: Horsham Y.M.C.A. (H) 7-0
Q1: Redhill (A) 3-3, (H) 1-3

88-89 PR: Chesham United (A) 1-1, (H) 5-6

89-90 PR: Merstham (A - *played away*) 2-1
Q1: Erith & Belvedere (H) 1-2

90-91 PR: Burnham Ramblers (A) 2-0
Q1: Biggleswade Town (A) 2-2, (H) 3-1
Q2: Chelmsford City (H) 1-2

91-92 PR: Ford United (A) 1-2

92-93 PR: Ruislip Manor (A) 0-1

HORNCHURCH & UPMINSTER

Currently: Merged with Upminster Wanderers
Playing as Hornchurch in Isthmian League
* - As Upminster F.C.
See also Hornchurch

47-48 * EX: Grays Athletic (H) 0-1

48-49 * EX: Sawbridgeworth (H) 2-2, (A) 2-1
PR: Crittall Athletic (A) 2-2, (H) 2-0
Q1: Romford (H) 1-2

49-50 * PR: Rainham Town (A) 2-1
Q1: Tilbury (A) 2-2, (H) 2-4

57-58 PR: Leytonstone (H) 1-1, (A) 3-3, 2-0
Q1: Leyton (H) 1-1, (A) 1-4

58-59 Q1: Briggs Sports (A) 4-4, (H) 3-2
Q2: Romford (A) 3-2
Q3: Hendon (H) 0-1

59-60 Q1: Clapton (A) 4-2
Q2: Hendon (A) 2-0
Q3: Walthamstow Avenue (A) 1-7

60-61 Q1: Ford United (H) 1-0
Q2: Clapton (H) 2-1
Q3: Romford (A) 0-3

HORNDEAN

Currently: Wessex League

81-82 Q1: Farnborough Town (A) 0-5

82-83 Q1: Eastbourne United (H) 1-1, (A) 2-3

83-84 PR: Whitehawk (A) 0-3

84-85 Q1: Epsom & Ewell (H) 1-3

85-86 PR: Calne Town (H) 1-1, (A) 0-0, (H) 2-1
Q1: Tooting & Mitcham United (H) 2-3

86-87 PR: Woking (H) 2-3

87-88 Q1: Tonbridge A.F.C. (H) 0-2

88-89 PR: Banstead Athletic (H) 2-3

89-90 PR: Flackwell Heath (A) 0-3

90-91 PR: Havant Town (A) 0-3

91-92 PR: Newbury Town (A) 0-1

HORSHAM

Currently: Isthmian League

45-46 PR: East Grinstead (A) 2-2, (H) 1-0
Q1: Worthing (H) 4-3
Q2: Hastings & St Leonards (A) 1-6

46-47 Q1: Southwick (A) 3-5

47-48 PR: Hastings & St Leonards (A) 2-1
Q1: Haywards Heath (H) 1-1, (A) 8-3
Q2: East Grinstead (H) 5-2
Q3: Worthing (H) 1-0
Q4: Redhill (H) 2-1
R1: Notts County (A) 1-9

48-49 PR: Lancing Athletic (H) *W/O*
Q1: Haywards Heath (A) 1-0
Q2: Bexhill Town (H) 4-0
Q3: Bognor Regis Town (H) 1-2

49-50 Q1: Eastbourne Comrades (A) 1-0
Q2: Hastings United (A) 1-4

50-51 PR: Hove (H) 4-2
Q1: Eastbourne (A) 2-3

51-52 PR: Eastbourne (H) 2-3

52-53 PR: Worthing (H) 1-4

53-54 PR: Littlehampton Town (H) 3-1
Q1: Hastings United (A) 1-4

54-55 PR: Shoreham (A) 6-1
Q1: Arundel (H) 2-0
Q2: Tunbridge Wells United (H) 2-3

55-56 PR: Redhill (H) 1-3

56-57 Q1: Wigmore Athletic (A) 4-1
Q2: Eastbourne (H) 2-0
Q3: Redhill (H) 2-1
Q4: Hastings United (H) 0-2

57-58 PR: Eastbourne United (A) 1-1, (H) 2-0
Q1: Redhill (H) 1-2

58-59 PR: Crawley Town (A) 1-0
Q1: Worthing (H) 5-2
Q2: Arundel (H) 5-1
Q3: Eastbourne United (H) 3-1
Q4: Tooting & Mitcham United (A) 0-4

59-60 PR: Hastings United (H) 1-3

60-61 Q1: Bognor Regis Town (H) 3-1
Q2: Southwick (H) 10-1
Q3: Littlehampton Town (H) 2-3

61-62 Q1: Littlehampton Town (A) 3-5

62-63 Q1: Lewes (A) 1-5

63-64 Q1: Littlehampton Town (H) 1-2

64-65 Q1: Haywards Heath (H) 3-3, (A) 2-1
Q2: Crawley Town (A) 0-5

65-66 Q1: Sutton United (H) 2-2, (A) 2-3

66-67 Q1: Dorking (A) 3-0
Q2: Fleet (H) 3-0
Q3: Woking (H) 2-1
Q4: Hastings United (H) 2-1
R1: Swindon Town (H) 0-3

67-68 Q1: Eastbourne United (A) 0-2

68-69 PR: Bognor Regis Town (H) 2-3

Above: *Horsham 'keeper Duncan Green cuts out a cross in the 1991 derby against Crawley. Photo: Roger Turner.*

69-70	PR: Lancing (H) 3-0 Q1: Haywards Heath (A) 2-1 Q2: Southwick (H) 2-0 Q3: Littlehampton Town (A) 2-3
70-71	PR: Chichester City (A) 2-5
71-72	Q1: Lewes (H) 2-0 Q2: Worthing (A) 3-1 Q3: Crawley Town (A) 1-3
72-73	Q1: Lewes (A) 0-1
73-74	PR: Rainham Town (A) 2-1 Q1: Carshalton Athletic (A) 3-0 Q2: Harrow Borough (A - *at Wealdstone*) 0-1
74-75	Q1: Bognor Regis Town (A) 2-1 Q2: Littlehampton Town (H) 1-0 Q3: Burgess Hill Town (H) 5-0 Q4: Chelmsford City (H) 1-3
75-76	Q1: Alton Town (A) 1-2
76-77	Q1: Selsey (H) 4-0 Q2: Basingstoke Town (A) 0-2
77-78	Q1: Worthing (H) 4-1 Q2: Andover (H) 3-2 Q3: Farnborough Town (H) 2-0 Q4: Enfield (H) 0-4
78-79	PR: Littlehampton Town (H) 4-0 Q1: Southwick (A) 2-1 Q2: Dorking (A) 2-0 Q3: Woking (A) 2-5
79-80	PR: Whitstable Town (H) 2-1 Q1: Chatham Town (A) 2-2, (H) 1-2
80-81	PR: Lewes (H) 1-6
81-82	Q1: Banstead Athletic (A) 0-2
82-83	Q1: Kingstonian (H) 0-3
83-84	PR: Burgess H. (H) 0-0, (A - *played home*) 2-0 Q1: Sittingbourne (A) 1-1, (H) 1-2
84-85	PR: Dover Athletic (A) 0-0, (H) 0-1
85-86	PR: Tonbridge A.F.C. (A) 0-3
86-87	Q1: Hastings United (A) 2-3
87-88	PR: Whitehawk (H) 0-0, (A) 0-2
88-89	Q1: Walton & Hersham (H) 1-5
89-90	PR: Herne Bay (A) 1-3
90-91	PR: Epsom & Ewell (H) 2-0 Q1: Tooting & Mitcham (A) 0-0, (H) 1-2
91-92	PR: Hungerford Town (H) 2-1 Q1: Buckingham Town (H) 1-0 Q2: Basingstoke T. (A) 1-1, (H) 2-1 Q3: Maidenhead United (H) 1-1, (A) 1-0 Q4: Crawley Town (H) 0-0, (A) 0-3
92-93	Q1: Dartford (H) *W/O* Q2: Deal Town (H) 1-6

HORSHAM Y.M.C.A.

Currently: Sussex County League

76-77	PR: Worthing (H) 2-0 Q1: Littlehampton Town (A) 1-0 Q2: Tunbridge W. (H) 1-1, (A) 3-0 *rep:* (A) 2-0 Q3: Lewes (A) 4-4, (H) 2-4
77-78	Q1: Ringmer (H) 1-0 Q2: Eastbourne United (H) 4-1 Q3: Folkestone & Shepway (H) 2-2, (A) 0-3
78-79	PR: Herne Bay (A) 1-1, (H) 1-0 Q1: Maidstone United (A) 0-2
79-80	Q1: Chichester City (H) 4-2 Q2: Salisbury (A) 1-3
80-81	Q1: Waterlooville (A) 0-2
81-82	PR: Uxbridge (H) 1-1, (A) 1-2
82-83	Q1: Ramsgate (H) 1-1, (A) 1-2
83-84	PR: Metropolitan Police (A) 1-0 Q1: Hertford Town (A) 1-1, (H) 2-2, (A) 0-2
84-85	Q1: Wokingham Town (H) 1-8
85-86	PR: Whyteleafe (H) 0-3
86-87	PR: Haringey Borough (H) 0-3
87-88	PR: Hornchurch (A) 0-7
88-89	Q1: Molesey (H) 1-2
89-90	PR: Hounslow (A) 2-2, (H) 0-1
90-91	PR: Darenth Heathside (H) 3-2 Q1: Andover (A) 0-3
91-92	PR: Erith & Belvedere (H) 1-2
92-93	PR: Eastbourne Town (H) 4-3 Q1: Havant Town (A) 1-2

HORWICH R.M.I.

Currently: Northern Premier League

46-47	PR: Great Harwood (A) 6-2 Q1: Darwen (A) 1-1, (H) 0-2
47-48	Q1: Leyland Motors (A) 2-1 Q2: Nelson (A) 1-4
48-49	Q1: Clitheroe (A) 1-3
49-50	PR: Rossendale United (A) 2-5
50-51	PR: Great Harwood (A) 4-1 Q1: Rossendale United (A) 5-6
51-52	PR: Chorley (A) 5-2 Q1: Rossendale United (A) 2-4
52-53	PR: Leyland Motors (A) 3-0 Q1: Chorley (H) 5-3 Q2: Ashton United (A) 1-2
53-54	Q1: Darwen (H) 1-1, (A) 2-3
54-55	PR: Skelmersdale United (H) 1-0 Q1: Darwen (A) 0-1
55-56	PR: Skelmersdale United (H) 3-2 Q1: Leyland Motors (A) 0-1
56-57	PR: Lytham (A) 7-1 Q1: Skelmersdale United (H) 2-1 Q2: Chorley (H) 3-0 Q3: Mossley (H) 1-0 Q4: Morecambe (A) 2-3
57-58	PR: Mossley (H) 1-1, (A) 1-2
58-59	PR: Crompton's Receation (A) 4-1 Q1: Chorley (A) 1-2
59-60	Q1: Bacup Borough (H) 1-2
60-61	Q1: Marine (A) 0-2
61-62	Q1: Ashton United (H) 0-2
62-63	Q1: Netherfield (H) 2-2, (A) 2-3
63-64	Q1: Burscough (H) 0-3
64-65	Q1: Accrington (H) 5-2 Q2: Lancaster City (H) 1-1, (A) 1-2
65-66	Q1: Burscough (H) 2-1 Q2: Fleetwood (H) 3-3, (A) 1-2
66-67	Q1: Chorley (A) 0-1
67-68	Q1: Wigan Rovers (H) 3-1 Q2: Hyde United (H) 0-3
68-69	Q1: Wigan Rovers (A) 1-1, (H) 2-0 Q2: Mossley (H) 1-5
69-70	Q1: Guinness Exports (H) 3-1 Q2: Formby (A) 2-1 Q3: Mossley (A) 1-2
70-71	Q1: Northwich Victoria (H) 2-0 Q2: Rossendale United (A) 1-3
71-72	Q1: Hyde United (H) 1-1, (A) 0-2
72-73	PR: Prestwich Heys (A) 3-3, (H) 4-1 Q1: Hyde United (H) 3-3, (A) 0-1
73-74	Q1: Skelmersdale United (H) 3-1 Q2: Congleton Town (H) 2-0 Q3: Altrincham (A) 0-4
74-75	Q1: Formby (A) 2-0 Q2: Ashton United (A) 2-0 Q3: Accrington Stanley (H) 0-2
75-76	PR: Farsley C. (H) 1-1, (A) 1-1, 2-1 Q1: Radcliffe Borough (A) 0-4
76-77	Q1: Worksop Town (H) 1-1, (A) 0-1
77-78	Q1: Barrow (H) 1-0 Q2: Chorley (A) 0-1
78-79	Q1: Leyland Motors (A) 2-1 Q2: Curzon Ashton (A) 2-1 Q3: Formby (A) 0-0, (H) 5-1 Q4: Morecambe (A) 1-3
79-80	Q1: Darwen (H) 4-1 Q2: Lancaster City (A) 0-4
80-81	Q1: North Ferriby United (A) 0-1
81-82	PR: Skelmersdale United (H) 4-0 Q1: Witton Albion (H) 2-0 Q2: Hyde United (H) 0-4
82-83	PR: South Liverpool (A) 4-1 Q1: New Mills (A) 3-0 Q2: Oswestry Town (H) 5-1 Q3: Caernarfon Town (H) 2-2, (A) 2-0 Q4: Runcorn (H) 2-2, (A) 1-0 R1: Blackpool (A) 0-3
83-84	Q1: Farsley Celtic (A) 4-1 Q2: Buxton (A) 1-0 Q3: Southport (H) 2-1 Q4: Macclesfield Town (H) 0-0, (A) 3-4
84-85	Q1: Appleby Frodingham Ath. (H) 3-0 Q2: Winsford United (A) 1-2
85-86	Q1: Skelmersdale United (A) 2-2, (H) 3-0 Q2: Congleton Town (A) 2-2, (H) 2-0 Q3: Rhyl (A) 0-2
86-87	Q1: Chorley (A) 1-2
87-88	Q1: South Liverpool (H) 1-1, (A) 4-3 Q2: St Helens Town (A) 0-0, (H) 2-3
88-89	Q1: Droylsden (H) 3-3, (A) 2-1 Q2: Emley (A) 0-5
89-90	Q1: Caernarfon Town (A) 1-3
90-91	Q1: Morecambe (A) 2-2, (H) 3-0 Q2: Irlam Town (A) 3-1 Q3: Colwyn Bay (H) 1-3
91-92	Q1: Ilkeston Town (H) 1-0 Q2: Emley (A) 2-4
92-93	Q1: Goole Town (A) 1-0 Q2: Worksop Town (H) 1-1, (A) 5-1 Q3: Macclesfield Town (A) 0-1

HOUGHTON RANGERS

Currently: Leicestershire Senior League

49-50 EX: Bedford Corinthians (H - *played away*) 4-1
PR: Hitchin Town (A) 0-5

HOUNSLOW

Currently: Merged with Feltham. Playing as Feltham & Hounslow Borough in Isthmian League
See also Feltham & Hounslow Borough
* - As Hounslow Town

45-46 * PR: Slough Utd (H) 4-4, (A) 1-3

46-47 * EX: Maidenhead United (H) 1-4

47-48 * EX: Wycombe Wanderers (A) 2-4

48-49 * PR: Farnham Town (A) 4-2
Q1: Tooting & Mitcham United (H) 1-3

49-50 * EX: Leatherhead (A) 6-2
PR: Wimbledon (H) 2-2, (A) 0-5

50-51 * PR: Metropolitan Police (A) 4-4, (H) 2-1
Q1: Carshalton Athletic (A) 0-1

51-52 * PR: Farnham Town (A) 5-3
Q1: Walton & Hersham (A) 6-0
Q2: Woking (A) 6-0
Q3: Sutton United (H) 1-4

52-53 * Q1: Sutton United (A) 2-3

53-54 * PR: Dover (A) 2-1
Q1: Dartford (H) 0-0, (A) 3-0
Q2: Epsom (H) 4-1
Q3: Kingstonian (H) 6-1
Q4: Hastings United (H) 1-2

54-55 * PR: Uxbridge (H) 2-2, (A) 7-1
Q1: Kingstonian (A) 4-3
Q2: Metropolitan Police (A) 4-2
Q3: Hayes (H) 2-1
Q4: Canterbury City (H) 3-0
R1: Hastings United (H) 2-4

55-56 * PR: Metropolitan Police (A) 3-3, (H) 4-0
Q1: Hemel Hempstead Town (A) 0-1

56-57 * Q1: Hayes (A) 2-0
Q2: Southall (A) 1-2

57-58 * PR: Harrow Town (H) 2-0
Q1: Hemel Hempstead Town (A) 2-1
Q2: Southall (H) 0-0, (A) 2-0
Q3: Yiewsley (H) 3-1
Q4: Wisbech Town (H) 2-3

58-59 * Q1: Yiewsley (H) 0-2

59-60 * Q1: Wembley (H) 6-0
Q2: Hayes (A) 0-1

60-61 * Q1: Barnet (A) 1-5

61-62 * Q1: Barnet (H) 2-4

62-63 * R1: Mansfield Town (H) 3-3, (A) 2-9

63-64 Q1: Finchley (A) 0-4

64-65 Q1: Finchley (H) 1-4

65-66 Q1: Southall (H) 2-3

66-67 Q1: St Albans City (H) 2-0
Q2: Oxford City (H) 0-3

67-68 Q1: Ware (A) 2-3

68-69 Q1: Finchley (A) 2-2, (H) 4-2
Q2: Ware (A) 2-3

69-70 Q1: Hazells (H) 6-1
Q2: Braintree & Crittall (H) 2-2, (A) 0-2

70-71 Q1: Harrow (H) 0-1 *void - Harrow ineligible player,* (H) 2-2, (H) 1-1, (*at Southall*) 2-3

71-72 Q1: Uxbridge (H) 0-2

72-73 Q1: Leytonstone (A) 0-1

73-74 Q1: Edgware (H) 2-0
Q2: Epping Town (H) 1-2

74-75 Q1: Uxbridge (A) 1-2

75-76 Q1: Boreham Wood (A) 0-2

76-77 Q1: Hatfield Town (A) 0-2

77-78 PR: Molesey (H) 2-1
Q1: Erith & Belvedere (A) 2-4

78-79 Q1: St Albans City (H) 1-1, (A) 2-4

79-80 Q1: Carshalton Athletic (H) 2-0
Q2: Woking (H) 2-3

80-81 Q1: Metropolitan Police (A) 3-2
Q2: Slough Town (H) 1-3

81-82 PR: Kingstonian (H) 1-3

82-83 PR: Cray Wanderers (H) 2-5

83-84 Q1: Slough Town (H) 0-3

84-85 Q1: Wealdstone (H) 2-5

85-86 PR: Crockenhill (A) 1-0
Q1: Leyton-Wingate (H) 1-2

86-87 Q1: Sutton United (A) 0-2

87-88 PR: Sudbury Town (A) 1-1, (H) 1-3

88-89 PR: Leatherhead (A) 1-1, (H) 1-2

89-90 PR: Horsham Y.M.C.A. (H) 2-2, (A) 1-0
Q1: Rayners Lane (A) 2-1
Q2: Hampton (A) 0-2

90-91 PR: Wootton Blue Cross (A) 3-1
Q1: Basildon United (H) 4-3
Q2: Bishop's Stortford (H) 1-5

HOVE

Currently: Defunct

46-47 PR: Bexhill Town (H - *played away*) 2-5

48-49 PR: Shoreham (A) 1-2

49-50 PR: Newhaven (H) 3-2
Q1: Hastings United (H - *played away*) 2-14

50-51 PR: Horsham (A) 2-4

HOYLAKE ATHLETIC

Currently: Defunct

49-50 EX: Southport Leyland Road (H) 9-5
PR: St Helens Town (H) 0-3

50-51 PR: Prescot Cables (H) 2-7

HOYLAND COMMON ATH.

Currently: Defunct

48-49 EX: Staveley Welfare (H) 5-1
PR: Steel, Peech & Tozer S.S. (A) 1-2

49-50 PR: Kilnhurst Colliery (H) 2-1
Q1: Cresswell Colliery (H) 1-1, (A) 2-0
Q2: Beighton Miners Welfare (H) 3-2
Q3: Rawmarsh Welfare (A) 2-4

HUCKNALL TOWN

Currently: Northern Counties (East) League

92-93 PR: Grantham Town (H) 2-1
Q1: Clitheroe (A) 3-1
Q2: Macclesfield Town (H) 1-1, (A) 1-3

HUDDERSFIELD TOWN

Currently: Football League

45-46 R3: Sheffield Utd (H) 1-1, (A) 0-2 (*agg: 1-3*)

46-47 R3: Barnsley (H) 3-4

47-48 R3: Colchester United (A) 0-1

48-49 R3: Queens Park Rangers (A) 0-0, (H) 5-0
R4: Newport County (A) 3-3, (H) 1-3

49-50 R3: Sunderland (A) 0-6

50-51 R3: Tottenham Hotspur (H) 2-0
R4: Preston North End (A) 2-0
R5: Wolverhampton Wanderers (A) 0-2

51-52 R3: Tranmere Rovers (H) 1-2

52-53 R3: Bristol Rovers (H) 2-0
R4: Blackpool (A) 0-1

53-54 R3: West Ham United (A) 0-4

54-55 R3: Coventry City (H) 3-3, (A) 2-1
R4: Torquay United (A) 1-0
R5: Liverpool (A) 2-0
R6: Newcastle United (H) 1-1, (A) 0-2

55-56 R3: Bolton Wanderers (A) 0-3

56-57 R3: Sheffield Utd (H) 0-0, (A) 1-1, 2-1
R4: Peterborough United (H) 3-1
R5: Burnley (H) 1-2

57-58 R3: Charlton Athletic (H) 2-2, (A) 0-1

58-59 R3: Ipswich Town (A) 0-1

59-60 R3: West Ham United (H) 1-1, (A) 5-1
R4: Luton Town (H) 0-1

60-61 R3: Wolverhampton W. (A) 1-1, (H) 2-1
R4: Barnsley (H) 1-1, (A) 0-1

61-62 R3: Rotherham United (H) 4-3
R4: Aston Villa (A) 1-2

62-63 R3: Manchester United (A) 0-5

63-64 R3: Plymouth Argyle (A) 1-0
R4: Chelsea (A) 2-1
R5: Burnley (A) 0-3

64-65 R3: Doncaster Rovers (A) 1-0
R4: Swansea Town (A) 0-1

65-66 R3: Hartlepools United (H) 3-1
R4: Plymouth Argyle (A) 2-0
R5: Sheffield Wednesday (H) 1-2

66-67 R3: Chelsea (H) 1-2

67-68 R3: Tranmere Rovers (A) 1-2

68-69 R3: Bury (A) 2-1
R4: West Ham United (H) 0-2

69-70 R3: Aldershot (H) 1-1, (A) 1-3

70-71 R3: Birmingham City (H) 1-1, (A) 2-0
R4: Stoke (A) 3-3, (H) 0-0, (*at Man. Utd*) 0-1

71-72 R3: Burnley (A) 1-0
R4: Fulham (H) 3-0
R5: West Ham United (H) 4-2
R6: Birmingham City (A) 1-3

72-73 R3: Carlisle United (A) 2-2, (H) 0-1

73-74 R1: Wigan Athletic (H) 2-0
R2: Chester (A) 2-3

74-75 R1: Grimsby Town (A) 0-1

75-76 R1: Walsall (A) 1-0
R2: Port Vale (H) 2-1
R3: Fulham (A) 3-2
R4: Bolton Wanderers (H) 0-1

76-77 R1: Mansfield Town (H) 0-0, (A) 1-2

77-78 R1: Barnsley (A) 0-1

78-79 R1: Doncaster Rovers (A) 1-2

79-80 R1: Darlington (A) 1-1, (H) 0-1

80-81 R1: Northwich Victoria (A) 1-1, (H) 6-0
R2: Tranmere Rovers (A) 3-0
R3: Shrewsbury Town (H) 0-3

81-82 R1: Workington (A) 1-1, (H) 5-0
R2: Chesterfield (A) 1-0
R3: Carlisle United (A) 3-2
R4: Orient (H) 1-1, (A) 0-2

82-83 R1: Mossley (H) 1-0
R2: Altrincham (A) 1-0
R3: Chelsea (H) 1-1, (A) 0-2

Opposite: *A scare for Huddersfield Town, and the best part of a 7,599 crowd at their Leeds Road ground; Mossley forward Mal Wagstaffe beats goalkeeper Brian Cox, but was ruled offside, and the Football club eventually triumphed 1-0 with a controversial goal of their own.*

83-84 R3: Queens Park Rangers (H) 2-1
R4: Notts County (H) 1-2

84-85 R3: Wolverhampton W. (A) 1-1, (H) 3-1
R4: Luton Town (A) 0-2

85-86 R3: Reading (H) 0-0, (A) 1-2

86-87 R3: Norwich City (A) 1-1, (H) 2-4

87-88 R3: Manchester C. (H) 2-2, (A) 0-0, (H) 0-3

88-89 R1: Rochdale (H) 1-1, (A) 4-3
R2: Chester City (H) 1-0
R3: Sheffield United (H) 0-1

89-90 R1: Hartlepool United (A) 2-0
R2: Chesterfield (A) 2-0
R3: Grimsby Town (H) 3-1
R4: Crystal Palace (A) 0-4

90-91 R1: Altrincham (A) 2-1
R2: Blackpool (H) 0-2

91-92 R1: Lincoln United (H) 7-0

R2: Rochdale (A) 2-1
R3: Millwall (H) 0-4

92-93 R1: Scunthorpe United (A) 0-0, (H) 2-1
R2: Bradford City (A) 2-0
R3: Gillingham (A) 0-0, (H) 2-1
R4: Southend United (H) 1-2

HULL AMATEUR

Currently: Defunct

46-47 Q1: Portrack Shamrocks (A) 1-5

HULL BRUNSWICK

Currently: Defunct * - As Brunswick Institute

49-50 * EX: Ferrybridge Amateur (H) 7-3
PR: Farsley Celtic (H) 0-3

50-51 * EX: Ossett Town (A) 2-5

51-52 * Q1: Norton Woodseats (H) 0-2

52-53 * Q1: Beighton Miners Welfare (H) 0-2

53-54 * Q1: Bentley Colliery (H) 0-4

54-55 * Q1: Beighton Miners Welfare (A) 0-6

55-56 * Q1: Worksop Town (A) 0-8

65-66 Q1: Yorkshire Amateur (A) 4-2
Q2: Bridlington Town (A) 0-6

66-67 Q1: Goole Town (A) 1-3

67-68 Q1: Barton Town (A) 2-5

68-69 Q1: Bridlington Town (A) 1-1, (H) 3-2
Q2: Selby Town (A) 1-2

69-70 Q1: Winterton Rangers (H) 2-0
Q2: Barton Town (H) 1-1, (A) 2-1
Q3: Scarborough (A) 1-5

71-72 Q1: Whitby Town (H) 1-3

HULL CITY

Currently: Football League

46-47 R1: New Brighton (H) 0-0, (A) 2-1
R2: Darlington (A) 2-1
R3: Blackburn Rovers (A) 1-1, (H) 0-3

47-48 R1: Southport (H) 1-1, (A) 3-2
R2: Cheltenham Town (H) 4-2
R3: Middlesbrough (H) 1-3

48-49 R1: Accrington Stanley (H) 3-1
R2: Reading (H) 0-0, (A) 2-1
R3: Blackburn Rovers (A) 2-1
R4: Grimsby Town (A) 3-2
R5: Stoke City (A) 2-0
R6: Manchester United (H) 0-1

49-50 R3: Southport (A) 0-0, (H) 5-0
R4: Stockport County (A) 0-0, (H) 0-2

50-51 R3: Everton (H) 2-0
R4: Rotherham United (H) 2-0
R5: Bristol Rovers (A) 0-3

51-52 R3: Manchester United (A) 2-0
R4: Blackburn Rovers (A) 0-2

52-53 R3: Charlton Athletic (H) 3-1
R4: Gateshead (H) 1-2

53-54 R3: Brentford (A) 0-0, (H) 2-2, (*at Doncaster Rovers*) 5-2
R4: Blackburn Rovers (A) 2-2, (H) 2-1
R5: Tottenham Hotspur (H) 1-1, (A) 0-2

54-55 R3: Birmingham City (H) 0-2

55-56 R3: Aston Villa (A) 1-1, (H) 1-2

56-57 R1: Gateshead (H) 4-0
R2: York City (H) 2-1
R3: Bristol Rovers (H) 3-4

57-58 R1: Crewe Alexandra (H) 2-1
R2: Port Vale (A) 2-2, (H) 4-3
R3: Barnsley (H) 1-1, (A) 2-0
R4: Sheffield Wednesday (A) 3-4

58-59 R1: Stockport County (H) 0-1

59-60 R3: Fulham (A) 0-5

60-61 R1: Sutton Town (H) 3-0
R2: Darlington (A) 1-1, (H) 1-1, 1-1, 0-0, 3-0
R3: Bolton Wanderers (H) 0-1

61-62 R1: Rhyl (H) 5-0
R2: Bradford City (H) 0-2

62-63 R1: Crook Town (H) 5-4
R2: Workington (H) 2-0
R3: Leyton Orient (A) 1-1, (H) 0-2

63-64 R1: Crewe Alexandra (H) 2-2, (A) 3-0
R2: Wrexham (A) 2-0
R3: Everton (H) 1-1, (A) 1-2

64-65 R1: Kidderminster Harriers (A) 4-1
R2: Lincoln City (H) 1-1, (A) 1-3

65-66 R1: Bradford (Park Avenue) (A) 3-2
R2: Gateshead (A) 4-0
R3: Southampton (H) 1-0
R4: Nottingham Forest (H) 2-0
R5: Southport (H) 2-0
R6: Chelsea (A) 2-2, (H) 1-3

66-67 R3: Portsmouth (H) 1-1, (A) 2-2, 1-3

67-68 R3: Middlesbrough (A) 1-1, (H) 2-2, 0-1

68-69 R3: Wolverhampton Wanderers (H) 1-3

69-70 R3: Manchester City (H) 0-1

70-71 R3: Charlton Athletic (H) 3-0
R4: Blackpool (H) 2-0
R5: Brentford (H) 1-0
R6: Stoke City (H) 2-3

71-72 R3: Norwich City (A) 3-0
R4: Coventry City (A) 1-0
R5: Stoke City (A) 1-4

72-73 R3: Stockport County (A) 0-0, (H) 2-0
R4: West Ham United (H) 1-0
R5: Coventry City (A) 0-3

73-74 R3: Bristol City (A) 1-1, (H) 0-1

74-75 R3: Fulham (A) 1-1, (H) 2-2, (*at Leicester*) 0-1

75-76 R3: Plymouth Argyle (H) 1-1, (A) 4-1
R4: Sunderland (A) 0-1

76-77 R3: Port Vale (H) 1-1, (A) 1-3

77-78 R3: Leicester City (H) 0-1

78-79 R1: Stafford Rangers (H) 2-1
R2: Carlisle United (A) 0-3

79-80 R1: Carlisle United (A) 3-3, (H) 0-2

80-81 R1: Halifax Town (H) 2-1
R2: Blyth Spartans (H) 1-1, (A) 2-2, (*at Leeds United*) 2-1
R3: Doncaster Rovers (H) 1-0
R4: Tottenham Hotspur (A) 0-2

81-82 R1: Rochdale (A) 2-2, (H) 2-2, (*at Leeds*) 1-0
R2: Hartleppol United (H) 2-0
R3: Chelsea (A) 0-0, (H) 0-2

82-83 R1: Sheffield United (H) 1-1, (A) 0-2

83-84 R1: Penrith (A) 2-0
R2: Rotherham United (A) 1-2

84-85 R1: Bolton Wanderers (H) 2-1
R2: Tranmere Rovers (A) 3-0
R3: Brighton & Hove Albion (A) 0-1

85-86 R3: Plymouth Argyle (H) 2-2, (A) 1-0
R4: Brighton & Hove Albion (H) 2-3

86-87 R3: Shrewsbury Town (A) 2-1
R4: Swansea City (A) 1-0
R5: Wigan Athletic (A) 0-3

87-88 R3: Watford (A) 1-1, (H) 2-2, (A) 0-1

88-89 R3: Cardiff City (A) 2-1
R4: Bradford City (A) 2-1
R5: Liverpool (H) 2-3

89-90 R3: Newcastle United (H) 0-1

90-91 R3: Notts County (H) 2-5

91-92 R1: Morecambe (A) 1-0
R2: Blackpool (A) 1-0
R3: Chelsea (H) 0-2

92-93 R1: Darlington (A) 2-1
R2: Rotherham United (A) 0-1

HUNGERFORD TOWN

Currently: Isthmian League

73-74 Q1: Trowbridge Town (H) 1-1, (A) 2-4

74-75 Q1: Westbury United (A) 3-1
Q2: Bath City (A) 1-6

75-76 Q1: Glastonbury (A) 1-2

76-77 Q1: Farnborough Town (H) 0-3

77-78 Q1: Gosport Borough (A) 0-0, (H) 3-0
Q2: Salisbury (H) 0-1

78-79 PR: Swaythling (H) 5-1
Q2: Yeovil Town (H) 4-4, (A) 0-3

79-80 Q1: Calne Town (H) 3-1
Q2: Trowbridge Town (A) 2-0
Q3: Barry Town (H) 3-1
Q4: Bridgend Town (A) 1-1, (H) 5-0
R1: Slough Town (A) 1-3

80-81 Q1: Wick (H) 5-1
Q2: Sutton United (A) 0-2

81-82 PR: Chippenham Town (H) 4-0
Q1: Dorchester Town (H) 1-2

82-83 Q1: Merthyr Tydfil (H) 0-3

83-84 Q1: Newbury Town (H) 2-1
Q2: Waterlooville (H) 3-3, (A) 0-3

84-85 PR: Thame United (A) 11-2
Q1: Gosport Borough (H) 2-1
Q2: Salisbury (A) 0-0, (H) 3-0
Q3: Farnborough Town (H) 3-3, (A) 1-4

85-86 Q1: Andover (A) 3-1
Q2: Poole Town (A) 2-3

86-87 PR: Trowbridge Town (A) 0-4

87-88 PR: Yate Town (H) 1-1, (A) 0-1

88-89 PR: Eastleigh (H) 0-0, (A) 1-0
Q1: Abingdon United (A) 2-1
Q2: Waterlooville (H) 0-2

89-90 Q1: Gosport Borough (A) 0-2

90-91 PR: Fareham Town (H) 1-0
Q1: Salisbury (A) 0-2

91-92 PR: Horsham (A) 1-2

92-93 PR: Welton Rovers (A) 1-4

HUNTINGDON UNITED

Currently: Huntingdonshire League

Season	Results
49-50	EX: Arlesey Town (A) 5-4 PR: Bedford Avenue (H) 4-2 Q1: Baldock Town (H) 2-3
50-51	EX: Shefford Town (A) 3-3, (H) 5-4 PR: Baldock Town (A) 3-1 Q1: Hitchin Town (H) 1-5
51-52	Q1: Wisbech Town (H) 0-2
52-53	Q1: Cambridge City (H) 0-3
53-54	PR: St Neots & District (A) 1-4
54-55	Q1: King's Lynn (A) 0-9

HUNTLEY & PALMERS
RECREATION (READING)

Currently: Defunct

Season	Results
47-48	EX: Pressed Steel (A) 3-0 PR: Aylesbury United (H) 4-1 Q1: Maidenhead United (A) 2-5
48-49	EX: Northern A.C. Ath. (A - *at Banbury S.*) 3-2 PR: Aylesbury United (H) 3-2 Q1: Oxford City (A) 1-2
49-50	EX: Headington Utd (H - *played away*) 4-9
50-51	EX: Northern Alumium Co. Ath. (A) 5-1 PR: Banbury Spencer (H) 1-2
51-52	PR: Abingdon Town (H) 6-2 Q1: Banbury Spencer (A) 1-2
52-53	PR: Witney Town (H) 4-2 Q1: Wycombe Wanderers (A) 2-4
53-54	PR: Chesham United (A) 1-3
54-55	PR: Banbury Spencer (H) 0-3
56-57	PR: Maidenhead United (A) 1-5
57-58	PR: Windsor & Eton (H) 4-2 Q1: Marlow (A) 1-4
58-59	PR: Chesham United (A) 0-3
59-60	PR: Maidenhead United (A) 1-4
60-61	Q1: Oxford City (A) 1-6
61-62	Q1: Abingdon Town (A) 0-2
62-63	Q1: Aylesbury United (A) 0-6
63-64	Q1: Banbury Spencer (A) 0-4
64-65	Q1: Hemel Hempstead Town (H) 0-6
65-66	Q1: Aylesbury United (A) 3-3, (H) 1-0 Q2: Oxford City (H) 1-4
66-67	Q1: Hemel Hempstead Town (A) 0-1
67-68	Q1: Barking (H) 1-2
68-69	Q1: Walton & Hersham (A) 0-5
69-70	Q1: Molesey (A) 1-1, (H) 3-1 Q2: Walton & Hersham (H) 0-9

HURST

See Ashton United

HYDE UNITED

Currently: Northern Premier League

Season	Results
46-47	PR: Buxton (A) 2-2, (H) 2-3 *Buxton expelled* Q1: Ellesmere Port Town (H) 1-2
47-48	PR: Fodens Motor Works (A) 2-1 Q1: Altrincham (A) 1-4
48-49	PR: Ashton United (H) 2-1 Q1: Barnton (A) 2-0 Q2: Winsford United (A) 0-4
49-50	PR: Glossop (A) 2-1 Q1: Buxton (A) 0-3
50-51	PR: Atherton Collieries (H) 5-0 Q1: Stalybridge Celtic (A) 6-2 Q2: Runcorn (A) 1-1, (H) 3-0 Q3: Altrincham (H) 1-1, (A) 2-1 Q4: Nelson (H) 2-2, (A) 0-3
51-52	PR: Buxton (A) 1-2
52-53	Q1: Stalybridge Celtic (A) 2-3

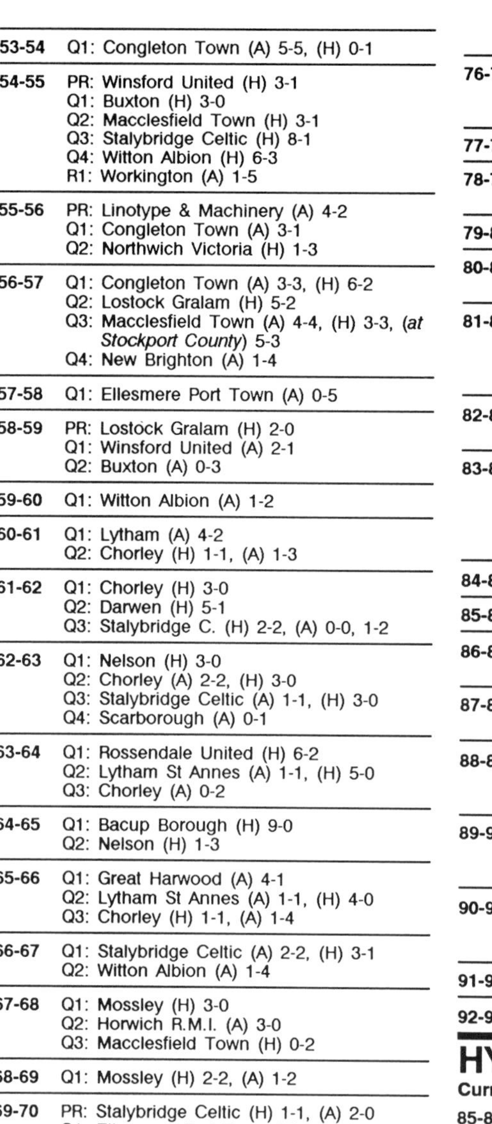

Season	Results
53-54	Q1: Congleton Town (A) 5-5, (H) 0-1
54-55	PR: Winsford United (H) 3-1 Q1: Buxton (H) 3-0 Q2: Macclesfield Town (H) 3-1 Q3: Stalybridge Celtic (H) 8-1 Q4: Witton Albion (H) 6-3 R1: Workington (A) 1-5
55-56	PR: Linotype & Machinery (A) 4-2 Q1: Congleton Town (A) 3-1 Q2: Northwich Victoria (H) 1-3
56-57	Q1: Congleton Town (A) 3-3, (H) 6-2 Q2: Lostock Gralam (H) 5-2 Q3: Macclesfield Town (A) 4-4, (H) 3-3, (*at Stockport County*) 5-3 Q4: New Brighton (A) 1-4
57-58	Q1: Ellesmere Port Town (A) 0-5
58-59	PR: Lostock Gralam (H) 2-0 Q1: Winsford United (A) 2-1 Q2: Buxton (A) 0-3
59-60	Q1: Witton Albion (A) 1-2
60-61	Q1: Lytham (A) 4-2 Q2: Chorley (H) 1-1, (A) 1-3
61-62	Q1: Chorley (H) 3-0 Q2: Darwen (H) 5-1 Q3: Stalybridge C. (H) 2-2, (A) 0-0, 1-2
62-63	Q1: Nelson (H) 3-0 Q2: Chorley (A) 2-2, (H) 3-0 Q3: Stalybridge Celtic (A) 1-1, (H) 3-0 Q4: Scarborough (A) 0-1
63-64	Q1: Rossendale United (H) 6-2 Q2: Lytham St Annes (A) 1-1, (H) 5-0 Q3: Chorley (A) 0-2
64-65	Q1: Bacup Borough (H) 9-0 Q2: Nelson (H) 1-3
65-66	Q1: Great Harwood (A) 4-1 Q2: Lytham St Annes (A) 1-1, (H) 4-0 Q3: Chorley (H) 1-1, (A) 1-4
66-67	Q1: Stalybridge Celtic (A) 2-2, (H) 3-1 Q2: Witton Albion (A) 1-4
67-68	Q1: Mossley (H) 3-0 Q2: Horwich R.M.I. (A) 3-0 Q3: Macclesfield Town (H) 0-2
68-69	Q1: Mossley (H) 2-2, (A) 1-2
69-70	PR: Stalybridge Celtic (H) 1-1, (A) 2-0 Q1: Ellesmere Port Town (A) 1-1, (H) 1-0 Q2: Burscough (H) 0-1
70-71	Q1: Guinness Exports (H) 3-1 Q2: Formby (A) 0-1
71-72	PR: Kirkby Town (H) 2-2, (A) 2-1 Q1: Horwich R.M.I. (A) 1-1, (H) 2-0 Q2: Mossley (A) 0-0, (H) 2-0 Q3: Ashton United (A) 2-2, (H) 3-1 Q4: Bangor City (H) 1-3
72-73	Q1: Horwich R.M.I. (A) 3-3, (H) 1-0 Q2: Ashton United (A) 1-1, (H) 2-2, 1-2
73-74	PR: New Brighton (A) 1-1, (H) 2-1 Q1: Congleton Town (A) 0-2
74-75	Q1: New Mills (A) 1-0 Q2: Runcorn (A) 0-3
75-76	Q1: Accrington Stanley (A) 3-2 Q2: Droylsden (A) 2-3
76-77	PR: Leek Town (H) 2-1 Q1: Ashton United (H) 4-1 Q2: Burton Albion (H) 0-1
77-78	Q1: Hednesford Town (A) 0-1
78-79	Q1: Skelmersdale Utd (H) 1-1, (A) 1-0 Q2: Formby (H) 2-2, (A) 1-2
79-80	PR: Ashton United (H) 1-3
80-81	Q1: Lancaster City (A) 1-1, (H) 3-1 Q2: Burscough (H) 1-2
81-82	Q1: Fleetwood Town (A) 1-1, (H) 2-1 Q2: Horwich R.M.I. (A) 4-0 Q3: Marine (H) 3-1 Q4: Horden Colliery Welfare (A) 0-2
82-83	Q1: Ossett Albion (A) 2-1 Q2: Macclesfield Town (H) 2-5
83-84	Q1: Darwen (H) 3-0 Q2: Runcorn (H) 3-0 Q3: Stalybridge Celtic (H) 2-0 Q4: Blyth Spartans (H) 1-1, (A) 4-2 R1: Burnley (H) 0-2
84-85	Q1: Ashton United (A) 0-0, (H) 2-4
85-86	Q1: Eastwood Hanley (A) 0-0, (H) 1-2
86-87	Q1: Rhyl (H) 1-1, (A) 4-3 Q2: Emley (A) 2-2, (H) 1-4
87-88	Q1: Mossley (H - *at Curzon Ashton*) 1-0 Q2: Leek Town (A) 1-2
88-89	Q1: Radcliffe Borough (A) 2-0 Q2: Chadderton (A) 5-1 Q3: Northwich Victoria (H) 1-1, (A) 0-3
89-90	Q1: Sheffield (A) 1-0 Q2: Bangor City (H) 2-1 Q3: Marine (H) 0-1
90-91	Q1: Oakham United (A) 2-1 Q2: Hednesford Town (A) 2-2, (H) 5-2 Q3: S. Liverpool (H) 1-1, (A - *at Bootle*) 1-3
91-92	Q1: Warrington Town (A) 0-1
92-93	Q1: Accrington Stanley (H) 1-5

HYTHE TOWN

Currently: Defunct

Season	Results
85-86	PR: Lancing (A) 3-0 Q1: Ashford Town (H) 1-0 Q2: Croydon (H) 1-5
86-87	Q1: Southwick (A) 0-1
87-88	Q1: Eastbourne United (A) 2-6
88-89	PR: Feltham (A) 1-1, (H) 2-5
89-90	Q1: Three Bridges (A) 2-0 Q2: Molesey (H) 2-1 Q3: Whitstable Town (H) 2-0 Q4: Hayes (H) 0-0, (A) 0-3
90-91	Q1: Tonbridge A.F.C. (A) 1-3
91-92	PR: Croydon Athletic (H) 4-4, (A) 1-2
92-93	PR: Dorking (A) *Scratched*

Right: *Hythe Town's brief F.A. Cup history ended with a surprise replay defeat away to Croydon Athletic in 1991. Here a foray by Jason Wheeler is curtailed by a good tackle from the home captain Noel Kidney.*
Photo: Dave West.

IBSTOCK PENISTONE ROVERS

Currently: Defunct

46-47 Q2: Coalville Town Amateurs (A) 0-14

47-48 Q1: Tamworth (A) 0-6

48-49 PR: Bedworth Town (H) 1-4

49-50 PR: Tamworth (H) 0-2

50-51 PR: Tamworth (H) 3-0
Q1: Hinckley Athletic (A) 0-4

51-52 Q1: Moira United (A) 1-5

52-53 Q1: Brush Sports (A) 0-5

ILFORD

Currently: Merged with Leytonstone
Subsequently merged with Walthamstow Avenue and Dagenham, and playing as Dagenham & Redbridge in the Alliance Premier League
See also Leytonstone-Ilford, Redbridge Forest and Dagenham & Redbridge.

45-46 Q4: Barnet (A) 2-5

46-47 PR: Harwich & Parkeston (A) 2-3

47-48 PR: Grays Athletic (A) 2-3

48-49 PR: Chingford Town (H) 2-3

49-50 PR: Ford Sports (H) 4-1
Q1: Grays Athletic (H) 1-2

50-51 PR: Chingford Town (A) 0-1

51-52 PR: Brentwood & W. (H) 1-1, (A) 3-3, 2-3

52-53 PR: Barking (A) 1-1, (H) 4-2
Q1: Tilbury (A) 0-1

53-54 Q1: Leyton (A) 2-0
Q2: Briggs Sports (H) 1-1, (A) 0-5

54-55 PR: Aveley (A) 0-0, (H) 3-0
Q1: Dagenham (H) 3-3, (A) 4-3
Q2: Leyton (A) 1-2

55-56 PR: Briggs Sports (H) 0-3

56-57 PR: Chelmsford City (A) 0-1

57-58 PR: Tilbury (A) 0-0, (H) 2-1
Q1: Grays Athletic (H) 4-3
Q2: Rainham Town (A) 3-4

58-59 R1: Norwich City (A) 1-3

59-60 Q1: Rainham Town (H) 4-1
Q2: Grays Athletic (A) 2-2, (H) 2-4

60-61 Q1: Rainham Town (A) 3-2
Q2: Brentwood & Warley (H) 0-2

61-62 Q1: Aveley (A) 2-2, (H) 3-0
Q2: Grays Athletic (A) 1-3

62-63 Q1: Barking (A) 4-0
Q2: Brentwood & Warley (H) 4-1
Q3: Tilbury (A) 0-1

63-64 Q1: Woodford Town (A) 3-1
Q2: Barking (A) 2-1
Q3: Aveley (A) 1-0
Q4: Maidenhead United (H) 1-3

64-65 Q1: Hornchurch (H) 3-4

65-66 Q1: Barking (H) 2-4

66-67 Q1: Barnet (H) 0-2

67-68 Q1: Grays Athletic (H) 1-0
Q2: Walthamstow Avenue (A) 0-1

68-69 Q1: Edmonton (H) 0-1

69-70 Q1: Leyton (H) 2-0
Q2: Edmonton (A) 1-2

70-71 Q1: Hoddesdon Town (A) 1-1, (H) 2-0
Q2: Cray Wanderers (H) 3-0
Q3: Slough Town (A) 2-4

71-72 PR: Staines Town (H) 2-3

72-73 PR: Tilbury (A) 1-2

73-74 Q1: Redhill (A) 1-0
Q2: Leatherhead (H) 1-1, (A) 0-2

74-75 R1: Romford (A) 2-0
R2: Southend United (H) 0-2

75-76 Q4: Leatherhead (A) 0-1

76-77 Q4: Enfield (A) 2-2, (H) 0-4

77-78 PR: Woking (H) 1-0
Q1: Hayes (A) 2-0
Q2: Chertsey Town (A) 1-1, (H) 6-1
Q3: Hampton (A) 1-1, (H) 1-1, (A) 0-2

78-79 PR: Hariney Borough (A) 3-1
Q1: Bye
Q2: Dulwich Hamlet (A) 0-4

ILFRACOMBE TOWN

Currently: Western League

49-50 PR: Truro City (A) 6-2
Q1: St Austell (H) 2-3

50-51 PR: St Blazey (A) 6-0
Q1: Newquay (A) 2-5

51-52 PR: Ilminster Town (A) 3-4

52-53 PR: Newton Abbot (A) 1-1, (H) 2-1
Q1: Bideford (H) 3-0
Q2: St Blazey (H) 2-0
Q3: Barnstaple Town (A) 0-0, (H) 1-0
Q4: Llanelly (A) 0-1

53-54 PR: Tiverton Town (A) 3-2
Q1: Bideford (H) 0-4

54-55 PR: St Blazey (A) 1-1, (H) 5-2
Q1: Newquay Amateur (H) 2-0
Q2: Barnstaple Town (A) 0-2

55-56 PR: Bodmin Town (A) 3-4

56-57 Q1: Bideford (H) 1-2

57-58 PR: Barnstaple Town (H) 1-7

58-59 Q1: Wadebridge Town (H) 4-4, (A) 1-2

59-60 Q1: Truro City (H) *Scratched*

89-90 PR: Clevedon Town (A) 1-0
Q1: Exmouth Town (A) 0-2

90-91 PR: Barnstaple Town (H) 4-0
Q1: Tiverton Town (A) 1-5

91-92 PR: Clandown (A) 1-0
Q1: Saltash United (A) 0-6

92-93 PR: Truro City (H) 3-4

ILKESTON TOWN

Currently: West Midlands (Regional) League

47-48 PR: Boots Athletic (A) 4-0
Q1: Ransome & Marles (H) 2-1
Q2: Boston United (H) 1-0
Q3: Grantham (A) 1-11

48-49 PR: Sherwood Colliery (H) 3-0
Q1: Linby Colliery (H) 0-3

49-50 EX: Sutton Town (H) 2-3

50-51 EX: Sherwood Colliery (A) 8-0
PR: Long Eaton Town (H) 0-4

51-52 Q1: Gedling Colliery (H) 7-3
Q2: Long Eaton Town (A) 3-0
Q3: Newhall United (H) 6-1
Q4: Grantham (H) 2-1
R1: Rochdale (H) 0-2

52-53 Q1: Long Eaton Town (H) 7-2
Q2: Gresley Rovers (A) 5-0
Q3: Boots Athletic (A) 4-0
Q4: Gainsborough Trinity (A) 1-5

53-54 Q1: Gresley Rovers (A) 2-3

54-55 Q1: Boots Athletic (A) 6-0
Q2: South Normanton Welfare (A) 5-1
Q3: Gresley Rovers (A) 2-2, (H) 5-4
Q4: Kettering Town (H) 1-1, (A) 2-4

55-56 Q2: South Normanton Welfare (H) 3-1
Q3: Boots Athletic (A) 9-0
Q4: Peterborough United (H) 1-3

56-57 Q2: Boots Athletic (H) 2-0
Q3: Clay Cross & Danesmoor M.W. (A) 8-1
Q4: Sutton Town (H) 2-2, (A) 2-1
R1: Blyth Spartans (H) 1-5

57-58 Q1: South Normanton Welf. (A) 2-2, (H) 2-0
Q2: Belper Town (H) 2-4

58-59 Q1: Long Eaton United (A) 0-2

59-60 Q1: Tamworth (A) 2-2, (H) 2-1
Q2: Atherstone Town (A) 2-0
Q3: Brush Sports (H) 1-1, (A) 2-1
Q4: Matlock Town (H) 2-6

60-61 Q1: Burton Albion (H) 3-1
Q2: Tamworth (H) 3-1
Q3: Loughborough United (H) 0-3

61-62 Q1: Hinckley Athletic (H) 1-1, (A) 1-2

62-63 Q1: Atherstone Town (A) 1-1, (H) 1-2

63-64 Q2: Loughborough United (H) 1-1, (A) 0-4

64-65 Q1: Long Eaton United (A) 3-1
Q2: Atherstone Town (A) 2-4

65-66 Q1: Gresley Rovers (A) 2-0
Q2: Long Eaton United (A) 2-3

66-67 Q1: Sutton Town (A) 0-1

67-68 Q1: Norton Woodseats Amateur (A) 1-2

68-69 PR: Wombwell Sporting (H) 1-1, (A) 5-1
Q1: Eastwood (Hanley) (A) 3-2
Q2: Buxton (A) 0-1

69-70 PR: Matlock Town (H) 1-2

70-71 Q1: Long Eaton United (A) 1-1, (H) 0-0, 0-2

71-72 Q1: Bedworth United (H) 1-2

72-73 Q1: Heanor Town (A) 0-0, (H) 0-2

73-74 Q1: Brereton Social (H) 2-2, (A) 1-1, 1-0
Q2: Atherstone Town (H) 2-0
Q3: Tamworth (H) 2-3

74-75 Q1: Arnold (A) 0-0, (H) 0-1

75-76 Q1: Belper Town (A) 0-1

76-77 Q1: Hednesford (A) 0-1

77-78 PR: Tamworth (H) 0-0, (A) 0-1

80-81 Q1: Holbeach United (H) 0-0, (A) 0-1

81-82 Q1: Hinckley Athletic (H) 2-0
Q2: Worksop Town (A) 3-2
Q3: Corby Town (A) 1-8

82-83 PR: Witton Albion (A) 0-2

83-84 Q1: Gainsborough Trinity (A) 0-6

84-85 PR: Arnold (A) 4-1
Q1: Accrington Stanley (A) 1-2

85-86 PR: Lincoln United (H) 5-0
Q1: Buxton (H) 2-2, (A) 1-4

86-87 PR: Emley (H) 1-3

87-88 Q1: St Helens (H) 1-1, (A) 1-1, (*E. Hanley*) 1-4

88-89 PR: Radcliffe Borough (A) 1-2

89-90 PR: Colwyn Bay (A - *at Rhyl*) 1-5

90-91 Q1: Bootle (H) 2-3

91-92 PR: Grantham Town (A) 5-1
Q1: Horwich R.M.I. (A) 0-1

92-93 PR: Harrogate Railway Athletic (H) 7-0
Q1: Heanor Town (A) 1-2

ILMINSTER TOWN

Currently: Somerset Senior League

48-49 EX: Bideford (H) 1-5

49-50 PR: Street (H) 4-1
Q1: Bideford (A) 0-6

51-52 PR: Ilfracombe Town (H) 4-3
Q1: Bridgwater Town (H) 1-1, (A) 2-4

52-53 Q1: Lymington (H) 2-1
Q2: Dorchester Town (A) 1-6

53-54 Q1: Poole Town (H) 3-2
Q2: Bournemouth Gasworks Athletic (H) 0-4

55-56 Q2: Portland United (A) 0-5

56-57 Q2: Portland United (A) 0-9

57-58 Q2: Bridport (H) 1-2

58-59 Q1: Portland United (A) 0-7

59-60 Q2: Bridgwater Town (H) 1-3

76-77 Q1: Wadebridge Town (H) 1-1, (A) 1-0
Q2: Yeovil Town (A) 1-10

77-78 Q1: Swaythling (H) 0-2

78-79 PR: Poole Town (H) 1-0
Q1: Tiverton Town (A) 0-1

79-80 PR: Shepton Mallet Town (H) 0-0, (A) 1-0
Q1: Saltash United (A) 0-3

80-81 Q1: Melksham Town (A) 0-7

81-82 Q1: Torrington (H) 0-2

IMMINGHAM TOWN

Currently: Northern Counties (East) League

92-93 PR: Clitheroe (A) 1-2

IPSWICH TOWN

Currently: F.A. Premier League

45-46 R1: Wisbech T. (A) 3-0, (H) 5-0 *(agg: 8-0)*
R2: Q.P.R. (A) 0-4, (H) 0-2 *(agg: 0-6)*

46-47 R1: Torquay United (H) 2-0
R2: Walsall (A) 1-1, (H) 1-1, 0-1

47-48 R1: Swindon Town (A) 2-4

48-49 R1: Aldershot (H) 0-3

49-50 R1: Brighton & Hove Albion (H) 2-1
R2: Chelmsford City (A) 1-1, (H) 1-0
R3: West Ham United (A) 1-5

50-51 R1: Leyton Orient (A) 2-1
R2: Brighton & Hove Albion (A) 0-2

51-52 R1: Merthyr Tydfil (A) 2-2, (H) 1-0
R2: Exeter City (H) 4-0
R3: Gateshead (H) 2-2, (A) 3-3, 1-2

52-53 R1: Bournemouth & B. (H) 2-2, (A) 2-2, 3-2
R2: Bradford City (A) 1-1, (H) 5-1
R3: Everton (A) 2-3

53-54 R1: Reading (H) 4-1
R2: Walthamstow Avenue (H) 2-2, (A) 1-0
R3: Oldham Athletic (H) 3-3, (A) 1-0
R4: Birmingham City (H) 1-0
R5: Preston North End (A) 1-6

54-55 R3: Bishop Auckland (H) 2-2, (A) 0-3

55-56 R1: Peterborough United (A) 1-3

56-57 R1: Hastings United (H) 4-0
R2: Watford (A) 3-1
R3: Fulham (H) 2-3

57-58 R3: Crystal Palace (A) 1-0
R4: Manchester United (A) 0-2

58-59 R3: Huddersfield Town (H) 1-0
R4: Stoke City (A) 1-0
R5: Luton Town (H) 2-5

59-60 R3: Peterborough United (H) 2-3

60-61 R3: Southampton (A) 1-7

61-62 R3: Luton Town (H) 1-1, (A) 1-1, 5-1
R4: Norwich City (A) 1-1, (H) 1-2

62-63 R3: Mansfield Ton (A) 3-2
R4: Leicester City (A) 1-3

63-64 R3: Oldham Athletic (H) 6-3
R4: Stoke City (H) 1-1, (A) 0-1

64-65 R3: Swindon Town (A) 2-1
R4: Tottenham Hotspur (A) 0-5

65-66 R3: Southport (A) 0-0, (H) 2-3

66-67 R3: Shrewsbury Town (H) 4-1
R4: Carlisle United (H) 2-0
R5: Manchester City (A) 1-1, (H) 0-3

67-68 R3: Chelsea (A) 0-3

68-69 R3: Everton (A) 1-2

69-70 R3: Manchester United (H) 0-1

70-71 R3: Newcastle United (A) 1-1, (H) 2-1
R4: West Bromwich Albion (A) 1-1, (H) 3-0
R5: Stoke City (A) 0-0, (H) 0-1

71-72 R3: Peterborough United (A) 2-0
R4: Birmingham City (A) 0-1

72-73 R3: Chelmsford City (A) 3-1
R4: Chelsea (A) 0-2

73-74 R3: Sheffield United (H) 3-2
R4: Manchester United (A) 1-0
R5: Liverpool (A) 0-2

74-75 R3: Wolverhampton Wanderers (A) 2-1
R4: Liverpool (H) 1-0
R5: Aston Villa (H) 3-2
R6: Leeds Utd (H) 0-0, (A) 1-1, *(both at Leic. City)* 0-0, 3-2
SF: West Ham United *(at Aston V.)* 0-0, *(at Chelsea)* 1-2

75-76 R3: Halifax Town (H) 3-1
R4: Wolverhampton W. (H) 0-0, (A) 0-1

76-77 R3: Bristol City (H) 4-1
R4: Wolverhampton W. (H) 2-2, (A) 0-1

77-78 R3: Cardiff City (A) 2-0
R4: Hartlepool United (H) 4-1
R5: Bristol Rovers (A) 2-2, (H) 3-0
R6: Millwall (A) 6-1
SF: West Bromwich A. *(at Arsenal F.C.)* 3-1
F: Arsenal *(at Wembley)* 1-0

Above: *Wembley delight for Ipswich after Roger Osborne's late winner against Arsenal in 1978. Photo: Colorsport*

78-79 R3: Carlisle United (H) 3-2
R4: Orient (H) 0-0, (A) 2-0
R5: Bristol Rovers (H) 6-1
R6: Liverpool (H) 0-1

79-80 R3: Preston North End (A) 3-0
R4: Bristol City (A) 2-1
R5: Chester (H) 2-1
R6: Everton (A) 1-2

80-81 R3: Aston Villa (H) 1-0
R4: Shrewsbury Town (A) 0-0, (H) 3-0
R5: Charlton Athletic (H) 2-0
R6: Nottingham Forest (A) 3-3, (H) 1-0
SF: Manchester City *(at Aston Villa)* 0-1

81-82 R3: Birmingham City (A) 3-2
R4: Luton Town (A) 3-0
R5: Shrewsbury Town (A) 1-2

82-83 R3: Charlton Athletic (A) 3-2
R4: Grimsby Town (H) 2-0
R5: Norwich City (A) 0-1

83-84 R3: Cardiff City (A) 3-0
R4: Shrewsbury Town (A) 0-2

84-85 R3: Bristol Rovers (A) 2-1
R4: Gillingham (H) 3-2
R5: Sheffield Wednesday (H) 3-2
R6: Everton (A) 2-2, (H) 0-1

85-86 R3: Bradford C. (H) 4-4, (A - *at Leeds*) 1-0
R4: West Ham (A) 0-0, (H) 1-1, (H) 0-1

86-87 R3: Birmingham City (H) 0-1

87-88 R3: Manchester United (H) 1-2

88-89 R3: Nottingham Forest (A) 0-3

89-90 R3: Leeds United (A) 1-0
R4: Barnsley (A) 0-2

90-91 R3: Southampton (A) 2-3

91-92 R3: Hartlepool United (H) 1-1, (A) 2-0
R4: A.F.C. Bournemouth (H) 3-0
R5: Liverpool (H) 0-0, (A) 2-3

92-93 R3: Plymouth Argyle (H) 3-1
R4: Tranmere Rovers (A) 2-1
R5: Grimsby Town (H) 4-0
R6: Arsenal (H) 2-4

IRLAM TOWN

Currently: North West Counties League

86-87 PR: Chadderton (A) 1-0
Q1: Lancaster City (H) 1-1, (A) 1-2

87-88 Q1: Radcliffe Borough (H) 1-0
Q2: Alfreton Town (A) 0-2

88-89 PR: Oakham United (H) 3-1
Q1: Bangor City (A) 2-2, (H) 1-4

89-90 PR: Congleton Town (A) 1-1, (H) 0-2

90-91 PR: Formby (H) 2-0
Q1: Vauxhall G.M. (A) 2-0
Q2: Horwich R.M.I. (H) 1-3

91-92 PR: Curzon Ashton (H) 0-0, (A) 1-4

92-93 PR: Atherton Laburnum Rovers (H) 1-2

IRTHLINGBOROUGH DIAMONDS

Currently: Merged with Rushden Town
Playing as Rushden & Diamonds in Southern League.
See also Rushden & Diamonds

69-70 Q1: Letchworth Town (A) 3-2
Q2: Newmarket Town (A) 1-3

70-71 Q1: Histon (H) 2-1
Q2: Rothwell Town (A) 1-1, (H) 5-0
Q3: Cambridge City (H) 2-2, (A) 0-3

71-72 PR: Desborough Town (A) 2-1
Q1: Corby Town (A) 1-0
Q2: Witney Town (A) 0-3

72-73 Q1: Hinckley Athletic (H) 1-1, (A) 2-1
Q2: Long Eaton United (H) 2-1
Q3: Enderby Town (H) 0-4

73-74 Q1: St Neots Town (A) 1-3

74-75 Q1: Rothwell Town (H) 3-1
Q2: Potton United (A) 3-5

75-76 Q1: A.P. Leamington (H) 1-2

76-77 Q1: Soham Town Rangers (H) 2-2, (A) 3-4

77-78 Q1: Stamford (H) 3-1
Q2: Corby Town (H) 1-2

78-79 Q1: Friar Lane Old Boys (H) 3-0
Q2: Atherstone Town (A) 3-1

Q3: Hinckley Athletic (A) 2-1
Q4: Dagenham (A) 0-0, (H) 1-2

79-80 Q1: Corby Town (A) 0-1

80-81 PR: Histon (A) 0-3

81-82 PR: Harefield United (H) 2-1
Q1: Chesham United (H) 1-0
Q2: Tring Town (H) 1-1, (A) 0-1

82-83 PR: Spalding United (A) 1-0
Q1: Felixstowe Town (A) 1-1, (H) 3-1
Q2: Skegness Town (A) 0-0, (H) 1-0
Q3: King's Lynn (H) 1-2

83-84 Q1: Dudley Town (A) 1-3

84-85 PR: Stamford (A) 2-0
Q1: Leicester United (H) 3-0
Q2: Nuneaton Borough (H) 0-5

85-86 Q1: Shepshed Charterhouse (H) 3-2
Q2: Wellingborough Town (A) 1-1, (H) 4-2
Q3: Halesowen Town (A) 2-2, (H) 1-2

86-87 Q1: Corby Town (A) 0-3

87-88 Q1: Banbury United (H) 3-1
Q2: Barnet (H) 0-4

88-89 PR: Northampton Spencer (A) 1-0
Q1: Moor Green (H) 1-1, (A) 3-4

89-90 PR: M.K. Wolverton Town (A) 1-2

90-91 PR: Buckingham Town (H) 3-4

91-92 PR: Wednesfield (H) 2-2, (A) 3-3, (H) 1-2

JARROW

Currently: Defunct

48-49 EX: Morpeth Town (H) 2-1
PR: Newburn (H) 0-3

49-50 EX: Lynemouth Welfare (A) 2-6

JUMP HOME GUARD

Currently: Defunct

49-50 EX: Parkhouse Colliery (A) 0-6

50-51 PR: Parkhouse Colliery (H) 3-3, (A) 1-7

KELLS WELFARE CENTRE

Currently: Defunct

45-46 Q2: Milnthorpe Corinthians (A) 5-4
Q3: Netherfield (H) 1-2

46-47 PR: William Colliery (H) 4-0
Q1: Lowca (H) 1-2

47-48 PR: Bowthorn United (A) 2-2 (H) 1-3

48-49 PR: Netherfield (H) 1-5

49-50 Q1: Cockermouth (A) 3-1
Q2: Netherfield (A) 0-2

50-51 Q1: Frizington United (A) *scratched*

KEMPSTON ROVERS

Currently: United Counties League

47-48 PR: Bedford Avenue (H) 4-1
Q1: Biggleswade Town (A) 5-4
Q2: Vauxhall Motors (H) 1-2

48-49 PR: Bedford Town (A) 1-7

49-50 PR: Bedford Town (H - *played away*) 0-2

50-51 EX: St Ives Town (A) 1-2

77-78 PR: Potton United (H) 2-1
Q1: Aylesbury United (A) 3-0
Q2: Hertford Town (A) 0-1

78-79 Q1: Grays Athletic (A) 2-0
Q2: Valley Sports (Rugby) (H) 3-1
Q3: Willenhall Town (A) 2-0
Q4: Wealdstone (A) 0-1

79-80 Q1: St Albans City (A) 2-0
Q2: Tring Town (A) 0-5

80-81 Q1: Hertford Town (H) 3-0
Q2: Witney Town (H) 2-1
Q3: Hayes (H) 0-2

81-82 Q1: Highgate United (A) 2-2, (H) 1-2

82-83 PR: Wootton Blue Cross (A) 0-2

87-88 PR: Finchley (A) 0-1

88-89 PR: Beckenham Town (H) 0-1

92-93 Q1: Wivenhoe Town (H) 3-4

KETTERING TOWN

Currently: Alliance Premier League

45-46 Q1: Peterborough Westwood Works (H) 5-0
Q2: Wellingborough Town (A) 5-2
Q3: Peterborough United (H) 2-1
Q4: Coalville Town (H) 2-1
R1: Grantham (H) 1-5, (A) 2-2 (*agg: 3-7*)

46-47 Q1: Rushden Town (H) 2-0
Q2: Stewart & Lloyds (A) 1-1, (H) 4-2
Q3: Peterborough United (A) 1-4

47-48 Q2: Rushden Town (A) 2-1
Q3: Peterborough United (H) 3-4

48-49 Q1: Rushden Town (H) 2-2, (A) 1-0
Q2: Desborough Town (H) 2-2, (A) 3-0
Q3: Peterborough United (A) 1-2

49-50 Q1: Northampton Amateur (H) 5-1
Q2: Peterborough United (H) 0-5

50-51 Q1: Rushden Town (A) 2-2, (H) 4-0
Q2: Peterborough United (H) 2-2, (A) 2-1
Q3: Corby Town (A) 5-1
Q4: Bromsgrove Rovers (A) 2-3

51-52 Q1: Spalding United (A) 7-1
Q2: Corby Town (A) 2-1
Q3: Desborough Town (H) 2-0
Q4: Bedworth Town (H) 4-2
R1: Bristol Rovers (A) 0-3

52-53 Q1: Rushden Town (H) 1-0
Q2: Corby Town (A) 1-1, (H) 0-2

53-54 Q1: Rushden Town (A) 1-1, (H) 3-1
Q2: Desborough Town (A) 4-0
Q3: Stamford (A) 3-3, (H) 12-0
Q4: Buxton (A) 3-0
R1: Leyton Orient (A) 0-3

54-55 Q4: Ilkeston Town (A) 1-1, (H) 4-2
R1: Bishop Auckland (A) 1-5

55-56 Q1: Corby Town (A) 1-2

56-57 Q1: Spalding United (A) 2-3

57-58 Q1: Stamford (H) 4-1
Q2: Corby Town (A) 1-3

58-59 Q1: Spalding United (A) 6-4
Q2: Corby Town (H) 5-1
Q3: Rushden Town (A) 1-0
Q4: Oswestry Town (A) 3-1
R1: Peterborough United (A) 2-2, (H) 2-3

59-60 Q4: Boston United (H) 1-0
R1: Margate (H) 1-1, (A) 2-3

60-61 Q1: Corby Town (A) 2-1
Q2: Stamford (H) 3-0
Q3: St Neots Town (H) 2-0
Q4: Boston United (H) 1-1, (A) 3-1
R1: Wycombe Wanderers (A) 2-1
R2: Reading (A) 2-4

61-62 Q4: Heanor Town (H) 2-0
R1: Swindon Town (A) 2-2, (H) 3-0
R2: Northampton Town (A) 0-3

62-63 Q4: Boston United (A) 0-2

63-64 Q4: Grantham (H) 3-1
R1: Millwall (H) 1-1, (A) 3-2
R2: Oxford United (A) 1-2

64-65 Q4: Lowestoft Town (A) 3-1
R1: Millwall (A) 0-2

65-66 Q4: Wisbech Town (A) 1-6

66-67 Q4: Lowestoft Town (A) 1-3

67-68 Q1: Newmarket Town (A) 1-0
Q2: Wellingborough Town (H) 1-1, (A) 2-1
Q3: Cambridge United (A) 0-3

68-69 Q1: Cambridge United (H) 1-0
Q2: Soham Town Rangers (A) 1-0
Q3: Wellingborough Town (H) 4-1
Q4: Atherstone Town (H) 2-0
R1: Waterlooville (A) 2-1
R2: Dartford (H) 5-0
R3: Bristol Rovers (A) 1-1, (H) 1-2

69-70 Q4: Braintree & Crittall Athletic (H) 4-0
R1: Swansea Town (H) 0-2

70-71 Q4: Wycombe Wanderers (A) 0-5

71-72 Q1: Cambridge City (H) 6-1
Q2: Chatteris Town (H) 2-0
Q3: Wellingborough Town (H) 2-1
Q4: Chelmsford City (H) 4-1
R1: Barnet (H) 2-4

72-73 PR: Spalding United (A) 2-0
Q1: Louth United (H) 4-0
Q2: Bourne Town (A) 5-1
Q3: Skegness Town (H) 7-0
Q4: Ely City (A) 2-1
R1: Walsall (A) 3-3, (H) 1-2

73-74 Q4: Grantham (A) 1-3

74-75 Q4: Bedford T. (H) 3-3, (A) 0-0, (A) 2-0
R1: Swansea City (A) 1-1, (H) 3-1
R2: Wimbledon (A) 0-2

75-76 Q4: Boston United (H) 3-4

Above: *In 1988-89 Kettering Town enjoyed one of the most memorable runs of all time by a non-League team. Here Robbie Cooke is pictured towering high above the Halifax Town defence in the Third Round tie at Rockingham Road. Photo: Mick Cheney.*

76-77	Q4: Darlaston (A) 1-1, (H) 2-0 R1: Oxford United (H) 1-1, (A) 1-0 R2: Tooting & Mitcham United (H) 1-0 R3: Colchester United (H) 2-3
77-78	Q4: Hitchin Town (A) 2-2, (H) 2-1 R1: Tilbury (A) 1-0 *void*, (A) 2-2, (H) 2-3
78-79	Q4: Boston United (H) 1-3
79-80	R1: Reading (A) 2-4
80-81	Q4: Banbury United (H) 3-0 R1: Maidstone U. (H) 1-1, (A) 0-0, (A) 1-3
81-82	Q4: King's Lynn (H) 2-1 R1: Boston United (A) 1-0 R2: Blackpool (H) 0-3
82-83	Q4: A.P. Leamington (H) 3-1 R1: Walsall (A) 0-3
83-84	Q4: Sutton Coldfield Town (H) 3-2 R1: Swindon Town (H) 0-7
84-85	Q4: Harrow Borough (H) 1-1, (A) 2-0 R1: A.F.C. Bournemouth (H) 0-0, (A) 2-3
85-86	Q4: Chelmsford City (A) 0-1
86-87	Q1: Lowestoft Town (H) 2-1 Q2: Tiptree United (A) 3-0 Q3: Corby Town (H) 2-0 Q4: Windsor & Eton (H) 1-0 R1: Gillingham (H) 0-3
87-88	Q1: Wisbech Town (A) 0-2
88-89	Q1: Ware (A) 3-0 Q2: Great Yarmouth Town (A) 3-0 Q3: Boreham Wood (H) 4-0 Q4: Wycombe Wanderers (A) 2-1 R1: Dartford (H) 2-1 R2: Bristol Rovers (H) 2-1 R3: Halifax Town (H) 1-1, (A) 3-2 R4: Charlton Ath. (A - *at Crystal Pal.*) 1-2
89-90	R1: Northampton Town (H) 0-1
90-91	Q4: Chelmsford City (A) 0-0, (H) 1-2
91-92	Q1: Wisbech Town (A) 3-0 Q2: Braintree Town (H) 3-1 Q3: Heybridge Swifts (H) 3-0 Q4: Stafford Rangers (H) 0-0, (A) 2-0 R1: Wycombe Wanderers (H) 1-1, (A) 2-0 R2: Maidstone United (A) 2-1 R3: Blackburn Rovers (A) 1-4
92-93	Q4: Corby Town (H) 2-1 R1: Gillingham (A) 2-3

KEYNSHAM TOWN

Currently: Western League

90-91	PR: Melksham Town (A) 1-2
91-92	PR: Glastonbury (A) 0-1

KIDDERMINSTER HARRIERS

Currently: Alliance Premier League

Above: *The Kidderminster attack forces Exeter City goalkeeper Kevin Miller into a full length dive, but the Harriers slip to defeat in a competition in which they have enjoyed comparatively little success. Photo: Paul Dennis.*

45-46	Q4: Wellington Town (A) 2-5
46-47	Q4: Wellington Town (A) 1-3
47-48	Q4: Cheltenham Town (H) 2-4
48-49	Q4: Brush Sports (H) 5-2 R1: Hereford United (H) 0-3
49-50	PR: Stourbridge (A) 0-0, (H) 2-3
50-51	PR: Halesowen Town (H) 3-0 Q1: Hereford United (H) 0-1
51-52	Q1: Stafford Rangers (H) 3-2 Q2: Brierley Hill Alliance (A) 2-1 Q3: Wellington Town (A) 2-3
52-53	PR: Dudley Town (H) 4-0 Q1: Oswestry Town (H) 2-0 Q2: Brierley Hill Alliance (H) 1-1, (A) 2-1 Q3: Bromsgrove Rovers (A) 2-0 Q4: Bedworth Town (H) 1-1, (A) 2-0 R1: Finchley (H) 0-1
53-54	Q1: Bilston (A) 2-0 Q2: Bromsgrove Rovers (H) 2-1 Q3: Brierley Hill Alliance (H) 2-0 Q4: Wellington Town (H) 1-2
54-55	PR: Halesowen Town (A) 4-1 Q1: Hednesford (A) 2-3
55-56	PR: Brierley Hill Alliance (A) 1-1, (H) 4-2 Q1: Wellington Town (H) 2-1 Q2: Worcester City (H) 2-0 Q3: Halesowen Town (H) 0-0, (A) 0-1
56-57	PR: Dudley Town (A) 3-0 Q1: Redditch (H) 1-0 Q2: Bromsgrove Rovers (A) 0-4
57-58	PR: Wellington Town (H) 0-2
58-59	Q1: Oswestry Town (A) 3-5
59-60	Q1: Bournville Athletic (H) 7-1 Q2: Oswestry Town (H) 0-2
60-61	Q1: Moor Green (A) 3-2 Q2: Oswestry Town (H) 2-1 Q3: Wellington Town (H) 0-1
61-62	Q1: Oswestry Town (A) 1-1, (H) 1-1, 4-0 Q2: Bromsgrove Rovers (H) 0-2
62-63	Q1: Sankey of Wellington (H) 1-0 Q2: Bromsgrove Rovers (A) 0-0, (H) 1-3
63-64	Q1: Stafford Rangers (H) 4-1 Q2: Moor Green (A) 2-1 Q3: Worcester City (A) 1-4
64-65	Q1: Redditch (H) 1-0 Q2: Sankey of Wellington (H) 3-0 Q3: Dudley Town (H) 2-1 Q4: Rugby Town (H) 5-1 R1: Hull City (H) 1-4
65-66	Q1: Reddtich (H) 3-0 Q2: Stafford Rangers (A) 2-0 Q3: Worcester City (H) 2-2, (A) 2-1 Q4: Oswestry Town (A) 4-3 R1: Peterborough United (A) 1-2
66-67	Q4: Hereford United (A) 1-1, (H) 2-4
67-68	Q4: Burton Albion (A) 4-1 R1: Walthamstow Avenue (A) 1-2
68-69	Q4: Nuneaton Borough (A) 1-1, (H) 3-0 R1: Brighton & Hove A. (A) 2-2, (H) 0-1
69-70	Q4: Telford United (A) 1-2
70-71	Q1: Worcester City (H) 1-0 Q2: Bilston (A) 2-2, (H) 7-1 Q3: Bromsgrove Rovers (A) 2-2, (H) 2-1 Q4: Hereford United (A) 0-5
71-72	PR: Lye Town (H) 3-1 Q1: Highgate United (A) 1-3
72-73	PR: Nuneaton Borough (A) 1-1, (H) 0-1
73-74	Q1: Cinderford Town (A) 1-1, (H) 1-3
74-75	Q1: Brierley Hill Alliance (A) 2-1 Q2: Highgate United (H) 5-2 Q3: Redditch Utd (H) 1-1, (A) 2-2, 3-0 Q4: Wigan Athletic (A) 0-4
75-76	PR: Bedworth United (H) 0-1
76-77	PR: Redditch United (H) 1-2
77-78	PR: Sutton Coldfield Town (H) 5-2 Q1: Alvechurch (A) 2-2, (H) 1-1, 1-0 Q2: Highgate United (A) 2-0 Q3: A.P. Leamington (H) 1-2
78-79	PR: Moor Green (H) 5-0 Q1: Stratford Town (A) 2-2, (H) 7-0 Q2: Dudley Town (A) 0-2
79-80	Q1: Friar Lane Old Boys (H) 2-0 Q2: Long Eaton United (A) 1-0 Q3: Lye Town (H) 2-1 Q4: Sutton Coldfield T. (A) 3-3, (H) 3-2 R1: Blackburn Rovers (H) 0-2
80-81	Q1: Hednesford Town (H) 3-0 Q2: Halesowen Town (A) 4-1 Q3: Buckingham Town (H) 2-1 Q4: Nuneaton Borough (H) 1-0 R1: Millwall (H) 1-1, (A) 0-1
81-82	Q1: Shepshed Charterhouse (H) 1-2
82-83	PR: Redditch United (H) 0-0, (A) 3-2 Q1: Banbury United (A) 2-0 Q2: Mile Oak Rovers & Youth (A) 7-2 Q3: Corby Town (H) 1-3
83-84	Q1: Barton Rovers (A) 1-0 Q2: Bedworth United (A) 1-2
84-85	Q1: Rushall Olympic (A) 2-1 Q2: Rothwell Town (A) 4-1 Q3: Bridgnorth Town (H) 3-2 Q4: King's Lynn (H) 1-1, (A) 0-1
85-86	Q1: Stevenage Borough (A) 2-0 Q2: Hednesford Town (A) 5-1 Q3: Tamworth (H) 4-3 Q4: Bishop's Stortford (H) 3-4
86-87	Q1: Hinckley Athletic (A) 1-0 Q2: Wigston Fields (A) 5-0 Q3: Malvern Town (A) 2-0 Q4: Chelmsford City (A) 1-2
87-88	R1: Halesowen Town (A) 2-2, (H) 4-0 R2: Maidstone United (A) 1-1, (H) 2-2, (H) 0-0, (A) 1-2
88-89	Q4: Stafford Rangers (A) 1-2
89-90	Q4: Chelmsford City (H) 2-2, (A) 3-1 R1: Swansea City (H) 2-3
90-91	Q4: Bromsgrove Rovers (A) 2-1 R1: Woking (A) 0-0, (H) 1-1, (H) 1-2
91-92	R1: Aylesbury United (H) 0-1
92-93	Q4: Atherstone United (H) 2-0 R1: Exeter City (A) 0-1

KIDLINGTON

Currently: Hellenic League

50-51	EX: Headington United (H) 0-6

KILNHURST COLLIERY

Currently: Defunct

48-49	PR: Denaby United (A) 0-1
49-50	PR: Hoyland Common Athletic (A) 1-2
50-51	PR: Beighton Miners Welfare (H) 0-3

KINGSBURY TOWN

Currently: Isthmian League

83-84 PR: Addlestone & Weybridge Town (H) 0-1

84-85 PR: Tring Town (A) 1-3

85-86 PR: Leyton-Wingate (H) 1-1, (A) 0-3

86-87 PR: Erith & Belvedere (H) 0-0, (A) 0-1

87-88 PR: Lowestoft Town (A) 1-0
Q1: Billericay Town (A) 3-0
Q2: Harlow T. (A) 1-1, (H) 2-2, (H) 3-2
Q3: Leytonstone-Ilford (H) 0-1

88-89 Q1: Wokinghham Town (A) 1-2

89-90 Q1: Bromley (A) 1-1, (H) 2-2, (H) 0-2

90-91 PR: Ford United (A) 1-3

91-92 PR: Leighton Town (A) 2-3

92-93 PR: Oakwood (H) 4-3
Q1: Beckenham Town (H) 2-3

KINGS LANGLEY

Currently: Herts Senior County League

45-46 PR: Hemel Hempstead United (A) 7-4
Q1: Harrow Town (A) 1-7

KING'S LYNN

Currently: Southern League

45-46 Q2: Cambridge Town (A) 1-4

46-47 Q2: Cambridge Town (H) 0-2

47-48 Q1: Cambridge Town (A) 1-3

48-49 PR: Royston Town (A) 6-1
Q1: Bury Town (H) 7-0
Q2: Histon Institute (A) 4-3
Q3: Cambridge Town (H) 4-5

49-50 Q1: March Town United (H) 3-2
Q2: Histon Institute (A) 2-2, (H) 5-2
Q3: Cambridge Town (H) 3-1
Q4: Dartford (H) 1-1, (A) 2-1
R1: Nuneaton Borough (A) 1-2

50-51 Q1: Abbey United (H) 2-2, (A) 1-0
Q2: March Town United (H) 6-0
Q3: Histon Institute (H) 3-1
Q4: Dartford (H) 1-1, (A) 0-3

51-52 Q1: Chatteris Town (H) 14-1
Q2: Wisbech Town (H) 2-0
Q3: March Town United (A) 4-1
Q4: Sudbury Town (H) 1-0
R1: Exeter City (H) 1-3

52-53 Q1: St Neots & District (H) 4-1
Q2: Cambridge City (A) 3-3, (H) 5-1
Q3: Cambridge United (A) 0-0, (H) 4-0
Q4: Grays Athletic (A) 0-0, (H) 0-2

53-54 Q1: March Town United (A) 1-3

54-55 PR: Wisbech Town (A) 1-1, (H) 8-1
Q1: Huntingdon United (H) 9-0
Q2: Holbeach United (A) 2-2, (H) 3-1
Q3: March Town United (H) 1-3

55-56 PR: Histon (H) 6-1
Q1: Chatteris Town (A) 4-2
Q2: March Town United (H) 1-1, (A) 0-1

56-57 Q1: St Neots & District (H) 4-0
Q2: March Town United (A) 1-4

57-58 PR: Holbeach United (H) 3-1
Q1: Cambridge City (A) 6-1
Q2: Wisbech Town (H) 2-2, (A) 1-4

58-59 Q1: Lowestoft Town (A) 1-0
Q2: Gorleston (H) 6-1
Q3: Great Yarmouth Town (A) 1-0
Q4: Cheshunt (A) 6-0
R1: Merthyr Tydfil (H) 2-1
R2: Brentford (A) 0-3

59-60 Q4: Letchworth Town (A) 4-3
R1: Aldershot (H) 3-1
R2: Reading (A) 2-4

60-61 Q4: Bedford Town (A) 4-1
R1: Loughborough United (A) 0-0, (H) 3-0
R2: Bristol City (H) 2-2, (A) 0-3

61-62 Q4: Dulwich Hamlet (A) 2-1
R1: Chelmsford City (A) 2-1
R2: Coventry City (A) 2-1
R3: Everton (A) 0-4

62-63 Q4: Corby Town (H) 2-1
R1: Boston United (A) 2-1
R2: Oxford United (H) 1-2

63-64 Q4: Harwich & Parkeston (A) 0-4

64-65 Q4: St Neots Town (H) 8-0
R1: Shrewsbury Town (H) 0-1

65-66 Q4: Corby Town (A) 1-2

66-67 Q1: Skegness Town (H) 4-3
Q2: Boston (H) 2-1
Q3: Boston United (H) 2-5

67-68 Q1: Skegness Town (A) 2-0
Q2: Bourne Town (H) 3-1
Q3: Boston United (A) 0-2

68-69 Q1: Skegness Town (A) 3-0
Q2: Louth United (H) 3-1
Q3: Wisbech Town (H) 5-3
Q4: Lowestoft Town (H) 3-0
R1: Southend United (A) 0-9

69-70 Q1: Boston (A) 3-2
Q2: Skegness Town (H) 2-1
Q3: Boston United (H) 2-1
Q4: Oxford City (A) 0-2

70-71 Q1: Ely City (A) 2-1
Q2: Wisbech Town (H) 4-0
Q3: Soham Town Rangers (A) 6-0
Q4: Chelmsford City (A) 0-2

71-72 Q1: Skegness Town (H) 4-1
Q2: Wisbech Town (A) 4-0
Q3: Bourne Town (A) 3-0
Q4: Bury Town (A) 3-1
R1: Hereford United (H) 0-0, (A) 0-1

72-73 PR: Thetford Town (A) 1-2

73-74 Q1: Sudbury Town (H) 1-0
Q2: Clacton Town (H) 3-1
Q3: Harwich & Parkeston (A) 2-1
Q4: Stamford Town (H) 3-1
R1: Wimbledon (H) 1-0
R2: Alvechurch (A) 1-6

74-75 Q1: Parson Drove United (H) 9-0
Q2: Bourne Town (A) 2-2, (H) 1-0
Q3: Boston (H) 1-0
Q4: Stafford Rangers (H) 1-3

75-76 PR: Gorleston (H) 2-0
Q1: Spalding Utd (A) 3-3, (H) 1-1, 2-5

76-77 Q1: Parson Drove (H) 3-2
Q2: Boston (A) 1-2

77-78 Q1: Wisbech Town (H) 1-2

78-79 PR: Bury Town (A) 2-1
Q1: St Neots Town (A) 0-1

79-80 Q1: Gorleston (H) 2-0
Q2: Sudbury Town (A) 2-1
Q3: Parson Drove (H) 0-1

80-81 Q1: Soham Town Rangers (A) 1-1, (H) 2-1
Q2: Enderby Town (H) 2-0
Q3: Hinckley Athletic (H) 5-1
Q4: Stafford Rangers (H) 1-3

81-82 Q1: Thetford Town (H) 0-0, (A) 1-0
Q2: Bury Town (A) 5-0
Q3: Great Yarmouth Town (H) 5-1
Q4: Kettering Town (A) 1-2

82-83 Q1: Gorleston (A) 3-2
Q2: Lowestoft Town (H) 2-1
Q3: Irthlingborough Diamonds (A) 2-1
Q4: Shepshed Charterhouse (A) 1-2

83-84 Q1: Halesowen Town (A) 0-6

84-85 Q1: Hemel Hempstead (A) 2-0
Q2: Saffron Walden Town (A) 0-0, (H) 2-1
Q3: Corby Town (H) 0-0, (A) 3-0
Q4: Kidderminster H. (A) 1-1, (H) 1-0
R1: Bristol Rovers (A) 1-2

85-86 Q1: Chalfont St Peter (A) 1-1, (H) 1-2

86-87 Q1: Haverhill Rovers (H) *W/O*
Q2: Hornchurch (A) 1-1, (H) 2-0
Q3: Cambridge City (H) 1-0
Q4: Woodford Town (H) 1-3

87-88 Q1: March Town United (H) 1-2

88-89 PR: Evesham United (A) 0-3

89-90 PR: Oldbury United (A) 1-1, (H) 3-1
Q1: Bromsgrove Rovers (H) 0-3

90-91 PR: Boston (A) 0-2

91-92 PR: Haverhill Rovers (H) 5-2
Q1: Cambridge City (H) 3-3, (A) 2-1
Q2: Purfleet (H) 4-2
Q3: Harlow Town (H) 2-3

92-93 Q1: Boston United (A) 1-2

KINGSTONIAN

Currently: Isthmian League

45-46 PR: Tooting & Mitcham United (A) 2-5

46-47 Q1: Vickers Armstrong (A) 1-1, (H) 3-2
Q2: Sutton United (A) 1-3

47-48 Q1: Epsom (H) 10-1
Q2: Tooting & Mitcham United (H) 0-2

48-49 Q4: Tooting & Mitcham (A) 1-1, (H) 2-4

49-50 PR: Sutton United (A) 1-0
Q1: Wimbledon (A) 0-0, (H) 1-1, 6-3
Q2: Epsom (A) 3-1
Q3: Tooting & Mitcham United (H) 5-3
Q4: Romford (A) 0-3

50-51 PR: Farnham Town (H) 6-1
Q1: Dorking (H) 4-0
Q2: Carshalton Athletic (A) 1-1, (H) 2-4

51-52 Q1: Tooting & Mitcham United (H) 3-1
Q2: Sutton United (A) 2-2, (H) 2-3

52-53 PR: Erith & Belvedere (H) 5-0
Q1: Carshalton Athletic (A) 0-3

53-54 PR: Woking (H) 3-1
Q1: Wimbledon (A) 1-1, (H) 4-2
Q2: Margate (H) 2-1
Q3: Hounslow Town (A) 1-6

54-55 PR: Finchley (A) 3-3, (H) 3-1
Q1: Hounslow Town (H) 3-4

55-56 PR: Berkhamsted Town (A) 2-2, (H) 6-0
Q1: Southall (A) 1-1, (H) 0-1

56-57 PR: Tonbridge (H) 2-2, (A) 1-6

57-58 PR: Woking (H) 3-5

58-59 PR: Carshalton Athletic (H) 1-5

59-60 PR: Walton & Hersham (A) 2-0
Q1: Carshalton Athletic (A) 4-2
Q2: Woking (H) 0-3

60-61 Q1: Bromley (A) 3-2
Q2: Walton & Hersham (A) 1-3

61-62 Q1: Leatherhead (A) 2-2, (H) 4-2
Q2: Bromley (H) 2-1
Q3: Walton & Hersham (H) 4-1
Q4: Harwich & Parkeston (A) 0-6

62-63 Q1: Walton & Hersham (H) 5-0
Q2: Metropolitan Police (A) 2-1
Q3: Wimbledon (A) 2-3

63-64 Q1: Walton & Hersham (H) 3-1
Q2: Leatherhead (A) 2-3

64-65 Q1: Dorking (H) 2-0
Q2: Leatherhead (H) 1-1, (A) 0-1

65-66 Q1: Guildford City (A) 2-3

66-67 Q1: Aveley (H) 5-2
Q2: Metropolitan Police (A) 2-2, (H) 2-1
Q3: Sutton United (H) 0-2

67-68 Q1: Hemel Hempstead Town (A) 0-1

68-69 Q1: Hampton (A) 5-1
Q2: Southall (A) 0-0, (H) 3-1
Q3: Edmonton (A) 1-1, (H) 2-0
Q4: Chelmsford City (H) 3-3, (A) 3-5

69-70 Q1: Enfield (H) 1-3 *protest upheld*, (A) 0-3

70-71 Q1: Hemel Hempstead Town (H) 2-0
Q2: Slough Town (A) 0-3

71-72 PR: Leighton Town (H) 4-2
Q1: Hayes (A) 0-2

72-73 Q1: Tilbury (A) 0-0, (H) 1-2

73-74 PR: Grays Athletic (H) 4-0
Q1: Clapton (A) 1-0
Q2: Dartford (A) 3-1
Q3: Dagenham (A) 2-3

74-75 Q1: Woking (A) 2-2, (H) 1-2

75-76 Q1: Carshalton Athletic (A) 2-0
Q2: Egham Town (A) 1-0
Q3: Tonbridge (H) 0-0, (H) 3-1

Q4: Wimbledon (A) 1-6

76-77 PR: Edmonton & Haringey (A) 1-0
Q1: Walthamstow Avenue (A) 4-1
Q2: Wealdstone (H) 0-2

77-78 PR: Tilbury (H) 0-1

78-79 Q1: Tring Town (H) 1-0
Q2: Uxbridge (H) 3-0
Q3: Hillingdon Borough (H) 0-0, (A) 2-3

79-80 Q1: Ruislip Manor (H) 2-0
Q2: Cray Wanderers (H) 1-0
Q3: Woking (H) 0-2

80-81 PR: Arundel (A) 2-0
Q1: Banstead Athletic (H) 1-0
Q2: Egham Town (H) 2-1
Q3: Windsor & Eton (A) 1-1, (H) 2-3

81-82 PR: Hounslow (A) 3-1
Q1: Boreham Wood (H) 2-0
Q2: Hampton (H) 1-0
Q3: Thame United (A) 2-1
Q4: Bideford (A) 0-1

82-83 Q1: Horsham (A) 3-0
Q2: Three Bridges (H) 4-3
Q3: Wokingham (A) 2-2, (H) 1-1, (A) 0-2

83-84 Q1: Steyning Town (H) 2-0
Q2: Worthing (H) 3-2
Q3: Farnborough Town (H) 2-4

84-85 PR: Chichester City (A) 1-0
Q1: Dulwich Hamlet (A) 2-0
Q2: Tooting & Mitcham (A) 2-2, (H) 0-4

85-86 Q1: Whitehawk (H) 1-0
Q2: Walton & Hersham (H) 3-1
Q3: Carshalton Athletic (H) 2-0
Q4: Slough T. (A) 2-2, (H) 1-1, (A) 1-2

86-87 Q1: Cray Wanderers (H) 2-0
Q2: Boreham Wood (A) 2-2, (H) 0-1

87-88 Q1: Carshalton Athletic (A) 0-1

88-89 Q1: Folkestone (H) 4-1
Q2: Feltham (A) 0-0, (H) 3-0
Q3: Fisher Athletic (A) 1-1, (H) 1-4

89-90 Q1: Woking (H) 1-5

90-91 Q1: Staines Town (H) 2-1
Q2: Havant Town (A) 4-0
Q3: Hailsham Town (H) 4-0
Q4: Hayes (A) 0-2

91-92 Q1: Herne Bay (A) 2-0
Q2: Lewes (H) 3-2
Q3: Tooting & Mitcham Utd (H) 0-0, (A) 3-2
Q4: Slough Town (A) 1-2

92-93 Q1: Dulwich Hamlet (H) 4-0
Q2: Langney S. (H) 2-2, (A) 1-1, (H) 3-2
Q3: Chertsey Town (A) 3-1
Q4: Welling United (H) 2-1
R1: Peterborough Utd (H) 1-1, (A) 1-9 *declared void due to missile throwing*, (A) 0-1

Below: *Peterborough goalkeeper Ian Bennett is beaten by a glorious 25-yard drive from John Finch for Kingstonian's only goal in the F.A. Cup match at London Road on 25th December 1992. Peterborough won 9-1, but the match was replayed, behind closed doors, because Kingstonian goalkeeper Adrian Blake had been injured by a missile thrown from the crowd. Photo: Francis Short.*

KIRKBY TOWN

Currently: Defunct

66-67 Q1: Marine (H) 2-0
Q2: Bangor City (H) 0-1

67-68 Q1: Nantwich (A) 2-1
Q2: Winsford United (A) 0-3

68-69 Q1: New Brighton (H) 3-1
Q2: Winsford United (A) 4-2
Q3: Northwich Victoria (A) 2-4

69-70 Q1: Linotype & Machinery (A) 1-0
Q2: New Brighton (A) 2-1
Q3: Northwich Victoria (A) 2-0
Q4: South Liverpool (A) 0-0, (H) 4-3
R1: Bangor City (A) 0-6

70-71 Q1: Oswestry Town (A) 0-2

71-72 PR: Hyde United (A) 2-2, (H) 1-2

KIRKBY TOWN (2)

See Knowsley United

KIVETON PARK UNITED

Currently: (Kiveton Park F.C.) Central Midlands Lge
* - As Kiveton Park Colliery

46-47 * PR: Ossett Town (H) 1-2

47-48 * PR: Lysaght's Sports (A) 1-4

48-49 * PR: Wombwell Athletic (H) 1-1, (A) 1-4

49-50 * EX: Bolsover Colliery (A) 1-2

69-70 PR: Yorkshire Amateur (H) 1-3

KNOWSLEY UNITED

Currently: Northern Premier League
* - As Kirkby Town

86-87 * PR: Burscough (A) 0-2

87-88 * PR: Ashton United (A) 0-2

90-91 PR: Ossett Town (H) 1-1, (A) 3-2
Q1: Colwyn Bay (H) 0-0, (A) 0-3

91-92 PR: Atherton Laburnum Rovers (H) 5-1
Q1: Sheffield (H) 2-0
Q2: Accrington Stanley (A) 2-2, (H) 2-1
Q3: Curzon Ashton (H) 2-0
Q4: Telford United (A) 0-1

92-93 Q1: Chorley (A) 1-1, (H) 2-1
Q2: Stockton (H) 0-2

KNUTSFORD

Currently: Mid-Cheshire League

49-50 EX: Barnton (A) 2-2, (H) 2-1
PR: Northwich Victoria (H) 0-9

LACEBY

Currently: Defunct

48-49 EX: Appleby Frodingham Athletic (A) 4-2
PR: Selby Town (A) 2-4

49-50 EX: Pilkington Recreation (A) 1-2

(CITY OF) LANCASTER

Currently: Northern Premier League

45-46 Q4: Netherfield (A) 0-2

46-47 Q4: Darwen (A) 5-2
R1: Spennymoor United (H) 1-0
R2: Gateshead (A) 0-4

47-48 Q4: Nelson (H) 5-1
R1: Oldham Athletic (A) 0-6

48-49 Q4: Workington (A) 1-1, (H) 1-1, 1-2

49-50 Q4: Fleetwood (A) 1-4

50-51 PR: Barnoldswick & District (H) 5-1
Q1: Nelson (A) 2-5

51-52 Q1: Bacup Borough (H) 2-0
Q2: Fleetwood (H) 2-3

52-53 Q1: Burscough (A) 0-1

53-54 Q1: Great Harwood (A) 4-1
Q2: Burscough (A) 1-2

54-55 Q1: Milnthorpe Corinthians (H) 8-1
Q2: Burscough (H) 2-3

55-56 Q1: Burscough (H) 2-0
Q2: Penrith (H) 2-0
Q3: Fleetwood (A) 1-1, (H) 3-1
Q4: Netherfield (A) 0-2

56-57 Q1: Fleetwood (A) 0-3

57-58 Q1: Morecambe (H) 1-2

58-59 Q1: Morecambe (A) 2-5

59-60 Q1: Burscough (H) 2-4

60-61 Q1: Morecambe (A) 4-7

61-62 Q1: Burscough (A) 0-2

62-63 Q1: Clitheroe (A) 1-4

63-64 Q1: Corinthians (Milnthorpe) (A) 5-0
Q2: Fleetwood (A) 2-1
Q3: Netherfield (A) 0-2

64-65 Q1: Burscough (H) 1-1, (A) 2-1
Q2: Horwich R.M.I. (A) 1-1, (H) 2-1
Q3: Morecambe (A) 2-1
Q4: Bangor City (H) 2-3

65-66 Q1: Clitheroe (A) 0-2

66-67 Q1: Clitheroe (H) 1-1, (A) 1-0
Q2: Rossendale United (A) 3-3, (H) 2-1
Q3: Chorley (A) 0-3

67-68 Q1: Milnthorpe Corinthians (H) 3-0
Q2: Penrith (A) 3-0
Q3: Great Harwood (A) 1-3

68-69 Q1: Lytham St Annes (H) 7-3
Q2: Morecambe (H) 2-4

69-70 Q1: Darwen (H) 1-0
Q2: Corinthians (Milnthorpe) (H) 3-0
Q3: Fleetwood (A) 1-3

70-71 Q1: Netherfield (A) 3-1
Q2: Great Harwood (H) 1-1, (A) 0-3

71-72 Q1: Penrith (H) 6-1
Q2: Fleetwood (A) 2-0
Q3: Rossendale United (H) 1-4

72-73 Q1: Fleetwood (H) 3-1
Q2: Bacup Borough (H) 2-1
Q3: Great Harwood (H) 1-0
Q4: Barrow (H) 3-1
R1: Boston United (A) 2-1
R2: Notts County (A) 1-2

73-74 Q4: Altrincham (H) 1-1, (A) 0-1

74-75 Q1: Burscough (A) 1-0
Q2: Netherfield (H) 2-1
Q3: Darwen (H) 3-0
Q4: Bishop Auckland (H) 1-1, (A) 1-2

75-76 Q1: Clitheroe (A) 2-1
Q2: Fleetwood (A) 1-1, (H) 2-1
Q3: Rossendale United (A) 1-2

76-77 PR: Evenwood Town (A) 1-1, (H) 4-0
Q1: Bishop Auckland (H) 1-1, (A) 0-2

77-78 Q1: Formby (A) 0-1

78-79 PR: Accrington Stanley (A) 2-1
Q1: Penrith (A) 4-0

Q2: Fleetwood Town (A) 1-1, (H) 0-1

79-80 PR: Witton Albion (H) 3-1
Q1: Skelmersdale United (A) 4-1
Q2: Horwich R.M.I. (H) 4-0
Q3: Droylsden (H) 0-0, (A) 0-2

80-81 Q1: Hyde United (H) 1-1, (A) 1-3

81-82 PR: Percy Main Amateurs (H) 3-1
Q1: Billingham Synthonia (H) 1-0
Q2: Ashington (H) 1-3

82-83 PR: Consett (A) 3-0
Q1: Blue Star (A) 2-1
Q2: Barrow (H) 0-0, (A) 0-1

83-84 Q1: Billingham Synthonia (A) 1-0
Q2: Yorkshire Amateur (H) 2-2, (A) 2-0
Q3: Whitby Town (H) 2-2, (A) 3-7

84-85 PR: Chester-le-Street (A) 0-3

85-86 PR: Willington (H) 1-0
Q1: Gretna (H) 0-4

86-87 PR: Accrington Stanley (A) 1-0
Q1: Irlam Town (A) 1-1, (H) 2-1
Q2: Southport (H) 1-1, (A) 1-3

87-88 PR: Darwen (H) 0-4

88-89 PR: Clitheroe (A) 2-2, (H) 1-0
Q1: Barrow (A) 1-3

89-90 PR: Darwen (A) 3-0
Q1: Durham City (H) 0-1

90-91 PR: Thackley (H) 2-0
Q1: Darwen (H) 1-0
Q2: Newcastle Blue Star (H) 0-2

91-92 PR: Winsford United (H) 1-5

92-93 PR: Chadderton (A) 1-2

LANCING

Currently: Sussex County League
* - As Lancing Athletic

48-49 * PR: Horsham (H) *withdrew*

50-51 * PR: Hastings United (H) 2-3

51-52 * PR: Southwick (A) 1-1, (H) 0-1

52-53 * PR: Eastbourne (H) 6-6, (A) 2-1
Q1: Bexhill Town (A) 2-1
Q2: East Grinstead (A) 1-0
Q3: Worthing (H) 2-0
Q4: Newport Isle of Wight (H) 1-5

53-54 * PR: Newhaven (H) 2-1
Q1: Haywards Heath (A) 3-1
Q2: Ashford Town (H) 1-3

55-56 * PR: Worthing (A) 0-5

56-57 * PR: Littlehampton Town (A) 2-1
Q1: Bognor Regis Town (H) 0-2

57-58 * Q1: Newhaven (A) 0-1

58-59 * PR: Southwick (A) 1-3

59-60 * PR: Newhaven (H) 2-1
Q1: Arundel (H) 2-3

60-61 * Q1: Littlehampton Town (A) 3-6

61-62 * Q1: Haywards Heath (H) 1-4

62-63 Q1: Haywards Heath (A) 0-4

63-64 Q1: Worthing (A) 0-0, (H) 3-2
Q2: Lewes (A) 0-3

65-66 Q1: Lewes (H) 3-1
Q2: Carshalton Athletic (H) 0-2

66-67 Q1: Eastbourne (A) 0-2

67-68 Q1: Worthing (A) 1-0
Q2: Haywards Heath (H) 1-1, (A) 1-1, 3-0
Q3: Eastbourne (A) 0-5

68-69 Q1: Eastbourne United (A) 0-2

69-70 PR: Horsham (A) 0-3

70-71 Q1: Carshalton Athletic (H) 1-2

83-84 PR: Faversham Town (H) 3-1
Q1: Hastings United (H) 2-2, (A) 0-2

84-85 PR: Chertsey Town (A) 0-0, (H) 1-0
Q1: Carshalton Town (A) 0-4

85-86 PR: Hythe Town (H) 0-3

86-87 PR: Peacehaven & Telscombe (H) 4-0
Q1: Woking (H) 2-4

87-88 PR: Hastings Town (A) 1-0
Q1: Whyteleafe (A) 0-2

88-89 PR: Whitehawk (A) 0-2

89-90 PR: Canterbury City (H) 0-1

90-91 PR: Lewes (H) 0-3

91-92 PR: Wick (H) 4-1
Q1: Hampton (H) 1-3

92-93 PR: Littlehampton Town (H) 2-3

LANGFORD

Currently: South Midlands League

89-90 PR: Canvey Island (H) 0-3

90-91 PR: Great Yarmouth Town (A) 2-2, (H) 0-1

91-92 PR: Walthamstow Pennant (A) 2-3

92-93 PR: Newmarket Town (A) 0-4

LANGLEY PARK

Currently: (Langley Pk S.&S. Utd) Northern Lge

85-86 PR: Horden Colliery Welfare (H) 2-6

86-87 PR: Evenwood Town (H) 0-0, (A) 1-2

87-88 PR: Ferryhill Athletic (A) 0-3

88-89 PR: Emley (A) 1-4

89-90 PR: Guiseley (H) 5-4
Q1: Brandon United (H) 3-1
Q2: Bishop Auckland (H) 2-5

90-91 PR: Washington (H) 2-0
Q1: Tow Law Town (H) 2-1
Q2: Easington Colliery (A) 1-1, (H) 0-1

91-92 PR: Clitheroe (A) 4-4, (H - *Consett*) 1-1, (A) 1-0
Q1: Northallerton Town (A) 0-1

92-93 PR: Northallerton Town (A) 1-6

LANGLEY PARK COLL. WELF.

Currently: Reformed as Langley Park (above)

46-47 EX: Evenwood Town (H) 0-2

47-48 PR: Seaham Colliery Welfare (A) 1-5

48-49 EX: Eppleton Colliery Welfare (H) 3-4

49-50 EX: Chilton Athletic (A) 1-4

50-51 EX: Evenwood Town (A) 2-5

LANGNEY SPORTS

Currently: Sussex County League

90-91 PR: Portfield (H) 3-0
Q1: Havant Town (A) 0-4

91-92 PR: Southwick (H) 0-1

92-93 PR: Worthing United (A) 4-1
Q1: Littlehampton Town (H) 3-1
Q2: Kingstonian (A) 2-2, (H) 1-1, (A) 2-3

LANGOLD W.M.C.

Currently: Defunct

49-50 EX: Raleigh Athletic (H) 3-3, (A) 2-0
PR: Gedling Colliery (A) 0-2

50-51 EX: Basford United (A) 5-1
PR: Holbeach United (H) 2-1
Q1: Long Eaton Town (H) 5-1
Q2: Spalding United (A) 2-2, (H) 1-2

51-52 Q1: Brodsworth Main Colliery (H) 3-2
Q2: Rawmarsh Welfare (A) 0-2

52-53 Q1: Bentley Colliery (H) 2-0
Q2: Norton Woodseats (H) 0-4

53-54 Q1: Beighton Miners Welfare (A) 2-5

54-55 Q1: Worksop Town (A) 0-4

55-56 Q1: Brodsworth Main Colliery (A) 2-1
Q2: Bentley Colliery (H) 1-2

LANGWITH MINERS WELF.

Currently: Defunct

54-55 Q1: South Kirkby Colliery (A) 6-3
Q2: Denaby United (A) 0-6

55-56 Q1: Hallam (H) 1-2

56-57 Q1: Cresswell Colliery (H) 1-2

LARKHALL ATHLETIC

Currently: Western League

77-78 Q1: Forest Green Rovers (A) 2-3

78-79 Q1: Paulton Rovers (H) 3-3, (A) 1-2

LEAMINGTON

Currently: Defunct
* - As Lockheed Leamington
\+ - As A.P. Leamington

48-49 * EX: Sutton Coldfield Town (A) 0-1

50-51 * PR: Moira United (A) 2-0
Q1: Atherstone Town (A) 4-2
Q2: Hinckley Athletic (A) 0-7

52-53 * PR: Nuneaton Borough (H) 1-2

53-54 * PR: Boldmere St Michaels (H) 7-0
Q1: Nuneaton Borough (A) 0-1

54-55 * PR: Bourneville Athletic (H) 7-1
Q1: Moor Green (H) 4-5

55-56 * Q1: Moor Green (H) 2-1
Q2: Sutton Coldfield Town (H) 3-4

56-57 * Q1: Rugby Town (H) 3-1
Q2: Atherstone Town (A) 4-4, (H) 2-1
Q3: Bedworth Town (A) 4-2
Q4: Hereford United (H) 1-4

57-58 * PR: Brierley Hill Alliance (H) 1-4

58-59 * PR: Bilston (A) 1-6

59-60 * PR: Bilston (A) 2-3

60-61 * Q1: Rugby Town (H) 4-0
Q2: Bilston (A) 3-1
Q3: Halesowen Town (H) 6-1
Q4: Hereford United (H) 1-2

61-62 * Q1: Rugby Town (H) 1-2

62-63 * Q2: Nuneaton Borough (A) 1-2

63-64 * Q1: Stourbridge (A) 1-0
Q2: Rugby Town (A) 1-1, (H) 2-2, 2-1
Q3: Nuneaton Borough (A) 2-0
Q4: Corby Town (H) 2-2, (A) 0-2

64-65 * Q1: Hednesford (H) 4-3
Q2: Halesowen Town (A) 4-2
Q3: Rugby Town (H) 2-3

65-66 * Q1: Nuneaton Borough (H) 3-1
Q2: Brierley Hill Alliance (H) 2-3

66-67 * Q1: Tamworth (A) 2-4

67-68 * Q1: Stourbridge (H) 0-1

68-69 * PR: Hednesford (H) 2-2, (A) 1-4

69-70 * PR: Telford United (A) 1-3

70-71 * PR: Bromsgrove Rovers (H) 1-3

71-72 * Q1: Stourbridge (H) 2-1
Q2: Highgate United (H) 0-2

72-73 * Q1: Nuneaton Borough (A) 1-4

73-74 + PR: Redditch United (A) 3-1
Q1: Bedworth United (A) 0-1

74-75 + Q1: Dudley Town (A) 3-1
Q2: Lye Town (H) 3-1
Q3: Worcester City (H) 2-1
Q4: Corby Town (H) 1-0
R1: Southend United (H) 1-2

75-76 + Q1: Irthlingborough Diamonds (A) 2-1
Q2: Aylesbury United (H) 3-1
Q3: Milton Keynes City (A) 1-0
Q4: Tividale (H) 3-2
R1: Stafford Rangers (H) 2-3

76-77 + PR: Moor Green (H) 1-0
Q1: Rothwell Town (A) 0-0, (H) 2-0
Q2: Bromsgrove Rovers (H) 1-1, (A) 1-2

77-78 + Q1: Tividale (H) 3-1
Q2: Dudley Town (A) 2-0
Q3: Kidderminster Harriers (A) 2-1
Q4: Boston United (A) 2-1
R1: Enderby Town (H) 6-1
R2: Southend United (H) 0-0, (A) 0-4

78-79 + Q4: Hednesford Town (H) 0-0, (A) 3-2
R1: Dartford (A) 2-1

R2: Torquay United (H) 0-1

79-80 + Q4: Boston (A) 2-2, (H) 1-0
R1: Tranmere Rovers (A) 0-9

80-81 + Q4: Barton Rovers (H) 0-1

81-82 + Q4: Stafford Rangers (A) 0-3

82-83 + Q1: Coventry Sporting (A) 4-0
Q2: Bridgnorth Town (H) 6-1
Q3: Stourbridge (A) 1-1, (H) 2-0
Q4: Kettering Town (A) 1-3

83-84 + Q1: Tividale (A) 5-0
Q2: Lye Town (A) 4-4, (H) 4-0
Q3: Corby Town (A) 2-2, (H) 3-0
Q4: Wellingborough Town (H) 3-0
R1: Gillingham (H) 0-1

84-85 + Q1: Wembley (A) 1-3

85-86 PR: Stevenage Borough (A) 1-2

86-87 PR: Mile Oak Rovers & Y. (A) 1-1, (H) 1-0
Q1: Wigston Fields (A) 1-2

87-88 Q1: Coventry Sporting (H) 2-1
Q2: Worcester City (H) 0-6

LEATHERHEAD

Currently: Isthmian League

47-48 PR: Woking (A) 0-2

48-49 PR: Cobham (A - *played home*) 6-2
Q1: Sutton United (H) 0-2

49-50 EX: Hounslow Town (H) 2-6

50-51 PR: Walton & Hersham (H) 1-3

59-60 Q1: Sutton United (A) 0-6

60-61 Q1: Dorking (H) 1-2

61-62 Q1: Kingstonian (H) 2-2, (A) 2-4

62-63 Q1: Wimbledon (H) 1-4

63-64 Q2: Kingstonian (H) 3-2
Q3: Guildford City (A) 1-5

64-65 Q1: Petter Sports (A) 5-0
Q2: Kingstonian (A) 1-1, (H) 1-0
Q3: Guildford City (H) 1-2

65-66 Q1: Chertsey Town (H) 3-3, (A) 5-2
Q2: Guildford City (H) 2-2, (A) 0-3

66-67 Q1: Barking (H) 1-0
Q2: Maidenhead United (A) 2-0
Q3: Corinthian-Casuals (H) 2-1
Q4: Chesham United (H) 1-2

67-68 Q1: Clapton (A) 1-2

68-69 Q1: Molesey (H) 5-0
Q2: Walton & Hersham (A) 1-4

69-70 Q1: Walton & Hersham (H) 0-1

70-71 Q1: Barking (H) 3-1
Q2: Tooting & Mitcham United (A) 2-1
Q3: Grays Athletic (H) 3-0
Q4: Wimbledon (H) 1-2

71-72 Q1: Erith & Belvedere (A) 2-2, (H) 3-0
Q2: Bexley United (A) 2-3

72-73 Q1: Worthing (H) 3-0
Q2: Bognor Regis Town (A) 0-2

73-74 Q1: Erith & Belvedere (A) 6-1
Q2: Ilford (A) 1-1, (H) 2-0
Q3: Leytonstone (H) 0-0, (A) 0-1

74-75 Q1: Croydon (A) 2-0
Q2: Hornchurch (H) 5-0
Q3: Dagenham (H) 0-0, (A) 3-1
Q4: Walton & Hersham (A) 7-1
R1: Bishop's Stortford (A) 0-0, (H) 2-0
R2: Colchester United (H) 1-0
R3: Brighton & Hove Albion (A) 1-0
R4: Leicester City (H - *played away*) 2-3

75-76 Q4: Ilford (H) 1-0
R1: Cambridge United (H) 2-0
R2: Tooting (H) 0-0, (A) 1-1 *ab. 57m.*, (A) 1-2

76-77 Q4: Chelmsford City (A) 4-0
R1: Northampton Town (H) 2-0
R2: Wimbledon (H) 1-3

77-78 Q4: Cheshunt (H) 4-1
R1: Swansea City (H) 0-0, (A) 1-2

78-79 R1: Merthyr Tydfil (H) 2-1
R2: Colchester United (H) 1-1, (A) 0-4

79-80 Q4: Croydon (H) 1-1, (A) 0-3

80-81 Q4: Bath City (H) 1-0
R1: Exeter City (A) 0-5

81-82 Q4: Dover (A) 1-1, (H) 0-1

82-83 Q4: Wokingham Town (A) 0-1

83-84 Q1: Littlehampton Town (A) 2-0
Q2: Egham Town (A) 5-1
Q3: Fisher Athletic (H) 0-4

84-85 Q1: Pagham (A) 5-0
Q2: Dover Athletic (A) 4-1
Q3: Hastings United (H) 1-2

85-86 Q1: Redhill (H) 0-2

86-87 PR: Eastbourne T. (H) 1-1, (A - *E'bourne U.*) 1-3

87-88 PR: Darenth Heathside (A) 1-2

88-89 PR: Hounslow (H) 1-1, (A) 2-1
Q1: Stowmarket Town (H) 1-0
Q2: Barnet (A) 3-4

89-90 Q1: Folkestone (A) 1-2

90-91 PR: Ashford Town (A) 1-3

91-92 PR: Corinthian-Casuals (H) 3-1
Q1: Dorking (H) 1-2

92-93 PR: Lewes (A) 0-1

LEAVESDEN

Currently: Defunct

46-47 EX: Hertford Town (A) 2-6

47-48 EX: Willesden (H) 7-1
PR: Twickenham (A) 3-1
Q1: St Albans City (H) 2-1
Q2: Harrow Town (H) 3-2
Q3: Wealdstone (H) 1-3

48-49 PR: Stevenage Town (A) 3-2
Q1: St Albans City (H) 1-4

50-51 EX: Morris Motors (H) 8-1
PR: Yiewsley (H) 1-2

LEEDS UNITED

Currently: F.A. Premier League

45-46 R3: Middlesbrough (H) 4-4, (A) 2-7 (*agg: 6-11*)

46-47 R3: West Bromwich Albion (A) 1-2

47-48 R3: Blackpool (A) 0-4

48-49 R3: Newport County (H) 1-3

49-50 R3: Carlisle United (A) 5-2
R4: Bolton Wanderers (H) 1-1, (A) 3-2
R5: Cardiff City (H) 3-1
R6: Arsenal (A) 0-1

50-51 R3: Middlesbrough (H) 1-0
R4: Manchester United (A) 0-4

Above: *Scorer Chris Kelly (front left) and manager Billy Miller celebrate Leatherhead's win at Brighton.*

Right: *An historic F.A. Cup moment; Leatherhead celebrate the Chris Kelly goal that put them two up at First Division Leicester. Photo: Colorsport.*

Above: *Jack Charlton lifts the F.A. Cup for Leeds United in 1972. Photo: Colorsport*

51-52	R3: Rochdale (A) 2-0 R4: Bradford (Park Avenue) (H) 2-0 R5: Chelsea (H) 1-1, (A) 1-1, 1-5
52-53	R3: Brentford (A) 1-2
53-54	R3: Tottenham Hotspur (H) 3-3, (A) 0-1
54-55	R3: Torquay United (H) 2-2, (A) 0-4
55-56	R3: Cardiff City (H) 1-2
56-57	R3: Cardiff City (H) 1-2
57-58	R3: Cardiff City (H) 1-2
58-59	R3: Luton Town (A) 1-5
59-60	R3: Aston Villa (A) 1-2
60-61	R3: Sheffield Wednesday (A) 0-2
61-62	R3: Derby County (H) 2-2, (A) 1-3
62-63	R3: Stoke City (H) 3-1 R4: Middlesbrough (A) 2-0 R5: Nottingham Forest (A) 0-3
63-64	R3: Cardiff City (A) 1-0 R4: Everton (H) 1-1, (A) 0-2
64-65	R3: Southport (H) 3-0 R4: Everton (H) 1-1, (A) 2-1 R5: Shrewsbury Town (H) 2-0 R6: Crystal Palace (A) 3-0 SF: Manchester Utd (*at Sheffield Wed.*) 0-0, (*at Nottingham Forest*) 1-0 F: Liverpool (*at Wembley*) 1-2
65-66	R3: Bury (H) 6-0 R4: Chelsea (A) 0-1
66-67	R3: Crystal Palace (H) 3-0 R4: West Bromwich Albion (H) 5-0 R5: Sunderland (A) 1-1, (H) 1-1, 2-1 R6: Manchester City (H) 1-0 SF: Chelsea (*at Aston Villa*) 0-1
67-68	R3: Derby County (H) 2-0 R4: Nottingham Forest (H) 2-1 R5: Bristol City (H) 2-0 R6: Sheffield United (H) 1-0 SF: Everton (**N**) 0-1
68-69	R3: Sheffield Wednesday (A) 1-1, (H) 1-3
69-70	R3: Swansea Town (H) 2-1 R4: Sutton United (A) 6-0 R5: Mansfield Town (A) 2-0 R6: Swindon Town (A) 2-0 SF: Manchester Utd (*at Sheffield Wed.*) 0-0, (*at Aston Villa*) 0-0, (*at Bolton*) 1-0 F: Chelsea (*Wembley*) 2-2, (*at Man. U.*) 1-2
70-71	R3: Rotherham United (A) 0-0, (H) 3-0 R4: Swindon Town (H) 4-0 R5: Colchester United (A) 2-3
71-72	R3: Bristol Rovers (H) 4-1 R4: Liverpool (A) 0-0, (H) 2-0 R5: Cardiff City (A) 2-0 R6: Tottenham Hotspur (H) 2-1 SF: Birmingham City (*at Sheffield Wed.*) 3-0 F: Arsenal (*at Wembley*) 1-0
72-73	R3: Norwich (A) 1-1, (H) 1-1, (*at Aston V.*) 5-0 R4: Plymouth Argyle (H) 2-1 R5: West Bromwich Albion (H) 2-0 R6: Derby County (A) 1-0 SF: Wolverhampton Wdrs (*at Man. City*) 1-0 F: Sunderland (*at Wembley*) 0-1
73-74	R3: Wolverhampton W. (A) 1-1, (H) 1-0 R4: Peterborough United (A) 4-1 R5: Bristol City (A) 1-1, (H) 0-1
74-75	R3: Cardiff City (H) 4-1 R4: Wimbledon (H) 0-0, (A - *at Crystal P.*) 1-0 R5: Derby County (A) 1-0 R6: Ipswich Town (A) 0-0, (H) 1-1, (*at Leic. City*) 0-0, (*at Leic. City*) 2-3
75-76	R3: Notts County (A) 1-0 R4: Crystal Palace (H) 0-1
76-77	R3: Norwich City (H) 5-2 R4: Birmingham City (A) 2-1 R5: Manchester City (H) 1-0 R6: Wolverhampton Wanderers (A) 1-0 SF: Manchester Utd (*at Sheff. Wed.*) 1-2
77-78	R3: Man. City (H) 1-2 *aband. - score valid*
78-79	R3: Hartlepool United (A) 6-2 R4: W. Brom. (H - *played away*) 3-3, (A) 0-2
79-80	R3: Nottingham Forest (H) 1-4
80-81	R3: Coventry City (H) 1-1, (A) 0-1
81-82	R3: Wolverhampton Wanderers (A) 3-1 R4: Tottenham Hotspur (A) 0-1
82-83	R3: Preston North End (H) 3-0 R4: Arsenal (A) 1-1, (H) 1-1, (A) 1-2
83-84	R3: Scunthorpe (H) 1-1, (A) 1-1, (A) 2-4
84-85	R3: Everton (H) 0-2
85-86	R3: Peterborough United (A) 0-1
86-87	R3: Telford United (*at West Brom.*) 2-1 R4: Swindon Town (A) 2-1 R5: Queens Park Rangers (H) 2-1 R6: Wigan Athletic (A) 2-0 SF: Coventry City (*at Sheffield Wed.*) 2-3
87-88	R3: Aston Villa (H) 1-2
88-89	R3: Brighton & Hove Albion (A) 2-1 R4: Nottingham Forest (A) 0-2
89-90	R3: Ipswich Town (H) 0-1
90-91	R3: Barnsley (A) 1-1, (H) 4-0 R4: Arsenal (A) 0-0, (H) 1-1, (A) 0-0, (H) 1-2
91-92	R3: Manchester United (H) 0-1
92-93	R3: Charlton Athletic (H) 1-1, (A) 3-1 R4: Arsenal (A) 2-2, (H) 2-3

LEEK TOWN

Currently: Northern Premier League

56-57	PR: Lostock Gralam (A) 1-2
72-73	Q1: Ellesmere Port Town (A) 1-2
73-74	Q1: Sandbach Ramblers (A) 4-0 Q2: Macclesfield Town (H) 2-2, (A) 2-4
74-75	Q1: Nantwich Town (H) 1-2
75-76	Q1: Armitage (A) 3-0 Q2: Congleton Town (A) 3-1 Q3: Northwich Victoria (A) 1-1, (H) 1-0 Q4: Grantham (A) 0-4
76-77	PR: Hyde United (A) 1-2
77-78	PR: Heanor Town (A) 2-2, (H) 2-0 Q1: Alfreton Town (A) 1-0 Q2: Telford United (A) 0-3
78-79	PR: Bangor City (H) 2-2, (A) 2-1 Q1: Stalybridge Celtic (A) 1-3
79-80	PR: Tamworth (H) 0-3
80-81	Q1: Mexborough Town Athletic (A) 2-1 Q2: Northwich Victoria (H) 1-1, (A) 0-1
81-82	Q1: Runcorn (A) 0-3
82-83	Q1: Shifnal Town (A) 0-1
83-84	Q1: Goole Town (H) 1-1, (A) 0-4
84-85	Q1: Runcorn (H) 2-1 Q2: Burscough (A) 0-2
85-86	PR: Armitage (H) 0-0, (A) 2-0 Q1: Winsford United (H) 2-0 Q2: G.K.N. Sankey (A) 1-1, (H) 5-4 Q3: St Helens Town (H) 0-1
86-87	Q1: Buxton (A) 0-1
87-88	PR: G.K.N. Sankey (H) 3-3, (A) 3-2 Q1: Eastwood Hanley (A) 0-0, (H) 2-0 Q2: Hyde United (H) 2-1 Q3: Brigg Town (A) 2-3
88-89	PR: Heanor Town (H) 3-0 Q1: South Liverpool (A) 1-1, (H) 2-1 Q2: Mossley (H) 2-0 Q3: Warrington Town (A) 2-1 Q4: Guisborough (H) 0-0, (A) 0-0, (A) 0-1
89-90	Q1: Boston United (A) 3-3, (H) 0-3
90-91	R1: Scarborough (A) 2-0 R2: Chester (H) 1-1, (A - *at Macclesfield*) 0-4
91-92	Q4: Lincoln United (H) 0-2
92-93	Q1: Burton Albion (H) 3-2 Q2: Rushall Olympic (H) 0-1

LEICESTER CITY

Currently: Football League

45-46	R3: Chelsea (A) 1-1, (H) 0-2 (*agg: 1-3*)
46-47	R3: West Ham United (A) 2-1 R4: Brentford (A) 0-0, (H) 0-0, 4-1 R5: Newcastle United (A) 1-1, (H) 1-2
47-48	R3: Bury (H) 1-0 R4: Sheffield Wednesday (H) 2-1 R5: Tottenham Hotspur (A) 2-5
48-49	R3: Birmingham C. (A) 1-1, (H) 1-1, 2-1 R4: Preston North End (H) 2-0 R5: Luton Town (A) 5-5, (H) 5-3 R6: Brentford (A) 2-0 SF: Portsmouth (*at Arsenal F.C.*) 3-1 F: Wolverhampton W. (*at Wembley*) 1-3
49-50	R3: Sheffield United (A) 1-3
50-51	R3: Preston North End (H) 0-3
51-52	R3: Coventry City (H) 1-1, (A) 1-4
52-53	R3: Notts County (H) 2-4
53-54	R3: Middlesbrough (A) 0-0, (H) 3-2 R4: Stoke City (A) 0-0, (H) 3-1 R5: Norwich City (A) 2-1

R6: Preston North End (H) 1-1, (A) 2-2, (*at Sheffield Wednesday*) 1-3

54-55 R3: Rotherham United (A) 0-1

55-56 R3: Luton Town (A) 4-0
R4: Stoke City (H) 3-3, (A) 1-2

56-57 R3: Tottenham Hotspur (A) 0-2

57-58 R3: Tottenham Hotspur (A) 0-4

58-59 R3: Lincoln City (H) 2-2, (A) 2-0
R4: Luton Town (H) 1-1, (A) 1-4

59-60 R3: Wrexham (A) 2-1
R4: Fulham (H) 2-1
R5: West Bromwich Albion (H) 2-1
R6: Wolverhampton Wanderers (H) 1-2

60-61 R3: Oxford United (H) 3-1
R4: Bristol City (H) 5-1
R5: Birmingham City (A) 1-1, (H) 2-1
R6: Barnsley (H) 0-0, (A) 2-1
SF: Sheffield United (*at Leeds United*) 0-0, (*at Nottm F.*) 0-0, (*at Birmingham C.*) 2-0
F: Tottenham Hotspur (*at Wembley*) 0-2

61-62 R3: Stoke City (H) 1-1, (A) 2-5

62-63 R3: Grimsby Town (A) 3-1
R4: Ipswich Town (H) 3-1
R5: Leyton Orient (H) 1-0
R6: Norwich City (A) 2-0
SF: Liverpool (*at Sheffield Wed.*) 1-0
F: Manchester United (*at Wembley*) 1-3

63-64 R3: Leyton Orient (H) 2-3

64-65 R3: Blackburn Rovers (H) 2-2, (A) 2-1
R4: Plymouth Argyle (H) 5-0
R5: Middlesbrough (A) 3-0
R6: Liverpool (H) 0-0, (A) 0-1

65-66 R3: Aston Villa (A) 2-1
R4: Birmingham City (A) 2-1
R5: Manchester City (A) 2-1, (H) 0-1

66-67 R3: Manchester City (A) 1-2

67-68 R3: Barrow (A) 2-1
R4: Manchester City (A) 0-0, (H) 4-3
R5: Rotherham United (A) 1-1, (H) 2-0
R6: Everton (A) 1-3

68-69 R3: Barnsley (A) 1-1, (H) 2-1
R4: Millwall (A) 1-0
R5: Liverpool (A) 0-0, (H) 1-0
R6: Mansfield Town (A) 1-0
SF: West Bromwich A. (*at Sheff. Wed.*) 1-0
F: Manchester City (*at Wembley*) 0-1

69-70 R3: Sunderland (H) 1-0
R4: Southampton (A) 1-1, (H) 4-2
R5: Liverpool (A) 0-0, (H) 0-2

70-71 R3: Notts County (H) 2-0
R4: Torquay United (H) 3-0
R5: Oxford United (H) 1-1, (A) 3-1
R6: Arsenal (H) 0-0, (A) 0-1

71-72 R3: Wolverhampton Wdrs (A) 1-1, (H) 2-0
R4: Orient (H) 0-2

72-73 R3: Arsenal (A) 2-2, (H) 1-2

73-74 R3: Tottenham Hotspur (H) 1-0
R4: Fulham (A) 1-1, (H) 2-1
R5: Luton Town (A) 4-0
R6: Queens Park Rangers (A) 2-0
SF: Liverpool (*at Manchester United*) 0-0, (*at Aston Villa*) 1-3
TP: Burnley (H) 0-1

74-75 R3: Oxford United (H) 3-1
R4: Leatherhead (A - *played home*) 3-2
R5: Arsenal (A) 0-0, (H) 1-1, 0-1

Right: *Alan Birchenall bursts past Leatherhead's John Doyle on the afternoon that Leicester City broke the hearts of all football romantics when they recovered from a two goal deficit against their non-League visitors. Photo: Colorsport.*

75-76 R3: Sheffield United (H) 3-0
R4: Bury (H) 1-0
R5: Manchester United (H) 1-2

76-77 R3: Aston Villa (H) 0-1

77-78 R3: Hull City (A) 1-0
R4: Walsall (A) 0-1

78-79 R3: Norwich City (H) 3-0
R4: Oldham Athletic (A) 1-3

79-80 R3: Harlow Town (H) 1-1, (A) 0-1

80-81 R3: Cardiff City (H) 3-0
R4: Exeter City (H) 1-1, (A) 1-3

81-82 R3: Southampton (H) 3-1
R4: Hereford United (A) 1-0
R5: Watford (H) 2-0
R6: Shrewsbury Town (H) 5-2
SF: Tottenham Hotspur (*at Aston Villa*) 0-2

82-83 R3: Notts County (H) 2-3

83-84 R3: Crystal Palace (A) 0-1

84-85 R3: Burton Albion (A - *at Derby*) 6-1 - *replay ordered behind closed doors because of crowd trouble* (*at Coventry City*) 1-0
R4: Carlisle United (H) 1-0
R5: Millwall (A) 0-2

85-86 R3: Bristol Rovers (A) 1-3

86-87 R3: Queens Park Rangers (A) 2-5

87-88 R3: Oxford United (A) 0-2

88-89 R3: Manchester City (A) 0-1

89-90 R3: Barnsley (H) 1-2

90-91 R3: Millwall (A) 1-2

91-92 R3: Crystal Palace (H) 1-0
R4: Bristol City (H) 1-2

92-93 R3: Barnsley (H) 2-2, (A) 1-1 (*4-5 pens*)

LEICESTER UNITED

Currently: Southern League
* - As Enderby Town

72-73 * Q1: Desborough Town (A) 2-1
Q2: Wellingborough Town (H) 2-1
Q3: Irthlingborough Diamonds (A) 4-0
Q4: Telford United (H) 0-2

73-74 * Q1: Worksop Town (H) 2-4

74-75 * Q1: Long Eaton United (H) 3-1
Q2: Arnold (A) 0-0, (H) 1-0
Q3: Eastwood Town (H) 1-0
Q4: Boston United (H) 1-2

75-76 * PR: Atherstone Town (H) 2-1
Q1: Moor Green (A) 1-0
Q2: Tividale (H) 0-1

76-77 * Q1: Desborough Town (A) 1-0
Q2: Redditch United (A) 0-0, (H) 1-0
Q3: Dudley Town (H) 0-1

77-78 * Q1: Coventry Sporting (A) 1-1, (H) 1-0
Q2: Rothwell Town (H) 5-0
Q3: Corby Town (A) 2-1
Q4: Letchworth G.C. (A) 0-0, (H) 1-0
R1: A.P. Leamington (A) 1-6

78-79 * Q1: Gainsborough Trinity (H) 3-4

79-80 * Q1: Saffron Walden Town (H) 5-0
Q2: V.S. Rugby (A) 1-0
Q3: Bedworth United (H) 0-0, (A) 1-0
Q4: Northwich Victoria (H) 0-1

80-81 * Q1: Tividale (H) 3-1
Q2: King's Lynn (A) 0-2

81-82 * Q1: Corby Town (A) 1-2

82-83 * Q1: Sutton Coldfield Town (H) 1-4

83-84 Q1: Eastwood Hanley (A) 2-0
Q2: Bridgnorth Town (A) 1-2

84-85 Q1: Irthlingborough Diamonds (A) 0-3

85-86 Q1: Witton Albion (H) 0-1

86-87 PR: Friar Lane O.B. (H - *played away*) 2-0
Q1: North Ferriby United (A) 3-3, (H - *at Leicester City*) 4-2
Q2: Goole Town (H) 0-1

87-88 Q1: Wellingborough Town (A) 1-1, (H) 1-0
Q2: Halesowen Town (A) 1-5

88-89 Q1: Rushden Town (H) 4-1
Q2: Shepshed Charterhouse (H) 1-0
Q3: Stafford Rangers (A) 1-1, (H) 2-3

89-90 PR: Hitchin Town (A) 1-3

90-91 PR: North Ferriby United (A) 2-1
Q1: Rocester (H) 1-0
Q2: Droylsden (H) 0-0, (A) 2-2, (H) 4-3
Q3: Marine (H) 0-2

91-92 Q1: Hinckley Town (A) 0-2

92-93 PR: Dudley Town (H) 3-0
Q1: Nuneaton Borough (A) 1-3

LEIGHTON TOWN

Currently: Isthmian League
* - As Leighton United

45-46 * Q2: Letchworth Town (A) 0-3

46-47 * Q1: Eynesbury Rovers (H) 2-1
Q2: Bedford Town (H) 2-5

47-48 * PR: Arlesey Town (A) 0-2

48-49 * PR: St Neots & District (H) 2-0
Q1: Hitchin Town (A) 2-4

49-50 * PR: Baldock Town (A) 0-2

50-51 * PR: Bedford Queens Works (H) 5-0
Q1: Bedford Town (H) 2-8

69-70 Q1: Stevenage Athletic (A) 3-1
Q2: Dunstable Town (A) 1-3

70-71 Q1: Biggleswade Town (A) 4-1
Q2: Wealdstone (H) 1-1, (A) 1-0
Q3: St Albans City (A) 1-2

71-72 PR: Kingstonian (A) 2-4

88-89 PR: Wolverton Town (M.K.) (H) 2-0
Q1: Banbury United (H) 0-0, (A) 1-2

89-90 Q1: Newmarket Town (A) 0-1

90-91 PR: Spalding United (H) 0-1

91-92 PR: Kingsbury Town (H) 3-2
Q1: Tilbury (A) 1-1, (H) 1-0
Q2: Berkhamsted Town (A) 0-2

92-93 PR: Harwich & Parkeston (A) 3-3, (H) 2-0
Q1: Aveley (H) 2-4

LEISTON

Currently: Suffolk & Ipswich League

45-46 Q2: Bye
Q3: Lowestoft T. (H) 2-2 *Lowestoft expelled*
Q4: Chelmsford City (A) 0-9

46-47 Q2: Great Yarmouth Town (H) 3-1
Q3: Gothic (A) 4-4, (H) 0-2

47-48 Q1: Old Grammarians (H) 8-2
Q2: Gothic (A) 1-3

48-49 PR: Stoke United (A) 1-1, (H) 6-0
Q1: Gothic (A) 2-5

49-50 PR: Achilles (A - *played home*) 0-5

50-51 PR: Bungay Town (A) 4-1
Q1: Lowestoft Town (H) 0-1

51-52 Q1: Whitton United (A) 1-4

52-53 Q1: Bury Town (A) 1-9

53-54 Q1: Stowmarket (A) 0-2

54-55 Q1: Sudbury Town (H) 2-3

55-56 Q1: Sudbury Town (A) 1-14

56-57 Q1: Lowestoft Town (A) 1-8

57-58 Q1: Bury Town (H) 1-8

58-59 Q1: Whitton United (H) 2-6

LETCHWORTH GARDEN CITY

Currently: South Midlands League
* - As Letchworth Town

45-46 * Q2: Letchworth Town (H) 3-0
Q3: Bedford Avenue (A) 0-1

46-47 * Q1: Hitchin Town (H) 0-2

47-48 * PR: Bedford Queens Works (Bedford) (A) 8-1
Q1: Vauxhall Motors (A) 2-2, (H) 1-5

48-49 * PR: Luton Amateur (H) 3-0
Q1: Biggleswade T. (A) 4-4, (H) 3-3, 0-4

49-50 * PR: St Neots St Mary's (A) 6-1
Q1: St Neots & District (A) 1-3

50-51 * EX: Arlesey Town (H) 3-2
PR: Biggleswade Town (H) 2-2, (A) 2-3

51-52 * PR: Clapton (H) 0-2

52-53 * Q1: Eton Mnr (A) 1-1, (H) 1-1, (*at Barnet*) 0-3

53-54 * Q1: Hitchin Town (A) 3-3, (H) 0-1

54-55 * PR: Shefford Town (A) 0-1

55-56 * PR: Enfield (A) 1-3

56-57 * PR: St Albans City (H) 1-0
Q1: Hertford Town (H) 0-0, (A) 0-3

57-58 * PR: Barnet (H) 2-1
Q1: Tufnell Park Edmonton (H) 1-1, (A) 1-0
Q2: Ware (A) 0-3

58-59 * Q1: Stevenage Town (A) 2-3

59-60 * Q1: Dunstable Town (H) 5-0
Q2: Biggleswade Town (A) 2-1
Q3: Wolverton Town & B.R. (H) 3-2
Q4: King's Lynn (H) 3-4

60-61 * Q1: Stevenage Town (A) 2-2, (H) 2-6

61-62 * Q1: Bedford Town (A) 0-6

62-63 * Q1: Biggleswade (A) 3-3, (H) 1-1 *abandoned after 106 minutes*, (H) 0-3

63-64 * Q2: Hitchin Town (H) 1-2

64-65 * Q1: St Albans City (A) 2-3

65-66 * Q1: Hitchin Town (A) 1-4

66-67 * Q1: Cambridge City (A) 3-5

67-68 * Q1: Marlow (A) 1-3

68-69 * Q1: Banbury United (H) 2-3

69-70 * Q1: Irthlingborough Diamonds (A) 2-3

70-71 * Q1: Bedford Town (H) 0-3

71-72 * Q1: Romford (H) 1-2

72-73 * Q1: Egham Town (H) 1-2

73-74 * PR: Ely City (H) 2-1
Q1: Biggleswade Town (A) 0-2

74-75 * Q1: Hatfield Town (H) 1-0
Q2: St Albans City (A) 0-1

75-76 * Q1: Histon (A) 2-0
Q2: Cambridge City (H) 0-1

76-77 PR: Maidenhead United (H) 5-1
Q1: Addlestone (H) 1-0
Q2: Dulwich Hamlet (H) 0-1

77-78 Q1: Rushden Town (H) 3-0
Q2: Hemel Hempstead (A) 2-2, (H) 4-3
Q3: Hertford Town (A) 3-0
Q4: Enderby Town (H) 0-0, (A) 0-1

78-79 Q1: Felixstowe Town (H) 5-1
Q2: Billericay Town (A) 1-5

79-80 Q1: Haverhill Rovers (H) 1-1, (A) 0-1

80-81 Q1: Sudbury Town (A) 3-0
Q2: Wembley (H) 0-0, (A) 1-3

81-82 Q1: Newmarket Town (A) 0-1

82-83 Q1: Harrow Borough (H) 0-6

83-84 PR: Lowestoft Town (A) 0-2

84-85 PR: Addlestone & Weybridge Town (A) 0-7

85-86 Q1: Corby Town (H) 2-3

86-87 Q1: Burton Albion (H) 1-1, (A) 1-5

87-88 Q1: Gorleston (H) 1-0
Q2: Bury Town (A) 1-1, (H) 3-1
Q3: March Town United (H) 2-2, (A) 3-2
Q4: Chelmsford City (H) 0-1

88-89 Q1: Cheshunt (H) 1-2

89-90 PR: Royston Town (H) 1-3

90-91 PR: Baker Perkins (A) 2-5

91-92 PR: Potton United (H) 1-1, (A) 0-2

92-93 PR: Haverhill Rovers (H) 1-1, (A) 4-3
Q1: Braintree Town (H) 0-4

LEWES

Currently: Isthmian League

62-63 Q1: Horsham (H) 5-1
Q2: Littlehampton Town (H) 6-2
Q3: Haywards Heath (A) 3-0
Q4: Gravesend & Northfleet (A) 0-1

63-64 Q1: Bognor Regis Town (A) 4-0
Q2: Lancing (H) 3-0
Q3: Crawley Town (A) 2-0
Q4: Gravesend & Northfleet (A) 1-2

64-65 Q1: Littlehampton Town (A) 3-1
Q2: Redhill (H) 2-2, (A) 3-4

65-66 Q1: Lancing (A) 1-3

71-72 Q1: Horsham (A) 0-2

72-73 PR: Eastbourne United (H) 3-0
Q1: Horsham (H) 1-0
Q2: Peacehaven & Telscombe (A) 1-0
Q3: Bognor Regis Town (H) 1-1, (A) 1-3

73-74 Q1: Whitstable Town (H) 4-1
Q2: Dover (H) 1-1, (A) 2-1
Q3: Folkestone (A) 1-5

74-75 Q1: Ringmer (H) 2-4

75-76 Q1: Ashford Town (A) 1-2

76-77 Q1: Eastbourne Town (A) 3-0
Q2: Bexhill Town (A) 3-0
Q3: Horsham Y.M.C.A. (H) 4-4, (A) 4-2
Q4: Harwich & Parkeston (H) 1-1, (A) 1-3

77-78 Q1: Ashford Town (H) 1-0
Q2: Tonbridge A.F.C. (A) 0-1

78-79 Q1: Ramsgate (H) 1-1, (A) 0-3

79-80 Q1: Folkestone & Shepway (H) 2-1
Q2: Ramsgate (A) 0-1

80-81 PR: Horsham (A) 6-1
Q1: Ringmer (A) 3-3, (H) 6-2
Q2: Gosport Borough (A) 1-2

81-82 PR: Chertsey Town (A) 5-2
Q1: Cheshunt (A) 2-2, (H) 3-3, (A) 2-0
Q2: Wembley (H) 1-2

82-83 Q1: Tooting & Mitcham United (H) 2-3

83-84 PR: Tunbridge Wells (H) 2-2, (A) 3-0
Q1: Dover Athletic (A) 4-1
Q2: Fisher Athletic (H) 0-2

84-85 PR: Banstead Athletic (A) 3-2
Q1: Ashford Town (A) 2-1
Q2: Worthing (A) 0-3

85-86 PR: Three Bridges (A) 3-2
Q1: Tonbridge A.F.C. (H) 0-1

86-87 PR: Thanet United (A) 2-0
Q1: Eastleigh (A) 1-1, (H) 1-2

87-88 Q1: Wokingham Town (A) 0-3

88-89 Q1: Carshalton Athletic (A) 1-3

89-90 PR: Hanwell Town (H) 2-1
Q1: Epsom & Ewell (H) 2-0
Q2: Dulwich Hamlet (A) 1-4

90-91 PR: Lancing (A) 3-0
Q1: Herne Bay (A) 1-0
Q2: Hailsham Town (H) 0-3

91-92 PR: Three Bridges (H) 4-3
Q1: Eastbourne United (A) 4-1
Q2: Kingstonian (A) 2-3

92-93 PR: Leatherhead (H) 1-0
Q1: Metropolitan Police (A) 1-2

LEYLAND DAF-S.G.L.

Currently: (Leyland DAF F.C.) West Lancs Lge
* - As Leyland Motors

45-46 * Q1: Skelmersdale United (H) 1-2

46-47 * PR: Lytham (A) 1-1, (H) *score unknown - 'Lytham Standard' says Leyland 'won easily'*
Q1: Skelmersdale United (A) 3-4

47-48 * Q1: Horwich R.M.I. (H) 1-2

48-49 * PR: Chorley (H) 1-0
Q1: Rossendale United (H) 2-2, (A) 2-4

49-50 * PR: Morecambe (A) 5-4
Q1: Rossendale United (A) 1-5

50-51 * PR: Clitheroe (A) 1-1, (H) 2-0
Q1: Fleetwood (H) 1-1, (A) 4-2
Q2: Nelson (A) 1-4

51-52 * Q1: Mossley (A) 0-3

52-53 * PR: Horwich R.M.I. (H) 0-3

53-54 * PR: Ashton United (H) 1-5

54-55 * Q1: Nelson (A) 2-8

55-56 * PR: Bacup Borough (H) 2-1
Q1: Horwich R.M.I. (H) 1-0
Q2: Ashton United (A) 1-2

56-57 * Q1: Darwen (A) 0-1

57-58 * PR: Crompton's Recreation (H) 2-2, (A) 1-5

58-59 * PR: Ashton United (A) 1-4

61-62 * Q1: Nelson (A) 0-4

62-63 * Q1: Rossendale United (H) 1-5

65-66 * Q1: Skelmersdale United (A) 2-2, (H) 1-2

66-67 * Q1: Netherfield (A) 0-4

67-68 * Q1: Great Harwood (A) 1-3

68-69 * Q1: Stalybridge Celtic (H) 2-3

69-70 * Q1: Burscough (A) 2-5

70-71 * Q1: Great Harwood (A) 2-5

71-72 * Q1: Ormskirk (H) 1-4

72-73 * Q1: Runcorn (H) 0-8

73-74 * PR: Ormskirk (A) 0-2

75-76 * Q1: Rossendale United (H) 1-8

78-79 * Q1: Horwich R.M.I. (H) 1-2

79-80 * Q1: Curzon Ashton (H) 1-4

80-81 * Q1: Lytham (A) 2-0
Q2: St Helens Town (H) 0-4

81-82 * Q1: Netherfield (A) 2-3

82-83 * PR: Clitheroe (A) 1-0
Q1: Ashton United (A) 2-6

83-84 * Q1: Congleton Town (H) 1-3

84-85 * Q1: Southport (H) 0-4

85-86 * PR: Colwyn Bay (A) 1-3

86-87 * Q1: Emley (H) 0-2

87-88 * PR: Evenwood Town (A) 2-0
Q1: Easington Colliery (A) 1-2

88-89 * PR: Bridlington Trinity (H) 0-1

89-90 * PR: Rossendale United (H) 0-1

90-91 PR: Whitby Town (A) 0-2

91-92 PR: Burscough (A) *scratched*

LEYTON

Currently: Merged with Wingate (Herts)
Playing as Leyton F.C. in Isthmian League.
See also Leyton (2).

45-46 Q1: Grays Athletic (H) 1-1, (A) 3-0
Q2: Ford Sports (H) 6-2
Q3: Romford (H) 1-4

46-47 PR: Hoffmann Ath. (Chelmsford) (H) 3-0
Q1: Tilbury (A) 1-4

47-48 PR: Harwich & Parkeston (H) 1-2

48-49 PR: Tilbury (H) 2-0
Q1: Chingford Town (H) 3-2
Q2: Barking (A) 0-3

49-50 PR: Tilbury (A) 2-2, (H) 2-3

50-51 EX: Bishop's Stortford (A) 1-2

51-52 Q1: Cheshunt (A) 2-1
Q2: Eton Manor (A) 1-0
Q3: Woodford Town (H) 3-2
Q4: Walthamstow Avenue (H) 0-0, (A) 2-1
R1: Chippenham Town (H) 3-0
R2: Chester (A) 2-5

52-53 R1: Hereford United (H) 0-0, (A) 2-3

53-54 PR: Tilbury (H) 2-1
Q1: Ilford (H) 0-2

54-55 PR: Grays Athletic (H) 2-0
Q1: Romford (H) 4-2
Q2: Ilford (H) 2-1
Q3: Chelmsford City (H) 0-1

55-56 PR: Barking (A) 2-2, (H) 1-0
Q1: Aveley (H) 3-0
Q2: Clacton Town (H) 4-0
Q3: Briggs Sports (A) 2-1
Q4: Hitchin Town (H) 3-1
R1: Bedford Town (A) 0-3

56-57 PR: Briggs Sports (A) 0-4

57-58 PR: Woodford Town (H) 5-0
Q1: Hornchurch & Upm. (A) 1-1, (H) 4-1
Q2: Chelmsford City (A) 0-5

58-59 Q1: Brentwood & Warley (H) 2-2, (H) 1-2

59-60 Q1: Woodford Town (A) 1-1, (H) 1-0
Q2: Leytonstone (A) 3-1
Q3: Grays Athletic (H) 1-1, (A) 2-6

60-61 Q1: Clapton (A) 0-1

61-62 Q1: Hendon (A) 1-9

62-63 Q1: Dagenham (A) 3-0
Q2: Hornchurch (A) 2-1
Q3: Hendon (A) 1-4

63-64 Q1: Dagenham (A) 1-2

64-65 Q1: Hendon (H) 2-3

65-66 Q1: Woodford Town (H) 3-2
Q2: Dagenham (H) 3-2
Q3: Leytonstone (H) 0-3

66-67 Q1: Enfield (A) 0-7

67-68 Q1: Walthamstow Avenue (A) 0-2

68-69 Q1: Hemel Hempstead Town (H) 3-2
Q2: Edmonton (H) 1-1, (A) 1-2

69-70 Q1: Ilford (A) 0-2

70-71 Q1: Boreham Wood (H) 2-4

72-73 Q1: Finchley (A) 0-2

73-74 Q1: Crawley Town (H) 2-2, (A) 2-3

74-75 Q1: Erith & Belvedere (A) 0-5

LEYTON

Currently: Isthmian League
See also Leyton (1) and Wingate (Herts)
* - As Leyton-Wingate

75-76 * Q1: Tilbury (H) 1-1, (A) 0-11

76-77 * PR: Hayes (A) 0-2

77-78 * PR: Uxbridge (H) 2-0
Q1: Hornchurch (A) 1-0
Q2: Dulwich Hamlet (A) 1-1, (H) 2-1
Q3: Enfield (A) 0-4

78-79 * Q1: Tilbury (H) 1-0
Q2: Grays Athletic (H) 2-0
Q3: Edgware (H) 1-1, (A) 1-3

79-80 * PR: Barton Rovers (H) 3-1
Q1: Ware (A) 1-2

80-81 * Q1: Harefield United (H) 0-3

81-82 * PR: Histon (A) 4-1
Q1: Stowmarket Town (A) 3-2
Q2: St Albans City (H) 2-2, (A) 1-4

82-83 * Q1: Dulwich Hamlet (H) 2-2, (A) 0-2

83-84 * Q1: St Albans City (H) 1-2

84-85 * PR: Burnham (H) 1-0
Q1: Chesham United (H) 2-2, (A) 0-1

85-86 * PR: Kingsbury Town (A) 1-1, (H) 3-0
Q1: Hounslow (A) 2-1
Q2: Harrow Borough (H) 2-2, (A) 3-2
Q3: Crawley Town (A) 3-2
Q4: Gresley Rovers (H) 2-0
R1: Swansea City (A) 0-2

86-87 * Q1: Faversham Town (H) 1-1, (A) 1-0
Q2: Dover Athletic (A) 1-2

87-88 * Q1: Stevenage Borough (H) 1-1, (A) 3-2
Q2: Dunstable (A) 1-0
Q3: Wembley (A) 2-2, (H) 5-1
Q4: Atherstone United (H) 0-0, (A) 2-4

88-89 * Q1: Hampton (H) 1-1, (A) 1-0
Q2: Halstead Town (H) 7-1
Q3: Sudbury Town (H) 1-2

89-90 * Q1: Tring Town (A) 4-0
Q2: Ware (H) 2-1
Q3: Wivenhoe Town (H) 0-0, (A) 0-2

90-91 * Q1: Billericay Town (H) 0-0, (A) 0-1

91-92 * PR: Eynesbury Rovers (H) 6-0
Q1: Harlow Town (A - *at Ware*) 1-4

92-93 PR: Felixstowe Town (H) 5-4
Q1: Lowestoft Town (H) 4-2
Q2: Gorleston (A) 2-1
Q3: Cambridge City (H) 3-0
Q4: Sutton Coldfield Town (A) 1-6

LEYTON ORIENT

Currently: Football League
* - As Clapton Orient
+ - As Orient

45-46 * R1: Newport I.O.W. (H) 2-1, (A) 0-2 (*agg: 2-3*)

46-47 R1: Notts County (H) 1-2

47-48 R1: Gillingham (A) 0-1

48-49 R1: Dartford (A) 3-2
R2: Darlington (A) 0-1

49-50 R1: Southend United (H) 0-2

50-51 R1: Ipswich Town (H) 1-2

51-52 R1: Gorleston (H) 2-2, (A) 0-0, 5-4
R2: Wrexham (A) 1-1, (H) 3-2
R3: Everton (H) 0-0, (A) 3-1
R4: Birmingham City (A) 1-0
R5: Arsenal (H) 0-3

52-53 R1: Bristol Rovers (H) 1-1, (A) 0-1

53-54 R1: Kettering Town (H) 3-0
R2: Weymouth (H) 4-0
R3: Tranmere Rovers (A) 2-2, (H) 4-1
R4: Fulham (H) 2-1
R5: Doncaster Rovers (H) 3-1
R6: Port Vale (H) 0-1

54-55 R1: Frome Town (A) 3-0
R2: Workington (H) 0-1

55-56 R1: Lovells Athletic (H) 7-1
R2: Brentford (H) 4-1
R3: Plymouth Argyle (H) 1-0
R4: Birmingham City (H) 0-4

56-57 R3: Chelsea (H) 0-2

57-58 R3: Reading (H) 1-0
R4: Cardiff City (A) 1-4

58-59 R3: Blackburn Rovers (A) 2-4

59-60 R3: Liverpool (A) 1-2

60-61 R3: Gillingham (A) 6-2
R4: Southampton (A) 1-0
R5: Sheffield Wednesday (H) 0-2

61-62 R3: Brentford (A) 1-1, (H) 2-1
R4: Burnley (A) 1-1, (H) 0-1

62-63 R3: Hull City (H) 1-1, (A) 2-0
R4: Derby County (H) 3-0
R5: Leicester City (A) 0-1

63-64 R3: Leicester City (A) 3-2
R4: West Ham United (A) 1-1, (H) 0-3

64-65 R3: Southampton (A) 1-3

65-66 R3: Norwich City (H) 1-3

66-67 R1: Lowestoft Town (H) 2-1
R2: Brentford (H) 0-0, (A) 1-3

67-68 R1: Weymouth (A) 2-0
R2: Boston United (A) 1-1, (H) 2-1
R3: Bury (H) 1-0
R4: Birmingham City (A) 0-3

68-69 R1: Gillingham (H) 1-1, (A) 1-2

69-70 + R1: Walsall (A) 0-0, (H) 0-2

70-71 + R3: Sunderland (A) 3-0
R4: Nottm F. (A) 1-1, (H) 0-0 *ab. 45m.*, (H) 0-1

71-72 + R3: Wrexham (H) 3-0
R4: Leicester City (A) 2-0
R5: Chelsea (H) 3-2
R6: Arsenal (H) 0-1

72-73 + R3: Coventry City (H) 1-4

73-74 + R3: A.F.C. Bournemouth (H) 2-1
R4: Portsmouth (A) 0-0, (H) 1-1, (*at Crystal Palace*) 0-2

74-75 + R3: Derby County (H) 2-2, (A) 1-2

75-76 + R3: Cardiff City (H) 0-1

76-77 + R3: Darlington (A) 2-2, (H) 0-0, (*at Tottenham Hotspur*) 3-0
R4: Blackburn Rovers (A) 0-3

77-78 + R3: Norwich City (H) 1-1, (A) 1-0
R4: Blackburn Rovers (H) 3-1
R5: Chelsea (H) 0-0, (A) 2-1
R6: Middlesbrough (A) 0-0, (H) 2-1
SF: Arsenal (*at Chelsea F.C.*) 0-3

78-79 + R3: Bury (H) 3-2
R4: Ipswich Town (A) 0-0, (H) 0-2

79-80 + R3: Altrincham (A) 1-1, (H) 2-1
R4: West Ham United (H) 2-3

Opposite: *A scare for Orient as Altrincham's Graham Heathcote fires a free-kick at goal. The East Londoners pulled through by the odd goal in three to set up a Fourth Round derby against West Ham, the eventual cup winners. Photo: John Rooney.*

80-81 + R3: Luton Town (H) 1-3

81-82 + R3: Charlton Athletic (H) 1-0
R4: Huddersfield Town (A) 1-1, (H) 2-0
R5: Crystal Palace (A) 0-0, (H) 0-1

82-83 + R1: Bristol City (H) 4-1
R2: Newport County (A) 0-1

83-84 + R1: Wimbledon (A) 1-2

84-85 + R1: Buckingham Town (A) 2-0
R2: Torquay United (H) 3-0
R3: West Bromwich Albion (H) 2-1
R4: Southampton (H) 0-2

85-86 + R1: V.S. Rugby (A) 2-2, (H) 4-1
R2: Slough Town (H) 2-2, (A) 3-2
R3: Oldham Athletic (A) 2-1
R4: Sheffield Wednesday (A) 0-5

86-87 + R1: Woodford Town (A) 1-0
R2: A.F.C. Bournemouth (A) 1-0
R3: West Ham United (H) 1-1, (A) 1-4

87-88 R1: Exeter City (H) 2-0
R2: Swansea City (H) 2-0
R3: Stockport County (A) 2-1
R4: Nottingham Forest (H) 1-2

88-89 R1: Enfield (A) 1-1, (H) 2-2, (H) 0-1

89-90 R1: Birmingham City (H) 0-1

90-91 R1: Southend United (H) 3-2
R2: Colchester United (A) 0-0, (H) 4-1
R3: Swindon (H) 1-1, (A) 1-1 *ab. 56 m.*, (A) 0-1

91-92 R1: Welling United (H) 2-1
R2: West Bromwich Albion (H) 2-1
R3: Oldham Athletic (A) 1-1, (H) 4-2
R4: Portsmouth (A) 0-2

92-93 R1: Dagenham & Redbridge (A) 5-4
R2: Reading (A) 0-3

LEYTONSTONE

Currently: Merged with Ilford
Subsequently merged with Walthamstow Avenue and Dagenham, and playing as Dagenham & Redbridge in the Alliance Premier League.
See also Leytonstone-Ilford, Redbridge Forest and Dagenham & Redbridge.

45-46 Q4: Slough United (H) 3-3, (A) 1-3

46-47 Q4: Barking (A) 4-1
R1: Walsall (H) 1-6

47-48 R1: Bristol Rovers (A) 2-3

48-49 R1: Watford (H) 2-1
R2: Newport County (H) 3-4

49-50 Q4; Hayes (H) 3-2
R1: Chelmsford City (H) 1-2

50-51 Q4: Bromley (A) 1-3

51-52 Q4: Chelmsford City (H) 2-1
R1: Shrewsbury Town (H) 2-0
R2: Newport County (H) 2-2, (A) 0-3

52-53 Q4: Gorleston (A) 4-1
R1: Watford (H) 0-2

53-54 Q4: Hitchin Town (H) 0-1

54-55 PR: Briggs Sports (A) 4-1
Q1: Chelmsford City (H) 0-0, (A) 1-2

55-56 PR: Harwich & Parkeston (H) 4-1
Q1: Dagenham (H) 0-3

56-57 PR: Aveley (H) 6-2
Q1: Clacton Town (A) 1-1, (H) 0-1

57-58 PR: Hornchurch & U. (A) 1-1, (H) 3-3, 0-2

58-59 Q1: Rainham Town (A) 1-2

59-60 PR: Aveley (A) 2-1
Q1: Barking (A) 1-0
Q2: Leyton (H) 1-3

60-61 Q1: Dagenham (H) 3-0
Q2: Romford (H) 1-3

61-62 Q1: Clapton (H) 1-1, (A) 2-1
Q2: Romford (A) 1-3

62-63 Q1: Hendon (A) 0-1

63-64 Q1: Hendon (A) 2-4

64-65 Q1: Ruislip Manor (H) 7-1
Q2: Dagenham (H) 4-0
Q3: Hendon (A) 1-2

65-66 Q1: Clapton (A) 6-0
Q2: Rainham Town (H) 5-0
Q3: Leyton (A) 3-0
Q4: Walthamstow Avenue (A) 6-2
R1: Hereford United (H) 0-1

66-67 Q1: Ashford (H) 2-2, (A) 0-4

67-68 Q1: Chesham United (A) 3-0
Q2: Erith & Belvedere (H) 4-0
Q3: Hitchin Town (H) 2-1
Q4: Slough Town (A) 2-2, (H) 2-1
R1: Walsall (H) 0-1

68-69 R1: Walsall (H) 0-1

69-70 Q4: Dagenham (H) 0-4

70-71 Q1: Staines Town (A) 1-0
Q2: Ford United (A) 2-0
Q3: Hornchurch (A) 2-1
Q4: Aveley (A) 0-0, (H) 2-3

71-72 PR: Hertford Town (A) 1-1, (H) 2-1
Q1: Hatfield Town (A) 4-0
Q2: Maidenhead United (A) 0-1

72-73 Q1: Hounslow (H) 1-0
Q2: Walton & Hersham (H) 2-2, (A) 0-1

73-74 Q1: Windsor & Eton (H) 2-0
Q2: Sutton United (H) 3-2
Q3: Leatherhead (A) 0-0, (H) 1-0
Q4: Margate (H) 0-0, (A) 3-1
R1: Hendon (A) 0-3

74-75 Q1: Carshalton Athletic (A) 1-0
Q2: Harrow Borough (H) 1-0
Q3: Romford (H) 0-1

75-76 Q1: Bromley (A) 1-3

76-77 Q1: Harrow Borough (H) 2-0
Q2: Slough Town (H) 1-1, (A) 0-1

77-78 PR: Didcot Town (A) 2-2, (H) 1-0
Q1: Aveley (A) 2-0
Q2: St Albans City (A) 0-2

78-79 Q1: Hornchurch (A) 1-1, (H) 4-1
Q2: Barking (H) 1-2

LEYTONSTONE-ILFORD

Currently: Merged with Walthamstow Avenue
Subsequently merged with Dagenham, and playing as Dagenham & Redbridge in the Alliance Premier Lge.
See also Leytonstone, Ilford, Redbridge Forest and Dagenham & Redbridge.

79-80 Q1: Southall & Ealing Borough (A) 3-0
Q2: Walthamstow Avenue (A) 2-2, (H) 3-1
Q3: Hillingdon Borough (H) 2-1
Q4: Dartford (A) 2-0
R1: Harlow Town (A) 1-2

80-81 Q1: Wembley (H) 0-1

81-82 Q1: Erith & Belvedere (A) 2-2, (H) 3-0
Q2: Woodford Town (H) 2-1
Q3: Billericay Town (A) 0-0, (H) 1-0
Q4: Carshalton Athletic (H) 2-0
R1: Aldershot (A) 0-2

82-83 Q1: Royston Town (A) 5-0
Q2: Tilbury (H) 1-1, (A) 2-2, (H) 2-1
Q3: Chelmsford City (A) 0-0, (H) 0-0, (A) 1-2

83-84 Q1: Basildon United (A) 0-1

84-85 Q1: Tunbridge Wells (A) 2-0
Q2: Metropolitan Police (A) 1-3

85-86 PR: Clapton (A) 2-3 - *Clapton expelled*
Q1: Marlow (H) 0-2

86-87 PR: Merstham (A) 6-0
Q1: Chertsey (A) 1-1, (H - *at Leyton-Win.*) 0-1

87-88 Q1: St Albans City (H) 2-0
Q2: Histon (A) 2-1
Q3: Kingsbury Town (A) 1-0
Q4: Worcester City (H) 0-1

88-89 Q1: Clapton (A) 1-0
Q2: Walton & Hersham (A) 2-3

LINBY COLLIERY

Currently: (Linby Colliery M.W.) Notts Alliance

48-49 EX: Heanor Athletic (A) 1-0
PR: Stamford (H) 3-2
Q1: Ilkeston Town (A) 3-0
Q2: Grantham (H) 1-2

49-50 PR: Grantham (H) 1-2

50-51 EX: Parliament Street Methodists (A) 4-3
PR: Retford Town (H) 3-0
Q1: Shirebrook (H) 2-0
Q2: Boston United (A) 4-0
Q3: Spalding United (A) 2-2, (H) 3-1
Q4: Nuneaton Borough (H) 3-1
R1: Gillingham (H) 1-4

51-52 PR: Sutton Town (A) 2-2, (H) 1-0
Q1: Parliament Street Methodists (A) 3-2
Q2: Ransome & Marles (H) 5-1
Q3: Cresswell Colliery (A) 0-2

52-53 PR: Parliament Street Methodists (A) 6-0
Q1: Bestwood Colliery (H) 3-0
Q2: Players Athletic (H) 6-0
Q3: Cresswell Colliery (H) 0-0, (A) 0-0, 5-0
Q4: Selby Town (A) 2-4

53-54 Q1: Sutton Town (A) 2-3

54-55 Q1: Bestwood Colliery (H) 5-0
Q2: Shirebrook Miners Welfare (A) 4-0
Q3: Cresswell Colliery (A) 1-3

55-56 Q2: Sutton Town (H) 3-3, (A) 2-3

56-57 Q2: Sutton Town (H) 0-3

LINCOLN CITY

Currently: Football League

45-46 R1: Yorks Amateur (A) 0-1, (H) 5-1 (*agg: 5-2*)
R2: Rotherham U. (A) 1-2, (H) 1-1 (*agg: 2-3*)

46-47 R1: Stockton (A) 4-2
R2: Wrexham (A) 3-3, (A) 1-1, 2-1
R3: Nottingham Forest (H) 0-1

47-48 R1: Workington (H) 0-2

48-49 R3: West Bromwich Albion (H) 0-1

49-50 R1: Carlisle United (A) 0-1

50-51 R1: Southport (H) 1-1, (A) 2-3

51-52 R1: Crewe Alexandra (A) 4-2
R2: Grimsby Town (H) 3-1
R3: Portsmouth (A) 0-4

52-53 R3: Southampton (H) 1-1, (A) 1-2

53-54 R3: Walsall (H) 1-1, (A) 1-1, (*at Nottm F.*) 2-1
R4: Preston North End (H) 0-2

54-55 R3: Liverpool (H) 1-1, (A) 0-1

55-56 R3: Southend United (H) 2-3

56-57 R3: Peterborough United (A) 2-2, (H) 4-5

57-58 R3: Wolverhampton Wanderers (H) 0-1

58-59 R3: Leicester City (A) 2-2, (H) 0-2

59-60 R3: Burnley (H) 1-1, (A) 0-2

60-61	R3: West Bromwich Albion (H) 3-1 R4: Sheffield United (A) 1-3
61-62	R1: Crewe Alexandra (A) 0-2
62-63	R1: Darlington (H) 1-1, (A) 2-1 R2: Halifax Town (H) 1-0 R3: Coventry City (H) 1-5
63-64	R1: Hartlepools United (A) 1-0 R2: Southport (H) 2-0 R3: Sheffield United (H) 0-4
64-65	R1: Tranmere Rovers (A) 0-0, (H) 1-0 R2: Hull City (A) 1-1, (H) 3-1 R3: Rotherham United (A) 1-5
65-66	R1: Barnsley (H) 1-3
66-67	R1: Scunthorpe United (H) 3-4
67-68	R1: Southport (A) 1-3
68-69	R1: Macclesfield Town (A) 3-1 R2: Chester (A) 1-1, (H) 2-1 R3: Birmingham City (A) 1-2
69-70	R1: Southport (H) 2-0 R2: Bradford City (A) 0-3
70-71	R1: Barrow (H) 2-1 R2: Bradford City (H) 2-2, (A) 2-2, 4-1 R3: Torquay United (A) 3-4
71-72	R1: Bury (H) 1-2
72-73	R1: Blackburn Rovers (H) 2-2, (A) 1-4
73-74	R1: Doncaster Rovers (A) 0-1
74-75	R1: Port Vale (A) 2-2, (H) 2-0 R2: Hartlepool United (A) 0-0, (H) 1-0 R3: Swindon Town (A) 0-2
75-76	R1: Boston United (A) 1-0 R2: Mansfield Town (A) 2-1 R3: Aldershot (A) 2-1 R4: West Bromwich Albion (A) 2-3
76-77	R1: Morecambe (H) 1-0 R2: Nuneaton Borough (H) 6-0 R3: Burnley (A) 2-2, (H) 0-1
77-78	R1: Preston North End (A) 2-3
78-79	R1: Blackpool (A) 1-2
79-80	R1: Sheffield Wednesday (A) 0-3
80-81	R1: Gateshead (H) 1-0 R2: Bury (A) 0-2
81-82	R1: Port Vale (H) 2-2, (A) 0-0, (A) 0-2
82-83	R1: Hartlepool United (A) 0-3
83-84	R1: Port Vale (A) 2-1 R2: Sheffield United (H) 0-0, (A) 0-1
84-85	R1: Telford United (H) 1-1, (A) 1-2
85-86	R1: Blackpool (H) 0-1
86-87	R1: Wigan Athletic (A) 1-3
87-88	Q4: Brigg Town (A - *played home*) 4-1 R1: Crewe Alexandra (H) 2-1 R2: Mansfield Town (A) 3-4
88-89	R1: Altrincham (A) 2-3
89-90	R1: Billingham Synthonia (H) 1-0 R2: Rochdale (A) 0-3
90-91	R1: Crewe Alexandra (H) 1-4
91-92	R1: Stockport County (A) 1-3
92-93	R1: Stafford Rangers (H) 0-0, (A) 1-2

LINCOLN UNITED

Currently: Northern Counties (East) League

70-71	Q1: Stamford (A) 5-2 Q2: Boston United (A) 0-1
71-72	PR: Louth United (H - *played away*) 1-0 Q1: Gainsborough Trinity (A) 3-2 Q2: Winterton Rangers (A) 1-3
84-85	Q1: Gresley Rovers (A) 1-6
85-86	PR: Ilkeston Town (A) 0-5
91-92	PR: Dudley Town (A) 4-1 Q1: Gainsborough Trinity (H) 3-1 Q2: Oakham United (H) 2-0 Q3: Frickley Athletic (A) 0-0, (H) 3-2 Q4: Leek Town (A) 2-0 R1: Huddersfield Town (A) 0-7
92-93	Q1: Frickley Athletic (A) 0-0, (H) 0-1

Above: *Lincoln United, then of the Websters Central Midlands League, enjoyed a fantastic cup run in 1991-92 when, eliminating three 'H.F.S. Loans' Northern Premier League clubs en route, they reached the First Round Proper for the first time. Ironically, they almost did not enter the competition for financial reasons. Here the Lincoln players applaud their large travelling support after a memorable afternoon at Huddersfield Town's Leeds Road ground. Photo: Barry Lockwood.*

LINOTYPE & MACHINERY

Currently: (Linotype F.C.) Mid-Cheshire League

51-52	Q1: Northwich Victoria (A) 2-6
54-55	PR: Lostock Gralam (A) 0-5
55-56	PR: Hyde United (H) 2-4
56-57	Q1: Winsford United (H) 1-1, (A) 1-2
57-58	Q1: Northwich Victoria (H) 3-6
58-59	PR: Witton Albion (H) 1-2
59-60	PR: Lostock Gralam (A) 1-0 Q1: Buxton (A) 1-4
60-61	Q1: Buxton (A) 3-1 Q2: Macclesfield Town (A) 1-1, (H) 0-3
61-62	Q1: Buxton (H) 1-1, (A) 1-6
62-63	Q1: Mossley (H) 1-2
66-67	Q1: Runcorn (A) 2-5
67-68	Q1: Runcorn (H) 1-3
68-69	Q1: Northwich Victoria (A) 0-3
69-70	Q1: Kirkby Town (H) 0-1

LISKEARD ATHLETIC

Currently: Western League

78-79	PR: Barnstaple Town (H) 1-0 Q1: Wadebridge Town (A) 2-0 Q2: Taunton Town (A) 0-6
79-80	Q1: Bideford (H) 3-1 Q2: Yeovil Town (H) 0-1
80-81	Q1: Falmouth Town (A) 1-1, (H) 2-3
81-82	Q1: Bridport (A) 2-2, (H) 3-1 Q2: Glastonbury (H) 2-0 Q3: Taunton Town (A) 0-2
82-83	PR: Ottery St Mary (H) 1-0 Q1: Tiverton Town (A) 2-2, (H) 2-1 Q2: Chard Town (H) 3-0 Q3: Bideford (H) 1-2
90-91	Q1: Wimborne Town (H) 5-2 Q2: Dorchester Town (H) 5-1 Q3: Tiverton Town (A) 0-1
91-92	Q1: St Austell (A) 3-2 Q2: Falmouth Town (H) 5-1 Q3: Tiverton Town (H) 1-3

LITTLEHAMPTON TOWN

Currently: Sussex County League

46-47	PR: Bognor Regis Town (H) 1-2
48-49	PR: Southwick (H) 7-2 Q1: Bognor Regis Town (A) 0-8
49-50	PR: Bexhill Town (A) 4-3 Q1: Worthing (A) 0-5
50-51	PR: East Grinstead (A) 1-6
51-52	PR: Tonbridge (H) 1-7
52-53	PR: Bognor Regis Town (H) 4-3 Q1: Worthing (H) 0-3
53-54	PR: Horsham (A) 1-3
54-55	PR: Southwick (H) 3-1 Q1: Eastbourne (A) 3-5
55-56	PR: Bexhill Town (A) 3-2 Q1: Southwick (A) 1-2
56-57	PR: Lancing Athletic (H) 1-2
57-58	PR: Bexhill Town (H) 3-1 Q1: Bognor Regis Town (H) 3-3, (A) 4-5
58-59	PR: Bognor Regis Town (A) 1-5
59-60	PR: Arundel (H) 1-2
60-61	Q1: Lancing Athletic (H) 6-3 Q2: Arundel (H) 3-2 Q3: Horsham (A) 3-2 Q4: Dover (A) 1-2
61-62	Q1: Horsham (H) 5-3 Q2: Bognor Regis Town (A) 1-1, (H) 0-2
62-63	Q2: Lewes (A) 2-6
63-64	Q1: Horsham (A) 2-1 Q2: Crawley Town (H) 0-4
64-65	Q1: Lewes (H) 1-3
65-66	Q1: Basingstoke Town (A) 0-6
66-67	Q1: Bognor Regis Town (H) 3-3, (A) 4-1 Q2: Woking (A) 1-2
67-68	Q1: Eastbourne (A) 1-1, (H) 1-2
68-69	Q1: Eastbourne United (H) 1-2
69-70	PR: Eastbourne United (H) 3-0 Q1: Bognor Regis Town (H) 1-0 Q2: Eastbourne (H) 2-0 Q3: Horsham (H) 3-2 Q4: Margate (H) 0-1
70-71	Q1: Southwick (A) 3-2

Above: *Cup fever hits Littlehampton in 1990, 'Bighampton' (Northampton) being the visitors. Photo: Roger Turner.*

Q2: Carshalton Athletic (H) 2-3

71-72 Q1: Worthing (H) 0-1

72-73 Q1: Haywards Heath (A) 2-2, (H) 1-2

73-74 Q1: Southwick (A) 3-0
Q2: Eastbourne Town (H) 2-2, (A) 1-0
Q3: Worthing (H) 0-2

74-75 Q1: Fareham Town (A) 1-1, (H) 1-1, 1-0
Q2: Horsham (A) 0-1

75-76 PR: Chichester City (H) 1-1, (A) 2-0
Q1: Waterlooville (A) 2-2, (H) 1-3

76-77 Q1: Horsham Y.M.C.A. (H) 0-1

77-78 PR: Three Bridges (H) 0-1

78-79 PR: Horsham (A) 0-4

79-80 Q1: Fareham Town (H) 0-8

80-81 Q1: Redhill (A) 2-0
Q2: Croydon (H) 0-3

81-82 Q1: Carshalton Athletic (H) 0-3

82-83 PR: Newport Isle of Wight (H) 0-3

83-84 Q1: Leatherhead (H) 0-2

84-85 PR: Canterbury City (H) 1-1, (A) 0-6

85-86 PR: Rainham Town (A) 2-1
Q1: Gravesend & N'flt (H - *played away*) 1-2

86-87 Q1: Road Sea Southampton (A) 1-7

87-88 Q1: Whitehawk (A) 2-1
Q2: Thanet United (H) 0-3

88-89 Q1: Southwick (A) 0-5

89-90 PR: Calne Town (H) 1-1, (A) 1-0
Q1: Waterlooville (H) 3-1
Q2: Witney Town (H) 0-4

90-91 PR: Chipstead (A) 3-2
Q1: Dulwich Hamlet (H) 2-0
Q2: Tooting & Mitcham United (A) 2-1
Q3: Tonbridge A.F.C. (H) 0-0, (A) 3-2
Q4: Romsey Town (A) 2-1
R1: Northampton Town (H) 0-4

91-92 Q1: Walton & Hersham (A) 1-1, (H) 2-1
Q2: Hampton (H) 1-3

92-93 PR: Lancing (A) 3-2
Q1: Langney Sports (A) 1-3

LIVERPOOL

Currently: F.A. Premier League

45-46 R3: Chester (A) 2-0, (H) 2-1 (*agg: 4-1*)
R4: Bolton Wdrs (A) 0-5, (H) 2-0 (*agg: 2-5*)

46-47 R3: Walsall (A) 5-2
R4: Grimsby Town (H) 2-0
R5: Derby County (H) 1-0
R6: Birmingham City (H) 4-1
SF: Burnley (*at Blackburn*) 0-0, (*at Man. C.*) 0-1

47-48 R3: Nottingham Forest (H) 4-1
R4: Manchester United (A) 0-3

48-49 R3: Nottingham Forest (A) 2-2, (H) 4-0
R4: Notts County (H) 1-0
R5: Wolverhampton Wanderers (A) 1-3

49-50 R3: Blackburn Rovers (A) 0-0, (H) 2-1
R4: Exeter City (H) 3-1
R5: Stockport County (A) 2-1
R6: Blackpool (H) 2-1
SF: Everton (*at Manchester City*) 2-0
F: Arsenal (*at Wembley*) 0-2

50-51 R3: Norwich City (A) 1-3

51-52 R3: Workington (H) 1-0
R4: Wolverhampton Wanderers (H) 2-1
R5: Burnley (A) 0-2

52-53 R3: Gateshead (A) 0-1

53-54 R3: Bolton Wanderers (A) 0-1

54-55 R3: Lincoln City (A) 1-1, (H) 1-0
R4: Everton (A) 4-0
R5: Huddersfield Town (H) 0-2

55-56 R3: Accrington Stanley (H) 2-0
R4: Scunthorpe United (H) 3-3, (A) 2-1
R5: Manchester City (A) 0-0, (H) 1-2

56-57 R3: Southend United (A) 1-2

57-58 R3: Southend United (H) 1-1, (A) 3-2
R4: Northampton Town (H) 3-1
R5: Scunthorpe United (A) 1-0
R6: Blackburn Rovers (A) 1-2

58-59 R3: Worcester City (A) 1-2

59-60 R3: Leyton Orient (H) 2-1
R4: Manchester United (H) 1-3

60-61 R3: Coventry City (H) 3-2
R4: Sunderland (H) 0-2

61-62 R3: Chelsea (H) 4-3
R4: Oldham Athletic (A) 2-1
R5: Preston N.E. (H) 0-0, (A) 0-0, 0-1

62-63 R3: Wrexham (A) 3-0
R4: Burnley (A) 1-1, (H) 2-1
R5: Arsenal (A) 2-1
R6: West Ham United (H) 1-0
SF: Leicester City (*at Sheffield Wed.*) 0-1

63-64 R3: Derby County (H) 5-0
R4: Port Vale (H) 0-0, (A) 2-1
R5: Arsenal (A) 1-0
R6: Swansea Town (A) 1-2

64-65 R3: West Bromwich Albion (H) 2-1
R4: Stockport County (H) 1-1, (A) 2-0
R5: Bolton Wanderers (A) 1-0
R6: Leicester City (A) 0-0, (H) 1-0
SF: Chelsea (*at Aston Villa*) 2-0
F: Leeds United (*at Wembley*) 2-1

65-66 R3: Chelsea (H) 1-2

66-67 R3: Watford (A) 0-0, (H) 3-1
R4: Aston Villa (H) 1-0
R5: Everton (A) 0-1

67-68 R3: A.F.C. Bournemouth (A) 0-0, (H) 4-1
R4: Walsall (A) 0-0, (H) 5-2
R5: Tottenham Hotspur (A) 1-1, (H) 2-1
R6: West Bromwich (A) 0-0, (H) 1-1, 1-2

68-69 R3: Doncaster Rovers (H) 2-0
R4: Burnley (H) 2-1
R5: Leicester City (H) 0-0, (A) 0-1

69-70 R3: Coventry City (A) 1-1, (H) 3-0
R4: Wrexham (H) 3-1
R5: Leicester City (H) 0-0, (A) 2-0
R6: Watford (A) 0-1

70-71 R3: Aldershot (H) 1-0
R4: Swansea City (H) 3-0
R5: Southampton (H) 1-0
R6: Tottenham Hotspur (H) 0-0, (A) 1-0
SF: Everton (*at Manchester United*) 2-1
F: Arsenal (*at Wembley*) 1-2

71-72 R3: Oxford United (A) 3-0
R4: Leeds United (H) 0-0, (A) 0-2

72-73 R3: Burnley (A) 0-0, (H) 3-0
R4: Manchester City (H) 0-0, (A) 0-2

73-74 R3: Doncaster Rovers (H) 2-2, (A) 2-0
R4: Carlisle United (H) 0-0, (A) 2-0
R5: Ipswich Town (H) 2-0
R6: Bristol City (A) 1-0
SF: Leicester City (*at Manchester United*) 0-0, (*at Aston Villa*) 3-1
F: Newcastle United (*at Wembley*) 3-0

74-75 R3: Stoke City (H) 2-0
R4: Ipswich Town (A) 0-1

75-76 R3: West Ham United (A) 2-0
R4: Derby County (A) 0-1

76-77 R3: Crystal Palace (H) 0-0, (A) 3-2
R4: Carlisle United (H) 3-0
R5: Oldham Athletic (H) 3-1
R6: Middlesbrough (H) 2-0
SF: Everton (*both at Manchester C.*) 2-2, 3-0
F: Manchester United (*at Wembley*) 1-2

77-78 R3: Chelsea (A) 2-4

78-79 R3: Southend United (A) 0-0, (H) 3-0
R4: Blackburn Rovers (H) 1-0
R5: Burnley (H) 3-0
R6: Ipswich Town (A) 1-0
SF: Man. U. (*at Man. C.*) 2-2, (*at Everton*) 0-1

79-80 R3: Grimsby Town (H) 5-0
R4: Nottingham Forest (A) 2-0
R5: Bury (H) 2-0
R6: Tottenham Hotspur (A) 1-0
SF: Arsenal (*at Sheffield Wed.*) 0-0, (*at Aston Villa*) 1-1, (*at Aston Villa*) 1-1, (*at Coventry City*) 0-1

80-81 R3: Altrincham (H) 4-1
R4: Everton (A) 1-2

Below: *Sammy Lee (right) evades Altrincham's Stan Allan as Liverpool beat their non-League opposition 4-1 at Anfield. Photo: Bob Thomas.*

Above: *Ian Rush (far right) beats Bobby Mimms for Liverpool's third goal in the 1986 final. Photo: Colorsport*

81-82 R3: Swansea City (A) 4-0
R4: Sunderland (A) 3-0
R5: Chelsea (A) 0-2

82-83 R3: Blackburn Rovers (A) 2-1
R4: Stoke City (H) 2-0
R5: Brighton & Hove Albion (H) 1-2

83-84 R3: Newcastle United (H) 4-0
R4: Brighton & Hove Albion (A) 0-2

84-85 R3: Aston Villa (H) 3-0
R4: Tottenham Hotspur (H) 1-0
R5: York City (A) 1-1, (H) 7-0
R6: Barnsley (A) 4-0
SF: Man. U. (*at Everton*) 2-2, (*at Man. C.*) 1-2

85-86 R3: Norwich City (H) 5-0
R4: Chelsea (A) 2-1
R5: York City (A) 1-1, (H) 3-1
R6: Watford (H) 0-0, (A) 2-1
SF: Southampton (*at Tottenham Hotspur*) 2-0
F: Everton (*at Wembley*) 3-1

86-87 R3: Luton Town (A) 0-0, (H) 0-0, (A) 0-3

87-88 R3: Stoke City (A) 0-0, (H) 1-0
R4: Aston Villa (A) 2-0
R5: Everton (A) 1-0
R6: Manchester City (A) 4-0
SF: Nottingham F. (*at Sheffield Wed.*) 2-1
F: Wimbledon (*at Wembley*) 0-1

88-89 R3: Carlisle United (A) 3-0
R4: Millwall (A) 2-0
R5: Hull City (A) 3-2
R6: Brentford (H) 4-0
SF: Nottingham Forest (*at Sheffield Wed.*) 0-0 - *abandoned in 1st half*), (*at Man. Utd*) 3-1
F: Everton (*at Wembley*) 3-2

89-90 R3: Swansea City (A) 0-0, (H) 8-0
R4: Norwich City (A) 0-0, (H) 3-1
R5: Southampton (H) 3-0
R6: Queens Park Rangers (A) 2-2, (H) 1-0
SF: Crystal Palace (*at Aston Villa*) 3-4

90-91 R3: Blackburn Rovers (A) 1-1, (H) 3-0
R4: Brighton & Hove A. (H) 2-2, (A) 3-2
R5: Everton (H) 0-0, (A) 4-4, (A) 0-1

91-92 R3: Crewe Alexandra (A) 4-0
R4: Bristol Rov. (A - *at Bath*) 1-1, (H) 2-1
R5: Ipswich Town (A) 0-0, (H) 3-2
R6: Aston Villa (H) 1-0
SF: Portsmouth (*at Arsenal F.C.*) 1-1, (*at Aston Villa*) 0-0 (*3-1 pens*)
F: Sunderland (*at Wembley*) 2-0

92-93 R3: Bolton Wanderers (A) 2-2, (H) 0-2

LIVERPOOL POLICE

Currently: (Merseyside Police) West Cheshire Lge

50-51 EX: Flint Town United (A) 2-4

51-52 PR: Marine (A) 0-4

LIVERSEDGE

Currently: Central Midlands League

48-49 EX: Farsley Celtic (A) 0-6

91-92 PR: Maine Road (H) 3-1
Q1: Marine (A) 0-4

92-93 PR: Arnold Town (A - *at Kimberley T.*) 0-4

LLANDUDNO

Currently: Cymru Alliance

46-47 PR: Northwich Victoria (H) 3-4

47-48 PR: Earle (H) 2-7

48-49 PR: Newton Y.M.C.A. (H) 0-1

49-50 PR: Rhyl (A) 0-2

50-51 PR: Flint Town United (A) 0-2

51-52 PR: Prescot Cables (A) 1-3

52-53 PR: Bootle Athletic (H) 1-1, (A) 0-1

54-55 PR: New Brighton (H) 6-2
Q1: Runcorn (A) 0-6

55-56 PR: Bangor City (A) 3-3, (H) 1-0
Q1: New Brighton (A) 0-4

56-57 Q1: Earlestown (H) 0-2

57-58 Q1: St Helens Town (A) 5-3
Q2: Stork (A) 1-1, (H) 0-2

58-59 PR: Stork (H) 7-0
Q1: St Helens Town (H) 3-0
Q2: Prescot Cables (H) 5-4
Q3: New Brighton (H) 0-1

59-60 Q1: Runcorn (A) 2-3

60-61 Q1: New Brighton (A) 1-3

61-62 PR: Ellesmere Port Town (A) 3-5

62-63 Q1: Runcorn (H) 2-3

63-64 Q1: Runcorn (H) 0-4

64-65 Q1: New Brighton (A) 3-8

66-67 Q1: Bangor City (H) 0-1

LLANELLI

Currently: League of Wales
***** - As Llanelly

45-46 * Q1: Aberaman (A) *W/O*
Q2: Monmouth Town (H) 7-0
Q3: Barry Town (H) 1-7

46-47 * PR: Ebbw Vale (A) 2-2, (H) 5-2
Q1: Merthyr Tydfil (A) 2-8

47-48 * PR: Cardiff Corinthians (A) 3-0
Q1: Ebbw Vale (A) 2-3

48-49 * Q1: Cardiff Corinthians (H) 1-1, (A) 2-0
Q2: Barry Town (A) 1-3

49-50 * EX: Hoffmann Ath. (Stonehouse) (H) 6-1
PR: Stonehouse (H) 4-1
Q1: Merthyr Tydfil (H) 0-3

50-51 * PR: Ebbw Vale (H) 2-0
Q1: Clevedon (A) 2-2, (H) 7-1
Q2: Merthyr Tydfil (H) 5-5, (A) 2-1
Q3: Barry Town (H) 2-1
Q4: Weymouth (H) 5-0
R1: Bristol Rovers (A) 1-1, (H) 1-1, 1-3

51-52 * Q1: Lovells Athletic (H) 2-0
Q2: Barry Town (A) 2-2, (H) 2-2, 0-4

52-53 * PR: Gloucester City (A) 1-1, (H) 5-0
Q1: Lovells Athletic (A) 1-0
Q2: Ebbw Vale (A) 3-0
Q3: Barry Town (A) 1-1, (H) 3-0
Q4: Ilfracombe Town (H) 1-0
R1: Grays Athletic (A) 5-0
R2: Colchester United (A) 2-3

53-54 * Q4: Portland United (H) 6-5
R1: Northampton Town (A) 0-3

54-55 * Q1: Merthyr Tydfil (H) 1-2

55-56 * Q1: Cinderford Town (H) 5-0
Q2: Lovells Athletic (H) 0-3

56-57 * Q1: Merthyr Tydfil (H) 5-1
Q2: Cinderford Town (H) 3-0
Q3: Cheltenham Town (A) 0-4

57-58 * Q1: Ebbw Vale (A) 5-5, (H) 3-2
Q2: Lovells Athletic (H) 2-1
Q3: Barry Town (H) 1-1, (A) 0-1

58-59 * Q1: Lovells Athletic (A) 1-1, (H) 1-1, 2-3

59-60 * Q1: Stonehouse (A) 5-0
Q2: Barry Town (A) 0-2

60-61 * Q1: Lovells Athletic (A) 3-2
Q2: Barry Town (H) 0-0, (A) 2-1
Q3: Cheltenham Town (A) 0-2

61-62 * Q1: Merthyr Tydfil (A) 0-5

62-63 * Q1: Cheltenham Town (A) 2-3

63-64 * Q1: Stonehouse (A) 1-1, (H) 1-0
Q2: Barry Town (A) 1-0
Q3: Cheltenham Town (A) 1-0
Q4: Bridgwater Town (A) 0-0, (H) 0-1

64-65 * Q1: Lovells Athletic (A) 1-1, (H) 2-1
Q2: Gloucester City (A) 1-0
Q3: Merthyr Tydfil (H) 2-7

65-66 * Q1: Gloucester City (A) 0-1

66-67 * Q1: Cinderford Town (A) 0-2

67-68 * Q1: Abergavenny Thursdays (A) 2-0
Q2: Barry Town (H) 0-0, (A) 0-4

68-69 * Q1: Ton Pentre (H) 2-1
Q2: Cinderford Town (A) 0-3

69-70 * Q1: Stonehouse (H) 1-2

70-71 * Q1: Barry Town (H) 1-0
Q2: Merthyr Tydfil (A) 1-1, (H) 0-2

71-72 * PR: Merthyr Tydfil (H) 0-3

72-73 * Q1: Barry Town (H) 0-1

73-74 * Q1: Weston-super-Mare (H) 1-0
Q2: Mangotsfield United (H) 1-2

74-75 Q1: Cheltenham Town (A) 2-3

75-76 PR: Mangotsfield United (H) 0-2

76-77 PR: Everwarm (A) 1-0
Q1: Calne Town (H) 2-1
Q2: Cinderford Town (H) 3-2
Q3: Merthyr Tydfil (H) 3-6

77-78 Q1: Worcester City (H) 1-1, (A) 0-2

78-79 Q1: Shepton Mallet Town (H) 1-3

79-80 PR: Weston-super-Mare (H) 0-2

80-81 Q1: Clandown (H) 2-0
Q2: Worcester City (H) 0-3

81-82 PR: Cinderford Town (A) 2-1
Q1: Haverfordwest County (H) 1-2

82-83 Q1: Gloucester City (A) 0-1

83-84 PR: Clevedon Town (H) 3-0
Q1: Basingstoke Town (A) 1-2

84-85 Q1: Gloucester City (H) 2-5

85-86 PR: Minehead (H) 2-3

86-87 PR: Maesteg Park (A) 3-2
Q1: Sharpness (A) 1-4

87-88 PR: Barnstaple Town (H) 1-2

LLOYDS (SITTINGBOURNE)
See Bowater Lloyds

LOCKHEED LEAMINGTON
See Leamington

LONDON TRANSPORT (CENTRAL BUSES)
Currently: Defunct

46-47 EX: Barking (H - *played away*) 0-9
47-48 PR: Dagenham British Legion (A) 1-4
48-49 EX: Eton Manor (H - *played away*) 0-5

LONG BUCKBY
Currently: United Counties League

91-92 PR: Stourbridge (A) 0-1
92-93 PR: Histon (A) 2-1
Q1: Rushden & Diamonds (H) 0-1

LONG EATON UNITED
Currently: Central Midlands League
* - As Long Eaton Town

50-51 * EX: Teversal & Silverhill (A) 2-2, (H) 3-2
PR: Ilkeston Town (A) 4-0
Q1: Langold W.M.C. (A) 1-5
51-52 * Q1: Gresley Rovers (H) 1-1, (A) 2-0
Q2: Ilkeston Town (H) 0-3
52-53 * Q1: Ilkeston Town (A) 2-7
54-55 * Q1: Hinckley Athletic (H) 1-7
55-56 * Q1: Whitwick Colliery (H) 2-3
56-57 * Q1: Players Athletic (A - *played home*) 9-0
Q2: Hinckley Athletic (H) 3-4
57-58 * Q2: Hinckley Athletic (A) 4-4, (H) 1-9
58-59 * Q1: Ilkeston Town (H) 2-0
Q2: Brush Sports (A) 1-2
59-60 PR: Brush Sports (A) 1-2
60-61 Q1: Loughborough United (A) 1-5
61-62 Q1: Atherstone Town (A) 2-3
62-63 Q1: Burton Albion (A) 1-1, (H) 0-3
63-64 Q1: Atherstone Town (H) 2-2, (A) 3-1
Q2: Tamworth (A) 1-3
64-65 Q1: Ilkeston Town (H) 1-3
65-66 Q1: Atherstone Town (H) 7-2
Q2: Ilkeston Town (H) 3-2
Q3: Burton Albion (H) 1-2
66-67 Q1: Matlock Town (H) 2-4
67-68 Q1: Gresley Rovers (H) 2-0
Q2: Bedworth Town (H) 2-0
Q3: Arnold (A) 0-1
68-69 PR: Loughborough United (H) 2-1
Q1: Atherstone Town (A) 2-4
69-70 PR: Gresley Rovers (A) 0-3
70-71 Q1: Ilkeston Town (H) 1-1, (A) 0-0, 2-0
Q2: Atherstone Town (H) 2-1
Q3: Burton Albion (H) 1-3
71-72 Q1: Sutton Coldfield Town (H) 3-1
Q2: Nuneaton Borough (A) 0-2
72-73 PR: Rushden Town (A) 1-0
Q1: Loughborough United (H) 3-0
Q2: Irthlingborough Diamonds (A) 1-2
73-74 Q1: Bilston (H) 1-3
74-75 Q1: Enderby Town (A) 1-3
75-76 Q1: Arnold (A) 1-2
76-77 Q1: Heanor Town (H) 3-0
Q2: New Mills (H) 3-0
Q3: Burton Albion (A) 0-5
77-78 Q1: Stalybridge Celtic (H) 0-2
78-79 Q1: Hinckley Athletic (A) 0-5
79-80 PR: Tividale (H) 3-1
Q1: Oldbury United (A) 1-0
Q2: Kidderminster Harriers (H) 0-1
80-81 Q1: Grantham (H) 0-0, (A) 2-2, (H) 0-3
81-82 PR: Halesowen Town (H) 1-3
82-83 PR: Wednesfield Social (H) 1-0
Q1: Holbeach United (A) 1-3
83-84 Q1: Lye Town (H) 1-1, (A) 3-4
84-85 PR: Curzon Ashton (H) 3-0
Q1: Hednesford Town (H) 1-3
85-86 Q1: Denaby United (A) 0-0, (H) 1-0
Q2: South Liverpool (H) 2-3
86-87 Q1: Northwich Victoria (H) 1-4
87-88 PR: Sutton Town (H) 1-3
88-89 PR: Bridgnorth Town (H) 0-5
89-90 PR: North Ferriby United (A) 0-1
90-91 PR: Oakham (A - *played home*) 1-1, (H) 0-1

LONGFLEET ST MARY'S
Currently: Defunct

47-48 EX: Weymouth (A) 1-4
48-49 EX: Portland United (A) 4-2
PR: Winchester City (H) 4-2
Q1: Thornycroft Athletic (H) 4-0
Q2: Weymouth (H) 0-4
49-50 PR: Portland United (H) 0-1
50-51 EX: Hamworthy (H) 1-1, (A) 0-1

LONG MELFORD
Currently: Essex & Suffolk Border League

57-58 Q1: Whitton United (A) 0-2
58-59 Q1: Haverhill Rovers (H) 2-2, (A) 2-4

LOSTOCK GRALAM
Currently: Mid-Cheshire League

47-48 PR: Ellesmere Port Town (A) 0-3
48-49 EX: Wheelock Albion (H) 4-0
PR: Buxton (H) 1-4
49-50 PR: Buxton (H) 1-2
54-55 PR: Linotype & Machinery (H) 5-0
Q1: Macclesfield Town (H) 2-5
55-56 Q1: Buxton (A) 1-2
56-57 PR: Leek Town (H) 2-1
Q1: Witton Albion (H) 1-0
Q2: Hyde United (A) 2-5
57-58 PR: Altrincham (H) 3-4
58-59 PR: Hyde United (A) 0-2
59-60 PR: Linotype & Machinery (H) 0-1
60-61 Q1: Congleton Town (H) 0-0, (A) 0-2
61-62 Q1: Congleton Town (A) 2-4
62-63 Q1: Northwich Victoria (H) 3-1
Q2: Winsford United (H) 0-3
63-64 Q1: Witton Albion (H) 4-1
Q2: Northwich Victoria (H) 4-4, (A) 0-4
64-65 Q1: Witton Albion (A) 0-4
66-67 Q1: Winsford United (H) 3-2
Q2: Skelmersdale United (H) 1-1, (A) 1-5
67-68 Q1: New Brighton (H) 1-1, (A) 2-1
Q2: Runcorn (A) 0-5
68-69 Q1: Nantwich (H) 4-2
Q2: Northwich Victoria (A) 1-2
69-70 Q1: Sandbach Ramblers (A) 1-0
Q2: Northwich Victoria (H) 0-5
70-71 PR: Stalybridge Celtic (H) 0-7

LOUGHBOROUGH UNITED
Currently: Defunct
* - As Brush Sports

46-47 * Q2: Gresley Rovers (H) 7-0
Q3: Coalville Town Amateurs (H) 3-1
Q4: Shrewsbury Town (H) 5-1
R1: Southend United (H) 1-6
47-48 * Q1: Moira United (A) 3-1
Q2: Tamworth (H) 3-1
Q3: Gresley Rovers (H) 5-1
Q4: Bromsgrove Rovers (A) 2-5
48-49 * Q1: Coalville Town Amateurs (A) 4-0
Q2: Tamworth (H) 4-3
Q3: Whitwick Colliery (A) 2-1
Q4: Kidderminster Harriers (A) 2-5
49-50 * Q1: Tamworth (H) 2-0
Q2: Gresley Rovers (A) 2-3
50-51 * PR: Coalville Town (A) 2-2, (H) 2-1
Q1: Whitwick Colliery (H) 5-2
Q2: Bedworth Town (H) 3-2
Q3: Hinckley Athletic (A) 1-0
Q4: Gainsborough Trinity (A) 1-3
51-52 * Q1: Whitwick Colliery (A) 3-0
Q2: Moira United (H) 2-0
Q3: Hinckley Athletic (A) 3-2
Q4: Wellington Town (H) 3-1
R1: Weymouth (H) 2-3
52-53 * Q1: Ibstock Penistone Rovers (H) 5-0
Q2: Coalville Town (H) 3-1
Q3: South Normanton Welfare (H) 3-1
Q4: Hereford United (H) 0-1
53-54 * Q1: Coalville Town (H) 2-0
Q2: Whitwick Colliery (A) 5-3
Q3: Hinckley Athletic (H) 2-1
Q4: Hereford United (H) 2-2, (A) 0-3
54-55 * Q1: Players Athletic (H) 2-0
Q2: Hinckley Athletic (H) 3-4
55-56 * Q2: Heanor Town (A) 2-1
Q3: Whitwick Colliery (H) 1-0
Q4: Burton Albion (H) 0-2
56-57 * Q1: Hinckley Athletic (H) 2-2, (A) 1-5
57-58 * Q1: Hinckley Athletic (H) 0-1
58-59 * Q1: Hinckley Athletic (A) 2-1
Q2: Long Eaton Town (H) 2-1
Q3: Nuneaton Borough (A) 1-2
59-60 * PR: Long Eaton United (H) 2-1
Q1: Hinckley Athletic (A) 1-0
Q2: Nuneaton Borough (H) 4-3
Q3: Ilkeston Town (A) 1-1, (H) 1-2
60-61 Q1: Long Eaton United (H) 5-1
Q2: Hinckley Athletic (H) 2-1
Q3: Ilkeston Town (A) 3-0
Q4: Holbeach United (A) 2-1
R1: King's Lynn (H) 0-0, (A) 0-3
61-62 Q1: Burton Albion (H) 1-3
62-63 Q1: Hinckley Athletic (A) 2-4
63-64 Q1: Gresley Rovers (A) 3-1
Q2: Ilkeston Town (A) 1-1, (H) 4-0
Q3: Tamworth (A) 0-0, (H) 2-0
Q4: Worcester City (A) 4-1
R1: Netherfield (A) 1-6
64-65 Q1: Nuneaton Borough (H) 1-2
65-66 Q1: Burton Albion (A) 0-1
66-67 Q1: Bedworth Town (H) 1-1, (A) 2-1
Q2: Nuneaton Borough (A) 2-8
67-68 PR: Rugby Town (A) 0-3
68-69 Q1: Long Eaton United (A) 1-2
69-70 PR: Bedworth United (H) 1-1, (A) 1-2
70-71 PR: Burton Albion (A) 0-1
71-72 Q1: Nuneaton Borough (H) 0-5
72-73 Q1: Long Eaton United (A) 0-3

LOUTH UNITED
Currently: Northern Counties (East) League

56-57 Q1: Ashby Institute (A) 0-0, (H) 5-0
Q2: Alford United (H) 1-1, (A) 1-2
57-58 Q1: Gainsborough Trinity (A) 2-4
58-59 Q1: Boston United (A) 2-5
59-60 Q1: Bourne Town (A) 1-4
60-61 Q1: Spalding United (H) 1-0
Q2: Holbeach United (H) 0-3
61-62 Q1: Boston United (A) 4-3
Q2: Grantham (A) 1-2

62-63 Q1: Grantham (A) 2-5

63-64 Q1: Grantham (A) 0-3

64-65 Q1: Holbeach United (H) 2-5

65-66 Q1: Holbeach United (A) 0-2

66-67 Q1: Boston (H) 0-3

67-68 Q1: Boston (A) 0-0, (H) 4-0
Q2: Boston United (H) 0-1

68-69 Q1: Boston (H) 3-1
Q2: King's Lynn (A) 1-3

69-70 Q1: Skegness Town (H) 0-1

70-71 Q1: Boston (H) 0-1

71-72 PR: Lincoln United (A - *played home*) 0-1

72-73 Q1: Kettering Town (A) 0-4

73-74 PR: Retford Town (A) 1-2

74-75 Q1: Bourne Town (A) 0-1

75-76 PR: Barton Town (H) 0-0, (A) 3-1
Q1: Selby Town (A) 0-1

76-77 PR: Wisbech Town (H) 2-2, (A) 0-2

77-78 Q1: Goole Town (A) 1-6

78-79 PR: Holbeach United (A) 3-0
Q1: Skegness Town (A) 1-0
Q2: Gainsborough Trinity (A) 1-1, (H) 1-2

79-80 Q1: Alfreton Town (H) 2-2, (A) 2-4

88-89 PR: Walsall Wood (A) 0-0, (H) 1-3

89-90 Q1: Grantham Town (A) 1-2

90-91 PR: Princes End United (H) 1-1, (A) 0-1

92-93 PR: Harrogate Town (A) 3-4

LOVELLS ATHLETIC

Currently: Defunct

45-46 Q1: Barry Town (A) 5-1
R1: Bournemouth (H) 4-1, (A) 2-3 (*agg: 6-4*)
R2: Bath City (H) 2-1, (A) 5-2 (*agg: 7-3*)
R3: Wolverhampton (H) 2-4, (A) 1-8 (*agg: 3-12*)

46-47 Q1: Aberaman & Aberdare Athletic (H) 1-0
Q2: Merthyr Tydfil (A) 2-4

47-48 PR: St Philips Marsh Adult School (A) 5-1
Q1: Weston-super-Mare St Johns (A) 4-1
Q2: Merthyr Tydfil (A) 1-2

48-49 Q1: Troedyrhiw (A) 2-1
Q2: Merthyr Tydfil (H) 3-1
Q3: Barry Town (A) 3-1
Q4: Yeovil Town (H) 2-3

49-50 PR: Weston-super-Mare St Johns (A) 7-2
Q1: Mount Hill Enterprise (H) 4-1
Q2: Merthyr Tydfil (H) 1-0
Q3: Gloucester City (H) 0-3

50-51 PR: Stonehouse (H) 2-2, (A) 0-1

51-52 Q1: Llanelly (A) 0-2

52-53 Q1: Llanelly (H) 0-1

53-54 PR: Cinderford Town (H) 1-3

54-55 PR: Ebbw Vale (H) 3-2
Q1: Stonehouse (H) 7-1
Q2: Merthyr Tydfil (A) 1-3

55-56 Q1: Cheltenham Town (A) 2-1
Q2: Llanelly (A) 3-0
Q3: Barry Town (A) 3-1
Q4: Merthyr Tydfil (H) 2-0
R1: Leyton Orient (A) 1-7

56-57 PR: Cheltenham Town (A) 0-3

57-58 PR: Merthyr Tydfil (H) 3-2
Q1: Cheltenham Town (A) 0-0, (H) 0-0, 4-2
Q2: Llanelly (A) 1-2

58-59 Q1: Llanelly (H) 1-1, (A) 1-1, 3-2
Q2: Gloucester City (H) 2-3

59-60 PR: Cheltenham Town (A) 0-1

60-61 Q1: Llanelly (H) 2-3

61-62 Q1: Barry Town (H) 2-3

62-63 Q1: Ebbw Vale (A) 1-1, (H) 4-1
Q2: Cheltenham Town (A) 1-5

63-64 Q1: Barry Town (A) 1-1, (H) 1-3

64-65 Q1: Llanelly (H) 1-1, (A) 1-2

65-66 Q1: Barry Town (H) 6-1
Q2: Gloucester City (H) 1-2

66-67 Q1: Cheltenham Town (H) 0-3

67-68 Q1: Gloucester City (H) 0-4

68-69 Q1: Cheltenham Town (A) 1-2

LOWCA

Currently: Defunct

46-47 PR: Distington (A) 7-1
Q1: Kells Centre (A) 2-1
Q2: Cleator Moor Celtic (A) 3-3, (H) 5-0
Q3: Netherfield (H) 0-1

47-48 PR: Penrith (H) 3-2
Q1: Bowthorn United (A) 2-4

48-49 PR: Parton United (H) 0-1

LOWER GORNAL ATH.

See Gornal Athletic

LOWESTOFT TOWN

Currently: Eastern Counties League

45-46 Q2: Bye
Q3: Leiston (A) 2-2 *expelled*

46-47 Q2: Gothic (H) 2-5

47-48 Q1: Whitton United (A) 5-3
Q2: Great Yarmouth Town (H) 2-3

48-49 PR: Sheringham (H) 6-0
Q1: Gorleston (H) 3-1
Q2: Great Yarmouth Town (A) 0-2

49-50 Q1: Gothic (A) 3-1
Q2: Great Yarmouth Town (H) 3-2
Q3: Gorleston (H) 0-3

50-51 PR: Whitton United (A) 3-1
Q1: Leiston (A) 1-0
Q2: Eastern Coachworks (A) 1-1, (H) 2-1
Q3: Great Yarmouth Town (H) 1-2

51-52 Q1: Thetford Town (A) 4-4, (H) 5-0
Q2: Bury Town (A) 0-2

52-53 Q1: Diss Town (A) 4-1
Q2: Sudbury Town (A) 0-4

53-54 Q1: Bury Town (H) 2-1
Q2: Sudbury Town (H) 3-0
Q3: Stowmarket (A) 2-4

54-55 Q1: Whitton United (H) 3-0
Q2: Sudbury Town (A) 1-3

55-56 Q1: Haverhill Rovers (H) 9-0
Q2: Bury Town (A) 3-2
Q3: Sudbury Town (H) 0-0, (A) 1-4

56-57 Q1: Leiston (H) 8-1
Q2: Sudbury Town (H) 0-1

57-58 Q1: Haverhill Rovers (A) 4-2
Q2: Bury Town (A) 1-2

58-59 Q1: King's Lynn (H) 0-1

59-60 Q1: Sheringham (H) 6-2
Q2: Great Yarmouth Town (A) 2-6

60-61 PR: Sheringham (H) 5-1
Q1: Great Yarmouth Town (H) 4-1
Q2: Clacton Town (A) 2-6

61-62 Q1: Sheringham (A) 5-3
Q2: Great Yarmouth Town (A) 0-2

62-63 Q1: Clacton Town (H) 4-2
Q2: Stowmarket Town (A) 2-1
Q3: Harwich & Parkeston (H) 4-0
Q4: Cambridge United (A) 0-4

63-64 Q1: Gorleston (H) 5-0
Q2: Harwich & Parkeston (A) 2-3

64-65 Q2: Harwich & Parkeston (A) 3-2
Q3: Sudbury Town (A) 5-0
Q4: Kettering Town (H) 1-3

65-66 Q1: Thetford Town (H) 10-2
Q2: Great Yarmouth Town (H) 4-2
Q3: Harwich & Parkeston (A) 2-4

66-67 Q1: Gothic (H) 6-0
Q2: Sudbury Town (A) 2-1
Q3: Haverhill Rovers (A) 4-4, (H) 6-4
Q4: Kettering Town (H) 3-1
R1: Leyton Orient (A) 1-2

67-68 Q1: Great Yarmouth Town (H) 3-0
Q2: Sudbury Town (H) 3-1
Q3: Bury Town (A) 1-0
Q4: Cambridge United (H) 2-2, (A) 2-1
R1: Watford (H) 0-1

68-69 Q4: King's Lynn (A) 0-3

69-70 Q1: Haverhill Rovers (H) 6-1
Q2: Harwich & Parkeston (A) 1-0
Q3: Bury Town (A) 3-1
Q4: Brentwood Town (A) 0-1

70-71 Q1: Newmarket Town (A) 3-3, (H) 3-0
Q2: Gorleston (H) 4-2
Q3: Clacton Town (H) 2-1
Q4: Barnet (H) 0-0, (A) 0-2

71-72 PR: Harwich & Parkeston (A) 2-2, (H) 1-2

72-73 Q1: Thetford Town (A) 2-4

73-74 PR: Soham Town Rangers (A) 2-1
Q1: Clacton Town (A) 1-2

74-75 Q1: Great Yarmouth Town (A) 3-3, (H) 3-2
Q2: Clacton Town (A) 0-3

75-76 PR: Harwich & Parkeston (H) 4-3
Q1: Stowmarket (A) 1-0
Q2: Potton United (H) 3-3, (A) 3-1
Q3: Cambridge City (H) 1-0
Q4: Bedford Town (A) 1-6

76-77 Q1: Gorleston (A) 1-1, (H) 2-0
Q2: Bury Town (A - *played home*) 3-2
Q3: Harwich & Parkeston (H) 0-3

77-78 Q1: Newmarket Town (H) 4-1
Q2: Great Yarmouth Town (H) 5-1
Q3: Wisbech Town (A) 3-0
Q4: Bishop's Stortford (H) 2-0
R1: Cambridge United (H) 0-2

78-79 PR: Haverhill Rovers (A) 0-0, (H) 2-0
Q1: Stowmarket (A) 1-0
Q2: Ely City (A) 2-1
Q3: Gorleston (A) 1-3

79-80 PR: Harlow Town (A) 1-2

80-81 Q1: Harwich & Parkeston (H) 0-2

81-82 Q1: Stamford (H) 1-0
Q2: Great Yarmouth Town (A) 1-3

82-83 Q1: Ely City (A) 3-1
Q2: King's Lynn (A) 1-2

83-84 PR: Letchworth Garden City (H) 2-0
Q1: Haverhill Rovers (A) 1-0
Q2: Felixstowe Town (H) 3-0
Q3: Walthamstow Avenue (A) 0-0, (H) 0-2

84-85 Q1: Epping Town (A) 4-3
Q2: Gorleston (A) 0-1

85-86 PR: Bury Town (H) 2-0
Q1: Braintree Town (H) 1-2

86-87 Q1: Kettering Town (A) 1-2

87-88 PR: Kingsbury Town (H) 0-1

88-89 PR: Ware (A) 0-2

89-90 PR: Gorleston (H) 2-1
Q1: Arlesey Town (H) 1-1, (A) 4-0
Q2: Hendon (A) 0-7

90-91 PR: Mirrlees Blackstone (H) 1-0
Q1: Boston United (A) 0-7

91-92 PR: Rainham Town (A - *played home*) 1-0
Q1: Boreham Wood (H) 2-1
Q2: Harwich & Parkeston (H) 1-0
Q3: Grays Athletic (H) 1-2

Opposite: *Lowestoft's most recent cup run of note was in 1991 when they reached the Third Qualifying Round. Here two home defenders (dark shirts) shut out Grays' Nicky Crown in the tie on October 12th.*
Photo: Francis Short.

92-93 Q1: Leyton (A) 2-4

LUDDENDEN FOOT

Currently: Defunct

47-48 PR: Bradford United (A) 0-1

LUDDINGTON (SCUNTHORPE)

Currently: Defunct

48-49	EX: New Waltham (A) 1-3
49-50	PR: Brigg Town (H) 1-7

LUTON AMATEURS

Currently: Defunct

46-47	PR: Vauxhall Motors (A) 4-2 Q1: Bedford Town (H) 1-5
47-48	PR: Wolverton Town (A) 2-4
48-49	EX: Wolverton Town (A) 5-1 PR: Letchworth Town (A) 0-3
49-50	EX: Potton United (A) 2-1 PR: Stewartby Works (A) 6-3 Q1: Bedford Town (A) 0-2
51-52	Q1: Wolverton Town (A) 1-6
52-53	Q1: Hitchin Town (A) 0-5
53-54	PR: Dunstable Town (H) 1-3

LUTON TOWN

Currently: Football League

45-46	R3: Derby County (H) 0-6, (A) 0-3 *(agg: 0-9)*
46-47	R3: Notts County (H) 6-0 R4: Swansea Town (H) 2-0 R5: Burnley (H) 0-0, (A) 0-3
47-48	R3: Plymouth Argyle (A) 4-2 R4: Coventry City (H) 3-2 R5: Queens Park Rangers (A) 1-3
48-49	R3: West Ham United (H) 3-1 R4: Walsall (H) 4-0 R5: Leicester City (H) 5-5, (A) 3-5
49-50	R3: Grimsby Town (H) 3-4
50-51	R3: Portsmouth (H) 2-0 R4: Bristol Rovers (H) 1-2
51-52	R3: Charlton Athletic (H) 1-0 R4: Brentford (H) 2-2, (A) 0-0, 3-2 R5: Swindon Town (H) 3-1 R6: Arsenal (H) 2-3
52-53	R3: Blackburn Rovers (H) 6-1 R4: Manchester City (A) 1-1, (H) 5-1 R5: Bolton Wanderers (H) 0-1
53-54	R3: Blackpool (A) 1-1, (H) 0-0, *(at Aston Villa)* 1-1, 0-2
54-55	R3: Workington (H) 5-0 R4: Rotherham United (A) 5-1 R5: Manchester City (H) 0-2
55-56	R3: Leicester City (H) 0-4
56-57	R3: Aston Villa (H) 2-2, (A) 0-2
57-58	R3: Stockport County (A) 0-3
58-59	R3: Leeds United (H) 5-1 R4: Leicester City (A) 1-1, (H) 4-1 R5: Ipswich Town (A) 5-2 R6: Blackpool (A) 1-1, (H) 1-0 SF: Norwich City *(at Tottenham Hotspur)* 1-1, *(at Birmingham City)* 1-0 F: Nottingham Forest *(at Wembley)* 1-2
59-60	R3: Exeter City (A) 2-1 R4: Huddersfield Town (A) 1-0 R5: Wolverhampton Wanderers (H) 1-4
60-61	R3: Northampton Town (H) 4-0 R4: Manchester C. (H) 2-6 *abandoned*, (H) 3-1 R5: Barnsley (A) 0-1
61-62	R3: Ipswich Town (A) 1-1, (H) 1-1, 1-5
62-63	R3: Swindon Town (H) 0-2
63-64	R1: Bridgwater Town (A) 3-0 R2: Reading (H) 2-1 R3: Fulham (A) 1-4
64-65	R1: Southend United (H) 1-0 R2: Gillingham (H) 1-0 R3: Sunderland (H) 0-3
65-66	R1: Romford (A) 1-1, (H) 1-0 R2: Corby Town (A) 2-2, (H) 0-1
66-67	R1: Exeter City (A) 1-1, (H) 2-0 R2: Bristol Rovers (A) 2-3
67-68	R1: Oxford City (A) 2-1 R2: Swindon Town (A) 2-3
68-69	R1: Ware (H) 6-1 R2: Gillingham (H) 3-1 R3: Manchester City (A) 0-1
69-70	R1: A.F.C. Bournemouth (A) 1-1, (H) 3-1 R2: Hillingdon Borough (A) 1-2
70-71	R3: Nottingham Forest (A) 1-1, (H) 3-4
71-72	R3: West Ham United (A) 1-2
72-73	R3: Crewe Alexandra (H) 2-0 R4: Newcastle United (A) 2-0 R5: Bolton Wanderers (A) 1-0 R6: Sunderland (A) 0-2
73-74	R3: Port Vale (A) 1-1, (H) 4-2 R4: Bradford City (H) 3-0 R5: Leicester City (H) 0-4
74-75	R3: Birmingham City (H) 0-1
75-76	R3: Blackburn Rovers (H) 2-0 R4: Norwich City (A) 0-2
76-77	R3: Halifax Town (A) 1-0 R4: Chester (A) 0-1
77-78	R3: Oldham Athletic (H) 1-1, (A) 2-1 R4: Millwall (A) 0-4
78-79	R3: York City (A) 0-2
79-80	R3: Swindon Town (H) 0-2
80-81	R3: Orient (A) 3-1 R4: Newcastle United (A) 1-2
81-82	R3: Swindon Town (H) 2-1 R4: Ipswich Town (H) 0-3
82-83	R3: Peterborough United (H) 3-0 R4: Manchester United (H) 0-2
83-84	R3: Watford (H) 2-2, (A) 3-4
84-85	R3: Stoke City (H) 1-1, (A) 3-2 R4: Huddersfield Town (H) 2-0 R5: Watford (H) 0-0, (A) 2-2, (H) 1-0 R6: Millwall (H) 1-0 SF: Everton *(at Aston Villa)* 1-2
85-86	R3: Crystal Palace (A) 2-1 R4: Bristol Rovers (H) 4-0 R5: Arsenal (H) 2-2, (A) 0-0, (H) 3-0 R6: Everton (H) 2-2, (A) 0-1
86-87	R3: Liverpool (H) 0-0, (A) 0-0, (H) 3-0 R4: Queens Park Rangers (H) 1-1, (A) 1-2
87-88	R3: Hartlepool United (A) 2-1 R4: Southampton (H) 2-1 R5: Queens Park Rangers (A) 1-1, (H) 1-0 R6: Portsmouth (H) 3-1 SF: Wimbledon *(at Tottenham Hotspur)* 1-2
88-89	R3: Millwall (A) 2-3
89-90	R3: Brighton & Hove Albion (A) 1-4
90-91	R3: Sheffield United (A) 3-1 R4: West Ham United (H) 1-1, (A) 0-5
91-92	R3: Sheffield United (A) 0-4
92-93	R3: Bristol City (H) 2-0 R4: Derby County (H) 1-5

LYE TOWN

Currently: West Midlands (Regional) League

48-49	EX: Boldmere St Michaels (H) 2-5
49-50	PR: Brierley Hill Alliance (H) 2-0 Q1: Cradley Heath (A) 0-1
50-51	EX: Moor Green (H) 2-2, (A) 3-1 PR: Boldmere St Michaels (H) 2-1 Q1: Oswestry Town (A) 1-2
51-52	PR: Brierley Hill Alliance (A) 2-4
52-53	Q1: Brierley Hill Alliance (H) 1-3
53-54	PR: Worcester City (H) 3-5
54-55	PR: Cradley Heath (H) 3-2 Q1: Bilston (A) 2-4
57-58	PR: Dudley Town (H) 6-0 Q1: Boldmere St Michaels (H) 4-2 Q2: Oswestry Town (H) 1-4
58-59	PR: Bournville Athletic (H) 1-0 Q1: Bromsgrove Rovers (A) 2-4
68-69	Q1: Stourbridge (A) 4-7
69-70	Q1: Alvechurch (H) 2-3
70-71	Q1: Moor Green (A) 2-2, (H) 2-0 Q2: Nuneaton Borough (H) 0-3
71-72	PR: Kidderminster Harriers (A) 1-3
72-73	Q1: Redditch United (H) 1-0 Q2: Alvechurch (A) 0-4
73-74	PR: Oldbury United (A) 1-0 Q1: Gornal Athletic (A) 0-0, (H) 5-0 Q2: Highgate United (A) 0-1
74-75	Q1: Halesowen Town (A) 2-1 Q2: A.P. Leamington (A) 1-3
75-76	Q1: Banbury United (A) 0-1
76-77	Q1: Gornal Athletic (A) 3-1 Q2: Nuneaton Borough (A) 0-2
77-78	Q1: Banbury United (H) 3-3, (A) 1-2
78-79	PR: Bromsgrove Rovers (A) 1-3
79-80	Q1: Alvechurch (H) 1-1, (A) 2-1 Q2: Hednesford Town (H) 1-0 Q3: Kidderminster Harriers (A) 1-2
80-81	PR: Mangotsfield United (H) 2-0 Q1: Chippenham Town (H) 1-1, (A) 2-0 Q2: Barry Town (A) 1-1, (H) 1-2
81-82	Q1: Wellingborough Town (H) 2-1 Q2: Nuneaton Borough (H) 1-2
82-83	PR: Bridgnorth Town (H) 0-2
83-84	PR: Willenhall Town (H) 1-0 Q1: Long Eaton United (A) 1-1, (H) 4-3 Q2: A.P. Leamington (H) 4-4, (A) 0-4
84-85	Q1: Formby (A) 2-5
85-86	PR: Sutton Coldfield (H - *played away*) 2-1 Q1: Stafford Rangers (H) 1-3

86-87 PR: Bilston Town (A) 2-1
Q1: Brigg Town (A) 2-0
Q2: G.K.N. Sankey (H) 4-1
Q3: Goole Town (H) 1-3

87-88 Q1: Evesham United (H) 1-0
Q2: Atherstone United (A) 0-1

88-89 Q1: Hinckley Town (H) 0-3

89-90 PR: Hednesford Town (A) 2-0
Q1: Stourbridge (H) 2-0
Q2: Desborough Town (A) 1-1, (H) 5-2
Q3: Stafford Rangers (H) 1-2

90-91 Q1: Shepshed Charterhouse (A) 1-3

91-92 PR: Tamworth (A) 2-2, (H) 1-3

92-93 PR: Barwell (H - *at Dudley T.*) 1-1, (A) 3-1
Q1: Halesowen Harriers (A) 1-2

(A.F.C.) LYMINGTON

Currently: Wessex League
See also Lymington (below)

90-91 PR: Chichester City (A) 5-1
Q1: Chippenham Town (A) 1-1, (H) 1-0
Q2: Wokingham (H) 1-1, (A - *at Reading*) 1-2

91-92 PR: A.F.C. Totton (A) 2-2, (H) 3-2
Q1: Bashley (H) 2-4

92-93 PR: Minehead (A) 2-2, (H) 2-1
Q1: Bristol M.F. (H) 3-3, (A - *at Keynsham*) 2-0
Q2: Dorchester Town (H) 1-1, (A) 4-2
Q3: Cheltenham Town (H) 0-1

LYMINGTON

Currently: Merged with Wellworthy Athletic
Playing as A.F.C. Lymington in Wessex League
See also A.F.C. Lymington

47-48 EX: Portland United (H) 1-2

48-49 EX: R.A.O.C. Hilsea (A) 0-3

49-50 EX: Cowes (A) 0-4

51-52 Q1: Blandford United (A) 3-1
Q2: Poole Town (H) 3-2
Q3: Portland United (H) 1-1, (A) 2-1
Q4: Barnstaple Town (H) 1-1, (A) 1-3

52-53 Q1: Ilminster Town (A) 1-2

53-54 Q1: Dorchester Town (A) 0-9

LYNEMOUTH WELFARE

Currently: Defunct

48-49 EX: Shilbottle Colliery Welfare (H) 1-2

49-50 EX: Jarrow (H) 6-2
PR: South Shields (A) 2-9

50-51 EX: West Stanley (H) 2-9

54-55 PR: Heaton Stannington (A) 3-3, (H) 2-3

LYNTON WORKS (BEDFORD)

Currently: Defunct

50-51 EX: Bedford Queens Works (A) 5-6

LYONS CLUB (GREENFORD)

Currently: Defunct

45-46 EX: Uxbridge (A) 1-11

46-47 PR: Slough United (A) 2-4

47-48 EX: Henley Town (A) 7-1
PR: Maidenhead United (A) 2-7

48-49 EX: Wood Green Town (H) 3-1
PR: Enfield (H) 0-5

49-50 EX: Pinner (H) 3-2
PR: Crown & Manor (H) 0-4

LYSAGHT'S SPORTS (SCUNTHORPE)

Currently: Defunct

45-46 Q2: Bye
Q3: Scunthorpe United (A) 1-4

46-47 PR: Brodsworth Main Colliery (A) 1-9

47-48 PR: Kiveton Park Colliery (H) 4-1
Q1: Grimethorpe Athletic (A) 2-4

48-49 PR: Frickley Colliery (A) 0-4

49-50 EX: Thorne Colliery (H) 3-1
PR: Selby Town (H) 0-5

50-51 EX: Brigg Town (A) 1-3

51-52 Q1: Holbeach United (A) 0-5

52-53 Q1: Skegness Town (H) 1-9

53-54 Q1: Barton Town (H) 2-2, (A) 4-1 *ab.*, 2-1
Q2: Boston United (H) 0-4

54-55 Q1: Skegness Town (A) 0-4

LYTHAM

Currently: West Lancashire League
* - As Lytham St Annes

46-47 PR: Leyland Mtrs (H) 1-1, (A) *see page 137*

47-48 PR: Bacup Borough (H) 0-1

48-49 PR: Atherton Collieries (A) 1-4

49-50 PR: Clitheroe (A) 2-4

50-51 PR: Fleetwood (A) 1-3

51-52 Q1: Darwen (H) 1-3

52-53 PR: Droylsden (H) 2-0
Q1: Mossley (A) 1-3

53-54 Q1: Droylsden (A) 4-2
Q2: Skelmersdale United (H) 1-2

54-55 PR: Nelson (A) 0-3

55-56 PR: Mossley (A) 1-1, (H) 1-0
Q1: Chorley (H) 1-4

56-57 PR: Horwich R.M.I. (H) 1-7

57-58 PR: Bacup Borough (A) 0-3

58-59 PR: Rossendale United (A) 0-1

59-60 PR: Rossendale United (A) 4-4, (H) 2-1
Q1: Nelson (A) 2-2, (H) 2-0
Q2: Bacup Borough (H) 2-1
Q3: Altrincham (H) 1-1, (A) 0-3

60-61 Q1: Hyde United (H) 2-4

61-62 * Q1: Darwen (A) 1-3

62-63 * Q1: Chorley (A) 2-10

63-64 * Q2: Hyde United (H) 1-1, (A) 0-5

64-65 * Q1: Nelson (A) 1-2

65-66 * Q1: Bacup Borough (H) 2-0
Q2: Hyde United (H) 1-1, (A) 0-4

66-67 * Q1: Nelson (H) 0-1

68-69 * Q1: Lancaster City (A) 3-7

69-70 * Q1: Milnethorpe Corinthians (A) 1-1, (H) 1-5

77-78 Q1: Rossendale United (H) 0-1

78-79 PR: Barrow (H) 0-2

79-80 PR: Rossendale United (H) 1-1, (A) 0-4

80-81 Q1: Leyland Motors (H) 0-2

81-82 Q1: Ashton United (A) 1-1, (H) 3-1
Q2: Marine (A) 0-0, (H) 0-6

82-83 PR: Southport (H) 1-2

83-84 PR: Prescot Cables (A) 0-0, (H) 0-3

84-85 PR: Colwyn Bay (A) 0-1

MABLETHORPE UNITED

Currently: Defunct

50-51 EX: Ransome & Marles (A) 0-6

MACCLESFIELD TOWN

Currently: Alliance Premier League

47-48 PR: Buxton (A) 1-6

48-49 EX: Shell (H) 6-3
PR: Northwich Victoria (H) 0-3

49-50 PR: Port Sunlight (H) 3-2
Q1: Congleton Town (H) 1-2

50-51 PR: Droylsden (A) 5-5, (H) 7-2
Q1: Altrincham (A) 1-3

51-52 Q1: Buxton (H) 0-0, (A) 0-2

52-53 Q1: Congleton Town (H) 3-0
Q2: Winsford United (A) 0-1

53-54 Q1: Stalybridge Celtic (A) 0-1

54-55 Q1: Lostock Gralam (A) 5-2
Q2: Hyde United (A) 1-3

55-56 Q1: Northwich Victoria (H) 0-4

56-57 PR: Ellesmere Port Town (H) 2-1
Q1: Altrincham (A) 3-1
Q2: Winsford United (A) 2-2, (H) 4-1
Q3: Hyde Utd (H) 4-4, (A) 3-3, (*at Stockport County*) 3-5

57-58 PR: Winsford United (H) 5-4
Q1: Altrincham (A) 3-4

58-59 PR: Ellesmere Port Town (H) 1-3

59-60 Q1: Ellesmere Port Town (H) 2-3

60-61 Q1: Northwich Victoria (A) 3-0
Q2: Linotype & Machinery (H) 1-1, (A) 3-0
Q3: Congleton Town (A) 3-0
Q4: Nelson (A) 3-2
R1: Southport (A) 2-7

61-62 Q1: Droylsden (H) 4-0
Q2: Northwich Victoria (A) 0-1

62-63 Q1: Droylsden (A) 3-3, (H) 2-2 *ab. in E.T.*, 2-3

63-64 Q1: Winsford United (H) 1-0
Q2: Mossley (A) 5-0
Q3: Northwich Victoria (A) 1-1, (H) 1-0
Q4: Frickley Colliery (H) 1-3

64-65 Q1: Oswestry Town (H) 2-0
Q2: Northwich Victoria (H) 4-1
Q3: Witton Albion (H) 2-1
Q4: Ellesmere Port Town (H) 2-1
R1: Wrexham (H) 1-2

65-66 Q1: Winsford Town (H) 7-0
Q2: Witton Albion (H) 9-0
Q3: Oswestry Town (A) 2-3

66-67 Q1: Alfreton Town (H) 2-1
Q2: Matlock Town (A) 2-2, (H) 6-1
Q3: Worksop Town (H) 3-1
Q4: Nuneaton Borough (H) 1-1, (A) 0-2

67-68 Q1: Bacup Borough (H) 7-0
Q2: Witton Albion (A) 2-0
Q3: Hyde United (A) 2-0
Q4: Wigan Athletic (A) 1-1, (H) 3-0
R1: Stockport County (A) 1-1, (H) 2-1
R2: Spennymoor United (H) 2-0
R3: Fulham (A) 2-4

68-69 Q4: Retford Town (A) 2-0
R1: Lincoln City (H) 1-3

69-70 Q4: Altrincham (H) 2-0
R1: Scunthorpe United (H) 1-1, (A) 2-4

70-71 R1: Bradford City (A) 2-3

71-72 Q4: Ellesmere Port Town (H) 1-2

72-73 Q1: Emley (A) 2-1
Q2: Glossop (H) 3-0
Q3: Bradford (Park Avenue) (H) 1-0
Q4: South Liverpool (H) 0-1

73-74 Q1: Ashton United (A) 3-0
Q2: Leek Town (A) 2-2, (H) 4-2
Q3: Stalybridge Celtic (H) 2-1
Q4: Merthyr Tydfil (H) 0-0, (A) 1-2

74-75 Q1: Congleton Town (H) 2-0
Q2: Stafford Rangers (A) 0-3

75-76 Q1: Sutton Town (H) 0-0, (A) 4-0
Q2: Sutton Coldfield T. (A) 2-0
Q3: Arnold (H) 3-1
Q4: Mexborough Town (A) 2-1
R1: Sheffield Wednesday (A) 1-3

76-77 Q1: Rhyl (A) 1-1, (H) 1-2

77-78 Q1: Mossley (H) 0-2

78-79 PR: Marine (H) 2-4

79-80 PR: New Brighton (A) 7-1
Q1: St Helens Town (A) 2-1
Q2: Mossley (H) 0-0, (A) 2-3

80-81 Q1: Stourbridge (A) 2-6

81-82 PR: Witton Albion (A) 1-3

82-83 Q1: Bangor City (H) 3-1

Q2: Hyde United (A) 5-2
Q3: Ashton United (A) 2-0
Q4: Stafford Rangers (H) 3-1
R1: Worcester City (H) 1-5

83-84 Q1: Tamworth (A) 6-1
Q2: Marine (A) 3-0
Q3: Congleton Town (H) 6-0
Q4: Horwich R.M.I. (A) 0-0, (H) 4-3
R1: York City (H) 0-0, (A) 0-2

84-85 Q4: Bishop Auckland (A) 2-1
R1: Port Vale (H) 1-2

85-86 Q4: South Bank (H) 3-1
R1: Hartlepool United (H) 1-2

86-87 Q4: Southport (H) 0-1

87-88 Q1: Stalybridge Celtic (A) 1-1, (H) 5-1
Q2: Chadderton (H) 5-0
Q3: Marine (H) 0-0, (A) 2-1
Q4: Whitby Town (H) 3-1
R1: Carlisle United (H) 4-2
R2: Rotherham United (H) 4-0
R3: Port Vale (A) 0-1

Right: *John Askey hits a shot at the Port Vale goal in front of a huge crowd gathered for the 1988 Third Round tie.*
Photo: John Rooney.

88-89 Q4: Altrincham (H) 0-0, (A) 0-4

89-90 R1: Chester (H) 1-1, (A) 2-3

90-91 Q4: Altrincham (H) 2-2, (H) 0-3

91-92 Q1: Skelmersdale United (A) 4-0
Q2: Borrowash Victoria (H) 1-2

92-93 Q1: Glossop North End (A) 1-0
Q2: Hucknall Town (A) 1-1, (H) 3-1
Q3: Horwich R.M.I. (H) 1-0
Q4: Netherfield (A) 1-1, (H) 5-0
R1: Chesterfield (H) 0-0, (A) 2-2 (*3-2 pens*)
R2: Stockport County (H) 0-2

MAESTEG PARK ATH.

Currently: League of Wales

85-86 PR: Forest Green Rovers (H) 0-1

86-87 PR: Llanelli (H) 2-3

87-88 Q1: Tiverton Town (H) 0-1

88-89 Q1: Shortwood United (H) 1-0
Q2: Dorchester Town (H) 0-2

89-90 PR: Glastonbury (A) 1-0
Q1: Trowbridge Town (H) 0-2

90-91 PR: Sharpness (A) *W/O*
Q1: Weston-super-Mare (A) 2-2, (H) 0-4

91-92 PR: Dawlish Town (A) 2-1
Q1: Frome Town (H) 4-0
Q2: Bath City (A) 2-5

MAIDENHEAD UNITED

Currently: Isthmian League

45-46 PR: Hayes (A) 1-4

46-47 EX: Hounslow Town (A) 4-1
PR: Yiewsley (A) 3-3, (H) 3-0
Q1: Uxbridge (A) 1-2

47-48 EX: Marlow (A) 2-0
PR: Lyons Club (H) 7-2
Q1: Huntley & Palmers Recreation (H) 5-2
Q2: Banbury Spencer (A) 0-4

48-49 PR: Chesham United (A) 4-1
Q1: Wallingford Town (A) 3-1
Q2: Oxford City (A) 0-8

49-50 PR: Osberton Radiator (H) 1-1, (A) 0-1

50-51 EX: Windsor & Eton (A) 1-1, (H) 2-1
PR: Wycombe Wanderers (H) 0-2

51-52 PR: Yiewsley (H) 4-1
Q1: St Albans City (A) 1-3

52-53 PR: Banbury Spencer (A) 1-1, (H) 3-0
Q1: Bicester Town (H) 2-0
Q2: Headington United (A) 0-2

53-54 PR: Bicester Town (A) 5-0
Q1: Witney Town (A) 1-0
Q2: Headington United (A) 0-4

54-55 PR: Marlow (H) 2-2, (A) 2-0
Q1: Bicester Town (H) 3-2
Q2: Chesham United (A) 5-5, (H) 5-3
Q3: Oxford City (A) 1-4

55-56 PR: Marlow (A) 2-1
Q1: Wycombe Wanderers (A) 2-4

56-57 PR: Huntley & Palmers Recreation (H) 5-1
Q1: Oxford City (H) 2-3

57-58 PR: Abingdon Town (A) 0-1

58-59 PR: Abingdon Town (A) 2-0
Q1: Witney Town (H) 7-2
Q2: Wokingham Town (H) 4-0
Q3: Headington United (H) 1-6

59-60 PR: Huntley & Palmers Recreation (H) 4-1
Q1: Abingdon Town (A) 1-1, (H) 3-1
Q2: Wokingham Town (H) 5-0
Q3: Oxford City (A) 0-3

60-61 Q1: Windsor & Eton (A) 4-2
Q2: Uxbridge (H) 4-0
Q3: Edgware Town (H) 3-3, (A) 2-0
Q4: Harrow Town (A) 3-2
R1: Colchester United (A) 0-5

61-62 Q1: Hayes (H) 8-2
Q2: Edgware Town (H) 1-0
Q3: Yiewsley (H) 2-3

62-63 Q1: Windsor & Eton (H) 2-1
Q2: Yiewsley (H) 3-2
Q3: Finchley (H) 3-1
Q4: Tilbury (H) 2-1
R1: Wycombe Wanderers (H) 0-3

63-64 Q1: Aylesbury United (A) 3-2
Q2: Banbury Spencer (A) 3-2
Q3: Hemel Hempstead Town (H) 2-1
Q4: Ilford (A) 3-1
R1: Bath City (H) 0-2

64-65 Q4: Guildford City (A) 0-9

65-66 Q1: Oxford City (A) 2-5

66-67 Q1: Grays Athletic (A) 0-0, (H) 3-1
Q2: Leatherhead (H) 0-2

67-68 Q1: Aylesbury United (A) 2-2, (H) 4-2
Q2: Banbury United (H) 1-3

68-69 Q1: Bletchley (A) 0-0, (H) 1-0
Q2: Aylesbury United (A) 1-2

69-70 PR: Marlow (A) 1-4

70-71 Q1: Dunstable Town (H) 0-1

71-72 Q1: Wycombe Wanderers (H) 2-0
Q2: Leytonstone (H) 1-0
Q3: Aveley (A) 1-1, (H) 3-2
Q4: Walton & Hersham (H) 2-1
R1: Enfield (A) 0-2

72-73 Q1: Woking (H) 0-1

73-74 PR: Hemel Hempstead Town (H) 2-0
Q1: Dorking (A) 2-0
Q2: Gravesend & Northfleet (A) 3-2
Q3: Epping Town (A) 0-3

74-75 Q1: Windsor & Eton (H) 4-1
Q2: Wimbledon (A) 0-4

75-76 Q1: Biggleswade Town (A) 1-0
Q2: Enfield (A) 0-6

76-77 PR: Letchworth Garden City (A) 1-5

77-78 Q1: Windsor & Eton (H) 3-0
Q2: Feltham (A) 2-3

78-79 PR: Farnborough Town (A) 0-1

79-80 Q1: Clapton (H) 1-0
Q2: Hendon (H) 2-2, (A) 3-0
Q3: Metropolitan Police (A) 1-0
Q4: Merthyr Tydfil (A) 1-2

80-81 Q1: Thame United (H) 1-0
Q2: Harefield United (A) 0-0, (H) 5-1
Q3: Addlestone & Weybridge (H) 0-0, (A) 0-5

81-82 Q1: Egham Town (H) 5-0
Q2: Harrow Borough (H) 0-2

82-83 Q1: Chichester City (H) 4-2
Q2: Dorchester Town (A) 1-1, (H) 0-2

83-84 Q1: Fareham Town (A) 1-1, (H) 0-1

84-85 PR: Southall (A) 2-1
Q1: Potton United (H) 0-2

85-86 PR: Tilbury (A - *at Aveley*) 0-2

86-87 PR: Redhill (A) 2-3

87-88 PR: Tunbridge Wells (H) 1-1, (A) 3-4

88-89 PR: Sheppey United (A) 1-1, (H) 0-1

89-90 Q1: Banbury United (A) 3-1
Q2: Stroud (H) 2-0
Q3: Abingdon Town (A) 1-3

90-91 Q1: Wycombe Wanderers (A) 0-3

91-92 PR: Sholing Sports (A) 6-0
Q1: Newport Isle of Wight (A) 3-0
Q2: Bashley (A) 1-1, (H) 1-0
Q3: Horsham (A) 1-1, (H) 0-1

92-93 Q1: Buckingham Town (A) 1-1, (H) 2-1
Q2: Abingdon Town (A) 0-2

MAIDSTONE UNITED

Currently: Defunct

46-47 PR: Margate (H) 3-1
Q1: Ashford (H) 3-5

47-48 PR: Ramsgate Athletic (H) 3-4

50-51 PR: Ramsgate Athletic (H) 5-2
Q1: Sittingbourne (A) 0-2

51-52 PR: Gravesend & Northfleet (A) 2-2, (H) 0-3

52-53 PR: Bromley (H) 0-6

53-54 PR: Sheppey United (A) 2-2, (H) 3-1
Q1: Margate (H) 1-3

54-55 PR: Bromley (H) 1-3

55-56 PR: Sheppey United (H) 1-1, (A) 4-0
Q1: Tonbridge (A) 1-0
Q2: Margate (H) 1-4

56-57 PR: Betteshanger Colliery Welfare (A) 0-1

57-58 PR: Whitstable (H) 1-3

58-59 PR: Tunbridge Wells United (A) 1-3

59-60 Q1: Tunbridge Wells Utd (A) 1-1, (H) 2-3

60-61 Q1: Gravesend & Northfleet (H) 2-1
Q2: Dartford (H) 1-3

61-62 Q1: Tunbridge Wells United (A) 0-1

62-63 Q1: Hastings United (A) 0-0, (H) 3-2
Q2: Bexhill Town (H) 5-0
Q3: Tunbridge Wells United (A) 1-0
Q4: Dartford (A) 0-2

63-64 Q1: Bexhill Town (H) 1-0
Q2: Tunbridge Wells United (A) 2-1
Q3: Tonbridge (H) 1-6

64-65 Q1: Hastings United (H) 1-3

65-66 Q1: Bexhill Town (H) 4-0
Q2: Hastings United (H) 1-5

66-67 Q1: Eastbourne (H) 2-2, (A) 3-1
Q2: Crawley Town (A) 0-1

67-68 Q1: Chatham Town (A) 2-4

68-69 Q1: Ashford Town (H) 1-2

69-70 Q1: Tonbridge (H) 5-4
Q2: Ashford Town (A) 0-1

70-71 Q1: Sittingbourne (A) 5-0
Q2: Hastings United (H) 0-2

71-72 Q1: Tunbridge Wells (H) 6-1
Q2: Herne Bay (H) 3-0
Q3: Folkestone (A) 0-2

72-73 PR: Tonbridge (A) 1-1, (H) 1-2

73-74 Q1: Canterbury City (H) 4-2
Q2: Ashford Town (H) 1-1, (A) 2-0
Q3: Ramsgate (H) 3-1
Q4: Wimbledon (A) 0-1

74-75 Q1: Eastbourne Town (A) 0-0, (H) 5-3
Q2: Hastings United (H) 6-0
Q3: Medway (H) 7-0
Q4: Hendon (A) 2-0
R1: Nuneaton Borough (A) 2-2, (H) 2-0
R2: Swindon Town (A) 1-3

75-76 PR: Eastbourne United (H) 5-0
Q1: Ringmer (A) 1-1, (H) 3-1
Q2: Ramsgate (H) 1-2

76-77 Q1: Gravesend & Northfleet (A) 0-0, (H) 3-0
Q2: Cray Wanderers (A) 1-2

77-78 Q1: Dover (A) 1-0
Q2: Burgess Hill Town (H) 5-0
Q3: Crawley (H) 1-1, (A) 1-1, (*at Bromley*) 4-1
Q4: Wealdstone (A) 1-2

78-79 Q1: Horsham Y.M.C.A. (H) 2-0
Q2: Dover (A) 0-0, (H) 1-0
Q3: Ramsgate (A) 3-1
Q4: Waterlooville (A) 2-1
R1: Wycombe Wanderers (H) 1-0
R2: Exeter City (A) 1-0
R3: Charlton Athletic (A) 1-1, (H) 1-2

79-80 Q4: Chesham United (A) 1-3

80-81 Q1: Ramsgate (H) 6-0
Q2: Folkestone (A) 2-0
Q3: Bromley (H) 2-0
Q4: Barking (H) 2-0
R1: Kettering Town (A) 1-1, (H) 0-0, (A) 3-1
R2: Gillingham (A) 0-0, (H) 0-0, (A) 2-0
R3: Exeter City (H) 2-4

81-82 Q4: Barking (H) 0-1

82-83 Q4: Gravesend & Northfleet (A) 2-1
R1: Weymouth (A) 3-4

83-84 Q4: Sutton United (H) 1-1, (A) 3-1
R1: Exeter City (A) 1-1, (H) 2-1
R2: Worcester City (H) 3-2
R3: Darlington (A) 1-4

84-85 Q4: Bishop's Stortford (A) 0-1

85-86 Q4: Bromley (A) 2-0
R1: Fareham Town (A) 3-0
R2: Plymouth Argyle (A) 0-3

86-87 Q4: Southwick (A) 1-1, (H) 1-1, (H) 2-2, (A) 5-1
R1: Welling United (A) 1-1, (H) 4-1
R2: Cambridge United (H) 1-0

Above: *Steve Galloway (centre) gives Maidstone the lead away to First Division Watford. Photo: Photo-News.*

R3: Watford (A) 1-3

87-88 Q4: Dartford (H) 2-0
R1: Dagenham (A) 2-0
R2: Kidderminster Harriers (H) 1-1, (A) 2-2, (A) 0-0, (H) 2-1
R3: Sheffield United (A) 0-1

88-89 R1: Newport County (A) 2-1
R2: Reading (A) 1-1, (H - *at Dartford*) 1-2

89-90 R1: Yeovil Town (H - *at Dartford*) 2-1
R2: Exeter City (H) 1-1, (A) 2-3

90-91 R1: Torquay United (H - *at Dartford*) 4-1
R2: Aldershot (A) 1-2

91-92 R1: Sutton United (H - *at Dartford*) 1-0
R2: Kettering Town (H - *at Dartford*) 1-2

MAINE ROAD

Currently: North West Counties League

89-90 PR: Glossop (A) 4-0
Q1: Burscough (A) 2-1
Q2: Colywn Bay (A - *at Rhyl F.C.*) 1-2

90-91 PR: Burscough (A) 3-0
Q1: Glossop (H) 1-0
Q2: Altrincham (H) 0-1

Below: *Maine Road 'keeper Jamie Irvine punches clear under pressure against Altrincham.*
Photo: Rob Ruddock.

68-69 Q1: Clapton (A) 1-1, (H) 2-1
Q2: Windsor & Eton (A) 2-2, (H) 3-2
Q3: Walton & Hersham (A) 0-4

69-70 Q1: Windsor & Eton (H) 4-0
Q2: Barking (H) 2-2, (A) 0-4

MALDEN VALE

Currently: Isthmian League

87-88 Q1: Witham Town (H) 1-3

88-89 PR: Redhill (A) 1-0
Q1: St Albans City (A) 0-1

89-90 Q1: Eastbourne United (A) 2-1
Q2: Whyteleafe (A) 0-2

90-91 PR: Banstead Athletic (A) 0-1

91-92 PR: Selsey (A) 1-2

92-93 PR: Merstham (A) 0-0, (H) 3-1
Q1: Deal Town (A) 0-4

MALTBY MAIN

Currently: Reformed at Maltby M.W. (see below)

46-47 PR: Denaby United (A) 1-4

47-48 PR: Appleby Frodingham Athletic (H) 1-4

48-49 EX: Beighton Miners Welfare (H) 1-3

91-92 PR: Liversedge (A) 1-3

92-93 Q1: Morecambe (H) 2-1
Q2: Seaham R.S. (A) 1-1, (H) 1-1, (H) 0-5

MALDEN TOWN

Currently: Defunct

66-67 Q1: Feltham (H) 1-0
Q2: Corinthian-Casuals (A) 1-1, (H) 2-3

67-68 Q1: Windsor & Eton (A) 1-3

49-50 EX: Cresswell Colliery (A) 0-3

50-51 PR: Steel, Peech & Tozer S.S. (A) 0-2

MALTBY MINERS WELFARE

Currently: Northern Counties (East) League

91-92 PR: Harworth Colliery Institute (A) 1-2

92-93 PR: Nantwich Town (A) 1-1, (H) 2-3

MALVERN TOWN

Currently: West Midlands (Regional) League

80-81 Q1: Worcester City (A) 1-1, (H) 0-2

81-82 Q1: Dudley Town (A) 2-0
Q2: Highgate United (H) 2-1
Q3: Bromsgrove Rovers (A) 1-4

82-83 PR: R.C. Warwick (H) 0-0, (A) 3-4

84-85 PR: Redditch United (H) 1-5

85-86 Q1: Oxford City (A) 2-7

86-87 Q1: Matlock Town (A) 3-1
Q2: Banbury United (H) 2-1
Q3: Kidderminster Harriers (H) 0-2

87-88 Q1: Atherstone United (A) 1-1, (H) 0-2

88-89 Q1: Willenhall (A) 3-3, (H) 0-0, (A) 1-0
Q2: Moor Green (H) 0-2

89-90 PR: Evesham United (A) 1-0
Q1: Barry Town (H) 1-5

90-91 PR: Soham Town Rangers (H) 3-0
Q1: Chalfont St Peter (A) 6-2
Q2: Tamworth (H) 3-3, (A) 1-5

91-92 PR: Halesowen Harriers (H) 3-2
Q1: Evesham United (A) 4-2
Q2: Alvechurch (A) 0-3

92-93 PR: Sandwell Borough (A) 0-4

MANCHESTER CITY

Currently: F.A. Premier League

45-46 R3: Barrow (H) 6-2, (A) 2-2 (*agg: 8-4*)
R4: Bradford P.A. (A) 3-1, (H) 2-8 (*agg: 5-9*)

46-47 R3: Gateshead (H) 3-0
R4: Bolton Wanderers (A) 3-3, (H) 1-0
R5: Birmingham City (A) 0-5

47-48 R3: Barnsley (H) 2-1
R4: Chelsea (H) 2-0
R5: Preston North End (H) 0-1

48-49 R3: Everton (A) 0-1

49-50 R3: Derby County (H) 3-5

50-51 R3: Birmingham City (A) 0-2

51-52 R3: Wolverhampton W. (H) 2-2, (A) 1-4

52-53 R3: Swindon Town (H) 7-0
R4: Luton Town (H) 1-1, (A) 1-5

53-54 R3: Bradford (Park Avenue) (A) 5-2
R4: Tottenham Hotspur (H) 0-1

54-55 R3: Derby County (A) 3-1
R4: Manchester United (H) 2-0
R5: Luton Town (A) 2-0
R6: Birmingham City (A) 1-0
SF: Sunderland (*at Aston Villa*) 1-0
F: Newcastle United (*at Wembley*) 1-3

55-56 R3: Blackpool (H) 2-1
R4: Southend United (A) 1-0
R5: Liverpool (H) 0-0, (A) 2-1
R6: Everton (H) 2-1
SF: Tottenham Hotspur (*at Aston Villa*) 1-0
F: Birmingham City (*at Wembley*) 3-1

56-57 R3: Newcastle United (A) 1-1, (H) 4-5

57-58 R3: West Bromwich Albion (A) 1-5

58-59 R3: Grimsby Town (A) 2-2, (H) 1-2

59-60 R3: Southampton (H) 1-5

60-61 R3: Cardiff City (A) 1-1, (H) 0-0, 2-0
R4: Luton Town (A) 6-2 *abandoned*, (A) 1-3

61-62 R3: Notts County (A) 1-0
R4: Everton (A) 0-2

62-63 R3: Walsall (A) 1-0
R4: Bury (H) 1-0
R5: Norwich City (H) 1-2

63-64 R3: Swindon Town (A) 1-2

64-65 R3: Shrewsbury Town (H) 1-1, (A) 1-3

65-66 R3: Blackpool (A) 1-1, (H) 3-1
R4: Grimsby Town (H) 2-0
R5: Leicester City (H) 2-2, (A) 1-0
R6: Everton (H) 0-0, (A) 0-0, 0-2

66-67 R3: Leicester City (H) 2-1
R4: Cardiff City (A) 1-1, (H) 3-1
R5: Ipswich Town (H) 1-1, (A) 3-0
R6: Leeds United (A) 0-1

Above: *Bert Trautman saves heroically for Manchester City in the 1956 final against Birmingham City.*
Photo: Colorsport

67-68 R3: Reading (H) 0-0, (A) 7-0
R4: Leicester City (H) 0-0, (A) 3-4

68-69 R3: Luton Town (H) 1-0
R4: Newcastle United (H) 0-0, (A) 2-0
R5: Blackburn Rovers (H) 4-1
R6: Tottenham Hotspur (H) 1-0
SF: Everton (*at Aston Villa*) 1-0
F: Leicester City (*at Wembley*) 1-0

69-70 R3: Hull City (A) 1-0
R4: Manchester Utd (A) 0-3

70-71 R3: Wigan Athletic (H) 1-0
R4: Chelsea (A) 3-0
R5: Arsenal (A) 1-2

71-72 R3: Middlesbrough (H) 1-1, (A) 0-1

72-73 R3: Stoke City (H) 3-2
R4: Liverpool (A) 0-0, (H) 2-0
R5: Sunderland (H) 2-2, (A) 1-3

73-74 R3: Oxford United (A) 5-2
R4: Nottingham Forest (A) 1-4

74-75 R3: Newcastle United (A) 0-2

75-76 R3: Hartlepool United (H) 6-0
R4: Stoke City (A) 0-1

76-77 R3: West Bromwich Albion (H) 1-1, (A) 1-0
R4: Newcastle United (A) 3-1
R5: Leeds United (A) 0-1

77-78 R3: Leeds (A) 2-1 *abandoned - score valid*
R4: Nottingham Forest (A) 1-2

78-79 R3: Rotherham United (H) 0-0, (A) 4-2
R4: Shrewsbury Town (A) 0-2

79-80 R3: Halifax Town (A) 0-1

80-81 R3: Crystal Palace (H) 4-0
R4: Norwich City (H) 6-0
R5: Peterborough United (A) 1-0
R6: Everton (A) 2-2, (H) 3-1
SF: Ipswich Town (*at Aston Villa*) 1-0
F: Tottenham H. (*both at Wembley*) 1-1, 2-3

81-82 R3: Cardiff City (H) 3-1
R4: Coventry City (H) 1-3

82-83 R3: Sunderland (A) 0-0, (H) 2-1
R4: Brighton & Hove Albion (A) 0-4

83-84 R3: Blackpool (A) 1-2

84-85 R3: Coventry City (A) 1-2

85-86 R3: Walsall (A) 3-1
R4: Watford (H) 1-1, (A) 0-0, (H) 1-3

86-87 R3: Manchester United (A) 0-1

87-88 R3: Huddersfield (A) 2-2, (H) 0-0, (A) 3-0
R4: Blackpool (A) 1-1, (H) 2-1
R5: Plymouth Argyle (H) 3-1
R6: Liverpool (H) 0-4

88-89 R3: Leicester City (H) 1-0
R4: Brentford (A) 1-3

89-90 R3: Millwall (H) 0-0, (A) 1-1, (A) 1-3

90-91 R3: Burnley (A) 1-0
R4: Port Vale (A) 2-1
R5: Notts County (A) 0-1

91-92 R3: Middlesbrough (A) 1-2

92-93 R3: Reading (H) 1-1, (A) 4-0
R4: Queens Park Rangers (A) 2-1
R5: Barnsley (H) 2-0
R6: Tottenham Hotspur (H) 2-4

MANCHESTER UNITED

Currently: F.A. Premier League

45-46 R3: Accrington S. (A) 2-2, (H) 5-1 (*agg: 7-3*)
R4: Preston N.E. (H) 1-0, (A) 1-3 (*agg: 2-3*)

46-47 R3: Bradford (Park Avenue) (A) 3-0
R4: Nottingham Forest (H) 0-2

47-48 R3: Aston Villa (A) 6-4
R4: Liverpool (H) 3-0
R5: Charlton Athletic (H) 2-0
R6: Preston North End (H) 4-1
SF: Derby Co. (*at Sheffield Wednesday*) 3-1
F: Blackpool (*at Wembley*) 4-2

48-49 R3: Bournemouth & Boscombe Ath. (H) 6-0
R4: Bradford P.A. (H) 1-1, (A) 1-1, 5-0
R5: Yeovil Town (H - *at Manchester C.*) 8-0
R6: Hull City (A) 1-0
SF: Wolves (*at Sheff. W.*) 1-1, (*at Everton*) 0-1

49-50 R3: Weymouth (H) 4-0
R4: Watford (A) 1-0
R5: Portsmouth (H) 3-3, (A) 3-1
R6: Chelsea (A) 0-2

50-51 R3: Oldham Athletic (H) 4-1
R4: Leeds United (H) 4-0
R5: Arsenal (H) 1-0
R6: Birmingham City (A) 0-1

51-52 R3: Hull City (H) 0-2

52-53 R3: Millwall (A) 1-0
R4: Walthamstow (H) 1-1, (A - *at Arsenal*) 5-2
R5: Everton (A) 1-2

53-54 R3: Burnley (A) 3-5

54-55 R3: Reading (A) 1-1, (H) 4-1
R4: Manchester City (A) 0-2

55-56 R3: Bristol Rovers (A) 0-4

56-57 R3: Hartlepools United (A) 4-3
R4: Wrexham (A) 5-0
R5: Everton (H) 1-0
R6: Bournemouth & Boscombe Ath. (A) 2-1
SF: Birmingham C. (*at Sheffield Wed.*) 2-0
F: Aston Villa (*at Wembley*) 1-2

57-58 R3: Workington (A) 3-1
R4: Ipswich Town (H) 2-0
R5: Sheffield Wednesday (H) 3-0
R6: West Bromwich Albion (A) 2-2, (H) 1-0
SF: Fulham (*at A. Villa*) 2-2, (*at Arsenal*) 5-3
F: Bolton Wanderers (*at Wembley*) 0-2

58-59 R3: Norwich City (A) 0-3

59-60 R3: Derby County (A) 4-2
R4: Liverpool (A) 3-1
R5: Sheffield Wednesday (H) 0-1

60-61 R3: Middlesbrough (H) 3-0
R4: Sheffield Wednesday (A) 1-1, (H) 2-7

61-62 R3: Bolton Wanderers (H) 2-1
R4: Arsenal (H) 1-0
R5: Sheffield Wednesday (H) 0-0, (A) 2-0
R6: Preston North End (A) 0-0, (H) 2-1
SF: Tottenham H. (*at Sheffield Wed.*) 1-3

62-63 R3: Huddersfield Town (H) 5-0
R4: Aston Villa (H) 1-0
R5: Chelsea (H) 2-1
R6: Coventry City (A) 3-1
SF: Southampton (*at Aston Villa*) 1-0
F: Leicester City (*at Wembley*) 3-1

63-64 R3: Southampton (A) 3-2
R4: Bristol Rovers (H) 4-1
R5: Barnsley (A) 4-0
R6: Sunderland (A) 3-3, (H) 2-2, 5-1
SF: West Ham Utd (*at Sheff. Wed.*) 1-3

64-65 R3: Chester (H) 2-1
R4: Stoke City (A) 0-0, (H) 1-0
R5: Burnley (H) 2-1
R6: Wolverhampton Wanderers (A) 5-3
SF: Leeds United (*at Sheffield Wednesday*) 0-0, (*at Nottingham Forest*) 0-1

65-66 R3: Derby County (A) 5-2
R4: Rotherham United (H) 0-0, (A) 1-0
R5: Wolverhampton Wanderers (A) 4-2
R6: Preston North End (A) 1-1, (H) 3-1
SF: Everton (*at Bolton Wanderers*) 0-1

66-67 R3: Stoke City (H) 2-0
R4: Norwich City (H) 1-2

67-68 R3: Tottenham Hotspur (H) 2-2, (A) 0-1

68-69 R3: Exeter City (A) 3-1
R4: Watford (H) 1-1, (A) 2-0
R5: Birmingham City (A) 2-2, (H) 6-2
R6: Everton (H) 0-1

69-70 R3: Ipswich Town (A) 1-0
R4: Manchester City (H) 3-0
R5: Northampton Town (A) 8-2
R6: Middlesbrough (A) 1-1, (H) 2-1
SF: Leeds United (*at Sheffield Wednesday*) 0-0, (*at Aston Villa*) 0-0, (*at Bolton W.*) 0-1
TP: Watford (*at Arsenal*) 2-0

70-71 R3: Middlesbrough (H) 0-0, (A) 1-2

71-72 R3: Southampton (A) 1-1, (H) 4-1
R4: Preston North End (A) 2-0
R5: Middlesbrough (H) 0-0, (A) 3-0
R6: Stoke City (H) 1-1, (A) 1-2

72-73 R3: Wolverhampton Wanderers (A) 0-1

73-74 R3: Plymouth Argyle (H) 1-0
R4: Ipswich Town (H) 0-1

74-75 R3: Walsall (H) 0-0, (A) 2-3

75-76 R3: Oxford United (H) 2-1
R4: Peterborough United (H) 3-1
R5: Leicester City (A) 2-1
R6: Wolverhampton W. (H) 1-1, (A) 3-2
SF: Derby County (*at Sheffield Wed.*) 2-0
F: Southampton (*at Wembley*) 0-1

76-77 R3: Walsall (H) 1-0
R4: Queens Park Rangers (H) 1-0
R5: Southampton (A) 2-2, (H) 2-1
R6: Aston Villa (H) 2-1
SF: Leeds United (*at Sheffield Wed.*) 2-1
F: Liverpool (*at Wembley*) 2-1

77-78 R3: Carlisle United (A) 1-1, (H) 4-2
R4: West Bromwich Albion (H) 1-1, (A) 2-3

Above: *Manchester United captain Bryan Robson (centre) tussles with Brighton's Michael Robinson during the thrilling draw with Brighton & Hove Albion at Wembley in 1983. Photo: Colorsport*

78-79 R3: Chelsea (H) 3-0
R4: Fulham (A) 1-1, (H) 1-0
R5: Colchester United (A) 1-0
R6: Tottenham Hotspur (A) 1-1, (H) 2-0
SF: Liverpool (*at Manchester City*) 2-2, (*at Everton*) 1-0
F: Arsenal (*at Wembley*) 2-3

79-80 R3: Tottenham Hotspur (A) 1-1, (H) 0-1

80-81 R3: Brighton & Hove A. (H) 2-2, (A) 2-0
R4: Nottingham Forest (A) 0-1

81-82 R3: Watford (A) 0-1

82-83 R3: West Ham United (H) 2-0
R4: Luton Town (A) 2-0
R5: Derby County (A) 1-0
R6: Everton (H) 1-0
SF: Arsenal (*at Aston Villa*) 2-1
F: Brighton (*both at Wembley*) 2-2, 4-0

83-84 R3: A.F.C. Bournemouth (A) 0-2

84-85 R3: A.F.C. Bournemouth (H) 3-0
R4: Coventry City (H) 2-1
R5: Blackburn Rovers (A) 2-0
R6: West Ham United (H) 4-2
SF: Liverpool (*at Everton*) 2-2, (*at Manchester City*) 2-1
F: Everton (*at Wembley*) 1-0

85-86 R3: Rochdale (H) 2-0
R4: Sunderland (A) 0-0, (H) 3-0
R5: West Ham United (A) 1-1, (H) 0-2

86-87 R3: Manchester City (H) 1-0
R4: Coventry City (H) 0-1

87-88 R3: Ipswich Town (A) 2-1
R4: Chelsea (H) 2-0
R5: Arsenal (A) 1-2

88-89 R3: Queens P.R. (H) 0-0, (A) 2-2, (H) 3-0
R4: Oxford United (H) 4-0
R5: A.F.C. Bournemouth (A) 1-1, (H) 1-0
R6: Nottingham Forest (H) 0-1

89-90 R3: Nottingham Forest (A) 1-0
R4: Hereford United (A) 1-0
R5: Newcastle United (A) 3-2
R6: Sheffield United (A) 1-0
SF: Oldham Ath. (*both at Man City*) 3-3, 2-1
F: Crystal Pal. (*both at Wembley*) 3-3, 1-0

90-91 R3: Queens Park Rangers (H) 2-1
R4: Bolton Wanderers (H) 1-0
R5: Norwich City (A) 1-2

91-92 R3: Leeds United (A) 1-0
R4: Southampton (A) 0-0, (H) 2-2 (*2-4 pens*)

92-93 R3: Bury (H) 2-0
R4: Brighton & Hove Albion (H) 1-0
R5: Sheffield United (A) 1-2

MANGOTSFIELD UNITED

Currently: Western League

73-74 PR: Welton Rovers (A) 4-1
Q1: Bridgend Town (A) 4-0
Q2: Llanelly (A) 2-1
Q3: Merthyr Tydfil (A) 0-2

74-75 Q1: Trowbridge Town (H) 2-1
Q2: Chippenham Town (A) 2-0
Q3: Bath City (H) 1-3

75-76 PR: Llanelli (A) 2-0
Q1: Merthyr Tydfil (H) 0-1

76-77 Q1: Frome Town (A) 5-1
Q2: Devizes Town (A) 1-0
Q3: Worcester Town (H) 0-2

77-78 PR: Clevedon Town (A) 0-4

78-79 PR: Barry Town (A) 0-2

79-80 Q1: Clevedon Town (H) 2-6

80-81 PR: Lye Town (A) 0-2

81-82 Q1: Bath City (A) 0-3

82-83 PR: Newbury Town (H) 3-2
Q1: Bridgwater Town (A) 1-1, (H) 1-2

83-84 PR: Ton Pentre (H) 3-1
Q1: Melksham Town (H) 4-0
Q2: Barry Town (A) 2-4

84-85 Q1: Highgate United (H) 0-0, (A) 3-1
Q2: Barry Town (H) 1-1, (A) 1-3

85-86 PR: Welton Rovers (A) 3-1
Q1: Frome Town (H) 1-3

86-87 Q1: Witney Town (A) 3-2
Q2: Clevedon Town (A) 0-2

87-88 Q1: Yate Town (H) 1-0
Q2: Cheltenham Town (H) 1-1, (A) 0-2

88-89 Q1: Torrington (H) 6-0
Q2: Worcester City (H) 0-1

89-90 PR: Ton Pentre (A) 2-2, (H) 1-0 *aband. after 41 minutes*, (H) 1-1, (A) 3-3, (H) 3-1
Q1: Gloucester City (A) 0-4

90-91 PR: Cwmbran Town (A - *played away*) 4-0
Q1: Bashley (H) 2-2, (A) 3-6

91-92 Q1: Cwmbran Town (H) 4-2
Q2: Trowbridge Town (A) 0-3

92-93 Q1: Dorchester Town (H) 0-1

MANSFIELD TOWN

Currently: Football League

45-46 R1: Gainsborough (H) 3-0, (A) 2-4 *(agg: 5-4)*
R2: Grantham (A) 2-1, (H) 2-1 *(agg: 4-2)*
R3: Sheffield Wed. (A) 0-5, (H) 0-0 *(agg: 0-5)*

46-47 R1: Northampton Town (A) 0-2

47-48 R1: Wimbledon (A) 1-0
R2: Oldham Athletic (A) 1-0
R3: Stoke City (H) 2-4

48-49 R1: Gloucester City (H) 4-0
R2: Northampton Town (H) 2-1
R3: Preston North End (A) 1-2

49-50 R1: Walsall (H) 4-1
R2: Doncaster Rovers (A) 0-1

50-51 R1: Walthamstow Avenue (H) 1-0
R2: Chelmsford City (A) 4-1
R3: Swansea Town (H) 2-0
R4: Sheffield United (A) 0-0, (H) 2-1
R5: Blackpool (A) 0-2

51-52 R1: Stockton (A) 1-1, (H) 0-2

52-53 R1: Scarborough (A) 8-0
R2: Accrington Stanley (A) 2-0
R3: Nottingham Forest (H) 0-1

53-54 R1: Hartlepools United (A) 1-1, (H) 0-3

54-55 R1: Bradford City (A) 1-3

55-56 R1: Stockport County (H) 2-0
R2: York City (A) 1-2

56-57 R1: Workington (H) 1-1, (A) 1-2

57-58 R1: Halifax Town (H) 2-0
R2: Wigan Athletic (A) 1-1, (H) 3-1
R3: Bristol Rovers (A) 0-5

58-59 R1: Bradford City (H) 3-4

59-60 R1: Accrington Stanley (A) 2-1
R2: Chester (H) 2-0
R3: Blackpool (A) 0-3

60-61 R1: Blyth Spartans (H) 3-1
R2: Accrington Stanley (A) 0-3

61-62 R1: Grimsby Town (H) 3-2
R2: Southport (A) 2-4

62-63 R1: Hounslow (A) 3-3, (H) 9-2
R2: Crystal Palace (A) 2-2, (H) 7-2
R3: Ipswich Town (H) 2-3

63-64 R1: Oldham Athletic (A) 2-3

64-65 R1: Oxford United (A) 1-0
R2: Newport County (A) 0-3

65-66 R1: Oldham Athletic (H) 1-3

66-67 R1: Bangor City (H) 4-1
R2: Scunthorpe United (H) 2-1
R3: Middlesbrough (H) 2-0
R4: Sheffield Wednesday (A) 0-4

67-68 R1: Tow Law Town (A) 1-5

68-69 R1: Tow Law Town (H) 4-1
R2: Rotherham United (A) 2-2, (H) 1-0
R3: Sheffield United (H) 2-1
R4: Southend United (H) 2-1
R5: West Ham United (H) 3-0
R6: Leicester City (H) 0-1

69-70 R1: Bury (A) 2-2, (H) 2-0
R2: Shrewsbury Town (A) 2-1
R3: Barnsley (H) 3-2
R4: Blackpool (A) 2-0
R5: Leeds United (H) 0-2

70-71 R1: Wrexham (H) 2-0
R2: Scunthorpe United (A) 0-3

71-72 R1: Chester (A) 1-1, (H) 4-3
R2: Tranmere Rovers (H) 2-2, (A) 2-4

72-73 R1: York City (A) 1-2

73-74 R1: York City (A) 0-0, (H) 5-3
R2: Scunthorpe United (H) 1-1, (A) 0-1

74-75 R1: Wrexham (H) 3-1
R2: Wigan Athletic (A) 1-1, (H) 3-1
R3: Cambridge United (H) 1-0
R4: Bury (A) 2-1
R5: Carlisle United (H) 0-1

75-76 R1: Wrexham (H) 1-1, (A) 1-1, *(at Aston V.)* 2-1
R2: Lincoln City (H) 1-2

76-77 R1: Huddersfield Town (A) 0-0, (H) 2-1
R2: Matlock Town (H) 2-5

77-78 R3: Plymouth Argyle (H) 1-0
R4: Bolton Wanderers (A) 0-1

78-79 R1: Shrewsbury Town (H) 0-2

79-80 R1: Blyth Spartans (A) 2-0
R2: Doncaster Rovers (A) 2-1
R3: Brighton & Hove Albion (H) 0-2

80-81 R1: Rochdale (H) 3-1
R2: Mossley (A) 3-1
R3: Carlisle United (H) 2-2, (A) 1-2

81-82 R1: Doncaster Rovers (H) 0-1

82-83 R1: Stockport County (H) 3-2
R2: Bradford City (H) 1-1, (A) 2-3

83-84 R1: Doncaster Rovers (H) 3-0
R2: Bolton Wanderers (A) 0-2

84-85 R1: Rotherham United (H) 2-1
R2: Bradford City (A) 1-2

85-86 R1: Port Vale (H) 1-1, (A) 0-1

86-87 R1: Darlington (A) 1-2

87-88 R1: Preston North End (A) 1-1, (H) 4-2
R2: Lincoln City (H) 4-3
R3: Bath City (H) 4-0
R4: Wimbledon (H) 1-2

88-89 R1: Sheffield United (H) 1-1, (A) 1-2

89-90 R1: Wigan Athletic (A) 0-2

90-91 R1: Preston North End (A) 1-0
R2: York City (H) 2-1
R3: Sheffield Wednesday (H) 0-2

91-92 R1: Preston (H) 1-1 *ab. 32 mins - fog,* (H) 0-1

92-93 R1: Shrewsbury Town (A) 1-3

MARCH TOWN UNITED

Currently: Eastern Counties League

47-48 PR: Wisbech Town (H) 4-2
Q1: Newmarket Town (A) 3-2
Q2: Histon Institute (H) 1-0
Q3: Bury Town (A) 0-3

48-49 Q1: Histon Institute (A) 1-2

49-50 PR: Parson Drove United (H) 4-1
Q1: King's Lynn (A) 2-3

50-51 Q1: Wisbech Town (A) 2-0
Q2: King's Lynn (A) 0-6

51-52 Q1: Cambridge United (H) 1-1, (A) 4-3
Q2: St Neots & District (H) 1-0
Q3: King's Lynn (H) 1-4

52-53 Q1: Cambridge United (A) 1-3

53-54 Q1: King's Lynn (H) 3-1
Q2: Wisbech Town (A) 1-4

54-55 PR: Chatteris Town (A) 3-1
Q1: Cambridge City (H) 1-0
Q2: Thetford Town (A) 3-0
Q3: King's Lynn (A) 3-1
Q4: Bedford Town (A) 2-5

55-56 PR: Cambridge City (A) 2-2, (H) 3-1
Q1: St Neots & District (H) 3-1
Q2: King's Lynn (A) 1-1, (H) 1-0
Q3: Wisbech Town (A) 1-1, (H) 2-0
Q4: Great Yarmouth Town (H) 1-0
R1: Brentford (A) 0-4

56-57 PR: Newmarket Town (A) 6-1
Q1: Wisbech Town (A) 0-0, (H) 2-1
Q2: King's Lynn (H) 4-1
Q3: Ely City (A) 0-2

57-58 PR: Thetford Town (H) 3-1
Q1: Soham Town Rangers (H) 4-2
Q2: Cambridge United (H) 4-1
Q3: Wisbech Town (H) 1-2

58-59 PR: Chatteris Town (H) 5-2
Q1: St Neots Town (H) 0-1

59-60 Q1: Chatteris Town (A) 2-1
Q2: Cambridge City (A) 1-5

60-61 Q1: Histon (A) 2-1
Q2: Cambridge United (A) 3-7

61-62 Q1: Newmarket Town (H) 0-2

62-63 Q1: Ely City (H) 4-1
Q2: Sudbury Town (H) 1-3

63-64 Q1: Chatteris Town (A) 0-4

64-65 Q1: Wisbech Town (H) 1-3

65-66 Q1: Bury Town (H) 1-2

66-67 Q1: Chatteris Town (H) 4-3
Q2: Rushden Town (A) 0-4

67-68 Q1: Cambridge United (A) 0-6

68-69 PR: Cambridge United (H) 1-1, (A) 0-5

69-70 PR: Newmarket Town (H) 1-1, (A) 0-3

70-71 Q1: Chatteris Town (H) 2-1
Q2: Soham Town Rangers (A) 0-2

71-72 PR: Skegness Town (H) 1-2

72-73 Q1: Wisbech Town (H) 1-1, (A) 0-3

73-74 Q1: Great Yarmouth (H) 2-2, (A) 2-2, 0-1

74-75 Q1: Soham Town Rangers (H) 2-1
Q2: St Neots Town (A) 3-2
Q3: Corby Town (H) 0-4

75-76 Q1: Cambridge City (A) 1-5

76-77 PR: Stowmarket (H) 0-3

77-78 Q1: Skegness Town (H) 2-1
Q2: Arnold (H) 3-8

78-79 Q1: Chatteris Town (H) 4-1
Q2: Harwich & Parkeston (A) 1-1, (H) 2-1
Q3: St Neots Town (A) 3-2
Q4: Southall & Ealing Borough (H) 2-1
R1: Swindon Town (A) 0-2

79-80 Q1: Felixstowe Town (A) 2-3

80-81 PR: Stamford (H) 2-1
Q1: Gainsborough Trinity (H) 1-2

81-82 PR: Soham Town Rangers (H) 1-1, (A) 4-0
Q1: St Neots Town (H) 1-0
Q2: Newmarket Town (H) 5-5, (A) 2-0
Q3: Wisbech Town (A) 1-2

82-83 PR: Cambridge City (A) 0-0, (H) 3-2
Q1: Skegness Town (A) 0-3

83-84 PR: Bromsgrove Rovers (H) 3-2
Q1: Walsall Borough (A) 2-1
Q2: Dudley Town (H) 3-2
Q3: Wellingborough Town (A) 0-1

84-85 Q1: Aveley (A) 0-5

85-86 PR: Royston Town (A) 7-2
Q1: Rushden Town (A) 3-2
Q2: Hinckley Athletic (H) 1-2

86-87 PR: Histon (H) 1-1, (A) 1-1, (H) 3-2
Q1: Wootton Blue Cross (A) 2-1
Q2: Bedworth United (H) 1-0
Q3: Bromsgrove Rovers (A) 0-1

87-88 Q1: King's Lynn (A) 2-1
Q2: Haverhill Rovers (A) 1-0
Q3: Letchworth G.C. (A) 2-2, (H) 2-3

88-89 PR: Berkhamsted Town (A) 2-2, (H) 4-2
Q1: Alvechurch (H) 1-2

89-90 PR: Chatteris Town (H) 5-0
Q1: Rothwell Town (A) 2-0
Q2: Bromsgrove Rovers (A) 0-4

90-91 Q1: Sandwell B. (H) 1-1, (A) 2-2, (A) 0-1

91-92 PR: Histon (H) 1-1, (A) 1-2

92-93 PR: Braintree Town (H) 1-3

MARGATE

Currently: Southern League
* - As Thanet United

46-47 PR: Maidstone United (A) 1-3

47-48 PR: Chatham Town (H) 3-0
Q1: Dartford (H) 0-3

48-49 EX: Canterbury City (H) 3-1
PR: Sheppey United (A) 4-5

49-50 EX: Faversham Town (H) 1-3

50-51 EX: Ashford Town (H) 1-2

51-52 PR: Canterbury City (H) 6-1
Q1: Folkestone (A) 1-3

52-53 PR: Gravesend & Northfleet (H) 1-4

53-54 PR: Gravesend & Northfleet (H) 5-1
Q1: Maidstone United (A) 3-1
Q2: Kingstonian (A) 1-2

54-55 PR: Erith & Belvedere (A) 4-0
Q1: Bromley (H) 4-2
Q2: Tonbridge (A) 2-2, (H) 0-1

55-56 PR: Bromley (A) 1-0
Q1: Gravesend & Northfleet (A) 2-1
Q2: Maidstone United (A) 4-1
Q3: Epsom (A) 3-1
Q4: Headington United (A) 4-2
R1: Walsall (H) 2-2, (A) 1-6

56-57 PR: Sheppey United (H) 8-1
Q1: Snowdown C.W. (A) 2-2, (H) 1-0
Q2: Canterbury City (H) 2-0
Q3: Sittingbourne (A) 3-2
Q4: Wycombe Wanderers (A) 4-2
R1: Dunstable Town (H) 3-1
R2: Millwall (A) 0-4

57-58 Q4: Headington United (A) 2-0
R1: Crystal Palace (H) 2-3

58-59 Q4: Gravesend & Northfleet (A) 0-0, (H) 4-3
R1: Headington United (A) 2-3

59-60 Q4: Guildford City (H) 1-0
R1: Kettering Town (A) 1-1, (H) 3-2
R2: Crystal Palace (H) 0-0, (A) 0-3

60-61 Q4: Ashford Town (A) 1-1, (H) 1-2

61-62 Q4: Guildford City (H) 6-2
R1: Bournemouth & Boscombe Athletic (A) 3-0
R2: Notts County (H) 1-1, (A) 1-3

62-63 Q4: Ashford Town (H) 2-0
R1: Millwall (A) 1-3

63-64 Q4: Tonbridge (H) 2-1
R1: Brentford (A) 2-2, (H) 0-2

64-65 Q4: Gravesend & Northfleet (A) 0-1

65-66 Q1: Folkestone Town (A) 1-2

66-67 Q1: Chatham Town (H) 2-1
Q2: Tunbridge Wells Rangers (A) 4-0
Q3: Ashford Town (A) 0-1

67-68 Q1: Hastings United (A) 1-0
Q2: Deal Town (A) 4-1
Q3: Ramsgate Athletic (H) 6-4
Q4: Eastbourne (A) 9-0
R1: Yeovil Town (A) 3-1
R2: Peterborough United (H) 0-4

68-69 Q1: Folkestone (H) 3-1
Q2: Sheppey United (A) 6-0
Q3: Hastings United (H) 4-0
Q4: Walton & Hersham (H) 1-0
R1: Northampton Town (A) 1-3

69-70 Q4: Littlehampton Town (A) 1-0
R1: Aldershot (H) 2-7

70-71 Q4: Herne Bay (A) 1-0
R1: Dagenham (A) 0-2

71-72 Q4: Wimbledon (H) 1-0
R1: A.F.C. Bournemouth (A) 0-11

72-73 Q4: Sutton United (H) 2-0
R1: Swansea City (H) 1-0
R2: Walton & Hersham (A) 1-0
R3: Tottenham Hotspur (H) 0-6

73-74 Q4: Leytonstone (A) 0-0, (H) 1-3

74-75 Q4: Wycombe Wanderers (A) 1-2

75-76 Q1: Bexhill Town (A) 8-0
Q2: Eastbourne Town (A) 2-0
Q3: Canterbury City (A) 0-2

76-77 PR: Sittingbourne (H) 2-2, (A) 1-0
Q1: Sheppey United (A) 2-2, (H) 2-0
Q2: Folkestone (H) 2-2, (A) 4-2, rep: (A) 4-3
Q3: Dover (A) 2-3

77-78 Q1: Hastings United (A) 2-2, (H) 1-2

78-79 PR: Redhill (H) 2-0
Q1: Three Bridges (A) 2-0
Q2: Croydon (A) 2-0
Q3: Folkestone & Shepway (A) 2-0
Q4: Woking (H) 1-7

79-80 Q1: Bromley (H) 4-1
Q2: Dulwich Hamlet (H) 1-0
Q3: Chatham Town (A) 1-0
Q4: Harlow Town (A) 0-1

80-81 Q1: Sittingbourne (H) 1-1, (A) 4-3
Q2: Epsom & Ewell (A) 1-3

81-82 * PR: Southwick (A) 1-0
Q1: Deal Town (H) 2-2, (A) 1-2

82-83 * Q1: Hailsham Town (A) 3-0
Q2: Hastings United (A) 2-1
Q3: Bognor Regis Town (A) 0-3

83-84 * Q1: Pagham (H) 1-1, (A) 1-0
Q2: Tooting & Mitcham (H) 0-7

84-85 * Q1: Sittingbourne (H) 2-3

85-86 * PR: Chichester City (H) 3-1
Q1: Bromley (H) 2-2, (A) 1-2

86-87 * PR: Lewes (H) 0-2

87-88 * PR: Canterbury City (H) 3-0
Q1: Merstham (A) 3-1
Q2: Littlehampton Town (A) 3-0
Q3: Woking (H) 1-1, (A) 2-0
Q4: Bognor Regis Town (H) 0-4

88-89 * Q1: Portfield (H) 1-0
Q2: Fisher Athletic (H) 1-3

89-90 PR: Wick (H) 2-1
Q1: Egham Town (A) 1-0
Q2: Wokingham Town (A) 0-1

90-91 PR: Ramsgate (A) 1-0
Q1: Gravesend & Northfleet (H) 2-2, (A) 4-1
Q2: Whitehawk (A) 1-0
Q3: Peacehaven & Telscombe (A) 0-1

91-92 Q1: Tooting & Mitcham United (A) 1-2

92-93 PR: Tunbridge Wells (A) 4-0
Q1: Corinthian (H) 0-0, (A) 1-1, (A) 4-0
Q2: Chertsey Town (H) 1-4

MARINE

Currently: Northern Premier League

45-46 Q4: Witton Albion (A) 3-2
R1: Stalybridge (H) 4-0, (A) 3-3 *(agg: 7-3)*
R2: Port Vale (A) 1-3, (H) 1-1 *(agg: 2-4)*

46-47 Q4: Haydock C. & B. Rec. (H) 7-0
R1: Wrexham (A) 0-5

47-48 Q4: Wigan Athletic (H) 3-1
R1: New Brighton (A) 0-4

48-49 PR: Burscough (A) 2-4

49-50 EX: Formby (H) 1-0
PR: Burscough (A) 1-2

50-51 PR: Stoneycroft (A) 5-3
Q1: Crompton's Recreation (H) 0-1

51-52 PR: Liverpool Police (H) 4-0
Q1: Runcorn (A) 1-2

52-53 PR: Ellesmere Port Town (H) 3-3, (A) 1-2

53-54 Q1: Pwllheli & District (H) 1-1, (A) 0-4

54-55 PR: Earlestown (H) 4-0
Q1: Ellesmere Port Town (H) 1-0
Q2: Flint Town United (A) 1-5

55-56 PR: Prescot Cables (A) 3-4

56-57 PR: St Helens Town (A) 2-2, (H) 2-1
Q1: New Brighton (H) 1-3

57-58 Q1: Stork (H) 0-1

58-59 PR: Flint Town United (A) 3-4

59-60 PR: New Brighton (A) 0-1

60-61 Q1: Horwich R.M.I. (H) 2-0
Q2: Wigan Athletic (H) 1-5

61-62 Q1: Altrincham (A) 3-3, (H) 2-2, 0-1

62-63 Q1: Altrincham (A) 0-1

63-64 Q1: Skelmersdale United (H) 2-2, (A) 0-3

64-65 Q1: Altrincham (H) 1-3

65-66 Q1: Droylsden (A) 3-3, (H) 1-0
Q2: Altrincham (A) 0-4

66-67 Q1: Kirkby Town (A) 0-2

67-68 Q1: Oswestry Town (H) 2-3

68-69 Q1: Rhyl (H) 0-0, (A) 1-0
Q2: South Liverpool (A) 1-2

69-70 Q1: South Liverpool (H) 2-3

70-71 PR: Prescot Town (H) 2-1
Q1: Sandbach Ramblers (A) 2-0
Q2: Skelmersdale United (A) 1-2

71-72 Q1: Chorley (A) 0-3

72-73 Q1: New Brighton (A) 4-1
Q2: Oswestry Town (H) 3-1
Q3: South Liverpool (H) 0-2

73-74 Q1: Blaenau Ffestiniog (H) 0-0, (A) 0-0, 1-0
Q2: Runcorn (A) 0-0, (H) 0-1

74-75 PR: Ormskirk (A) *W/O*
Q1: Witton Albion (H) 4-1
Q2: Winsford United (H) 1-1, (A) 4-1
Q3: Sandbach Ramblers (A) 1-0
Q4: Telford United (H) 2-1
R1: Rochdale (A) 0-0, (H) 1-2

75-76 Q1: Formby (A) 1-0
Q2: Bangor City (H) 1-0
Q3: Runcorn (A) 0-0, (H) 1-0
Q4: Worksop Town (A) 0-0, (H) 4-0
R1: Barnsley (H) 3-1
R2: Hartlepool United (H) 1-1, (A) 3-6

76-77 Q4: Barrow (H) 1-1, (A) 1-3

77-78 Q4: Wigan Athletic (H) 0-3

78-79 PR: Macclesfield Town (H) 4-2
Q1: Porthmadog (A) 1-3

79-80 Q1: Congleton Town (H) 4-0
Q2: Mexborough Town Athletic (A) 1-0
Q3: Ashton United (H) 4-0
Q4: Blyth Spartans (A) 2-2, (H) 0-5

80-81 Q1: Rhyl (H) 3-0
Q2: Colwyn Bay (A) 2-2, (H) 4-0
Q3: Chorley (H) 3-0
Q4: Gateshead (H) 1-0 *expelled*

81-82 PR: Prestwich Heys (H) 2-0
Q1: Formby (H) 4-0
Q2: Lytham (H) 0-0, (A) 6-2
Q3: Hyde United (A) 1-3

82-83 Q1: Prescot Cables (A) 1-2

83-84 Q1: Heanor Town (H) 3-2
Q2: Macclesfield Town (H) 0-3

84-85 Q1: Bootle (A) 2-0
Q2: Barrow (H) 3-0
Q3: Denaby United (A) 1-0
Q4: Whitby Town (H) 0-1

85-86 Q1: Sutton Town (A) 2-2, (H) 6-0
Q2: Radcliffe Borough (A) 4-0
Q3: Goole Town (A) 5-0
Q4: Chorley (A) 2-4

86-87 Q1: Caernarfon Town (A) 0-2

87-88 Q1: Bangor City (A) 2-2, (H) 3-1
Q2: Bootle (A) 2-2, (H) 1-0
Q3: Macclesfield Town (A) 0-0, (H) 1-2

88-89 Q1: Thackley (H) 5-0
Q2: Fleetwood Town (H) 2-4

89-90 Q1: Eastwood Hanley (H) 1-1, (A) 2-1
Q2: Rossendale United (H) 2-1
Q3: Hyde United (A) 1-0
Q4: Chorley (A) 1-1, (H) 0-0, (H) 3-0
R1: Rochdale (H - *at Liverpool F.C.*) 0-1

90-91 Q1: Willenhall (A) 0-0, (H) 2-2, (H) 4-1
Q2: Worksop Town (A - *at Gainsborough*) 3-1
Q3: Leicester United (A) 2-0
Q4: Stafford Rangers (H) 1-1, (A) 1-2

91-92 Q1: Liversedge (H) 4-0
Q2: Warrington Town (A) 0-0, (H) 1-0
Q3: Colwyn Bay (A) 3-4

92-93 Q1: Emley (H) 5-0
Q2: Heanor Town (H) 2-0
Q3: Nantwich Town (A) 1-0
Q4: Runcorn (A) 4-1
R1: Halifax Town (H) 4-1
R2: Stafford Rangers (H) 3-2
R3: Crewe Alexandra (A) 1-3

Opposite: *Marine battled their way through to the Third Round in 1992-93 but were unfortunate to draw Crewe who were neither a glamour side nor a 'push-over'. They fell behind to three early goals at Gresty Road, but fought back and here goalkeeper Dean Greygoose is seen clutching the ball under pressure from Marine forward Chris Camden (left). Photo: Keith Clayton.*

MARLOW

Currently: Isthmian League

45-46 PR: Yiewsley (H) 3-4

46-47 EX: Wycombe Wanderers (A) 0-2

47-48 EX: Maidenhead United (H) 0-2

48-49 EX: Slough Centre (H) 2-3

49-50 EX: Hemel Hempstead Town (A) 0-6

50-51 EX: Aylesbury United (H) 2-4

51-52 PR: Hemel Hempstead Town (H) 4-3
Q1: Aylesbury United (A) 1-4

52-53 PR: Headington United (H) 0-8

53-54 Q1: Chesham United (A) 0-2

54-55 PR: Maidenhead United (A) 2-2, (H) 0-2

55-56 PR: Maidenhead United (H) 1-2

56-57 Q1: Windsor & Eton (H) 6-1
Q2: Witney Town (A) 1-1, (H) 0-4

57-58 Q1: Huntley & Palmers Recreation (H) 4-1
Q2: Chesham United (A) 2-2, (H) 5-1
Q3: Headington United (A) 0-1

58-59 PR: Windsor & Eton (A) 3-4

59-60 Q1: Banbury Spencer (H) 0-3

60-61 Q1: Slough Town (H) 0-1

61-62 Q1: Tooting & Mitcham United (A) 1-7

62-63 Q1: Carshalton Athletic (A) 0-4

63-64 Q1: Tooting & Mitcham United (A) 0-5

64-65 Q1: Epsom & Ewell (H) 1-7

65-66 Q1: Metropolitan Police (H) 0-4

66-67 Q1: Finchley (A) 1-4

67-68 Q1: Letchworth Town (H) 3-1
Q2: Wembley (H) 0-3

68-69 PR: Banbury United (H) 1-4

69-70 PR: Maidenhead United (H) 4-1
Q1: Dunstable Town (A) 2-4

70-71 Q1: St Albans City (A) 0-2

71-72 Q1: Wembley (H) 0-3

72-73 Q1: Sutton United (A) 1-5

73-74 PR: Wealdstone (A) 0-2

74-75 PR: Aylesbury Utd (H) 3-3, (A) 1-1, 1-0
Q1: Wycombe Wanderers (H) 0-1

75-76 Q1: Wokingham Town (H) 2-0
Q2: Tonbridge (A) 2-2, (H) 1-3

76-77 PR: Milton Keynes City (H) 0-0, (A) 1-0
Q1: Carshalton Athletic (H) 1-2

77-78 PR: Hatfield Town (A) 2-1
Q1: Basingstoke Town (A) 0-2

78-79 Q1: Feltham (H) 1-1, (A) 0-3

79-80 PR: Bracknell Town (H) 2-3

Above: *Marlow scorer David Lay is 'collared' by Tottenham's Dean Austin as the Diadora Isthmian League club enjoy an unforgettable afternoon at White Hart Lane on 2nd January 1993. Photo: Dennis Nicholson.*

80-81 Q1: Harrow Borough (H) 1-2

81-82 PR: Egham T. (A) 1-1, (H) 1-1, (A) 4-7

82-83 PR: A.F.C. Totton (A) 0-1

83-84 PR: Tonbridge A.F.C. (A) 0-3

84-85 PR: Salisbury (A) 1-3

85-86 Q1: Leytonstone-Ilford (A) 2-0
Q2: Ware (H) 2-3

86-87 Q1: Wokingham Town (A) 0-4

87-88 Q1: Tunbridge Wells (H) 5-1
Q2: Basingstoke Town (H) 1-1, (A) 1-2

88-89 Q1: Ruislip (A) 1-1, (H) 3-0
Q2: Dulwich Hamlet (A) 0-1

89-90 Q1: Pagham (A) 1-0
Q2: Andover (H) 3-2
Q3: Newport Isle of Wight (A) 1-0
Q4: Basingstoke Town (A) 1-1, (H) 1-2

90-91 Q1: Merstham (H) 3-0
Q2: Royston Town (H) 2-2, (A) 2-0
Q3: Andover (A) 1-0
Q4: Yeovil Town (A) 1-3

91-92 Q1: Camberley Town (A) 3-1
Q2: Havant Town (H) 2-1
Q3: Romsey Town (H) 2-0
Q4: Worcester City (A) 2-1
R1: West Bromwich Albion (A) 0-6

92-93 Q4: Sittingbourne (A) 1-1, (H) 2-1
R1: Salisbury (H) 3-3, (A) 2-2, (*4-3 pens*)
R2: V.S. Rugby (A) 0-0, (H) 2-0
R3: Tottenham Hotspur (H - *played away*) 1-5

MARSDEN

Currently: West Riding County Amateur League

50-51 EX: Meltham (H) 3-2
PR: Yorkshire Amateur (A) 0-2

MARSTON SHELTON ROVERS

Currently: Bedford & District League

50-51 EX: Bedford Corinthians (H) 3-0
PR: Hitchin Town (A) 1-2

MATLOCK TOWN

Currently: Northern Premier League

46-47 PR: Sheffield (H) 2-5

47-48 EX: Armthorpe Welfare (A) 1-3

48-49 PR: Congleton Town (H) 3-8

49-50 EX: Port Sunlight (H) 0-2

50-51 PR: Stalybridge Celtic (H) 2-4

51-52 Q1: Newhall United (A) 0-4

52-53 Q1: Newhall United (A) 2-3

53-54 Q1: Boots Athletic (A) 5-0
Q2: Gresley Rovers (A) 0-2

54-55 Q1: Gedling Colliery (H) 1-1, (A) 1-6

57-58 Q1: Gresley Rovers (H) 2-3

58-59 Q1: Norton Woodseats Amateur (A) 1-4

59-60 Q1: Stocksbridge Works (A) 3-1
Q2: Worksop Town (H) 3-1
Q3: Belper Town (A) 3-2
Q4: Ilkeston Town (A) 6-2
R1: Crook Town (A) 2-2, (H) 0-1

60-61 PR: Cresswell Colliery Welfare (H) 6-0
Q1: Heanor Town (H) 0-1

61-62 Q1: Arnold St Mary's (A) 5-1
Q2: Heanor Town (A) 2-4

62-63 Q1: Arnold St Mary's (A) 2-3

63-64 Q1: Arnold St Mary's (H) 4-1
Q2: Belper Town (A) 3-2
Q3: Heanor Town (H) 0-1

64-65 Q1: Creswell Colliery (H) 4-1
Q2: Arnold (H) 1-3

65-66 Q1: Arnold (A) 1-1, (H) 2-2, 2-1
Q2: Worksop Town (H) 1-3

66-67 Q1: Long Eaton United (A) 4-2
Q2: Macclesfield Town (H) 2-2, (A) 1-6

67-68 Q1: Alfreton Town (A) 2-1
Q2: Eastwood (Hanley) (H) 4-1
Q3: Tamworth (H) 2-0

Q4: Nuneaton Borough (A) 0-1

68-69 Q1: Alfreton Town (A) 2-1
Q2: Sutton Town (A) 1-0
Q3: Buxton (A) 3-0
Q4: Bilston (A) 0-2

69-70 PR: Ilkeston Town (A) 2-1
Q1: Eastwood (Hanley) (A) 3-2
Q2: Rawmarsh Welfare (H) 2-2, (A) 2-3

70-71 Q1: Retford Town (A) 1-2

71-72 Q1: Sutton Town (H) 1-3

72-73 Q1: Sutton Town (H) 1-1, (A) 2-3

73-74 PR: Heanor Town (H) 3-0
Q1: Arnold (A) 1-1, (H) 3-4

74-75 Q1: Brigg Town (A) 1-0
Q2: Gainsborough Trinity (H) 2-1
Q3: Worksop Town (H) 6-2
Q4: Bangor City (H) 3-0
R1: Blackburn Rovers (H) 1-4

75-76 R1: Wigan Athletic (A) 1-4

76-77 Q4: Telford United (A) 5-2
R1: Wigan Athletic (H) 2-0
R2: Mansfield Town (A) 5-2
R3: Carlisle United (A) 1-5

77-78 Q4: Goole Town (A) 1-2

78-79 Q4: Nuneaton (A) 2-2, (H) 2-2, (*Stafford*) 1-2

79-80 Q1: Buxton (A) 1-3

80-81 Q1: Oldbury United (A) 0-4

81-82 PR: Colwyn B. (A) 3-3, (H) 2-2, (*Mossley*) 4-1
Q1: Shifnal Town (H) 1-1, (A) 0-2

82-83 PR: Dudley Town (H) 0-2

83-84 Q1: Winsford United (H) 2-2, (A) 1-2

84-85 Q1: Boston (A) 4-1
Q2: Eastwood Town (H) 2-0
Q3: Goole Town (A) 2-4

85-86 Q1: Spalding (A) 2-2, (H) 0-0, (H) 3-2
Q2: Alfreton Town (A) 0-2

86-87 Q1: Malvern Town (H) 1-3

87-88 Q1: Gainsborough Trinity (H) 3-3, (A) 3-0
Q2: Arnold (A) 3-2
Q3: Moor Green (A) 2-3

88-89 Q1: Walsall Wood (H) 2-3

89-90 Q1: Rushall Olympic (A) 1-0
Q2: Willenhall Town (H) 5-0
Q3: Boston United (H) 1-1, (A) 1-0
Q4: Enfield (H) 3-1
R1: Scunthorpe United (A) 1-4

90-91 Q1: West Midlands Police (A) 6-0
Q2: Corby Town (A) 0-2

91-92 Q1: Bridgnorth Town (A) 2-1
Q2: Solihull Borough (H) 2-1
Q3: Tamworth (H) 0-2

92-93 Q1: Rothwell Town (A) 2-0
Q2: Nuneaton Borough (A) 1-2

McLAREN SPORTS

See Petter Sports

MEASHAM IMPERIAL

Currently: Defunct

49-50 EX: Boots Athletic (A) 2-1
PR: Sutton Town (A) 2-3

MEDWAY

See Chatham Town

MELKSHAM TOWN

Currently: Wiltshire League
* - As Melksham F.C.

46-47 * EX: Spencer Moulton (A) 4-2
PR: Swindon Victoria (H) 4-1
Q1: Swindon G.W.R. Corinthians (H) 3-2
Q2: Hoffmann Ath. (Stonehouse) (A) 1-5

47-48 * PR: Swindon Victoria (A) 2-4

48-49 * EX: Devizes Town (A) 1-2

49-50 * PR: Swindon Corinthians (H) 2-1

Q1: Paulton Rovers (H) 3-8

51-52 PR: Calne & Harris United (A) 0-4

52-53 PR: Warminster Town (H) 0-2

53-54 PR: Andover (H) 1-5

54-55 Q1: Westbury United (A) 2-1
Q2: Swindon Victoria (H) 4-2
Q3: Frome Town (H) 0-2

55-56 PR: Warminster Town (A) 1-3

56-57 Q1: Westbury United (H) 2-2, (A) 2-4

57-58 Q1: Frome Town (H) 0-0, (A) 3-2
Q2: Warminster Town (H) 7-2
Q3: Trowbridge Town (H) 0-6

58-59 Q1: Chippenham United (H) 1-6

59-60 Q1: Trowbridge Town (H) 2-4

60-61 Q1: Westbury United (H) 3-2
Q2: Chippenham United (H) 2-5

61-62 Q1: Calne & Harris United (H) 6-0
Q2: Cheltenham Town (A) 2-5

62-63 Q1: Devizes Town (H) 0-5

63-64 Q1: Chippenham Town (H) 0-2

64-65 Q1: Cheltenham Town (H) 0-4

65-66 Q1: Chippenham Town (A) 1-5

66-67 Q1: Trowbridge Town (H) 0-4

67-68 Q2: Poole Town (A) 0-5

68-69 PR: Poole Town (A) 0-4

69-70 PR: Glastonbury (A) 1-5

71-72 Q1: Andover (H) 1-3

72-73 PR: Welton Rovers (A) 0-2

73-74 Q1: Chippenham Town (H) 4-2
Q2: Basingstoke Town (H) 0-6

74-75 Q1: Chippenham Town (A) 0-3

75-76 PR: Devizes Town (H) 2-0
Q1: Weston-super-Mare (A) 0-3

76-77 Q1: Cinderford Town (A) 1-1, (H) 0-1

77-78 PR: Welton Rovers (H) 1-0
Q1: Barry Town (A) 1-4

78-79 Q1: Gloucester City (H) 1-0
Q2: Cheltenham Town (A) 0-6

79-80 PR: Trowbridge Town (H) 1-3

80-81 Q1: Ilminster Town (H) 7-0
Q2: Ton Pentre (H) 0-3

81-82 Q1: Gosport Borough (A) 1-0
Q2: Eastleigh (A) 1-3

82-83 PR: Cinderford Town (A) 0-3

83-84 Q1: Mangotsfield United (A) 0-4

84-85 Q1: Road Sea Southampton (H) 0-3

85-86 PR: Newbury Town (A) 1-2

86-87 PR: Shortwood United (A) 3-2
Q1: Trowbridge Town (A) 2-3

87-88 PR: Andover (H) 2-0
Q1: Wimborne Town (H) 1-3

88-89 Q1: Gloucester City (H) 0-5

89-90 Q1: Swanage Town & Herston (A) 0-4

90-91 PR: Keynsham Town (H) 2-1
Q1: Calne Town (H) 2-1
Q2: Newport Isle of Wight (H) 0-2

91-92 PR: Welton Rovers (H) 1-1, (A) 2-1
Q1: Worcester City (H) 1-8

92-93 PR: Swanage Town & Herston (H) 1-5

MELTHAM

Currently: Defunct
* - As Meltham Mills F.C.

45-46 * Q1: South Kirkby Colliery (H) 1-7

46-47 * PR: Selby Town (A) 0-6

47-48 * PR: Ossett Town (A) 1-5

48-49 * EX: Hessle Old Boys (A) 3-2
PR: Yorkshire Amateur (A) 1-2

49-50 EX: Brodsworth (H - *played away*) 2-3

50-51 EX: Marsden (A) 2-3

MERSTHAM

Currently: Combined Counties League

82-83 Q1: Hendon (H) 0-2

83-84 PR: Hoddesdon Town (A - *at Ware*) 0-1

84-85 PR: Haywards Heath (A) 0-2

85-86 Q1: Slough Town (H) 0-4

86-87 PR: Leytonstone-Ilford (H) 0-6

87-88 Q1: Thanet United (H) 1-3

88-89 PR: Clapton (H) 3-3, (A) 1-2

89-90 PR: Hornchurch (H - *played away*) 1-2

90-91 PR: Harefield United (A) 1-0
Q1: Marlow (A) 0-3

91-92 PR: Corinthian (A) 0-6

92-93 PR: Malden Vale (H) 0-0, (A) 1-3

Below: *Merstham put the Malden Vale defence under intense pressure during an August bank holiday Monday afternoon F.A. Cup replay at Grand Drive. However, the home side triumphed 3-1. Photo: Dave West.*

MERTHYR TYDFIL

Currently: Alliance Premier League

Season	Results
46-47	PR: Cardiff Corinthians (H) 4-1
	Q1: Llanelly (H) 8-2
	Q2: Lovells Athletic (H) 4-2
	Q3: Barry Town (H) 3-0
	Q4: Bath City (H) 7-1
	R1: Bristol Rovers (H) 3-1
	R2: Reading (H) 1-3
47-48	PR: Clevedon (H) 2-1
	Q1: Hanham Athletic (H) 9-0
	Q2: Lovells Athletic (H) 2-1
	Q3: Barry Town (A) 4-3
	Q4: Bath City (H) 2-1
	R1: Norwich City (A) 0-3
48-49	Q2: Lovells Athletic (A) 1-3
49-50	PR: Ebbw Vale (H) 5-1
	Q1: Llanelly (A) 3-0
	Q2: Lovells Athletic (A) 0-1
50-51	PR: Bristol St George (H) 11-3
	Q1: Hoffmann Ath. (Stonehouse) (H) 7-0
	Q2: Llanelly (A) 5-5, (H) 1-2
51-52	Q4: Cheltenham Town (A) 3-2
	R1: Ipswich Town (H) 2-2, (A) 0-1
52-53	Q4: Yeovil Town (A) 0-1
53-54	Q1: Cheltenham Town (H) 3-2
	Q2: Ebbw Vale (H) 3-0
	Q3: Barry Town (H) 3-3, (A) 3-2
	Q4: Yeovil Town (A) 1-2
54-55	Q1: Llanelly (A) 2-1
	Q2: Lovells Athletic (H) 3-1
	Q3: Gloucester City (A) 1-0
	Q4: Bath City (H) 3-1
	R1: Wellington Town (H) 1-1, (A) 6-1
	R2: Bradford City (A) 1-7
55-56	Q4: Lovells Athletic (A) 0-2
56-57	Q1: Llanelly (A) 1-5
57-58	PR: Lovells Athletic (A) 2-3
58-59	Q1: Barry Town (H) 4-1
	Q2: Stonehouse (A) 3-2
	Q3: Gloucester City (H) 2-1
	Q4: Taunton (H) 2-1
	R1: King's Lynn (A) 1-2
59-60	Q1: Cinderford Town (A) 1-1, (H) 2-0
	Q2: Cheltenham Town (A) 2-2, (H) 0-1
60-61	Q1: Stonehouse (H) 5-2
	Q2: Cheltenham Town (A) 0-4
61-62	Q1: Llanelly (H) 5-0
	Q2: Ebbw Vale (A) 2-1
	Q3: Barry Town (A) 0-2
62-63	Q1: Gloucester City (A) 2-3
63-64	Q1: Gloucester City (A) 2-2, (H) 2-3
64-65	Q1: Cinderford Town (H) 4-1
	Q2: Barry Town (H) 4-0
	Q3: Llanelly (A) 7-2
	Q4: Bath City (A) 1-4
65-66	Q1: Cinderford Town (A) 1-1, (H) 4-0
	Q2: Stonehouse (H) 6-2
	Q3: Gloucester C. (H) 1-1, (A) 1-1, 1-0
	Q4: Stourbridge (A) 5-1
	R1: Swindon Town (A) 1-5
66-67	Q1: Barry Town (A) 1-0
	Q2: Cheltenham Town (H) 1-3
67-68	PR: Stonehouse (A) 6-0
	Q1: Cheltenham Town (A) 1-2
68-69	Q1: Cinderford Town (H) 1-4
69-70	Q1: Barry Town (H) 2-1
	Q2: Abergavenny Thursdays (H) 3-2
	Q3: Ton Pentre (A) 2-4
70-71	Q1: Stonehouse (A) 2-1
	Q2: Llanelly (H) 1-1, (A) 2-0
	Q3: Ton Pentre (H) 2-0
	Q4: Minehead (H) 0-2
71-72	PR: Llanelly (A) 3-0
	Q1: Gloucester City (A) 3-2
	Q2: Stonehouse (A) 2-0
	Q3: Ton Pentre (A) 1-2
72-73	PR: Ton Pentre (A) 3-3, (H) 1-0
	Q1: Minehead (H) 1-0
	Q2: Barry Town (A) 0-1
73-74	Q1: Barry Town (A) 3-0
	Q2: Glastonbury (A) 0-0, (H) 3-1
	Q3: Mangotsfield United (H) 2-0
	Q4: Macclesfield Town (A) 0-0, (H) 2-1
	R1: Weymouth (A) 1-0
	R2: Hendon (H) 0-3
74-75	Q1: Gloucester City (A) 2-3
75-76	Q1: Mangotsfield United (A) 1-0
	Q2: Barry Town (A) 2-5
76-77	Q1: Gloucester City (H) 4-1
	Q2: Cheltenham T. (H) 3-3, (A) 1-1, 4-0
	Q3: Llanelli (A) 6-3
	Q4: Wycombe Wanderers (A) 1-3
77-78	PR: Glastonbury (A) 1-0
	Q1: Evesham United (A) 0-0, (H) 2-1
	Q2: Calne Town (A) 4-0
	Q3: Bridgend Town (A) 3-1
	Q4: Bath City (H) 1-2
78-79	Q1: Bridgend Town (H) 4-0
	Q2: Cinderford Town (A) 1-0
	Q3: Barry Town (A) 2-0
	Q4: Minehead (H) 2-0
	R1: Leatherhead (A) 1-2
79-80	Q1: Chippenham Town (A) 3-0
	Q2: Cheltenham Town (A) 2-0
	Q3: Weston-super-Mare (A) 2-2, (H) 3-1
	Q4: Maidenhead United (H) 2-1
	R1: Fareham Town (A) 3-2
	R2: Chesham United (A) 1-1, (H) 1-3
80-81	Q4: Farnborough Town (H) 0-1
81-82	Q4: Yeovil Town (A) 0-3
82-83	Q1: Hungerford Town (A) 3-0
	Q2: Barry Town (H) 3-1
	Q3: Bridgend Town (A) 3-1
	Q4: Wimborne Town (A) 0-1
83-84	Q1: Cinderford Town (A) 2-1
	Q2: Bath City (A) 1-0
	Q3: Gloucester City (H) 3-2
	Q4: Corinthian-Casuals (A) 0-1
84-85	Q1: Saltash United (A) 0-0, (H) 1-0
	Q2: Dorchester Town (A) 0-0, (H) 3-0
	Q3: Cheltenham Town (H) 4-1
	Q4: Barry T. (H) 1-1, (A) 1-1, (A) 2-3
85-86	Q1: Bideford (A) 1-1, (H) 1-1, (A) 0-2
86-87	PR: Ottery St Mary (A) 1-0
	Q1: Saltash United (A) 0-1
87-88	Q1: Paulton Rovers (H) 2-0
	Q2: Barry Town (A) 1-0
	Q3: Forest Green Rovers (H) 3-1
	Q4: Croydon (H) 3-0
	R1: Bristol Rovers (A - *at Bath City*) 0-6
88-89	Q1: Sharpness (H) 3-0
	Q2: Tiverton Town (A) 1-0
	Q3: Gloucester City (A) 1-0
	Q4: Crawley Town (A) 3-3, (H) 3-1
	R1: Yeovil Town (A) 2-3
89-90	Q4: Dulwich (A - *at Fisher A.*) 1-1, (H) 4-2
	R1: Redditch United (A) 3-1
	R2: Hereford United (A) 2-3
90-91	Q4: Dover Athletic (A) 0-0, (H) 2-0
	R1: Sutton United (H) 1-1, (A) 1-0
	R2: Woking (A) 1-5
91-92	Q4: Windsor & Eton (H) 1-1, (A) 0-1
92-93	Q4: Abingdon Town (A) 0-0, (H) 2-1
	R1: Wycombe Wanderers (A) 1-3

Above: *Merthyr 'keeper Steve Morris claims the ball during the 1992 visit to Abingdon Town. Photo: Francis Short*

METAL & PRODUCE RECOVERY DEPOT (OXFORD)

Currently: Defunct

Season	Results
46-47	EX: Chesham United (H) 1-1, (A) 0-5
47-48	PR: Bicester Town (A) 3-1
	Q1: Banbury Spencer (H) 0-3
48-49	EX: Wallingford Town (H) 1-3

METROPOLITAN POLICE

Currently: Isthmian League

Season	Results
45-46	PR: Banstead Hospital (A) 2-0
	Q1: Woking (H) 1-4
46-47	PR: Epsom (A) 5-0
	Q1: Sutton United (A) 0-7
47-48	PR: Walton & Hersham (H) 4-6
48-49	PR: Camberley (H) 7-2
	Q1: Woking (H) 0-2
49-50	PR: Woking (A) 0-1
50-51	EX: Surbiton Town (H) 2-1
	PR: Hounslow Town (H) 4-4, (A) 1-2
51-52	PR: Tooting & Mitcham United (H) 2-3
53-54	Q1: Epsom (H) 1-2
54-55	PR: Harrow Town (H) 1-1, (A) 5-1
	Q1: Hemel Hempstead T. (A) 0-0, (H) 3-2
	Q2: Hounslow Town (H) 2-4
55-56	PR: Hounslow Town (H) 3-3, (A) 0-4
56-57	PR: Bromley (A) 3-5
57-58	PR: Dulwich Hamlet (A) 0-8
58-59	Q1: Carshalton Athletic (A) 0-5
59-60	PR: Carshalton Athletic (H) 1-3
60-61	Q1: Walton & Hersham (A) 1-5
61-62	Q1: Bromley (A) 0-4
62-63	Q1: Dorking (A) 3-2
	Q2: Kingstonian (H) 1-2
64-65	Q1: Slough Town (A) 1-4
65-66	Q1: Marlow (A) 4-0
	Q2: Slough Town (A) 1-0
	Q3: Wokingham Town (H) 3-2
	Q4: Wycombe Wanderers (H) 2-3
66-67	Q1: Hampton (A) 2-0
	Q2: Kingstonian (H) 2-2, (A) 1-2
67-68	Q1: Uxbridge (A) 1-3
68-69	Q1: Carshalton Athletic (H) 5-4

Q2: Uxbridge (A) 2-2, (H) 3-3 *aband. after 90 minutes*, 3-1
Q3: Brentwood Town (A) 1-2

69-70 Q1: Guildford City (H) 1-0
Q2: Carshalton Athletic (H) 1-4

70-71 Q1: Erith & Belvedere (H) 0-1

71-72 PR: Hornchurch (A) 4-1
Q1: Hoddesdon Town (A) 1-2

72-73 PR: Walton & Hersham (A) 1-1, (H) 1-6

73-74 PR: Sutton United (A) 0-3

74-75 Q1: Hornchurch (A) 1-2

76-77 Q1: Sutton United (H) 0-3

77-78 PR: Clapton (A) 1-4

78-79 Q1: Harlow Town (H) 1-0
Q2: Edgware Town (A) 0-1

79-80 Q1: Willesden (H) 1-1, (A) 1-1, 3-0
Q2: Burnham (H) 1-1, (A) 3-3, 1-0
Q3: Maidenhead United (H) 0-1

80-81 Q1: Hounslow (H) 2-3

81-82 PR: Worthing (H) 1-2

82-83 PR: Sittingbourne (H) 1-2

83-84 PR: Horsham Y.M.C.A. (H) 0-1

84-85 PR: Chatham Town (A) 3-2
Q1: Ware (H) 5-0
Q2: Leytonstone-Ilford (H) 3-1
Q3: Welling United (H) 3-1
Q4: Harlow Town (A) 3-1
R1: Dartford (H) 0-3

85-86 Q1: Newport Isle of Wight (A) 2-3

86-87 PR: Chesham United (A) 8-1
Q1: Feltham (A) 5-0
Q2: Hampton (H) 2-2, (A) 0-2

87-88 PR: Sheppey United (A) 3-1
Q1: Dover Athletic (H) 3-1
Q2: Epsom & Ewell (H) 3-0
Q3: Croydon (H) 0-1

88-89 PR: Purfleet (A) 1-0
Q1: Arlesey Town (H) 1-1, (A) 0-2

89-90 PR: Epsom & Ewell (H) 0-0, (H) 0-2

90-91 PR: Hemel Hempstead (A) 2-1
Q1: Hendon (H) 1-3

91-92 PR: Hastings Town (H) 2-4

92-93 PR: Ford United (H) 0-0, (A) 2-0
Q1: Lewes (H) 2-1
Q2: Slough Town (H) 0-1

Below: *Paul Richardson of Metropolitan Police is hotly pursued by George Friel of Slough. Friel scored the only goal of the Second Qualifying Round tie.*
Photo: Dennis Nicholson.

MEXBOROUGH TOWN

Currently: Defunct
* - As Mexborough Town Athletic

64-65 Q1: Worksop Town (A) 1-2

65-66 Q1: Goole Town (A) 2-4

66-67 Q1: Denaby United (H) 0-2

67-68 Q1: Retford Town (A) 1-2

68-69 PR: Denaby United (H) 1-1, (A) 2-3

69-70 Q1: Worksop Town (H) 3-3, (A) 1-6

70-71 Q1: Norton Woodseats Amateur (A) 3-7

71-72 PR: Frickley Colliery (A) 2-3

72-73 Q1: Glossop (A) 2-3

73-74 Q1: Bridlington Trinity (H) 3-2
Q2: Bradford Park Avenue (H) 1-1, (A) 2-4

74-75 Q1: Gainsborough Trinity (A) 1-5

75-76 Q1: Ashby Institute (A) 1-0
Q2: Brigg Town (A) 3-2
Q3: Retford Town (A) 2-1
Q4: Macclesfield Town (H) 1-2

76-77 Q1: Frickley Athletic (H) 2-0
Q2: Bridlington Trinity (H) 3-2
Q3: Goole Town (A) 1-7

77-78 Q1: Buxton (H) 1-3

78-79 PR: Alfreton Town (A) 5-2
Q1: Winsford United (A) 0-3

79-80 * PR: Yorkshire Amateur (H) 6-1
Q1: Worsborough Bridge M.W. Ath. (A) 2-0
Q2: Marine (H) 0-1

80-81 * Q1: Leek Town (H) 1-2

81-82 * PR: Farsley Celtic (A) 1-1, (H) 2-1
Q1: Goole Town (H) 1-6

82-83 * Q1: Belper Town (A) 1-1, (H) 0-3

MICKLEOVER R.B.L.

Currently: Central Midlands League

92-93 PR: Belper Town (H - *played away*) 0-2

MIDDLESBROUGH

Currently: Football League

45-46 R3: Leeds Utd (A) 4-4, (H) 7-2 (*agg: 11-6*)
R4: Blackpool (A) 2-3, (H) 3-2 (*agg: 5-5*), 1-0
R5: Bolton Wdrs (A) 0-1, (H) 1-1 (*agg: 1-2*)

46-47 R3: Queens Park Rgrs (A) 1-1, (H) 3-1
R4: Chesterfield (H) 2-1
R5: Nottingham Forest (A) 2-2, (H) 6-2
R6: Burnley (H) 1-1, (A) 0-1

47-48 R3: Hull City (A) 3-1
R4: Brentford (A) 2-1
R5: Derby County (H) 1-2

48-49 R3: Brentford (A) 2-3

49-50 R3: Aston Villa (A) 2-2, (H) 0-0, 3-0
R4: Chesterfield (A) 2-3

50-51 R3: Leeds United (A) 0-1

51-52 R3: Derby County (H) 2-2, (A) 2-0
R4: Doncaster Rovers (H) 1-4

52-53 R3: Aston Villa (A) 1-3

53-54 R3: Leicester City (H) 0-0, (A) 2-3

54-55 R3: Notts County (H) 1-4

55-56 R3: Bradford (Park Avenue) (A) 4-0
R4: Tottenham Hotspur (A) 1-3

56-57 R3: Charlton Athletic (H) 1-1, (A) 3-2
R4: Aston Villa (H) 2-3

57-58 R3: Derby County (H) 5-0
R4: Stoke City (A) 1-3

58-59 R3: Birmingham City (H) 1-1, (A) 0-1

59-60 R3: Sheffield Wednesday (A) 1-2

60-61 R3: Manchester United (A) 0-3

61-62 R3: Cardiff City (H) 1-0
R4: Shrewsbury Town (A) 2-2, (H) 5-1
R5: Blackburn Rovers (A) 1-2

62-63 R3: Blackburn Rovers (A) 1-1, (H) 3-1
R4: Leeds United (H) 0-2

63-64 R3: Brentford (A) 1-2

64-65 R3: Oldham Athletic (H) 6-2
R4: Charlton Athletic (A) 1-1, (H) 2-1
R5: Leicester City (H) 0-3

65-66 R3: Tottenham Hotspur (A) 0-4

66-67 R1: Chester (A) 5-2
R2: York City (H) 1-1, (A) 0-0, 4-1
R3: Mansfield Town (A) 0-2

67-68 R3: Hull City (H) 1-1, (A) 2-2, 1-0
R4: Bristol City (H) 1-1, (A) 1-2

68-69 R3: Millwall (H) 1-1, (A) 0-1

69-70 R3: West Ham United (H) 2-1
R4: York City (H) 4-1
R5: Carlisle United (H) 2-1
R6: Manchester United (H) 1-1, (A) 1-2

70-71 R3: Manchester United (A) 0-0, (H) 2-1
R4: Everton (A) 0-3

71-72 R3: Manchester City (A) 1-1, (H) 1-0
R4: Millwall (A) 2-2, (H) 2-1
R5: Manchester United (A) 0-0, (H) 0-3

72-73 R3: Plymouth Argyle (A) 0-1

73-74 R3: Grantham (A) 2-0
R4: Wrexham (A) 0-1

74-75 R3: Wycombe Wanderers (A) 0-0, (H) 1-0
R4: Sunderland (H) 3-1
R5: Peterborough (A) 1-1, (H) 2-0
R6: Birmingham City (A) 0-1

Opposite: *David Armstrong (far right) slots home the only goal against non-League Wycombe Wanderers in a tie that proved to be a surprisingly difficult struggle for Middlesbrough.*

75-76 R3: Bury (H) 0-0, (A) 2-3

76-77 R3: Wimbledon (A) 0-0, (H) 1-0
R4: Hereford United (H) 4-0
R5: Arsenal (H) 4-1
R6: Liverpool (A) 0-2

77-78 R3: Coventry City (H) 3-0
R4: Everton (H) 3-2
R5: Bolton Wanderers (H) 2-0
R6: Orient (H) 0-0, (A) 1-2

78-79 R3: Crystal Palace (H) 1-1, (A) 0-1

79-80 R3: Portsmouth (A) 1-1, (H) 3-0
R4: Birmingham City (A) 1-2

80-81 R3: Swansea City (A) 5-0
R4: West Bromwich Albion (H) 1-0
R5: Barnsley (H) 2-1
R6: Wolverhampton W. (H) 1-1, (A) 1-3

81-82 R3: Queens Park Rgrs (A) 1-1, (H) 2-3

82-83 R3: Bishop's Stortford (H) 2-2, (A) 2-1
R4: Notts County (H) 2-0
R5: Arsenal (H) 1-1, (A) 2-3

83-84 R3: Arsenal (H) 3-2
R4: A.F.C. Bournemouth (H) 2-0
R5: Notts County (A) 0-1

84-85 R3: Darlington (H) 0-0, (A) 1-2

85-86 R3: Southampton (H) 1-3

86-87 R1: Blackpool (H) 3-0
R2: Notts County (A) 1-0
R3: Preston North End (H) 0-1

87-88 R3: Sutton United (A) 1-1, (H) 1-0
R4: Everton (A) 1-1, (H) 2-2, (A) 1-2

88-89 R3: Grimsby Town (H) 1-2

89-90 R3: Everton (H) 0-0, (A) 1-1, (A) 0-1

90-91 R3: Plymouth Argyle (H) 0-0, (A) 2-1
R4: Cambridge United (A) 0-2

91-92 R3: Manchester City (H) 2-1
R4: Sheffield Wednesday (A) 2-1
R5: Portsmouth (A) 1-1, (H) 2-4

92-93 R3: Chelsea (H) 2-1
R4: Nottingham Forest (A) 1-1, (H) 0-3

MILE OAK ROVERS & YTH

Currently: Midland Combination

82-83 Q1: Buckingham Town (H) 2-0
Q2: Kidderminster Harriers (H) 2-7

83-84 Q1: Corby Town (H) 0-1

84-85 PR: Blakenall (A) 0-2

85-86 Q1: Bridgnorth Town (A) 1-0
Q2: Grantham (H) 1-3

86-87 PR: Leamington (H) 1-1, (A) 0-1

87-88 Q1: Brigg Town (H) 1-2

88-89 PR: Rothwell Town (A) 5-1
Q1: Goole Town (H) 3-1
Q2: Boston United (A) 0-5

89-90 PR: Warrington Town (H) 1-2

90-91 PR: Stourbridge (H) 0-5

MILLOM TOWN

Currently: Defunct

50-51 PR: Florence & Ullcoats United (H) 2-3

MILLWALL

Currently: Football League

45-46 R3: Northampton (A) 2-2, (H) 3-0 (*agg: 5-2*)
R4: Aston Villa (H) 2-4, (A) 1-9 (*agg: 3-13*)

46-47 R3: Port Vale (H) 0-3

47-48 R3: Preston North End (H) 1-2

48-49 R1: Tooting & Mitcham United (H) 1-0
R2: Crewe Alexandra (A) 2-3

49-50 R1: Exeter City (H) 3-5

50-51 R1: Crystal Palace (A) 4-1
R2: Bradford (Park Avenue) (H) 1-1, (A) 1-0
R3: Queens Park Rangers (A) 4-3
R4: Fulham (H) 0-1

Above: *Millwall's Peter Anderson (centre) prepares to tackle Dagenham's Joey Dunwell during the 1981 tie at Victoria Road. Photo: Greater London & Essex Newspapers.*

51-52 R1: Plymouth Argyle (H) 1-0
R2: Scunthorpe United (H) 0-0, (A) 0-3

52-53 R1: Aldershot (A) 0-0, (H) 7-1
R2: Barrow (A) 2-2, (H) 4-1
R3: Manchester United (H) 0-1

53-54 R1: Colchester United (A) 1-1, (H) 4-0
R2: Headington United (H) 3-3, (A) 0-1

54-55 R1: Exeter City (H) 3-2
R2: Accrington Stanley (H) 3-2
R3: Bolton Wanderers (A) 1-3

55-56 R1: Northampton Town (A) 1-4

56-57 R1: Brighton & Hove A. (A) 1-1, (H) 3-1
R2: Margate (H) 4-0
R3: Crystal Palace (H) 2-0
R4: Newcastle United (H) 2-1
R5: Birmingham City (H) 1-4

57-58 R1: Brentford (H) 1-0
R2: Gillingham (H) 1-1, (A) 1-6

58-59 R1: Hitchin Town (A) 1-1, (H) 2-1
R2: Worcester City (A) 2-5

59-60 R1: Bath City (A) 1-3

60-61 R1: Reading (A) 2-6

61-62 R1: Northampton Town (A) 0-2

62-63 R1: Margate (H) 3-1
R2: Coventry City (H) 0-0, (A) 1-2

63-64 R1: Kettering Town (A) 1-1, (H) 2-3

64-65 R1: Kettering Town (H) 2-0
R2: Port Vale (H) 4-0
R3: Fulham (A) 3-3, (H) 2-0
R4: Shrewsbury Town (H) 1-2

65-66 R1: Wealdstone (H) 3-1
R2: Hereford United (A) 0-1

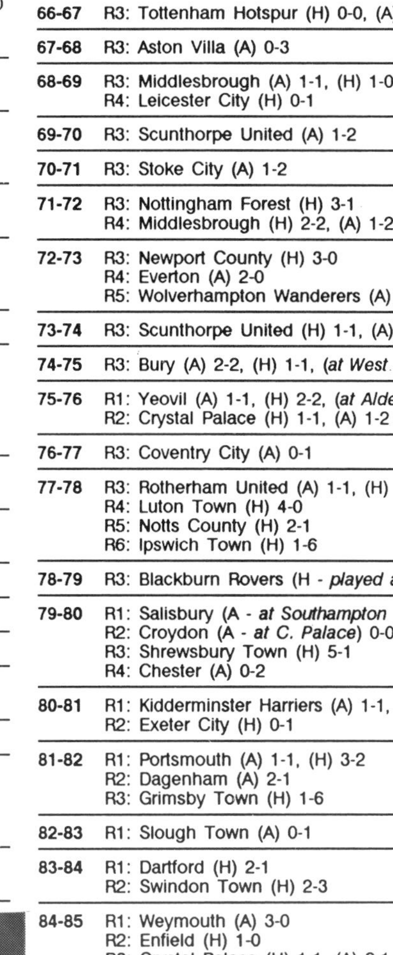

66-67 R3: Tottenham Hotspur (H) 0-0, (A) 0-1

67-68 R3: Aston Villa (A) 0-3

68-69 R3: Middlesbrough (A) 1-1, (H) 1-0
R4: Leicester City (H) 0-1

69-70 R3: Scunthorpe United (A) 1-2

70-71 R3: Stoke City (A) 1-2

71-72 R3: Nottingham Forest (H) 3-1
R4: Middlesbrough (H) 2-2, (A) 1-2

72-73 R3: Newport County (H) 3-0
R4: Everton (A) 2-0
R5: Wolverhampton Wanderers (A) 0-1

73-74 R3: Scunthorpe United (H) 1-1, (A) 0-1

74-75 R3: Bury (A) 2-2, (H) 1-1, (*at West Brom.*) 0-2

75-76 R1: Yeovil (A) 1-1, (H) 2-2, (*at Aldershot*) 1-0
R2: Crystal Palace (H) 1-1, (A) 1-2

76-77 R3: Coventry City (A) 0-1

77-78 R3: Rotherham United (A) 1-1, (H) 2-0
R4: Luton Town (H) 4-0
R5: Notts County (H) 2-1
R6: Ipswich Town (H) 1-6

78-79 R3: Blackburn Rovers (H - *played away*) 1-2

79-80 R1: Salisbury (A - *at Southampton F.C.*) 2-1
R2: Croydon (A - *at C. Palace*) 0-0, (H) 3-2
R3: Shrewsbury Town (H) 5-1
R4: Chester (A) 0-2

80-81 R1: Kidderminster Harriers (A) 1-1, (H) 1-0
R2: Exeter City (H) 0-1

81-82 R1: Portsmouth (A) 1-1, (H) 3-2
R2: Dagenham (A) 2-1
R3: Grimsby Town (H) 1-6

82-83 R1: Slough Town (A) 0-1

83-84 R1: Dartford (H) 2-1
R2: Swindon Town (H) 2-3

84-85 R1: Weymouth (A) 3-0
R2: Enfield (H) 1-0
R3: Crystal Palace (H) 1-1, (A) 2-1
R4: Chelsea (A) 3-2
R5: Leicester City (H) 2-0
R6: Luton Town (A) 0-1

85-86 R3: Wimbledon (H) 3-1
R4: Aston Villa (A) 1-1, (H) 1-0
R5: Southampton (A) 0-0, (H) 0-1

86-87 R3: Cardiff C. (H) 0-0, (A) 2-2, (A) 0-1

87-88 R3: Arsenal (A) 0-2

88-89 R3: Luton Town (H) 3-2
R4: Liverpool (H) 0-2

89-90 R3: Manchester C. (A) 0-0, (H) 1-1, (H) 3-1
R4: Cambridge United (H) 1-1, (A) 0-1

90-91 R3: Leicester City (H) 2-1
R4: Sheffield Wednesday (H) 4-4, (A) 0-2

91-92 R3: Huddersfield Town (A) 4-0
R4: Norwich City (A) 1-2

92-93 R3: Southend United (A) 0-1

MILNTHORPE CORINTHIANS
Currently: Defunct

45-46 Q2: Kells Centre (H) 4-5

46-47 Q1: Moss Bay (A) 3-2
Q2: Netherfield (A) 2-6

47-48 PR: Appleby (A) 9-3
Q1: William Colliery (A) 4-3
Q2: Netherfield (A) 1-4

48-49 PR: Frizington United (H) 8-2
Q1: Cockermouth (H) 11-0
Q2: Netherfield (H) 2-9

49-50 Q1: Aspatria Spartans (A) 1-6

50-51 PR: Bowthorn United (H) 5-2
Q1: Netherfield (H) 0-5

54-55 Q1: Lancaster City (A) 1-8

55-56 Q1: Morecambe (H) 5-2
Q2: Fleetwood (A) 0-0, (H) 2-5

56-57 Q1: Burscough (H) 2-1
Q2: Morecambe (H) 1-4

57-58 Q1: Clitheroe (A) 0-4

58-59 Q1: Penrith (H) 2-0
Q2: Netherfield (H) 1-2

59-60 Q1: Netherfield (H) 0-3

60-61 Q1: Burscough (A) 1-2

61-62 Q1: Fleetwood (A) 0-5

62-63 Q1: Wigan Athletic (A) 0-5

63-64 Q1: Lancaster City (H) 0-5

64-65 Q1: Fleetwood (A) 0-3

65-66 Q1: Fleetwood (H) 1-7

66-67 Q1: Morecambe (A) 0-7

67-68 Q1: Lancaster City (A) 0-3

68-69 PR: Fleetwood (A) 0-5

69-70 Q1: Lytham St Annes (H) 1-1, (A) 5-1
Q2: Lancaster City (A) 0-3

MILTON KEYNES BOROUGH
Currently: South Midlands League

85-86 Q1: Hednesford Town (A) 1-2

86-87 PR: Stevenage Borough (A) 2-3

87-88 PR: Bourne Town (A) 4-1
Q1: Haverhill Rovers (A) 1-1, (H) 0-4

88-89 Q1: Great Yarmouth Town (A) 0-3

91-92 PR: Ware (A) 1-5

92-93 PR: Eynesbury Rovers (A) 5-4
Q1: Bourne Town (A) 2-3

MILTON KEYNES CITY
Currently: Defunct
* - As Bletchley
+ - As Bletchley Town United
See also Bletchley & W.I.P.A.C. Sports

63-64 + Q1: St Albans City (A) 0-3

64-65 + Q1: Wolverton Town & B.R. (A) 1-0
Q2: Cheshunt (A) 1-1, (H) 1-0
Q3: Hitchin Town (A) 4-0
Q4: Wisbech Town (A) 2-3

65-66 * Q1: Vauxhall Motors (H) 3-2
Q2: Wolverton Town & B.R. (H) 2-1
Q3: St Albans City (A) 1-0
Q4: Guildford City (A) 0-4

66-67 * Q1: Hoddesdon Town (A) 7-0
Q2: Finchley (A) 0-0, (H) 0-1

67-68 * Q1: Wembley (H) 3-4

68-69 * Q1: Maidenhead United (H) 0-0, (A) 0-1

69-70 * PR: Wealdstone (A) 1-2

70-71 * Q1: Witney Town (H) 1-0
Q2: Dunstable Town (A) 0-1

71-72 * Q1: Hampton (A) 1-2

72-73 * Q1: Slough Town (A) 0-0, (H) 0-3

73-74 * Q1: Potton United (H) 3-0
Q2: St Neots Town (A) 3-0
Q3: Hitchin Town (H) 1-1, (A) 0-2

74-75 Q1: Wolverton Town & B.R. (A) 2-1
Q2: Wycombe Wanderers (A) 0-2

75-76 PR: Didcot Town (H) 3-1
Q1: Wellingborough Town (A) 1-0
Q2: Witney Town (H) 2-1
Q3: A.P. Leamington (H) 0-1

76-77 PR: Marlow (A) 0-0, (H) 0-1

77-78 PR: Rushden Town (H) 0-2

78-79 Q1: Coventry Sporting (H) 2-0
Q2: Darlaston (A) 0-5

79-80 PR: Wokingham Town (H) 4-1
Q1: Uxbridge (A) 0-1

80-81 PR: Southall (H) 0-2

81-82 PR: Tividale (A) 0-3

82-83 PR: Friar Lane Old Boys (A) 1-1, (H) 1-4

83-84 PR: Stevenage Borough (A) 0-2

84-85 PR: Rothwell Town (H) 0-3

MINEHEAD
Currently: Western League

51-52 PR: Bridgwater Town (A) 1-2

52-53 PR: Bideford (H) 1-4

53-54 PR: Newquay Amateur (A) 1-2

54-55 PR: Dartmouth United (H) 3-3, (A) 5-3
Q1: Bodmin Town (A) 3-3, (H) 2-2, 3-2
Q2: Tavistock (A) 2-4

55-56 Q1: Bideford (A) 0-4

56-57 PR: Wadebridge Town (H) 2-3

57-58 Q1: Barnstaple Town (A) 1-5

58-59 PR: Bideford (H) 3-4

59-60 Q1: Bridgwater Town (A) 1-2

60-61 Q2: Bridgwater Town (A) 1-4

61-62 Q2: Frome Town (H) 3-0
Q3: Borough of Weston-super-Mare (A) 0-1

62-63 Q2: Frome Town (A) 2-2, (H) 4-0
Q3: Bridgwater Town (A) 3-1
Q4: Cheltenham Town (H) 0-1

63-64 Q1: Frome Town (A) 3-1
Q2: Borough of Weston-super-Mare (H) 3-1
Q3: Bridgwater Town (H) 0-1

64-65 Q1: Borough of Weston-super-Mare (H) 2-1
Q2: Frome Town (A) 3-1
Q3: Welton Rovers (H) 0-3

65-66 Q1: Borough of Weston-super-Mare (A) 1-2

66-67 Q1: Taunton (A) 4-1
Q2: Barnstaple Town (A) 2-1
Q3: Bideford (H) 5-0
Q4: Poole Town (A) 0-1

67-68 Q1: Street (H) 4-1
Q2: Frome Town (A) 1-1, (H) 2-1
Q3: Taunton (H) 2-2, (A) 2-1
Q4: Falmouth Town (H) 1-2

68-69 Q1: Frome Town (H) 1-2

69-70 PR: Trowbridge Town (A) 3-2
Q1: Bridgwater Town (H) 2-0
Q2: Bridport (H) 2-0
Q3: Bath City (H) 3-0
Q4: Yeovil T. (H) 0-0, (A) 0-0, 0-5

70-71 Q1: Bridgwater Town (H) 1-1, (A) 3-2
Q2: Taunton Town (A) 2-1
Q3: Glastonbury (H) 1-0
Q4: Merthyr Tydfil (A) 2-0
R1: Shrewsbury Town (H) 1-2

71-72 PR: Poole Town (H) 1-2

72-73 Q1: Merthyr Tydfil (A) 0-1

73-74 Q1: Barnstaple Town (A) 1-2

74-75 Q1: St Blazey (A) 1-1, (H) 4-1
Q2: Falmouth Town (H) 3-2
Q3: Bideford (H) 2-1
Q4: Weymouth (H) 0-3

75-76 Q1: Bridgwater Town (A) 2-1
Q2: Glastonbury (A) 4-0
Q3: Yeovil Town (A) 0-1

76-77 Q1: Bridport(A) 4-2
Q2: Barnstaple Town (A) 2-1
Q3: Taunton Town (H) 2-1
Q4: Falmouth Town (A) 1-1, (H) 3-0
R1: Swansea City (A) 1-0
R2: Portsmouth (A) 1-2

77-78 Q4: Salisbury (A) 1-1, (H) 2-1
R1: Wycombe Wanderers (H) 2-0
R2: Exeter City (H) 0-3

78-79 Q4: Merthyr Tydfil (A) 0-2

79-80 Q4: Witney Town (H) 1-0
R1: Chesham United (H) 1-2

80-81 Q4: Sutton United (H) 2-0
R1: Barnet (H) 2-2, (A) 1-2

81-82 Q4: Worcester City (H) 1-0
R1: Dorchester Town (A) 3-3, (H) 0-4

82-83 Q4: Worthing (A) 2-2, (H) 0-3

83-84 Q4: Yeovil Town (A) 2-2, (H) 2-4

84-85 Q1: Wadebridge Town (A) 2-0
Q2: Bath City (H) 0-0, (A) 0-3

85-86 PR: Llanelli (A) 3-2
Q1: Cheltenham Town (H) 1-1, (A) 2-1
Q2: Barry Town (A) 1-5

86-87 Q1: Tiverton Town (H) 1-0
Q2: Barnstaple Town (H) 2-1
Q3: Exmouth Town (A) 4-3
Q4: Ton Pentre (A) 1-5

87-88 Q1: Barnstaple Town (H) 1-1, (A) 0-1

88-89 PR: Sharpness (H) 0-4

89-90 PR: Taunton Town (A) 1-9

90-91 PR: Barry Town (A) 1-2

91-92 PR: St Blazey (A) 3-0
Q1: Falmouth Town (A) 0-2

92-93 PR: A.F.C. Lymington (H) 2-2, (A) 1-2

MIRRLEES BLACKSTONE
Currently: United Counties League

90-91 PR: Lowestoft Town (A) 0-1

91-92 PR: Great Yarmouth Town (H) 2-1
Q1: Bishop's Stortford (A) 1-1, (H) 2-0
Q2: Heybridge Swifts (A) 1-1, (H) 0-1

92-93 PR: Rainham Town (A - *at Purfleet*) 0-2

MOIRA UNITED
Currently: Defunct

47-48 Q1: Brush Sports (H) 1-3

48-49 PR: Rugby Town (A) 8-3
Q1: Tamworth (A) 2-6

49-50 PR: Rugby Town (A) 3-2
Q1: Nuneaton Borough (A) 1-7

50-51 PR: Lockheed Leamington (H) 0-2

51-52 Q1: Ibstock Penistone Rovers (H) 5-1
Q2: Brush Sports (A) 0-2

52-53 Q1: Coalville Town (A) 1-7

54-55 Q1: Raleigh Athletic (A) 2-3

MOLESEY
Currently: Isthmian League

68-69 Q1: Leatherhead (A) 0-5

69-70 Q1: Huntley & Palmers (H) 1-1, (A) 1-3

72-73 Q1: Carshalton Athletic (A) 0-0, (H) 4-1
Q2: Hampton (H) 0-0, (A) 0-1

73-74 Q1: Chatham Town (A) 0-3

74-75 Q1: Harrow Borough (A) 0-0, (H) 0-1

75-76 Q1: Willesden (H) 4-1
Q2: Walthamstow Avenue (A) 2-1
Q3: Croydon (H) 0-4

76-77 PR: St Albans City (H) 2-1
Q1: Burnham (H) 2-1

Above: *Molesey's Benny Penfold dummies Barry Rake of Chesham United, but the visitors still comfortably won the Second Qualifying Round tie on 26th October 1992. Photo: Dave West.*

Q2: Hillingdon Borough (H) 1-1, (A) 1-2

77-78 PR: Hounslow (A) 1-2

78-79 Q1: Hillingdon Borough (H) 2-2, (A) 1-2

79-80 Q1: Addlestone (H) 2-3

80-81 PR: Egham Town (A) 1-3

81-82 PR: Burgess Hill Town (A) 0-4

82-83 PR: Tooting & Mitcham United (A) 1-3

83-84 PR: Erith & Belvedere (H) 0-2

84-85 PR: Tonbridge A.F.C. (A) 1-4

85-86 Q1: Staines Town (A) 1-3

86-87 PR: Wick (H) 0-3

87-88 Q1: Epsom & Ewell (H) 1-2

88-89 PR: Herne Bay (H) 7-0
Q1: Horsham Y.M.C.A. (A) 2-1
Q2: Woking (H) 1-1, (A) 0-1

89-90 PR: Ringmer (A - *played away*) 1-0
Q1: Peacehaven & Telscombe (A) 1-0
Q2: Hythe Town (A) 1-2

90-91 PR: Vauxhall Motors (H) 1-1, (A) 5-0
Q1: Banstead Athletic (H) 3-3, (A) 2-0
Q2: Dagenham (H) 1-2

91-92 PR: Ringmer (H) 1-0
Q1: Crawley Town (H) 1-5

92-93 PR: Northwood (H) 3-1
Q1: East Thurrock United (H) 4-2
Q2: Chesham United (H) 0-4

MONCKTON ATHLETIC

Currently: Defunct

45-46 Q1: Upton Colliery (H) 6-2
Q2: Rawmarsh Welfare (A) 1-2

47-48 EX: Brodsworth Main Colliery (H) 1-2

48-49 PR: Firbeck Colliery (H) 1-2

MONMOUTH TOWN

Currently: Gwent County League

45-46 Q2: Llanelli (A) 0-7

MOOR GREEN

Currently: Southern League

45-46 Q1: Hereford United (A) 8-0
Q2: Bournville Athletic (A) 5-6

46-47 Q1: Worcester City (A) 1-1, (H) 1-6

47-48 PR: Stafford Rangers (H) 2-7

48-49 PR: Darlaston (A) 1-2

49-50 EX: Boldmere St Michaels (H) 3-2
PR: Bromsgrove Rovers (H) 2-2, (A) 1-4

50-51 EX: Lye Town (A) 2-2, (H) 1-3

51-52 PR: Burton Albion (H) 2-4

52-53 PR: Burton Albion (H) 1-1, (A) 0-3

53-54 PR: Rugby Town (A) 1-5

54-55 Q1: Lockheed Leamington (A) 5-4
Q2: Burton Albion (A) 2-3

55-56 PR: Bloxwich Strollers (H) 2-2, (A) 2-0
Q1: Lockheed Leamington (A) 1-2

56-57 PR: Sutton Coldfield Town (A) 2-3

57-58 PR: Boldmere St Michael's (H) 0-1

58-59 PR: Cradley Heath (H) 5-3
Q1: Wellington Town (H) 0-8

59-60 Q1: Bromsgrove Rovers (H) 2-4

60-61 Q1: Kidderminster Harriers (H) 2-3

61-62 PR: Bromsgrove Rovers (A) 0-2

62-63 Q1: Stafford Rangers (H) 0-6

63-64 Q2: Kidderminster Harriers (H) 1-2

64-65 Q1: Rugby Town (A) 0-4

69-70 Q1: Highgate United (H) 1-1, (A) 2-3

70-71 Q1: Lye Town (H) 2-2, (A) 0-2

71-72 Q1: Alvechurch (A) 0-4

72-73 PR: Darlaston (H) 2-1
Q1: Dudley Town (H) 2-1
Q2: Burton Albion (A) 1-2

73-74 Q1: Bromsgrove Rovers (H) 1-1, (A) 0-1

74-75 Q1: Coventry Sporting (A) 0-1

75-76 Q1: Enderby Town (H) 0-1

76-77 PR: A.P. Leamington (A) 0-1

77-78 PR: Cheltenham Town (A) 1-4

78-79 PR: Kidderminster Harriers (A) 0-5

79-80 Q1: Tamworth (H) 2-1
Q2: Brereton Social (H) 2-1
Q3: Telford United (H) 2-1
Q4: Runcorn (H) 2-0
R1: Stafford Rangers (A) 2-3

80-81 Q1: Rothwell Town (H) 4-0
Q2: Dudley Town (A) 0-0, (H) 2-1
Q3: Banbury United (H) 0-2

81-82 PR: Hednesford Town (A) 0-3

82-83 Q1: Sutton Town (H) 4-0
Q2: Bromsgrove Rovers (A) 2-2, (H) 1-0
Q3: Holbeach United (A) 1-2

83-84 Q1: Stevenage Borough (A) 0-0, (H) 1-0
Q2: Thame United (A) 4-4, (H) 4-2
Q3: Bedworth U. (A) 0-0 *ab. 20 mins*, (A) 1-2

84-85 Q1: Baldock Town (H) 2-1
Q2: Sutton Coldfield Town (A) 3-0
Q3: Oxford City (A) 2-1
Q4: Frickley Athletic (A) 0-5

85-86 Q1: Wednesfield Social (H) 5-0
Q2: Nuneaton Borough (H) 1-4

86-87 PR: Rushall Olympic (A) 3-2
Q1: Atherstone United (A) 1-2

87-88 PR: Tividale (H) 3-1
Q1: Halesowen Harriers (A) 1-1, (H) 2-1
Q2: Stafford Rangers (A) 3-2
Q3: Matlock Town (H) 3-2
Q4: Hayes (A) 0-2

88-89 Q1: Irthlingborough B. (A) 1-1, (H) 4-3
Q2: Malvern Town (A) 2-0
Q3: Tamworth (H) 1-1, (A) 6-4
Q4: Bromsgrove Rovers (A) 0-2

89-90 Q1: Redditch United (H) 0-1

90-91 Q1: Tamworth (H) 1-2

91-92 Q1: Tamworth (H) 0-3

92-93 Q1: Barton Rovers (A) 3-2
Q2: Bourne Town (A) 8-4
Q3: V.S. Rugby (H) 1-2

MORECAMBE

Currently: Northern Premier League

46-47 PR: Nelson (A) 2-1
Q1: Wigan Athletic (H) 0-3

47-48 PR: De Havilland (Bolton) (A) 3-1
Q1: Bacup Borough (A) 3-2
Q2: Fleetwood (A) 0-2

48-49 PR: Fleetwood (H) 0-1

49-50 PR: Leyland Motors (H) 4-5

50-51 PR: Bacup Borough (H) 0-4

51-52 Q1: Burscough (A) 2-2, (H) 0-1

52-53 Q1: Great Harwood (H) 1-0
Q2: Clitheroe (A) 1-0
Q3: Netherfield (A) 1-3

53-54 Q1: Penrith (A) 6-1
Q2: Fleetwood (A) 2-1
Q3: Burscough (H) 0-1

54-55 Q1: Fleetwood (H) 2-2, (A) 1-3

55-56 Q1: Milnthorpe Corinthians (A) 2-5

56-57 Q2: Milnthorpe Corinthians (A) 4-1
Q3: Fleetwood (A) 3-3, (H) 2-1
Q4: Horwich R.M.I. (H) 3-2
R1: Accrington Stanley (A) 1-4

57-58 Q1: Lancaster City (A) 2-1
Q2: Clitheroe (H) 1-0
Q3: Burscough (H) 6-2
Q4: Prescot Cables (A) 0-3

58-59 Q1: Lancaster City (H) 5-2
Q2: Fleetwood (H) 4-2
Q3: Netherfield (A) 0-0, (H) 7-1
Q4: Chorley (H) 2-0
R1: Blyth Spartans (H) 1-2

59-60 Q1: Penrith (A) 0-1

60-61 Q1: Lancaster City (H) 7-4
Q2: Burscough (H) 2-2, (A) 2-1
Q3: Netherfield (A) 0-2

61-62 Q1: Clitheroe (H) 4-2
Q2: Penrith (A) 2-1
Q3: Burscough (A) 8-1
Q4: Wigan Athletic (H) 2-0
R1: South Shields (H) 2-1
R2: Chester (A) 1-0
R3: Weymouth (H) 0-1

62-63 Q4: Droylsden (H) 1-0
R1: Blyth Spartans (A) 1-2

63-64 Q4: Chorley (H) 3-4

64-65 Q1: Clitheroe (A) 2-1
Q2: Fleetwood (H) 6-1
Q3: Lancaster City (H) 1-2

65-66 Q1: Penrith (H) 2-0
Q2: Clitheroe (A) 1-2

66-67	Q1: Milnthorpe Corinthians (H) 7-0 Q2: Nelson (A) 4-0 Q3: Netherfield (H) 2-1 Q4: South Liverpool (A) 1-1, (H) 1-0 R1: York City (A) 0-0, (H) 1-1, 0-1
67-68	Q4: Spennymoor United (A) 0-1
68-69	Q1: Netherfield (H) 4-0 Q2: Lancaster City (A) 4-2 Q3: Fleetwood (H) 1-0 Q4: Mossley (A) 2-1 R1: Bangor City (A) 3-2 R2: York City (A) 0-2
69-70	Q4: Mossley (A) 1-4
70-71	Q1: Penrith (A) 1-3
71-72	Q1: Accrington Stanley (H) 2-0 Q2: Rossendale United (A) 2-2, (H) 0-1
72-73	Q1: Bacup Borough (A) 0-1
73-74	Q1: Darwen (H) 0-0, (A) 2-3
74-75	R1: Bishop Auckland (A) 0-5
75-76	Q4: Willington (A) 2-2, (H) 4-1 R1: Scarborough (A) 0-2
76-77	Q4: Great Harwood (H) 2-0 R1: Lincoln City (A) 0-1
77-78	Q4: Burscough (A) 0-0, (H) 0-1
78-79	Q4: Horwich R.M.I. (H) 3-1 R1: Stockport County (A) 1-5
79-80	Q4: Droylsden (H) 3-2 R1: Rotherham United (H) 1-1, (A) 0-2
80-81	Q4: Burscough (A) 0-2
81-82	Q1: Consett (H) 2-3
82-83	PR: Whitby Town (H) 2-0 Q1: Tow Law Town (A) 5-3 Q2: Chester-le-Street (A) 5-1 Q3: South Bank (H) 1-1, (A) 0-1
83-84	Q1: Guiseley (H) 1-0 Q2: North Shields (H) 2-2, (A) 2-4
84-85	Q1: Alfreton Town (H) 0-1
85-86	Q1: Harrogate Town (A) 2-0 Q2: Billingham Town (A) 5-0 Q3: Gretna (A) 2-0 Q4: St Helens Town (H) 1-1, (A) 1-0 R1: York C. (A) 0-0, (H - *at Man. City*) 0-2
86-87	Q1: Esh Winning (H) 8-0 Q2: Bridlington Town (A) 1-0 Q3: Bishop Auckland (H) 1-2
87-88	Q1: Newcastle Blue Star (A) 0-1
88-89	Q1: Skelmersdale Utd (H) 3-3, (A) 2-1 Q2: Northallerton Town (H) 3-2 Q3: Barrow (H) 0-0, (A) 1-5
89-90	Q1: Colwyn Bay (A - *at Rhyl*) 1-4
90-91	Q1: Horwich R.M.I. (H) 2-2, (A) 0-3
91-92	Q1: Great Harwood Town (H) 1-0 Q2: Durham City (A) 4-1 Q3: Penrith (A) 3-0 Q4: Colwyn Bay (A) 2-0 R1: Hull City (H) 0-1
92-93	Q1: Maine Road (A) 1-2

Below: *Morecambe's John Coleman tries a spectacular overhead kick at Maine Road. Photo: Andrew Mollit.*

MORESBY WELFARE CENTRE

Currently: Defunct

48-49	PR: Cockermouth (A) 3-6

MORETON TOWN

Currently: Hellenic League

79-80	PR: Ton Pentre (H) 0-2
80-81	Q1: Dudley Town (H) 0-1
81-82	Q1: Worcester City (A) 2-5
82-83	PR: Ton Pentre (H) 2-2, (A) 1-4
83-84	Q1: Witney Town (A) 1-2
84-85	Q1: Haverfordwest (A) 2-2, (H) 1-1, (H) 3-5

MORPETH TOWN

Currently: Northern Alliance

48-49	EX: Jarrow (A) 1-2
49-50	PR: Gosforth & Coxlodge (H) 2-2, (A) 1-3
50-51	EX: Boldon Colliery Welfare (H) 1-3
56-57	Q1: North Shields (H) 0-5
57-58	Q2: Durham City (H) 1-2
58-59	Q1: Ferryhill Athletic (A) 1-1, (H) 0-2

MORRIS MOTORS (OXFORD)

Currently: Defunct

45-46	EX: Pressed Steel (A) 0-1
46-47	EX: Aylesbury United (A) 1-2
50-51	EX: Leavesden (A) 1-8

MORRIS SPTS (LOUGHBORO.)

Currently: Defunct

48-49	PR: Hinckley Athletic (H) 1-5
49-50	PR: Hinckley Athletic (A) 0-11
50-51	PR: Bedworth Town (A) 1-3

MOSS BAY

Currently: Defunct

46-47	PR: Scalegill (A) 4-2 Q1: Milnthorpe Corinthians (H) 2-3
47-48	PR: Scalegill (A) 0-1
48-49	PR: Cleator Moor Celtic (H) 6-2 Q1: High Duty Alloys (H) 2-3
50-51	PR: Penrith (A) 0-12

MOSSLEY

Currently: Northern Premier League

48-49	EX: Ashton United (A) 0-3
49-50	EX: Ashton United (H) 2-1 PR: Altrincham (A) 3-2 Q1: Northwich Victoria (H) 3-2 Q2: Buxton (H) 2-1 Q3: Droylsden (A) 3-1 Q4: Runcorn (H) 0-0, (A) 1-0 R1: Witton Albion (A) 1-0 R2: Nuneaton Borough (A) 0-0, (H) 0-3
50-51	PR: Runcorn (A) 1-3
51-52	Q1: Leyland Motors (H) 3-0 Q2: Darwen (A) 0-1
52-53	Q1: Lytham (H) 3-1 Q2: Rossendale United (H) 1-0 Q3: Ashton United (A) 1-2
53-54	Q1: Ashton United (H) 3-2 Q2: Darwen (H) 2-0 Q3: Skelmersdale United (A) 3-1 Q4: Rhyl (H) 1-1, (A) 0-2
54-55	Q1: Droylsden (A) 2-1 Q2: Darwen (A) 1-3
55-56	PR: Lytham (H) 1-1, (A) 0-1
56-57	PR: Rossendale United (A) 1-0 Q1: Bacup Borough (A) 8-2 Q2: Darwen (A) 1-1, (H) 3-0 Q3: Horwich R.M.I. (A) 0-1
57-58	PR: Horwich R.M.I. (A) 1-1, (H) 2-1 Q1: Bacup Borough (A) 1-1, (H) 3-1 Q2: Chorley (H) 1-4
58-59	PR: Chorley (A) 0-1
59-60	PR: Skelmersdale United (A) 0-0, (H) 3-0 Q1: Chorley (H) 2-1 Q2: Altrincham (A) 2-3
60-61	PR: Rossendale Utd (A) 1-1 *abandoned after 51 minutes*, (H) 1-1, (A) 5-1 Q1: Chorley (H) 0-1
61-62	PR: Congleton Town (H) 1-2
62-63	Q1: Linotype & Machinery (A) 2-1 Q2: Droylsden (A) 0-0, (H) 1-2
63-64	Q2: Macclesfield Town (H) 0-5
64-65	Q1: Northwich Victoria (A) 2-5
65-66	Q1: Northwich Victoria (H) 1-4
66-67	Q1: Prescot Town (H) 6-2 Q2: Northwich Victoria (H) 1-1, (A) 1-3
67-68	Q1: Hyde United (A) 0-3
68-69	PR: Guinness Exports (H) 1-0 Q1: Hyde United (A) 2-2, (H) 2-1 Q2: Horwich R.M.I. (A) 5-1 Q3: Witton Albion (H) 2-0 Q4: Morecambe (H) 1-2
69-70	Q1: New Mills (A) 1-0 Q2: Rossendale United (H) 0-0, (A) 1-0 Q3: Horwich R.M.I. (H) 2-1 Q4: Morecambe (H) 4-1 R1: Stockport County (A) 1-1, (H) 0-1
70-71	PR: Eastwood (Hanley) (H) 0-1
71-72	Q1: Prestwich Heys (H) 2-2, (A) 2-1 Q2: Hyde United (H) 0-0, (A) 0-2
72-73	Q1: Stalybridge Celtic (H) 1-1, (A) 3-4
73-74	Q1: Yorkshire Amateur (H) 2-0 Q2: Prestwich Heys (H) 1-1, (A) 3-2 Q3: Buxton (A) 1-2
74-75	Q1: Eastwood Hanley (A) 3-1 Q2: Nantwich Town (H) 5-1 Q3: Runcorn (H) 1-0 Q4: Oswestry Town (H) 1-3
75-76	PR: Emley (H) 2-0 Q1: Worksop Town (A) 0-1
76-77	Q1: Chorley (H) 5-2 Q2: Great Harwood (A) 0-6
77-78	Q1: Macclesfield Town (A) 2-0 Q2: Curzon Ashton (H) 1-0 Q3: Winsford (A) 1-1, (H) 3-3, (*Altrincham*) 2-0 Q4: Appleby Frodingham Athletic (A) 2-0 R1: Rotherham United (A) 0-3
78-79	PR: Burscough (H) 2-1 Q1: Witton Albion (A) 2-4
79-80	Q1: Fleetwood (A) 4-1 Q2: Macclesfield Town (A) 0-0, (H) 3-2 Q3: Winsford United (A) 1-0 Q4: Goole Town (H) 2-1 R1: York City (A) 2-5
80-81	R1: Crewe Alexandra (H) 1-0 R2: Mansfield Town (H) 1-3

Opposite: *Leo Skeete drives home Mossley's only goal at home to Mansfield.*

81-82 Q4: South Bank (A) 1-0
R1: Stockport County (A) 1-3

82-83 Q4: South Bank (H) 1-0
R1: Huddersfield Town (A) 0-1

83-84 Q4: Workington (A) 0-0, (H) 1-0
R1: Darlington (A) 0-5

84-85 Q4: Goole Town (H) 0-1

85-86 Q1: Rossendale United (A) 2-1
Q2: Burscough (A) 3-0
Q3: Runcorn (H) 0-2

86-87 Q1: Eastwood T. (H) 3-3, (A) 1-1, (A) 0-2

87-88 Q1: Hyde United (A - *at Curzon Ashton*) 0-1

88-89 Q1: Bridgnorth T. (H - *at Curzon Ashton*) 2-0
Q2: Leek Town (A) 0-2

89-90 Q1: South Liverpool (H) 0-0, (A) 3-0
Q2: Accrington Stanley (H) 3-1
Q3: Curzon Ashton (A) 1-1, (H) 3-1
Q4: Bishop Auckland (H) 1-1, (A) 0-3

90-91 Q1: Chorley (A) 0-4

91-92 Q1: Flixton (A) 1-1, (H) 2-1
Q2: Winsford United (H) 1-1, (A) 0-6

92-93 Q1: Borrowash Victoria (H) 0-0, (A) 1-0
Q2: Pelsall Villa (H) 1-2

MOUNT HILL ENTERPRISE

Currently: Defunct

49-50 EX: St Philips Marsh Adult School (A) 2-1
PR: Cardiff Corinthians (A) 1-0
Q1: Lovells Athletic (A) 1-4

50-51 PR: Hoffmann (Stonehouse) (H) 1-1, (A) 1-2

MURTON

Currently: Northern League
* - As Murton Colliery Welfare

46-47 * PR: South Shields (H) 3-2
Q1: Ashington (H) 1-3

47-48 * EX: Stanley United (H) 2-2, (A) 2-2, 2-1
PR: Crook Colliery Welfare (A) 2-1
Q1: Easington Colliery Welfare (H) 2-3

48-49 * EX: Shildon (H) 6-2
PR: West Auckland Town (A) 1-0
Q1: South Hetton Colliery Welfare (A) 1-0
Q2: Annfield Plain (H) 1-2

50-51 * EX: Wingate Welfare (A) 2-4

51-52 * Q1: Silksworth Colliery Welfare (H) 3-2
Q2: Horden Colliery Welfare (H) 0-3

52-53 * Q1: Silksworth Colliery Welfare (A) 0-7

53-54 * Q1: Blackhall Colliery Welfare (H) 2-1
Q2: Ushaw Moor (H) 1-1, (A) 1-4

54-55 * Q1: Blackhall Colliery Welfare (A) 0-2

55-56 * Q1: Blackhall Colliery Welfare (H) 4-2
Q2: Ferryhill Athletic (H) 0-2

59-60 * Q1: Billingham Synthonia (A) 5-3
Q2: Scarborough (H) 2-5

60-61 * Q1: Shotton Colliery Welfare (A) 2-2, (H) 3-1
Q2: Bridlington Town (A) 0-5

61-62 * Q1: Evenwood Town (A) 3-3, (H) 2-3

64-65 * Q1: North Shields (H) 2-5

65-66 * Q1: Consett (A) 0-7

66-67 * Q1: Durham City (H) 4-2
Q2: Annfield Plain (A) 0-4

67-68 * Q1: Shildon (A) 3-3, (H) 1-1, 2-1
Q2: Durham City (A) 0-3

68-69 * Q1: Ferryhill Athletic (H) 1-0
Q2: North Shields (H) 0-4

69-70 * Q1: Wingate (A) 0-3

72-73 * Q1: Shildon (A) 4-3
Q2: Gateshead (H) 2-4

73-74 * Q1: Annfield Plain (A) 1-0
Q2: Ashington (A) 1-2

86-87 PR: Bridlington Town (A) 0-2

87-88 Q1: Seaham Red Star (H) 0-1

88-89 PR: Workington (A) 1-1, (H) 2-4

89-90 PR: Penrith (A) 3-2
Q1: Blyth Spartans (H) 0-3

90-91 PR: Netherfield (A) 3-0
Q1: Harrogate Railway Athletic (A) 0-2

91-92 Q1: Darlington Cleveland Bridge (A) 3-1
Q2: Garforth Town (H) 3-1
Q3: Gretna (A) 0-3

92-93 Q1: Guisborough Town (H) 1-2

NANPEAN ROVERS

Currently: East Cornwall Premier League

68-69 Q1: St Blazey (A) 2-2, (H) 1-1, 2-0
Q2: Wadebridge Town (A) 1-1, (H) 0-7

69-70 Q1: Wadebridge Town (A) 0-8

NANTWICH TOWN

Currently: North West Counties League
* - As Nantwich F.C.

46-47 * PR: Ellesmere Port Town (A) 0-9

47-48 * PR: Altrincham (H) 1-8

48-49 * EX: Barnton (A) 1-5

49-50 * PR: Droylsden (A) 1-10

50-51 * PR: Ellesmere Port Town (H) 4-3
Q1: Runcorn (A) 1-4

51-52 * Q1: Congleton Town (H) 2-2, (A) 2-3

54-55 * Q1: Stalybridge Celtic (H) 1-2

55-56 * PR: Congleton Town (H) 0-1

66-67 * Q1: Skelmersdale United (A) 3-4

67-68 * Q1: Kirkby Town (H) 1-2

68-69 * PR: Sandbach Ramblers (H) 5-4
Q1: Lostock Gralam (A) 2-4

69-70 * Q1: Northwich Victoria (H) 2-3

70-71 * Q1: New Brighton (A) 1-1, (H) 0-2

71-72 * Q1: New Mills (H) 3-1
Q2: Witton Albion (A) 1-0
Q3: Altrincham (A) 1-1, (H) 1-4

72-73 * Q1: Connah's Quay Nomads (H) 3-2
Q2: South Liverpool (H) 1-1, (A) 0-1

73-74 Q1: Ellesmere Port Town (H) 5-0
Q2: Altrincham (H) 0-3

74-75 Q1: Leek Town (A) 2-1
Q2: Mossley (A) 1-5

75-76 Q1: Chorley (A) 0-1

76-77 Q1: Northwich Victoria (H) 0-1

77-78 Q1: Bangor City (H) 1-1, (A) 1-4

78-79 PR: Prescot Town (H) 1-2

79-80 Q1: Colwyn Bay (H) 2-0
Q2: Oswestry Town (A) 0-2

80-81 PR: Winterton Rangers (H) 0-0, (A) 1-0
Q1: Eastwood Town (H) 0-0, (A) 0-1

81-82 Q1: Armitage (A) 2-0
Q2: Prescot Cables (A) 1-1, (H) 0-1

82-83 Q1: Witton Albion (H) 0-3

83-84 Q1: Emley (H) 1-1, (A) 2-6

84-85 PR: Droylsden (H) 0-0, (A) 0-2

85-86 PR: Glossop (H) 1-0
Q1: Emley (A) 0-1

91-92 PR: Radcliffe Borough (A) 1-0
Q1: Winsford United (A) 0-3

92-93 PR: Maltby Miners Welfare (H) 1-1, (A) 3-2
Q1: Congleton Town (A) 0-0, (H) 2-1
Q2: Blakenall (H) 1-0
Q3: Marine (H) 0-1

NELSON

Currently: North West Counties League

46-47 PR: Morecambe (H) 1-2

47-48 Q1: Chorley (H) 2-1
Q2: Horwich R.M.I. (H) 4-1
Q3: Fleetwood (A) 1-1, (H) 2-1
Q4: Lancaster City (A) 1-5

48-49 PR: De Havilland (Bolton) (A) 1-0
Q1: Fleetwood (A) 0-1

49-50 PR: Barnoldswick & District (A) 3-1
Q1: Darwen (A) 5-0
Q2: Fleetwood (A) 2-3

50-51 Q1: Lancaster City (H) 5-2
Q2: Leyland Motors (H) 4-1
Q3: Bacup Borough (A) 2-0
Q4: Hyde United (A) 2-2, (H) 3-0
R1: Witton Albion (A) 2-1
R2: Port Vale (A) 2-3

51-52 Q4: Skelmersdale United (A) 3-0
R1: Oldham Athletic (H) 0-4

52-53 Q4: Rhyl (H) 1-3

53-54 Q4: Winsford United (H) 1-0
R1: Witton Albion (A) 1-4

54-55 PR: Lytham (H) 3-0
Q1: Leyland Motors (H) 8-2
Q2: Chorley (A) 2-4

55-56 Q1: Ashton United (A) 1-1, (H) 1-4

56-57 Q1: Chorley (A) 1-4

57-58 Q1: Chorley (A) 1-5

58-59 Q1: Bacup Borough (A) 3-2
Q2: Skelmersdale United (A) 0-2

59-60 PR: Ashton United (H) 0-0, (A) 2-1
Q1: Lytham (H) 2-2, (A) 0-2

60-61 Q1: Stalybridge Celtic (H) 6-2
Q2: Bacup Borough (A) 3-0
Q3: Chorley (H) 7-4
Q4: Macclesfield Town (H) 2-3

61-62 Q1: Leyland Motors (H) 4-0
Q2: Stalybridge Celtic (A) 0-1

62-63 Q1: Hyde United (A) 0-3

63-64 Q1: Bacup Borough (H) 5-1
Q2: Chorley (A) 1-6

64-65 Q1: Lytham St Annes (H) 2-1
Q2: Hyde United (A) 3-1
Q3: Stalybridge Celtic (H) 2-3

65-66 Q1: Chorley (A) 0-6

66-67 Q1: Lytham St Annes (A) 1-0
Q2: Morecambe (H) 0-4

67-68 Q1: Penrith (A) 0-4

68-69 PR: Netherfield (H) 0-4

NETHERFIELD

Currently: Northern Premier League

45-46 Q2: Bye
Q3: Kells Welfare (A) 2-1
Q4: Lancaster City (H) 2-0
R1: Barrow (A) 0-1, (H) 2-2 *(agg: 2-3)*

46-47 Q1: Frizington United (H) 7-2
Q2: Milnthorpe Corinthians (H) 6-2
Q3: Lowca (A) 1-0
Q4: Workington (H) 1-3

47-48 PR: Cockermouth (H) 10-2
Q1: Scalegill (H) 5-1
Q2: Corinthians (Milnthorpe) (H) 4-1
Q3: Parton United (A) 4-1
Q4: Workington (A) 1-2

48-49 PR: Kells Welfare Centre (A) 5-1
Q1: Florence & Ullcoats United (H) 10-0
Q2: Corinthians (Milnthorpe) (A) 9-2
Q3: Penrith (H) 2-1
Q4: Rossendale United (H) 3-1
R1: Gateshead (A) 0-3

49-50 Q1: Penrith (A) 3-2
Q2: Kells Welfare Centre (H) 2-0
Q3: Aspatria Spartans (A) 4-2
Q4: Workington (H) 2-0
R1: North Shields (H) 4-3
R2: Watford (A) 0-6

50-51 Q1: Milnthorpe Corinthians (A) 5-0
Q2: Frizington United (A) 2-1
Q3: Cleator Moor Celtic (A) 1-2

51-52 Q1: Clitheroe (H) 2-0
Q2: Burscough (H) 4-2
Q3: Fleetwood (A) 0-3

52-53 Q1: Bacup Borough (H) 5-0
Q2: Burscough (A) 4-2
Q3: Morecambe (H) 3-1
Q4: Wigan Athletic (A) 3-2
R1: Gainsborough Trinity (A) 1-1, (H) 1-2

53-54 Q1: Fleetwood (A) 1-3

54-55 Q1: Great Harwood (A) 3-2
Q2: Fleetwood (H) 7-0
Q3: Burscough (A) 1-0
Q4: Chorley (A) 4-1
R1: Wrexham (H) 3-3, (A) 0-4

55-56 Q4: Lancaster City (H) 2-0
R1: Grimsby Town (H) 1-5

56-57 Q4: Wigan Athletic (A) 2-2, (H) 3-3, 0-2

57-58 Q1: Penrith (H) 5-2
Q2: Burscough (H) 0-2

58-59 Q1: Burscough (A) 2-2, (H) 2-1
Q2: Corinthians (Milnthorpe) (A) 2-1
Q3: Morecambe (H) 0-0, (A) 1-7

59-60 Q1: Corinthians (Milnthorpe) (A) 3-0
Q2: Burscough (A) 1-4

60-61 Q1: Penrith (H) 5-0
Q2: Fleetwood (A) 4-0
Q3: Morecambe (H) 2-0
Q4: Bangor City (A) 0-1

61-62 Q1: Penrith (H) 2-3

62-63 Q1: Horwich R.M.I. (A) 2-2, (H) 3-2
Q2: Clitheroe (A) 4-0
Q3: Wigan Athletic (H) 0-3

63-64 Q1: Clitheroe (A) 1-0
Q2: Burscough (H) 2-0
Q3: Lancaster City (H) 2-0
Q4: Horden Colliery Welfare (A) 3-0
R1: Loughborough United (H) 6-1
R2: Chesterfield (H) 1-1, (A) 1-4

64-65 Q4: Gateshead (A) 4-1
R1: Barnsley (H) 1-3

65-66 Q4: Scarborough (A) 1-5

66-67 Q1: Leyland Motors (H) 4-0
Q2: Fleetwood (H) 2-1
Q3: Morecambe (A) 1-2

67-68 Q1: Fleetwood (A) 3-2
Q2: Great Harwood (H) 1-2

68-69 PR: Nelson (A) 4-0
Q1: Morecambe (A) 0-4

69-70 Q1: Great Harwood (A) 3-1
Q2: Fleetwood (A) 0-3

70-71 Q1: Lancaster City (H) 1-3

71-72 Q1: Rossendale United (H) 2-4

72-73 Q1: Penrith (H) 3-0
Q2: Great Harwood (A) 0-5

73-74 Q1: Rossendale United (H) 3-2
Q2: Accrington Stanley (H) 2-1
Q3: Chorley (A) 1-0
Q4: Blyth Spartans (A) 0-2

74-75 Q1: Fleetwood (A) 2-0
Q2: Lancaster City (A) 2-1

75-76 Q1: Ashington (A) 2-0
Q2: Boldon C.W. (A) 1-1, (H) 3-2
Q3: Spennymoor United (A) 0-3

76-77 Q1: Ferryhill Athletic (A) 1-0
Q2: Annfield Plain (A) 1-1, (H) 6-0
Q3: Durham City (H) 1-1, (A) 2-1
Q4: Crook Town (A) 1-2

77-78 Q1: Willington (H) 4-0
Q2: Bishop Auckland (H) 1-1, (A) 1-1, (H) 3-4

78-79 Q1: Fleetwood T. (A) 0-0, (H) 1-1, (A) 0-2

79-80 Q1: Accrington Stanley (H) 4-0
Q2: Burscough (H) 0-2

80-81 PR: Washington (H) 3-2
Q1: Bridlington Trinity (H) 1-2

81-82 PR: Clitheroe (A) 1-0
Q1: Leyland Motors (H) 3-2
Q2: Droylsden (H) 1-1, (A) 1-3

82-83 Q1: Frickley Athletic (H) 0-2

83-84 PR: Peterlee Newtown (A) 0-3

84-85 Q1: South Bank (H) 0-4

85-86 PR: Bridlington Trinity (A) 0-4

86-87 PR: Thackley (A) 0-1

87-88 Q1: Crook Town (H) 1-1, (A) 1-2

88-89 PR: Farsley Celtic (A) 2-2, (H) 0-3

89-90 PR: Northallerton (A) 3-3, (H) 2-1
Q1: Ryhope Community Association (H) 3-1
Q2: Billingham Sythonia (A) 0-0, (H) 1-2

90-91 PR: Murton (H) 0-3

91-92 PR: Esh Winning (A) 3-1
Q1: Billingham Synthonia (H) 3-2
Q2: Newcastle Blue Star (H) 2-1
Q3: Gateshead (A) 0-0, (H) 0-3

92-93 Q1: Ossett Albion (A) 3-1
Q2: Consett (A) 1-1 *ab. (fog) 58m.*, (A) 4-3
Q3: Guisborough Town (H) 4-1
Q4: Macclesfield Town (H) 1-1, (A) 0-5

NEVILLE'S ATHLETIC

Currently: Defunct

50-51 EX: Rufford Colliery (A) 3-7

NEWBIGGIN CENTRAL WELF.

Currently: Northern Alliance

47-48 PR: West Stanley (H) 1-5

48-49 PR: North Shields (H) 2-5

49-50 EX: Amble (A) 2-0
PR: Cramlington Welfare (H) 3-0
Q1: North Shields (H) 0-3

50-51 EX: Alnwick Town (A) 0-4

NEW BRIGHTON

Currently: Defunct
* - As New Brighton Rakers

46-47 R1: Hull City (A) 0-0, (H) 1-2

47-48 R1: Marine (H) 4-0
R2: Bristol Rovers (A) 0-4

48-49 R1: Carlisle United (H) 1-0
R2: Bradford City (A) 0-0, (H) 1-0
R3: Sheffield United (A) 2-5

49-50 R1: Doncaster Rovers (A) 1-5

50-51 R1: Port Vale (A) 2-3

51-52 Q4: Bangor City (A) 1-2

52-53 Q1: Bootle Athletic (A) 1-1, (H) 1-0
Q2: Bangor City (A) 0-2

53-54 PR: Runcorn (A) 1-3

54-55 PR: Llandudno (A) 2-6

55-56 Q1: Llandudno (H) 4-0
Q2: Pwllheli & District (H) 4-2
Q3: Runcorn (H) 1-0
Q4: Rhyl (A) 1-3

56-57 PR: Prescot Cables (H) 2-1
Q1: Marine (A) 3-1
Q2: Earlestown (A) 6-1
Q3: South Liverpool (H) 6-1
Q4: Hyde United (H) 4-1
R1: Stockport County (H) 3-3, (A) 3-2
R2: Derby County (A) 3-1
R3: Torquay United (H) 2-1
R4: Burnley (A) 0-9

57-58 Q4: Rhyl (H) 2-3

58-59 Q1: Bangor City (A) 0-0, (H) 3-2
Q2: Flint Town United (H) 3-0
Q3: Llandudno (A) 1-0
Q4: Buxton (A) 0-4

59-60 PR: Marine (H) 1-0
Q1: Bangor City (A) 2-3

60-61 Q1: Llandudno (H) 3-1
Q2: Ellesmere Port Town (H) 0-0, (A) 1-0
Q3: Bangor City (A) 0-3

61-62 Q1: Flint Town United (H) 7-0
Q2: Ellesmere Port Town (H) 1-2

62-63 Q1: Bangor City (A) 0-4

63-64 Q1: Stork (A) 2-2, (H) 2-2, 3-0
Q2: Borough United (A) 1-1, (H) 3-1
Q3: Bangor City (A) 0-2

64-65 Q1: Llandudno (H) 8-3
Q2: Ellesmere Port Town (A) 0-4

65-66 Q1: Holyhead Town (A) 2-0
Q2: Borough United (A) 0-3

66-67 Q1: Colwyn Bay (H) 3-1
Q2: Oswestry Town (A) 4-2
Q3: Bangor City (A) 6-6, (H) 0-1

67-68 Q1: Lostock Gralam (A) 1-1, (H) 1-2

68-69 Q1: Kirkby Town (A) 1-3

69-70 Q1: Winsford United (H) 2-1
Q2: Kirkby Town (H) 1-2

70-71 Q1: Nantwich (H) 1-1, (A) 2-0
Q2: Ellesmere Port Town (A) 1-3

71-72 Q1: Runcorn (A) 0-2

72-73 Q1: Marine (H) 1-4

73-74 PR: Hyde United (H) 1-1, (A) 1-2

74-75 Q1: Porthmadog (H) 2-1
Q2: Oswestry Town (A) 1-2

75-76 PR: Bacup Borough (H) 3-1
Q1: Winsford United (A) 1-4

76-77 * PR: Skelmersdale United (H) 1-1, (A) 2-0
Q1: Porthmadog (A) 4-3
Q2: Rhyl (H) 1-3

77-78 * Q1: St Helens Town (H) 1-0
Q2: Winsford United (H) 1-3

78-79 Q1: Prestwich Heys (H) 1-3

79-80 PR: Macclesfield Town (H) 1-7

80-81 PR: Worsborough Bridge M.W. Ath. (H) 1-3

NEWBURN

Currently: Defunct

45-46 Q1: Amble (H) 3-1
Q2: Throckley Welfare (H) 0-0, (A) *W/O*

46-47 Q1: Annfield Plain (A) 2-1
Q2: Ashington (H) 3-3, (A) 1-6

47-48 Q1: Gosforth & Coxlodge (H) 2-0
Q2: Blyth Spartans (H) 1-5

48-49 PR: Jarrow (A) 3-0
Q1: South Shields (A) 2-5

49-50 EX: Shankhouse (A) 4-1
PR: North Shields (A) 0-7

50-51 EX: Wardley Welfare (H) 3-1
PR: Alnwick Town (A) 2-10

51-52 Q1: Blyth Spartans (H) 1-1, (A) 0-1

52-53 Q1: Shankhouse (H) 4-1
Q2: Alnwick Town (A) 1-0
Q3: Ashington (H) 1-4

53-54 Q1: Amble (A) 3-3 - *then Amble withdrew*
Q2: West Sleekburn Colliery Welf. (A) 1-0
Q3: Hexham Hearts (A) 4-5

54-55 PR: Ashington (H) 1-6

55-56 Q1: Cramlington Welfare (H) 1-2

57-58 Q2: Alnwick Town (H) 0-2

58-59 Q2: Evenwood Town (A) 2-7

59-60 Q2: North Shields (A) 0-5

60-61 Q1: Ashington (H - *played away*) 1-2

61-62 Q1: South Bank (A) 3-0
Q2: Willington (A) 2-3

NEWBURY TOWN

Currently: Isthmian League

45-46 PR: Banbury Spencer (H) 0-8

61-62 Q1: Cowes Isle of Wight (A) 1-3

62-63 Q1: Chichester City (A) 3-2
Q2: Alton Town (H) 1-9

63-64 Q1: Hemel Hempstead Town (H) 0-0, (A) 0-6

64-65 Q1: Abingdon Town (H) 2-0
Q2: Oxford City (H) 0-2

65-66 Q1: Salisbury (A) 0-4

66-67 Q1: Andover (H) 0-3

77-78 Q1: Bridgwater Town (H) 0-1

78-79 PR: Andover (A) 1-1, (H) 1-2

79-80 Q1: Didcot Town (H) 2-1
Q2: Barry Town (H) 1-2

80-81 PR: Pagham (H) 1-0
Q1: Chichester City (H) 2-0
Q2: Bognor Regis Town (A) 2-1
Q3: Farnborough Town (A) 1-4

81-82 PR: Burnham (A - *played home*) 4-3
Q1: Camberley Town (A) 2-0
Q2: Wealdstone (H) 1-6

82-83 PR: Mangotsfield United (A) 2-3

83-84 PR: Devizes Town (H) 4-2
Q1: Hungerford Town (A) 1-2

84-85 Q1: Slough Town (H) 1-5

85-86 PR: Melksham Town (H) 2-1
Q1: A.F.C. Totton (H) 3-3, (A) 0-2

86-87 Q1: Petersfield United (H) 2-1
Q2: Fareham Town (H) 0-5

87-88 PR: Welton Rovers (H) 2-2, (A) 4-2
Q1: Radstock Town (A) 0-5

88-89 PR: Salisbury (A) 2-4

89-90 PR: Bristol Manor Farm (H) 2-2, (A) 1-3

90-91 PR: Eastleigh (H) 2-1
Q1: Trowbridge Town (A) 0-3

91-92 PR: Horndean (H) 1-0
Q1: Romsey Town (A) 1-2

92-93 PR: Cinderford Town (A) 0-3

NEWCASTLE BLUE STAR

Currently: Northern League
* - As Blue Star F.C.

78-79 * Q1: Washington (A) 2-3

79-80 * PR: Guisborough Town (A) 2-3

80-81 * Q1: Bridlington Town (H) 3-1
Q2: Thackley (H) 2-0
Q3: Penrith (A) 0-1

81-82 * PR: Whitley Bay (H) 0-0, (A) 1-3

82-83 * Q1: Lancaster City (H) 1-2

83-84 * PR: Fleetwood Town (A) 1-2

84-85 * Q1: Horden Colliery Welfare (H) 3-0
Q2: Billingham Synthonia (H) 1-0
Q3: Gateshead (A) 1-1, (H) 3-1
Q4: Burscough (A) 0-0, (H) 4-0
R1: York City (A) 0-2

85-86 * Q1: Guisborough Town (H) 2-1
Q2: Bishop Auckland (H) 1-3

86-87 PR: Norton & Stockton Ancients (A) 1-1, (H - *at North Shields*) 6-0
Q1: Farsley Celtic (A) 3-1
Q2: South Bank (H) 0-0, (A) 2-1
Q3: Workington (H) 1-1, (A) 1-0
Q4: Whitby Town (A) 0-2

87-88 Q1: Morecambe (H) 1-0
Q2: Ryhope Community Association (A) 2-0
Q3: Easington Colliery (A) 0-3

88-89 Q1: Norton & Stocton & Ancients (H) 4-0
Q2: Billingham Town (A) 1-2

89-90 Q1: Stockton (H) 1-1, (A) 3-1
Q2: North Shields (H) 1-1, (A) 2-4

90-91 Q1: Whitby Town (A) 7-4
Q2: Lancaster City (A) 2-0
Q3: Consett (H) 3-0
Q4: Runcorn (A) 0-1

91-92 Q1: Hebburn (H) 5-1
Q2: Netherfield (A) 1-2

92-93 PR: Whickham (H) 0-0, (A) 2-0
Q1: Annfield Plain (A) 1-0
Q2: Bishop Auckland (H) 0-1

NEWCASTLE TOWN

Currently: North West Counties League

91-92 PR: Ossett Albion (H) 2-0
Q1: Bootle (A) 1-2

92-93 PR: Bilston Town (A) 3-1
Q1: Gresley Rovers (H) 0-1

NEWCASTLE UNITED

Currently: F.A. Premier League

45-46 R3: Barnsley (H) 4-2, (A) 0-3 (*agg: 4-5*)

46-47 R3: Crystal Palace (H) 6-2
R4: Southampton (H) 3-1
R5: Leicester City (H) 1-1, (A) 2-1
R6: Sheffield United (A) 2-0
SF: Charlton Athletic (*at Leeds Utd*) 0-4

47-48 R3: Charlton Athletic (A) 1-2

48-49 R3: Bradford (Park Avenue) (H) 0-2

49-50 R3: Oldham Athletic (A) 7-2
R4: Chelsea (A) 0-3

50-51 R3: Bury (H) 4-1
R4: Bolton Wanderers (H) 3-2
R5: Stoke City (A) 4-2
R6: Bristol Rovers (H) 0-0, (A) 3-1
SF: Wolves (*at Sheff. W.*) 0-0, (*Hud'field*) 2-1
F: Blackpool (*at Wembley*) 2-0

51-52 R3: Aston Villa (H) 4-2
R4: Tottenham Hotspur (A) 3-0
R5: Swansea Town (A) 1-0
R6: Portsmouth (A) 4-2
SF: Blackburn (*at Sheff. W.*) 0-0, (*at Leeds*) 2-1
F: Arsenal (*at Wembley*) 1-0

52-53 R3: Swansea Town (H) 3-0
R4: Rotherham United (H) 1-3

53-54 R3: Wigan Athletic (H) 2-2, (A) 3-2
R4: Burnley (A) 1-1, (H) 1-0
R5: West Bromwich Albion (A) 2-3

54-55 R3: Plymouth Argyle (A) 1-0
R4: Brentford (H) 3-2
R5: Nottingham Forest (A) 1-1, (H) 2-2, 2-1
R6: Huddersfield Town (A) 1-1, (H) 2-0
SF: York (*at Sheff. W.*) 1-1, (*Sunderland*) 2-0
F: Manchester City (*at Wembley*) 3-1

55-56 R3: Sheffield Wednesday (A) 3-1
R4: Fulham (A) 5-4
R5: Stoke City (H) 2-1
R6: Sunderland (H) 0-2

56-57 R3: Manchester City (H) 1-1, (A) 5-4
R4: Millwall (A) 1-2

57-58 R3: Plymouth Argyle (A) 6-1

Above: *Newcastle United's Frank Clark (left) challenges Tony Jennings in the 1974 home draw with Hendon.*

	R4: Scunthorpe United (H) 1-3
58-59	R3: Chelsea (H) 1-4
59-60	R3: Wolverhampton Wdrs (H) 2-2, (A) 2-4
60-61	R3: Fulham (H) 5-0 R4: Stockport County (H) 4-0 R5: Stoke City (H) 3-1 R6: Sheffield United (H) 1-3
61-62	R3: Peterborough United (H) 0-1
62-63	R3: Bradford City (A) 6-1 R4: Norwich City (A) 0-5
63-64	R3: Bedford Town (H) 1-2
64-65	R3: Swansea Town (A) 0-1
65-66	R3: Chester (A) 3-1 R4: Sheffield Wednesday (H) 1-2
66-67	R3: Coventry City (A) 4-3 R4: Nottingham Forest (A) 0-3
67-68	R3: Carlisle United (H) 0-1
68-69	R3: Reading (H) 4-0 R4: Manchester City (A) 0-0, (H) 0-2
69-70	R3: Southampton (A) 0-3
70-71	R3: Ipswich Town (H) 1-1, (A) 1-2
71-72	R3: Hereford United (H) 2-2, (A) 1-2
72-73	R3: A.F.C. Bournemouth (H) 2-0 R4: Luton Town (H) 0-2
73-74	R3: Hendon (H) 1-1, (A - *at Watford*) 4-0 R4: Scunthorpe United (H) 1-1, (A) 3-0 R5: West Bromwich Albion (A) 3-0 R6: Nottm Forest (H) 4-3 *replay ordered*, (*at Everton*) 0-0, (*at Everton*) 1-0 SF: Burnley (*at Sheffield Wednesday*) 2-0 F: Liverpool (*at Wembley*) 0-3
74-75	R3: Manchester City (H) 2-0 R4: Walsall (A) 0-1
75-76	R3: Queens Park Rangers (A) 0-0, (H) 2-1 R4: Coventry City (A) 1-1, (H) 5-0 R5: Bolton Wanderers (A) 3-3, (H) 0-0, (*at Leeds United*) 2-1 R6: Derby County (A) 2-4
76-77	R3: Sheffield United (A) 0-0, (H) 3-1 R4: Manchester City (H) 1-3
77-78	R3: Peterborough United (A) 1-1, (H) 2-0 R4: Wrexham (H) 2-2, (A) 1-4
78-79	R3: Torquay United (H) 3-1 R4: Wolverhampton W. (H) 1-1, (A) 0-1
79-80	R3: Chester (H) 0-2
80-81	R3: Sheffield Wednesday (H) 2-1 R4: Luton Town (H) 2-1 R5: Exeter City (H) 1-1, (A) 0-4
81-82	R3: Colchester United (H) 1-1, (A) 4-3 R4: Grimsby Town (H) 1-2
82-83	R3: Brighton & Hove A. (A) 1-1, (H) 0-1
83-84	R3: Liverpool (A) 0-4
84-85	R3: Nottingham Forest (A) 1-1, (H) 1-3
85-86	R3: Brighton & Hove Albion (H) 0-2
86-87	R3: Northampton Town (H) 2-1 R4: Preston North End (H) 2-0 R5: Tottenham Hotspur (A) 0-1
87-88	R3: Crystal Palace (H) 1-0 R4: Swindon Town (H) 5-0 R5: Wimbledon (H) 1-3
88-89	R3: Watford (H) 0-0, (A) 2-2, (H) 0-0, (A) 0-1
89-90	R3: Hull City (A) 1-0 R4: Reading (A) 3-3, (H) 4-1 R5: Manchester United (H) 2-3
90-91	R3: Derby County (H) 2-0 R4: Nottingham Forest (H) 2-2, (A) 0-3
91-92	R3: A.F.C. Bournemouth (A) 0-0, (H) 0-0 - *ab. (fog) after 17 mins*, (H) 2-2 (*3-4 pens*)
92-93	R3: Port Vale (H) 4-0 R4: Rotherham United (A) 1-1, (H) 2-0 R5: Blackburn Rovers (A) 0-1

NEWHALL UNITED

Currently: Central Midlands League

50-51	PR: Hinckley Athletic (H) 2-2, (A) 1-2
51-52	Q1: Matlock Town (H) 4-0 Q2: Basford United (A) 1-1, (H) 3-0 Q3: Ilkeston Town (A) 1-6
52-53	Q1: Matlock Town (H) 3-2 Q2: Boots Athletic (A) 2-2, (H) 2-3
53-54	Q1: Basford United (A) 0-0, (H) 2-3
54-55	Q1: South Normanton Welfare (A) 1-2
70-71	Q1: Hinckley Athletic (A) 1-1, (H) 4-1 Q2: Burton Albion (H) 1-3
71-72	Q1: Heanor Town (A) 0-1

NEWHAVEN

Currently: Sussex County League

45-46	Q1: Haywards Heath (H) 2-2, (A) 0-5
46-47	PR: Eastbourne (A) 1-4
47-48	PR: East Grinstead (A) 2-5
49-50	PR: Hove (A) 2-3
50-51	PR: Eastbourne Comrades (A) 0-0, (H) 3-0 Q1: East Grinstead (H) 1-2
52-53	PR: Ashford Town (H) 2-4
53-54	PR: Lancing Athletic (A) 1-2
54-55	PR: Eastbourne (H) 2-2, (A) 0-3
55-56	PR: East Grinstead (A) 1-2
56-57	PR: Bognor Regis Town (H) 1-5
57-58	PR: Eastbourne (H) 2-1 Q1: Lancing Athletic (H) 1-0 Q2: Bognor Regis Town (A) 1-5
58-59	Q1: Arundel (A) 3-5
59-60	PR: Lancing Athletic (A) 1-2
60-61	Q1: Eastbourne (A) 1-2
61-62	Q2: Eastbourne United (H) 1-6
62-63	Q1: Bexhill T. (A - *played home*) 0-0, (H) 0-2

NEWMARKET TOWN

Currently: Eastern Counties League

45-46	Q1: Chatteris Town (A) 1-0 Q2: Wisbech Town (A) 0-5
46-47	Q2: Chatteris Town (H) 0-2
47-48	Q1: March Town United (H) 2-3
48-49	PR: Chatteris Town (H) 6-2 Q1: Parson Drove United (A) 2-3
49-50	PR: Chatteris Town (H) 4-4, (A) 4-1 Q1: Abbey United (H) 1-0 Q2: Cambridge Town (A) 0-1
50-51	Q1: Chatteris Town (A) 2-0 Q2: Histon Institute (H) 1-3
54-55	PR: Somersham Town (A) 0-3
55-56	PR: Holbeach United (A) 0-6
56-57	PR: March Town United (H) 1-6
57-58	PR: Wisbech Town (A) 0-6
58-59	Q1: Stowmarket (A) 1-3
59-60	Q1: Clacton Town (H) 1-4
60-61	Q1: Cambridge United (A) 0-5
61-62	Q1: March Town United (A) 2-0 Q2: Bury Town (H) 2-6
65-66	Q1: Wisbech Town (A) 1-5
66-67	Q1: Bury Town (H) 1-1, (A) 1-2
67-68	Q1: Kettering Town (H) 0-1
68-69	Q1: Ely City (A) 1-4
69-70	PR: March Town United (A) 1-1, (H) 3-0 Q1: Eynesbury Rovers (A) 3-2 Q2: Irthlingborough Diamonds (H) 3-1 Q3: Cambridge United (A) 0-6
70-71	Q1: Lowestoft Town (H) 3-3, (A) 0-3
71-72	Q1: Thetford Town (H) 1-4
76-77	Q1: Harwich & Parkeston (H) 1-1, (A) 1-8
77-78	Q1: Lowestoft Town (A) 1-4
78-79	PR: Olney Town (H) 1-2
79-80	PR: Sudbury Town (H) 1-3
80-81	PR: Wellingborough Town (H) 1-0 Q1: Hayes (H) 1-1, (A) 0-5
81-82	Q1: Letchworth Garden City (H) 1-0 Q2: March Town United (A) 5-5, (H) 0-2
82-83	Q1: Boreham Wood (H) 0-3
83-84	PR: Rothwell Town (A) 0-2
84-85	Q1: Wellingborough Town (H) 1-2
85-86	PR: Chatteris Town (A) 3-0 Q1: Stamford (H - *played away*) 1-6
86-87	Q1: Great Yarmouth Town (H) 2-0 Q2: Cambridge City (H) 1-2
87-88	PR: Dunstable (H) 0-3
88-89	PR: Staines Town (A) 0-3
89-90	PR: Braintree Town (A) 1-1, (H) 1-0 Q1: Leighton Town (H) 1-0 Q2: Barnet (A) 2-4
90-91	PR: Cheshunt (H) 2-1 Q1: Cambridge City (H) 1-2
91-92	PR: Biggleswade T. (H) 1-1, (A) 2-2, (A) 0-1
92-93	PR: Langford (H) 4-0 Q1: Tilbury (A) 1-1, (H) 1-0 Q2: Baldock Town (H) 2-2, (A) 6-2 Q3: Grays Athletic (H) 1-0 Q4: Hayes (H) 0-2

Below: *Jerry Rose scores Newmarket's first goal in the 2-2 draw against Baldock on Saturday 26th September 1992. The 'Jockeys' won the replay and enjoyed their best post-war cup run. Photo: Clive Pearson.*

NEW MILLS

Currently: Manchester League

69-70 Q1: Mossley (H) 0-1

70-71 PR: Chorley (H) 0-2

71-72 PR: Sandbach Ramblers (H) 3-1
Q1: Nantwich (A) 1-3

72-73 Q1: Radcliffe Borough (H) 1-3

73-74 Q1: Stalybridge Celtic (H) 0-2

74-75 Q1: Hyde United (H) 0-1

75-76 Q1: Oswestry Town (H) 1-1, (A) 3-5

76-77 Q1: Brereton Social (H) 5-2
Q2: Long Eaton United (A) 0-3

77-78 Q1: Curzon Ashton (H) 1-2

78-79 Q1: Denaby United (H) 2-0
Q2: Hednesford Town (A) 0-4

79-80 Q1: Glossop (H) 1-2

80-81 Q1: Northwich Victoria (A) 0-1

81-82 PR: Shifnal Town (A) 0-5

82-83 Q1: Horwich R.M.I. (H) 0-3

NEWPORT A.F.C.

Currently: Southern League

92-93 PR: Dawlish Town (A) 3-0
Q1: Forest Green Rovers (A) 2-1
Q2: Worcester City (H - *at Gloucester*) 3-0
Q3: Clevedon Town (H - *at Gloucester*) 1-1, (A) 1-1, (H - *at Gloucester*) 4-2
Q4: Sutton United (H - *at Gloucester*) 1-4

NEWPORT COUNTY

Currently: Defunct

45-46 R1: Torquay Utd (A) 1-0, (H) 1-1 (*agg: 2-1*)
R2: Exeter City (H) 5-1, (A) 3-1 (*agg: 8-2*)
R3: Southampton (A) 3-4, (H) 1-2 (*agg: 4-6*)

46-47 R3: Coventry City (A) 2-5

47-48 R1: Southend United (H) 3-2
R2: Reading (A) 0-3

48-49 R1: Brighton & Hove Albion (H) 3-1
R2: Leytonstone (A) 4-3
R3: Leeds United (A) 3-1
R4: Huddersfield Town (H) 3-3, (A) 3-1
R5: Portsmouth (A) 2-3

49-50 R1: Crystal Palace (A) 3-0
R2: Gateshead (H) 1-1, (A) 2-1
R3: Port Vale (H) 1-2

50-51 R1: Walsall (H) 4-2
R2: Hereford United (A) 3-0
R3: Reading (H) 3-2
R4: Norwich City (H) 0-2

51-52 R1: Barry Town (H) 4-0
R2: Leytonstone (A) 2-2, (H) 3-0
R3: Sheffield United (A) 0-2

52-53 R1: Walsall (H) 2-1
R2: Gainsborough Trinity (H) 2-1
R3: Sheffield United (H) 1-4

53-54 R1: Cambridge United (A) 2-2, (H) 1-2

54-55 R1: Gillingham (A) 0-2

55-56 R1: Brighton & Hove Albion (A) 1-8

56-57 R1: Walsall (A) 1-0
R2: Gillingham (A) 2-1
R3: Southampton (H) 3-3, (A) 1-0
R4: Arsenal (H) 0-2

57-58 R1: Northampton Town (A) 0-3

58-59 R1: Wisbech Town (A) 2-2, (H) 4-1
R2: Hereford United (A) 2-0
R3: Torquay United (H) 0-0, (A) 1-0
R4: Tottenham Hotspur (A) 1-4

59-60 R1: Hereford United (H) 4-2
R2: Salisbury (A) 1-0
R3: Tottenham Hotspur (H) 0-4

60-61 R1: Shrewsbury Town (A) 1-4

61-62 R1: Reading (A) 1-1, (H) 1-0
R2: Weymouth (A) 0-1

62-63 R1: Queens Park Rangers (A) 2-3

63-64 R1: Hereford United (A) 1-1, (H) 4-0
R2: Watford (H) 2-0
R3: Sheffield Wednesday (H) 3-2
R4: Burnley (A) 1-2

64-65 R1: Spalding United (H) 5-3
R2: Mansfield Town (H) 3-0
R3: Reading (A) 2-2, (H) 0-1

65-66 R1: Bath City (A) 0-2

66-67 R1: Brighton & Hove Albion (H) 1-2

67-68 R1: Gillingham (H) 3-0
R2: Guildford City (A) 1-0
R3: Southampton (A) 1-1, (H) 2-3

68-69 R1: Exeter City (A) 0-0, (H) 1-3

69-70 R1: Colchester United (H) 2-1
R2: Hereford United (H) 2-1
R3: Gillingham (A) 0-1

70-71 R1: Barnet (A) 1-6

71-72 R1: Notts County (A) 0-6

72-73 R1: Alton Town (H) 5-1
R2: Torquay United (A) 1-0
R3: Millwall (A) 0-3

73-74 R1: Wycombe Wanderers (A) 1-3

74-75 R1: Exeter City (A) 2-1
R2: Walsall (H) 1-3

75-76 R1: Swindon Town (H) 2-2, (A) 0-3

76-77 R1: A.F.C. Bournemouth (A) 0-0, (H) 3-0
R2: Southend United (A) 0-3

77-78 R1: Exeter City (H) 1-1, (A) 2-4

78-79 R1: Hereford United (A) 1-0
R2: Worcester City (H) 0-0, (A) 2-1
R3: West Ham United (H) 2-1
R4: Colchester United (H) 0-0, (A) 0-1

79-80 R1: Portsmouth (A) 0-1

80-81 R1: Plymouth Argyle (A) 0-2

81-82 R1: Colchester United (A) 0-2

82-83 R1: Enfield (A) 0-0, (H) 4-2
R2: Orient (H) 1-0
R3: Everton (H) 1-1, (A) 1-2

83-84 R1: Poole Town (A) 0-0, (H) 3-1
R2: Harrow Borough (A) 3-1
R3: Plymouth Argyle (A) 2-2, (H) 0-1

84-85 R1: Aldershot (H) 1-1, (A) 0-4

85-86 R1: Southend United (A) 1-0
R2: Torquay United (H) 1-1, (A) 3-2
R3: Sunderland (A) 0-2

86-87 R1: Bromsgrove Rovers (A) 1-0
R2: Fulham (A) 0-2

87-88 R1: Northampton Town (A) 1-2

88-89 Q4: Weymouth (H) 2-1
R1: Maidstone United (H) 1-2

NEWPORT ISLE OF WIGHT

Currently: Southern League

45-46 Q1: Totton (A) 4-0
Q2: Gosport Borough Athletic (H) 2-0
Q3: Cowes (H) 0-1 *Cowes expelled*
Q4: Guildford City (A) 2-1
R1: Clapton Orient (A) 1-2, (H) 2-0 (*agg: 3-2*)
R2: Aldershot (A) 0-7, (H) 0-5 (*agg: 0-12*)

46-47 PR: Sandown (A) 3-3, (H) 3-2
Q1: Bournemouth Gasworks Athletic (H) 0-1

47-48 EX: Cowes (A) 3-1
PR: Weymouth (H) 5-2
Q1: Salisbury (A) 0-0, (H) 2-0
Q2: Gosport Borough Athletic (A) 2-5

48-49 PR: Bitterne Nomads (A - *played home*) 4-0
Q1: Weymouth (H) 2-4

49-50 EX: Winchester City (A) 2-1
PR: Ryde Sports (A) 1-1, (H) 3-5

50-51 EX: Totton (H) 4-0
PR: Winchester City (H) 5-1
Q1: Poole Town (H) 6-6, (A) 0-1

51-52 Q1: Gosport Borough Athletic (A) 3-2
Q2: Totton (H) 6-1
Q3: Alton Town (H) 5-1
Q4: Chippenham Town (A) 1-3

52-53 Q1: Cowes (A) 1-0
Q2: Winchester City (A) 3-1
Q3: Basingstoke Town (A) 4-2
Q4: Lancing Athletic (A) 5-1
R1: Swindon Town (A) 0-5

53-54 Q1: Basingstoke Town (A) 5-0
Q2: Winchester City (H) 7-0
Q3: Cowes (H) 4-2
Q4: Chippenham United (H) 3-1
R1: Swindon Town (A) 1-2

54-55 Q4: Wells City (A) 4-1
R1: Hinckley Athletic (A) 3-4

55-56 Q4: Dorchester Town (A) 0-3

56-57 Q4: Poole Town (A) 3-0
R1: Watford (H) 0-6

57-58 Q4: Portland United (H) 5-0
R1: Hereford United (H) 0-3

58-59 Q4: Portland United (A) 2-2, (H) 3-1
R1: Shrewsbury Town (H) 0-0, (A) 0-5

59-60 Q1: Cowes (A) 0-2

60-61 Q1: Cowes (H) 1-2

61-62 Q1: Fareham Town (A) 3-2
Q2: Cowes (H) 0-0, (A) 1-5

62-63 Q1: Alton Town (A) 0-2

63-64 Q1: Andover (A) 0-2

64-65 Q1: Fareham Town (H) 1-5

65-66 Q1: Bognor Regis Town (H) 2-1
Q2: Cowes (A) 3-3, (H) 0-3

66-67 Q1: Fareham Town (A) 1-5

67-68 Q1: Andover (H) 4-3
Q2: Selsey (A) 3-1
Q3: Salisbury (A) 0-3

68-69 Q1: Selsey (H) 3-2
Q2: Waterlooville (A) 0-3

69-70 Q1: Andover (A) 1-4

70-71 Q1: Ryde Sports (A) 3-0
Q2: Basingstoke Town (H) 2-2, (A) 0-1

71-72 PR: Gosport Borough (A) 0-0, (H) 4-0
Q1: Fleet (A) 1-1, (H) 5-2
Q2: Thornycroft Athletic (A) 1-4

72-73 PR: Cowes (H) 2-0
Q1: Fareham Town (H) 2-6

73-74 PR: Fareham Town (H) 1-1, (A) 1-0
Q1: Arundel (A) 2-0
Q2: Bognor Regis Town (A) 0-1

74-75 Q1: Alton Town (A) 2-3

75-76 Q1: Bognor Regis Town (A) 3-1
Q2: Gosport Borough (A) 2-2, (H) 1-1, 0-2

76-77 PR: Wigmore Athletic (H) 2-0
Q1: Swaythling (A) 0-4

77-78 Q1: Waterlooville (H) 0-0, (A) 1-0
Q2: Farnborough Town (A) 0-3

78-79 Q1: Basingstoke Town (H) 0-1

79-80 PR: Selsey (H) 4-0
Q1: Salisbury (A) 3-4

80-81 Q1: Fareham Town (A) 0-2

81-82 PR: Woking (A) 0-1

82-83 PR: Littlehampton Town (A) 3-0
Q1: Eastleigh (A) 2-2, (H) 1-3

83-84 PR: Wick (A) 1-2

84-85 Q1: Salisbury (A) 1-4

85-86 Q1: Metropolitan Police (H) 3-2
Q2: Pagham (A) 5-3
Q3: Worthing (A) 0-4

86-87 Q1: Gosport Borough (A) 1-1, (H) 3-2
Q2: Sheppey United (A) 1-1, (H) 1-0
Q3: Southwick (A) 0-2

87-88 Q1: A.F.C. Totton (H) 2-0
Q2: Chertsey Town (A) 1-0
Q3: Bracknell Town (A) 1-4

88-89 Q1: Bashley (H) 1-1, (A) 0-1

89-90 PR: Abingdon United (A) 4-1
Q1: Flackwell Heath (A) 2-0
Q2: A.F.C. Totton (A) 3-1
Q3: Marlow (H) 0-1

90-91 Q1: Waterlooville (A) 1-1, (H) 3-0
Q2: Melksham Town (A) 2-0
Q3: Romsey Town (H) 0-1

91-92 Q1: Maidenhead United (H) 0-3

92-93 PR: Eastleigh (A) 2-1
Q1: Wimborne Town (H) 2-3

NEWQUAY

Currently: South Western League
* - As Newquay Amateurs

50-51 PR: St Austell (H) 3-0
Q1: Ilfracombe Town (H) 5-2
Q2: Street (H) 1-2

51-52 PR: Wadebridge Town (H) 3-1
Q1: Dartmouth United (A) 1-3

52-53 PR: Truro City (H) 7-1
Q1: St Blazey (H) 1-3

53-54 * PR: Minehead (H) 2-1
Q1: St Blazey (A) 2-4

54-55 * PR: Bideford (H) 5-1
Q1: Ilfracombe Town (A) 0-2

55-56 * PR: Penzance (A) 2-4

56-57 Q1: Tavistock (A) 4-3
Q2: Bideford (A) 0-4

57-58 PR: St Austell (H) 2-0
Q1: Truro City (A) 1-3

58-59 Q1: St Blazey (A) 1-2

59-60 Q1: Barnstaple Town (H) 3-3 *then withdrew*

71-72 Q1: St Blazey (A) 0-4

72-73 Q1: Truro City (A) 1-2

73-74 Q1: Wadebridge Town (H) 1-0
Q2: Bideford (H) 1-1, (A) 1-6

74-75 Q1: Falmouth Town (A) 0-2

75-76 Q1: Falmouth Town (A) 1-5

76-77 * Q1: St Blazey (H) 0-0, (A) 3-1
Q2: Falmouth Town (A) 0-8

77-78 * Q1: Falmouth Town (A) 1-0
Q2: Bideford (H) 2-3

78-79 PR: Penzance (H) 2-2, (A) 1-2

79-80 Q1: Penzance (A) 4-1
Q2: Tiverton Town (A) 3-3, (H) 0-1

80-81 PR: Ottery St Mary (H) 8-0
Q1: Saltash United (A) 0-4

81-82 Q1: Falmouth Town (A) 0-2

NEWTON ABBOT

Currently: Defunct

51-52 PR: Truro City (A) 3-5

52-53 PR: Ilfracombe Town (H) 1-1, (A) 1-2

54-55 PR: Wadebridge Town (H) 1-3

NEWTON ABBOT SPURS

Currently: South Devon League

47-48 PR: Oak Villa (A) 2-1
Q1: Wells City (A) 1-0
Q2: Street (H) 2-4

48-49 PR: Wells City (A) 2-4

49-50 PR: Bideford (A) 1-1, (H) 2-4

64-65 Q1: Falmouth Town (H) 1-1, (A) 2-3

NEWTON Y.M.C.A.

Currently: (Newton F.C.) West Cheshire League

46-47 Q1: Orrell (A) 2-1
Q2: Haydock C. & B. Rec. (A) 1-1, (H) 1-3

47-48 PR: Orrell (H) 1-2

48-49 PR: Llandudno (A) 1-0
Q1: Rhyl (H) 1-4

49-50 EX: Earle (H) 3-4

NEWTOWN

Currently: League of Wales

90-91 PR: Eastwood Town (H) 1-1, (A) 1-2

91-92 PR: Glossop (H) 4-2
Q1: Rhyl (A) 0-1

NEW WALTHAM

Currently: Defunct

48-49 EX: Luddington (H) 3-1
PR: Bradford United (A) 4-8

NORMANBY PARK WORKS

Currently: Defunct

79-80 PR: Whitby Town (H) 1-3

80-81 PR: Sutton Town (H) 0-0, (A) 3-2
Q1: Desborough Town (H) 0-4

NORTHALLERTON TOWN

Currently: Northern League

85-86 PR: Garforth Town (A) 2-1
Q1: Shotton Comrades (H) 1-2

86-87 PR: Guiseley (H) 0-4

87-88 PR: Rossendale United (A) 0-3

88-89 PR: Ossett Albion (A) 2-2, (H) 2-1
Q1: Easington Colliery (H) 2-0
Q2: Morecambe (A) 2-3

89-90 PR: Netherfield (H) 3-3, (A) 1-2

90-91 PR: Clitheroe (H) 4-2
Q1: Billingham Synthonia (H) 2-0
Q2: Horden Colliery Welfare (A) 3-0
Q3: Spennymoor United (A) 0-2

91-92 Q1: Langley Park (H) 1-0
Q2: Bridlington Town (A) 0-4

92-93 PR: Langley Park (H) 6-1
Q1: Darwen (A) 6-1
Q2: Fleetwood Town (A) 2-1
Q3: Dunston F.B. (A) 3-0
Q4: Accrington Stanley (A) 1-3

Below: *Northallerton goalkeeper Michael Devine punches clear an Accrington corner under pressure from Paul Beck during the thrilling Fourth Qualifying Round tie on October 24th 1992. Photo: Colin Stevens.*

88-89 PR: Irthlingborough Diamonds (H) 0-1

89-90 PR: Paget Rangers (H) 3-3, (A) 0-2

90-91 PR: Sandwell Borough (A) 1-4

91-92 PR: Hednesford (A) 1-1, (H) 1-1, (A) 0-1

92-93 PR: Rushall Olympic (H) 1-1, (A) 2-3

NORTHAMPTON TOWN

Currently: Football League

45-46 R1: Chelmsford (H) 5-1, (A) 5-0 *(agg: 10-1)*
R2: Notts County (H) 3-1, (A) 0-1 *(agg: 3-2)*
R3: Millwall (H) 2-2, (A) 0-3 *(agg: 2-5)*

46-47 R1: Mansfield Town (H) 2-0
R2: Peterborough U. (A) 1-1, (H) 1-1, 8-1
R3: Preston North End (H) 1-2

47-48 R1: Exeter City (A) 1-1, (H) 2-0
R2: Torquay Utd (H) 1-1, (A) 1-1, 0-2

48-49 R1: Dulwich Hamlet (H) 2-1
R2: Mansfield Town (A) 1-2

49-50 R1: Walthamstow Avenue (H) 4-1
R2: Torquay United (H) 4-2
R3: Southampton (H) 1-1, (A) 3-2
R4: Bournemouth & B.A. (A) 1-1, (H) 2-1
R5: Derby County (A) 2-4

50-51 R3: Barnsley (H) 3-1
R4: Arsenal (A) 2-3

51-52 R1: Norwich City (A) 2-3

52-53 R1: Hendon (A) 0-0, (H) 2-0
R2: Swindon Town (A) 0-2

53-54 R1: Llanelly (H) 3-0
R2: Hartlepools Utd (H) 1-1, (A) 0-1

54-55 R1: Coventry City (H) 0-1

55-56 R1: Millwall (H) 4-1
R2: Hastings United (H) 4-1
R3: Blackburn Rovers (H) 1-2

56-57 R1: Southampton (A) 0-2

57-58 R1: Newport County (H) 3-0
R2: Bournemouth & Boscombe Ath. (H) 4-1
R3: Arsenal (H) 3-1
R4: Liverpool (A) 1-3

58-59 R1: Wycombe Wanderers (H) 2-0
R2: Tooting & Mitcham United (A) 1-2

59-60 R1: Torquay United (A) 1-7

60-61 R1: Hastings United (H) 2-1
R2: Romford (A) 5-1
R3: Luton Town (A) 0-4

61-62 R1: Millwall (H) 2-0
R2: Kettering Town (H) 3-0
R3: Port Vale (A) 1-3

NORTHAMPTON AMATEUR

Currently: Northampton Town League

48-49 PR: Symington's Recreation (H) 1-4

49-50 Q1: Kettering Town (A) 1-5

NORTHAMPTON SPENCER

Currently: United Counties League

87-88 PR: Atherstone United (H) 2-5

62-63	R1: Torquay United (H) 1-2
63-64	R3: Sunderland (A) 0-2
64-65	R3: Chelsea (A) 1-4
65-66	R3: Nottingham Forest (H) 1-2
66-67	R3: West Bromwich Albion (H) 1-3
67-68	R1: Bournemouth & Boscombe Ath. (A) 0-2
68-69	R1: Margate (H) 3-1 R2: Brighton & Hove Albion (A) 2-1 R3: Bolton Wanderers (A) 1-2
69-70	R1: Weymouth (H) 0-0, (A) 3-1 R2: Exeter City (H) 1-1, (A) 0-0, 2-1 R3: Brentwood Town (A) 1-0 R4: Tranmere Rovers (A) 0-0, (H) 2-1 R5: Manchester United (H) 2-8
70-71	R1: Hereford United (A) 2-2, (H) 1-2
71-72	R1: Basingstoke Town (A) 5-1 R2: Hereford Utd (A) 0-0, (H) 2-2, (*at West Bromwich Albion*) 1-2
72-73	R1: Peterborough United (A) 0-1
73-74	R1: Banbury United (A) 0-0, (H) 3-2 R2: Bristol Rovers (H) 1-2
74-75	R1: Torquay United (A) 1-0 R2: Rotherham United (A) 1-2
75-76	R1: Brentford (A) 0-2
76-77	R1: Leatherhead (A) 0-2
77-78	R1: Tooting & Mitcham United (A) 2-1 R2: Enfield (H) 0-2
78-79	R1: Portsmouth (A) 0-2
79-80	R1: Hereford United (A) 0-1
80-81	R1: Peterborough United (H) 1-4
81-82	R1: Weymouth (A) 0-0, (H) 6-2 R2: Bristol City (A) 0-3
82-83	R1: Wimbledon (H) 2-2, (A) 2-0 R2: Gillingham (A) 1-1, (H) 3-2 R3: Aston Villa (H) 0-1
83-84	R1: Waterlooville (H) 1-1, (A) 1-1, (H) 2-0 R2: Telford United (H) 1-1, (A) 2-3
84-85	R1: V.S. Rugby (H) 2-2, (A) 1-0 R2: Brentford (A) 2-2, (H) 0-0 *aban.*, (H) 0-2
85-86	R1: Gillingham (A) 0-3
86-87	R1: Peterborough United (H) 3-0 R2: Southend United (A) 4-4, (H) 3-2 R3: Newcastle United (A) 1-2
87-88	R1: Newport County (H) 2-1 R2: Brighton & Hove Albion (H) 1-2
88-89	R1: Swansea City (A) 1-3
89-90	R1: Kettering Town (A) 1-0 R2: Aylesbury United (H) 0-0, (A) 1-0 R3: Coventry City (H) 1-0 R4: Rochdale (A) 0-3
90-91	R1: Littlehampton Town (A) 4-0 R2: Barnet (A) 0-0, (H) 0-1
91-92	R1: Crawley Town (A) 2-4
92-93	R1: Fulham (H) 3-1 R2: Bath City (A) 2-2, (H) 3-0 R3: Rotherham United (H) 0-1

NORTHERN ALUMINIUM CO. ATHLETIC (BANBURY)

Currently: (Alcan United) Banbury & Dist. League

48-49	EX: Huntley & Palmers Recreation (H - *at Banbury Spencer*) 2-3
49-50	PR: Oxford City (A) 2-5

Right: *The N.A.C. Athletic side of 1949-50. Photo courtesy of V. Bradley.*

50-51	EX: Huntley & Palmers Recreation (H) 1-5

NORTH FERRIBY UNITED

Currently: Northern Counties (East) League

77-78	Q1: Frickley Athletic (A) 1-3
78-79	PR: Selby Town (H) 2-0 Q1: Winterton Rangers (A) 0-0, (H) 0-1
79-80	Q1: Eastwood Town (H) 2-1 Q2: Boston (H) 1-3
80-81	Q1: Horwich R.M.I. (H) 1-0 Q2: Stalybridge Celtic (H) 0-0, (A) 0-3
81-82	Q1: Bourne Town (A) 2-1 Q2: Boston (A) 2-1 Q3: Boston United (A) 0-4
82-83	PR: Goole Town (A) 0-1
83-84	PR: Formby (A) 1-2
84-85	Q1: Winsford United (H) 2-2, (A) 1-3
85-86	PR: Radcliffe Borough (A) 2-2, (H) 1-2
86-87	Q1: Leicester U. (H) 3-3, (A - *at Leic. C.*) 2-4
87-88	Q1: Droylsden (H) 2-3
88-89	Q1: Grantham (H) 3-2 Q2: Witton Albion (H) 2-2, (A) 1-3
89-90	PR: Long Eaton United (H) 1-0 Q1: Warrington Town (A) 0-1
90-91	PR: Leicester United (H) 1-2
91-92	PR: Ossett Town (A) 0-2
92-93	PR: Salford City (A) 1-0 Q1: Garforth Town (H) 1-0 Q2: Brigg Town (H) 0-2

NORTH SHIELDS

Currently: Defunct (reformed in Wearside Lge)

45-46	Q4: Scarborough (A) 4-2 R1: Carlisle U. (A) 1-5, (H) 2-3 (*agg: 3-8*)
46-47	Q4: Ashington (H) 1-1, (A) 3-1 R1: Hartlepools United (A) 0-6
47-48	Q4: Bishop Auckland (A) 2-3
48-49	PR: Newbiggin Colliery Welfare (A) 5-2 Q1: Hexham Hearts (H) 0-0, (A) 2-1 Q2: Blyth Spartans (A) 1-2
49-50	PR: Newburn (H) 7-0 Q1: Newbiggin Colliery Welfare (A) 3-0 Q2: South Shields (H) 2-0 Q3: Blyth Spartans (A) 5-1 Q4: Scarborough (H) 1-1, (A) 3-1 R1: Netherfield (A) 3-4
50-51	Q4: Stockton (A) 1-0 R1: Crewe Alexandra (A) 0-4
51-52	Q4: Billingham Synthonia Recreation (A) 1-2
52-53	Q4: Consett (A) 3-1 R1: Stockport County (H) 3-6
53-54	Q4: Blyth Spartans (A) 2-4
54-55	PR: South Shields (A) 4-1 Q1: Shankhouse (A) 5-1 Q2: Ashington (A) 0-2
55-56	Q1: Hexham Hearts (A) 4-2 Q2: Ashington (H) 3-1 Q3: South Shields (H) 1-0 Q4: Scarborough (A) 3-4
56-57	Q1: Morpeth Town (A) 5-0 Q2: Ashington (H) 1-0 Q3: South Shields (H) 1-1, (A) 1-2
57-58	Q1: Annfield Plain (H) 4-1 Q2: Ashington (H) 0-0, (A) 1-3
58-59	Q2: Horden Colliery Welfare (H) 4-1 Q3: Evenwood Town (A) 0-1
59-60	Q1: Horden Colliery Welfare (A) 2-2, (H) 3-1 Q2: Newburn (H) 5-0 Q3: Shildon (A) 0-2
60-61	Q1: Spennymoor United (H) 6-2 Q2: Consett (A) 2-3
61-62	Q1: Easington Colliery Welfare (H) 3-0 Q2: Bridlington Town (A) 2-1 Q3: Willington (A) 4-2 Q4: Blyth Spartans (H) 1-2
62-63	Q2: Consett (A) 1-1, (H) 5-2 Q3: Shildon (A) 3-3, (H) 5-2 Q4: Stockton (H) 2-2, (A) 3-3, 4-2 R1: Workington (H) 2-2, (A) 2-7
63-64	Q1: Consett (H) 3-2 Q2: Scarborough (A) 1-2
64-65	Q1: Murton Colliery Welfare (A) 5-2 Q2: Bishop Auckland (A) 3-2 Q3: Horden Colliery Welfare (H) 0-2
65-66	Q1: Spennymoor United (A) 0-2
66-67	Q1: Ashington (A) 2-2, (H) 2-4
67-68	PR: Horden Colliery Welfare (A) 0-1
68-69	Q1: Boldon Colliery Welfare (H) 3-0 Q2: Murton Colliery Welfare (A) 4-0 Q3: Shildon (H) 2-1 Q4: Tow Law Town (H) 1-3
69-70	R1: Hartlepools United (A) 0-3
70-71	Q1: Bishop Auckland (H) 2-0 Q2: Washington (A) 0-1
71-72	Q1: Wingate (A) 1-0 Q2: Ferryhill Athletic (H) 3-1 Q3: Gateshead (A) 1-0 Q4: Scarborough (A) 0-1
72-73	Q1: Horden Colliery Welfare (A) 2-0 Q2: Spennymoor Utd (A) 1-1, (H) 2-2, 0-1
73-74	Q1: Spennymoor United (H) 2-0 Q2: Whitley Bay (H) 0-0, (A) 1-1, 2-2, 3-0 Q3: Willington (A) 0-3
74-75	Q1: Whitley Bay (A) 1-1, (H) 1-3
75-76	Q1: Bishop Auckland (A) 1-0 Q2: Eppleton Colliery Wel. (A) 1-1, (H) 0-1
76-77	PR: Spennymoor United (H) 0-0, (A) 1-4
77-78	PR: West Auckland Town (H) 1-1, (A) 1-2
78-79	Q1: Evenwood Town (A) 2-2, (H) 1-0 Q2: Spennymoor United (H) 0-3

79-80 Q1: Ferryhill Athletic (H) 4-2
Q2: Consett (H) 3-0
Q3: Ashington (H) 2-1
Q4: Brandon United (H) 1-2

80-81 Q1: Tow Law Town (H) 0-0, (A) 2-4

81-82 Q1: Wingate (H) 2-1
Q2: Seaham Colliery Welfare Red Star (A) 1-0
Q3: Spennymoor United (A) 2-2, (H) 1-5

82-83 Q1: Eppleton Colliery Welfare (H) 6-0
Q2: Horden Colliery Welfare (A) 1-0
Q3: Gateshead (A) 4-2
Q4: Barrow (H) 2-1
R1: Halifax Town (A) 1-0
R2: Walsall (H) 0-3

83-84 Q1: Evenwood Town (A) 3-0
Q2: Morecambe (A) 2-2, (H) 4-2
Q3: Brandon United (H) 2-0
Q4: Frickley Athletic (A) 0-1

84-85 Q1: Billingham Town (H) 7-2
Q2: Whitby Town (A) 1-1, (H) 2-2, (H) 1-1, (A) 0-2

85-86 Q1: Fleetwood (A) 2-2, (H) 2-1
Q2: Peterlee Newtown (A) 1-2

86-87 PR: Denaby United (H) 3-1
Q1: Whitley Bay (A) 3-2
Q2: Bishop Auckland (H) 0-0, (A) 2-4

87-88 Q1: Barrow (H) 1-1, (A) 0-3

88-89 Q1: Bridlington Town (H) 1-1, (A) 1-1, (A) 1-2

89-90 PR: Esh Winning (A) 6-2
Q1: Whickham (H) 1-0
Q2: Newcastle Blue Star (A) 1-1, (H) 4-2
Q3: Blyth Spartans (A) 3-0
Q4: Billingham Synthonia (A) 1-2

90-91 PR: Whickham (H) 2-0
Q1: Gateshead (H) 1-1, (A) 1-0
Q2: Prudhoe East End (A) 1-0
Q3: Fleetwood Town (A) 0-2

91-92 Q1: Annfield Plain (A) 4-0
Q2: Consett (H) 3-1
Q3: Bridlington Town (H) 0-2

92-93 Q1: South Bank (A) *scratched*

NORTH SKELTON ATH.

Currently: Defunct

54-55 Q1: Bridlington Trinity United (H) 9-1
Q2: Bridlington Central United (A) 6-1
Q3: Scarborough (H) 0-4

55-56 Q1: Bridlington Central United (A) 0-3

56-57 Q2: Billingham Synthonia Recreation (H) 1-3

NORTH WALSHAM ATH.

Currently: Anglian Combination

54-55 Q1: Bungay Town (H) 3-2
Q2: Gorleston (H) 1-4

NORTHWICH VICTORIA

Currently: Alliance Premier League

45-46 Q1: Fodens Motor Works (H) 0-4

46-47 PR: Llandudno (A) 4-3
Q1: Stalybridge Celtic (A) 3-4

47-48 PR: Wheelock Albion (H) 8-1
Q1: Buxton (A) 0-2

48-49 EX: Ellesmere Port Town (A) 2-0
PR: Macclesfield Town (A) 3-0
Q1: Port Sunlight (H) 5-0
Q2: Witton Albion (H) 1-3

49-50 PR: Knutsford (A) 9-0
Q1: Mossley (A) 2-3

50-51 Q4: Witton Albion (A) 2-4

51-52 Q1: Linotype & Machinery (H) 6-2
Q2: Congleton Town (A) 0-1

52-53 Q1: Winsford United (H) 1-1, (A) 2-4

53-54 Q1: Winsford Utd (H) 0-0, (A) 2-2, 0-2

54-55 PR: Congleton Town (A) 5-2
Q1: Altrincham (A) 2-3

55-56 PR: Altrincham (H) 2-2, (A) 2-0
Q1: Macclesfield Town (A) 4-0
Q2: Hyde United (A) 3-1
Q3: Winsford United (H) 2-2, (A) 2-1
Q4: Denaby United (H) 3-1
R1: Boston United (A) 2-3

56-57 PR: Altrincham (A) 3-4

57-58 PR: Buxton (H) 4-2
Q1: Linotype & Machinery (A) 6-3
Q2: Witton Albion (A) 2-3

58-59 Q1: Ellesmere Port Town (A) 1-3

59-60 PR: Winsford United (A) 3-0
Q1: Congleton Town (A) 3-0
Q2: Ellesmere Port Town (H) 0-3

60-61 Q1: Macclesfield Town (H) 0-3

61-62 Q1: Witton Albion (H) 2-1
Q2: Macclesfield Town (H) 1-0
Q3: Congleton Town (A) 2-1
Q4: Ellesmere Port Town (H) 1-0
R1: Southport (A) 0-1

62-63 Q1: Lostock Gralam (A) 1-3

63-64 Q1: Droylsden (H) 2-1
Q2: Lostock Gralam (A) 4-4, (H) 4-0
Q3: Macclesfield Town (H) 1-1, (A) 0-1

64-65 Q1: Mossley (H) 5-2
Q2: Macclesfield Town (A) 1-4

65-66 Q1: Mossley (A) 4-1
Q2: Oswestry Town (A) 1-3

66-67 Q1: Congleton Town (H) 5-0
Q2: Mossley (A) 1-1, (H) 3-1
Q3: Witton Albion (H) 1-6

67-68 Q1: Winsford United (A) 0-1

68-69 Q1: Linotype & Machinery (H) 3-0
Q2: Lostock Gralam (H) 2-1
Q3: Kirkby Town (H) 4-2
Q4: Skelmersdale United (H) 1-3

69-70 Q1: Nantwich (A) 3-2
Q2: Lostock Gralam (A) 5-0
Q3: Kirkby Town (H) 0-2

70-71 PR: Buxton (H) 2-0
Q1: Horwich R.M.I. (A) 0-2

71-72 Q1: South Liverpool (A) 0-1

72-73 PR: Winsford United (A) 1-3

73-74 PR: Oswestry Town (A) 3-1
Q1: Eastwood Hanley (A) 1-1, (H) 4-1
Q2: Stalybridge Celtic (A) 1-3

74-75 Q1: Sandbach Ramblers (H) 2-3

75-76 Q1: Buxton (H) 2-0
Q2: Oswestry Town (H) 3-1
Q3: Leek Town (H) 1-1, (A) 0-1

76-77 Q1: Nantwich (A) 1-0
Q2: Witton Albion (A) 3-1
Q3: Rhyl (H) 0-0, (A) 3-1
Q4: Burton Albion (A) 1-0
R1: Rochdale (H) 1-1, (A) 0-0, (*at Manchester City*) 2-1
R2: Peterborough United (H) 0-1 *abandoned after 25 minutes*, (H) 4-0
R3: Watford (H) 3-2
R4: Oldham Ath. (H - *at Manchester C.*) 1-3

77-78 Q4: Stafford Rangers (H) 2-2, (A) 1-2

78-79 Q4: Southport (H) 0-0, (A) 0-2

79-80 Q1: Caernarvon Town (A) 0-0, (H) 4-0
Q2: Formby (A) 1-1, (H) 2-0
Q3: Oswestry Town (A) 1-1, (H) 4-1
Q4: Enderby Town (A) 1-0
R1: Nuneaton Borough (A) 3-3, (H) 3-0
R2: Wigan Athletic (H) 0-3 *abandoned after 67 minutes*, (H) 2-2, (A) 0-1

Right: *Frank Sromek (8) of Northwich Victoria and Wigan's Colin Methven challenge for a high ball in the abandoned Second Round replay on Christmas Eve 1979. Photo: Netstretcher Magazine.*

80-81 Q1: New Mills (H) 1-0
Q2: Leek Town (A) 1-1, (H) 1-0
Q3: Alfreton Town (H) 3-2
Q4: Runcorn (H) 2-1
R1: Huddersfield Town (H) 1-1, (A) 0-6

81-82 Q4: Penrith (A) 0-1

82-83 Q4: Blyth Spartans (H) 3-0
R1: Chester (A) 1-1, (H) 3-1
R2: Scunthorpe United (A) 1-2

83-84 R1: Bangor City (H) 1-1, (A) 0-1

84-85 R1: Crewe Alexandra (H) 3-1
R2: Wigan Athletic (A) 1-2

85-86 Q4: Frickley Athletic (A) 1-2

86-87 Q1: Long Eaton United (A) 4-1
Q2: Worksop Town (A) 2-0
Q3: Skelmersdale United (A) 3-2
Q4: Stafford Rangers (H) 0-1

87-88 Q1: Warrington Town (A) 1-1, (H) 5-1
Q2: Droylsden (H) 2-1
Q3: St Helens Town (H) 3-2
Q4: Easington Colliery (H) 3-0
R1: Colwyn Bay (H) 1-0
R2: Blackpool (H) 0-2

88-89 Q1: Arnold (A) 5-0
Q2: Eastwood Hanley (A) 1-0
Q3: Hyde United (A) 1-1, (H) 3-0
Q4: Billingham Synthonia (H) 2-0
R1: Frickley Athletic (A) 2-0
R2: Tranmere Rovers (H) 1-2

89-90 Q4: Goole Town (H) 2-0
R1: Darlington (A) 2-6

90-91 Q4: Spennymoor United (H) 1-1, (A) 1-2

91-92 Q1: Eastwood Hanley (A) 1-2

92-93 Q1: Winsford United (H) 4-1
Q2: Raunds Town (H) 0-2

NORTHWOOD

Currently: Spartan League

89-90 PR: Hampton (H) 1-3

90-91 PR: Ruislip Manor (A) 1-2

91-92 PR: Hertford Town Town (A) 2-3

92-93 PR: Molesey (A) 1-3

NORTON & STOCKTON ANCIENTS

Currently: Northern League

85-86 PR: Shotton Com. (H) 1-1, (A) 2-2, (A) 2-5

86-87 PR: Newcastle Blue Star (H) 1-1, (A - *at Nth Shields*) 0-6

87-88 PR: Farsley Celtic (H) 4-5

88-89 PR: Darwen (H) 1-0
Q1: Newcastle Blue Star (A) 0-4

89-90 PR: South Bank (H) 1-7

90-91 PR: Bedlington Terriers (A) 4-0
Q1: Gretna (A) 1-5

91-92 Q1: Guiseley (H) 0-4

92-93 PR: Crook Town (A) 3-0
Q1: Dunston F.B. (A) 0-7

NORTON WOODSEATS

Currently: Central Midlands League
* - As Norton Woodseats Amateur

45-46 Q1: Rawmarsh Welfare (A) 1-3

46-47 PR: Scunthorpe United (A) 2-5

47-48 PR: Armthorpe Welfare (A) 4-1
Q1: Harworth Colliery Athletic (A) 1-0
Q2: Grimethorpe Athletic (H) 7-1
Q3: Scunthorpe United (A) 1-2

48-49 PR: Grimethorpe Athletic (H) 2-1
Q1: Firbeck Main Colliery (H) 2-1
Q2: Dinnington Athletic (A) 3-3, (H) 2-1
Q3: Harworth Colliery Welfare (A) 6-1
Q4: Gainsborough Trinity (H) 2-4

49-50 PR: Dinnington Athletic (H) 3-1
Q1: Stocksbridge Works (A) 1-2

50-51 PR: Rawmarsh Welfare (A) 0-0, (H) 4-2
Q1: Steel, Peech & Tozer (H) 9-0
Q2: Worksop Town (H) 1-3

51-52 Q1: Brunswick Institute (A) 2-0
Q2: Worksop Town (A) 0-1

52-53 * Q1: Brodsworth Main Colliery (A) 5-0
Q2: Langold W.M.C. (A) 4-0
Q3: Beighton Miners Welfare (A) 1-1, (H) 1-3

53-54 * Q1: Rawmarsh Welfare (A) 1-1, (H) 6-2
Q2: Beighton Miners Welfare (A) 1-2

54-55 * Q1: Brodsworth Miners Welfare (A) 4-0
Q2: Worksop Town (A) 3-3, (H) 1-2

55-56 * Q1: Beighton Miners Welfare (H) 1-2

56-57 * Q1: Hallam (A) 2-2, (H) 0-0, 3-1
Q2: Sheffield (H) 2-1
Q3: Stocksbridge Works (A) 2-3

57-58 * Q2: Beighton Miners Welfare (A) 2-1
Q3: Hallam (H) 4-0
Q4: Witton Albion (H) 2-2, (A) 1-6

58-59 * Q1: Matlock Town (H) 4-1
Q2: Hallam (H) 4-1
Q3: Sheffield (A) 0-2

59-60 * Q1: Boots Athletic (H) 2-1
Q2: Belper Town (A) 2-3

61-62 * Q1: Gainsborough Trinity (A) 0-6

62-63 * Q1: Worksop Town (H) 1-3

63-64 * Q2: Gainsborough Trinity (H) 1-6

64-65 * Q1: Retford Town (A) 1-5

65-66 * Q1: Frickley Colliery (H) 0-3

67-68 * Q1: Ilkeston Town (H) 2-1
Q2: Tamworth (H) 0-2

68-69 * Q1: Buxton (H) 0-3

69-70 * PR: Buxton (H) 1-0
Q1: Wombwell Sporting (H) 1-3

70-71 * Q1: Mexborough Town (H) 7-3
Q2: Frickley Colliery (H) 0-0, (A) 1-2

71-72 * Q1: Winterton Rangers (H) 0-3

72-73 * PR: Heanor Town (H) 0-0, (A) 1-2

73-74 * Q1: Denaby United (H) 0-4

NORWICH C.E.Y.M.S.

Currently: Anglian Combination

47-48 PR: Cromer (H) 0-0, (A) 3-1
Q1: Great Yarmouth Town (H) 1-6

48-49 PR: Cromer (H) 2-0
Q1: Achilles (H) 3-4

NORWICH CITY

Currently: F.A. Premier League

45-46 R3: Brighton (H) 1-2, (A) 1-4 *(agg: 2-6)*

46-47 R1: Brighton & Hove Albion (H) 7-2
R2: Queens Park Rangers (H) 4-4, (A) 0-2

47-48 R1: Merthyr Tydfil (H) 3-0
R2: Walsall (H) 2-2, (A) 2-2, 2-3

48-49 R1: Wellington Town (H) 1-0
R2: Torquay United (A) 1-3

Above: *Norwich City's Malcolm Allen, scorer of four goals, is pursued by Sutton United defender Rolyn Jones in the tie at Carrow Road on 28th January 1989.*

49-50 R1: Gloucester City (A) 3-2
R2: Hartlepools United (A) 1-1, (H) 5-1
R3: Portsmouth (A) 1-1, (H) 0-2

50-51 R1: Watford (H) 2-0
R2: Rhyl (A) 1-0
R3: Liverpool (H) 3-1
R4: Newport County (A) 2-0
R5: Sunderland (A) 1-3

51-52 R1: Northampton Town (H) 3-2
R2: Chesterfield (H) 3-1
R3: Arsenal (H) 0-5

52-53 R1: Tonbridge (A) 2-2, (H) 1-0
R2: Brighton & Hove Albion (A) 0-2

53-54 R1: Yeovil Town (A) 2-0
R2: Barnsley (H) 2-1
R3: Hastings United (A) 3-3, (H) 3-0
R4: Arsenal (A) 2-1
R5: Leicester City (H) 1-2

54-55 R1: Headington United (H) 4-2
R2: Brighton & Hove A. (H) 0-0, (A) 1-5

55-56 R1: Dorchester Town (H) 4-0
R2: Brighton & Hove Albion (A) 2-1
R3: Sunderland (A) 2-4

56-57 R1: Bedford Town (H) 2-4

57-58 R1: Redhill (H) 6-1
R2: Brighton & Hove A. (H) 1-1, (A) 2-1
R3: Darlington (H) 1-2

58-59 R1: Ilford (H) 3-1
R2: Swindon Town (A) 1-1, (H) 1-0
R3: Manchester United (H) 3-0
R4: Cardiff City (H) 3-2
R5: Tottenham Hotspur (A) 1-1, (H) 1-0
R6: Sheffield United (A) 1-1, (H) 3-2
SF: Luton *(at Tottenham)* 1-1, *(Birm. C.)* 0-1

59-60 R1: Reading (H) 1-1, (A) 1-2

60-61 R3: York City (A) 1-1, (H) 1-0
R4: Scunthorpe United (A) 4-1
R5: Sunderland (H) 0-1

61-62 R3: Wrexham (H) 3-1
R4: Ipswich Town (H) 1-1, (A) 2-1
R5: Sheffield United (A) 1-3

62-63 R3: Blackpool (A) 1-1, (H) 3-1
R4: Newcastle United (H) 5-0
R5: Manchester City (A) 2-1
R6: Leicester City (H) 0-2

63-64 R3: Bristol Rovers (A) 1-2

64-65 R3: Nottingham Forest (A) 0-1

65-66 R3: Leyton Orient (A) 3-1
R4: Walsall (H) 3-2
R5: Blackburn Rovers (H) 2-2, (A) 2-3

66-67 R3: Derby County (H) 3-0
R4: Manchester United (A) 2-1
R5: Sheffield Wednesday (H) 1-3

67-68 R3: Sunderland (H) 1-1, (A) 1-0
R4: Chelsea (A) 0-1

68-69 R3: West Bromwich Albion (A) 0-3

69-70 R3: Wrexham (H) 1-2

70-71 R3: Wolverhampton Wanderers (A) 1-5

71-72 R3: Hull City (H) 0-3

72-73 R3: Leeds (H) 1-1, (A) 1-1, *(at Aston V.)* 0-5

73-74 R3: Arsenal (H) 0-1

74-75 R3: Coventry City (A) 0-2

75-76 R3: Rochdale (H) 1-1, (A) 0-0, (H) 2-1
R4: Luton Town (H) 2-0
R5: Bradford City (H) 1-2

76-77 R3: Leeds United (A) 2-5

77-78 R3: Orient (A) 1-1, (H) 0-1

78-79 R3: Leicester City (A) 0-3

79-80 R3: Yeovil Town (A) 3-0
R4: Wolverhampton Wdrs (A) 1-1, (H) 2-3

80-81 R3: Cambridge United (H) 1-0
R4: Manchester City (A) 0-6

81-82 R3: Stoke City (A) 1-0
R4: Doncaster Rovers (H) 2-1
R5: West Bromwich Albion (A) 0-1

82-83 R3: Swansea City (H) 2-1
R4: Coventry City (A) 2-2, (H) 2-1
R5: Ipswich Town (H) 1-0
R6: Brighton & Hove Albion (A) 0-1

83-84 R3: Aston Villa (A) 1-1, (H) 3-0
R4: Tottenham Hotspur (A) 0-0, (H) 2-1
R5: Derby County (A) 1-2

84-85 R3: Birm. City (A) 0-0, (H) 1-1, (A) 1-1, (H) 1-0
R4: West Ham United (A) 1-2

85-86 R3: Liverpool (A) 0-5

86-87 R3: Huddersfield Town (H) 1-1, (A) 4-2
R4: Wigan Athletic (A) 0-1

87-88 R3: Swindon Town (A) 0-0, (H) 0-2

88-89 R3: Port Vale (A) 3-1
R4: Sutton United (H) 8-0
R5: Sheffield United (H) 3-2
R6: West Ham United (A) 0-0, (H) 3-1
SF: Everton *(at Aston Villa)* 0-1

89-90 R3: Exeter City (A) 1-1, (H) 2-0
R4: Liverpool (H) 0-0, (A) 1-3

90-91 R3: Bristol City (H) 2-1
R4: Swindon Town (H) 3-1
R5: Manchester United (H) 2-1
R6: Nottingham Forest (H) 0-1

91-92 R3: Barnsley (H) 1-0
R4: Millwall (H) 2-1
R5: Notts County (H) 3-0
R6: Southampton (A) 0-0, (H) 2-1
SF: Sunderland *(at Sheffield Wednesday)* 0-1

92-93 R3: Coventry City (H) 1-0
R4: Tottenham Hotspur (H) 0-2

NORWICH UNITED

Currently: Eastern Counties League

92-93 PR: Edgware Town (H) 1-0
Q1: Barking (H) 2-1
Q2: Cambridge City (A) 1-6

NOTTINGHAM FOREST

Currently: Football League

45-46 R3: Watford (H) 1-1, (A) 1-1, 0-1 *(agg: 2-3)*

46-47 R3: Lincoln City (A) 1-0
R4: Manchester United (A) 2-0
R5: Middlesbrough (H) 2-2, (A) 2-6

47-48 R3: Liverpool (A) 1-4

48-49 R3: Liverpool (H) 2-2, (A) 0-4

49-50 R1: Bristol City (H) 1-0
R2: Stockport County (H) 0-2

50-51 R1: Torquay United (H) 6-1
R2: Rotherham United (A) 1-3

51-52 R3: Blackburn Rovers (H) 2-2, (A) 0-2

52-53 R3: Mansfield Town (A) 1-0
R4: Everton (A) 1-4

53-54 R3: Plymouth Argyle (A) 0-2

54-55 R3: Sheffield United (A) 3-1
R4: Hartlepools United (A) 1-1, (H) 2-1
R5: Newcastle Utd (H) 1-1, (A) 2-2, 1-2

55-56 R3: Doncaster Rovers (A) 0-3

56-57 R3: Goole Town (H) 6-0
R4: Portsmouth (A) 3-1
R5: Barnsley (A) 2-1
R6: Birmingham City (A) 0-0, (H) 0-1

57-58 R3: Gillingham (H) 2-0
R4: West Bromwich Albion (A) 3-3, (H) 1-5

58-59 R3: Tooting & Mitcham Utd (A) 2-2, (H) 3-0
R4: Grimsby Town (H) 4-1
R5: Birmingham City (A) 1-1, (H) 1-1, 5-0
R6: Bolton Wanderers (H) 2-1
SF: Aston Villa *(at Sheffield Wed.)* 1-0
F: Luton Town *(at Wembley)* 2-1

59-60 R3: Reading (H) 1-0
R4: Sheffield United (A) 0-3

60-61 R3: Birmingham City (H) 0-2

61-62 R3: Workington (A) 2-1
R4: Sheffield Wednesday (H) 0-2

62-63 R3: Wolverhampton Wanderers (H) 4-3
R4: West Bromwich Albion (A) 0-0, (H) 2-1
R5: Leeds United (H) 3-0
R6: Southampton (H) 1-1, (A) 3-3, 0-5

63-64 R3: Preston North End (H) 0-0, (A) 0-1

64-65 R3: Norwich City (H) 1-0
R4: Sunderland (A) 3-1
R5: Crystal Palace (A) 1-3

65-66 R3: Northampton Town (A) 2-1
R4: Hull City (A) 0-2

66-67 R3: Plymouth Argyle (H) 2-1
R4: Newcastle United (H) 3-0
R5: Swindon Town (H) 0-0, (A) 1-1, 3-0
R6: Everton (H) 3-2
SF: Tottenham Hotspur *(at Sheff. Wed.)* 1-2

67-68 R3: Bolton Wanderers (H) 4-2
R4: Leeds United (A) 1-2

68-69 R3: Preston North End (A) 0-3

69-70 R3: Carlisle United (H) 0-0, (A) 1-2

70-71 R3: Luton Town (H) 1-1, (A) 4-3
R4: Orient (H) 1-1, (A) 0-0 *abandoned after 45 minutes*, (A) 1-0
R5: Tottenham Hotspur (A) 1-2

71-72 R3: Millwall (A) 1-3

72-73 R3: West Bromwich Albion (A) 1-1, (H) 0-0, *(at Leicester City)* 1-3

73-74 R3: Bristol Rovers (H) 4-3
R4: Manchester City (H) 4-1
R5: Portsmouth (H) 1-0
R6: Newcastle (A) 3-4 *replay ordered*, *(at Everton)* 0-0, *(at Everton)* 0-1

74-75 R3: Tottenham Hotspur (H) 1-1, (A) 1-0
R4: Fulham (A) 0-0, (H) 1-1, 1-1, 1-2

75-76 R3: Peterborough United (H) 0-0, (A) 0-1

76-77 R3: Bristol Rovers (H) 1-1, (A) 1-1, *(at Aston Villa)* 6-0
R4: Southampton (H) 3-3, (A) 1-2

77-78 R3: Swindon Town (H) 4-1
R4: Manchester City (H) 2-1
R5: Queens P.R. (A) 1-1, (H) 1-1, (H) 3-1
R6: West Bromwich Albion (A) 0-2

78-79 R3: Aston Villa (H) 2-0
R4: York City (H) 3-1
R5: Arsenal (H) 0-1

79-80 R3: Leeds United (A) 4-1
R4: Liverpool (H) 0-2

80-81 R3: Bolton Wanderers (H) 3-3, (A) 1-0
R4: Manchester United (H) 1-0
R5: Bristol City (H) 2-1
R6: Ipswich Town (H) 3-3, (A) 0-1

81-82 R3: Wrexham (H) 1-3

82-83 R3: Derby County (A) 0-2

83-84 R3: Southampton (H) 1-2

84-85 R3: Newcastle United (H) 1-1, (A) 3-1
R4: Wimbledon (H) 0-0, (A) 0-1

85-86 R3: Blackburn Rovers (H) 1-1, (A) 2-3

86-87 R3: Crystal Palace (A) 0-1

87-88 R3: Halifax Town (A) 4-0
R4: Leyton Orient (A) 2-1
R5: Birmingham City (A) 1-0
R6: Arsenal (A) 2-1
SF: Liverpool *(at Sheffield Wednesday)* 1-2

88-89 R3: Ipswich Town (H) 3-0
R4: Leeds United (H) 2-0
R5: Watford (A) 3-0
R6: Manchester United (A) 1-0
SF: Liverpool *(at Sheffield Wednesday)* 0-0 *abandoned in 1st half*, *(at Man. U.)* 1-3

89-90 R3: Manchester United (H) 0-1

90-91 R3: Crystal Palace (A) 0-0, (H) 2-2, (H) 3-0
R4: Newcastle United (A) 2-2, (H) 3-0
R5: Southampton (A) 1-1, (H) 3-1
R6: Norwich City (A) 1-0
SF: West Ham United *(at Aston Villa)* 4-0
F: Tottenham Hotspur *(at Wembley)* 1-2

91-92 R3: Wolverhampton Wanderers (H) 1-0
R4: Hereford United (H) 2-0
R5: Bristol City (H) 4-1
R6: Portsmouth (A) 0-1

92-93 R3: Southampton (H) 2-1
R4: Middlesbrough (H) 1-1, (A) 3-0
R5: Arsenal (A) 0-2

Above: *Tom Wilson (out of picture) scores for Forest in the 1959 final against Luton Town. Photo: Colorsport*

NOTTS COUNTY

Currently: Football League

45-46 R1: Bradford C. (H) 2-2, (A) 2-1 *(agg: 4-3)*
R2: Northampton (A) 1-3, (H) 1-0 *(agg: 2-3)*

46-47 R1: Leyton Orient (A) 2-1
R2: Swindon Town (H) 2-1
R3: Luton Town (A) 0-6

47-48 R1: Horsham (H) 9-1
R2: Stockton (H) 1-1, (A - *at Mid'brough*) 4-1
R3: Birmingham City (A) 6-0
R4: Swindon Town (A) 0-1

48-49 R1: Port Vale (H) 2-1
R2: Barrow (H) 3-2
R3: Plymouth Argyle (A) 1-0
R4: Liverpool (A) 0-1

49-50 R1: Tilbury (H) 4-0
R2: Rochdale (A) 2-1
R3: Burnley (H) 1-4

50-51 R3: Southampton (H) 3-4

51-52 R3: Stockton (H) 4-0
R4: Portsmouth (H) 1-3

52-53 R3: Leicester City (A) 4-2
R4: Bolton Wanderers (A) 1-1, (H) 2-2, 0-1

53-54 R3: Everton (A) 1-2

54-55 R3: Middlesbrough (A) 4-1
R4: Sheffield Wednesday (A) 1-1, (H) 1-0
R5: Chelsea (H) 1-0
R6: York City (H) 0-1

55-56 R3: Fulham (H) 0-1

56-57 R3: Rhyl (H) 1-3

57-58 R3: Tranmere Rovers (H) 2-0
R4: Bristol City (H) 1-2

58-59 R1: Barrow (H) 1-2

59-60 R1: Hastings United (A) 2-1
R2: Bath City (H) 0-1

60-61 R1: Aldershot (A) 0-2

61-62 R1: Yeovil Town (H) 4-2
R2: Margate (A) 1-1, (H) 3-1
R3: Manchester City (H) 0-1

62-63 R1: Peterborough United (H) 0-3

63-64 R1: Frickley Colliery (H) 2-1
R2: Doncaster Rovers (A) 1-1, (H) 1-2

64-65 R1: Chelmsford City (H) 2-0
R2: Brentford (A) 0-4

65-66 R1: Southend United (A) 1-3

66-67 R1: Oldham Athletic (A) 1-3

67-68 R1: Runcorn (A) 0-1

68-69 R1: Doncaster Rovers (A) 0-1

69-70 R1: Rotherham United (H) 0-3

70-71 R1: Port Vale (H) 1-0
R2: Bury (A) 1-1, (H) 3-0
R3: Leicester City (A) 0-2

71-72 R1: Newport County (H) 6-0
R2: South Shields (A) 3-1
R3: Watford (A) 4-1

R4: Derby County (A) 0-6

72-73 R1: Altrincham (A) 1-0
R2: Lancaster City (H) 2-1
R3: Sunderland (H) 1-1, (A) 0-2

73-74 R3: West Bromwich Albion (A) 0-4

74-75 R3: Portsmouth (H) 3-1
R4: Queens Park Rangers (A) 0-3

75-76 R3: Leeds United (H) 0-1

76-77 R3: Arsenal (H) 0-1

77-78 R3: Charlton Athletic (A) 2-0
R4: Brighton & Hove Albion (A) 2-1
R5: Millwall (A) 1-2

78-79 R3: Reading (H) 4-2
R4: Arsenal (A) 0-2

79-80 R3: Wolverhampton Wanderers (H) 1-3

80-81 R3: Blackburn Rovers (H) 2-1
R4: Peterborough United (H) 0-1

81-82 R3: Aston Villa (H) 0-6

82-83 R3: Leicester City (A) 3-2
R4: Middlesbrough (A) 0-2

83-84 R3: Bristol City (H) 2-2, (A) 2-0
R4: Huddersfield Town (A) 2-1
R5: Middlesbrough (H) 1-0
R6: Everton (H) 1-2

84-85 R3: Grimsby Town (H) 2-2, (A) 2-4

85-86 R1: Scarborough (H) 6-1
R2: Wrexham (H) 2-2, (A) 3-0
R3: Stoke City (A) 2-0
R4: Tottenham Hotspur (H) 1-1, (A) 1-5

86-87 R1: Carlisle United (H) 1-1, (A) 3-0
R2: Middlesbrough (H) 0-1

87-88 R1: Chesterfield (H) 3-3, (A) 1-0
R2: Port Vale (A) 0-2

88-89 R1: Darlington (A) 2-1
R2: Hartlepool United (A) 0-1

89-90 R1: Doncaster Rovers (A) 0-1

90-91 R3: Hull City (A) 5-2
R4: Oldham Athletic (H) 2-0
R5: Manchester City (H) 1-0
R6: Tottenham Hotspur (A) 1-2

91-92 R3: Wigan Athletic (H) 2-0
R4: Blackburn Rovers (H) 2-1
R5: Norwich City (A) 0-3

92-93 R3: Sunderland (H) 0-2

NUNEATON BOROUGH

Currently: Southern League

45-46 Q1: Hednesford (A) 2-2, (H) 5-2
Q2: Worcester City (H) 1-0
Q3: Bournville Athletic (H) 8-1 *expelled*

46-47 PR: Darlaston (H) 3-1
Q1: Atherstone Town (A) 4-1
Q2: Dudley Town (H) 2-1
Q3: Hereford United (A) 0-5

47-48 Q1: Gresley Rovers (A) 2-3

48-49 PR: Whitwick Colliery (A) 0-2

49-50 PR: Bedworth Town (A) 3-1
Q1: Moira United (H) 7-1
Q2: Atherstone Town (A) 2-2, (H) 1-1, 2-1
Q3: Gresley Rovers (H) 2-2, (A) 3-2
Q4: Wellington Town (A) 4-3
R1: King's Lynn (H) 2-1
R2: Mossley (H) 0-0, (A) 3-0
R3: Exeter City (A) 0-3

50-51 Q4: Linby Colliery (A) 1-3

51-52 Q1: Burton Albion (H) 2-2, (A) 4-2
Q2: Sutton Coldfield Town (H) 5-1
Q3: Bedworth Town (A) 1-1, (H) 1-2

52-53 PR: Lockheed Leamington (A) 2-1
Q1: Hednesford (A) 1-1, (H) 2-5

53-54 Q1: Lockheed Leamington (H) 1-0
Q2: Rugby Town (A) 2-1
Q3: Burton Albion (A) 1-1, (H) 3-1
Q4: Gresley Rovers (H) 4-1
R1: Watford (H) 3-0
R2: Queens Park Rangers (A) 1-1, (H) 1-2

54-55 Q4: Hereford United (H) 3-2
R1: Brentford (A) 1-2

55-56 Q4: Hereford United (A) 1-8

56-57 Q4: Bromsgrove Rovers (H) 1-2

57-58 PR: Sutton Coldfield T. (A) 2-2, (H) 3-1
Q1: Bilston (H) 2-0
Q2: Brierley Hill Alliance (A) 2-4

58-59 Q1: Burton Albion (A) 3-0
Q2: Tamworth (A) 1-1, (H) 1-0
Q3: Brush Sports (H) 2-1
Q4: Hereford United (H) 2-2, (A) 1-3

59-60 Q1: Burton Albion (A) 4-1
Q2: Brush Sports (A) 3-4

60-61 Q1: Tamworth (H) 1-4

61-62 Q1: Tamworth (H) 2-0
Q2: Burton Albion (H) 1-0
Q3: Hinckley Ath. (A) 2-2, (H) 1-1, 1-3

62-63 Q1: Halesowen Town (H) 6-0
Q2: Lockheed Leamington (H) 2-1
Q3: Rugby Town (A) 0-1

63-64 Q1: Hednesford (A) 4-3
Q2: Halesowen Town (H) 2-1
Q3: Lockheed Leamington (H) 0-2

64-65 Q1: Loughborough United (A) 2-1
Q2: Tamworth (H) 2-1
Q3: Atherstone Town (A) 1-1, (H) 2-5

65-66 Q1: Lockheed Leamington (A) 1-3

66-67 Q1: Atherstone Town (A) 6-1
Q2: Loughborough United (H) 8-2
Q3: Burton Albion (A) 1-0
Q4: Macclesfield Town (A) 1-1, (H) 2-0
R1: Wealdstone (A) 2-0
R2: Swansea Town (H) 2-0
R3: Rotherham United (H) 1-1, (A) 0-1

67-68 Q4: Matlock Town (H) 1-0
R1: Exeter City (H) 0-0, (A) 0-0, 0-1

68-69 Q4: Kidderminster Harriers (H) 1-1, (A) 0-3

69-70 Q4: Tamworth (H) 2-4

70-71 Q1: Hednesford (A) 2-1
Q2: Lye Town (A) 3-0
Q3: Stourbridge (H) 2-1
Q4: Tamworth (A) 1-1, (H) 2-2, 1-3

71-72 Q1: Loughborough United (A) 5-0
Q2: Long Eaton United (H) 2-0
Q3: Alfreton Town (A) 4-0
Q4: Tamworth (H) 3-1
R1: Torquay United (A) 0-1

72-73 PR: Kidderminster Harriers (H) 1-1, (A) 1-0
Q1: Lockheed Leamington (H) 4-1
Q2: Rugby Town (A) 1-0
Q3: Alvechurch (H) 2-0
Q4: Alfreton Town (A) 2-0
R1: Telford United (A) 2-3

73-74 Q1: Gresley Rovers (H) 3-0
Q2: Hednesford (H) 1-0
Q3: Highgate United (H) 1-4

74-75 Q1: Banbury Rovers (H) 3-0
Q2: Alvechurch (A) 3-1
Q3: Atherstone Town (A) 1-1, (H) 2-0
Q4: Grantham (H) 1-1, (A) 3-2
R1: Maidstone United (H) 2-2, (A) 0-2

75-76 Q1: Tamworth (H) 2-1
Q2: Dudley Town (A) 1-0
Q3: Gornal Athletic (H) 1-1, 3-0
Q4: Cheltenham Town (H) 2-1
R1: Wimbledon (H) 0-1

76-77 PR: Racing Club Warwick (H) 2-1
Q1: Brierley Hill Alliance (H) 2-0
Q2: Lye Town (H) 2-0
Q3: Bromsgrove Rovers (H) 2-0
Q4: Barton Rovers (A) 3-2
R1: Crook Town (A) 4-1
R2: Lincoln City (A) 0-6

77-78 Q4: Hednesford Town (H) 2-1
R1: Oxford United (H) 2-0
R2: Tilbury (H) 1-2

78-79 Q4: Matlock (H) 2-2, (A) 2-2, (*at Stafford*) 2-1
R1: Crewe Alexandra (H) 0-2

79-80 Q4: Boston United (A) 1-1, (H) 2-1
R1: Northwich Victoria (H) 3-3, (A) 0-3

80-81 Q4: Kidderminster Harriers (A) 0-1

81-82 Q1: Rushden Town (H) 6-0
Q2: Lye Town (A) 2-1
Q3: Tividale (H) 5-2
Q4: Bromsgrove Rovers (H) 2-1
R1: Bishop Auckland (A) 1-4

82-83 Q1: Stamford (A) 1-1, (H) 5-0
Q2: Gainsborough Trinity (H) 3-3, (A) 0-2

83-84 Q1: Oldbury United (H) 1-2

84-85 Q1: Wisbech Town (A) 6-2
Q2: Irthlingborough Diamonds (A) 5-0
Q3: Gainsborough Trinity (H) 2-0
Q4: Hednesford Town (A) 4-0
R1: Scunthorpe United (H) 1-1, (A) 1-2

85-86 Q1: Hemel Hempstead (A) 3-1
Q2: Moor Green (A) 4-1
Q3: Hinckley Athletic (H) 0-0, (A) 1-0
Q4: Dunstable (A) 2-0
R1: Burnley (H) 2-3

86-87 Q4: Goole Town (A) 2-1
R1: Rochdale (H) 0-3

87-88 Q4: V.S. Rugby (A) 0-3

88-89 Q1: Stamford (H) 2-0
Q2: Banbury United (H) 1-1, (A) 0-1

89-90 PR: Willenhall Town (H) 1-1, (A) 0-1

90-91 PR: Hinckley Town (H) 4-1
Q1: Goole Town (H) 1-0
Q2: Blakenall (A) 3-3, (H) 3-0
Q3: Frickley Athletic (A) 0-1

91-92 Q1: Chalfont St Peter (A) 4-0
Q2: Corby Town (H) 2-2, (A) 0-1

92-93 PR: Boldmere St Michaels (H) 2-1
Q1: Leicester United (H) 3-1
Q2: Matlock Town (H) 2-1
Q3: Raunds Town (H) 4-0
Q4: Wembley (A) 1-1, (H) 0-0, (A) 2-1
R1: Woking (A) 2-3

OAKHAM UNITED

Currently: Central Midlands League

87-88 PR: Brigg Town (A) 0-4

88-89 PR: Irlam Town (A) 1-3

89-90 PR: Worksop Town (H) 4-2
Q1: Walsall Wood (A) 1-0
Q2: Rhyl (A) 0-2

90-91 PR: Long Eaton (H - *played away*) 1-1, (A) 1-0
Q1: Hyde United (H) 1-2

91-92 PR: Rocester (A) 3-1
Q1: Goole Town (A) 1-0
Q2: Lincoln United (A) 0-2

92-93 PR: Alfreton Town (A) 1-2

OAK VILLA

Currently: (Weston Mill Oak Villa) Devon Co. Lge

47-48 PR: Newton Spurs (H) 1-2

48-49 PR: Bideford (A) 0-6

49-50 PR: St Austell (A) 1-4

50-51 PR: Barnstaple Town (H) 2-6

51-52 PR: Dartmouth United (A) 1-4

OAKWOOD

Currently: Sussex County League

90-91 PR: Camberley Town (A - *played home*) 5-0
Q1: Pagham (A) 0-4

91-92 PR: Havant Town (H) 0-3

92-93 PR: Kingsbury Town (A) 3-4

ODD DOWN

Currently: Western League

46-47 PR: Soundwell (H) 0-3

47-48 EX: Chippenham Town (A) 2-4

48-49 EX: Welton Rovers (A) 1-5

OLDBURY UNITED

Currently: West Midlands (Regional) League

72-73 Q1: Alvechurch (A) 1-3

73-74 PR: Lye Town (H) 0-1

74-75 Q1: Highgate United (A) 1-2

75-76 Q1: Coventry Sporting (H) 0-0, (A) 1-3

76-77 Q1: Tividale (H) 0-4

77-78 PR: Halesowen Town (A) 1-2

78-79 Q1: Willenhall Town (H) 1-1, (A) 0-2

79-80 Q1: Long Eaton United (H) 0-1

80-81 Q1: Matlock Town (H) 4-0
Q2: Sutton Coldfield Town (H) 0-3

81-82 Q1: Willenhall Town (H) 0-2

82-83 Q1: Burton Albion (H) 0-0, (A) 0-1

83-84 Q1: Nuneaton Borough (A) 2-1
Q2: Halesowen Town (H) 2-0
Q3: Burton Albion (H) 0-3

84-85 Q1: Chalfont S.P. (A) 0-0, (H) 1-1, (A) 3-1
Q2: Oxford City (A) 0-3

85-86 PR: Desborough Town (A) 3-2
Q1: Grantham (H) 1-1, (A) 1-2

86-87 Q1: Eastwood Hanley (H) 0-0, (A) 1-0
Q2: Buxton (H) 3-1
Q3: Rossendale United (A) 2-1
Q4: Halesowen Town (A) 2-2, (H) 1-2

87-88 Q1: Rushall Olympic (A) 2-0
Q2: Hinckley Town (H) 5-2
Q3: Willenhall Town (H) 0-1

88-89 Q1: Dudley Town (H) 2-3

89-90 PR: King's Lynn (H) 1-1, (A) 1-3

90-91 PR: Wolverton (H) 0-0, (A) 1-2

91-92 PR: Blakenall (H) 1-2

92-93 PR: Pelsall Villa (A) 0-0, (H) 4-4, (A) 0-1

OLD GRAMMARIANS (IPSWICH)

Currently: Defunct

46-47 Q1: Great Yarmouth Town (A) 1-5

47-48 Q1: Leiston (A) 2-8

48-49 PR: Achilles (H) 1-9

OLDHAM ATHLETIC

Currently: F.A. Premier League

45-46 R1: Southport (A) 2-1, (H) 3-1 *(agg: 5-2)*
R2: Accrington S. (H) 2-1, (A) 1-3 *(agg: 3-4)*

46-47 R1: Tranmere Rovers (H) 1-0
R2: Doncaster Rovers (H) 1-2

47-48 R1: Lancaster City (H) 6-0
R2: Mansfield Town (H) 0-1

48-49 R1: Wrexham (A) 3-0
R2: Walthamstow Avenue (A) 2-2, (H) 3-1
R3: Cardiff City (H) 2-3

49-50 R1: Stockton (H) 4-0
R2: Crewe Alexandra (A) 1-1, (H) 0-0, 3-0
R3: Newcastle United (H) 2-7

50-51 R1: Bradford City (A) 2-2, (H) 2-1
R2: Hartlepools United (A) 2-1
R3: Manchester United (A) 1-4

51-52 R1: Nelson (A) 4-0
R2: Southend United (A) 0-5

52-53 R1: Boston United (A) 2-1
R2: Port Vale (A) 3-0
R3: Birmingham City (H) 1-3

53-54 R3: Ipswich Town (A) 3-3, (H) 0-1

54-55 R1: Crewe Alexandra (H) 1-0
R2: Bournemouth & Boscombe Ath. (A) 0-1

55-56 R1: Bradford City (A) 1-3

56-57 R1: Halifax Town (A) 3-2
R2: Accrington Stanley (A) 1-2

57-58 R1: Bradford (Park Avenue) (H) 2-0
R2: Workington (H) 1-5

58-59 R1: Denaby United (A) 2-0
R2: South Shields (H) 2-0
R3: Stoke City (A) 1-5

59-60 R1: Shildon (A) 1-1, (H) 3-0
R2: Bury (A) 1-2

60-61 R1: Rhyl (A) 1-0
R2: Chesterfield (A) 4-4, (H) 0-3

61-62 R1: Shildon (H) 5-2
R2: Chesterfield (A) 2-2, (H) 4-2
R3: Bristol Rovers (A) 1-1, (H) 2-0
R4: Liverpool (H) 1-2

62-63 R1: Bradford City (H) 2-5

63-64 R1: Mansfield Town (H) 3-2
R2: Bradford (Park Avenue) (H) 2-0
R3: Ipswich Town (A) 3-6

64-65 R1: Hereford United (H) 4-0
R2: Crook Town (A) 1-0
R3: Middlesbrough (A) 2-6

65-66 R1: Mansfield Town (A) 3-1
R2: Darlington (A) 1-0
R3: West Ham United (H) 2-2, (A) 1-2

66-67 R1: Notts County (H) 3-1
R2: Grantham (A) 4-0
R3: Wolverhampton W. (H) 2-2, (A) 1-4

67-68 R1: Barrow (A) 0-2

68-69 R1: Wrexham (A) 2-4

69-70 R1: Grantham (H) 3-1
R2: South Shields (A) 0-0, (H) 1-2

70-71 R1: Rochdale (A) 0-2

71-72 R1: Chesterfield (A) 0-3

72-73 R1: Scarborough (H) 1-1, (A) 1-2

73-74 R1: Formby (A) 2-0
R2: Halifax Town (A) 1-0
R3: Cambridge U. (A) 2-2, (H) 3-3, *(at Nottm Forest)* 2-1
R4: Burnley (H) 1-4

74-75 R3: Aston Villa (H) 0-3

75-76 R3: Sunderland (A) 0-2

76-77 R3: Plymouth Argyle (H) 3-0
R4: Northwich Vic. (A - *at Man. City*) 3-1
R5: Liverpool (A) 1-3

77-78 R3: Luton Town (A) 1-1, (H) 1-2

78-79 R3: Stoke City (A) 0-2 *ab. 45m.*, (A) 1-0
R4: Leicester City (H) 3-1
R5: Tottenham Hotspur (H) 0-1

79-80 R3: Coventry City (H) 0-1

80-81 R3: Wimbledon (A) 0-0, (H) 0-1

81-82 R3: Gillingham (A) 1-2

82-83 R3: Fulham (H) 0-2

83-84 R3: Shrewsbury Town (A) 0-3

84-85 R3: Brentford (H) 2-1
R4: Sheffield Wednesday (A) 1-5

85-86 R3: Orient (H) 1-2

86-87 R3: Bradford City (H) 1-1, (A) 1-5

87-88 R3: Tottenham Hotspur (H) 2-4

88-89 R3: Charlton Ath. (A - *at Crystal Palace*) 1-2

89-90 R3: Birmingham City (A) 1-1, (H) 1-0
R4: Brighton & Hove Albion (H) 2-1
R5: Everton (H) 2-2, (A) 1-1, (H) 2-1
R6: Aston Villa (H) 3-0
SF: Manchester Utd *(at Manchester City)* 3-3, *(at Manchester City)* 1-2

90-91 R3: Brentford (H) 3-1
R4: Notts County (A) 0-2

91-92 R3: Leyton Orient (H) 1-1, (A) 2-4

92-93 R3: Tranmere Rovers (H) 2-2, (A) 0-3

OLDSWINFORD F. & S.C.

Currently: (Brierley Hill Town) W. Mids (Reg.) Lge

84-85 PR: Chatteris Town (A) 4-1
Q1: Gainsborough Trinity (A) 0-3

85-86 PR: Highgate United (H) 2-1
Q1: Gresley Rovers (H) 2-2, (A) 3-5

86-87 PR: Boldmere St Michaels (H) 3-3, (A) 1-3

87-88 PR: Racing Club Warwick (H) 0-1

OLLERTON COLLIERY

Currently: (Ollerton & Bevercotes M.W.) Notts All.

45-46 Q2: Boston United (H) 4-2
Q3: Grantham (A) 1-2

46-47 Q1: Basford United (A) 1-2

47-48 PR: Spalding United (A) 2-3

48-49 PR: Basford United (A) 3-0
Q1: Ransome & Marles (A) 1-2

49-50 EX: Gedling Colliery (H) 0-4

OLNEY TOWN

Currently: United Counties League

78-79 PR: Newmarket Town (A) 2-1
Q1: Rothwell Town (A) 1-1, (H) 0-1

79-80 Q1: Bedworth United (H) 0-4

ORIENT

See Leyton Orient

ORMSKIRK

Currently: Defunct
* - As Guinness Exports

68-69 * PR: Mossley (A) 0-1

69-70 * Q1: Horwich R.M.I. (A) 1-3

70-71 * Q1: Hyde United (A) 1-3

71-72 Q1: Leyland Motors (A) 4-1
Q2: Ellesmere Port Town (H) 0-1

72-73 PR: Chorley (H) 3-3, (A) 0-1

73-74 PR: Leyland Motors (H) 2-0
Q1: Clitheroe (A) 4-1
Q2: South Liverpool (A) 1-0
Q3: Formby (A) 0-1

74-75 PR: Marine (H) *scratched*

ORRELL (LIVERPOOL)

Currently: Defunct

46-47 Q1: Newton Y.M.C.A. (H) 1-2

47-48 PR: Newton Y.M.C.A. (A) 2-1
Q1: Prescot Cables (H) 0-6

48-49 EX: Bangor City (H) 1-8

49-50 PR: Earle (A) *withdrew*

OSBERTON RADIATOR (OXFORD)

Currently: Defunct

45-46 PR: Aylesbury United (A) 0-5

46-47 PR: Aylesbury United (A) 2-6

47-48 PR: Banbury Spencer (A) 2-8

48-49 EX: Headington United (A) 2-4

49-50 EX: Abingdon Town (H) 5-0
PR: Maidenhead United (A) 1-1, (H) 1-0
Q1: Southall (H) 1-3

50-51 EX: Pressed Steel (H) 1-2

OSSETT ALBION

Currently: Northern Counties (East) League

62-63 Q1: Selby Town (A) 5-1
Q2: Farsley Celtic (H) 2-1
Q3: Scarborough (H) 1-2

63-64 Q1: Frickley Colliery (A) 0-3

64-65 Q1: Harrogate Town (H) 3-0
Q2: Scarborough (A) 1-2

65-66 Q1: Bridlington Town (H) 0-0, (A) 2-1
Q2: Harrogate Town (H) 1-1, (A) 3-2
Q3: Bridlington Trinity (H) 2-0
Q4: South Liverpool (A) 0-3

66-67 Q1: Gainsborough Trinity (A) 0-3

67-68 Q1: Denaby United (A) 0-4

81-82 Q1: Bishop Auckland (A) 0-4

82-83 Q1: Hyde United (H) 1-2

83-84 PR: Radcliffe Borough (A) 1-2

84-85 PR: Formby (H) 1-4

85-86 Q1: Radcliffe Borough (A) 0-0, (H) 0-3

86-87 PR: Ashton United (A) 2-3

87-88 PR: Chester-le-Street Town (H) 1-1, (A) 1-2

88-89 PR: Northallerton Town (H) 2-2, (A) 1-2

89-90 PR: Prescot Cables (A) 1-2

90-91 PR: Farsley Celtic (A) 1-1, (H) 0-2

91-92 PR: Newcastle Town (A) 0-2

92-93 Q1: Netherfield (H) 1-3

OSSETT TOWN

Currently: Northern Counties (East) League

45-46 PR: Thorne Colliery (H) 1-3

46-47 PR: Kiveton Park Colliery (A) 2-1
Q1: South Kirkby Colliery (H) 0-2

47-48 PR: Meltham Mills (H) 5-1
Q1: Goole Town (A) 1-3

48-49 EX: David Brown Athletic (A) 11-0
PR: Pilkington Recreation (A) 5-2
Q1: Farsley Celtic (H) 3-2
Q2: Selby Town (H) 1-4

49-50 PR: Pilkington Recreation (H) 7-0
Q1: Brodsworth Main Colliery (H) 1-3

50-51 EX: Brunswick Institute (H) 5-2
PR: Winterton Rangers (A) 3-1
Q1: Selby Town (H) 1-3

51-52 Q1: Bradford United (H) *W/O*
Q2: Goole Town (H) 2-3

52-53 Q1: Farsley Celtic (A) 0-1

53-54 Q1: Goole Town (A) 2-4

54-55 Q2: Farsley Celtic (A) 1-2

55-56 Q1: Yorkshire Amateur (A) 2-1
Q2: Farsley Celtic (H) 3-2
Q3: Goole Town (A) 1-2

56-57 Q1: Harrogate & District Railway (A) 2-3

57-58 Q2: Stocksbridge Works (A) 1-1, (H) 3-4

90-91 PR: Knowsley United (A) 1-1, (H) 2-3

91-92 PR: North Ferriby United (H) 2-0
Q1: Southport (H) 0-1

92-93 PR: Dunston F.B. (H) 1-2

OSWESTRY TOWN

Currently: Welsh League (Wrexham Area)

47-48 PR: Bromsgrove Rovers (H) 1-4

48-49 PR: Bromsgrove Rovers (A) 0-5

49-50 EX: Bilston (A) 0-1

50-51 EX: Hednesford (H) 2-1
PR: Shrewsbury Town (A) *W/O*
Q1: Lye Town (H) 2-1
Q2: Dudley Town (A) 1-0
Q3: Hereford United (H) 1-2

51-52 PR: Dudley Town (H) 5-2
Q1: Stourbridge (A) 0-4

52-53 Q1: Kidderminster Harriers (A) 0-2

53-54 PR: Stourbridge (A) 0-2

54-55 PR: Redditch (A) 1-0
Q1: Bromsgrove Rovers (H) 1-1, (A) 0-3

55-56 PR: Stourbridge (A) 0-6

56-57 Q1: Stafford Rangers (A) 1-1, (H) 0-4

57-58 PR: Tamworth (A) 2-1
Q1: Stafford Rangers (H) 3-0
Q2: Lye Town (A) 4-1
Q3: Wellington Town (H) 2-2, (A) 1-0
Q4: Burton Albion (H) 5-1
R1: Bournemouth & Boscombe Ath. (H) 1-5

58-59 Q1: Kidderminster Harriers (H) 5-3
Q2: Bromsgrove Rovers (H) 3-0
Q3: Wellington Town (A) 3-2
Q4: Kettering Town (H) 1-3

59-60 Q1: Wellington Town (A) 1-1, (H) 3-1
Q2: Kidderminster Harriers (A) 2-0
Q3: Bromsgrove Rovers (H) 3-1
Q4: Evesham United (H) 4-1
R1: Southend United (A) 0-6

60-61 PR: Stourbridge (A) 4-1
Q1: Bromsgrove Rovers (H) 3-2
Q2: Kidderminster Harriers (A) 1-2

61-62 Q1: Kidderminster (H) 1-1, (A) 1-1, 0-4

62-63 Q1: Bromsgrove Rovers (A) 1-7

64-65 Q1: Macclesfield Town (A) 0-2

65-66 Q1: Congleton Town (H) 6-0
Q2: Northwich Victoria (H) 3-1
Q3: Macclesfield Town (H) 3-2
Q4: Kidderminster Harriers (H) 3-4

66-67 Q1: Borough United (A) 3-2
Q2: New Brighton (H) 2-4

67-68 Q1: Marine (A) 3-2
Q2: Rhyl (A) 0-4

68-69 Q1: South Liverpool (A) 2-4

69-70 Q1: Runcorn (H) 0-1

70-71 Q1: Kirkby Town (H) 2-0
Q2: Winsford United (A) 0-0, (H) 1-0
Q3: Rhyl (H) 1-1, (A) 1-2

71-72 Q1: Portmadoc (H) 2-1
Q2: Connah's Quay Nomads (H) 3-1
Q3: South Liverpool (H) 2-0
Q4: Altrincham (H) 0-3

72-73 Q1: Blaenau Ffestiniog (A) 2-1
Q2: Marine (A) 1-3

73-74 PR: Northwich Victoria (H) 1-3

74-75 Q1: Blaenau Ffestiniog (A) 0-0, (H) 1-0
Q2: New Brighton (H) 2-1
Q3: Rhyl (H) 2-1
Q4: Mossley (A) 3-1
R1: Doncaster Rovers (H) 1-3

75-76 Q1: New Mills (A) 1-1, (H) 5-3
Q2: Northwich Victoria (A) 1-3

76-77 Q1: Bethesda Athletic (A) 1-2

77-78 Q1: Porthmadog (H) 2-0
Q2: Rhyl (H) 1-2

78-79 Q1: St Helens (H) 1-1, (A) 0-0, (*at Winsford United*) 3-2
Q2: Winsford United (H) 0-1

79-80 PR: Radcliffe Borough (H) 1-0
Q1: Prestwich Heys (A) 1-0
Q2: Nantwich Town (H) 2-0
Q3: Northwich Victoria (H) 1-1, (A) 1-4

80-81 Q1: Colwyn Bay (H) 0-1

81-82 PR: Telford United (A) 0-4

82-83 Q1: Burscough (H) 2-1
Q2: Horwich R.M.I. (A) 1-5

83-84 Q1: Wren Rovers (A) 2-0
Q2: Congleton Town (A) 0-3

84-85 Q1: Chadderton (A) 0-0, (H) 4-0
Q2: Radcliffe Borough (A) 1-0
Q3: Frickley Athletic (H) 1-1, (A) 0-2

85-86 Q1: G.K.N. Sankey (H) 1-1, (A) 0-1

86-87 Q1: Prescot Cables (H) 1-0 *expelled*

OTTERY ST MARY

Currently: Western League

80-81 PR: Newquay (A) 0-8

81-82 PR: Bridport (A) 0-5

82-83 PR: Liskeard Athletic (A) 0-1

85-86 Q1: Exmouth Town (A) 0-2

86-87 PR: Merthyr Tydfil (H) 0-1

87-88 PR: Chippenham Town (H) 1-0
Q1: Sharpness (A) 4-1
Q2: Saltash United (A) 1-7

OXFORD CITY

Currently: Isthmian League

45-46 PR: Uxbridge (H) 4-0
Q1: Aylesbury United (A) 2-1
Q2: Southall (H) 2-1
Q3: Slough United (A) 1-3

46-47 PR: Windsor & Eton (A) 2-4

47-48 EX: Banbury Spencer (A) 0-5

48-49 EX: Henley Town (H) 9-1
PR: Bicester Town (H) 6-1
Q1: Huntley & Palmers Rec. (H) 2-1
Q2: Maidenhead United (H) 8-0
Q3: Banbury Spencer (A) 3-2
Q4: Hereford United (A) 3-4

49-50 PR: N.A.C. Athletic (H) 5-2
Q1: Slough Town (H) 1-1, (A) 2-4

50-51 PR: Pressed Steel (H) 5-4
Q1: Slough Town (A) 2-2, (H) 1-2

51-52 PR: Headington United (A) 2-2, (H) 0-3

52-53 PR: Wycombe Wanderers (H) 1-4

53-54 PR: Abingdon Town (A) 5-0
Q1: Banbury Spencer (A) 0-2

54-55 PR: Witney Town (H) 4-3
Q1: Slough Town (A) 3-2
Q2: Wycombe Wanderers (H) 4-1
Q3: Maidenhead United (H) 4-1
Q4: Tunbridge Wells United (A) 1-3

55-56 Q1: Chesham United (H) 2-1
Q2: Banbury Spencer (A) 1-3

56-57 Q1: Maidenhead United (A) 3-2
Q2: Aylesbury United (A) 0-2

57-58 Q1: Slough Town (A) 2-1
Q2: Headington United (H) 0-2

58-59 PR: Banbury Spencer (A) 3-0
Q1: Chesham United (H) 5-2
Q2: Headington United (A) 2-3

59-60 PR: Witney Town (A) 1-0
Q1: Aylesbury United (A) 4-1
Q2: Banbury Spencer (H) 5-1
Q3: Maidenhead United (H) 3-0
Q4: Wycombe Wanderers (A) 0-1

60-61 Q1: Huntley & Palmers Rec. (H) 6-1
Q2: Abingdon Town (H) 1-1, (A) 1-2

61-62 Q1: Aylesbury United (H) 5-2
Q2: Wokingham Town (A) 3-0
Q3: Banbury Spencer (A) 1-3

62-63 Q1: Banbury Spencer (A) 2-0
Q2: Harrow Town (H) 4-2
Q3: Hemel Hempstead Town (H) 4-3
Q4: Wimbledon (A) 1-6

63-64 Q1: Chesham United (H) 5-0
Q2: Hemel Hempstead Town (A) 0-5

64-65 Q1: Banbury Spencer (H) 2-1
Q2: Newbury Town (A) 2-0
Q3: Hemel Hempstead Town (A) 1-1, (H) 4-2
Q4: Chelmsford City (A) 2-6

65-66 Q1: Maidenhead United (H) 5-2
Q2: Huntley & Palmers Rec. (A) 4-1
Q3: Hemel Hempstead Town (A) 1-0
Q4: Wealdstone (A) 0-2

66-67 Q1: Addlestone (H) 8-0
Q2: Hounslow (A) 3-0
Q3: Wolverton Town & B.R. (H) 3-2
Q4: Finchley (H) 5-1
R1: Bristol Rovers (H) 2-2, (A) 0-4

67-68 Q4: Ware (A) 2-0
R1: Luton Town (H) 1-2

68-69 Q4: Romford (H) 7-1
R1: Swansea Town (H) 2-3

69-70 Q4: King's Lynn (H) 2-0
R1: Cheltenham Town (A) 2-0
R2: Swansea Town (H) 1-5

70-71 Q4: Cambridge City (H) 4-1
Q1: A.F.C. Bournemouth (H) 1-1, (A) 1-8

71-72 Q4: Alvechurch (A) 2-2, (H) 1-1, (*at Birmingham C.*) 1-1, (*at Oxford U.*) 0-0, (*at Oxford U.*) 0-0, (*at Aston Villa*) 0-1

72-73 Q1: Aylesbury United (A) 1-1, (H) 3-0
Q2: Witney Town (H) 0-4

73-74 Q1: Witney Town (H) 0-1

74-75 Q1: Witney Town (H) 1-1, (A) 0-0, 1-0
Q2: Chesham United (A) 1-4

75-76 Q1: Wolverton Town & B.R. (H) 2-0
Q2: Rothwell Town (A) 1-0

	Q3: Cheltenham Town (H) 0-0, (A) 0-2
76-77	Q1: Didcot Town (A) 1-3
77-78	Q1: Racing Club Warwick (H) 2-0 Q2: Bromsgrove Rovers (H) 2-1 Q3: Banbury United (A) 0-1
78-79	PR: Burton Albion (A) 1-0 Q1: Sutton Coldfield Town (A) 0-3
79-80	Q1: Bridgend Town (H) 0-0, (A) 2-5
80-81	PR: Cheltenham Town (H) 0-2
81-82	Q1: Harrow Borough (A) 2-4
82-83	Q1: Dorchester Town (H) 2-2, (A) 0-1
83-84	PR: Road Sea Southampton (A) 1-4
84-85	Q1: Ampthill Town (A) 4-1 Q2: Oldbury United (H) 3-0 Q3: Moor Green (H) 1-2
85-86	Q1: Malvern Town (H) 7-2 Q2: Gosport Borough (H) 2-1 Q3: Poole Town (H) 4-1 Q4: Windsor & Eton (A) 2-2, (H) 0-1
86-87	Q1: Fareham Town (A) 1-2
87-88	PR: Abingdon United (A) 1-1, (H) 3-0 Q1: Calne Town (A) 5-1 Q2: Wimborne Town (A) 1-2
88-89	PR: Pagham (H) *scratched*
92-93	PR: Devizes Town (H) 2-3

OXFORD UNITED

Currently: Football League
* - As Headington United

45-46 *	EX: Banbury Spencer (A) 1-8
46-47 *	EX: Bicester Town (A) 3-2 PR: Banbury Spencer (H) 3-2 Q1: Aylesbury United (A) 3-2 Q2: Uxbridge (A) 2-5
47-48 *	PR: Wallingford Town (H) 4-0 Q1: Southall (A) 1-2
48-49 *	EX: Osberton Radiators (H) 4-2 PR: Banbury Spencer (H) 1-3
49-50 *	EX: Huntley & Palmers (A - *played home*) 9-4 PR: Hemel Hempstead Town (A) 1-3
50-51 *	EX: Kidlington (A) 6-0 PR: Slough Town (H) 3-4
51-52 *	PR: Oxford City (H) 2-2, (A) 3-0 Q1: Chesham United (H) 5-2 Q2: Wycombe Wanderers (H) 3-2 *expelled*
52-53 *	PR: Marlow (A) 8-0 Q1: Aylesbury United (H) 4-2 Q2: Maidenhead United (H) 2-0 Q3: Wycombe Wanderers (H) 6-2 Q4: Guildford City (A) 1-2
53-54 *	Q1: Aylesbury United (A) 2-1 Q2: Maidenhead United (H) 4-0 Q3: Chesham United (H) 2-0 Q4: Wealdstone (A) 3-0 R1: Harwich & Parkeston (A) 3-2 R2: Millwall (A) 3-3, (H) 1-0 R3: Stockport County (A) 0-0, (H) 1-0 R4: Bolton Wanderers (H) 2-4
54-55 *	Q4: Tonbridge (H) 1-0 R1: Norwich City (A) 2-4
55-56 *	Q4: Margate (H) 2-4
56-57 *	Q4: Guildford City (H) 0-2
57-58 *	PR: Aylesbury United (H) 3-0 Q1: Banbury Spencer (H) 1-0 Q2: Oxford City (A) 2-0 Q3: Marlow (H) 1-0 Q4: Margate (H) 0-2
58-59 *	Q1: Windsor & Eton (H) 7-0 Q2: Oxford City (H) 3-2 Q3: Maidenhead United (A) 6-1 Q4: Wealdstone (A) 4-2 R1: Margate (H) 3-2 R2: Peterborough United (A) 2-4
59-60 *	Q4: Cambridge City (A) 3-2 R1: Enfield (A) 3-4
60-61	Q4: Brentwood & Warley (A) 4-1 R1: Hendon (A) 2-2, (H) 3-2 R2: Bridgwater Town (H) 2-1 R3: Leicester City (A) 1-3
61-62	Q4: Salisbury (H) 3-2 R1: Brentford (A) 0-3
62-63	R1: Falmouth Town (A) 2-1 R2: King's Lynn (A) 2-1 R3: Arsenal (A) 1-5
63-64	R1: Folkestone (H) 2-0 R2: Kettering Town (H) 2-1 R3: Chesterfield (H) 1-0 R4: Brentford (H) 2-2, (A) 2-1 R5: Blackburn Rovers (H) 3-1 R6: Preston North End (H) 1-2
64-65	R1: Mansfield Town (H) 0-1
65-66	R1: Port Vale (H) 2-2, (A) 2-3
66-67	R1: Yeovil Town (A) 3-1 R2: Bedford Town (H) 1-1, (A) 0-1
67-68	R1: Chelmsford City (A) 3-3, (H) 3-3, 0-1
68-69	R3: Southampton (H) 1-1, (A) 0-2
69-70	R3: Stoke City (H) 0-0, (A) 2-3
70-71	R3: Burnley (H) 3-0 R4: Watford (H) 1-1, (A) 2-1 R5: Leicester City (A) 1-1, (H) 1-3
71-72	R3: Liverpool (H) 0-3
72-73	R3: York City (A) 1-0 R4: Queens Park Rangers (H) 0-2
73-74	R3: Manchester City (H) 2-5
74-75	R3: Leicester City (A) 1-3
75-76	R3: Manchester United (A) 1-2
76-77	R1: Kettering Town (A) 1-1, (H) 0-1
77-78	R1: Nuneaton Borough (A) 0-2
78-79	R1: Colchester United (A) 2-4
79-80	R1: Barking (A) 0-1
80-81	R1: Aldershot (H) 1-0 R2: Plymouth Argyle (A) 0-3
81-82	R1: Dover Athletic (A) 2-0 R2: Aldershot (A) 2-2, (H) 4-2 R3: A.F.C. Bournemouth (A) 2-0 R4: Brighton & Hove Albion (A) 3-0 R5: Coventry City (A) 0-4
82-83	R1: Folkestone (H) 5-2 R2: Worthing (H) 4-0 R3: Torquay United (H) 1-1, (A) 1-2
83-84	R1: Peterborough United (H) 2-0 R2: Reading (A) 1-1, (H) 3-0 R3: Burnley (A) 0-0, (H) 2-1 R4: Blackpool (H) 2-1 R5: Sheffield Wednesday (H) 0-3
84-85	R3: Shrewsbury Town (A) 2-0 R4: Blackburn Rovers (H) 0-1
85-86	R3: Tottenham Hotspur (H) 1-1, (A) 1-2
86-87	R3: Aldershot (A) 0-3
87-88	R3: Leicester City (H) 2-0 R4: Bradford City (A) 2-4
88-89	R3: Sunderland (A) 1-1, (H) 2-0 R4: Manchester United (A) 0-4
89-90	R3: Plymouth Argyle (A) 1-0 R4: Southampton (A) 0-1
90-91	R3: Chelsea (A) 3-1 R4: Tottenham Hotspur (A) 2-4
91-92	R3: Tranmere Rovers (H) 3-1 R4: Sunderland (H) 2-3
92-93	R3: Swansea C. (A) 1-1, (H) 2-2 (*4-5 pens*)

PAGET RANGERS

Currently: West Midlands (Regional) League

84-85	Q1: Dudley Town (A) 1-1, (H) 2-3
85-86	PR: Rushall Olympic (H) 2-2, (A) 0-3
86-87	Q1: Willenhall Town (A) 0-1
87-88	Q1: Tamworth (H) 1-4
88-89	PR: Gresley Rovers (A) 0-2
89-90	PR: Northampton Spencer (A) 3-3, (H) 2-0 Q1: Ely City (H) 2-1 Q2: Redditch United (A) 0-5
90-91	PR: Boldmere St Michaels (H) 2-0 Q1: Princes End United (H) 1-2
91-92	PR: Stamford (A) 1-2
92-93	Q1: Gainsborough Trinity (H) 1-3

PAGHAM

Currently: Sussex County League

72-73	Q1: Chichester City (A) 0-0, (H) 1-2
73-74	Q1: Worthing (H) 0-0, (A) 1-3
74-75	Q1: Chichester City (H) 3-3, (A) 4-5
75-76	Q1: Southwick (H) 1-1, (A) 1-3
79-80	PR: Wigmore Athletic (H) 0-0, (A) 2-0 Q1: Tunbridge Wells (A) 2-2, (H) 1-2
80-81	PR: Newbury Town (A) 0-1
81-82	PR: Waterlooville (H - *played away*) 3-0 Q1: Andover (H - *played away*) 2-1 Q2: Banstead Athletic (H) 2-2, (A) 1-7
82-83	Q1: Hastings United (H) 1-3
83-84	Q1: Thanet United (A) 1-1, (H) 0-1
84-85	Q1: Leatherhead (H) 0-5
85-86	PR: Devizes Town (A) 2-2, (H) 4-1

	Q1: Petersfield United (H) 2-0 Q2: Newport Isle of Wight (H) 3-5
87-88	Q1: Worthing (H) 2-2, (A) 2-0 Q2: Tooting & Mitcham (A) 0-0, (H) 3-4
88-89	PR: Oxford City (A) *W/O* Q1: Salisbury (A) 3-2 Q2: Bashley (A) 3-4
89-90	Q1: Marlow (H) 0-1
90-91	PR: Sheppey United (A) 2-0 Q1: Oakwood (H) 4-0 Q2: Windsor & Eton (H) 0-3
91-92	Q1: Basingstoke Town (H) 1-3
92-93	PR: Whyteleafe (A) 1-5

PARKGATE WELFARE

Currently: Defunct

50-51	PR: Denaby United (H) 2-0 Q1: Stocksbridge Works (H) 0-2

PARKHOUSE COLLIERY

Currently: Defunct

49-50	EX: Jump Home Guard (H) 6-0 PR: Rawmarsh Welfare (A) 3-6
50-51	PR: Jump Home Guard (A) 3-3, (H) 7-1 Q1: Cresswell Colliery (H) 1-2

PARLIAMENT STREET METHODISTS (NOTTINGHAM)

Currently: Defunct

49-50	EX: Teversal Colliery Welfare (H) 2-5
50-51	EX: Linby Colliery (H) 3-4
51-52	Q1: Linby Colliery (H) 2-3
52-53	PR: Linby Colliery (H) 0-6
53-54	Q1: Shirebrook Miners Welfare (A) 1-5
54-55	Q1: Cresswell Colliery (H) 2-5

PARSON DROVE UNITED

Currently: Defunct

47-48	Q1: Histon Institute (A) 2-3
48-49	PR: Sawston United (A) 8-2 Q1: Newmarket Town (H) 3-2 Q2: Cambridge Town (H) 1-3
49-50	PR: March Town United (A) 1-4
50-51	PR: Wimblington Old Boys (H) 4-1 Q1: Histon Institute (A) 0-1
74-75	Q1: King's Lynn (A) 0-9
75-76	Q1: Thetford Town (H) 5-5, (A) 0-5
76-77	Q1: King's Lynn (A) 2-3
77-78	Q1: Boston (H) 0-2
78-79	Q1: Histon (A) 1-3
79-80	Q1: Chelmsford City (H) 2-0 Q2: Felixstowe Town (H) 2-0 Q3: King's Lynn (A) 1-0 Q4: Burton Albion (A) 0-1
80-81	Q1: Stowmarket (H) 0-1
81-82	Q1: Great Yarmouth Town (A) 2-3

PARTON UNITED

Currently: Local football

46-47	Q1: Cleator Moor Celtic (H) 2-4
47-48	PR: Cleator Moor Celtic (H) 3-1 Q1: Frizington United (H) 3-2 Q2: Bowthorn United (A) 4-3 Q3: Netherfield (H) 1-4
48-49	PR: Lowca (A) 1-0 Q1: Penrith (H) 1-3

PAULTON ROVERS

Currently: Western League

45-46	Q1: Swindon Corinthians (H) 4-3 Q2: Westbury United (H) 4-0 Q3: Trowbridge Town (A) 0-7
46-47	PR: Hoffmann Ath. (Stonehouse) (H) 2-4
47-48	PR: Radstock Town (H) 5-1 Q1: Clandown (H) 4-3, *replayed after protest over size of pitch,* (A) 1-4
48-49	EX: Frome Town (A) 0-2
49-50	PR: Purton (H) 4-0 Q1: Melksham (A) 8-3 Q2: Trowbridge Town (H) 1-4
50-51	PR: Trowbridge Town (H) 1-1, (A) 1-4
51-52	PR: Hanham Athletic (A) 7-0 Q1: Clandown (A) 1-3
52-53	PR: Hanham Athletic (A) 1-0 Q1: Bath City (H) 2-7
53-54	PR: Hanham Athletic (A) 1-4
78-79	Q1: Larkhall Athletic (A) 3-3, (H) 2-1 Q2: Barry Town (H) 1-2
79-80	Q1: Cheltenham Town (H) 0-2
80-81	PR: Weston-super-Mare (H) 0-3
81-82	PR: Bridgend Town (A) 0-6
82-83	PR: Bristol Manor Farm (H) 0-2
83-84	PR: Wellington (H) 2-1 Q1: Welton Rovers (A) 0-2
84-85	PR: Taunton Town (H) 2-1 Q1: Wimborne Town (H) 0-4
85-86	Q1: Barry Town (A) 2-2, (H) 0-2
86-87	PR: Clevedon Town (A) 0-1
87-88	PR: Devizes Town (A) 0-0, (H) 1-0 Q1: Merthyr Tydfil (A) 0-2
88-89	PR: Barnstaple Town (H) 2-1 Q1: Saltash United (H) 1-4
89-90	PR: Radstock Town (H) 4-2 Q1: Shortwood United (H) 2-3
90-91	PR: Calne Town (A) 0-2
91-92	PR: Cwmbran Town (A) 0-1
92-93	PR: Bristol Manor Farm (H) 0-2

PEACEHAVEN & TELSCOMBE

Currently: Sussex County League
* - As Peacehaven & Telscombe Cliffs

72-73	Q1: Burgess Hill Town (A) 3-1 Q2: Lewes (H) 0-1
73-74	Q1: Eastbourne Town (A) 2-3
74-75	Q1: Crawley Town (A) 0-3
75-76	Q1: Dover (A) 1-4
76-77	Q1: Hastings United (A) 0-5
77-78	Q1: Ramsgate (H) 1-1, (A) 0-1
79-80	PR: Ashford Town (H) 0-0, (A) 1-2
80-81	PR: Tilbury (H) 0-1
81-82	Q1: Uxbridge (A) 2-2, (H) 1-3
82-83 *	PR: Faversham Town (A) 0-2
83-84	PR: Chertsey Town (A) 5-0 Q1: Fisher Athletic (H) 0-3
86-87	PR: Lancing (A) 0-4
87-88	PR: Bracknell Town (A) 0-1
88-89	PR: Ramsgate (H) 0-1
89-90	PR: Corinthian-C. (H) 0-0, (A - *at Leatherhead*) 2-1 Q1: Molesey (H) 0-1
90-91	PR: Selsey (H) 8-1 Q1: Southwick (H) 4-1 Q2: Bognor Regis Town (H) 3-1 Q3: Margate (H) 1-0 Q4: Tiverton Town (A) 2-3
91-92	Q1: Hastings Town (H) 2-1 Q2: Tooting & Mitcham United (A) 0-2
92-93	PR: Walton & Hersham (A) 1-2

PEASEDOWN MINERS WELF.

Currently: (Peasedown Ath.) Somerset Senior Lge

45-46	Q2: Welton Rovers (A) 7-3 Q3: Radstock Town (H) 5-1 Q4: Cheltenham Town (A) 1-1, (H) 0-1
46-47	Q1: Glastonbury (H) 1-0 Q2: Dartmouth United (H) 1-1, (A) 1-3
47-48	PR: Clandown (H) 2-3
48-49	EX: Calne & Harris United (A) 3-1 PR: Frome Town (A) 3-7
49-50	PR: Clandown (A) 1-3
51-52	PR: Bristol St George (H) 3-1 Q1: Wells City (A) 2-2, (H) 0-2
52-53	PR: Clevedon (H) 6-2 Q1: Radstock Town (H) 3-0 Q2: Glastonbury (H) 0-1
53-54	Q1: Street (H) 1-4
54-55	Q1: Chippenham United (H) 3-1 Q2: Radstock Town (A) 3-4
55-56	Q1: Wells City (A) 1-2
56-57	Q1: Glastonbury (H) 0-2

PELSALL VILLA

Currently: West Midlands (Regional) League

92-93	PR: Oldbury Utd (H) 0-0, (A) 4-4, (H) 1-0 Q1: Willenhall Town (H) 1-0 Q2: Mossley (A) 2-1 Q3: Gainsborough Trinity (A) 2-4

Above: *Peacehaven & Telscombe's best F.A. Cup showing was a Fourth Qualifying Round trip to Tiverton Town in 1990. Here Adie Chipper stoops to score the visitors' first in the 64th minute, but Tiverton ultimately ran out 3-2 winners. Photo: Francis Short.*

PENRITH

Currently: North West Counties League

46-47 PR: Cleator Moor Celtic (H) 1-5

47-48 PR: Lowca (A) 2-3

48-49 PR: Bowthorn United (H) 9-2
Q1: Parton United (A) 3-1
Q2: High Duty Alloys (A) 4-4, (H) 3-2
Q3: Netherfield (A) 1-2

49-50 Q1: Netherfield (H) 2-3

50-51 PR: Moss Bay (H) 12-0
Q1: Cleator Moor Celtic (H) 1-2

52-53 PR: Burscough (H) 4-4, (A) 1-3

53-54 Q1: Morecambe (H) 1-6

54-55 Q1: Burscough (A) 0-4

55-56 Q2: Lancaster City (A) 0-2

56-57 Q2: Fleetwood (A) 1-2

57-58 Q1: Netherfield (A) 0-5

58-59 Q1: Milnethorpe Corinthians (A) 0-2

59-60 Q1: Morecambe (H) 1-0
Q2: Clitheroe (A) 3-6

60-61 Q1: Netherfield (A) 1-4

61-62 Q1: Netherfield (A) 3-2
Q2: Morecambe (H) 1-2

62-63 Q1: Stockton (A) 1-2

63-64 Q1: Scarborough (H) 1-3

64-65 Q1: Willington (H) 4-2
Q2: Evenwood Town (H) 3-1
Q3: Consett (H) 3-3, (A) 0-1

65-66 Q1: Morecambe (A) 0-2

66-67 Q1: Fleetwood (A) 1-3

67-68 Q1: Nelson (H) 4-0
Q2: Lancaster City (H) 0-3

68-69 Q1: Fleetwood (A) 0-0, (H) 0-5

69-70 PR: Darwen (A) 0-3

70-71 Q1: Morecambe (H) 3-1
Q2: Clitheroe (A) 2-0
Q3: Great Harwood (A) 2-3

71-72 Q1: Lancaster City (A) 1-6

72-73 Q1: Netherfield (A) 0-3

73-74 Q1: Chorley (H) 0-1

74-75 Q1: Darwen (H) 0-3

75-76 Q1: Whitley Bay (H) 1-0
Q2: Spennymoor United (A) 0-2

76-77 Q1: Crook Town (H) 0-2

77-78 Q1: Washington (H) 3-3, (A) 0-1

78-79 Q1: Lancaster City (H) 0-4

79-80 Q1: Rossendale United (H) 0-1

80-81 Q1: Durham City (H) 6-0
Q2: Goole Town (H) 2-0
Q3: Blue Star (H) 1-0
Q4: Burton Albion (A) 0-1

81-82 Q1: Rossendale United (H) 2-1
Q2: Chorley (A) 1-0
Q3: Droylsden (H) 3-2
Q4: Northwich Victoria (H) 1-0
R1: Chester (H) 1-0
R2: Doncaster Rovers (A) 0-3

82-83 Q4: Workington (A) 2-2, (H) 0-2

83-84 Q4: Horden Colliery Welfare (H) 3-0
R1: Hull City (H) 0-2

84-85 Q4: Formby (H) 3-2
R1: Burnley (H) 0-9

85-86 Q1: Peterlee Newtown (H) 1-3

86-87 PR: Glossop (H) 6-2
Q1: Warrington Town (A) 2-0
Q2: Chorley (H) 1-2

87-88 PR: Horden Colliery Welfare (H) 7-0
Q1: Brandon United (H) 2-1
Q2: Easington Colliery (H) 1-2

88-89 Q1: Southport (A) 0-1

89-90 PR: Murton (H) 2-3

90-91 PR: Harrogate Railway Athletic (H) 0-5

91-92 PR: Ferryhill Athletic (H) 1-0
Q1: Billingham Town (H) 4-2
Q2: Dunston F.B. (A) 2-2, (H) 6-6, (H) 2-1
Q3: Morecambe (H) 0-3

92-93 Q1: Blyth Spartans (H) 1-2

PENZANCE

Currently: South Western League

52-53 PR: St Blazey (A) 1-3

53-54 Q1: Barnstaple Town (H) 0-6

54-55 PR: St Austell (A) 1-3

55-56 PR: Newquay Amateur (H) 4-2
Q1: Truro City (H) 3-1
Q2: Bodmin Town (H) 4-3
Q3: Bideford (H) 2-2, (A) 0-2

56-57 Q1: Truro City (A) 4-3
Q2: Taunton (H) 1-1, (A) 3-3, 1-1, 2-3

57-58 Q1: Tavistock (A) 3-1
Q2: Bideford (A) 1-5

58-59 PR: Wadebridge Town (A) 1-4

59-60 Q1: Bideford (H) 3-5

60-61 Q2: Bideford (A) 2-5

61-62 Q2: Barnstaple Town (H) 2-3

67-68 Q1: Falmouth Town (A) 1-4

68-69 Q1: Falmouth Town (H) 3-4

69-70 Q2: Falmouth Town (A) 0-1

70-71 Q1: St Blazey (A) 3-3, (H) 1-2

72-73 Q1: Bideford (A) 2-3

73-74 PR: Truro City (A) 2-0
Q1: Bideford (A) 1-4

74-75 Q1: Bideford (H) 1-2

75-76 PR: Bideford (H) 5-1
Q1: Tiverton Town (A) 3-1
Q2: Wadebridge Town (H) 2-1
Q3: Falmouth Town (H) 0-3

76-77 PR: Yeovil Town (H) 2-7

77-78 Q1: Tiverton Town (H) 2-2, (A) 1-3

78-79 PR: Newquay (A) 2-2, (H) 2-1
Q1: Saltash United (A) 1-8

79-80 Q1: Newquay (H) 1-4

80-81 Q1: St Blazey (A) 2-1
Q2: Taunton Town (H) 2-3

81-82 PR: Falmouth (A) 2-2, (H) 2-2, (A) 0-1

82-83 PR: Wellington (H) 2-1
Q1: Chard Town (A) 1-2

PERCY MAIN AMATEURS

Currently: Northern Alliance

81-82 PR: Lancaster City (A) 1-3

PETERBOROUGH CITY

Currently: Defunct
* - As Baker Perkins F.C.
+ - As A.P.V. Peterbrough City F.C.

87-88 * PR: Rushall Olympic (H) 2-2, (A) 0-3

88-89 * PR: Bourne Town (A) 1-1, (H) 0-1

89-90 * Q1: M.K. Wolverton Town (A) 1-2

90-91 * PR: Letchworth Garden City (H) 5-2
Q1: Boreham Wood (A) 0-0, (H) 1-2

91-92 + Q1: Alvechurch (H) 0-0, (A) 2-3

92-93 PR: Bourne Town (A) 3-4

PETERBOROUGH UNITED

Currently: Football League

45-46 Q2: Rushden Town (A) 9-1
Q3: Kettering Town (A) 1-2

46-47 Q1: Wellingborough Town (H) 6-0
Q2: Peterborough Westwood Works (H) 3-0
Q3: Kettering Town (H) 4-1
Q4: Hitchin Town (H) 4-1
R1: Yeovil Town (A) 2-2, (H) 1-0
R2: Northampton Town (H) 1-1, (A) 1-1, 1-8

47-48 Q1: Westwood Works (A) 5-1
Q2: Desborough Town (A) 2-1
Q3: Kettering Town (A) 4-3
Q4: Vauxhall Motors (A) 1-2

48-49 Q1: Symington's Recreation (H) 4-0
Q2: Wellingborough Town (A) 3-2
Q3: Kettering Town (H) 2-1
Q4: Ransome & Marles (H) 3-1
R1: Torquay United (H) 0-1

49-50 Q1: Desborough Town (H) 5-1
Q2: Kettering Town (A) 5-0
Q3: Corby Town (A) 0-1

50-51 Q1: Symington's Recreation (H) 3-0
Q2: Kettering Town (A) 2-2, (H) 1-2

51-52 Q4: Hereford United (H) 1-1, (A) 0-1

52-53 Q1: Symington's Recreation (A) 5-2
Q2: Spalding United (A) 2-2, (H) 3-0
Q3: Corby Town (A) 0-0, (H) 5-3
Q4: Bedford Town (H) 2-1
R1: Torquay United (H) 2-1
R2: Bristol Rovers (H) 0-1

53-54 Q4: Grays Athletic (H) 4-1
R1: Hitchin Town (A) 3-1
R2: Aldershot (H) 2-1
R3: Cardiff City (A) 1-3

54-55 Q4: Boston United (H) 1-2

55-56 Q4: Ilkeston Town (A) 3-1
R1: Ipswich Town (H) 3-1
R2: Swindon Town (A) 1-1, (H) 1-2.

56-57 Q4: Corby Town (A) 5-1
R1: Yeovil Town (A) 3-1
R2: Bradford (Park Avenue) (H) 3-0
R3: Lincoln City (H) 2-2, (H) 5-4
R4: Huddersfield Town (A) 1-3

57-58 Q4: Wolverton Town & B.R. (H) 7-0
R1: Torquay United (H) 3-3, (A) 0-1

58-59 Q4: Walthamstow Avenue (H) 3-0
R1: Kettering Town (H) 3-3, (A) 3-2
R2: Headington United (H) 4-2
R3: Fulham (A) 0-0, (H) 0-1

59-60 Q4: Bury Town (H) 7-1
R1: Shrewsbury Town (H) 4-3
R2: Walsall (A) 3-2
R3: Ipswich Town (A) 3-2
R4: Sheffield Wednesday (A) 0-2

60-61 R1: Dover (A) 4-1
R2: Torquay United (A) 3-1
R3: Portsmouth (A) 2-1
R4: Aston Villa (H) 1-1, (A) 1-2

61-62 R1: Colchester Utd (H) 3-3, (A) 2-2, 3-0
R2: Torquay United (A) 4-1
R3: Newcastle United (A) 1-0
R4: Sheffield United (H) 1-3

62-63 R1: Notts County (A) 3-0
R2: Enfield (H) 1-0
R3: Derby County (A) 0-2

63-64 R1: Watford (H) 1-1, (A) 1-2

64-65 R1: Salisbury (H) 5-1
R2: Queens Park Rangers (A) 3-3, (H) 2-1
R3: Chesterfield (A) 3-0
R4: Arsenal (H) 2-1
R5: Swansea Town (H) 0-0, (A) 2-0
R6: Chelsea (A) 1-5

65-66 R1: Kidderminster Harriers (H) 2-1
R2: Shrewsbury Town (A) 2-3

66-67 R1: Hereford United (H) 4-1
R2: Colchester United (A) 3-0
R3: Bedford Town (A) 6-2
R4: Sunderland (A) 1-7

67-68 R1: Falmouth Town (H) 5-2
R2: Margate (A) 4-0
R3: Portsmouth (H) 0-1

68-69 R1: Bristol Rovers (A) 1-3

69-70 R1: Falmouth Town (A) 4-1
R2: Plymouth Argyle (H) 2-0

R3: Rotherham United (H) 1-0
R4: Gillingham (A) 1-5

70-71 R1: Wimbledon (H) 3-1
R2: Wigan Athletic (A) 1-2

71-72 R1: Redditch (A) 1-1, (H) 6-0
R2: Enfield (H) 4-0
R3: Ipswich Town (H) 0-2

72-73 R1: Northampton Town (H) 1-0
R2: Bishop's Stortford (A) 2-2, (H) 3-1
R3: Derby County (H) 0-1

73-74 R1: Colchester United (A) 3-2
R2: Wycombe Wanderers (A) 3-1
R3: Southend United (H) 3-1
R4: Leeds United (H) 1-4

74-75 R1: Weymouth (H) 0-0, (A) 3-3, (H) 3-0
R2: Charlton Athletic (H) 3-0
R3: Tranmere Rovers (H) 1-0
R4: Stafford Rangers (A) 2-1
R5: Middlesbrough (H) 1-1, (A) 0-2

75-76 R1: Winsford United (H) 4-1
R2: Coventry Sporting (A - *at Cov. City*) 4-0
R3: Nottingham Forest (A) 0-0, (H) 1-0
R4: Manchester United (A) 1-3

76-77 R1: Tranmere Rovers (A) 4-0
R2: Northwich V. (A) 1-0 *aban. 45m.*, (A) 0-4

77-78 R1: Barnet (A) 2-1
R2: Gillingham (A) 1-1, (H) 2-0
R3: Newcastle United (H) 1-1, (A) 0-2

78-79 R1: Southend United (A) 2-3

79-80 R1: A.F.C. Bournemouth (H) 1-2

80-81 R1: Northampton Town (A) 4-1
R2: Barnet (A) 1-0
R3: Chesterfield (H) 1-1, (A) 2-1
R4: Notts County (A) 1-0
R5: Manchester City (H) 0-1

81-82 R1: Halifax Town (A) 3-0
R2: Walsall (H) 2-1
R3: Bristol City (H) 0-1

82-83 R1: Chesterfield (A) 2-2, (H) 2-1
R2: Doncaster Rovers (H) 5-2
R3: Luton Town (A) 0-3

83-84 R1: Oxford United (A) 0-2

84-85 R1: Cambridge United (A) 2-0
R2: Dagenham (A) 0-1

85-86 R1: Bishop's Stortford (A) 2-2, (H) 3-1
R2: Bath City (H) 1-0
R3: Leeds United (H) 1-0
R4: Carlisle United (H) 1-0
R5: Brighton & Hove Albion (H) 2-2, (A) 0-1

86-87 R1: Northampton Town (A) 0-3

87-88 R1: Cardiff City (H) 2-1
R2: Sutton United (H) 1-3

88-89 R1: Gillingham (A) 3-3, (H) 1-0
R2: Brentford (H) 0-0, (A) 2-3

89-90 R1: Hayes (H) 1-1, (A) 1-0
R2: Swansea City (A) 1-3

90-91 R1: Hereford United (A) 1-1, (H) 2-1
R2: Wycombe Wanderers (A) 1-1, (H) 2-0
R3: Port Vale (A) 1-2

91-92 R1: Harlow Town (H) 7-0
R2: Reading (H) 0-0, (A) 0-1

92-93 R1: Kingstonian (A) 1-1, (H) 9-1 *declared void due to missile throwing*, (H) 1-0
R2: Plymouth Argyle (A) 2-3

PETERLEE NEWTOWN

Currently: Northern League

79-80 Q1: Eppleton Colliery Welfare (H) 2-1
Q2: South Bank (A) 2-3

80-81 PR: West Auckland Town (H) 1-1, (A) 4-3
Q1: Farsley Celtic (H) 0-2

81-82 PR: South Bank (H) 0-2

82-83 Q1: Gateshead (H) 1-2

83-84 PR: Netherfield (H) 3-0
Q1: Easington Colliery (A) 1-2

84-85 PR: Eppleton Colliery Welfare (H) 5-1
Q1: Evenwood Town (H) 4-0
Q2: Gretna (H) 0-0, (A) 0-2

85-86 Q1: Penrith (A) 3-1
Q2: North Shields (H) 2-1
Q3: Wingate (H) 2-1
Q4: Whitby Town (A) 2-2, (H) 0-1

86-87 Q1: Bridlington Trinity (A) 1-1, (H) 2-0
Q2: Wren Rovers (A) 2-2, (H) 2-0
Q3: Spennymoor United (A) 0-1

87-88 PR: Denaby United (H) 1-3

88-89 PR: Droylsden (H) 1-2

89-90 PR: Alnwick Town (A) 1-1, (H) 1-2

90-91 PR: Darwen (A) 0-2

91-92 PR: Seaham Red Star (A) 2-3

92-93 PR: Evenwood Town (H) 1-0
Q1: Bamber Bridge (A) 1-1, (H) 0-2

PETERSFIELD UNITED

Currently: Reformed as P'field Town in Wessex Lge

84-85 PR: Fleet Town (A) 1-1, (H) 1-3

85-86 Q1: Pagham (A) 0-2

86-87 PR: Hailsham Town (H) 2-1
Q1: Newbury Town (A) 1-2

87-88 PR: Wick (H) 1-1, (A) 3-4

88-89 PR: Chichester City (A) 1-2

89-90 PR: Poole Town (H) 0-4

92-93 PR: Chippenham Town (H) 0-1

PETTER SPORTS

Currently: Defunct * - As McLaren Sports

48-49 * EX: Farnham Town (A - *played home*) 2-4

49-50 * EX: Camberley (H) 3-1
PR: Vickers Armstrong (A) 2-7

62-63 Q1: Woking (H) 0-2

63-64 Q1: Guildford City (H - *played away*) 2-8

64-65 Q1: Leatherhead (H) 0-5

PEWSEY VALE

Currently: Western League * - As Pewsey Y.M.

45-46 * Q1: Trowbridge Town (H) 1-3

46-47 * PR: Warminster Town (A) 6-4
Q1: Westbury United (A) 1-2

47-48 EX: Wootton Bassett Town (A) 2-0
PR: Swindon G.W.R. Corinthians (A) 1-2

PICA

Currently: Defunct

47-48 EX: Cockermouth (A) 1-6

PILKINGTON RECREATION

Currently: Doncaster Senior League

47-48 EX: Harworth Colliery Athletic (A) 3-7

48-49 PR: Ossett Town (H) 2-5

49-50 EX: Laceby (H) 2-1
PR: Ossett Town (A) 0-7

50-51 EX: Thorne Colliery (A) 2-2, (H) 3-5

51-52 Q1: Yorkshire Amateur (A) 2-5

PINNER

Currently: Defunct

45-46 PR: Wealdstone (H) 1-2

46-47 EX: Hendon (H) 2-3

47-48 EX: Saffron Walden Town (H) 2-0
PR: Edgware Town (A) 0-7

48-49 EX: Hoddesdon Town (H) 0-7

49-50 EX: Lyons Club (Greenford) (A) 2-3

50-51 EX: Enfield (A) 0-5

PIRELLI GENERAL CABLES

Currently: (Pirelli General F.C.) Hampshire Lge

47-48 EX: Andover (A) 0-7

48-49 EX: Romsey Town (H) 2-5

49-50 PR: Cowes (H) 3-4

50-51 EX: Thornycroft Athletic (A) 5-5, (H) 3-2
PR: Hamworthy (H) 1-2

PLAYERS ATHLETIC

Currently: (John Player F.C.) Notts Alliance

51-52 Q1: Ransome & Marles (A) 1-4

52-53 Q1: Shirebrook Miners Welfare (H) 8-5
Q2: Linby Colliery (A) 0-6

53-54 Q1: Hinckley Athletic (A) 0-5

54-55 Q1: Brush Sports (A) 0-2

55-56 Q2: Whitwick Colliery (H) 1-4

56-57 Q1: Long Eaton Utd (H - *played away*) 0-9

57-58 Q2: Heanor Town (H) 0-5

58-59 Q1: Worksop Town (H) 0-4

PLYMOUTH ARGYLE

Currently: Football League

45-46 R3: Aldershot (A) 0-2, (H) 0-1 (*agg: 0-3*)

46-47 R3: Chester (A) 0-2

47-48 R3: Luton Town (H) 2-4

48-49 R3: Notts County (H) 0-1

49-50 R3: Wolverhampton W. (H) 1-1, (A) 0-3

50-51 R1: Gainsborough Trinity (A) 3-0
R2: Crewe Alexandra (A) 2-2, (H) 3-0
R3: Wolverhampton Wanderers (H) 1-2

51-52 R1: Millwall (A) 0-1

52-53 R3: Coventry City (H) 4-1
R4: Barnsley (H) 1-0
R5: Gateshead (H) 0-1

53-54 R3: Nottingham Forest (H) 2-0
R4: Doncaster Rovers (H) 0-2

54-55 R3: Newcastle United (H) 0-1

55-56 R3: Leyton Orient (A) 0-1

56-57 R1: Exeter City (A) 2-0
R2: Torquay United (A) 0-1

57-58 R1: Watford (H) 6-2
R2: Dorchester Town (H) 5-2
R3: Newcastle United (H) 1-6

58-59 R1: Gillingham (H) 2-2, (A) 4-1
R2: Coventry City (A) 3-1
R3: Cardiff City (H) 0-3

59-60 R3: West Bromwich Albion (A) 2-3

60-61 R3: Bristol City (H) 0-1

61-62 R3: West Ham United (H) 3-0
R4: Tottenham Hotspur (H) 1-5

62-63 R3: West Bromwich Albion (H) 1-5

63-64 R3: Huddersfield Town (H) 0-1

64-65 R3: Derby County (H) 4-2
R4: Leicester City (A) 0-5

65-66 R3: Corby Town (H) 6-0
R4: Huddersfield Town (H) 0-2

66-67 R3: Nottingham Forest (A) 1-2

67-68 R3: Sheffield Wednesday (A) 0-3

68-69 R1: Reading (A) 0-3

69-70 R1: Brentford (A) 0-0, (H) 2-0
R2: Peterborough United (A) 0-2

70-71 R1: Walsall (A) 0-3

71-72 R1: Gillingham (A) 2-3

72-73 R1: Hendon (H) 1-0
R2: Yeovil Town (A) 2-0
R3: Middlesbrough (H) 1-0
R4: Leeds United (A) 1-2

73-74 R1: Brentford (H) 2-1
R2: Walsall (H) 1-0
R3: Manchester United (A) 0-1

74-75 R1: Dartford (A) 3-2

Above: *Plymouth's David Phillips takes on the Watford defence at Villa Park in 1984. Photo: Colorsport*

R2: Crystal Palace (H) 2-1
R3: Blackpool (H) 2-0
R4: Everton (H) 1-3

75-76 R3: Hull City (A) 1-1, (H) 1-4

76-77 R3: Oldham Athletic (A) 0-3

77-78 R1: Bath City (A) 0-0, (H) 2-0
R2: Cambridge United (H) 1-0
R3: Mansfield Town (A) 0-1

78-79 R1: Worcester City (A) 0-2

79-80 R1: Colchester United (A) 1-1, (H) 0-1

80-81 R1: Newport County (H) 2-0
R2: Oxford United (H) 3-0
R3: Charlton Athletic (H) 1-2

81-82 R1: Gillingham (H) 0-0, (A) 0-1

82-83 R1: Exeter City (H) 2-0
R2: Bristol Rovers (A) 2-2, (H) 1-0
R3: Watford (A) 0-2

83-84 R1: Southend United (A) 0-0, (H) 2-0
R2: Barking (H) 2-1
R3: Newport County (H) 2-2, (A) 1-0
R4: Darlington (H) 2-1
R5: West Bromwich Albion (A) 1-0
R6: Derby County (H) 0-0, (A) 1-0
SF: Watford (*at Aston Villa*) 0-1

84-85 R1: Barnet (H) 3-0
R2: Hereford United (H) 0-0, (A) 0-2

85-86 R1: Aldershot (H) 1-0
R2: Maidstone United (H) 3-0
R3: Hull City (A) 2-2, (H) 0-1

86-87 R3: Bristol City (A) 1-1, (H) 3-1
R4: Arsenal (A) 1-6

87-88 R3: Colchester United (H) 2-0
R4: Shrewsbury Town (H) 1-0
R5: Manchester City (A) 1-3

88-89 R3: Cambridge United (H) 2-0
R4: Everton (H) 1-1, (A) 0-4

89-90 R3: Oxford United (H) 0-1

90-91 R3: Middlesbrough (A) 0-0, (H) 1-2

91-92 R3: Bristol Rovers (A - *at Bath City*) 0-5

92-93 R1: Dorking (A) 3-2
R2: Peterborough United (H) 3-2
R3: Ipswich Town (A) 1-3

PLYMOUTH UNITED

Currently: Defunct

46-47 Q1: Dartmouth United (A) 2-5

47-48 Q1: Dartmouth United (H) 1-2

POLYTECHNIC

Currently: Southern Amateur League

46-47 EX: Finchley (H - *played away*) 0-2

48-49 EX: Ware (H) 1-0
PR: St Albans City (H - *played away*) 0-3

49-50 EX: Wood Green Town (A) 0-1

50-51 EX: Hertford Town (H) 2-6

POOLE TOWN

Currently: Southern League

46-47 PR: Bournemouth (A) 4-2
Q1: East Cowes Victoria (H) 1-0
Q2: Gosport Borough (H) 3-0
Q3: Bournemouth Gas. (H) 4-2 *protest*, (H) 3-2
Q4: Trowbridge Town (H) 2-0
R1: Queens Park Rangers (A) 2-2, (H) 0-6

47-48 PR: Bournemouth (H) 3-2
Q1: Andover (H) 2-1
Q2: Ryde Sports (A) 1-2

48-49 PR: Romsey Town (H) 5-3
Q1: Ryde Sports (A) 1-0
Q2: East Cowes Victoria (A) 2-1
Q3: Weymouth (A) 2-4

49-50 PR: R.A.O.C. Hilsea (H) 9-0
Q1: East Cowes Victoria (H) 5-1
Q2: Weymouth (A) 0-4

50-51 PR: R.A.O.C. Hilsea (A) 5-0
Q1: Newport I.O.W. (A) 6-6, (H) 1-0
Q2: Dorchester Town (H) 1-3

51-52 Q1: Shaftesbury (A) 4-1
Q2: Lymington (A) 2-3

52-53 Q1: Bournemouth Gasworks Athletic (A) 0-3

53-54 Q1: Ilminster Town (A) 2-3

54-55 Q1: Dorchester Town (A) 1-2

55-56 Q2: Bridport (H) 3-1
Q3: Portland United (H) 4-1
Q4: Weymouth (H) 2-3

56-57 Q3: Portland United (H) 2-0
Q4: Newport Isle of Wight (H) 0-3

57-58 Q2: Portland United (A) 1-3

58-59 Q1: Frome Town (H) 7-1
Q2: Salisbury (H) 2-1
Q3: Portland United (A) 0-1

59-60 Q2: Bridport (H) 4-0
Q3: Salisbury (H) 0-1

60-61 Q1: Bridport (H) 6-3
Q2: Frome Town (H) 4-1
Q3: Weymouth (A) 1-1, (H) 3-4

61-62 Q2: Dorchester Town (H) 0-1

62-63 Q1: Swanage Town (A) 8-0
Q2: Warminster Town (H) 10-1
Q3: Dorchester Town (A) 3-0
Q4: Weymouth (H) 0-0, (A) 2-0
R1: Watford (A) 2-2, (H) 1-2

63-64 Q1: Dorchester Town (A) 0-1

64-65 Q1: Bridport (H) 2-0
Q2: Salisbury (A) 1-1, (H) 0-1

65-66 Q1: Bridport (H) 3-2
Q2: Portland United (H) 0-2

66-67 Q1: Bridport (H) 7-0
Q2: Portland United (A) 2-0
Q3: Dorchester Town (A) 1-0
Q4: Minehead (H) 1-0
R1: Queens Park Rangers (A) 2-3

67-68 Q1: Devizes Town (A) 4-0
Q2: Melksham Town (H) 5-0
Q3: Dorchester Town (A) 2-3

68-69 PR: Melksham Town (H) 4-0
Q1: Dorchester Town (A) 5-2
Q2: Westbury United (H) 4-0
Q3: Gloucester City (H) 1-1, (A) 2-1
Q4: Weymouth (A) 1-1, (H) 0-1

69-70 PR: Devizes Town (H) 6-1
Q1: Welton Rovers (H) 1-1, (A) 1-2

70-71 Q1: Devizes Town (H) 5-1
Q2: Salisbury (A) 1-0
Q3: Bath City (H) 1-0
Q4: Yeovil Town (H) 1-2

71-72 PR: Minehead (A) 2-1
Q1: Glastonbury (A) 1-2

72-73 Q1: Welton Rovers (A) 0-2

73-74 Q1: Weymouth (H) 0-3

74-75 Q1: Bridport (A) 6-1
Q2: Taunton (H) 2-0
Q3: Weymouth (H) 0-3

75-76 Q1: Worthing (H) 1-0
Q2: Waterlooville (A) 0-3

76-77 Q1: Dorchester Town (H) 2-0
Q2: Farnborough Town (A) 1-1, (H) 3-1
Q3: Fareham Town (A) 1-0
Q4: Weymouth (H) 2-3

77-78 Q1: Selsey (H) 4-1
Q2: Frome Town (H) 0-2

78-79 PR: Ilminster Town (A) 0-1

79-80 Q1: Epsom & Ewell (H) 3-1
Q2: Waterlooville (H) 0-0, (A) 2-0
Q3: Salisbury (A) 0-3

80-81 PR: Bracknell Town (A) 5-1
Q1: Wokingham Town (A) 1-0
Q2: Andover (A) 2-0
Q3: Sutton United (A) 1-4

81-82 PR: Chichester City (A) 5-1
Q1: Eastleigh (A) 1-2

82-83 PR: Basingstoke Town (H) 0-0, (A) 0-2
Q1: Slough Town (A) 0-2

83-84 Q1: Saltash United (A) 1-0
Q2: St Blazey (A) 3-0
Q3: Frome Town (A) 3-2
Q4: Slough Town (H) 3-0
R1: Newport County (H) 0-0, (A) 1-3

Opposite: *Poole Town score their consolation goal in the First Round replay at Newport County.*
Photo: Mike Joss.

84-85 Q1: Shepton Mallet Town (H) 2-1
Q2: Witney (H) 1-1, (A) 0-0, (*at Andover*) 1-3

85-86 PR: Bridgend Town (A) 1-0
Q1: Weston-super-Mare (H) 5-1
Q2: Hungerford Town (H) 3-2
Q3: Oxford City (A) 1-4

86-87 Q1: Chippenham Town (A) 1-3

87-88 PR: Frome Town (A) 0-1

88-89 PR: Taunton Town (A) 1-1, (H) 1-0
Q1: Chard Town (A) 3-0
Q2: Forest Green Rovers (H) 2-4

89-90 PR: Petersfield United (A) 4-0
Q1: Salisbury (A) 1-1, (H) 3-1
Q2: Romsey Town (A) 2-1
Q3: Gosport Borough (H) 1-0
Q4: Bath City (H) 2-2, (A) 0-3

90-91 Q1: Saltash U. (A) 1-1, (H) 2-2, (A) 1-3

91-92 Q1: Westbury United (H) 3-1
Q2: Salisbury (A) 0-2

92-93 PR: Abingdon United (H) 0-1

PORTFIELD

Currently: Sussex County League

86-87 PR: Eastbourne United (A) 1-1, (H) 1-0
Q1: Ashford Town (H) 1-7

87-88 PR: Egham Town (A) 1-1, (H) 1-3

88-89 Q1: Thanet United (A) 0-1

89-90 PR: Ruislip Manor (A) 0-0, (H) 0-2

90-91 PR: Langney Sports (A) 0-3

91-92 PR: Bracknell Town (A) 2-2, (H) 2-1
Q1: Havant Town (H) 1-2

92-93 PR: Faversham Town (H) 2-4

Right: *Sean Forry stretches to put Portfield 1-0 up at home to Faversham Town on 29th August 1992, but the Kent side fought back to win. Photo: Graham Cotterill.*

PORTHMADOG

Currently: League of Wales
* - As Portmadoc

67-68 * Q1: Holyhead Town (A) 0-4

68-69 * Q1: Pwllheli & District (A) 5-0
Q2: Bangor City (H) 1-8

69-70 * Q1: Rhyl (H) 1-3

70-71 * Q1: Holyhead Town (H) 6-0
Q2: Rhyl (A) 1-2

71-72 * Q1: Oswestry Town (A) 1-2

72-73 * Q1: South Liverpool (H) 0-0, (A) 1-2

73-74 * Q1: Winsford United (A) 2-1
Q2: Connah's Quay Nomads (H) 2-0
Q3: Runcorn (H) 0-2

74-75 Q1: New Brighton (A) 1-2

75-76 PR: Bethesda Athletic (H) 3-2
Q1: Runcorn (A) 3-5

76-77 Q1: New Brighton Rakers (H) 3-4

77-78 Q1: Oswestry Town (A) 0-2

78-79 Q1: Marine (H) 3-1
Q2: Droylsden (A) 1-3

79-80 Q1: Formby (H) 0-2

80-81 PR: Skelmersdale United (H) 1-1, (A) 1-3

PORTLAND UNITED

Currently: Dorset Combination

47-48 EX: Lymington (A) 2-1
PR: Bournemouth Gasworks Athletic (A) 0-4

48-49 EX: Longfleet St Mary's (H) 2-4

49-50 EX: Hamworthy (A) 1-0
PR: Longfleet St Mary's (A) 1-0
Q1: Bournemouth (A) 1-3

50-51 EX: Dorchester Town (A) 3-6

51-52 Q1: Dorchester Town (H) 1-1, (A) 3-2
Q2: Bournemouth Gasworks Athletic (A) 3-1
Q3: Lymington (A) 1-1, (H) 1-2

52-53 Q1: Shaftesbury (H) 3-1
Q2: Bournemouth Gasworks Athletic (A) 1-5

53-54 Q1: Shaftesbury (H) 11-1
Q2: Dorchester Town (A) 3-1
Q3: Bournemouth Gasworks Athletic (H) 4-1
Q4: Llanelly (A) 5-6

54-55 Q2: Bridport (H) 4-2
Q3: Dorchester Town (H) 1-5

55-56 Q2: Ilminster Town (H) 5-0
Q3: Poole Town (A) 1-4

56-57 Q2: Ilminster Town (H) 9-0
Q3: Poole Town (A) 0-2

57-58 Q2: Poole Town (H) 3-1
Q3: Bridport (H) 2-1
Q4: Newport Isle of Wight (A) 0-5

58-59 Q1: Ilminster Town (H) 7-0
Q2: Warminster Town (H) 3-0
Q3: Poole Town (H) 1-0
Q4: Newport I.O.W. (H) 2-2, (A) 1-3

59-60 Q1: Salisbury (H) 2-3

60-61 Q1: Warminster Town (A) 1-3

61-62 Q2: Bridport (H) 4-3
Q3: Dorchester Town (H) 0-3

62-63 Q1: Bridport (A) 5-1
Q2: Dorchester Town (H) 1-3

63-64 Q1: Bridport (H) 2-4

64-65 Q2: Warminster Town (A) 3-1
Q3: Salisbury (A) 1-5

65-66 Q1: Dorchester Town (H) 4-1
Q2: Poole Town (A) 2-0
Q3: Salisbury (A) 3-0
Q4: Yeovil Town (H) 1-1, (A) 0-3

66-67 Q1: Glastonbury (A) 2-2, (H) 4-2
Q2: Poole Town (H) 0-2

67-68 Q1: Bridport (H) 3-1
Q2: Taunton (A) 0-2

68-69 Q1: Trowbridge Town (A) 0-3

69-70 Q1: Frome Town (H) 1-1, (A) 0-2

70-71 Q1: Salisbury (A) 0-3

PORTRACK SHAMROCKS

Currently: Defunct

46-47 Q1: Hull Amateur (H) 5-1
Q2: Billingham Synthonia Recreation (H) 2-1
Q3: Stockton (A) 1-9

47-48 Q1: Billingham Synthonia Recreation (A) 3-1
Q2: Whitby United (A) 0-1

48-49 Q1: Filey Town (A) 4-1
Q2: South Bank (A) 3-1
Q3: Billingham Synthonia Recreation (A) 0-5

49-50 Q1: Bridlington Central United (H) 1-0
Q2: South Bank St Peters (A) 2-2, (H) 2-1
Q3: Billingham Synthonia Recreation (A) 1-3

PORTSMOUTH

Currently: Football League

45-46 R3: Birmingham (A) 0-1, (H) 0-0 (*agg: 0-1*)

46-47 R3: Doncaster Rovers (A) 3-2
R4: Birmingham City (A) 0-1

47-48 R3: Brighton & Hove Albion (H) 4-1
R4: Preston North End (H) 1-3

48-49 R3: Stockport County (H) 7-0
R4: Sheffield Wednesday (H) 2-1
R5: Newport County (H) 3-2
R6: Derby County (H) 2-1
SF: Leicester City (*at Arsenal F.C.*) 1-3

49-50 R3: Norwich City (H) 1-1, (A) 2-0
R4: Grimsby Town (H) 5-0
R5: Manchester United (A) 3-3, (H) 1-3

50-51 R3: Luton Town (A) 0-2

51-52 R3: Lincoln City (H) 4-0
R4: Notts County (A) 3-1
R5: Doncaster Rovers (H) 4-0
R6: Newcastle United (H) 2-4

52-53 R3: Burnley (H) 1-1, (A) 1-3

53-54 R3: Charlton Athletic (H) 3-3, (A) 3-2
R4: Scunthorpe Utd (A) 1-1, (H) 2-2, 4-0
R5: Bolton Wanderers (A) 0-0, (H) 1-2

54-55 R3: Bristol Rovers (A) 1-2

55-56 R3: Grimsby Town (H) 3-1
R4: West Bromwich Albion (A) 0-2

56-57 R3: Bury (A) 3-1
R4: Nottingham Forest (H) 1-3

57-58 R3: Aldershot (H) 5-1
R4: Wolverhampton Wanderers (A) 1-5

58-59 R3: Swansea Town (H) 3-1
R4: Accrington Stanley (A) 0-0, (H) 4-1
R5: Burnley (A) 0-1

59-60 R3: Sheffield United (A) 0-3

60-61 R3: Peterborough United (H) 1-2

61-62 R1: Crystal Palace (A) 0-3

62-63 R3: Scunthorpe United (H) 1-1, (A) 2-1
R4: Coventry City (H) 1-1, (A) 2-2, 1-2

63-64 R3: Stoke City (A) 1-4

64-65 R3: Wolverhampton W. (H) 0-0, (A) 2-3

65-66 R3: Grimsby Town (A) 0-0, (H) 1-3

66-67 R3: Hull City (A) 1-1, (H) 2-2, 3-1
R4: Tottenham Hotspur (A) 1-3

67-68 R3: Peterborough United (A) 1-0
R4: Fulham (A) 0-0, (H) 1-0
R5: West Bromwich Albion (H) 1-2

68-69 R3: Chesterfield (H) 3-0
R4: Blackburn Rovers (A) 0-4

69-70 R3: Tranmere Rovers (H) 1-2

70-71 R3: Sheffield United (H) 2-0
R4: Arsenal (H) 1-1, (A) 2-3

71-72 R3: Boston United (A) 1-0
R4: Swansea City (H) 2-0
R5: Birmingham City (A) 1-3

72-73 R3: Bristol City (H) 1-1, (A) 1-4

73-74 R3: Swindon Town (H) 3-3, (A) 1-0
R4: Orient (H) 0-0, (A) 1-1, (*at Crystal P.*) 2-0
R5: Nottingham Forest (A) 0-1

74-75 R3: Notts County (A) 1-3

75-76 R3: Birmingham City (H) 1-1, (A) 1-0
R4: Charlton Athletic (A) 1-1, (H) 0-3

76-77 R1: Aldershot (A) 1-1, (H) 2-1
R2: Minehead (H) 2-1
R3: Birmingham City (A) 0-1

77-78 R1: Bideford (H) 3-1
R2: Swansea City (H) 2-2, (A) 1-2

78-79 R1: Northampton Town (H) 2-0
R2: Reading (H) 0-1

79-80 R1: Newport County (H) 1-0
R2: Wimbledon (A) 0-0, (H) 3-3, 1-0
R3: Middlesbrough (H) 1-1, (A) 0-3

80-81 R1: Colchester United (A) 0-3

81-82 R1: Millwall (H) 1-1, (A) 2-3

82-83 R1: Hereford United (H) 4-1
R2: Aldershot (H) 1-3

83-84 R3: Grimsby Town (H) 2-1
R4: Southampton (H) 0-1

84-85 R3: Blackburn Rovers (H) 0-0, (A) 1-2

85-86 R3: Aston Villa (H) 2-2, (A) 2-3

86-87 R3: Blackburn Rovers (H) 2-0
R4: Wimbledon (A) 0-4

87-88 R3: Blackburn Rovers (A) 2-1
R4: Sheffield United (H) 2-1
R5: Bradford City (H) 3-0
R6: Luton Town (A) 1-3

88-89 R3: Swindon Town (H) 1-1, (A) 0-2

89-90 R3: Crystal Palace (A) 1-2

90-91 R3: Barnet (A) 5-0
R4: A.F.C. Bournemouth (H) 5-1
R5: Tottenham Hotspur (H) 1-2

91-92 R3: Exeter City (A) 2-1
R4: Leyton Orient (H) 2-0
R5: Middlesbrough (H) 1-1, (A) 4-2
R6: Nottingham Forest (H) 1-0
SF: Liverpool (*at Arsenal*) 1-1, (*at Aston Villa*) 0-0 (*1-3 pens*)

Right: *Darren Anderton (left) gets in a cross for Second Division Portsmouth in their 1992 Semi-Final replay against Liverpool at Villa Park. It was a sad day not only for Pompey, but for traditionalists who feel the essence of the F.A. Cup is to keep playing until a winner has been determined. Photo: Colorsport*

92-93 R3: Brighton & Hove Albion (A) 0-1

PORTSMOUTH ELECTRICITY

Currently: Defunct

46-47 PR: East Cowes Victoria (A) 1-4

PORT SUNLIGHT

Currently: Defunct

48-49 PR: Wilmslow Albion (A) 6-0
Q1: Northwich Victoria (A) 0-5

49-50 EX: Matlock Town (A) 2-0
PR: Macclesfield Town (A) 2-3

PORT VALE

Currently: Football League

45-46 R1: Wellington T. (H) 4-0, (A) 2-0 (*agg: 6-0*)
R2: Marine (H) 3-1, (A) 4-1 (*agg: 7-2*)
R3: Bradford P.A. (A) 1-2, (H) 1-1 (*agg: 2-3*)

46-47 R1: Finchley (H) 5-0
R2: Watford (A) 1-1, (H) 2-1
R3: Millwall (A) 3-0
R4: Blackburn Rovers (A) 0-2

47-48 R1: Crystal Palace (A) 1-2

48-49 R1: Notts County (A) 1-2

49-50 R1: Wealdstone (H) 1-0
R2: Tranmere Rovers (H) 1-0
R3: Newport County (A) 2-1
R4: Burnley (A) 1-2

50-51 R1: New Brighton (H) 3-2
R2: Nelson (H) 3-2
R3: Stoke City (A) 2-2, (H) 0-1

51-52 R1: Colchester United (A) 1-3

52-53 R1: Exeter City (H) 2-1
R2: Oldham Athletic (H) 0-3

53-54 R1: Darlington (A) 3-1
R2: Southport (A) 1-1, (H) 2-0
R3: Queens Park Rangers (A) 1-0
R4: Cardiff City (A) 2-0
R5: Blackpool (H) 2-0
R6: Leyton Orient (A) 1-0
SF: West Bromwich A. (*at Aston Villa*) 1-2

54-55 R3: West Ham United (A) 2-2, (H) 3-1
R4: Tottenham Hotspur (A) 2-4

55-56 R3: Walsall (A) 1-0
R4: Everton (H) 2-3

56-57 R3: Barnsley (A) 3-3, (H) 0-1

57-58 R1: Shrewsbury Town (H) 2-1
R2: Hull City (H) 2-2, (A) 3-4

58-59 R1: Torquay United (A) 0-1

59-60 R1: Dorchester Town (A) 2-1
R2: Queens Park Rangers (A) 3-3, (H) 2-1
R3: Cardiff City (A) 2-0
R4: Scunthorpe United (A) 1-0
R5: Aston Villa (H) 1-2

60-61 R1: Chelmsford City (A) 3-2
R2: Carlisle United (H) 2-1
R3: Swansea Town (A) 0-3

61-62 R1: Bradford (Park Avenue) (A) 1-0
R2: Crewe Alexandra (A) 1-1, (H) 3-0
R3: Northampton Town (H) 3-1
R4: Sunderland (A) 0-0, (H) 3-1
R5: Fulham (A) 0-1

62-63 R1: Bristol Rovers (A) 2-0
R2: Aldershot (H) 2-0
R3: Gillingham (A) 4-2
R4: Sheffield United (H) 1-2

63-64 R1: Bradford City (A) 2-1
R2: Workington (H) 2-1
R3: Birmingham City (A) 2-1
R4: Liverpool (A) 0-0, (H) 1-2

64-65 R1: Hendon (H) 2-1
R2: Millwall (A) 0-4

65-66 R1: Oxford United (A) 2-2, (H) 3-2
R2: Dartford (H) 1-0
R3: Cardiff City (A) 1-2

66-67 R1: Bradford City (A) 2-1
R2: Barnsley (A) 1-1, (H) 1-3

67-68 R1: Chester (H) 1-2

68-69 R1: Shrewsbury Town (A) 1-1, (H) 3-1
R2: Workington (H) 0-0, (A) 2-1
R3: Watford (A) 0-2

69-70 R1: Wigan (A) 1-1, (H) 2-2, (*at Man. Utd*) 1-0
R2: Tranmere Rovers (H) 2-2, (A) 1-3

70-71 R1: Notts County (A) 0-1

71-72 R1: Blackburn Rovers (A) 1-1, (H) 3-1
R2: Darlington (H) 1-0
R3: Birmingham City (A) 0-3

72-73 R1: Southport (H) 2-1
R2: Wrexham (H) 1-0
R3: West Ham United (H) 0-1

73-74 R1: Stockport County (A) 1-0
R2: Scarborough (H) 2-1
R3: Luton Town (H) 1-1, (A) 2-4

74-75 R1: Lincoln City (H) 2-2, (A) 0-2

75-76 R1: Grantham (A) 2-2, (H) 4-1
R2: Huddersfield Town (A) 1-2

76-77 R1: Southport (A) 2-1
R2: Barnsley (H) 3-0
R3: Hull City (A) 1-1, (H) 3-1
R4: Burnley (H) 2-1
R5: Aston Villa (A) 0-3

77-78 R1: Arnold (A) 0-0, (H) 5-2
R2: Walsall (A) 1-1, (H) 1-3

Opposite: *A potentially dangerous Cup assignment for Port Vale in the small town of Arnold in 1977. Vale, under pressure here, held their Midland League opponents to a draw before safely coming through the replay. Photo: 'Studio Arnold'.*

78-79 R1: Bradford City (A) 0-1

79-80 R1: Doncaster Rovers (H) 1-3

80-81 R1: Bradford City (H) 4-2
R2: Burnley (A) 1-1, (H) 2-0
R3: Enfield (H) 1-1, (A) 0-3

81-82 R1: Lincoln (A) 2-2, (H) 0-0, (H) 2-0
R2: Stockport County (H) 4-1
R3: Shrewsbury Town (A) 0-1

82-83 R1: Bradford City (H) 0-1

83-84 R1: Lincoln City (H) 1-2

84-85 R1: Macclesfield Town (A) 2-1
R2: Scunthorpe United (H) 4-1
R3: West Ham United (A) 1-4

85-86 R1: Mansfield Town (A) 1-1, (H) 1-0
R2: Walsall (H) 0-0, (A) 1-2

86-87 R1: Stafford Rangers (H) 1-0
R2: Walsall (A) 0-5

87-88 R1: Tranmere Rovers (A) 2-2, (H) 3-1
R2: Notts County (H) 2-0
R3: Macclesfield Town (H) 1-0
R4: Tottenham Hotspur (H) 2-1
R5: Watford (H) 0-0, (A) 0-2

88-89 R1: Southport (A) 2-0
R2: Bolton Wanderers (A) 2-1
R3: Norwich City (H) 1-3

89-90 R3: Derby County (H) 1-1, (A) 3-2
R4: Aston Villa (A) 0-6

90-91 R3: Peterborough United (H) 2-1
R4: Manchester City (H) 1-2

91-92 R3: Sunderland (A) 0-1

92-93 R1: Stoke City (A) 0-0, (H) 3-1
R2: Altrincham (A) 4-1
R3: Newcastle United (A) 0-4

POST OFFICE TELECOMS (WALLINGTON)

Currently: Defunct
* - as Post Office Engineers

46-47 * PR: Vickers Armstrong (A) 0-5

48-49 EX: Cobham (A) 2-2, (H) 1-6

POTTON UNITED

Currently: United Counties League

48-49 PR: Waterlows (H) 2-1
Q1: Stewartby Works (A) 6-1
Q2: Hitchin Town (H) 1-1, (A) 1-3

49-50 EX: Luton Amateurs (H) 1-2

50-51 PR: Bedford Town (H) 2-6

51-52 Q1: Vauxhall Motors (A) 0-0, (H) 4-3
Q2: Wolverton Town (H) 2-5

52-53 Q1: Bedford Town (A) 0-6

53-54 Q1: Bedford Town (H) 1-5

54-55 Q1: Vauxhall Motors (H) 1-0
Q2: Biggleswade Town (H) 2-5

55-56 Q1: Eynesbury Rovers (H) 0-2

68-69 Q1: Wellingborough Town (H) 1-2

69-70 Q1: Soham Town Rangers (A) 2-2, (H) 2-1
Q2: Cambridge United (H) 0-10

70-71 Q1: Rothwell Town (A) 0-1

71-72 Q1: Witney Town (H) 0-1

72-73 Q1: Histon (A) 3-1
Q2: Cambridge City (A) 1-3

73-74 Q1: Bletchley Town (A) 0-3

74-75 Q1: Biggleswade Town (A) 0-0, (H) 2-1
Q2: Irthlingborough Diamonds (H) 5-3
Q3: Bedford Town (H) 1-2

75-76 Q1: Sudbury Town (H) 2-1
Q2: Lowestoft Town (A) 3-3, (H) 1-3

76-77 Q1: Histon (A) 4-1
Q2: Bedford Town (A) 1-4

77-78 PR: Kempston Rovers (A) 1-2

78-79 Q1: Rushden Town (H) 0-1

79-80 PR: Chatteris Town (H) 1-1, (A) 2-1
Q1: Stamford (A) 0-2

80-81 PR: Wisbech Town (H) 0-1

81-82 Q1: Bedford Town (H) 1-1, (A) 1-4

84-85 Q1: Maidenhead United (A) 2-0
Q2: Tring Town (H) 0-2

86-87 PR: Basildon United (A) 1-3

87-88 PR: Hertford Town (A) 1-1, (H) 1-2

88-89 PR: Welwyn Garden City (H) 2-0
Q1: Cambridge City (A) 1-5

89-90 Q1: Wivenhoe Town (A) 0-3

90-91 PR: Holbeach United (A) 2-1
Q1: Stourbridge (H) 1-1, (A) 0-7

91-92 PR: Letchworth Garden City (A) 1-1, (H) 2-0
Q1: Harwich & Parkeston (A) 1-2

92-93 PR: Royston Town (A) 2-1
Q1: Sudbury Town (A) 2-3

PRESCOT A.F.C.

Currently: North West Counties League
* - As Prescot Cables
\+ - As Prescot Town

46-47 * Q1: St Helens Town (A) *W/O*
Q2: Earle (A) 3-0
Q3: Haydock C. & B. (H) 2-2, (A) 0-1

47-48 * PR: St Helens Town (A) 1-0
Q1: Orrell (A) 6-0
Q2: Skelmersdale United (H) 1-1, (A) 3-0
Q3: Wigan Athletic (A) 0-3

48-49 * PR: Stoneycroft (A) 7-0
Q1: Wigan Athletic (A) 2-1
Q2: Rhyl (A) 1-2

49-50 * PR: Skelmersdale United (H) 3-0
Q1: Bootle Athletic (A) 1-2

50-51 * PR: Hoylake Athletic (A) 7-2
Q1: Skelmersdale United (A) 2-6

51-52 * PR: Llandudno (H) 3-1
Q1: St Helens Town (A) 1-1, (H) 2-1
Q2: Flint Town United (H) 3-1
Q3: Bangor City (A) 0-1

52-53 * PR: Earlestown (A) 2-0
Q1: Flint Town United (H) 1-1, (A) 0-3

53-54 * Q1: Bangor City (A) 2-1
Q2: Pwllheli & District (H) 0-1

54-55 * PR: Pwllheli & District (A) 0-7

55-56 * PR: Marine (H) 4-3
Q1: Pwllheli & District (A) 1-4

56-57 * PR: New Brighton (A) 1-2

57-58 * PR: Earlestown (A) 6-1
Q1: Runcorn (A) 1-0
Q2: Bangor City (H) 4-2
Q3: Stork (A) 3-1
Q4: Morecambe (H) 3-0
R1: Hartlepools United (A) 0-5

58-59 * PR: Earlestown (H) 4-3
Q1: Pwllheli & District (H) 8-0
Q2: Llandudno (A) 4-5

59-60 * Q1: Flint Town United (H) 4-0
Q2: Earlestown (A) 1-0
Q3: Bangor City (H) 4-1
Q4: Altrincham (H) 1-0
R1: Darlington (A) 0-4

60-61 * PR: Wigan Athletic (A) 0-2

61-62 * Q1: St Helens Town (H) 3-1
Q2: Wigan Athletic (A) 1-1, (H) 1-3

62-63 * Q1: Ashton United (A) 0-2

63-64 * Q1: South Liverpool (A) 0-3

64-65 * Q1: St Helens Town (A) 1-4

65-66 + Q1: Altrincham (H) 1-2

66-67 + Q1: Mossley (A) 2-6

67-68 + Q1: Stalybridge Celtic (A) 1-1, (H) 0-1

68-69 + PR: Rhyl (A) 1-5

69-70 + PR: Runcorn (H) 1-6

70-71 + PR: Marine (A) 1-2

71-72 + Q1: Great Harwood (A) 1-7

72-73 + Q1: Winsford United (A) 0-1

73-74 + Q1: Connah's Quay Nomads (A) 1-5

74-75 + Q1: Winsford United (A) 1-5

75-76 + Q1: Stalybridge Celtic (H) 1-1, (A) 2-1
Q2: Great Harwood (A) 1-5

76-77 + PR: St Helens Town (H) 4-1
Q1: Bangor City (A) 0-6

77-78 + Q1: Darwen (H) 0-1

78-79 + PR: Nantwich Town (A) 2-1
Q1: Rhyl (A) 0-2

79-80 + Q1: Emley (H) 1-0
Q2: Droylsden (H) 2-2, (A) 0-1

80-81 * PR: South Liverpool (H) 2-1
Q1: Glossop (H) 2-0
Q2: Curzon Ashton (A) 4-1
Q3: Burscough (A) 0-4

81-82 * PR: St Helens Town (H) 4-1
Q1: Bootle (H) 3-1
Q2: Nantwich Town (H) 1-1, (A) 1-0
Q3: Runcorn (A) 1-4

82-83 * Q1: Marine (H) 2-1
Q2: Caernarfon Town (A) 1-4

83-84 * PR: Lytham (H) 0-0, (A) 3-0
Q1: Rhyl (H) 0-5

84-85 * PR: Ashton United (H) 0-0, (A) 1-3

85-86 * Q1: Runcorn (H) 1-2

86-87 * Q1: Oswestry Town (A) 0-1 *awarded tie*
Q2: Rossendale United (A) 1-2

87-88 * Q1: Colwyn Bay (H) 0-1

88-89 * PR: Glossop (A) 0-0, (H) 1-0

Q1: Eastwood Hanley (A) 0-2

89-90 * PR: Ossett Albion (H) 2-1
Q1: Curzon Ashton (A) 0-2

90-91 PR: Emley (H) 1-1, (A) 1-2

91-92 PR: Chadderton (H) 3-2
Q1: Accrington Stanley (H) 0-5

92-93 PR: Great Harwood Town (A) 1-2

PRESCOT B.I.C.C.

Currently: St Helens Combination

48-49 EX: St Helens Town (A) 2-4

49-50 EX: Haydock C. & B. (A) 2-5

PRESSED STEEL

Currently: (Pressed Steel Fisher) Oxon Senior Lge

45-46 EX: Morris Motors (H) 1-0
PR: Windsor & Eton (A) 1-11

46-47 PR: Hayes (A) 1-7

47-48 EX: Huntley & Palmers Recreation (H) 0-3

48-49 EX: Aylesbury United (A) 1-4

49-50 EX: Henley Town (A) 2-4

50-51 EX: Osberton Radiator (A) 2-1
PR: Oxford City (A) 4-5

PRESTON NORTH END

Currently: Football League

45-46 R3: Everton (H) 2-1, (A) 2-2 (*agg: 4-3*)
R4: Manchester U. (A) 0-1, (H) 3-1 (*agg: 3-2*)
R5: Charlton Ath. (H) 1-1, (A) 0-6 (*agg: 1-7*)

46-47 R3: Northampton Town (A) 2-1
R4: Barnsley (H) 6-0
R5: Sheffield Wednesday (A) 2-0
R6: Charlton Athletic (A) 1-2

47-48 R3: Millwall (A) 2-1
R4: Portsmouth (A) 3-1
R5: Manchester City (A) 1-0
R6: Manchester United (A) 1-4

48-49 R3: Mansfield Town (H) 2-1
R4: Leicester City (A) 0-2

49-50 R3: Watford (A) 2-2, (H) 0-1

50-51 R3: Leicester City (A) 3-0
R4: Huddersfield Town (H) 0-2

51-52 R3: Bristol Rovers (A) 0-2

52-53 R3: Wolverhampton Wanderers (H) 5-2
R4: Tottenham Hotspur (H) 2-2, (A) 0-1

53-54 R3: Derby County (A) 2-0
R4: Lincoln City (A) 2-0
R5: Ipswich Town (H) 6-1
R6: Leicester (A) 1-1, (H) 2-2, (*at Sheff. W.*) 3-1
SF: Sheffield Wed. (*at Manchester C.*) 3-1
F: West Bromwich Albion (*at Wembley*) 2-3

54-55 R3: Fulham (A) 3-2
R4: Sunderland (H) 3-3, (A) 0-2

55-56 R3: West Ham United (A) 2-5

56-57 R3: Sheff. W. (H) 0-0, (A) 2-2, (*at Everton*) 5-1
R4: Bristol Rovers (A) 4-1
R5: Arsenal (H) 3-3, (A) 1-2

57-58 R3: Bolton Wanderers (H) 0-3

58-59 R3: Derby County (A) 2-2, (H) 4-2
R4: Bradford City (H) 3-2
R5: Bolton Wanderers (A) 2-2, (H) 1-1, 0-1

59-60 R3: Stoke City (A) 1-1, (H) 3-1
R4: Bristol Rovers (A) 3-3, (H) 5-1
R5: Brighton & Hove Albion (H) 2-1
R6: Aston Villa (A) 0-2

60-61 R3: Accrington Stanley (H) 1-1, (A) 4-0
R4: Swansea Town (A) 1-2

61-62 R3: Watford (H) 3-2
R4: Weymouth (H) 2-0
R5: Liverpool (A) 0-0, (H) 0-0, 1-0
R6: Manchester United (H) 0-0, (A) 1-2

62-63 R3: Sunderland (H) 1-4

63-64 R3: Nottingham Forest (A) 0-0, (H) 1-0
R4: Bolton Wanderers (A) 2-2, (H) 2-1
R5: Carlisle United (A) 1-0

Preston North End attracted big crowds to Northern League grounds for cup ties in the season 1974-75. **Above:** The legendary Bobby Charlton (second left) fires in a shot at Blyth Spartans. **Below:** Goalkeeper Roy Tunks is challenged by Bishop Auckland's Terry Boylan in the Second Round tie. Photos: Galdon Photographers.

R6: Oxford United (A) 2-1
SF: Swansea Town (*at Aston Villa*) 2-1
F: West Ham United (*at Wembley*) 2-3

64-65 R3: Barnet (A) 3-2
R4: Bolton Wanderers (H) 1-2

65-66 R3: Charlton Athletic (A) 3-2
R4: Bolton Wanderers (A) 1-1, (H) 3-2
R5: Tottenham Hotspur (H) 2-1
R6: Manchester United (H) 1-1, (A) 1-3

66-67 R3: Aston Villa (H) 0-1

67-68 R3: Queens Park Rangers (A) 3-1
R4: Tottenham Hotspur (A) 1-3

68-69 R3: Nottingham Forest (H) 3-0
R4: Chelsea (H) 0-0, (A) 1-2

69-70 R3: Derby County (H) 1-1, (A) 1-4

70-71 R1: Chester (H) 1-1, (A) 0-1

71-72 R3: Bristol City (H) 4-2
R4: Manchester United (H) 0-2

72-73 R3: Grimsby Town (A) 0-0, (H) 0-1

73-74 R3: Fulham (A) 0-1

74-75 R1: Blyth Spartans (A) 1-1, (H) 5-1
R2: Bishop Auckland (A) 2-0
R3: Carlisle United (H) 0-1

75-76 R1: Scunthorpe United (H) 2-1
R2: Scarborough (A) 2-3

76-77 R1: Crewe (A) 1-1, (H) 2-2, (*at Liverpool*) 3-0
R2: Halifax Town (A) 0-1

77-78 R1: Lincoln City (H) 3-2
R2: Wrexham (H) 0-2

78-79 R3: Derby County (H) 3-0
R4: Southampton (H) 0-1

79-80 R3: Ipswich Town (H) 0-3

80-81 R3: Bristol Rovers (H) 3-4

81-82 R1: Chesterfield (A) 1-4

82-83 R1: Shepshed Charterhouse (H) 5-1
R2: Blackpool (H) 2-1
R3: Leeds United (A) 0-3

83-84 R1: Scunthorpe United (A) 0-1

84-85 R1: Bury (H) 4-3
R2: Telford United (H) 1-4

85-86 R1: Walsall (A) 3-7

86-87 R1: Bury (H) 5-1
R2: Chorley (A - *at Blackburn*) 0-0, (H) 5-1

R3: Middlesbrough (A) 1-0
R4: Newcastle United (A) 0-2

87-88 R1: Mansfield Town (H) 1-1, (A) 2-4

88-89 R1: Tranmere Rovers (H) 1-1, (A) 0-3

89-90 R1: Tranmere Rovers (H) 1-0
R2: Whitley Bay (A) 0-2

90-91 R1: Mansfield Town (H) 0-1

91-92 R1: Mansfield (A) 1-1 *ab. (fog) 32m.*, (A) 1-0
R2: Witton Albion (H) 5-1
R3: Sheffield Wednesday (H) 0-2

92-93 R1: Bradford City (A) 1-1, (H) 4-5

PRESTWICH HEYS

Currently: Manchester League

70-71 Q1: Burscough (H) 2-3

71-72 Q1: Mossley (A) 2-2, (H) 1-2

72-73 PR: Horwich R.M.I. (H) 3-3, (A) 1-4

73-74 PR: Stocksbridge Wks Social (A) 4-4, (H) 6-0
Q1: Droylsden (A) 4-1
Q2: Mossley (A) 1-1, (H) 2-3

74-75 Q1: Chorley (H) 0-0, (A) 1-6

75-76 Q1: Great Harwood (H) 0-1

76-77 Q1: Runcorn (H) 0-1

77-78 Q1: Great Harwood (A) 1-1, (H) 1-5

78-79 Q1: New Brighton (A) 3-1
Q2: Stalybridge Celtic (H) 1-1, (A) 1-4

79-80 Q1: Oswestry Town (H) 0-1

80-81 Q1: Burscough (A) 1-2

81-82 PR: Marine (A) 0-2

82-83 PR: Skelmersdale United (A) 4-0
Q1: Eastwood Town (A) 2-4

83-84 PR: Droylsden (A) 2-1
Q1: St Helens Town (A) 1-0
Q2: Southport (H) 0-1

PRINCES END UNITED

Currently: Defunct

89-90 PR: Alfreton Town (H) 0-2

90-91 PR: Louth Town (A) 1-1, (H) 1-0
Q1: Paget Rangers (A) 2-1
Q2: Frickley Athletic (H) 0-4

PRUDHOE EAST END

Currently: Northern League

89-90 PR: Harrogate Town (H) 1-0
Q1: Seaham Red Star (H) 0-0, (A) 2-3

90-91 PR: Ashington (A) 4-1
Q1: Durham City (A) 3-0
Q2: North Shields (H) 0-1

91-92 PR: Bedlington Terriers (H) 0-2

92-93 PR: Bamber Bridge (A) 0-4

PURFLEET

Currently: Isthmian League

88-89 PR: Metropolitan Police (H) 0-1

89-90 PR: Stamford (H) 1-1, (A) 2-1
Q1: Canvey Island (A) 0-3

90-91 PR: Alma Swanley (A) 2-1
Q1: Egham Town (A) 1-2

91-92 PR: Gorleston (H) 3-1
Q1: Collier Row (H) 2-2, (A) 1-0
Q2: King's Lynn (A) 2-4

92-93 PR: Great Yarmouth Town (H) 4-1
Q1: Watton United (H) 6-1
Q2: Corby Town (H) 2-2, (A) 0-1

PURTON

Currently: Hellenic League

45-46 PR: Swindon Corinthians (H) 0-4

46-47 PR: Clandown (A) 3-8

47-48 PR: Devizes Town (A) 0-4

48-49 EX: Salisbury (A) 0-1

49-50 PR: Paulton Rovers (A) 0-4

50-51 PR: Chippenham United (A) 1-4

PWLLHELI & DISTRICT

Currently: Gwynedd League

53-54 PR: Bootle Athletic (A) 2-0
Q1: Marine (A) 1-1, (H) 4-0
Q2: Prescot Cables (A) 1-0
Q3: Runcorn (H) 2-2, (A) 0-3

54-55 PR: Prescot Cables (H) 7-0
Q1: Bangor City (H) 2-1
Q2: Runcorn (A) 1-0
Q3: Flint Town United (A) 3-2
Q4: Rhyl (H) 0-3

55-56 PR: St Helens Town (A) 1-1, (H) 3-1
Q1: Prescot Cables (H) 4-1
Q2: New Brighton (A) 2-4

56-57 PR: Bangor City (A) 2-2, (H) 4-1
Q1: South Liverpool (H) 1-4

57-58 PR: Runcorn (A) 0-3

58-59 Q1: Prescot Cables (A) 0-8

59-60 PR: South Liverpool (A) 4-3
Q1: Earlestown (A) 2-5

60-61 PR: South Liverpool (A) 5-1
Q1: Ellesmere Port Town (H) 1-4

61-62 Q1: Ellesmere Port Town (A) 0-2

62-63 Q1: Ellesmere Port Town (A) 0-3

63-64 Q1: Borough United (A) 2-7

67-68 Q1: Bangor City (A) 0-6

68-69 Q1: Portmadoc (H) 0-5

69-70 Q1: Bethesda Athletic (H) 0-6

70-71 Q1: Rhyl (H) 0-6

71-72 Q1: Connah's Quay Nomads (H) 0-3

75-76 Q1: Bangor City (A) 0-2

QUEENS PARK RANGERS

Currently: F.A. Premier League

45-46 R1: Barnet (A) 6-2, (H) 2-1 *(agg: 8-3)*
R2: Ipswich Town (H) 4-0, (A) 2-0 *(agg: 6-0)*
R3: Crystal Palace (H) 0-0, (A) 0-0 *abandoned in extra-time*, (H) 1-0 *(agg: 1-0)*
R4: Southampton (A) 1-0, (H) 4-3 *(agg: 5-3)*
R5: Brentford (H) 1-3, (A) 0-0 *(agg: 1-3)*

46-47 R1: Poole Town (H) 2-2, (A) 6-0
R2: Norwich City (A) 4-4, (H) 2-0
R3: Middlesbrough (H) 1-1, (A) 1-3

47-48 R3: Gillingham (A) 1-1, (H) 3-1
R4: Stoke City (H) 3-0
R5: Luton Town (H) 3-1
R6: Derby County (H) 1-1, (A) 0-5

48-49 R3: Huddersfield Town (A) 0-0, (H) 0-5

49-50 R3: Everton (H) 0-2

50-51 R3: Millwall (H) 3-4

51-52 R3: Brentford (A) 1-3

52-53 R1: Shrewsbury T. (H) 2-2, (A) 2-2, 1-4

53-54 R1: Shrewsbury Town (H) 2-0
R2: Nuneaton Borough (H) 1-1, (A) 2-1
R3: Port Vale (H) 0-1

54-55 R1: Walthamstow Ave. (H) 2-2, (A) 2-2, 0-4

55-56 R1: Southend United (A) 0-2

56-57 R1: Dorcester Town (H) 4-0
R2: Tooting & Mitcham United (A) 2-0
R3: Sunderland (A) 0-4

57-58 R1: Clapton (A) 1-1, (H) 3-1
R2: Hereford United (A) 1-6

58-59 R1: Walsall (A) 1-0
R2: Southampton (H) 0-1

59-60 R1: Colchester United (A) 3-2
R2: Port Vale (H) 3-3, (A) 1-2

60-61 R1: Walthamstow Avenue (H) 3-2
R2: Coventry City (H) 1-2

61-62 R1: Barry Town (A) 1-1, (H) 7-0
R2: Ashford Town (A) 3-0
R3: Burnley (A) 1-6

62-63 R1: Newport County (H) 3-2
R2: Hinckley Athletic (H) 7-2
R3: Swansea Town (A) 0-2

63-64 R1: Gillingham (H) 4-1
R2: Colchester United (A) 1-0
R3: Carlisle United (A) 0-2

64-65 R1: Bath City (H) 2-0
R2: Peterborough United (H) 3-3, (A) 1-2

65-66 R1: Colchester United (A) 3-3, (H) 4-0
R2: Guildford City (H) 3-0
R3: Shrewsbury Town (H) 0-0, (A) 0-1

66-67 R1: Poole Town (H) 3-2
R2: Bournemouth & Boscombe Ath. (H) 2-0
R3: Sheffield Wednesday (A) 0-3

67-68 R3: Preston North End (H) 1-3

68-69 R3: Aston Villa (A) 1-2

69-70 R3: South Shields (H) 4-1
R4: Charlton Athletic (A) 3-2
R5: Derby County (H) 1-0
R6: Chelsea (A) 2-4

70-71 R3: Swindon Town (H) 1-2

71-72 R3: Fulham (H) 1-1, (A) 1-2

72-73 R3: Barnet (H) 0-0, (A) 3-0
R4: Oxford United (A) 2-0
R5: Derby County (A) 2-4

73-74 R3: Chelsea (A) 0-0, (H) 1-0
R4: Birmingham City (H) 2-0
R5: Coventry City (A) 0-0, (H) 3-2
R6: Leicester City (H) 0-2

74-75 R3: Southend United (A) 2-2, (H) 2-0
R4: Notts County (H) 3-0
R5: West Ham United (A) 1-2

75-76 R3: Newcastle United (H) 0-0, (A) 1-2

76-77 R3: Shrewsbury Town (H) 2-1
R4: Manchester United (A) 0-1

77-78 R3: Wealdstone (H) 4-0
R4: West Ham United (A) 1-1, (H) 6-1
R5: Nottm F. (H) 1-1, (A) 1-1, (A) 1-3

78-79 R3: Fulham (A) 0-2

79-80 R3: Watford (H) 1-2

80-81 R3: Tottenham Hotspur (H) 0-0, (A) 1-3

81-82 R3: Middlesbrough (H) 1-1, (A) 3-2
R4: Blackpool (A) 0-0, (H) 5-1
R5: Grimsby Town (H) 3-1
R6: Crystal Palace (H) 1-0
SF: West Bromwich A. *(at Arsenal F.C.)* 1-0
F: Tottenham H. *(both at Wembley)* 1-1, 0-1

82-83 R3: West Bromwich Albion (A) 2-3

83-84 R3: Huddersfield Town (A) 1-2

84-85 R3: Doncaster Rovers (A) 0-1

85-86 R3: Carlisle United (A) 0-1

86-87 R3: Leicester City (H) 5-2
R4: Luton Town (A) 1-1, (H) 2-1
R5: Leeds United (A) 1-2

87-88 R3: Yeovil Town (A) 3-0
R4: West Ham United (H) 3-1
R5: Luton Town (H) 1-1, (A) 0-1

88-89 R3: Manchester U. (A) 0-0, (H) 2-2, (A) 0-3

89-90 R3: Cardiff City (A) 0-0, (H) 2-0
R4: Arsenal (A) 0-0, (H) 2-0
R5: Blackpool (A) 2-2, (H) 0-0, (H) 3-0
R6: Liverpool (H) 2-2, (A) 0-1

90-91 R3: Manchester United (A) 1-2

91-92 R3: Southampton (A) 0-2

92-93 R3: Swindon Town (H) 3-0
R4: Manchester City (H) 1-2

RACING CLUB WARWICK

Currently: Southern League

76-77 PR: Nuneaton Borough (A) 1-2

77-78 Q1: Oxford City (A) 0-2

78-79 Q1: Tamworth (H) 1-1, (A) 0-1

79-80 Q1: Gornal Athletic (H) 1-1, (A) 3-2
Q2: Sutton Coldfield Town (A) 0-3

80-81 PR: V.S. Rugby (H) 1-2

81-82 Q1: Gresley Rovers (A) 1-1, (H) 1-3

82-83 PR: Malvern Town (A) 0-0, (H) 4-3
Q1: Tamworth (A) 1-2

83-84 PR: Banbury United (H) 3-1
Q1: Alvechurch (H) 2-2, (A) 1-5

84-85 PR: Desborough Town (A) 0-3

85-86 Q1: Halesowen Town (A) 0-2

86-87 PR: Coventry Sporting (A) 1-3

87-88 PR: Oldswinford (A) 1-0
Q1: Desborough Town (A) 2-2, (H) 4-0
Q2: Bedworth United (A) 2-1
Q3: Halesowen Town (H) 1-3

88-89 PR: Chatteris Town (A) 2-2, (H) 6-0
Q1: Tamworth (A) 0-3

89-90 PR: Haverhill Rovers (H) 1-1, (A) 0-1

90-91 Q1: Evesham United (H) 0-0, (A) 1-5

91-92 PR: Rushall Olympic (H) 2-1
Q1: Willenhall Town (A) 1-2

92-93 Q1: Eastwood Hanley (H) 0-2

RADCLIFFE BOROUGH

Currently: Northern Premier League

71-72 Q1: Burscough (H) 2-3

72-73 Q1: New Mills (A) 3-1
Q2: Altrincham (A) 2-3

73-74 Q1: Emley (H) 1-2

74-75 Q1: Accrington Stanley (A) 1-1, (H) 0-1

75-76 Q1: Horwich R.M.I. (H) 4-0
Q2: Rossendale United (H) 2-2, (A) 1-4

76-77 PR: Darwen (A) 1-3

77-78 Q1: South Liverpool (H) 2-6

78-79 Q1: Runcorn (H) 0-6

79-80 PR: Oswestry Town (A) 0-1

83-84 PR: Ossett Albion (H) 2-1
Q1: Southport (H) 1-3

84-85 PR: Clitheroe (H) 1-0
Q1: Farsley Celtic (H) 5-2
Q2: Oswestry Town (H) 0-1

85-86 PR: North Ferriby United (H) 2-2, (A) 2-1
Q1: Ossett Albion (H) 0-0, (A) 3-0
Q2: Marine (H) 0-4

86-87 PR: Eastwood Hanley (H) 3-3, (A) 0-1

87-88 PR: Skelmersdale United (H) 1-0
Q1: Irlam Town (A) 0-1

88-89 PR: Ilkeston Town (H) 2-1
Q1: Hyde United (H) 0-2

89-90 PR: Bridgnorth Town (H) 2-2, (A) 2-0
Q1: Rhyl (H) 1-2

90-91 PR: Chadderton (A) 2-1
Q1: Emley (H) 0-0, (A) 0-1

91-92 PR: Nantwich Town (H) 0-1

92-93 PR: Thackley (A) 1-2

RADCLIFFE WELFARE UTD

Currently: Defunct

47-48 PR: South Shields (A) 0-13

48-49 PR: Shankhouse (H) 1-5

RADSTOCK TOWN

Currently: Western League

45-46 Q2: Bye
Q3: Peasedown Miners Welfare (A) 1-5

46-47 Q1: Welton Rovers (A) 4-2
Q2: Street (H) 2-1
Q3: Dartmouth United (H) 1-3

47-48 PR: Paulton Rovers (A) 1-5

48-49 EX: Chippenham United (A) 1-6

51-52 PR: Wells City (H) 1-3

52-53 Q1: Peasedown Miners Welfare (A) 0-3

53-54 PR: Bristol St George (A) 3-4

54-55 Q1: Hanham Athletic (H) 4-1
Q2: Peasedown Miners Welfare (H) 4-3
Q3: Wells City (A) 0-4

55-56 Q1: Borough of Weston-super-Mare (H) 2-3

86-87 PR: Havant Town (A) 1-1, (H) 0-1

87-88 Q1: Newbury Town (H) 5-0
Q2: Weymouth (A) 0-3

88-89 PR: Cwmbran (A - *played home*) 2-2, (H) 1-0
Q1: Cheltenham Town (H) 0-2

89-90 PR: Paulton Rovers (A) 2-4

90-91 PR: Weston-super-Mare (H) 0-3

91-92 PR: Devizes Town (H) 0-2

RAINHAM TOWN

Currently: Isthmian League

47-48 EX: Clapton (H - *played away*) 1-2

48-49 EX: Tilbury (A) 0-2

49-50 EX: Woodford Town (H) 2-1
PR: Upminster (H) 1-2

50-51 PR: Crittall Athletic (H) 0-0, (A) 1-2

54-55 PR: Brentwood & Warley (A) 1-0
Q1: Barking (A) 1-1, (H) 1-2

55-56 PR: Clacton Town (H) 1-3

56-57 PR: Woodford Town (A) 5-0
Q1: Chelmsford City (A) 0-6

57-58 PR: Aveley (H) 2-1
Q1: Brentwood & Warley (H) 2-0
Q2: Ilford (H) 4-3
Q3: Chelmsford City (A) 0-6

58-59 Q1: Leytonstone (H) 2-1
Q2: Brentwood & Warley (H) 3-1
Q3: Woodford Town (A) 0-2

59-60 Q1: Ilford (A) 1-4

60-61 Q1: Ilford (H) 2-3

61-62 Q1: Barking (H) 0-1

62-63 Q1: Brentwood & Warley (A) 2-3

63-64 Q1: Barking (A) 1-3

65-66 Q1: Ruislip Manor (A) 5-1
Q2: Leytonstone (A) 0-5

66-67 Q1: Ruislip Manor (A) 2-1
Q2: Cheshunt (A) 2-5

67-68 Q1: Wolverton Town & B.R. (A) 1-4

68-69 Q1: Corinthian-Casuals (A) 4-6

69-70 Q1: Wolverton Town & B.R. (H) 1-0
Q2: Hendon (H) 1-1, (A) 2-7

70-71 Q1: Romford (A) 0-11

72-73 Q1: Barking (A) 0-1

73-74 PR: Horsham (H) 1-2

76-77 PR: Medway (A) 3-3, (H) 2-1
Q1: Aveley (H) 1-2

77-78 Q1: Walthamstow Avenue (H) 0-5

78-79 Q1: Walthamstow Avenue (H) 0-4

79-80 Q1: Walton & Hersham (H) 2-2, (A) 2-5

80-81 PR: Uxbridge (H) 3-4

81-82 PR: Erith & Belvedere (A) 1-2

82-83 PR: Chalfont St Peter (A) 1-2

83-84 Q1: Felixstowe Town (A) 1-3

84-85 PR: Erith & Belvedere (A) 2-2, (H) 3-1
Q1: Fisher Athletic (A) 1-6

85-86 PR: Littlehampton Town (H) 1-2

86-87 PR: Cheshunt (A) 2-1
Q1: Sudbury Town (A) 1-4

87-88 PR: Sittingbourne (H) 1-1, (A) 3-2
Q1: Saffron Walden Town (A) 1-2

88-89 PR: Collier Row (A) 3-0
Q1: Burnham (A) 2-2, (H) 1-1, (A) 1-3

89-90 PR: Southwick (A) 0-3

90-91 PR: Royston Town (A) 1-1, (H) 1-2

91-92 PR: Lowestoft Town (H - *played away*) 0-1

92-93 PR: Mirrlees Blackstone (H - *at Purfleet*) 2-0
Q1: Corby Town (H - *at Purfleet*) 0-1

RALEIGH ATHLETIC

Currently: Defunct

48-49 EX: Rufford Colliery (A) 2-0
PR: Bourne Town (A) 5-0
Q1: Grantham (A) 0-6

49-50 EX: Langold W.M.C. (A) 3-3, (H) 0-2

50-51 EX: South Lawford (A) 1-1, (H) 5-2
PR: Gedling Colliery (H) 1-1, (A) 1-8

51-52 Q1: Cresswell Colliery (H) 2-4

52-53 PR: Ransome & Marles (H) 1-4

53-54 Q2: Hinckley Athletic (H) 0-3

54-55 Q1: Moira United (H) 3-2
Q2: Whitwick Colliery (H) 0-1

RAMSGATE

Currently: Kent League
* - As Ramsgate Athletic

45-46 * Q2: Lloyds (Sittingbourne) (H) 3-3, (A) 1-3

46-47 * PR: Dover (H) 9-0
Q1: Folkestone Town (A) 1-2

47-48 * PR: Maidstone United (A) 4-3
Q1: Sheppey United (H) 4-2
Q2: Folkestone Town (A) 1-4

48-49 * PR: Betteshanger Colliery Welfare (H) 6-1
Q1: Ashford (H) 4-0
Q2: Dartford (A) 0-2

49-50 * PR: Betteshanger Colliery Welfare (H) 6-0
Q1: Gravesend & Northfleet (H) 0-0, (A) 1-2

50-51 * PR: Maidstone United (A) 2-5

51-52 * PR: Bowater Lloyds (A) 2-2, (H) 7-0
Q1: Dover (A) 0-4

52-53 * PR: Snowdown Colliery Welfare (H) 4-2
Q1: Betteshanger Colliery Welfare (A) 2-1
Q2: Dover (A) 3-5

53-54 * PR: Bowater Lloyds (A) *W/O*
Q1: Deal Town (A) 0-0, (H) 1-0
Q2: Guildford City (H) 2-4

54-55 * PR: Sittingbourne (H) 1-1, (A) 1-2

55-56 * PR: Chatham Town (A) 6-1
Q1: Ashford Town (A) 5-2
Q2: Canterbury City (H) 1-1, (A) 5-2
Q3: Sittingbourne (A) 1-1, (H) 3-2
Q4: Guildford City (A) 2-2, (H) 3-2
R1: Watford (A) 3-5

56-57 * PR: Chatham Town (A) 4-2
Q1: Sittingbourne (H) 1-2

57-58 * PR: Chatham Town (H) 5-1
Q1: Betteshanger Colliery Welfare (A) 0-1

58-59 * Q1: Folkestone Town (H) 3-2
Q2: Canterbury City (H) 0-2

59-60 * PR: Betteshanger C.W. (A) 2-2, (H) 0-1

60-61 * Q1: Folkestone Town (H) 1-1, (A) 1-4

61-62 * Q2: Canterbury City (H) 2-1
Q3: Dover (A) 2-3

62-63 * Q2: Dover (A) 1-4

63-64 * Q1: Deal Town (H) 4-2
Q2: Canterbury City (A) 1-0
Q3: Folkestone Town (H) 1-3

64-65 * Q1: Folkestone Town (H) 1-2

65-66 * Q1: Canterbury City (A) 1-2

66-67 * Q1: Dover (H) 2-1

Q2: Sittingbourne (A) 3-1
Q3: Hastings United (A) 1-2

67-68 * Q1: Snowdown Colliery Welfare (A) 4-0
Q2: Bexhill Town (H) 4-1
Q3: Margate (A) 4-6

68-69 * Q1: Hastings United (A) 1-1, (H) 0-1

69-70 * Q1: Snowdown Colliery Welfare (H) 8-1
Q2: Folkestone (A) 1-1, (H) 1-0
Q3: Hastings United (H) 2-1
Q4: Carshalton Athletic (A) 0-1

70-71 * Q1: Sheppey United (A) 2-1
Q2: Herne Bay (H) 0-0, (A) 1-3

71-72 * PR: Sittingbourne (H) 1-1, (A) 1-0
Q1: Dover (A) 1-2

72-73 * Q1: Tonbridge (A) 1-1, (H) 0-3

73-74 PR: Herne Bay (H) 2-1
Q1: Bexhill Town (A) 2-0
Q2: Sittingbourne (A) 1-1, (H) 2-0
Q3: Maidstone United (A) 1-3

74-75 Q1: Folkestone & Shepway (A) 0-0, (H) 2-0
Q2: Canterbury City (A) 1-2

75-76 Q1: Sittingbourne (H) 4-1
Q2: Maidstone United (A) 2-1
Q3: Dover (H) 0-2

76-77 Q1: Herne Bay (H) 2-1
Q2: Southwick (H) 1-1, (A) 2-1
Q3: Hastings United (A) 0-2

77-78 Q1: Peacehaven & Tels. (A) 1-1, (H) 1-0
Q2: Haywards Heath (H) 2-0
Q3: Tonbridge A.F.C. (A) 0-2

78-79 Q1: Lewes (A) 1-1, (H) 3-0
Q2: Canterbury City (H) 1-0
Q3: Maidstone United (H) 1-3

79-80 PR: Snowdown Colliery Welfare (H) 3-1
Q1: Sheppey United (A) 1-1, (H) 5-2
Q2: Lewes (H) 1-0
Q3: Gravesend & Northfleet (H) 2-2, (A) 1-2

80-81 Q1: Maidstone United (A) 0-6

82-83 Q1: Horsham Y.M.C.A. (A) 1-1, (H) 2-1
Q2: Corinthian-Casuals (A - *at Dulwich*) 0-1

83-84 Q1: Dulwich Hamlet (A) 0-5

87-88 Q1: Shoreham (H) 2-0
Q2: Croydon (H) 0-1

88-89 PR: Peacehaven & Telscombe (A) 1-0
Q1: Fisher Athletic (H) 0-2

89-90 Q1: Redhill (A) 0-1

90-91 PR: Margate (H) 0-1

RANSOME & MARLES

Currently: Defunct

46-47 Q1: Boots Athletic (H) 3-1
Q2: Basford United (A) 7-0
Q3: Boston United (A) 1-3

47-48 Q1: Ilkeston Town (A) 1-2

48-49 PR: Boots Athletic (A) 6-0
Q1: Ollerton Colliery (H) 2-1
Q2: Spalding United (A) 1-0
Q3: Grantham (H) 2-0
Q4: Peterborough United (A) 1-3

49-50 PR: Stanton Ironwicks (A) 5-3
Q1: Gedling Colliery (H) 4-6

50-51 EX: Mablethorpe United (H) 6-0
PR: Spalding United (H) 0-1

51-52 Q1: Players Athletic (H) 4-1
Q2: Linby Colliery (A) 1-5

52-53 PR: Raleigh Athletic (A) 4-1
Q1: Cinderhill Colliery (H) 1-0
Q2: Cresswell Colliery (A) 0-3

53-54 Q1: Cresswell Colliery (A) 0-1

54-55 Q1: Sutton Town (H) 0-3

55-56 Q1: Cresswell Colliery (H) 6-1
Q2: Shirebrook Miners Welfare (A) 1-3

56-57 Q2: Cresswell Colliery (A) 6-0
Q3: Sutton Town (A) 1-4

57-58 Q1: Worksop Town (H) 2-1
Q2: Cresswell Colliery (H) 3-4

58-59 Q1: Heanor Town (H) 1-5

59-60 Q1: South Normanton Welfare (A) 0-3

60-61 Q2: Skegness Town (A) 1-5

61-62 Q1: Alford United (H) 2-5

R.A.O.C. (HILSEA)

Currently: Defunct

46-47 EX: Trafalgar Sports (A) 6-2
PR: Cowes (H) 4-3
Q1: Thornycroft Athletic (A) 2-1
Q2: Bournemouth Gasworks (H) 2-2, (A) 2-6

48-49 EX: Lymington (H) 3-0
PR: Thornycroft Athletic (H) 2-3

49-50 PR: Poole Town (A) 0-9

50-51 PR: Poole Town (H) 0-5

RAWMARSH WELFARE

Currently: County Senior League

45-46 Q1: Norton Woodseats (H) 3-1
Q2: Monckton Athletic (H) 2-1
Q3: Denaby United (H) 5-1
Q4: Gainsborough Trinity (H) 1-3

46-47 PR: Firbeck Main Colliery (H) 5-1
Q1: Grimethorpe Rovers (H) 4-0
Q2: Scunthorpe United (H) 0-3

47-48 PR: Brodsworth Main Colliery (A) 4-3
Q1: Scunthorpe United (A) 0-8

48-49 PR: Harworth Colliery Athletic (H) 1-4

49-50 EX: Steel, Peech & Tozer (A) 4-1
PR: Parkhouse Colliery (H) 6-3
Q1: Staveley Welfare (H) 3-2
Q2: Stocksbridge Works (H) 2-1
Q3: Hoyland Common Athletic (H) 4-2
Q4: Witton Albion (A) 0-3

50-51 PR: Norton Woodseats (H) 0-0, (A) 2-4

51-52 Q1: Beighton Miners Welfare (H) 2-0
Q2: Langold W.M.C. (H) 2-0
Q3: Worksop Town (H) 2-1
Q4: Skegness Town (H) 4-2
R1: Buxton (H) 1-4

52-53 Q1: Worksop Town (A) 3-3, (H) 3-2
Q2: Beighton Miners Welfare (A) 0-6

53-54 Q1: Norton Woodseats Amtr (H) 1-1, (A) 2-6

54-55 Q1: Bentley Colliery (H) 2-1
Q2: Beighton Miners Welfare (H) 1-0
Q3: Worksop Town (H) 0-3

68-69 Q1: Sutton Town (H) 0-0, (A) 1-4

69-70 Q1: Heanor Town (H) 1-1, (A) 1-0
Q2: Matlock Town (A) 2-2, (H) 3-2
Q3: Alfreton Town (A) 1-3

70-71 Q1: Dinnington Athletic (H) 0-1

71-72 Q1: Yorkshire Amateur (H) 1-1, (A) 2-4

72-73 PR: Glossop (H) 0-1

73-74 PR: Hatfield Main (H) 2-1
Q1: Bridlington Town (A) 0-5

RAUNDS TOWN

Currently: United Counties League

91-92 PR: Walsall Wood (A) 1-1, (H) 3-1
Q1: Gresley Rovers (H) 1-1, (A) 0-2

92-93 PR: Rocester (H) 2-2, (A) 4-3
Q1: Stratford Town (H) 0-0, (A) 2-1
Q2: Northwich Victoria (A) 2-0
Q3: Nuneaton Borough (A) 0-4

RAYNERS LANE

Currently: Hellenic League

86-87 PR: Hillingdon & B. (A - *played home*) 1-0
Q1: Boreham Wood (H) 2-5

87-88 Q1: Darenth Heathside (H) 1-2

88-89 PR: Stevenage Borough (A) 1-6

89-90 PR: Wembley (H) 1-0
Q1: Hounslow (H) 1-2

90-91 PR: Hoddesdon Town (H) 2-1
Q1: Harlow Town (H) 0-3

91-92 PR: Yeading (A) 0-8

92-93 PR: Ashford Town (Middx) (H) 2-2, (A) 1-0
Q1: Uxbridge (H) 1-1, (A) 1-0
Q2: St Albans City (A) 1-5

READING

Currently: Football League

45-46 R1: Aldershot (A) 3-7, (H) 3-1 (*agg: 6-8*)

46-47 R1: Colchester United (H) 5-0
R2: Merthyr Tydfil (A) 3-1
R3: Grimsby Town (H) 2-2, (A) 1-3

47-48 R1: Bromley (A) 3-3, (H) 3-0
R2: Newport County (H) 3-0
R3: West Bromwich Albion (A) 0-2

48-49 R1: Colchester United (A) 4-2
R2: Hull City (A) 0-0, (H) 1-2

49-50 R3: Doncaster Rovers (H) 2-3

50-51 R1: Cheltenham Town (H) 3-1
R2: Dartford (H) 4-0
R3: Newport County (A) 2-3

51-52 R1: Walsall (H) 1-0
R2: Southport (H) 1-1, (A) 1-1, 2-0
R3: Swansea Town (H) 0-3

52-53 R1: Crystal Palace (A) 1-1, (H) 1-3

53-54 R1: Ipswich Town (A) 1-4

54-55 R1: Colchester United (H) 3-3, (A) 2-1
R2: Gillingham (A) 1-1, (H) 5-3
R3: Manchester United (H) 1-1, (A) 1-4

55-56 R1: Bournemouth & Boscombe Ath. (H) 1-0
R2: Aldershot (H) 2-2, (A) 0-3

56-57 R1: Cheltenham Town (A) 2-1
R2: Bedford Town (H) 1-0
R3: Wrexham (A) 1-1, (H) 1-2

57-58 R1: Swindon Town (H) 1-0
R2: Wisbech Town (H) 2-1
R3: Leyton Orient (A) 0-1

58-59 R1: Watford (A) 1-1, (H) 0-2

59-60 R1: Norwich City (A) 1-1, (H) 2-1
R2: King's Lynn (H) 4-2
R3: Nottingham Forest (A) 0-1

60-61 R1: Millwall (H) 6-2
R2: Kettering Town (H) 4-2
R3: Barnsley (H) 1-1, (A) 1-3

61-62 R1: Newport County (H) 1-1, (A) 0-1

62-63 R1: Swindon Town (A) 2-4

63-64 R1: Enfield (H) 2-2, (A) 4-2
R2: Luton Town (A) 1-2

64-65 R1: Watford (H) 3-1
R2: Aldershot (A) 3-1
R3: Newport County (H) 2-2, (A) 1-0
R4: Burnley (H) 1-1, (A) 0-1

65-66 R1: Bristol Rovers (H) 3-2
R2: Brentford (H) 5-0
R3: Sheffield Wednesday (H) 2-3

66-67 R1: Hendon (A) 3-1
R2: Aldershot (A) 0-1

67-68 R1: Aldershot (H) 6-2
R2: Dagenham (H) 1-1, (A) 1-0
R3: Manchester City (A) 0-0, (H) 0-7

68-69 R1: Plymouth Argyle (H) 3-0
R2: Torquay United (H) 0-0, (A) 2-1
R3: Newcastle United (A) 0-4

69-70 R1: Brentwood Town (A) 0-1

70-71 R1: Bishop's Stortford (H) 6-1
R2: Shrewsbury Town (A) 2-2, (H) 1-0
R3: Watford (A) 0-5

71-72 R1: Bridgwater Town (A) 3-0
R2: Aldershot (H) 1-0
R3: Blyth Spartans (A) 2-2, (H) 6-1
R4: Arsenal (H) 1-2

72-73 R1: Gillingham (A) 2-1
R2: Hayes (H) 0-0, (A) 1-0
R3: Doncaster Rovers (H) 2-0
R4: Sunderland (A) 1-1, (H) 1-3

73-74 R1: Slough Town (H) 3-0
R2: Southend United (A) 0-2

74-75 R1: Swindon Town (A) 0-4

75-76 R1: Hendon (A) 0-1

76-77 R1: Wealdstone (H) 1-0
R2: Wycombe Wanderers (A) 2-1
R3: Hereford United (A) 0-1

77-78 R1: Aldershot (H) 3-1
R2: Wealdstone (A) 1-2

78-79 R1: Gillingham (A) 0-0, (A) 2-1
R2: Portsmouth (A) 1-0
R3: Notts County (A) 2-4

79-80 R1: Kettering Town (H) 4-2
R2: Barking (H) 3-1
R3: Colchester United (H) 2-0
R4: Swansea City (A) 1-4

Right: *Richie Bowman scores from the spot for Reading against Isthmian League Barking in 1979. Photo: Reading Evening Post.*

80-81 R1: Fulham (H) 1-2

81-82 R1: A.F.C. Bournemouth (A) 0-1

82-83 R1: Bishop's Stortford (H) 1-2

83-84 R1: Hereford United (H) 2-0
R2: Oxford United (H) 1-1, (A) 0-3

84-85 R1: Barry Town (A) 2-1
R2: Bognor Regis Town (H) 6-2
R3: Barnsley (A) 3-4

85-86 R1: Wealdstone (H) 1-0
R2: Hereford United (H) 2-0
R3: Huddersfield Town (A) 0-0, (H) 2-1
R4: Bury (H) 1-1, (A) 0-3

86-87 R3: Arsenal (H) 1-3

87-88 R3: Southampton (H) 0-1

88-89 R1: Hendon (H) 4-2
R2: Maidstone United (H) 1-1, (A) 2-1
R3: Tranmere Rovers (A) 1-1, (H) 2-1
R4: Grimsby Town (A) 1-1, (H) 1-2

89-90 R1: Bristol Rovers (A - *at Bath*) 1-1, (H) 1-1, (A - *at Bath*) 1-0
R2: Welling (H) 0-0, (A) 1-1, (H) 0-0, (A) 2-1
R3: Sunderland (H) 2-1
R4: Newcastle United (H) 3-3, (A) 1-4

90-91 R1: Colchester United (A) 1-2

91-92 R1: Slough Town (A) 3-3, (H) 2-1
R2: Peterborough United (A) 0-0, (H) 1-0
R3: Bolton Wanderers (A) 0-2

92-93 R1: Birmingham City (H) 1-0
R2: Leyton Orient (H) 3-0
R3: Manchester City (A) 1-1, (H) 0-4

REDBRIDGE FOREST

Currently: Merged with Dagenham. Playing as Dagenham & Redbridge in Alliance Premier Lge. See also Leytonstone, Ilford, Leytonstone-Ilford, Walthamstow Avenue and Dagenham & Redbridge.

89-90 Q1: Dartford (H) 2-4

90-91 Q1: Barkingside (A) 3-1
Q2: Harwich & Parkeston (A) 3-1
Q3: Bishop's Stortford (A) 1-2

91-92 Q1: Haringey Borough (H) 5-0
Q2: Grays Athletic (A) 1-3

Right: *Redbridge goalkeeper Kevin Foster deals confidently with a high ball in the comfortable home win over Haringey Borough on 14th September 1991. Photo: Francis Short.*

REDCAR ALBION

Currently: (Redcar Works B.S.C.) Teesside League

58-59 Q2: West Auckland Town (A) 0-3

59-60 Q2: Shildon (A) 0-4

REDDITCH UNITED

Currently: Southern League
* - As Redditch F.C.

54-55 * PR: Oswestry Town (H) 0-1

55-56 * PR: Worcester City (H) 0-1

56-57 * PR: Hednesford (H) 4-1
Q1: Kidderminster Harriers (A) 0-1

60-61 * Q1: Cradley Heath (A) 3-1
Q2: Wellington Town (H) 0-3

61-62 * Q1: Bromsgrove Rovers (A) 0-4

64-65 * Q1: Kidderminster Harriers (A) 0-1

65-66 * Q1: Kidderminster Harriers (A) 0-3

66-67 * Q1: Stratford Town Amateur (H) 0-2

67-68 * Q1: Halesowen Town (H) 2-3

68-69 * Q1: Alvechurch (A) 2-3

69-70 Q1: Stourbridge (H) 0-0, (A) 0-3

70-71 Q1: Stratford Town Amateur (A) 2-1
Q2: Bromsgrove Rovers (H) 2-2, (A) 0-3

71-72 Q1: Hednesford (A) 2-0
Q2: Lower Gornal Athletic (A) 0-0, (H) 3-1
Q3: Highgate United (H) 3-0
Q4: Ton Pentre (H) 3-0
R1: Peterborough United (H) 1-1, (A) 0-6

72-73 Q1: Lye Town (A) 0-1

73-74 PR: A.P. Leamington (H) 1-3

74-75 Q1: Gornal Athletic (H) 2-1
Q2: Bilston (A) 2-0
Q3: Kidderminster H. (A) 1-1, (H) 2-2, 0-3

75-76 Q1: Aylesbury United (A) 1-2

76-77 PR: Kidderminster Harriers (A) 2-1
Q1: Alvechurch (H) 2-0
Q2: Enderby Town (H) 0-0, (A) 0-1

77-78 Q1: Wellingborough Town (H) 1-3

78-79 Q1: Tividale (H) 3-2
Q2: Alvechurch (H) 1-0
Q3: Brereton Social (H) 0-0, (A) 1-0
Q4: Stafford Rangers (A) 1-2

79-80 Q1: Cinderford Town (A) 2-1
Q2: Bridgend Town (A) 0-0, (H) 2-3

80-81 PR: Witton Albion (H) 0-0, (A) 1-5

81-82 PR: Gresley Rovers (A) 1-2

82-83 PR: Kidderminster H. (A) 0-0, (H) 2-3

83-84 Q1: Bridgend Town (A) 0-1

84-85 PR: Malvern Town (A) 5-1
Q1: Bridgnorth Town (A) 2-3

85-86 Q1: Road Sea Southampton (H) 1-1, (A) 2-3

86-87 Q1: Frome Town (A) 2-0
Q2: Stourbridge (A) 1-2

87-88 Q1: Alvechurch (A) 1-1, (H) 1-3

88-89 Q1: Evesham United (H) 2-1
Q2: Atherstone United (H) 2-1
Q3: Banbury United (A) 3-2
Q4: Hayes (A) 0-1

89-90 Q1: Moor Green (A) 1-0
Q2: Paget Rangers (H) 5-0
Q3: Hitchin Town (A) 2-0
Q4: Bedworth United (H) 1-1, (A) 2-0
R1: Merthyr Tydfil (H) 1-3

90-91 Q1: Barton Rovers (A) 2-0
Q2: Histon (A) 1-1, (H) 1-0
Q3: Tamworth (A) 0-2

Opposite: *An agonising moment for Redditch United goalkeeper Dennis Burke as he cannot quite keep out an effort from Tamworth's Terry Knight (out of picture). Redditch were beaten 0-2 in this Third Qualifying Round tie on 13th October 1990. Photo: Paul Barber.*

91-92 Q1: Edgware Town (H) 5-1
Q2: Sutton Coldfield Town (A) 3-1
Q3: Bromsgrove Rovers (A) 0-2

92-93 Q1: Chasetown (A) 0-1

REDFORD SPORTS (HIGH WYCOMBE)

Currently: Defunct

46-47 EX: Yiewsley (H) 3-7

47-48 EX: Southall (H) 0-5

REDHILL

Currently: Sussex County League

45-46 Q1: Tooting & Mitcham United (H) 1-5

46-47 PR: Tooting & Mitcham United (H) 3-9

47-48 PR: Guildford (H) 9-0
Q1: Walton & Hersham (A) 2-2, (H) 2-1
Q2: Carshalton Athletic (H) 5-2
Q3: Tooting & Mitcham United (H) 1-0
Q4: Horsham (A) 1-2

48-49 PR: Brookwood Hospital (H) 11-1
Q1: Walton & Hersham (A) 2-1
Q2: Woking (H) 4-3
Q3: Tooting & Mitcham United (A) 1-5

49-50 PR: Dorking (H) 7-3
Q1: Walton & Hersham (A) 0-1

50-51 EX: Vickers Armstrong (H) 2-2, (A) 2-4

51-52 PR: Chichester City (H) 3-0
Q1: Ashford Town (H) 2-3

52-53 PR: East Grinstead (A) 2-4

53-54 PR: Bognor Regis Town (H) 2-0
Q1: Eastbourne (H) 0-1

54-55 PR: Bognor Regis Town (A) 2-3

55-56 PR: Horsham (A) 3-1
Q1: Eastbourne (A) 2-0
Q2: Bognor Regis Town (A) 2-2, (H) 4-0
Q3: Worthing (A) 4-1
Q4: Hastings United (H) 2-2, (A) 0-4

56-57 Q1: Worthing (A) 2-2, (H) 7-2
Q2: Bognor Regis Town (H) 3-0
Q3: Horsham (A) 1-2

57-58 Q1: Horsham (A) 2-1
Q2: Southwick (H) 3-0
Q3: Bognor Regis Town (A) 3-0
Q4: Tooting & Mitcham United (A) 3-1
R1: Norwich City (A) 1-6

58-59 PR: Walton & Hersham (H) 3-2
Q1: Dulwich Hamlet (H) 1-0
Q2: Tooting & Mitcham United (A) 1-7

59-60 PR: Bromley (A) 0-5

60-61 Q1: Sutton United (A) 0-4

61-62 Q1: Carshalton Athletic (H) 1-0
Q2: Slough Town (A) 0-2

62-63 Q1: Dulwich Hamlet (A) 1-6

63-64 Q1: Carshalton Athletic (A) 0-2

64-65 Q1: Bognor Regis Town (A) 3-1
Q2: Lewes (A) 2-2, (H) 4-3
Q3: Crawley Town (H) 1-6

65-66 Q1: Carshalton Athletic (H) 2-2, (A) 0-3

66-67 Q1: Dulwich Hamlet (A) 1-2

67-68 Q1: Dagenham (A) 0-1

68-69 Q1: Ford United (H) 3-0
Q2: Cray Wanderers (H) 1-0
Q3: Dartford (H) 2-4

69-70 Q1: Gravesend & Northfleet (A) 1-0
Q2: Romford (A) 0-2

70-71 Q1: Southall (A) 4-2
Q2: Hornchurch (H) 0-0, (A) 1-2

71-72 Q1: Feltham (A) 3-1
Q2: Dulwich Hamlet (A) 1-0
Q3: Sutton United (H) 0-2

72-73 Q1: Southwick (H) 1-0
Q2: Chichester City (A) 2-1
Q3: Haywards Heath (A) 2-1
Q4: Hillingdon Borough (A) 0-0, (H) 0-1

73-74 Q1: Ilford (H) 0-1

74-75 Q1: Epsom & Ewell (H) 3-0
Q2: Dagenham (A) 0-3

75-76 Q1: Burgess Hill Town (H) 1-0
Q2: Tunbridge Wells (H) 4-1
Q3: Crawley Town (H) 1-1, (A) 0-1

76-77 Q1: Bromley (H) 0-1

77-78 Q1: Eastbourne Town (H) 0-1

78-79 PR: Margate (A) 0-2

79-80 Q1: Bognor Regis Town (H) 0-5

80-81 Q1: Littlehampton Town (H) 0-2

81-82 PR: Dartford (A) 2-2, (H) 1-0
Q1: Hertford Town (H) 1-2

82-83 Q1: Deal Town (A) 1-3

83-84 Q1: Eastbourne United (H) 1-1, (A) 1-2

84-85 PR: Steyning Town (A) 2-1
Q1: Ringmer (H - *played away*) 3-2
Q2: Folkestone (H) 0-3

85-86 Q1: Leatherhead (A) 2-0
Q2: Fisher Athletic (H) 0-2

86-87 PR: Maidenhead United (H) 3-2
Q1: Whyteleafe (A) 2-0
Q2: Buckingham Town (H) 2-4

87-88 Q1: Hornchurch (H) 3-3, (A) 3-1
Q2: Sutton United (A) 1-3

88-89 PR: Malden Vale (H) 0-1

89-90 Q1: Ramsgate (H) 1-0
Q2: Folkestone (A) 1-1, (H) 0-1

90-91 Q1: Whitehawk (H) 2-3

91-92 PR: Tooting & Mitcham United (A) 0-2

92-93 PR: Boreham Wood (H) 1-5

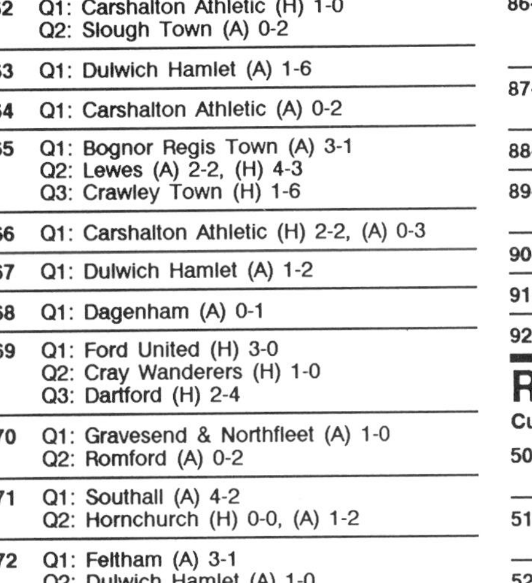

RETFORD TOWN

Currently: Defunct

50-51 EX: Boots Athletic (H) 2-0
PR: Linby Colliery (A) 0-3

51-52 Q1: Bourne Town (A) 4-2
Q2: Boston United (A) 1-6

52-53 PR: Holbeach United (H) 2-1
Q1: Brigg Town (H) 8-2
Q2: Boston United (H) 1-4

53-54 Q1: Upton Colliery (H) 3-4

54-55 Q1: Denaby United (H) 1-4

55-56 Q1: Denaby United (A) 0-5

56-57 Q1: Denaby United (H) 3-3, (A) 0-3

57-58 Q2: Frickley Colliery (A) 0-1

58-59 Q1: Shirebrook Miners Welfare (A) 1-0
Q2: Heanor Town (H) 1-1, (A) 1-7

59-60 Q1: Heanor Town (H) 2-2, (A) 0-4

60-61 Q1: East End Park W.M.C. (A) 2-0
Q2: Selby Town (H) 1-2

61-62 Q1: Denaby United (H) 5-0
Q2: Stocksbridge Works (A) 0-0, (H) 2-5

62-63 Q1: Denaby United (A) 0-4

63-64 Q1: Cresswell Colliery (H) 4-0
Q2: Worksop Town (A) 0-2

64-65 Q1: Norton Woodseats Amateur (H) 5-1
Q2: Goole Town (A) 1-0
Q3: Frickley Colliery (H) 3-0
Q4: South Liverpool (H) 2-3

65-66 Q1: Gainsborough Trinity (A) 0-1

66-67 Q1: Frickley Colliery (H) 4-0
Q2: Farsley Celtic (A) 0-2

67-68 Q1: Mexborough Town (H) 2-1
Q2: Frickley Colliery (H) 2-0
Q3: Farsley Celtic (A) 1-0
Q4: Grantham (H) 4-4, (A) 1-3

68-69 Q1: Farsley Celtic (A) 2-1
Q2: Hatfield Main (A) 2-2, (H) 1-0
Q3: Frickley (A) 0-0, (H) 0-0, 3-0
Q4: Macclesfield Town (H) 0-2

69-70 Q1: Yorkshire Amateur (H) 4-0
Q2: Frickley Colliery (H) 1-1, (A) 0-3

70-71 Q1: Matlock Town (H) 2-1
Q2: Heanor Town (H) 1-2

71-72 Q1: Eastwood Town (A) 2-2, (H) 0-3

72-73 Q1: Worksop Town (H) 1-2

73-74 PR: Louth United (H) 2-1
Q1: Brigg Town (A) 0-1

74-75 Q1: Denaby United (H) 3-0
Q2: Worksop Town (A) 0-1

75-76 Q1: Skegness Town (H) 0-0, (A) 2-0
Q2: Selby Town (A) 2-0
Q3: Mexborough Town (H) 1-2

76-77 Q1: Winterton Rangers (H) 0-3

77-78 Q1: Worksop Town (H) 1-2

78-79 Q1: Stamford (H) 2-1
Q2: Boston United (H) 1-4

79-80 Q1: Skegness Town (H) 0-3

RHYL

Currently: Cymru Alliance

45-46 Q1: Bangor City (A) 1-4 *Bangor expelled*
Q2: Fodens Motor Works (H) 5-1
Q3: Witton Albion (H) 2-2, (A) 1-3

46-47 Q1: Glossop (A) 6-2
Q2: Ellesmere Port Town (H) 4-4, (A) 3-1
Q3: Bangor City (A) 3-5

47-48 PR: Crossens (H) 10-0
Q1: Burscough (A) 3-0
Q2: Wigan Athletic (A) 1-2

48-49 PR: Earlestown (H) 2-1
Q1: Newton Y.M.C.A. (A) 4-1
Q2: Prescot Cables (H) 2-1
Q3: Bangor City (A) 2-0
Q4: South Liverpool (H) 3-0
R1: Scarborough (H) 0-2

49-50 PR: Llandudno (H) 2-0
Q1: Earle (A) 3-1
Q2: Bangor City (H) 4-1
Q3: Wigan Athletic (H) 2-0
Q4: Stalybridge Celtic (H) 6-0
R1: Rochdale (H) 0-3

50-51 Q4: Wigan Athletic (H) 0-0, (A) 3-2
R1: Scarborough (A) 2-1
R2: Norwich City (H) 0-1

51-52 Q4: Fleetwood (H) 7-2
R1: Hartlepools United (A) 0-2

52-53 Q4: Nelson (A) 3-1
R1: Bradford City (A) 0-4

53-54 Q4: Mossley (A) 1-1, (H) 2-0
R1: Halifax Town (A) 0-0, (H) 4-3
R2: Bristol City (H) 0-3

54-55 Q4: Pwllheli & District (A) 3-0
R1: Selby Town (A) 1-2

55-56 Q4: New Brighton (H) 3-1
R1: Bradford (Park Avenue) (H) 0-3

56-57 Q4: Frickley Colliery (H) 2-0
R1: Scarborough (H) 3-2
R2: Bishop Auckland (H) 3-1
R3: Notts County (A) 3-1
R4: Bristol City (A) 0-3

57-58 Q4: New Brighton (A) 3-2
R1: Carlisle United (A) 1-5

58-59 Q4: Wigan Athletic (H) 1-0
R1: Chesterfield (A) 0-3

59-60 Q4: Wigan Athletic (A) 1-1, (H) 3-1
R1: Grimsby Town (H) 1-2

60-61 Q4: Wigan Athletic (A) 0-0, (H) 2-1
R1: Oldham Athletic (H) 0-1

61-62 Q4: Stalybridge Celtic (H) 4-0
R1: Hull City (A) 0-5

62-63 Q4: Altrincham (A) 3-2
R1: Barnsley (A) 0-4

63-64 Q4: Altrincham (A) 1-3

64-65 Q1: Ellesmere Port Town (A) 1-6

65-66 Q1: Borough United (H) 1-1, (A) 0-1

66-67 Q1: St Helens Town (H) 5-1
Q2: Runcorn (H) 3-3, (A) 2-2, 3-1
Q3: Skelmersdale United (H) 2-0
Q4: Witton Albion (A) 2-4

67-68 Q1: South Liverpool (H) 2-1
Q2: Oswestry Town (H) 4-0
Q3: Bangor City (A) 0-4

68-69 PR: Prescot Town (H) 5-1
Q1: Marine (A) 0-0, (H) 0-1

69-70 Q1: Portmadoc (A) 3-1
Q2: Bethesda Ath. (A) 2-2 *ab. 70m.*, (A) 3-1
Q3: South Liverpool (A) 0-2

70-71 Q1: Pwllheli & District (A) 6-0
Q2: Portmadoc (H) 2-1
Q3: Oswestry Town (A) 1-1, (H) 2-1
Q4: South Liverpool (H) 3-3, (A) 2-2, 1-0
R1: Hartlepool United (H) 1-0
R2: Barnsley (H) 0-0, (A) 1-1, 2-0
R3: Swansea City (A) 1-6

71-72 Q4: Wigan Athletic (A) 1-2

72-73 Q4: Skelmersdale United (A) 4-0
R1: Chesterfield (A) 2-4

73-74 Q4: Frickley Colliery (H) 0-4

74-75 Q1: Ellesmere Port Town (H) *W/O*
Q2: Bethesda Athletic (A) 2-2, (H) 2-2, 3-0
Q3: Oswestry Town (A) 1-2

75-76 Q1: St Helens Town (H) 4-2
Q2: Runcorn (A) 1-4

76-77 Q1: Macclesfield Town (H) 1-1, (A) 2-1
Q2: New Brighton Rakers (A) 3-1
Q3: Northwich Victoria (A) 0-0, (H) 1-3

77-78 Q1: Congleton Town (H) 0-0, (A) 2-0
Q2: Oswestry Town (A) 2-1
Q3: Bangor City (A) 0-1

78-79 Q1: Prescot Town (H) 2-0
Q2: Buxton (A) 0-2

79-80 PR: Winsford United (H) 1-5

80-81 Q1: Marine (A) 0-3

81-82 PR: Winsford United (H) 0-1

82-83 Q1: Curzon Ashton (A) 1-4

83-84 Q1: Prescot Cables (A) 5-0
Q2: Stalybridge Celtic (A) 0-2

84-85 Q1: Belper Town (A) 1-1, (H) 1-0
Q2: Frickley Athletic (H) 0-2

85-86 Q1: Wren Rovers (H) 3-1
Q2: Formby (H) 5-0
Q3: Horwich R.M.I. (H) 2-0
Q4: Runcorn (H) 0-2

86-87 Q1: Hyde United (A) 1-1, (H) 3-4

87-88 Q1: Buxton (A) 3-6

88-89 Q1: Ashtree Highfield (H) 4-1
Q2: Warrington Town (H) 1-1, (A) 0-2

89-90 Q1: Radcliffe Borough (A) 2-1
Q2: Oakham United (H) 2-0
Q3: Southport (H) 0-3

90-91 Q1: Altrincham (A) 2-3

91-92 PR: Ashton United (A) 0-0, (H) 1-0
Q1: Newtown (H) 1-0
Q2: Colwyn Bay (A) 0-2

RICKMANSWORTH TOWN

Currently: Defunct

48-49 EX: Berkhamsted Town (A) 1-3

49-50 EX: Yiewsley (H) 2-2, (A) 0-2

RINGMER

Currently: Sussex County League

70-71 Q1: Arundel (H) 5-2
Q2: Chichester City (H) 4-0
Q3: Bognor Regis Town (A) 2-1
Q4: Waterlooville (A) 3-2
R1: Colchester United (A) 0-3

71-72 Q1: East Grinstead (A) 0-2

72-73 PR: Haywards Heath (H) 0-1

73-74 PR: Tunbridge Wells (A) 1-5

74-75 Q1: Lewes (A) 4-2
Q2: Crawley Town (A) 2-2, (H) 2-1
Q3: Southwick (H) 1-3

75-76 Q1: Maidstone United (H) 1-1, (A) 1-3

76-77 Q1: Haywards Heath (A) 1-3

77-78 Q1: Horsham Y.M.C.A. (A) 0-1

78-79 Q1: Hastings United (H) 0-2

79-80 Q1: Eastbourne Town (H) 3-3, (A) 0-2

80-81 PR: Tunbridge Wells (H) 3-1
Q1: Lewes (H) 3-3, (A) 2-6

81-82 PR: Croydon (A) 0-1

82-83 Q1: Addlestone & Weybridge Town (H) 2-1
Q2: Folkestone (H) 0-2

83-84 PR: Sittingbourne (H - *played away*) 0-3

84-85 Q1: Redhill (A - *played home*) 2-3

85-86 PR: Whitstable Town (H) 2-1
Q1: Woking (H) 1-3

86-87 PR: Arundel (A) 0-0, (H) 0-3 *ab. in E.T.*, (H) 0-3

87-88 PR: Eastbourne United (H) 1-5

88-89 PR: Folkestone (A) 0-2

89-90 PR: Molesey (H - *played away*) 0-1

90-91 PR: Slade Green (A) 0-2

91-92 PR: Molesey (A) 0-1

92-93 PR: Andover (A) 0-5

ROAD SEA SOUTHAMPTON

Currently: Defunct

83-84 Pr: Oxford City (H) 4-1
Q1: Waterlooville (H) 0-0, (A) 1-2

84-85 Q1: Melksham Town (A) 3-0
Q2: Chippenham Town (A) 2-2, (H) 1-2

85-86 Q1: Redditch United (A) 1-1, (H) 3-2
Q2: Clandown (A) 2-1
Q3: Ton Pentre (A) 1-1, (H) 1-2

86-87 Q1: Littlehampton Town (H) 7-1
Q2: Devizes Town (A) 2-0
Q3: Fareham Town (H) 0-3

ROCESTER

Currently: West Midlands (Regional) League

89-90 Q1: Alfreton Town (A) 0-1

90-91 PR: Sutton Town (A) 2-2, (H) 1-0
Q1: Leicester United (A) 0-1

91-92 PR: Oakham United (H) 1-3

92-93 PR: Raunds Town (A) 2-2, (H) 3-4

ROCHDALE

Currently: Football League

45-46 R1: Stockport C. (A) 2-1, (H) 1-1 *(agg: 3-2)*
R2: Tranmere R. (A) 1-3, (H) 3-0 *(agg: 4-3)*
R3: Bury (A) 3-3, (H) 2-4 *(agg: 5-7)*

46-47 R1: Bishop Auckland (H) 6-1
R2: Hartlepools United (H) 6-1
R3: Charlton Athletic (A) 1-3

47-48 R1: York City (A) 1-0
R2: Gillingham (H) 1-1, (A) 1-1, 0-3

48-49 R1: Barrow (H) 1-1, (A) 0-2

49-50 R1: Rhyl (A) 3-0
R2: Notts County (H) 1-2

50-51 R1: Willington (H) 3-1
R2: Ashington (A) 2-1
R3: Chelsea (H) 2-3

51-52 R1: Ilkeston Town (A) 2-0
R2: Gillingham (A) 3-0
R3: Leeds United (H) 0-2

52-53 R1: Bradford (Park Avenue) (A) 1-2

53-54 R1: Grimsby Town (A) 0-2

54-55 R1: Tranmere Rovers (A) 3-3, (H) 1-0
R2: Hinckley Athletic (H) 2-1
R3: Charlton Athletic (H) 1-3

55-56 R1: York City (H) 0-1

56-57 R1: Scunthorpe United (A) 0-1

57-58 R1: Darlington (H) 0-2

58-59 R1: Hartlepools U. (A) 1-1, (H) 3-3, 1-2

59-60 R1: Carlisle United (H) 2-2, (A) 3-1
R2: Bradford City (H) 1-1, (A) 1-2

60-61 R1: Crewe Alexandra (A) 1-1, (H) 1-2

61-62 R1: Halifax Town (H) 2-0
R2: Wrexham (H) 1-2

62-63 R1: York City (A) 0-0, (H) 1-2

63-64 R1: Chorley (H) 2-1
R2: Barnsley (A) 1-3

64-65 R1: Workington (A) 0-2

65-66 R1: Fleetwood (A) 2-2, (H) 5-0
R2: Altrincham (H) 1-3

66-67 R1: Barrow (H) 1-3

67-68 R1: Tranmere Rovers (A) 1-5

68-69	R1: Barnsley (A) 0-0, (H) 0-1
69-70	R1: Workington (A) 1-2
70-71	R1: Oldham Athletic (H) 2-0 R2: Darlington (A) 2-0 R3: Coventry City (H) 2-1 R4: Colchester United (H) 3-3, (A) 0-5
71-72	R1: Barnsley (H) 1-3
72-73	R1: Bangor City (H) 1-2
73-74	R1: South Shields (H) 2-0 R2: Grantham (A) 1-1, (H) 3-5
74-75	R1: Marine (H) 0-0, (A) 2-1 R2: Tranmere Rangers (H) 1-1, (A) 0-1
75-76	R1: Workington (A) 1-1, (H) 2-1 R2: Gateshead United (A) 1-1, (H) 3-1 R3: Norwich C. (A) 1-1, (H) 0-0, (A) 1-2
76-77	R1: Northwich Victoria (H) 1-1, (A) 0-0, (*at Manchester City*) 1-2
77-78	R1: Scarborough (A) 2-4
78-79	R1: Droylsden (H) 0-1
79-80	R1: Scunthorpe United (H) 2-1 R2: Tranmere Rovers (A) 2-2, (H) 2-1 R3: Bury (H) 1-1, (A) 2-3
80-81	R1: Mansfield Town (A) 1-3
81-82	R1: Hull C. (H) 2-2, (A) 2-2, (*at Leeds U.*) 0-1
82-83	R1: Altrincham (A) 1-2
83-84	R1: Crewe Alexandra (H) 1-0 R2: York City (A) 2-0 R3: Telford United (H) 1-4
84-85	R1: Doncaster Rovers (H) 1-2
85-86	R1: Darlington (H) 2-1 R2: Scunthorpe United (A) 2-2, (H) 2-1 R3: Manchester United (A) 0-2
86-87	R1: Nuneaton Borough (A) 3-0 R2: Wrexham (H) 1-4
87-88	R1: Wrexham (H) 0-2
88-89	R1: Huddersfield Town (A) 1-1, (H) 3-4
89-90	R1: Marine (A - *at Liverpool F.C.*) 1-0 R2: Lincoln City (H) 3-0 R3: Whitley Bay (H) 1-0 R4: Northampton Town (H) 3-0 R5: Crystal Palace (A) 0-1
90-91	R1: Scunthorpe United (H) 1-1, (A) 1-2
91-92	R1: Gretna (A) 0-0, (H) 3-1 R2: Huddersfield Town (H) 1-2

Right: *Rochdale's Alex Jones (right) wins an aerial challenge against Chris Pickford during the excursion north of the border to play Gretna. Photo: Alan Watson.*

92-93	R1: Blackpool (A) 1-1, (H) 1-0 R2: Bolton Wanderers (A) 0-4

ROMFORD

Currently: Defunct (reformed in Essex Senior Lge)

45-46	Q1: Eton Manor (A) 1-1, (H) 4-3 Q2: Crittall Athletic (H) 7-1 Q3: Leyton (A) 4-1 Q4: Dulwich Hamlet (A) 2-1 R1: Brighton (A) 1-3, (H) 1-1 (*agg: 2-4*)
46-47	PR: Grays Athletic (H) 2-1 Q1: Ekco (Southend) (H) 3-0 Q2: Tilbury (A) 1-2
47-48	PR: Barking (H) 1-3
48-49	EX: Ford Sports (H) 5-0 PR: Grays Athletic (H) 3-0 Q1: Upminster (A) 2-1 Q2: Brentwood & Warley (H) 3-1 Q3: Barking (H) 3-2 Q4: Gillingham (H) 2-1 R1: Yeovil Town (A) 0-4
49-50	Q4: Kingstonian (H) 3-0 R1: Yeovil Town (A) 1-4
50-51	PR: Grays Athletic (H) 7-1 Q1: Tilbury (H) 5-1 Q2: Briggs Sports (H) 2-2, (A) 2-1 Q3: Woodford Town (A) 2-2, (H) 1-1, 1-2
51-52	Q1: Barking (H) 1-0 Q2: Briggs Sports (A) 1-1, (H) 6-2 Q3: Brentwood & Warley (H) 3-1 Q4: Gorleston (A) 0-1
52-53	Q1: Clacton Town (A) 1-1, (H) 1-3
53-54	Q1: Chelmsford City (A) 2-3
54-55	PR: Harwich & Parkeston (H) 3-1 Q1: Leyton (A) 2-4
55-56	PR: Dagenham (A) 1-2
56-57	PR: Grays Athletic (H) 4-2 Q1: Briggs Sports (A) 1-0 Q2: Chelmsford City (A) 0-4
57-58	PR: Clacton Town (H) 1-1, (A) 2-2, 2-4
58-59	Q1: Eton Manor (A) 9-2 Q2: Hornchurch & Upminster (H) 2-3
59-60	Q1: Finchley (H) 1-3
60-61	Q1: Wembley (H) 7-0 Q2: Leytonstone (A) 3-1 Q3: Hornchurch & Upminster (H) 3-0 Q4: Enfield (H) 2-1 R1: Sutton United (A) 2-2, (H) 5-0 R2: Northampton Town (H) 1-5
61-62	Q1: Wembley (H) 6-2 Q2: Leytonstone (H) 3-1 Q3: Dagenham (A) 1-1, (H) 4-1 Q4: Cambridge United (H) 2-1 R1: Walthamstow Avenue (A) 3-2 R2: Watford (H) 1-3
62-63	Q4: Chelmsford City (A) 0-2
63-64	Q4: Chelmsford City (A) 0-2
64-65	Q4: Wimbledon (A) 1-1, (H) 2-1 R1: Enfield (H) 0-0, (A) 0-0, 2-4
65-66	Q4: Chelmsford City (H) 2-1 R1: Luton Town (H) 1-1, (A) 0-1
66-67	Q4: Bedford Town (A) 1-1, (H) 1-2
67-68	Q4: Hendon (A) 2-1 R1: Wimbledon (A) 0-3
68-69	Q4: Oxford City (A) 1-7
69-70	Q1: Ford United (H) 2-2, (A) 4-2 Q2: Redhill (H) 2-0 Q3: Dagenham (H) 1-2
70-71	Q1: Rainham Town (H) 11-0 Q2: Erith & Belvedere (H) 0-0, (A) 1-1, 1-0 Q3: Walton & Hersham (H) 1-1, (A) 3-3, 2-3
71-72	PR: St Albans City (H) 3-0 Q1: Letchworth Town (A) 2-1 Q2: Slough Town (A) 1-0 Q3: Braintree & Crittall Athletic (A) 2-0 Q4: Folkestone (A) 2-0 R1: Witney Town (A) 3-0 R2: Gillingham (H) 0-1
72-73	Q4: Tonbridge (A) 0-0, (H) 1-2
73-74	Q1: Dulwich Hamlet (A) 1-0 Q2: Bexley United (H) 2-2, (A) 1-3
74-75	Q1: Gravesend & Northfleet (H) 2-0 Q2: Wembley (A) 3-2 Q3: Leytonstone (A) 1-0 Q4: Clacton Town (A) 2-1 R1: Ilford (H) 0-2
75-76	Q1: Ware (H) 3-1 Q2: Clacton Town (A) 1-1, (H) 3-2 Q3: Cheshunt (H) 1-0 Q4: Hitchin Town (A) 1-0 R1: Tooting & Mitcham United (H) 0-1
76-77	PR: Hertford Town (A) 1-1, (H) 1-2
77-78	PR: Walthamstow Avenue (H) 1-1, (A) 2-3

ROMSEY TOWN

Currently: Hampshire League

48-49	EX: Pirelli General Cable Works (A) 5-2 PR: Poole Town (A) 3-5
49-50	PR: Dorchester Town (H) 1-4
50-51	PR: East Cowes Victoria (H) 3-2 Q1: Dorchester Town (H) 1-1, (A) 0-2
83-84	PR: Chippenham Town (H) 1-1, (A) 1-0 Q1: Gosport Borough (H) 0-2
88-89	PR: Trowbridge Town (A) 0-2
89-90	PR: Westbury United (H) 5-1 Q1: Fareham Town (H) 1-1, (A) 2-1 Q2: Poole Town (H) 1-2
90-91	PR: Frome Town (H) 1-0 Q1: Chard Town (A) 4-4, (H) 3-0 Q2: Stroud (H) 1-0 Q3: Newport Isle of Wight (A) 1-0 Q4: Littlehampton Town (H) 1-2
91-92	Q1: Newbury Town (H) 2-1 Q2: Selsey (A) 6-1 Q3: Marlow (A) 0-2
92-93	Q1: Bognor Regis Town (A) 2-9

ROSSENDALE UNITED

Currently: North West Counties League

48-49 PR: Bacup Borough (H) 2-0
Q1: Leyland Motors (A) 2-2, (H) 4-2
Q2: Darwen (H) 4-0
Q3: Fleetwood (A) 1-0
Q4: Netherfield (A) 1-3

49-50 PR: Horwich R.M.I. (H) 5-2
Q1: Leyland Motors (H) 5-1
Q2: Chorley (A) 3-2
Q3: Fleetwood (A) 0-5

50-51 Q1: Horwich R.M.I. (H) 6-5
Q2: Bacup Borough (A) 2-3

51-52 Q1: Horwich R.M.I. (H) 4-2
Q2: Skelmersdale United (H) 1-1, (A) 0-3

52-53 Q1: Darwen (H) 2-0
Q2: Mossley (A) 0-1

53-54 PR: Darwen (A) 0-2

54-55 PR: Bacup Borough (A) 0-1

55-56 Q1: Droylsden (H) 4-3
Q2: Chorley (H) 2-1
Q3: Ashton United (A) 0-1

56-57 PR: Mossley (H) 0-1

57-58 Q1: Ashton United (H) 2-2, (A) 0-1

58-59 PR: Lytham (H) 1-0
Q1: Darwen (A) 1-3

59-60 PR: Lytham (H) 4-4, (A) 1-2

60-61 PR: Mossley (H) 1-1 *ab. 51m.*, (A) 1-1, (H) 1-5

61-62 Q1: Stalybridge Celtic (H) 1-2

62-63 Q1: Leyland Motors (A) 5-1
Q2: Stalybridge Celtic (H) 2-4

63-64 Q1: Hyde United (A) 2-6

64-65 Q1: Great Harwood (H) 1-0
Q2: Stalybridge Celtic (H) 0-3

65-66 Q1: Darwen (H) 3-2
Q2: Chorley (A) 1-1, (H) 0-3

66-67 Q1: Burscough (A) 3-2
Q2: Lancaster City (H) 3-3, (A) 1-2

67-68 Q1: Witton Albion (A) 1-6

68-69 Q1: Bacup Borough (A) 1-0
Q2: Witton Albion (A) 3-4

69-70 Q1: Witton Albion (H) 2-1
Q2: Mossley (A) 0-0, (H) 0-1

70-71 Q1: St Helens Town (A) 2-0
Q2: Horwich R.M.I. (H) 3-1
Q3: South Liverpool (H) 1-3

71-72 Q1: Netherfield (A) 4-2
Q2: Morecambe (H) 2-2, (A) 1-0
Q3: Lancaster City (A) 4-1
Q4: Stafford Rangers (H) 6-3
R1: Altrincham (H) 1-0
R2: Bolton Wanderers (H - *at Bury*) 1-4

72-73 Q4: Bangor City (H) 1-2

73-74 Q1: Netherfield (A) 2-3

74-75 Q1: Barrow (A) 0-1

75-76 Q1: Leyland Motors (A) 8-1
Q2: Radcliffe Borough (A) 2-2, (H) 4-1
Q3: Lancaster City (H) 2-1
Q4: Blyth Spartans (A) 0-0, (H) 1-0
R1: Shrewsbury Town (H) 0-1

76-77 Q1: Buxton (H) 0-5

77-78 Q1: Lytham (A) 1-0
Q2: Runcorn (H) 1-2

79-80 PR: Lytham (A) 1-1, (H) 4-0
Q1: Penrith (A) 1-0
Q2: Curzon Ashton (H) 2-0
Q3: Burscough (H) 0-4

80-81 PR: Worksop Town (H) 1-1, (A) 1-3

81-82 Q1: Penrith (A) 1-2

82-83 Q1: Chorley (H) 0-3

84-85 PR: Denaby United (H) 1-2

85-86 PR: Guiseley (H) 1-0
Q1: Mossley (H) 1-2

86-87 PR: Colwyn Bay (A) 1-1, (H) 3-2
Q1: Bridgnorth Town (A) 1-1, (H) 3-2
Q2: Prescot Cables (H) 2-1
Q3: Oldbury United (H) 1-2

87-88 PR: Northallerton Town (H) 3-0
Q1: Worksop Town (H) 1-1, (A) 4-2
Q2: Guisborough Town (H) 2-3

88-89 PR: Ashington (A) 4-2
Q1: Blyth Spartans (A) 0-1

89-90 PR: Leyland Motors (A) 1-0
Q1: Vauxhall G.M. (H) 2-1
Q2: Marine (A) 0-2

90-91 PR: Atherton Laburnum Rovers (A) 1-3

91-92 PR: Heanor Town (H) 2-4

92-93 PR: Sheffield (A - *played home*) 2-2, (H) 1-2

ROTHERHAM UNITED

Currently: Football League

45-46 R1: Doncaster (A) 1-0, (H) 2-1 (*agg: 1-3*)
R2: Lincoln C. (H) 2-1, (A) 1-1 (*agg: 3-2*)
R3: Gateshead (H) 2-2, (A) 2-0 (*agg: 4-2*)
R4: Barnsley (A) 0-3, (H) 2-1 (*agg: 2-4*)

46-47 R1: Crewe Alexandra (H) 2-0
R2: Scunthorpe United (H) 4-1
R3: Wolverhampton Wanderers (A) 0-3

47-48 R3: Brentford (H) 0-3

48-49 R3: Darlington (H) 4-2
R4: Burnley (H) 0-1

49-50 R3: Bury (A) 4-5

50-51 R1: Darlington (A) 7-2
R2: Nottingham Forest (H) 3-1
R3: Doncaster Rovers (H) 2-1
R4: Hull City (A) 0-2

51-52 R3: Bury (H) 2-1
R4: Swansea Town (A) 0-3

52-53 R3: Colchester United (H) 2-2, (A) 2-0
R4: Newcastle United (A) 3-1
R5: Aston Villa (H) 1-3

53-54 R3: Bristol City (A) 3-1
R4: West Bromwich Albion (A) 0-4

54-55 R3: Leicester City (H) 1-0
R4: Luton Town (H) 1-5

55-56 R3: Scunthorpe United (H) 1-1, (A) 2-4

56-57 R3: Bristol City (A) 1-4

57-58 R3: Blackburn Rovers (H) 1-4

58-59 R3: Aston Villa (A) 1-2

59-60 R3: Arsenal (H) 2-2, (A) 1-1, 2-0
R4: Brighton (H) 1-1, (A) 1-1, 0-6

60-61 R3: Watford (H) 1-0
R4: Birmingham City (A) 0-4

61-62 R3: Huddersfield Town (A) 3-4

62-63 R3: Watford (A) 0-2

63-64 R3: Burnley (A) 1-1, (H) 2-3

64-65 R3: Lincoln City (H) 5-1
R4: Wolverhampton W. (A) 0-0, (H) 0-3

65-66 R3: Southend United (H) 3-2
R4: Manchester United (A) 0-0, (H) 0-1

66-67 R3: Nuneaton Borough (A) 1-1, (H) 1-0
R4: Birmingham City (H) 0-0, (A) 1-2

67-68 R3: Wolverhampton Wanderers (H) 1-0
R4: Aston Villa (A) 1-0
R5: Leicester City (H) 1-1, (A) 0-2

68-69 R1: Hartlepool Utd (A) 1-1, (H) 3-0
R2: Mansfield Town (H) 2-2, (A) 0-1

69-70 R1: Notts County (A) 3-0
R2: Workington (H) 3-0
R3: Peterborough United (H) 0-1

70-71 R1: Great Harwood (A) 6-2
R2: Grantham (A) 4-1
R3: Leeds United (H) 0-0, (A) 0-3

71-72 R1: Frickley Colliery (A) 2-2, (H) 4-0
R2: York City (H) 1-1, (A) 3-2
R3: Bury (A) 1-1, (H) 2-1
R4: Tottenham Hotspur (A) 0-2

72-73 R1: South Shields (H) 4-0
R2: Stockport County (H) 0-1

73-74 R1: Southport (H) 2-1
R2: Wrexham (A) 0-3

74-75 R1: Chester (H) 1-0
R2: Northampton Town (H) 2-1
R3: Stafford Rangers (A) 0-0, (H) 0-2

75-76 R1: Crewe Alexandra (H) 2-1
R2: Bradford City (H) 0-3

76-77 R1: Altrincham (H) 5-0
R2: York City (H) 0-0, (A) 1-1, 2-1
R3: Wolverhampton Wanderers (A) 2-3

77-78 R1: Mossley (H) 3-0
R2: Spennymoor United (H) 6-0
R3: Millwall (H) 1-1, (A) 0-2

78-79 R1: Workington (H) 3-0
R2: Barnsley (A) 1-1, (H) 2-1
R3: Manchester City (A) 0-0, (H) 2-4

79-80 R1: Morecambe (H) 1-1, (H) 2-0
R2: Altrincham (H) 0-2

80-81 R1: Boston United (A) 4-0
R2: Barnsley (H) 0-1

81-82 R3: Sunderland (H) 1-1, (A) 0-1

82-83 R3: Shrewsbury Town (A) 1-2

83-84 R1: Hartlepool United (H) 0-0, (A) 1-0
R2: Hull City (H) 2-1
R3: West Bromwich Albion (H) 0-0, (A) 0-3

84-85 R1: Mansfield Town (A) 1-2

85-86 R1: Wolverhampton Wanderers (H) 6-0
R2: Burnley (H) 4-1
R3: Frickley Athletic (A) 3-1
R4: Arsenal (A) 1-5

Below: *Rotherham United goalkeeper Kelham O'Hanlon dives the right way for Will Foley's penalty as the Millers win 3-1 away to local non-League rivals Frickley Athletic in the Third Round. Photo: South Yorkshire Times.*

86-87 R1: Chester City (A) 1-1, (H) 1-1, (A) 0-1

87-88 R1: Doncaster Rovers (A) 1-1, (H) 2-0
R2: Macclesfield Town (A) 0-4

88-89 R1: Barrow (H) 3-1
R2: Grimsby Town (A) 2-3

89-90 R1: Bury (H) 0-0, (A) 2-1
R2: Walsall (A) 0-1

90-91 R1: Stockport County (H) 1-0
R2: Halifax Town (H) 1-1, (A) 2-1
R3: Swansea City (A) 0-0, (H) 4-0
R4: Crewe Alexandra (A) 0-1

91-92 R1: Scunthorpe (A) 1-1, (H) 3-3 (*7-6 pens*)
R2: Burnley (A) 0-2

92-93 R1: Walsall (H) 4-0
R2: Hull City (H) 1-0
R3: Northampton Town (A) 1-0
R4: Newcastle United (H) 1-1, (A) 0-2

ROTHWELL TOWN

Currently: United Counties League

49-50 PR: Corby Town (A) 1-7

55-56 Q1: Desborough Town (A) 0-0, (H) 5-0
Q2: Rushden Town (A) 3-3, (H) 3-2
Q3: Corby Town (A) 1-3

56-57 Q1: Corby Town (H) 0-1

57-58 Q1: Corby Town (A) 1-2

58-59 Q1: Rushden Town (A) 2-5

59-60 Q1: Wellingborough Town (A) 2-3

60-61 Q1: Rushden Town (H) 0-2

61-62 Q1: Eynesbury Town (H) 6-2
Q2: Bourne Town (H) 1-2

63-64 Q1: Rushden Town (H) 0-3

64-65 Q1: Rushden Town (A) 3-2
Q2: Eynesbury Rovers (A) 1-3

65-66 Q1: Eynesbury Rovers (A) 2-0
Q2: Bourne Town (A) 1-3

67-68 Q1: Biggleswade Town (A) 1-1, (H) 5-2
Q2: Cambridge City (H) 1-7

68-69 Q1: Biggleswade Town (H) 2-3

69-70 PR: Rushden Town (H) 0-2

70-71 Q1: Potton United (H) 1-0
Q2: Irthlingborough Diamonds (H) 1-1, (A) 0-5

71-72 PR: Histon (A) 2-4

72-73 Q1: Wellingborough Town (H) 1-5

73-74 Q1: Vauxhall Motors (H) 3-2
Q2: Hitchin Town (H) 1-7

74-75 Q1: Irthlingborough Diamonds (A) 1-3

75-76 Q1: Bedworth United (H) 1-0
Q2: Oxford City (H) 0-1

76-77 Q1: A.P. Leamington (H) 0-0, (A) 0-2

77-78 Q1: Bourne Town (H) 4-1
Q2: Enderby Town (A) 0-5

78-79 Q1: Olney Town (H) 1-1, (A) 1-0
Q2: Bedford Town (A) 2-5

79-80 PR: Willenhall Town (H) 0-2

80-81 Q1: Moor Green (A) 0-4

81-82 Q1: Tring Town (H) 1-3

82-83 Q1: Darlaston (H) 3-0
Q2: Worcester City (A) 1-3

83-84 PR: Newmarket Town (H) 2-0
Q1: Burton Albion (H) 1-5

84-85 PR: Milton Keynes City (A) 3-0
Q1: Wolverton Town (H) 2-1
Q2: Kidderminster Harriers (H) 1-4

85-86 PR: Hemel Hempstead (H) 3-3, (A) 0-1

86-87 PR: Tividale (H) 3-2
Q1: Boldmere St Michaels (A) 1-0
Q2: Grantham (H) 0-1

87-88 PR: Dudley Town (A - *at Tividale F.C.*) 1-1, (H) 2-1
Q1: Rushden Town (A) 4-1
Q2: Alvechurch (H) 1-2

88-89 PR: Mile Oak Rovers & Youth (H) 1-5

89-90 PR: Soham Town Rangers (A) 1-0
Q1: March Town United (H) 0-2

90-91 PR: Stamford (H) 7-2
Q1: Histon (A) 1-2

91-92 PR: Evesham United (A) 1-3

92-93 Q1: Matlock Town (H) 0-2

ROUNDWAY HOSP. (DEVIZES)

Currently: Defunct
* - As Wiltshire County Mental Hospital

47-48 * PR: Dilton Rovers (H) 4-0
Q1: Swindon Victoria (H) 5-3
Q2: Westbury United (H) 1-3

48-49 * PR: Salisbury (H) 0-3

49-50 PR: Bath City (H - *played away*) 2-7

ROYSTON TOWN

Currently: Isthmian League

47-48 EX: Tufnell Park (A) 3-4

48-49 PR: King's Lynn (H) 1-6

49-50 PR: Bury Town (H) 0-6

54-55 PR: Barnet (A) 0-11

82-83 Q1: Leytonstone-Ilford (H) 0-5

83-84 PR: Epping Town (H) 4-1
Q1: Hampton (H) 1-7

84-85 Q1: Chelmsford City (H) 0-3

85-86 PR: March Town United (H) 2-7

86-87 PR: Finchley (H) 2-3

87-88 PR: Watton United (A) 1-0
Q1: Ruislip Manor (A) 2-3

88-89 Q1: Stevenage Borough (H) 0-1

89-90 PR: Letchworth Garden City (A) 3-1
Q1: Feltham (H) 2-1
Q2: Bromley (A) 0-3

90-91 PR: Rainham Town (H) 1-1, (A) 2-1
Q1: Yeading (H) 3-2
Q2: Marlow (A) 2-2, (H) 0-2

91-92 PR: East Thurrock United (A) 0-1

92-93 PR: Potton United (H) 1-2

RUFFORD COLLIERY

Currently: (Rainworth M.W.) Notts Alliance

48-49 EX: Raleigh Athletic (H) 0-2

49-50 EX: Bourne Town (H - *played away*) 3-5

50-51 EX: Neville's Athletic (H) 7-3
PR: Shirebrook (H) 0-2

RUGBY TOWN

Currently: Defunct (reformed in Midland Comb.)

48-49 PR: Moira United (A) 3-8

49-50 PR: Moira United (H) 2-3

51-52 PR: Bedworth Town (A) 2-2, (H) 1-6

52-53 PR: Boldmere St Michaels (A) 2-2, (H) 2-1
Q1: Bournville Athletic (A) 2-0
Q2: Atherstone Town (A) 0-2

53-54 PR: Moor Green (H) 5-1
Q1: Sutton Coldfield Town (A) 1-1, (H) 4-1
Q2: Nuneaton Borough (H) 1-2

54-55 PR: Bedworth Town (A) 3-2
Q1: Boldmere St Michaels (H) 5-1
Q2: Atherstone Town (A) 1-2

55-56 Q1: Bedworth Town (H) 2-2, (A) 2-2, 1-3

56-57 Q1: Lockheed Leamington (A) 1-3

57-58 Q1: Worcester City (A) 1-1, (H) 0-2

58-59 Q1: Bilston (A) 1-2

59-60 Q1: Brierley Hill All. (A) 2-2, (H) 1-0
Q2: Bilston (A) 1-5

60-61 Q1: Lockheed Leamington (A) 0-4

61-62 Q1: Lockheed Leamington (A) 2-1
Q2: Bilston (H) 1-0
Q3: Brierley Hill Alliance (A) 1-2

62-63 Q1: Stourbridge (H) 2-1
Q2: Hednesford (H) 2-0
Q3: Nuneaton Borough (H) 1-0
Q4: Wellington Town (H) 1-1, (A) 0-4

63-64 Q1: Bilston (A) 4-1
Q2: Lockheed Leamington (H) 1-1, (A) 2-2, 1-2

64-65 Q1: Moor Green (H) 4-0
Q2: Stourbridge (H) 5-0
Q3: Lockheed Leamington (A) 3-2
Q4: Kidderminster Harriers (A) 1-5

65-66 Q1: Bilston (A) 1-2

66-67 Q1: Bromsgrove Rovers (H) 4-2
Q2: Stratford Town Amateur (A) 2-0
Q3: Tamworth (H) 2-2, (A) 1-2

67-68 PR: Loughborough United (H) 3-0
Q1: Bedworth Town (A) 0-2

68-69 Q1: Bedworth Town (A) 3-3, (H) 0-2

69-70 Q1: Atherstone Town (A) 2-1
Q2: Arnold (A) 3-0
Q3: Burton Albion (H) 1-0
Q4: Hereford United (A) 1-3

70-71 Q1: Burton Albion (H) 0-2

72-73 Q1: Bedworth United (A) 3-0
Q2: Nuneaton Borough (H) 0-1

RUISLIP

Currently: Defunct
See also Ruislip Town

88-89 PR: Crockenhill (H) 2-0
Q1: Marlow (H) 1-1, (A) 0-3

RUISLIP MANOR

Currently: Isthmian League

48-49 EX: Tufnell Park (H) 6-2
PR: Wingate (H) 4-3
Q1: Enfield (H) 3-5

49-50 EX: Acton Town (A - *played home*) 4-2
PR: St Albans City (H) 1-2

62-63 Q1: Tooting & Mitcham United (H) 0-2

64-65 Q1: Leytonstone (A) 1-7

65-66 Q1: Rainham Town (H) 1-5

66-67 Q1: Rainham Town (H) 1-2

67-68 Q1: Hornchurch (H) 0-1

68-69 Q1: Dagenham (A) 2-2, (H) 1-6

69-70 PR: Egham Town (A) 1-1, (H) 1-2

75-76 Q1: Clacton Town (H) 0-2

76-77 PR: Wokingham Town (H) 2-2, (A) 1-3

77-78 PR: Windsor & Eton (H) 1-3

78-79 Q1: Southall & Ealing Borough (H) 0-3

79-80 PR: Hoddesdon Town (A) 2-1
Q1: Kingstonian (A) 0-2

80-81 Q1: Witney Town (A) 1-2

81-82 Q1: Addlestone & Weybridge Town (A) 1-3

82-83 PR: Saffron Walden Town (A) 2-5

84-85 PR: Horley Town (A) 3-0
Q1: Crawley Town (A) 1-2

85-86 Q1: Hendon (H) 1-0
Q2: Bromley (A) 2-3

86-87 Q1: St Albans City (A) 2-1
Q2: Staines Town (A) 0-0, (H) 0-2

87-88 Q1: Royston Town (H) 3-2
Q2: Wembley (A) 1-1, (H) 0-5

88-89 PR: Hailsham Town (A) 0-0, (H) 0-2

89-90 PR: Portfield (H) 0-0, (A) 2-0
Q1: Ashford Town (H) 1-3

90-91 PR: Northwood (H) 2-1
Q1: Cray Wanderers (A) 3-2
Q2: Hendon (H) 2-1

Q3: Wealdstone (H) 1-0
Q4: Halesowen Town (A) 2-5

91-92 Q1: Yeading (A) 1-3

92-93 PR: Hornchurch (H) 1-0
Q1: Basildon United (H) 3-1
Q2: Stevenage Borough (H) 1-3

RUISLIP TOWN

Currently: Merged with Southall Corinthians, and subsequently Coteford, to form Ruislip F.C. (now defunct)
See also Ruislip

48-49 EX: Stevenage Town (H) 2-4

49-50 EX: Hatfield Town (A) 2-6

RUNCORN

Currently: Alliance Premier League

45-46 Q4: Stalybridge Celtic (A) 0-3

46-47 Q4: Witton Albion (A) 2-1
R1: Carlisle United (A) 0-4

47-48 Q4: South Liverpool (A) 3-2
R1: Scunthorpe United (H) 4-2
R2: Barrow (H) 0-1

48-49 Q4: Stalybridge Celtic (H) 4-1
R1: York City (A) 1-2

49-50 Q4: Mossley (A) 0-0, (H) 0-1

50-51 PR: Mossley (H) 3-1
Q1: Nantwich (H) 4-1
Q2: Hyde United (H) 1-1, (A) 0-3

51-52 Q1: Marine (H) 2-1
Q2: Bangor City (A) 0-1

52-53 PR: Bangor City (H) 2-2, (A) 2-3

53-54 PR: New Brighton (H) 3-1
Q1: Earlestown (A) 4-1
Q2: Flint Town United (A) 3-1
Q3: Pwllheli & District (A) 2-2, (H) 3-0
Q4: Witton Albion (A) 0-2 *expelled*

54-55 Q1: Llandudno (H) 6-0
Q2: Pwllheli & District (H) 0-1

55-56 Q1: Flint Town United (A) 0-0, (H) 4-3
Q2: South Liverpool (H) 1-1, (A) 3-1
Q3: New Brighton (A) 0-1

56-57 PR: Flint Town United (H) 1-1, (A) 2-1
Q1: Stork (A) 2-2, (H) 3-2
Q2: South Liverpool (H) 0-1

57-58 PR: Pwllheli & District (H) 3-0
Q1: Prescot Cables (H) 0-1

58-59 PR: South Liverpool (H) 7-1
Q1: Flint Town United (H) 0-1

59-60 PR: Stork (A) 2-1
Q1: Llandudno (H) 3-2
Q2: Bangor City (A) 1-4

60-61 Q1: Stork (H) 6-0
Q2: Bangor City (H) 1-2

61-62 Q1: Bangor City (H) 2-0
Q2: South Liverpool (A) 0-0, (H) 2-0
Q3: Ellesmere Port Town (A) 3-4

62-63 Q1: Llandudno (A) 3-2
Q2: Borough United (H) 0-1

63-64 Q1: Llandudno (A) 4-0
Q2: Bangor City (H) 1-2

64-65 Q1: Holyhead Town (H) 5-2
Q2: Borough United (H) 0-2

65-66 Q1: Ellesmere Port Town (A) 1-3

66-67 Q1: Linotype & Michinery (H) 5-2
Q2: Rhyl (A) 3-3, (H) 2-2, 1-3

67-68 Q1: Linotype & Machinery (A) 3-1
Q2: Lostock Gralam (H) 5-0
Q3: Winsford United (H) 7-1
Q4: Ellesmere Port Town (A) 2-1
R1: Notts County (H) 1-0
R2: Southport (A) 2-4

68-69 Q4: Bangor City (H) 1-4

69-70 PR: Prescot Town (A) 6-1
Q1: Oswestry Town (A) 1-0
Q2: South Liverpool (H) 1-1, (A) 0-5

70-71 Q1: Winsford United (H) 0-2

71-72 Q1: New Brighton (H) 2-0
Q2: South Liverpool (A) 0-1

72-73 Q1: Leyland Motors (A) 8-0
Q2: Accrington Stanley (A) 1-1, (H) 2-1
Q3: Burscough (A) 2-2, (H) 2-3

73-74 Q1: Witton Albion (H) 2-0
Q2: Marine (H) 0-0, (A) 1-0
Q3: Portmadoc (A) 2-0
Q4: Bangor City (H) 2-2, (A) 2-1
R1: Grimsby Town (H) 0-1

74-75 Q1: Buxton (A) 1-0
Q2: Hyde United (H) 3-0
Q3: Mossley (A) 0-1

75-76 Q1: Porthmadog (H) 5-3
Q2: Rhyl (H) 4-1
Q3: Marine (H) 0-0, (A) 0-1

76-77 Q1: Prestwich Heys (A) 1-0
Q2: Winsford United (A) 0-1

77-78 PR: Bacup Borough (H) 4-0
Q1: Droylsden (A) 2-0
Q2: Rossendale United (A) 2-1
Q3: Darwen (H) 2-0
Q4: Altrincham (H) 2-1
R1: Southport (A) 2-2, (H) 1-0
R2: Hartlepool United (A) 2-4

78-79 Q1: Radcliffe Borough (A) 6-0
Q2: Witton Albion (H) 3-1
Q3: Buxton (H) 1-1, (A) 4-0
Q4: Spennymoor United (A) 0-0, (H) 2-1
R1: Chester (A) 1-1, (H) 0-5

79-80 Q4: Moor Green (A) 0-2

80-81 Q4: Northwich Victoria (A) 1-2

81-82 Q1: Leek Town (H) 3-0
Q2: Shifnal Town (A) 3-0
Q3: Prescot Cables (H) 4-1
Q4: Spennymoor United (A) 1-0
R1: Burnley (A) 0-0, (H) 1-2

82-83 Q1: Thackley (A) 0-0, (H) 2-1
Q2: Curzon Ashton (H) 3-0
Q3: Chorley (A) 2-2, (H) 4-0
Q4: Horwich R.M.I. (A) 2-2, (H) 0-1

83-84 Q1: Ashton United (A) 1-0
Q2: Hyde United (A) 0-3

84-85 Q1: Leek Town (A) 1-2

85-86 Q1: Prescot Cables (A) 2-1
Q2: Accrington Stanley (A) 1-1, (H) 9-1
Q3: Mossley (A) 2-0
Q4: Rhyl (A) 2-0
R1: Boston United (H) 2-2, (A) 1-1, (H) 4-1
R2: Wigan Athletic (H) 1-1, (A) 0-4

86-87 R1: Boston United (H) 1-1, (A) 2-1
R2: Scunthorpe United (A) 0-1

87-88 Q4: Barrow (H) 2-1
R1: Chester City (A) 1-0
R2: Stockport County (H) 0-1

88-89 Q4: Fleetwood Town (A) 3-1
R1: Wrexham (H) 2-2, (A) 3-2
R2: Crewe Alexandra (H) 0-3

89-90 Q4: Darlington (A) 2-4

90-91 Q4: Newcastle Blue Star (H) 1-0
R1: Hartlepool United (H) 0-3

91-92 Q4: Gateshead (H) 1-0
R1: Tranmere Rovers (H - *played away*) 0-3

92-93 Q4: Marine (H) 1-4

RUSHALL OLYMPIC

Currently: West Midlands (Regional) League

81-82 PR: Bilston (A) 0-0, (H) 1-3

82-83 Q1: Dudley Town (H) 1-1, (A) 1-0
Q2: Holbeach United (A) 0-1

83-84 Q1: Grantham (H) 1-1, (A) 0-3

84-85 Q1: Kidderminster Harriers (H) 1-2

85-86 PR: Paget Rangers (A) 2-2, (H) 3-0
Q1: Wellingborough Town (H) 0-2

86-87 PR: Moor Green (H) 2-3

87-88 PR: Baker Perkins (A) 2-2, (H) 3-0
Q1: Oldbury United (H) 0-2

88-89 PR: Tividale (A) 4-1
Q1: Brackley Town (A) 2-1
Q2: Stafford Rangers (A) 0-1

89-90 PR: Sutton Town (A) 1-1, (H) 3-0
Q1: Matlock Town (H) 0-1

90-91 PR: Alfreton Town (A) 2-2, (H) 3-0
Q1: Blakenall (A) 2-3

91-92 PR: Racing Club Warwick (A) 1-2

92-93 PR: Northampton Spencer (A) 1-1, (H) 3-2
Q1: Sandwell Borough (H) 3-0
Q2: Leek Town (A) 1-0
Q3: Sutton C'field (A) 0-0, (H) 1-1, (H) 1-2

RUSHDEN & DIAMONDS

Currently: Southern League
See also Rushden Town and Irthlingborough Diamonds

92-93 PR: Desborough Town (H) 2-0
Q1: Long Buckby (A) 1-0
Q2: Hednesford Town (A) 1-4

RUSHDEN TOWN

Currently: Merged with Irthlingborough Diamonds. Playing as Rushden & Diamonds in Southern Lge.
See also Rushden & Diamonds

45-46 Q2: Peterborough United (H) 1-9

46-47 Q1: Kettering Town (A) 0-2

47-48 Q1: Wellingborough Town (A) 3-0
Q2: Kettering Town (H) 1-2

48-49 Q1: Kettering Town (A) 2-2, (H) 0-1

49-50 Q1: Symington's Recreation (H) 0-3

50-51 Q1: Kettering Town (H) 2-2, (A) 0-4

51-52 Q1: Corby Town (H) 0-6

52-53 PR: Wellingborough Town (H) 3-1
Q1: Kettering Town (A) 0-1

53-54 Q1: Kettering Town (H) 1-1, (A) 1-3

54-55 Q1: Desborough Town (H) 3-1
Q2: Wellingborough Town (A) 1-2

55-56 Q1: Stamford (A) 5-1
Q2: Rothwell Town (H) 3-3, (A) 2-3

56-57 Q1: Stamford (H) 3-1
Q2: Spalding United (H) 0-3

57-58 Q1: Spalding United (H) 2-2, (A) 0-8

58-59 Q1: Rothwell Town (H) 5-2
Q2: Wellingborough Town (H) 1-0
Q3: Kettering Town (H) 0-1

59-60 Q1: Stamford (H) 3-2
Q2: Wellingborough Town (A) 2-0
Q3: Corby Town (A) 2-2, (H) 2-1
Q4: Enfield (A) 0-3

60-61 Q1: Rothwell Town (H) 1-0
Q2: St Neots Town (H) 0-5

61-62 Q1: Bourne Town (A) 1-2

62-63 Q1: Bourne Town (A) 1-4

63-64 Q1: Rothwell Town (A) 3-0
Q2: Wellingborough Town (H) 0-2

64-65 Q1: Rothwell Town (H) 2-3

65-66 Q1: Bourne Town (H) 4-4, (A) 1-4

66-67 Q1: Eynesbury Rovers (A) 0-0, (H) 6-3
Q2: March Town United (H) 4-0
Q3: St Neots Town (H) 0-3

67-68 Q1: Histon (H) 8-0
Q2: St Neots Town (H) 4-0
Q3: Cambridge City (A) 0-1

68-69 PR: St Neots Town (H) 0-1

69-70 PR: Rothwell Town (A) 2-0
Q1: Desborough Town (A) 2-1
Q2: Corby Town (H) 2-1
Q3: Cambridge City (A) 1-4

70-71 Q1: Soham Town Rangers (A) 0-1

71-72 Q1: Biggleswade Town (A) 1-2

72-73 PR: Long Eaton United (H) 0-1

73-74 PR: Stevenage Athletic (A) 1-6

74-75 Q1: Desborough Town (H) 2-1
Q2: Bedford Town (A) 0-2

Season	Results
75-76	Q1: Witney Town (H) 0-3
76-77	PR: Wolverton Town & B.R. (H) 1-0 Q1: Vauxhall Motors (A) 0-0, (H) 1-2
77-78	PR: Milton Keynes City (A) 2-0 Q1: Letchworth Garden City (A) 0-3
78-79	Q1: Potton United (A) 1-0 Q2: Barton Rovers (H) 1-1, (A) 1-3
79-80	Q1: Hinckley Athletic (H) 2-3
80-81	Q1: Hitchin Town (A) 0-3
81-82	Q1: Nuneaton Borough (A) 0-6
82-83	Q1: Bridgnorth Town (H) 0-2
83-84	PR: Ampthill Town (A) 1-2
84-85	Q1: Stafford Rangers (H) 3-3, (A) 3-1 Q2: Bridgnorth Town (H) 0-1
85-86	PR: Holbeach United (A) 1-1, (H) 3-3, (H) 1-0 Q1: March Town United (H) 2-3
86-87	PR: Spalding United (A) 0-0, (H) 2-4
87-88	Q1: Rothwell Town (H) 1-4
88-89	PR: Highgate United (A) 4-0 Q1: Leicester United (A) 1-4
89-90	PR: Halesowen Harriers (A) 5-2 Q1: Holbeach United (H) 4-5
90-91	Q1: Spalding United (A) 3-0 Q2: Boreham Wood (A) 0-1
91-92	PR: Friar Lane Old Boys (H) 3-2 Q1: Desborough Town (A) 4-2 Q2: Bromsgrove Rovers (A) 0-1

RYDE SPORTS

Currently: Wessex League

Season	Results
45-46	Q1: Cowes (H) 1-3
46-47	PR: Gosport Borough Athletic (H) 1-8
47-48	PR: Sandown (A) 2-2, (H) 4-1 Q1: Thornycroft Athletic (H) 3-0 Q2: Poole Town (H) 2-1 Q3: Gosport Borough Athletic (A) 2-1 Q4: Trowbridge Town (H) 0-1
48-49	PR: Dorchester Town (A) 2-0 Q1: Poole Town (H) 0-1
49-50	EX: Andover (H) 1-0 PR: Newport I.O.W. (H) 1-1, (A) 5-3 Q1: Weymouth (H) 2-6
50-51	EX: Andover (H) 2-1 PR: Dorchester Town (H) 3-3, (A) 2-4
51-52	Q1: Totton (A) 0-3
52-53	Q1: Alton Town (H) 3-4
58-59	PR: Fareham Town (A) 2-4
68-69	Q1: Salisbury (H) 1-7
69-70	PR: Salisbury (H) 1-1, (A) 2-3
70-71	Q1: Newport Isle of Wight (H) 0-3
71-72	Q1: Thornycroft Athletic (H) 1-4
72-73	Q1: Gosport Borough Athletic (A) 0-2
73-74	Q1: Bognor Regis Town (A) 0-3
74-75	Q1: Gosport Borough (A) 1-7
75-76	Q1: Guildford & Dorking United (H) 0-4

RYHOPE COLLIERY WELFARE

Currently: Merged with Sporting Club Vaux. Playing as Sunderland Vaux Ryhope C.W. in Wearside League. See also Sunderland Vaux Ryhope C.W.

Season	Results
61-62	Q1: Billingham Synthonia Recreation (H) 1-2
62-63	Q1: South Bank (A) 0-0, (H) 2-1 Q2: Ferryhill Athletic (A) 2-2, (H) 1-0 Q3: Stockton (H) 1-2
63-64	Q1: Shildon (A) 1-0 Q2: Ferryhill Athletic (A) 1-4
64-65	Q1: Stanley United (H) 3-2 Q2: Annfield Plain (H) 1-1, (A) 1-2
65-66	Q1: Blyth Spartans (A) 3-4
66-67	Q1: Stanley United (A) 0-1
67-68	Q1: Evenwood Town (A) 6-0 Q2: Stanley United (H) 1-0 Q3: Durham City (H) 4-3 Q4: Bishop Auckland (A) 2-2, (H) 4-1 R1: Workington (H) 0-1
68-69	Q1: Consett (A) 0-2
69-70	Q1: Ashington (H) 0-1
70-71	Q1: Shildon (A) 1-3
71-72	Q1: Bedlington Colliery Welfare (A) 1-5
72-73	Q1: Consett (A) 1-3

RYHOPE COMMUNITY ASSN.

Currently: Northern League

Season	Results
83-84	PR: Harrogate Town (H) 1-3
84-85	Q1: Spennymoor United (H) 4-2 Q2: Wren Rovers (A) 3-2 Q3: Whitby Town (H) 1-1, (A) 1-5
85-86	Q1: Whitley Bay (H) 1-3
86-87	PR: Farsley Celtic (H) 1-1, (A) 2-3
87-88	Q1: Ashington (H) 1-1, (A) 2-1 Q2: Newcastle Blue Star (H) 0-2
88-89	PR: Esh Winning (A) 1-1, (H) 2-3
89-90	Q1: Netherfield (A) 1-3
90-91	PR: Hebburn (A - *at Washington F.C.*) 2-0 Q1: Consett (H) 1-2

ST ALBANS CITY

Currently: Isthmian League

Season	Results
45-46	PR: Finchley (H) 4-3 Q1: Wealdstone (H) 2-2, (A) 0-3
46-47	PR: Apsley (H) 5-1 Q1: Hertford Town (H) 5-1 Q2: Harrow Town (H) 2-5
47-48	PR: Chipperfield (H) 1-0 Q1: Leavesden (A) 1-2
48-49	EX: De Havilland Vamps (A - *played home*) 5-0 PR: Polytechnic (A - *played home*) 3-0 Q1: Leavesden (A) 4-1 Q2: Wealdstone (H) 0-5
49-50	PR: Ruislip Manor (A) 2-1 Q1: Crown & Manor (H) 4-1 Q2: Wealdstone (H) 0-1
50-51	PR: Finchley (H) 1-0 Q1: Wealdstone (A) 5-1 Q2: Enfield (A) 0-2
51-52	Q1: Maidenhead United (H) 3-1 Q2: Slough Town (H) 1-1, (A) 0-4
52-53	Q1: Barnet (A) 2-1 Q2: Hendon (H) 1-1, (A) 1-3
53-54	Q1: Slough Centre (A) 1-0 Q2: Wealdstone (A) 0-2
54-55	PR: Eton Manor (A) 1-0 Q1: Clapton (A) 1-1, (H) 0-1
55-56	PR: Hertford Town (A) 2-1 Q1: Clapton (A) 0-0, (H) 4-1 Q2: Enfield (A) 2-4
56-57	PR: Letchworth Town (A) 0-1
57-58	PR: Hoddesdon Town (A) 2-2, (H) 4-1 Q1: Clapton (A) 1-3
58-59	Q1: Barnet (A) 2-1 Q2: Cheshunt (H) 1-2 *ab. 45 mins* (H) 2-3
59-60	Q1: Hoddesdon Town (A) 0-2
60-61	Q1: Dunstable Town (H) 2-1 Q2: Stevenage Town (A) 1-1, (H) 2-2, 3-2 Q3: Hitchin Town (A) 0-4
61-62	Q1: Cambridge City (H) 1-2
62-63	Q1: Cambridge City (A) 0-3
63-64	Q1: Bletchley Town United (H) 3-0 Q2: Biggleswade Town (A) 4-5
64-65	Q1: Letchworth Town (H) 3-2 Q2: Hitchin Town (A) 0-4
65-66	Q1: Dunstable Town (H) 3-0 Q2: Hitchin Town (H) 2-0 Q3: Bletchley (H) 0-1
66-67	Q1: Hounslow (A) 0-2
67-68	Q1: Hitchin Town (H) 0-0, (A) 1-3
68-69	Q1: Wycombe Wanderers (A) 0-0, (H) 1-0 Q2: Erith & Belvedere (H) 3-2 Q3: Hitchin Town (A) 2-0 Q4: Corby Town (A) 1-0 R1: Wealdstone (A) 1-1, (H) 1-0 R2: Walsall (H) 1-1, (A) 1-3
69-70	Q1: Erith & Belvedere (A) 1-2
70-71	Q1: Marlow (H) 2-0 Q2: Bedford Town (H) 1-1, (A) 3-2 Q3: Leighton Town (H) 2-1 Q4: Hendon (A) 0-0, (H) 1-2
71-72	PR: Romford (A) 0-3
72-73	Q1: Gravesend & Northfleet (A) 1-1, (H) 1-0 Q2: Addlestone (A) 1-0 Q3: Barking (A) 2-3
73-74	Q1: Dartford (A) 1-4
74-75	Q1: Epping Town (A) 1-1, (H) 2-2, 2-1 Q2: Letchworth Town (H) 1-0 Q3: Hitchin Town (A) 1-2
75-76	Q1: Tooting & Mitcham Utd (H) 3-3, (A) 0-4
76-77	PR: Molesey (A) 1-2
77-78	Q1: Carshalton Athletic (A) 3-2 Q2: Leytonstone (H) 2-0

Above: *Allan Cockram scores from the spot as St Albans win at Telford on 24th October 1992 to secure a place in the First Round Proper for the first time in twelve years. Photo: John Sherwood.*

Q3: Barnet (H) 2-4

78-79 Q1: Hounslow (A) 1-1, (H) 4-2
Q2: Wokingham Town (H) 0-0, (A) 1-4

79-80 Q1: Kempston Rovers (H) 0-2

80-81 Q1: Chesham United (A) 1-0
Q2: Harrow Borough (A) 4-3
Q3: Dulwich Hamlet (H) 2-1
Q4: Harwich & Parkeston (A) 2-2, (H) 3-0
R1: Gravesend & Northfleet (A) 2-1
R2: Torquay United (H) 1-1, (A) 1-4

81-82 Q1: Grays Athletic (H) 2-1
Q2: Leyton-Wingate (A) 2-2, (H) 4-1
Q3: Dunstable (H) 1-5

82-83 Q1: Abingdon Town (H) 4-1
Q2: Hampton (H) 1-3

83-84 PR: Banstead Athletic (H) 10-0
Q1: Leyton-Wingate (A) 2-1
Q2: Hornchurch (H) 3-0
Q3: Windsor & Eton (A) 1-4

84-85 Q1: Grays Athletic (A) 0-3

85-86 PR: Wolverton Town (H) 1-1, (A) 2-0
Q1: Woodford Town (A) 0-1

86-87 Q1: Ruislip Manor (H) 1-2

87-88 Q1: Leytonstone-Ilford (A) 0-2

88-89 Q1: Malden Vale (H) 1-0
Q2: Dartford (A) 1-1, (H) 2-4

89-90 Q1: Wealdstone (H) 1-2

90-91 Q1: Ford United (A) 1-3

91-92 Q1: Thetford Town (A) 2-0
Q2: Brimsdown Rovers (H) 1-1, (A) 0-2

92-93 Q1: Brimsdown Rovers (H) 3-1
Q2: Rayners Lane (H) 5-1
Q3: Stevenage Borough (A) 3-3, (H) 2-1
Q4: Telford United (A) 2-1
R1: Cheltenham Town (H) 1-2

ST AUSTELL

Currently: South Western League

47-48 Q1: Glastonbury (H) 2-1
Q2: Dartmouth United (H) 5-2
Q3: Street (H) 1-2

48-49 PR: Soundwell (A) 3-4

49-50 PR: Oak Villa (H) 4-1
Q1: Ilfracombe Town (A) 3-2
Q2: Dartmouth United (A) 1-2

50-51 PR: Newquay (A) 0-3

51-52 PR: Tavistock (H) 3-0
Q1: Bideford (H) 1-1, (A) 0-5

52-53 PR: Wadebridge Town (A) 5-4
Q1: Bridgwater Town (H) 2-3

53-54 PR: Dartmouth United (A) 1-2

54-55 PR: Penzance (H) 3-1
Q1: Tavistock (H) 3-6

55-56 PR: Truro City (H) 1-8

57-58 PR: Newquay (A) 0-2

63-64 Q1: Barnstaple Town (A) 2-4

64-65 Q1: Bideford (H) 3-5

66-67 Q1: St Blazey (A) 2-0
Q2: Bideford (A) 0-5

67-68 Q2: Bideford (A) 0-2

90-91 PR: Falmouth Town (H) 0-4

91-92 Q1: Liskeard Athletic (H) 2-3

ST BLAZEY

Currently: South Western League

50-51 PR: Ilfracombe Town (H) 0-6

52-53 PR: Penzance (H) 3-1
Q1: Newquay (A) 3-1
Q2: Ilfracombe Town (A) 0-2

53-54 PR: Taunton (A) 2-0
Q1: Newquay Amateur (H) 4-2
Q2: Bideford (A) 3-1
Q3: Barnstaple Town (H) 3-5

54-55 PR: Ilfracombe Town (H) 1-1, (A) 2-5

55-56 PR: Tavistock (H) 3-1
Q1: Taunton (A) 2-0
Q2: Bideford (A) 1-4

56-57 PR: Bideford (H) 2-5

57-58 PR: Tavistock (A) 3-4

58-59 Q1: Newquay (H) 2-1
Q2: Wadebridge Town (H) 2-2, (A) 1-3

59-60 Q1: Wadebridge Town (A) 2-3

60-61 Q1: Wadebridge Town (A) 7-2
Q2: Barnstaple Town (A) 1-1, (H) 1-2

62-63 Q2: Falmouth Town (A) 0-1

63-64 Q2: Wadebridge Town (A) 1-1, (H) 8-1
Q3: Bideford (A) 1-3

64-65 Q1: Wadebridge Town (A) 6-2
Q2: Falmouth Town (H) 2-1
Q3: Bideford (H) 0-3

65-66 Q2: Falmouth Town (H) 4-1
Q3: Bideford (H) 2-2, (A) 0-3

66-67 Q1: St Austell (H) 0-2

67-68 Q1: Bideford (A) 2-3

68-69 Q1: Nanpean Rovers (H) 2-2, (A) 1-1, 0-2

69-70 Q1: Barnstaple Town (A) 1-3

70-71 Q1: Penzance (H) 3-3, (A) 2-1
Q2: Falmouth Town (H) 3-2
Q3: Bideford (H) 2-6

71-72 Q1: Newquay (H) 4-0
Q2: Wadebridge Town (A) 1-6

72-73 Q1: Wadebridge Town (H) 1-2

73-74 Q1: Falmouth Town (H) 1-3

74-75 Q1: Minehead (H) 1-1, (A) 1-4

75-76 Q1: Barnstaple Town (A) 1-9

76-77 Q1: Newquay (A) 0-0, (H) 1-3

77-78 Q1: Bideford (H) 0-1

78-79 Q1: Taunton Town (H) 0-3

79-80 Q1: Barnstaple Town (H) 0-2

80-81 Q1: Penzance (H) 1-2

81-82 Q1: Bideford (A) 1-4

82-83 PR: Clandown (H) 3-1
Q1: Clevedon Town (A) 2-0
Q2: Wimborne Town (A) 2-3

83-84 Q1: Bridgwater Town (H) 3-1
Q2: Poole Town (H) 0-3

84-85 PR: Barnstaple Town (A) 1-4

85-86 PR: Shepton Mallet Town (H) 1-0
Q1: Clevedon Town (H) 2-4

86-87 Q1: Barnstaple (H) 1-1, (A) 0-0, (H) 0-2

87-88 PR: Tiverton Town (H) 4-4, (A) 2-5

88-89 PR: Frome Town (A) 1-4

89-90 Q1: Falmouth Town (A) 1-1, (H) 1-0
Q2: Weymouth (A) 0-2

90-91 PR: Shortwood United (A) 2-1
Q1: Weymouth (H) 0-2

91-92 PR: Minehead (H) 0-3

92-93 PR: Falmouth Town (H) 1-4

ST FRIDESWIDES (OXFORD)

Currently: Defunct

48-49 EX: Abingdon Town (A) 3-4

ST HELENS TOWN

Currently: North West Counties League

46-47 Q1: Prescot Cables (H) *withdrew*

47-48 PR: Prescot Cables (H) 0-1

48-49 EX: Prescot B.I.C.C. (H) 4-2
PR: Earle (A) 2-1
Q1: Formby (A) 1-0
Q2: Bangor City (H) 0-3

49-50 PR: Hoylake Athletic (A) 3-0
Q1: Bangor City (H) 0-3

50-51 EX: Burscough (A) 1-3

51-52 Q1: Prescot Cables (H) 1-1, (A) 1-2

52-53 Q1: Bangor City (A) 0-2

53-54 PR: Bangor City (H) 2-2, (A) 1-5

54-55 Q1: Flint Town United (H) 2-2, (A) 2-5

55-56 PR: Pwllheli & District (H) 1-1, (A) 1-3

56-57 PR: Marine (H) 2-2, (A) 1-2

57-58 Q1: Llandudno (H) 3-5

58-59 Q1: Llandudno (A) 0-3

59-60 PR: Earlestown (H) 0-2

60-61 Q1: Skelmersdale United (A) 2-3

61-62 Q1: Prescot Cables (A) 1-3

62-63 Q1: Earlestown (A) 3-1
Q2: South Liverpool (H) 2-1
Q3: Altrincham (H) 1-3

63-64 Q1: Ashton United (A) 2-5

64-65 Q1: Prescot Cables (H) 4-1
Q2: Altrincham (A) 1-4

65-66 Q1: Ashton United (A) 4-2
Q2: Skelmersdale United (H) 0-3

66-67 Q1: Rhyl (A) 1-5

67-68 Q1: Chorley (A) 1-1, (H) 0-3

68-69 Q1: Chorley (H) 0-0, (A) 1-0
Q2: Skelmersdale United (H) 0-1

69-70 Q1: Droylsden (A) 0-1

70-71 Q1: Rossendale United (H) 0-2

74-75 Q1: Skelmersdale United (H) 0-1

75-76 Q1: Rhyl (A) 2-4

76-77 PR: Prescot Town (A) 1-4

77-78 Q1: New Brighton Rakers (A) 0-1

78-79 Q1: Oswestry (A) 1-1, (H) 0-0, (*at Winsford United*) 2-3

79-80 Q1: Macclesfield Town (H) 1-2

80-81 Q1: Southport (A) 3-1
Q2: Leyland Motors (A) 4-0
Q3: Fleetwood Town (H) 0-1

81-82 PR: Prescot Cables (A) 1-4

82-83 Q1: Bootle (H) 0-4

83-84 Q1: Prestwich Heys (H) 0-1

84-85 PR: Coleshill Town (H) 6-1
Q1: Congleton Town (H) 2-0
Q2: Formby (A) 0-1

85-86 Q1: Colwyn Bay (A) 3-0
Q2: Eastwood Hanley (H) 2-0
Q3: Leek Town (A) 1-0
Q4: Morecambe (A) 1-1, (H) 0-1

86-87 Q1: Heanor Town (H) 6-0
Q2: Armthorpe Welfare (A) 1-1, (H) 0-1

87-88 PR: Curzon Ashton (H) 6-2
Q1: Ilkeston (A) 1-1, (H) 1-1, (*E. Hanley*) 4-1
Q2: Horwich R.M.I. (H) 0-0, (A) 3-2
Q3: Northwich Victoria (A) 2-3

88-89 PR: Ashton United (H) 0-1

89-90 PR: Brigg Town (A) 2-0
Q1: Sandwell Borough (H) 0-1

90-91 PR: Belper Town (A) 3-2
Q1: Curzon Ashton (H) 0-3

Opposite: *St Helens defend a corner as they lose at home to Curzon Ashton in the First Qualifying Round. Photo: Colin Stevens.*

91-92 PR: Borrowash Victoria (H) 1-3

92-93 PR: Tow Law Town (H) 3-2
Q1: Stockton (H) 3-4

ST IVES TOWN

Currently: United Counties League

50-51 EX: Kempston Rovers (H) 2-1
PR: St Neots & District (A) 2-5

ST NEOTS ST MARY

Currently: Defunct

48-49 EX: Baldock Town (H) 0-4

49-50 PR: Letchworth Town (H) 1-6

ST NEOTS TOWN

Currently: Defunct
* - As St Neots & District

47-48 * PR: Biggleswade Town (A) 1-9

48-49 * PR: Leighton United (A) 0-2

49-50 * PR: Vauxhall Motors (H) 3-2
Q1: Letchworth Town (H) 3-1
Q2: Bedford Town (A) 0-3

50-51 * PR: St Ives Town (H) 5-2
Q1: Wolverton Town (A) 2-3

51-52 * Q1: Histon Institute (H) 6-3
Q2: March Town United (A) 0-1

52-53 * Q1: King's Lynn (A) 1-4

53-54 * PR: Huntingdon United (H) 4-1
Q1: Cambridge United (H) 0-3

54-55 * PR: Holbeach United (A) 1-4

55-56 * Q1: March Town United (A) 1-3

56-57 * PR: Chatteris Town (A) 3-1
Q1: King's Lynn (A) 0-4

57-58 PR: Somersham Town (H) 6-0
Q1: Cambridge United (A) 2-6

58-59 Q1: March Town United (A) 1-0
Q2: Wisbech Town (A) 0-4

59-60 Q1: Holbeach United (H) 1-1, (A) 2-3

60-61 Q1: Eynesbury Rovers (A) 9-1
Q2: Rushden Town (A) 5-0
Q3: Kettering Town (A) 0-2

61-62 Q1: Corby Town (H) 0-2

62-63 Q1: Eynesbury Rovers (A) 5-0
Q2: Corby Town (A) 0-1

63-64 Q1: Corby Town (A) 0-3

64-65 Q1: Wellingborough Town (A) 2-0
Q2: Desborough Town (H) 3-0
Q3: Eynesbury Rovers (H) 7-0
Q4: King's Lynn (A) 0-8

65-66 Q1: Desborough Town (A) 0-3

66-67 Q1: Ely City (H) 4-2
Q2: Desborough Town (A) 2-1
Q3: Rushden Town (A) 3-0
Q4: Wisbech Town (H) 2-0
R1: Walsall (A) 0-2

67-68 PR: Stamford (A) 4-0
Q1: Chatteris Town (A) 2-1
Q2: Rushden Town (A) 0-4

68-69 PR: Rushden Town (A) 1-0
Q1: Cambridge City (A) 0-0, (H) 3-3, 0-3

69-70 PR: Chatteris Town (H) 3-0
Q1: Biggleswade Town (H) 2-3

70-71 PR: Corby Town (H) 1-4

71-72 Q1: Wellingborough Town (H) 1-3

72-73 Q1: Sudbury Town (H) 1-1, (A) 1-6

73-74 Q1: Irthlingborough Diamonds (H) 3-1
Q2: Bletchley Town (H) 0-3

74-75 Q1: Chatteris Town (A) 2-0
Q2: March Town United (H) 2-3

75-76 Q1: Bury Town (A) 1-1, (H) 2-0
Q2: Great Yarmouth Town (A) 2-3

76-77 Q1: Stowmarket (H) 1-0
Q2: Corby Town (H) 3-0
Q3: Bedford Town (A) 0-3

77-78 Q1: Thetford Town (H) 2-1
Q2: Wisbech Town (H) 4-4, (A) 1-2

78-79 Q1: King's Lynn (H) 1-0
Q2: Histon (A) 1-0
Q3: March Town United (H) 2-3

79-80 Q1: Grantham (H) 4-2
Q2: Wisbech Town (A) 2-5

80-81 PR: Thetford Town (H) 3-1
Q1: Great Yarmouth Town (H) 0-1

81-82 Q1: March Town United (A) 0-1

ST PHILIPS
MARSH ADULT SCHOOL

Currently: Gloucestershire County League

46-47 Q1: Gloucester City (H) 2-0
Q2: Barry Town (H) 1-6

47-48 PR: Lovells Athletic (H) 1-5

49-50 EX: Mount Hill Enterprise (H) 1-2

50-51 PR: Cinderford Town (A) 1-2

SAFFRON WALDEN TOWN

Currently: Isthmian League

46-47 EX: Ware (H) 4-2
PR: Hertford Town (A) 2-7

47-48 EX: Pinner (A) 0-2

48-49 EX: Woodford Town (A) 1-6

49-50 EX: Colchester Casuals (H) 2-3

79-80 Q1: Enderby Town (A) 0-5

80-81 Q1: Dartford (A) 1-4

81-82 PR: Great Yarmouth Town (A) 0-4

82-83 PR: Ruislip Manor (H) 5-2
Q1: Hayes (A) 1-2

83-84 Q1: Stowmarket Town (H) 3-0
Q2: Basildon United (H) 2-4

84-85 Q1: Bury Town (A) 2-0
Q2: King's Lynn (H) 0-0, (A) 1-2

85-86 Q1: Witney Town (A) 0-3

86-87 PR: Barton Rovers (A) 1-1, (H) 3-1
Q1: Baldock Town (A) 0-1

87-88 Q1: Rainham Town (H) 2-1
Q2: Carshalton Athletic (H) 1-5

88-89 PR: Ely City (H) 2-0
Q1: Barton Rovers (A) 0-1

89-90 PR: Burnham Ramblers (H) 2-1
Q1: Stowmarket Town (A) 3-5

90-91 PR: Stowmarket Town (A) 1-1, (H) 2-1
Q1: Wealdstone (H) 0-4

91-92 PR: Collier Row (A) 2-2, (H) 2-3

92-93 PR: Sudbury Town (A) 1-6

SALFORD CITY

Currently: North West Counties League

90-91 PR: Warrington Town (H) 0-3

91-92 PR: Warrington Town (H) 0-0, (A) 0-1

92-93 PR: North Ferriby United (H) 0-1

SALISBURY

Currently: (Salisbury City) Southern League

47-48 EX: Winchester City (A) 1-0
PR: Basingstoke Town (H) 5-1
Q1: Newport Isle of Wight (H) 0-0, (A) 0-2

48-49 EX: Purton (H) 1-0
PR: Wilts County Mental Hospital (A) 3-0
Q1: Frome Town (H) 3-2
Q2: Trowbridge Town (A) 1-4

49-50 PR: Warminster Town (H) 8-0
Q1: Bath City (A) 2-0
Q2: Clandown (A) 1-6

50-51 PR: Westbury United (A) 6-1
Q1: Chippenham United (H) 2-1
Q2: Clandown (H) 4-2
Q3: Trowbridge Town (H) 1-0
Q4: Gloucester City (A) 1-2

51-52 Q1: Calne & Harris United (H) 2-0
Q2: Frome Town (A) 3-2
Q3: Chippenham Town (H) 1-1, (A) 1-2

52-53 PR: Welton Rovers (H) 7-1
Q1: Westbury United (H) 4-1
Q2: Chippenham Town (H) 3-1
Q3: Trowbridge Town (H) 0-2

53-54 Q1: Andover (H) 2-1
Q2: Chippenham Town (A) 2-4

54-55 Q1: Frome Town (H) 2-3

55-56 Q1: Devizes Town (A) 2-0
Q2: Bulford United (H) 3-0
Q3: Frome Town (H) 3-0
Q4: Chippenham United (A) 6-2
R1: Weymouth (A) 2-3

56-57 Q1: Warminster Town (A) 6-1
Q2: Chippenham Town (H) 1-2

57-58 PR: Westbury United (H) 4-2
Q1: Trowbridge Town (H) 0-3

58-59 Q1: Bridport (A) 5-2
Q2: Poole Town (A) 1-2

59-60 Q1: Portland United (A) 3-2
Q2: Warminster Town (A) 5-0
Q3: Poole Town (A) 1-0
Q4: Basingstoke Town (H) 2-2, (A) 2-1
R1: Barnet (H) 1-0
R2: Newport County (H) 0-1

60-61 Q4: Weymouth (A) 1-1, (H) 0-2

61-62 Q4: Oxford United (A) 2-3

62-63 Q1: Chippenham Town (H) 2-2, (A) 1-3

63-64 Q2: Warminster Town (A) 2-2, (H) 4-0
Q3: Dorchester Town (A) 1-1, (H) 1-3

64-65 Q1: Dorchester Town (H) 3-3, (A) 3-1
Q2: Poole Town (H) 1-1, (A) 1-0
Q3: Portland United (H) 5-1
Q4: Yeovil Town (H) 2-1
R1: Peterborough United (A) 1-5

65-66 Q1: Newbury Town (H) 4-0
Q2: Andover (A) 3-0
Q3: Portland United (H) 0-3

66-67 Q1: Cowes Isle of Wight (H) 4-1
Q2: Waterlooville (A) 2-0
Q3: Fareham Town (A) 2-2, (H) 1-2

67-68 Q1: Fareham Town (A) 2-2, (H) 5-1
Q2: Cowes Isle of Wight (A) 1-1, (H) 5-1
Q3: Newport Isle of Wight (H) 3-0
Q4: Dorchester Town (A) 2-1
R1: Swindon Town (A) 0-4

68-69 Q1: Ryde Sports (A) 7-1
Q2: Thornycroft Athletic (H) 4-0
Q3: Waterlooville (A) 2-4

69-70 PR: Ryde Sports (A) 1-1, (H) 3-2
Q1: Thornycroft Athletic (A) 4-3
Q2: Fareham Town (H) 1-0
Q3: Andover (A) 0-0, (H) 3-0
Q4: Weymouth (H) 0-1

70-71 Q1: Portland United (H) 3-0
Q2: Poole Town (H) 0-1

71-72 Q1: Westbury United (H) 4-0
Q2: Bath City (H) 2-1
Q3: Basingstoke Town (A) 2-5

72-73 Q1: Westbury United (H) 9-1
Q2: Andover (A) 1-0
Q3: Frome Town (A) 0-0, (H) 0-1

73-74 PR: Westbury United (A) 2-0
Q1: Bridport (A) 1-0
Q2: Weymouth (A) 0-2

74-75 Q1: Cowes Isle of Wight (H) 3-0
Q2: Basingstoke Town (A) 1-1, (H) 3-1
Q3: Alton Town (A) 3-1
Q4: Cheltenham Town (A) 1-4

75-76 Q1: Trowbridge Town (H) 3-1
Q2: Swaythling (A) 1-0
Q3: Frome Town (H) 1-0
Q4: Weymouth (H) 4-5

76-77 PR: Farnborough Town (A) 0-4

77-78 Q1: Cowes Isle of Wight (H) 5-1
Q2: Hungerford Town (A) 1-0
Q3: Frome Town (A) 2-2, (H) 1-0
Q4: Minehead (H) 1-1, (A) 1-2

78-79 Q1: Welton Rovers (H) 4-0
Q2: Bath City (H) 0-2

79-80 Q1: Newport Isle of Wight (H) 4-3
Q2: Horsham Y.M.C.A. (H) 3-1
Q3: Poole Town (H) 3-0
Q4: Worcester City (H) 2-1
R1: Millwall (H - *at Southampton F.C.*) 1-2

80-81 Q1: Trowbridge Town (H) 1-1, (A) 1-2

81-82 Q1: Wealdstone (A) 0-4

82-83 PR: Calne Town (H) 3-2
Q1: Slough Town (A) 0-2

83-84 PR: Flackwell Heath (H) 1-0
Q1: Sholing Sports (A) 1-2

84-85 PR: Marlow (H) 3-1
Q1: Newport Isle of Wight (H) 4-1
Q2: Hungerford Town (H) 0-0, (A) 0-3

85-86 Q1: Fareham Town (A) 2-2, (H) 0-5

86-87 Q1: Bridgend Town (H) 2-1
Q2: Trowbridge Town (A) 0-2

87-88 PR: Barry Town (H) 0-1

88-89 PR: Newbury Town (H) 4-2
Q1: Pagham (H) 2-3

89-90 PR: Sholing Sports (H) 6-0
Q1: Poole Town (H) 1-1, (A) 1-3

90-91 PR: Uxbridge Town (H) 1-1, (A) 2-1
Q1: Hungerford Town (H) 2-0
Q2: Bournemouth (H) 4-0
Q3: Farnborough Town (H) 0-3

91-92 Q1: Thatcham Town (A) 1-1, (H) 3-0
Q2: Poole Town (H) 2-0
Q3: Thame United (A) 4-0
Q4: Farnborough Town (H) 1-7

92-93 Q1: Trowbridge Town (H) 6-2
Q2: Thatcham Town (H) 4-0
Q3: Brockenhurst (A) 3-1
Q4: Witney Town (A) 2-1
R1: Marlow (A) 3-3, (H) 2-2 (*3-4 pens*)

SALISBURY CORINTHIANS

Currently: Defunct

45-46 Q1: Gosport Borough Ath. (H) 1-1, (A) 2-6

46-47 PR: Basingstoke T. (A) 1-1, (H) 2-2, 2-1
Q1: Gosport Borough Ath. (H) 2-2, (A) 1-2

47-48 PR: Andover (H) 1-2

48-49 PR: Devizes Town (A) 0-3

SALTASH UNITED

Currently: Western League

70-71 Q1: Wadebridge Town (A) 3-1
Q2: Bideford (A) 1-3

71-72 Q1: Wadebridge Town (H) 2-3

78-79 Q1: Penzance (H) 8-1
Q2: Bideford (A) 0-2

79-80 Q1: Ilminster Town (H) 3-0
Q2: Glastonbury (H) 4-0
Q3: Yeovil Town (H) 3-3, (A) 1-2

80-81 PR: Wadebridge Town (H) 5-0
Q1: Newquay (H) 4-0
Q2: Falmouth Town (A) 1-2

81-82 Q1: Taunton Town (A) 0-1

83-84 PR: Barnstaple Town (H) 3-1
Q1: Poole Town (H) 0-1

84-85 Q1: Merthyr Tydfil (H) 0-0, (A) 0-1

85-86 PR: Barnstaple Town (H) 1-0
Q1: Sharpness (H) 1-2

86-87 PR: Gloucester City (H) 0-0, (A) 2-0
Q1: Merthyr Tydfil (H) 1-0
Q2: Bideford (H) 1-2

87-88 Q1: Taunton Town (A) 3-0
Q2: Ottery St Mary (H) 7-1
Q3: Tiverton Town (H) 3-0
Q4: Farnborough Town (A) 2-4

88-89 Q1: Paulton Rovers (A) 4-1
Q2: Falmouth Town (A) 2-2, (H) 5-0
Q3: Exmouth Town (H) 2-2, (A) 3-4

89-90 Q1: Cheltenham Town (A) 0-1

90-91 PR: Torrington (H) 1-1, (A) 5-2
Q1: Poole Town (H) 1-1, (A) 2-2, (H) 3-1
Q2: Tiverton Town (A) 2-4

91-92 Q1: Ilfracombe Town (H) 6-0
Q2: Tiverton Town (A) 0-0, (H) 1-2

92-93 Q1: Weymouth (A) 0-1

SANDBACH RAMBLERS

Currently: Defunct

68-69 PR: Nantwich (A) 4-5

69-70 Q1: Lostock Gralam (H) 0-1

70-71 Q1: Marine (H) 0-2

71-72 PR: New Mills (A) 1-3

72-73 Q1: Witton Albion (H) 0-7

73-74 Q1: Leek Town (H) 0-4

74-75 Q1: Northwich Victoria (A) 3-2
Q2: Skelmersdale United (H) 2-1
Q3: Marine (H) 0-1

SANDOWN

Currently: Defunct

45-46 Q1: East Cowes Victoria (A) 1-9

46-47 PR: Newport I.O.W. (H) 3-3, (A) 2-3

47-48 PR: Ryde Sports (H) 2-2, (A) 1-4

48-49 EX: East Cowes Victoria (A) 1-6

49-50 EX: Thornycroft Athletic (A) 0-5

SANDWELL BOROUGH

Currently: Midland Combination
* - As Ashtree Highfield

87-88 * PR: Wolverton Town (A) 2-0
Q1: Halesowen Town (A) 1-1, (H) 0-1

88-89 * Q1: Rhyl (A) 1-4

89-90 Q1: St Helens Town (A) 1-0
Q2: Buxton (A) 1-1, (H) 1-1, (A) 2-3

90-91 PR: Northampton Spencer (H) 4-1
Q1: March Town United (A) 1-1, (H) 2-2, (H) 1-0
Q2: Bromsgrove Rovers (H) 0-2

Opposite: *Sandwell Borough's best ever F.A. Cup run culminated in a Second Qualifying Round home tie against local non-League 'giants' Bromsgrove Rovers. Here a run by Sandwell's Neil Mahoney is ended by a sliding tackle from Paul Webb. Photo: Paul Williamson.*

91-92 PR: Alfreton Town (H) 1-2

92-93 PR: Malvern Town (H) 4-0
Q1: Rushall Olympic (A) 0-3

SANKEY OF WELLINGTON

See G.K.N. Sankey

SAWBRIDGEWORTH TOWN

Currently: Essex Senior League

47-48 EX: Crown & Manor (H) 4-1
PR: Berkhamsted Town (H) 1-6

48-49 EX: Upminster (A) 2-2, (H) 1-2

49-50 EX: Tilbury (H) 0-6

SAWSTON UNITED

Currently: Defunct

48-49 PR: Parson Drove United (H) 2-8

SCALEGILL

Currently: Defunct

46-47 PR: Moss Bay (H) 2-4

47-48 PR: Moss Bay (H) 1-0
Q1: Netherfield (A) 1-5

48-49 PR: High Duty Alloys (H) 3-8

49-50 PR: Florence & Ullcoats United (H) 6-4
Q1: High Duty Alloys (H) *W/O*
Q2: Aspatria Spartans (A) 0-1

SCARBOROUGH

Currently: Football League

45-46 Q4: North Shields (H) 2-4

46-47 Q4: Stockton (A) 1-5

47-48 Q4: South Shields (H) 2-3

48-49 Q4: Bishop Auckland (H) 3-0
R1: Rhyl (A) 2-0
R2: Gateshead (A) 0-3

49-50 Q4: North Shields (A) 1-1, (H) 1-3

50-51 Q1: Bridlington Trinity United (H) 7-2
Q2: South Bank (H) 3-2
Q3: Whitby Town (H) 3-0
Q4: Billingham Synthonia Recreation (A) 3-0
R1: Rhyl (H) 1-2

51-52 Q4: Blackhall Colliery Welf. (H) 0-0, (A) 3-5

52-53 Q4: Stockton (H) 5-1
R1: Mansfield Town (H) 0-8

53-54 Q4: Stockton (H) 6-1
R1: Wigan Athletic (A) 0-4

54-55 Q1: Head Wrightsons (H) 3-0
Q2: South Bank (H) 4-1
Q3: North Skelton Athletic (A) 4-0
Q4: Ashington (A) 3-2
R1: York City (A) 2-3

55-56 Q4: North Shields (H) 4-3
R1: Workington (A) 2-4

56-57 Q4: Worksop Town (A) 4-1
R1: Rhyl (A) 2-3

57-58 Q4: Selby Town (H) 2-2, (A) 2-2, (H) 1-0
R1: Bradford City (A) 0-6

58-59 Q4: Heanor Town (A) 2-2, (H) 2-3

59-60 Q1: Ashington (H) 2-2, (A) 0-0, 1-0
Q2: Murton Colliery Welfare (A) 5-2
Q3: Annfield Plain (A) 3-2
Q4: Bishop Auckland (A) 2-1
R1: Bradford Park Avenue (A) 1-6

60-61 Q1: Whitley Bay (H) 4-1
Q2: Willington (H) 5-2
Q3: Consett (A) 2-1
Q4: Ferryhill Athletic (H) 1-0
R1: Bradford City (A) 0-0, (H) 1-3

61-62 Q4: Ashington (H) 2-2, (A) 0-2

62-63 Q1: Bridlington Town (A) 1-1, (H) 5-2
Q2: Harrogate Town (H) 5-1
Q3: Ossett Albion (A) 2-1
Q4: Hyde United (H) 1-0
R1: Crewe Alexandra (A) 1-1, (H) 2-3

63-64 Q1: Penrith (A) 3-1
Q2: North Shields (H) 2-1
Q3: Tow Law Town (H) 0-2

64-65 Q1: Farsley Celtic (A) 0-0, (H) 0-0, (H) 5-0
Q2: Ossett Albion (H) 2-1
Q3: Bridlington Town (H) 3-1
Q4: Blyth Spartans (H) 4-3
R1: Bradford City (H) 1-0
R2: Doncaster Rovers (A) 0-0, (H) 1-2

65-66 Q4: Netherfield (H) 5-1
Q1: Altrincham (A) 0-6

66-67 Q1: Bridlington Trinity (H) 1-2

67-68 Q1: Goole Town (H) 1-1, (A) 1-2

68-69 Q1: Bridlington Trinity (H) 0-0, (A) 1-1, (H) 3-1
Q2: Goole Town (H) 0-2

69-70 Q1: Brigg Town (A - *played home*) 4-1
Q2: Ashby Institute (A) 2-0
Q3: Hull Brunswick (H) 5-1
Q4: Whitby Town (A) 1-3

70-71 Q1: Bridlington Town (H) 1-0
Q2: Winterton Rangers (A) 2-1
Q3: Bridlington Trinity (H) 2-2, (A) 5-0
Q4: Ferryhill Athletic (H) 3-0
R1: Workington (H) 2-3

71-72 Q1: Ashby Institute (A) 6-0
Q2: Whitby Town (A) 2-0
Q3: Goole Town (H) 2-0
Q4: North Shields (H) 1-0
R1: Hartlepool United (A) 1-6

72-73 Q1: Goole Town (A) 0-0, (H) 1-0
Q2: Farsley Celtic (A) 1-0
Q3: Yorkshire Amateur (H) 2-2, (A) 2-0
Q4: Blyth Spartans (H) 2-1
R1: Oldham Athletic (A) 1-1, (H) 2-1
R2: Doncaster Rovers (H) 1-2

73-74 R1: Crewe Alexandra (A) 0-0, (H) 2-1
R2: Port Vale (A) 1-2

74-75 Q4: Blyth Spartans (A) 1-3

75-76 R1: Morecambe (H) 2-0
R2: Preston North End (H) 3-2
R3: Crystal Palace (H) 1-2

76-77 R1: Darlington (H) 0-0, (A) 1-4

77-78 R1: Rochdale (H) 4-2
R2: Crewe Alexandra (A) 0-0, (H) 2-0
R3: Brighton & Hove Albion (A) 0-3

78-79 R1: Chorley (A) 1-0
R2: York City (A) 0-3

79-80 R1: Halifax Town (A) 0-2

80-81 R1: Burnley (A) 0-1

81-82 Q4: Blyth Spartans (H) 2-3

82-83 Q4: Spennymoor United (H) 4-2
R1: Tranmere Rovers (A) 2-4

83-84 Q4: Bangor City (A) 1-2

84-85 Q4: Tow Law Town (A) 0-1

85-86 Q1: Bridlington Town (A) 1-0
Q2: Crook Town (A) 1-0
Q3: Blyth Spartans (A) 1-1, (H) 3-1
Q4: Bishop Auckland (H) 4-1
R1: Notts County (A) 1-6

86-87 Q1: Goole Town (A) 1-2

87-88 R1: Grimsby Town (H) 1-2

88-89 R1: Stockport County (H) 2-1
R2: Carlisle United (H) 0-1

89-90 R1: Whitley Bay (H) 0-1

90-91 R1: Leek Town (H) 0-2

91-92 R1: Wigan Athletic (H) 0-2

92-93 R1: Burnley (A) 1-2

SCUNTHORPE UNITED

Currently: Football League

45-46 Q2: Bye
Q3: Lysaght's Sports (H) 4-1
Q4: Yorkshire Amateur (H) 1-2

46-47 PR: Norton Woodseats (H) 5-2
Q1: Harworth Colliery Athletic (H) 5-2
Q2: Rawmarsh Welfare (A) 3-0
Q3: Wombwell Athletic (A) 5-2
Q4: Boston United (H) 4-1
R1: York City (A) 1-0
R2: Rotherham United (A) 1-4

47-48 PR: Sheffield (H) 5-1
Q1: Rawmarsh Welfare (H) 8-0
Q2: Denaby United (H) 1-0
Q3: Norton Woodseats (H) 2-1
Q4: Gainsborough Trinity (H) 4-2
R1: Runcorn (A) 2-4

48-49 Q4: Selby Town (H) 2-1
R1: Halifax Town (A) 0-0, (H) 1-0
R2: Stockport County (H) 0-1

49-50 Q4: Goole Town (H) 0-0, (A) 1-3

50-51 Q4: Hereford United (A) 0-1

51-52 R1: Billingham Synthonia Recreation (H) 5-0
R2: Millwall (A) 0-0, (H) 3-0
R3: Tottenham Hotspur (H) 0-3

52-53 R1: Carlisle United (H) 1-0
R2: Hereford United (A) 0-0, (H) 2-1
R3: Sunderland (A) 1-1, (H) 1-2

53-54 R1: Boston United (H) 9-0
R2: Bournemouth & Boscombe Ath. (H) 1-0
R3: Wrexham (A) 3-3, (H) 3-0
R4: Portsmouth (H) 1-1, (A) 2-2, 0-4

54-55 R1: Horden Colliery Welfare (A) 1-0
R2: Coventry City (A) 0-4

55-56 R1: Shildon (H) 3-0
R2: Bishop Auckland (A) 0-0, (H) 2-0
R3: Rotherham United (A) 1-1, (H) 4-2
R4: Liverpool (A) 3-3, (H) 1-2

56-57 R1: Rochdale (H) 1-0
R2: Wrexham (H) 0-0, (A) 2-6

57-58 R1: Goole Town (H) 2-1
R2: Bury (H) 2-0
R3: Bradford City (H) 1-0
R4: Newcastle United (A) 3-1
R5: Liverpool (H) 0-1

58-59 R3: Bolton Wanderers (H) 0-2

59-60 R3: Crystal Palace (H) 1-0
R4: Port Vale (H) 0-1

60-61 R3: Blackpool (H) 6-2
R4: Norwich City (H) 1-4

61-62 R3: Charlton Athletic (A) 0-1

62-63 R3: Portsmouth (A) 1-1, (H) 1-2

63-64 R3: Barnsley (H) 2-2, (A) 2-3

64-65 R1: Darlington (H) 1-2

65-66 R1: Crewe Alexandra (A) 0-3

66-67 R1: Lincoln City (A) 4-3
R2: Mansfield Town (A) 1-2

67-68 R1: Skelmersdale United (H) 2-0
R2: Halifax Town (A) 0-1

68-69 R1: Workington (A) 0-2

69-70 R1: Macclesfield Town (A) 1-1, (H) 4-2
R2: Stockport County (A) 0-0, (H) 4-0
R3: Millwall (H) 2-1
R4: Sheffield Wednesday (A) 2-1
R5: Swindon Town (A) 1-3

70-71 R1: Tranmere (A) 1-1, (H) 0-0, (*at Everton*) 1-0
R2: Mansfield Town (H) 3-0
R3: West Bromwich Albion (A) 0-0, (H) 1-3

71-72 R1: South Shields (A) 3-3, (H) 2-3

72-73 R1: Hartlepool United (A) 0-0, (H) 0-0, (*at Sunderland*) 2-1
R2: Halifax Town (H) 3-2
R3: Cardiff City (H) 2-3

73-74 R1: Darlington (H) 1-0
R2: Mansfield Town (A) 1-1, (H) 1-0
R3: Millwall (A) 1-1, (H) 1-0

Above: *Scunthorpe United were denied a trip to Anfield to face Liverpool when they lost a replay at non-League Altrincham in 1980 by a single goal. Here Barry Whitbread almost gets a second for the Alliance Premier Leaguers from a cross by Barry Howard. Photo: John Rooney.*

R4: Newcastle United (A) 1-1, (H) 0-3

74-75 R1: Altrincham (H) 1-1, (A) 1-3

75-76 R1: Preston North End (A) 1-2

76-77 R1: Chesterfield (H) 1-2

77-78 R1: Stockport County (A) 0-3

78-79 R1: Sheffield Wednesday (H) 1-1, (A) 0-1

79-80 R1: Rochdale (A) 1-2

80-81 R1: Hartlepool United (H) 3-1
R2: Altrincham (H) 0-0, (A) 0-1

81-82 R1: Bradford City (H) 1-0
R2: Crewe Alexandra (A) 3-1
R3: Hereford United (H) 1-1, (A) 1-4

82-83 R1: Darlington (A) 1-0
R2: Northwich Victoria (H) 2-1
R3: Grimsby Town (H) 0-0, (A) 0-2

83-84 R1: Preston North End (H) 1-0
R2: Bury (H) 2-0
R3: Leeds Utd (A) 1-1, (H) 1-1, (H) 4-2
R4: West Bromwich Albion (A) 0-1

84-85 R1: Nuneaton Borough (A) 1-1, (H) 2-1
R2: Port Vale (A) 1-4

85-86 R1: Halifax Town (A) 3-1
R2: Rochdale (H) 2-2, (A) 1-2

86-87 R1: Southport (H) 2-0
R2: Runcorn (H) 1-0
R3: Tottenham Hotspur (A) 2-3

87-88 R1: Bury (H) 3-1
R2: Sunderland (H) 2-1
R3: Blackpool (H) 0-0, (A) 0-1

88-89 R1: Blackpool (A) 1-2

89-90 R1: Matlock Town (H) 4-1
R2: Burnley (H) 2-2, (A) 1-1, (A) 0-5

90-91 R1: Rochdale (A) 1-1, (H) 2-1
R2: Tranmere Rovers (H) 3-2
R3: Brighton & Hove Albion (A) 2-3

91-92 R1: Rotherham Utd (H) 1-1, (A) 3-3 (*6-7 pens*)

92-93 R1: Huddersfield Town (H) 0-0, (A) 1-2

SEAHAM COLLIERY WELF.

Currently: Defunct

45-46 Q1: Blackhall C.W. (A) 2-4

46-47 PR: Dawdon Colliery (H) 7-0
Q1: West Auckland Town (A) 3-0
Q2: Brandon C.W. (A) 1-1, (H) 2-0
Q3: Spennymoor United (H) 0-4

47-48 PR: Langley Park C.W. (H) 5-1
Q1: Evenwood Town (A) 1-3

48-49 EX: Shotton Colliery Welfare (A) 4-1
PR: Tow Law Town (A) 1-0
Q1: Evenwood Town (A) 1-3

49-50 PR: Shildon (H) 1-1, (A) 3-2
Q1: Easington Colliery Welf. (H) 1-1, (A) 1-2

50-51 EX: Eppleton Colliery Welfare (H) 1-2

51-52 Q1: Horden Colliery Welfare (A) 1-9

52-53 Q1: Horden Colliery Welfare (H) 1-3

53-54 Q1: Chilton Athletic (H) 2-2, (A) 2-0
Q2: Horden Colliery Welfare (H) 0-2

54-55 Q1: Annfield Plain (H) 1-2

55-56 Q1: Easington Colliery Welfare (H) 1-3

SEAHAM RED STAR

Currently: Northern League
* - As Seaham Colliery Welfare Red Star

81-82 * Q1: Guisborough Town (A) 3-2
Q2: North Shields (H) 0-1

82-83 * Q1: Billingham Synthonia (A) 1-0
Q2: Spennymoor United (A) 1-2

83-84 * PR: Bridlington Trinity (H) 7-0
Q1: Gateshead (H) 1-3

84-85 * Q1: Tow Law Town (H) 3-3, (A) 1-3

85-86 * PR: Farsley Celtic (A) 0-2

86-87 * PR: Ashington (A) 2-3

87-88 PR: Shildon (H) 2-0
Q1: Murton (A) 1-0
Q2: Bishop Auckland (H) 0-1

88-89 Q1: Accrington Stanley (H) 0-0, (A) 1-2

89-90 PR: Easington Colliery (H) 1-0
Q1: Prudhoe East End (A) 0-0, (H) 3-2
Q2: Bridlington Town (A) 1-2

90-91 Q1: Evenwood Town (H) 1-1, (A) 1-0
Q2: Consett (H) 1-1, (A) 0-2

91-92 PR: Peterlee Newtown (H) 3-2
Q1: Shildon (H) 3-0 *expelled*

92-93 PR: Yorkshire Amateur (A) 3-1
Q1: Eccleshill United (H) 3-2
Q2: Maine Road (H) 1-1, (A) 1-1, (A) 5-0
Q3: Stockton (H) 1-2

SEAHAM UNITED

Currently: Defunct

48-49 EX: Tow Law Town (A) 2-7

49-50 EX: Willington (A) 0-8

SELBY TOWN

Currently: Northern Counties (East) League

46-47 PR: Meltham Mills (H) 6-0
Q1: Thorne Colliery (H) 0-0, (A) 1-2

47-48 Q1: Frickley Colliery (A) 3-1
Q2: Bradford United (H) 3-1
Q3: Goole Town (H) 0-5

48-49 PR: Laceby (H) 4-2
Q1: Yorkshire Amateur (A) 4-0
Q2: Ossett Town (A) 4-1
Q3: Frickley Colliery (H) 2-0
Q4: Scunthorpe United (A) 1-2

49-50 PR: Lysaght's Sports (A) 5-0
Q1: Brigg Town (H) 2-1
Q2: Brodsworth Main Colliery (H) 0-1

50-51 PR: South Kirkby Colliery (H) 4-1
Q1: Ossett Town (A) 3-1
Q2: Farsley Celtic (H) 2-3

51-52 Q1: Farsley Celtic (H) 1-1, (A) 2-4

52-53 Q2: Yorkshire Amateur (H) 2-1
Q3: Goole Town (H) 4-1
Q4: Linby Colliery (H) 4-2
R1: Bishop Auckland (H) 1-5

53-54 Q2: Yorkshire Amateur (A) 3-3, (H) 4-1
Q3: Goole Town (A) 3-1
Q4: Frickley Colliery (H) 2-1
R1: Bradford (Park Avenue) (H) 0-2

54-55 Q4: Gainsborough Trinity (H) 4-2
R1: Rhyl (H) 2-1
R2: Hastings United (H) 0-2

55-56 Q4: Goole Town (H) 2-4

56-57 Q4: Stocksbridge Works (H) 3-1
R1: Hartlepools United (A) 1-3

57-58 Q4: Scarborough (A) 2-2, (H) 2-2, (A) 0-1

58-59 Q1: Farsley Celtic (A) 3-1
Q2: Stocksbridge Works (A) 1-1, (H) 1-2

59-60 Q1: Denaby United (H) 1-3

60-61 Q1: Yorkshire Amateur (H) 3-2
Q2: Retford Town (A) 2-1
Q3: Frickley Colliery (H) 1-3

61-62 Q1: Frickley Colliery (H) 4-1
Q2: Harrogate Town (A) 2-1
Q3: Goole Town (A) 2-2, (H) 1-0
Q4: Gateshead (H) 1-1, (H) 0-3

62-63 Q1: Ossett Albion (H) 1-5

63-64 Q1: Goole Town (H) 0-0, (A) 2-3

64-65 Q1: Bridlington Trinity (H) 1-6

65-66 Q1: Bridlington Trinity (A) 2-3

66-67 Q1: Bridlington Town (A) 0-4

67-68 PR: Thorne Colliery (A) 4-3
Q1: Bridlington Trinity (A) 2-1
Q2: Goole Town (A) 0-2

68-69 Q1: Ashby Institute (A) 3-0
Q2: Hull Brunswick (H) 2-1
Q3: Goole Town (A) 0-5

69-70 PR: Winterton Rangers (A) 2-5

70-71 Q1: Winterton Rangers (A) 1-3

71-72 Q1: Goole Town (A) 0-3

72-73 Q1: Yorkshire Amateur (H) 0-2

75-76 Q1: Louth United (H) 1-0
Q2: Retford Town (H) 0-2

76-77 Q1: Bridlington Trinity (H) 0-2

77-78 Q1: Denaby United (H) 3-1
Q2: Goole Town (A) 0-7

78-79 PR: North Ferriby United (A) 0-2

79-80 Q1: Bridlington Trinity (H) 0-1

SELSEY

Currently: Sussex County League

67-68 Q1: Waterlooville (A) 2-2, (H) 3-2
Q2: Newport Isle of Wight (H) 1-3

68-69 PR: Andover (H) 1-0
Q1: Newport Isle of Wight (A) 2-3

69-70 Q1: Waterlooville (H) 3-4

70-71 Q1: Chichester City (H) 2-4

71-72 Q1: Fareham Town (A) 2-8

76-77 Q1: Horsham (A) 0-4

Above: *Bruising early season Qualifying Round action as Unijet Sussex County League side Selsey attack during their surprise win over Diadora Isthmian club Malden Vale on 31st August 1991. Photo: Graham Cotterill.*

77-78 Q1: Poole Town (A) 1-4

78-79 Q1: Tunbridge Wells (H) 2-3

79-80 PR: Newport Isle of Wight (A) 0-4

90-91 PR: Peacehaven & Telscombe (A) 1-8

91-92 PR: Malden Vale (H) 2-1
Q1: Andover (H) 2-1
Q2: Romsey Town (H) 1-6

92-93 PR: Egham Town (A) 1-2

SEVERALLS ATHLETIC

Currently: Defunct

45-46 PR: Barking (A) *withdrew*

SHAFTESBURY

Currently: Dorset Combination

50-51 EX: Bournemouth Gasworks Athletic (A) 2-1
PR: Alton Town (H) 1-5

51-52 Q1: Poole Town (H) 1-4

52-53 Q1: Portland United (A) 1-3

53-54 Q1: Portland United (A) 1-11

SHANKHOUSE

Currently: Northern Alliance

45-46 Q1: Consett (A) 0-6

48-49 EX: Alnwick Town (H) 4-1
PR: Radcliffe Welfare United (A) 5-1
Q1: Annfield Plain (A) 1-7

49-50 EX: Newburn (H) 1-4

50-51 EX: Cramlington Welfare (H) 2-6

51-52 Q1: Amble (A) 4-3
Q2: Alnwick Town (A) 0-2

52-53 Q1: Newburn (A) 1-4

53-54 Q1: Alnwick Town (A) 0-9

54-55 PR: Alnwick Town (H) 5-1
Q1: North Shields (H) 1-5

SHARPNESS

Currently: Gloucestershire Senior League (North)

85-86 PR: Shortwood Utd (A) 1-1, (H) 1-1, (H) 5-1
Q1: Saltash United (A) 2-1
Q2: Chippenham Town (H) 2-3

86-87 Q1: Llanelli (H) 4-1
Q2: Ton Pentre (H) 0-1

87-88 Q1: Ottery St Mary (H) 1-4

88-89 PR: Minehead (A) 4-0
Q1: Merthyr Tydfil (A) 0-3

89-90 PR: Chippenham Town (H) 1-1, (A) 0-1

90-91 PR: Maestep Park Athletic (H) *withdrew*

SHEFFIELD

Currently: Northern Counties (East) League

46-47 PR: Matlock Town (A) 5-2
Q1: Wombwell Athletic (H) 2-4

47-48 PR: Scunthorpe United (A) 1-5

48-49 PR: Cresswell Colliery (A) 0-2

49-50 PR: Denaby United (A) 1-3

50-51 PR: Worksop Town (A) 1-2

51-52 Q1: Upton Colliery (A) 3-3, (H) 0-2

52-53 Q1: Grimethorpe Athletic (A) 1-3

53-54 Q1: Stocksbridge (H) 2-2, (A) 0-0, 1-1, 3-1
Q2: Frickley Colliery (A) 1-2

54-55 Q1: Hallam (A) 3-1
Q2: Upton Colliery (A) 2-3

55-56 Q1: Stocksbridge Works (A) 2-8

56-57 Q2: Norton Woodseats Amateur (A) 1-2

57-58 Q2: Hallam (A) 2-5

58-59 Q1: Belper Town (A) 3-2
Q2: South Normanton Welfare (A) 4-1
Q3: Norton Woodseats Amateur (H) 2-0
Q4: Boston United (H) 0-3

59-60 Q1: Worksop Town (H) 2-3

89-90 PR: Armthorpe Welfare (H) 1-0
Q1: Hyde United (H) 0-1

90-91 PR: Armthorpe Welfare (A) 0-3

91-92 PR: Congleton Town (H) 2-0
Q1: Knowsley United (A) 0-2

92-93 PR: Rossendale (H - *played away*) 2-2, (A) 2-1
Q1: Thackley (H - *played away*) 3-1
Q2: Altrincham (A) 1-3

SHEFFIELD UNITED

Currently: F.A. Premier League

45-46 R3: Huddersfield (A) 1-1, (H) 2-0 (*agg: 3-1*)
R4: Stoke City (A) 0-2, (H) 3-2 (*agg: 3-4*)

46-47 R3: Carlisle United (H) 3-0
R4: Wolverhampton W. (A) 0-0, (H) 2-0
R5: Stoke City (A) 1-0
R6: Newcastle United (H) 0-2

47-48 R3: Crewe Alexandra (A) 1-3

48-49 R3: New Brighton (H) 5-2
R4: Wolverhampton Wanderers (H) 0-3

49-50 R3: Leicester City (H) 3-1
R4: Wolverhampton W. (A) 0-0, (H) 3-4

50-51 R3: Gateshead (H) 1-0
R4: Mansfield Town (H) 0-0, (A) 1-2

51-52 R3: Newport County (H) 2-0
R4: West Ham United (A) 0-0, (H) 4-2
R5: Southend United (A) 2-1
R6: Chelsea (H) 0-1

52-53 R3: Newport County (A) 4-1
R4: Birmingham City (H) 1-1, (A) 1-3

53-54 R3: Sheffield Wednesday (A) 1-1, (H) 1-3

54-55 R3: Nottingham Forest (H) 1-3

55-56 R3: Barrow (H) 5-0
R4: Bolton Wanderers (A) 2-1
R5: Sunderland (H) 0-0, (A) 0-1

56-57 R3: Huddersfield T. (A) 0-0, (H) 1-1, 1-2

57-58 R3: Grimsby Town (H) 5-1
R4: Tottenham Hotspur (A) 3-0
R5: West Bromwich A. (H) 1-1, (A) 1-4

58-59 R3: Crystal Palace (H) 2-0
R4: Worcester City (A) 2-0
R5: Arsenal (A) 2-2, (H) 3-0
R6: Norwich City (H) 1-1, (A) 2-3

59-60 R3: Portsmouth (H) 3-0
R4: Nottingham Forest (H) 3-0
R5: Watford (H) 3-2
R6: Sheffield Wednesday (H) 0-2

60-61 R3: Everton (A) 1-0
R4: Lincoln City (H) 3-1
R5: Blackburn Rovers (H) 2-1
R6: Newcastle United (A) 3-1
SF: Leicester City (*at Leeds United*) 0-0, (*at Nottm Forest*) 0-0, (*at Birm'ham C.*) 0-2

61-62 R3: Bury (A) 0-0, (H) 2-2, 2-0
R4: Peterborough United (A) 3-1
R5: Norwich City (H) 3-1
R6: Burnley (H) 0-1

62-63 R3: Bolton Wanderers (H) 3-1
R4: Port Vale (A) 2-1
R5: Southampton (A) 0-1

63-64 R3: Lincoln City (A) 4-0
R4: Swansea Town (H) 1-1, (A) 0-4

64-65 R3: Bristol City (A) 1-1, (H) 3-0
R4: Aston Villa (H) 0-2

65-66 R3: Fulham (H) 3-1
R4: Wolverhampton Wanderers (A) 0-3

66-67 R3: Charlton Athletic (A) 1-0
R4: Fulham (A) 1-1, (H) 3-1
R5: Chelsea (A) 0-2

67-68 R3: Watford (A) 1-0
R4: Blackpool (H) 2-1
R5: West Ham United (A) 2-1
R6: Leeds United (A) 0-1

68-69 R3: Mansfield Town (A) 1-2

69-70 R3: Everton (H) 2-1
R4: Derby County (A) 0-3

70-71 R3: Portsmouth (A) 0-2

71-72 R3: Cardiff City (H) 1-3

72-73 R3: Watford (A) 1-0
R4: Carlisle United (A) 1-2

73-74 R3: Ipswich Town (A) 2-3

74-75 R3: Bristol City (H) 2-0
R4: Aston Villa (A) 1-4

75-76 R3: Leicester City (A) 0-3

76-77 R3: Newcastle United (H) 0-0, (A) 1-3

77-78 R3: Arsenal (H) 0-5

78-79 R3: Aldershot (H) 0-0, (A) 0-1

79-80 R1: Burscough (A - *played home*) 3-0
R2: Grimsby Town (A) 0-2

80-81 R1: Stockport County (A) 0-0, (H) 3-2
R2: Chesterfield (H) 1-1, (A) 0-1

81-82 R1: Altrincham (H) 2-2, (A) 0-3

82-83 R1: Hull City (A) 1-1, (H) 2-0
R2: Boston United (A) 1-1, (H) 5-1
R3: Stoke City (H) 0-0, (A) 2-3

83-84 R1: Wrexham (A) 5-1
R2: Lincoln City (A) 0-0, (H) 1-0
R3: Birmingham City (H) 1-1, (A) 0-2

84-85 R3: Watford (A) 0-5

Above: *Jamie Hoyland celebrates as Sheffield United surprise Man United in February 1993. Photo: Colorsport*

85-86 R3: Fulham (H) 2-0
R4: Derby County (H) 0-1

86-87 R3: Brighton & Hove A. (H) 0-0, (A) 2-1
R4: West Ham United (A) 0-4

87-88 R3: Maidstone United (H) 1-0
R4: Portsmouth (A) 1-2

88-89 R1: Mansfield Town (A) 1-1, (H) 2-1
R2: Doncaster Rovers (A) 3-1
R3: Huddersfield Town (A) 1-0
R4: Colchester United (H) 3-3, (A) 2-0
R5: Norwich City (A) 2-3

89-90 R3: A.F.C. Bournemouth (H) 2-0
R4: Watford (H) 1-1, (A) 2-1
R5: Barnsley (H) 2-2, (A) 0-0, (A) 1-0
R6: Manchester United (H) 0-1

90-91 R3: Luton Town (H) 1-3

91-92 R3: Luton Town (H) 4-0
R4: Charlton (A - *at West Ham*) 0-0, (H) 3-1
R5: Chelsea (A) 0-1

92-93 R3: Burnley (H) 2-2, (A) 4-2
R4: Hartlepool United (H) 1-0
R5: Manchester United (H) 2-1
R6: Blackburn (A) 0-0, (H) 2-2 (*5-4 pens*)
SF: Sheffield Wednesday (*at Wembley*) 1-2

SHEFFIELD WEDNESDAY

Currently: F.A. Premier League

45-46 R3: Mansfield T. (A) 0-0, (H) 5-0 (*agg: 5-0*)
R4: York City (H) 5-1, (A) 6-1 (*agg: 11-2*)
R5: Stoke City (A) 0-2, (H) 0-0 (*agg: 0-2*)

46-47 R3: Blackpool (H) 4-1
R4: Everton (H) 2-1
R5: Preston North End (H) 0-2

47-48 R3: Cardiff City (A) 2-1
R4: Leicester City (A) 1-2

48-49 R3: Southampton (H) 2-1
R4: Portsmouth (A) 1-2

49-50 R3: Arsenal (A) 0-1

50-51 R3: Fulham (A) 0-1

51-52 R3: Bradford (Park Avenue) (A) 1-2

52-53 R3: Blackpool (H) 1-2

53-54 R3: Sheffield United (H) 1-1, (A) 3-1
R4: Chesterfield (H) 0-0, (A) 4-2
R5: Everton (H) 3-1
R6: Bolton Wanderers (H) 1-1, (A) 2-0
SF: Preston N.E. (*at Manchester City*) 0-2

54-55 R3: Hastings United (H) 2-1
R4: Notts County (H) 1-1, (A) 0-1

55-56 R3: Newcastle United (H) 1-3

56-57 R3: Preston (A) 0-0, (H) 2-2, (*at Everton*) 1-5

57-58 R3: Hereford United (A) 3-0
R4: Hull City (H) 4-3

R5: Manchester United (A) 0-3

58-59 R3: West Bromwich Albion (H) 0-2

59-60 R3: Middlesbrough (H) 2-1
R4: Peterborough United (H) 2-0
R5: Manchester United (A) 1-0
R6: Sheffield United (A) 2-0
SF: Blackburn Rovers (*at Manchester C.*) 1-2

60-61 R3: Leeds United (H) 2-0
R4: Manchester United (H) 1-1, (A) 7-2
R5: Leyton Orient (A) 2-0
R6: Burnley (H) 0-0, (A) 0-2

61-62 R3: Swansea Town (H) 1-0
R4: Nottingham Forest (A) 2-0
R5: Manchester United (A) 0-0, (H) 0-2

62-63 R3: Shrewsbury Town (A) 1-1, (H) 2-1
R4: Arsenal (A) 0-2

63-64 R3: Newport County (A) 2-3

64-65 R3: Everton (A) 2-2, (H) 0-3

65-66 R3: Reading (A) 3-2
R4: Newcastle United (A) 2-1
R5: Huddersfield Town (A) 2-1
R6: Blackburn Rovers (A) 2-1
SF: Chelsea (*at Aston Villa*) 2-0
F: Everton (*at Wembley*) 2-3

66-67 R3: Queens Park Rangers (H) 3-0
R4: Mansfield Town (H) 4-0
R5: Norwich City (A) 3-1
R6: Chelsea (A) 0-1

67-68 R3: Plymouth Argyle (H) 3-0
R4: Swindon Town (H) 2-1
R5: Chelsea (H) 2-2, (A) 0-2

68-69 R3: Leeds United (H) 1-1, (A) 3-1
R4: Birmingham City (H) 2-2, (A) 1-2

69-70 R3: West Bromwich Albion (H) 2-1
R4: Scunthorpe United (H) 1-2

70-71 R3: Tottenham Hotspur (A) 1-4

71-72 R3: Sunderland (A) 0-3

72-73 R3: Fulham (H) 2-0
R4: Crystal P. (H) 1-1, (A) 1-1, (*at Aston V.*) 3-2
R5: Chelsea (H) 1-2

73-74 R3: Coventry City (H) 0-0, (A) 1-3

74-75 R3: Chelsea (A) 2-3

75-76 R1: Macclesfield Town (H) 3-1
R2: Wigan Athletic (H) 2-0
R3: Charlton Athletic (A) 1-2

76-77 R1: Stockport County (H) 2-0
R2: Darlington (A) 0-1

77-78 R1: Bury (H) 1-0
R2: Wigan Athletic (A) 0-1

78-79 R1: Scunthorpe United (A) 1-1, (H) 1-0
R2: Tranmere Rovers (A) 1-1, (H) 4-0
R3: Arsenal (A) 1-1, (H) 1-1, (*at Leicester*) 2-2, 3-3 (*at Leicester*), (*at Leicester*) 0-2

79-80 R1: Lincoln City (H) 3-0
R2: Carlisle United (A) 0-3

80-81 R3: Newcastle United (A) 1-2

81-82 R3: Coventry City (A) 1-3

82-83 R3: Southend U. (A) 0-0, (H) 2-2, (H) 2-1
R4: Torquay United (A) 3-2
R5: Cambridge United (A) 2-1
R6: Burnley (A) 1-1, (H) 5-0
SF: Brighton & Hove Albion (*at Arsenal*) 1-2

83-84 R3: Barnsley (H) 1-0
R4: Coventry City (H) 3-2
R5: Oxford United (A) 3-0
R6: Southampton (H) 0-0, (A) 1-5

84-85 R3: Fulham (A) 3-2
R4: Oldham Athletic (H) 5-1
R5: Ipswich Town (A) 2-3

85-86 R3: West Bromwich Albion (H) 2-2, (A) 3-2
R4: Orient (H) 5-0
R5: Derby County (A) 1-1, (H) 2-0
R6: West Ham United (H) 2-1
SF: Everton (*at Aston Villa*) 1-2

86-87 R3: Derby County (H) 1-0
R4: Chester City (A) 1-1, (H) 3-1
R5: West Ham United (H) 1-1, (A) 2-0
R6: Coventry City (H) 1-3

87-88 R3: Everton (H) 1-1, (A) 1-1, (A) 1-1, (H) 0-5

88-89 R3: Torquay United (H) 5-1

Above: *David Hirst scores Wednesday's Cup Final equaliser against Arsenal in May 1993. Photo: Colorsport*

R4: Blackburn Rovers (A) 1-2

89-90 R3: Wolverhampton Wanderers (A) 2-1
R4: Everton (H) 1-2

90-91 R3: Mansfield Town (A) 2-0
R4: Millwall (A) 4-4, (H) 2-0
R5: Cambridge United (A) 0-4

91-92 R3: Preston North End (A) 2-0
R4: Middlesbrough (H) 1-2

92-93 R3: Cambridge United (A) 2-1
R4: Sunderland (H) 1-0
R5: Southend United (H) 2-0
R6: Derby County (A) 3-3, (H) 1-0
SF: Sheffield United *(at Wembley)* 2-1
F: Arsenal *(both at Wembley)* 1-1, 1-2

SHEFFORD TOWN

Currently: South Midlands League

50-51 EX: Huntingdon United (H) 3-3, (A) 4-5

54-55 PR: Letchworth Town (H) 1-0
Q1: Hoddesdon Town (H) 2-5

55-56 PR: Ware (A) 2-7

56-57 Q1: Hitchin Town (H) 2-6

57-58 PR: Clapton (H) 2-8

SHELL (ELLESMERE PORT)

Currently: West Cheshire League

48-49 EX: Macclesfield Town (A) 3-6

49-50 EX: Atherton Collieries (H) 5-1
PR: Congleton Town (H) 3-6

SHEPPEY UNITED

Currently: Kent League

45-46 Q1: Bromley (H) 1-5

46-47 PR: Dartford (A) 5-2
Q1: Woolwich Polytechnic (A) 0-0, (H) 1-3

47-48 PR: Bexley (H) 3-2
Q1: Ramsgate Athletic (A) 2-4

48-49 PR: Margate (H) 5-4
Q1: Dover (H) 2-4

49-50 EX: Ashford (H) 1-0
PR: Gravesend & Northfleet (A) 0-4

50-51 PR: Gravesend & Northfleet (A) 2-5

51-52 PR: Betteshanger Colliery Welfare (H) 1-3

52-53 PR: Bowater Lloyds (H) 5-1
Q1: Dover (A) 0-2

53-54 PR: Maidstone United (H) 2-2, (A) 1-3

54-55 PR: Tonbridge (A) 0-6

55-56 PR: Maidstone United (A) 1-1, (H) 0-4

56-57 PR: Margate (A) 1-8

57-58 PR: Sittingbourne (H) 2-5

58-59 Q1: Gravesend & Northfleet (H) 2-6

59-60 PR: Chatham Town (A) 3-0
Q1: Dartford (A) 1-4

60-61 Q1: Sittingbourne (H) 1-4

61-62 Q1: Erith & Belvedere (H) 2-2, (A) 1-2

62-63 Q1: Dover (H) 0-1

63-64 Q1: Dover (A) 2-1
Q2: Folkestone Town (A) 0-2

64-65 Q1: Ashford Town (H) 0-1

65-66 Q1: Cray Wanderers (A) 1-0
Q2: Bexley United (H) 1-3

67-68 Q1: Deal Town (A) 0-2

68-69 Q1: Herne Bay (H) 1-1, (A) 5-3
Q2: Margate (H) 0-6

69-70 Q1: Bretts Sports (H) 3-1
Q2: Hastings United (H) 0-6

70-71 Q1: Ramsgate Athletic (H) 1-4

71-72 Q1: Folkestone (A) 2-6

72-73 PR: Dover (H) 2-2, (A) 0-1

73-74 Q1: Faversham Town (H) 2-3

74-75 Q1: Dover (H) 1-3

75-76 Q1: Whitstable Town (H) 5-1
Q2: Canterbury City (A) 2-6

76-77 Q1: Margate (H) 2-2, (A) 0-2

77-78 PR: Bexhill Town (H) 1-2

78-79 Q1: Canterbury City (H) 1-4

79-80 Q1: Ramsgate (H) 1-1, (A) 2-5

80-81 Q1: Welling United (A) 2-4

81-82 PR: Whitstable Town (A) 2-2, (H) 1-2

82-83 PR: Ashford Town (A) 2-0
Q1: Welling United (A) 0-2

83-84 Q1: Egham Town (A) 1-2

84-85 Q1: Whitehawk (H) 2-0
Q2: Hastings United (H) 0-1

85-86 PR: Fleet Town (A) 2-0
Q1: Fisher Ath. (H) 1-1, (A) 2-2, (H) 0-4

86-87 PR: Chichester City (H) 2-1
Q1: Waterlooville (A) 1-0
Q2: Newport I.O.W. (H) 1-1, (A) 0-1

87-88 PR: Metropolitan Police (H) 1-3

88-89 PR: Maidenhead United (H) 1-1, (A) 1-0
Q1: Bromley (H) 1-4

89-90 PR: Egham Town (A) 1-4

90-91 PR: Pagham (H) 0-2

91-92 PR: Shoreham (A) 3-0
Q1: Hailsham Town (A) 1-1, (H) 4-1
Q2: Crawley Town (A) 0-2

92-93 PR: Croydon (H - *at Faversham Town*) 0-1

SHEPSHED ALBION

Currently: Midland Combination
***** - As Shepshed Charterhouse

49-50 PR: Atherstone Town (H) 0-0, (A) 2-8

81-82 * Q1: Kidderminster Harriers (A) 2-1
Q2: Tamworth (A) 2-2, (H) 3-1
Q3: Willenhall Town (H) 1-5

82-83 * PR: Denaby United (A) 3-1
Q1: Alfreton Town (A) 4-0
Q2: Goole Town (A) 2-0
Q3: Gainsborough Trinity (H) 3-2
Q4: King's Lynn (H) 2-1
R1: Preston North End (A) 1-5

83-84 * Q1: Hinckley Athletic (A) 1-0
Q2: Winsford United (A) 1-3

84-85 * Q1: Bromsgrove Rovers (A) 5-2
Q2: Gainsborough Trinity (H) 2-5

85-86 * Q1: Irthlingborough Diamonds (A) 2-3

86-87 * Q1: Stafford Rangers (H) 0-1

87-88 * Q1: Stourbridge (H) 2-0
Q2: Boldmere St Michaels (A) 2-1
Q3: Tamworth (A) 2-3

88-89 * Q1: Witney Town (H) 3-2
Q2: Leicester United (A) 0-1

89-90 * Q1: Brackley Town (A) 1-2

90-91 * Q1: Lye Town (H) 3-1
Q2: Buckingham Town (A) 4-2
Q3: Atherstone United (H) 2-3

91-92 Q1: Stourbridge (H) 2-0
Q2: Hinckley Town (A) 3-3, (H) 3-2
Q3: Burton Albion (A) 2-3

92-93 Q1: Arlesey Town (A) 1-0
Q2: Stourbridge (A) 0-0, (H) 4-2
Q3: Hednesford Town (H) 1-2

SHEPTON MALLET TOWN

Currently: Somerset Senior League

78-79 Q1: Llanelli (A) 3-1
Q2: Trowbridge Town (H) 1-2

79-80 PR: Ilminster Town (A) 0-0, (H) 0-1

80-81 PR: Welton Rovers (H) 2-1
Q1: Clevedon Town (H) 0-4

81-82 Q1: Devizes Town (A) 0-1

82-83 Q1: Torrington (H) 3-0
Q2: Bideford (A) 1-3

83-84 Q1: Bath City (A) 0-4

84-85 PR: Chard Town (A) 2-0
Q1: Poole Town (A) 1-2

85-86 PR: St Blazey (A) 0-1

SHERINGHAM

Currently: Anglian Combination

47-48 Q1: Gothic (A) 1-3

48-49 PR: Lowestoft Town (A) 0-6

49-50 PR: Stowmarket (H) 0-1

50-51 EX: Felixstowe United (H) 3-1
PR: Gothic (H) 0-3

51-52 Q1: Gothic (H) 0-2

52-53 Q2: Beccles (H) 2-2, (A) 1-2

53-54 Q1: Beccles (A) 1-7

54-55 Q1: Gorleston (A) 0-4

55-56 Q1: Great Yarmouth Town (H) 0-0, (A) 2-3

56-57 Q2: Great Yarmouth Town (H) 0-2

57-58 Q2: Gorleston (A) 0-3

58-59 Q1: Bungay Town (A) 3-4

59-60 Q1: Lowestoft Town (A) 2-6

60-61 PR: Lowestoft Town (A) 1-5

61-62 Q1: Lowestoft Town (H) 3-5

SHERWOOD COLLIERY

Currently: Defunct

48-49 PR: Ilkeston Town (A) 0-3

49-50 EX: South Normanton Welfare (H) 0-3

50-51 EX: Ilkeston Town (H) 0-8

SHIFNAL TOWN

Currently: Midland Combination

81-82 PR: New Mills (H) 5-0
Q1: Matlock Town (A) 1-1, (H) 2-0
Q2: Runcorn (H) 0-3

82-83 Q1: Leek Town (H) 1-0
Q2: Burton Albion (A) 4-2
Q3: Witton Albion (A) 2-0
Q4: Boston United (A) 1-4

83-84 Q1: Bourne Town (A) 4-1
Q2: Sutton Coldfield Town (A) 4-5

84-85 PR: Chadderton (H) 2-2, (A) 1-2

85-86 PR: Arnold (A - *at Eastwood Town*) 0-4

SHILBOTTLE COLLIERY WELF.

Currently: Northern Alliance

48-49 EX: Lynemouth Welfare (A) 2-1
PR: South Shields (H) 1-4

49-50 EX: Gosforth & Coxlodge (H) 2-3

50-51 PR: Blyth Spartans (H) 1-6

SHILDON

Currently: Northern League

45-46 PR: Usworth Colliery (H) 7-1
Q1: Ferryhill Athletic (A) 3-1
Q2: Blackhall Colliery Welfare (H) 6-1
Q3: Spennymoor United (H) 3-2
Q4: Willington (A) 2-3

46-47 PR: Easington Colliery Welfare (H) 2-2, (A) 4-2
Q1: Spennymoor United (H) 3-3, (A) 2-4

47-48 PR: Chilton Athletic (A) 3-2
Q1: Ferryhill Athletic (A) 0-1

48-49 EX: Murton Colliery Welfare (A) 2-6

49-50 PR: Seaham Colliery Welfare (A) 1-1, (H) 2-3

50-51 EX: Cockfield (A) 3-0
PR: Evenwood Town (H) 3-5

51-52 Q1: Stanley United (H) 3-0
Q2: Spennymoor United (H) 0-2

52-53 Q1: Crook Town (H) 0-4

53-54 Q1: Tow Law Town (H) 4-0
Q2: Willington (A) 0-3

54-55 Q1: Willington (H) 1-2

55-56 Q1: Stockton (H) 3-0
Q2: Willington (A) 3-3, (H) 7-3
Q3: West Auckland Town (A) 1-1, (H) 5-3
Q4: Blyth Spartans (A) 4-2
R1: Scunthorpe United (A) 0-3

56-57 Q1: West Auckland Town (H) 2-2, (A) 1-2

57-58 Q1: Shotton Colliery Welfare (A) 3-0
Q2: Bridlington Central United (A) 3-0
Q3: Willington (H) 1-2

58-59 Q1: Horden Colliery Welfare (H) 2-6

59-60 Q2: Redcar Albion (H) 4-0
Q3: North Shields (H) 2-0
Q4: Denaby United (H) 6-1
R1: Oldham Athletic (H) 1-1, (A) 0-3

60-61 Q2: Annfield Plain (A) 4-1
Q3: Horden Colliery Welfare (A) 1-5

61-62 Q1: Tow Law Town (H) 3-3, (A) 5-1
Q2: Evenwood Town (H) 4-2
Q3: Horden Colliery Welfare (H) 1-0
Q4: Crook Town (A) 2-1
R1: Oldham Athletic (A) 2-5

62-63 Q1: Durham City (H) 3-1
Q2: Bedlington Mechanics (H) 4-0
Q3: North Shields (H) 3-3, (A) 2-5

63-64 Q1: Ryhope Colliery Welfare (H) 0-1

64-65 Q1: Bishop Auckland (A) 1-4

65-66 Q1: Horden Colliery Welfare (H) 0-4

66-67 Q1: South Bank (A) 3-4

67-68 Q1: Murton C.W. (H) 3-3, (A) 1-1, 1-2

68-69 Q1: Whitley Bay (A) 1-0
Q2: Durham City (H) 3-1
Q3: North Shields (A) 1-2

69-70 Q1: Horden Colliery Welfare (A) 1-0
Q2: Crook Town (A) 4-0
Q3: Bishop Auckland (A) 1-2

70-71 Q1: Ryhope Colliery Welfare (H) 1-0
Q2: Stanley United (A) 0-1

71-72 Q1: Evenwood Town (H) 1-1, (A) 3-4

72-73 Q1: Murton Colliery Welfare (H) 3-4

73-74 Q1: Ferryhill Athletic (H) 2-1
Q2: Bishop Auckland (H) 1-3

74-75 Q1: Boldon Colliery Welfare (A) 3-2
Q2: Willington (H) 2-4

75-76 Q1: Billingham Synthonia (A) 1-1, (H) 3-2
Q2: Easington Colliery Welfare (A) 3-1
Q3: Tow Law Town (A) 1-4

76-77 Q1: Heaton Stannington (A) 3-0
Q2: Barrow (A) 1-2

77-78 Q1: Blyth Spartans (H) 0-3

78-79 Q1: Whitley Bay (H) 3-1
Q2: South Bank (H) 2-1
Q3: Gateshead (H) 1-8

79-80 PR: Wingate (H) 2-2, (A) 3-4

80-81 Q1: Brandon United (A) 0-0, (H) 1-0
Q2: Evenwood Town (A) 0-2

81-82 PR: Guisborough Town (A) 1-3

82-83 PR: Frickley Athletic (A) 3-5

83-84 PR: Chester-le-Street (A) 0-2

84-85 PR: Crook Town (H) 0-1

85-86 PR: Esh Winning (H) 3-1
Q1: Billingham Town (H) 1-2

86-87 PR: Durham City (A) 1-2

87-88 PR: Seaham Red Star (A) 0-2

88-89 PR: Willington (H) 6-2
Q1: Whitley Bay (H) 1-5

89-90 Q1: South Bank (A) 0-2

90-91 PR: Garforth Town (H) 3-1
Q1: Cleator Moor Celtic (H) 2-1
Q2: Fleetwood Town (H) 0-4

91-92 PR: Washington (A - *played home*) 3-1
Q1: Seaham R.S. (A) 0-3 *Seaham expelled*
Q2: Guiseley (A) 1-5

92-93 PR: Blackpool (Wren) Rovers (H) 2-0
Q1: Whitby Town (H) 0-2

SHIREBROOK MINERS WELFARE

Currently: Defunct
* - As Shirebrook F.C.

50-51 * EX: Sutton Town (A) 1-0
PR: Rufford Colliery (A) 2-0
Q1: Linby Colliery (A) 0-2

51-52 * Q1: Cinderhill Colliery (H) 5-1
Q2: Cresswell Colliery (H) 2-2, (A) 0-1

52-53 * Q1: Players Athletic (A) 5-8

53-54 Q1: Parliament Street Methodists (H) 5-1
Q2: Sutton Town (A) 1-1, (H) 4-3
Q3: Cresswell Colliery (A) 4-3
Q4: Boston United (H) 2-5

54-55 Q1: Cinderhill Colliery (H) 5-0
Q2: Linby Colliery (H) 0-4

55-56 Q2: Ransome & Marles (H) 3-1
Q3: Sutton Town (A) 1-4

56-57 Q1: Sutton Town (A) 2-3

57-58 Q2: Sutton Town (H) 2-3

58-59 Q1: Retford Town (H) 0-1

59-60 Q1: Sutton Town (H) 1-1, (A) 4-3
Q2: South Normanton Welfare (A) 1-6

60-61 Q1: Alfreton Town (H) *Scratched*

61-62 Q1: Alfreton Town (H) 1-8

SHOLING SPORTS

Currently: Suspended playing

83-84 Q1: Salisbury (H) 2-1
Q2: Gosport Borough (H) 0-0, (A) 0-4

84-85 Q1: Chippenham Town (A) 0-3

85-86 PR: A.F.C. Totton (A) 0-2

86-87 PR: Andover (A) 0-1

87-88 Q1: Swanage Town & Herston (H) 1-3

88-89 PR: Devizes Town (A) 2-3

89-90 PR: Salisbury (A) 0-6

90-91 PR: Abingdon United (H) 1-3

91-92 PR: Maidenhead United (H) 0-6

92-93 PR: Bemerton Heath Harlequins (H) 1-2

SHOREHAM

Currently: Sussex County League

46-47 PR: East Grinstead (A) 0-11

47-48 Q1: Bognor Regis Town (A) 1-1, (H) 2-5

48-49 PR: Hove (H) 2-1
Q1: Bexhill Town (H - *played away*) 1-5

49-50 PR: Hastings United (A) 0-3

50-51 PR: Eastbourne (A) 1-2

51-52 PR: Worthing (A) 2-3

52-53 PR: Bexhill Town (A) 0-2

53-54 PR: Hastings United (H) 0-3

54-55 PR: Horsham (H) 1-6

55-56 PR: Bognor Regis Town (H) 1-6

86-87 PR: Camberley Town (A) 0-4

87-88 PR: Faversham Town (A) 1-1, (H) 2-0
Q1: Ramsgate (A) 0-2

88-89 PR: Eastbourne (H) 1-3

89-90 Q1: Salisbury (A) 0-5

90-91 PR: Tonbridge A.F.C. (A) 1-2

91-92 PR: Sheppey UNited (H) 0-3

92-93 PR: Witney Town (H) 0-3

SHORTS SPORTS

Currently: Defunct

45-46 Q4: Bromley (A) 0-2

46-47 PR: Lloyds (Sittingbourne) (A) 2-4

SHORTWOOD UNITED

Currently: Hellenic League

85-86 PR: Sharpness (H) 1-1, (A) 1-1, (A) 1-5

86-87 PR: Melksham Town (H) 2-3

87-88 PR: Waterlooville (H) 1-6

88-89 PR: Bideford (A) 1-1, (H) 2-1
Q1: Maesteg Park Athletic (A) 0-1

89-90 Q1: Paulton Rovers (A) 3-2
Q2: Worcester City (A) 0-3

90-91 PR: St Blazey (H) 1-2

91-92 PR: Weston-super-Mare (H) 3-0
Q1: Gloucester City (A) 1-4

92-93 PR: Brockenhurst (H) 0-4

SHOTTON COLLIERY WELF.

Currently: Defunct

47-48 EX: Easington Colliery Welfare (A) 1-4

48-49 EX: Seaham Colliery Welfare (H) 1-4

49-50 EX: Spennymoor United (H) 2-2, (A) 2-4

50-51 PR: Consett (H) 1-8

54-55 Q1: Trimdon Grange Colliery Welfare (H) 5-1
Q2: Wolsingham Welfare (A) 2-2, (H) 2-3

56-57 Q1: Wingate Welfare (H) 4-2
Q2: Boldon Colliery Welfare (H) 3-0
Q3: Annfield Plain (H) 2-3

57-58 Q1: Shildon (H) 0-3

58-59 Q1: Willington (A) 0-6

59-60 Q1: Spennymoor United (H) 0-2

60-61 Q1: Murton Colliery Welfare (H) 2-2, (A) 1-3

61-62 Q1: Willington (A) 2-2, (H) 2-3

SHOTTON COMRADES

Currently: Northern League

85-86 PR: Norton & S.A. (A) 1-1, (H) 2-2, (H) 5-2
Q1: Northallerton Town (A) 2-1
Q2: Wingate (H) 0-2

87-88 PR: Garforth Town. (H) 2-1
Q1: Darlington Cleveland Bridge (A) 1-2

88-89 Q1: South Bank (H) 1-1, (A) 1-3

89-90 PR: Annfield Plain (A) 3-2
Q1: Bridlington Town (H) 0-5

90-91 PR: Esh Winning (H) 1-2

91-92 PR: Brandon United (A) 1-7

92-93 PR: Easington Colliery (A) 1-2

SHREWSBURY TOWN

Currently: Football League

45-46 Q4: Bournville Athletic (H) 6-2
R1: Walsall (H) 5-0, (A) 1-4 (*agg: 6-4*)
R2: Wrexham (H) 0-1, (A) 1-1 (*agg: 1-2*)

46-47 Q4: Brush Sports (A) 1-5

47-48 Q4: Wellington Town (A) 1-0
R1: Great Yarmouth Town (A) 4-1
R2: Stockport (A) 1-1, (H) 1-1, 2-2, 2-2, 2-3

48-49 Q4: Witton Albion (A) 0-4

49-50 Q4: Bromsgrove Rovers (A) 2-5

50-51 PR: Oswestry Town (H) *scratched*

51-52 R1: Leytonstone (A) 0-2

52-53 R1: Queens Park R. (A) 2-2, (H) 2-2, 4-1
R2: Chesterfield (H) 0-0, (A) 4-2
R3: Finchley (H) 2-0
R4: Southampton (H) 1-4

53-54	R1: Queens Park Rangers (A) 0-2
54-55	R1: Walsall (A) 2-5
55-56	R1: Gillingham (A) 1-1, (H) 4-1 R2: Torquay United (H) 0-0, (A) 1-5
56-57	R1: Weymouth (A) 0-1
57-58	R1: Port Vale (A) 1-2
58-59	R1: Newport I.O.W. (A) 0-0, (H) 5-0 R2: Crystal Palace (A) 2-2, (H) 2-2, 1-4
59-60	R1: Peterborough United (A) 3-4
60-61	R1: Newport County (H) 4-1 R2: Swindon Town (A) 1-0 R3: Aldershot (A) 1-1, (H) 2-2, 0-2
61-62	R1: Banbury Spencer (H) 7-1 R2: Brierley Hill Alliance (H) 3-0 R3: Southport (A) 3-1 R4: Middlesbrough (H) 2-2, (A) 1-5
62-63	R1: Chelmsford City (A) 6-2 R2: Torquay United (H) 2-1 R3: Sheffield Wednesday (H) 1-1, (A) 1-2
63-64	R1: Exeter City (A) 1-2
64-65	R1: King's Lynn (A) 1-0 R2: Exeter City (A) 2-1 R3: Manchester City (A) 1-1, (H) 3-1 R4: Millwall (A) 2-1 R5: Leeds United (A) 0-2
65-66	R1: Torquay United (H) 2-1 R2: Peterborough United (H) 3-2 R3: Queens Park Rangers (A) 0-0, (H) 1-0 R4: Carlisle Utd (H) 0-0, (A) 1-1, 4-3 R5: Chelsea (A) 2-3
66-67	R1: Hartlepools United (H) 5-2 R2: Wrexham (H) 5-1 R3: Ipswich Town (A) 1-4
67-68	R1: Darlington (H) 3-0 R2: Tow Law Town (A) 1-1, (H) 6-2 R3: Arsenal (H) 1-1, (A) 0-2
68-69	R1: Port Vale (H) 1-1, (A) 1-3
69-70	R1: Yeovil Town (A) 3-2 R2: Mansfield Town (H) 1-2
70-71	R1: Minehead (A) 2-1 R2: Reading (H) 2-2, (A) 0-1
71-72	R1: Colchester United (A) 4-1 R2: Guildford City (H) 2-1 R3: Derby County (A) 0-2
72-73	R1: Spennymoor United (A) 1-1, (H) 3-1 R2: Bolton Wanderers (A) 0-3
73-74	R1: Wrexham (A) 1-1, (H) 0-1
74-75	R1: Wigan Athletic (H) 1-1, (A) 1-2
75-76	R1: Rossendale United (A) 1-0 R2: Chester (H) 3-1 R3: Bradford City (H) 1-2
76-77	R1: Doncaster Rovers (A) 2-2, (H) 4-3 R2: Bury (A) 0-0, (H) 2-1 R3: Queens Park Rangers (A) 1-2
77-78	R1: Doncaster Rovers (A) 1-0 R2: Stockport County (H) 1-1, (A) 2-1 R3: Blackburn Rovers (A) 1-2
78-79	R1: Mansfield Town (A) 2-0 R2: Doncaster Rovers (A) 3-0 R3: Cambridge United (H) 3-1 R4: Manchester City (H) 2-0 R5: Aldershot (A) 2-2, (H) 3-1 R6: Wolverhampton W. (A) 1-1, (H) 1-3
79-80	R3: Millwall (A) 1-5
80-81	R3: Huddersfield Town (A) 3-0 R4: Ipswich Town (H) 0-0, (A) 0-3
81-82	R3: Port Vale (H) 1-0 R4: Burnley (H) 1-0 R5: Ipswich Town (H) 2-1 R6: Leicester City (A) 2-5
82-83	R3: Rotherham United (H) 2-1 R4: Everton (A) 1-2
83-84	R3: Oldham Athletic (H) 3-0 R4: Ipswich Town (H) 2-0 R5: Everton (A) 0-3
84-85	R3: Oxford United (H) 0-2
85-86	R3: Chelsea (H) 0-1
86-87	R3: Hull City (H) 1-2
87-88	R3: Bristol Rovers (H) 2-1 R4: Plymouth Argyle (A) 0-1
88-89	R3: Colchester United (H) 0-3
89-90	R1: Chesterfield (H) 2-3
90-91	R1: Bradford City (A) 0-0, (H) 2-1 R2: Chorley (H) 1-0 R3: Watford (H) 4-1 R4: Wimbledon (H) 1-0 R5: Arsenal (H) 0-1
91-92	R1: Hartlepool United (A) 2-3
92-93	R1: Mansfield Town (H) 3-1 R2: Burnley (A) 1-1, (H) 1-2

SIDLEY UNITED

Currently: Sussex County League

73-74	PR: Waterlooville (A) 0-4
74-75	Q1: Haywards Heath (H) 1-3
75-76	Q1: Canterbury City (H) 0-2
76-77	Q1: Folkestone & S. (H - *played away*) 0-3
77-78	Q1: Tonbridge A.F.C. (H) 0-0, (A) 1-8
78-79	Q1: Medway (A) 1-4

SILKSWORTH COLLIERY WELFARE

Currently: Defunct (reformed as Silksworth F.C. in Wearside League)

48-49	EX: Willington (H) 4-3 PR: Stanley United (A) 1-3
49-50	EX: Cockfield (H) 1-0 PR: West Auckland Town (H) 3-3, (A) 5-2 Q1: South Hetton C.W. (H) 0-0, (A) 2-0 Q2: Consett (H) 2-1 Q3: Horden Colliery Welfare (A) 1-3
50-51	PR: Tow Law Town (H) 3-3, (A) 0-2
51-52	Q1: Murton Colliery Welfare (A) 2-3
52-53	Q1: Murton Colliery Welfare (H) 7-0 Q2: Ushaw Moor (A) 1-4
53-54	Q1: Horden Colliery Welfare (A) 0-1
54-55	Q1: Boldon Colliery Welfare (A) 0-2
55-56	Q1: Annfield Plain (H) 9-5 Q2: Easington Colliery Welfare (A) 2-4
60-61	Q2: Ashington (A) 1-6
61-62	Q1: Ashington (A) 1-4

SITTINGBOURNE

Currently: Southern League

47-48	EX: Bexley (H) 3-4
48-49	PR: Gravesend & Northfleet (A) 1-3
49-50	EX: Erith & Belvedere (H) 0-2
50-51	PR: Canterbury City (A) 1-0 Q1: Maidstone United (H) 2-0 Q2: Tonbridge (A) 1-3
51-52	PR: Deal Town (H) 2-2, (A) 3-1 Q1: Snowdown Colliery Welfare (A) 2-4
52-53	PR: Faversham Town (H) 3-1 Q1: Tunbridge Wells (A) 4-2 Q2: Gravesend & Northfleet (A) 0-3
53-54	PR: Carshalton Athletic (H) 2-1 Q1: Guildford City (A) 0-2
54-55	PR: Ramsgate Athletic (A) 1-1, (H) 2-1 Q1: Tooting & Mitcham United (H) 2-1 Q2: Snowdown Colliery Welfare (H) 2-1 Q3: Canterbury City (A) 1-2
55-56	PR: Bexleyheath & Welling (H) 4-2 Q1: Tunbridge Wells United (H) 2-0 Q2: Carshalton Athletic (H) 0-0, (A) 2-1 Q3: Ramsgate Athletic (H) 1-1, (A) 2-3
56-57	PR: Deal Town (A) 5-3 Q1: Ramsgate Athletic (A) 2-1 Q2: Gravesend & Northfleet (H) 1-0 Q3: Margate (H) 2-3
57-58	PR: Sheppey United (A) 5-2 Q1: Gravesend & Northfleet (A) 1-3
58-59	Q1: Erith & Belvedere (A) 4-0 Q2: Tonbridge (A) 2-0 Q3: Gravesend & Northfleet (H) 4-4, (A) 0-2
59-60	Q1: Bexleyheath & Welling (A) 1-5
60-61	Q1: Sheppey United (A) 4-1 Q2: Bexleyheath & Welling (A) 0-1
61-62	Q1: Dartford (A) 0-5
62-63	Q1: Whitstable (A - *played home*) 10-0 Q2: Folkestone Town (H) 2-2, (A) 2-1 Q3: Dover (H) 2-1 Q4: Guildford City (A) 0-0, (H) 1-0 R1: Hinckley Athletic (A) 0-3
63-64	Q1: Erith & Belvedere (H) 3-3, (A) 2-1 Q2: Cray Wanderers (H) 1-1, (A) 1-0 Q3: Bexley United (H) 0-2
64-65	Q1: Bexley United (H) 0-3
65-66	Q1: Faversham Town (H) 9-0 Q2: Bromley (A) 2-0 Q3: Bexley United (A) 2-4
66-67	Q1: Deal Town (A) 1-1, (H) 6-2 Q2: Ramsgate Athletic (H) 1-3
67-68	Q1: Whitstable Town (A) 1-1, (H) 3-3, 2-3

***Below:** Gary Hackett curls a shot beyond Ipswich's Paul Cooper to give Second Division Shrewsbury a surprise lead in 1984. Photo: Mike Joss.*

68-69 Q1: Chatham Town (A) 6-1
Q2: Canterbury City (A) 0-2

69-70 Q1: Tunbridge Wells (H) 0-1

70-71 Q1: Maidstone United (H) 0-5

71-72 PR: Ramsgate Athletic (A) 1-1, (H) 0-1

72-73 Q1: Whitstable Town (H) 2-0
Q2: Bexhill Town (A) 0-0, (H) 1-0
Q3: Tonbridge (A) 1-4

73-74 Q1: Hastings United (A) 5-3
Q2: Ramsgate Athletic (H) 1-1, (A) 0-2

74-75 Q1: Ashford Town (A) 0-0, (H) 1-2

75-76 Q1: Ramsgate (A) 1-4

76-77 PR: Margate (A) 2-2, (H) 0-1

77-78 Q1: Haywards Heath (H) 0-2

78-79 Q1: Eastbourne United (H) 1-4

79-80 Q1: Welling United (H) 2-2, (A) 0-5

80-81 Q1: Margate (A) 1-1, (H) 3-4

81-82 Q1: Finchley (A) 3-4

82-83 PR: Metropolitan Police (A) 2-1
Q1: Southall (A) 1-1, (H) 1-3

83-84 PR: Ringmer (A - *played home*) 3-0
Q1: Horsham (H) 1-1, (A) 2-1
Q2: Three Bridges (H) 3-0
Q3: Dartford (A) 2-2, (H) 1-4

84-85 Q1: Thanet United (A) 3-2
Q2: Haywards Heath (A) 3-0
Q3: Staines Town (H) 1-1, (A) 0-3

85-86 Q1: Banstead Athletic (H) 1-2

86-87 PR: Dorking (H) 1-1, (A) 1-2

87-88 PR: Rainham Town (A) 1-1, (H) 2-3

88-89 PR: Hastings Town (H) 2-3

89-90 Q1: Whyteleafe (A) 0-1

90-91 PR: Burgess Hill Town (H) 2-0
Q1: Whitstable Town (H) 1-1, (A) 4-1
Q2: Dover Athletic (A) 0-2

91-92 Q1: Southwick (A) 3-1
Q2: Tonbridge A.F.C. (H) 1-2

92-93 PR: Whitstable Town (A) 2-1
Q1: Whitehawk (A) 1-0
Q2: Fareham Town (H) 3-2
Q3: Havant Town (H) 3-2
Q4: Marlow (H) 1-1, (A) 1-2

SKEGNESS TOWN

Currently: Lincolnshire League

49-50 EX: Alford United (A) 4-6

51-52 PR: Ashby Institute (A) 6-3
Q1: Alford United (A) 3-1
Q2: Holbeach United (H) 4-0
Q3: Boston United (H) 2-1
Q4: Rawmarsh Welfare (A) 2-4

52-53 Q1: Lysaght's Sports (A) 9-1
Q2: Grantham (H) 2-0
Q3: Boston United (A) 2-3

53-54 Q1: Brigg Town (A) 1-4

54-55 Q1: Lysaght's Sports (H) 4-0
Q2: Alford United (A) 2-2, (H) 5-2
Q3: Boston United (H) 2-6

55-56 Q1: Barton Town (H) 9-2
Q2: Brigg Town (H) 3-1
Q3: Grantham (A) 3-3, (H) 3-0
Q4: Gainsborough Trinity (H) 1-1, (A) 2-0
R1: Worksop Town (H) 0-4

56-57 Q1: Grantham (A) 1-2

57-58 Q1: Grantham (H) 1-1, (A) 0-2

58-59 Q1: Bourne Town (A) 2-1
Q2: Boston United (H) 0-3

59-60 Q1: Grantham (H) 5-0
Q2: Brigg Town (A) 3-0
Q3: Gainsborough Trinity (H) 0-0, (A) 0-3

60-61 Q1: Grantham (A) 4-3
Q2: Ransome & Marles (H) 5-1
Q3: Holbeach United (A) 0-1

61-62 Q1: Spalding United (H) 1-1, (A) 3-0
Q2: Alford United (H) 6-1
Q3: Grantham (A) 1-3

62-63 Q2: Holbeach United (A) 3-2
Q3: Boston United (A) 0-1

63-64 Q2: Stamford (H) 2-4

64-65 Q1: Stamford (A) 1-1, (H) 4-0
Q2: Spalding United (H) 0-3

65-66 Q1: Boston United (H) 3-2
Q2: Holbeach United (H) 2-2, (A) 1-0
Q3: Grantham (H) 0-7

66-67 Q1: King's Lynn (A) 3-4

67-68 Q1: King's Lynn (H) 0-2

68-69 Q1: King's Lynn (H) 0-3

69-70 Q1: Louth United (A) 1-0
Q2: King's Lynn (A) 1-2

70-71 Q1: Spalding United (A) 1-1, (H) 1-2

71-72 PR: March Town United (A) 2-1
Q1: King's Lynn (A) 1-4

72-73 Q1: Stamford (H) 3-1
Q2: Corby Town (A) 2-0
Q3: Kettering Town (A) 0-7

73-74 Q1: Wisbech Town (H) 2-3

74-75 Q1: Holbeach United (H) 3-0
Q2: Boston (A) 1-1, (H) 1-2

75-76 Q1: Retford Town (A) 0-0, (H) 0-2

76-77 Q1: Wisbech Town (H) 0-2

77-78 Q1: March Town United (A) 1-2

78-79 Q1: Louth United (H) 0-1

79-80 PR: Holbeach United (A) 2-2, (H) 2-1
Q1: Retford Town (A) 3-0
Q2: Gainsborough Trinity (H) 2-0
Q3: Boston (H) 1-1, (A) 2-2, 0-1

80-81 Q1: Boston United (A) 0-3

81-82 Q1: Worksop Town (A) 1-2

82-83 Q1: March Town United (H) 3-0
Q2: Irthlingborough D. (H) 0-0, (A) 0-1

83-84 PR: Tividale (H) 2-4

85-86 Q1: Goole Town (A) 2-3

SKELMERSDALE UNITED

Currently: North West Counties League

45-46 Q1: Leyland Motors (A) 2-1
Q2: Darwen (A) 2-2, (H) 2-3

46-47 Q1: Leyland Motors (H) 4-3
Q2: Chorley (H) 1-1, (A) 1-1, 1-0
Q3: Darwen (H) 1-1, (A) 4-6

47-48 PR: Stoneycroft (H) 8-0
Q1: Earle (H) 3-2
Q2: Prescot Cables (A) 1-1, (H) 0-3

48-49 PR: Wigan Athletic (A) 1-2

49-50 PR: Prescot Cables (A) 0-3

50-51 EX: Crossens (A) 12-0
PR: Bangor City (H) 1-0
Q1: Prescot Cables (H) 6-2
Q2: Burscough (A) 2-3

51-52 Q1: Ashton United (H) 5-1
Q2: Rossendale United (A) 1-1, (H) 3-0
Q3: Darwen (H) 1-1, (A) 1-0
Q4: Nelson (H) 0-3

52-53 Q1: Ashton United (A) 2-7

53-54 Q1: Chorley (H) 1-1, (A) 2-0
Q2: Lytham (A) 2-1
Q3: Mossley (H) 1-3

54-55 PR: Horwich R.M.I. (A) 0-1

55-56 PR: Horwich R.M.I. (A) 2-3

56-57 PR: Ashton United (H) 5-0
Q1: Horwich R.M.I. (A) 1-2

57-58 PR: Ashton United (A) 1-3

58-59 Q1: Ashton United (A) 3-1
Q2: Nelson (H) 2-0
Q3: Chorley (H) 2-2, (A) 0-3

59-60 PR: Mossley (H) 0-0, (A) 0-3

60-61 Q1: St Helens Town (H) 3-2
Q2: Earlestown (A) 4-2
Q3: Wigan Athletic (H) 0-0, (A) 1-2

61-62 Q1: Wigan Athletic (H) 0-4

62-63 Q1: South Liverpool (A) 1-3

63-64 Q1: Marine (A) 2-2, (H) 3-0
Q2: Altrincham (H) 0-3

64-65 Q1: Droylsden (H) 0-0, (A) 2-1
Q2: South Liverpool (H) 2-2, (A) 3-5

65-66 Q1: Leyland Motors (H) 2-2, (A) 2-1
Q2: St Helens Town (A) 3-0
Q3: Altrincham (A) 1-4

66-67 Q1: Nantwich (H) 4-3
Q2: Lostock Gralam (A) 1-1, (H) 5-1
Q3: Rhyl (A) 0-2

67-68 R1: Scunthorpe United (A) 0-2

68-69 PR: Droylsden (A) 3-0
Q1: Darwen (A) 4-1
Q2: St Helens Town, (A) 1-0
Q3: Stalybridge Celtic (H) 3-1
Q4: Northwich Victoria (A) 3-1
R1: Chesterfield (A) 0-2

69-70 Q4: Wigan Athletic (A) 0-2

70-71 Q1: Congleton Town (H) 3-0
Q2: Marine (H) 2-1
Q3: Ellesmere Port Town (A) 1-0
Q4: Wigan Athletic (H) 1-1, (A) 0-5

71-72 R1: Tranmere Rovers (H) 0-4

72-73 Q4: Rhyl (H) 0-4

73-74 Q1: Horwich R.M.I. (A) 1-3

74-75 Q1: St Helens Town (A) 1-0
Q2: Sandbach Ramblers (A) 1-2

75-76 Q1: Ashton United (A) 2-1
Q2: Chorley (A) 1-3

76-77 PR: New Brighton Rakers (A) 1-1, (H) 0-2

77-78 PR: Accrington Stanley (H) 0-3

78-79 Q1: Hyde United (A) 1-1, (H) 0-1

79-80 PR: Lancaster City (H) 1-4

80-81 PR: Porthmadog (A) 1-1, (H) 3-1
Q1: Chorley (H) 0-1

81-82 PR: Horwich R.M.I. (A) 0-4

82-83 PR: Prestwich Heys (H) 0-4

84-85 Q1: Burscough (A) 0-3

85-86 Q1: Horwich R.M.I. (H) 2-2, (A) 0-3

86-87 PR: Walsall Wood (A) 1-0
Q1: Sutton Town (H) 1-0
Q2: Hednesford Town (H) 2-1
Q3: Northwich Victoria (H) 2-3

87-88 PR: Radcliffe Borough (A) 0-1

88-89 Q1: Morecambe (A) 3-3, (H) 1-2

89-90 PR: Curzon Ashton (H) 1-1, (A) 0-2

90-91 PR: Glossop (A) 1-1, (H) 0-2

Opposite: *Patrick Coggins (white shirt in centre of photo) heads Skelmersdale United into a 1-0 lead away to Glossop in the Preliminary Round tie on 1st September 1990. Skem's joy was short-lived, however. The Bass North West Counties Division Two side equalised and then forced a 2-0 away win in the replay.*
Photo: Barry Lockwood.

91-92 Q1: Macclesfield Town (H) 0-4

92-93 PR: Warrington Town (A) 1-6

SKINNINGROVE WORKS

Currently: Defunct

50-51 PR: Whitby Town (H) 0-5

51-52 Q1: Billingham Synthonia Recreation (A) 0-6

52-53 Q1: Ferryhill Athletic (A) 0-7

53-54 Q1: Ferryhill Athletic (A) 0-18

SLADE GREEN

Currently: Kent League

90-91 PR: Ringmer (H) 2-0
Q1: Whyteleafe (A) 1-2

91-92 PR: Cove (A) 1-2

92-93 Q1: Harlow Town (H) *W/O*
Q2: Wembley (A) 2-3

SLOUGH CENTRE

Currently: Defunct

48-49 EX: Marlow (A) 3-2
PR: Southall (A) 2-2, (H) 0-2

49-50 EX: Slough Town (A) 0-1

50-51 EX: Abingdon Town (H) 2-2, (A) 3-4

52-53 PR: Slough Town (H) 2-1
Q1: Edgware Town (A) 1-2

53-54 PR: Slough Town (H) 4-1
Q1: St Albans City (H) 0-1

54-55 Q1: Wycombe Wanderers (H) 1-3

55-56 PR: Aylesbury United (A) 1-3

Above: *Slough Town's Andy Sayer just misses with a spectacular shot during the Rebels' Second Qualifying Round win away to Metropolitan Police in 1992-93. Photo: Dennis Nicholson.*

SLOUGH TOWN

Currently: Alliance Premier League
* - As Slough United

45-46 * PR: Hounslow Town (A) 4-4, (H) 3-1
Q1: Yiewsley (A) 2-2, (H) 2-0
Q2: Banbury Spencer (A) 5-2
Q3: Oxford City (H) 3-1
Q4: Leytonstone (A) 3-3, (H) 3-1
R1: Bromley (A) 1-2 *abandoned after 80 mins,*
(A) 1-6, (H) 1-0 *(agg: 2-6)*

46-47 * PR: Lyons Club (Greenford) (H) 4-2
Q1: Windsor & Eton (H) 3-3, (A) 4-2
Q2: Hayes (A) 3-6

47-48 * PR: Southall (H) 0-1

48-49 EX: Hayes (H) 2-1
PR: Berkhamsted Town (A) 1-3

49-50 EX: Slough Centre (H) 1-0
PR: Aylesbury United (H) 3-2
Q1: Oxford City (A) 1-1, (H) 4-2
Q2: Hayes (H) 1-2

50-51 PR: Headington United (A) 4-3
Q1: Oxford City (H) 2-2, (A) 2-1
Q2: Banbury Spencer (A) 5-1
Q3: Wycombe Wanderers (H) 1-1, (A) 0-2

51-52 Q1: Barnet (H) 2-2, (A) 6-1
Q2: St Albans City (A) 1-1, (H) 4-0
Q3: Wealdstone (A) 0-5

52-53 PR: Slough Centre (A) 1-2

53-54 PR: Slough Centre (A) 1-4

54-55 PR: Windsor & Eton (H) 6-2
Q1: Oxford City (H) 2-3

55-56 PR: Bicester Town (H) 4-0
Q1: Abingdon Town (A) 3-0
Q2: Wycombe Wanderers (H) 3-3, (A) 0-1

56-57 Q1: Aylesbury United (A) 0-3

57-58 PR: Witney Town (H) 5-2
Q1: Oxford City (H) 1-2

58-59 Q1: Wokingham Town (A) 2-3

59-60 PR: Wokingham Town (A) 2-5

60-61 Q1: Marlow (A) 1-0
Q2: Carshalton Athletic (A) 2-5

61-62 Q1: Sutton United (H) 4-1
Q2: Redhill (H) 2-0
Q3: Dulwich Hamlet (A) 1-5

62-63 Q1: Epsom & Ewell (A) 3-1
Q2: Tooting & Mitcham United (H) 0-4

63-64 Q1: Epsom & Ewell (A) 1-2

64-65 Q1: Metropolitan Police (H) 4-1
Q2: Carshalton Athletic (H) 2-0
Q3: Epsom & Ewell (A) 1-0
Q4: Hendon (A) 1-3

65-66 Q1: Wembley (H) 5-3
Q2: Metropolitan Police (H) 0-1

66-67 Q1: Dagenham (H) 2-0
Q2: Clapton (A) 2-0
Q3: Finchley (A) 2-3

67-68 Q1: Corinthian-Casuals (A) 3-0
Q2: Hertford Town (H) 3-0
Q3: Bishop's Stortford (H) 5-1
Q4: Leytonstone (H) 2-2, (A) 1-2

68-69 Q1: Feltham (H) 2-1
Q2: Hendon (H) 2-1
Q3: Bishop's Stortford (H) 2-0
Q4: Wealdstone (H) 1-1, (A) 0-2

69-70 Q1: Hertford Town (A) 0-1

70-71 Q1: Tilbury (A) 1-1, (H) 2-0
Q2: Kingstonian (H) 3-0
Q3: Ilford (H) 4-2
Q4: Hillingdon Borough (H) 2-2, (A) 2-0
R1: Wycombe Wanderers (A) 1-1, (H) 1-0
R2: Barnet (H) 0-1

71-72 Q1: Woking (H) 1-1, (A) 2-0
Q2: Romford (H) 0-1

72-73 PR: Bedford Town (H) 1-0
Q1: Bletchley (H) 0-0, (A) 3-0
Q2: Banbury United (A) 1-2

73-74 R1: Reading (A) 0-3

74-75 Q4: Sutton United (H) 1-0
R1: Brentford (H) 1-4

75-76 Q4: Walton & Hersham (H) 1-2

76-77 Q1: Finchley (H) 2-2, (A) 4-0
Q2: Leytonstone (A) 1-1, (H) 1-0
Q3: Barnet (A) 1-0
Q4: Woking (A) 0-0, (H) 0-1

77-78 PR: Hillingdon Borough (A) 3-3, (H) 0-1

78-79 Q1: Farnborough Town (H) 2-0
Q2: Carshalton Athletic (A) 2-1
Q3: Southall & Ealing Borough (A) 0-1

79-80 Q1: Crawley Town (A) 0-0, (H) 3-0
Q2: Hayes (A) 4-2
Q3: Walton & Hersham (A) 2-0
Q4: Tooting & Mitcham United (H) 4-0
R1: Hungerford Town (H) 3-1
R2: Yeovil Town (A) 0-1

80-81 Q1: Ware (H) 5-1
Q2: Hounslow (A) 3-1
Q3: Barton Rovers (H) 0-1

81-82 PR: Wootton Blue Cross (A) 2-2, (H) 4-2
Q1: Chalfont St Peter (H) 2-1
Q2: Wokingham Town (H) 1-5

82-83 Q1: Salisbury (H) 2-0
Q2: Basingstoke Town (A) 2-2, (H) 2-0
Q3: Frome Town (H) 3-0
Q4: Bideford (H) 7-1
R1: Millwall (H) 1-0
R2: Bishop's Stortford (H) 1-4

83-84 Q1: Hounslow (A) 3-0
Q2: Whyteleafe (A) 5-0
Q3: Hampton (H) 3-2
Q4: Poole Town (A) 0-3

84-85 Q1: Newbury Town (A) 5-1
Q2: Fareham Town (H) 2-0
Q3: Chippenham Town (A) 0-1

85-86 Q1: Merstham (A) 4-0
Q2: Woking (A) 5-1
Q3: Welling United (A) 0-0, (H) 2-1
Q4: Kingstonian (H) 2-2, (A) 1-1, (H) 2-1
R1: Aylesbury (H) 2-2, (A - *at Tring T.*) 5-2
R2: Orient (A) 2-2, (H) 2-3

86-87 Q4: Dover Athletic (H) 1-1, (A) 3-2
R1: Bognor Regis Town (H) 1-1, (A) 1-0
R2: Swansea City (A) 0-3

87-88 Q4: Bath City (A) 1-3

88-89 Q4: Dartford (H) 1-2

89-90 Q1: Walthamstow Pennant (H) 5-1
Q2: Carshalton Athletic (A) 2-0
Q3: Uxbridge (H) 0-0, (A) 2-1
Q4: Abingdon Town (A) 3-0
R1: Woking (H) 1-2

90-91 Q1: Feltham (H) 8-0
Q2: Farnborough Town (H) 2-3

91-92 Q1: Croydon (H) 2-2, (A) 3-0
Q2: Yeading (A) 0-0, (H) 1-0
Q3: Berkhamsted Town (A) 4-1
Q4: Kingstonian (H) 2-1
R1: Reading (H) 3-3, (A) 1-2

92-93 Q1: Corinthian-Casuals (A) 1-1, (H) 4-3
Q2: Metropolitan Police (A) 1-0
Q3: Yeading (H) 2-1
Q4: Ashford Town (A) 2-1
R1: Colchester United (A) 0-4

Above: *Paul McKinnon (left) beats Ashford's Neil Cugley to head Slough Town's first goal in the Fourth Qualifying Round win on 24th October 1992. Photo: Paul Dennis.*

SMITH'S DOCK

Currently: Defunct

48-49 PR: South Bank St Peter's (A) 2-0
Q1: South Bank East End (H) 2-1
Q2: Billingham Synthonia Recreation (H) 2-5

50-51 PR: Bridlington Central United (H) 3-6

SNOWDOWN COLLIERY WELF.

Currently: Kent County League

49-50 EX: Whitstable (H) 2-1
PR: Folkestone Town (A) 1-1, (H) 2-1
Q1: Dover (A) 0-2

50-51 PR: Dover (A) 2-1
Q1: Bowater Lloyds (A) 1-1, (H) 2-0
Q2: Betteshanger C.W. (A) 0-0, (H) 1-0
Q3: Tonbridge (A) 1-1, (H) 3-6

51-52 PR: Faversham Town (A) 3-0
Q1: Sittingbourne (H) 4-2
Q2: Betteshanger Colliery Welfare (H) 0-2

52-53 PR: Ramsgate Athletic (A) 2-4

53-54 PR: Guildford City (H) 1-3

54-55 Q1: Ashford Town (A) 1-1, (H) 5-0
Q2: Sittingbourne (A) 1-2

55-56 PR: Walton & Hersham (H) 4-0
Q1: Carshalton Athletic (H) 0-1

56-57 PR: Dover (H) 0-0, (A) 2-1
Q1: Margate (H) 2-2, (A) 0-1

57-58 PR: Betteshanger Colliery Welfare (A) 0-2

58-59 Q1: Ashford Town (A) 0-6

59-60 Q1: Canterbury City (A) 0-1

60-61 Q1: Whitstable (H) 6-1
Q2: Dover (A) 3-5

67-68 Q1: Ramsgate Athletic (H) 0-4

68-69 Q1: Deal Town (A) 2-2, (H) 2-1
Q2: Hastings United (H) 3-7

69-70 Q1: Ramsgate Athletic (A) 1-8

70-71 PR: Folkestone (A) 3-4

71-72 Q1: Whitstable Town (H) 1-4

77-78 Q1: Cray Wanderers (H) 2-1
Q2: Hastings United (A) 1-5

78-79 Q1: Tonbridge A.F.C. (H) 0-3

79-80 PR: Ramsgate (A) 1-3

SOHAM TOWN RANGERS

Currently: Eastern Counties League

57-58 PR: Warboys Town (H) 4-2
Q1: March Town United (A) 2-4

58-59 PR: Warboys Town (H) 4-1
Q1: Holbeach United (H) 1-3

64-65 Q1: Bury Town (A) 1-2

65-66 Q1: Canterbury City (A) 1-8

66-67 Q1: Bishop's Stortford (A) 0-2

67-68 PR: Wellingborough Town (A) 1-3

68-69 Q1: Eynesbury Rovers (H) 6-0
Q2: Kettering Town (H) 0-1

69-70 PR: Ely City (H) 1-1, (A) 3-2
Q1: Potton United (H) 2-2, (A) 1-2

70-71 Q1: Rushden Town (H) 1-0
Q2: March Town United (H) 2-0
Q3: King's Lynn (H) 0-6

71-72 Q1: Chatteris Town (A) 0-3

72-73 PR: Histon (H) 0-2

73-74 PR: Lowestoft Town (H) 1-2

74-75 Q1: March Town United (A) 1-2

75-76 Q1: Wisbech Town (H) 1-0
Q2: Spalding United (A) 2-8

76-77 Q1: Irthlingborough D. (A) 2-2, (H) 4-3
Q2: Barton Rovers (A) 0-5

77-78 Q1: Great Yarmouth Town (H) 0-2

78-79 Q1: Sudbury Town (H) 2-0
Q2: Gorleston (H) 0-3

79-80 Q1: V.S. Rugby (H) 0-0, (A) 0-3

80-81 Q1: King's Lynn (H) 1-1, (A) 1-2

81-82 PR: March Town United (A) 1-1, (H) 0-4

82-83 Q1: Ware (A) 1-1, (H) 4-2
Q2: Billericay Town (A) 3-5

83-84 PR: Harwich & Parkeston (H) 1-0
Q1: Heybridge Swifts (A) 0-1

84-85 Q1: Stevenage Borough (A) 1-2

85-86 PR: Histon (A) 0-3

86-87 PR: Hertford Town (H) 0-1

87-88 PR: Hemel Hempstead (H) 0-0, (A) 0-1

88-89 PR: Watton United (H) 0-1

89-90 PR: Rothwell Town (H) 0-1

90-91 PR: Malvern Town (A) 0-3

SOLIHULL BOROUGH

Currently: Southern League

90-91 PR: Banbury (H) 0-0, (A) 1-1, (H) 2-2, (A) 4-3
Q1: Corby Town (A) 0-3

91-92 PR: Spalding United (H) 1-0
Q1: Wednesfield (H) 3-0
Q2: Matlock Town (A) 1-2

92-93 Q1: Hemel Hempstead Town (A) 2-1
Q2: Cheshunt (A) 0-0, (H) 4-0
Q3: Braintree Town (H) 4-1
Q4: Chesham United (H) 3-1
R1: V.S. Rugby (H) 2-2, (A) 1-3

SOMERSHAM TOWN

Currently: Eastern Counties League

54-55 PR: Newmarket Town (H) 3-0
Q1: Holbeach United (H) 1-7

57-58 PR: St Neots Town (A) 0-6

58-59 Q1: Wisbech Town (A) 0-7

SOMERTON AMATEUR

Currently: (Somerton F.C.) Yeovil & District Lge

46-47 Q1: Street (A) 0-2

47-48 Q1: Street (A) 1-9

48-49 EX: Coleford Athletic (H) 0-4

SOUNDWELL

Currently: Merged with Victoria Park
Playing as Soundwell Victoria in Avon Premier Combination.

46-47 EX: Hanham Athletic (H - *played away*) 2-1
PR: Odd Down (A) 3-0
Q1: Trowbridge Town (H - *played away*) 2-6

47-48 EX: Bristol Aero Company (H) 2-0
PR: Barry Town (H) 0-10

48-49 EX: Stonehouse (H) 9-3
PR: St Austell (H) 4-3
Q1: Glastonbury (A) 3-4

49-50 PR: Barry Town (A) 0-3

50-51 PR: Barry Town (A) 0-4

SOUTHALL

Currently: Isthmian League
* - As Southall & Ealing Borough

45-46 PR: Wycombe Wanderers (A) 2-0
Q1: Hayes (A) 1-1, (H) 2-1
Q2: Oxford City (A) 1-2

46-47 PR: Wycombe Wanderers (H) 2-5

47-48 EX: Redford Sports (A) 5-0
PR: Slough United (A) 1-0
Q1: Headington United (H) 2-1
Q2: Wycombe Wanderers (A) 3-3, (H) 2-1
Q3: Banbury Spencer (H) 3-4

48-49 EX: Windsor & Eton (H) 3-1
PR: Slough Centre (H) 2-2, (A) 2-0
Q1: Uxbridge (A) 0-1

49-50 EX: Berkhamsted Town (H) 1-0
PR: Wycombe Wanderers (H) 6-2
Q1: Osberton Radiator (A) 3-1
Q2: Uxbridge (H) 4-1
Q3: Hayes (A) 1-4

50-51 PR: Hayes (A) 0-3

51-52 PR: Wealdstone (A) 1-2

52-53 PR: Edgware Town (H) 1-3

53-54 PR: Edgware Town (A) 1-0
Q1: Wealdstone (A) 1-2

54-55 PR: Yiewsley (A) 0-1

55-56 PR: Yiewsley (A) 0-0, (H) 2-1
Q1: Kingstonian (H) 1-1, (A) 1-0
Q2: Wealdstone (A) 2-1
Q3: Finchley (H) 3-0
Q4: Sudbury Town (A) 4-4, (H) 2-2, 7-2
R1: Hastings United (A) 1-6

56-57 Q1: Harrow Town (A) 3-0
Q2: Hounslow Town (H) 2-1
Q3: Yiewsley (H) 0-1

57-58 PR: Edgware Town (H) 4-0
Q1: Uxbridge (A) 2-1
Q2: Hounslow Town (A) 0-0, (H) 0-2

58-59 Q1: Hayes (H) 0-2

59-60 Q1: Harrow Town (H) 1-0
Q2: Yiewsley (H) 1-1, (A) 2-1
Q3: Hayes (H) 1-1, (A) 1-4

Season	Results
60-61	Q1: Hayes (H) 2-1 Q2: Edgware Town (H) 2-2, (A) 2-3
61-62	Q1: Edgware Town (A) 1-2
62-63	Q1: Finchley (A) 0-4
63-64	Q1: Yiewsley (A) 2-2, (H) 0-3
64-65	Q1: Uxbridge (A) 3-0 Q2: Finchley (A) 0-4
65-66	Q1: Hounslow (A) 3-2 Q2: Finchley (A) 2-2, (H) 2-1 Q3: Corinthian-Casuals (H) 2-2, (A) 2-3
66-67	Q1: Dunstable Town (H) 3-0 Q2: Chesham United (A) 3-4
67-68	Q1: Hampton (A) 0-2
68-69	Q1: Grays Athletic (A) 4-1 Q2: Kingstonian (H) 0-0, (A) 1-3
69-70	PR: Enfield (A) 1-1, (H) 1-1, 2-6
70-71	Q1: Redhill (H) 2-4
71-72	Q1: Gravesend & Northfleet (A) 2-2, (H) 3-1 Q2: Aveley (A) 1-1, (H) 3-3, 1-2
72-73	PR: Dulwich Hamlet (H) 0-1
73-74	PR: Wembley (A) 1-0 Q1: Bromley (A) 1-0 Q2: Wimbledon (A) 1-2
74-75	Q1: Tooting & Mitcham U. (H) 0-0, (A) 1-3
75-76 *	Q1: Epsom & Ewell (H) 1-1, (A) 3-3, 5-1 Q2: Tilbury (H) 2-1 Q3: Dulwich Hamlet (H) 2-2, (A) 2-1 Q4: Tooting & Mitcham United (H) 1-4
76-77 *	Q1: Hornchurch (H) 2-1 Q2: Dagenham (H) 0-1
77-78 *	PR: Harwich & Parkeston (A) 0-4
78-79 *	Q1: Ruislip Manor (A) 3-0 Q2: Camberley Town (H) 2-2, (A) 3-1 Q3: Slough Town (H) 1-0 Q4: March Town United (A) 1-2
79-80 *	Q1: Leytonstone-Ilford (H) 0-3
80-81	PR: Milton Keynes City (A) 2-0 Q1: Dulwich Hamlet (H) 0-8
81-82	Q1: Hitchin Town (A) 2-1 Q2: Witney Town (A) 1-4
82-83	Q1: Sittingbourne (H) 1-1, (A) 3-1 Q2: Chatham Town (H) 2-2, (A) 2-4
83-84	Q1: Carshalton Athletic (H) 3-3, (A) 4-3 Q2: Corinthian-Cas. (A - *at Leatherhead*) 2-3
84-85	PR: Maidenhead United (H) 1-2
85-86	PR: Chatham Town (A) 1-1, (H) 2-0 Q1: Hampton (A) 1-3
86-87	PR: Alma Swanley (A) 0-4
87-88	PR: Hoddesdon Town (A - *at Ware*) 0-2
90-91	PR: Tilbury (A) 0-0, (H) 1-3
91-92	PR: Edgware Town (A) 0-4
92-93	PR: Uxbridge (A) 2-4

SOUTHAMPTON

Currently: F.A. Premier League

Season	Results
45-46	R3: Newport Co. (H) 4-3, (A) 2-1 (*agg: 6-4*) R4: Queens P.R. (H) 0-1, (A) 3-4 (*agg: 3-5*)
46-47	R3: Bury (H) 5-1 R4: Newcastle United (A) 1-3
47-48	R3: Sunderland (H) 1-0 R4: Blackburn Rovers (H) 3-2 R5: Swindon Town (H) 3-0 R6: Tottenham Hotspur (H) 0-1
48-49	R3: Sheffield Wednesday (A) 1-2
49-50	R3: Northampton Town (A) 1-1, (H) 2-3
50-51	R3: Notts County (A) 4-3 R4: Sunderland (A) 0-2
51-52	R3: Southend United (A) 0-3
52-53	R3: Lincoln City (A) 1-1, (H) 2-1 R4: Shrewsbury Town (A) 4-1 R5: Blackpool (A) 1-1, (H) 1-2
53-54	R1: Bournemouth & B.A. (H) 1-1, (A) 1-3
54-55	R1: Barnet (A) 4-1 R2: Grimsby Town (A) 1-4
55-56	R1: Crystal Palace (A) 0-0, (H) 2-0 R2: Walsall (A) 1-2
56-57	R1: Northampton Town (H) 2-0 R2: Weymouth (H) 3-2 R3: Newport County (A) 3-3, (H) 0-1
57-58	R1: Walton & Hersham (A) 6-1 R2: Crystal Palace (A) 0-1
58-59	R1: Woking (H) 4-1 R2: Queens Park Rangers (A) 1-0 R3: Blackpool (H) 1-2
59-60	R1: Coventry City (A) 1-1, (H) 5-1 R2: Southend United (H) 3-0 R3: Manchester City (A) 5-1 R4: Watford (H) 2-2, (A) 0-1
60-61	R3: Ipswich Town (H) 7-1 R4: Leyton Orient (H) 0-1
61-62	R3: Sunderland (H) 2-2, (A) 0-2
62-63	R3: York City (H) 5-0 R4: Watford (H) 3-1 R5: Sheffield United (H) 1-0 R6: Nottingham F. (A) 1-1, (H) 3-3, 5-0 SF: Manchester United (*at Aston Villa*) 0-1
63-64	R3: Manchester United (H) 2-3
64-65	R3: Leyton Orient (H) 3-1 R4: Crystal Palace (H) 1-2
65-66	R3: Hull City (A) 0-1
66-67	R3: Barrow (A) 2-2, (H) 3-0 R4: Bristol City (A) 0-1
67-68	R3: Newport County (H) 1-1, (A) 3-2 R4: West Bromwich Albion (A) 1-1, (H) 2-3
68-69	R3: Oxford United (A) 1-1, (H) 2-0 R4: Aston Villa (H) 2-2, (A) 1-2
69-70	R3: Newcastle United (H) 3-0 R4: Leicester City (H) 1-1, (A) 2-4
70-71	R3: Bristol City (H) 3-0 R4: York City (A) 3-3, (H) 3-2 R5: Liverpool (A) 0-1
71-72	R3: Manchester United (H) 1-1, (A) 1-4
72-73	R3: Crystal Palace (A) 0-2
73-74	R3: Blackpool (H) 2-1 R4: Bolton Wanderers (H) 3-3, (A) 2-0 R5: Wrexham (H) 0-1
74-75	R3: West Ham United (H) 1-2
75-76	R3: Aston Villa (H) 1-1, (A) 2-1 R4: Blackpool (H) 3-1 R5: West Bromwich Albion (A) 1-1, (H) 4-0 R6: Bradford City (A) 1-0 SF: Crystal Palace (*at Chelsea*) 2-0 F: Manchester United (*at Wembley*) 1-0
76-77	R3: Chelsea (H) 1-1, (A) 3-0 R4: Nottingham Forest (A) 3-3, (H) 2-1 R5: Manchester United (H) 2-2, (A) 1-2
77-78	R3: Grimsby T. (A) 0-0, (H) 0-0, (*at Leicester City*) 4-1 R4: Bristol Rovers (A) 0-2
78-79	R3: Wimbledon (A) 2-0 R4: Preston North End (A) 1-0 R5: West Bromwich Albion (A) 1-1, (H) 2-1 R6: Arsenal (H) 1-1, (A) 0-2
79-80	R3: Birmingham City (A) 1-2
80-81	R3: Chelsea (H) 3-1 R4: Bristol Rovers (H) 3-1 R5: Everton (H) 0-0, (A) 0-1
81-82	R3: Leicester City (A) 1-3
82-83	R3: Tottenham Hotspur (A) 0-1
83-84	R3: Nottingham Forest (A) 2-1 R4: Portsmouth (A) 1-0 R5: Blackburn Rovers (A) 1-0 R6: Sheffield Wednesday (A) 0-0, (H) 5-1 SF: Everton (*at Arsenal*) 0-1
84-85	R3: Sunderland (H) 4-0 R4: Orient (A) 2-0 R5: Barnsley (H) 1-2
85-86	R3: Middlesbrough (A) 3-1 R4: Wigan Athletic (H) 3-0 R5: Millwall (H) 0-0, (A) 1-0 R6: Brighton & Hove Albion (A) 2-0 SF: Liverpool (*at Tottenham Hotspur*) 0-2
86-87	R3: Everton (A) 1-2
87-88	R3: Reading (A) 1-0 R4: Luton Town (A) 1-2
88-89	R3: Derby County (A) 1-1, (H) 1-2
89-90	R3: Tottenham Hotspur (A) 3-1 R4: Oxford United (H) 1-0 R5: Liverpool (A) 0-3
90-91	R3: Ipswich Town (H) 3-2 R4: Coventry City (A) 1-1, (H) 2-0 R5: Nottingham Forest (H) 1-1, (A) 1-3
91-92	R3: Queens Park Rangers (H) 2-0 R4: Manchester U. (H) 0-0, (A) 2-2 (*4-2 pens*) R5: Bolton Wanderers (A) 2-2, (H) 3-2 R6: Norwich City (H) 0-0, (A) 1-2
92-93	R3: Nottingham Forest (A) 1-2

Left: *Second Division Southampton with the F.A. in 1975-76 after their remarkable Wembley triumph against Manchester United. Photo: Colorsport*

SOUTH BANK

Currently: Suspended playing

46-47 Q4: Spennymoor United (H) 0-3

47-48 Q1: Stockton (H) 2-3

48-49 Q1: Bridlington Central United (H) 10-0
Q2: Portrack Shamrocks (H) 1-3

49-50 Q1: Whitby Albion Rangers (A) 2-1
Q2: Billingham Synthonia Recreation (H) 0-1

50-51 Q1: South Bank St Peter's (A) 4-1
Q2: Scarborough (A) 2-3

51-52 Q1: Ferryhill Athletic (A) 4-3
Q2: Whitby Town (A) 2-3

52-53 Q1: Billingham Synthonia Recreation (A) 2-3

53-54 Q1: Bridlington Central United (A) 0-4

54-55 Q1: Whitby Town (H) 2-1
Q2: Scarborough (A) 1-4

55-56 Q2: Billingham Synthonia Recreation (H) 0-1

56-57 Q2: Whitby Town (A) 1-5

57-58 Q1: Alnwick Town (A) 3-8

58-59 Q1: West Auckland Town (H) 0-1

59-60 Q2: Spennymoor United (A) 1-3

60-61 Q2: Ferryhill Athletic (H) 3-4

61-62 PR: Annfield Plain (H) 4-2
Q1: Newburn (H) 0-3

62-63 Q1: Ryhope Colliery Welfare (H) 0-0, (A) 1-2

63-64 Q1: Spennymoor United (H) 2-5

64-65 Q1: Evenwood Town (H) 1-4

65-66 Q1: Bishop Auckland (A) 1-5

66-67 Q1: Shildon (H) 4-3
Q2: Bishop Auckland (A) 1-3

67-68 Q1: Tow Law Town (A) 1-5

69-70 Q1: Spennymoor United (A) 0-1

70-71 Q1: Washington (H) 2-2, (A) 0-1

74-75 Q1: Bridlington Town (A) 0-1

75-76 Q1: West Auckland Town (H) 2-0
Q2: Tow Law Town (A) 1-2

76-77 Q1: Carlisle City (H) 3-0
Q2: Crook Town (A) 0-1

77-78 PR: Eppleton Colliery Welfare (A) 0-1

78-79 PR: Crook Town (A) 2-1
Q1: Wingate (A) 0-0, (H) 1-1, (*at Billingham Synthonia*) 0-0, (*at Billingham Syn.*) 2-1
Q2: Stockton (A) 1-2

79-80 PR: Whitley Bay (H) 4-1
Q1: West Auckland Town (A) 3-1
Q2: Peterlee Newtown (H) 3-2
Q3: Brandon United (H) 1-2

80-81 PR: Easington Colliery Welfare (A) 2-0
Q1: Whitby Town (A) 0-3

81-82 PR: Peterlee Newtown (A) 2-0
Q1: Barrow (H) 3-2
Q2: Durham City (H) 4-1
Q3: Whitley Bay (A) 2-0
Q4: Mossley (H) 0-1

82-83 Q1: Emley (A) 6-3
Q2: Brandon United (H) 2-1
Q3: Morecambe (A) 1-1, (H) 1-0
Q4: Mossley (A) 0-1

83-84 Q1: Clitheroe (A) 0-0, (H) 0-0, (A) 0-1

84-85 Q1: Netherfield (A) 4-0
Q2: West Auckland Town (A) 6-0
Q3: Tow Law Town (H) 1-2

85-86 Q1: Darlington Cleveland Bridge (H) 4-0
Q2: Chester-le-Street (H) 2-0
Q3: Gateshead (H) 2-2, (A) 1-1, (A) 2-1
Q4: Macclesfield Town (A) 1-3

86-87 Q1: Billingham Town (H) 1-1, (A) 2-0
Q2: Newcastle Blue Star (A) 0-0, (H) 1-2

87-88 Q1: Spennymoor United (H) 1-0
Q2: Darlington Cleveland Bridge (A) 1-2

88-89 PR: West Auckland Town (A) 0-0, (H) 2-0
Q1: Shotton Comrades (A) 1-1, (H) 3-1
Q2: Barrow (H) 0-0, (A) 0-1

89-90 PR: Norton & Stockton Ancients (A) 7-1
Q1: Shildon (H) 2-0
Q2: Hebburn (A) 0-0, (H) 3-0
Q3: Bishop Auckland (A) 1-1, (H) 1-3

90-91 Q1: Ferryhill Athletic (A) 1-1, (H) 1-0
Q2: Harrogate Railway Athletic (A) 0-1

91-92 PR: Durham City (A) 1-4

92-93 PR: Bedlington Terriers (H) 5-0
Q1: North Shields (H) *W/O*
Q2: Dunston F.B. (A) 0-2

SOUTH BANK EAST END

Currently: Defunct

47-48 PR: Filey Town (A) 2-3

48-49 Q1: Smith's Dock (A) 1-2

49-50 PR: Whitby United (H) 2-5

50-51 PR: Bridlington Trinity Utd (H) 1-1, (A) 2-4

SOUTH BANK ST PETER'S

Currently: Defunct

47-48 PR: Whitby Albion Rangers (A) 0-2

48-49 PR: Smith's Dock (H) 0-2

49-50 Q1: Filey Town (H) 4-2
Q2: Portrack Shamrocks (H) 2-2, (A) 1-2

50-51 Q1: South Bank (H) 1-4

SOUTHEND UNITED

Currently: Football League

45-46 R1: Watford (A) 1-1, (H) 0-3 (*agg: 1-4*)

46-47 R1: Brush Sports (A) 6-1
R2: Barnet (A) 9-2
R3: Everton (A) 2-4

47-48 R1: Newport County (A) 2-3

48-49 R1: Swansea City (H) 1-2

49-50 R1: Leyton Orient (H) 0-2
R2: Wrexham (A) 2-2, (H) 2-0
R3: Blackpool (A) 0-4

50-51 R1: Swindon Town (H) 0-3

51-52 R1: Bournemouth & Boscombe Ath. (H) 6-1
R2: Oldham Athletic (H) 5-0
R3: Southampton (H) 3-0
R4: Bristol Rovers (H) 2-1
R5: Sheffield United (H) 1-2

52-53 R1: Bath City (A) 1-3

53-54 R1: Finchley (A) 3-1
R2: Chesterfield (H) 1-2

54-55 R1: Bristol City (A) 2-1
R2: Bradford (Park Avenue) (A) 3-2
R3: Everton (A) 1-3

55-56 R1: Queens Park Rangers (H) 2-0
R2: Weymouth (A) 1-0
R3: Lincoln City (A) 3-2
R4: Manchester City (H) 0-1

56-57 R1: Colchester United (A) 4-1
R2: Hereford United (A) 3-2
R3: Liverpool (H) 2-1
R4: Birmingham City (H) 1-6

57-58 R1: Trowbridge Town (A) 2-0
R2: Torquay United (A) 1-1, (H) 2-1
R3: Liverpool (A) 1-1, (H) 2-3

58-59 R1: Yeovil Town (H) 0-0, (A) 0-1

59-60 R1: Oswestry Town (H) 6-0
R2: Southampton (A) 0-3

60-61 R1: Clacton Town (A) 3-1
R2: Gillingham (A) 2-3

61-62 R1: Watford (H) 0-2

62-63 R1: Brighton & Hove Albion (H) 2-1
R2: Watford (H) 0-2

63-64 R1: Yeovil Town (A) 0-1

64-65 R1: Luton Town (A) 0-1

65-66 R1: Notts County (H) 3-1
R2: Watford (H) 2-1
R3: Rotherham United (A) 2-3

66-67 R1: Watford (A) 0-1

67-68 R1: Brighton & Hove Albion (A) 0-1

68-69 R1: King's Lynn (H) 9-0
R2: Brentwood Town (H) 10-1
R3: Swindon Town (A) 2-0
R4: Mansfield Town (A) 1-2

69-70 R1: Gillingham (H) 0-0, (A) 1-2

70-71 R1: Weymouth (H) 7-0
R2: Dagenham (H) 1-0
R3: Carlisle United (H) 0-3

71-72 R1: Aston Villa (H) 1-0
R2: A.F.C. Bournemouth (A) 0-2

72-73 R1: Aldershot (H) 0-2

73-74 R1: Boreham Wood (H) 3-0
R2: Reading (H) 2-0
R3: Peterborough United (A) 1-3

74-75 R1: A.P. Leamington (A) 2-1
R2: Ilford (A) 2-0
R3: Queens Park Rangers (H) 2-2, (A) 0-2

75-76 R1: Swansea City (H) 2-0
R2: Dover (H) 4-1
R3: Brighton & Hove Albion (H) 2-1
R4: Cardiff City (H) 2-1
R5: Derby County (A) 0-1

76-77 R1: Exeter City (A) 1-1, (H) 2-1
R2: Newport County (H) 3-0
R3: Chester (H) 0-4

77-78 R1: Torquay United (A) 2-1
R2: A.P. Leamington (A) 0-0, (H) 4-0
R3: Derby County (A) 2-3

78-79 R1: Peterborough United (H) 3-2
R2: Watford (A) 1-1, (H) 1-0
R3: Liverpool (H) 0-0, (A) 0-3

79-80 R1: Wealdstone (A) 1-0
R2: Harlow Town (H) 1-1, (A) 0-1

80-81 R1: Hereford United (H) 0-1

81-82 R1: Hereford United (A) 1-3

82-83 R1: A.F.C. Bournemouth (A) 2-0
R2: Yeovil Town (H) 3-0
R3: Sheffield W. (H) 0-0, (A) 2-2, (A) 1-2

83-84 R1: Plymouth Argyle (H) 0-0, (A) 0-2

84-85 R1: Colchester United (H) 2-2, (A) 2-3

85-86 R1: Newport County (H) 0-1

86-87 R1: Halesowen Town (H) 4-1
R2: Northampton Town (H) 4-4, (A) 2-3

87-88 R1: Walsall (H) 0-0, (A) 1-2

88-89 R1: Bristol City (A) 1-3

89-90 R1: Aylesbury United (A) 0-1

90-91 R1: Leyton Orient (A) 2-3

91-92 R3: Everton (A) 0-1

92-93 R3: Millwall (H) 1-0
R4: Huddersfield Town (A) 2-1
R5: Sheffield Wednesday (A) 0-2

SOUTH HETTON COLLIERY WELFARE

Currently: Defunct

48-49 EX: Eldon Albion (A) 6-0
PR: Ferryhill Athletic (H) 1-1, (A) 2-1
Q1: Murton Colliery Welfare (H) 0-1

49-50 PR: Chilton Athletic (H) 5-1
Q1: Silksworth C.W. (A) 0-0, (H) 0-2

50-51 EX: Stanley United (H) 2-1
PR: West Auckland Town (A) 0-4

SOUTH KIRKBY COLLIERY

Currently: Doncaster Senior League

45-46 Q1: Meltham Mills (A) 7-1
Q2: Frickley Colliery (H) 0-2

46-47 Q1: Ossett Town (A) 2-0
Q2: Frickley Colliery (H) 2-1
Q3: Yorkshire Amateur (H) 1-2

47-48	Q1: Bradford United (A) 2-4
48-49	EX: Armthorpe Welfare (A) 5-2 PR: Bentley Colliery (A) 3-1 Q1: Frickley Colliery (A) 0-3
49-50	PR: Brodsworth Main Colliery (A) 0-2
50-51	PR: Selby Town (A) 1-4
51-52	Q1: Grimethorpe Colliery (H) 4-0 Q2: Upton Colliery (A) 2-2, (H) 2-3
52-53	Q1: Hallam (H) 2-1 Q2: Frickley Colliery (A) 0-4
53-54	Q1: Hallam (H) 1-2
54-55	Q1: Langwith Miners Welfare (H) 3-6

SOUTH LAWFORD

Currently: Defunct

50-51	EX: Raleigh Athletic (H) 1-1, (A) 2-5

SOUTH LIVERPOOL

Currently: Defunct (reformed and merged with Cheshire Lines F.C., and playing as Cheshire Lines South Liverpool in Liverpool County Comb.)

45-46	R1: Tranmere R. (H) 1-1, (A) 1-6 *(agg: 2-7)*
46-47	Q4: Bangor City (H) 2-2, (A) 4-0 R1: Workington (H) 2-1 R2: Carlisle United (H) 2-3
47-48	Q4: Runcorn (H) 2-3
48-49	Q4: Rhyl (A) 0-3
49-50	PR: Wigan Athletic (H) 0-1
50-51	PR: Wigan Athletic (H) 0-0, (A) 2-3
51-52	PR: Bangor City (H) 1-1, (A) 1-2
52-53	Q1: Ellesmere Port Town (A) 0-4
54-55	PR: Bangor City (H) 1-3
55-56	PR: Ellesmere Port Town (H) 4-2 Q1: Earlestown (A) 1-1, (H) 3-1 Q2: Runcorn (A) 1-1, (H) 1-3
56-57	PR: Earle (H) 7-0 Q1: Pwllheli & District (A) 4-1 Q2: Runcorn (A) 1-0 Q3: New Brighton (A) 1-6
57-58	PR: Stork (A) 2-3
58-59	PR: Runcorn (A) 1-7
59-60	PR: Pwllheli & District (H) 3-4
60-61	PR: Pwllheli & District (H) 1-5
61-62	Q1: Stork (H) 4-0 Q2: Runcorn (H) 0-0, (A) 0-2
62-63	Q1: Skelmersdale United (H) 3-1 Q2: St Helens Town (A) 1-2
63-64	Q1: Prescot Cables (H) 3-0 Q2: Ashton United (A) 2-2, (H) 3-1 Q3: Altrincham (A) 0-3
64-65	Q1: Ashton United (H) 2-1 Q2: Skelmersdale United (A) 2-2, (H) 5-3 Q3: Altrincham (A) 3-0 Q4: Retford Town (A) 3-2 R1: Halifax Town (A) 2-2, (H) 4-2 R2: Workington (H) 0-2
65-66	Q4: Ossett Albion (H) 3-0 R1: Wrexham (A) 1-4
66-67	Q4: Morecambe (H) 1-1, (A) 0-1
67-68	Q1: Rhyl (A) 1-2
68-69	Q1: Oswestry Town (H) 4-2 Q2: Marine (H) 2-1 Q3: Bangor City (A) 1-3
69-70	Q1: Marine (A) 3-2 Q2: Runcorn (A) 1-1, (H) 5-0 Q3: Rhyl (H) 2-0 Q4: Kirkby Town (H) 0-0, (A) 3-4
70-71	Q1: Stalybridge Celtic (H) 1-1, (A) 2-0 Q2: Burscough (A) 3-0 Q3: Rossendale United (A) 3-1 Q4: Rhyl (A) 3-3, (H) 2-2, 0-1
71-72	Q1: Northwich Victoria (H) 1-0 Q2: Runcorn (H) 1-0 Q3: Oswestry Town (A) 0-2

Above: *South Liverpool's last ever F.A. Cup tie. Their goalkeeper John Routledge saves bravely from Kevin Stonehouse of Bishop Auckland. Photo: Tony Smith.*

72-73	Q1: Portmadoc (A) 0-0, (H) 2-1 Q2: Nantwich (A) 1-1, (H) 1-0 Q3: Marine (A) 2-0 Q4: Macclesfield Town (A) 1-0 R1: Tranmere Rovers (H) 0-2
73-74	Q1: Great Harwood (A) 1-0 Q2: Ormskirk (H) 0-1
74-75	Q1: Bethesda Athletic (A) 0-1
75-76	Q1: Witton Albion (H) 0-3
76-77	PR: Winsford United (H) 0-4
77-78	Q1: Radcliffe Borough (A) 6-2 Q2: Bangor City (H) 2-2, (A) 0-1
78-79	Q1: Formby (H) 0-3
79-80	Q1: Winsford United (H) 2-2, (A) 1-3
80-81	PR: Prescot Cables (A) 1-2
81-82	PR: Accrington Stanley (A) 1-2
82-83	PR: Horwich R.M.I. (H) 1-4
83-84	Q1: Chadderton (A) 4-1 Q2: Emley (A) 3-1 Q3: Bangor City (A) 0-1
84-85	Q1: Bilston Town (A - *at Darlaston*) 2-3
85-86	Q1: Boldmere St Michael (A) 1-1, (H) 5-0 Q2: Long Eaton United (A) 3-2 Q3: Witton Albion (H) 5-0 Q4: Bangor City (A) 1-1, (H) 3-2 R1: Whitby Town (A) 0-1
86-87	Q1: G.K.N. Sankey (H) 2-3
87-88	Q1: Horwich R.M.I. (A) 1-1, (H) 3-4
88-89	Q1: Leek Town (H) 1-1, (A) 1-2
89-90	Q1: Mossley (A) 0-0, (H) 0-3
90-91	Q1: Warrington T. (H - *at Bootle F.C.*) 2-0 Q2: Curzon Ashton (H - *at Bootle F.C.*) 1-0 Q3: Hyde U. (A) 1-1, (H - *at Bootle F.C.*) 3-1 Q4: Bishop Auckland (A) 0-1

SOUTH LYNN

Currently: Defunct

49-50	PR: Wimblington Old Boys (H) 4-0 Q1: Histon Institute (A) 2-4
50-51	PR: Chatteris Town (H) 0-1

SOUTH NORMANTON WELF.

Currently: Defunct

48-49	PR: Holbeach United (H) 5-1 Q1: Spalding United (H) 1-3
49-50	EX: Sherwood Colliery (A) 3-0 PR: Worksop Town (H) 1-1, (A) 2-1 Q1: Bourne Town (H) 3-2 Q2: Grantham (H) 0-3
50-51	PR: Boston United (A) 2-3
51-52	Q1: Coalville Town (H) 6-0 Q2: Hinckley Athletic (A) 2-2, (H) 1-2
52-53	Q1: Barwell Athletic (H) 4-0 Q2: Whitwick Colliery (H) 3-0 Q3: Brush Sports (A) 1-3
53-54	Q1: Gedling Colliery (H) 1-1, (A) 4-2 Q2: Basford United (A) 5-0 Q3: Gresley Rovers (A) 1-5
54-55	Q1: Newhall United (H) 2-1 Q2: Ilkeston United (H) 1-5
55-56	Q2: Ilkeston Town (A) 1-3
56-57	Q1: Clay Cross & Danesmoor M.W. (H) 3-5
57-58	Q1: Ilkeston Town (H) 2-2, (A) 0-2
58-59	Q1: Clay Cross & Danesmoor M.W. (A) 3-2 Q2: Sheffield (H) 1-4
59-60	Q1: Ransome & Marles (H) 3-0 Q2: Shirebrook Miners Welfare (H) 6-1 Q3: Heanor Town (A) 1-2
60-61	Q1: Belper Town (A) 2-3
61-62	Q1: Sutton Town (H) 2-6

SOUTHPORT

Currently: Alliance Premier League

45-46	R1: Oldham Ath. (H) 1-2, (A) 1-3 *(agg: 2-5)*
46-47	R1: Stockport County (A) 0-2
47-48	R1: Hull City (A) 1-1, (H) 2-3
48-49	R1: Horden Colliery Welfare (H) 2-1 R2: York City (H) 2-2, (A) 2-0 R3: Derby County (A) 1-4
49-50	R1: Barrow (H) 1-1, (A) 1-0 R2: Bradford City (H) 2-1 R3: Hull City (H) 0-0, (A) 0-5
50-51	R1: Lincoln City (A) 1-1, (H) 3-2 R2: Carlisle United (H) 1-3
51-52	R1: Bangor City (A) 2-2, (H) 3-0 R2: Reading (A) 1-1, (H) 1-1, 0-2
52-53	R1: Bangor City (H) 3-1 R2: Halifax Town (A) 2-4
53-54	R1: Carlisle United (H) 1-0 R2: Port Vale (H) 1-1, (A) 0-2
54-55	R1: Bradford (Park Avenue) (A) 0-2
55-56	R1: Ashton United (H) 6-1 R2: Grimsby Town (H) 0-0, (A) 2-3
56-57	R1: York City (H) 0-0, (A) 1-2
57-58	R1: Wigan Athletic (H) 1-2
58-59	R1: Halifax Town (H) 0-2

59-60 R1: Workington (H) 2-2, (A) 0-3

60-61 R1: Macclesfield Town (H) 7-2
R2: Bangor City (A) 1-1, (H) 3-1
R3: Stockport County (A) 1-3

61-62 R1: Northwich Victoria (H) 1-0
R2: Mansfield Town (H) 4-2
R3: Shrewsbury Town (H) 1-3

62-63 R1: Wrexham (H) 1-1, (A) 2-3

63-64 R1: Walsall (H) 2-1
R2: Lincoln City (A) 0-2

64-65 R1: Annfield Plain (H) 6-1
R2: Wrexham (A) 3-2
R3: Leeds United (A) 0-3

65-66 R1: Halifax Town (H) 2-0
R2: Stockport County (H) 3-3, (A) 2-0
R3: Ipswich Town (H) 0-0, (A) 3-2
R4: Cardiff City (H) 2-0
R5: Hull City (A) 0-2

66-67 R1: Barnsley (A) 1-3

67-68 R1: Lincoln City (H) 3-1
R2: Runcorn (H) 4-2
R3: Everton (H) 0-1

68-69 R1: Tranmere Rovers (A) 1-0
R2: Doncaster Rovers (A) 1-2

69-70 R1: Lincoln City (A) 0-2

70-71 R1: Boston United (H) 0-2

71-72 R1: Workington (H) 1-3

72-73 R1: Port Vale (A) 1-2

73-74 R1: Rotherham United (A) 1-2

74-75 R1: Bury (A) 2-4

75-76 R1: Spennymoor United (A) 1-4

76-77 R1: Port Vale (H) 1-2

77-78 R1: Runcorn (H) 2-2, (A) 0-1

78-79 Q4: Northwich Victoria (A) 0-0, (H) 2-0
R1: Altrincham (A) 3-4

79-80 Q4: Workington (H) 1-3

80-81 Q1: St Helens Town (H) 1-3

81-82 Q1: Droylsden (A) 0-1

82-83 PR: Lytham (A) 2-1
Q1: Darwen (A) 0-2

83-84 Q1: Radcliffe Borough (A) 3-1
Q2: Prestwich Heys (A) 1-0
Q3: Horwich R.M.I. (A) 1-2

84-85 Q1: Leyland Motors (A) 4-0
Q2: Alfreton Town (H) 1-1, (A) 0-3

85-86 Q1: Clitheroe (H) 4-2
Q2: Stalybridge Celtic (H) 2-0
Q3: Chorley (H) 1-3

86-87 Q1: Garforth (H) 1-1, (A) 1-1 *abandoned in extra-time*, (H) 2-1
Q2: Lancaster City (A) 1-1, (H) 3-1
Q3: Emley (H) 3-3, (A) 4-4, (H) 2-0
Q4: Macclesfield Town (A) 1-0
R1: Scunthorpe United (A) 0-2

87-88 Q1: Emley (A) 0-2

88-89 Q1: Penrith (H) 1-0
Q2: Harworth Colliery Institute (H) 2-0
Q3: Bangor City (H) 3-0
Q4: Tow Law Town (H) 2-1
R1: Port Vale (H) 0-2

89-90 Q1: Stalybridge Celtic (H) 3-2
Q2: Arnold Town (H) 2-1
Q3: Rhyl (A) 3-0
Q4: Whitley Bay (H) 1-3

90-91 Q1: Armthorpe Welfare (A) 2-1
Q2: Bootle (A) 0-2

91-92 Q1: Ossett Town (A) 1-0
Q2: Stalybridge Celtic (H) 1-2

92-93 Q1: Buxton (H) 0-0, (A) 2-1
Q2: Chadderton (H) 2-0

Q3: Brigg Town (A) 1-0
Q4: Barrow (A) 0-0, (H) 3-2
R1: Blyth Spartans (A) 2-1
R2: Hartlepool United (A) 0-4

SOUTHPORT LEYLAND ROAD

Currently: Defunct

49-50 EX: Hoylake Athletic (A) 5-9

SOUTH SHIELDS

See Gateshead United

SOUTH SHIELDS EX-SCHOOLBOYS

Currently: Defunct

50-51 EX: Annfield Plain (A) 1-1, (H) 1-3

SOUTHWICK

Currently: Sussex County League

45-46 Q1: Bognor Regis Town (H) 4-1
Q2: Haywards Heath (A) 1-5

46-47 Q1: Horsham (H) 5-3
Q2: Eastbourne (H) 5-5, (A) 1-4

48-49 PR: Littlehampton Town (A) 2-7

50-51 PR: Worthing (H) 1-2

51-52 PR: Lancing Athletic (H) 1-1, (A) 1-0
Q1: Worthing (H) 6-7

52-53 PR: Haywards Heath (A) 2-2, (H) 0-1

53-54 PR: East Grinstead (A) 2-4

54-55 PR: Littlehampton Town (A) 1-3

55-56 Q1: Littlehampton Town (H) 2-1
Q2: Worthing (H) 1-2

56-57 PR: Worthing (A) 2-3

57-58 Q1: Worthing (H) 3-2
Q2: Redhill (A) 0-3

58-59 PR: Lancing Athletic (H) 3-1
Q1: Eastbourne United (A) 1-3

59-60 PR: Crawley Town (A) 1-6

60-61 Q1: Worthing (H) 2-2, (A) 3-2
Q2: Horsham (A) 1-10

68-69 Q1: Worthing (H) 1-1, (A) 5-3
Q2: Eastbourne (H) 1-2

69-70 Q1: Arundel (H) 2-1
Q2: Horsham (A) 0-2

70-71 Q1: Littlehampton Town (H) 2-3

71-72 Q1: Hastings Utd (A) 1-1, (H) 1-1, 1-2

72-73 Q1: Redhill (A) 0-1

73-74 Q1: Littlehampton Town (H) 0-3

74-75 Q1: Bexhill Town (A) 6-0
Q2: Haywards Heath (H) 3-2
Q3: Ringmer (A) 3-1
Q4: Hayes (H) 2-1
R1: A.F.C. Bournemouth (A) 0-5

75-76 Q1: Pagham (A) 1-1, (H) 3-1
Q2: Guildford & Dorking Utd (A) 2-2, (H) 3-2
Q3: Basingstoke Town (H) 2-1
Q4: Wealdstone (A) 1-3

76-77 Q1: Deal Town (H) 2-0
Q2: Ramsgate (A) 1-1, (H) 1-2

77-78 PR: Waterlooville (H) 0-1

78-79 Q1: Horsham (H) 1-2

79-80 PR: Worthing (H) 2-3

80-81 Q1: Croydon (A) 0-1

81-82 PR: Thanet United (H) 0-1

82-83 Q1: Banstead Athletic (H) 2-2, (A) 1-0
Q2: Carshalton Athletic (A) 1-3

83-84 Q1: Worthing (H) 1-2

84-85 PR: Egham Town (H) 1-1, (A) 1-2

85-86 PR: Deal Town (A) 4-1
Q1: Folkestone (H) 1-1, (A) 1-1, (H) 3-1
Q2: Dulwich Hamlet (A) 1-1, (H) 2-1
Q3: Croydon (H) 0-1

86-87 Q1: Hythe Town (H) 1-0
Q2: Ashford Town (A) 0-0, (H) 1-0
Q3: Newport Isle of Wight (H) 2-0
Q4: Maidstone (H) 1-1, (A) 1-1, (A) 2-2, (H) 1-5

87-88 Q1: Croydon (H) 1-3

88-89 Q1: Littlehampton Town (H) 5-0
Q2: Whyteleafe (H) 0-1

89-90 PR: Rainham Town (H) 3-0
Q1: Shoreham (H) 5-0
Q2: Woking (A) 1-4

90-91 PR: Corinthian (H) 1-0
Q1: Peacehaven & Telscombe (A) 1-4

91-92 PR: Langney Sports (A) 1-0
Q1: Sittingbourne (H) 1-3

92-93 PR: Ryde Sports (A) 2-1
Q1: Witney Town (H) 2-5

SPALDING UNITED

Currently: United Counties League

47-48 PR: Ollerton Colliery (H) 3-2
Q1: Grantham (H) 0-4

48-49 PR: Boston United (H) 2-1
Q1: South Normanton Welfare (A) 3-1
Q2: Ransome & Marles (H) 0-1

49-50 EX: Stamford (H) 1-0
PR: Heanor Athletic (H) 3-2
Q1: Sutton Town (A) 4-0
Q2: Gedling Colliery (H) 5-2

Right: *A far-cry from their Football League days - Southport visit Armthorpe Welfare, and forwards Reggie McGuire and Steve Holden apply the pressure.*
Photo: S Jackson.

Q3: Grantham (H) 0-2

50-51 PR: Ransome & Marles (A) 1-0
Q1: Gedling Colliery (H) 8-0
Q2: Langold W.M.C. (H) 2-2, (A) 2-1
Q3: Linby Colliery (H) 2-2, (A) 1-3

51-52 Q1: Kettering Town (H) 1-7

52-53 Q1: Stamford (H) 1-0
Q2: Peterborough United (H) 2-2, (A) 0-3

53-54 Q1: Corby Town (A) 2-6

54-55 Q1: Corby Town (H) 2-3

55-56 Q1: Wellingborough Town (A) 9-1
Q2: Corby Town (H) 1-3

56-57 Q1: Kettering Town (H) 3-2
Q2: Rushden Town (A) 3-0
Q3: Corby Town (A) 1-3

57-58 Q1: Rushden Town (A) 2-2, (H) 8-0
Q2: Wellingborough Town (A) 1-1, (H) 4-1
Q3: Corby Town (H) 4-0
Q4: Belper Town (H) 2-1
R1: Durham City (A) 1-3

58-59 Q1: Kettering Town (H) 4-6

59-60 Q2: Corby Town (H) 1-2

60-61 Q1: Louth United (A) 0-1

61-62 Q1: Skegness Town (A) 1-1, (H) 0-3

62-63 Q1: Boston United (H) 1-3

64-65 Q1: Boston United (A) 14-0
Q2: Skegness Town (A) 3-0
Q3: Grantham (H) 4-0
Q4: Hinckley Athletic (H) 3-1
R1: Newport County (A) 3-5

65-66 Q1: Grantham (A) 0-3

66-67 Q1: Holbeach United (H) 5-2
Q2: Boston United (A) 0-2

67-68 PR: Wisbech Town (A) 1-1, (H) 2-3

68-69 Q1: Holbeach United (A) 1-1, (H) 2-5

69-70 Q1: Boston United (H) 0-4

70-71 Q1: Skegness Town (H) 1-1, (A) 2-1
Q2: Boston (H) 2-2, (A) 0-3

71-72 Q1: Wisbech Town (H) 0-1

72-73 PR: Kettering Town (H) 0-2

73-74 PR: Thetford Town (A) 0-3

74-75 Q1: Boston (A) 0-4

75-76 Q1: King's Lynn (H) 3-3, (A) 1-1, 5-2
Q2: Soham Town Rangers (H) 8-2
Q3: Great Yarmouth Town (H) 2-0
Q4: Coventry Sporting (A) 0-2

76-77 Q1: Corby Town (H) 0-3

77-78 PR: Arnold (H) 2-3

78-79 Q1: Brigg Town (A) 1-1, (H) 3-4

79-80 PR: Wisbech Town (H) 1-3

80-81 Q1: Boston (A) 1-6

81-82 PR: Bury Town (A) 0-2

82-83 PR: Irthlingborough Diamonds (H) 0-1

83-84 Q1: Sutton Coldfield Town (A) 1-2

84-85 PR: Coventry Sporting (A) 0-0, (H) 2-3

85-86 PR: Coventry Sp. (H) 1-2 *Coventry expelled*
Q1: Matlock T. (H) 2-2, (A) 0-0, (A) 2-3

86-87 PR: Rushden Town (H) 0-0, (A) 4-2
Q1: Stevenage Borough (A) 0-1

87-88 PR: Wellingborough Town (A) 2-3

88-89 PR: Brackley Town (A) 0-1

89-90 PR: Chasetown (A) 2-2, (H) 3-0
Q1: Willenhall Town (A) 1-1, (H) 0-2

90-91 PR: Leighton Town (A) 1-0
Q1: Rushden Town (H) 0-3

91-92 PR: Solihull Borough (A) 0-1

92-93 PR: Cheshunt (A) 0-0, (H) 0-5

SPENCER MOULTON

Currently: (Avon (Bradford) F.C.) Trowbridge Lge

46-47 EX: Melksham (H) 2-4

48-49 EX: West End Rovers (H) 10-3
PR: Westbury United (A) 1-2

49-50 EX: Devizes Town (H) 1-3

51-52 PR: Chippenham Town (A) 0-4

52-53 Q1: Chippenham Town (H) 0-3

53-54 PR: Westbury United (H) 6-2
Q1: Welton Rovers (H) 3-5

69-70 Q1: Weston-super-Mare (A) 2-11

SPENNYMOOR UNITED

Currently: Northern Premier League

45-46 Q1: Tow Law Town (H) 4-1
Q2: Stanley United (H) 6-1
Q3: Shildon (A) 2-3

46-47 PR: Willington (H) 7-2
Q1: Shildon (A) 3-3, (H) 4-2
Q2: Ferryhill Athletic (H) 2-0
Q3: Seaham Colliery Welfare (A) 4-0
Q4: South Bank (A) 3-0
R1: Lancaster City (A) 0-1

47-48 PR: Horden Colliery Welfare (A) 0-2

48-49 EX: Blackhall Colliery Welfare (H) 3-0
PR: Dawdon Colliery Welfare (A) 3-1
Q1: Horden Colliery Welfare (A) 1-3

49-50 EX: Shotton Colliery Welfare (A) 2-2, (H) 4-2
PR: Willington (A) 2-2, (H) 2-4

50-51 EX: Blackhall Colliery Welfare (H) 1-2

51-52 Q1: West Auckland Town (A) 4-2
Q2: Shildon (A) 2-0
Q3: Crook Town (A) 2-0
Q4: Goole Town (A) 3-4

52-53 Q1: Stanley United (A) 4-2
Q2: Crook Town (A) 2-1
Q3: Evenwood Town (A) 1-1, (H) 4-1
Q4: Bishop Auckland (H) 1-1, (A) 1-2

53-54 Q1: West Auckland Town (H) 6-0
Q2: Stanley United (H) 2-1
Q3: Willington (H) 2-1
Q4: Bishop Auckland (H) 3-1
R1: Barrow (H) 0-3

54-55 Q4: Horden Colliery Welfare (A) 0-1

55-56 Q4: Crook Town (H) 2-2, (A) 0-5

56-57 Q1: Blackhall C.W. (H) 1-1, (A) 4-0
Q2: Durham City (H) 3-1
Q3: Horden Colliery Welfare (A) 0-3

57-58 Q1: Ferryhill Athletic (H) 2-2, (A) 2-4

58-59 Q1: Stockton (A) 5-4
Q2: Ferryhill Athletic (H) 3-3, (A) 1-2

59-60 Q1: Shotton Colliery Welfare (A) 2-0
Q2: South Bank (H) 3-1
Q3: Stockton (A) 1-1, (H) 1-0
Q4: Blyth Spartans (A) 0-4

60-61 Q1: North Shields (A) 2-6

61-62 PR: Ashington (A) 2-3

62-63 Q1: Consett (A) 0-2

63-64 Q1: South Bank (A) 5-2
Q2: Whitby Town (A) 2-2, (H) 0-2

65-66 Q1: North Shields (H) 2-0
Q2: Bishop Auckland (H) 0-0, (A) 4-1
Q3: Whitby Town (A) 3-4

66-67 Q1: Horden Colliery Welfare (H) 0-2

67-68 PR: Boldon Colliery Welfare (H) 5-0
Q1: Stockton (A) 3-0
Q2: Ferryhill Athletic (A) 0-0, (H) 4-2
Q3: Whitby Town (A) 1-0
Q4: Morecambe (H) 1-0
R1: Goole Town (A) 0-0, (H) 3-1
R2: Macclesfield Town (A) 0-2

68-69 Q1: Blyth Spartans (A) 3-4

69-70 Q1: South Bank (H) 1-0
Q2: Gateshead (H) 2-2, (A) 1-0
Q3: Whitley Bay (A) 3-2
Q4: Tow Law Town (H) 1-0
R1: Wrexham (H) 1-4

70-71 Q1: Bedlington Terriers (H) 2-0
Q2: Gateshead (H) 0-1

71-72 Q1: Horden Colliery Welfare (H) 4-2
Q2: Durham City (A) 0-2

72-73 Q1: Stockton (H) 5-1
Q2: North Shields (H) 1-1, (A) 2-2, 1-0
Q3: Gateshead (A) 4-0
Q4: Willington (A) 2-0
R1: Shrewsbury Town (H) 1-1, (A) 1-3

73-74 Q1: North Shields (A) 0-2

74-75 PR: Evenwood Town (A) 2-2, (H) 4-0
Q1: Durham City (H) 6-2
Q2: Wingate (H) 3-0
Q3: Bishop Auckland (A) 2-4

75-76 Q1: Crook Town (H) 1-1, (A) 2-1
Q2: Penrith (H) 2-0
Q3: Netherfield (H) 3-0
Q4: Tow Law Town (A) 2-0
R1: Southport (H) 4-1
R2: Bury (A) 0-3

76-77 PR: North Shields (A) 0-0, (H) 4-1
Q1: Whitby Town (A) 0-3

77-78 PR: Horden Colliery Welfare (A) 2-2, (H) 3-1
Q1: Ferryhill Athletic (A) 4-2
Q2: Durham City (A) 2-1
Q3: Whitley Bay (A) 2-2, (H) 4-1
Q4: Bangor City (H) 2-1
R1: Goole Town (H) 3-1
R2: Rotherham United (A) 0-6

78-79 Q1: Carlisle City (H) 2-1
Q2: North Shields (A) 3-0
Q3: Consett (H) 0-0, (A) 2-1
Q4: Runcorn (H) 0-0, (A) 1-2

79-80 Q1: Brandon United (A) 2-3

80-81 Q1: Wallsend Town (A) 2-0
Q2: Horden Colliery Welfare (H) 1-2

81-82 Q1: Gateshead (A) 1-1, (H) 3-0
Q2: Chester-le-Street (A) 1-1, (H) 1-0
Q3: North Shields (H) 2-2, (A) 5-1
Q4: Runcorn (H) 0-1

82-83 Q1: Fleetwood Town (A) 2-1
Q2: Seaham Colliery Welfare Red Star (H) 2-1
Q3: Frickley A. (A) 1-1, (H) 1-1, (A) 3-2
Q4: Scarborough (A) 2-4

83-84 Q1: Yorkshire Amateur (A) 1-4

84-85 Q1: Ryhope Community Association (A) 2-4

85-86 Q1: Eppleton Colliery Welfare (A) 4-2
Q2: Gateshead (H) 1-2

86-87 Q1: Tow Law Town (A) 2-0
Q2: Evenwood Town (A) 5-0
Q3: Peterlee Newtown (H) 1-0
Q4: Gretna (H) 2-0
R1: Tranmere Rovers (H) 2-3

87-88 Q1: South Bank (A) 0-1

88-89 Q1: Bridlington Trinity (H) 3-0
Q2: Ferryhill Athletic (A) 2-0
Q3: Tow Law T. (A) 2-2, (H) 2-2, (H) 1-2

89-90 Q1: Billingham Town (A) 1-1, (H) 2-1
Q2: Whitley Bay (H) 2-4

90-91 Q1: Stockton (A - *played home*) 2-0
Q2: Esh Winning (A) 3-1
Q3: Northallerton Town (H) 2-0
Q4: Northwich Victoria (A) 1-1, (H) 2-1
R1: Chesterfield (A) 2-3

91-92 PR: Easington Colliery (H) 1-0
Q1: Bedlington Terriers (H) 0-1

92-93 PR: Ferryhill Athletic (A) 3-2
Q1: Gretna (H) 4-0
Q2: Bamber Bridge (A) 4-0
Q3: Gateshead (H) 0-7

STAFFORD RANGERS

Currently: Alliance Premier League

47-48 PR: Moor Green (A) 7-2
Q1: Hereford United (A) 1-2

48-49 PR: Sutton Coldfield Town (H) 2-1
Q1: Darlaston (H) 4-3
Q2: Hereford United (H) 3-5

49-50 PR: Worcester City (H) 3-0
Q1: Stourbridge (A) 3-0
Q2: Dudley Town (H) 2-2, (A) 0-1

50-51 PR: Dudley Town (H) 1-2

51-52 Q1: Kidderminster Harriers (A) 2-3

52-53 PR: Bilston (H) 0-1

53-54 PR: Halesowen Town (A) 2-1
Q1: Bromsgrove Rovers (H) 2-3

54-55 PR: Dudley Town (H) 3-1
Q1: Stourbridge (H) 0-1

55-56 PR: Bilston (A) 5-1
Q1: Worcester City (H) 1-2

56-57 PR: Halesowen Town (A) 3-2
Q1: Oswestry Town (H) 1-1, (A) 4-0
Q2: Wellington Town (A) 1-4

57-58 Q1: Oswestry Town (A) 0-3

58-59 PR: Dudley Town (A - *played home*) 11-0
Q1: Stourbridge (H) 4-1
Q2: Wellington Town (A) 1-3

59-60 PR: Bromsgrove Rovers (A) 1-2

60-61 Q1: Wellington Town (H) 0-1

61-62 Q1: Sankey of Wellington (H) 2-2, (A) 1-5

62-63 Q1: Moor Green (A) 6-0
Q2: Wellington Town (H) 0-2

63-64 Q1: Kidderminster Harriers (A) 1-4

64-65 Q1: Sankey of Wellington (H) 3-3, (A) 0-3

65-66 Q1: Bromsgrove Rovers (H) 1-1, (A) 2-1
Q2: Kidderminster Harriers (H) 0-2

67-68 PR: Lower Gornal Athletic (H) 0-1

68-69 Q1: Bromsgrove Rovers (A) 1-1, (H) 2-1
Q2: Darlaston (H) 2-0
Q3: Bilston (A) 2-3

69-70 Q1: Bilston (A) 1-0
Q2: Tamworth (A) 3-3, (H) 0-2

70-71 PR: Brierley Hill Alliance (H) 1-2

71-72 Q1: Gresley Rovers (A) 4-0
Q2: Burton Albion (A) 2-1
Q3: Sutton Town (H) 2-0
Q4: Rossendale United (A) 3-6

72-73 R1: Crewe Alexandra (A) 0-1

73-74 Q4: Alvechurch (H) 1-1, (A) 0-2

74-75 Q1: Belper Town (A) 0-0, (H) 4-0
Q2: Macclesfield Town (H) 3-0
Q3: Burton Albion (A) 0-0, (H) 2-0
Q4: King's Lynn (A) 3-1
R1: Stockport County (A) 0-0, (H) 1-0
R2: Halifax Town (H) 2-1
R3: Rotherham United (H) 0-0, (A) 2-0
R4: Peterborough United (H) 1-2

75-76 Q4: Alvechurch (H) 1-1, (A) 2-1
R1: A.P. Leamington (A) 3-2
R2: Halifax Town (H) 1-3

76-77 R1: Halifax Town (H) 0-0, (A) 0-1

77-78 Q4: Northwich Victoria (A) 2-2, (H) 2-1
R1: Carlisle United (A) 0-2

78-79 Q4: Redditch United (H) 2-1
R1: Hull City (A) 1-2

79-80 R1: Moor Green (H) 3-2
R2: Blackburn Rovers (A) 0-2

80-81 Q4: King's Lynn (A) 3-1
R1: Walsall (A) 0-3

81-82 Q4: A.P. Leamington (H) 3-0
R1: York City (H) 1-2

82-83 Q4: Macclesfield Town (A) 1-3

83-84 Q4: Boston United (A) 1-3

84-85 Q1: Rushden Town (A) 3-3, (H) 1-3

85-86 Q1: Lye Town (A) 2-0
Q2: Halesowen Town (A) 2-3

86-87 Q1: Shepshed Charterhouse (A) 1-0
Q2: Atherstone United (A) 4-2
Q3: Wolverton Town (A) 4-1
Q4: Northwich Victoria (A) 1-0

Above: *In 1988 Stafford Rangers became embroiled in a memorable local derby with Crewe. They fell two behind only to battle back and force a replay. Then, away from home, they took a two goal lead themselves only to see it frittered away. Here goalkeeper Ryan Price comes out to claim the ball ahead of Crewe's Mark Gardiner in the match at Marston Road. Photo: Staffordshire Newsletter.*

R1: Port Vale (A) 0-1

87-88 Q1: Walsall Wood (A) 3-0
Q2: Moor Green (H) 2-3

88-89 Q1: Halesowen Harriers (H) 2-0
Q2: Rushall Olympic (H) 1-0
Q3: Leicester United (H) 1-1, (A) 3-2
Q4: Kidderminster Harriers (H) 2-1
R1: Crewe Alexandra (H) 2-2, (A) 2-3

89-90 Q1: Hinckley Town (H) 1-0
Q2: M.K. Wolverton Town (H) 2-0
Q3: Lye Town (A) 2-1
Q4: Wycombe Wanderers (H) 4-1
R1: Halifax Town (H) 2-3

90-91 Q4: Marine (A) 1-1, (H) 2-1
R1: Burnley (H) 1-3

91-92 Q4: Kettering Town (A) 0-0, (H) 0-2

92-93 Q1: Alfreton Town (A) 0-0, (H) 3-0
Q2: Bedworth United (A) 1-1, (H) 1-0
Q3: Frickley Athletic (H) 3-0
Q4: Bromsgrove Rovers (H) 3-0
R1: Lincoln City (A) 0-0, (H) 2-1
R2: Marine (A) 2-3

STAFFORDSHIRE CASUALS

Currently: (Wolverhampton Casuals) West Midlands (Regional) League

48-49 EX: Thynnes Athletic (H) *scratched*

49-50 PR: Sutton Coldfield Town (A) 0-4

STAINES TOWN

Currently: Isthmian League

58-59 PR: Harrow Town (H) 2-2, (A) 3-2
Q1: Wembley (H) 3-6

59-60 Q1: Hayes (H) 1-2

60-61 Q1: Dulwich Hamlet (H) 0-2

67-68 Q1: Carshalton Ath. (A) 2-2, (H) 1-1, 2-3

68-69 Q1: Croydon Amateurs (H) 0-4

69-70 Q1: Hayes (A) 2-2, (H) 1-0
Q2: Whyteleafe (A) 2-1
Q3: Carshalton Athletic (H) 1-2

70-71 Q1: Leytonstone (H) 0-1

71-72 PR: Ilford (A) 3-2
Q1: Ford United (A) 4-1
Q2: Windsor & Eton (A) 1-2

72-73 Q1: Walton & Hersham (A) 0-3

73-74 Q1: Croydon (H) 2-0
Q2: Egham Town (H) 2-0
Q3: Wimbledon (H) 1-1, (A) 3-4

74-75 Q1: Farnborough Town (A) 1-1, (H) 0-1

75-76 Q1: Tring Town (H) 2-0
Q2: Sutton United (A) 1-5

76-77 Q1: Hayes (H) 3-1
Q2: Ware (A) 3-1
Q3: Hillingdon Borough (A) 0-2

77-78 PR: Gravesend & Northfleet (A) 0-4

78-79 Q1: Willesden (H) 2-1
Q2: Windsor & Eton (H) 0-0, (A) 0-1

79-80 PR: Wellingborough Town (H) 0-1

80-81 PR: Willesden (H) 0-1

81-82 PR: Edgware Town (A) 1-3

82-83 Q1: Dorking Town (H - *played away*) 5-0
Q2: Wokingham Town (H - *played away*) 0-2

83-84 Q1: Grays Athletic (H) 1-0
Q2: Windsor & Eton (H) 2-2, (A) 0-2

84-85 Q1: Whyteleafe (A) 1-0
Q2: Carshalton Athletic (H) 4-2
Q3: Sittingbourne (A) 1-1, (H) 3-0
Q4: Hastings United (A) 1-1, (H) 2-1
R1: Burton Albion (A) 0-2

85-86 Q1: Molesey (H) 3-1
Q2: Welling United (H) 0-3

86-87 PR: Burgess Hill Town (A) 2-0
Q1: Chatham Town (A) 2-1
Q2: Ruislip Manor (H) 0-0, (A) 2-0
Q3: Wembley (H) 1-1, (A) 1-4

87-88 PR: Ware (H) 0-0, (A) 1-1, (A) 2-4

88-89 PR: Newmarket Town (H) 3-0
Q1: Harrow Borough (H) 2-0
Q2: Cheshunt (A) 2-1
Q3: Wycombe Wanderers (H) 0-1

89-90 Q1: Crawley Town (A) 1-0
Q2: Dunstable (H) 1-0 *Dunstable w'drew 38m.*
Q3: Burnham (A) 1-0
Q4: Yeovil Town (H) 0-3

90-91 Q1: Kingstonian (A) 1-2

91-92 Q1: Hertford Town (A) 0-2

92-93 Q1: Yeading (H) 0-3

STALYBRIDGE CELTIC

Currently: Alliance Premier League

45-46 Q4: Runcorn (H) 3-0
R1: Marine (A) 0-4, (H) 3-3 (*agg: 3-7*)

46-47 Q1: Northwich Victoria (H) 4-3
Q2: Bangor City (A) 1-4

47-48 Q4: Witton Albion (A) 3-2
R1: Tranmere Rovers (A) 0-2

48-49 Q4: Runcorn (A) 1-4

49-50 Q4: Rhyl (A) 0-6

50-51 PR: Matlock Town (A) 4-2
Q1: Hyde United (H) 2-6

51-52 PR: Darwen (H) 2-2, (A) 0-2

52-53 Q1: Hyde United (H) 3-2
Q2: Altrincham (H) 2-2, (A) 1-2

53-54 Q1: Macclesfield Town (H) 1-0
Q2: Altrincham (A) 1-2

54-55 Q1: Nantwich (A) 2-1
Q2: Altrincham (H) 2-1
Q3: Hyde United (A) 1-8

55-56 Q1: Winsford United (H) 1-1, (A) 0-6

57-58 PR: Congleton Town (A) 0-2

58-59 PR: Winsford United (H) 1-1, (A) 1-5

59-60 PR: Witton Albion (A) 3-3, (H) 1-2

60-61 Q1: Nelson (A) 2-6

61-62 Q1: Rossendale United (A) 2-1
Q2: Nelson (H) 1-0
Q3: Hyde United (A) 2-2, (H) 0-0, 2-1
Q4: Rhyl (A) 0-4

62-63 Q1: Bacup Borough (A) 3-0
Q2: Rossendale United (A) 4-2
Q3: Hyde United (H) 1-1, (A) 0-3

63-64 Q1: Chorley (A) 1-2

64-65 Q1: Chorley (H) 5-1
Q2: Rossendale United (A) 3-0
Q3: Nelson (A) 3-2
Q4: Wigan Athletic (H) 2-4

65-66 Q1: Witton Albion (A) 0-4

66-67 Q1: Hyde United (H) 2-2, (A) 1-3

67-68 Q1: Prescot Town (H) 1-1, (A) 1-0
Q2: Burscough (H) 1-1, (A) 1-3

68-69 Q1: Leyland Motors (A) 3-2
Q2: Burscough (H) 2-2, (A) 3-2
Q3: Skelmersdale United (A) 1-3

69-70 PR: Hyde United (A) 1-1, (H) 0-2

70-71 PR: Lostock Gralam (A) 7-0
Q1: South Liverpool (A) 1-1, (H) 0-2

71-72 Q1: Witton Albion (H) 0-1

72-73 Q1: Mossley (A) 1-1, (H) 4-3
Q2: Bradford (Park Avenue) (A) 1-2

73-74 Q1: New Mills (A) 2-0
Q2: Northwich Victoria (H) 3-1
Q3: Macclesfield Town (A) 1-2

74-75 Q1: Frickley Colliery (A) 2-2, (H) 2-0
Q2: Emley (A) 1-3

75-76 Q1: Prescot Town (A) 1-1, (H) 1-2

76-77 PR: Witton Albion (H) 1-3

77-78 Q1: Long Eaton United (A) 2-0
Q2: Sutton Town (H) 6-0
Q3: Hednesford (H) 1-1, (A) 1-2

78-79 Q1: Leek Town (H) 3-1
Q2: Prestwich Heys (A) 1-1, (H) 4-1
Q3: Droylsden (H) 1-1, (A) 1-3

79-80 Q1: Ashton United (H) 1-2

80-81 Q1: Droylsden (A) 1-1, (H) 2-1
Q2: North Ferriby Utd (A) 0-0, (H) 3-0
Q3: Worksop Town (H) 0-0, (A) 2-1
Q4: Fleetwood Town (A) 0-1

81-82 Q1: Yorkshire Amateur (H) 2-1
Q2: Buxton (A) 0-1

82-83 PR: Burscough (H) 1-1, (A) 1-4

83-84 PR: Warrington Town (A) 3-0
Q1: Formby (H) 8-1
Q2: Rhyl (H) 2-0
Q3: Hyde United (A) 0-2

84-85 Q1: Hinckley Athletic (A) 3-1
Q2: Dudley Town (A) 1-1, (H) 3-1
Q3: Winsford United (H) 5-0
Q4: Workington (H) 1-0
R1: Frickley Athletic (A) 1-2

85-86 Q1: Ashton United (A) 1-0
Q2: Southport (A) 0-2

86-87 PR: Sutton Town (A) 2-6

87-88 PR: Congleton Town (H) 2-0
Q1: Macclesfield Town (H) 1-1, (A) 1-5

88-89 Q1: Chadderton (H) 1-4

89-90 Q1: Southport (A) 2-3

90-91 Q1: Droylsden (A) 1-1, (H) 1-2

91-92 Q1: Worksop Town (H) 4-0
Q2: Southport (A) 2-1
Q3: Eastwood Hanley (A) 2-1
Q4: Gretna (A) 2-3

Above: *Mark Burrell of Stalybridge holds off Ian Wheaton of Eastwood Hanley during the tie on 12th October 1991*
Photo: Colin Stevens.

92-93 Q1: Stocksbridge Park Steels (A) 4-0
Q2: Warrington Town (A) 3-0
Q3: Accrington Stanley (H) 1-2

STAMFORD

Currently: United Counties League

47-48 PR: Bourne Town (H) 4-0
Q1: Basford United (A) 1-3

48-49 PR: Linby Colliery (A) 2-3

49-50 EX: Spalding United (A) 0-1

50-51 EX: Boston United (H) 1-1, (A) 2-10

51-52 Q1: Wellingborough Town (H) 5-3
Q2: Desborough Town (A) 1-2

52-53 Q1: Spalding United (A) 0-1

53-54 Q1: Wellingborough Town (H) 5-0
Q2: Corby Town (H) 3-2
Q3: Kettering Town (H) 3-3, (A) 0-12

54-55 Q1: Wellingborough Town (H) 2-2, (A) 0-2

55-56 Q1: Rushden Town (H) 1-5

56-57 Q1: Rushden Town (A) 1-3

57-58 Q1: Kettering Town (A) 1-4

58-59 Q1: Corby Town (A) 2-7

59-60 Q1: Rushden Town (A) 2-3

60-61 Q1: Wellingborough Town (H) 2-1
Q2: Kettering Town (A) 0-3

61-62 Q1: Wellingborough Town (H) 5-0
Q2: Corby Town (H) 1-1, (A) 1-3

62-63 Q2: Bourne Town (A) 1-5

63-64 Q2: Skegness Town (A) 4-2
Q3: Grantham (A) 2-4

64-65 Q1: Skegness Town (H) 1-1, (A) 0-4

65-66 Q1: Boston (H) 0-1

66-67 Q1: Boston United (A) 0-4

67-68 PR: St Neots Town (H) 0-4

68-69 Q1: Desborough Town (A) 4-0
Q2: Bedford Town (H) 1-0
Q3: Biggleswade Town (A) 2-1
Q4: Bury Town (H) 0-2

69-70 Q1: Cambridge City (A) 0-7

70-71 Q1: Lincoln United (H) 2-5

71-72 Q1: Holbeach United (A) 4-1
Q2: Bourne Town (A) 1-3

72-73 Q1: Skegness Town (A) 1-3

73-74 Q1: Desborough Town (H) 1-0
Q2: Holbeach United (H) 3-1
Q3: Wisbech Town (H) 4-2
Q4: King's Lynn (A) 1-3

74-75 Q1: Histon (H) 1-3

75-76 Q1: Corby Town (H) 3-2
Q2: Thetford Town (H) 2-0
Q3: Bedford Town (H) 0-2

76-77 Q1: Holbeach United (H) 3-2
Q2: Wisbech Town (A) 1-1, (H) 3-0
Q3: Boston (A) 0-1

77-78 Q1: Irthlingborough Diamonds (A) 1-3

78-79 Q1: Retford Town (A) 1-2

79-80 Q1: Potton United (H) 2-0
Q2: Boston United (H) 0-5

80-81 PR: March Town United (A) 1-2

81-82 Q1: Lowestoft Town (A) 0-1

82-83 PR: Nuneaton Borough (H) 1-1, (A) 0-5

83-84 Q1: Stourbridge (A) 1-2

84-85 PR: Irthlingborough Diamonds (H) 0-2

85-86 Q1: Newmarket Town (A - *played home*) 6-1
Q2: Berkhamsted Town (H) 3-0
Q3: Stourbridge (A) 0-4

86-87 Q1: Bury Town (H) 2-3

87-88 PR: Vauxhall Motors (H) 0-0, (A) 2-3

88-89 Q1: Nuneaton Borough (A) 0-2

89-90 PR: Purfleet (A) 1-1, (H) 1-2

90-91 PR: Rothwell Town (A) 2-7

91-92 PR: Paget Rangers (H) 2-1
Q1: V.S. Rugby (A) 0-2

STANLEY UNITED

Currently: Wearside League

45-46 Q1: West Auckland Town (H) 5-0
Q2: Spennymoor United (A) 1-6

46-47 PR: Brandon C.W. (A) 3-3, (H) 1-3

47-48 EX: Murton C.W. (A) 2-2, (H) 2-2, 1-2

48-49 EX: Consett (H) 3-3, (A) 1-2 *protest upheld,* (H) 3-2
PR: Silksworth Colliery Welfare (H) 3-1
Q1: Easington Colliery Welfare (H) 3-2
Q2: South Shields (H) 2-3 *Shields expelled*
Q3: Horden Colliery Welfare (H) 1-3

49-50 PR: Evenwood Town (A) 1-5

50-51 EX: South Hetton Colliery Welfare (A) 1-2

51-52 Q1: Shildon (A) 0-3

52-53 Q1: Spennymoor United (H) 2-4

53-54 Q1: Crook Town (A) 1-0
Q2: Spennymoor United (A) 1-2

54-55 Q1: Tow Law Town (A) 1-0
Q2: Willington (A) 1-0
Q3: Ferryhill Athletic (H) 3-1
Q4: Wolsingham Welfare (H) 5-1
R1: Crook Town (A) 3-5

55-56 Q1: West Auckland Town (H) 0-1

56-57 Q1: Cockfield (A) 3-2
Q2: West Auckland Town (A) 0-0, (H) 2-0
Q3: Evenwood Town (A) 1-5

57-58 Q1: Chilton Athletic (H) 3-1
Q2: Wingate Welfare (A) 11-2
Q3: Crook Town (A) 1-1, (H) 0-4

58-59 Q2: Chilton Athletic (H) 4-2
Q3: West Auckland Town (A) 3-3, (H) 2-0
Q4: Bishop Auckland (A) 1-4

59-60	Q2: Stockton (A) 2-4
61-62	Q1: Durham City (H) 5-1 Q2: Ashington (H) 1-4
62-63	Q1: Easington Colliery Welfare (A) 5-1 Q2: Hebburn (H) 0-1
63-64	Q1: Annfield Plain (A) 2-1 Q2: Ashington (H) 3-0 Q3: Whitby Town (H) 2-0 Q4: Crook Town (H) 0-2
64-65	Q1: Ryhope Colliery Welfare (A) 2-3
65-66	Q1: Ferryhill Athletic (A) 3-1 Q2: Whitley Bay (H) 2-2, (A) 0-1
66-67	Q1: Ryhope Colliery Welfare (H) 1-0 Q2: Stockton (H) 4-4, (A) 1-3
67-68	Q1: Whitley Bay (H) 3-2 Q2: Ryhope Colliery Welfare (A) 0-1
68-69	Q1: West Auckland Town (A) 2-3
69-70	Q1: Whitley Bay (A) 1-2
70-71	Q1: Horden C.W. (A) 0-0, (H) 1-1, (A) 2-1 Q2: Shildon (H) 1-0 Q3: Washington (H) 0-2
71-72	Q1: Bishop Auckland (A) 1-4
72-73	Q1: Billingham Synthonia (A) 2-3
73-74	Q1: Willington (H) 1-6
74-75	Q1: Bishop Auckland (H) *scratched*

STANSTED

Currently: Essex Senior League

49-50	EX: Grays Athletic (H) 0-5

STANTON IRONWORKS

Currently: (Stanton Ilkeston) Central Mids League

49-50	EX: Basford United (A) 1-0 PR: Ransome & Marles (H) 3-5

STAVELEY WELFARE

Currently: Defunct

48-49	EX: Hoyland Common Athletic (A) 1-5
49-50	PR: Firbeck Colliery (A) 3-2 Q1: Rawmarsh Welfare (A) 2-3
50-51	PR: Cresswell Colliery (A) 0-9

STEEL, PEECH & TOZER SOCIAL SERVICES

Currently: Defunct

48-49	EX: Bolsover Colliery (H) 4-2 PR: Hoyland Common Athletic (H) 2-1 Q1: Harworth Colliery Athletic (H) 0-2
49-50	EX: Rawmarsh Welfare (H) 1-4
50-51	PR: Maltby Main (H) 2-0 Q1: Norton Woodseats (A) 0-9

STEVENAGE ATHLETIC

Currently: Defunct

69-70	Q1: Leighton Town (H) 1-3
70-71	Q1: Woodford Town (H) 3-1 Q2: Cheshunt (A) 1-3
71-72	Q1: Finchley (A) 1-0 Q2: Bromley (A) 1-1, (H) 2-4
72-73	Q1: Ware (H) 1-0 Q2: Wimbledon (A) 1-3
73-74	PR: Rushden Town (H) 6-1 Q1: Hitchin Town (A) 1-1, (H) 1-1, 2-3
74-75	Q1: Enfield (H) 1-0 Q2: Ware (A) 3-0 Q3: Harlow Town (A) 0-0, (H) 0-2
75-76	Q1: Barking (H) 2-1 Q2: Tooting & Mitcham Utd (H) 2-2, (A) 0-2
76-77	Q1: Dagenham (H) *scratched*

STEVENAGE BOROUGH

Currently: Isthmian League

83-84	PR: Milton Keynes City (H) 2-0 Q1: Moor Green (H) 0-0, (A) 0-1
84-85	PR: Holbeach United (H) 8-0 Q1: Soham Town Rangers (H) 2-1 Q2: Burton Albion (H) 0-2
85-86	PR: Leamington (H) 2-1 Q1: Kidderminster Harriers (H) 0-2
86-87	PR: Milton Keynes Borough (H) 3-2 Q1: Spalding United (H) 1-0 Q2: Dudley Town (H) 2-0 Q3: Halesowen Town (H) 1-3
87-88	Q1: Leyton-Wingate (A) 1-1, (H) 2-3
88-89	PR: Rayners Lane (H) 6-1 Q1: Royston Town (A) 1-0 Q2: Burnham (H) 3-2 *expelled*
89-90	PR: Great Yarmouth Town (A) 2-0 Q1: Cambridge City (H) 3-5
90-91	PR: East Thurrock United (A) 1-0 Q1: Bishop's Stortford (H) 2-3
91-92	PR: Waltham Abbey (A) 1-0 Q1: Sutton Coldfield Town (H) 0-2
92-93	Q1: Fisher Athletic (A - *played home*) 7-1 Q2: Ruislip Manor (A) 3-1 Q3: St Albans City (H) 3-3, (A) 1-2

STEVENAGE TOWN

Currently: Defunct

48-49	EX: Ruislip (A) 4-2 PR: Leavesden (H) 2-3
49-50	EX: Willesden (H) 2-2, (A) 2-7
50-51	EX: Finchley (A) 0-5
51-52	PR: Woodford Town (H) 1-4
52-53	Q1: Woodford Town (A) 1-2
53-54	Q1: Cheshunt (H) 6-1 Q2: Tufnell Park Edmonton (A) 1-2
54-55	PR: Welwyn Garden City (H) 5-2 Q1: Enfield (H) 1-2
55-56	PR: Barnet (H) 1-3
56-57	PR: Barnet (A) 1-2
57-58	Q1: Ware (A) 0-3
58-59	Q1: Letchworth Town (H) 3-2 Q2: Hitchin Town (H) 1-1, (A) 3-4
59-60	Q1: Vauxhall Motors (H) 0-1
60-61	Q1: Letchworth Town (H) 2-2, (A) 6-2 Q2: St Albans City (H) 1-1, (A) 2-2, 2-3
62-63	Q1: Enfield (H) 0-2
63-64	Q1: Barnet (A) 2-4
64-65	Q1: Hatfield Town (H) 5-0 Q2: Bishop's Stortford (H) 4-1 Q3: Barnet (A) 0-2
65-66	Q1: Bishop's Stortford (A) 1-1, (H) 2-0 Q2: Ware (H) 1-1, (A) 4-1 Q3: Wealdstone (A) 5-6
66-67	Q1: Erith & Belvedere (H) 0-0, (A) 3-0 Q2: Walthamstow Avenue (A) 2-0 Q3: Enfield (A) 2-2, (H) 1-1, 0-2
67-68	Q1: Epsom & Ewell (A) 3-1 Q2: Bexley United (A) 2-1 Q3: Sutton United (H) 2-3

STEWARTS & LLOYDS (1)

See Corby Town

STEWARTS & LLOYDS

Currently: United Counties League

92-93	PR: Evesham United (H) 4-2 Q1: Sutton Coldfield Town (H) 1-3

STEWARTBY WORKS

Currently: Defunct

47-48	PR: Vauxhall Motors (A) 1-7
48-49	PR: Bedford Queens Works (A) 2-1 Q1: Potton United (H) 1-6
49-50	PR: Luton Amateur (H) 3-6
50-51	EX: Vauxhall Motors (A) 0-5

STEYNING TOWN

Currently: Sussex County League
* - As Steyning F.C.

80-81	* Q1: Sutton United (A) 1-3
81-82	PR: Three Bridges (H) 0-0, (A) 3-1 Q1: Dulwich Hamlet (H) 1-1, (A) 0-3
82-83	Q1: Dover Athletic (H) 3-4
83-84	Q1: Kingstonian (A) 0-2
84-85	PR: Redhill (H) 1-2
86-87	PR: Ashford Town (A) 0-1
87-88	PR: Haywards Heath (A) 0-4
88-89	Q1: Corinthian (H) 5-1 Q2: Whitehawk (H) 1-3
89-90	PR: Eastbourne Utd (H - *played away*) 2-5
90-91	PR: Whitehawk (H) 1-2
91-92	PR: Chatham Town (A) 3-1 Q1: Bognor Regis Town (A) 0-1
92-93	PR: Hailsham Town (A) 1-3

Right: *Stevenage Borough attack during their tie at Ruislip Manor in the 1992-93 Second Qualifying Round. Photo: Eric Marsh.*

STOCKPORT COUNTY

Currently: Football League

45-46 R1: Rochdale (H) 1-2, (A) 1-1 (*agg: 2-3*)

46-47 R1: Southport (H) 2-0
R2: Halifax Town (A) 1-1, (H) 2-1
R3: Bolton Wanderers (A) 1-5

47-48 R1: Accrington Stanley (H) 3-1
R2: Shrewsbury (H) 1-1, (A) 1-1, 2-2, 2-2, 3-2
R3: Torquay United (H) 3-0
R4: Charlton Athletic (A) 0-3

48-49 R1: Workington (A) 3-0
R2: Scunthorpe United (A) 1-0
R3: Portsmouth (A) 0-7

49-50 R1: Billingham Synthonia (H) 3-0
R2: Nottingham Forest (A) 2-0
R3: Barnsley (H) 4-2
R4: Hull City (H) 0-0, (A) 2-0
R5: Liverpool (H) 1-2

50-51 R3: Brentford (H) 2-1
R4: Blackpool (A) 1-2

51-52 R1: Gateshead (H) 2-2, (A) 1-1, 1-2

52-53 R1: North Shields (A) 6-3
R2: Gillingham (H) 3-1
R3: Walthamstow Avenue (A) 1-2

53-54 R1: Chester (H) 4-2
R2: Workington (H) 2-1
R3: Headington United (H) 0-0, (A) 0-1

54-55 R1: Carlisle United (H) 0-1

55-56 R1: Mansfield Town (A) 0-2

56-57 R1: New Brighton (A) 3-3, (H) 2-3

57-58 R1: Barrow (H) 2-1
R2: Hartlepools United (H) 2-1
R3: Luton Town (H) 3-0
R4: West Ham United (A) 2-3

58-59 R1: Hull City (A) 1-0
R2: Blyth Spartans (A) 4-3
R3: Burnley (H) 1-3

59-60 R1: West Auckland Town (A) 6-2
R2: Crewe Alexandra (H) 0-0, (A) 0-2

60-61 R1: Workington (H) 1-0
R2: Bishop Auckland (H) 2-0
R3: Southport (H) 3-1
R4: Newcastle United (A) 0-4

61-62 R1: Accrington Stanley (H) 0-1

62-63 R1: Chesterfield (A) 1-4

63-64 R1: Barnsley (A) 0-1

64-65 R1: Wigan Athletic (H) 2-1
R2: Grimsby Town (H) 0-0, (A) 1-0
R3: Bristol Rovers (A) 0-0, (H) 3-2
R4: Liverpool (A) 1-1, (H) 0-2

65-66 R1: Tranmere Rovers (A) 1-0
R2: Southport (A) 3-3, (H) 0-2

66-67 R1: Darlington (A) 0-0, (H) 1-1, 2-4

67-68 R1: Macclesfield Town (H) 1-1, (A) 1-2

68-69 R1: Bradford (Park Avenue) (H) 3-0
R2: Barrow (H) 2-0
R3: Blackburn Rovers (A) 0-2

69-70 R1: Mossley (H) 1-1, (A) 1-0
R2: Scunthorpe United (H) 0-0, (A) 0-4

70-71 R1: Grantham (A) 1-2

71-72 R1: Doncaster Rovers (A) 2-1
R2: Blyth Spartans (A) 0-1

72-73 R1: Workington (H) 1-0
R2: Rotherham United (A) 1-0
R3: Hull City (H) 0-0, (A) 0-2

73-74 R1: Port Vale (H) 0-1

74-75 R1: Stafford Rangers (H) 0-0, (A) 0-1

75-76 R1: Hartlepool United (A) 0-3

76-77 R1: Sheffield Wednesday (A) 0-2

77-78 R1: Scunthorpe United (H) 3-0
R2: Shrewsbury Town (A) 1-1, (H) 1-2

78-79 R1: Morecambe (H) 5-1
R2: Bradford City (H) 4-2
R3: Wrexham (A) 2-6

79-80 R1: Walsall (A) 0-2

80-81 R1: Sheffield United (H) 0-0, (A) 2-3

81-82 R1: Mossley (H) 3-1
R2: Port Vale (A) 1-4

82-83 R1: Mansfield Town (A) 2-3

83-84 R1: Telford United (A) 0-3

84-85 R1: Walsall (H) 1-2

85-86 R1: Telford United (H) 0-1

86-87 R1: Caernarfon Town (A) 0-1

87-88 R1: Telford United (A) 1-1, (H) 2-0
R2: Runcorn (A) 1-0
R3: Leyton Orient (H) 1-2

88-89 R1: Scarborough (A) 1-2

89-90 R1: Burnley (A) 1-1, (H) 1-2

90-91 R1: Rotherham United (A) 0-1

91-92 R1: Lincoln City (H) 3-1
R2: Wigan Athletic (A) 0-2

92-93 R1: York City (A) 3-1
R2: Macclesfield Town (A) 2-0
R3: Derby County (A) 1-2

STOCKSBRIDGE PARK STEELS

Currently: Northern Counties (East) League
See also Stocksbridge Works

92-93 Q1: Stalybridge Celtic (H) 0-4

STOCKSBRIDGE WORKS

Currently: Merged with Oxley Park. Playing as Stocksbridge Park Steels in Northern Counties (East) League.
See also Stocksbridge Park Steels.

49-50 EX: Wombwell Athletic (H) 4-1
PR: Harworth Colliery Ath. (A) 2-2, (H) 8-4
Q1: Norton Woodseats (H) 2-1
Q2: Rawmarsh Welfare (H) 1-2

50-51 PR: Grimethorpe Athletic (A) 2-1
Q1: Parkgate Welfare (A) 2-0
Q2: Cresswell Colliery (H) 6-3
Q3: Worksop Town (A) 2-1
Q4: Worcester City (H) 2-2, (A) 0-3

51-52 Q1: Denaby United (H) 1-1, (A) 1-2

52-53 Q1: Denaby United (A) 1-2

53-54 Q1: Sheffield (A) 2-2, (H) 0-0, 1-1, 1-3

55-56 Q1: Sheffield (H) 8-2
Q2: Denaby United (A) 2-3

56-57 Q2: Beighton Miners Welfare (H) 4-3
Q3: Norton Woodseats Amateur (H) 3-2
Q4: Selby Town (A) 1-3

57-58 Q2: Ossett Town (H) 1-1, (A) 4-3
Q3: Yorkshire Amateur (H) 2-3

58-59 Q1: Frickley Colliery (H) 3-3, (A) 3-0
Q2: Selby Town (H) 1-1, (A) 2-1
Q3: Denaby United (A) 1-2

59-60 Q1: Matlock Town (H) 1-3

61-62 Q2: Retford Town (H) 0-0, (A) 5-2
Q3: Worksop Town (A) 1-3

62-63 Q1: Gainsborough Trinity (A) 1-3

63-64 Q1: Gainsborough Trinity (A) 0-5

64-65 Q1: Frickley Colliery (H) 1-4

65-66 Q1: Denaby United (H) 1-4

72-73 Q1: Bradford (Park Avenue) (H) 1-3

73-74 PR: Prestwich Heys (H) 4-4, (A) 0-6

74-75 Q1: Farsley Celtic (H) 1-3

75-76 Q1: Denaby United (A) 1-4

STOCKTON

Currently: Defunct

45-46 Q2: Whitby United (H) 4-0
Q3: Billingham Synthonia Recreation (H) 4-1
Q4: Consett (A) 3-2
R1: Darlington (A) 0-2, (H) 1-4 (*agg: 1-6*)

46-47 Q2: Whitby United (A) 2-0
Q3: Portrack Shamrock (H) 9-1
Q4: Scarborough (H) 5-1
R1: Lincoln City (H) 2-4

47-48 Q1: South Bank (A) 3-2
Q2: Whitby Albion Rovers (H) 8-1
Q3: Whitby United (A) 3-1
Q4: Ferryhill Athletic (A) 3-1
R1: Grantham (H) 2-1
R2: Notts Co. (A) 1-1, (H - *at Middlesbrough F.C.*) 1-4

48-49 Q4: Horden Colliery Welfare (H) 1-2

49-50 Q4: Bishop Auckland (H) 7-0
R1: Oldham Athletic (A) 0-4

50-51 Q4: North Shields (H) 0-1

51-52 Q4: Consett (H) 2-0
R1: Mansfield Town (H) 1-1, (A) 2-0
R2: Folkestone (H) 2-1
R3: Notts County (A) 0-4

52-53 Q4: Scarborough (A) 1-5

53-54 Q4: Scarborough (A) 1-6

54-55 Q1: Evenwood Town (A) 0-4

55-56 Q1: Shildon (A) 0-3

57-58 Q1: Willington (A) 0-1

58-59 Q1: Spennymoor United (H) 4-5

59-60 Q2: Stanley United (H) 4-2
Q3: Spennymoor United (H) 1-1, (A) 0-1

60-61 Q1: Whitby Town (A) 2-1
Q2: Boldon C.W. (H) 2-2, (A) 1-3

61-62 Q1: Bridlington Town (H) 2-3

62-63 Q1: Penrith (H) 2-1
Q2: Ashington (H) *W/O*
Q3: Ryhope Colliery Welfare (A) 2-1
Q4: North Shields (A) 2-2, (H) 3-3, 2-4

63-64 Q1: Tow Law Town (A) 0-4

64-65 Q2: Consett (H) 2-3

65-66 Q1: Evenwood Town (H) 3-0
Q2: Ashington (H) 3-1
Q3: Consett (A) 0-2

66-67 Q1: Boldon Colliery Welfare (H) 2-2, (A) 0-0, 4-1
Q2: Stanley United (A) 4-4, (H) 3-1
Q3: Blyth Spartans (A) 2-4

67-68 Q1: Spennymoor United (H) 0-3

68-69 Q1: Crook Town (A) 3-2
Q2: West Auckland Town (H) 2-1
Q3: Consett (H) 0-3

69-70 Q1: Blyth Spartans (H) 3-3, (A) 2-8

70-71 Q1: West Auckland Town (A) 0-1

71-72 Q1: Whitley Bay (H) 2-2, (A) 2-5

72-73 Q1: Spennymoor United (A) 1-5

73-74 Q1: Tow Law Town (H) 2-4

74-75 Q1: Goole Town (A) 0-3

STOCKTON

Currently: Northern League

87-88 Q1: Denaby United (H) 1-0
Q2: Emley (H) 0-1

88-89 PR: Harrogate Town (H - *played away*) 1-1, (A) 1-2

89-90 Q1: Newcastle Blue Star (A) 1-1, (H) 1-3

90-91 Q1: Spennymoor Utd (H - *played away*) 0-2

91-92 PR: Billingham Town (H) 2-4

92-93 PR: Washington (A - *played home*) 3-1
Q1: St Helens Town (A) 4-3
Q2: Knowsley United (A) 2-0
Q3: Seaham Red Star (A) 2-1
Q4: Blyth Spartans (A) 1-1, (H) 1-2

STOCKTON HEATH

See Warrington Town

STOKE CITY

Currently: Football League

45-46 R3: Burnley (H) 3-1, (A) 1-2 *(agg: 4-3)*
R4: Sheffield Utd (H) 2-0, (A) 2-3 *(agg: 4-3)*
R5: Sheffield W. (H) 2-0, (A) 0-0 *(agg: 2-0)*
R6: Bolton Wdrs (H) 0-2, (A) 0-0, *(agg: 0-2)*

46-47 R3: Tottenham Hotspur (A) 2-2, (H) 1-0
R4: Chester (A) 0-0, (H) 3-2
R5: Sheffield United (H) 0-1

47-48 R3: Mansfield Town (A) 4-2
R4: Queens Park Rangers (A) 0-3

48-49 R3: Swindon Town (A) 3-1
R4: Blackpool (H) 1-1, (A) 1-0
R5: Hull City (H) 0-2

49-50 R3: Tottenham Hotspur (H) 0-1

50-51 R3: Port Vale (H) 2-2, (A) 1-0
R4: West Ham United (H) 1-0
R5: Newcastle United (H) 2-4

51-52 R3: Sunderland (A) 0-0, (H) 3-1
R4: Swindon Town (A) 1-1, (H) 0-1

52-53 R3: Wrexham (H) 2-1
R4: Halifax Town (A) 0-1

53-54 R3: Hartlepools United (H) 6-2
R4: Leicester City (H) 0-0, (A) 1-3

54-55 R3: Bury (A) 1-1, (H) 1-1, 3-3, 2-2, 3-2
R4: Swansea Town (A) 1-3

55-56 R3: Exeter City (A) 0-0, (H) 3-0
R4: Leicester City (A) 3-3, (H) 2-1
R5: Newcastle United (A) 1-2

56-57 R3: Arsenal (A) 2-4

57-58 R3: Aston Villa (H) 1-1, (A) 3-3, 2-0
R4: Middlesbrough (H) 3-1
R5: Bolton Wanderers (A) 1-3

58-59 R3: Oldham Athletic (H) 5-1
R4: Ipswich Town (H) 0-1

59-60 R3: Preston North End (H) 1-1, (A) 1-3

60-61 R3: West Ham United (A) 2-2, (H) 1-0
R4: Aldershot (H) 0-0, (A) 0-0, 3-0
R5: Newcastle United (A) 1-3

61-62 R3: Leicester City (A) 0-0, (H) 5-2
R4: Blackburn Rovers (H) 0-1

62-63 R3: Leeds United (A) 1-3

63-64 R3: Portsmouth (H) 4-1
R4: Ipswich Town (A) 1-1, (H) 1-0
R5: Swansea Town (H) 2-2, (A) 0-2

64-65 R3: Blackpool (H) 4-1
R4: Manchester United (H) 0-0, (A) 0-1

65-66 R3: Walsall (H) 0-2

66-67 R3: Manchester United (A) 0-2

67-68 R3: Cardiff City (H) 4-1
R4: West Ham United (H) 0-3

68-69 R3: York City (A) 2-0
R4: Halifax Town (H) 1-1, (A) 3-0
R5: Chelsea (A) 2-3

69-70 R3: Oxford United (A) 0-0, (H) 3-2
R4: Watford (A) 0-1

70-71 R3: Millwall (H) 2-1
R4: Huddersfield Town (H) 3-3, (A) 0-0, *(at Manchester United)* 1-0
R5: Ipswich Town (H) 0-0, (A) 1-0
R6: Hull City (A) 3-2
SF: Arsenal *(at Sheff. W.)* 2-2, *(at Aston V.)* 0-2
TP: Everton *(at Crystal Palace)* 3-2

71-72 R3: Chesterfield (H) 2-1
R4: Tranmere Rovers (A) 2-2, (H) 2-0
R5: Hull City (H) 4-1
R6: Manchester United (A) 1-1, (H) 2-1
SF: Arsenal *(at Aston V.)* 1-1, *(at Everton)* 1-2

72-73 R3: Manchester City (A) 2-3

73-74 R3: Bolton Wanderers (A) 2-3

74-75 R3: Liverpool (A) 0-2

75-76 R3: Tottenham Hotspur (A) 1-1, (H) 2-1
R4: Manchester City (H) 1-0
R5: Sunderland (H) 0-0, (A) 1-2

76-77 R3: Everton (A) 0-2

77-78 R3: Tilbury (H) 4-0
R4: Blyth Spartans (H) 2-3

78-79 R3: Oldham A. (H) 2-0 *ab. after 45m.*, (H) 0-1

79-80 R3: Burnley (A) 0-1

80-81 R3: Wolverhampton Wdrs (H) 2-2, (A) 1-2

81-82 R3: Norwich City (H) 0-1

82-83 R3: Sheffield United (A) 0-0, (H) 3-2
R4: Liverpool (A) 0-2

83-84 R3: Everton (H) 0-2

84-85 R3: Luton Town (A) 1-1, (H) 2-3

85-86 R3: Notts County (H) 0-2

86-87 R3: Grimsby Town (A) 1-1, (H) 1-1, (H) 6-0
R4: Cardiff City (H) 2-1
R5: Coventry City (H) 0-1

87-88 R3: Liverpool (H) 0-0, (A) 0-1

88-89 R3: Crystal Palace (H) 1-0
R4: Barnsley (H) 3-3, (A) 1-2

89-90 R3: Arsenal (H) 0-1

90-91 R1: Telford United (A) 0-0, (H) 1-0
R2: Burnley (A) 0-2

91-92 R1: Telford United (H) 0-0, (A) 1-2

92-93 R1: Port Vale (H) 0-0, (A) 1-3

STOKE UNITED

Currently: Defunct

48-49 PR: Leiston (H) 1-1, (A) 0-6

STONEHOUSE

Currently: (Stonehouse Freeway) Gloucestershire Northern Senior League

47-48 PR: Weston-s-Mare St Johns (H) 4-7

48-49 EX: Soundwell (A) 3-9

49-50 PR: Llanelly (A) 1-4

50-51 PR: Lovells Athletic (A) 2-2, (H) 1-0
Q1: Troedrhiw (H) 3-1
Q2: Barry Town (H) 2-3

51-52 Q1: Gloucester City (H) 1-2

52-53 Q1: Ebbw Vale (H) 0-1

53-54 Q1: Barry Town (H) 0-6

54-55 Q1: Lovells Athletic (A) 1-7

55-56 Q1: Barry Town (H) 3-4

56-57 Q1: Cinderford Town (H) 1-4

57-58 Q1: Barry Town (H) 0-2

58-59 Q1: Ebbw Vale (A - *played home*) 1-0
Q2: Merthyr Tydfil (H) 2-3

59-60 Q1: Llanelly (H) 0-5

60-61 Q1: Merthyr Tydfil (A) 2-5

61-62 Q1: Gloucester City (A) 1-5

62-63 Q1: Barry Town (A) 0-2

63-64 Q1: Llanelly (H) 1-1, (A) 0-1

64-65 Q1: Barry Town (H) 1-2

65-66 Q1: Abergavenny Thursdays (H) 2-1
Q2: Merthyr Tydfil (A) 2-6

66-67 Q1: Borough of Weston-super-Mare (H) 3-2
Q2: Trowbridge Town (A) 0-5

67-68 PR: Merthyr Tydfil (H) 0-6

68-69 Q1: Abergavenny Thursdays (A) 1-4

69-70 Q1: Llanelly (A) 2-1
Q2: Ton Pentre (A) 0-2

70-71 Q1: Merthyr Tydfil (H) 1-2

71-72 Q1: Weston-super-Mare (H) 4-2
Q2: Merthyr Tydfil (H) 0-2

72-73 PR: Cinderford Town (H) 4-0
Q1: Glastonbury (H) 0-1

73-74 Q1: Gloucester City (H) 1-1, (A) 1-0
Q2: Cinderford Town (H) 1-2

74-75 Q1: Everwarm (H) 1-1, (A) 1-4

75-76 Q1: Yeovil Town (H) 0-6

STONYCROFT

Currently: Liverpool I. Zingari League

47-48 PR: Skelmersdale United (A) 0-8

48-49 PR: Prescot Cables (H) 0-7

49-50 EX: Bootle Athletic (A) 1-5

50-51 PR: Marine (H) 3-5

STORK

Currently: West Cheshire League

49-50 EX: Droylsden (H) 2-5

56-57 Q1: Runcorn (H) 2-2, (A) 2-3

57-58 PR: South Liverpool (H) 3-2
Q1: Marine (A) 1-0
Q2: Llandudno (H) 1-1, (A) 2-0
Q3: Prescot Cables (H) 1-3

58-59 PR: Llandudno (A) 0-7

59-60 PR: Runcorn (H) 1-2

60-61 Q1: Runcorn (A) 0-6

61-62 Q1: South Liverpool (A) 0-4

62-63 Q1: Borough United (A) 0-4

63-64 Q1: New Brighton (H) 2-2, (A) 2-2, 0-3

64-65 Q1: Borough United (H) 0-4

65-66 Q1: Colwyn Bay (H) 0-2

Below: *Sammy McIlroy (left) tackles Everton's Peter Reid as Stoke City lose 0-2 in 1984. Photo: Colorsport*

STOURBRIDGE

Currently: Southern League

46-47 PR: Birmingham City Transport (A) 5-0
Q1: Dudley Town (A) 1-1, (H) 0-1

47-48 PR: Dudley Town (H) 1-0
Q1: Hednesford (A) 3-2
Q2: Hereford United (H) 4-0
Q3: Bromsgrove Rovers (A) 0-2

48-49 PR: Dudley Town (H) 3-1
Q1: Bromsgrove Rovers (A) 2-3

49-50 PR: Kidderminster Harriers (H) 0-0, (A) 2-1
Q1: Stafford Rangers (H) 0-3

50-51 EX: Sutton Coldfield Town (H) 3-0
PR: Cradley Heath (A) 1-0
Q1: Dudley Town (A) 0-0, (H) 1-3

51-52 PR: Bilston (H) 5-0
Q1: Oswestry Town (H) 4-0
Q2: Wellington Town (H) 1-3

52-53 PR: Darlaston (A) 1-2

53-54 PR: Oswestry Town (H) 2-0
Q1: Brierley Hill Alliance (H) 0-5

54-55 PR: Brierley Hill Alliance (A) 3-0
Q1: Stafford Rangers (A) 1-0
Q2: Bromsgrove Rovers (A) 1-3

55-56 PR: Oswestry Town (H) 6-0
Q1: Darlaston (A) 7-2
Q2: Halesowen Town (A) 0-3

56-57 PR: Brierley Hill Alliance (A) 2-0
Q1: Wellington Town (A) 2-8

57-58 Q1: Bournville Athletic (H) 3-1
Q2: Wellington Town (H) 2-3

58-59 Q1: Stafford Rangers (A) 1-4

59-60 Q1: Cradley Heath (A) 5-0
Q2: Bromsgrove Rovers (A) 0-4

60-61 PR: Oswestry Town (H) 1-4

61-62 Q1: Wellington Town (H) 1-0
Q2: Sankey of Wellington (H) 0-2

62-63 Q1: Rugby Town (A) 1-2

63-64 Q1: Lockheed-Leamington (H) 0-1

64-65 Q1: Brierley Hill Alliance (H) 3-2
Q2: Rugby Town (A) 0-5

65-66 Q1: Bedworth Town (H) 8-0
Q2: Bilston (A) 1-0
Q3: Brierley Hill Alliance (A) 2-1
Q4: Merthyr Tydfil (H) 1-5

66-67 Q1: Dudley Town (H) 5-3
Q2: Brierley Hill Alliance (A) 0-5

67-68 Q1: Lockheed-Leamington (A) 1-0
Q2: Wellington Town (A) 2-2, (H) 1-0
Q3: Worcester City (H) 4-0
Q4: Arnold (A) 2-4

68-69 Q1: Lye Town (H) 7-4
Q2: Wellington Town (H) 0-2

69-70 PR: Stratford Town Amateur (H) 5-1
Q1: Redditch (A) 0-0, (H) 3-0
Q2: Alvechurch (H) 1-1, (A) 3-1
Q3: Telford United (A) 0-3

70-71 Q1: Brierley Hill Alliance (H) 3-0
Q2: Dudley Town (A) 2-1
Q3: Nuneaton Borough (A) 1-2

71-72 Q1: Lockheed-Leamington (A) 1-2

72-73 Q1: Worcester City (H) 2-1
Q2: Bilston (A) 2-3

73-74 Q1: Hinckley Athletic (A) 4-2
Q2: Bedworth United (H) 5-2
Q3: Alvechurch (A) 2-3

74-75 Q1: Bilston (A) 0-3

75-76 Q1: Dudley Town (H) 0-1

76-77 Q1: Bromsgrove Rovers (H) 1-3

77-78 PR: Tividale (H) 1-1, (A) 0-1

78-79 Q1: Highgate United (A) 1-2

79-80 Q1: Ton Pentre (H) 2-1
Q2: Clevedon Town (H) 2-3

80-81 Q1: Macclesfield Town (H) 6-2
Q2: Burton Albion (H) 1-1, (A) 1-2

81-82 PR: Dudley Town (A) 0-3

82-83 Q1: Friar Lane Old Boys (H) 3-0
Q2: Tamworth (H) 3-2
Q3: A.P. Leamington (H) 1-1, (A) 0-2

83-84 Q1: Stamford (H) 2-1
Q2: Wellingborough Town (H) 2-3

84-85 Q1: Sutton Town (H) 2-0
Q2: Wigston Fields (A) 6-1
Q3: Halesowen Town (H) 1-1, (A) 4-3
Q4: V.S. Rugby (H) 1-1, (A) 0-2

85-86 Q1: Sudbury Town (A) 0-0, (H) 1-0
Q2: Witney Town (A) 0-0, (H) 1-0
Q3: Stamford (H) 4-0
Q4: V.S. Rugby (H) 1-1, (A) 1-3

86-87 Q1: Abingdon Utd (H) 1-1, (A) 0-0, (H) 2-1
Q2: Redditch United (H) 2-1
Q3: Trowbridge Town (A) 1-1, (H) 0-4

87-88 Q1: Shepshed Charterhouse (A) 0-2

88-89 PR: Hinckley Town (A) 0-2

89-90 PR: Tividale (A) 3-1
Q1: Lye Town (A) 0-2

90-91 PR: Mile Oak & Rovers & Youth (A) 5-0
Q1: Potton United (A) 1-1, (H) 7-0
Q2: Sutton Coldfield Town (H) 1-2

91-92 PR: Long Buckby (H) 1-0
Q1: Shepshed Albion (A) 0-2

92-93 PR: Stourport Swifts (A) 5-0
Q1: Boston (A) 4-3
Q2: Shepshed Albion (H) 0-0, (A) 2-4

STOURPORT SWIFTS

Currently: West Midlands (Regional) League

92-93 PR: Stourbridge (H) 0-5

STOWMARKET TOWN

Currently: Eastern Counties League
* - As Stowmarket F.C.
+ - As Stowmarket Corinthians

48-49 + PR: City of Norwich School O.B.U. (H) 8-0
Q1: Great Yarmouth Town (A) 2-3

49-50 * PR: Sheringham (A) 1-0
Q1: City of Norwich Sch. O.B.U. (A - *played home*) 3-3, (H) 3-3, 3-0
Q2: Gorleston (A) 2-4

50-51 * PR: Beccles (H) 7-3
Q1: Thetford Town (H) 5-0
Q2: Great Yarmouth Town (A) 1-2

51-52 * Q1: Bury Town (H) 0-3

52-53 * Q1: Thetford Town (H) 4-0
Q2: Bury Town (A) 1-1, (H) 2-4

53-54 * Q1: Leiston (H) 2-0
Q2: Whitton United (H) 4-1
Q3: Lowestoft Town (H) 4-2
Q4: Cambridge United (H) 0-5

54-55 * Q1: Diss Town (A) 3-1
Q2: Bury Town (H) 2-3

55-56 * Q1: Diss Town (H) 7-0
Q2: Sudbury Town (A) 0-4

57-58 * Q1: Sudbury Town (A) 3-1
Q2: Whitton United (A) 4-2
Q3: Bury Town (H) 2-3

58-59 * Q1: Newmarket Town (H) 3-1
Q2: Haverhill Rovers (H) 5-1
Q3: Harwich & Parkeston (A) 0-1

59-60 * Q1: Sudbury Town (H) 0-3

60-61 * Q1: Sudbury Town (H) 2-3

61-62 * Q1: Harwich & Parkeston (H) 2-2, (A) 2-7

62-63 * Q1: Gorleston (H) 3-1
Q2: Lowestoft Town (H) 1-2

75-76 * Q1: Lowestoft Town (H) 0-1

76-77 * PR: March Town United (A) 3-0
Q1: St Neots Town (A) 0-1

77-78 * Q1: Harlow Town (A) 0-5

78-79 * Q1: Lowestoft Town (H) 0-1

79-80 * Q1: Sudbury Town (H) 0-1

80-81 * Q1: Parson Drove United (A) 1-0
Q2: Harwich & Parkeston (A) 1-2

81-82 * Q1: Leyton-Wingate (H) 2-3

82-83 * Q1: Tilbury (A) 2-3

83-84 * PR: Cheshunt (H) 1-0
Q1: Saffron Walden Town (A) 0-3

84-85 * PR: Gorleston (H) 1-1, (A) 0-3

85-86 * PR: Flackwell Heath (H) 3-0
Q1: V.S. Rugby (H) 2-2, (A) 2-3

86-87 PR: Billericay Town (A) 2-0
Q1: Harwich & Parkeston (A) 2-2, (H) 1-3

87-88 Q1: Dunstable (H) 1-3

88-89 PR: Canvey Island (A) 3-2
Q1: Leatherhead (A) 0-1

89-90 PR: Basildon United (A) 1-0
Q1: Saffron Walden Town (H) 5-3
Q2: Sudbury Town (A) 2-3

90-91 PR: Saffron Walden Town (H) 1-1, (A) 1-2

91-92 Q1: Hendon (H) 1-4

92-93 PR: Ware (A) 2-1
Q1: Flackwell Heath (A) 5-0
Q2: Dagenham & Redbridge (A) 1-6

STRATFORD TOWN

Currently: Midland Combination
* - As Stratford Town Amateur

66-67 * Q1: Redditch (A) 2-0
Q2: Rugby Town (H) 0-2

67-68 * Q1: Worcester City (A) 0-2

68-69 * PR: Wellington Town (H) 1-3

69-70 * PR: Stourbridge (A) 1-5

70-71 * Q1: Redditch (H) 1-2

76-77 Q1: Dudley Town (H) 0-2

77-78 Q1: Burton Albion (A) 0-1

78-79 Q1: Kidderminster Harriers (H) 2-2, (A) 0-7

89-90 PR: Wellingborough Town (H) 0-0, (A) 4-3
Q1: Histon (H) 2-0
Q2: Bedworth United (A) 0-3

90-91 PR: Highgate United (H) 3-1
Q1: Buxton (H) 1-4

91-92 PR: Banbury United (A) 1-4

92-93 PR: Hinckley Athletic (H) 6-2
Q1: Raunds Town (A) 0-0, (H) 1-2

STREET

Currently: Somerset Senior League

46-47 PR: Wells City (H) 2-2, (A) 2-1
Q1: Somerton Amateur (H) 2-0
Q2: Radstock Town (A) 1-2

47-48 Q1: Somerton Amateur (H) 9-1
Q2: Newton Abbot Spurs (A) 4-1
Q3: St Austell (A) 2-1
Q4: Yeovil Town (H) 2-1
R1: Cheltenham Town (A) 0-5

48-49 PR: Tavistock Town (H) 6-1
Q1: Bideford (H) 4-1
Q2: Hanham Athletic (A) 5-2
Q3: Gloucester City (A) 1-4

49-50 PR: Ilminster Town (A) 1-4

50-51 PR: Tiverton Town (H) 7-0
Q1: Taunton (H) 3-0
Q2: Newquay (A) 2-1
Q3: Glastonbury (H) 0-1

51-52 Q1: Chippenham United (H) 0-3

52-53 PR: Bristol St George (H) 2-0
Q1: Glastonbury (H) 1-2

53-54 Q1: Peasedown Miners Welfare (A) 4-1
Q2: Glastonbury (H) 2-1
Q3: Chippenham United (A) 1-4

54-55 PR: Borough of Weston-super-Mare (H) 3-2

	Q1: Clandown (A) 0-2
55-56	Q1: Glastonbury (A) 1-0 Q2: Chippenham United (H) 3-6
56-57	PR: Wells City (A) 1-1, (H) 0-0, 2-0 Q1: Chippenham United (H) 1-2
57-58	Q1: Glastonbury (A) 0-5
58-59	Q1: Bridgwater Town (A) 0-2
59-60	Q1: Glastonbury (A) 1-2
60-61	Q1: Borough of Weston-super-Mare (H) 0-8
61-62	Q1: Frome Town (H) 0-2
66-67	Q1: Frome Town (H) 1-1, (A) 3-1 Q2: Dorchester Town (A) 0-2
67-68	Q1: Minehead (A) 1-4
68-69	Q1: Bridgwater Town (H) 2-2, (A) 1-3
69-70	PR: Frome Town (H) 1-3
70-71	Q1: Taunton Town (A) 2-6
71-72	Q1: Trowbridge Town (H) 2-4

STROUD

See Forest Green Rovers

SUDBURY TOWN

Currently: Southern League

50-51	EX: Churchman Sports (H) 4-0 PR: Cromer (A) 4-0 Q1: Eastern Coachworks (A) 2-2, (H) 0-1
51-52	Q1: Diss Town (A) 4-0 Q2: Whitton United (A) 2-1 Q3: Bury Town (A) 1-1, (H) 2-2, 4-2 Q4: King's Lynn (A) 0-1
52-53	Q1: Whitton United (A) 4-0 Q2: Lowestoft Town (H) 4-0 Q3: Bury Town (A) 0-3
53-54	Q1: Diss Town (H) 2-1 Q2: Lowestoft Town (A) 0-3
54-55	Q1: Leiston (A) 3-2 Q2: Lowestoft Town (H) 3-1 Q3: Bury Town (H) 3-1 Q4: Walthamstow Avenue (H) 0-2
55-56	Q1: Leiston (H) 14-1 Q2: Stowmarket (H) 4-0 Q3: Lowestoft Town (A) 0-0, (H) 4-1 Q4: Southall (H) 4-4, (A) 2-2, 2-7
56-57	Q2: Lowestoft Town (A) 1-0 Q3: Bury Town (A) 0-0, (H) 3-1 Q4: Ely City (A) 0-1
57-58	Q1: Stowmarket (H) 1-3
58-59	Q1: Harwich & Parkeston (A) 1-1, (H) 0-2
59-60	Q1: Stowmarket (A) 3-0 Q2: Harwich & Parkeston (A) 2-4
60-61	Q1: Stowmarket (A) 3-2 Q2: Bungay Town (A) 2-4
61-62	Q1: Ely City (H) 5-3 Q2: Cambridge United (A) 1-5
62-63	Q2: March Town United (A) 3-1 Q3: Cambridge United (A) 0-6
63-64	Q2: Cambridge City (H) 2-4
64-65	Q1: Great Yarmouth Town (H) 1-0 Q2: Clacton Town (A) 0-0, (H) 4-2 Q3: Lowestoft Town (H) 0-5
65-66	Q1: Haverhill Rovers (H) 3-0 Q2: Harwich & Parkeston (H) 1-2
66-67	Q1: Gorleston (A) 3-1 Q2: Lowestoft Town (H) 1-2
67-68	PR: Thetford Town (A) 2-2, (H) 2-0 Q1: Gorleston (A) 2-0 Q2: Lowestoft Town (A) 1-3
68-69	Q1: Gothic (H) 4-0 Q2: Bury Town (H) 1-1, (A) 2-3
69-70	PR: Gorleston (H) 1-3
70-71	PR: Harwich & Parkeston (A) 2-1 Q1: Thetford Town (A) 1-1, (H) 0-1
71-72	Q1: Gorleston (A) 3-0 Q2: Bury Town (A) 0-2
72-73	Q1: St Neots Town (A) 1-1, (H) 6-1 Q2: Bury Town (A) 1-1, (H) 1-3
73-74	Q1: King's Lynn (A) 0-1
74-75	Q1: Ely City (H) 5-0 Q2: Bury Town (A) 2-0 Q3: Clacton Town (A) 1-2
75-76	Q1: Potton United (A) 1-2
76-77	Q1: Great Yarmouth Town (H) 1-1, (A) 1-0 Q2: Harwich & Parkeston (A) 1-3
77-78	PR: Bury Town (H) 1-1, (A) 0-2
78-79	Q1: Soham Town Rangers (A) 0-2
79-80	PR: Newmarket Town (A) 3-1 Q1: Stowmarket (A) 1-0 Q2: King's Lynn (H) 1-2
80-81	Q1: Letchworth Town (H) 0-3
81-82	PR: Epping Town (H) 3-3, (A) 4-2 Q1: Dunstable (H) 1-1, (A) 1-2
82-83	Q1: Chelmsford City (H) 1-1, (A) 1-3
83-84	Q1: Walthamstow Avenue (H) 1-1, (A) 0-2
84-85	PR: Edgware Town (H) 8-1 Q1: Flackwell Heath (H) 2-0 Q2: Wembley (H) 0-0, (A) 2-2, (H) 0-3
85-86	PR: Tiptree Town (H) 2-0 Q1: Stourbridge (H) 0-0, (A) 0-1
86-87	PR: Gorleston (H) 5-0 Q1: Rainham Town (H) 4-1 Q2: Bury Town (H) 0-2
87-88	PR: Hounslow (H) 1-1, (A) 3-1 Q1: Braintree Town (A) 4-0 Q2: Aylesbury United (H) 1-1, (A) 1-2
88-89	Q1: Harlow Town (H) 3-1 Q2: Cambridge City (H) 2-1 Q3: Leyton-Wingate (A) 2-1 Q4: Aylesbury United (A) 1-1, (H) 0-1
89-90	Q1: Clapton (A) 2-1 Q2: Stowmarket Town (H) 3-2 Q3: Hendon (H) 1-2
90-91	Q1: Heybridge Swifts (H) 1-3
91-92	PR: Barking (H) 2-2, (A) 2-2, (H) 2-1 Q1: Histon (H) 1-0 Q2: Billericay Town (A) 1-3
92-93	PR: Saffron Walden Town (H) 6-1 Q1: Potton United (H) 3-2 Q2: Grays Athletic (A) 0-1

Below: *David Rush skips over a Norwich City tackle as Sunderland defeat their First Division opponents 1-0 at Villa Park to reach a Wembley F.A. Cup final for the first time since 1973. Photo: Colorsport.*

SUNDERLAND

Currently: Football League

45-46	R3: Grimsby Town (A) 3-1, (H) 2-1 (*agg: 5-2*) R4: Bury (H) 3-1, (A) 4-5 (*agg: 7-6*) R5: Birmingham C. (H) 1-0, (A) 1-3 (*agg: 2-3*)
46-47	R3: Chesterfield (A) 1-2
47-48	R3: Southampton (A) 0-1
48-49	R3: Crewe Alexandra (A) 2-0 R4: Yeovil Town (A) 1-2
49-50	R3: Huddersfield Town (H) 6-0 R4: Tottenham Hotspur (A) 1-5
50-51	R3: Coventry City (H) 2-0 R4: Southampton (H) 2-0 R5: Norwich City (H) 3-1 R6: Wolverhampton W. (H) 1-1, (A) 1-3
51-52	R3: Stoke City (H) 0-0, (A) 1-3
52-53	R3: Scunthorpe United (H) 1-1, (A) 2-1 R4: Burnley (A) 0-2
53-54	R3: Doncaster Rovers (H) 0-2
54-55	R3: Burnley (H) 1-0 R4: Preston North End (A) 3-3, (H) 2-0 R5: Swansea Town (A) 2-2, (H) 1-0 R6: Wolverhampton Wanderers (H) 2-0 SF: Manchester City (*at Aston Villa*) 0-1
55-56	R3: Norwich City (H) 4-2 R4: York City (A) 0-0, (H) 2-1 R5: Sheffield United (A) 0-0, (H) 1-0 R6: Newcastle United (A) 2-0 SF: Birmingham City (*at Sheffield Wed.*) 0-3
56-57	R3: Queens Park Rangers (H) 4-0 R4: West Bromwich Albion (A) 2-4
57-58	R3: Everton (H) 2-2, (A) 1-3
58-59	R3: Everton (A) 0-4
59-60	R3: Blackburn Rovers (H) 1-1, (A) 1-4
60-61	R3: Arsenal (H) 2-1 R4: Liverpool (A) 2-0 R5: Norwich City (A) 1-0 R6: Tottenham Hotspur (H) 1-1, (A) 0-5
61-62	R3: Southampton (A) 2-2, (H) 3-0 R4: Port Vale (H) 0-0, (A) 1-3
62-63	R3: Preston North End (A) 4-1 R4: Gravesend & Northfleet (A) 1-1, (H) 5-2 R5: Coventry City (A) 1-2
63-64	R3: Northampton Town (H) 2-0 R4: Bristol City (H) 6-1 R5: Everton (H) 3-1 R6: Manchester Utd (H) 3-3, (A) 2-2, 1-5
64-65	R3: Luton Town (A) 3-0 R4: Nottingham Forest (H) 1-3
65-66	R3: Everton (A) 0-3
66-67	R3: Brentford (H) 5-2

R4: Peterborough United (H) 7-1
R5: Leeds United (H) 1-1, (A) 1-1, 1-2

67-68 R3: Norwich City (A) 1-1, (H) 0-1

68-69 R3: Fulham (H) 1-4

69-70 R3: Leicester City (A) 0-1

70-71 R3: Orient (H) 0-3

71-72 R3: Sheffield Wednesday (H) 3-0
R4: Cardiff (A) 1-1, (H) 1-1, (*at Man. C.*) 1-3

72-73 R3: Notts County (A) 1-1, (H) 2-0
R4: Reading (H) 1-1, (A) 3-1
R5: Manchester City (A) 2-2, (H) 3-1
R6: Luton Town (H) 2-0
SF: Arsenal (*at Sheffield Wednesday*) 2-1
F: Leeds United (*at Wembley*) 1-0

73-74 R3: Carlisle United (A) 0-0, (H) 0-1

74-75 R3: Chesterfield (H) 2-0
R4: Middlesbrough (A) 1-3

75-76 R3: Oldham Athletic (H) 2-0
R4: Hull City (H) 1-0
R5: Stoke City (A) 0-0, (H) 2-1
R6: Crystal Palace (H) 0-1

76-77 R3: Wrexham (H) 2-2, (A) 0-1

77-78 R3: Bristol Rovers (H) 0-1

78-79 R3: Everton (H) 2-1
R4: Burnley (A) 1-1, (H) 0-3

79-80 R3: Bolton Wanderers (H) 0-1

80-81 R3: Birmingham City (A) 1-1, (H) 1-2

81-82 R3: Rotherham United (A) 1-1, (H) 1-0
R4: Liverpool (H) 0-3

82-83 R3: Manchester City (H) 0-0, (A) 1-2

83-84 R3: Bolton Wanderers (A) 3-0
R4: Birmingham City (H) 1-2

84-85 R3: Southampton (A) 0-4

85-86 R3: Newport County (H) 2-0
R4: Manchester United (H) 0-0, (A) 0-3

86-87 R3: Wimbledon (A) 1-2

87-88 R1: Darlington (H) 2-0
R2: Scunthorpe United (A) 1-2

88-89 R3: Oxford United (H) 1-1, (A) 0-2

89-90 R3: Reading (A) 1-2

90-91 R3: Arsenal (A) 1-2

91-92 R3: Port Vale (H) 3-0
R4: Oxford United (A) 3-2
R5: West Ham United (H) 1-1, (A) 3-2
R6: Chelsea (A) 1-1, (H) 2-1
SF: Norwich City (*at Aston Villa*) 1-0
F: Liverpool (*at Wembley*) 0-2

92-93 R3: Notts County (A) 2-0
R4: Sheffield Wednesday (A) 0-1

SURBITON TOWN

Currently: Surrey County Premier League

50-51 EX: Metropolitan Police (A) 1-2

SUTTON COLDFIELD TOWN

Currently: Southern League

48-49 EX: Lockheed-Leamington (H) 1-0
PR: Stafford Rangers (A) 1-2

49-50 EX: Halesowen Town (H) 3-0
PR: Staffordshire Casuals (H) 4-0
Q1: Dudley Town (A) 0-0, (H) 0-1

50-51 EX: Stourbridge (A) 0-3

51-52 Q1: Boldmere St Michaels (H) 2-0
Q2: Nuneaton Borough (A) 1-5

52-53 Q1: Atherstone Town (H) 1-2

53-54 PR: Bournville Athletic (H) 3-2
Q1: Rugby Town (H) 1-1, (A) 1-4

54-55 PR: Bloxwich Strollers (H) 0-3

55-56 PR: Boldmere St Michaels (A) 2-2, (H) 4-2
Q1: Bournville Athletic (H) 2-2, (A) 4-1
Q2: Lockheed-Leamington (A) 4-3
Q3: Burton Albion (H - *played away*) 3-6

56-57 PR: Moor Green (H) 3-2
Q1: Tamworth (H) 1-7

57-58 PR: Nuneaton Borough (H) 2-2, (A) 1-3

58-59 Q1: Bedworth Town (A) 1-1, (H) 2-3

59-60 Q1: Hednesford (H) 2-3

71-72 Q1: Long Eaton United (A) 1-3

72-73 PR: Highgate United (H) 0-0, (A) 0-2

73-74 PR: Eastwood Town (H) 0-2

74-75 Q1: Alvechurch (A) 0-3

75-76 Q1: Hednesford (H) 1-0
Q2: Macclesfield Town (H) 0-2

76-77 Q1: Friar Lane Old Boys (H) 3-0
Q2: Coventry Sporting (H) 2-1
Q3: Darlaston (A) 0-1

77-78 PR: Kidderminster Harriers (A) 2-5

78-79 Q1: Oxford City (H) 3-0
Q2: Brereton Social (A) 2-3

79-80 Q1: Willenhall Town (H) 3-2
Q2: Racing Club Warwick (H) 3-0
Q3: Dudley Town (H) 4-1
Q4: Kidderminster Harriers (H) 3-3, (A) 2-3

80-81 Q1: Telford United (H) 1-0
Q2: Oldbury United (A) 3-0
Q3: Witton Albion (H) 2-1
Q4: Hitchin Town (A) 1-0
R1: Doncaster Rovers (H) 0-2

81-82 Q1: Buckingham Town (H) 2-1
Q2: Bromsgrove Rovers (A) 0-1

82-83 PR: Walsall Borough (H) 4-2
Q1: Enderby Town (A) 4-1
Q2: V.S. Rugby (H) 2-1
Q3: Worcester City (H) 2-4

83-84 Q1: Spalding United (H) 2-1
Q2: Shifnal Town (H) 5-4
Q3: Buckingham Town (H) 2-1
Q4: Kettering Town (A) 2-3

84-85 Q1: Hertford Town (A) 2-2, (H) 2-1
Q2: Moor Green (H) 0-3

85-86 PR: Lye Town (A - *played home*) 1-2

86-87 PR: Wellingborough Town (A) 3-1
Q1: Wisbech Town (A) 2-0
Q2: Gainsborough Trinity (H) 0-1

87-88 Q1: Hinckley Town (H) 1-1, (A) 1-2

88-89 Q1: Worksop Town (A) 2-1
Q2: Eastwood Town (H) 1-0
Q3: Dudley Town (H) 0-1

89-90 PR: Harrisons (H) 7-0
Q1: Gainsborough Trinity (A) 2-1
Q2: Brackley Town (A) 2-1
Q3: Bedworth United (H) 1-2

90-91 Q1: Bedworth United (A) 5-1
Q2: Stourbridge (A) 2-1
Q3: Bromsgrove Rovers (H) 0-0, (A) 2-4

91-92 Q1: Stevenage Borough (A) 2-0
Q2: Redditch United (H) 1-3

92-93 PR: West Bromwich Town (H) 0-0, (A) 2-0
Q1: Stewarts & Lloyds (A) 3-1
Q2: Eastwood Hanley (H) 2-1
Q3: Rushall Olympic (H) 0-0, (A) 1-1, (A) 2-1
Q4: Leyton (H) 6-1
R1: Bolton Wanderers (A) 1-2

SUTTON TOWN

Currently: (Ashfield Utd) Northern Co's (East) Lge

49-50 EX: Ilkeston Town (A) 3-2
PR: Measham Imperial (H) 3-2
Q1: Spalding United (H) 0-4

50-51 EX: Shirebrook (H) 0-1

51-52 PR: Linby Colliery (H) 2-2, (A) 0-1

52-53 Q1: Cresswell Colliery (A) 0-2

53-54 Q1: Linby Colliery (H) 3-2
Q2: Shirebrook Miners Welf. (H) 1-1, (A) 3-4

54-55 Q1: Ransome & Marles (A) 3-0
Q2: Cresswell Colliery (A) 0-6

55-56 Q2: Linby Colliery (A) 3-3, (H) 3-2
Q3: Shirebrook Miners Welfare (H) 4-1
Q4: Boston United (H) 2-8

56-57 Q1: Shirebrook Miners Welfare (H) 3-2
Q2: Linby Colliery (A) 3-0
Q3: Ransome & Marles (H) 4-1
Q4: Ilkeston Town (A) 2-2, (H) 1-2

57-58 Q2: Shirebrook Miners Welfare (A) 3-2
Q3: Cresswell Colliery (H) 2-1
Q4: Frickley Colliery (H) 0-1

58-59 Q1: Cresswell Colliery (A) 3-0
Q2: Worksop Town (A) 3-3, (H) 4-3
Q3: Heanor Town (H) 1-3

59-60 Q1: Shirebrook Miners Welf. (A) 1-1, (H) 3-4

60-61 Q1: Worksop Town (A) 2-2, (H) 3-0
Q2: Heanor Town (H) 4-2
Q3: Belper Town (A) 2-1
Q4: Frickley Colliery (H) 2-1
R1: Hull City (A) 0-3

61-62 Q1: South Normanton Welfare (A) 6-2
Q2: Alfreton Town (H) 5-0
Q3: Heanor Town (A) 1-5

62-63 Q1: Buxton (A) 1-2

63-64 Q1: Buxton (A) 1-1, (H) 2-0
Q2: Heanor Town (A) 1-5

64-65 Q1: Arnold (H) 2-2, (A) 0-2

65-66 Q1: Worksop Town (H) 2-2, (A) 2-6

66-67 Q1: Ilkeston Town (H) 1-0
Q2: Worksop Town (A) 0-3

67-68 PR: Tamworth (A) 1-5

68-69 Q1: Rawmarsh Welfare (A) 0-0, (H) 4-1
Q2: Matlock Town (H) 0-1

69-70 Q1: Alfreton Town (A) 1-2

70-71 PR: Gainsborough Trinity (A) 1-2

71-72 Q1: Matlock Town (A) 3-1
Q2: Bedworth United (H) 2-2, (A) 1-0
Q3: Stafford Rangers (A) 0-2

72-73 Q1: Matlock Town (A) 1-1, (H) 3-2
Q2: Alfreton Town (A) 0-3

73-74 Q1: Gainsborough Trinity (A) 2-1
Q2: Brigg Town (H) 1-1, (A) 1-0
Q3: Frickley Colliery (A) 1-2

74-75 Q1: Eastwood Town (H) 0-2

75-76 Q1: Macclesfield Town (A) 0-0, (H) 0-4

76-77 Q1: Denaby United (H) 0-1

77-78 PR: Belper Town (H) 2-1
Q1: Gresley Rovers (A) 2-2, (H) 2-1
Q2: Stalybridge Celtic (A) 0-6

78-79 Q1: Boston United (H) 0-0, (A) 0-4

79-80 Q1: Winterton Rangers (H) 2-0
Q2: Burton Albion (H) 1-1, (A) 2-3

80-81 PR: Normanby Park Works (A) 0-0, (H) 2-3

81-82 Q1: Boston United (A) 1-2

82-83 PR: Heanor Town (H) 2-1
Q1: Moor Green (A) 0-4

83-84 Q1: Bridgnorth Town (H) 0-2

84-85 Q1: Stourbridge (A) 0-2

85-86 Q1: Marine (H) 2-2, (A) 0-6

86-87 PR: Stalybridge Celtic (H) 6-2
Q1: Skelmersdale United (A) 0-1

87-88 PR: Long Eaton United (A) 3-1
Q1: Goole Town (H) 1-2

88-89 PR: Boston (A) 0-2

89-90 PR: Rushall Olympic (H) 1-1, (A) 0-3

90-91 PR: Rocester (H) 2-2, (A) 0-1

SUTTON UNITED

Currently: Isthmian League

45-46 PR: Guildford (H) 6-0
Q1: Wimbledon (H) 7-0
Q2: Walton & Hersham (H) 4-0
Q3: Tooting & Mitcham Utd (A) 3-3, (H) 5-1
Q4: Gillingham (A) 9-3

R1: Walthamstow A. (H) 1-4, (A) 2-7 (*agg: 3-11*)

46-47 Q1: Metropolitan Police (H) 7-0
Q2: Kingstonian (H) 3-1
Q3: Tooting & Mitcham United (A) 5-3
Q4: Bromley (H) 2-0
R1: Barnet (A) 0-3

47-48 Q1: Carshalton Athletic (H) 1-3

48-49 PR: Epsom (A) 2-2, (H) 2-0
Q1: Leatherhead (A) 2-0
Q2: Tooting & Mitcham United (H) 0-1

49-50 PR: Kingstonian (H) 0-1

50-51 EX: Banstead Athletic (H) 3-1
PR: Tooting & Mitcham (H) 0-0, (A) 0-1

51-52 PR: Carshalton Athletic (H) 3-3, (A) 3-2
Q1: Erith & Belvedere (H) 2-2, (A) 1-1, 3-0
Q2: Kingstonian (H) 2-2, (A) 3-2
Q3: Hounslow Town (A) 4-1
Q4: Folkestone Town (A) 1-1, (H) 1-3

52-53 Q1: Hounslow Town (H) 3-2
Q2: Carshalton Athletic (H) 0-2

53-54 Q1: Deal Town (H) 3-5

54-55 PR: Canterbury City (A) 0-3

55-56 PR: Canterbury City (A) 1-2

56-57 PR: Erith & Belvedere (A) 3-4

57-58 PR: Dorking (A) 1-1, (H) 5-0
Q1: Walton & Hersham (A) 3-3, (H) 0-4

58-59 Q1: Dorking (A) 4-1
Q2: Carshalton Athletic (H) 1-1, (A) 4-3
Q3: Tooting & Mitcham United (H) 1-8

59-60 Q1: Leatherhead (H) 6-0
Q2: Wimbledon (A) 1-0
Q3: Woking (H) 3-3, (A) 3-1
Q4: Hastings United (H) 2-3

60-61 Q1: Redhill (H) 4-0
Q2: Dulwich Hamlet (H) 4-2
Q3: Carshalton Ath. (A) 2-2, (H) 3-0
Q4: Bexleyheath & Welling (A) 3-1
R1: Romford (H) 2-2, (A) 0-5

61-62 Q1: Slough Town (A) 1-4

62-63 Q1: Cray Wanderers (H) 4-1
Q2: Gravesend & Northfleet (A) 1-2

63-64 Q1: Aldershot (H) 0-4

64-65 Q1: Erith & Belvedere (A) 4-0
Q2: Bexley United (H) 1-1, (A) 1-2

65-66 Q1: Horsham (A) 2-2, (H) 3-2
Q2: Crawley Town (H) 0-1

66-67 Q1: Hatfield Town (H) 4-0
Q2: Crittall Athletic (A) 2-1
Q3: Kingstonian (A) 2-0
Q4: Eastbourne United (H) 7-2
R1: Bath City (A) 0-1

67-68 Q1: Tooting & Mitcham United (A) 3-1
Q2: Hillingdon Borough (H) 5-1
Q3: Stevenage Town (A) 3-2
Q4: Barnet (H) 2-2, (A) 1-3

68-69 Q1: Bexley United (A) 0-1

69-70 R1: Dagenham (A) 1-0
R2: Barnet (A) 2-0
R3: Hillingdon Borough (A) 0-0, (H) 4-1
R4: Leeds United (H) 0-6

70-71 Q4: Walton & Hersham (A) 0-1

71-72 Q1: Grays Athletic (A) 4-2
Q2: Uxbridge (A) 3-1
Q3: Redhill (A) 2-0
Q4: Witney Town (H) 0-1

72-73 PR: Corinthian-Casuals (H) 3-1
Q1: Marlow (H) 5-1
Q2: Aveley (A) 2-1
Q3: Wimbledon (H) 3-1
Q4: Margate (A) 0-2

73-74 PR: Metropolitan Police (H) 3-0
Q1: Hornchurch (A) 0-0, (H) 2-0
Q2: Leytonstone (A) 2-3

74-75 Q1: Dulwich Hamlet (H) 4-2
Q2: Cray Wanderers (A) 5-1
Q3: Erith & Belvedere (A) 5-1
Q4: Slough Town (A) 0-1

75-76 Q1: Barnet (H) 1-1, (A) 2-1
Q2: Staines Town (H) 5-1

The Sutton United glory years of the late 1980's..... **Above:** *The team celebrate their 3-1 win at Aldershot in 1987. Photo: Eric Marsh.* **Below:** *Mark Golley, on the line, and Francis Awaritefe and Mark's brother Nigel, celebrate the former's bullet header that gave Sutton a draw against Middlesbrough, also in 1987-88. Photo: Sutton Herald.* **Bottom:** *The most famous goal of all - Matthew Hanlon (11) gets the winner against First Division Coventry City the following season.*

Q3: Chesham United (H) 3-1
Q4: Waterlooville (H) 1-1, (A) 3-1
R1: A.F.C. Bournemouth (H) 1-1, (A) 0-1

76-77 Q1: Metropolitan Police (A) 3-0
Q2: Barking (A) 1-1, (H) 1-4

77-78 Q1: Medway (A) 1-0
Q2: Croydon (H) 2-0
Q3: Hastings United (H) 1-0
Q4: Tooting & Mitcham United (A) 0-3

78-79 Q1: Hertford Town (H) 2-1
Q2: Chalfont St Peter (A) 2-0
Q3: Windsor & Eton (A) 1-0
Q4: Dartford (H) 0-2

79-80 Q1: Banstead Athletic (A) 2-0

Q2: Addlestone (H) 0-0, (H) 0-3

80-81 Q1: Steyning (H) 3-1
Q2: Hungerford Town (H) 2-0
Q3: Poole Town (H) 4-1
Q4: Minehead (A) 0-2

81-82 R1: Bishop's Stortford (A) 2-2, (H) 2-1
R2: Swindon Town (A) 1-2

82-83 Q4: Wealdstone (A) 1-3

83-84 Q4: Maidstone United (A) 1-1, (H) 1-3

84-85 Q1: Harefield United (A) 3-0
Q2: Grays Athletic (A) 1-3

85-86 Q1: Beckenham Town (H) 5-0
Q2: Gravesend & Northfleet (H) 0-1

86-87 Q1: Hounslow (H) 2-0
Q2: Yeading (A) 1-4

87-88 Q1: Wivenhoe Town (A) 3-0
Q2: Redhill (H) 3-1
Q3: Bromley (H) 0-0, (A) 2-1
Q4: Basingstoke Town (H) 3-0
R1: Aldershot (H) 3-0
R2: Peterborough United (A) 3-1
R3: Middlesbrough (H) 1-1, (A) 0-1

88-89 Q4: Walton & Hersham (H) 1-1, (A) 3-0
R1: Dagenham (A) 4-0
R2: Aylesbury United (A) 1-0
R3: Coventry City (H) 2-1
R4: Norwich City (A) 0-8

89-90 R1: Torquay United (H) 1-1, (A) 0-4

90-91 R1: Merthyr Tydfil (A) 1-1, (H) 0-1

91-92 Q4: Weymouth (A) 1-1, (H) 3-0
R1: Maidstone United (A - *at Dartford*) 0-1

92-93 Q4: Newport A.F.C. (A - *at Gloucester*) 4-1
R1: Hereford United (H) 1-2

SWANAGE TOWN

Currently: Merged with Herston. Playing as Swanage Town & Herston in Wessex League.
See also Swanage Town & Herston

61-62 Q1: Bridport (A) 1-3

62-63 Q1: Poole Town (H) 0-8

SWANAGE
TOWN & HERSTON

Currently: Wessex League
See also Swanage Town

87-88 PR: Eastleigh (A) 1-1, (H) 3-1
Q1: Sholing Sports (A) 3-1
Q2: Fareham Town (H) 0-2

88-89 Q1: Yate Town (H) 2-1
Q2: Exmouth Town (H) 1-1, (A) 0-3

89-90 PR: Wimborne Town (A) 2-0
Q1: Melksham Town (H) 4-0
Q2: Gosport Borough (A) 1-1, (H) 0-2

90-91 PR: Devizes Town (H) 4-0
Q1: Taunton Town (A) 2-1
Q2: Weymouth (H) 1-1, (A) 1-2

91-92 Q1: Waterlooville (H) 1-1, (A) 0-2

92-93 PR: Melksham Town (A) 5-1
Q1: Cinderford Town (H) 1-2

SWANSEA CITY

Currently: Football League
* - As Swansea Town

45-46 * R3: Bristol City (A) 1-5, (H) 2-2 (*agg: 3-7*)

46-47 * R3: Gillingham (H) 4-1
R4: Luton Town (A) 0-2

47-48 * R3: Bristol Rovers (A) 0-3

48-49 * R1: Southend United (A) 2-1
R2: Bristol City (A) 1-3

49-50 * R3: Birmingham City (H) 3-0
R4: Arsenal (A) 1-2

50-51 * R3: Mansfield Town (A) 0-2

51-52 * R3: Reading (A) 3-0
R4: Rotherham United (H) 3-0
R5: Newcastle United (H) 0-1

52-53 * R3: Newcastle United (A) 0-3

53-54 * R3: Barrow (A) 2-2, (H) 4-2
R4: Everton (A) 0-3

54-55 * R3: Blackburn Rovers (A) 2-0
R4: Stoke City (H) 3-1
R5: Sunderland (H) 2-2, (A) 0-1

55-56 * R3: York City (H) 1-2

56-57 * R3: Wolverhampton Wanderers (A) 3-5

57-58 * R3: Burnley (A) 2-4

58-59 * R3: Portsmouth (A) 1-3

59-60 * R3: Gillingham (A) 4-1
R4: Burnley (H) 0-0, (A) 1-2

60-61 * R3: Port Vale (H) 3-0
R4: Preston North End (H) 2-1
R5: Burnley (A) 0-4

61-62 * R3: Sheffield Wednesday (A) 0-1

62-63 * R3: Queens Park Rangers (H) 2-0
R4: West Ham United (A) 0-1

63-64 * R3: Barrow (H) 4-1
R4: Sheffield United (A) 1-1, (H) 4-0
R5: Stoke City (A) 2-2, (H) 2-0
R6: Liverpool (H) 2-1
SF: Preston North End (*at Aston Villa*) 1-2

64-65 * R3: Newcastle United (H) 1-0
R4: Huddersfield Town (H) 1-0
R5: Peterborough United (A) 0-0, (H) 0-2

65-66 * R1: Walsall (A) 3-6

66-67 * R1: Folkestone (A) 2-2, (H) 7-2
R2: Nuneaton Borough (A) 0-2

67-68 * R1: Enfield (H) 2-0
R2: Brighton & Hove Albion (H) 2-1
R3: Doncaster Rovers (A) 2-0
R4: Arsenal (H) 0-1

68-69 * R1: Oxford City (A) 3-2
R2: Weymouth (A) 1-1, (H) 2-0
R3: Halifax Town (H) 0-1

69-70 * R1: Kettering Town (A) 2-0
R2: Oxford City (A) 5-1
R3: Leeds United (A) 1-2

70-71 R1: Exeter City (H) 4-1
R2: Telford United (H) 6-2
R3: Rhyl (H) 6-1
R4: Liverpool (A) 0-3

71-72 R1: Brentford (H) 1-1, (A) 3-2
R2: Exeter City (H) 0-0, (A) 1-0
R3: Gillingham (H) 1-0
R4: Portsmouth (A) 0-2

72-73 R1: Margate (A) 0-1

73-74 R1: Walsall (A) 0-1

74-75 R1: Kettering Town (H) 1-1, (A) 1-3

75-76 R1: Southend United (A) 0-2

76-77 R1: Minehead (H) 0-1

77-78 R1: Leatherhead (A) 0-0, (H) 2-1
R2: Portsmouth (A) 2-2, (H) 2-1
R3: Walsall (A) 1-4

78-79 R1: Hillingdon Borough (H) 4-1
R2: Woking (H) 2-2, (A) 5-3
R3: Bristol Rovers (H) 0-1

79-80 R3: Crystal Pal. (H) 2-2, (A) 3-3, (*at Cardiff City*) 2-1
R4: Reading (H) 4-1
R5: West Ham United (A) 0-2

80-81 R3: Middlesbrough (H) 0-5

81-82 R3: Liverpool (H) 0-4

82-83 R3: Norwich City (A) 1-2

83-84 R3: Brighton & Hove Albion (A) 0-2

84-85 R1: Bognor Regis Town (H) 1-1, (A) 1-3

85-86 R1: Leyton-Wingate (H) 2-0
R2: Bristol Rovers (H) 1-2

86-87 R1: Wealdstone (A) 1-1, (H) 2-1 *aband. after 54 minutes*, (H) 4-1
R2: Slough Town (H) 3-0
R3: West Bromwich Albion (H) 3-2
R4: Hull City (H) 0-1

87-88 R1: Hayes (A) 1-0
R2: Leyton Orient (A) 0-2

88-89 R1: Northampton Town (H) 3-1
R2: Colchester United (A) 2-2, (H) 1-3

89-90 R1: Kidderminster Harriers (A) 3-2
R2: Peterborough United (H) 3-1
R3: Liverpool (H) 0-0, (A) 0-8

90-91 R1: Welling United (H) 5-2
R2: Walsall (H) 2-1
R3: Rotherham United (H) 0-0, (A) 0-4

91-92 R1: Cardiff City (H) 2-1
R2: Exeter City (A) 0-0, (H) 1-2

92-93 R1: Bye
R2: Exeter (A) 2-1 *aband. (floodlight failure) after 86 mins*, (A) 5-2
R3: Oxford Utd (H) 1-1, (A) 2-2 (*5-4 pens*)
R4: Grimsby Town (H) 0-0, (A) 0-2

Below: *Swansea City fall behind to a first-half goal from Terry Robbins (10) of G.M.V. Conference side Welling United. However, things turned out well for the Swans as they ran in four second-half goals to record a 5-2 win in November 1990. Photo: Keith Gillard.*

SWAYTHLING

See Eastleigh

SWINDON BRITISH RAIL

Currently: Defunct
* - As Swindon G.W.R. Corinthians

45-46 * PR: Purton (A) 4-0
Q1: Paulton Rovers (A) 3-4

46-47 * PR: Wootton Bassett Town (H) 5-1
Q1: Melksham (A) 2-3

47-48 * PR: Pewsey Vale (H) 2-1
Q1: Westbury United (H) 1-4

48-49 * EX: Wootton Bassett Town (H) 6-3
PR: Welton Rovers (H) 2-3

49-50 * EX: Calne & Harris United (H) 3-2
PR: Melksham (A) 1-2

50-51 PR: Welton Rovers (H) 1-5

SWINDON TOWN

Currently: F.A. Premier League

45-46 R1: Bristol R. (H) 1-0, (A) 1-4 *(agg: 2-4)*

46-47 R1: Cambridge Town (H) 4-1
R2: Notts County (A) 1-2

47-48 R1: Ipswich Town (H) 4-2
R2: Aldershot (A) 0-0, (H) 0-0, 2-0
R3: Burnley (A) 2-0
R4: Notts County (H) 1-0
R5: Southampton (A) 0-3

48-49 R3: Stoke City (H) 1-3

49-50 R1: Bristol Rovers (H) 1-0
R2: Carlisle United (A) 0-2

50-51 R1: Southend United (A) 3-0
R2: Exeter City (A) 0-3

51-52 R1: Bedford Town (H) 2-0
R2: Torquay Utd (H) 3-3, (A) 1-1, 3-1
R3: Cardiff City (A) 1-1, (H) 1-0
R4: Stoke City (H) 1-1, (A) 1-0
R5: Luton Town (A) 1-3

52-53 R1: Newport Isle of Wight (H) 5-0
R2: Northampton Town (H) 2-0
R3: Manchester City (A) 0-7

53-54 R1: Newport Isle of Wight (H) 2-1
R2: Hastings United (A) 1-4

54-55 R1: Crystal Palace (H) 0-2

55-56 R1: Hereford United (H) 4-0
R2: Peterborough United (H) 1-1, (A) 2-1
R3: Worksop Town (H) 1-0
R4: Charlton Athletic (A) 1-2

56-57 R1: Coventry City (H) 2-1
R2: Bournemouth & Boscombe Ath. (H) 0-1

57-58 R1: Reading (A) 0-1

58-59 R1: Aldershot (H) 5-0
R2: Norwich City (H) 1-1, (A) 0-1

59-60 R1: Walsall (H) 2-3

60-61 R1: Bath City (H) 2-2, (A) 6-4
R2: Shrewsbury Town (H) 0-1

61-62 R1: Kettering Town (H) 2-2, (A) 0-3

62-63 R1: Reading (H) 4-2
R2: Yeovil Town (A) 2-0
R3: Luton Town (A) 2-0
R4: Everton (H) 1-5

63-64 R3: Manchester City (H) 2-1
R4: Aldershot (A) 2-1
R5: West Ham United (A) 1-3

64-65 R3: Ipswich Town (H) 1-2

65-66 R1: Merthyr Tydfil (H) 5-1
R2: Grantham (A) 6-1
R3: Coventry City (H) 1-2

66-67 R1: Horsham (A) 3-0
R2: Ashford Town (H) 5-0
R3: West Ham United (A) 3-3, (H) 3-1
R4: Bury (H) 2-1
R5: Nottingham F. (A) 0-0, (H) 1-1, 0-3

67-68 R1: Salisbury (H) 4-0
R2: Luton Town (H) 3-2
R3: Blackburn Rovers (H) 1-0
R4: Sheffield Wednesday (A) 1-2

68-69 R1: Canterbury City (A) 1-0
R2: Grantham (A) 2-0
R3: Southend United (H) 0-2

69-70 R3: Blackburn Rovers (A) 4-0
R4: Chester (H) 4-2
R5: Scunthorpe United (H) 3-1
R6: Leeds United (H) 0-2

70-71 R3: Queens Park Rangers (A) 2-1
R4: Leeds United (A) 0-4

71-72 R3: Arsenal (H) 0-2

72-73 R3: Birmingham City (H) 2-0
R4: West Bromwich Albion (A) 0-2

73-74 R3: Portsmouth (A) 3-3, (H) 0-1

74-75 R1: Reading (H) 4-0
R2: Maidstone United (H) 3-1
R3: Lincoln City (H) 2-0
R4: West Ham United (A) 1-1, (H) 1-2

75-76 R1: Newport County (A) 2-2, (H) 3-0
R2: Hendon (A) 1-0
R3: Tooting & Mitcham Utd (H) 2-2, (A) 1-2

76-77 R1: Bromley (H) 7-0
R2: Hitchin Town (A) 1-1, (H) 1-0 *abandoned (fog) after 67 minutes*, (H) 3-1
R3: Fulham (A) 3-3, (H) 5-0
R4: Everton (H) 2-2, (A) 1-2

77-78 R1: Boreham Wood (A) 0-0, (H) 2-0
R2: Brentford (H) 2-1
R3: Nottingham Forest (A) 1-4

78-79 R1: March Town United (H) 2-0
R2: Enfield (H) 3-0
R3: Cardiff City (H) 3-0
R4: Aldershot (A) 1-2

79-80 R1: Brentford (H) 4-1
R2: Torquay United (A) 3-3, (H) 3-2
R3: Luton Town (A) 2-0
R4: Tottenham Hotspur (H) 0-0, (A) 1-2

80-81 R1: Weymouth (H) 3-2
R2: Wimbledon (A) 0-2

81-82 R1: Taunton Town (A - *played home*) 2-1
R2: Sutton United (H) 2-1
R3: Luton Town (A) 1-2

82-83 R1: Wealdstone (H) 2-0
R2: Brentford (H) 2-2, (A) 3-1
R3: Aldershot (H) 7-0
R4: Burnley (A) 1-3

83-84 R1: Kettering Town (A) 7-0
R2: Millwall (A) 3-2
R3: Carlisle United (A) 1-1, (H) 3-1
R4: Blackburn Rovers (H) 1-2

Above: *Swindon Town goalkeeper Jim Barron punches the ball clear under pressure from Hendon's John Baker and Rod Haider during a 1-0 win at Claremont Road in 1976. Photo: John Hutton.*

84-85 R1: Dagenham (A) 0-0, (H) 1-2

85-86 R1: Bristol City (H) 0-0, (A) 2-4

86-87 R1: Farnborough Town (A - *played home*) 4-0
R2: Enfield (H) 3-0
R3: Fulham (A) 1-0
R4: Leeds United (H) 1-2

87-88 R3: Norwich City (H) 0-0, (A) 2-0
R4: Newcastle United (A) 0-5

88-89 R3: Portsmouth (A) 1-1, (H) 2-0
R4: West Ham United (H) 0-0, (A) 0-1

89-90 R3: Bristol City (A) 1-2

90-91 R3: Leyton Orient (A) 1-1, (H) 1-1 *abandoned after 56 mins - frozen pitch*, (H) 1-0
R4: Norwich City (A) 1-3

91-92 R3: Watford (H) 3-2
R4: Cambridge United (A) 3-0
R5: Aston Villa (H) 1-2

92-93 R3: Queens Park Rangers (A) 0-3

SWINDON VICTORIA

Currently: Merged with Malmesbury Town. Playing as Malmesbury Victoria in Wiltshire League.

45-46 Q1: Westbury United (A) 3-4

46-47 PR: Melksham (A) 1-4

47-48 PR: Melksham (H) 4-2
Q1: Wiltshire County Mental Hospital (A) 3-5

48-49 PR: Warminster Town (A) 1-3

49-50 EX: Coleford Athletic (A) 5-2
PR: Trowbridge Town (H) 0-7

54-55 PR: Welton Rovers (A) 7-3
Q1: Bulford United (H) 2-2, (A) 2-1
Q2: Melksham (A) 2-4

SYMINGTON'S RECREATION (MARKET HARBOROUGH)

Currently: Defunct

48-49 PR: Northampton Amateurs (A) 4-1
Q1: Peterborough United (A) 0-4

49-50 Q1: Rushden Town (A) 3-0
Q2: Corby Town (A) 1-6

50-51 Q1: Peterborough United (A) 0-3

51-52 Q1: Desborough Town (H) 1-3

52-53 Q1: Peterborough United (H) 2-5

53-54 Q1: Desborough Town (H) 0-3

54-55 Q1: Bourne Town (A) 2-3

TAMWORTH

Currently: Southern League

45-46	Q1: Bournville Athletic (H) 2-5
47-48	Q1: Ibstock Penistone Rovers (H) 6-0 Q2: Brush Sports (A) 1-3
48-49	Q1: Moira United (H) 6-2 Q2: Brush Sports (A) 3-4
49-50	PR: Ibstock Penistone Rovers (A) 2-0 Q1: Brush Sports (A) 0-2
50-51	PR: Ibstock Penistone Rovers (A) 0-3
51-52	PR: Bournville Athletic (A) 3-1 Q1: Hednesford (A) 0-0, (H) 2-4
52-53	PR: Hednesford (H) 0-2
53-54	Q1: Atherstone Town (H) 0-1
54-55	PR: Burton Albion (A) 0-1
55-56	Q1: Burton Albion (A) 0-2
56-57	Q1: Sutton Coldfield Town (A) 7-1 Q2: Bedworth Town (H) 1-4
57-58	PR: Oswestry Town (H) 1-2
58-59	Q1: Gresley Rovers (A) 3-1 Q2: Nuneaton Borough (H) 1-1, (A) 0-1
59-60	Q1: Ilkeston Town (H) 2-2, (A) 1-2
60-61	Q1: Nuneaton Borough (A) 4-1 Q2: Ilkeston Town (A) 1-3
61-62	Q1: Nuneaton Borough (A) 0-2
62-63	Q1: Gresley Rovers (A) 2-2, (H) 4-1 Q2: Hinckley Athletic (A) 0-0, (H) 0-1
63-64	Q1: Burton Albion (A) 1-0 Q2: Long Eaton United (H) 3-1 Q3: Loughborough United (H) 0-0, (A) 0-2
64-65	Q1: Burton Albion (H) 2-0 Q2: Nuneaton Borough (A) 1-2
65-66	Q1: Hinckley Athletic (H) 1-1, (A) 2-4
66-67	Q1: Lockheed Leamington (H) 4-2 Q2: Worcester City (A) 1-0 Q3: Rugby Town (A) 2-2, (H) 2-1 Q4: Hednesford (H) 1-1, (A) 3-1 R1: Gillingham (A) 1-4
67-68	PR: Sutton Town (H) 5-1 Q1: Congleton Town (A) 5-0 Q2: Norton Woodseats Amateur (A) 2-0 Q3: Matlock Town (A) 0-2
68-69	Q1: Darlaston (H) 1-2
69-70	Q1: Lower Gornal Athletic (A) 1-1, (H) 4-2 Q2: Stafford Rangers (H) 3-3, (A) 2-0 Q3: Dudley Town (H) 3-0 Q4: Nuneaton Borough (A) 4-2 R1: Torquay United (H) 2-1 R2: Gillingham (A) 0-6
70-71	Q4: Nuneaton Borough (H) 1-1, (A) 2-2, 3-1 R1: York City (H) 0-0, (A) 0-5
71-72	Q4: Nuneaton Borough (A) 1-3
72-73	Q1: Brierley Hill Alliance (A) 1-2
73-74	Q1: Dudley Town (A) 2-1 Q2: Belper Town (H) 3-0 Q3: Ilkeston Town (A) 3-2 Q4: Banbury United (A) 0-2
74-75	Q1: Alfreton Town (A) 1-1, (H) 1-0 Q2: Eastwood Town (H) 1-1, (A) 3-5
75-76	Q1: Nuneaton Borough (A) 1-2
76-77	Q1: Coventry Sporting (H) 1-1, (A) 0-2
77-78	PR: Ilkeston Town (A) 0-0, (H) 1-0 Q1: Hinckley Athletic (A) 0-0, (H) 1-1, 1-2
78-79	Q1: Racing Club Warwick (A) 1-1, (H) 1-0 Q2: Halesowen Town (H) 0-2
79-80	PR: Leek Town (A) 2-0 Q1: Moor Green (A) 1-2
80-81	PR: Wolverton Town (H) 3-0 Q1: Histon (H) 3-0 Q2: Hinckley Athletic (A) 1-2
81-82	PR: Brereton Social (A) 3-0 Q1: Darlaston (A) 2-1 Q2: Shepshed Charterhouse (H) 2-2, (A) 1-3
82-83	Q1: Racing Club Warwick (H) 2-1 Q2: Stourbridge (A) 2-3
83-84	Q1: Macclesfield Town (H) 1-6
84-85	PR: Brigg Town (A) 2-0 Q1: Eastwood Town (A) 0-1
85-86	PR: Blakenall (A) 4-0 Q1: Walsall Borough (H) 2-1 Q2: Wisbech Town (H) 2-1 Q3: Kidderminster Harriers (A) 3-4
86-87	PR: Bourne Town (A) 2-0 Q1: Wolverton Town (A) 0-0 (H) 2-2, (H) 0-2
87-88	PR: Gresley Rovers (H) 3-2 Q1: Paget Rangers (A) 4-1 Q2: Wisbech Town (A) 3-2 Q3: Shepshed Chartershouse (H) 3-2 Q4: Wealdstone (H) 2-0 R1: Colchester United (A) 0-3
88-89	Q1: Racing Club Warwick (H) 3-0 Q2: Chasetown (A) 1-0 Q3: Moor Green (A) 1-1, (H) 4-6
89-90	Q1: Boldmere St Michaels (A) 3-2 Q2: Holbeach United (H) 1-0 Q3: Bromsgrove Rovers (A) 0-2
90-91	Q1: Moor Green (A) 2-1 Q2: Malvern Town (A) 3-3, (H) 5-1 Q3: Redditch United (H) 2-0 Q4: Burton Albion (A) 0-0, (H) 3-2 R1: Whitley Bay (H) 4-6
91-92	PR: Lye Town (H) 2-2, (A) 3-1 Q1: Moor Green (A) 3-0 Q2: Boston United (A) 1-1, (H) 1-0 Q3: Matlock Town (A) 2-0 Q4: Bromsgrove Rovers (H) 0-1
92-93	Q1: Hednesford Town (A) 1-1, (H) 2-4

TAUNTON TOWN

Currently: Western League
* - As Taunton F.C.

48-49	* EX: Tavistock Town (A) 2-7
49-50	* PR: Bridgwater Town (A) 1-1, (H) 1-3
50-51	* PR: Wells City (H) 3-2 Q1: Street (A) 0-3
51-52	* PR: Bideford (H) 1-1, (A) 2-8
52-53	* PR: Tiverton Town (A) 2-1 Q1: Barnstaple Town (A) 1-1, (H) 3-5
53-54	* PR: St Blazey (H) 0-2
54-55	* PR: Barnstaple Town (H) 3-3, (A) 0-6
55-56	* PR: Barnstaple Town (H) 2-1 Q1: St Blazey (H) 0-2

Tamworth enjoyed two fine Cup runs in the early Nineties, but both ended in narrow home defeats. **Above:** *Donovan Gethfield powers in a header during the ten-goal thriller against Whitley Bay in 1990, and* **Below:** *Bobby Parker (7) and Roy Green fail to get on the end of a corner against Bromsgrove in 1991. Photos: Paul Barber.*

56-57 * Q1: Wadebridge Town (A) 6-0
Q2: Penzance (A) 1-1, (H) 3-3, 1-1, 3-2
Q3: Bideford (H) 1-7

58-59 * Q1: Clandown (A) 3-1
Q2: Glastonbury (A) 1-1, (H) 4-0
Q3: Bridgwater Town (A) 2-1
Q4: Merthyr Tydfil (A) 1-2

59-60 * Q1: Borough of Weston-super-Mare (H) 7-0
Q2: Glastonbury (H) 0-0, (A) 1-2

62-63 * Q2: Bridgwater Town (A) 1-5

63-64 * Q2: Bridgwater Town (H) 1-3

64-65 * Q1: Frome Town (H) 0-1

65-66 * Q1: Bridgwater Town (A) 0-1

66-67 * Q1: Minehead (H) 1-4

67-68 * Q1: Warminster Town (A) 9-0
Q2: Portland United (H) 2-0
Q3: Minehead (A) 2-2, (H) 1-2

69-70 * Q1: Bath City (H) 2-4

70-71 * Q1: Street (H) 6-2
Q2: Minehead (H) 1-2

71-72 Q1: Dorchester Town (A) 2-3

72-73 Q1: Weston-super-Mare (H) 3-1
Q2: Bridgwater Town (A) 4-0
Q3: Barry Town (A) 0-0, (H) 2-0
Q4: Yeovil Town (A) 1-4

73-74 Q1: Devizes Town (H) 3-1
Q2: Bridgwater Town (H) 1-0
Q3: Weymouth (H) 1-2

74-75 Q1: Glastonbury (A) 2-2, (H) 4-0
Q2: Poole Town (A) 0-2

75-76 Q1: Wadebridge Town (H) 2-3

76-77 Q1: Weston-super-Mare (H) 1-0
Q2: Bideford (H) 4-2
Q3: Minehead (A) 1-2

77-78 PR: Bath City (H) 1-2

78-79 Q1: St Blazey (A) 3-0
Q2: Liskeard Athletic (H) 6-0
Q3: Bideford (H) 3-0
Q4: Weymouth (H) 0-2

79-80 Q1: Trowbridge Town (H) 0-1

80-81 Q1: Tiverton Town (A) 5-0
Q2: Penzance (A) 3-2
Q3: Falmouth Town (H) 1-0
Q4: Weymouth (A) 0-0, (H) 0-3

81-82 Q1: Saltash United (H) 1-0
Q2: Bridgwater Town (A) 1-1, (H) 1-0
Q3: Liskeard Athletic (H) 2-0
Q4: Addlestone & W. (A) 2-2, (H) 0-0, (H) 4-2
R1: Swindon Town (H - *played away*) 1-2

Right: *Taunton Town's only post-War appearance in the competition proper was in 1981 when, after an epic four-match struggle against fellow Southern Leaguers Addlestone, they earned the right to play Swindon Town. The tie was switched from Wordsworth Drive to the County Ground, Swindon, and here Taunton 'keeper Norman Stevens clears the ball under pressure from Andy Rowlands. The Taunton defenders in the picture are Eddie Aherne and Dave Awcock (5). Photo: 'Epix'.*

82-83 Q1: Bath City (A) 2-2, (H) 2-4

83-84 PR: Chard Town (A) 1-2

84-85 PR: Paulton Rovers (A) 1-2

85-86 Q1: Bath City (A) 1-4

86-87 PR: Welton Rovers (A) 0-1

87-88 PR: Clandown (H) 2-0
Q1: Saltash United (H) 0-3

88-89 PR: Poole Town (H) 1-1, (A) 0-1

89-90 PR: Minehead (H) 9-1
Q1: Bideford (H) 3-0
Q2: Exmouth (H) 0-0, (A) 2-2, (H) 0-0, (A) 1-2

90-91 Q1: Swanage Town & Herston (H) 1-2

91-92 Q1: Devizes Town (H) 2-0
Q2: Cheltenham Town (A) 0-8

92-93 PR: Barri (H) 0-3

TAVISTOCK

Currently: South Western League
* - As Tavistock Town

48-49 * EX: Taunton (H) 7-2
PR: Street (A) 1-6

49-50 * PR: Barnstaple Town (H) 0-4

51-52 * PR: St Austell (A) 0-3

52-53 PR: Bridgwater Town (H) 1-2

53-54 PR: Barnstaple Town (H) 1-3

54-55 PR: Tiverton Town (H) 5-2
Q1: St Austell (A) 6-3
Q2: Minehead (H) 4-2
Q3: Barnstaple Town (A) 1-12

55-56 PR: St Blazey (A) 1-3

56-57 Q1: Newquay (H) 3-4

57-58 PR: St Blazey (H) 4-3
Q1: Penzance (H) 1-3

58-59 Q1: Bideford (A) 0-3

59-60 PR: Bideford (A) 3-4

TELFORD UNITED

Currently: Alliance Premier League
* - As Wellington Town

45-46 * Q4: Kidderminster Harriers (H) 5-2
R1: Port Vale (A) 0-4, (H) 0-2 (*agg: 0-6*)

46-47 * Q4: Kidderminster Harriers (H) 3-1
R1: Watford (H) 1-1, (A) 0-1

47-48 * Q4: Shrewsbury Town (H) 0-1

48-49 * Q4: Cheltenham Town (H) 2-1
R1: Norwich City (A) 0-1

49-50 * Q4: Nuneaton Borough (H) 3-4

50-51 * PR: Bilston (A) 3-1
Q1: Brierley Hill Alliance (H) 3-1
Q2: Hereford United (H) 1-4

51-52 * PR: Halesowen Town (H) 4-0
Q1: Worcester City (A) 4-3
Q2: Stourbridge (A) 3-1
Q3: Kidderminster Harriers (H) 3-2
Q4: Brush Sports (A) 1-3

52-53 * Q4: Worcester City (H) 1-0
R1: Gillingham (H) 1-1, (A) 0-3

53-54 * Q4: Kidderminster Harriers (A) 2-1
R1: Aldershot (A) 3-5

54-55 * Q4: Burton Albion (A) 1-0
R1: Merthyr Tydfil (A) 1-1, (H) 1-6

55-56 * Q1: Kidderminster Harriers (A) 1-2

56-57 * PR: Bilston (A) 1-1, (H) 3-2
Q1: Stourbridge (H) 8-2
Q2: Stafford Rangers (H) 4-1
Q3: Bromsgrove Rovers (A) 0-1

57-58 * PR: Kidderminster Harriers (A) 2-0
Q1: Cradley Heath (H) 7-1
Q2: Stourbridge (A) 3-2
Q3: Oswestry Town (A) 2-2, (H) 0-1

58-59 * Q1: Moor Green (A) 8-0
Q2: Stafford Rangers (H) 3-1
Q3: Oswestry Town (H) 2-3

59-60 * Q1: Oswestry Town (H) 1-1, (A) 1-3

60-61 * Q1: Stafford Rangers (A) 1-0
Q2: Redditch (A) 3-0
Q3: Kidderminster Harriers (H) 1-0
Q4: Worcester City (H) 1-1, (A) 2-3

61-62 * Q1: Stourbridge (A) 0-1

62-63 * Q1: Congleton Town (A) 1-1, (H) 2-0
Q2: Stafford Rangers (A) 2-0
Q3: Bromsgrove Rovers (H) 2-0
Q4: Rugby Town (A) 1-1, (H) 4-0
R1: Bristol City (A) 2-4

63-64 * Q1: Bromsgrove Rovers (A) 3-1
Q2: Worcester City (H) 0-1

64-65 * Q1: Dudley Town (H) 1-3

65-66 * Q1: Dudley Town (A) 0-0, (H) 1-2

66-67 * Q1: Brierley Hill Alliance (A) 1-2

67-68 * Q1: Hednesford (A) 5-0
Q2: Stourbridge (H) 2-2, (A) 0-1

68-69 * PR: Stratford Town Amateur (A) 3-1
Q1: Halesowen Town (A) 1-0
Q2: Stourbridge (A) 2-0
Q3: Worcester City (H) 2-3

69-70 PR: Lockheed-Leamington (H) 3-1
Q1: Halesowen Town (H) 7-3
Q2: Hednesford (H) 4-3
Q3: Stourbridge (H) 3-0
Q4: Kidderminster Harriers (H) 2-1
R1: Bristol Rovers (H) 0-3

70-71 R1: Walton & Hersham (A) 5-2
R2: Swansea City (A) 2-6

71-72 R1: Bristol Rovers (A) 0-3

72-73 Q4: Enderby Town (A) 2-0
R1: Nuneaton Borough (H) 3-2
R2: Chelmsford City (A) 0-5

73-74 Q4: Highgate United (H) 2-0
R1: Chester (A) 0-1

74-75 Q4: Marine (A) 1-2

75-76 Q4: Winsford United (H) 1-1, (A) 4-5

76-77 Q1: Gresley Rovers (H) 3-1
Q2: Tividale (A) 3-0
Q3: Hednesford (A) 0-0, (H) 3-0
Q4: Matlock Town (H) 2-5

77-78 Q1: Friar Lane Old Boys (A) 2-1
Q2: Leek Town (H) 3-0
Q3: Hinckley Athletic (H) 1-0
Q4: Arnold (A) 0-3

78-79 Q1: Halesowen Town (H) 0-1

79-80 Q1: Bilston (A) 2-1
Q2: Coventry Sporting (A) 4-2
Q3: Moor Green (A) 1-2

80-81 Q1: Sutton Coldfield Town (A) 0-1

81-82 PR: Oswestry Town (H) 4-0
Q1: Belper Town (A) 6-0
Q2: Burscough (H) 3-0
Q3: Caernarfon Town (H) 1-2

82-83 Q1: Buxton (H) 3-0
Q2: Congleton Town (H) 3-2
Q3: Eastwood Town (A) 2-2, (H) 4-0
Q4: Grantham (H) 3-0
R1: Wigan Athletic (A) 0-0, (H) 2-1
R2: Tranmere Rovers (H) 1-1, (A) 1-2

83-84 R1: Stockport County (H) 3-0
R2: Northampton Town (A) 1-1, (H) 3-2
R3: Rochdale (A) 4-1
R4: Derby County (A) 2-3

84-85 R1: Lincoln City (A) 1-1, (H) 2-1
R2: Preston North End (A) 4-1
R3: Bradford City (H) 2-1
R4: Darlington (A) 1-1, (H) 3-0
R5: Everton (A) 0-3

Right: *Gola League Telford United were the last side from the ranks of non-League football to reach the last sixteen. Their run in 1984-85 saw them dispose of four Football League clubs, most notably a Bradford City side who were to go on to be Third Division champions that season.* **Top:** *Tony Turner (centre) and Mark Hancock (left) in the thick of the action in the crushing victory at Preston.* **Bottom:** *Colin Williams (8) challenges Darlington goalkeeper Fred Barber at Feethams in Round Four. On the fringe of the action are Darlo's Graeme Aldred (2) and Telford's Steve Eaton (right).*

85-86 R1: Stockport County (A) 1-0
R2: Derby County (A) 1-6

86-87 R1: Burnley (H) 3-0
R2: Altrincham (H) 1-0
R3: Leeds U. (H - *at West Bromwich A.*) 1-2

87-88 R1: Stockport County (H) 1-1, (A) 0-2

88-89 R1: Carlisle United (H) 1-1, (A) 1-4

89-90 R1: Walsall (H) 0-3

90-91 Q4: Egham Town (H) 2-0
R1: Stoke City (H) 0-0, (A) 0-1

91-92 Q4: Knowsley United (H) 1-0
R1: Stoke City (A) 0-0, (H) 2-1
R2: Wrexham (A) 0-1

92-93 Q4: St Albans City (H) 1-2

TEVERSAL & SILVERHILL COLLIERY WELF.

Currently: Defunct
* - As Teversal Colliery Welfare

49-50 * EX: Parliament Street Methodists (A) 5-2
PR: Boston United (A) 1-2

50-51 EX: Long Eaton Town (H) 2-2, (A) 2-3

THACKLEY

Currently: Northern Counties (East) League

69-70 Q1: Gainsborough Trinity (H) 1-4

79-80 Q1: Whitby Town (H) 2-2, (A) 0-2

80-81 PR: Wingate (H) 1-1, (A) 1-0
Q1: Crook Town (H) 1-0
Q2: Blue Star (A) 0-2

81-82 PR: Bridlington Town (A) 3-1
Q1: Emley (A) 1-2

82-83 Q1: Runcorn (H) 0-0, (A) 1-2

83-84 Q1: Bishop Auckland (A) 2-2, (H) 1-4

84-85 PR: Darwen (H) 0-2

85-86 PR: Fleetwood Town (H) 0-1

86-87 PR: Netherfield (H) 1-0
Q1: Wren Rovers (A) 1-3

87-88 Q1: Guisborough T. (H) 1-1, (A) 0-0, (A) 0-1

88-89 Q1: Marine (A) 0-5

89-90 PR: Cleator Moor Celtic (A) 1-1, (H) 1-3

90-91 PR: Lancaster City (A) 0-2

91-92 PR: Blackpool Wren Rovers (A) 2-3

92-93 PR: Radcliffe Borough (H) 2-1
Q1: Sheffield (A - *played at home*) 1-3

THAME UNITED

Currently: Isthmian League

76-77 Q1: Witney Town (H) 1-0
Q2: Chesham United (H) 0-1

77-78 Q1: Bromsgrove Rovers (H) 1-3

78-79 PR: Banbury United (A) 2-4

79-80 Q1: Bracknell Town (H) 6-5
Q2: Witney Town (H) 0-1

80-81 Q1: Maidenhead United (A) 0-1

81-82 PR: Haringey Borough (H) 1-0
Q1: Edgware (A) 3-1
Q2: Feltham (H) 1-1, (A) 2-1
Q3: Kingstonian (H) 1-2

82-83 Q1: Cheltenham Town (H) 2-3

83-84 Q1: Ampthill Town (H) 2-1
Q2: Moor Green (H) 4-4, (A) 2-4

84-85 PR: Hungerford Town (H) 2-11

88-89 Q1: Westbury United (H) 3-1
Q2: Gosport Borough (H) 1-3

89-90 PR: Frome Town (H) 7-0
Q1: Abingdon Town (H) 0-3

90-91 PR: Feltham (A) 0-2

91-92 PR: Eastleigh (H) 1-1, (A) 2-0
Q1: Abingdon Town (H) 2-0
Q2: Waterlooville (A) 3-3, (H) 3-2
Q3: Salisbury (H) 0-4

Below: *An extra-time penalty from Paul Rayson gives Thame United, then of the Campri South Midlands League, the most significant win of their F.A. Cup history; 3-2 against Beazer Homes Southern League Premier Division side Waterlooville. Photo: Steve Daniels.*

92-93 Q1: Bashley (H) 2-3

THANET UNITED
See Margate

THATCHAM TOWN
Currently: Wessex League

87-88 PR: Worthing (H) 0-3

88-89 PR: Calne Town (A) 1-0
Q1: Gosport Borough (H) 1-3

89-90 PR: Welton Rovers (A) 5-0
Q1: Stroud (H) 2-2, (A) 1-2

90-91 PR: Bournemouth (A) 0-1

91-92 PR: Fareham Town (A) 5-1
Q1: Salisbury (H) 1-1, (A) 0-3

92-93 PR: Westbury United (A) 5-0
Q1: Chippenham Town (A) 2-1
Q2: Salisbury (A) 0-4

THETFORD TOWN
Currently: Eastern Counties League

50-51 PR: Holt United (A) 5-1
Q1: Stowmarket (A) 0-5

51-52 Q1: Lowestoft Town (H) 4-4, (A) 0-5

52-53 Q1: Stowmarket (A) 0-4

54-55 PR: Ely City (A) 8-0
Q1: Histon (A) 2-1
Q2: March Town United (H) 0-3

55-56 Q1: Ely City (A) 3-4

56-57 Q1: Cambridge City (H) 0-2

57-58 PR: March Town United (A) 1-3

58-59 Q1: Great Yarmouth Town (A) 4-4, (H) 3-3, 4-5

59-60 Q1: Great Yarmouth Town (H) 2-4

65-66 Q1: Lowestoft Town (A) 2-10

67-68 PR: Sudbury Town (H) 2-2, (A) 0-2

68-69 Q1: Clacton Town (A) 2-4

69-70 Q1: Clacton Town (A) 1-2

70-71 Q1: Sudbury Town (H) 1-1, (A) 1-0
Q2: Clacton Town (A) 0-2

71-72 Q1: Newmarket Town (A) 4-1
Q2: Harwich & Parkeston (H) 3-3, (A) 0-1

72-73 PR: King's Lynn (H) 2-1
Q1: Lowestoft Town (H) 4-2
Q2: Ely City (A) 0-2

73-74 PR: Spalding United (H) 3-0
Q1: Bury Town (A) 4-0
Q2: Wisbech Town (A) 1-3

74-75 Q1: Bury Town (A) 1-4

75-76 Q1: Parson Drove United (A) 5-5, (H) 5-0
Q2: Stamford (A) 0-2

76-77 PR: Harwich & Parkeston (A) 2-4

77-78 Q1: St Neots Town (A) 1-2

78-79 Q1: Gorleston (H) 1-5

79-80 Q1: Wisbech Town (H) 1-2

80-81 PR: St Neots Town (A) 1-3

81-82 Q1: King's Lynn (A) 0-0, (H) 0-1

82-83 PR: Heybridge Swifts (A) 0-1

83-84 Q1: Billericay Town (A) 0-3

88-89 PR: Harlow Town (H) 2-2, (A) 1-4

91-92 Q1: St Albans City (H) 0-2

THORNE COLLIERY
Currently: Websters Central Midlands League

45-46 PR: Ossett Town (A) 3-1
Q1: East Bierley (A) 3-3, (H) 1-6

46-47 PR: Bradford United (H) 0-0, (A) 2-1
Q1: Selby Town (A) 0-0, (H) 2-1
Q2: Yorkshire Amateur (A) 0-1

47-48 Q1: Yorkshire Amateur (A) 0-0, (H) 4-3
Q2: Goole Town (A) 0-2

48-49 EX: Barton Town (H) 2-0
PR: Farsley Celtic (A) 1-2

49-50 EX: Lysaght's Sports (A) 1-3

50-51 EX: Pilkington Recreation (H) 2-2, (A) 5-3
PR: Ashby Institute (A) 1-2

67-68 PR: Selby Town (H) 3-4

THORNYCROFT ATHLETIC
Currently: Defunct
* - As Thornycroft (Basingstoke)

45-46 * PR: Totton (H) *scratched*

46-47 PR: Andover (H) 2-0
Q1: R.A.O.C. Hilsea (H) 1-2

47-48 PR: Bitterne Nomads (A) 3-2
Q1: Ryde Sports (A) 0-3

48-49 PR: R.A.O.C. Hilsea (A) 3-2
Q1: Longfleet St Mary's (A) 0-4

49-50 EX: Sandown (H) 5-0
PR: Bournemouth (A) 2-5

50-51 EX: Pirelli General Cable Wks (H) 5-5, (A) 2-3

67-68 Q1: Cowes Isle of Wight (A) 1-2

68-69 Q1: Cowes Isle of Wight (A) 1-0
Q2: Salisbury (A) 0-4

69-70 Q1: Salisbury (H) 3-4

70-71 PR: Fareham Town (A) 2-1
Q1: Waterlooville (A) 1-1, (H) 0-0, 0-1

71-72 Q1: Ryde Sports (A) 4-1
Q2: Newport Isle of Wight (H) 4-1
Q3: Fareham Town (A) 1-5

THREE BRIDGES
Currently: Sussex County League

76-77 Q1: Faversham Town (H) 3-3, (A) 1-2

77-78 PR: Littlehampton Town (A) 1-0
Q1: Andover (A) 0-2

78-79 Q1: Margate (H) 0-2

79-80 Q1: Ashford Town (H) 0-2

80-81 PR: Wokingham Town (H) 0-1

81-82 PR: Steyning Town (A) 0-0, (H) 1-3

82-83 Q1: Uxbridge (H) 0-0, (A) 2-1
Q2: Kingstonian (A) 3-4

83-84 PR: Hemel Hempstead (H) 3-2
Q1: Croydon (H) 5-1
Q2: Sittingbourne (A) 0-3

84-85 Q1: Dover Athletic (A) 0-1

85-86 PR: Lewes (H) 2-3

86-87 PR: Epsom & Ewell (A) 2-1
Q1: Haringey Borough (A) 0-1

87-88 PR: Gravesend & Northfleet (H) 0-0, (A) 1-2

88-89 Q1: Dulwich Hamlet (A) 0-1

89-90 PR: Banstead Athletic (H) 1-0
Q1: Hythe Town (H) 0-2

90-91 PR: Wick (H) 1-3

91-92 PR: Lewes (A) 3-4

92-93 PR: Alma Swanley (H) 0-3

THRELKELD
Currently: Defunct

50-51 PR: Frizington United (A) 1-5

THROCKLEY WELFARE
Currently: Defunct

45-46 Q1: Gosforth & Coxlodge (A) 2-0
Q2: Newburn (H) 0-0 (A) *W/O*
Q3: Consett (H) 2-4

46-47 Q1: Crook Colliery Welfare (H) 2-5

47-48 Q1: Blyth Spartans (A) 0-4

THURNSCOE VICTORIA
Currently: Defunct

46-47 PR: Wombwell Athletic (H) 0-5

47-48 PR: Grimethorpe Athletic (H) *scratched*

THYNNES ATHLETIC
Currently: Defunct

47-48 PR: Hereford United (A) 0-11

48-49 EX: Staffordshire Casuals (A) *W/O*
PR: Hednesford (A) 0-10

49-50 EX: Darlaston (H) 0-6

TILBURY
Currently: Isthmian League

46-47 EX: Brentwood & Warley (A) 4-3
PR: Clacton Town (H) 3-0
Q1: Leyton (H) 4-1
Q2: Romford (H) 2-1
Q3: Barking (A) 0-3

47-48 PR: Crittall Athletic (A) 2-3

48-49 EX: Rainham Town (H) 2-0
PR: Leyton (A) 0-2

49-50 EX: Sawbridgeworth Town (A) 6-0
PR: Leyton (H) 2-2, (A) 3-2
Q1: Upminster (H) 2-2, (A) 4-2
Q2: Harwich & Parkston (A) 2-0
Q3: Barking (A) 2-1
Q4: Gorleston (A) 1-1, (H) 2-1
R1: Notts County (A) 0-4

50-51 PR: Brentwood & Warley (A) 1-0
Q1: Romford (A) 1-5

51-52 PR: Briggs Sports (H) 0-4

52-53 Q1: Ilford (H) 1-0

Q2: Clacton Town (A) 2-6

53-54 PR: Leyton (A) 1-2

54-55 PR: Dagenham (A) 1-3

55-56 PR: Woodford Town (A) 2-4

56-57 PR: Barking (A) 1-4

57-58 PR: Ilford (H) 0-0, (A) 1-2

58-59 Q1: Barking (A) 1-3

59-60 PR: Brentwood & Warley (A) 2-1
Q1: Grays Athletic (A) 1-2

60-61 Q1: Woodford Town (H) 2-2, (A) 2-1
Q2: Barking (A) 3-3, (H) 3-1
Q3: Brentwood & Warley (H) 1-3

61-62 Q1: Woodford Town (H) 6-0
Q2: Barking (H) 2-0
Q3: Grays Athletic (A) 1-1, (H) 2-1
Q4: Wycombe Wanderers (A) 1-3

62-63 Q1: Grays Athletic (A) 2-1
Q2: Aveley (H) 2-1
Q3: Ilford (H) 1-0
Q4: Maidenhead United (A) 1-2

63-64 Q1: Grays Athletic (A) 3-1
Q2: Aveley (H) 3-3, (A) 1-2

64-65 Q1: Aveley (H) 1-1, (A) 0-2

65-66 Q1: Brentwood & Warley (A) 2-0
Q2: Walthamstow Avenue (H) 0-0, (A) 4-5

66-67 Q1: Crittall Athletic (A) 0-1

67-68 Q1: Bexley (A) 0-2

68-69 Q1: Epsom & Ewell (H) 1-0
Q2: Hillingdon Borough (H) 0-3

69-70 Q1: Epsom & Ewell (A) 1-0
Q2: Walthamstow Ave. (A) 2-2, (H) 2-2, 3-1
Q3: Hillingdon Borough (H) 1-2

70-71 Q1: Slough Town (H) 1-1 (A) 0-2

71-72 Q1: Hitchin Town (A) 2-2, (H) 3-2
Q2: Addlestone (H) 3-0
Q3: Bexley United (A) 1-1, (H) 2-1
Q4: Enfield (H) 0-3

72-73 PR: Ilford (H) 2-1
Q1: Kingstonian (H) 0-0, (A) 2-1
Q2: Dartford (A) 3-4

73-74 Q1: Wycombe Wanderers (H) 0-3

74-75 Q1: Dagenham (A) 1-3

75-76 Q1: Leyton-Wingate (A) 1-1, (H) 11-0
Q2: Southall & Ealing Borough (A) 1-2

76-77 Q1: Enfield (H) 2-2, (A) 0-3

77-78 PR: Kingstonian (A) 1-0
Q1: Bracknell Town (A) 2-1
Q2: Witney Town (A) 3-0
Q3: Feltham (H) 4-1
Q4: Tonbridge A.F.C. (H) 4-3
R1: Kettering T. (H) 0-1 (*void*), (H) 2-2, (A) 3-2
R2: Nuneaton Borough (A) 2-1
R3: Stoke City (A) 0-4

78-79 Q1: Leyton-Wingate (A) 0-1

79-80 Q1: Epping Town (H) 3-0
Q2: Barking (H) 0-1

80-81 PR: Peacehaven & Telscombe (A) 1-0
Q1: Cray Wanderers (H) 4-1
Q3: Canterbury City (A) 1-2

81-82 Q1: Hayes (A) 1-1, (H) 0-0, (A) 0-0, (H) 1-1, (A) 0-4

82-83 Q1: Stowmarket (H) 3-2
Q2: Leytonstone-Ilf. (A) 1-1, (H) 2-2, (A) 1-2

83-84 Q1: Chesham United (H) 0-1

84-85 PR: Epping Town (H) 0-1

85-86 PR: Maidenhead United (H - *at Aveley*) 2-0
Q1: Tunbridge Wells (H - *at Grays Ath.*) 2-1
Q2: Hayes (H) 0-0, (A) 2-1
Q3: Fisher Athletic (A) 1-2

86-87 Q1: Witham Town (H) 3-1
Q2: Harlow Town (H) 2-1 *expelled*

87-88 PR: Great Yarmouth Town (A) 0-0, (H) 0-2

88-89 PR: Cray Wanderers (A) 4-1

Q1: Tring Town (A) 1-2

89-90 Q1: Dorking (A) 2-1
Q2: Hailsham T. (H) 2-2, (A) 1-2 *abandoned in extra-time*, (*at Tonbridge*) 2-3

90-91 PR: Southall (H) 0-0, (A) 3-1
Q1: Witney Town (H) 1-1, (A) 1-2

91-92 PR: Cheshunt (A) 3-0
Q1: Leighton Town (H) 1-1, (A) 0-1

92-93 PR: Collier Row (H) 3-2
Q1: Newmarket Town (H) 1-1, (A) 0-1

TIMSBURY ATHLETIC

Currently: Somerset Senior League

49-50 EX: Chippenham Town (H) 0-7

TIPTREE UNITED

Currently: Eastern Counties League

80-81 PR: Wootton Blue Cross (H) 3-0
Q1: Edgware (H) 0-1

81-82 PR: Billericay Town (A) 0-1

82-83 Q1: Feltham (A) 0-3

83-84 PR: Bury Town (A) 3-3, (H) 0-1

84-85 Q1: Harlow Town (H) 0-4

85-86 PR: Sudbury Town (A) 0-2

86-87 PR: Berkhamsted Town (A) 1-1, (H) 2-1
Q1: Ely City (A) 4-1
Q2: Kettering Town (H) 0-3

87-88 PR: Aveley (H) 0-4

88-89 PR: Dunstable (H) 1-1, (A) 1-1, (H) 0-0, (A) 1-0
Q1: Grays Athletic (A) 0-5

89-90 PR: Ware (A) 1-2

90-91 PR: Harlow Town (H) 0-1

91-92 PR: Hitchin Town (A) 1-1, (H) 1-0
Q1: Dagenham (H) 1-0
Q2: Harlow Town (H) 0-6

92-93 PR: Wealdstone (A - *at Watford*) 1-2

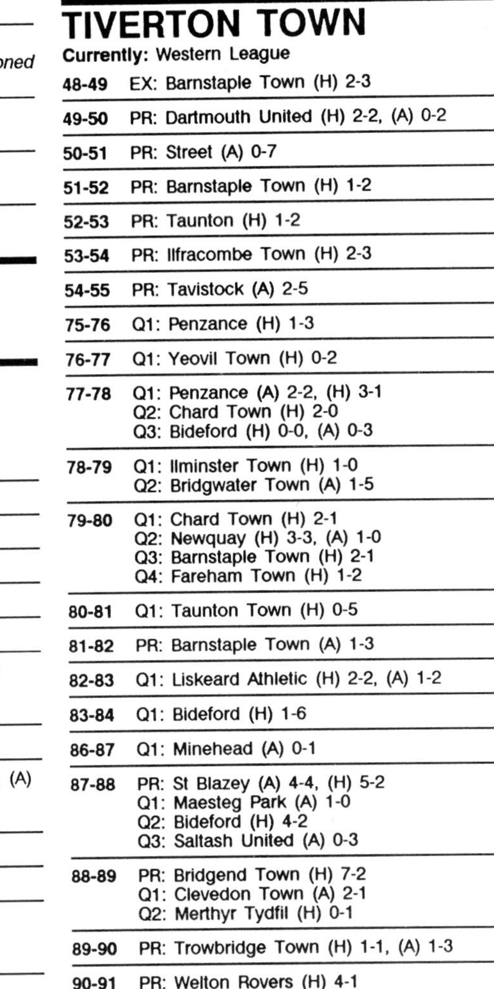

TIVERTON TOWN

Currently: Western League

48-49 EX: Barnstaple Town (H) 2-3

49-50 PR: Dartmouth United (H) 2-2, (A) 0-2

50-51 PR: Street (A) 0-7

51-52 PR: Barnstaple Town (H) 1-2

52-53 PR: Taunton (H) 1-2

53-54 PR: Ilfracombe Town (H) 2-3

54-55 PR: Tavistock (A) 2-5

75-76 Q1: Penzance (H) 1-3

76-77 Q1: Yeovil Town (H) 0-2

77-78 Q1: Penzance (A) 2-2, (H) 3-1
Q2: Chard Town (H) 2-0
Q3: Bideford (H) 0-0, (A) 0-3

78-79 Q1: Ilminster Town (H) 1-0
Q2: Bridgwater Town (A) 1-5

79-80 Q1: Chard Town (H) 2-1
Q2: Newquay (H) 3-3, (A) 1-0
Q3: Barnstaple Town (H) 2-1
Q4: Fareham Town (H) 1-2

80-81 Q1: Taunton Town (H) 0-5

81-82 PR: Barnstaple Town (A) 1-3

82-83 Q1: Liskeard Athletic (H) 2-2, (A) 1-2

83-84 Q1: Bideford (H) 1-6

86-87 Q1: Minehead (A) 0-1

87-88 PR: St Blazey (A) 4-4, (H) 5-2
Q1: Maesteg Park (A) 1-0
Q2: Bideford (H) 4-2
Q3: Saltash United (A) 0-3

88-89 PR: Bridgend Town (H) 7-2
Q1: Clevedon Town (A) 2-1
Q2: Merthyr Tydfil (H) 0-1

89-90 PR: Trowbridge Town (H) 1-1, (A) 1-3

90-91 PR: Welton Rovers (H) 4-1

Above: *In 1992 Tiptree United appeared at a Football League ground in the F.A. Cup for the first time. However, their opponents were fellow Pyramid side Wealdstone, groundsharers at Watford F.C. Here Tiptree's Chris Guy is felled by Gary Nash. A penalty resulted. Photo: Dave West.*

Tiverton Town created a piece of history in 1990 when they became the first Western League team since Wimborne Town in 1982 to reach the First Round Proper. Coincidently, as with Wimborne, Tiverton were drawn away to Aldershot. **Above:** *Four Tiverton players (Hedley Steele, Martin Rogers, Dave Cadwallader and John Durham) celebrate the Fourth Qualifying Round win over Peacehaven. Photo: Francis Short.* **Below:** *Ian Nott makes a brave save from from Aldershot's leading scorer Dave Puckett at the 'Rec'. Photo: Eric Marsh.*

Q1: Ilfracombe Town (H) 5-1
Q2: Saltash United (H) 4-2
Q3: Liskeard Athletic (H) 1-0
Q4: Peacehaven & Telscombe (H) 3-2
R1: Aldershot (A) 2-6

91-92 Q1: Torrington (A) 2-2, (H) 3-2
Q2: Saltash United (H) 0-0, (A) 2-1
Q3: Liskeard Athletic (A) 3-1
Q4: Dover Athletic (H) 1-0
R1: Barnet (A) 0-5

92-93 Q4: Bath City (H) 0-0, (A) 1-2

TIVIDALE

Currently: West Midlands (Regional) League

75-76 Q1: Heanor Town (A) 6-2
Q2: Enderby Town (A) 1-0
Q3: Alfreton Town (H) 0-0, (A) 1-0
Q4: A.P. Leamington (A) 2-3

76-77 PR: Hinckley Athletic (A) 1-0
Q1: Oldbury United (A) 4-0
Q2: Telford United (H) 0-3

77-78 PR: Stourbridge (A) 1-1, (H) 1-0
Q1: A.P. Leamington (A) 1-3

78-79 Q1: Redditch United (A) 2-3

79-80 PR: Long Eaton United (A) 1-3

80-81 Q1: Enderby Town (A) 1-3

81-82 PR: Milton Keynes City (H) 3-0
Q1: Walsall Wood (H) 3-0
Q2: V.S. Rugby (H) 2-2, (A) 2-0
Q3: Nuneaton Borough (A) 2-5

82-83 Q1: Bromsgrove Rovers (H) 0-1

83-84 PR: Skegness Town (A) 4-2
Q1: A.P. Leamington (H) 0-5

84-85 Q1: Worksop Town (H) 1-2

85-86 Q1: Arnold (A) 1-6

86-87 PR: Rothwell Town (A) 2-3

87-88 PR: Moor Green (A) 1-3

88-89 PR: Rushall Olympic (H) 1-4

89-90 PR: Stourbridge (H) 1-3

90-91 PR: Wellingborough Town (A) 0-1

TONBRIDGE A.F.C.

Currently: Southern League
* - As Tonbridge F.C.

48-49 * EX: Bexley (A - *played home*) 5-0
PR: Dover (A) 2-4

49-50 * PR: Woolwich Poly (A - *played home*) 5-1
Q1: Erith & Belvedere (A) 0-3

50-51 * PR: Aylesford Paper Mills (A) 3-0
Q1: Gravesend & Northfleet (H) 1-0
Q2: Sittingbourne (H) 3-1
Q3: Snowdown Colliery Welf. (H) 1-1, (A) 6-3
Q4: Hendon (H) 3-3, (A) 3-1
R1: Chelmsford City (A) 2-2, (H) 0-1

51-52 * PR: Littlehampton Town (A) 7-1
Q1: Bexhill Town (A) 4-0
Q2: Worthing (H) 11-1
Q3: Ashford Town (A) 1-1, (H) 4-0
Q4: Wealdstone (H) 2-0
R1: Aldershot (H) 0-0, (A) 2-3

52-53 * Q4: Folkestone (A) 0-0, (H) 4-4, 2-0
R1: Norwich City (H) 2-2, (A) 0-1

53-54 * Q4: Guildford City (A) 0-4

54-55 * PR: Sheppey United (H) 6-0
Q1: Gravesend & Northfleet (A) 2-1
Q2: Margate (H) 2-2, (A) 1-0
Q3: Dover (H) 3-2
Q4: Headington United (A) 0-1

55-56 * PR: Betteshanger Colliery Welfare (A) 8-2
Q1: Maidstone United (H) 0-1

56-57 * PR: Kingstonian (A) 2-2, (H) 6-1
Q1: Tooting & Mitcham Utd (H) 3-3, (A) 1-2

57-58 * PR: Bexleyheath & Welling (A) 0-1

58-59 * Q1: Bexleyheath & Welling (A) 1-1 (H) 6-5
Q2: Sittingbourne (H) 0-2

59-60 * PR: Erith & Belvedere (A) 2-0
Q1: Gravesend & Northfleet (A) 0-2

60-61 * Q1: Bexhill Town (H) 2-2, (A) 2-1
Q2: Tunbridge Wells United (A) 2-1
Q3: Hastings United (H) 1-2

61-62 * Q2: Tunbridge Wells United (H) 1-3

62-63 * Q1: Eastbourne United (A) 3-4

63-64 * Q1: Eastbourne United (A) 1-0
Q2: Hastings United (A) 5-2
Q3: Maidstone United (A) 6-1
Q4: Margate (A) 1-2

64-65 * Q1: Tunbridge Wells Rangers (A) 3-1
Q2: Eastbourne (H) 2-0
Q3: Hastings United (H) 3-0
Q4: Dartford (A) 1-3

65-66 * Q1: Eastbourne (A) 4-1
Q2: Tunbridge Wells Rangers (H) 4-1
Q3: Hastings United (A) 1-1, (H) 3-1
Q4: Dartford (H) 0-0, (A) 2-6

66-67 * Q1: Hastings United (A) 0-1

67-68 * Q1: Canterbury City (A) 2-1
Q2: Chatham Town (H) 2-1
Q3: Dover (H) 4-2
Q4: Folkestone Town (H) 5-1
R1: Dagenham (A) 0-1

68-69 * Q1: Dover (H) 2-5

69-70 * Q1: Maidstone United (A) 4-5

70-71 * Q1: Tunbridge Wells (H) 5-0
Q2: Gravesend & Northfleet (A) 1-0
Q3: Herne Bay (A) 1-4

71-72 * Q1: Deal Town (A) 1-1, (H) 2-0
Q2: Ashford Town (A) 1-3

72-73 * PR: Maidstone United (H) 1-1, (A) 2-1
Q1: Ramsgate Athletic (H) 1-1 (A) 3-0
Q2: Folkestone (A) 1-0
Q3: Sittingbourne (H) 4-1
Q4: Romford (H) 0-0, (A) 2-1
R1: Charlton Athletic (H) 0-5

73-74 * PR: Woking (A) 1-2

74-75 * Q1: Hastings United (A) 0-0, (H) 1-2

75-76 * Q1: Hatfield Town (H) 5-0
Q2: Marlow (H) 2-2 (A) 3-1
Q3: Kingstonian (H) 0-0 (A) 1-3

76-77 * Q1: Croydon (H) 0-1

77-78 Q1: Sidley United (A) 0-0, (H) 8-1
Q2: Lewes (H) 1-0
Q3: Ramsgate (H) 2-0
Q4: Tilbury (A) 3-4

78-79 Q1: Snowdown Colliery Welfare (A) 3-0
Q2: Folkestone & Shepway (H) 2-3

79-80 Q1: Worthing (H) 2-3

80-81 PR: Herne Bay (A) 3-0
Q1: Chatham Town (H) 1-1, (A) 0-1

81-82 PR: Eastbourne United (A) 2-0
Q1: Whitstable Town (H) 3-1
Q2: Dover (H) 2-2 (A) 2-5

82-83 Q1: Walton & Hersham (H) 2-0
Q2: Dartford (H) 2-3

83-84 PR: Marlow (H) 3-0
Q1: Chichester City (A) 2-1
Q2: Farnborough Town (H) 1-2

84-85 PR: Molesey (H) 4-1
Q1: Folkestone (H) 0-1

85-86 PR: Horsham (H) 3-0
Q1: Lewes (A) 1-0
Q2: Carshalton Athletic (H) 0-2

86-87 PR: Haywards Heath (H) 2-0
Q1: Whitstable Town (A) 1-2

87-88 PR: Folkestone (H) 5-2
Q1: Horndean (A) 2-0

Q2: Eastbourne United (A) 0-0, (H) 3-1
Q3: Wokingham Town (H) 0-0, (A) 1-2

88-89 PR: Canterbury City (H) 2-3

89-90 Q1: Hailsham Town (A) 0-2

90-91 PR: Shoreham (H) 2-1
Q1: Hythe Town (H) 3-1
Q2: Whyteleafe (A) 2-0
Q3: Littlehampton Town (A) 0-0, (H) 2-3

Right: *Tonbridge goalkeeper Baldwin cut outs a dangerous cross during the Third Qualifying Round goalless draw at Littlehampton in 1990-91.*
Photo: Dennis Nicholson.

91-92 Q1: Croydon Athletic (H) 2-1
Q2: Sittingbourne (A) 2-1
Q3: Hampton (A) 2-2, (H) 2-1 *abondoned (f'light failure) after 81 mins,* (H) 3-0
Q4: Yeovil Town (H) 1-2

92-93 Q1: Dover Athletic (H) 0-0, (A) 1-2

TON PENTRE

Currently: League of Wales

68-69 Q1: Llanelly (A) 1-2

69-70 Q1: Gloucester City (H) 2-2, (A) 1-0
Q2: Stonehouse (H) 2-0
Q3: Merthyr Tydfil (H) 4-2
Q4: Falmouth Town (A) 1-1, (H) 1-1, 0-1

70-71 Q1: Abergavenny Thursdays (H) 4-1
Q2: Cinderford Town (A) 1-0
Q3: Merthyr Tydfil (A) 0-2

71-72 Q1: Cinderford Town (A) 1-1, (H) 3-1
Q2: Abergavenny Thursdays (A) 2-0
Q3: Merthyr Tydfil (H) 2-1
Q4: Redditch United (A) 0-3

72-73 PR: Merthyr Tydfil (H) 3-3, (A) 0-1

73-74 Q1: Glastonbury (H) 1-2

74-75 Q1: Cinderford Town (A) 2-3

75-76 Q1: Worcester City (H) 4-3
Q2: Alvechurch (A) 0-1

76-77 Q1: Cheltenham Town (H) 1-1, (A) 0-4

77-78 Q1: Weston-super-Mare (H) 2-2, (A) 2-3

78-79 Q1: Barry Town (H) 0-1

79-80 PR: Moreton Town (A) 2-0
Q1: Stourbridge (A) 1-2

80-81 Q1: Bridgend Town (A) 1-0
Q2: Melksham Town (A) 3-0
Q3: Bath City (H) 1-3

81-82 PR: Barry Town (A) 0-2

82-83 PR: Moreton Town (A) 2-2, (H) 4-1
Q1: Trowbridge Town (A) 1-2

83-84 PR: Mangotsfield United (A) 1-3

84-85 Q1: Trowbridge Town (H) 1-1, (A) 3-0
Q2: Cheltenham Town (H) 2-3

85-86 Q1: Gloucester City (A) 0-0, (H) 3-3, (H) 2-1
Q2: Frome Town (H) 2-1
Q3: R.S. Southampton (H) 1-1, (A) 2-1
Q4: Weymouth (H) 1-3

86-87 Q1: Basingstoke Town (A) 2-0
Q2: Sharpness (A) 1-0
Q3: Clevedon Town (A) 4-0
Q4: Minehead (H) 5-1
R1: Cardiff City (H) 1-4

87-88 Q1: Gloucester City (A) 2-1
Q2: Weston-super-Mare (H) 1-2

88-89 Q1: Exmouth Town (H) 0-1

89-90 PR: Mangotsfield United (H) 2-2, (A) 0-1 - *aban. 41 mins,* (A) 1-1, (H) 3-3, (A) 1-3

90-91 PR: Bridgend Town (A) 1-2

91-92 PR: Barry Town (H) 1-3

TOOTING & MITCHAM UTD

Currently: Isthmian League

45-46 PR: Kingstonian (H) 5-2
Q1: Redhill (A) 5-1
Q2: Woking (A) 2-1
Q3: Sutton United (H) 3-3, (A) 1-5

46-47 PR: Redhill (A) 9-3
Q1: Walton & Hersham (A) 1-1, (H) 2-1
Q2: Wimbledon (H) 1-0
Q3: Sutton United (H) 3-5

47-48 Q1: Woking (A) 3-2
Q2: Kingstonian (A) 2-0
Q3: Redhill (A) 0-1

48-49 PR: Guildford (A - *played home*) 6-1
Q1: Hounslow Town (A) 3-1
Q2: Sutton United (A) 1-0
Q3: Redhill (H) 5-1
Q4: Kingstonian (H) 1-1, (A) 4-2
R1: Millwall (A) 0-1

49-50 PR: Farnham Town (H) 4-0
Q1: Vickers Armstrong (A) 4-2
Q2: Walton & Hersham (H) 1-1, (A) 2-1
Q3: Kingstonian (A) 3-5

50-51 PR: Sutton United (A) 0-0, (H) 1-0
Q1: Camberley (H) 3-2
Q2: Walton & Hersham (H) 2-1
Q3: Carshalton Athletic (A) 3-1
Q4: Great Yarmouth Town (H) 5-3
R1: Brighton & Hove Albion (H) 2-3

51-52 PR: Metropolitan Police (A) 3-2
Q1: Kingstonian (A) 1-3

52-53 PR: Walton & Hersham (A) 1-0
Q1: Dulwich Hamlet (A) 1-2

53-54 PR: Chatham Town (A) 3-1
Q1: Betteshanger Colliery Welfare (A) 0-1

54-55 PR: Bexleyheath & Welling (A) 3-3, (H) 4-1
Q1: Sittingbourne (A) 1-2

55-56 PR: Ashford Town (A) 0-1

56-57 PR: Wimbledon (A) 5-1
Q1: Tonbridge (A) 3-3 (H) 2-1
Q2: Tunbridge Wells (A) 3-2
Q3: Bromley (H) 4-0
Q4: Aylesbury United (H) 3-1
R1: Bromgrove Rovers (H) 2-1
R2: Queens Park Rangers (H) 0-2

57-58 Q4: Redhill (H) 1-3

58-59 Q1: Bromley (A) 2-2, (H) 5-1
Q2: Redhill (H) 7-1
Q3: Sutton United (A) 8-1
Q4: Horsham (H) 4-0
R1: Bournemouth & Boscombe Ath. (H) 3-1
R2: Northampton Town (H) 2-1
R3: Nottingham Forest (H) 2-2, (A) 0-3

59-60 Q4: Wisbech Town (H) 1-2

60-61 Q4: Wycombe Wanderers (A) 1-2

61-62 Q1: Marlow (H) 7-1
Q2: Dulwich Hamlet (A) 1-3

62-63 Q1: Ruislip Manor (A) 2-0
Q2: Slough Town (A) 4-0
Q3: Dulwich Hamlet (H) 5-1
Q4: Enfield (H) 2-3

63-64 Q1: Marlow (H) 5-0
Q2: Carshalton Athletic (A) 3-0
Q3: Walthamstow Avenue (A) 6-3
Q4: Hayes (A) 2-1
R1: Gravesend & Northfleet (H) 1-2

64-65 Q1: Carshalton Athletic (H) 1-4

65-66 Q1: Dulwich Hamlet (A) 2-3

66-67 Q1: Brentwood Town (H) 2-3

67-68 Q1: Sutton United (H) 1-3

68-69 Q1: Aveley (A) 1-0
Q2: Bexley United (H) 0-1

69-70 PR: Canvey Island (A) 0-0, (H) 4-1
Q1: Hillingdon Borough (A) 0-0, (H) 1-2

70-71 Q1: Vauxhall Motors (A) 2-1
Q2: Leatherhead (H) 1-2

71-72 Q1: Windsor & Eton (H) 1-1, (A) 0-2

72-73 Q1: Wycombe Wanderers (H) 1-3

73-74 Q1: Harrow Boro. (A - *at Wealdstone*) 1-2

74-75 Q1: Southall (A) 0-0, (H) 3-1
Q2: Farnborough Town (A) 2-2, (H) 6-1
Q3: Wealdstone (H) 1-0
Q4: Harlow Town (H) 3-0
R1: Crystal Palace (H) 1-2

75-76 Q1: St Albans (A) 3-3 (H) 4-0

Q2: Stevenage Athletic (A) 2-2, (H) 2-0
Q3: Addlestone (H) 4-2
Q4: Southall & Ealing Borough (A) 4-1
R1: Romford (A) 1-0
R2: Leatherhead (A) 0-0, (H) 1-1 *ab. after 57 minutes*, (H) 2-1
R3: Swindon Town (A) 2-2, (H) 2-1
R4: Bradford City (A) 1-3

Right: *Tooting's 1975-76 cup run was one of the most notable in non-League history.* **Top:** *Right-back Alan Berrecloth (centre) gets in a header at Swindon watched by team-mates Steve Grubb (left) and Dave Juneman. Photo: Neil McGuinn.* **Bottom:** *After-match scenes in the Tooting dressing room after the replay win. Photo: Tom Morris.*

76-77	Q4: Barking (H) 1-1, (A) 2-1 R1: Dartford (H) 4-2 R2: Kettering Town (A) 0-1
77-78	Q4: Sutton United (H) 3-0 R1: Northampton Town (H) 1-2
78-79	Q4: Hillingdon Borough (A) 1-2
79-80	Q4: Slough Town (A) 0-4
80-81	Q1: Windsor & Eton (H) 0-3
81-82	Q1: Basingstoke Town (A) 1-2
82-83	PR: Molesey (H) 3-1 Q1: Lewes (A) 3-2 Q2: Canterbury City (H) 2-0 Q3: Deal Town (H) 8-1 Q4: Dagenham (A) 0-2
83-84	Q1: Hastings Town (A) 4-3 Q2: Thanet United (A) 7-0 Q3: Whitehawk (H) 3-0 Q4: Dartford (A) 0-2
84-85	Q1: Bracknell Town (A) 3-0 Q2: Kingstonian (H) 2-2, (A) 4-0 Q3: Egham Town (A) 0-0, (H) 1-0 Q4: Windsor & Eton (A) 2-5
85-86	Q1: Horndean (A) 3-2 Q2: Worthing (A) 1-5
86-87	Q1: Hampton (H) 1-2
87-88	Q1: Wick (A) 1-1, (H) 3-0 Q2: Pagham (H) 0-0, (A) 4-3 Q3: Basingstoke Town (H) 0-0, (A) 1-4
88-89	Q1: Whytleafe (A) 1-2
89-90	PR: Worthing (H) 2-2, (A) 1-0 Q1: Canterbury City (A) 0-2
90-91	PR: Hastings Town (H) 1-1, (A) 2-1 Q1: Horsham (H) 0-0, (A) 2-1 Q2: Littlehampton Town (H) 1-2
91-92	PR: Redhill (H) 2-0 Q1: Margate (H) 2-1 Q2: Peacehaven & Telscombe (H) 2-0 Q3: Kingstonian (A) 0-0, (H) 2-3
92-93	Q1: Fareham Town (A) 0-2

TORQUAY UNITED

Currently: Football League

45-46	R1: Newport Co. (H) 0-1, (A) 1-1 (*agg: 1-2*)
46-47	R1: Ipswich Town (A) 0-2
47-48	R1: Watford (A) 1-1, (H) 3-0 R2: Northampton T. (A) 1-1, (H) 1-1, 2-0 R3: Stockport County (A) 0-3
48-49	R1: Peterborough United (A) 1-0 R2: Norwich City (H) 3-1 R3: Coventry City (H) 1-0 R4: Brentford (A) 0-1
49-50	R1: Gravesend & Northfleet (A) 3-1 R2: Northampton Town (A) 2-4
50-51	R1: Nottingham Forest (A) 1-6
51-52	R1: Bromley (H) 3-2 R2: Swindon T. (A) 3-3, (H) 1-1, 1-3
52-53	R1: Peterborough United (A) 1-2
53-54	R1: Bristol City (H) 1-3
54-55	R1: Cambridge United (H) 4-0 R2: Blyth Spartans (A) 3-1 R3: Leeds United (A) 2-2, (H) 4-0 R4: Huddersfield Town (H) 0-1
55-56	R1: Colchester United (H) 2-0 R2: Shrewsbury Town (A) 0-0, (H) 5-1 R3: Birmingham City (H) 1-7
56-57	R1: Ely City (A) 6-2 R2: Plymouth Argyle (H) 1-0 R3: New Brighton (A) 1-2
57-58	R1: Peterborough United (A) 3-3, (H) 1-0 R2: Southend United (H) 1-1, (A) 1-2
58-59	R1: Port Vale (H) 1-0 R2: Watford (H) 2-0 R3: Newport County (A) 0-0, (H) 0-1
59-60	R1: Northampton Town (H) 7-1 R2: Gillingham (A) 2-2, (H) 1-2
60-61	R1: Weymouth (A) 3-1 R2: Peterborough United (H) 1-3
61-62	R1: Harwich & Parkeston (H) 5-1 R2: Peterborough United (H) 1-4
62-63	R1: Northampton Town (A) 2-1 R2: Shrewsbury Town (A) 1-2
63-64	R1: Barnet (H) 6-2 R2: Aldershot (H) 2-3
64-65	R1: Canterbury City (A) 6-0 R2: Colchester United (H) 2-0 R3: Tottenham Hotspur (H) 3-3, (A) 1-5
65-66	R1: Shrewsbury Town (A) 1-2
66-67	R1: Aldershot (A) 1-2
67-68	R1: Colchester United (H) 1-1, (A) 1-2
68-69	R1: Hereford United (A) 0-0, (H) 4-2 R2: Reading (A) 0-0, (H) 1-2
69-70	R1: Tamworth (A) 1-2
70-71	R1: Aston Villa (H) 3-1 R2: Chelmsford City (A) 1-0 R3: Lincoln City (H) 4-3 R4: Leicester City (A) 0-3
71-72	R1: Nuneaton Borough (H) 1-0 R2: Barnet (A) 4-1 R3: Bolton Wanderers (A) 1-2
72-73	R1: Hereford United (H) 3-0 R2: Newport County (H) 0-1
73-74	R1: Hereford United (A) 1-3
74-75	R1: Northampton Town (H) 0-1
75-76	R1: Hereford United (A) 0-2
76-77	R1: Hillingdon Borough (H) 1-2

Right: *Torquay supporters, and players Jimmy Smith (2), Daral Pugh (7) and Mark Loram show just how much it means to score in an F.A. Cup derby. Loram had just put United ahead in the match at Yeovil on 10th December 1988. Photo: Nigel Andrews.*

77-78 R1: Southend United (H) 1-2

78-79 R1: Walsall (A) 2-0
R2: A.P. Leamington (A) 1-0
R3: Newcastle United (A) 1-3

79-80 R1: Gravesend & Northfleet (A) 1-0
R2: Swindon Town (H) 3-3, (A) 2-3

80-81 R1: Barton Rovers (H) 2-0
R2: St Albans City (A) 1-1, (H) 4-1
R3: Barnsley (A) 1-2

81-82 R1: Bristol City (A) 0-0, (H) 1-2

82-83 R1: Colchester United (A) 2-0
R2: Carshalton Athletic (H) 4-1
R3: Oxford United (A) 1-1, (H) 2-1
R4: Sheffield Wednesday (H) 2-3

83-84 R1: Colchester United (H) 1-2

84-85 R1: Yeovil Town (H) 2-0
R2: Orient (A) 0-3

85-86 R1: Windsor & Eton (A) 1-1, (H) 3-0
R2: Newport County (A) 1-1, (H) 2-3

86-87 R1: Aldershot (A) 0-1

87-88 R1: Bognor Regis Town (A) 3-0
R2: Bristol City (A) 1-0
R3: Coventry City (A) 0-2

88-89 R1: Fareham Town (H) 2-2, (A) 3-2
R2: Yeovil Town (A) 1-1, (H) 1-0
R3: Sheffield Wednesday (A) 1-5

89-90 R1: Sutton United (A) 1-1, (H) 4-0
R2: Basingstoke Town (A) 3-2
R3: West Ham United (H) 1-0
R4: Blackpool (A) 0-1

90-91 R1: Maidstone Utd (A - *at Dartford*) 1-4

91-92 R1: Birmingham City (H) 3-0
R2: Farnborough Town (H) 1-1, (A) 3-4

92-93 R1: Yeovil Town (H) 2-5

TORRINGTON

Currently: Western League

81-82 Q1: Ilminster Town (A) 2-0
Q2: Falmouth Town (A) 0-1

82-83 Q1: Shepton Mallet Town (A) 0-3

83-84 Q1: Frome Town (A) 1-1, (H) 0-3

84-85 Q1: Frome Town (H) 0-1

86-87 PR: Weston-super-Mare (A) 0-1

87-88 PR: Glastonbury (H) 3-0
Q1: Forest Green Rovers (H) 0-3

88-89 Q1: Mangotsfield United (A) 0-6

89-90 PR: Falmouth Town (H) 1-1, (A) 2-4

90-91 PR: Saltash United (A) 1-1, (H) 2-5

91-92 PR: Barnstaple Town (H) 3-1
Q1: Tiverton Town (H) 2-2, (A) 2-3

92-93 PR: Bideford (H) 1-0
Q1: Truro City (A) 0-2

TOTTON

Currently: Merged with Totton Athletic. Playing as A.F.C. Totton in Wessex League.
See also A.F.C. Totton.

45-46 PR: Thornycroft Athletic (A) *W/O*
Q1: Newport Isle of Wight (H) 0-4

49-50 EX: Basingstoke Town (H) 3-0
PR: Weymouth (A) 3-6

50-51 EX: Newport Isle of Wight (A) 0-4

51-52 Q1: Ryde Sports (H) 3-0
Q2: Newport Isle of Wight (A) 1-6

52-53 Q1: Basingstoke Town (A) 1-3

(A.F.C.) TOTTON

Currently: Wessex League
See also Totton F.C.

82-83 PR: Marlow (H) 1-0
Q1: Brockenhurst (A) 2-1
Q2: Gosport Borough (A) 2-2, (H) 2-1
Q3: Dorchester Town (H) 1-0
Q4: Windsor & Eton (H) 0-0, (A) 0-1

83-84 Q1: Andover (A) 3-1
Q2: Fareham Town (A) 3-0
Q3: Waterlooville (H) 1-0 *abandoned after 65 minutes*, (H) 1-1, (A) 0-3

84-85 Q1: Eastleigh (A) 2-0
Q2: Farnborough Town (H) 1-1, (A) 1-5

85-86 PR: Sholing Sports (H) 2-0
Q1: Newbury Town (A) 3-3, (H) 2-0
Q2: Basingstoke Town (H) 1-1, (A) 2-1
Q3: Fareham Town (A) 0-0, (H) 0-3

86-87 Q1: Calne Town (H) 1-0
Q2: Havant Town (A) 1-1, (H) 1-0
Q3: Wimborne Town (H) 0-0, (A) 0-1

87-88 Q1: Newport Isle of Wight (A) 0-2

88-89 Q1: Worthing (A) 2-3

89-90 PR: Haywards Heath (A) 2-1
Q1: Whitehawk (H) 4-2
Q2: Newport Isle of Wight (H) 1-3

90-91 PR: Warminster Town (H) 2-3

91-92 PR: A.F.C. Lymington (H) 2-2, (A) 2-3

92-93 PR: Havant Town (H) 0-1

TOTTENHAM HOTSPUR

Currently: F.A. Premier League

45-46 R3: Brentford (H) 2-2, (A) 0-2 (*agg: 0-2*)

46-47 R3: Stoke City (H) 2-2, (A) 0-1

47-48 R3: Bolton Wanderers (A) 2-0
R4: West Bromwich Albion (H) 3-1
R5: Leicester City (H) 5-2
R6: Southampton (A) 1-0
SF: Blackpool (*at Aston Villa*) 1-3

48-49 R3: Arsenal (A) 0-3

49-50 R3: Stoke City (A) 1-0
R4: Sunderland (H) 5-1
R5: Everton (A) 0-1

50-51 R3: Huddersfield Town (A) 0-2

51-52 R3: Scunthorpe United (A) 3-0
R4: Newcastle United (H) 0-3

52-53 R3: Tranmere Rovers (A) 1-1, (H) 9-1
R4: Preston North End (A) 2-2, (H) 1-0
R5: Halifax Town (A) 3-0
R6: Birmingham City (A) 1-1, (H) 2-2, 1-0
SF: Blackpool (*at Aston Villa*) 1-2

53-54 R3: Leeds United (A) 3-3, (H) 1-0
R4: Manchester City (A) 1-0
R5: Hull City (A) 1-1, (H) 2-0
R6: West Bromwich Albion (A) 0-3

54-55 R3: Gateshead (A) 2-0
R4: Port Vale (H) 4-2
R5: York City (A) 1-3

55-56 R3: Boston United (H) 4-0
R4: Middlesbrough (H) 3-1
R5: Doncaster Rovers (A) 2-0
R6: West Ham United (H) 3-3, (A) 2-1
SF: Manchester City (*at Aston Villa*) 0-1

56-57 R3: Leicester City (H) 2-0
R4: Chelsea (H) 4-0
R5: Bournemouth & Boscombe Ath. (A) 1-3

57-58 R3: Leicester City (H) 4-0
R4: Sheffield United (H) 0-3

58-59 R3: West Ham United (H) 2-0
R4: Newport County (H) 4-1
R5: Norwich City (H) 1-1, (A) 0-1

Right: *A.F.C. Totton player Eddie Holdaway loses a boot as he shoots at the Havant goal. His side also lost this 1992 Preliminary Round tie. Photo: Jon Hollaway.*

Above: *Bobby Smith and Danny Blanchflower on their lap of honour after Tottenham's 1961 final triumph against Leicester City. Photo: Colorsport.*

59-60 R3: Newport County (A) 4-0
R4: Crewe Alexandra (A) 2-2, (H) 13-2
R5: Blackburn Rovers (H) 1-3

60-61 R3: Charlton Athletic (H) 3-2
R4: Crewe Alexandra (H) 5-1
R5: Aston Villa (A) 2-0
R6: Sunderland (A) 1-1, (H) 5-0
SF: Burnley (*at Aston Villa*) 3-0
F: Leicester City (*at Wembley*) 2-0

61-62 R3: Birmingham City (A) 3-3, (H) 4-2
R4: Plymouth Argyle (A) 5-1
R5: West Bromwich Albion (A) 4-2
R6: Aston Villa (H) 2-0
SF: Manchester Utd (*at Sheffield Wed.*) 3-1
F: Burnley (*at Wembley*) 3-1

62-63 R3: Burnley (H) 0-3

63-64 R3: Chelsea (H) 1-1, (A) 0-2

64-65 R3: Torquay United (A) 3-3, (H) 5-1
R4: Ipswich Town (H) 5-0
R5: Chelsea (A) 0-1

65-66 R3: Middlesbrough (H) 4-0
R4: Burnley (H) 4-3
R5: Preston North End (A) 1-2

66-67 R3: Millwall (A) 0-0, (H) 1-0
R4: Portsmouth (H) 3-1
R5: Bristol City (H) 2-0
R6: Birmingham City (A) 0-0, (H) 6-0
SF: Nottingham F. (*at Sheffield Wed.*) 2-1
F: Chelsea (*at Wembley*) 2-1

67-68 R3: Manchester United (A) 2-2, (H) 1-0
R4: Preston North End (H) 3-1
R5: Liverpool (H) 1-1, (A) 1-2

68-69 R3: Walsall (A) 1-0
R4: Wolverhampton Wanderers (H) 2-1
R5: Aston Villa (H) 3-2
R6: Manchester City (A) 0-1

69-70 R3: Bradford City (A) 2-2, (H) 5-0
R4: Crystal Palace (H) 0-0, (A) 0-1

70-71 R3: Sheffield Wednesday (H) 4-1
R4: Carlisle United (A) 3-2
R5: Nottingham Forest (H) 2-1
R6: Liverpool (A) 0-0, (H) 0-1

71-72 R3: Carlisle United (H) 1-1, (A) 3-1
R4: Rotherham United (H) 2-0
R5: Everton (A) 2-0
R6: Leeds United (A) 1-2

72-73 R3: Margate (A) 6-0
R4: Derby County (A) 1-1, (H) 3-5

73-74 R3: Leicester City (A) 0-1

74-75 R3: Nottingham Forest (A) 1-1, (H) 0-1

75-76 R3: Stoke City (H) 1-1, (A) 1-2

76-77 R3: Cardiff City (A) 0-1

77-78 R3: Bolton Wanderers (H) 2-2, (A) 1-2

78-79 R3: Altrincham (H) 1-1, (A - *at Man. City*) 3-0
R4: Wrexham (H) 3-3, (A) 3-2
R5: Oldham Athletic (A) 1-0
R6: Manchester United (H) 1-1, (A) 0-2

79-80 R3: Manchester United (H) 1-1, (A) 1-0
R4: Swindon Town (A) 0-0, (H) 2-1
R5: Birmingham City (H) 3-1
R6: Liverpool (H) 0-1

80-81 R3: Queens Park Rangers (A) 0-0, (H) 3-1
R4: Hull City (H) 2-0
R5: Coventry City (H) 3-1
R6: Exeter City (H) 2-0
SF: Wolves (*at Sheff W.*) 2-2, (*at Arsenal*) 3-0
F: Manchester C. (*both at Wembley*) 1-1, 3-2

81-82 R3: Arsenal (H) 1-0
R4: Leeds United (H) 1-0
R5: Aston Villa (H) 1-0
R6: Chelsea (A) 3-2
SF: Leicester City (*at Aston Villa*) 2-0
F: Queens Pk Rgrs (*both at Wembley*) 1-1, 1-0

82-83 R3: Southampton (H) 1-0
R4: West Bromwich Albion (H) 2-1
R5: Everton (A) 1-2

83-84 R3: Fulham (A) 0-0, (H) 2-0
R4: Norwich City (H) 0-0, (A) 1-2

84-85 R3: Charlton Athletic (H) 1-1, (A) 2-1
R4: Liverpool (A) 0-1

85-86 R3: Oxford United (A) 1-1, (H) 2-1
R4: Notts County (A) 1-1, (H) 5-0
R5: Everton (H) 1-2

86-87 R3: Scunthorpe United (H) 3-2
R4: Crystal Palace (H) 4-0
R5: Newcastle United (H) 1-0
R6: Wimbledon (A) 2-0
SF: Watford (*at Aston Villa*) 4-1
F: Coventry City (*at Wembley*) 2-3

87-88 R3: Oldham Athletic (A) 4-2
R4: Port Vale (A) 1-2

88-89 R3: Bradford City (A) 0-1

89-90 R3: Southampton (H) 1-3

90-91 R3: Blackpool (A) 1-0
R4: Oxford United (H) 4-2
R5: Portsmouth (A) 2-1
R6: Notts County (H) 2-1
SF: Arsenal (*at Wembley*) 3-1
F: Nottingham Forest (*at Wembley*) 2-1

91-92 R3: Aston Villa (A) 0-0, (H) 0-1

92-93 R3: Marlow (A - *played home*) 5-1
R4: Norwich City (A) 2-0
R5: Wimbledon (H) 3-2
R6: Manchester City (A) 4-2
SF: Arsenal (*at Wembley*) 0-1

TOW LAW TOWN

Currently: Northern League

45-46 Q1: Spennymoor United (A) 1-4

46-47 PR: Chilton & Windlestone Snr Boys (H) 1-3

47-48 PR: Evenwood Town (H) 4-6

48-49 EX: Seaham United (H) 7-2
PR: Seaham Colliery Welfare (H) 0-1

49-50 EX: Blackhall Colliery Welfare (A) 0-1

50-51 PR: Silksworth Colliery Welf. (A) 3-3 (H) 2-0
Q1: West Auckland Town (H) 3-2
Q2: Blackhall Colliery Welf. (H) 0-0, (A) 0-3

51-52 Q1: Willington (A) 4-4, (H) 1-2

52-53 Q1: Evenwood Town (A) 0-1

53-54 Q1: Shildon (A) 0-4

54-55 Q1: Stanley United (H) 0-1

55-56 Q1: Evenwood Town (H) 3-1
Q2: West Auckland Town (H) 1-4

56-57 Q1: Evenwood Town (A) 0-4

57-58 Q1: Whitby Town (H) 2-2, (A) 1-5

58-59 Q1: Billingham Synthonia Recreation (A) 4-2
Q2: Boldon Colliery Welfare (H) 4-1
Q3: Ferryhill Athletic (H) 2-0
Q4: South Shields (H) 2-3

59-60 Q1: Whitby Town (H) 2-1
Q2: West Auckland Town (H) 4-4, (A) 2-5

61-62 Q1: Shildon (A) 3-3, (H) 1-5

63-64 Q1: Stockton (H) 4-0
Q2: Whitley Bay (H) 3-1
Q3: Scarborough (A) 2-0
Q4: Blyth Spartans (A) 0-1

64-65 Q2: Ashington (A) 0-0, (H) 0-0, 2-1
Q3: Annfield Plain (A) 2-3

65-66 Q1: Boldon Colliery Welfare (A) 1-2

66-67 Q1: West Auckland Town (H) 5-0
Q2: Blyth Spartans (A) 3-3, (H) 2-3

67-68 Q1: South Bank (H) 5-1
Q2: Crook Town (H) 2-0
Q3: Ashington (H) 3-2
Q4: South Shields (A) 2-2 (H) 1-0
R1: Mansfield Town (H) 5-1
R2: Shrewsbury Town (H) 1-1, (A) 2-6

68-69 Q4: North Shields (A) 3-1
R1: Mansfield Town (A) 1-4

69-70 Q4: Spennymoor United (A) 0-1

70-71 Q1: Evenwood Town (A) 0-3

71-72 Q1: Gateshead (A) 0-3

72-73 Q1: Boldon Colliery Welfare (H) 1-1, (A) 3-0
Q2: Crook Town (A) 2-4

73-74 Q1: Stockton (A) 4-2
Q2: Evenwood Town (A) 2-2, (H) 1-0
Q3: Bishop Auckland (A) 1-3

74-75 Q1: Ferryhill Athletic (A) 3-0
Q2: Ashington (H) 0-4

75-76 Q1: Bridlington Trinity (H) 1-0
Q2: South Bank (H) 2-1
Q3: Shildon (H) 4-1
Q4: Spennymoor United (H) 0-2

76-77 Q1: Wingate (H) 3-1
Q2: Durham City (H) 1-2

77-78 Q1: Whitby Town (H) 0-4

78-79 PR: Billingham Synthonia (A) 1-2

79-80 Q1: Guisborough Town (H) 1-0
Q2: Brandon United (H) 0-4

80-81 Q1: North Shields (A) 0-0, (H) 4-2
Q2: Gateshead (A) 0-2

81-82 PR: Boldon Community Association (A) 5-1
Q1: Evenwood Town (H) 4-2
Q2: Horden Colliery Welfare (H) 1-4

82-83 Q1: Morecambe (H) 3-5

83-84 Q1: Fleetwood Town (A) 2-1
Q2: Easington Coll. (A) 0-0, (H) 1-1, (A) 0-1

84-85 Q1: Seaham C.W. Red Star (A) 3-3, (H) 3-1
Q2: Guisborough Town (H) 4-3
Q3: South Bank (A) 2-1
Q4: Scarborough (H) 1-0
R1: Bradford City (A) 2-7

85-86 Q1: Consett (H) 1-0
Q2: Gretna (H) 0-1

86-87 Q1: Spennymoor United (H) 0-2

87-88 Q1: Darwen (A) 2-2, (H) 3-2
Q2: Farsley Celtic (H) 2-1
Q3: Darlington Cleveland Bridge (H) 4-0
Q4: Colwyn Bay (A) 1-2

88-89 Q1: Consett (H) 2-0
Q2: Gateshead (H) 3-2
Q3: Spennymoor (H) 2-2, (A) 2-2, (A) 2-1
Q4: Southport (A) 1-2

89-90 Q1: Gretna (A) 5-3
Q2: Crook Town (H) 4-2
Q3: Bridlington Town (A) 0-0, (H) 0-0, (H) 3-2
Q4: Altrincham (H) 2-0
R1: Bishop Auckland (A) 0-2

90-91 Q1: Langley Park (A) 1-2

91-92 Q1: Durham City (A) 0-1

92-93 PR: St Helens Town (A) 2-3

TRAFALGAR SPORTS
(PORTSMOUTH)

Currently: Defunct

46-47 EX: R.A.O.C. Hilsea (H) 2-6

TRANMERE ROVERS

Currently: Football League

45-46 R1: S. Liverpool (A) 1-1, (H) 6-1 *(agg: 7-2)*
R2: Rochdale (H) 3-1, (A) 0-3 *(agg: 3-4)*

46-47 R1: Oldham Athletic (A) 0-1

47-48 R1: Stalybridge Celtic (H) 2-0
R2: Chester (H) 0-1

48-49 R1: Darlington (H) 1-3

49-50 R1: Halifax Town (H) 2-1
R2: Port Vale (A) 0-1

50-51 R1: Cleator Moor C. (A - *at Workington*) 5-0
R2: York City (A) 1-2

51-52 R1: Goole Town (H) 4-2
R2: Blyth (H) 1-1, (A) 1-1 *ab. in E.T.*, 2-2, 5-1
R3: Huddersfield Town (A) 2-1
R4: Chelsea (A) 0-4

52-53 R1: Ashington (H) 8-1
R2: Hartlepools United (H) 2-1
R3: Tottenham Hotspur (H) 1-1, (A) 1-9

53-54 R1: Gateshead (A) 2-1
R2: Accrington Stanley (A) 2-2, (H) 5-1
R3: Leyton Orient (H) 2-2, (A) 1-4

54-55 R1: Rochdale (H) 3-3, (A) 0-1

55-56 R1: Easington Colliery Welfare (A) 2-0
R2: Barrow (H) 0-3

56-57 R1: Bishop Auckland (A) 1-2

57-58 R1: Witton Albion (H) 2-1
R2: Durham City (A) 3-0
R3: Notts County (A) 0-2

58-59 R1: Bishop Auckland (H) 8-1
R2: Doncaster Rovers (H) 1-2

59-60 R1: Chester (H) 0-1

60-61 R1: Bury (H) 1-0
R2: York City (H) 1-1, (A) 1-2

61-62 R1: Gateshead (H) 2-3

62-63 R1: Chester (A) 2-0
R2: Doncaster Rovers (A) 4-1
R3: Chelsea (H) 2-2, (A) 1-3

63-64 R1: Doncaster Rovers (A) 0-3

64-65 R1: Lincoln City (H) 0-0, (A) 0-1

65-66 R1: Stockport County (H) 0-1

66-67 R1: Wigan Athletic (H) 1-1, (A) 1-0
R2: Barrow (A) 1-2

67-68 R1: Rochdale (H) 5-1
R2: Bradford Park Avenue (A) 3-2
R3: Huddersfield Town (H) 2-1
R4: Coventry City (A) 1-1, (H) 2-0
R5: Everton (A) 0-2

68-69 R1: Southport (H) 0-1

69-70 R1: Chesterfield (H) 3-0
R2: Port Vale (A) 2-2, (H) 3-1
R3: Portsmouth (A) 2-1
R4: Northampton Town (H) 0-0, (A) 1-2

70-71 R1: Scunthorpe United (H) 1-1, (A) 0-0, (*at Everton*) 0-1

71-72 R1: Skelmersdale United (A) 4-0
R2: Mansfield Town (A) 2-2, (H) 4-2
R3: Charlton Athletic (A) 0-0, (H) 4-2
R4: Stoke City (H) 2-2, (A) 0-2

72-73 R1: South Liverpool (A) 2-0
R2: Bradford City (A) 1-2

73-74 R1: Bury (H) 2-1
R2: Doncaster Rovers (A) 0-3

74-75 R1: Farsley Celtic (A - *at Leeds Utd*) 2-0
R2: Rochdale (A) 1-1, (H) 1-0
R3: Peterborough United (A) 0-1

75-76 R1: Coventry Sporting (A - *at Cov. City*) 0-2

76-77 R1: Peterborough United (H) 0-4

77-78 R1: Hartlepool United (H) 1-1, (A) 1-3

78-79 R1: Boston United (H) 2-1
R2: Sheffield Wednesday (H) 1-1, (A) 0-4

79-80 R1: A.P. Leamington (H) 9-0
R2: Rochdale (H) 2-2, (A) 1-2

80-81 R1: York City (H) 0-0, (A) 2-1
R2: Huddersfield Town (H) 0-3

81-82 R1: Bury (H) 1-1, (A) 1-3

82-83 R1: Scarborough (H) 4-2
R2: Telford United (A) 1-1, (H) 2-1
R3: Wolverhampton Wanderers (H) 0-1

83-84 R1: Bolton Wanderers (H) 2-2, (A) 1-4

84-85 R1: Bangor City (A) 1-1, (H) 7-0
R2: Hull City (H) 0-3

85-86 R1: Chesterfield (H) 2-2, (A) 1-0
R2: Bury (H) 1-1, (A) 1-2

86-87 R1: Spennymoor United (A) 3-2
R2: Bolton Wanderers (A) 0-2

87-88 R1: Port Vale (H) 2-2, (A) 1-3

88-89 R1: Preston North End (A) 1-1, (H) 3-0
R2: Northwich Victoria (A) 2-1
R3: Reading (H) 1-1, (A) 1-2

89-90 R1: Preston North End (A) 0-1

90-91 R1: Halesowen Town (A) 2-1
R2: Scunthorpe United (A) 2-3

91-92 R1: Runcorn (A - *played home*) 3-0
R2: York City (A) 1-1, (H) 2-1
R3: Oxford United (A) 1-3

92-93 R3: Oldham Athletic (A) 2-2, (H) 3-0
R4: Ipswich Town (H) 1-2

Below: *Tranmere Rovers (white shirts) attract a large crowd to the Grove for their tie against non-League Halesowen Town in 1990. Photo: Mal Cobley.*

TRIMDON GRANGE
COLLIERY WELFARE

Currently: Defunct

46-47 PR: Evenwood Town (H) 3-3, (A) 1-2

54-55 Q1: Shotton Colliery Welfare (A) 1-5

TRING TOWN

Currently: Isthmian League

75-76 Q1: Staines Town (A) 0-2

76-77 Q1: Chesham United (H) 0-3

77-78 Q1: Hertford Town (A) 1-1, (H) 2-3

78-79 Q1: Kingstonian (A) 0-1

79-80 Q1: Wellingborough Town (H) 2-1
Q2: Kempston Rovers (H) 5-0
Q3: Witney Town (H) 0-2

80-81 Q1: Woking (A) 0-2

81-82 Q1: Rothwell Town (A) 3-1
Q2: Irthlingborough D. (A) 1-1, (H) 1-0
Q3: Hendon (A) 0-4

82-83 Q1: Dunstable (H) 1-0
Q2: Hornchurch (H) 2-2, (A) 0-0, (A) 3-0
Q3: Boreham Wood (A) 0-3

83-84 Q1: Hornchurch (A) 2-3

84-85 PR: Kingsbury Town (H) 3-1
Q1: Hampton (H) 1-0
Q2: Potton United (A) 2-0
Q3: Fisher Athletic (H) 1-1, (A) 0-5

85-86 Q1: Abingdon Town (A) 1-0
Q2: Dunstable (A) 2-3

86-87 PR: Chertsey Town (H) 1-3

87-88 PR: Harlow Town (H) 0-2

88-89 Q1: Tilbury (H) 2-1
Q2: Crawley Town (H) 1-2

89-90 PR: Felixstowe Town (A) 2-0
Q1: Leyton-Wingate (H) 0-4

90-91 PR: Flackwell Heath (A) 0-5

91-92 PR: Hemel Hempstead (H) 0-3

92-93 PR: Basildon United (A) 0-1

TROEDRHIW

Currently: Merthyr Tydfil League

48-49 Q1: Lovells Athletic (H) 1-2

49-50 PR: Bristol Aero. Company (H) 3-0
Q1: Clevedon (A) 1-2

50-51 PR: Hanham Athletic (A) 2-0
Q1: Stonehouse (A) 1-3

51-52 Q1: Barry Town (H) 1-3

52-53 Q1: Barry Town (H) 3-8

53-54 Q1: Ebbw Vale (H) 2-3

TROWBRIDGE TOWN

Currently: Southern League

45-46 Q1: Pewsey Y.M. (A) 3-1
Q2: Chippenham Town (H) 3-1
Q3: Paulton Rovers (H) 7-0
Q4: Haywards Heath (H) 6-0
R1: Exeter C. (H) 1-3, (A) 2-7 *(agg: 3-10)*

46-47 PR: Chippenham Town (H) 6-0
Q1: Soundwell (A - *played home*) 6-2
Q2: Westbury United (A) 4-0
Q3: Hoffman Ath. (Stonehouse) (A) 4-3
Q4: Poole Town (A) 0-2

47-48 PR: Welton Rovers (A) 2-0
Q1: Devizes Town (H) 4-1
Q2: Clandown (H) 4-3
Q3: Westbury United (A) 3-0
Q4: Ryde Sports (A) 1-0
R1: Brighton & Hove A. (H) 1-1, (A) 0-5

48-49 PR: Chippenham United (A) 2-1
Q1: Warminster Town (H) 4-1
Q2: Salisbury (H) 4-1
Q3: Westbury United (H) 8-0
Q4: Weymouth (A) 0-2

49-50 PR: Swindon Victoria (A) 7-0
Q1: Chippenham Town (H) 3-1
Q2: Paulton Rovers (A) 4-1
Q3: Clandown (H) 1-0
Q4: Weymouth (A) 3-3, (H) 1-2

50-51 PR: Paulton Rovers (A) 1-1, (H) 4-1
Q1: Corsham Town (H) 6-1
Q2: Welton Rovers (A) 2-0
Q3: Salisbury (A) 0-1

51-52 Q1: Chippenham Town (H) 2-2, (A) 1-2

52-53 PR: Calne & Harris United (A) 4-0
Q1: Warminster Town (A) 1-1, (H) 4-1
Q2: Devizes Town (A) 3-0
Q3: Salisbury (A) 2-0
Q4: Bath City (A) 0-3

53-54 PR: Devizes Town (A) 11-2
Q1: Warminster Town (A) 2-2, (H) 8-2
Q2: Welton Rovers (A) 3-0
Q3: Chippenham Town (A) 2-3

54-55 Q1: Devizes Town (A) 5-2
Q2: Frome Town (H) 1-1, (A) 0-4

55-56 PR: Frome Town (A) 3-4

56-57 Q1: Frome Town (H) 5-0
Q2: Westbury United (H) 5-2
Q3: Chippenham Town (A) 1-4

57-58 Q1: Salisbury (A) 3-0
Q2: Chippenham Town (A) 1-1, (H) 3-0
Q3: Melksham Town (A) 6-0
Q4: Cowes (A) 2-2, (H) 4-1
R1: Southend United (H) 0-2

58-59 Q1: Calne & Harris United (A) 7-2
Q2: Chippenham United (A) 2-1
Q3: Chippenham Town (A) 2-2, (H) 3-0
Q4: Bath City (A) 1-3

59-60 Q1: Melksham Town (A) 4-2
Q2: Westbury United (A) 3-1
Q3: Calne & Harris United (A) 6-1
Q4: Barnstaple Town (A) 0-1

60-61 Q1: Chippenham Town (H) 1-1, (A) 1-0
Q2: Devizes Town (H) 2-2, (A) 3-2
Q3: Chippenham United (H) 2-1
Q4: Yeovil Town (H) 0-4

61-62 Q1: Devizes Town (H) 2-2, (A) 2-0
Q2: Chippenham Town (A) 1-1, (H) 0-2

62-63 Q2: Devizes Town (A) 3-2
Q3: Chippenham Town (A) 1-0
Q4: Yeovil Town (A) 0-4

63-64 Q1: Devizes Town (A) 5-0
Q2: Chippenham Town (H) 1-1, (A) 4-2
Q3: Welton Rovers (H) 3-0
Q4: Bideford (H) 2-2, (A) 4-2
R1: Coventry City (H) 1-6

64-65 Q1: Chippenham Town (H) 3-1
Q2: Cheltenham Town (H) 1-3

65-66 Q1: Westbury United (A) 3-1
Q2: Devizes Town (A) 2-3

66-67 Q1: Melksham Town (A) 4-0
Q2: Stonehouse (H) 5-0
Q3: Welton Rovers (H) 0-3

67-68 Q1: Frome Town (A) 0-1

68-69 Q1: Portland United (H) 3-0
Q2: Bridgwater Town (H) 2-3

69-70 PR: Minehead (H) 2-3

70-71 Q1: Westbury United (A) 3-1
Q2: Bath City (A) 0-3

71-72 Q1: Street (A) 4-2
Q2: Glastonbury (H) 0-0, (A) 5-0
Q3: Bridgwater Town (A) 1-2

72-73 Q1: Gloucester City (A) 2-2, (H) 2-0
Q2: Cheltenham Town (A) 0-4

73-74 Q1: Hungerford Town (A) 1-1, (H) 4-2
Q2: Bath City (H) 0-0, (A) 4-2
Q3: Basingstoke Town (A) 1-0
Q4: Bideford (A) 2-2, (H) 1-1, 1-1, 2-3

74-75 Q1: Mangotsfield United (A) 1-2

75-76 Q1: Salisbury (A) 1-3

76-77 PR: Gloucester City (A) 1-1, (H) 1-2

77-78 PR: Weston-super-Mare (H) 1-1, (A) 1-2

78-79 Q1: Forest Green Rovers (H) 1-0
Q2: Shepton Mallet Town (A) 2-1
Q3: Cheltenham Town (H) 0-4

79-80 PR: Melksham Town (A) 3-1
Q1: Taunton Town (A) 1-0
Q2: Hungerford Town (H) 0-2

80-81 Q1: Salisbury (A) 1-1, (H) 2-1
Q2: Gloucester City (A) 1-0
Q3: Bideford (H) 2-3

81-82 Q1: Frome Town (A) 1-2

82-83 Q1: Ton Pentre (H) 2-0
Q2: Bristol Manor Farm (H) 3-0
Q3: Cheltenham Town (H) 1-1, (A) 0-1

83-84 Q1: Clandown (A) 2-4

84-85 Q1: Ton Pentre (A) 1-1, (H) 0-3

85-86 Q1: Chippenham Town (H) 1-3

86-87 PR: Hungerford Town (H) 4-0
Q1: Melksham Town (H) 3-2
Q2: Salisbury (H) 2-0
Q3: Stourbridge (H) 1-1, (A) 4-0
Q4: Fareham Town (H) 0-0, (A) 1-4

87-88 Q1: Fareham Town (A) 0-1

88-89 PR: Romsey Town (H) 2-0
Q1: Weymouth (H) 1-2

89-90 PR: Tiverton Town (A) 1-1, (H) 3-1
Q1: Maesteg Park (A) 2-1
Q2: Dorchester Town (A) 0-0, (H) 0-2

90-91 PR: Clandown (H) 7-1
Q1: Newbury Town (H) 3-0
Q2: Wycombe Wanderers (H) 0-0, (A) 1-2

91-92 Q1: Glastonbury (A) 4-0
Q2: Mangotsfield United (H) 3-0
Q3: Dorchester Town (A) 0-1

92-93 Q1: Salisbury (A) 2-6

TRURO CITY

Currently: South Western League

49-50 PR: Ilfracombe Town (H) 2-6

50-51 PR: Green Waves (A) 3-2
Q1: Glastonbury (H) 2-4

51-52 PR: Newton Abbot (H) 5-3
Q1: Barnstaple Town (H) 2-3 *expelled*

52-53 PR: Newquay (A) 1-7

54-55 Q1: Barnstaple Town (H) 1-3

55-56 PR: St Austell (A) 8-1
Q1: Penzance (A) 1-3

56-57 Q1: Penzance (H) 3-4

57-58 Q1: Newquay (H) 3-1
Q2: Barnstaple Town (H) 2-5

58-59 Q1: Barnstaple Town (A) 0-3

59-60 Q1: Ilfracombe Town (A) *W/O*
Q2: Bideford (A) 2-6

60-61 Q1: Bideford (H) 2-2, (A) 2-4

61-62 Q1: Bideford (A) 3-5

62-63 Q1: Bideford (H) 0-3

70-71 Q1: Falmouth Town (A) 1-5

71-72 Q1: Falmouth Town (A) 2-3

72-73 PR: Falmouth Town (H) 1-0
Q1: Newquay (H) 2-1
Q2: Bideford (A) 0-8

73-74 PR: Penzance (H) 0-2

92-93 PR: Ilfracombe Town (A) 4-3
Q1: Torrington (H) 2-0
Q2: Weymouth (A) 2-3

TUFNELL PARK

Currently: Merged with Edmonton Borough
Playing as Haringey Borough in London Spartan Lge
See also Haringey Borough

45-46 PR: Welywn Garden City (H) 11-1
Q1: Barnet (H) 1-1, (A) 1-3

46-47 PR: Wealdstone (A) 1-6

47-48 EX: Royston Town (H) 4-3
PR: Harrow Town (A) 0-4

48-49 EX: Ruislip Manor (A) 2-6

49-50 EX: Crown & Manor (A - *at Ilford F.C.*) 1-2

50-51 EX: Harrow Town (H) 6-3
PR: Edgware Town (H) 0-2

TUFNELL PARK EDMONTON

See Haringey Borough

TUNBRIDGE WELLS

Currently: Kent League
* - As Tunbridge Wells United
\+ - As Tunbridge Wells Rangers

52-53 * PR: Canterbury City (H) 2-1
Q1: Sittingbourne (H) 2-4

53-54 * PR: Canterbury City (A) 2-0
Q1: Dulwich Hamlet (H) 3-1
Q2: Betteshanger Colliery Welfare (A) 2-1
Q3: Guildford City (H) 0-2

54-55 * PR: East Grinstead (H) 5-0
Q1: Haywards Heath (H) 4-0
Q2: Horsham (A) 3-2
Q3: Bognor Regis Town (H) 4-0
Q4: Oxford City (H) 3-1
R1: Brighton & Hove Albion (A) 0-5

55-56 * Q1: Sittingbourne (A) 0-2

56-57 * PR: Dorking (A) 1-0
Q1: Woking (H) 3-0
Q2: Tooting & Mitcham United (H) 2-3

57-58 * PR: Erith & Belvedere (A) 3-1
Q1: Bexleyheath & Welling (H) 1-4

58-59 * PR: Maidstone United (H) 3-1
Q1: Dartford (A) 3-3, (H) 1-2

59-60 * Q1: Maidstone United (H) 1-1, (A) 3-2
Q2: Dartford (A) 2-0
Q3: Gravesend & Northfleet (H) 0-3

60-61 * Q1: Eastbourne United (A) 2-1
Q2: Tonbridge (H) 1-2

61-62 * Q1: Maidstone United (H) 1-0
Q2: Tonbridge (A) 3-1
Q3: Eastbourne United (A) 5-1
Q4: Crawley Town (A) 2-1
R1: Aldershot (A) 1-3

62-63 * Q1: Eastbourne (A) 4-3
Q2: Eastbourne United (A) 1-0
Q3: Maidstone United (H) 0-1

63-64 * Q1: Eastbourne (A) 1-1, (H) 2-0
Q2: Maidstone United (H) 1-2

64-65 + Q1: Tonbridge (H) 1-3

65-66 + Q1: Ashford Town (H) 4-1
Q2: Tonbridge (A) 1-4

66-67 + Q1: Bromley (A) 1-0
Q2: Margate (H) 0-4

69-70 PR: Whitstable Town (H) 2-1
Q1: Sittingbourne (A) 1-0
Q2: Canterbury City (H) 3-4

70-71 PR: Deal Town (H) 2-1
Q1: Tonbridge (A) 0-5

71-72 Q1: Maidstone United (A) 1-6

72-73 Q1: Herne Bay (A) 0-5

73-74 PR: Ringmer (H) 5-1
Q1: Dover (A) 0-5

74-75 Q1: Faversham Town (H) 0-0, (A) 2-3

75-76 Q1: Medway (A) 3-1
Q2: Redhill (A) 1-4

76-77 Q1: Crawley Town (H) 2-0
Q2: Horsham Y.C.M.A. (A) 1-1, (H) 0-3 - *replay ordered* (H) 0-2

77-78 PR: Canterbury City (H) 5-0
Q1: Croydon (A) 3-3, (H) 0-2

78-79 Q1: Selsey (A) 3-2
Q2: Woking (H) 0-2

79-80 Q1: Pagham (H) 2-2, (A) 2-1
Q2: Fareham Town (H) 1-2

80-81 PR: Ringmer (A) 1-3

81-82 Q1: Hillingdon Borough (A) 2-7

82-83 PR: Canterbury City (H) 0-3

83-84 PR: Lewes (A) 2-2, (H) 0-3

84-85 Q1: Leytonstone-Ilford (H) 0-2

85-86 Q1: Tilbury (A - *at Grays Athletic*) 1-2

86-87 PR: Dover Athletic (A) 0-0, (H) 1-2

87-88 PR: Maidenhead United (A) 1-1, (H) 4-3
Q1: Marlow (A) 1-5

88-89 PR: Gravesend & Northfleet (A) 1-2

89-90 PR: Deal Town (H) 1-1, (A) 1-2

90-91 PR: Eastbourne United (A) 5-6

91-92 PR: Burgess Hil Town (H) 0-2

92-93 PR: Margate (H) 0-4

TWICKENHAM
Currently: Defunct

46-47 EX: Acton Town (H) 1-2

47-48 PR: Leavesden (H) 1-3

48-49 PR: Walton & Hers. (H - *played away*) 1-11

U.G.B. (ST HELENS)
Currently: Defunct

48-49 EX: Earlestown (A) 1-5

49-50 EX: Wigan Athletic (A) 0-2

50-51 EX: Crompton's Recreation (A) 0-3

UPMINSTER
See Hornchurch & Upminster

UPTON COLLIERY
Currently: Defunct

45-46 Q1: Monckton Athletic (A) 2-6

46-47 PR: Harworth Colliery Athletic (A) 1-8

47-48 PR: Goole Town (H) 1-3

48-49 EX: Bentley Colliery (A) 1-3

49-50 EX: Bentley Colliery (A) 1-9

50-51 EX: Barton Town (A) 3-5

51-52 Q1: Sheffield (H) 3-3, (A) 2-0
Q2: South Kirkby Colliery (H) 2-2, (A) 3-2
Q3: Frickley Colliery (A) 0-5

52-53 Q1: Frickley Colliery (A) 2-2, (H) 0-2

53-54 Q1: Retford Town (A) 4-3
Q2: Hallam (A) 5-0
Q3: Frickley Colliery (H) 2-3

54-55 Q1: Frickley Colliery (H) 4-3
Q2: Sheffield (H) 3-2
Q3: Denaby United (A) 0-2

55-56 Q1: Frickley Colliery (H) 0-3

56-57 Q2: Bentley Colliery (A) 1-2

57-58 Q1: Denaby United (A) 1-5

58-59 Q1: East End Park W.M.C. (A) 0-1

59-60 Q1: Farsley Celtic (A) 2-5

USHAW MOOR
Currently: Defunct

50-51 EX: Brandon Colliery Welfare (A) 1-0
PR: Crook Town (A) 2-2, (H) 3-2
Q1: Blackhall Colliery Welfare (H) 1-3

51-52 Q1: Blackhall Colliery Welfare (A) 1-2

52-53 Q1: Chilton Athletic (H) 2-0
Q2: Silksworth Colliery Welfare (H) 4-1
Q3: Horden Colliery Welfare (A) 1-4

53-54 Q2: Murton Colliery Welfare (A) 1-1, (H) 4-1
Q3: Horden Colliery Welfare (A) 2-4

54-55 Q1: Durham City (A) 3-4

USWORTH COLLIERY
Currently: Defunct

45-46 PR: Shildon (A) 1-7

49-50 EX: Boldon Colliery (H) 0-2

UXBRIDGE
Currently: Isthmian League

45-46 EX: Lyons Club (H) 11-1
PR: Oxford City (A) 0-4

46-47 EX: Henley Town (A) 6-6, (H) 3-1
PR: Chesham United (H) 7-2
Q1: Maidenhead United (H) 2-1
Q2: Headington United (H) 5-2
Q3: Hayes (A) 2-3

47-48 PR: Wycombe Wanderers (A) 1-3

48-49 EX: Yiewsley (H) 1-1, (A) 3-3, (*at Hayes*) 3-0
PR: Wycombe Wanderers (H) 4-3
Q1: Southall (H) 1-0
Q2: Banbury Spencer (A) 1-3

49-50 PR: Chesham United (H) 2-0
Q1: Hemel Hempstead Town (A) 4-1
Q2: Southall (A) 1-4

50-51 PR: Aylesbury United (A) 2-2, (H) 1-1, 1-4

51-52 PR: Harrow Town (H) 3-2
Q1: Wealdstone (A) 1-2

52-53 PR: Harrow Town (A) 8-1
Q1: Hayes (A) 3-0
Q2: Edgware Town (H) 2-1
Q3: Hendon (A) 1-3

53-54 PR: Hayes (H) 2-2, (A) 3-2
Q1: Yiewsley (H) 0-1

54-55 PR: Hounslow Town (A) 2-2, (H) 1-7

55-56 PR: Harrow Town (A) 3-3, (H) 1-2

56-57 PR: Berkhamsted Town (H) 3-2
Q1: Yiewsley (H) 1-4

57-58 Q1: Southall (H) 1-2

58-59 Q1: Wealdstone (A) 1-2

59-60 Q1: Yiewsley (A) 1-2

60-61 Q1: Yiewsley (H) 4-1
Q2: Maidenhead United (A) 0-4

61-62 Q1: Finchley (H) 1-2

62-63 Q1: Hayes (A) 0-3

63-64 Q1: Edgware Town (A) 2-1
Q2: Yiewsley (H) 0-0, (A) 1-2

64-65 Q1: Southall (H) 0-3

65-66 Q1: Finchley (H) 1-7

66-67 Q1: Edgware Town (H) 1-2

67-68 Q1: Metropolitan Police (H) 3-1
Q2: Brentwood Town (H) 1-4

68-69 Q1: Banstead Athletic (A) 1-1, (H) 3-1
Q2: Metropolitan Police (H) 2-2, (A) 3-3 *aban. after 90 minutes*, (A) 1-3

69-70 PR: Guildford City (A) 1-4

70-71 PR: Bromley (H) 0-0, (A) 1-3

71-72 Q1: Hounslow (A) 2-0
Q2: Sutton United (H) 1-3

72-73 Q1: Harlow Town (A) 0-1

73-74 Q1: Fleet (H) 1-1, (A) 1-3

74-75 Q1: Hounslow (H) 2-1
Q2: Wealdstone (A) 0-2

75-76 Q1: Wembley (H) 1-2

76-77 Q1: Bracknell Town (H) 0-1

77-78 PR: Leyton-Wingate (A) 0-2

78-79 Q1: Berkhamsted Town (H) 2-1
Q2: Kingstonian (A) 0-3

79-80 Q1: Milton Keynes City (H) 1-0
Q2: Edgware Town (H) 0-2

80-81 PR: Rainham Town (A) 4-3
Q1: Epping Town (H) 1-0
Q2: Aylesbury United (A) 0-6

81-82 PR: Horsham Y.M.C.A. (A) 1-1, (H) 2-1
Q1: Peacehaven & Tel. (H) 2-2, (A) 3-1
Q2: Carshalton Athletic (H) 0-3

82-83 Q1: Three Bridges (A) 0-0, (H) 1-2

83-84 Q1: Chalfont St Peter (H) 4-2
Q2: Hampton (H) 0-1

84-85 Q1: Welling United (H) 0-1

85-86 PR: Corinthian-Casuals (H) 3-0
Q1: Buckingham Town (H) 0-1

86-87 Q1: Desborough Town (H) 4-0
Q2: Hayes (H) 3-1
Q3: Yeading (A) 0-1

87-88 PR: Haringey Borough (H) 2-2, (A) 3-2
Q1: Barking (H) 4-1
Q2: Baldock Town (H) 1-0
Q3: Great Yarmouth Town (H) 0-2

88-89 PR: Barkingside (A) 2-1
Q1: Halstead Town (H) 0-2

89-90 Q1: Hemel Hempstead (H) 1-0
Q2: Yeading (H) 1-0
Q3: Slough Town (A) 0-0, (H) 1-2

90-91 PR: Salisbury (A) 1-1, (H) 1-2

91-92 PR: Wolverton (A) 0-1

92-93 PR: Southall (H) 4-2
Q1: Rayners Lane (A) 1-1, (H) 0-1

VAUXHALL G.M.
Currently: Defunct

89-90 Q1: Rossendale United (A) 1-2

90-91 PR: Bridgnorth Town (A) 1-1, (H) 4-1
Q1: Irlam Town (H) 0-2

91-92 PR: Armthorpe Welfare (A) 1-1, (H) 1-2

VAUXHALL MOTORS
Currently: Defunct

45-46 Q1: Hitchin Town (A) 2-3

46-47 PR: Luton Amateurs (H) 2-4

47-48 PR: Stewartby Works (H) 7-1
Q1: Letchworth Town (H) 2-2, (A) 5-1
Q2: Kempston Rovers (A) 2-1
Q3: Bedford Town (H) 1-1, (A) 2-0
Q4: Peterborough United (H) 2-1
R1: Walsall (H - *at Luton Town*) 1-2

48-49 PR: Baldock Town (H) 1-1, (A) 5-2
Q1: Bedford Town (A) 2-1
Q2: Biggleswade Town (A) 4-1
Q3: Hitchin Town (H) 2-1
Q4: Walthamstow Avenue (H) 0-2

49-50 PR: St Neots & District (A) 2-3

50-51 EX: Stewartby Works (H) 5-0
PR: Wolverton Town (A) 3-6

51-52 Q1: Potton United (H) 0-0, (A) 3-4

52-53 Q1: Eynesbury Rovers (H) 2-4

53-54 Q1: Eynesbury Rovers (H) 6-2
Q2: Dunstable Town (A) 2-3

54-55 Q1: Potton United (A) 0-1

56-57 Q1: Biggleswade Town (A) 3-2
Q2: Dunstable Town (A) 0-3

57-58	Q2: Dunstable Town (A) 6-1 Q3: Wolverton Town & B.R. (A) 1-2
58-59	Q1: Biggleswade Town (A) 2-1 Q2: Eynesbury Rovers (A) 3-0 Q3: Hitchin Town (H) 0-2
59-60	Q1: Stevenage Town (A) 1-0 Q2: Wolverton Town & B.R. (A) 1-5
60-61	Q1: Wolverton Town & B.R. (H) 2-0 Q2: Hitchin Town (A) 0-3
61-62	Q1: Wolverton Town & B.R. (H) 2-2, (A) 3-0 Q2: Cambridge City (H - *played away*) 0-7
62-63	Q1: Hitchin Town (A) 0-0 (H) 0-3
63-64	Q1: Hitchin Town (A) 2-4
64-65	Q1: Cheshunt (H) 0-2
65-66	Q1: Bletchley (A) 2-3
66-67	Q1: Corinthian-Casuals (A) 1-2
67-68	Q1: Crittall Athletic (A) 1-3
68-69	Q1: Harrow Borough (H) 6-1 Q2: Hoddesdon Town (H) 1-0 Q3: Ware (H) 3-3, (A) 1-2
69-70	Q1: Hoddesdon Town (A) 2-4
70-71	Q1: Tooting & Mitcham United (H) 1-2
72-73	Q1: Edmonton (H) 0-0, (A) 2-0 Q2: Harlow Town (H) 2-1 Q3: Bishop's Stortford (A) 0-2
73-74	Q1: Rothwell Town (A) 2-3
74-75	Q1: Chesham United (A) 0-1
75-76	Q1: Dunstable Town (H) 0-1
76-77	Q1: Rushden Town (H) 0-0, (A) 2-1 Q2: Wellingborough Town (H) 1-3
77-78	Q1: Finchley (A) 0-1
86-87	PR: Chatham Town (A) 0-0 (H) 0-2
87-88	PR: Stamford (A) 0-0 (H) 3-2 Q1: Boreham Wood (A) 0-2
88-89	Q1: Wealdstone (A) 1-2
89-90	Q1: Dunstable (A) 0-3
90-91	PR: Molesey (A) 1-1, (H) 0-5
91-92	PR: Desborough Town (A) *withdrew*

VICKERS (WEYBRIDGE)

Currently: Defunct
* - Vickers Armstrong

46-47 *	PR: P.O. Engineers (Wallington) (H) 5-0 Q1: Kingstonian (H) 1-1, (A) 2-3
49-50 *	PR: McLaren Sports (H) 7-2 Q1: Tooting & Mitcham United (H) 2-4
50-51 *	EX: Redhill (A) 2-2 (H) 4-2 PR: Carshalton Athletic (A) 2-4
54-55	PR: Dartford (H) 0-6

VIKING SPORTS

Currently: Combined Counties League

92-93	PR: Bishop's Stortford (H) 0-1

V.S. RUGBY

Currently: Southern League
* - As Valley Sports (Rugby)

76-77 *	Q1: Bilston (H) 1-4
77-78 *	PR: Bedworth United (H) 0-0, (A) 1-0 Q1: Corby Town (A) 1-1, (H) 0-2
78-79 *	Q1: Dunstable (H) 2-0 Q2: Kempston Rovers (A) 1-3
79-80	PR: Histon (A) 2-0 Q1: Soham Town Rangers (A) 0-0, (H) 3-0 Q2: Enderby Town (H) 0-1
80-81	PR: Racing Club Warwick (A) 2-1 Q1: Darlaston (H) 3-1 Q2: Banbury United (A) 3-3, (H) 1-3
81-82	Q1: Wolverton Town (H) 5-0 Q2: Tividale (A) 2-2, (H) 0-2

Above: *Gary Fitzpatrick (left) prepares to challenge Enfield's Mark Keen as V.S. Rugby suffer a disappointing Fourth Qualifying Round defeat. Photo: Dennis Nicholson.*

82-83	Q1: Highgate United (H) 3-1 Q2: Sutton Coldfield Town (A) 1-2
83-84	Q1: Bury Town (A) 2-0 Q2: Heybridge Swifts (A) 2-2, (H) 2-0 Q3: Chelmsford City (A) 2-2, (H) 1-2
84-85	Q1: Berkhamsted Town (A) 0-0, (H) 3-1 Q2: Alvechurch (H) 5-0 Q3: Wembley (A) 5-1 Q4: Stourbridge (A) 1-1, (H) 2-0 R1: Northampton Town (A) 2-2, (H) 0-1
85-86	Q1: Stowmarket (A) 2-2, (H) 3-2 Q2: Hitchin Town (A) 0-0, (H) 3-1 Q3: Corby Town (H) 2-0 Q4: Stourbridge (A) 1-1, (H) 3-1 R1: Orient (H) 2-2, (A) 1-4
86-87	Q4: Wycombe Wanderers (A) 5-1 R1: Bristol City (A) 1-3
87-88	Q4: Nuneaton Borough (H) 3-0 R1: Atherstone United (H) 0-0, (A) 2-0 R2: Bristol Rovers (H) 1-1, (A) 0-4
88-89	Q4: Hendon (H) 1-1, (A) 0-2
89-90	Q4: Bromsgrove Rovers (A) 0-1
90-91	Q1: Haverhill Rovers (A) 1-1, (H) 5-0 Q2: Boston United (A) 1-3
91-92	Q1: Stamford (H) 2-0 Q2: Gresley Rovers (A) 3-3, (H) 3-0 Q3: Chasetown (A) 0-0, (H) 3-0 Q4: Enfield (A) 1-2
92-93	Q1: Alvechurch (H) *W/O* Q2: Hitchin Town (H) 3-0 Q3: Moor Green (A) 2-1 Q4: Halesowen Town (A) 2-1 R1: Solihull Borough (A) 2-2, (H) 3-1 R2: Marlow (H) 0-0, (A) 0-2

WADEBRIDGE TOWN

Currently: South Western League

51-52	PR: Newquay (A) 1-3
52-53	PR: St Austell (H) 4-5
53-54	PR: Newton Abbot (A) 3-1 Q1: Dartmouth United (A) 3-2 Q2: Barnstaple Town (A) 2-2, (H) 3-4
54-55	PR: Bodmin Town (A) 0-2
55-56	Q1: Bodmin Town (H) 2-5
56-57	PR: Minehead (A) 3-2 Q1: Taunton (H) 0-6
57-58	Q1: Bideford (H) 0-2
58-59	PR: Penzance (H) 4-1 Q1: Ilfracombe Town (A) 4-4, (H) 2-1 Q2: St Blazey (A) 2-2, (H) 3-1 Q3: Bideford (A) 1-7
59-60	Q1: St Blazey (H) 3-2 Q2: Barnstaple Town (A) 1-9
60-61	Q1: St Blazey (H) 2-7
61-62	Q2: Bideford (H) 1-4
62-63	Q2: Bideford (A) 0-0, (H) 2-5
63-64	Q2: St Blazey (H) 1-1, (A) 1-8
64-65	Q1: St Blazey (H) 2-6
67-68	Q1: Barnstaple Town (H) 7-1 Q2: Falmouth Town (A) 0-6
68-69	Q2: Nanpean Rovers (H) 1-1, (A) 7-0 Q3: Falmouth Town (H) 2-2, (A) 1-3
69-70	Q1: Nanpean Rovers (H) 8-0 Q2: Barnstaple Town (H) 4-2 Q3: Falmouth Town (H) 0-5
70-71	Q1: Saltash United (H) 1-3
71-72	Q1: Saltash United (A) 3-2 Q2: St Blazey (H) 6-1 Q3: Bideford (A) 1-4
72-73	Q1: St Blazey (A) 2-1 Q2: Barnstaple Town (A) 0-3
73-74	Q1: Newquay (A) 0-1
74-75	Q1: Barnstaple Town (A) 4-0 Q2: Bideford (H) 3-3 (A) 2-4
75-76	Q1: Taunton Town (A) 3-2 Q2: Penzance (A) 1-2
76-77	Q1: Ilminster Town (H) 1-1, (A) 0-1
77-78	PR: Barnstaple Town (H) 0-7
78-79	Q1: Liskeard Athletic (H) 0-2
79-80	Q1: Dorchester Town (A) 0-2
80-81	PR: Saltash United (A) 0-5
84-85	Q1: Minehead (H) 0-2

WALLASEY TRANSPORT

Currently: Defunct

50-51	EX: Ellesmere Port Town (H) *scratched*

WALLINGFORD TOWN

Currently: Hellenic League

47-48	EX: Chesham United (H) 4-2 PR: Headington United (A) 0-4
48-49	EX: Metal & Produce Recovery Depot (A) 3-1 PR: Abingdon Town (A) 2-2, (H) 2-0 Q1: Maidenhead United (H) 1-3

WALLSEND TOWN

Currently: Defunct

77-78	PR: Whitby Town (H) 2-3
78-79	Q1: Ferryhill Athletic (H) 1-0 Q2: Gateshead (A) 0-6
79-80	Q1: Billingham Synthonia (H) 1-4
80-81	Q1: Spennymoor United (H) 0-2
81-82	PR: Evenwood Town (H) 1-4

WALSALL

Currently: Football League

45-46 R1: Shrewsbury (A) 0-5, (H) 4-1 *(agg: 4-6)*

46-47 R1: Leytonstone (A) 6-1
R2: Ipswich Town (H) 1-1, (A) 1-1, 1-0
R3: Liverpool (H) 2-5

47-48 R1: Vauxhall Motors (A - *at Luton Town*) 2-1
R2: Norwich City (A) 2-2, (H) 2-2, 3-2
R3: Coventry City (A) 1-2

48-49 R1: Bristol Rovers (H) 2-1
R2: Gainsborough Trinity (H) 4-3
R3: Fulham (A) 1-0
R4: Luton Town (A) 0-4

49-50 R1: Mansfield Town (A) 1-4

50-51 R1: Newport County (A) 2-4

51-52 R1: Reading (A) 0-1

52-53 R1: Newport County (A) 1-2

53-54 R1: Bath City (A) 3-0
R2: Crewe Alexandra (H) 3-0
R3: Lincoln City (A) 1-1, (H) 1-1, *(at Nottm Forest)* 1-2

54-55 R1: Shrewsbury Town (H) 5-2
R2: Wrexham (A) 2-1
R3: Chelsea (A) 0-2

55-56 R1: Margate (A) 2-2, (H) 6-1
R2: Southampton (H) 2-1
R3: Port Vale (H) 0-1

56-57 R1: Newport County (H) 0-1

57-58 R1: Brighton & Hove Albion (A) 1-2

58-59 R1: Queens Park Rangers (H) 0-1

59-60 R1: Swindon Town (A) 3-2
R2: Peterborough United (H) 2-3

60-61 R1: Yeovil Town (H) 0-1

61-62 R3: Bristol City (A) 0-0, (H) 4-1
R4: Fulham (A) 2-2, (H) 0-2

62-63 R3: Manchester City (H) 0-1

63-64 R1: Southport (A) 1-2

64-65 R1: Bristol Rovers (H) 0-2

65-66 R1: Swansea Town (H) 6-3
R2: Aldershot (A) 2-0
R3: Stoke City (A) 2-0
R4: Norwich City (A) 2-3

66-67 R1: St Neots Town (H) 2-0
R2: Gillingham (H) 3-1
R3: Bury (A) 0-2

67-68 R1: Leytonstone (A) 1-0
R2: Exeter City (A) 3-1
R3: Crystal Palace (H) 1-1, (A) 2-1
R4: Liverpool (H) 0-0, (A) 2-5

68-69 R1: Leytonstone (A) 1-0
R2: St Albans City (A) 1-1, (H) 3-1
R3: Tottenham Hotspur (H) 0-1

69-70 R1: Orient (H) 0-0, (A) 2-0
R2: Brighton & Hove Albion (A) 1-1, (H) 1-1, (N) 0-0, *(at Coventry City)* 2-1
R3: Crystal Palace (A) 0-2

70-71 R1: Plymouth Argyle (H) 3-0
R2: Brentford (A) 0-1

71-72 R1: Dagenham (H) 4-1
R2: Brighton & Hove A. (A) 1-1, (H) 2-1
R3: A.F.C. Bournemouth (H) 1-0
R4: Everton (A) 1-2

72-73 R1: Kettering Town (H) 3-3, (A) 2-1
R2: Charlton Athletic (H) 1-2

73-74 R1: Swansea City (H) 1-0
R2: Plymouth Argyle (A) 0-1

74-75 R1: Ashford Town (A) 3-1
R2: Newport County (A) 3-1
R3: Manchester United (A) 0-0, (H) 3-2
R4: Newcastle United (H) 1-0
R5: Birmingham City (A) 1-2

75-76 R1: Huddersfield Town (H) 0-1

76-77 R1: Bradford City (H) 0-0, (A) 1-0
R2: Chesterfield (A) 1-1, (H) 0-0, *(at Derby County)* 1-0
R3: Manchester United (A) 0-1

77-78 R1: Dagenham (H) 1-0
R2: Port Vale (H) 1-1, (A) 3-1
R3: Swansea City (H) 4-1
R4: Leicester City (H) 1-0
R5: Arsenal (A) 1-4

78-79 R1: Torquay United (H) 0-2

79-80 R1: Stockport County (H) 2-0
R2: Halifax (H) 1-1, (A) 1-1, (A) 0-2

80-81 R1: Stafford Rangers (H) 3-0
R2: Carlisle United (A) 0-3

81-82 R1: Blyth Spartans (A) 2-1
R2: Peterborough United (A) 1-2

82-83 R1: Kettering Town (H) 3-0
R2: North Shields (A) 3-0
R3: Birmingham City (H) 0-0, (A) 0-1

83-84 R1: A.F.C. Bournemouth (A) 0-4

84-85 R1: Stockport County (A) 2-1
R2: Chesterfield (H) 1-0
R3: York City (A) 0-3

85-86 R1: Preston North End (H) 7-3
R2: Port Vale (A) 0-0, (H) 2-1
R3: Manchester City (H) 1-3

86-87 R1: Chesterfield (H) 2-0
R2: Port Vale (H) 5-0
R3: Charlton Athletic (A - *at Crystal Pal.*) 2-1
R4: Birmingham City (H) 1-0
R5: Watford (H) 1-1, (A) 4-4, (H) 0-1

87-88 R1: Southend United (A) 0-0, (H) 2-1
R2: Gillingham (A) 1-2

88-89 R3: Brentford (H) 1-1, (A) 0-1

89-90 R1: Telford United (A) 3-0
R2: Rotherham United (H) 1-0
R3: Hereford United (A) 1-2

90-91 R1: Aylesbury United (A) 1-0
R2: Swansea City (A) 1-2

91-92 R1: Yeovil Town (A) 1-1, (H) 0-1

92-93 R1: Rotherham United (A) 0-4

WALSALL WOOD

Currently: Merged with Walsall Sportsco. Playing as Walsall Wood in West Mids (Regional) League.
See also Walsall Wood (2)

80-81 PR: Winsford United (H) 0-3

81-82 Q1: Tividale (A) 0-3

WALSALL WOOD

Currently: West Mids (Regional) League
* - As Walsall Borough
See also Walsall Wood (1)

82-83 * PR: Sutton Coldfield Town (A) 2-4

83-84 * Q1: March Town United (H) 1-2

84-85 * PR: Gresley Rovers (H) 1-4

85-86 * Q1: Tamworth (A) 1-2

86-87 PR: Skelmersdale United (H) 0-1

87-88 PR: Holbeach United (A) 4-1
Q1: Stafford Rangers (H) 0-3

88-89 PR: Louth United (H) 0-0, (A) 3-1
Q1: Matlock Town (A) 3-2
Q2: Dudley Town (A) 1-2

89-90 PR: Winsford United (H) 2-0
Q1: Oakham United (H) 0-1

90-91 PR: Brackley Town (A) 0-1

91-92 PR: Raunds Town (H) 1-1, (A) 1-3

92-93 PR: Bedworth United (A) 0-1

WALTHAM ABBEY

Currently: Spartan League

90-91 PR: Cray Wanderers (A) 1-3

91-92 PR: Stevenage Borough (H) 0-1

92-93 PR: Halstead Town (H - *played away*) 1-1, (A) 4-3
Q1: Baldock Town (H - *played away*) 2-3

WALTHAMSTOW AVENUE

Currently: Merged with Leytonstone-Ilford
Subsequently merged with Dagenham, and playing as Dagenham & Redbridge in Alliance Premier Lge. See also Redbridge Forest and Dagenham & Redbridge.

45-46 Q4: Clapton (H) 4-0
R1: Sutton U. (A) 4-1, (H) 7-2 *(agg: 11-3)*
R2: Brighton (H) 1-1, (A) 2-4 *(agg: 3-5)*

46-47 Q4: Gravesend & Northfleet (A) 0-1

47-48 Q4: Dartford (H) 0-1

48-49 Q4: Vauxhall Motors (A) 2-0
R1: Cambridge Town (H) 3-2
R2: Oldham Athletic (H) 2-2, (A) 1-3

49-50 Q4: Dulwich Hamlet (H) 3-3, (A) 3-1
R1: Northampton Town (A) 1-4

50-51 Q4: Eastbourne (H) 2-0
R1: Mansfield Town (A) 0-1

51-52 Q4: Leyton (A) 0-0, (H) 1-2

52-53 R1: Wimbledon (H) 2-2, (A) 3-0
R2: Watford (H) 1-1, (A) 2-1
R3: Stockport County (H) 2-1
R4: Manchester U. (A) 1-1, (H - *at Arsenal*) 2-5

53-54 R1: Gillingham (H) 1-0
R2: Ipswich Town (A) 2-2, (H) 0-1

54-55 Q4: Sudbury Town (A) 2-0
R1: Queens Park R. (A) 2-2, (H) 2-2, 4-0
R2: Darlington (H) 0-3

55-56 Q4: Bedford Town (A) 0-6

56-57 Q4: Great Yarmouth Town (H) 6-0
R1: Crystal Palace (A) 0-2

57-58 Q4: Bedford Town (A) 1-1, (H) 1-0
R1: Coventry City (A) 0-1

58-59 Q4: Peterborough United (A) 0-3

59-60 Q1: Dagenham (A) 1-1, (H) 4-0
Q2: Finchley (H) 4-0
Q3: Hornchurch & Upminster (H) 7-1
Q4: Great Yarmouth Town (H) 2-1
R1: Bournemouth & Boscombe Ath. (H) 2-3

60-61 Q4: Walton & Hersham (H) 4-1
R1: Queens Park Rangers (A) 2-3

61-62 R1: Romford (H) 2-3

62-63 Q4: Wycombe Wanderers (H) 1-1, (A) 1-3

63-64 Q1: Dulwich Hamlet (A) 3-0
Q2: Epsom & Ewell (A) 6-0
Q3: Tooting & Mitcham (H) 3-6

64-65 Q1: Barking (A) 2-1
Q2: Brentwood & Warley (H) 1-0
Q3: Hornchurch (H) 3-1
Q4: Barnet (A) 3-3, (H) 1-4

65-66 Q1: Aveley (H) 4-0
Q2: Tilbury (A) 0-0, (H) 5-4
Q3: Grays Athletic (A) 3-1
Q4: Leytonstone (H) 2-6

66-67 Q1: Chertsey Town (A) 3-0
Q2: Stevenage Town (H) 0-2

67-68 Q1: Leyton (H) 2-0
Q2: Ilford (H) 1-0
Q3: Hampton (A) 5-4
Q4: Brentwood Town (A) 3-1
R1: Kidderminster Harriers (H) 2-1
R2: Bournemouth & Boscombe Ath. (H) 1-3

68-69 Q4: Ware (A) 0-1

69-70 Q1: Bexley United (H) 1-1, (A) 2-2, 2-0
Q2: Tilbury (H) 2-2, (A) 2-2, 1-3

70-71 Q1: Bromley (H) 1-4

71-72 Q1: Woodford Town (H) 1-0
Q2: Hoddesdon Town (H) 2-0
Q3: Boreham Wood (A) 2-2, (H) 2-1
Q4: Dover (H) 0-0, (A) 0-1

72-73 Q1: Hornchurch (A) 8-0
Q2: Bexley United (A) 0-1

73-74 Q1: Gravesend & Northfleet (A) 1-5

74-75 Q1: Cray Wanderers (A) 0-2

75-76 Q1: Gravesend & Northfleet (H) 2-1
Q2: Molesey (H) 1-2

76-77 Q1: Kingstonian (H) 1-4

77-78 PR: Romford (A) 1-1, (H) 3-2
Q1: Rainham Town (A) 5-0
Q2: Corinthian-Casuals (A) 2-0
Q3: Billericay Town (A) 1-3

78-79 Q1: Rainham Town (A) 4-0
Q2: Gravesend & Northfleet (H) 2-3

79-80 PR: Windsor & Eton (H) 4-2
Q1: Wembley (A) 1-0
Q2: Leytonstone-Ilford (H) 2-2, (A) 1-3

80-81 PR: Hornchurch (A) 3-2
Q1: Clapton (H) 5-0
Q2: Aveley (A) 0-2

81-82 Q1: Basildon United (A) 2-1
Q2: Dunstable (A) 2-3

82-83 Q1: Wootton Blue Cross (H) 2-0
Q2: Aveley (A) 3-1
Q3: Woodford Town (H) 2-0
Q4: Carshalton Athletic (H) 1-1, (A) 1-2

83-84 Q1: Sudbury Town (A) 1-1, (H) 2-0
Q2: Billericay (A) 2-2, (H) 0-0, (H) 2-1
Q3: Lowestoft Town (H) 0-0, (A) 2-0
Q4: Burton Albion (H) 0-0, (A) 1-3

84-85 Q1: Herne Bay (A) 3-0
Q2: Crawley Town (H) 1-0
Q3: Folkestone (A) 0-1

85-86 Q1: Barton Rovers (A) 2-1
Q2: Wembley (A) 3-1
Q3: Dunstable (H) 0-0, (A) 0-2

86-87 Q1: Heybridge S. (H - *at B. Stortford*) 3-2
Q2: Harwich & Parkeston (A) 1-4

87-88 PR: Felixstowe Town (A) 2-1
Q1: Histon (A) 1-2

WALTHAMSTOW PENNANT

Currently: Spartan League

89-90 PR: Beckenham Town (A) 5-0
Q1: Slough Town (A) 1-5

90-91 PR: Arlesey Town (A) 4-0
Q1: Chelmsford City (H) 0-3

91-92 PR: Langford (H) 3-2
Q1: Enfield (A) 0-4

92-93 PR: Flackwell Heath (A) 0-2

WALTON & HERSHAM

Currently: Isthmian League

45-46 Q1: Epsom Town (H) 11-0
Q2: Sutton United (A) 0-4

46-47 PR: Guildford (H) 11-0
Q1: Tooting & Mitcham Utd (H) 1-1, (A) 1-2

47-48 PR: Metropolitan Police (A) 6-4
Q1: Redhill (H) 2-2, (A) 1-2

48-49 PR: Twickenham (A - *played at home*) 11-1
Q1: Redhill (H) 1-2

49-50 PR: Carshalton Athletic (H) 2-2, (A) 8-0
Q1: Redhill (H) 1-0
Q2: Tooting & Mitcham Utd (A) 1-1, (H) 1-2

50-51 PR: Leatherhead (A) 3-1
Q1: Wimbledon (A) 2-0
Q2: Tooting & Mitcham United (A) 1-2

51-52 Q1: Hounslow Town (H) 0-6

52-53 PR: Tooting & Mitcham United (H) 0-1

53-54 PR: Betteshanger Colliery Welfare (A) 2-3

54-55 PR: Chatham Town (H) 1-1, (A) 4-0
Q1: Carshalton Athletic (H) 0-0, (A) 0-2

55-56 PR: Snowdown Colliery Welfare (A) 0-4

57-58 PR: Wimbledon (A) 3-1
Q1: Sutton United (H) 3-3, (A) 4-0
Q2: Bromley (H) 1-0
Q3: Bexleyheath & Welling (H) 3-1
Q4: Hastings United (H) 3-1
R1: Southampton (H) 1-6

58-59 PR: Redhill (A) 2-3

59-60 PR: Kingstonian (H) 0-2

60-61 Q1: Metropolitan Police (H) 5-1
Q2: Kingstonian (H) 3-1
Q3: Dorking (A) 1-1, (H) 2-1
Q4: Walthamstow Avenue (A) 1-4

61-62 Q1: Dorking (H) 2-2, (A) 3-1
Q2: Wimbledon (A) 2-1
Q3: Kingstonian (A) 1-4

62-63 Q1: Kingstonian (A) 0-5

63-64 Q1: Kingstonian (A) 1-3

64-65 Q1: Chertsey Town (H) 4-1
Q2: Guildford City (H) 1-5

65-66 Q1: Dorking (A) 1-1, (H) 4-1
Q2: Woking (H) 0-4

66-67 Q1: Clapton (A) 2-3

67-68 Q1: Barnet (A) 2-3

68-69 Q1: Huntley & Palmers Rec. (H) 5-0
Q2: Leatherhead (H) 4-1
Q3: Malden Town (H) 4-0
Q4: Margate (A) 0-1

69-70 Q1: Leatherhead (A) 1-0
Q2: Huntley & Palmers Rec. (A) 9-0
Q3: Barking (H) 4-1
Q4: Ashford Town (A) 1-0
R1: Barnet (H) 0-1

70-71 Q1: Chertsey Town (H) 5-0
Q2: Hitchin Town (A) 1-1, (H) 3-0
Q3: Romford (A) 1-1, (H) 3-3, 3-2
Q4: Sutton United (H) 1-0
R1: Telford United (H) 2-5

71-72 Q1: Dartford (A) 1-1, (H) 1-0
Q2: Carshalton Athletic (A) 0-0, (H) 5-1
Q3: Windsor & Eton (H) 2-2, (A) 1-0
Q4: Maidenhead United (A) 1-2

72-73 PR: Metropolitan Police (H) 1-1, (A) 6-1
Q1: Staines Town (H) 3-0
Q2: Leytonstone (A) 2-2, (H) 1-0
Q3: Wycombe Wanderers (H) 1-0
Q4: Dartford (H) 2-2, (A) 1-0
R1: Exeter City (H) 2-1
R2: Margate (H) 0-1

73-74 R1: Brighton & H.A. (H) 0-0, (A) 4-0
R2: Hereford United (A) 0-3

74-75 Q4: Leatherhead (H) 1-7

75-76 Q4: Slough Town (A) 2-1
R1: Crystal Palace (A) 0-1

76-77 Q4: Bromley (A) 3-9

77-78 Q1: Cheshunt (A) 2-3

78-79 Q1: Camberley Town (H) 2-3

79-80 PR: Harefield United (A) 4-1
Q1: Rainham Town (A) 2-2, (H) 5-2
Q2: Hampton (H) 1-1, (A) 5-1
Q3: Slough Town (H) 0-2

80-81 PR: Woodford Town (H) 3-0
Q1: Chertsey Town (H) 1-0
Q2: Barton Rovers (A) 0-1

81-82 Q1: Windsor & Eton (A) 4-3
Q2: Burgess Hill Town (A) 1-2

82-83 PR: Epsom & Ewell (A) 2-1
Q1: Tonbridge A.F.C. (A) 0-2

83-84 PR: Fleet Town (H) 1-1, (A) 4-0
Q1: Welling United (H) 1-0
Q2: Whitehawk (A) 1-4

84-85 PR: Eastbourne United (H) 1-0
Q1: Gravesend & Northfleet (H) 0-1

85-86 PR: Horley Town (A) 5-0
Q1: Hastings United (H) *W/O*
Q2: Kingstonian (A) 1-3

86-87 Q1: Erith & Belvedere (H) 2-2 (A) 1-0
Q2: Fisher Athletic (H) 0-0, (A) 2-3

87-88 Q1: Finchley (H) 3-0
Q2: Welling United (A) 1-2

88-89 Q1: Horsham (A) 5-1
Q2: Leytonstone-Ilford (H) 3-2
Q3: Wembley (H) 2-1
Q4: Sutton United (A) 1-1, (H) 0-3

89-90 Q1: Hastings Town (A) 3-0
Q2: Whitstable Town (H) 0-1

90-91 PR: Chertsey Town (A) 3-0
Q1: Bromley (H) 2-3

91-92 PR: Epsom & Ewell (A) 5-1
Q1: Littlehampton Town (H) 1-1, (A) 1-2

92-93 PR: Peacehaven & Telscombe (H) 2-1
Q1: Wokingham Town (H) 2-0
Q2: Dorking (A) 2-4

WANDSWORTH & NORWOOD

See Croydon Athletic

WARBOYS TOWN

Currently: Eastern Counties League

54-55 PR: Histon (A) 2-4

55-56 PR: Wisbech Town (A) 0-7

56-57 PR: Cambridge City (A) 1-2

57-58 PR: Soham Town Rangers (A) 2-4

58-59 PR: Soham Town Rangers (A) 1-4

WARDLEY WELFARE

Currently: Defunct

49-50 EX: Ashington (H - *played away*) 2-5

50-51 EX: Newburn (A) 1-3

WARE

Currently: Isthmian League

46-47 EX: Saffron Walden Town (A) 2-4

47-48 EX: Edmonton Borough (H) 2-3

48-49 EX: Polytechnic (A) 0-1

49-50 EX: Wembley (A) 2-2, (H) 2-2, 5-1
PR: Wingate (A) 5-1
Q1: Edgware Town (H) 0-2

50-51 EX: Wood Green Town (H) 4-0
PR: Cheshunt (A) 1-2

54-55 PR: Hitchin Town (H) 2-3

55-56 PR: Shefford Town (H) 7-2
Q1: Hitchin Town (A) 0-5

56-57 PR: Hitchin Town (H) 1-1, (A) 2-5

57-58 PR: Hitchin Town (H) 3-1
Q1: Stevenage Town (H) 3-0
Q2: Letchworth Town (H) 3-0
Q3: Clapton (A) 0-2

58-59 PR: Hemel Hempstead Town (H) 2-2, (A) 0-1

59-60 Q1: Enfield (H) 1-7

60-61 Q1: Hertford Town (A) 1-5

61-62 Q1: Wealdstone (H - *played away*) 0-5

62-63 Q1: Bishop's Stortford (A) 0-1

63-64 Q1: Harlow Town (A) 2-2, (H) 0-0, 2-1
Q2: Harrow Town (H) 2-1
Q3: Barnet (H) 1-6

64-65 Q1: Bishop's Stortford (H) 1-3

65-66 Q1: Cheshunt (H) 3-1
Q2: Stevenage Town (A) 1-1, (H) 1-4

66-67 Q1: Carshalton Athletic (A) 4-2
Q2: Edgware Town (H) 2-2, (A) 0-1

67-68 Q1: Hounslow (H) 3-2
Q2: Harrow Borough (H) 4-1
Q3: Crittall Athletic (A) 2-1
Q4: Oxford City (H) 0-2

68-69 Q1: Crittall Athletic (A) 1-1, (H) 2-1
Q2: Hounslow (H) 3-2
Q3: Vauxhall Motors (A) 3-3, (H) 2-1
Q4: Walthamstow Avenue (H) 1-0
R1: Luton Town (A) 1-6

69-70 PR: Hazells (A) 2-3

70-71 PR: Grays Athletic (H) 0-1

71-72 Q1: Cray Wanderers (A) 0-3

72-73 Q1: Stevenage Athletic (A) 0-1

73-74 Q1: Dunstable Town (H) 2-0
Q2: Aylesbury United (H) 1-0
Q3: Hertford Town (H) 0-0, (A) 1-3

74-75 Q1: Edmonton & Haringey (A) 1-0
Q2: Stevenage Athletic (H) 0-3

75-76 Q1: Romford (A) 1-3

76-77 Q1: Edgware (H) 2-0
Q2: Staines Town (A) 1-3

77-78 Q1: Haringey Boro. (A) 2-2, (H) 3-3, (H) 0-1

78-79 Q1: Barking (H) 0-2

79-80 Q1: Leyton-Wingate (H) 2-1
Q2: Hillingdon Borough (H) 1-1, (A) 0-3

80-81 Q1: Slough Town (A) 1-5

81-82 Q1: Clacton Town (A) 0-1

82-83 Q1: Soham Town Rangers (H) 1-1, (A) 2-4

83-84 Q1: Harrow Borough (A) 0-9

84-85 Q1: Metropolitan Police (A) 0-5

85-86 Q1: Billericay Town (H) 1-0
Q2: Marlow (A) 3-2
Q3: Chelmsford City (A) 0-1

86-87 Q1: Finchley (H) 5-2
Q2: Corby Town (H) 1-2

87-88 PR: Staines Town (A) 0-0, (H) 1-1, (H) 4-2
Q1: Hendon (H) 0-1

88-89 PR: Lowestoft Town (H) 2-0
Q1: Kettering Town (H) 0-3

89-90 PR: Tiptree United (H) 2-1
Q1: Cheshunt (H) 2-0
Q2: Leyton-Wingate (A) 1-2

90-91 PR: Corinthian-Cas. (H) 0-0, (A - *played home*) 0-1

91-92 PR: Milton Keynes Borough (H) 5-1
Q1: Dartford (A) 1-5

92-93 PR: Stowmarket Town (H) 1-2

WARLEY

Currently: Defunct

71-72 Q1: Darlaston (A) 1-2

72-73 Q1: Gresley Rovers (A) 1-0
Q2: Brierley Hill Alliance (A) 2-5

WARLEY COUNTY BOROUGH

Currently: Defunct

74-75 Q1: Evesham United (H) 2-0
Q2: Worcester City (A) 0-5

75-76 Q1: Halesowen Town (A) 1-2

76-77 PR: Friar Lane Old Boys (A) 0-2

WARMINSTER TOWN

Currently: Western League

46-47 EX: Calne & Harris United (A) 4-3
PR: Pewsey Y.M. (H) 4-6

47-48 EX: Clandown (H) 3-4

48-49 PR: Swindon Victoria (H) 3-1
Q1: Trowbridge Town (A) 1-4

49-50 EX: Wootton Bassett Town (A) 5-4
PR: Salisbury (A) 0-8

50-51 PR: Corsham Town (A) 2-3

51-52 PR: Corsham Town (H) 3-5

52-53 PR: Melksham Town (A) 2-0
Q1: Trowbridge Town (H) 1-1, (A) 1-4

53-54 Q1: Trowbridge Town (H) 2-2, (A) 2-8

54-55 PR: Westbury United (A) 0-2

55-56 PR: Melksham Town (H) 3-1
Q1: Frome (A) 1-2

56-57 Q1: Salisbury (H) 1-6

57-58 Q1: Calne & Harris United (A) 2-1
Q2: Melksham Town (A) 2-7

58-59 Q2: Portland United (A) 0-3

59-60 Q1: Frome Town (H) 1-1, (A) 2-1
Q2: Salisbury (H) 0-5

60-61 Q1: Portland United (H) 3-1
Q2: Weymouth (A) 1-5

61-62 Q1: Dorchester Town (H) 1-6

62-63 Q2: Poole Town (A) 1-10

63-64 Q2: Salisbury (H) 2-2, (A) 0-4

64-65 Q2: Portland United (H) 1-3

65-66 Q1: Andover (H) 0-4

66-67 Q1: Dorchester Town (A) 0-5

67-68 Q1: Taunton (H) 0-9

68-69 Q1: Bridport (A) 1-9

69-70 Q1: Bridport (A) 3-9

85-86 PR: Brockenhurst (A) 3-1
Q1: Wokingham Town (H) 1-1, (A) 2-3

90-91 PR: A.F.C. Totton (A) 3-2
Q1: Wokingham Town (H) 0-1

WARRINGTON TOWN

Currently: Northern Premier League
* - As Stockton Heath

56-57 * PR: Winsford United (H) 4-5

57-58 * PR: Ellesmere Port Town (A) 0-3

58-59 * Q1: Witton Albion (A) 4-2
Q2: Ellesmere Port Town (H) 0-2

59-60 * PR: Congleton Town (H) 0-3

83-84 PR: Stalybridge Celtic (H) 0-3

85-86 PR: Eastwood Town (H) 3-1
Q1: Formby (H) 1-3

86-87 Q1: Penrith (H) 0-2

87-88 PR: Burscough (A - *at Southport*) 2-1
Q1: Northwich Victoria (H) 1-1, (A) 1-5

88-89 PR: Curzon Ashton (H) 3-2
Q1: Bilston Town (A) 0-0, (H) 3-2
Q2: Rhyl (A) 1-1, (H) 2-0
Q3: Leek Town (H) 1-2

89-90 PR: Mile Oak Rovers & Youth (A) 2-1
Q1: North Ferriby United (H) 1-0
Q2: Witton Athletic (A) 0-2

90-91 PR: Salford City (A) 3-0
Q1: South Liverpool (A - *at Bootle*) 0-2

91-92 PR: Salford City (A) 0-0, (H) 1-0
Q1: Hyde United (H) 1-0
Q2: Marine (H) 0-0, (A) 0-1

Below: *Warrington attack during the goalless derby tie against Marine.*

92-93 PR: Skelmersdale United (H) 6-1
Q1: Harrogate Town (A) 2-1
Q2: Stalybridge Celtic (H) 0-3

WASHINGTON

Currently: Northern League

69-70 Q1: Bishop Auckland (A) 1-4

70-71 Q1: South Bank (A) 2-2, (H) 1-0
Q2: North Shields (H) 1-0
Q3: Stanley United (A) 2-0
Q4: Bradford (Park Avenue) (H) 0-3

71-72 Q1: Willington (H) 1-1, (A) 0-1

76-77 PR: West Auckland Town (H) 3-1
Q1: Barrow (H) 0-2

77-78 Q1: Penrith (A) 3-3, (H) 1-0
Q2: Consett (H) 0-3

78-79 Q1: Blue Star (H) 3-2
Q2: Boldon Community Association (A) 2-3

79-80 Q1: Wingate (H) 3-2
Q2: Horden Colliery Welfare (H) 0-5

80-81 PR: Netherfield (A) 2-3

89-90 PR: Chester-le-Street T. (H) 0-0, (A) 1-2

90-91 PR: Langley Park (A) 0-2

91-92 PR: Shildon (H - *played away*) 1-3

92-93 PR: Stockton (H - *played away*) 1-3

WATERLOOVILLE

Currently: Southern League

66-67 Q1: Chichester City (A) 2-2, (H) 4-1
Q2: Salisbury (H) 0-2

67-68 Q1: Selsey (H) 2-2, (A) 2-3

68-69 Q1: Basingstoke Town (H) 2-1
Q2: Newport Isle of Wight (H) 3-0
Q3: Salisbury (H) 4-2
Q4: Falmouth Town (A) 2-2, (H) 1-1, 2-0
R1: Kettering Town (H) 1-2

69-70 Q1: Selsey (A) 4-3
Q2: Andover (A) 1-2

70-71 Q1: Thornycroft Ath. (H) 1-1, (A) 0-0, 1-0
Q2: Gosport Borough (A) 3-2
Q3: Basingstoke Town (A) 0-0, (H) 1-0
Q4: Ringmer (H) 2-3

73-74 PR: Sidley United (H) 4-0
Q1: Haywards Heath (A) 1-1, (H) 3-1
Q2: Worthing (A) 1-2

74-75 Q1: Basingstoke Town (A) 1-3

75-76 Q1: Littlehampton Town (H) 2-2, (A) 3-1
Q2: Poole Town (H) 3-0
Q3: Gosport Borough (H) 4-0
Q4: Sutton United (A) 1-1, (H) 1-3

76-77 Q1: Cowes (H) 9-0
Q2: Swaythling (A) 3-0
Q3: Basingstoke Town (A) 2-1
Q4: Hendon (H) 4-1
R1: Wycombe Wanderers (H) 1-2

77-78 PR: Southwick (A) 1-0
Q1: Newport I.O.W. (A) 0-0, (H) 0-1

78-79 Q1: Fareham Town (H) 2-0
Q2: Bognor Regis Town (A) 2-0
Q3: Worthing (A) 1-1, (H) 3-0
Q4: Maidstone United (H) 1-2

79-80 Q1: Camberley Town (A) 2-1
Q2: Poole Town (A) 0-0, (H) 0-2

80-81 Q1: Horsham Y.M.C.A. (H) 2-0
Q2: Windsor & Eton (H) 0-0, (A) 1-4

81-82 PR: Pagham (A - *played home*) 0-3

82-83 PR: Bracknell Town (H) 1-2

83-84 Q1: Road Sea Southampton (A) 0-0, (H) 2-1
Q2: Hungerford Town (A) 3-3, (H) 3-0
Q3: A.F.C. Totton (A) 0-1 *abandoned after 65 minutes*, (A) 1-1, (H) 3-0
Q4: Wokingham Town (H) 3-2
R1: Northampton T. (A) 1-1, (H) 1-1, (A) 0-2

84-85 Q1: Clevedon Town (A) 2-3

85-86 Q1: Worthing (A) 0-3

86-87 Q1: Sheppey United (H) 0-1

87-88 PR: Shortwood United (A) 6-1
Q1: Havant Town (A) 2-0
Q2: Yeovil Town (H) 1-1, (A) 2-3

88-89 Q1: Chippenham Town (H) 2-0
Q2: Hungerford Town (A) 2-0
Q3: Gosport Borough (A) 1-0
Q4: Farnborough Town (A) 3-2
R1: Aylesbury United (H) 1-4

89-90 Q1: Littlehampton Town (A) 1-3

90-91 Q1: Newport I.O.W. (H) 1-1, (A) 0-3

91-92 Q1: Swanage Town & Herston (A) 1-1, (H) 2-0
Q2: Thame United (H) 3-3, (A) 2-3

92-93 Q1: Cheltenham Town (H) 0-0, (A) 0-2

WATERLOWS (DUNSTABLE)

Currently: Defunct

46-47 PR: Eynesbury Rovers (A) 0-1

47-48 PR: Hitchin Town (A) 0-8

48-49 PR: Potton United (A) 1-2

50-51 EX: Wootton Blue Cross (A) 0-5

WATFORD

Currently: Football League

45-46 R1: Southend U. (H) 1-1, (A) 3-0 (*agg: 4-1*)
R2: Bromley (A) 3-1, (H) 1-1 (*agg: 4-2*)
R3: Nottm F. (A) 1-1, (H) 1-1, 1-0 (*agg: 3-2*)
R4: Birmingham (A) 0-5, (A) 1-1 (*agg: 1-6*)

46-47 R1: Wellington Town (A) 1-1, (H) 1-0
R2: Port Vale (H) 1-1, (A) 1-2

47-48 R1: Torquay United (H) 1-1, (A) 0-3

48-49 R1: Leytonstone (A) 1-2

49-50 R1: Bromley (A) 2-1
R2: Netherfield (H) 6-0
R3: Preston North End (H) 2-2, (A) 1-0
R4: Manchester United (H) 0-1

50-51 R1: Norwich City (A) 0-2

51-52 R1: Aylesbury United (A) 5-0
R2: Hartlepools United (H) 1-2

52-53 R1: Leytonstone (A) 2-0
R2: Walthamstow Avenue (A) 1-1, (H) 1-2

53-54 R1: Nuneaton Borough (A) 0-3

54-55 R1: Corby Town (A) 2-0
R2: Carlisle United (A) 2-2, (H) 4-1
R3: Doncaster Rovers (H) 1-2

55-56 R1: Ramsgate Athletic (H) 5-3
R2: Bedford Town (A) 2-3

56-57 R1: Newport Isle of Wight (A) 6-0
R2: Ipswich Town (H) 1-3

57-58 R1: Plymouth Argyle (A) 2-6

58-59 R1: Reading (H) 1-1, (A) 2-0
R2: Torquay United (A) 0-2

59-60 R1: Cheltenham Town (A) 0-0, (H) 3-0
R2: Wycombe Wanderers (H) 5-1
R3: Birmingham City (H) 2-1
R4: Southampton (A) 2-2, (H) 1-0
R5: Sheffield United (A) 2-3

60-61 R1: Brentford (H) 2-2, (A) 2-0
R2: Crystal Palace (A) 0-0, (H) 1-0
R3: Rotherham United (A) 0-1

61-62 R1: Southend United (A) 2-0
R2: Romford (A) 3-1
R3: Preston North End (A) 2-3

62-63 R1: Poole Town (H) 2-2, (A) 2-1
R2: Southend United (A) 2-0
R3: Rotherham United (H) 2-0
R4: Southampton (A) 1-3

63-64 R1: Peterborough United (A) 1-1, (H) 2-1
R2: Newport County (A) 0-2

64-65 R1: Reading (A) 1-3

65-66 R1: Corinthian-Casuals (A) 5-1
R2: Southend United (A) 1-2

66-67 R1: Southend United (H) 1-0
R2: Enfield (A) 4-2
R3: Liverpool (H) 0-0, (A) 1-3

67-68 R1: Lowestoft Town (A) 1-0
R2: Hereford United (H) 3-0
R3: Sheffield United (H) 0-1

68-69 R1: Cheltenham Town (A) 4-0
R2: Brentford (H) 1-0
R3: Port Vale (H) 2-0
R4: Manchester United (A) 1-1, (H) 0-2

69-70 R3: Bolton Wanderers (A) 2-1
R4: Stoke City (H) 1-0
R5: Gillingham (H) 2-1
R6: Liverpool (H) 1-0
SF: Chelsea (*at Tottenham Hotspur*) 1-5
TP: Manchester United (*at Arsenal*) 0-2

70-71 R3: Reading (H) 5-0
R4: Oxford United (A) 1-1, (H) 1-2

71-72 R3: Notts County (H) 1-4

72-73 R1: Guildford City (H) 4-2
R2: Aldershot (H) 2-0
R3: Sheffield United (H) 0-1

73-74 R1: Chelmsford City (H) 2-1
R2: A.F.C. Bournemouth (H) 0-1

74-75 R1: Colchester United (H) 0-1

75-76 R1: Brighton & Hove Albion (H) 0-3

76-77 R1: Gillingham (A) 1-0
R2: Hillingdon Borough (A) 3-2
R3: Northwich Victoria (A) 2-3

77-78 R1: Hendon (H) 2-0
R2: Colchester United (H) 2-0
R3: West Ham United (A) 0-1

78-79 R1: Dagenham (H) 3-0
R2: Southend United (H) 1-1, (A) 0-1

79-80 R3: Queens Park Rangers (A) 2-1
R4: Harlow Town (H) 4-3
R5: Wolverhampton Wanderers (A) 3-0
R6: Arsenal (H) 1-2

80-81 R3: Colchester United (A) 1-0
R4: Wolverhampton W. (H) 1-1, (A) 1-2

81-82 R3: Manchester United (H) 1-0
R4: West Ham United (H) 2-0
R5: Leicester City (A) 0-2

82-83 R3: Plymouth Argyle (H) 2-0
R4: Fulham (H) 1-1, (A) 2-1
R5: Aston Villa (A) 1-4

83-84 R3: Luton Town (A) 2-2, (H) 4-3
R4: Charlton Athletic (A) 2-0
R5: Brighton & Hove Albion (H) 3-1
R6: Birmingham City (A) 3-1
SF: Plymouth Argyle (*at Aston Villa*) 1-0
F: Everton (*at Wembley*) 0-2

84-85 R3: Sheffield United (H) 5-0
R4: Grimsby Town (A) 3-1
R5: Luton T. (A) 0-0, (H) 2-2, (A) 0-1

85-86 R3: Coventry City (A) 3-1
R4: Manchester C. (A) 1-1, (H) 0-0, (A) 3-1
R5: Bury (H) 1-1, (A) 3-0
R6: Liverpool (A) 0-0, (H) 1-2

86-87 R3: Maidstone United (H) 3-1
R4: Chelsea (H) 1-0
R5: Walsall (A) 1-1, (H) 4-4, (A) 1-0
R6: Arsenal (A) 3-1
SF: Tottenham Hotspur (*at Aston Villa*) 1-4

87-88 R3: Hull City (H) 1-1, (A) 2-2, (H) 1-0
R4: Coventry City (A) 1-0
R5: Port Vale (A) 0-0, (H) 2-0
R6: Wimbledon (A) 1-2

88-89 R3: Newcastle Utd (H) 0-0, (A) 2-2, (A) 0-0, (H) 1-0
R4: Derby County (H) 2-1
R5: Nottingham Forest (H) 0-3

89-90 R3: Wigan Athletic (H) 2-0
R4: Sheffield United (A) 1-1, (H) 1-2

90-91 R3: Shrewsbury Town (A) 1-4

91-92 R3: Swindon Town (A) 2-3

92-93 R3: Wolverhampton Wanderers (H) 1-4

Opposite: *Two great headers for Watford at Vicarage Road.* **Top:** *Barry Endean heads the goal that gave the Hornets their most famous F.A. Cup win, against Liverpool in 1970.* **Bottom:** *Alan Garner nets against non-League Hendon seven years later.*

WATTON UNITED

Currently: Eastern Counties League

87-88	PR: Royston Town (H) 0-1
88-89	PR: Soham Town Rangers (A) 1-0 Q1: Witham Town (A) 1-2
91-92	PR: Haringey Borough (A) 0-5
92-93	PR: Burnham Ramblers (H) 1-0 Q1: Purfleet (A) 1-6

WEALDSTONE

Currently: Southern League

45-46	PR: Pinner (A) 2-1 Q1: St Albans City (A) 2-2, (H) 3-0 Q2: Harrow Town (A) 1-1, (H) 6-1 Q3: Barnet (A) 0-3
46-47	PR: Tufnell Park (H) 6-1 Q1: Harrow Town (A) 3-4
47-48	PR: Enfield (H) 2-0 Q1: Finchley (H) 5-4 Q2: Edgware Town (A) 2-1 Q3: Leavesden (A) 3-1 Q4: Bromley (H) 0-2
48-49	PR: Willesden (H) 4-0 Q1: Harrow Town (H) 2-1 Q2: St Albans City (A) 5-0 Q3: Hendon (A) 2-4
49-50	PR: Hendon (A) 4-0 Q1: Enfield (A) 0-0, (H) 2-0 Q2: St Albans City (A) 1-0 Q3: Edgware Town (A) 1-0 Q4: Colchester United (H) 1-0 R1: Port Vale (A) 0-1
50-51	PR: Hertford Town (A) 3-1 Q1: St Albans City (H) 1-5
51-52	PR: Southall (H) 2-1 Q1: Uxbridge (H) 2-1 Q2: Hayes (H) 2-0 Q3: Slough Town (H) 5-0 Q4: Tonbridge (A) 0-2
52-53	PR: Windsor & Eton (A) 4-0 Q1: Hendon (H) 0-1
53-54	PR: Barnet (A) 2-1 Q1: Southall (H) 2-1 Q2: St Albans City (H) 2-0 Q3: Yiewsley (A) 3-0 Q4: Headington United (H) 0-3
54-55	PR: Wimbledon (H) 2-4
55-56	PR: Wembley (A) 3-2 Q1: Harrow Town (A) 7-0 Q2: Southall (H) 1-2
56-57	PR: Hayes (H) 2-4
57-58	PR: Hendon (H) 0-5
58-59	Q1: Uxbridge (H) 2-1 Q2: Hayes (H) 1-4 *aban. 82 mins*, (A) 2-1 Q3: Yiewsley (A) 2-1 Q4: Headington United (H) 2-4
59-60	PR: Hayes (A) 1-2
60-61	Q1: Harrow Town (H) 1-2
61-62	Q1: Ware (A - *played home*) 5-0 Q2: Barnet (H) 1-1, (A) 0-8
62-63	Q1: Harlow Town (A) 2-0 Q2: Bishop's Stortford (A) 2-0 Q3: Enfield (H) 1-5
63-64	Q1: Hertford Town (H) 0-1
65-66	Q1: Hertford Town (A) 2-1 Q2: Harlow Town (H) 5-1 Q3: Stevenage Town (H) 6-5 Q4: Oxford City (H) 2-0 R1: Millwall (A) 1-3
66-67	R1: Nuneaton Borough (H) 0-2
67-68	PR: Wembley (A) 0-2
68-69	Q1: Dunstable Town (H) 3-2 Q2: Banbury United (H) 3-1 Q3: Aylesbury United (H) 2-1 Q4: Slough Town (A) 1-1, (H) 2-0 R1: St Albans City (H) 1-1, (A) 0-1
69-70	PR: Bletchley (H) 2-1 Q1: Aylesbury United (H) 0-0, (A) 3-1 Q2: Banbury United (H) 1-0 Q3: Dunstable Town (H) 4-0 Q4: Enfield (H) 0-1
70-71	PR: Hatfield Town (H) 2-0 Q1: Wembley (A) 2-0 Q2: Leighton Town (A) 1-1, (H) 0-1
71-72	Q1: Harrow Borough (A) 1-0 Q2: Boreham Wood (A) 1-1, (H) 0-2
72-73	Q1: Windsor & Eton (H) 0-0, (A) 3-0 Q2: Finchley (A) 2-0 Q3: Hayes (A) 1-3
73-74	PR: Marlow (H) 2-0 Q1: Chesham United (A) 1-1, (H) 2-4
74-75	Q1: Hampton (A) 2-2, (H) 2-0 Q2: Uxbridge (H) 2-0 Q3: Tooting & Mitcham United (A) 0-1
75-76	Q1: Woking (H) 1-1, (A) 5-3 Q2: Burnham (A) 2-0 Q3: Dagenham (H) 2-0 Q4: Southwick (H) 3-1 R1: Aldershot (A) 3-4

Above: *Wealdstone's Brian Greenaway in action at Reading in the First Round in 1985.*

76-77 Q1: Clapton (H) 5-1
Q2: Kingstonian (A) 2-0
Q3: Dulwich Hamlet (A) 2-0
Q4: Bishop's Stortford (H) 3-2
R1: Reading (A) 0-1

77-78 Q4: Maidstone United (H) 2-1
R1: Hereford United (H) 0-0, (A) 3-2
R2: Reading (H) 2-1
R3: Queens Park Rangers (A) 0-4

78-79 Q4: Kempston Rovers (H) 1-0
R1: Enfield (H) 0-5

79-80 Q4: Woking (H) 1-0
R1: Southend United (H) 0-1

80-81 Q4: Harlow Town (A) 1-1, (H) 0-1

81-82 Q1: Salisbury (H) 4-0
Q2: Newbury Town (A) 6-1
Q3: Harrow Borough (H) 1-4

82-83 Q1: Hertford Town (H) 5-0
Q2: Hendon (A) 1-1, (H) 3-2
Q3: Dulwich Hamlet (A) 0-0, (H) 2-1
Q4: Sutton United (H) 3-1
R1: Swindon Town (A) 0-2

83-84 Q1: Cambridge City (A) 2-1
Q2: Aveley (A) 1-1, (H) 2-0
Q3: Basildon United (H) 3-1
Q4: Bishop's Stortford (H) 1-0
R1: Enfield (H) 1-1, (A) 2-2, (H) 2-0
R2: Colchester United (A) 0-4

84-85 Q1: Hounslow (A) 5-2
Q2: Dunstable (H) 6-0
Q3: Grays Athletic (A) 1-2

85-86 R1: Reading (A) 0-1

86-87 Q4: Dagenham (A) 3-0
R1: Swansea C. (H) 1-1, (A) 1-2 *abandoned after 54 minutes*, (A) 1-4

87-88 Q4: Tamworth (A) 0-2

88-89 Q1: Vauxhall Motors (A) 2-1
Q2: Arlesey Town (A) 1-0
Q3: Hayes (H) 1-2

89-90 Q1: St Albans City (A) 2-1
Q2: Wivenhoe Town (H) 0-1

90-91 Q1: Saffron Walden Town (A) 4-0
Q2: Wivenhoe Town (A) 0-0, (H) 2-1
Q3: Ruislip Manor (A) 0-1

91-92 Q1: Witham Town (A) 3-1
Q2: Chesham United (H - *at Watford*) 2-4

92-93 PR: Tiptree United (H - *at Watford*) 2-1
Q1: Witham Town (H - *at Watford*) 2-1
Q2: Wivenhoe (H - *at Watford*) 1-1, (A) 2-0
Q3: Dagenham & Redb. (H - *at Watford*) 1-6

WEDNESFIELD

Currently: West Midlands (Regional) League
* - As Wednesfield Social

82-83 * PR: Long Eaton United (A) 0-1

83-84 * Q1: Ely City (H) 4-0
Q2: Burton Albion (H) 1-2

84-85 * PR: Friar Lane (H) 0-0, (A) 0-0, (H) 1-2

85-86 * Q1: Moor Green (A) 0-5

86-87 * Q1: Grantham (A) 1-5

87-88 * PR: Hinckley Athletic (H) 0-1

88-89 * PR: Chasetown (H) 2-3

90-91 PR: Arnold Town (A) 1-1, (H) 1-0
Q1: Bilston Town (A) 0-6

91-92 PR: Irthlingborough (A) 2-2, (H) 3-3, (A) 2-1
Q1: Solihull Borough (A) 0-3

92-93 PR: Halesowen Harriers (A) 2-2, (H) 2-3

WELLINGBOROUGH TOWN

Currently: United Counties League

45-46 Q2: Kettering Town (H) 2-5

46-47 Q1: Peterborough United (A) 0-6

47-48 Q1: Rushden Town (H) 0-3

48-49 Q1: Stewarts & Lloyds (H) 1-0
Q2: Peterborough United (H) 2-3

49-50 Q1: Corby Town (H) 0-5

50-51 Q1: Desborough Town (H) 2-0
Q2: Corby Town (A) 0-5

51-52 Q1: Stamford (A) 3-5

52-53 PR: Rushden Town (A) 1-3

53-54 Q1: Stamford (A) 0-5

54-55 Q1: Stamford (A) 2-2, (H) 2-0
Q2: Rushden Town (H) 2-1
Q3: Corby Town (A) 0-8

55-56 Q1: Spalding United (H) 1-9

56-57 Q2: Corby Town (A) 0-6

57-58 Q2: Spalding United (H) 1-1, (A) 1-4

58-59 Q2: Rushden Town (A) 0-1

59-60 Q1: Rothwell Town (H) 3-2
Q2: Rushden Town (H) 0-2

60-61 Q1: Stamford (A) 1-2

61-62 Q1: Stamford (A) 0-5

62-63 Q1: Corby Town (H) 0-0, (A) 0-1

63-64 Q1: Eynesbury Rovers (H) 3-0
Q2: Rushden Town (A) 2-0
Q3: Corby Town (A) 1-3

64-65 Q1: St Neots Town (H) 0-2

65-66 Q1: Biggleswade Town (H) 3-0
Q2: Desborough Town (A) 2-1
Q3: Bourne Town (A) 2-2, (H) 3-2
Q4: Harwich & Parkeston (H) 1-0
R1: Aldershot (A) 1-2

66-67 Q1: Desborough Town (A) 1-2

67-68 PR: Soham Town Rangers (H) 3-1
Q1: Eynesbury Rovers (A) 4-0
Q2: Kettering Town (A) 1-1, (H) 1-2

68-69 Q1: Potton United (A) 2-1
Q2: Ely City (H) 3-1
Q3: Kettering Town (A) 1-4

69-70 Q1: Cambridge United (A) 0-7

70-71 Q1: Corby Town (H) 4-1
Q2: Cambridge City (A) 2-2, (H) 2-3 *aband.*, (H - *at Peterborough United*) 1-2

71-72 Q1: St Neots Town (A) 3-1
Q2: Ely City (H) 4-2
Q3: Kettering Town (A) 1-2

72-73 Q1: Rothwell Town (A) 5-1
Q2: Enderby Town (A) 1-2

73-74 Q1: Corby Town (A) 0-1

74-75 Q1: Bedford Town (A) 1-2

75-76 Q1: Milton Keynes City (H) 0-1

76-77 Q1: Ely City (H) 3-1
Q2: Vauxhall Motors (A) 3-1
Q3: Barton Rovers (A) 1-1 (H) 1-2

77-78 Q1: Redditch United (A) 3-1
Q2: Banbury United (H) 1-2

78-79 Q1: Arnold (H) 1-1, (A) 1-2

79-80 PR: Staines Town (A) 1-0
Q1: Tring Town (A) 1-2

80-81 PR: Newmarket Town (A) 0-1

81-82 PR: Brierley Hill Alliance (A) *W/O*
Q1: Lye Town (A) 1-2

82-83 PR: Basildon United (H) 5-2
Q1: Hitchin Town (A) 4-0
Q2: Great Yarmouth Town (A) 1-1, (H) 2-0
Q3: Billericay Town (H) 1-1, (A) 2-1
Q4: Worcester City (A) 1-2

83-84 Q1: Chatteris Town (A) 2-0
Q2: Stourbridge (A) 3-2
Q3: March Town United (H) 1-0
Q4: A.P. Leamington (A) 0-3

84-85 Q1: Newmarket Town (A) 2-1
Q2: Corby Town (H) 1-4

85-86 PR: Wigston Fields (H) 4-0
Q1: Rushall Olympic (A) 2-0
Q2: Irthlingborough D. (H) 1-1, (A) 2-4

86-87 PR: Sutton Coldfield Town (H) 1-3

87-88 PR: Spalding United (H) 3-2
Q1: Leicester United (H) 1-1, (A) 0-1

88-89 Q1: Chasetown (H) 1-2

89-90 PR: Stratford Town (A) 0-0, (H) 3-4

90-91 PR: Tividale (H) 1-0
Q1: Alvechurch (A) 1-4

91-92 PR: Willenhall Town (A) 1-6

92-93 PR: Wisbech Town (A) 0-10

WELLINGTON

Currently: Western League

81-82 PR: Almondsbury Greenway (A) 1-1, (H) 3-0
Q1: Bridgwater Town (A) 0-2

82-83 PR: Penzance (A) 1-2

83-84 PR: Paulton Rovers (A) 1-2

84-85 PR: Devizes Town (H) 5-1
Q1: Glastonbury (H) 2-3

WELLINGTON TOWN

See Telford United

WELLING UNITED

Currently: Alliance Premier League

78-79 Q1: Gravesend & Northfleet (H) 1-2

79-80 PR: Hastings United (A) 4-0
Q1: Sittingbourne (A) 2-2, (H) 5-0
Q2: Erith & Belvedere (H) 1-0
Q3: Addlestone (H) 3-1
Q4: Gravesend & Northfleet (A) 1-2

80-81 Q1: Sheppey United (H) 4-2
Q2: Dover (A) 0-2

81-82 Q1: Aveley (A) 1-1, (H) 1-1, (A) 0-0, (H) 3-2
Q2: Billericay Town (A) 1-3

82-83 Q1: Sheppey United (H) 2-0
Q2: Egham Town (A) 0-2

83-84 Q1: Walton & Hersham (A) 0-1

84-85 Q1: Uxbridge (A) 1-0
Q2: Addlestone & Weybridge Town (H) 2-1
Q3: Metropolitan Police (A) 1-3

85-86 Q1: Dorking (A) 7-1
Q2: Staines Town (A) 3-0
Q3: Slough Town (H) 0-0, (A) 1-2

86-87 Q1: Darenth Heathside (H) 6-0
Q2: Bracknell Town (H) 2-1
Q3: Hendon (A) 1-0
Q4: Wembley (A) 3-2
R1: Maidstone United (H) 1-1, (A) 1-4

87-88 Q1: Camberley (A) 2-0
Q2: Walton & Hersham (H) 2-1
Q3: Burnham (H) 3-1
Q4: Boston United (A) 1-1, (H) 3-2
R1: Carshalton Athletic (H) 3-2
R2: Bath City (H) 0-1

88-89 Q4: Hinckley Town (H) 1-1, (A) 3-0
R1: Bromsgrove Rovers (H) 3-0
R2: Bath City (A) 0-0, (H) 3-2
R3: Blackburn Rovers (H) 0-1

Right: *Welling's most prolific Cup run was in 1988-89.* **Top:** *Ray Burgess (right) equalises in the Second Round replay at home to Bath.* **Bottom:** *John Glover leaps high above the Blackburn defence in the next round. Incredibly, Rovers were the first Football League club drawn by Welling despite having been 'in the hat' with the big boys on five previous occasions.*
Photos: Keith Gillard.

89-90 Q4: Bromley (H) 5-2
R1: Gillingham (A) 0-0, (H) 1-0
R2: Reading (A) 0-0, (H) 1-1, (A) 0-0, (H) 1-2

90-91 Q4: Bashley (H) 1-0
R1: Swansea City (A) 2-5

91-92 Q4: Alvechurch (H) 5-1
R1: Leyton Orient (A) 1-2

92-93 Q4: Kingstonian (A) 1-2

WELLS AMATEUR

Currently: Defunct

48-49 EX: Clevedon (H) *withdrew*

WELLS CITY

Currently: Somerset Senior League

46-47 PR: Street (A) 2-2, (H) 1-2

47-48 Q1: Newton Spurs (H) 0-1

48-49 PR: Newton Spurs (H) 4-2
Q1: Hanham Athletic (A) 3-4

49-50 PR: Glastonbury (A) 4-1
Q1: Barnstaple Town (H) 1-0
Q2: Bideford (H) 1-1, (A) 2-3

50-51 PR: Taunton (A) 2-3

51-52 PR: Radstock Town (A) 3-1
Q1: Peasedown Miners Welfare (H) 2-2 (A) 2-0
Q2: Chippenham United (H) 1-5

52-53 Q1: Chippenham United (A) 2-2, (H) 3-1
Q2: Bath City (A) 0-2

53-54 PR: Clandown (A) 0-1

54-55 Q1: Bridgwater Town (H) 2-1
Q2: Clandown (A) 2-0
Q3: Radstock Town (H) 4-0
Q4: Newport Isle of Wight (H) 1-4

55-56 PR: Bridgwater Town (H) 2-1
Q1: Peasedown Miners Welfare (H) 2-1
Q2: Borough of Weston-super-Mare (A) 1-5

56-57 PR: Street (H) 1-1, (A) 0-0, 0-2

57-58 Q1: Chippenham United (H) 2-1
Q2: Glastonbury (A) 0-3

58-59 Q1: Borough of Weston-super-Mare (A) 1-2

WELTON ROVERS

Currently: Western League

45-46 Q2: Peasedown Miners Welfare (H) 3-7

46-47 Q1: Radstock Town (H) 2-4

47-48 EX: Frome Town (A) 2-1
PR: Trowbridge Town (H) 0-2

48-49 EX: Odd Down (H) 5-1
PR: Swindon G.W.R. Corinthians (A) 3-2
Q1: Clandown (A) 1-2

50-51 PR: Swindon British Rail (A) 5-1
Q1: Bath City (H) 2-1
Q2: Trowbridge Town (H) 0-2

51-52 Q1: Westbury United (H) 2-2, (A) 3-0
Q2: Chippenham Town (A) 1-5

52-53 PR: Salisbury (A) 1-7

53-54 Q1: Spencer Moulton (A) 5-3
Q2: Trowbridge Town (H) 0-3

54-55 PR: Swindon Victoria (H) 3-7

55-56 PR: Bulford United (A) 1-1, (H) 1-3

63-64 Q2: Westbury United (A) 3-0
Q3: Trowbridge Town (A) 0-3

64-65 Q2: Glastonbury (H) 4-0
Q3: Minehead (A) 3-0
Q4: Bridgwater Town (H) 1-0
R1: Weymouth (H) 1-1, (A) 3-4

65-66 Q2: Boro. of Weston-s-Mare (H) 1-1, (A) 3-0
Q3: Frome Town (H) 4-1
Q4: Bath City (A) 1-3

66-67 Q1: Devizes Town (H) 2-0
Q2: Chippenham Town (A) 4-0
Q3: Trowbridge Town (A) 3-0
Q4: Fareham Town (H) 4-1
R1: Bournemouth & Boscombe Ath. (A) 0-3

67-68 Q4: Yeovil Town (A) 0-2

68-69 Q1: Chippenham Town (A) 4-2
Q2: Gloucester City (H) 1-2

69-70 Q1: Poole Town (A) 1-1, (H) 2-1
Q2: Chippenham Town (H) 2-2, (A) 1-2

70-71 PR: Frome Town (H) 5-1
Q1: Weston-super-Mare (A) 2-1
Q2: Glastonbury (A) 0-1

71-72 Q1: Basingstoke Town (A) 1-2

72-73 PR: Melksham Town (H) 2-0
Q1: Poole Town (H) 2-0
Q2: Frome Town (A) 1-1, (H) 0-1

73-74 PR: Mangotsfield United (H) 1-4

74-75 Q1: Frome Town (H) 1-1, (A) 2-1
Q2: Weymouth (A) 1-7

75-76 Q1: Alvechurch (H) 1-3

76-77 Q1: Bideford (H) 1-2

77-78 PR: Melksham Town (A) 0-1

78-79 Q1: Salisbury (A) 0-4

79-80 Q1: Weston-super-Mare (H) 0-4

80-81 PR: Shepton Mallet Town (A) 1-2

81-82 Q1: Clevedon Town (A) 1-3

82-83 Q1: Bristol Manor Farm (H) 0-0, (A) 0-1

83-84 Q1: Paulton Rovers (H) 2-0
Q2: Gloucester City (H) 1-4

84-85 PR: Clevedon Town (H) 0-0, (A) 0-1

85-86 PR: Mangotsfield United (H) 1-3

86-87 PR: Taunton Town (H) 1-0
Q1: Weston-super-Mare (A) 0-1

87-88 PR: Newbury Town (A) 2-2, (H) 2-4

88-89 PR: Exmouth Town (H) 0-5

89-90 PR: Thatcham Town (H) 0-5

90-91 PR: Tiverton Town (A) 1-4

91-92 PR: Melksham Town (A) 1-1, (H) 1-2

92-93 PR: Hungerford Town (H) 4-1
Q1: Calne Town (H) 1-4

WELWYN GARDEN CITY

Currently: South Midlands League

45-46 PR: Tufnell Park (A) 1-11

46-47 EX: Berkhamsted Town (H) 2-2, (A) 2-4

47-48 EX: Enfield (H) 1-5

48-49 EX: Hendon (H) 0-3

49-50 PR: Edgware Town (H) 0-2

54-55 PR: Stevenage Town (A) 2-5

55-56 PR: Clapton (H) 0-3

88-89 PR: Potton United (A) 0-2

89-90 PR: Halstead Town (H) 1-1, (A) 2-4

90-91 PR: Chalfont St Peter (H) 1-2

91-92 PR: Witham Town (A) 1-3

92-93 PR: Wembley (A) 0-5

WEMBLEY

Currently: Isthmian League

49-50 EX: Ware (H) 2-2, (A) 2-2, 1-5

55-56 PR: Wealdstone (H) 2-3

56-57 PR: Edgware Town (H) 4-1
Q1: Finchley (A) 0-1

57-58 PR: Berkhamsted Town (H) 3-0
Q1: Yiewsley (H) 0-1

58-59 Q1: Staines Town (A) 6-3
Q2: Yiewsley (A) 1-3

59-60 Q1: Hounslow Town (A) 0-6

60-61 Q1: Romford (A) 0-7

61-62 Q1: Romford (A) 2-6

62-63 Q1: Ford United (A) 1-8

63-64 Q1: Hornchurch (H) 0-2

64-65 Q1: Dagenham (H) 2-2, (A) 0-3

65-66 Q1: Slough Town (A) 3-5

66-67 Q1: Chesham United (A) 0-1

67-68 PR: Wealdstone (H) 2-0
Q1: Bletchley (A) 4-3
Q2: Marlow (A) 3-0
Q3: Banbury United (A) 2-3

68-69 Q1: Aylesbury United (A) 0-1

69-70 Q1: Banbury United (A) 1-2

70-71 Q1: Wealdstone (H) 0-2

71-72 Q1: Marlow (A) 3-0
Q2: Hayes (H) 1-6

72-73 PR: Hayes (H) 1-3

73-74 PR: Southall (H) 0-1

74-75 Q1: Corinthian-Casuals (A) 2-1
Q2: Romford (H) 2-3

75-76 Q1: Uxbridge (A) 2-1
Q2: Dunstable Town (A) 2-0
Q3: Enfield (H) 1-0
Q4: Dartford (H) 0-1

76-77 Q1: Wokingham Town (H) 1-1, (A) 1-1, 0-1

77-78 Q1: Enfield (A) 0-6

78-79 Q1: Grays Athletic (H) 0-0, (A) 1-4

79-80 Q1: Walthamstow Avenue (H) 0-1

80-81 Q1: Leytonstone-Ilford (A) 1-0
Q2: Letchworth G.C. (A) 0-0, (H) 3-1
Q3: Chelmsford City (H) 3-1
Q4: Dover (H) 1-1, (A) 3-2
R1: Enfield (A) 0-3

81-82 Q1: East Grinstead (H) 2-1
Q2: Lewes (A) 2-1
Q3: Basingstoke Town (H) 5-1
Q4: Hastings United (A) 0-2

82-83 Q1: Erith & Belvedere (A) 2-1
Q2: Windsor & Eton (H) 1-3

83-84 Q1: Hayes (A) 3-1
Q2: Chesham United (H) 0-0, (A) 2-3

84-85 PR: Bourne Town (H) 2-1
Q1: A.P. Leamington (H) 3-1
Q2: Sudbury Town (A) 0-0, (H) 2-2, (A) 3-0
Q3: V.S.Rugby (H) 1-5

85-86 Q1: Boreham Wood (H) 2-0
Q2: Walthamstow Avenue (H) 1-3

86-87 Q1: Dorking (H) 1-0
Q2: Dulwich Hamlet (H) 2-1
Q3: Staines Town (A) 1-1, (H) 4-1
Q4: Welling United (H) 2-3

87-88 Q1: Hoddesdon Town (A) 3-1
Q2: Ruislip Manor (H) 1-1, (A) 5-0
Q3: Leyton-Wingate (H) 2-2, (A) 1-5

88-89 Q1: Burgess Hill Town (H) 3-1
Q2: Hanwell Town (A) 1-0
Q3: Walton & Hersham (A) 1-2

89-90 PR: Rayners Lane (A) 0-1

90-91 PR: Bury Town (H) 1-0
Q1: Bourne Town (H) 4-1
Q2: Heybridge Swifts (H) 2-2, (A) 1-3

91-92 PR: Egham Town (A) 1-0
Q1: Windsor & Eton (H) 1-2

92-93 PR: Welwyn Garden City (H) 5-0
Q1: Barkingside (A) 3-1
Q2: Slade Green (H) 3-2
Q3: Hendon (H) 1-0
Q4: Nuneaton Boro. (H) 1-1, (A) 0-0, (H) 1-2

Below: *Frank Omere, the Wembley forward, heads the ball into the Welwyn Garden City area and follows up to score his side's third in the Preliminary Round tie on August 28th 1992. Photo: Paul Dennis.*

WEST AUCKLAND TOWN

Currently: Northern League

45-46 Q1: Stanley United (A) 0-5

46-47 Q1: Seaham Colliery Welfare (H) 0-3

47-48 PR: Blackhall Colliery Welfare (H) 5-3
Q1: Horden Colliery Welfare (H) 1-0
Q2: Easington Colliery Welfare (H) 0-1

48-49 PR: Murton Colliery Welfare (H) 0-1

49-50 PR: Silksworth C.W. (A) 3-3, (H) 2-5

50-51 EX: Chilton Athletic (H) 2-1
PR: South Hetton C.W. (H) 4-0
Q1: Tow Law Town (A) 2-3

51-52 Q1: Spennymoor United (H) 2-4

52-53 Q1: Willington (A) 4-2
Q2: Evenwood Town (H) 1-2

53-54 Q1: Spennymoor United (A) 0-6

55-56 Q1: Stanley United (A) 1-0
Q2: Tow Law Town (A) 4-1
Q3: Shildon (H) 1-1, (A) 3-5

56-57 Q1: Shildon (A) 2-2, (H) 2-1
Q2: Stanley United (H) 0-0, (A) 0-2

57-58 Q1: Whitley Bay Athletic (H) 1-2

58-59 Q1: South Bank (A) 1-0
Q2: Redcar Albion (H) 3-0
Q3: Stanley United (H) 3-3, (A) 0-2

59-60 Q2: Tow Law Town (A) 4-4, (H) 5-2
Q3: Willington (A) 2-0
Q4: Durham City (H) 2-2, (A) 0-0, 4-1
R1: Stockport County (H) 2-6

60-61 Q1: Annfield Plain (H) 2-4

61-62 R1: Barnsley (H) 3-3, (A) 0-2

62-63 Q4: Gateshead (A) 2-2, (H) 0-2

63-64 Q1: Boldon C.W. (A - *played home*) 4-1
Q2: Horden Colliery Welfare (A) 0-1

65-66 Q1: Ashington (A) 1-3

66-67 Q1: Tow Law Town (A) 0-5

67-68 Q1: Annfield Plain (A) 2-2, (H) 2-0
Q2: Ashington (H) 0-1

68-69 Q1: Stanley United (H) 3-2
Q2: Stockton (A) 1-2

69-70 PR: Whitby Town (A) 0-1

70-71 Q1: Stockton (H) 1-0
Q2: Blyth Spartans (A) 1-6

72-73 Q1: Gateshead (A) 0-1

73-74 Q1: Whitley Bay (H) 1-1, (A) 1-4

74-75 PR: Boldon Colliery Welfare (A) 0-4

75-76 Q1: South Bank (A) 0-2

76-77 PR: Washington (A) 1-3

77-78 PR: North Shields (A) 1-1, (H) 2-1
Q1: Bishop Auckland (A) 0-3

78-79	Q1: Easington Colliery Welfare (A) 1-2
79-80	Q1: South Bank (H) 1-3
80-81	PR: Peterlee Newtown (A) 1-1, (H) 3-4
81-82	PR: Chester-le-Street (A) 0-1
82-83	PR: Harrogate Town (A) 0-3
83-84	Q1: Horden Colliery Welfare (A) 1-5
84-85	Q1: Guiseley (A) 1-1, (H) 3-1 Q2: South Bank (H) 0-6
85-86	PR: Ferryhill Athletic (A) 2-2, (H) 1-2
86-87	PR: Darwen (A) 0-2
87-88	PR: Annfield Plain (A) 4-0 Q1: Fleetwood Town (A) 2-3
88-89	PR: South Bank (H) 0-0, (A) 0-2
89-90	Q1: Crook Town (A) 1-5
90-91	PR: Annfield Plain (H) 4-2 Q1: Accrington Stanley (A) 0-3
91-92	PR: Denaby United (H) 3-5
92-93	PR: Workington (A) 2-3

Above: *Jeff Astle rejoices after scoring an injury-time cup-winning goal for Albion in 1968. Photo: Colorsport*

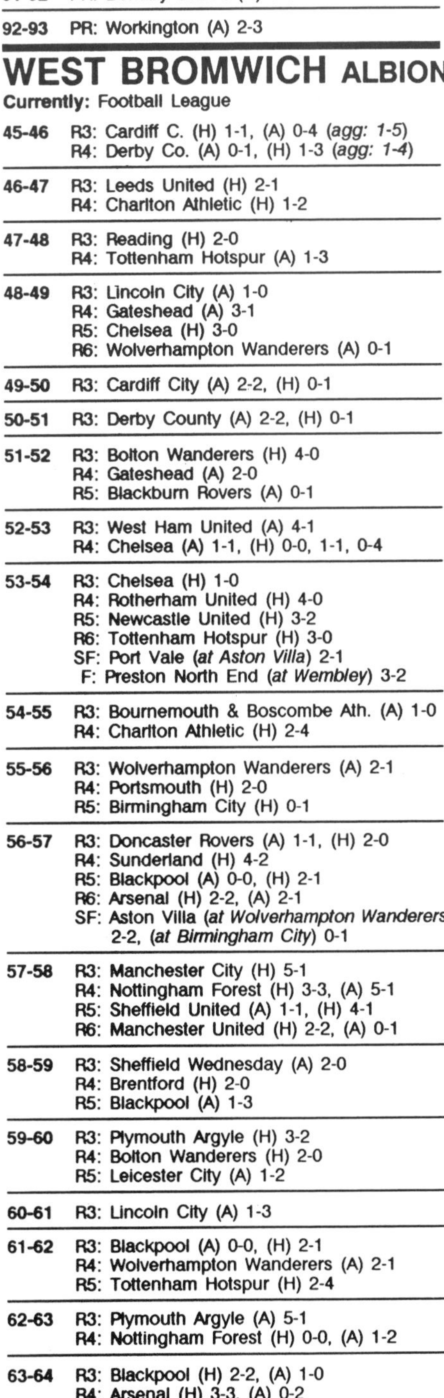

WEST BROMWICH ALBION

Currently: Football League

45-46	R3: Cardiff C. (H) 1-1, (A) 0-4 *(agg: 1-5)* R4: Derby Co. (A) 0-1, (H) 1-3 *(agg: 1-4)*
46-47	R3: Leeds United (H) 2-1 R4: Charlton Athletic (H) 1-2
47-48	R3: Reading (H) 2-0 R4: Tottenham Hotspur (A) 1-3
48-49	R3: Lincoln City (A) 1-0 R4: Gateshead (A) 3-1 R5: Chelsea (H) 3-0 R6: Wolverhampton Wanderers (A) 0-1
49-50	R3: Cardiff City (A) 2-2, (H) 0-1
50-51	R3: Derby County (A) 2-2, (H) 0-1
51-52	R3: Bolton Wanderers (H) 4-0 R4: Gateshead (A) 2-0 R5: Blackburn Rovers (A) 0-1
52-53	R3: West Ham United (A) 4-1 R4: Chelsea (A) 1-1, (H) 0-0, 1-1, 0-4
53-54	R3: Chelsea (H) 1-0 R4: Rotherham United (H) 4-0 R5: Newcastle United (H) 3-2 R6: Tottenham Hotspur (H) 3-0 SF: Port Vale *(at Aston Villa)* 2-1 F: Preston North End *(at Wembley)* 3-2
54-55	R3: Bournemouth & Boscombe Ath. (A) 1-0 R4: Charlton Athletic (H) 2-4
55-56	R3: Wolverhampton Wanderers (A) 2-1 R4: Portsmouth (H) 2-0 R5: Birmingham City (H) 0-1
56-57	R3: Doncaster Rovers (A) 1-1, (H) 2-0 R4: Sunderland (H) 4-2 R5: Blackpool (A) 0-0, (H) 2-1 R6: Arsenal (H) 2-2, (A) 2-1 SF: Aston Villa *(at Wolverhampton Wanderers)* 2-2, *(at Birmingham City)* 0-1
57-58	R3: Manchester City (H) 5-1 R4: Nottingham Forest (H) 3-3, (A) 5-1 R5: Sheffield United (A) 1-1, (H) 4-1 R6: Manchester United (H) 2-2, (A) 0-1
58-59	R3: Sheffield Wednesday (A) 2-0 R4: Brentford (H) 2-0 R5: Blackpool (A) 1-3
59-60	R3: Plymouth Argyle (H) 3-2 R4: Bolton Wanderers (H) 2-0 R5: Leicester City (A) 1-2
60-61	R3: Lincoln City (A) 1-3
61-62	R3: Blackpool (A) 0-0, (H) 2-1 R4: Wolverhampton Wanderers (A) 2-1 R5: Tottenham Hotspur (H) 2-4
62-63	R3: Plymouth Argyle (A) 5-1 R4: Nottingham Forest (H) 0-0, (A) 1-2
63-64	R3: Blackpool (H) 2-2, (A) 1-0 R4: Arsenal (H) 3-3, (A) 0-2
64-65	R3: Liverpool (A) 1-2
65-66	R3: Bolton Wanderers (A) 0-3
66-67	R3: Northampton Town (A) 3-1 R4: Leeds United (A) 0-5
67-68	R3: Colchester United (A) 1-1, (H) 4-0 R4: Southampton (H) 1-1, (A) 3-2 R5: Portsmouth (A) 2-1 R6: Liverpool (H) 0-0, (A) 1-1, 2-1 SF: Birmingham City (N) 2-0 F: Everton *(at Wembley)* 1-0
68-69	R3: Norwich City (H) 3-0 R4: Fulham (H) 2-1 R5: Arsenal (H) 1-0 R6: Chelsea (A) 2-1 SF: Leicester City *(at Sheffield Wed.)* 0-1
69-70	R3: Sheffield Wednesday (A) 1-2
70-71	R3: Scunthorpe United (H) 0-0, (A) 3-1 R4: Ipswich Town (H) 1-1, (A) 0-3
71-72	R3: Coventry City (H) 1-2
72-73	R3: Nottingham Forest (H) 1-1, (A) 0-0, *(at Leicester City)* 3-1 R4: Swindon Town (H) 2-0 R5: Leeds United (A) 0-2
73-74	R3: Notts County (H) 4-0 R4: Everton (A) 0-0, (H) 1-0 R5: Newcastle United (H) 0-3
74-75	R3: Bolton Wanderers (A) 0-0, (H) 4-0 R4: Carlisle United (A) 2-3
75-76	R3: Carlisle United (H) 3-1 R4: Lincoln City (H) 3-2 R5: Southampton (H) 1-1, (A) 0-4
76-77	R3: Manchester City (A) 1-1, (H) 0-1
77-78	R3: Blackpool (H) 4-1 R4: Manchester United (A) 1-1, (H) 3-2 R5: Derby County (A) 3-2 R6: Nottingham Forest (H) 2-0 SF: Ipswich Town *(at Arsenal F.C.)* 1-3
78-79	R3: Coventry City (A) 2-2, (H) 4-0 R4: Leeds Utd *(A - played home)* 3-3, (H) 2-0 R5: Southampton (H) 1-1, (A) 1-2
79-80	R3: West Ham United (H) 1-1, (A) 1-2
80-81	R3: Grimsby Town (H) 3-0 R4: Middlesbrough (A) 0-1
81-82	R3: Blackburn Rovers (H) 3-2 R4: Gillingham (A) 1-0 R5: Norwich City (H) 1-0 R6: Coventry City (H) 2-0 SF: Queens Park Rangers *(at Arsenal)* 0-1
82-83	R3: Queens Park Rangers (H) 3-2 R4: Tottenham Hotspur (A) 1-2
83-84	R3: Rotherham United (A) 0-0, (H) 3-0 R4: Scunthorpe United (H) 1-0 R5: Plymouth Argyle (H) 0-1
84-85	R3: Orient (A) 1-2
85-86	R3: Sheffield Wednesday (A) 2-2, (H) 2-3
86-87	R3: Swansea City (A) 2-3
87-88	R3: Wimbledon (A) 1-4
88-89	R3: Everton (H) 1-1, (A) 0-1
89-90	R3: Wimbledon (H) 2-0 R4: Charlton Athletic (H) 1-0 R5: Aston Villa (H) 0-2
90-91	R3: Woking (H) 2-4
91-92	R1: Marlow (H) 6-0 R2: Orient (A) 1-2
92-93	R1: Aylesbury United (H) 8-0 R2: Wycombe Wanderers (A) 2-2, (H) 1-0 R3: West Ham United (H) 0-2

WEST BROMWICH TOWN

Currently: West Midlands (Regional) League

92-93	PR: Sutton Coldfield Town (A) 0-0, (H) 0-2

WESTBURY UNITED

Currently: Western League

45-46	Q1: Swindon Victoria (H) 4-3 Q2: Paulton Rovers (A) 0-4
46-47	PR: Devizes Town (A) 2-1 Q1: Pewsey Y.M. (H) 2-1 Q2: Trowbridge Town (H) 0-4
47-48	PR: Chippenham Town (H) 3-0 Q1: Swindon G.W.R. Corinthians (A) 4-1 Q2: Wilts County Mental Hospital (A) 3-1 Q3: Trowbridge Town (H) 0-3
48-49	PR: Spencer Moulton (H) 3-1 Q1: Devizes Town (H) 3-2 Q2: Clandown (A) 0-0, (H) 2-1 Q3: Trowbridge Town (A) 0-8
49-50	PR: Chippenham United (H) 1-2
50-51	PR: Salisbury (H) 1-6
51-52	PR: Andover (H) 5-1 Q1: Welton Rovers (A) 2-2, (H) 0-3
52-53	Q1: Salisbury (A) 1-4
53-54	PR: Spencer Moulton (A) 2-6
54-55	PR: Warminster Town (H) 2-0 Q1: Melksham (H) 1-2
55-56	Q1: Chippenham Town (H) 1-1, (A) 1-0 Q2: Frome Town (A) 2-2, (H) 1-2
56-57	Q1: Melksham Town (A) 2-2, (H) 4-2 Q2: Trowbridge Town (A) 2-5

57-58	PR: Salisbury (A) 2-4
58-59	Q2: Chippenham Town (A) 0-3
59-60	Q1: Chippenham Town (H) 3-1 Q2: Trowbridge Town (H) 1-3
60-61	Q1: Melksham Town (A) 2-3
61-62	Q1: Borough of Weston-super-Mare (A) 3-5
62-63	Q2: Chippenham Town (A) 1-4
63-64	Q2: Welton Rovers (H) 0-3
64-65	Q2: Devizes Town (H) 0-3
65-66	Q1: Trowbridge Town (H) 1-3
66-67	Q1: Chippenham Town (A) 2-4
67-68	Q1: Chippenham Town (H) 0-0, (A) 2-3
68-69	Q1: Glastonbury (H) 3-1 Q2: Poole Town (A) 0-4
69-70	Q1: Chippenham Town (A) 2-3
70-71	Q1: Trowbridge Town (H) 1-3
71-72	Q1: Salisbury (A) 0-4
72-73	Q1: Salisbury (A) 1-9
73-74	PR: Salisbury (H) 0-2
74-75	Q1: Hungerford Town (H) 1-3
86-87	PR: Brockenhurst (A) 0-2
87-88	PR: Gloucester City (A) 0-7
88-89	Q1: Thame United (A) 1-3
89-90	PR: Romsey Town (A) 1-5
90-91	PR: Stroud (H) 1-1, (A) 0-3
91-92	PR: Calne Town (A) 2-1 Q1: Poole Town (A) 1-3
92-93	PR: Thatcham Town (H) 0-5

WEST END ROVERS

Currently: Defunct

48-49	EX: Spencer Moulton (A) 3-10

WEST HAM UNITED

Currently: F.A. Premier League

45-46	R3: Arsenal (H) 6-0, (A) 0-1 *(agg: 6-1)* R4: Chelsea (A) 0-2, (H) 1-0 *(agg: 1-2)*
46-47	R3: Leicester City (H) 1-2
47-48	R3: Blackburn Rovers (A) 0-0, (H) 0-0, 2-4
48-49	R3: Luton Town (A) 1-3
49-50	R3: Ipswich Town (H) 5-1 R4: Everton (H) 1-2
50-51	R3: Cardiff City (H) 2-1 R4: Stoke City (A) 0-1
51-52	R3: Blackpool (H) 2-1 R4: Sheffield United (H) 0-0, (A) 2-4
52-53	R3: West Bromwich Albion (H) 1-4
53-54	R3: Huddersfield Town (H) 4-0 R4: Blackpool (H) 1-1, (A) 1-3
54-55	R3: Port Vale (H) 2-2, (A) 1-3
55-56	R3: Preston North End (H) 5-2 R4: Cardiff City (H) 2-1 R5: Blackburn Rovers (H) 0-0, (A) 3-2 R6: Tottenham Hotspur (A) 3-3, (H) 1-2
56-57	R3: Grimsby Town (H) 5-3 R4: Everton (A) 1-2
57-58	R3: Blackpool (H) 5-1 R4: Stockport County (H) 3-2 R5: Fulham (H) 2-3
58-59	R3: Tottenham Hotspur (A) 0-2
59-60	R3: Hudddersfield Town (A) 1-1, (H) 1-5
60-61	R3: Stoke City (H) 2-2, (A) 0-1
61-62	R3: Plymouth Argyle (A) 0-3
62-63	R3: Fulham (H) 0-0, (A) 2-1 R4: Swansea Town (H) 1-0 R5: Everton (H) 1-0 R6: Liverpool (A) 0-1
63-64	R3: Charlton Athletic (H) 3-0 R4: Leyton Orient (H) 1-1, (A) 3-0 R5: Swindon Town (H) 3-1 R6: Burnley (H) 3-2 SF: Manchester Utd *(at Sheffield Wed.)* 3-1 F: Preston North End *(at Wembley)* 3-2
64-65	R3: Birmingham City (H) 4-2 R4: Chelsea (H) 0-1
65-66	R3: Oldham Athletic (A) 2-2, (H) 2-1 R4: Blackburn Rovers (H) 3-3, (A) 1-4
66-67	R3: Swindon Town (H) 3-3, (A) 1-3
67-68	R3: Burnley (A) 3-1 R4: Stoke City (A) 3-0 R5: Sheffield United (H) 1-2
68-69	R3: Bristol City (H) 3-2 R4: Huddersfield Town (A) 2-0 R5: Mansfield Town (A) 0-3
69-70	R3: Middlesbrough (A) 1-2
70-71	R3: Blackpool (A) 0-4
71-72	R3: Luton Town (H) 2-1 R4: Hereford United (A) 0-0, (H) 3-0 R5: Huddersfield Town (A) 2-4
72-73	R3: Port Vale (A) 1-0 R4: Hull City (A) 0-1
73-74	R3: Hereford United (H) 1-1, (A) 1-2
74-75	R3: Southampton (A) 2-1 R4: Swindon Town (H) 1-1, (A) 2-1 R5: Queens Park Rangers (H) 2-1 R6: Arsenal (A) 2-0 SF: Ipswich Town *(at Aston Villa)* 0-0, *(at Chelsea)* 2-1 F: Fulham *(at Wembley)* 2-0
75-76	R3: Liverpool (H) 0-2
76-77	R3: Bolton Wanderers (H) 2-1 R4: Aston Villa (A) 0-3
77-78	R3: Watford (H) 1-0 R4: Queens Park Rangers (H) 1-1, (A) 1-6
78-79	R3: Newport County (A) 1-2
79-80	R3: West Bromwich Albion (A) 1-1, (H) 2-1 R4: Orient (A) 3-2 R5: Swansea City (H) 2-0 R6: Aston Villa (H) 1-0 SF: Everton *(at Aston V.)* 1-1, *(at Leeds)* 2-1 F: Arsenal *(at Wembley)* 1-0
80-81	R3: Wrexham (H) 1-1, (A) 0-0, (A) 0-1
81-82	R3: Everton (H) 2-1 R4: Watford (A) 0-2
82-83	R3: Manchester United (A) 0-2
83-84	R3: Wigan Athletic (A) 1-0 R4: Crystal Palace (A) 1-1, (H) 2-0 R5: Birmingham City (A) 0-3
84-85	R3: Port Vale (H) 4-1 R4: Norwich City (H) 2-1 R5: Wimbledon (A) 1-1, (H) 5-1 R6: Manchester United (A) 2-4
85-86	R3: Charlton Ath. (A - *at Crystal Palace*) 1-0 R4: Ipswich Town (H) 0-0, (A) 1-1, (A) 1-0 R5: Manchester United (H) 1-1, (A) 2-0 R6: Sheffield Wednesday (A) 1-2
86-87	R3: Orient (A) 1-1, (H) 4-1 R4: Sheffield United (H) 4-0 R5: Sheffield Wednesday (A) 1-1, (H) 0-2
87-88	R3: Charlton Athletic (H) 2-0 R4: Queens Park Rangers (A) 1-3
88-89	R3: Arsenal (H) 2-2, (A) 1-0 R4: Swindon Town (A) 0-0, (H) 1-0 R5: Charlton Ath. (A - *at Crystal Palace*) 1-0 R6: Norwich City (H) 0-0, (A) 1-3
89-90	R3: Torquay United (A) 0-1
90-91	R3: Aldershot (A - *played home*) 0-0, (H) 6-1 R4: Luton Town (A) 1-1, (H) 5-0 R5: Crewe Alexandra (H) 1-0 R6: Everton (H) 2-1 SF: Nottingham Forest *(at Aston Villa)* 0-4
91-92	R3: Farnborough (A - *played home*) 1-1, (H) 1-0 R4: Wrexham (H) 2-2, (A) 1-0 R5: Sunderland (A) 1-1, (H) 2-3
92-93	R3: West Bromwich Albion (A) 2-0 R4: Barnsley (A) 1-4

Above: *West Ham's Paul Allen became the youngest player ever to play in an F.A. final when he starred for the victorious Second Division side against Arsenal in 1980. Here he is flanked by Gunners Liam Brady (left) and Brian Talbot. Photo: Colorsport*

WEST MIDLANDS POLICE

Currently: Midland Combination

90-91	PR: Eastwood Hanley (A) 2-0 Q1: Matlock Town (H) 0-6
91-92	Q1: Burton Albion (H) 0-1
92-93	PR: Bridgnorth Town (H) 5-2 Q1: Bedworth United (H) 1-2

WESTON-SUPER-MARE

Currently: Southern League
* - Borough of Weston-super-Mare

49-50	PR: Gloucester City (H) 2-3
51-52	PR: Chippenham United (A) 0-4
54-55 *	PR: Street (A) 2-3
55-56 *	Q1: Radstock Town (A) 3-2 Q2: Wells City (H) 5-1 Q3: Chippenham United (A) 2-3
57-58 *	Q1: Bath City (A) 0-5
58-59 *	Q1: Wells City (H) 2-1 Q2: Bridgwater Town (H) 1-3
59-60 *	Q1: Taunton (A) 0-7

60-61 * Q1: Street (A) 8-0
Q2: Glastonbury (A) 2-2, (H) 2-0
Q3: Bridgwater Town (H) 0-1

61-62 * Q1: Westbury United (H) 5-3
Q2: Glastonbury (A) 1-1, (H) 2-2, 3-0
Q3: Minehead (H) 1-0
Q4: Cheltenham Town (A) 1-0
R1: Bridgwater Town (A) 0-0, (H) 0-1

62-63 * Q1: Bridgwater Town (A) 1-1, (H) 0-0, 1-3

63-64 * Q1: Glastonbury (A) 5-2
Q2: Minehead (A) 1-3

64-65 * Q1: Minehead (A) 1-2

65-66 * Q1: Minehead (H) 2-1
Q2: Welton Rovers (A) 1-1, (H) 0-3

66-67 * Q1: Stonehouse (A) 2-3

69-70 Q1: Spencer Moulton (H) 11-2
Q2: Glastonbury (A) 1-3

70-71 Q1: Welton Rovers (H) 1-2

71-72 Q1: Stonehouse (A) 2-4

72-73 Q1: Taunton Town (A) 1-3

73-74 Q1: Llanelly (A) 0-1

74-75 Q1: Bath City (A) 0-3

75-76 Q1: Melksham Town (H) 3-0
Q2: Yeovil Town (H) 0-0, (A) 0-4

76-77 PR: Clevedon (A) 1-1, (H) 3-0
Q1: Taunton Town (A) 0-1

77-78 PR: Trowbridge Town (A) 1-1, (H) 2-1
Q1: Ton Pentre (A) 2-2, (H) 3-2
Q2: Forest Green Rovers (A) 2-0
Q3: Worcester City (A) 1-1, (H) 1-2

78-79 Q1: Bath City (H) 1-2

79-80 PR: Llanelli (A) 2-0
Q1: Welton Rovers (A) 4-0
Q2: Forest Green Rovers (H) 3-1
Q3: Merthyr Tydfil (H) 2-2, (A) 1-3

80-81 PR: Paulton Rovers (A) 3-0
Q1: Bath City (H) 1-2

81-82 Q1: Glastonbury (A) 1-3

82-83 Q1: Bideford (H) 1-4

83-84 PR: Haverfordwest County (A) 0-1

84-85 Q1: Dorchester Town (A) 2-4

85-86 PR: Wimborne Town (A) 5-2
Q1: Poole Town (A) 1-5

86-87 PR: Torrington (H) 1-0
Q1: Welton Rovers (H) 1-0
Q2: Exmouth Town (H) 2-3

87-88 PR: Bridgend Town (A) 3-1
Q1: Bristol Manor Farm (A) 3-0
Q2: Ton Pentre (A) 2-1
Q3: Cheltenham Town (H) 1-2

88-89 Q1: Wimborne Town (A) 5-3
Q2: Weymouth (H) 0-1

89-90 Q1: Chippenham Town (A) 2-1
Q2: Cheltenham Town (A) 0-7

90-91 PR: Radstock Town (A) 3-0
Q1: Maesteg Park (H) 2-2, (A) 4-0
Q2: Cheltenham Town (H) 0-2

91-92 PR: Shortwood United (A) 0-3

92-93 Q1: Gloucester City (A) 3-2
Q2: Clevedon Town (H) 0-4

WESTON-SUPER-MARE ST JOHNS

Currently: (Weston St Johns) Somerset Senior Lge

46-47 PR: Gloucester City (H) 0-5

47-48 PR: Stonehouse (A) 7-4
Q1: Lovells Athletic (H) 1-4

48-49 PR: Glastonbury (H) 1-1, (A) 0-9

49-50 PR: Lovells Athletic (H) 2-7

WEST SLEEKBURN WELFARE

Currently: Defunct

49-50 EX: Cramlington Welfare (A) 1-3

50-51 PR: Cramlington Welfare (A) 1-5

51-52 Q1: Hexham Hearts (H) 2-2, (A) 0-6

52-53 Q1: Alnwick Town (A) 1-4

53-54 Q1: Ashington (A) 2-1
Q2: Newburn (H) 0-1

54-55 Q1: Hexham Hearts (H) 3-2
Q2: Cramlington Welfare (A) 7-1
Q3: Ashington (A) 1-2

WEST STANLEY

Currently: Defunct

47-48 PR: Newbiggin Central Welfare (A) 5-1
Q1: Ashington (A) 3-4

48-49 PR: Ashington (H - *played away*) 0-1

49-50 PR: Hexham (H - *at Annfield P.*) 0-0, (A) 1-2

50-51 EX: Lynemouth Welfare (A) 9-2
PR: Boldon Colliery Welfare (A) 4-1
Q1: Ashington (A) 1-2

WEST THURROCK ATHLETIC

Currently: Defunct

47-48 EX: Ford Sports (H) 3-0
PR: Clapton (H) 4-1
Q1: Grays Athletic (A) 0-3

WESTWOOD WORKS (PETERBOROUGH)

Currently: Defunct

45-46 Q1: Kettering Town (A) 0-5

46-47 Q2: Peterborough United (A) 0-3

47-48 Q1: Peterborough United (H) 1-5

48-49 Q1: Desborough Town (H) *withdrew*

WEYMOUTH

Currently: Southern League

47-48 EX: Longfleet St Mary's (H) 4-1
PR: Newport Isle of Wight (A) 2-5

48-49 EX: Bournemouth (H) 8-3
PR: Andover (H) 3-0
Q1: Newport Isle of Wight (A) 4-2
Q2: Longfleet St Mary's (A) 4-0
Q3: Poole Town (H) 4-2
Q4: Trowbridge Town (H) 2-0
R1: Chelmsford City (H) 2-1
R2: Yeovil Town (H) 0-4

49-50 PR: Totton (H) 6-3
Q1: Ryde Sports (A) 6-2
Q2: Poole Town (H) 4-0
Q3: Cowes (A) 5-1
Q4: Trowbridge Town (H) 3-3, (A) 2-1
R1: Aldershot (H) 2-2, (A) 3-2
R2: Hereford United (H) 2-1
R3: Manchester United (A) 0-4

50-51 Q4: Llanelly (A) 0-5

51-52 Q4: Yeovil Town (A) 1-1, (H) 2-1
R1: Brush Sports (A) 3-2
R2: Bristol Rovers (A) 0-2

52-53 Q4: Dorchester Town (A) 5-1
R1: Colchester United (H) 1-1, (A) 0-4

53-54 Q4: Chippenham Town (A) 4-2
R1: Bedford Town (H) 2-0
R2: Leyton Orient (A) 0-4

54-55 Q4: Frome Town (A) 1-3

55-56 Q4: Poole Town (A) 3-2
R1: Salisbury (H) 3-2
R2: Southend United (H) 0-1

56-57 Q4: Chippenham Town (A) 0-0, (H) 4-1
R1: Shrewsbury Town (H) 1-0
R2: Southampton (A) 2-3

57-58 Q4: Dorchester Town (H) 2-2, (A) 1-2

58-59 Q4: Dorchester Town (H) 3-0
R1: Coventry City (H) 2-5

59-60 Q4: Dorchester Town (H) 0-1

60-61 Q2: Warminster Town (H) 5-1
Q3: Poole Town (H) 1-1, (A) 4-3
Q4: Salisbury (H) 1-1, (A) 2-1
R1: Torquay United (H) 1-3

61-62 Q4: Dorchester Town (A) 3-3, (H) 2-0
R1: Barnet (H) 1-0
R2: Newport County (H) 1-0
R3: Morecambe (A) 1-0
R4: Preston North End (A) 0-2

62-63 Q4: Poole Town (A) 0-0, (H) 0-2

63-64 Q4: Dorchester Town (H) 3-0
R1: Bedford Town (H) 1-1, (A) 0-1

64-65 Q4: Fareham Town (H) 3-2
R1: Welton Rovers (A) 1-1, (H) 4-3
R2: Bristol Rovers (A) 1-4

65-66 Q4: Bideford (H) 1-1, (A) 3-1
R1: Bournemouth & B.A. (A) 0-0, (H) 1-4

66-67 Q4: Bath City (A) 2-2, (H) 0-1

67-68 Q4: Bath City (H) 1-1, (A) 1-0
R1: Leyton Orient (H) 0-2

68-69 Q4: Poole Town (H) 1-1, (A) 1-0
R1: Yeovil Town (H) 2-1
R2: Swansea Town (H) 1-1, (A) 0-2

69-70 Q4: Salisbury (A) 1-0
R1: Northampton Town (A) 0-0, (H) 1-3

70-71 Q4: Bideford (H) 3-0
R1: Southend United (A) 0-7

71-72 Q4: Bideford (H) 3-1
R1: Cambridge United (A) 1-2

72-73 Q4: Barnstaple Town (A) 0-1

73-74 Q1: Poole Town (A) 3-0
Q2: Salisbury (H) 2-0
Q3: Taunton Town (A) 2-1
Q4: Yeovil Town (A) 1-1, (H) 2-2, 1-0
R1: Merthyr Tydfil (H) 0-1

74-75 Q1: Dorchester Town (A) 3-1
Q2: Welton Rovers (H) 7-1
Q3: Poole Town (A) 3-0
Q4: Minehead (A) 3-0
R1: Peterborough U. (A) 0-0, (H) 3-3, (A) 0-3

75-76 Q4: Salisbury (A) 5-4
R1: Gillingham (H) 0-2

76-77 Q4: Poole Town (A) 3-2
R1: Hitchin Town (H) 1-1, (A) 2-2, (*at Aldershot*) 3-3, (*At Salisbury*) 1-3

77-78 Q4: Worcester City (A) 2-2, (H) 2-1
R1: Gillingham (A) 1-1, (H) 0-1

78-79 Q4: Taunton Town (A) 2-0
R1: Aldershot (A) 1-1, (H) 0-2

79-80 Q4: Yeovil Town (A) 1-2

80-81 Q4: Taunton Town (H) 0-0, (A) 3-0
R1: Swindon (A) 2-3

81-82 Q4: Farnborough Town (H) 3-0
R1: Northampton Town (H) 0-0, (A) 2-6

82-83 Q4: Cheltenham Town (A) 0-0, (H) 4-0
R1: Maidstone United (H) 4-3
R2: Cardiff City (A) 3-2
R3: Cambridge United (A) 0-1

83-84 Q4: Farnborough Town (H) 1-1, (A) 2-3

84-85 Q4: Worcester City (H) 3-1
R1: Millwall (H) 0-3

85-86 Q4: Ton Pentre (A) 3-1
R1: Chelmsford City (A) 0-1

86-87 Q4: Woking (A) 0-1

87-88 Q1: Frome Town (A) 2-2, (H) 3-0
Q2: Radstock Town (H) 3-0
Q3: Fareham Town (H) 2-2, (A) 2-0
Q4: Yeovil Town (H) 1-3

88-89 Q1: Trowbridge Town (A) 2-1
Q2: Weston-super-Mare (A) 1-0
Q3: Forest Green Rovers (H) 3-0
Q4: Newport County (A) 1-2

89-90 Q1: Barnstaple Town (H) 6-2
Q2: St Blazey (H) 2-0
Q3: Exmouth Town (A) 0-2

90-91 Q1: St Blazey (A) 2-0
Q2: Swanage Town & Hers. (A) 1-1, (H) 2-1

Q3: Bashley (A) 2-2, (H) 2-3

91-92 Q1: Wimborne Town (A) 2-1
Q2: Barry Town (H) 1-1, (A) 3-2
Q3: Cheltenham Town (H) 4-0
Q4: Sutton United (H) 1-1, (A) 0-3

92-93 Q1: Saltash United (H) 1-0
Q2: Truro City (H) 3-2
Q3: Bath City (A) 0-2

WEYMOUTH S.A.A.
Currently: Defunct

46-47 PR: Bournemouth Gasworks Ath. (A) *withdrew*

WHEELOCK ALBION
Currently: Defunct

47-48 PR: Northwich Victoria (A) 1-8

48-49 EX: Lostock Gralam (A) 0-4

49-50 PR: Winsford United (A) 1-9

WHICKHAM
Currently: Northern League

89-90 Q1: North Shields (A) 0-1

90-91 PR: North Shields (A) 0-2

91-92 PR: Garforth Town (A) 1-4

92-93 PR: Newcastle Blue Star (A) 0-0, (H) 0-2

WHITBY ALBION RANGERS
Currently: Defunct

46-47 Q1: Whitby United (H) 2-6

47-48 PR: South Bank St Peter's (H) 2-0
Q1: Guisborough (A) 2-1
Q2: Stockton (A) 1-8

48-49 PR: Filey Town (A) 1-3

49-50 Q1: South Bank (H) 1-2

WHITBY TOWN
Currently: Northern League
* - Whitby United

45-46 * Q2: Stockton (A) 0-4

46-47 * Q1: Whitby Albion Rangers (A) 6-2
Q2: Stockton (H) 0-2

47-48 * Q1: Filey Town (H) 4-2
Q2: Portrack Shamrocks (H) 1-0
Q3: Stockton (H) 1-3

48-49 * PR: Bridlington Central United (A) 1-4

49-50 * PR: South Bank East End (A) 5-2
Q1: Billingham Synthonia (H) 2-2, (A) 0-5

50-51 PR: Skinningrove Works (A) 5-0
Q1: Cargo Fleet Works (H) 10-2
Q2: Head Wrightsons (H) 4-2
Q3: Scarborough (A) 0-3

51-52 Q1: Bridlington Central United (H) 6-2
Q2: South Bank (H) 3-2
Q3: Billingham Synthonia Recreation (H) 2-3

52-53 Q2: Ferryhill Athletic (A) 0-4

53-54 Q1: Billingham Synthonia Recreation (A) 1-2

54-55 Q1: South Bank (A) 1-2

55-56 Q2: Bridlington Central Utd (A) 4-4, (H) 0-1

56-57 Q2: South Bank (H) 5-1
Q3: Billingham Synthonia Recreation (H) 2-3

57-58 Q1: Tow Law Town (A) 2-2, (H) 5-1
Q2: Willington (A) 2-5

58-59 Q1: Consett (A) 1-2

59-60 Q1: Tow Law Town (A) 1-2

60-61 Q1: Stockton (H) 1-2

61-62 Q1: Bedlington Mechanics (A) 2-4

62-63 Q1: Bedlington Mechanics (A) 1-3

63-64 Q1: Willington (H) 4-2
Q2: Spennymoor United (H) 2-2, (A) 2-0
Q3: Stanley United (A) 0-2

65-66 Q1: Billingham Synthonia (A) 2-1
Q2: Willington (A) 2-1

Above: *Northern League Whitby Town attack against Chesterfield in 1984.*

Q3: Spennymoor United (H) 4-3
Q4: Crook Town (H) 1-1, (A) 1-4

66-67 Q1: Consett (A) 3-2
Q2: Billingham Synthonia (H) 1-1, (A) 0-1

67-68 Q1: Billingham Synthonia (A) 6-2
Q2: Blyth Spartans (H) 2-0
Q3: Spennymoor United (H) 0-1

68-69 Q1: Horden Colliery Welfare (A) 1-2

69-70 PR: West Auckland Town (H) 1-0
Q1: Bedlington Colliery Welfare (A) 1-0
Q2: Wingate (H) 3-1
Q3: Evenwood Town (A) 2-1
Q4: Scarborough (H) 3-1
R1: York City (A) 0-2

71-72 Q1: Hull Brunswick (A) 3-1
Q2: Scarborough (H) 0-2

72-73 PR: Goole Town (H) 0-1

73-74 Q1: Wingate (A) 1-2

74-75 Q1: Bridlington Trinity (H) 1-1, (A) 1-0
Q2: Winterton Rangers (A) 2-3

75-76 Q1: Wingate (H) 4-0
Q2: Willington (A) 0-2

76-77 Q1: Spennymoor United (H) 3-0
Q2: Whitley Bay (H) 2-0
Q3: Barrow (A) 2-2, (H) 3-4

77-78 PR: Wallsend Town (A) 3-2
Q1: Tow Law Town (A) 4-0
Q2: Boldon Community Association (A) 1-2

78-79 Q1: Worsborough B.M.W. (H) 3-3, (A) 1-0
Q2: Yorkshire Amateur (H) 1-2

79-80 PR: Normanby Park Works (A) 3-1
Q1: Thackley (A) 2-2, (H) 2-0
Q2: Frickley Athletic (H) 3-2
Q3: Goole Town (H) 2-2, (A) 1-2

80-81 PR: Yorkshire Amateur (H) 3-1
Q1: South Bank (H) 3-0
Q2: Barrow (A) 1-1, (H) 1-2

81-82 Q1: Frickley Athletic (A) 0-2

82-83 PR: Morecambe (A) 0-2

83-84 Q1: Harrogate Town (A) 4-2
Q2: Durham City (A) 3-1
Q3: Lancaster City (A) 2-2, (H) 7-3
Q4: Bishop Auckland (H) 4-2
R1: Halifax Town (A) 3-2
R2: Wigan Athletic (A) 0-1

84-85 Q1: Willington (A) 5-2
Q2: North Shields (H) 1-1, (A) 2-2, (A) 1-1, (H) 2-0
Q3: Ryhope C.A. (A) 1-1, (H) 5-1
Q4: Marine (A) 1-0
R1: Chesterfield (H) 1-3

85-86 Q4: Peterlee Newtown (H) 2-2, (A) 1-0
R1: South Liverpool (H) 1-0
R2: York City (A) 1-3

86-87 Q4: Newcastle Blue Star (H) 2-0
R1: Doncaster Rovers (H) 2-2, (A) 2-3

87-88 Q4: Macclesfield Town (A) 1-3

88-89 Q4: Barrow (A) 1-1, (H) 1-3

89-90 Q1: Hebburn (H) 1-3

90-91 PR: Leyland Daf-S.G.L. (H) 2-0
Q1: Newcastle Blue Star (H) 4-7

91-92 Q1: Garforth Town (H) 0-1

92-93 PR: Willington (A) 5-1
Q1: Shildon (A) 2-0
Q2: Gateshead (A) 2-5

WHITEHAWK
Currently: Sussex County League

82-83 PR: Dartford (A) 2-5

83-84 PR: Horndean (H) 3-0
Q1: Whitstable Town (A) 2-1
Q2: Walton & Hersham (H) 4-1
Q3: Tooting & Mitcham United (A) 0-3

84-85 Q1: Sheppey United (A) 0-2

85-86 Q1: Kingstonian (A) 0-1

86-87 Q1: Eastbourne Town (H) 2-3

87-88 PR: Horsham (A) 0-0, (H) 2-0
Q1: Littlehampton Town (H) 1-2

88-89 PR: Lancing (H) 2-0
Q1: Bracknell Town (A) 2-1
Q2: Steyning Town (A) 3-1
Q3: Windsor & Eton (A) 1-1, (H) 1-0
Q4: Bognor Regis Town (A) 2-2, (H - *at Brighton & Hove Albion*) 0-2

89-90 Q1: A.F.C. Totton (A) 2-4

90-91 PR: Steyning Town (A) 2-1
Q1: Redhill (A) 3-2
Q2: Margate (H) 0-1

91-92 Q1: Bromley (H) 0-2

92-93 PR: Chichester (H) 5-2 *extra-time erroneosly played*, (A) 3-1
Q1: Sittingbourne (H) 0-1

WHITLEY BAY
Currently: Northern Premier League
* - As Whitley Bay Athletic

56-57 * Q1: Ashington (H) 1-3

57-58 * Q1: West Auckland Town (A) 2-1
Q2: Crook Town (H) 0-5

58-59 * Q1: Annfield Plain (A) 1-1, (H) 2-1
Q2: Cramlington Welfare (A) 4-3
Q3: Blackhall Colliery Welf. (A) 2-2, (H) 5-0
Q4: Consett (A) 0-3

59-60 Q2: Willington (A) 1-4

60-61 Q1: Scarborough (A) 1-4

61-62 Q1: Boldon Colliery Welfare (H) 5-2
Q2: Horden Colliery Welfare (H) 0-4

62-63 Q2: Annfield Plain (A) 2-2, (H) 0-1

63-64 Q1: Durham City (H) 4-0
Q2: Tow Law Town (A) 1-3

65-66 Q1: Annfield Plain (H) 11-0

Q2: Stanley United (A) 2-2, (H) 1-0
Q3: Horden Colliery Welfare (A) 0-1

66-67 Q1: Blyth Spartans (A) 1-4

67-68 Q1: Stanley United (A) 2-3

68-69 Q1: Shildon (H) 0-1

69-70 Q1: Stanley United (H) 2-1
Q2: Annfield Plain (H) 7-1
Q3: Spennymoor United (H) 2-3

70-71 Q1: Billingham Synthonia (A) 4-2
Q2: Evenwood Town (A) 0-1

71-72 Q1: Stockton (A) 2-2, (H) 5-2
Q2: Evenwood Town (H) 3-1
Q3: Durham City (H) 3-1
Q4: Blyth Spartans (H) 1-1, (A) 1-2

72-73 Q1: Bishop Auckland (H) 0-1

73-74 Q1: West Auckland Town (A) 1-1, (H) 4-1
Q2: North Shields (A) 0-0, (H) 1-1, 2-2, 0-3

74-75 Q1: North Shields (H) 1-1, (A) 3-1
Q2: Bishop Auckland (H) 2-2, (A) 3-4

75-76 Q1: Penrith (A) 0-1

76-77 Q1: Boldon Community Association (H) 5-0
Q2: Whitby Town (A) 0-2

77-78 Q1: Easington C.W. (A) 4-4, (H) 3-2
Q2: Billingham Synthonia (H) 3-1
Q3: Spennymoor United (H) 2-2, (A) 1-4

78-79 Q1: Shildon (A) 1-3

79-80 PR: South Bank (A) 1-4

80-81 Q1: Goole Town (A) 0-1

81-82 PR: Blue Star (A) 0-0, (H) 3-1
Q1: Willington (H) 3-1
Q2: Consett (H) 1-0
Q3: South Bank (H) 0-2

82-83 PR: Bridlington Trinity (A) 1-3

83-84 PR: Easington Colliery (A) 0-2

84-85 Q1: Ashington (A) 1-3

85-86 Q1: Ryhope Community Association (A) 3-1
Q2: Blyth Spartans (H) 1-2

86-87 Q1: North Shields (H) 2-3

87-88 Q1: Clitheroe (A) 0-2

88-89 PR: Wren Rovers (A) 3-0
Q1: Shildon (A) 5-1
Q2: Gretna (A) 1-1, (H) 1-0
Q3: Brandon United (H) 0-1

89-90 PR: Horden Colliery Welfare (A) 3-0
Q1: Willington (H) 6-0
Q2: Spennymoor United (A) 4-2
Q3: Barrow (A) 2-2, (H) 3-1
Q4: Southport (A) 3-1
R1: Scarborough (A) 1-0
R2: Preston North End (H) 2-0
R3: Rochdale (A) 0-1

Below: *Whitley Bay's Warren Teasdale roasts the Rochdale defence. Photo: Alan Pearson.*

90-91 Q4: Colwyn Bay (A) 4-1
R1: Tamworth (A) 6-4
R2: Barrow (H) 0-1

91-92 Q4: Witton Albion (H) 1-4

92-93 Q4: Gatesead (A) 0-3

WHITSTABLE TOWN

Currently: Kent League
* - As Whitstable F.C.

46-47 * PR: Ashford (H) 3-10

47-48 * EX: Chatham (A) *W/O*
PR: Ashford (A) 1-4

48-49 * PR: Ashford (H) 0-1

49-50 * EX: Snowdown Colliery Welfare (A) 1-2

50-51 * EX: Chatham Town (H) 1-0
PR: Ashford Town (H) 0-2

51-52 * PR: Dover (H) 0-4

54-55 * Q1: Epsom (H) 0-0, (A) 4-1
Q2: Dover (A) 1-2

55-56 * PR: Dover (A) 1-5

56-57 * PR: Ashford Town (A) 1-3

57-58 * PR: Maidstone United (A) 3-1
Q1: Canterbury City (H) 2-2, (A) 5-1
Q2: Betteshanger Colliery Welfare (H) 2-0
Q3: Gravesend & Northfleet (H) 0-3

58-59 * Q1: Deal Town (A) 4-3
Q2: Ashford Town (H) 1-2

59-60 * Q1: Folkestone Town (H) 1-6

60-61 * Q1: Snowdown Colliery Welfare (A) 1-6

61-62 * Q1: Canterbury City (H - *played away*) 0-4

62-63 * Q1: Sittingbourne (H - *played away*) 0-10

63-64 * Q1: Canterbury City (A) 1-7

64-65 * Q1: Deal Town (H) 2-7

65-66 * Q1: Herne Bay (H) 1-3

67-68 Q1: Sittingbourne (H) 1-1, (A) 3-3, 3-2
Q2: Dover (H) 1-7

68-69 Q1: Canterbury City (A) 0-1

69-70 PR: Tunbridge Wells (A) 1-2

70-71 Q1: Folkestone (H) 2-7

71-72 Q1: Snowdon Colliery Welfare (A) 4-1
Q2: Dover (H) 0-5

72-73 Q1: Sittingbourne (A) 0-2

73-74 Q1: Lewes (A) 1-4

74-75 Q1: Medway (A) 2-4

75-76 Q1: Sheppey United (A) 1-5

76-77 PR: Herne Bay (A) 1-4

77-78 PR: Ashford Town (H) 0-1

78-79 Q1: Folkestone & Shepway (H) 1-1, (A) 0-5

79-80 PR: Horsham (A) 1-2

80-81 PR: Haywards Heath (A) 0-1

81-82 PR: Sheppey United (H) 2-2, (A) 2-1
Q1: Tonbridge A.F.C. (A) 1-3

82-83 Q1: Bromley (H) 1-0
Q2: Bognor Regis Town (H) 0-3

83-84 Q1: Whitehawk (H) 1-2

84-85 PR: Burgess Hill Town (H) 1-0
Q1: Croydon (H) 0-0, (A) 0-5

85-86 PR: Ringmer (A) 1-2

86-87 Q1: Tonbridge A.F.C. (H) 2-1
Q2: Folkestone (H) 2-1
Q3: Herne Bay (A) 0-1

89-90 Q1: Deal Town (A) 3-1
Q2: Walton & Hersham (A) 1-0
Q3: Hythe Town (A) 0-2

90-91 Q1: Sittingbourne (A) 1-1, (H) 1-4

91-92 PR: Eastbourne United (H) 0-1

92-93 PR: Sittingbourne (H) 1-2

WHITTON UNITED

Currently: Suffolk & Ipswich League

47-48 PR: Gorleston (A) 4-2
Q1: Lowestoft Town (H) 3-5

48-49 PR: Gorleston (A) 3-5

49-50 PR: Churchman Spts (A - *played home*) 3-0
Q1: Great Yarmouth Town (A) 1-4

50-51 PR: Lowestoft Town (H) 1-3

51-52 Q1: Leiston (H) 4-1
Q2: Sudbury Town (H) 1-2

52-53 Q1: Sudbury Town (H) 0-4

53-54 Q2: Stowmarket (A) 1-4

54-55 Q1: Lowestoft Town (A) 0-3

55-56 Q1: Bury Town (A) 2-4

56-57 Q1: Diss Town (A) 3-6

57-58 Q1: Long Melford (H) 2-0
Q2: Stowmarket (H) 2-4

58-59 Q1: Leiston (A) 6-2
Q2: Harwich & Parkeston (H) 0-2

59-60 Q1: Harwich & Parkeston (H) 1-2

WHITWICK COLLIERY

Currently: Defunct

48-49 PR: Nuneaton Borough (H) 2-1
Q1: Bedworth Town (A) 3-1
Q2: Gresley Rovers (A) 3-0
Q3: Brush Sports (H) 1-2

50-51 PR: Barwell Athletic (A) 2-1
Q1: Brush Sports (A) 2-5

51-52 Q1: Brush Sports (H) 0-3

52-53 Q1: Hinckley Athletic (A) 3-2
Q2: South Normanton (A) 0-3

53-54 Q2: Brush Sports (H) 3-5

54-55 PR: Heanor Town (A) 5-2
Q1: Coalville Town (H) 14-0
Q2: Raleigh Athletic (A) 1-0
Q3: Hinckley Athletic (H) 2-2 (A) 1-4

55-56 Q1: Long Eaton Town (A) 3-2
Q2: Players Athletic (A) 4-1
Q3: Brush Sports (A) 0-1

56-57 Q2: Heanor Town (A) 0-2

WHYTELEAFE

Currently: Isthmian League

69-70 Q1: Croydon Amateurs (H) 1-1, (A) 1-1, 1-0
Q2: Staines Town (H) 1-2

81-82 PR: Clapton (A) 0-1

82-83 Q1: Wokingham Town (H) 0-0, (A) 0-1

83-84 Q1: Feltham (A) 1-0
Q2: Slough Town (H) 0-5

84-85 Q1: Staines Town (H) 0-1

85-86 PR: Horsham Y.M.C.A. (A) 3-0
Q1: Eastbourne United (H) 2-1
Q2: Canterbury City (H) 1-2

86-87 Q1: Redhill (H) 0-2

87-88 Q1: Lancing (H) 2-0
Q2: Wokingham Town (H) 3-3, (A) 0-1

88-89 PR: Arundel (H) 6-0
Q1: Tooting & Mitcham United (H) 2-1
Q2: Southwick (A) 1-0
Q3: Woking (H) 0-2

89-90 Q1: Sittingbourne (H) 1-0
Q2: Malden Vale (H) 2-0
Q3: Wokingham Town (A) 1-1, (H) 1-2

90-91 Q1: Slade Green (H) 2-1
Q2: Tonbridge A.F.C. (H) 0-2

91-92 PR: Ashford Town (H) 2-0
Q1: Worthing (H) 1-2

92-93 PR: Pagham (H) 5-1
Q1: Windsor & Eton (H) 1-5

WICK

Currently: Sussex County League

80-81 Q1: Hungerford Town (A) 1-5

81-82 PR: Arundel (A) 4-1
Q1: Woking (H) 2-1
Q2: Farnborough Town (H) 2-2, (A) 0-3

82-83 Q1: Corinthian-Casuals (H) 1-2

83-84 PR: Newport Isle of Wight (H) 2-1
Q1: Farnborough Town (H) 1-2

84-85 Q1: Eastbourne Town (A) 2-9

86-87 PR: Molesey (A) 3-0
Q1: Dover Athletic (H) 0-4

87-88 PR: Petersfield United (A) 1-1 (H) 4-3
Q1: Tooting & Mitcham (H) 1-1, (A) 0-3

88-89 PR: Corinthian (A) 1-2

89-90 PR: Margate (A) 1-2

90-91 PR: Three Bridges (A) 3-1
Q1: Dorking (H) 0-3

Right: *The Wick defence have some trouble containing Dorking forward Steve Lunn (nearest camera) in the tie at Crabtree Park on 15th September 1990.*
Photo: Dennis Nicholson.

91-92 PR: Lancing (A) 1-4

92-93 PR: Ashford Town (H) 1-1, (A) 1-3

WIGAN ATHLETIC

Currently: Football League

45-46 Q2: Chorley (A) 2-5

46-47 PR: Crossens (A - *played home*) 3-2
Q1: Morecambe (A) 3-0
Q2: Darwen (H) 1-2

47-48 PR: Formby (A) 4-0
Q1: Earlestown (A) 1-0
Q2: Rhyl (H) 2-1
Q3: Prescot Cables (H) 3-0
Q4: Marine (A) 1-3

48-49 PR: Skelmersdale United (H) 2-1
Q1: Prescot Cables (H) 1-2

49-50 EX: U.G.B. St Helens (H) 2-0
PR: South Liverpool (A) 1-0
Q1: Burscough (H) 1-1, (A) 5-1
Q2: Bootle Athletic (H) 6-1
Q3: Rhyl (A) 0-2

50-51 PR: South Liverpool (A) 0-0, (H) 3-2
Q1: Flint Town United (H) 1-1, (A) 3-1
Q2: Crompton's Recreation (H) 1-0
Q3: Burscough (A) 2-0
Q4: Rhyl (A) 0-0, (H) 2-3

51-52 Q4: Witton Albion (H) 2-2, (A) 3-3, 1-2

52-53 Q4: Netherfield (H) 2-3

53-54 Q4: Burscough (H) 2-1
R1: Scarborough (H) 4-0
R2: Hereford United (H) 4-1
R3: Newcastle United (A) 2-2, (H) 2-3

54-55 Q4: Farsley Celtic (H) 3-1
R1: Barnsley (A) 2-3

55-56 Q4: Ashton United (A) 0-5

56-57 Q4: Netherfield (H) 2-2, (A) 3-3, 2-0
R1: Goole Town (H) 1-2

57-58 Q4: Chorley (A) 2-1
R1: Southport (A) 2-1
R2: Mansfield Town (H) 1-1, (A) 1-3

58-59 Q4: Rhyl (A) 0-1

59-60 Q4: Rhyl (H) 1-1, (A) 1-3

60-61 PR: Prescot Cables (H) 2-0
Q1: Ashton United (H) 3-2
Q2: Marine (A) 5-1
Q3: Skelmersdale United (A) 0-0, (H) 2-1
Q4: Rhyl (H) 0-0, (A) 1-2

61-62 Q1: Skelmersdale United (A) 4-0
Q2: Prescot Cables (H) 1-1, (A) 3-1
Q3: Altrincham (A) 1-1, (H) 3-1
Q4: Morecambe (A) 0-2

62-63 Q1: Milnthorpe Corinthians (H) 5-0
Q2: Fleetwood (H) 8-1
Q3: Netherfield (A) 3-0
Q4: Ellesmere Port Town (H) 2-0
R1: Gateshead (A) 1-2

63-64 Q4: Bangor City (H) 1-1, (A) 0-1

64-65 Q4: Stalybridge Celtic (A) 4-2
R1: Stockport County (A) 1-2

65-66 Q4: Chorley (H) 4-0
R1: Doncaster Rovers (A) 2-2, (H) 3-1
R2: Chester (A) 1-2

66-67 Q4: Altrincham (A) 4-2
R1: Tranmere Rovers (A) 1-1, (H) 0-1

67-68 Q4: Macclesfield Town (H) 1-1, (A) 0-3

68-69 Q4: Altrincham (A) 0-2

69-70 Q1: Chorley (H) 1-1, (A) 5-2
Q2: Droylsden (H) 4-1
Q3: Burscough (H) 1-1, (A) 3-2
Q4: Skelmersdale United (H) 2-0
R1: Pt Vale (H) 1-1, (A) 2-2, (*at Man. Utd*) 0-1

70-71 Q4: Skelmersdale United (A) 1-1 (H) 5-0
R1: South Shields (A) 1-1, (H) 2-0
R2: Peterborough United (H) 2-1
R3: Manchester City (A) 0-1

71-72 Q4: Rhyl (H) 2-1
R1: Halifax Town (H) 2-1
R2: Wrexham (A) 0-4

72-73 Q4: Burscough (A) 3-1
R1: Grimsby Town (A) 1-2

73-74 R1: Huddersfield Town (A) 0-2

74-75 Q4: Kidderminster Harriers (H) 4-0
R1: Shrewsbury Town (A) 1-1, (H) 2-1
R2: Mansfield Town (H) 1-1, (A) 1-3

75-76 R1: Matlock Town (H) 4-1
R2: Sheffield Wednesday (A) 0-2

76-77 R1: Matlock Town (A) 0-2

77-78 Q4: Marine (A) 3-0
R1: York City (H) 1-0
R2: Sheffield Wednesday (H) 1-0
R3: Birmingham City (A) 0-4

78-79 R1: Bury (H) 2-2, (A) 1-4

79-80 R1: Blackpool (A) 1-1, (H) 2-0
R2: Northwich Victoria (A) 3-0 *abandoned (fog) after 67 minutes*, (A) 2-2, (H) 1-0
R3: Chelsea (A) 1-0
R4: Everton (A) 0-3

80-81 R1: Chesterfield (H) 2-2, (A) 0-2

81-82 R1: Hartlepool United (H) 2-2, (A) 0-1

82-83 R1: Telford United (H) 0-0, (A) 1-2

83-84 R1: Bradford City (A) 0-0, (H) 4-2
R2: Whitby Town (H) 1-0
R3: West Ham (A) 0-1

84-85 R1: Wrexham (A) 2-0
R2: Northwich Victoria (H) 2-1
R3: Chelsea (A) 2-2, (H) 0-5

85-86 R1: Doncaster Rovers (H) 4-1
R2: Runcorn (A) 1-1, (H) 4-0
R3: A.F.C. Bournemouth (H) 3-0
R4: Southampton (A) 0-3

86-87 R1: Lincoln City (H) 3-1
R2: Darlington (A) 5-0
R3: Gillingham (H) 2-1
R4: Norwich City (H) 1-0
R5: Hull City (H) 3-0
R6: Leeds United (H) 0-2

87-88 R1: Altrincham (A) 2-0
R2: Wolverhampton Wanderers (H) 1-3

88-89 R1: Hartlepool United (A) 0-2

89-90 R1: Mansfield Town (H) 2-0
R2: Carlisle United (H) 2-0
R3: Watford (A) 0-2

90-91 R1: Carlisle United (H) 5-0
R2: Hartlepool United (H) 2-0
R3: Coventry City (A) 1-1, (H) 0-1

91-92 R1: Scarborough (A) 2-0
R2: Stockport County (H) 2-0
R3: Notts County (A) 0-2

92-93 R1: Carlisle United (H) 3-1
R2: Bury (H) 1-1, (A) 0-1

WIGAN ROVERS

Currently: Defunct

67-68 Q1: Horwich R.M.I. (A) 1-3

68-69 Q1: Horwich R.M.I. (H) 1-1, (A) 0-2

69-70 Q1: Formby (H) 0-6

72-73 Q1: Burscough (A) 0-2

WIGMORE ATHLETIC

See Worthing United

WIGSTON FIELDS

Currently: Midland Combination

83-84 PR: Coventry Sporting (H) 3-1
Q1: Buckingham Town (H) 1-4

84-85 Q1: Desborough T. (A) 0-0, (H) 1-1, (A) 2-1
Q2: Stourbridge (H) 1-6

85-86 PR: Wellingborough Town (A) 0-4

86-87 Q1: Leamington (H) 2-1
Q2: Kidderminster Harriers (H) 0-5

WILLENHALL TOWN

Currently: West Midlands (Regional) League

77-78 Q1: Highgate United (A) 1-2

78-79 Q1: Oldbury United (A) 1-1, (H) 2-0
Q2: Banbury United (H) 2-0
Q3: Kempston Rovers (H) 0-2

79-80 PR: Rothwell Town (A) 2-0
Q1: Sutton Coldfield Town (A) 2-3

80-81 Q1: Burton Albion (A) 2-2 (H) 1-2

81-82 Q1: Oldbury United (A) 2-0
Q2: Gresley Rovers (A) 3-3, (H) 1-0
Q3: Shepshed Charterhouse (A) 5-1
Q4: Burton Albion (H) 2-1
R1: Crewe Alexandra (H) 0-1

82-83 Q1: Armitage (A) 2-3

83-84 PR: Lye Town (A) 0-1

84-85 Q1: Banbury United (A) 4-1
Q2: Bedworth United (H) 3-0
Q3: Burton Albion (A) 1-2

85-86 Q1: Hinckley Athletic (A) 1-2

86-87 Q1: Paget Rangers (H) 1-0
Q2: Wolverton Town (A) 0-2

87-88 Q1: Bromsgrove Rovers (H) 3-2
Q2: Bilston Town (A) 3-0
Q3: Oldbury United (A) 1-0
Q4: Barnet (H) 0-6

88-89 Q1: Malvern Town (H) 3-3, (A) 0-0, (H) 0-2

89-90 PR: Nuneaton Borough (A) 1-1, (H) 1-0
Q1: Spalding United (H) 1-1, (A) 2-0
Q2: Matlock Town (A) 0-5

90-91 PR: Brigg Town (H) 1-1, (A) 1-1, (A) 3-1
Q1: Marine (H) 0-0, (A) 2-2, (A) 1-4

91-92 PR: Wellingborough Town (H) 6-1
Q1: Racing Club Warwick (H) 2-1
Q2: Burton Albion (A) 1-4

92-93 PR: Hinckley Town (A) 1-1, (H) 2-1
Q1: Pelsall Villa (A) 0-1

WILLESDEN

Currently: Defunct

47-48 EX: Leavesden (A) 1-7

48-49 EX: Chipperfield (H) 7-1
PR: Wealdstone (A) 0-4

49-50 EX: Stevenage Town (A) 2-2, (H) 7-2
PR: Wood Green Town (A) 1-0
Q1: Hatfield United (A) 1-4

50-51 PR: Enfield (A) 1-5

75-76 Q1: Molesey (A) 1-4

76-77 PR: Harrow Borough (A) 1-3

77-78 PR: Bedford Town (H) 4-3
Q1: Chesham United (A) 0-5

78-79 Q1: Staines Town (A) 1-2

79-80 PR: Haringey Borough (A) 1-0
Q1: Met. Police (A) 1-1, (H) 1-1, 0-3

80-81 PR: Staines Town (A) 1-0
Q1: Carshalton Athletic (H) 0-2

81-82 PR: Didcot Town (A) *scratched*

WILLIAM COLLIERY (WHITEHAVEN)

Currently: Defunct

46-47 PR: Kells Welfare Centre (A) 0-4

47-48 PR: Distington (H) 8-2
Q1: Milnthorpe Corinthians (H) 3-4

WILLINGTON

Currently: Northern League

45-46 Q4: Shildon (H) 3-2
R1: Bishop Auck. (H) 0-5, (A) 2-0 (*agg: 2-5*)

46-47 PR: Spennymoor United (A) 2-7

47-48 EX: Blackhall Colliery Welfare (A) 1-2

48-49 EX: Silksworth Colliery Welfare (A) 3-4

49-50 EX: Seaham United (H) 8-0
PR: Spennymoor United (H) 2-2, (A) 4-2
Q1: Horden Colliery Welfare (H) 2-2, (A) 0-4

50-51 R1: Rochdale (A) 1-3

51-52 Q1: Tow Law Town (A) 4-4, (H) 2-1
Q2: Crook Town (A) 1-2

52-53 Q1: West Auckland Town (H) 2-4

53-54 Q1: Evenwood Town (H) 2-0
Q2: Shildon (H) 3-0
Q3: Spennymoor United (A) 1-2

54-55 Q1: Shildon (A) 2-1
Q2: Stanley United (H) 0-1

55-56 Q1: Cockfield (H) 3-1
Q2: Shildon (H) 3-3, (A) 3-7

56-57 Q1: Wolsingham Welfare (A) 8-1
Q2: Evenwood Town (A) 1-2

57-58 Q1: Stockton (H) 1-0
Q2: Whitby Town (H) 5-2
Q3: Shildon (A) 2-1
Q4: Durham City (A) 0-2

58-59 Q1: Shotton Colliery Welfare (H) 6-0
Q2: Wolsingham Welfare (A) 4-1
Q3: Consett (A) 0-0, (H) 1-2

59-60 Q2: Whitley Bay (H) 4-1
Q3: West Auckland Town (H) 0-2

60-61 Q2: Scarborough (A) 2-5

61-62 Q1: Shotton C.W. (H) 2-2, (A) 3-2
Q2: Newburn (H) 3-2
Q3: North Shields (H) 2-4

62-63 Q1: Ashington (A) 3-4

63-64 Q1: Whitby Town (A) 2-4

64-65 Q1: Penrith (A) 2-4

65-66 Q1: Durham City (A) 8-0
Q2: Whitby Town (H) 1-2

66-67 Q1: Bishop Auckland (H) 0-3

67-68 Q1: Durham City (H) 1-3

68-69 Q1: Durham City (A) 0-1

69-70 Q1: Evenwood Town (H) 2-4

70-71 Q1: Blyth Spartans (A) 1-2

71-72 Q1: Washington (A) 1-1, (H) 1-0
Q2: Blyth Spartans (A) 1-3

72-73 Q1: Wingate (A) 4-1
Q2: Consett (A) 2-1
Q3: Ferryhill Athletic (A) 5-1
Q4: Spennymoor United (H) 0-2

73-74 Q1: Stanley United (A) 6-1
Q2: Durham City (H) 3-1
Q3: North Shields (H) 3-0
Q4: Ashington (H) 1-0
R1: Blackburn Rovers (H) 0-0, (A) 1-6

74-75 Q1: Consett (H) 4-1
Q2: Shildon (A) 4-2
Q3: Ashington (A) 2-2, (H) 1-5

75-76 Q1: Bridlington Town (H) 4-2
Q2: Whitby Town (H) 2-0
Q3: Easington Colliery Welfare (H) 2-1
Q4: Morecambe (H) 2-2, (A) 1-4

76-77 Q1: Durham City (H) 3-3, (A) 3-3, 2-3

77-78 Q1: Netherfield (A) 0-4

78-79 Q1: Billingham Synthonia (H) 0-1

79-80 PR: Ferryhill Athletic (A) 1-2

80-81 Q1: Horden Colliery Welfare (A) 0-1

81-82 PR: Eppleton C.W. (H) 0-0, (A) 2-0
Q1: Whitley Bay (A) 1-3

82-83 Q1: Brandon United (H) 0-5

83-84 Q1: Accrington Stanley (H) 1-1, (A) 0-3

84-85 Q1: Whitby Town (H) 2-5

85-86 PR: Lancaster City (A) 0-1

87-88 Q1: Harrogate Town (H) 0-3

88-89 PR: Shildon (A) 2-6

89-90 Q1: Whitley Bay (A) 0-6

90-91 PR: Cleator Moor Celtic (H) 0-1

91-92 PR: Consett (A) 0-5

92-93 PR: Whitby Town (H) 1-5

WILMSLOW ALBION

Currently: Mid-Cheshire League

47-48 EX: Droylsden (A) 0-2

48-49 PR: Port Sunlight (H) 0-6

49-50 EX: Congleton Town (A) 2-8

WILTS CO. MENTAL HOSP.

See Roundway Hospital

WIMBLEDON

Currently: F.A. Premier League

45-46 Q1: Sutton United (A) 0-7

46-47 PR: Carshalton Athletic (H) 3-0
Q1: Woking (A) 6-2
Q2: Tooting & Mitcham United (A) 0-1

47-48 R1: Mansfield Town (H) 0-1

48-49 Q4: Dartford (H) 1-2

49-50 PR: Hounslow Town (A) 2-2, (H) 5-0
Q1: Kingstonian (H) 0-0, (A) 1-1, 3-6

50-51 EX: Chertsey Town (A) 3-1
PR: Guildford (A) 9-3
Q1: Walton & Hersham (H) 0-2

51-52 PR: Erith & Belvedere (H) 0-1

52-53 PR: Metropolitan Police (A) 5-1
Q1: Woking (A) 2-1
Q2: Dulwich Hamlet (A) 3-3, (H) 5-2
Q3: Carshalton Athletic (A) 4-3
Q4: Gravesend & Northfleet (H) 4-2
R1: Walthamstow Avenue (A) 2-2, (H) 0-3

53-54 PR: Bromley United (H) 2-1
Q1: Kingstonian (H) 1-1, (A) 2-4

54-55 PR: Wealdstone (A) 4-2
Q1: Hayes (A) 1-1, (H) 0-2

55-56 PR: Edgware Town (H) 4-1
Q1: Finchley (H) 0-1

56-57 PR: Tooting & Mitcham United (H) 1-5

57-58 PR: Walton & Hersham (H) 1-3

58-59 PR: Dorking (A) 1-2

59-60 PR: Dorking (H) 6-0
Q1: Bromley (H) 3-0
Q2: Sutton United (H) 0-1

60-61 Q1: Woking (H) 5-1
Q2: Dorking (A) 3-4

61-62 Q1: Woking (H) 5-1
Q2: Walton & Hersham (H) 1-2

62-63 Q1: Leatherhead (A) 4-1
Q2: Woking (H) 4-2
Q3: Kingstonian (H) 3-2
Q4: Oxford City (H) 6-1
R1: Colchester United (H) 2-1
R2: Bristol City (A) 1-2

63-64 R1: Bexley United (A) 5-1
R2: Bath City (H) 2-2, (A) 0-4

64-65 Q4: Romford (H) 1-1, (A) 1-2

65-66 Q4: Fareham Town (A) 3-0
R1: Gravesend & Northfleet (H) 4-1
R2: Folkestone Town (H) 0-1

66-67 Q4: Dartford (A) 2-2, (H) 3-0
R1: Grantham (A) 1-2

67-68 Q4: Ashford Town (H) 3-0
R1: Romford (H) 3-0
R2: Bristol Rovers (H) 0-4

68-69 Q4: Woking (H) 0-2

69-70 Q4: Crawley Town (H) 0-0, (A) 0-0, 2-0
R1: Hillingdon Borough (A) 0-2

70-71 Q4: Leatherhead (A) 2-1
R1: Peterborough United (A) 1-3

71-72 Q4: Margate (A) 0-1

72-73 Q1: Cheshunt (A) 4-0
Q2: Stevenage Athletic (H) 3-1
Q3: Sutton United (A) 1-3

73-74 Q1: Epsom & Ewell (A) 5-1
Q2: Southall (H) 2-1
Q3: Staines Town (A) 1-1, (H) 4-3
Q4: Maidstone United (H) 1-0
R1: King's Lynn (A) 0-1

74-75 Q1: Bracknell Town (A) 3-1
Q2: Maidenhead United (H) 4-0
Q3: Wokingham Town (H) 2-0
Q4: Guildford & Dorking United (A) 3-0

R1: Bath City (H) 1-0
R2: Kettering Town (H) 2-0
R3: Burnley (A) 1-0
R4: Leeds U. (A) 0-0, (H - *at Crystal P.*) 0-1

75-76 Q4: Kingstonian (H) 6-1
R1: Nuneaton Borough (A) 1-0
R2: Brentford (H) 0-2

76-77 R1: Woking (H) 1-0
R2: Leatherhead (A) 3-1
R3: Middlesbrough (H) 0-0, (A) 0-1

Right: *Wimbledon force Woking 'keeper John Overton into a fine save during the 1976 tie.*
Photo: John McDonnell, Surrey Comet.

77-78 R1: Enfield (A) 0-3

78-79 R1: Gravesend & Northfleet (A) 0-0, (H) 1-0
R2: A.F.C. Bournemouth (H) 1-1, (A) 2-1
R3: Southampton (H) 0-2

Below right: *Wimbledon's Ray Goddard gathers the ball under pressure from Gravesend defender Peter Osborne (dark shirt). Photo: Gravesend & Dartford Reporter.*

79-80 R1: Gillingham (A) 0-0, (H) 4-2
R2: Portsmouth (H) 0-0, (A) 3-3, 0-1

80-81 R1: Windsor & Eton (H) 7-2
R2: Swindon Town (H) 2-0
R3: Oldham Athletic (H) 0-0, (A) 1-0
R4: Wrexham (A) 1-2

81-82 R1: Bedford Town (A) 2-0
R2: Enfield (A) 1-4

82-83 R1: Northampton Town (A) 2-2, (H) 0-2

83-84 R1: Orient (H) 2-1
R2: Brentford (A) 2-3

84-85 R3: Burnley (H) 3-1
R4: Nottingham Forest (A) 0-0, (H) 1-0
R5: West Ham United (H) 1-1, (A) 1-5

85-86 R3: Millwall (A) 1-3

86-87 R3: Sunderland (H) 2-1
R4: Portsmouth (H) 4-0
R5: Everton (H) 3-1
R6: Tottenham Hotspur (H) 0-2

87-88 R3: West Bromwich Albion (H) 4-1
R4: Mansfield Town (A) 2-1
R5: Newcastle United (A) 3-1
R6: Watford (H) 2-1
SF: Luton Town (*at Tottenham Hotspur*) 2-1
F: Liverpool (*at Wembley*) 1-0

88-89 R3: Birmingham City (A) 1-0
R4: Aston Villa (A) 1-0
R5: Grimsby Town (H) 3-1
R6: Everton (A) 0-1

89-90 R3: West Bromwich Albion (A) 0-2

90-91 R3: Aston Villa (A) 1-1, (H) 1-0
R4: Shrewsbury Town (A) 0-1

91-92 R3: Bristol C. (A) 1-1, (H - *at Crystal P.*) 0-1

92-93 R3: Everton (H - *at Crystal P.*) 0-0, (A) 2-1
R4: Aston V. (A) 1-1, (H - *at C.P.*) 0-0 (*6-5 pens*)
R5: Tottenham Hotspur (A) 2-3

WIMBLINGTON OLD BOYS

Currently: Defunct

49-50 PR: South Lynn (A) 0-4

50-51 PR: Parson Drove United (A) 1-4

WIMBORNE TOWN

Currently: Wessex League

82-83 PR: Bridport (A) 3-2
Q1: Falmouth Town (A) 2-1
Q2: St Blazey (H) 3-2
Q3: Bath City (H) 1-0
Q4: Merthyr Tydfil (H) 1-0
R1: Aldershot (A) 0-4

83-84 Q1: Forest Green Rovers (A) 0-6

84-85 Q1: Paulton Rovers (A) 4-0
Q2: Frome Town (H) 1-3

85-86 PR: Weston-super-Mare (H) 2-5

86-87 Q1: Clandown (H) 2-2, (A) 2-1
Q2: Chippenham Town (H) 1-1, (A) 1-0
Q3: A.F.C. Totton (A) 0-0 (H) 1-0
Q4: Bognor Regis Town (H) 2-5

87-88 Q1: Melksham Town (A) 3-1
Q2: Oxford City (H) 2-1
Q3: Yeovil Town (H) 0-4

88-89 Q1: Weston-super-Mare (H) 3-5

89-90 PR: Swanage Town & Herston (H) 0-2

90-91 PR: Bideford (H) 3-2
Q1: Liskeard Athletic (A) 2-5

91-92 Q1: Weymouth (H) 1-2

92-93 PR: Bournemouth (H) 1-1, (A) 3-1
Q1: Newport Isle of Wight (A) 3-2
Q2: Bashley (A) 1-3

WINCHESTER CITY

Currently: Hampshire League

47-48 EX: Salisbury (H) 0-1

48-49 EX: Botley (A) 3-1
PR: Longfleet St Mary's (A) 2-4

49-50 EX: Newport Isle of Wight (H) 1-2

50-51 PR: Newport Isle of Wight (A) 1-5

51-52 Q1: Alton Town (H) 2-2, (A) 1-3

52-53 Q1: Gosport Borough Athletic (H) 1-0
Q2: Newport Isle of Wight (H) 1-3

53-54 Q2: Newport Isle of Wight (A) 0-7

54-55 Q2: Basingstoke Town (A) 2-0
Q3: Gosport Borough Athletic (H) 3-0
Q4: Dorchester Town (H) 0-1

55-56 Q1: Chichester City (H) 2-2, (A) 3-1
Q2: Andover (A) 1-2

56-57 Q2: Gosport Borough Athletic (H) 3-0
Q3: Andover (H) 0-2

57-58 Q1: Cowes (A) 0-0, (H) 0-1

58-59 Q1: Andover (A) 1-4

59-60 Q1: Fareham Town (H) 1-4

72-73 Q1: Basingstoke (A) 1-1, (H) 1-1, 0-0, 0-3

WINDSOR & ETON

Currently: Isthmian League

45-46 PR: Pressed Steel (H) 11-1
Q1: Banbury Spencer (H) 0-3

46-47 PR: Oxford City (H) 4-2
Q1: Slough United (A) 3-3, (H) 2-4

47-48 EX: Yiewsley (A) 3-3, (H) 3-2
PR: Hayes (A) 1-3

48-49 EX: Southall (A) 1-3

49-50 EX: Hayes (H) 2-3

50-51 EX: Maidenhead United (H) 1-1, (A) 1-2

51-52 PR: Bicester Town (H) 3-2
Q1: Wycombe Wanderers (A) 1-6

52-53 PR: Wealdstone (H) 0-4

53-54 PR: Yiewsley (H) 3-3, (A) 1-2

54-55 PR: Slough Town (A) 2-6

55-56 PR: Chesham United (H) 2-2, (A) 0-2

56-57 Q1: Marlow (A) 1-6

57-58 PR: Huntley & Palmers (A) 2-4

58-59 PR: Marlow (H) 4-3
Q1: Headington United (A) 0-7

59-60 PR: Aylesbury United (H) 2-3

60-61 Q1: Maidenhead United (H) 2-4

61-62 Q1: Yiewsley (H) 0-2

62-63 Q1: Maidenhead United (A) 1-2

63-64 Q1: Hayes (A) 1-2

64-65 Q1: Corinthian-Casuals (H) 2-2 (A) 2-1
Q2: Hayes (H) 0-1

65-66 Q1: Hayes (A) 2-1
Q2: Corinthian-Casuals (H) 0-8

66-67 Q2: Hertford Town (H) 2-2, (A) 1-4

67-68 Q1: Malden Town (H) 3-1
Q2: Barking (H) 2-1
Q3: Barnet (A) 1-7

68-69 Q1: Barking (A) 1-0
Q2: Malden Town (H) 2-2, (A) 2-3

69-70 PR: Hatfield Town (A) 2-0
Q1: Malden Town (A) 0-4

70-71 Q1: Grays Athletic (H) 0-1

71-72 Q1: Tooting & Mitcham Utd (A) 1-1, (H) 2-0
Q2: Staines Town (H) 2-1
Q3: Walton & Hersham (A) 2-2, (H) 0-1

72-73 Q1: Wealdstone (A) 0-0, (H) 0-3

73-74 Q1: Leytonstone (A) 0-2

74-75 Q1: Maidenhead United (A) 1-4

75-76 Q1: Burnham (H) 1-1, (A) 0-1

76-77 Q1: Cheshunt (H) 3-2
Q2: Wokingham Town (A) 1-2

77-78 PR: Ruislip Manor (A) 3-1
Q1: Maidenhead United (A) 0-3

78-79 Q1: Hampton (H) 1-0
Q2: Staines Town (A) 0-0 (H) 1-0
Q3: Sutton United (H) 0-1

79-80 PR: Walthamstow Avenue (A) 2-4

80-81 Q1: Tooting & Mitcham United (A) 3-0
Q2: Waterlooville (A) 0-0, (H) 4-1
Q3: Kingstonian (H) 1-1, (A) 3-2
Q4: Gosport Borough (H) 2-0
R1: Wimbledon (A) 2-7

81-82 Q1: Walton & Hersham (H) 3-4

82-83 Q1: Hoddesdon Town (A) 2-0
Q2: Wembley (A) 3-1
Q3: Hampton (A) 2-1
Q4: A.F.C. Totton (A) 0-0, (H) 1-0
R1: Brentford (H - *played away*) 0-7

83-84 Q1: Edgware (A) 5-0
Q2: Staines Town (A) 2-2, (H) 2-0
Q3: St Albans City (H) 4-1
Q4: Cheltenham Town (H) 1-0
R1: Burton Albion (A) 2-1
R2: A.F.C. Bournemouth (H) 0-0, (A) 0-2

84-85 Q4: Tooting & Mitcham United (H) 5-2
R1: Gillingham (A) 1-2

85-86 Q4: Oxford City (H) 2-2, (A) 1-0
R1: Torquay United (H) 1-1, (A) 0-3

86-87 Q4: Kettering Town (A) 0-1

87-88 Q1: Woking (H) 0-0, (A) 3-6

88-89 Q1: Banstead Athletic (A) 2-0
Q2: Worthing (A) 4-0
Q3: Whitehawk (H) 1-1 (A) 0-1

89-90 Q1: Barton Rovers (A) 0-2

90-91 Q1: Cove (A) 3-1
Q2: Pagham (A) 3-0
Q3: Dover Athletic (H) 1-1, (A) 0-3

91-92 Q1: Wembley (A) 2-1
Q2: Fisher Athletic (H) 3-2
Q3: Hertford Town (A) 2-1
Q4: Merthyr Tydfil (A) 1-1, (H) 1-0
R1: Woking (H) 1-1 *ab. (fog) 69m.*, (H) 2-4

92-93 Q1: Whyteleafe (A) 3-1
Q2: Ashford Town (A) 2-2, (H) 2-3

Right: *A brave dive at the feet of Chris Yates by Bournemouth 'keeper Ian Leigh denies Windsor & Eton a shock Cup win, and a Third Round tie against Manchester United, in season 1983-84. Photo: Eric Marsh.*

WINGATE

Currently: Merged with Leyton.
Playing as Leyton in Isthmian League.
See also Leyton (2).

48-49 EX: Acton Town (A) 8-1
PR: Ruislip Manor (A) 3-4

49-50 EX: Harrow Town (A) 2-0
PR: Ware (H) 1-5

54-55 PR: Hemel Hempstead (A) 2-2, (H) 1-3

WINGATE

Currently: Merged with Billingham Cassell Mall.
Playing as Wingate Mall in Wearside League.
* - As Wingate Welfare

50-51 * EX: Murton Colliery Welfare (H) 4-2
PR: Easington Colliery Welfare (A) 1-3

56-57 * Q1: Shotton Colliery Welfare (A) 2-4

57-58 * Q2: Stanley United (H) 2-11

69-70 Q1: Murton Colliery Welfare (H) 3-0
Q2: Whitby Town (A) 1-3

71-72 Q1: North Shields (H) 0-1

72-73 Q1: Willington (H) 1-4

73-74 Q1: Whitby Town (H) 2-1
Q2: Horden Colliery Welfare (A) 2-3

74-75 Q1: Crook Town (A) 4-1
Q2: Spennymoor United (A) 0-3

75-76 Q1: Whitby Town (A) 0-4

76-77 PR: Horden Colliery Welfare (A) 3-2
Q1: Tow Law Town (A) 1-3

77-78 PR: Annfield Plain (H) 2-1
Q1: Consett (A) 1-1, (H) 1-4

78-79 Q1: South Bank (H) 0-0, (A) 1-1, (*both at Billingham Synthonia*) 0-0, 1-2

79-80 PR: Shildon (A) 2-2, (H) 4-3
Q1: Washington (A) 2-3

80-81 PR: Thackley (A) 1-1, (H) 0-1

81-82 Q1: North Shields (A) 1-2

82-83 Q1: Annfield Plain (H) 1-3

85-86 Q1: Workington (H) 4-2
Q2: Shotton Comrades (A) 2-0
Q3: Peterlee Newtown (A) 1-2

WINGATE & FINCHLEY

Currently: South Midlands League
See also Finchley

91-92 PR: Beckenham Town (A) 0-1

92-93 PR: Witham Town (A) 3-4

WINSFORD UNITED

Currently: Northern Premier League

47-48 PR: Ashton United (A) 0-2

48-49 PR: Glossop (H) 3-1
Q1: Congleton Town (A) 2-2, (H) 2-0
Q2: Hyde United (H) 4-0
Q3: Witton Albion (H) 0-1

49-50 PR: Wheelock Albion (H) 9-1
Q1: Droylsden (H) 2-3

50-51 PR: Ashton United (H) 2-0
Q1: Congleton Town (H) 4-0
Q2: Altrincham (A) 2-3

51-52 Q1: Altrincham (H) 2-0
Q2: Buxton (A) 0-4

52-53 Q1: Northwich Victoria (A) 1-1, (H) 4-2
Q2: Macclesfield Town (H) 1-0
Q3: Altrincham (H) 0-1

53-54 Q1: Northwich Victoria (A) 0-0, (H) 2-2, 2-0
Q2: Congleton Town (H) 1-0
Q3: Altrincham (H) 3-1
Q4: Nelson (A) 0-1

54-55 PR: Hyde United (A) 1-3

55-56 PR: Witton Albion (H) 4-1
Q1: Stalybridge Celtic (A) 1-1, (H) 6-0
Q2: Buxton (H) 5-1
Q3: Northwich Victoria (A) 2-2, (H) 1-2

56-57 PR: Stockton Heath (A) 5-4
Q1: Linotype & Machinery (A) 1-1, (H) 2-1
Q2: Macclesfield Town (H) 2-2, (A) 1-4

57-58 PR: Macclesfield Town (A) 4-5

58-59 PR: Stalybridge Celtic (A) 1-1, (H) 5-1
Q1: Hyde United (H) 1-2

59-60 PR: Northwich Victoria (H) 0-3

60-61 Q1: Witton Albion (H) 1-0
Q2: Congleton Town (A) 1-3

62-63 Q1: Witton Albion (H) 3-0
Q2: Lostock Gralam (A) 3-0
Q3: Droylsden (H) 0-1

63-64 Q1: Macclesfield Town (A) 0-1

64-65 Q1: Congleton Town (H) 2-1
Q2: Witton Albion (H) 1-1, (A) 1-2

65-66 Q1: Macclesfield Town (A) 0-7

66-67 Q1: Lostock Gralam (A) 2-3

67-68 Q1: Northwich Victoria (H) 1-0
Q2: Kirkby Town (H) 3-0
Q3: Runcorn (A) 1-7

68-69 Q1: Congleton Town (A) 1-0
Q2: Kirkby Town (H) 2-4

69-70 PR: Congleton Town (A) 6-0
Q1: New Brighton (A) 1-2

70-71 Q1: Runcorn (A) 2-0
Q2: Oswestry Town (H) 0-0, (A) 0-1

71-72 Q1: Eastwood (Hanley) (A) 0-1

72-73 PR: Northwich Victoria (H) 3-1
Q1: Prescot Town (H) 1-0
Q2: Ellesmere Port Town (A) 0-1

73-74 Q1: Portmadoc (H) 1-2

74-75 Q1: Prescot Town (H) 5-1
Q2: Marine (A) 1-1, (H) 1-4

75-76 Q1: New Brighton (H) 4-1
Q2: Witton Albion (H) 3-2
Q3: Chorley (H) 2-0
Q4: Telford United (A) 1-1, (H) 5-4

R1: Peterborough United (A) 1-4

76-77 PR: South Liverpool (A) 4-0
Q1: Burscough (H) 0-0, (A) 3-1
Q2: Runcorn (H) 1-0
Q3: Bangor City (H) 1-1, (A) 1-4

77-78 PR: Ashton United (H) 1-1, (A) 2-0
Q1: Glossop (A) 2-0
Q2: New Brighton Rakers (A) 3-1
Q3: Mossley (H) 1-1, (A) 3-3, (*at Altrincham*) 0-2

78-79 Q1: Mexborough Town (H) 3-0
Q2: Oswestry Town (A) 1-0
Q3: Hednesford Town (H) 1-2

79-80 PR: Rhyl (A) 5-1
Q1: South Liverpool (A) 2-2, (H) 3-1
Q2: Glossop (H) 2-0
Q3: Mossley (H) 0-1

80-81 PR: Walsall Wood (A) 3-0
Q1: Bilston (H) 4-2
Q2: Belper Town (A) 2-2, (H) 5-0
Q3: Burton Albion (A) 2-2, (H) 1-3

81-82 PR: Rhyl (A) 1-0
Q1: Caernarfon Town (H) 2-3

82-83 PR: Blakenall (H) 1-2

83-84 Q1: Matlock Town (A) 2-2, (H) 2-1
Q2: Shepshed Charterhouse (H) 3-1
Q3: Eastwood Town (H) 0-1

84-85 Q1: North Ferriby United (A) 2-2, (H) 3-1
Q2: Horwich R.M.I. (H) 2-1
Q3: Stalybridge Celtic (A) 0-5

85-86 Q1: Leek Town (A) 0-2

86-87 Q1: Droylsden (H) 2-0
Q2: Caernarfon Town (H) 1-3

87-88 PR: Colwyn Bay (A) 0-3

88-89 PR: Hinckley Athletic (A) 0-3

89-90 PR: Walsall Wood (A) 0-2

90-91 PR: Bootle (A) 0-1

91-92 PR: Lancaster City (A) 5-1
Q1: Nantwich Town (H) 3-0
Q2: Mossley (A) 1-1, (H) 6-0
Q3: Droylsden (H) 3-2
Q4: Altrincham (H) 3-2
R1: Wrexham (A) 2-5

92-93 Q1: Northwich Victoria (A) 1-4

WINTERTON RANGERS

Currently: Merged with Appleby Frodingham Athletic. Playing as Winterton Rgrs in Northern Co's (East) Lge.

47-48 EX: Bentley Colliery (A) 4-2
PR: Denaby United (H) 1-2

48-49 EX: Brigg Town (A) 2-3

49-50 EX: Ashby Institute (H) 1-4

50-51 PR: Ossett Town (H) 1-3

69-70 PR: Selby Town (H) 5-2
Q1: Hull Brunswick (A) 0-2

70-71 Q1: Selby Town (H) 3-1
Q2: Scarborough (H) 1-2

71-72 Q1: Norton Woodseats Amateur (A) 3-0
Q2: Lincoln United (H) 3-1
Q3: Eastwood Town (A) 2-1
Q4: Boston United (H) 0-1

72-73 PR: Frickley Colliery (H) 2-0
Q1: Gainsborough Trinity (H) 1-3

73-74 Q1: Goole Town (A) 0-2

74-75 Q1: Barton Town (A) 2-2, (H) 1-0
Q2: Whitby Town (H) 3-2
Q3: Bridlington Town (A) 1-1, (H) 0-2

75-76 Q1: Yorkshire Amateur (H) 4-2
Q2: Worksop Town (A) 3-4

76-77 PR: Frecheville Community (A) 1-0
Q1: Retford Town (A) 3-0
Q2: Denaby United (H) 2-1
Q3: Emley (A) 7-4
Q4: Droylsden (H) 3-3, (A) 2-3

77-78 PR: Appleby Frodingham Athletic (H) 0-1

78-79 Q1: North Ferriby United (H) 1-1, (A) 1-0
Q2: Bridlington Trinity (A) 2-2, (H) 2-1
Q3: Yorkshire Amateur (A) 0-1

79-80 PR: Heanor Town (A) 5-0
Q1: Sutton Town (A) 0-2

80-81 PR: Nantwich Town (A) 0-0, (H) 0-1

81-82 PR: Bridlington Trinity (A) 1-3

82-83 Q1: Bourne Town (H) 4-3
Q2: Grantham (H) 0-0, (A) 0-4

83-84 PR: Friar Lane Old Boys (H) 1-0
Q1: Eastwood Town (H) 0-3

WISBECH TOWN

Currently: Eastern Counties League

45-46 Q2: Newmarket Town (H) 5-0
Q3: Cambridge Town (H) 3-1
Q4: Colchester United (H) 5-0
R1: Ipswich Town (H) 0-3, (A) 0-5 (*agg: 0-8*)

47-48 PR: March Town United (A) 2-4

48-49 PR: Abbey United (A) 1-1, (H) 8-0
Q1: Cambridge Town (H) 4-4, (A) 2-5

49-50 PR: Abbey United (A) 1-2

50-51 PR: Bury Town (H) 1-0
Q1: March Town United (H) 0-2

51-52 Q1: Huntingdon United (A) 2-0
Q2: King's Lynn (A) 0-2

52-53 Q1: Histon (H) 3-0
Q2: Cambridge United (A) 0-0, (H) 2-3

53-54 Q1: Chatteris Town (H) 6-0
Q2: March Town United (H) 4-1
Q3: Cambridge United (A) 0-1

54-55 PR: King's Lynn (H) 1-1, (A) 1-8

55-56 PR: Warboys Town (H) 7-0
Q1: Holbeach United (H) 2-2, (A) 2-0
Q2: Ely City (H) 3-2
Q3: March Town United (H) 1-1, (A) 0-2

56-57 Q1: March Town United (H) 0-0, (A) 1-2

57-58 PR: Newmarket Town (H) 6-0
Q1: Chatteris Town (A) 5-0
Q2: King's Lynn (A) 2-2, (H) 4-1
Q3: March Town United (A) 2-1
Q4: Hounslow Town (A) 3-2
R1: Colchester United (H) 1-0
R2: Reading (A) 1-2

58-59 PR: Histon (A) 5-0
Q1: Somersham Town (H) 7-0
Q2: St Neots Town (H) 4-0
Q3: Holbeach United (H) 4-0
Q4: Bedford Town (A) 4-3
R1: Newport County (H) 2-2, (A) 1-4

59-60 Q4: Tooting & Mitcham United (A) 2-1
R1: Wycombe Wanderers (A) 2-4

60-61 Q4: Chelmsford City (A) 3-3, (H) 1-4

61-62 Q4: Chelmsford City (H) 3-3, (A) 0-1

62-63 Q4: Bedford Town (A) 0-1

64-65 Q1: March Town United (A) 3-1
Q2: Ely City (A) 2-0
Q3: Cambridge City (A) 2-1
Q4: Bletchley Town United (H) 3-2
R1: Brentford (H) 0-2

65-66 Q1: Newmarket Town (H) 5-1
Q2: Cambridge City (A) 1-1, (H) 1-0
Q3: Bury Town (A) 3-0
Q4: Kettering Town (H) 6-1
R1: Brighton & Hove Albion (A) 1-10

66-67 Q4: St Neots Town (A) 0-2

67-68 PR: Spalding United (H) 1-1, (A) 3-2
Q1: Bourne Town (A) 0-4

68-69 Q1: Bourne Town (A) 3-2
Q2: Holbeach United (H) 3-1
Q3: King's Lynn (A) 3-5

69-70 PR: Boston United (A) 1-2

70-71 Q1: Bourne Town (H) 2-1
Q2: King's Lynn (A) 0-4

71-72 Q1: Spalding United (A) 1-0
Q2: King's Lynn (H) 0-4

72-73 Q1: March Town United (A) 1-1, (H) 3-0
Q2: Chatteris Town (A) 1-3

73-74 Q1: Skegness Town (A) 3-2
Q2: Thetford Town (H) 3-1
Q3: Stamford Town (A) 2-4

74-75 Q1: Corby Town (A) 0-2

75-76 Q1: Soham Town Rangers (A) 0-1

76-77 PR: Louth United (A) 2-2, (H) 2-0
Q1: Skegness Town (A) 2-0
Q2: Stamford (H) 1-1, (A) 0-3

77-78 PR: Clacton Town (H) 5-0
Q1: King's Lynn (A) 2-1
Q2: St Neots Town (A) 4-4, (H) 2-1
Q3: Lowestoft Town (H) 0-3

78-79 Q1: Barton Rovers (H) 0-2

79-80 PR: Spalding United (A) 3-1
Q1: Thetford Town (A) 2-1
Q2: St Neots Town (H) 5-2
Q3: Boston United (H) 1-5

80-81 PR: Potton United (A) 1-0
Q1: Bury Town (H) 1-2

81-82 Q1: Harwich & Parkeston (A) 2-1
Q2: Heybridge Swifts (A) 2-2, (H) 2-1
Q3: March Town United (H) 2-1
Q4: Bedford Town (A) 0-3

82-83 Q1: Billericay Town (A) 1-3

83-84 Q1: Worksop Town (A) 2-1
Q2: Corby Town (H) 2-2, (A) 2-3

84-85 PR: Evesham United (H) 3-0
Q1: Nuneaton Borough (H) 2-6

85-86 Q1: Dudley Town (H) 2-0
Q2: Tamworth (A) 1-2

86-87 Q1: Sutton Coldfield Town (H) 0-2

87-88 PR: Brackley Town (H) 1-0
Q1: Kettering Town (H) 2-0
Q2: Tamworth (H) 2-3

88-89 PR: Histon (A) 1-0
Q1: Atherstone United (A) 0-4

89-90 PR: Eynesbury Rovers (H) 5-0
Q1: Hitchin Town (A) 2-3

90-91 PR: Barton Rovers (H) 1-1, (A) 1-2

91-92 PR: Burnham Ramblers (H) 4-3
Q1: Kettering Town (H) 0-3

92-93 PR: Wellingborough Town (H) 10-0
Q1: Hitchin Town (A) 2-4

WITHAM TOWN

Currently: Isthmian League

86-87 Q1: Tilbury (A) 1-3

87-88 PR: Burgess Hill Town (H) 1-0
Q1: Malden Vale (A) 3-1
Q2: Gravesend & Northfleet (A) 0-1

88-89 Q1: Watton United (H) 2-1
Q2: Bishop's Stortford (H) 2-3

89-90 PR: Clacton Town (H) 2-1
Q1: Finchley (H) 3-1
Q2: Dartford (A) 1-3

90-91 PR: Basildon United (H) 2-3

91-92 PR: Welwyn Garden City (H) 3-1
Q1: Wealdstone (H) 1-3

92-93 PR: Wingate & Finchley (H) 4-3
Q1: Wealdstone (A - *at Watford*) 1-2

WITNEY TOWN

Currently: Southern League

50-51 EX: Chesham United (A) 2-4

51-52 PR: Chesham United (H) 1-3

52-53 PR: Huntley & Palmers Rec. (A) 2-4

53-54 Q1: Maidenhead United (H) 0-1

54-55 PR: Oxford City (A) 3-4

55-56 PR: Wycombe Wanderers (H) 0-0, (A) 1-15

56-57 Q1: Banbury Spencer (H) 1-0
Q2: Marlow (H) 1-1, (A) 4-0
Q3: Aylesbury United (A) 0-7

57-58 PR: Slough Town (A) 2-5

58-59 Q1: Maidenhead United (A) 2-7

59-60 PR: Oxford City (H) 0-1

60-61 Q1: Wokingham Town (H) 2-5

61-62 Q1: Wokingham Town (H) 0-4

70-71 Q1: Bletchley (A) 0-1

71-72 Q1: Potton United (A) 1-0
Q2: Irthlingborough Diamonds (H) 3-0
Q3: Bedford Town (A) 2-2, (H) 2-0
Q4: Sutton United (A) 1-0
R1: Romford (H) 0-3

72-73 Q1: Chesham United (A) 1-0
Q2: Oxford City (A) 4-0
Q3: Banbury United (A) 0-0, (H) 1-2

73-74 Q1: Oxford City (A) 1-0
Q2: Banbury United (H) 1-2

74-75 Q1: Oxford City (A) 1-1, (H) 0-0, 0-1

75-76 Q1: Rushden Town (A) 3-0
Q2: Milton Keynes City (A) 1-2

76-77 PR: Dunstable (A) 4-0
Q1: Thame United (A) 0-1

77-78 Q1: Harrow Borough (A) 1-1, (H) 2-1
Q2: Tilbury (H) 0-3

78-79 Q1: Banbury United (H) 0-2

79-80 Q1: Harrow Borough (A) 3-1
Q2: Thame United (A) 1-0
Q3: Tring Town (A) 2-0
Q4: Minehead (A) 0-1

80-81 Q1: Ruislip Manor (H) 2-1
Q2: Kempston Rovers (A) 1-2

81-82 Q1: Didcot Town (H) 3-0
Q2: Southall (H) 4-1
Q3: Wokingham Town (H) 2-0
Q4: Wycombe Wanderers (H) 0-1

82-83 Q1: Frome Town (A) 1-1, (H) 2-2, (A) 1-2

83-84 Q1: Moreton Town (H) 2-1
Q2: Forest Green Rovers (H) 2-2, (A) 2-1
Q3: Basingstoke Town (H) 2-2, (A) 1-2

84-85 Q1: Bridgend Town (A) 2-0
Q2: Poole (H) 1-1, (A) 0-0, (*at Andover*) 3-1
Q3: Clevedon Town (A) 3-2
Q4: Yeovil Town (A) 1-3

85-86 Q1: Saffron Walden Town (H) 3-0
Q2: Stourbridge (H) 0-0, (A) 0-1

86-87 Q1: Mangotsfield United (H) 2-3

87-88 Q1: Barnet (H) 0-3

88-89 PR: Desborough Town (A) 2-2, (H) 1-0
Q1: Shepshed Chaterhouse (A) 2-3

89-90 PR: Chichester City (H) 4-1
Q1: Bournemouth (H) 1-0
Q2: Littlehampton Town (A) 4-0
Q3: Basingstoke Town (H) 0-2

90-91 Q1: Tilbury (A) 1-1, (H) 2-1
Q2: Egham Town (A) 0-1

91-92 PR: Chard Town (A) 2-1
Q1: Clevedon Town (A) 2-2, (H) 1-0
Q2: Dorchester Town (A) 2-3

92-93 PR: Shoreham (A) 3-0
Q1: Southwick (A) 5-2
Q2: Hampton (H) 3-1
Q3: Bemerton Heath Harlequins (H) 1-0
Q4: Salisbury (H) 1-2

WITTON ALBION

Currently: Alliance Premier League

45-46 Q1: Glossop (H) 8-2
Q2: Hurst (H) 6-1
Q3: Rhyl (A) 2-2, (H) 3-1
Q4: Marine (H) 2-3

46-47 Q4: Runcorn (H) 1-2

47-48 PR: Congleton Town (A) 3-3, (H) 7-0
Q1: Ashton United (A) 6-2
Q2: Buxton (H) 6-3
Q3: Altrincham (H) 4-2
Q4: Stalybridge Celtic (H) 2-3

48-49 PR: Altrincham (A) 4-0
Q1: Buxton (H) 3-0
Q2: Northwich Victoria (A) 3-1
Q3: Winsford United (A) 1-0
Q4: Shrewsbury Town (H) 4-0
R1: Gainsborough Trinity (A) 0-1

49-50 Q4: Rawmarsh Welfare (H) 3-0
R1: Mossley (H) 0-1

50-51 Q4: Northwich Victoria (H) 4-2
R1: Nelson (H) 1-2

51-52 Q4: Wigan Athletic (A) 2-2, (H) 3-3, 2-1
R1: Gainsborough Trinity (H) 2-1
R2: Workington (H) 3-3, (A) 0-1

52-53 Q4: Bangor City (H) 0-2

53-54 Q4: Runcorn (H) 2-0 *aban. - tie awarded*
R1: Nelson (H) 4-1
R2: Grimsby Town (H) 1-1, (A) 1-6

54-55 Q4: Hyde United (A) 3-6

55-56 PR: Winsford United (A) 1-4

56-57 PR: Buxton (H) 2-1
Q1: Lostock Gralam (A) 0-1

57-58 Q1: Congleton Town (H) 4-0
Q2: Northwich Victoria (H) 3-2
Q3: Altrincham (H) 3-2
Q4: Norton Woodseats Am. (A) 2-2, (H) 6-1
R1: Tranmere Rovers (A) 1-2

58-59 PR: Linotype & Machinery (A) 2-1
Q1: Stockton Heath (H) 2-4

59-60 PR: Stalybridge Celtic (H) 3-3, (A) 2-1
Q1: Hyde United (H) 2-1
Q2: Buxton (A) 2-1
Q3: Ellesmere Port Town (A) 1-4

60-61 Q1: Winsford United (A) 0-1

61-62 Q1: Northwich Victoria (A) 1-2

62-63 Q1: Winsford United (A) 0-3

63-64 Q1: Lostock Gralam (A) 1-4

64-65 Q1: Lostock Gralam (H) 4-0
Q2: Winsford United (A) 1-1, (H) 2-1
Q3: Macclesfield Town (A) 1-2

65-66 Q1: Stalybridge Celtic (H) 4-0
Q2: Macclesfield Town (A) 0-9

66-67 Q1: Ellesmere Port (A) 0-0, (H) 3-1
Q2: Hyde United (H) 4-1
Q3: Northwich Victoria (A) 6-1
Q4: Rhyl (H) 4-2
R1: Bradford Park Avenue (A) 2-3

67-68 Q1: Rossendale United (H) 6-1
Q2: Macclesfield Town (H) 0-2

68-69 Q1: Ashton United (A) 6-1
Q2: Rossendale United (H) 4-3
Q3: Mossley (A) 0-2

69-70 Q1: Rossendale United (A) 1-2

70-71 Q1: Chorley (H) 4-1
Q2: Droylsden (A) 3-2
Q3: Formby (A) 1-1, (H) 3-1
Q4: Bangor City (A) 1-1, (H) 2-3

71-72 Q1: Stalybridge Celtic (A) 1-0
Q2: Nantwich (H) 0-1

72-73 Q1: Sandbach Ramblers (A) 7-0
Q2: Eastwood Hanley (A) 0-3

73-74 Q1: Runcorn (A) 0-2

74-75 Q1: Marine (A) 1-4

75-76 Q1: South Liverpool (A) 3-0
Q2: Winsford United (A) 2-3

76-77 PR: Stalybridge Celtic (A) 3-1
Q1: Curzon Ashton (H) 3-1
Q2: Northwich Victoria (H) 1-3

77-78 PR: Bangor City (H) 1-1, (A) 1-2

78-79 Q1: Mossley (H) 4-2
Q2: Runcorn (A) 1-3

79-80 PR: Lancaster City (A) 1-3

80-81 PR: Redditch United (A) 0-0, (H) 5-1
Q1: Highgate United (H) 3-1
Q2: Bedworth United (A) 2-1
Q3: Sutton Coldfield Town (A) 1-2

81-82 PR: Macclesfield Town (H) 3-1
Q1: Horwich R.M.I. (A) 0-2

82-83 PR: Ilkeston Town (H) 2-0
Q1: Nantwich Town (A) 3-0
Q2: Bilston (H) 4-2
Q3: Shifnal Town (H) 0-2

83-84 Q1: Glossop (H) 1-1, (A) 0-2

84-85 Q1: Armitage (A) 4-0
Q2: Accrington Stanley (H) 4-0
Q3: Hednesford (A) 2-2, (H) 2-2, (H) 2-3

85-86 Q1: Leicester United (A) 1-0
Q2: Arnold (A) 2-0
Q3: South Liverpool (A) 0-5

86-87 Q1: Hednesford Town (H) 0-2

87-88 Q1: Alfreton Town (A) 2-4

88-89 Q1: Boston (H) 0-0, (A) 2-0
Q2: North Ferriby United (A) 2-2, (H) 3-1
Q3: Frickley Athletic (A) 1-3

89-90 Q1: Gresley Rovers (A) 2-2, (H) 1-0
Q2: Warrington Town (H) 2-0
Q3: Buxton (H) 1-1, (A) 6-4
Q4: Congleton Town (A) 0-1

90-91 Q1: Congleton Town (H) 2-0
Q2: Alvechurch (A) 7-2
Q3: Bilston Town (H) 4-0
Q4: Frickley Athletic (A) 2-0
R1: Bolton Wanderers (H) 1-2

91-92 Q4: Whitley Bay (A) 4-1
R1: Halifax Town (H) 1-1, (A) 2-1
R2: Preston North End (A) 1-5

92-93 R1: Bury (A) 0-2

Above: *Witton's Brendan Burke shields the ball during the First Round tie at Bury on November 14th 1992. Witton had been exempt to the Competition Proper on the strength of their appearance in the previous season's F.A. Trophy final. They showed tremendous spirit at Gigg Lane and were very unlucky to lose to two penalty strikes.*
Photo: Colin Stevens.

WIVENHOE TOWN

Currently: Isthmian League

87-88 PR: Erith & Belvedere (A) 0-0, (H) 4-2
Q1: Sutton United (H) 0-3

88-89 PR: Clacton Town (H) 3-0
Q1: Bury Town (A) 0-0, (H) 0-2

89-90 PR: Harwich & Parkeston (H) 2-0
Q1: Potton United (H) 3-0
Q2: Wealdstone (A) 1-0
Q3: Leyton-Wingate (A) 0-0, (H) 2-0
Q4: Halesowen Town (H) 0-0, (A) 2-3

90-91 Q1: Halstead Town (H) 3-1
Q2: Wealdstone (H) 0-0, (A) 1-2

91-92 Q1: Ford United (A) 1-3

92-93 Q1: Kempston Rovers (A) 4-3
Q2: Wealdstone (A - *at Watford*) 1-1, (H) 0-2

WOKING

Currently: Alliance Premier League

45-46 PR: Epsom (A) 8-1
Q1: Metropolitan Police (A) 4-1
Q2: Tooting & Mitcham United (H) 1-2

46-47 Q1: Wimbledon (H) 2-6

47-48 PR: Leatherhead (H) 2-0
Q1: Tooting & Mitcham United (H) 2-3

48-49 PR: Carshalton Athletic (H) 1-1, (A) 7-4
Q1: Metropolitan Police (A) 2-0
Q2: Redhill (A) 3-4

49-50 PR: Metropolitan Police (H) 1-0
Q1: Epsom (H) 1-2

50-51 EX: Carshalton Athletic (H) 2-2, (A) 4-7

51-52 PR: Epsom (A) 4-3
Q1: Dorking (H) 5-1
Q2: Hounslow Town (H) 0-6

52-53 PR: Dorking (H) 4-1
Q1: Wimbledon (H) 1-2

53-54 PR: Kingstonian (A) 1-3

54-55 PR: Dover (A) 1-2

55-56 PR: Folkestone Town (H) 1-1, (A) 1-2

56-57 PR: Dulwich Hamlet (A) 2-1
Q1: Tunbridge Wells United (A) 0-3

57-58 PR: Kingstonian (A) 5-3
Q1: Bromley (H) 1-5

58-59 R1: Southampton (A) 1-4

59-60 PR: Epsom (H) 3-0
Q1: Dulwich Hamlet (H) 3-0
Q2: Kingstonian (A) 3-0
Q3: Sutton United (A) 3-3, (H) 1-3

60-61 Q1: Wimbledon (A) 1-5

61-62 Q1: Wimbledon (A) 1-5

62-63 Q1: Petter Sports (A) 2-0
Q2: Wimbledon (A) 2-4

63-64 Q1: Dorking (A) 3-2
Q2: Guildford City (H) 0-2

64-65 Q1: Guildford City (H) 1-3

65-66 Q1: Addlestone (H) 9-0
Q2: Walton & Hersham (A) 4-0
Q3: Guildford City (A) 0-6

66-67 Q1: Basingstoke Town (A) 2-1
Q2: Littlehampton Town (H) 2-1
Q3: Horsham (A) 1-2

67-68 Q1: Basingstoke Town (A) 1-5

68-69 Q1: Crawley Town (H) 2-1
Q2: Addlestone (H) 5-2
Q3: Wokingham Town (H) 3-2
Q4: Wimbledon (A) 2-0
R1: Brentford (A) 0-2

69-70 PR: Chichester City (H) 4-0
Q1: Addlestone (H) 3-3, (A) 0-2

70-71 PR: East Grinstead (H) 2-0
Q1: Worthing (A) 2-0
Q2: Crawley Town (A) 1-3

71-72 Q1: Slough Town (A) 1-1, (H) 0-2

72-73 Q1: Maidenhead United (A) 1-0
Q2: Biggleswade Town (A) 2-0
Q3: Dartford (A) 2-3

73-74 PR: Tonbridge (H) 2-1
Q1: Farnborough T. (A) 2-2, (H) 2-2, 2-1
Q2: Wycombe Wanderers (A) 0-1

74-75 Q1: Kingstonian (H) 2-2, (A) 2-1
Q2: Wokingham Town (A) 1-2

75-76 Q1: Wealdstone (A) 1-1, (H) 3-5

76-77 Q1: Burgess Hill Town (H) 3-1
Q2: Croydon (A) 0-0, (H) 2-0
Q3: Aveley (A) 1-1, (H) 4-0
Q4: Slough Town (H) 0-0, (A) 1-0
R1: Wimbledon (A) 0-1

77-78 PR: Ilford (A) 0-1

78-79 Q1: Epsom & Ewell (H) 3-1
Q2: Tunbridge Wells (A) 2-0
Q3: Horsham (H) 5-2
Q4: Margate (A) 7-1
R1: Barnet (A) 3-3, (H) 3-3, (*at Brentford*) 3-0
R2: Swansea City (A) 2-2, (H) 3-5

Above: *Woking's great run of F.A. Cup success started in 1988 when they reached the First Round Proper as a Vauxhall Isthmian League Division One side. Here Shane Wye clenches his fist to acknowledge his goal against Cambridge at a packed Kingfield.*

79-80 Q1: Corinthian-Casuals (A) 6-1
Q2: Hounslow (A) 3-2
Q3: Kingstonian (A) 2-0
Q4: Wealdstone (A) 0-1

80-81 Q1: Tring Town (H) 2-0
Q2: Hendon (A) 1-1, (H) 1-4

81-82 PR: Newport Isle of Wight (H) 1-0
Q1: Wick (A) 1-2

82-83 PR: Chatham Town (H) 0-0, (A) 1-2

83-84 PR: Hailsham Town (A - *played home*) 1-2

84-85 Q1: Haywards Heath (A) 0-2

85-86 Q1: Ringmer (A) 3-1
Q2: Slough Town (H) 1-5

86-87 PR: Horndean (A) 3-2
Q1: Lancing (A) 4-2
Q2: Hastings Town (H) 4-0
Q3: Crawley Town (H) 3-1
Q4: Weymouth (H) 1-0
R1: Chelmsford City (H) 1-1, (A) 1-2

87-88 Q1: Windsor & Eton (A) 0-0, (H) 6-3
Q2: Banstead Athletic (A) 0-0, (H) 1-0
Q3: Thanet United (A) 1-1, (H) 0-2

88-89 Q1: Canterbury City (H) 3-0
Q2: Molesey (A) 1-1, (H) 1-0
Q3: Whyteleafe (A) 2-0
Q4: Exmouth Town (A) 5-1
R1: Cambridge United (H) 1-4

89-90 Q1: Kingstonian (A) 5-1
Q2: Southwick (H) 4-1
Q3: Erith & Belvedere (A) 1-1, (H) 5-0
Q4: Wokingham Town (A) 3-1
R1: Slough Town (A) 2-1
R2: Cambridge United (A) 1-3

90-91 Q4: Bath City (H) 2-1
R1: Kidderminster (H) 0-0, (A) 1-1, (A) 2-1
R2: Merthyr Tydfil (H) 5-1
R3: West Bromwich Albion (A) 4-2
R4: Everton (H - *played away*) 0-1

Below: *One of the greatest televised Cup shocks off all time. Tim Buzaglo scores one of his three goals at West Bromwich Albion. Photo: Barry O'Grady.*

91-92 R1: Windsor & E. (A) 1-1 *ab. 69m (fog)* (A) 4-2
R2: Yeovil Town (H) 3-0
R3: Hereford United (H) 0-0, (A) 1-2

92-93 R1: Nuneaton Borough (H) 3-2
R2: Brighton & Hove Albion (A) 1-1, (H) 1-2

WOKINGHAM TOWN

Currently: Isthmian League

58-59 PR: Aylesbury United (A) 2-2, (H) 4-2
Q1: Slough Town (H) 3-2
Q2: Maidenhead United (A) 0-4

59-60 PR: Slough Town (H) 5-2
Q1: Chesham United (H) 4-1
Q2: Maidenhead United (A) 0-5

60-61 Q1: Witney Town (A) 5-2
Q2: Chesham United (A) 1-1, (H) 1-2

61-62 Q1: Witney Town (A) 4-0
Q2: Oxford City (H) 0-3

62-63 Q1: Harrow Town (A) 2-5

64-65 Q1: Dulwich Hamlet (A) 0-0, (H) 2-0
Q2: Epsom & Ewell (H) 2-4

65-66 Q1: Bracknell Town (H) 6-0
Q2: Dulwich Hamlet (A) 2-1
Q3: Metropolitan Police (A) 2-3

66-67 Q1: Harrow Borough (H) 1-3

67-68 Q1: Fleet (H) 2-1
Q2: Crawley Town (H) 1-5

68-69 Q1: Fareham Town (A) 3-2
Q2: Chichester City (H) 5-0
Q3: Woking (A) 2-3

69-70 Q1: Basingstoke Town (A) 2-1
Q2: Addlestone (A) 1-0
Q3: Crawley Town (H) 2-5

70-71 Q1: Cray Wanderers (H) 1-3

72-73 Q1: Banbury United (A) 1-4

73-74 Q1: Hertford Town (A) 1-5

74-75 Q1: Addlestone (A) 0-0, (H) 1-1, 3-1
Q2: Woking (H) 2-1
Q3: Wimbledon (A) 0-2

75-76 Q1: Marlow (A) 0-2

76-77 PR: Ruislip Manor (A) 2-2, (H) 3-1
Q1: Wembley (A) 1-1, (H) 1-1, 1-0
Q2: Windsor & Eton (H) 2-1
Q3: Barking (A) 1-3

77-78 Q1: Hampton (A) 0-3

78-79 Q1: Aylesbury United (H) 2-0
Q2: St Albans City (A) 0-0, (H) 4-1
Q3: Barnet (H) 0-4

79-80 PR: Milton Keynes City (A) 1-4

80-81 PR: Three Bridges (A) 1-0
Q1: Poole Town (H) 0-1

81-82 Q1: Bracknell Town (A) 2-1
Q2: Slough Town (A) 5-1
Q3: Witney Town (H) 0-2

82-83 PR: Andover (H) 6-1
Q1: Whyteleafe (A) 0-0, (H) 1-0
Q2: Staines Town (A - *played home*) 2-0
Q3: Kingstonian (H) 2-2, (A) 1-1, (H) 2-0
Q4: Leatherhead (H) 1-0
R1: Cardiff City (H) 1-1, (A) 0-3

83-84 Q1: Abingdon Town (A) 3-0
Q2: Dorchester Town (H) 3-0
Q3: Gosport Borough (H) 2-1
Q4: Waterlooville (A) 2-3

84-85 Q1: Horsham Y.M.C.A. (A) 8-1
Q2: Bognor Regis Town (H) 1-2

85-86 Q1: Warminster Town (A) 1-1, (H) 3-2
Q2: Fareham Town (A) 2-3

86-87 Q1: Marlow (H) 4-0
Q2: Haringey Borough (A) 2-4

87-88 Q1: Lewes (H) 3-0
Q2: Whyteleafe (A) 3-3, (H) 1-0
Q3: Tonbridge A.F.C. (A) 0-0, (H) 2-1
Q4: Carshalton Athletic (A) 1-2

88-89 Q1: Kingsbury Town (H) 2-1
Q2: Hertford Town (H) 3-1
Q3: Dartford (H) 1-2

89-90 Q1: Croydon (A - *at Sutton United*) 3-0
Q2: Margate (H) 1-0
Q3: Whyteleafe (H) 1-1, (A) 2-1
Q4: Woking (H) 1-3

90-91 Q1: Warminster Town (A) 1-0
Q2: A.F.C. Lymington (A) 1-1, (H - *at Reading F.C.*) 2-1
Q3: Wycombe Wanderers (A) 1-4

91-92 Q1: Banstead Athletic (A) 2-1
Q2: Erith & Belvedere (H) 1-2

92-93 Q1: Walton & Hersham (A) 0-2

WOLSINGHAM WELFARE

Currently: Defunct

54-55 Q1: Chilton Athletic (H) 7-3
Q2: Shotton Colliery Welfare (H) 2-2, (A) 3-2
Q3: Durham City (A) 3-1
Q4: Stanley United (A) 1-5

55-56 Q2: Durham City (H) 2-2, (A) 0-2

56-57 Q1: Willington (H) 1-8

57-58 Q1: Easington Colliery Welfare (A) 2-11

58-59 Q2: Willington (H) 1-4

WOLVERHAMPTON WANDERERS

Currently: Football League

45-46 R3: Lovells Ath. (A) 4-2, (H) 8-1 (*agg: 12-3*)
R4: Charlton Ath. (A) 2-5, (H) 1-1, (*agg: 3-6*)

46-47 R3: Rotherham United (H) 3-0
R4: Sheffield United (H) 0-0, (A) 0-2

47-48 R3: Bournemouth & Boscombe Ath. (A) 2-1
R4: Everton (H) 1-1, (A) 2-3

48-49 R3: Chesterfield (H) 6-0
R4: Sheffield United (A) 3-0
R5: Liverpool (H) 3-1
R6: West Bromwich Albion (H) 1-0
SF: Manchester Utd (*at Sheffield Wednesday*) 1-1, (*at Everton*) 1-0
F: Leicester City (*at Wembley*) 3-1

49-50 R3: Plymouth Argyle (A) 1-1, (H) 3-0
R4: Sheffield United (H) 0-0, (A) 4-3
R5: Blackpool (H) 0-0, (A) 0-1

50-51 R3: Plymouth Argyle (A) 2-1
R4: Aston Villa (H) 3-1
R5: Huddersfield Town (H) 2-0
R6: Sunderland (A) 1-1, (H) 3-1
SF: Newcastle United (*at Sheffield Wednesday*) 0-0, (*at Huddersfield Town*) 1-2

51-52 R3: Manchester City (A) 2-2, (H) 4-1
R4: Liverpool (A) 1-2

52-53 R3: Preston North End (A) 2-5

53-54 R3: Birmingham City (H) 1-2

54-55 R3: Grimsby Town (A) 5-2
R4: Arsenal (H) 1-0
R5: Charlton Athletic (H) 4-1
R6: Sunderland (A) 0-2

55-56 R3: West Bromwich Albion (H) 1-2

56-57 R3: Swansea Town (H) 5-3
R4: Bournemouth & Boscombe Ath. (H) 0-1

57-58 R3: Lincoln City (A) 1-0
R4: Portsmouth (H) 5-1
R5: Darlington (H) 6-1
R6: Bolton Wanderers (A) 1-2

58-59 R3: Barrow (A) 4-2
R4: Bolton Wanderers (H) 1-2

59-60 R3: Newcastle United (A) 2-2, (H) 4-2
R4: Charlton Athletic (H) 2-1
R5: Luton Town (A) 4-1
R6: Leicester City (A) 2-1
SF: Aston Villa (*at West Bromwich A.*) 1-0
F: Blackburn Rovers (*at Wembley*) 3-0

60-61 R3: Huddersfield Town (H) 1-1, (A) 1-2

61-62 R3: Carlisle United (H) 3-1
R4: West Bromwich Albion (H) 1-2

62-63 R3: Nottingham Forest (A) 3-4

63-64 R3: Arsenal (A) 1-2

64-65 R3: Portsmouth (A) 0-0, (H) 3-2
R4: Rotherham United (H) 2-2, (A) 3-0
R5: Aston Villa (A) 1-1, (H) 0-0, 3-1
R6: Manchester United (H) 3-5

65-66 R3: Altrincham (H) 5-0
R4: Sheffield United (H) 3-0
R5: Manchester United (H) 2-4

66-67 R3: Oldham Athletic (A) 2-2, (H) 4-1
R4: Everton (H) 1-1, (A) 1-3

67-68 R3: Rotherham United (A) 0-1

68-69 R3: Hull City (A) 3-1
R4: Tottenham Hotspur (A) 1-2

69-70 R3: Burnley (A) 0-3

70-71 R3: Norwich City (H) 5-1
R4: Derby County (A) 1-2

71-72 R3: Leicester City (H) 1-1, (A) 0-2

72-73 R3: Manchester United (H) 1-0
R4: Bristol City (H) 1-0
R5: Millwall (H) 1-0
R6: Coventry City (H) 2-0
SF: Leeds United (*at Manchester City*) 0-1
TP: Arsenal (A) 3-1

73-74 R3: Leeds United (H) 1-1, (A) 0-1

74-75 R3: Ipswich Town (H) 1-2

75-76 R3: Arsenal (H) 3-0
R4: Ipswich Town (A) 0-0, (H) 1-0
R5: Charlton Athletic (H) 3-0
R6: Manchester United (A) 1-1, (H) 2-3

76-77 R3: Rotherham United (H) 3-2
R4: Ipswich Town (A) 2-2, (H) 1-0
R5: Chester (H) 1-0
R6: Leeds United (H) 0-1

77-78 R3: Exeter City (A) 2-2, (H) 3-1
R4: Arsenal (A) 1-2

78-79 R3: Brighton & Hove Albion (A) 3-2
R4: Newcastle United (A) 1-1, (H) 1-0
R5: Crystal Palace (A) 1-0
R6: Shrewsbury Town (H) 1-1, (A) 3-1
SF: Arsenal (*at Aston Villa*) 0-2

79-80 R3: Notts County (A) 3-1
R4: Norwich City (H) 1-1, (A) 3-2
R5: Watford (H) 0-3

80-81 R3: Stoke City (A) 2-2, (H) 2-1
R4: Watford (A) 1-1, (H) 2-1
R5: Wrexham (H) 3-1
R6: Middlesbrough (A) 1-1, (H) 3-1
SF: Tottenham Hotspur (*at Sheffield Wed.*) 2-2, (*at Arsenal*) 0-3

81-82 R3: Leeds United (H) 1-3

82-83 R3: Tranmere Rovers (A) 1-0
R4: Aston Villa (A) 0-1

83-84 R3: Coventry (A) 1-1, (H) 1-1, (A) 0-3

84-85 R3: Huddersfield Town (H) 1-1, (A) 1-3

85-86 R1: Rotherham United (A) 0-6

86-87 R1: Chorley (A - *at Bolton Wanderers*) 1-1, (H) 1-1, (A - *at Bolton Wanderers*) 0-3

87-88 R1: Cheltenham Town (H) 5-1
R2: Wigan Athletic (A) 3-1
R3: Bradford City (A) 1-2

88-89 R1: Grimsby Town (A) 0-1

89-90 R3: Sheffield Wednesday (H) 1-2

90-91 R3: Cambridge United (H) 0-1

91-92 R3: Nottingham Forest (A) 0-1

92-93 R3: Watford (A) 4-1
R4: Bolton Wanderers (H) 0-2

WOLVERTON

Currently: Defunct
* - As Wolverton Town & British Railways
x - As Wolverton Town
+ - As M.K. Wolverton Town

46-47 x PR: Bedford Town (A) 1-1, (H) 1-2

47-48 x PR: Luton Amateur (H) 4-2
Q1: Hitchin Town (H) 1-2

48-49 x EX: Luton Amateur (H) 1-5

49-50 x PR: Eynesbury Rovers (A) 1-2

50-51 x EX: Eynesbury Rovers (H) 3-2
PR: Vauxhall Motors (H) 6-3
Q1: St Neots & District (H) 3-2
Q2: Bedford Town (A) 1-3

51-52 x Q1: Luton Amateur (H) 6-1
Q2: Potton United (A) 5-2
Q3: Bedford Town (A) 1-5

52-53 * Q1: Biggleswade Town (A) 3-0
Q2: Hitchin Town (A) 2-6

53-54 * Q1: Biggleswade Town (H) 0-2

54-55 * Q1: Bletchley Town (H) 1-0
Q2: Eynesbury Rovers (A) 2-3

55-56 * Q1: Dunstable Town (H) 0-2

56-57 * Q2: Eynesbury Rovers (H) 4-3
Q3: Dunstable Town (A) 1-3

57-58 * Q2: Biggleswade Town (H) 7-0
Q3: Vauxhall Motors (H) 2-1
Q4: Peterborough United (A) 0-7

58-59 * Q1: Eynesbury Rovers (A) 0-3

59-60 * Q1: Hitchin Town (H) 2-1
Q2: Vauxhall Motors (H) 5-1
Q3: Letchworth Town (A) 2-3

60-61 * Q1: Vauxhall Motors (A) 0-2

61-62 * Q1: Vauxhall Motors (A) 2-2, (H) 0-3

62-63 * Q1: Bedford Town (A) 0-8

63-64 * Q1: Biggleswade Town (A) 1-4

64-65 * Q1: Bletchley Town United (H) 0-1

65-66 * Q1: Amersham Town (H) 2-2, (A) 2-0
Q2: Bletchley (A) 1-2

66-67 * Q1: Egham Town (A) 2-2, (H) 6-1
Q2: Harrow Borough (H) 4-1
Q3: Oxford City (A) 2-3

67-68 * Q1: Rainham Town (H) 4-1
Q2: Bishop's Stortford (H) 1-3

68-69 * Q1: Bishop's Stortford (A) 0-6

69-70 * PR: Chertsey Town (A) 2-0
Q1: Rainham Town (A) 0-1

70-71 * PR: Baldock Town (H) 1-0
Q1: Wycombe Wanderers (A) 1-8

74-75 * Q1: Milton Keynes City (H) 1-2

75-76 * Q1: Oxford City (A) 0-2

76-77 * PR: Rushden Town (A) 0-1

77-78 * PR: Banbury United (H) 1-1, (A) 1-4

78-79 * Q1: Alvechurch (H) 1-2

79-80 * PR: Haverhill Rovers (A) 0-4

80-81 x PR: Tamworth (A) 0-3

81-82 x Q1: V.S. Rugby (A) 0-5

84-85 x Q1: Rothwell Town (A) 1-2

85-86 x PR: St Albans City (A) 1-1, (H) 0-2

86-87 x PR: Gresley Rovers (A) 1-0
Q1: Tamworth (H) 0-0, (A) 2-2, (A) 2-0
Q2: Willenhall Town (H) 2-0
Q3: Stafford Rangers (H) 1-4

87-88 x PR: Ashtree Highfield (H) 0-2

88-89 + PR: Leighton Town (A) 0-2

89-90 + PR: Irthlingborough Diamonds (H) 2-1
Q1: Baker Perkins (H) 2-1
Q2: Stafford Rangers (A) 0-2

90-91 PR: Oldbury United (A) 0-0, (H) 2-1
Q1: Atherstone United (H) 2-2, (A) 1-4

91-92 PR: Uxbridge (H) 1-0
Q1: Chesham United (A) 0-2

WOMBWELL MAIN COLL.

Currently: Defunct

46-47 PR: Grimethorpe Rvrs (H) 2-2, (A) *scratched*

WOMBWELL SPORTING

Currently: Defunct

46-47 PR: Thurnscoe Victoria (A) 5-0
Q1: Sheffield (A) 4-2
Q2: Denaby United (H) 4-2
Q3: Scunthorpe United (H) 2-5

47-48 EX: Firbeck Main Colliery (H) 4-3
PR: Harworth Colliery Athletic (A) 1-4

48-49 PR: Kiveton Park Colliery (A) 1-1, (H) 4-1
Q1: Denaby United (A) 1-3

49-50 EX: Stocksbridge Works (A) 1-4

68-69 PR: Ilkeston Town (A) 1-1, (H) 1-5

69-70 Q1: Norton Woodseats Amateur (A) 3-1
Q2: Alfreton Town (H) 1-1, (A) 1-2

WOODFORD TOWN

Currently: London Spartan League

46-47 PR: Crittall Athletic (A) 2-4

47-48 PR: Brentwood & Warley (H) 1-8

48-49 EX: Saffron Walden Town (H) 6-1
PR: Bishop's Stortford (H) 3-2
Q1: Brentwood & Warley (A) 0-5

49-50 EX: Rainham Town (A) 1-2

50-51 PR: Clapton (H) 4-0
Q1: Harwich & Parkeston (H) 3-2
Q2: Chingford Town (H) 1-1, (A) 4-0
Q3: Romford (H) 2-2, (A) 1-1, 2-1
Q4: Colchester United (H) 1-7

51-52 PR: Stevenage Town (A) 4-1
Q1: Enfield (A) 2-0
Q2: Finchley (H) 3-1
Q3: Leyton (A) 2-3

52-53 PR: Enfield (A) 3-3, (H) 4-2
Q1: Stevenage Town (H) 2-1
Q2: Finchley (A) 0-2

53-54 PR: Chelmsford City (H) 0-3

54-55 PR: Barking (A) 2-3

55-56 PR: Tilbury (H) 4-2
Q1: Clacton Town (A) 0-3

56-57 PR: Rainham Town (H) 0-5

57-58 PR: Leyton (A) 0-5

58-59 Q1: Grays Athletic (A) 1-0
Q2: Barking (H) 2-1
Q3: Rainham Town (H) 2-0
Q4: Hitchin Town (A) 1-1, (H) 2-3

59-60 Q1: Leyton (H) 1-1, (A) 0-1

60-61 Q1: Tilbury (A) 2-2, (H) 1-2

61-62 Q1: Tilbury (A) 0-6

62-63 Q1: Aveley (A) 0-1

63-64 Q1: Ilford (H) 1-3

65-66 Q1: Leyton (A) 2-3

66-67 Q1: Bexley United (A) 1-5

68-69 Q1: Dulwich Hamlet (A) 1-0
Q2: Hitchin Town (A) 1-3

70-71 Q1: Stevenage Athletic (A) 1-3

71-72 Q1: Walthamstow Avenue (A) 0-1

80-81 PR: Walton & Hersham (A) 0-3

81-82 Q1: Hornchurch (A) 0-0, (H) 2-1
Q2: Leytonstone-Ilford (A) 1-2

82-83 Q1: Heybridge Swifts (H) 3-1
Q2: Edgware (A) 1-0
Q3: Walthamstow Avenue (A) 0-2

83-84 Q1: Aveley (H) 0-2

84-85 Q1: Hornchurch (A) 1-2

85-86 PR: Wootton Blue Cross (A) 1-0
Q1: St Albans City (H) 1-0
Q2: Felixstowe Town (H) 3-1
Q3: Harlow Town (A) 0-3

86-87 Q1: Hertford Town (H) 2-0
Q2: Grays Athletic (H) 2-1
Q3: Harwich & Parkeston (A) 2-1
Q4: King's Lynn (A) 3-1
R1: Orient (H) 0-1

87-88 Q1: Harlow Town (A) 0-1

WOOD GREEN TOWN

Currently: Defunct

46-47 EX: Enfield (A) 1-1, (H) 4-3
PR: Acton Town (H) 4-0
Q1: Finchley (H) 2-4

47-48 EX: Chipperfield (H) 1-4

48-49 EX: Lyons Club (Greenford) (A) 1-3

49-50 EX: Polytechnic (H) 1-0
PR: Willesden (H) 0-1

50-51 EX: Ware (A) 0-4

WOOLWICH POLYTECHNIC

Currently: (Thames Polytechnic) Kent County Lge

45-46 Q1: Lloyds (H) 1-1, (A) 0-4

46-47 PR: Callenders Athletic (A) 3-2
Q1: Sheppey United (H) 0-0, (A) 3-1
Q2: Folkestone (H) 0-3

47-48 PR: Betteshanger Colliery Welfare (A) 1-2

48-49 EX: Ashford (H - *played away*) 0-2

49-50 PR: Tonbridge (H - *played away*) 1-5

WOOTTON BASSETT TOWN

Currently: Hellenic League

46-47 EX: Dilton Rovers (H) 5-0
PR: Swindon G.W.R. Corinthians (A) 1-5

47-48 EX: Pewsey Vale (H) 0-2

48-49 EX: Swindon G.W.R. Corinthians (A) 3-6

49-50 EX: Warminster Town (H) 4-5

50-51 PR: Devizes Town (A) 0-4

WOOTTON BLUE CROSS

Currently: United Counties League

50-51 EX: Waterlows (H) 2-0
PR: Bedford Avenue (A) 4-0
Q1: Biggleswade Town (A) 2-1
Q2: Hitchin Town (H) 3-4

80-81 PR: Tiptree United (A) 0-3

81-82 PR: Slough Town (H) 2-2, (A) 2-4

82-83 PR: Kempston Rovers (H) 2-0
Q1: Walthamstow Avenue (A) 0-2

83-84 PR: Basildon United (H) 1-1, (A) 0-2

84-85 PR: Histon (H) 3-2
Q1: Burton Albion (H) 0-4

85-86 PR: Woodford Town (H) 0-1

86-87 Q1: March Town United (H) 1-2

87-88 PR: Berkhamsted Town (H) 0-0, (A) 0-2

88-89 PR: Finchley (A) 0-1

89-90 PR: Cheshunt (H) 0-2

90-91 PR: Hounslow (H) 1-3

WORCESTER CITY

Currently: Southern League

45-46 Q1: Birmingham City Transport (H) 8-0
Q2: Nuneaton Borough (A) 0-1

46-47 Q1: Moor Green (H) 1-1, (A) 6-1
Q2: Hereford United (A) 0-3

47-48 PR: Darlaston (A) 2-1
Q1: Bromsgrove Rovers (A) 2-3

48-49 PR: Birmingham City Transport (H) 4-0
Q1: Hednesford (A) 2-4

49-50 PR: Stafford Rangers (A) 0-3

50-51 Q4: Stocksbridge Works (A) 2-2, (H) 3-0
R1: Hartlepool United (H) 1-5

51-52 Q1: Wellington Town (H) 3-4

52-53 Q4: Wellington Town (A) 0-1

53-54 PR: Lye Town (A) 5-3
Q1: Darlaston (A) 0-0, (H) 3-1
Q2: Brierley Hill Alliance (A) 0-2

54-55 PR: Hednesford (H) 2-3

55-56 PR: Redditch (A) 1-0
Q1: Stafford Rangers (A) 2-1
Q2: Kidderminster Harriers (A) 0-2

56-57 PR: Darlaston (A) 7-0
Q1: Bromsgrove Rovers (H) 0-1

57-58 PR: Hednesford (H) 4-1

Q1: Rugby Town (H) 1-1, (A) 2-0
Q2: Bedworth Town (A) 1-1, (H) 3-0
Q3: Brierley Hill Alliance (H) 4-0
Q4: Bromsgrove Rovers (A) 3-3, (H) 2-1
R1: Aldershot (A) 0-0, (H) 2-2, 2-3

58-59 Q4: Brierley Hill Alliance (H) 3-0
R1: Chelmsford City (A) 0-0, (H) 3-1
R2: Millwall (H) 5-2
R3: Liverpool (H) 2-1
R4: Sheffield United (H) 0-2

Right: *Cup fever grips Worcester before the visit of Liverpool. Photo: Berrow's Newspapers.*

59-60 Q4: Hereford United (H) 0-3

60-61 Q4: Wellington Town (A) 1-1, (H) 3-2
R1: Coventry City (H) 1-4

61-62 Q4: Brierley Hill Alliance (H) 0-1

62-63 Q4: Hereford United (H) 0-2

63-64 Q1: Sankey of Wellington (A) 3-2
Q2: Wellington Town (A) 1-0
Q3: Kidderminster Harriers (H) 4-1
Q4: Loughborough United (H) 1-4

64-65 Q1: Bromsgrove Rovers (H) 4-0
Q2: Dudley Town (A) 1-3

65-66 Q1: Lower Gornal Athletic (H) 4-2
Q2: Dudley Town (A) 3-0
Q3: Kidderminster Harriers (A) 2-2, (H) 1-2

66-67 Q1: Hinckley Athletic (A) 4-0
Q2: Tamworth (H) 0-1

67-68 Q1: Stratford Town Amateur (H) 2-0
Q2: Halesowen Town (H) 1-1, (A) 0-0, 2-0
Q3: Stourbridge (A) 0-4

68-69 Q1: Hednesford (A) 2-1
Q2: Alvechurch (H) 0-0, (A) 1-0
Q3: Wellington Town (A) 3-2
Q4: Hereford United (A) 1-4

69-70 Q1: Hednesford (A) 1-2

70-71 PR: Highgate United (A) 1-1, (H) 5-0
Q1: Kidderminster Harriers (A) 0-1

71-72 Q1: Dudley Town (A) 1-0
Q2: Atherstone Town (H) 0-0, (A) 0-1

72-73 Q1: Stourbridge (A) 1-2

73-74 Q1: Highgate United (A) 1-1, (H) 1-2

74-75 Q1: Bromsgrove Rovers (A) 3-0
Q2: Warley County Borough (H) 5-0
Q3: A.P. Leamington (A) 1-2

75-76 Q1: Ton Pentre (A) 3-4

76-77 Q1: Glastonbury (H) 3-2
Q2: Evesham United (H) 3-1
Q3: Mangotsfield United (A) 2-0
Q4: Chesham United (A) 2-4

77-78 Q1: Llanelli (A) 1-1, (H) 2-0
Q2: Barry Town (H) 1-0
Q3: Weston-super-Mare (H) 1-1, (A) 2-1
Q4: Weymouth (H) 2-2, (A) 1-2

78-79 Q1: Bromsgrove Rovers (H) 1-0
Q2: Highgate United (A) 0-0, (H) 3-2
Q3: Darlaston (H) 7-1
Q4: Bath City (A) 1-1, (H) 2-1
R1: Plymouth Argyle (H) 2-0
R2: Newport County (A) 0-0, (H) 1-2

79-80 Q4: Salisbury (A) 1-2

80-81 Q1: Malvern Town (H) 1-1, (A) 2-0
Q2: Llanelli (A) 3-0
Q3: Barry Town (H) 1-1, (A) 3-2
Q4: Wycombe Wanderers (H) 1-1, (A) 0-1

81-82 Q1: Moreton Town (H) 5-2
Q2: Bridgend Town (A) 3-1
Q3: Devizes Town (H) 4-1
Q4: Minehead (A) 0-1

82-83 Q1: Alvechurch (A) 4-2
Q2: Rothwell Town (H) 3-1
Q3: Sutton Coldfield Town (A) 4-2
Q4: Wellingborough Town (H) 2-1
R1: Macclesfield Town (A) 5-1
R2: Wrexham (H) 2-1
R3: Coventry City (A) 1-3

Right: *Worcester City looked set for a major Cup shock when they took an early lead away to First Division Coventry City. However, despite this save by Phil Parkes, they were pegged back and lost 1-3. Photo: M Ward.*

83-84 Q4: Basingstoke Town (A) 1-1, (H) 3-1
R1: Aldershot (A) 1-1, (H) 2-1
R2: Maidstone United (A) 2-3

84-85 Q4: Weymouth (A) 1-3

85-86 Q4: Dartford (A) 0-2

87-88 Q1: Corby Town (A) 1-1, (H) 3-1
Q2: Leamington (A) 6-0
Q3: Boreham Wood (A) 3-1
Q4: Leytonstone-Ilford (A) 1-0
R1: Yeovil Town (H) 1-1, (A) 0-1

88-89 Q1: Barry Town (A) 2-0
Q2: Mangotsfield United (A) 1-0
Q3: Dorchester Town (H) 1-1, (A) 2-1
Q4: Yeovil Town (H) 1-2

89-90 Q1: Clandown (H) 3-0
Q2: Shortwood United (H) 3-0
Q3: Gloucester City (A) 2-4

90-91 Q1: Yate Town (A) 3-1
Q2: Bridgend Town (A) 7-1
Q3: Cheltenham Town (A) 2-4

91-92 Q1: Melksham Town (A) 8-1
Q2: Gloucester City (H) 2-1
Q3: Bath City (A) 2-1
Q4: Marlow (H) 1-2

92-93 Q1: Frome Town (A) 2-1
Q2: Newport A.F.C. (A - *at Gloucester C.*) 0-3

WORKINGTON

Currently: Northern Prmeier League

45-46 Q4: Chorley (H) 1-2

46-47 Q4: Netherfield (A) 3-1
R1: South Liverpool (A) 1-2

47-48 Q4: Netherfield (H) 2-1
R1: Lincoln City (A) 2-0
R2: Crewe Alexandra (H) 1-2

48-49 Q4: Lancaster City (H) 1-1, (A) 1-1, 2-1
R1: Stockport County (H) 0-3

49-50 Q4: Netherfield (A) 0-2

50-51 Q4: Cleator Moor Celtic (H) 0-1

51-52 R1: Blackhall Colliery Welfare (A) 5-2
R2: Witton Albion (A) 3-3, (H) 1-0
R3: Liverpool (A) 0-1

52-53 R1: Chesterfield (A) 0-1

53-54 R1: Ferryhill Athletic (H) 3-0
R2: Stockport County (A) 1-2

54-55 R1: Hyde United (H) 5-1
R2: Leyton Orient (A) 1-0
R3: Luton Town (A) 0-5

55-56 R1: Scarborough (H) 4-2
R2: Bradford Park Avenue (A) 3-4

56-57 R1: Mansfield Town (A) 1-1, (H) 2-1
R2: Goole Town (A) 2-2, (H) 0-1

57-58 R1: Crook Town (H) 8-1
R2: Oldham Athletic (A) 5-1
R3: Manchester United (H) 1-3

58-59 R1: Accrington Stanley (A) 1-5

59-60 R1: Southport (A) 2-2, (H) 3-0
R2: Halifax Town (H) 1-0
R3: Crewe Alexandra (A) 0-2

60-61 R1: Stockport County (A) 0-1

61-62 R1: Worksop Town (H) 2-0
R2: Gateshead (A) 2-0
R3: Nottingham Forest (H) 1-2

62-63 R1: North Shields (A) 2-2, (H) 7-2
R2: Hull City (A) 0-2

63-64 R1: Halifax Town (H) 4-1
R2: Port Vale (A) 1-2

64-65 R1: Rochdale (H) 2-0
R2: South Liverpool (A) 2-0
R3: Bolton Wanderers (A) 1-4

65-66 R1: Hartlepool United (A) 1-3

66-67 R1: South Shields (A) 4-1
R2: Bradford Park Avenue (A) 1-3

67-68 R1: Ryhope Colliery (A) 1-0
R2: Doncaster Rovers (A) 1-1, (H) 1-2

68-69 R1: Scunthorpe United (H) 2-0
R2: Port Vale (A) 0-0, (H) 1-2

69-70 R1: Rochdale (H) 2-1
R2: Rotherham United (A) 0-3

70-71 R1: Scarborough (A) 3-2
R2: Chesterfield (A) 0-0, (H) 3-2
R3: Brentford (H) 0-1

71-72 R1: Southport (A) 3-1
R2: Bury (H) 1-3

72-73 R1: Stockport County (A) 0-1

73-74 R1: Bradford City (A) 0-2

74-75 R1: Darlington (A) 0-1

75-76 R1: Rochdale (H) 1-1, (A) 1-2

76-77 R1: Bury (A) 0-6

77-78 R1: Grimsby Town (H) 0-2

78-79 Q4: Gateshead (A) 1-1, (H) 3-2
R1: Rotherham United (A) 0-3

79-80 Q4: Southport (A) 3-1
R1: Chester (A) 1-5

80-81 Q4: Bishop Auckland (H) 4-1
R1: Carlisle United (H) 0-0, (A) 1-4

81-82 Q4: Burton (H) 4-1
R1: Huddersfield Town (H) 1-1, (A) 0-5

82-83 Q4: Penrith (H) 2-2, (A) 2-0
R1: Doncaster Rovers (H) 1-2

83-84 Q4: Mossley (H) 0-0, (A) 0-1

84-85 Q4: Stalybridge Celtic (A) 0-1

83-86 Q1: Wingate (A) 2-4

86-87 Q1: Billingham Synthonia (H) 2-1
Q2: Brandon United (H) 0-0, (A) 1-0
Q3: Newcastle Blue Star (A) 1-1, (H) 0-1

87-88 Q1: Bishop Auckland (A) 2-5

88-89 PR: Murton (H) 1-1, (A) 4-2
Q1: Gateshead (H) 0-0 (A) 0-1

89-90 PR: Crook Town (A) 0-0, (H) 0-1

90-91 Q1: Horden Colliery Welfare (H) 1-1, (A) 1-2

91-92 Q1: Gateshead (H) 0-1

92-93 PR: West Auckland Town (H) 3-2
Q1: Easington Colliery (A) 1-1, (H) 1-0
Q2: Blyth Spartans (A) 0-6

Below: *The qualifying competitions have enjoyed television exposure in recent years via the B.B.C.'s 'Road to Wembley' series. Here Worthing take the field for their Third Qualifying Round tie against Canterbury City in 1992. Photo: Roger Turner*

WORKSOP TOWN

Currently: Northern Premier League

49-50 EX: Bestwood Colliery (A) 2-1
PR: South Normanton M.W. (A) 1-1, (H) 1-2

50-51 EX: Hallam (A) 4-2
PR: Sheffield (H) 2-1
Q1: Beighton M.W. (A) 1-1, (H) 5-3
Q2: Norton Woodseats (A) 3-1
Q3: Stocksbridge Works (H) 1-2

51-52 Q1: Bentley Colliery (H) 5-1
Q2: Norton Woodseats (H) 1-0
Q3: Rawmarsh Welfare (A) 1-2

52-53 Q1: Rawmarsh Welfare (H) 3-3, (A) 2-3

53-54 Q1: Brodsworth Main Colliery (A) 4-1
Q2: Bentley Colliery (A) 2-1
Q3: Beighton Miners Welfare (H) 3-2
Q4: Gainsborough Trinity (H) 2-2, (A) 1-2

54-55 Q1: Langold W.M.C. (H) 4-0
Q2: Norton Woodseats Am. (H) 3-3, (A) 2-1
Q3: Rawmarsh Welfare (A) 3-0
Q4: Corby Town (A) 1-3

55-56 Q1: Brunswick Institute (H) 8-0
Q2: Beighton M.W. (H) 3-0
Q3: Bentley Colliery (H) 9-2
Q4: Corby Town (H) 1-0
R1: Skegness Town (A) 4-0
R2: Bradford City (A) 2-2, (H) 1-0
R3: Swindon Town (A) 0-1

56-57 Q4: Scarborough (H) 1-4

57-58 Q1: Ransome & Marles (A) 1-2

58-59 Q1: Players Athletic (A) 4-0
Q2: Sutton Town (H) 3-3, (A) 3-4

59-60 Q1: Sheffield (A) 3-2
Q2: Matlock Town (A) 1-3

60-61 Q1: Sutton Town (H) 2-2, (A) 0-3

61-62 Q1: Cresswell Colliery (A) 2-1
Q2: Gainsborough Trinity (H) 4-3
Q3: Stocksbridge Works (H) 3-1
Q4: Corby Town (A) 2-2, (H) 2-1
R1: Workington (A) 0-2

62-63 Q1: Norton Woodseats Amateur (A) 3-1
Q2: Frickley Colliery (H) 1-0
Q3: Gainsborough Trinity (H) 0-0, (A) 1-3

63-64 Q1: Denaby United (A) 5-0
Q2: Retford Town (H) 2-0
Q3: Gainsborough Trinity (H) 1-3

64-65 Q1: Mexborough Town (H) 2-1
Q2: Frickley Colliery (A) 0-2

65-66 Q1: Sutton Town (A) 2-2, (H) 6-2
Q2: Matlock Town (A) 3-1
Q3: Heanor Town (A) 2-3

66-67 Q1: Buxton (A) 2-1
Q2: Sutton Town (H) 3-0
Q3: Macclesfield Town (A) 1-3

67-68 PR: Yorkshire Amateur (A) 0-1

68-69 Q1: Frickley Colliery (H) 2-4

69-70 Q1: Mexborough Town (A) 3-3, (H) 6-1
Q2: Gainsborough Trinity (A) 1-2

70-71 Q1: Gainsborough Trinity (H) 0-1

71-72 Q1: Glossop (A) 1-0
Q2: Denaby United (A) 2-1
Q3: Frickley Colliery (H) 1-1, (A) 1-3

72-73 Q1: Retford Town (A) 2-1
Q2: Bridlington Trinity (A) 1-0
Q3: Gainsborough Trinity (A) 0-1

73-74 Q1: Enderby Town (A) 4-2
Q2: Arnold (H) 1-0
Q3: Alfreton Town (A) 1-2

74-75 Q1: Ashby Institute (A) 1-0
Q2: Retford Town (H) 1-0
Q3: Matlock Town (A) 2-6

75-76 Q1: Mossley (H) 1-0
Q2: Winterton Rovers (H) 4-3
Q3: Frickley Colliery (H) 1-1, (A) 1-1, 2-0
Q4: Marine (H) 0-0, (A) 0-4

76-77 PR: Congleton Town (A) 2-1
Q1: Horwich R.M.I. (A) 1-1, (H) 1-0
Q2: Buxton (H) 3-0
Q3: Droylsden (A) 0-1

77-78 Q1: Retford Town (A) 2-1
Q2: Emley (H) 4-2
Q3: Goole Town (H) 2-2, (A) 2-2, *(at Doncaster Rovers)* 1-3

78-79 Q1: Eastwood Town (H) 2-1
Q2: Brigg Town (A) 1-1, (H) 1-1 *(at Gainsborough Trinity)* 2-0
Q3: Grantham (H) 0-0, (A) 3-0
Q4: Dudley Town (A) 1-0
R1: Barnsley (A) 1-5

79-80 Q1: Arnold (A) 3-2
Q2: Alfreton Town (A) 1-3

80-81 PR: Rossendale United (A) 1-1, (H) 3-1
Q1: Frickley Athletic (H) 3-2
Q2: Appleby Frodingham Athletic (A) 2-0
Q3: Stalybridge Celtic (A) 0-0, (H) 1-2

81-82 PR: Heanor Town (A) 3-1
Q1: Skegness Town (H) 2-1
Q2: Ilkeston Town (H) 2-3

82-83 PR: Gresley Rovers (A) 4-2
Q1: Glossop (A) 5-2
Q2: Eastwood Town (H) 1-1, (A) 1-3

83-84 Q1: Wisbech Town (H) 1-2

84-85 Q1: Tividale (A) 2-1
Q2: Halesowen Town (H) 0-3

85-86 Q1: Brigg Town (A) 1-0
Q2: Gresley Rovers (A) 0-1

86-87 Q1: Armitage (H) 7-0
Q2: Northwich Victoria (H) 0-2

87-88 Q1: Rossendale United (A) 1-1, (H) 2-4

88-89 Q1: Sutton Coldfield Town (H) 1-2

89-90 PR: Oakham United (A) 2-4

90-91 Q1: Gresley Rovers (H - *at Gainsborough*) 2-0
Q2: Marine (H - *at Gainsborough*) 1-3

91-92 PR: Brigg Town (H - *at Gainsborough*) 3-1
Q1: Stalybridge Celtic (A) 0-4

92-93 PR: Flixton (A) 1-1, (H) 3-0
Q1: Arnold Town (H) 5-3
Q2: Horwich R.M.I. (A) 1-1, (H) 1-5

WORSBOROUGH BRIDGE MINERS WELFARE & ATHLETIC

Currently: Northern Counties (East) League

78-79 Q1: Whitby Town (A) 3-3, (H) 0-1

79-80 Q1: Mexborough Town Athletic (H) 0-2

80-81 PR: New Brighton (A) 3-1
Q1: Fleetwood Town (H) 0-4

Opposite: *Workington goalkeeper Lee Copeland catches competently despite the attentions of Stephen Pyle (10) of Blyth Spartans. Photo: Colin Stevens*

WORTHING

Currently: Isthmian League

45-46 Q1: Horsham (A) 3-4

46-47 PR: Hastings & St Leo. (A) 3-3, (H) 2-2, 3-2
Q1: Eastbourne (H) 3-5

47-48 Q1: Chichester (H) 3-2
Q2: Bognor Regis Town (A) 3-1
Q3: Horsham (A) 0-1

48-49 PR: Eastbourne Comrades (H) 4-3
Q1: East Grinstead (H) 2-0
Q2: Bognor Regis Town (H) 1-4

49-50 Q1: Littlehampton Town (H) 5-0
Q2: Haywards Heath (H) 2-4

50-51 PR: Southwick (A) 2-1
Q1: Haywards Heath (H) 1-2

51-52 PR: Shoreham (H) 3-2
Q1: Southwick (A) 7-6
Q2: Tonbridge (A) 1-11

52-53 PR: Horsham (A) 4-1
Q1: Littlehampton Town (A) 3-0
Q2: Hastings United (H) 2-2, (A) 3-1
Q3: Lancing Athletic (A) 0-2

53-54 PR: Eastbourne (H) 2-4

54-55 Q1: Bognor Regis Town (H) 3-3, (A) 1-4

55-56 PR: Lancing Athletic (H) 5-0
Q1: Haywards Heath (H) 4-1
Q2: Southwick (A) 2-1
Q3: Redhill (H) 1-4

56-57 PR: Southwick (H) 3-2
Q1: Redhill (H) 2-2, (A) 2-7

57-58 PR: Haywards Heath (H) 1-1, (A) 3-3 *aban. in extra-time,* (A) 7-1
Q1: Southwick (A) 2-3

58-59 Q1: Horsham (A) 2-5

59-60 PR: Eastbourne United (H) 3-1
Q1: Crawley Town (H) 1-6

60-61 Q1: Southwick (A) 2-2, (H) 2-3

61-62 Q1: Crawley Town (A) 0-5

62-63 Q1: Bognor Regis Town (H) 1-2

63-64 Q1: Lancing (H) 0-0, (A) 2-3

66-67 Q1: Crawley Town (A) 0-4

67-68 Q1: Lancing (H) 0-1

68-69 Q1: Southwick (A) 1-1, (H) 3-5

69-70 Q1: Eastbourne (A) 1-5

70-71 Q1: Woking (H) 0-2

71-72 Q1: Littlehampton Town (A) 1-0
Q2: Horsham (H) 1-3

72-73 Q1: Leatherhead (A) 0-3

73-74 Q1: Pagham (A) 0-0, (H) 3-1
Q2: Waterlooville (H) 2-1
Q3: Littlehampton Town (A) 2-0
Q4: Wycombe Wanderers (H) 0-3

74-75 Q1: Burgess Hill Town (A) 0-2

75-76 Q1: Poole Town (A) 0-1

76-77 PR: Horsham Y.M.C.A. (A) 0-2

77-78 Q1: Horsham (A) 1-4

78-79 Q1: Alton Town (H) 4-1
Q2: Haywards Heath (A) 2-1
Q3: Waterlooville (H) 1-1, (A) 0-3

79-80 PR: Southwick (A) 3-2
Q1: Tonbridge A.F.C. (A) 3-2
Q2: Bognor Regis Town (H) 1-2

80-81 Q1: Basingstoke Town (H) 0-1

81-82 PR: Metropolitan Police (A) 2-1
Q1: Bognor Regis Town (H) 0-0, (A) 0-1

82-83 PR: Fleet Town (H) 7-1
Q1: Crawley Town (A) 2-1
Q2: Eastleigh (H) 3-1
Q3: Farnborough Town (H) 1-0
Q4: Minehead (H) 2-2, (A) 3-0
R1: Dartford (H) 2-1
R2: Oxford United (A) 0-4

83-84 Q1: Southwick (A) 2-1
Q2: Kingstonian (A) 2-3

84-85 Q1: Arundel (A) 2-2, (H) 4-1
Q2: Lewes (H) 3-0
Q3: Canterbury City (A) 1-2

85-86 Q1: Waterlooville (H) 3-0
Q2: Tooting & Mitcham United (H) 5-1
Q3: Newport Isle of Wight (H) 4-0
Q4: Bognor Regis Town (H) 1-2

86-87 Q1: Herne Bay (H) 0-1

87-88 PR: Thatcham Town (A) 3-0
Q1: Pagham (A) 2-2, (H) 0-2

88-89 Q1: A.F.C. Totton (H) 3-2
Q2: Windsor & Eton (H) 0-4

89-90 PR: Tooting & Mitcham Utd (A) 2-2, (H) 0-1

90-91 Q1: Chatham Town (H) 3-0
Q2: Crawley Town (H) 3-2
Q3: Dorking (A) 1-1, (H) 2-4

91-92 PR: Chertsey Town (A) 2-2, (H) 4-1
Q1: Whyteleafe (A) 2-1
Q2: Bromley (A) 1-3

92-93 PR: Chatham Town (H) 8-0
Q1: Egham Town (A) 1-1, (H) 7-1
Q2: Bromley (H) 2-1
Q3: Canterbury City (H) 3-1
Q4: Cheltenham Town (A) 2-3

WORTHING UNITED

Currently: Sussex County League
* - As Wigmore Athletic

54-55 * PR: Arundel (A) 0-4

55-56 * PR: Eastbourne (A) 2-4

56-57 * Q1: Horsham (H) 1-4

76-77 * PR: Newport Isle of Wight (A) 0-2

77-78 * PR: East Grinstead (H) 1-3

78-79 * Q1: Haywards Heath (A) 0-4

79-80 * PR: Pagham (A) 0-0, (H) 0-2

92-93 PR: Langney Sports (H) 1-4

WREN ROVERS

See Blackpool Rovers

WREXHAM

Currently: Football League

45-46 R1: Crewe Alex. (A) 2-4, (H) 3-0 (*agg: 5-4*)
R2: Shrewsbury T. (A) 1-0, (H) 1-1 (*agg: 2-1*)
R3: Blackpool (H) 1-4, (A) 1-4 (*agg: 2-8*)

46-47 R1: Marine (H) 5-0
R2: Lincoln City (A) 3-3, (H) 1-1, 1-2

47-48 R1: Halifax Town (H) 5-0
R2: Colchester United (A) 0-1

48-49 R1: Oldham Athletic (H) 0-3

49-50 R1: Grantham (H) 4-1
R2: Southend United (H) 2-2, (A) 0-2

50-51 R1: Accrington Stanley (H) 1-0
R2: Bristol City (A) 1-2

51-52 R1: Halifax Town (H) 3-0
R2: Leyton Orient (H) 1-1, (A) 2-3

52-53 R1: Beighton Miners Welfare (A) 3-0
R2: Great Yarmouth Town (A) 2-1
R3: Stoke City (A) 1-2

53-54 R1: Horden Colliery Welfare (A) 1-0
R2: Brighton (H) 1-1, (A) 1-1, 3-1
R3: Scunthorpe Utd (H) 3-3, (A) 0-3

54-55 R1: Netherfield (A) 3-3, (H) 4-0
R2: Walsall (H) 1-2

55-56 R1: Accrington Stanley (A) 1-3

56-57 R1: Crewe Alexandra (A) 2-2, (H) 2-1
R2: Scunthorpe Utd (A) 0-0, (H) 6-2
R3: Reading (H) 1-1, (A) 2-1
R4: Manchester United (H) 0-5

57-58 R1: Accrington Stanley (H) 0-1

58-59 R1: Darlington (H) 1-2

59-60 R1: Blyth Spartans (H) 2-1
R2: Grimsby Town (A) 3-2
R3: Leicester City (H) 1-2

60-61 R1: Bangor City (A) 0-1

61-62 R1: Barrow (H) 3-2
R2: Rochdale (A) 2-1
R3: Norwich City (A) 1-3

62-63 R1: Southport (A) 1-1, (H) 3-2
R2: Barrow (H) 5-2
R3: Liverpool (H) 0-3

63-64 R1: Altrincham (A) 1-1, (H) 0-0, 3-0
R2: Hull City (H) 0-2

64-65 R1: Macclesfield Town (A) 2-1
R2: Southport (H) 2-3

65-66 R1: South Liverpool (H) 4-1
R2: Hartlepools United (A) 0-2

66-67 R1: Chesterfield (H) 3-2
R2: Shrewsbury Town (A) 1-5

67-68 R1: Bradford City (A) 1-7

68-69 R1: Oldham Athletic (H) 4-2
R2: Chesterfield (A) 1-2

69-70 R1: Spennymoor United (A) 4-1
R2: Hartlepools United (A) 1-0
R3: Norwich City (A) 2-1
R4: Liverpool (A) 1-3

70-71 R1: Mansfield Town (A) 0-2

71-72 R1: Bradford City (H) 5-1
R2: Wigan Athletic (H) 4-0
R3: Orient (A) 0-3

72-73 R1: Darlington (A) 1-1, (H) 5-0
R2: Port Vale (A) 0-1

73-74 R1: Shrewsbury Town (H) 1-1, (A) 1-0
R2: Rotherham United (H) 3-0
R3: Crystal Palace (A) 2-0
R4: Middlesbrough (H) 1-0
R5: Southampton (A) 1-0
R6: Burnley (A) 0-1

74-75 R1: Mansfield Town (A) 1-3

75-76 R1: Mansfield Town (A) 1-1, (H) 1-1, (*at*

Aston Villa) 1-2

76-77 R1: Gateshead (H) 6-0
R2: Goole Town (H) 1-1, (A) 1-0
R3: Sunderland (A) 2-2, (H) 1-0
R4: Cardiff City (A) 2-3

77-78 R1: Burton Albion (H) 2-0
R2: Preston North End (A) 2-0
R3: Bristol City (A) 4-4, (H) 3-0
R4: Newcastle United (A) 2-2, (H) 4-1
R5: Blyth S. (H) 1-1, (A - *Newcastle Utd*) 2-1
R6: Arsenal (H) 2-3

78-79 R3: Stockport County (H) 6-2
R4: Tottenham Hotspur (A) 3-3, (H) 2-3

79-80 R3: Charlton Athletic (H) 6-0
R4: Carlisle United (A) 0-0, (H) 3-1
R5: Everton (A) 2-5

80-81 R3: West Ham U. (A) 1-1, (H) 0-0, (H) 1-0
R4: Wimbledon (H) 2-1
R5: Wolverhampton Wanderers (A) 1-3

81-82 R3: Nottingham Forest (A) 3-1
R4: Chelsea (A) 0-0, (H) 1-1, (H) 1-2

82-83 R1: Holbeach (A - *at Peterborough U.*) 4-0
R2: Worcester City (A) 1-2

83-84 R1: Sheffield United (H) 1-5

84-85 R1: Wigan Athletic (H) 0-2

85-86 R1: Bolton Wanderers (H) 3-1
R2: Notts County (A) 2-2, (H) 0-3

86-87 R1: Hartlepool United (H) 2-1
R2: Rochdale (A) 4-1
R3: Chester City (H) 1-2

87-88 R1: Rochdale (A) 2-0
R2: Bolton Wanderers (H) 1-2

88-89 R1: Runcorn (A) 2-2, (H) 2-3

89-90 R1: Carlisle United (A) 0-3

90-91 R1: Halifax Town (A) 2-3

91-92 R1: Winsford United (H) 5-2
R2: Telford United (H) 1-0
R3: Arsenal (H) 2-1
R4: West Ham United (A) 2-2, (H) 0-1

92-93 R1: Crewe Alexandra (A) 1-6

WYCOMBE WANDERERS

Currently: Football League

45-46 PR: Southall (H) 0-2

46-47 EX: Marlow (H) 2-0
PR: Southall (A) 5-2
Q1: Hayes (H) 3-4

47-48 EX: Hounslow Town (H) 4-2
PR: Uxbridge (H) 3-1
Q1: Hayes (H) 1-0
Q2: Southall (A) 3-3, (H) 1-2

48-49 PR: Uxbridge (A) 3-4

49-50 PR: Southall (A) 2-6

50-51 EX: Amersham Town (A) 13-0
PR: Maidenhead United (A) 2-0
Q1: Chesham United (A) 1-1, (H) 4-2
Q2: Aylesbury United (A) 2-0
Q3: Slough Town (A) 1-1, (H) 2-0
Q4: Chelmsford City (H) 0-4

51-52 Q1: Windsor & Eton (H) 6-1
Q2: Headington (A) 2-3 *Headington expelled*
Q3: Aylesbury United (H) 1-2

52-53 PR: Oxford City (A) 4-1
Q1: Huntley & Palmers Recreation (H) 4-2
Q2: Hemel Hempstead Town (A) 2-1
Q3: Headington United (A) 2-6

53-54 PR: Banbury Spencer (A) 1-2

54-55 PR: Aylesbury United (A) 1-0
Q1: Slough Centre (A) 3-1
Q2: Oxford City (A) 1-4

55-56 PR: Witney Town (A) 0-0, (H) 15-1
Q1: Maidenhead United (H) 4-2
Q2: Slough Town (A) 3-3, (H) 1-0
Q3: Banbury Spencer (A) 2-1
Q4: Fareham Town (H) 3-1
R1: Burton Albion (H) 1-3

56-57 Q4: Margate (H) 2-4

57-58 R1: Dorchester Town (A) 2-3

58-59 Q4: Hendon (A) 3-1
R1: Northampton Town (A) 0-2

59-60 Q4: Oxford City (H) 1-0
R1: Wisbech Town (H) 4-2
R2: Watford (A) 1-5

60-61 Q4: Tooting & Mitcham United (H) 2-1
R1: Kettering Town (H) 1-2

61-62 Q4: Tilbury (H) 3-1
R1: Ashford Town (H) 0-0, (A) 0-3

62-63 Q4: Walthamstow Avenue (A) 1-1, (H) 3-1
R1: Maidenhead United (A) 3-0
R2: Gravesend & Northfleet (A) 1-3

63-64 Q4: Barnet (A) 3-6

64-65 Q4: Hayes (A) 0-7

65-66 Q4: Metropolitan Police (A) 3-2
R1: Guildford City (A) 2-2, (H) 0-1

66-67 Q4: Cheshunt (H) 8-0
R1: Bedford T. (H) 1-1, (A) 3-3, 1-1, 2-3

67-68 Q4: Dagenham (H) 0-2

68-69 Q1: St Albans City (H) 0-0, (A) 0-1

69-70 Q1: Dulwich Hamlet (H) 2-1
Q2: Erith & Belvedere (H) 2-0
Q3: Hitchin Town (H) 1-0
Q4: Barnet (H) 0-0, (A) 0-3

70-71 Q1: Wolverton Town & B.R. (H) 8-1
Q2: Banbury United (A) 3-0
Q3: Dunstable Town (A) 4-0
Q4: Kettering Town (H) 5-0
R1: Slough Town (H) 1-1, (A) 0-1

71-72 Q1: Maidenhead United (A) 0-2

72-73 Q1: Tooting & Mitcham United (A) 3-1
Q2: Egham Town (A) 6-2
Q3: Walton & Hersham (A) 0-1

73-74 Q1: Tilbury (A) 3-0
Q2: Woking (H) 1-0
Q3: Chatham Town (A) 7-0
Q4: Worthing (A) 3-0
R1: Newport County (H) 3-1
R2: Peterborough United (H) 1-3

74-75 Q1: Marlow (A) 1-0
Q2: Milton Keynes City (H) 2-0
Q3: Chesham United (A) 3-1
Q4: Margate (H) 2-1
R1: Cheltenham Town (H) 3-1
R2: A.F.C. Bournemouth (H) 0-0, (A) 2-1
R3: Middlesbrough (H) 0-0, (A) 0-1

Below: *Tony Horseman (advertising his league sponsors' wares) leads the celebrations after Wycombe's magnificent replay triumph away to A.F.C. Bournemouth in 1974.*

75-76 Q4: Croydon (A) 2-2, (H) 5-2
R1: Bedford T. (H) 0-0, (A) 2-2, 2-1
R2: Cardiff City (A) 0-1

76-77 Q4: Merthyr Tydfil (H) 3-1
R1: Waterlooville (A) 2-1
R2: Reading (H) 1-2

77-78 R1: Minehead (A) 0-2

78-79 R1: Maidstone United (A) 0-1

79-80 Q4: Barnet (A) 2-0
R1: Croydon (H) 0-3

80-81 Q4: Worcester City (A) 1-1, (H) 1-0
R1: A.F.C. Bournemouth (H) 0-3

81-82 Q4: Witney Town (A) 1-0
R1: Hendon (A) 1-1, (H) 2-0
R2: Barnet (A) 0-2

82-83 R1: Bristol Rovers (A) 0-1

83-84 Q4: Eastwood Town (A) 2-2, (H) 2-1
R1: Chelmsford City (A) 0-0, (H) 1-2

84-85 Q4: Burton Albion (H) 1-1, (A) 1-2

85-86 Q4: Burton Albion (H) 1-0
R1: Colchester United (H) 2-0
R2: Chelmsford City (H) 2-0
R3: York City (A) 0-2

86-87 Q4: V.S. Rugby (H) 1-5

87-88 Q1: Aylesbury United (A) 0-2

88-89 Q1: Haverhill Rovers (H) 4-1
Q2: Finchley (A) 3-0
Q3: Staines Town (A) 1-0
Q4: Kettering Town (H) 1-2

89-90 Q1: Baldock Town (A) 2-0
Q2: Boreham Wood (H) 3-1
Q3: Gravesend & N. (H) 1-1, (A) 1-1, (A) 3-0
Q4: Stafford Rangers (A) 1-4

90-91 Q1: Maidenhead United (H) 3-0
Q2: Trowbridge Town (A) 0-0, (H) 2-1
Q3: Wokingham Town (H) 4-1
Q4: Basingstoke Town (H) 6-0
R1: Boston United (A) 1-1, (H) 4-0
R2: Peterborough United (H) 1-1, (A) 0-2

91-92 R1: Kettering Town (A) 1-1, (H) 0-2

92-93 R1: Merthyr Tydfil (H) 3-1
R2: West Bromwich Albion (H) 2-2, (A) 0-1

Opposite Right: *Wycombe's Andy Kerr directs a header at the West Bromwich Albion goal during the narrow replay defeat at the Hawthorns on Tuesday 15th December 1992. In the initial match at Adams Park, Wycombe had recovered from a two goal deficit, and only a late goal in the the replay cost them defeat in what turned out to be their last F.A. Cup tie as a non-League club. Photo: Paul Dennis.*

Right: *Yeovil Town's Ian McGinlay (centre) takes on Alan McDonald of Queens Park Rangers in the Third Round tie on 9th January 1988. Photo: Bob Thomas.*

WYMONDHAM TOWN

Currently: Anglian Combination

50-51 EX: City of Norwich School O.B.U. (H) 1-5

51-52 Q1: Cromer (H) 1-4

52-53 Q1: Gothic (A) 0-6

53-54 Q1: Bungay Town (H) 3-3, (A) 1-4

54-55 Q1: Beccles (A) 0-2

55-56 Q1: Cromer (A) 2-1
Q2: Beccles (A) 2-2, (H) 1-2

YATE TOWN

Currently: Southern League

86-87 Q1: Forest Green Rovers (A) 0-2

87-88 PR: Hungerford Town (A) 1-1, (H) 1-0
Q1: Mangotsfield United (A) 0-1

88-89 PR: Clandown (A) 2-0
Q1: Swanage Town & Herston (A) 1-2

89-90 PR: Chard Town (A) 1-2

90-91 PR: Glastonbury (H) 4-0
Q1: Worcester City (H) 1-3

91-92 PR: Bristol Manor Farm (H) 4-1
Q1: Barry Town (H) 0-3

92-93 PR: Clevedon Town (A) 1-4

YEADING

Currently: Isthmian League

86-87 PR: Clapton (A) 1-0
Q1: Alma Swan. (H) 4-4, (A - *at Greenwich Borough*) 1-0
Q2: Sutton United (H) 4-1
Q3: Uxbridge (H) 1-0
Q4: Aylesbury United (H) 1-3

87-88 Q1: Harrow Borough (A) 0-2

88-89 PR: Haywards Heath Town (H) 2-3

89-90 PR: Buckingham Town (H) 4-0
Q1: Chalfont St Peter (H) 0-0, (A) 5-0
Q2: Uxbridge (A) 0-1

90-91 Q1: Royston Town (A) 2-3

91-92 PR: Rayners Lane (H) 8-0
Q1: Ruislip Manor (H) 3-1
Q2: Slough Town (H) 0-0, (A) 0-1

92-93 Q1: Staines Town (A) 3-0
Q2: Alma Swanley (H) 7-1
Q3: Slough Town (A) 1-2

YEOVIL TOWN

Currently: Alliance Premier League
* - As Yeovil & Petters United

45-46 * R1: Bristol C. (H) 2-2, (A) 0-3 (*agg: 2-5*)

46-47 Q4: Dartmouth United (H) 10-2
R1: Peterborough United (H) 2-2, (A) 0-1

47-48 Q4: Street (A) 1-2

48-49 Q4: Lovells Athletic (A) 3-2
R1: Romford (H) 4-0
R2: Weymouth (A) 4-0
R3: Bury (H) 3-1
R4: Sunderland (H) 2-1
R5: Manchester Utd (A - *at Man. City*) 0-8

49-50 R1: Romford (H) 4-1
R2: Gillingham (H) 3-1
R3: Chesterfield (A) 1-3

50-51 Q4: Cheltenham Town (H) 2-4

51-52 Q4: Weymouth (H) 1-1, (A) 1-2

52-53 Q4: Merthyr Tydfil (H) 1-0
R1: Brighton & Hove Albion (H) 1-4

53-54 Q4: Merthyr Tydfil (H) 2-1
R1: Norwich City (H) 0-2

54-55 Q4: Barnstaple Town (A) 1-3

55-56 Q4: Bideford (A) 3-0
R1: Aldershot (H) 1-1, (A) 1-1, 0-3

56-57 Q4: Glastonbury (H) 3-1
R1: Peterborough United (H) 1-3

57-58 Q4: Bideford (H) 3-1
R1: Guildford City (A) 2-2, (H) 1-0
R2: Bath City (H) 2-0
R3: Fulham (A) 0-4

58-59 Q4: Bideford (A) 4-1
R1: Southend United (A) 0-0, (H) 1-0
R2: Colchester United (A) 1-1, (H) 1-7

59-60 Q4: Bath City (H) 0-2

60-61 Q4: Trowbridge Town (A) 4-0
R1: Walsall (A) 1-0
R2: Bournemouth & Boscombe Ath. (A) 1-2

61-62 Q4: Andover (H) 4-0
R1: Notts County (A) 2-4

62-63 Q4: Trowbridge Town (H) 4-0
R1: Dartford (H) 3-2
R2: Swindon Town (H) 0-2

63-64 Q4: Cowes Isle of Wight (A) 1-0
R1: Southend United (H) 1-0
R2: Crystal Palace (H) 3-1
R3: Bury (H) 0-2

64-65 Q4: Salisbury (A) 1-2

65-66 Q4: Portland United (A) 1-1, (H) 3-0
R1: Brentford (A) 1-2

66-67 Q4: Cheltenham Town (A) 3-3, (H) 3-1
R1: Oxford United (H) 1-3

67-68 Q4: Welton Rovers (H) 2-0
R1: Margate (H) 1-3

68-69 Q4: Bath City (A) 2-0
R1: Weymouth (A) 1-2

69-70 Q4: Minehead (A) 0-0, (H) 0-0, 5-0
R1: Shrewsbury Town (H) 2-3

70-71 Q4: Poole Town (A) 2-1
R1: Aveley (H) 1-0
R2: A.F.C. Bournemouth (A) 1-0
R3: Arsenal (H) 0-3

71-72 Q4: Bridgwater Town (A) 0-2

72-73 Q4: Taunton Town (H) 4-1
R1: Brentford (H) 2-1
R2: Plymouth Argyle (H) 0-2

73-74 Q4: Weymouth (H) 1-1, (A) 2-2, 0-1

74-75 Q4: Bath City (A) 1-2

75-76 Q1: Stonehouse (A) 6-0
Q2: Weston-super-Mare (A) 0-0, (H) 4-0
Q3: Minehead (H) 1-0
Q4: Falmouth Town (A) 5-1
R1: Millwall (H) 1-1, (A) 2-2, (*at Aldershot*) 0-1

76-77 PR: Penzance (A) 7-2
Q1: Tiverton Town (A) 2-0

Q2: Ilminster Town (H) 10-1
Q3: Falmouth Town (A) 0-2

77-78 PR: Alton Town (H) 2-2, (A) 4-0
Q1: Frome Town (A) 1-2

78-79 Q1: Andover (H) 4-0
Q2: Hungerford Town (A) 4-4, (H) 3-0
Q3: Dorchester Town (H) 2-1
Q4: Cheltenham Town (A) 2-1
R1: Barking (H) 0-1

79-80 Q1: Bridgwater Town (A) 0-0, (H) 2-0
Q2: Liskeard Athletic (A) 1-0
Q3: Saltash United (A) 3-3, (H) 2-1
Q4: Weymouth (H) 2-1
R1: Enfield (A) 1-0
R2: Slough Town (H) 1-0
R3: Norwich City (H) 0-3

80-81 Q4: Hayes (A) 1-1, (H) 2-0
R1: Farnborough Town (H) 2-1
R2: Colchester United (A) 1-1, (H) 0-2

81-82 Q4: Merthyr Tydfil (H) 3-0
R1: Dagenham (A) 2-2, (H) 0-1

82-83 Q4: Bognor Regis Town (H) 4-2
R1: Chesham United (A) 1-0
R2: Southend United (A) 0-3

83-84 Q4: Minehead (H) 2-2, (A) 4-2
R1: Harrow Borough (H) 0-1

84-85 Q4: Witney Town (H) 3-1
R1: Torquay United (A) 0-2

85-86 Q4: Barry Town (H) 4-1
R1: Hereford United (H) 2-4

86-87 Q4: Bath City (A) 1-2

87-88 Q1: Gosport Borough (A) 1-0
Q2: Waterlooville (A) 1-1, (H) 3-2
Q3: Wimborne Town (A) 4-0
Q4: Weymouth (A) 3-1
R1: Worcester City (A) 1-1, (H) 1-0
R2: Cambridge United (A) 1-0
R3: Queens Park Rangers (H) 0-3

88-89 Q4: Worcester City (A) 2-1
R1: Merthyr Tydfil (H) 3-2
R2: Torquay United (H) 1-1, (A) 0-1

89-90 Q4: Staines Town (A) 3-0
R1: Maidstone U. (A - *at Dartford*) 1-2

90-91 Q4: Marlow (H) 3-1
R1: Brentford (A) 0-5

91-92 Q4: Tonbridge A.F.C. (A) 2-1
R1: Walsall (H) 1-1, (A) 1-0
R2: Woking (A) 0-3

92-93 Q4: Crawley Town (A) 2-1
R1: Torquay United (A) 5-2
R2: Hereford United (H) 0-0, (A) 2-1
R3: Arsenal (H) 1-3

Right: *When Yeovil Town defeated Barclays League Third Division Hereford United in 1992-93 they regained from Altrincham the record for wins by a non-League club over over Football League opposition. Here Paul Sanderson holds off Hereford's Gareth Davis in the 0-0 draw at Huish Park. Photo: Dave West.*

YIEWSLEY

See Hillingdon Borough

YORK CITY

Currently: Football League

45-46 R1: Halifax T. (A) 0-1, (H) 4-2 (*agg: 4-3*)
R2: Bishop Auckland (A) 2-1, (H) 3-0 (*agg: 5-1*)
R3: Chesterfield (A) 1-1, (H) 3-2 (*agg: 4-3*)
R4: Sheffield Wed. (A) 1-5, (H) 1-6 (*agg: 2-11*)

46-47 R1: Scunthorpe United (H) 0-1

47-48 R1: Rochdale (H) 0-1

48-49 R1: Runcorn (H) 2-1
R4: Southport (A) 2-2, (H) 0-2

49-50 R1: Gateshead (A) 1-3

50-51 R1: Bishop Auckland (A) 2-2 (H) 2-1
R2: Tranmere Rovers (H) 2-1
R3: Bolton Wanderers (A) 0-2

51-52 R1: Bradford Park Ave. (H) 1-1, (A) 1-1, 0-4

52-53 R1: Barrow (H) 1-2

53-54 R1: Barnsley (A) 2-5

54-55 R1: Scarborough (H) 3-2
R2: Dorchester Town (A) 5-2
R3: Blackpool (A) 2-0
R4: Bishop Auckland (A) 3-1
R5: Tottenham Hotspur (H) 3-1
R6: Notts County (A) 1-0
SF: Newcastle United (*at Sheffield Wednesday*) 1-1, (*at Sunderland*) 0-2

55-56 R1: Rochdale (A) 1-0
R2: Mansfield Town (H) 2-1
R3: Swansea Town (A) 2-1
R4: Sunderland (H) 0-0, (A) 1-2

56-57 R1: Southport (A) 0-0, (H) 2-1
R2: Hull City (A) 1-2

57-58 R1: Chesterfield (H) 1-0
R2: South Shields (A) 3-1
R3: Birmingham City (H) 3-0
R4: Bolton Wanderers (H) 0-0, (A) 0-3

58-59 R1: Bury (A) 0-0, (H) 0-1

59-60 R1: Barrow (H) 3-1
R2: Crook Town (A) 1-0
R3: Bournemouth & Boscombe A. (A) 0-1

60-61 R1: Bradford Park Ave. (H) 0-0, (A) 2-0
R2: Tranmere Rovers (A) 1-1, (H) 2-1
R3: Norwich City (H) 1-1, (A) 0-1

61-62 R1: Bradford City (A) 0-1

62-63 R1: Rochdale (H) 0-0, (A) 2-1
R2: Crewe Alexandra (H) 2-1
R3: Southampton (A) 0-5

63-64 R1: Carlisle United (H) 2-5

64-65 R1: Bangor City (H) 5-1
R2: Chesterfield (A) 1-2

65-66 R1: South Shields (A) 1-3

66-67 R1: Morecambe (H) 0-0, (A) 1-1, 1-0
R2: Middlesbrough (A) 1-1, (H) 0-0, 1-4

67-68 R1: Doncaster Rovers (H) 0-1

68-69 R1: South Shields (A) 6-0
R2: Morecambe (H) 2-0
R3: Stoke City (H) 0-2

69-70 R1: Whitby Town (H) 2-0
R2: Bangor City (A) 0-0, (H) 2-0
R3: Cardiff C. (H) 1-1, (A) 1-1, (*at Birmingham City*) 3-1
R4: Middlesbrough (A) 1-4

70-71 R1: Tamworth (A) 0-0, (H) 5-0
R2: Boston United (A) 2-1
R3: Bolton Wanderers (H) 2-0
R4: Southampton (H) 3-3, (A) 2-3

71-72 R1: Grimsby Town (H) 4-2
R2: Rotherham United (A) 1-1, (H) 2-3

72-73 R1: Mansfield Town (H) 2-1
R2: Bangor City (A) 3-2
R3: Oxford United (H) 0-1

73-74 R1: Mansfield Town (H) 0-0, (A) 3-5

74-75 R3: Arsenal (A) 1-1, (H) 1-3

75-76 R3: Hereford United (H) 2-1
R4: Chelsea (H) 0-2

76-77 R1: Dudley Town (A) 1-1, (H) 4-1
R2: Rotherham U. (A) 0-0, (H) 1-1, 1-2

77-78 R1: Wigan Athletic (A) 0-1

78-79 R1: Blyth Spartans (H) 1-1, (A) 5-3
R2: Scarborough (H) 3-0
R3: Luton Town (H) 2-0
R4: Nottingham Forest (A) 1-3

79-80 R1: Mossley (H) 5-2
R2: Bury (A) 0-0, (H) 0-2

80-81 R1: Tranmere Rovers (A) 0-0, (H) 1-2

81-82 R1: Stafford Rangers (A) 2-1
R2: Altrincham (H) 0-0, (A) 3-4

82-83 R1: Bury (H) 3-1
R2: Hartlepool United (A) 1-1, (H) 4-0

	R3: Crystal Palace (A) 1-2
83-84	R1: Macclesfield Town (A) 0-0, (H) 2-0 R2: Rochdale (H) 0-2
84-85	R1: Blue Star (H) 2-0 R2: Hartlepool United (A) 2-0 R3: Walsall (H) 3-0 R4: Arsenal (H) 1-0 R5: Liverpool (H) 1-1, (A) 0-7
85-86	R1: Morecambe (H) 0-0, (A - *Man. City*) 2-0 R2: Whitby Town (H) 3-1 R3: Wycombe Wanderers (H) 2-0 R4: Altrincham (H) 2-0 R5: Liverpool (H) 1-1, (A) 1-3
86-87	R1: Crewe Alexandra (H) 3-1 R2: Caernarfon Town (A) 0-0, (H) 1-2
87-88	R1: Burton Albion (H) 0-0, (A) 2-1 R2: Hartlepool United (H) 1-1, (A) 1-3
88-89	R1: Halifax Town (A) 0-1
89-90	R1: Grimsby Town (H) 1-2
90-91	R1: Darlington (A) 1-1, (H) 1-0 R2: Mansfield Town (A) 1-2
91-92	R1: Bridlington Town (A) 2-1 R2: Tranmere Rovers (H) 1-1, (A) 1-2
92-93	R1: Stockport County (H) 1-3

YORKSHIRE AMATEUR

Currently: Northern Counties (East) League

45-46	Q1: Goole Town (A) 1-0 Q2: East Bierley (H) 3-0 Q3: Frickley Colliery (A) 4-0 Q4: Scunthorpe United (A) 2-1 R1: Lincoln City (H) 1-0, (A) 1-5 (*agg: 2-5*)
46-47	Q1: Goole Town (A) 4-2 Q2: Thorne Colliery (H) 1-0 Q3: South Kirkby Colliery (A) 2-1 Q4: Gainsborough Trinity (H) 3-3, (A) 2-6
47-48	Q1: Thorne Colliery (H) 0-0, (A) 3-4
48-49	PR: Meltham Mills (H) 2-1 Q1: Selby Town (H) 0-4
49-50	PR: Frickley Colliery (A) 0-1
50-51	EX: Harrogate Town (H) 4-1 PR: Marsden (H) 2-0 Q1: Goole Town (H) 0-4
51-52	Q1: Pilkington Recreation (H) 5-2 Q2: Farsley Celtic (A) 3-2 Q3: Goole Town (A) 0-3
52-53	Q2: Selby Town (A) 1-2
53-54	Q2: Selby Town (H) 3-3, (A) 1-4
55-56	Q1: Ossett Town (H) 1-2
56-57	Q2: Farsley Celtic (A) 0-1
57-58	Q2: Farsley Celtic (H) 1-1, (A) 2-1 Q3: Stocksbridge Works (A) 3-2 Q4: Goole Town (H) 1-2
58-59	Q1: Denaby United (A) 2-4
59-60	Q1: Goole Town (H) 1-3
60-61	Q1: Selby Town (A) 2-3
61-62	Q1: East End Park W.M.C. (A) 1-1, (H) 0-2
63-64	Q1: Farsley Celtic (A) 0-0, (H) 0-4
64-65	Q1: Bridlington Town (H) 0-1
65-66	Q1: Hull Brunswick (H) 2-4
66-67	Q1: Farsley Celtic (A) 0-1
67-68	PR: Worksop Town (H) 1-0 Q1: Frickley Colliery Welfare (A) 0-5
68-69	Q1: Hatfield Main (A) 0-5
69-70	PR: Kiveton Park United (A) 3-1 Q1: Retford Town (A) 0-4
70-71	Q1: Goole Town (H) 1-2
71-72	Q1: Rawmarsh Welfare (A) 1-1, (H) 4-2 Q2: Frickley Colliery (H) 0-0, (A) 1-3
72-73	Q1: Selby Town (A) 2-0 Q2: Hatfield Main (A) 2-1 Q3: Scarborough (A) 2-2, (H) 0-2
73-74	Q1: Mossley (A) 0-2
74-75	Q1: Droylsden (A) 1-1, (H) 4-4, 1-0 Q2: Farsley Celtic (H) 0-2
75-76	Q1: Winterton Rangers (A) 2-4
76-77	PR: Frickley Colliery (A) 0-3
77-78	PR: Barton Town (H) 0-2
78-79	Q1: Bridlington Town (H) 0-0, (A) 3-2 Q2: Whitby Town (A) 2-1 Q3: Winterton Rangers (H) 1-0 Q4: Chorley (A) 2-4
79-80	PR: Mexborough Town Athletic (A) 1-6
80-81	PR: Whitby Town (A) 1-3
81-82	Q1: Stalybridge Celtic (A) 1-2
82-83	Q1: Bishop Auckland (H) 0-1
83-84	Q1: Spennymoor United (H) 4-1 Q2: Lancaster City (A) 2-2, (H) 0-2
84-85	PR: Consett (H) 0-1
85-86	PR: Eppleton Colliery Welfare (A) 1-5
86-87	Q1: Guiseley (H) 0-1
92-93	PR: Seaham Red Star (H) 1-3

YOULGRAVE

Currently: (Youlgrave Utd) Hope Valley League

47-48	PR: Droylsden (H) 6-6, (A) 1-2

Above: *Andy Linighan heads Arsenal's sensational last gasp winner in the 1993 final replay. Photo: Colorsport*

APPENDIX I: ANNOTATION

SEASONS have been abbreviated by the removal of the '19'. Therefore season 1962-63 is shown as '62-63'. Rules across the page divide seaons in the club entries.

VENUES are shown in brackets '(H)' for home, '(A)' for away. Neutral venues are italicised.

SCORES. The score of the featured club is always given first, irrespective of venue.

ROUND ABBREVIATIONS

EX: - Extra Preliminary Round

PR: - Preliminary Round

Q1: - First Qualifying Round

Q2: - Second Qualifying Round

Q3: - Third Qualifying Round

Q4: - Fourth Qualifying Round

R1: - First Round Proper

R2: - Second Round Proper

R3: - Third Round Proper

R4: - Fourth Round Proper

R5: - Fifth Round Proper

R6: - Sixth Round Proper (Quarter-final)

SF: - Semi-final

F: - Final

OTHER COMMON ABBREVIATIONS

E.T.: - Extra Time

Ab., Aban., Aband.: Abandoned

Lge.: - League

Rvrs.: - Rovers

Rgrs.: - Rangers

Wdrs.: - Wanderers

Pl.: - Played

m/mins.: Minutes

Above: *West Bromwich Albion - Cup winners, 1968. Photo: Colorsport.*

APPENDIX II: Acknowledgements

MAJOR CONTRIBUTORS: TONY BROWN AND KERRY MILLER

WE ARE GREATLY INDEBTED TO THE FOLLOWING CONTRIBUTORS WHO HELPED US OBTAIN MISSING SCORES, AND SUPPILED INFORMATION ON THE CURRENT STATUS OF VARIOUS CLUBS.

Trevor Urban

Tony Angell

Jason Dickinson

John S. Roe (Lancing FC)

Tony Booth

Neil Harvey (Cambridge City)

Eddie Miller

J.M.Redpath

Martin Smith

Steve Taylor

A.Bayles (Northern League)

Michael Greaves

Pete Thomas (Burton Albion Sup. Club '91)

A.Bastin

Keith Iles

Mike Newcombe (St.Blazey FC)

Alan Eastwood

N.Webb (Purton FC)

Andy Molden

Graham Trimming

P.J.Clynes (Moor Green FC)

P Savage (Netherfield FC)

D.A.Christmas

Roger Tilbury

D.Hardy

Malcolm Clarke

J.D.Vause

M.W.Smith

John Powell

Steve Taylor

M.Jones

John Van Laer (Hayes FC)

V.Bradley

Ian Hay (Gosport Borough FC)

Bob Hotchkiss

Steve Taylor

Jonathan Rowse

Ken Hilton (Skelmersdale United)

A.E.Nicholas

Les Turland

Mark Bettany

J.Hooper (Trowbridge Town)

Roger Daniel

Neil Bennett (Shildon FC)

Paul Marsh

Mark Dell (Hoddesdon Town FC)

Brian Fear (Aberaman Athletic)

Ray Davies (Llanelli FC)

A.Proudlock (Bridlington Town)

W.Brogden (Penrith FC)

The staff of Darlington Library.

The staff of Durham Library.

The staff of British Newspaper Library, Colindale, North London.

All 'Association of Football Statisticians' members who helped Tony Brown with his research.

Steve Clark (Football Association).

All photographers (credits are given next to photos).

APPENDIX III: League Sponsors

AS MENTIONED IN THE INTRODUCTION, THE LEAGUE NAMES USED THROUGHOUT THIS BOOK ARE THEIR ORIGINAL TITLES. THIS IS BECAUSE IT IS HOPED THAT THIS BOOK WILL PROVIDE A SOURCE OF REFERENCE FOR MANY YEARS TO COME. IN ORDER THAT CURRENT LEAGUE SPONSORS RECEIVE THEIR DESERVED RECOGNITION A LIST OF LEAGUE SPONSORS, AS PER SEPTEMBER 1993, IS REPRODUCED BELOW.

FA Premier League: Carling Premership

Football League: Endsleigh Insurance F.L.

Alliance Premier League: G.M. Vauxhall Conference

North West Counties: Carling N.W.C.

Northern League: Federation Brewery N.L.

Wearside League: Vaux Wearside League

Northern Alliance: Courage N.A.

Central Midlands League: John Smith's Bitter C.M.L.

Leicestershire Senior League: Everards Brewery L.S.L.

Staffs Senior League: Refuge Assurance Midland League

Mid-Cheshire League: Green Insulation M.C.L.

West Cheshire League: Carlsberg Tetley W.C.L.

Midland Combination: Skol M.C.

Southern League: Beazer Homes League

Isthmian League: Diadora League

United Counties League: Hereward Sports U.C.L.

South Midlands League: Minerva Footballs S.M.L.

Eastern Counties League: Jewson E.C.L.

Suffolk & Ipswich League: British Sugar S & I.L.

Anglian Combination: Lovewell Blake A.C.

Combined Counties League: Parasol C.C.L.

Kent League: Winstonlead K.L.

Sussex County League: Unijet S.C.L.

Wessex League: Jewson W.L.

Hampshire League: CHB Hampshire League

Teesside League: GC Developments T.L.

County Senior League: Whitbread C.S.L.

Hellenic League: Spectre H.L.

Chiltonian League: Charrington C.L.

Western League: Great Mills League

South-Western League: Jewson S.W.L.

Devon County League: Westward Developments D.C.L.

Somerset Senior League: Colborne Trophies S.S.L.

Lincolnshire League: TSW Printers (Scunthorpe) L.L.

South Devon League: Mod-Dec Windows S.D.L.

East Cornwall Premier League: Cornish Guardian E.C.P.L.

Surrey Senior League: S.C.Johnson S.S.L.

Oxfordshire Senior League: Banbury Sports O.S.L.

Auckland & District League: Hathaway A&D.L.

League of Wales: Konica League of Wales

Welsh League: Abacus W.L.

Welsh Alliance: Stena Sealink W.A.

Welsh National League (Wrexham Area): Read Construction W.N.L. (W.A.)

APPENDIX IV: Still Missing?

DESPITE ALL THE EXTENSIVE RESEARCH THAT HAS BEEN UNDERTAKEN, FIVE RESULTS STILL HAVE NOT BEEN TRACED. BECAUSE THESE RESULTS DO NOT SEEM TO APPEAR IN ANY NEWSPAPERS, WE HAVE ASSUMED THAT THE MATCHES PROBABLY NEVER TOOK PLACE. THEREFORE "WALK-OVERS" HAVE BEEN ENTERED AS THE RESULTS. HOWEVER, IT IS POSSIBLE THAT SOMEONE OUT THERE DOES KNOW THE SCORELINES. THE MATCHES IN QUESTION ARE:

1945/46 Preliminary Round - Thornycrofts (Basingstoke) v Totton

1945/46 First Qualifying Round - Ebbw Vale v Cardiff Corinthians

1945/46 First Qualifying Round (Replay) - Frickley Colliery v Guiseley

1945/46 Second Qualifying Round (Replay) - Newburn v Throckley

1946/47 Preliminary Round (Replay) - Grimethorpe v Wombwell MW

THERE IS ONE RESULT MISSING FROM A GAME THAT WE KNOW WAS PLAYED. THAT IS THE 1946/47 PRELIMINARY ROUND REPLAY BETWEEN LEYLAND MOTORS AND LYTHAM. INFURIATINGLY, THE 'LYTHAM & FYLDE STANDARD' ALLUDES TO LEYLAND WINNING EASILY WITHOUT GIVING THE SCORE! IF ANYONE HAS THIS RESULT, OR ANY OF THE ONES ABOVE, PLEASE DO LET US KNOW BY WRITING TO ADDRESS ON PAGE TWO.

Ian St. John heads the winning goal for Liverpool in the 1965 Cup Final against Leeds United. Photo: Colorsport.

Sheffield United's Franz Carr loses out to Manchester United's Dennis Irwin, during Sheffield's shock defeat of the mighty Reds in the Fifth Round of the 1992/93 F.A. Cup competition. Photo: Colorsport.

Yeovil Town's Steve Rutter out-jumps Q.P.R.'s Gary Bannister, in Rangers' 3-0 victory at the Huish during the 1987/88 season. Photo: Bob Thomas.